Linux:
The Complete Reference
Fourth Edition

Richard Petersen

Osborne/**McGraw-Hill**

Berkeley New York St. Louis San Francisco
Auckland Bogotá Hamburg London Madrid
Mexico City Milan Montreal New Delhi Panama City
Paris São Paulo Singapore Sydney
Tokyo Toronto

Osborne/**McGraw-Hill**
2600 Tenth Street
Berkeley, California 94710
U.S.A.

For information on translations or book distributors outside the U.S.A., or to arrange bulk purchase discounts for sales promotions, premiums, or fund-raisers, please contact Osborne/**McGraw-Hill** at the above address.

Linux: The Complete Reference, Fourth Edition

1234567890 DOC DOC 01987654321
Book p/n 0-07-212939-5 and CD #1 p/n 0-07-212937-9 and CD #2 p/n 0-07-212938-7
parts of
ISBN 0-07-212940-9

Publisher
   Brandon A. Nordin

Vice President & Associate Publisher
   Scott Rogers

Senior Acquisitions Editor
   Jane K. Brownlow

Project Editors
   Betsy Manini
   Jody McKenzie

Acquisitions Coordinator
   Ross Doll

Technical Editors
   Nalneesh Gaur
   Kurt Wall

Copy Editors
   Robert Campbell
   Dennis Weaver

Proofreaders
   Linda Medoff
   Paul Medoff
   C^2 Editorial Services
   Pat Mannion

Indexer
   Jack Lewis

Computer Designers
   Jean Butterfield
   Roberta Steele

Illustrators
   Beth E. Young
   Lyssa Sieben-Wald
   Robert Hansen
   Michael Mueller

Series Design
   Peter F. Hancik

This book was composed with Corel VENTURA™ Publisher.

To my brothers,
George, Robert, and Mark

About the Author

Richard Petersen holds a master's degree in Library and Information Studies. He currently teaches Unix and C/C++ courses at the University of California in Berkeley.

About the Technical Reviewer

Nalneesh Gaur is a technical manager with the eRisk Solutions practice of Ernst & Young in Dallas, Texas. He is experienced with UNIX, Linux and Windows NT system administration, e-commerce architectures, UNIX/NT integration, e-commerce security, and Web application development.

Contents at a Glance

Part V
Servers

Part VI
Administration

Part VII
Network Administration

Part VIII
Programming

Part IX
Appendix

Contents

Part II

Environments

Part III

Internet

Part IV

Applications

Part V

Servers

Part VI

Administration

Part VIII

Programming

Part IX

Appendix

Acknowledgments

I would like to thank all those at Osborne/McGraw-Hill who made this book a reality, particularly Jane Brownlow, acquisitions editor, for her continued encouragement and analysis as well as management of such a complex project; Nalneesh Gaur and Kurt Wall, the technical editors, whose analysis and suggestions proved very insightful and helpful; Ross Doll, editorial assistant, who provided needed resources and helpful advice; Dennis Weaver and Robert Campbell, copy editors, for their excellent job editing as well as insightful comments; and project editors Betsy Manini and Jody McKenzie, who incorporated the large number of features found in this book as well as coordinating the intricate task of generating the final version. Thanks also to Scott Rogers who initiated the project.

Special thanks to Linus Torvalds, the creator of Linux, and to those who continue to develop Linux as an open, professional, and effective operating system accessible to anyone. Thanks also to the academic community whose special dedication has developed Unix as a flexible and versatile operating system. I would also like to thank professors and students at the University of California, Berkeley, for the experience and support in developing new and different ways of understanding operating system technologies.

I would also like to thank my parents, George and Cecelia, and my brothers, George, Robert, and Mark, for their support and encouragement with such a difficult project. Also Valerie and Marylou and my nieces and nephews, Aleina, Larisa, Justin, Christopher, and Dylan, for their support and deadline reminders.

Introduction

The Linux operating system has become one of the major Unix distributions, bringing to the PC all the power and flexibility of a Unix workstation as well as a complete set of Internet applications and a fully functional desktop interface. This book is designed not only to be a complete reference on Linux, but also to provide clear and detailed explanations of Linux features. No prior knowledge of Unix is assumed; Linux is an operating system anyone can use.

This book identifies seven major Linux topics: Environments, the Internet, Applications, Servers, Administration, Network Administration, and Programming. Gnome and the K Desktop Environment (KDE) have become standard desktop Graphical User Interfaces (GUI) for Linux, noted for their power, flexibility, and ease-of-use. These are complete desktop environments that are more flexible than either Windows or the Mac/OS. They support standard desktop features such as menus, taskbars, and drag-and-drop operations. But they also provide virtual desktops, panel applets and menus, and Internet-capable file managers. You can install both, run applications from one on the other, and easily switch from one to the other. Both Gnome and KDE were designed with software development in mind, providing a firm foundation that has encouraged the development of a massive number of new applications for these interfaces. They have become integrated components of Linux, with applications and tools for every kind of task and operation. Instead of treating

Gnome and KDE as separate entities, Gnome and KDE tools and applications are presented throughout the book. For example, Gnome and KDE mail clients are discussed in the chapter on Internet mailers, along with other mail clients. Gnome and KDE FTP clients, editors, graphic tools, and administration tools, among others, are also handled in those respective chapters.

Linux is also a fully functional Unix operating system. It has all the standard features of a powerful Unix system, including a complete set of Unix shells such as BASH, TCSH, and the Z shell. Those familiar with the Unix interface can use any of these shells, with the same Unix commands, filters, and configuration features.

For the Internet, Linux has become a platform for very powerful Internet applications. You can not only use the Internet but, with Linux, become a part of it, creating your own Web, FTP, and Gopher sites. Other users can access your Linux systems, several at the same time, using different services. You can also use very powerful Gnome, KDE, and Unix clients for mail and news. Linux systems are not limited to the Internet. You can use Linux on any local intranet, setting up an FTP or Web site for your network. The Red Hat and Caldera Linux systems provided on the CD-ROMs with this book come equipped with variety a of fully functional FTP and Web servers already installed and ready to use. All you need to do is add the files you want onto your site.

Linux has the same level of administration features that you find on standard Unix systems as well as several user-friendly GUI configuration tools that make any administration task a simple matter of choosing items on a menu or selecting a check box. It has the same multiuser and multitasking capabilities. You can set up accounts for different users, and each can access your system at the same time. Each user can have several programs running concurrently. With Linux, you can control access, set up network connections, and install new devices. Linux includes very powerful and easy-to-use, window- and Web-based configuration utilities like Linuxconf and Webmin, which you can use to perform system administration tasks such as installing printers, adding users, and establishing new network connections.

A wide array of applications operate on Linux. Many personal versions of commercial applications such as WordPerfect and the Sybase database are available for Linux free of charge. You can download them directly from the Internet. Numerous Gnome and KDE applications are continually released through their respective Web sites. The GNU public licensed software provides professional-level applications such as programming development tools, editors, and word processors, as well as numerous specialized applications such as those for graphics and sound. A massive amount of software is available at online Linux sites where you can download applications and then easily install them onto your system.

What many may not realize is that all standard Linux systems support a wide range of programming languages, enabling users to create their own programs easily. All Linux distributions include a large selection of programming platforms, including support for numerous kinds of shell programming, a variety of higher-level languages like Perl and Tcl/Tk, and extensive GUI programming for desktops like Gnome and KDE. Once Linux is installed, you can start creating your own programs.

Since this book is really six books in one—an Internet book, a Gnome and KDE book, a Server book, an Applications book, a Programming book, and an Administration book—how you choose to use it depends upon how you want to use your Linux system. Almost all Linux operations can be carried out using either the Gnome or KDE interface. You need to use the Unix command line interface very little, if at all. You can focus on the Gnome and KDE chapters and their corresponding tools and applications in the different chapters throughout the book. On the other hand, if you want to delve deeper into the Unix aspects of Linux, you can check out the shell chapters and the corresponding shell-based applications in other chapters. If you only want to use Linux for its Internet services, then concentrate on the Internet clients and servers, most of which are already installed for you. If you want to use Linux as a multiuser system servicing many users or integrate it into a local network, you can use the detailed system, file, and network administration information provided in the administration chapters. None of these tasks are in any way exclusive. If you are working in a business environment, you will probably make use of all three aspects. Single users may concentrate more on the desktops and the Internet features, whereas administrators may make more use of the Unix features.

This book is designed to help you start using Linux quickly. In **Part I,** after a streamlined installation procedure for both Red Hat and Caldera taking about 30 minutes or less, basic Gnome and KDE interface operations and system configuration task are discussed. Here you learn the essentials of using both Gnome and KDE. System configuration tasks like mounting CD-ROMs and adding new user accounts are presented with the easiest methods, without much of the complex detail described in the administration chapters that is unnecessary for basic operations. Basic network configuration tasks are discussed, such as setting up a connection to an Internet service provider (ISP) over a modem, and entering ISP network information, such as name server and gateway addresses. Finally, a brief discussion of network security methods shows you how to quickly set up simple protection for a single system connected to the Internet, as well as where to find out more if you have more complex security requirements.

In **Part II,** you are introduced to the different kinds of user environments available for Linux, starting with KDE 2.0 and Gnome. Different features such as applets, the Panel, and configuration tools are described in detail. With either of these interfaces, you can run all your applications using icons, menus, and windows. At any time, you can open up a terminal window through which you can enter standard Linux commands on a command line. This edition covers KDE 2.0, which has superseded the earlier KDE 1.1. Linux makes a distinction between a desktop and a window manager. A window manager controls basic window operations like window appearance, movement, and elements. You have a variety of very powerful Linux window managers to choose from, including AfterStep, WindowMaker, and Enlightenment. You can also choose to use just the standard Unix command line interface to run any of the standard Unix commands. The remaining chapters in this section discuss the BASH shell and its various file, directory, and filter commands.

In **Part III,** the book discusses in detail the many Internet applications you can use on your Linux system. Linux automatically installs mail, news, FTP, and Web browser applications, as well as FTP and Web servers. Both KDE and Gnome come with a full set of mail, news, and FTP clients and Web browsers. These are described in detail along with Netscape Communicator, now an integrated part of all Linux systems. On your CD-ROMs there are other mail clients, newsreaders, and Internet tools that you can easily install from your desktop. In addition, the book describes Internet clients like Balsa that you can download from Internet sites and install on your system.

Part IV reviews applications available for Linux, beginning with Office suites like KOffice and StarOffice. KOffice is now distributed as part of KDE 2.0 and can be found on most Linux distributions. The different database management systems available are also discussed, along with the Web site locations where you can download them. Software installation has been simplified with the Red Hat Package Management System (RPMS). There are several GUI tools such as the KDE kpackage and Gnome GnomeRPM that you can use to easily install and uninstall software, much as you would with the Windows Install Wizard. A variety of different text editors are also available, including several Gnome and KDE editors, as well as the Vim (enhanced VI), gvim (graphical Vi), and GNU Emacs editors.

Part V discusses Internet servers, including FTP, Web, Gopher, and DNS servers. Internet servers have become integrated components of most Linux systems. Both the standard wu-ftpd FTP server and the newer ProFTPD server with its directive format are presented. ProFTPD includes such features as guest and virtual FTP sites. The Apache Web server chapter covers standard configuration directives like those for automatic indexing as well as the newer virtual host directives. Apache GUI configuration tools like Comanche are also presented. Configuration files and features for the Domain Name System (DNS) and its BIND server are examined in detail along with features like virtual domains and IP aliases. With Linux, you can easily set up your own domain name server for a home or small local network. Both sendmail and POP mail servers are covered. The INN news server, the Squid proxy server, and the ht:/DIG and WAIS search servers are also examined.

Part VI discusses user, file system, devices, kernel, and X Window System administration, respectively. These chapters emphasize use of the GUI system management configuration tools Linuxconf and Webmin. There are also detailed descriptions of the configuration files used in administration tasks and how to make entries in them. First, basic system administration tasks are covered, such as selecting runlevels, monitoring your system, and scheduling shutdowns. Then aspects of setting up and controlling users and groups are discussed. Presentations include both the GUI tools you can use for these tasks and the underlying configuration files and commands. Next, different file system tasks are covered, such as mounting file systems, selecting device names, and accessing DOS files. Device configuration covers topics such as device files, installing printers, and using the kernel modules to support new devices. Using, updating, and configuring the Linux kernel with its modules is covered in detail along with procedures for installing new kernels. X Window System topics cover the

XFree86 servers, window manager configuration, X Window System startup methods such as the display manager, and X Window System configuration commands.

Part VII covers network administration, dealing with topics such as configuring remote file system access and setting up firewalls. Most network administration tasks can be performed using configuration tools such as Linuxconf and Webmin. These are discussed in detail first. Next, the various network file system interfaces such as NFS for Unix, Samba for Windows file systems, and Netatalk for AppleTalk networks are presented. Then the different aspects of network administration are discussed, such as network connections and routes, domain name services, hostname designations, IP virtual hosts, and IP masquerading. Network security topics cover firewalls and encryption using ipchains and Netfilter (iptables) to protect your system, the Secure Shell (SSH) to provide secure remote transmissions, and Kerberos to provide secure authentication. Netfilter is a feature of the 2.4 kernel and is discussed along with ipchains, which it replaces; ipchains, which is used for the 2.2 kernel and may still be installed on many systems, is also covered in detail.

Part VIII discusses programming topics beginning with shell programming for the BASH shell, where you can create complex shell scripts. Compilers, libraries, and programming tools are then covered, including such topics as using the GCC compiler, managing static and shared libraries, and using development tools such as **make**, the gdb debugger, and the RCS revision manager. Then, Perl programming is discussed, including file management, string manipulation, and control structures. Tcl, Tk, and Expect are also covered. You can use Tcl and Tk commands to quickly create and easily maintain your own GUI interfaces. Then, a discussion of Gawk shows you how to easily create powerful shell applications.

Finally, there is an **Appendix** covering what is available on the CD-ROMs included with this book.

The Complete Reference

Part I

Introduction

Chapter 1

Introduction to Linux

Linux is an operating system for PC computers and workstations that now features a fully functional *graphical user interface (GUI)*, just like Windows and the Mac (though more stable). Linux was developed in the early 1990s by Linus Torvald, along with other programmers around the world. As an operating system, Linux performs many of the same functions as UNIX, Mac, Windows, and Windows NT. However, Linux is distinguished by its power and flexibility. Most PC operating systems, such as Windows, began their development within the confines of small, restricted personal computers, which have only recently become more versatile machines. Such operating systems are constantly being upgraded to keep up with the ever-changing capabilities of PC hardware. Linux, on the other hand, was developed in a different context. Linux is a PC version of the UNIX operating system that has been used for decades on mainframes and minicomputers, and is currently the system of choice for workstations. Linux brings the speed, efficiency, and flexibility of UNIX to your PC, taking advantage of all the capabilities that personal computers can now provide. Along with its UNIX capabilities come powerful networking features, including support for Internet, intranets, Windows, and AppleTalk networking. As a standard, Linux is distributed with fast, efficient, and stable Internet servers, such as the Web, FTP, and Gopher servers, along with domain name, proxy, news, mail, and indexing servers. In other words, Linux has everything you need to set up, support, and maintain a fully functional network.

Now, with both the Gnome and K Desktop, Linux also provides GUI interfaces with that same level of flexibility and power. Unlike Windows and the Mac, you can choose the interface you want and then customize it further, adding panels, applets, virtual desktops, and menus, all with full drag-and-drop capabilities and Internet-aware tools. On your desktop, a file manager window can access any Internet site, enabling you to display Web pages and download files with a few simple mouse operations. To print a file, simply drag it to a Printer icon.

Linux does all this at a great price. Linux is free, including the network servers and GUI desktops. Unlike the official UNIX operating system, Linux is distributed freely under a GNU General Public License as specified by the Free Software Foundation, making it available to anyone who wants to use it. GNU stands for "Gnu's Not UNIX" and is a project initiated and managed by the Free Software Foundation to provide free software to users, programmers, and developers. Linux is copyrighted, and it is not public domain. However, a GNU public license has much the same effect as being in the public domain. The GNU public license is designed to ensure Linux remains free and, at the same time, standardized. Only one official Linux exists. The list of software available under the GNU public license is extensive, including environments, programming languages, Internet tools, and text editors. People sometimes have the mistaken impression that Linux is somehow less than a professional operating system because it is free. Linux is, in fact, a PC and workstation version of UNIX. Many consider it far more stable and much more powerful than Windows. This power and stability have made Linux an operating system of choice as a network server.

To appreciate Linux completely, you need to understand the special context in which the UNIX operating system was developed. UNIX, unlike most other operating systems, was developed in a research and academic environment. In universities, research laboratories, data centers, and enterprises, UNIX is the system of choice. Its development paralleled the entire computer and communications revolution over the past several decades. Computer professionals often developed new computer technologies on UNIX, such as those developed for the Internet. Although a sophisticated system, UNIX was designed from the beginning to be flexible. The UNIX system itself can be easily modified to create different versions. In fact, many different vendors maintain different official versions of UNIX. IBM, Sun, and Hewlett-Packard all sell and maintain their own versions of UNIX. The unique demands of research programs often require that UNIX be tailored to their own special needs. This inherent flexibility in the UNIX design in no way detracts from its quality. In fact, this flexibility attests to the ruggedness of UNIX, allowing it to adapt to practically any environment. This is the context in which Linux was developed. Linux is, in this sense, one other version of UNIX—a version for the PC. The development of Linux by computer professionals working in a research-like environment reflects the way UNIX versions have usually been developed. Linux is publicly licensed and free, and reflects the deep roots UNIX has in academic institutions, with their sense of public service and support. Linux is a top-rate operating system accessible to everyone, free of charge.

As a way of introducing Linux, this chapter discusses Linux as an operating system, the history of Linux and UNIX, the overall design of Linux, and Linux distributions. This chapter also discusses online resources for documentation, software, and newsgroups, plus Web sites with the latest news and articles on Linux. Web and FTP site listings are placed in tables at the end of this chapter for easy reference. Here you can find sites for different distributions, Linux publications, software repositories, and Linux development, as well as for office suites and commercial databases.

Operating Systems and Linux

An *operating system* is a program that manages computer hardware and software for the user. Operating systems were originally designed to perform repetitive hardware tasks. These tasks centered around managing files, running programs, and receiving commands from the user. You interact with an operating system through a user interface. This user interface allows the operating system to receive and interpret instructions sent by the user. You only need to send an instruction to the operating system to perform a task, such as reading a file or printing a document. An operating system's user interface can be as simple as entering commands on a line or as complex as selecting menus and icons on a desktop.

An operating system also manages software applications. To perform different tasks, such as editing documents or performing calculations, you need specific software applications. An *editor* is an example of a software application, which enables you to edit a document, making changes and adding new text. The editor itself is a program consisting of instructions to be executed by the computer. To use the program, it must first be loaded into computer memory, and then its instructions are executed. The operating system controls the loading and execution of all programs, including any software applications. When you want to use an editor, simply instruct the operating system to load the editor application and execute it.

File management, program management, and user interaction are traditional features common to all operating systems. Linux, like all versions of UNIX, adds two more features. Linux is a multiuser and multitasking system. As a multitasking system, you can ask the system to perform several tasks at the same time. While one task is being done, you can work on another. For example, you can edit a file while another file is being printed. You do not have to wait for the other file to finish printing before you edit. As a multiuser system, several users can log in to the system at the same time, each interacting with the system through his or her own terminal.

Operating systems were originally designed to support hardware efficiency. When computers were first developed, their capabilities were limited and the operating system had to make the most of them. In this respect, operating systems were designed with the hardware in mind, not the user. Operating systems tended to be rigid and inflexible, forcing the user to conform to the demands of hardware efficiency.

Linux, on the other hand, is designed to be flexible, reflecting its UNIX roots. As a version of UNIX, Linux shares the same flexibility designed for UNIX, a flexibility stemming from UNIX's research origins. The UNIX operating system was developed by Ken Thompson at AT&T Bell Laboratories in the late 1960s and early 1970s. The UNIX system incorporated many new developments in operating system design. Originally, UNIX was designed as an operating system for researchers. One major goal was to create a system that could support the researchers' changing demands. To do this, Thompson had to design a system that could deal with many different kinds of tasks. Flexibility became more important than hardware efficiency. Like UNIX, Linux has the advantage of being able to deal with the variety of tasks any user may face.

This flexibility allows Linux to be an operating system that is accessible to the user. The user is not confined to limited and rigid interactions with the operating system. Instead, the operating system is thought of as providing a set of highly effective tools available to the user. This user-oriented philosophy means you can configure and program the system to meet your specific needs. With Linux, the operating system becomes an operating environment.

History of Linux and UNIX

As a version of UNIX, the history of Linux naturally begins with UNIX. The story begins in the late 1960s when a concerted effort to develop new operating system techniques occurred. In 1968, a consortium of researchers from General Electric, AT&T Bell Laboratories, and the Massachusetts Institute of Technology carried out a special operating system research project called *MULTICS* (*MULTiplexed Information Computing*

System). MULTICS incorporated many new concepts in multitasking, file management, and user interaction. In 1969, Ken Thompson, Dennis Ritchie, and the researchers at AT&T Bell Laboratories developed the UNIX operating system, incorporating many of the features of the MULTICS research project. They tailored the system for the needs of a research environment, designing it to run on minicomputers. From its inception, UNIX was an affordable and efficient multiuser and multitasking operating system.

The UNIX system became popular at Bell Labs as more and more researchers started using the system. In 1973, Dennis Ritchie collaborated with Ken Thompson to rewrite the programming code for the UNIX system in the C programming language. Dennis Ritchie, a fellow researcher at Bell Labs, developed the C programming language as a flexible tool for program development. One of the advantages of C is it can directly access the hardware architecture of a computer with a generalized set of programming commands. Up until this time, an operating system had to be specially rewritten in a hardware-specific assembly language for each type of computer. The C programming language allowed Dennis Ritchie and Ken Thompson to write only one version of the UNIX operating system, which could then be compiled by C compilers on different computers. In effect, the UNIX operating system became transportable, able to run on a variety of different computers with little or no reprogramming.

UNIX gradually grew from one person's tailored design to a standard software product distributed by many different vendors, such as Novell and IBM. Initially, UNIX was treated as a research product. The first versions of UNIX were distributed free to the computer science departments of many noted universities. Throughout the 1970s, Bell Labs began issuing official versions of UNIX and licensing the systems to different users. One of these users was the Computer Science department of the University of California, Berkeley. Berkeley added many new features to the system that later became standard. In 1975, Berkeley released its own version of UNIX, known by its distribution arm, *Berkeley Software Distribution* (*BSD*). This BSD version of UNIX became a major contender to the AT&T Bell Labs version. Other independently developed versions of UNIX sprouted up. In 1980, Microsoft developed a PC version of UNIX called *Xenix*. AT&T developed several research versions of UNIX and, in 1983, it released the first commercial version, called System 3. This was later followed by System V, which became a supported commercial software product. You can find more information on UNIX in *UNIX: The Complete Reference*, written by the UNIX experts at AT&T labs, Kenneth Rosen, Doug Host, James Farber, and Richard Rosinski.

At the same time, the BSD version of UNIX was developing through several releases. In the late 1970s, BSD UNIX became the basis of a research project by the *Department of Defense's Advanced Research Projects Agency* (*DARPA*). As a result, in 1983, Berkeley released a powerful version of UNIX called BSD release 4.2. This release included sophisticated file management, as well as networking features based on TCP/IP network protocols—the same protocols now used for the Internet. BSD release 4.2 was widely distributed and adopted by many vendors, such as Sun Microsystems.

The proliferation of different versions of UNIX led to a need for a UNIX standard. Software developers had no way of knowing on what versions of UNIX their programs would actually run. In the mid-1980s, two competing standards emerged, one based on the AT&T version of UNIX and the other based on the BSD version. In bookstores today, you can find many different books on UNIX for one or the other version. Some specify System V UNIX, while others focus on BSD UNIX.

AT&T moved UNIX to a new organization, called UNIX System Laboratories, which could focus on developing a standard system, integrating the different major versions of UNIX. In 1991, UNIX System Laboratories developed System V release 4, which incorporated almost all the features found in System V release 3, BSD release 4.3, SunOS, and Xenix. In response to System V release 4, several other companies, such as IBM and Hewlett-Packard, established *the Open Software Foundation* (*OSF*) to create their own standard version of UNIX. Two commercial standard versions of UNIX existed then— the OSF version and System V release 4. In 1993, AT&T sold off its interest in UNIX to Novell. UNIX Systems Laboratories became part of Novell's UNIX Systems Group. Novell issued its own versions of UNIX based on System V release 4, called UNIXWare, designed to interact with Novell's NetWare system. UNIX Systems Laboratories is currently owned by the Santa Cruz Operation. With Solaris, Sun has introduced System V release 4 onto its Sun systems. Two competing GUIs for UNIX, called Motif and Open-Look, have been superseded by a new desktop standard called the *Common Desktop Environment* (*CDE*).

Throughout much of its development, UNIX remained a large and demanding operating system requiring a workstation or minicomputer to be effective. Several versions of UNIX were designed primarily for the workstation environment. SunOS was developed for Sun workstations and AIX was designed for IBM workstations. As personal computers became more powerful, however, efforts were made to develop a PC version of UNIX. Xenix and System V/386 are commercial versions of UNIX designed for IBM-compatible PCs. AUX is a UNIX version that runs on the Macintosh. A testament to UNIX's inherent portability is that it can be found on almost any type of computer: workstations, minicomputers, and even supercomputers. This inherent portability made possible an effective PC version of UNIX.

Linux was originally designed specifically for Intel-based personal computers. Linux started out as a personal project of a computer science student named Linus Torvald at the University of Helsinki. At that time, students were making use of a program called *Minix*, which highlighted different UNIX features. Minix was created by Professor Andrew Tannebaum and widely distributed over the Internet to students around the world. Linus's intention was to create an effective PC version of UNIX for Minix users. He called it Linux, and in 1991, Linus released version 0.11. Linux was widely distributed over the Internet and, in the following years, other programmers refined and added to it, incorporating most of the applications and features now found in standard UNIX systems. All the major window managers have been ported to Linux. Linux has all the Internet utilities, such as FTP file transfer support, Web browsers, and remote connections with PPP. It also has a full set of program development utilities, such as C++ compilers and debuggers. Given all its features, the Linux operating system remains small, stable, and fast. In its simplest format, Linux can run effectively on only 4MB of memory.

Although Linux has developed in the free and open environment of the Internet, it adheres to official UNIX standards. Because of the proliferation of UNIX versions in the previous decades, the *Institute of Electrical and Electronics Engineers (IEEE)* developed an independent UNIX standard for *the American National Standards Institute (ANSI).* This new ANSI-standard UNIX is called the *Portable Operating System Interface for Computer Environments (POSIX).* The standard defines how a UNIX-like system needs to operate, specifying details such as system calls and interfaces. POSIX defines a universal standard to which all UNIX versions must adhere. Most popular versions of UNIX are now POSIX-compliant. Linux was developed from the beginning according to the POSIX standard. Linux also adheres to the *Linux filesystem standard (FSSTND),* which specifies the location of files and directories in the Linux file structure. See **www.pathname.com/fhs** for more details.

Linux Overview

Like UNIX, Linux can be generally divided into three major components: the kernel, the environment, and the file structure. The *kernel* is the core program that runs programs and manages hardware devices, such as disks and printers. The *environment* provides an interface for the user. It receives commands from the user and sends those commands to the kernel for execution. The *file structure* organizes the way files are stored on a storage device, such as a disk. Files are organized into directories. Each directory may contain any number of subdirectories, each holding files. Together, the kernel, the environment, and the file structure form the basic operating system structure. With these three, you can run programs, manage files, and interact with the system.

An environment provides an interface between the kernel and the user. It can be described as an interpreter. An environment interprets commands entered by the user and sends them to the kernel. Linux provides several kinds of environments: desktops, window managers, and command line shells. Each user on a Linux system has his or her own user interface. Users can tailor their environments to their own special needs, whether they be shells, window managers, or desktops. In this sense, for the user, the operating system functions more as an operating environment, which the user can control.

The shell interface is simple and usually consists of a prompt at which you type a command, and then press ENTER. In a sense, you are typing the command on a line; this line is often referred to as the *command line.* You will find the commands entered on the command line can become quite complex. Over the years, several different kinds of shells have been developed and, currently, three major shells exist: Bourne, Korn, and C shell. The *Bourne shell* was developed at Bell Labs for System V. The *C shell* was developed for the BSD version of UNIX. The *Korn shell* is a further enhancement of the Bourne shell. Current versions of UNIX, including Linux, incorporate all three shells, enabling you to choose the one you prefer. However, Linux uses enhanced or public domain versions of these shells: the Bourne Again shell, the TC shell, and the Public Domain Korn shell. When you start your Linux system, you are placed in the *Bourne Again shell*, an updated version of the Bourne shell. From there, you can switch to other shells as you choose.

As an alternative to a command line interface, Linux provides both desktops and window managers. These use GUI based on the X Windows System developed for UNIX by the Open Group consortium (**www.opengroup.org**). A *window manager* is a reduced version of a desktop, supporting only window operation, but it still enables you to run any application. A desktop provides a complete GUI, much like Windows and the Mac. You have windows, icons, and menus, all managed through mouse controls. Currently, two desktops are freely available and both are included with most distributions of Linux: Gnome and KDE.

In Linux, files are organized into directories, much as they are in Windows. The entire Linux file system is one large interconnected set of directories, each containing files. Some directories are standard directories reserved for system use. You can create your own directories for your own files, as well as easily move files from one directory to another. You can even move entire directories, and share directories and files with other users on your system. With Linux, you can also set permissions on directories and files, allowing others to access them or restricting access to you alone. The directories of each user are, in fact, ultimately connected to the directories of other users. Directories are organized into a hierarchical tree structure, beginning with an initial root directory. All other directories are ultimately derived from this first root directory.

Desktops

With the *K Desktop Environment* (*KDE*) and the *GNU Network Object Model Environment* (*Gnome*), Linux now has a completely integrated GUI interface. You can perform all your Linux operations entirely from either interface. Previously, Linux did support window managers that provided some GUI functionality, but they were usually restricted to window operations. KDE and Gnome are fully operational desktops supporting drag-and-drop operations, enabling you to drag icons to your desktop and to set up your own menus on an Applications panel. Both rely on an underlying X Windows System, which means as long as they are both installed on your system, applications from one can run on the other desktop. You can run KDE programs like the KDE mailer or the newsreader on the Gnome desktop. Gnome applications like the Gftp FTP client can run on the KDE desktop. You can even switch file managers, running the KDE file manager on Gnome. You lose some desktop functionality, such as drag-and-drop operations, but the applications runs fine. Desktop and window manager sites are listed in Table 1-1. The Gnome and KDE sites are particularly helpful for documentation, news, and software you can download for those desktops.

URL	Internet Site
www.gnome.org	Gnome Web site
www.kde.org	K Desktop Environment Web site
www.x11.org	X Windows System Web site, with links
www.fvwm.org	FVWM window manager
www.windowmaker.org	WindowMaker window manager
www.enlightenment.org	Enlightenment window manager
www.afterstep.org	AfterStep window manager
www.blackbox.org	Blackbox window manager
www.lesstif.org	Hungry Programmers OSF/Motif
www.themes.org	Desktop and Window manager themes, including KDE and Gnome
www.xfree86.org	XFree86, GNU version of the X Windows System provided for Linux
www.themes.org	Themes for window managers and desktops
www.eazel.com	Eazel, Gnome software
www.helixcode.com	Helix Code, Gnome software

Table 1-1.   *X Desktops and Window Managers*

Both desktops can run any X Windows System program, as well as any cursor-based program like Emacs and Vi, which were designed to work in a shell environment. At the same time, a great many applications are written just for those desktops and included with your distributions. The K Desktop has a complete set of Internet tools, along with editors and graphic, multimedia, and system applications. Gnome has slightly fewer applications, but a great many are currently in the works. Check their Web sites at **www.gnome.org** and **www.kde.org** for new applications. As new versions are released, they include new software.

Open Source Software

Linux was developed as a cooperative effort over the Internet, so no company or institution controls Linux. Software developed for Linux reflects this background. Development often takes place when Linux users decide to work on a project together. When completed, the software is posted at an Internet site, and any Linux user can then access the site and download the software. The potential for Linux-based software is explosive. Linux software development has always operated in an Internet environment and it is global in scope, enlisting programmers from around the world. The only thing you need to start a Linux-based software project is a Web site.

Most Linux software is developed as open source software. This means that the source code for an application is freely distributed along with the application. Programmers over the internet can make their own contributions to a software's development, modifying and correcting the source code. Linux is considered open source. Its source code is included in all its distributions and is freely available on the Internet. Many major software development efforts are also open source projects such as the KDE and Gnome desktops along with most of their applications. The Netscape Communicator Web browser package has also become open source, with all its source code freely available. The Star Office office suite supported by Sun is now an open source project. Recently, many of the Tcl/TK development tools have become open source projects. Many of the open source applications that run on Linux have located their Web sites at Source Forge (**sourceforge.net**). Source Forge is a hosting site designed specifically to support open source projects. You can find more information about the open source movement and recent developments at both Linuxcare (**www.linuxcare.com**) and at **www.opensource.org**.

Open source software is protected by Public Licenses. These prevent commercial companies from taking control of open source software by adding a few modifications of their own, copyrighting those changes, and selling the software as their own product. The most popular Public License is the GNU Public License provided by the Free Software Foundation. This is the license under which Linux is distributed. The GNU Public License retains copyrights, freely licensing the software with the requirement that the software and any modifications made to it are always freely available. Other public licenses have also been created to support the demands of different kinds of open source projects. The Lesser GNU Public License (LGPL) lets commercial applications use GNU licensed software libraries. Netscape made its Netscape Communicator software available under a Netscape Public License (NPL) which covers modifications made directly to the Netscape source code. Additions made to Netscape are covered under the Mozilla Public License. The QT Public License (QPL) lets open source developers use the QT libaries essential to the KDE desktop. You can find a complete listing at **www.opensource.org**.

Linux is currently copyrighted under a GNU Public License provided by the Free Software Foundation, and is often referred to as GNU software (see **www.gnu.org**). GNU software is distributed free, provided it is freely distributed to others. GNU software has proven both reliable and effective. Many of the popular Linux utilities, such as C compilers, shells, and editors, are all GNU software applications. Installed with your Linux distribution are the GNU C++ and Lisp compilers, Vi and Emacs editors, BASH and TCSH shells, as well as TeX and Ghostscript document formatters. In addition there are many open source software projects that are licensed under the GNU Public License (GPL). Many of these software applications are available at different Internet sites, and these are listed in Table 1-2. Chapter 3 and Chapter 32 describe in detail the process of downloading software applications from Internet sites and installing them on your system.

Under the terms of the GNU General Public License, the original author retains the copyright, although anyone can modify the software and redistribute it, provided the source code is included. Also, no restriction exists on selling the software or giving it away free. One distributor could charge for the software, while another one could provide it free of charge.

Lately, major software companies are also developing Linux versions of their most popular applications. A Linux version of Sun's *Java Development Kit* (*JDK*) is also available through **ftp.blackdown.org**. Corel has developed a Linux version of WordPerfect, while Oracle provides a Linux version of its Oracle database. (At present, no plans seem in the works for Microsoft applications.) Until recently however, many of these lacked a true desktop interface, but this has changed dramatically with the introduction of KDE and Gnome. These desktops are not merely interfaces: they both provide extensive, flexible, and powerful development libraries that software developers can use to create almost any kind of application, which they are.

Linux Software

An great deal of Linux software is currently available from online sources. You can download applications for desktops, Internet servers, Office suites, programming packages, among others. Several centralized repositories make it easy to locate an application and find information about it. Of particular note are **sourceforge.net**, **freshmeat.net**, **rpmfind.net**, and **linuxapps.com**.

Software packages are distributed either in compressed archives or in RPM packages. RPM packages are those archived using the Red Hat Package Manager. Compressed archives have an extension such as **.tar.gz** or **.tar.Z**, whereas RPM packages have an **.rpm** extension. For Red Hat and Caldera, downloading the RPM package versions of software from their FTP sites is best. Whenever possible, you should try to download software from a distribution's FTP site, but you could also download the source version and compile it directly on your system. This has become a simple process, almost as simple as installing the compiled versions (see Chapter 4).

Distributions, such as Red Hat and Caldera, also have a large number of mirror sites from which you can download their software packages. Red Hat mirror sites are listed at **www.redhat.com/mirrors.html**. Most Linux Internet sites that provide extensive software archives have mirror sites, such as **www.kernel.org**, that hold the new Linux kernels. If you have trouble connecting to a main FTP site, try one of its mirrors.

The following tables list different sites for Linux software. Repositories and archives for Linux software are listed in Table 1-2, along with several specialized sites, such as those for commercial and game software. When downloading software packages, always check to see if versions are packaged for your particular distribution. For example, Red Hat will use RPM packages. Many sites provide packages for the different popular distributions, such as Red Hat, Caldera, and Debian. For others, first check the distribution FTP sites for a particular package. For example, a Red Hat package version for ProFTPD is located at the **ftp.redhat.com** FTP site. **rpmfind.net, freshmeat.net**, **sourceforge.net**, and **www.linuxapps.com** are also good places for locating RPM packages for particular distributions.

URL	Internet Site
www.linuxapps.com	Linux Software Repository
sourceforge.net	Source Forge, open source software development sites for Linux applications and software repository.
www.happypenguin.org/	Linux Game Tome
www.linuxgames.org	Linux games
www.linuxquake.com	Quake
http:// www.xnet.com/~blatura/linapps.shtml	Linux applications and utilities page
freshmeat.net	New Linux software
www.linuxlinks.com	Linux links
filewatcher.org	Linux FTP site watcher
www.linuxdoc.org/links.html	Linux links
rpmfind.net	RPM package repository
www.gnu.org	GNU archive
www.opensound.com	Open sound system drivers
www.blackdown.org	Web site for Linux Java
www.fokus.gmd.de/linux	Woven goods for Linux
metalab.unc.edu	Mirror site for Linux software and distributions
apps.kde.com	KDE Applications
www.gnome.org	Gnome Applications

Table 1-2. *Linux Software Archives, Repositories, and Links*

Linux Office and Database Software

Many professional level databases and office suites are now available for Linux. These include Oracle and IBM databases as well as the StarOffice and K Office office suites. Table 1-3 lists sites for office suites and databases. Many of these sites provide free personal versions of their software for Linux and others are entirely free. You can download from them directly and install on your Linux system.

URL	Databases
www.oracle.com	Oracle database
www.sybase.com	Sybase database
www.software.ibm.com/data/db2/linux	IBM database
www.informix.com/linux	Informix database
www.cai.com/products/ingres.htm	Ingress II
www.softwareag.com	Adabas D database
www.mysql.com	MySQL database
www.ispras.ru/~kml/gss	The GNU SQL database
www.postgresql.org	The PostgreSQL database
www.fship.com/free.html	Flagship (Interface for xBase database files)
koffice.kde.org	Katabase (KOffice desktop database)
gaby.netpedia.net	Gaby (Gnome desktop personal database)
Office Software	
koffice.kde.org	KOffice
linux.corel.com	WordPerfect
www.sun.com	Star Office (Sun Microsystems product)
www.gnome.org/gw.html	Gnome Workshop Project
www.redhat.com	Applixware (commercial)

Table 1-3.   *Database and Office Software*

Internet Servers

One of the most important features of Linux, as well as all UNIX systems, is its set of Internet clients and servers. The Internet was designed and developed on UNIX systems, and Internet clients and servers, such as those for FTP and the Web, were first implemented on BSD versions of UNIX. DARPANET, the precursor to the Internet, was set up to link UNIX systems at different universities across the nation. Linux contains a full set of Internet clients and servers including mail, news, FTP, and Web, as well as proxy clients and servers. Sites for Internet server software available for Linux are listed in Table 1-4. Most of these are already included on the Red Hat and Caldera CD-ROMs included with this book; however, you can obtain news, documentation, and recent releases directly from the server's Web sites.

URL	Servers
www.apache.org	Apache Web server
www.proftpd.org	ProFTPD FTP server
www.isc.org	Internet Software Consortium: BIND, INN, and DHCPD
www.sendmail.org	Sendmail mail server
www.squid.org	Squid proxy server
www.samba.org	Samba SMB (Windows network) sever
boombox.micro.umn.edu/pub/gopher	Gopher server
www.eudora.com/free/qpop.html	Qpopper pop3 mail server
netfilter.kernelnotes.org	IP Tables firewall server
netfilter.kernelnotes.org/ipchains	IP Chains firewall server
www.ssh.com	Secure Shell encryption
http://web.mit.edu/kerberos/www	Kerberos network authentication protocol
www.openssh.com	Open Secure Shell (free version of SSH)

Table 1-4. *Network Servers and Security*

URL	Internet Sites
www.linuxprogramming.org	Linux programming resources
www.gnu.org	Linux compilers and tools (gcc).
dev.scriptics.com	Tcl Developers Xchange, Tcl/TK Products
java.sun.com	Sun Java Web site
www.perl.com	Perl Web site with Perl software
www.blackdown.org	Sun's Java Development Kit for Linux
developer.gnome.org	Gnome developers Web site
www.openprojects.nu	Open Projects Network
developer.kde.org	Developer's library for KDE
www.linuxcare.org	Linux open source software support

Table 1-5.   *Linux Programming*

Development Resources

Linux has always provided strong support for programming languages and tools. All distributions include the GNU C and C++ compiler (gcc) with supporting tools such as Make. Most distributions come with full development support for the KDE and Gnome desktops letting you create your own Gnome and KDE applications. You can also download the Linux version of the Java Development Kit for creating Java programs. Perl and Tcl/TK versions of Linux are also included with most distributions. You can download current versions from their Web sites. Table 1-5 lists different sites of interest for Linux programming.

Online Information Sources

Extensive online resources are available on almost any Linux topic. The tables in this chapter list sites from which you can obtain software, display documentation, and read articles on the latest developments. Many Linux Web sites provide news, articles, and information about Linux. Several are based on popular Linux magazines, such as **www.linuxjournal.com** and **www.linuxgazette.com**. Others operate as Web portals for Linux such as **www.linux.com**, **www.linuxworld.org**, and **www.linux.org**. Some specialize in particular topics, such as **kernelnotes.org** for news on the Linux kernel and **www.linuxgames.org** for the latest games ported for Linux. Currently, many Linux Web sites provide news, information, and articles on Linux developments, as well as documentation, software links, and other resources. These are listed in Table 1-6.

Distribution FTP and Web sites, such as **www.redhat.com** and **ftp.redhat.com,** provide extensive Linux documentation and software. The **www.gnome.org** site holds software and documentation for the Gnome desktop, while **www.kde.org** holds software and documentation for the KDE desktop. The tables in this chapter list

URL	Internet Site
www.linuxdoc.org	Web site for Linux Documentation Project
www.lwn.net	Linux Weekly News
www.linux.com	Linux.com
www.linuxtoday.com	Linux Today
www.linuxpower.org	Linux Power
www.linuxfocus.org	Linux Focus
www.linuxworld.org	Linux World
www.linuxmall.com	Linux Mall
www.linuxjournal.com	Linux Journal
www.linuxgazette.com	Linux Gazette
www.magazine.com	Linux Magazine
www.linux.org	Linux Online
www.li.org	Linux International Web site
www.linux.org.uk	Linux European Web site
www.kernelnotes.org	Latest news on the Linux kernel
slashdot.org	Linux forum
webwatcher.org	Linux Web site watcher
www.opensource.org	Open source Information

Table 1-6.   *Linux Information and News Sites*

many of the available sites. You can find other sites through resource pages that hold links to other Web sites—for example, the Linux Web site on the World Wide Web at **www.linuxdoc.org/links.html**.

Documentation

Linux documentation has also been developed over the Internet. Much of the documentation currently available for Linux can be downloaded from Internet FTP sites. A special Linux project called the *Linux Documentation Project* (*LDP*), headed by Matt Welsh, is currently developing a complete set of Linux manuals. The documentation, at its current level, is available at the LDP home site at **www.linuxdoc.org**. Linux documentation provided by the LDP is listed in Table 1-7, along with the Internet sites.

Sites	Web Sites
www.linuxdoc.org	LDP Web site
ftp.linuxdoc.org	LDP FTP site
Guides	**Document Format**
Linux Installation and Getting Started Guide	DVI, PostScript, LaTeX, PDF, and HTML
Linux User's Guide	DVI, PostScript, HTML, LaTeX, and PDF
Linux System Administrator's Guide	PostScript, PDF, LaTeX, and HTML
Linux Network Administrator's Guide	DVI, PostScript, PDF, and HTML
Linux Programmer's Guide	DVI, PostScript, PDF, LaTeX, and HTML
The Linux Kernel	HTML, LaTeX, DVI, and PostScript
Linux Kernel Hacker's Guide	DVI, PostScript, and HTML
Linux HOWTOs	HTML, PostScript, SGML, and DVI
Linux FAQs	HTML, PostScript, and DVI
Linux Man Pages	Man page format

Table 1-7.   *Linux Documentation Project*

An extensive number of mirrors are maintained for the Linux Documentation Project. You can link to any of them through a variety of sources, such as the LDP home site **www.linuxdoc.org** and **www.linuxjournal.org**. The documentation includes a user's guide, an introduction, and administration guides. These are available in text, PostScript, or Web page format. Table 1-7 lists these guides. You can also find briefer explanations, in what are referred to as HOW-TO documents. HOW-TO documents are available for different subjects, such as installation, printing, and e-mail. The documents are available at Linux FTP sites, usually in the directory **/pub/Linux/doc/HOW-TO**.

You can find a listing of different Linux information sites in the file **META-FAQ** located at Linux FTP sites, usually in the directory **/pub/Linux/doc**. On the same site and directory, you can also download the *Linux Software Map* (*LSM*). This is a listing of most of the software currently available for Linux.

In addition to FTP sites, Linux Usenet newsgroups are also available. Through your Internet connection, you can access Linux newsgroups to read the comments of other Linux users and to post messages of your own. Several Linux newsgroups exist, each beginning with **comp.os.linux**. One of particular interest to the beginner is **comp.os.linux.help**, where you can post questions. Table 1-8 lists some of the Usenet Linux newsgroups you can check out, particularly for posting questions.

Most of the standard Linux software and documentation currently available is already included on your Red Hat and Caldera CD-ROMs. HOW-TO documents are all accessible in HTML format, so you can view them easily with your Web browser. In the future, though, you may need to access Linux Internet sites directly for current information and software.

Newsgroup	Title
comp.os.linux.announce	Announcements of Linux developments
comp.os.linux.devlopment.apps	For programmers developing Linux applications
comp.os.linux.devlopment.system	For programmers working on the Linux operating system
comp.os.linux.hardware	Linux hardware specifications
comp.os.linux.admin	System administration questions
comp.os.linux.misc	Special questions and issues

Table 1-8. *Usenet Newsgroups*

comp.os.linux.setup	Installation problems
comp.os.linux.answers	Answers to command problems
comp.os.linux.help	Questions and answers for particular problems
comp.os.linux.networking	Linux network questions and issues
linux.dev.*group*	There are an extensive number of development newsgroups beginning with **linux.dev** such as **linux.dev.admin** and **linux.dev.doc**.

Table 1-8.   *Usenet Newsgroups* (continued)

Linux Distributions

Although there is only one standard version of Linux, there are actually several different releases. Different companies and groups have packaged Linux and Linux software in slightly different ways. Each company or group then releases the Linux package, usually on a CD-ROM. Later releases may include updated versions of programs or new software. Some of the more popular releases are Red Hat, OpenLinux, SuSE, and Debian. The Linux kernel is, of course, centrally distributed through **www.kernel.org**. All distributions use this same kernel, although it may be configured differently.

Table 1-9 lists the Web sites for several of the more popular Linux distributions. Listed here also are Linux kernel sites where the newest releases of the official Linux kernel are provided. These sites have corresponding FTP sites where you can download updates and new releases, as well as third-party software packaged for these distributions (see Table 1-10). For those not listed, check their Web sites for FTP locations.

Note   *Several distributions, such as Caldera and Red Hat, also offer their systems bundled with commercial software.*

URL	Internet Site
www.redhat.com	Red Hat Linux
www.caldera.com	OpenLinux (Caldera)
www.suse.com	SuSE Linux
www.debian.org	Debian Linux
www.infomagic.com	Infomagic
www.linuxppc.com	LinuxPPC (Mac PowerPC version)
www.turbolinux.com	Turbo Linux (Pacific Hi-Tech)
www.slackware.com	Slackware Linux Project
www.kernel.org	The Linux Kernel
www.kernelnotes.org	Linux Kernel release information
www.linux-mandrake.com	Mandrake

Table 1-9. *Linux Distributions and Kernel Sites*

URL	Internet Site
ftp.redhat.com	Red Hat Linux and Updates
ftp.redhat.com/contrib	Software packaged for Red Hat Linux
ftp.caldera.com	OpenLinux (Caldera)
ftp.suse.com	SuSE Linux
ftp.debian.org	Debian Linux
ftp.linuxppc.com	LinuxPPC (Mac PowerPC version)
ftp.turbolinux.com	Turbo Linux (Pacific Hi-Tech)

Table 1-10. *Linux Distribution FTP Sites*

Red Hat

Red Hat Linux is currently the most popular Linux distribution. Red Hat originated the RPM package system used on several distributions, which automatically installs and removes software packages. Red Hat is also providing much of the software development for the Gnome desktop, and it is a strong supporter of KDE. Its distribution includes both Gnome and KDE. Red Hat maintains software alliances with major companies like Oracle, IBM, and Sun. The Red Hat distribution of Linux is available online at numerous FTP sites. It maintains its own FTP site at **ftp.redhat.com**, where you can download the entire current release of Red Hat Linux, as well as updates and third-party software. Red Hat was designed from its inception to work on numerous hardware platforms. Currently, Red Hat supports Sparc, Intel, Alpha, PPC, ARM, m68k, and SGI platforms. See **www.redhat.com** for more information, including extensive documentation such as Red Hat manuals, FAQs, and links to other Linux sites.

If you purchase Red Hat Linux from Red Hat, you are entitled to online support services. Although Linux is free, Red Hat as a company specializes in support services, providing customers with its expertise in developing solutions to problems that may arise or using Linux to perform any of several possible tasks, such as e-commerce or database operations.

Red Hat maintains an extensive library of Linux documentation that is freely accessible online. On its Web page, you can link to its support page, which lists the complete set of Red Hat manuals, all in Web page format for easy viewing with any Web browser. These include the Reference Guide, the Getting Started Guide, and the Installation Guide. Tip, HOW-TO, and FAQ documents are also provided. Of particular note is the Hardware Compatibility Lists. This documentation lists all the hardware compatible with Red Hat Linux. For PC users, this includes most hardware, with few exceptions. All the Red Hat documentation is freely available under the GNU public license.

OpenLinux

Caldera OpenLinux is designed for corporate commercial use. OpenLinux Linux system and software packages include all the GNU software packages, as well as the X Windows System managers, Internet servers, WordPerfect, and the K Desktop. However, it does not presently include Gnome. It is POSIX compliant, adhering to UNIX standards. Caldera distributes its OpenLinux system free of charge.

Caldera has organized its OpenLinux distribution into several different packages, each geared to different markets. These include the eDesktop package, which is designed for basic workstation operations, and the eServer package, which is designed for Linux servers. The eDesktop, included with this book, provides workstation software such as the KDE Desktop. The eServer installs server software such as the mail, FTP, and DNS servers. See the Caldera Web site at **www.caldera.com** for more information.

Caldera also offers a line of commercial and proprietary Linux packages. Such proprietary, licensed software packages are not freely distributable. They include such products as the Novell NetWare client. Recently Caldera merged with Santa Cruz Operation, which develops and distributes SCO UNIX.

SuSE

Originally a German language–based distribution, SuSE has become very popular throughout Europe and is currently one of the fastest growing distributions worldwide. Its current distribution includes both KDE and Gnome. Its distributions include WordPerfect, Star Office, and KOffice. It also bundles commercial products like AdabasD and the Linux Office Suite. Currently, it supports only Intel platforms. For more information, see **www.suse.com**.

Debian

Debian Linux is an entirely noncommercial project, maintained by a group of volunteer programmers. It does, however, incorporate support for commercial products in its distribution. Debian currently maintains software associations with Corel and Sun, among others. Currently it supports Alpha, Intel, Macintosh 68K, and Sparc platforms. For more information, see **www.debian.org**.

Slackware

Slackware is available from numerous Internet sites, and you can order the CD from Walnut Creek Software. It includes both Gnome and KDE. The Slackware distribution takes special care to remain as closely UNIX compliant as possible. Currently, it supports only Intel platforms. See **www.slackware.com** for more information.

Infomagic

Infomagic distributes bundled sets of Linux software. The Linux Developers Resource Set includes the four major distributions: Red Hat, OpenLinux, SuSE, and Slackware. The Linux Archive Set contains mirrors of Linux archive sites, including KDE, Gnome, XFree86, and GNU. Currently it supports only the Intel platform. See **www.infomagic.com** for more information.

LinuxPPC

The LinuxPPC distribution provides versions of Linux designed exclusively for use on PowerPC machines. The distribution will run on any PowerPC machine, including IBM, Motorola, and Apple systems (including G4 and iMac machines). It provides support for the USB on Mac systems. Its current distribution includes the Gnome desktop and the Enlightenment window manager. See **www.linuxppc.com** for more information.

TurboLinux

TurboLinux is distributed by Pacific HiTech, providing English, Chinese, and Japanese versions. It includes several of its own packages such as TurboPkg for automatically updating applications, the TurboDesk desktop, and the Cluster Web Server. Like Red Hat, it supports RPM packages. It is currently widely distributed in East Asia. Currently, TurboLinux supports only the Intel platform, but a PowerPC version is in development. See **www.turbolinux.com** for more information.

Mandrake

Mandrake Linux is another popular Linux distribution with many of the same features as Red Hat. It focuses on providing up-to-date enhancements and an easy-to-use installation and GUI configuration. You can learn more about Mandrake at **www.linux-mandrake.com**.

Chapter 2

Installing Red Hat Linux

T his chapter describes the installation procedure for Red Hat Linux. The installation includes the Linux operating system, a great many Linux applications, and a complete set of Internet servers. Different Linux distributions usually have their own installation programs. The Red Hat installation program is designed to be efficient and brief, while installing as many features as possible. Certain features, such as Web server support, would ordinarily require specialized and often complex configuration operations. Red Hat automatically installs and configures many of these features.

Red Hat provides a detailed installation manual at its Web site. The manual consists of Web pages you can view using any browser. They include detailed figures and step-by-step descriptions. Checking this manual before you install is advisable. This chapter presents all the steps in the installation process but is not as detailed as the Red Hat manual. On the Red Hat Web site at **www.redhat.com**, click Support and choose the link for your version of Red Hat, such as Red Hat Linux 7. This presents a list of links including the Official Red Hat Linux Installation Guide.

Installing Linux involves several steps. First, you need to determine whether your computer meets the basic hardware requirements. These days, most Intel-based PC computers do. If you want to have your Linux system share a hard drive with another operating system, you may need to repartition your hard disk. Several different options exist for partitioning your hard drive, depending on whether it already contains data you need to preserve.

Red Hat supports several methods for installing Linux. You can install from a local source such as a CD-ROM or a hard disk, or from a network or Internet source. For a network or Internet source, Red Hat supports NFS, FTP, and HTTP installations. With FTP, you can install from an FTP site. With HTTP, you can install from a Web site. NFS enables you to install over a local network. For a local source, you can install from a CD-ROM or a hard disk. In addition, you can start the installation process by booting from your CD-ROM, from a DOS system, or from boot disks that can then use the CD-ROM or hard disk repository. Red Hat documentation covers each of these methods in detail. This chapter deals with the installation using the CD-ROM provided by this book and a boot disk created from a boot image on the CD-ROM. This is the most common approach.

Once the installation program begins, you simply follow the instructions, screen by screen. Most of the time, you only need to make simple selections or provide yes and no answers. The installation program progresses through several phases. First, you create Linux partitions on your hard drive, and then you install the software packages. After that, you can configure your network connection, and then your X Window System for graphical user interface support. Both X Windows and network configurations can be performed independently at a later time.

Once your system is installed, you are ready to start it and log in. You will be logging in to a simple command line interface. From the command line, you can then invoke X Windows, which provides you with a full graphical user interface.

You have the option of installing just the operating system, the system with a standard set of applications, or all the software available on the CD-ROM. If you choose a standard installation, you can add the uninstalled software packages later. Chapter 4 and Chapter 19 describe how you can use the GnomeRPM utility or the Red Hat Package Manager to install, or even uninstall, the software packages.

Hardware, Software, Information Requirements

Before installing Linux, you must ensure that your computer meets certain minimum hardware requirements. You also need to have certain specific information ready concerning your monitor, video card, mouse, and CD-ROM drive. All the requirements are presented in detail in the following sections. Be sure to read them carefully before you begin installation. During the installation program, you need to provide responses based on the configuration of your computer.

Hardware Requirements

Listed here are the minimum hardware requirements for installing a Linux system:

■ A 32-bit Intel-based personal computer. An Intel or compatible 80386, 80486, or Pentium microprocessor is required.

■ A 3 1/2-inch floppy disk drive

■ At least 32MB RAM, though 64MB are recommended

■ At least 2GB free hard disk space; 2 to 4GB or more are recommended. The size usually increases with each new release. You need at least 3GB to load and make use of all the software packages on your CD-ROM. The Standard installation of basic software packages takes 2GB, plus 32 to 64MB for swap space. If you have less than 1GB, you can elect to perform a minimum install, installing only the Linux kernel without most of the applications. You could later install the applications you want, one at a time.

■ A 3 1/2-inch, DOS-formatted, high-density (HD) floppy disk drive, to be used to create a install disk.

■ A CD-ROM drive

■ Two empty DOS-formatted, 3 1/2-inch, high-density (HD) floppy disks

If you plan to use the X Windows graphical user interface, you will also need:

■ A video graphics card
■ A mouse or other pointing device

Software Requirements

Only a few software requirements exist. If you intend to install using the floppy disks, you need an operating system from which you can create the disks. The DOS operating system is required to enable you to prepare your installation disks. Using a DOS system, you can access the CD-ROM and issue DOS-like commands to create your installation disks. Any type of DOS will do. You can even use the same commands on OS/2. However, you do not need DOS to run Linux. Linux is a separate operating system in its own right.

If you want to have Linux share your hard disk with another operating system, like Windows, you need certain utilities to prepare the hard disk for sharing. This way one part of your hard disk could be used for Windows and another for Linux. For Windows, you need either the **defrag** and **fips** utilities or disk management software like Partition Magic 4.0. The **fips** utility is provided on your CD-ROM. This utility essentially frees space by reducing the size of your current extended or primary partition. Usually located in your dos directory, **defrag** and **fdisk** are standard DOS utilities. **Defrag** is used with **fips** to defragment your hard disk before **fips** partitions it. This collects all files currently on the partition into one area, leaving all the free space grouped in one large chunk. If you are installing on a new empty hard drive and you want to use part of it for Windows, you can use **fdisk** to set up your Windows partitions. All these tasks can also be carried out using Partition Magic 4.0, a commercial product that now supports Linux partitions.

Information Requirements

Part of adapting a powerful operating system like Linux to the PC entails making the most efficient use of the computer hardware at hand. To do so, Linux requires specific information about the computer components with which it is dealing. For example, special Linux configuration files are tailored to work with special makes and models of video cards and monitors. Before installing Linux, you need to have such information on hand. The information is usually available in the manual that came with your hardware peripherals or computer.

CD-ROM, Hard Disk, and Mouse Information

- For some older SCSI CD-ROM drives, you need the manufacturer's name and model.

- Decide how much of your hard drive (in megabytes) you want to dedicate to your Linux system. If you are sharing with Windows, decide how much you want for Windows and how much for Linux.

- Decide how much space you want for your swap partition. Your swap partition must be between 16MB and 64MB, with 32MB appropriate for most systems. Your swap partition is used by Linux as an extension of your computer's RAM.

- Find the make and model of the mouse you are using. Linux supports both serial and bus mice. Most mice are supported, including Microsoft, Logitech, and Mouse Systems.

- Know what time zone you are in and to what time zone your hardware clock is set. This can be either Greenwich Mean Time (GMT) or your local time zone.

- Know which serial port your mouse is using: COM1, COM2, or none, if you use the PS/2 mouse port (most newer systems use PS/2).

Video and Monitor Information

Although most monitors and video cards are automatically configured during installation, you still need to provide the manufacturer's make and model. Find out the manufacturer for your monitor and its model, such as Iiyama VisionMaster 450 or NEC E500. Do the same for your video card, for example, Matrox Millennium G400 or ATI XPERT@Play 98 (you can find a complete list of supported cards at www.xfree86.org). This should be listed on the manuals or registration information provided with your computer. For some of the most recent monitors and video cards, and some older, uncommon ones, you may need to provide certain hardware specifications. Having this information on hand, if possible, is advisable, just in case. At the end of the installation process, you are presented with lists of video cards and monitors from which to choose your own. These lists are extensive. In case your card or monitor is not on the list, however, you need to provide certain hardware information about them. If the configuration should fail, you can always do it later using an X Window System configuration utility such as Xconfigurator and XF86Setup. Of particular importance is the monitor information, including the vertical and horizontal refresh rates.

Video Card Information

- What is the make and model of your video card?

- What chipset does your video card use?

- How much memory is on your video card?

Monitor Information

What is the manufacturer and model of your monitor? Linux supports an extensive list of monitors, covering almost all current ones. You only have to select yours from the list. If, however, your monitor is not on this list, you need to provide the following information. Be sure this information is correct. Should you enter a horizontal or vertical refresh rate that is too high, you can seriously damage your monitor. You can choose a generic profile or you can enter information for a custom profile. To do that, you need the following information:

- The horizontal refresh rate in Hz
- The vertical refresh rate in Hz

Network Configuration Information

Except for deciding your hostname, you do not have to configure your network during installation. You can put configuration off until a later time and use network configuration utilities like Linuxconf or netcfg to perform network configuration. If the information is readily available, however, the installation procedure will automatically configure your network, placing needed entries in the appropriate configuration files.

If you are on a network, you must obtain most of this information from your network administrator, unless your network information is automatically provided by a DHCP server on your network. In this case, you will only need your system's host name. During the installation process, you will be given the option of either using DHCP or entering the network information manually.

If you are setting up a network yourself, you have to determine each piece of information. If you are using a dial-up Internet service provider, you configure your network access using a PPP dial-up utility, such as Kppp or Linuxconf, after you have installed the system. The installation program will prompt you to enter these values:

- Decide on a name for your computer (this is called a *hostname*). Your computer will be identified by this name on the Internet. Do not use "localhost"; that name is reserved for special use by your system. The host name should be a simple alphabetic word; it can include numbers but not punctuation such as periods and backslashes.

- Your domain name.

- The Internet Protocol (IP) address assigned to your machine. Every host on the Internet is assigned an IP address. This address is a set of four numbers, separated by periods, which uniquely identifies a single location on the Internet, allowing information from other locations to reach that computer.

- Your network IP address. This address is usually similar to the IP address, but with one or more zeros at the end.

- The netmask. This is usually 255.255.255.0 for class C IP addresses. If, however, you are part of a large network, check with your network administrator.

- The broadcast address for your network, if available. Usually, your broadcast address is the same as your IP address with the number 255 added at the end.

- If you have a gateway, you need the gateway (router) IP address for your network.

- The IP address of any name servers your network uses.

- The NIS domain and IP address if your network uses an NIS server.

Upgrade Information
for Currently Installed Linux Systems

If you have already installed a previous version of Red Hat Linux (kernel 2.0 and above), you may have personalized your system with different settings that you would like to keep. If you choose the Upgrade option, rather than Install, during the installation process, these settings will be kept. All your previous configuration files are saved in files with a **.rpmsave** extension. However, upgrade only works for Red Hat kernel 2.0 and above (Red Hat 5.0 and up).

For earlier Red Hat versions or other installed Linux distributions, you must save your settings first. You may want to back up these settings anyway as a precaution. These settings are held in configuration files that you can save to a floppy disk and then use on your new system, in effect, retaining your original configuration (if you use **mcopy**, be sure to use the **-t** option). You may want to preserve directories and files of data, such as Web pages used for a Web site. You may also want to save copies of software packages you have downloaded. For these and for large directories, using the following **tar** operation is best.

```
tar cvMf /dev/fd0   directory-or-package
```

Make copies of the following configuration files and any other files you want to restore. You only need to copy the files you want to restore.

Files	Description
/etc/XF86Config	X Windows configuration file
/etc/lilo.conf	Boot manager configuration file
/etc/hosts	IP addresses of connected systems
/etc/resolv.conf	Domain name server addresses
/etc/fstab	File systems mounted on your system
/etc/passwd	Names and passwords of all users on your system
/home/user	Any home directories of users with their files on your system, where *user* is the username. (For a large number of files, use **tar cfM/dev/fd0/home/user**)
.netscape	Each home directory has its own **.netscape** subdirectory with Netscape configuration files such as your bookmark entries
Web site pages and FTP files	You may want to save any pages used for a Web site or files on an FTP site you are running. On CND versions, these are located at **/home/httpd/** and **/home/ftpd**

Once you have installed your system, you can mount the floppy disk and copy the saved files from the floppy to your system, overwriting those initially set up. If you use the **/etc/XF86Config** file from your previous system, you needn't run XF86Setup to set up X Windows. The **/etc/XF86Config** file includes all the X Windows setup information.

If you want to restore the **/etc/lilo.conf** file from your previous system, you must also install it, using the following command.

```
# lilo /etc/lilo.conf
```

To restore archives that you saved on multiple disks using the **tar** operation, place the first disk in the floppy drive and use the following command.

```
tar xvMf  /dev/fd0
```

Opening Disk Space for Linux Partitions for Shared Hard Disks

If you are using an entire hard drive for your Linux system or if you are upgrading a currently installed Linux system and you want to use the same partitions, you can skip this section and go on to installing Linux. If, however, your Linux system is going to share a hard drive with your Windows or DOS system, you need to organize your hard drive so that part of it is used for DOS and the remaining part is free for Linux installation. How you go about this process depends on the current state of your hard disk. If you have a new hard disk and you are going to install both Windows and Linux on it, you need to be sure to install Windows on only part of the hard drive, leaving the rest free for Linux. This means specifying a size smaller than the entire hard disk for your Windows partition that you set up during the Windows install procedure. You could also use **fdisk** to create partitions manually for Windows that will take up only a part of the hard disk. If you want to install Linux on a hard disk that already has Windows installed on its entire area, however, you need to resize your primary or extended partition, leaving part of the disk free for Linux. The objective in each situation is to free space for Linux. When you install Linux, you will then partition and format that free space for use by Linux.

A hard disk is organized into partitions. The partitions are further formatted to the specifications of a given operating system. When you installed Windows, you first needed to create a primary partition for it on your hard disk. If you have only one disk on your hard drive, then you only have a primary partition. To add more partitions, you create an extended partition and then, within that, logical partitions. For example, if you have C, D, and E disks on your hard drive, your C disk is your primary partition and the D and E disks are logical partitions set up within your extended partition. You then used the DOS **format** operation to format each partition into a Windows disk, each identified by a letter. For example, you may have divided your disk into two partitions, one formatted as the C disk and the other as the D disk. Alternatively, you may have divided your hard disk into just one partition and formatted it as the C disk. To share your hard drive with Linux, you need to free some space by either deleting some of those partitions or reducing their size.

First, decide how much space you need for your Linux system. You probably need a minimum of 2GB, though more is recommended. As stated earlier, the basic set of Linux software packages takes up 500MB, whereas the entire set of software packages, including all their source code files, takes several GBs. In addition, you need space for a Linux swap partition used to implement virtual memory. This takes between 16 and 64MB.

Once you determine the space you need for your Linux system, you can then set about freeing that space on your hard drive. To see what options are best for you, you should first determine what your partitions are and their sizes. You can do this with the **fdisk** utility. To start this utility, type **fdisk** at the DOS prompt, and press ENTER.

```
C:\> fdisk
```

This brings up the menu of **fdisk** options. Choose Option 4 to display a list of all your current partitions and the size of each. Press ESC to leave the **fdisk** utility. You can use the DOS **defrag** and Linux **fips** utilities to reduce the size of the partitions, creating free space from unused space on your hard drive. You should still make a backup of your important data for safety's sake. First, check if you already have enough unused space on your hard drive that can be used for Linux. If you do not, you must delete some files. When Windows creates and saves files, it places them in different sectors on your hard disk. Your files are spread out across your hard disk with a lot of empty space in between. This has the effect of fragmenting the remaining unused space into smaller sections, separated by files. The **defrag** utility performs a defragmentation process that moves all the files into adjoining space on the hard disk, thereby leaving all the unused space as one large continuous segment. Once you have defragmented your disk, you can use the **fips** utility to create free space using part or all of the unused space. **fips** is a version of **fdisk** designed to detect continuous unused space and remove it from its current Windows partition, opening unpartitioned free space that can then be used by Linux. All your Windows partitions and drives remain intact with all their data and programs. They are just smaller.

To run the **defrag** utility, enter the command **defrag**. This is a DOS command usually found in the **dos** or **windows** directory. You can also run it from Windows.

```
C:\> windows\defrag
```

Defrag displays a screen with colored blocks representing the different sectors on your hard disk. It carries out an optimization of your hard disk, moving all your used sectors, your data and programs, together on the hard disk. This may take a few minutes. When it is complete, you will see the used sectors arranged together on the screen. You can then exit the **defrag** utility.

Now you are ready to run the **fips** utility to free space. **fips** is located on your Red Hat Linux CD-ROM, also in the directory named **dosutils**. Change to your CD-ROM drive and run the **fips** utility. In the following example, the CD-ROM drive is drive E.

```
C:\> e:
E:\> \dosutils\fips
```

The **fips** utility displays a screen showing the amount of free space. Use your arrow keys to make the space smaller if you do not need all your free space for Linux. You should leave some free space for your Windows programs. Then press ENTER to free the space.

Creating the Red Hat Boot Disks

You can install Red Hat using an install disk whose image is located on the Red Hat CD-ROM. You create the install disk using the MS-DOS program **rawrite** and an install disk image. The install disk has to be created on a computer that runs DOS. Install disk images exist for local installation (**boot.img**), installing from an network source like a Web site (**netimage.img**), and installing with PCMCIA support (**pcmcia.img**). Begin by first starting your computer and entering DOS. Then perform the following steps.

Insert the Red Hat CD-ROM into your CD-ROM drive. At your DOS prompt, change to your CD-ROM drive, using whatever the letter for that drive may be. For example, if your CD-ROM drive is the E drive, just type **e:** and press ENTER. Once you have changed to the CD-ROM drive, you then need to change to the **images** directory. The Install disk images are there, **boot.img**, **pcmia.img**, and **netboot.img**. The **rawrite** command is in the **dosutils** directory, **dosutils\rawrite**.

To create the install disk, insert a blank floppy disk into your floppy drive. Now start the **rawrite** command. The **rawrite** command will actually write the disk image to your floppy disk. The **rawrite** command first prompts you for the name of the disk image file you want to copy. Enter the full name of the install image file (in this example **boot.img**). The command then asks you to enter the letter of the floppy drive where you put your floppy disk. On many systems, this is the A drive.

```
E:\> cd images
E:\col\launch\floppy > e:\dosutils\rawrite
```

```
Enter source file name: boot.img
Enter destination drive (A or B) and press ENTER: a
```

Press ENTER to confirm that you have a blank floppy disk in the drive. **rawrite** will then copy the image file to your floppy disk, creating your install disk. When it finishes, remove your disk from the floppy drive. This is the disk that the installation procedure (described later) refers to as the Install diskette. If you need to create a network boot disk, use **netimage.img** instead. For PCMCIA support, use **pcmcia.img**.

Installing Linux

Installing Linux involves several processes, beginning with creating Linux partitions, and then loading the Linux software, configuring your X Windows interface, installing the Linux Loader (LILO) that will boot your system, and creating new user accounts. The installation program is a screen-based program that takes you through all these processes, step-by-step, as one continuous procedure. You can use either your mouse or the keyboard to make selections. When you finish with a screen, click the Next button at the bottom to move to the next screen. If you need to move back to the previous screen, click the Back button. You can also use the TAB, the arrow keys, SPACEBAR, and ENTER to make selections. You have little to do, other than make selections and choose options. Some screens provide a list of options from which you make a selection. In a few cases, you are asked for information you should already have if you followed the steps earlier in this chapter. You are now ready to begin installation. The steps for each part of the procedure are delineated in the following sections. This should not take more than an hour.

Starting the Installation Program

If you followed the instructions in the first part of the chapter, you have freed space on your hard drive, and created your install and module disks. Now you are ready to create your Linux partitions. To do this, you need to boot your computer using the install disk you made earlier. When you start your computer, the installation program will begin and, during the installation, you can create your Linux partitions.

You can start the installation using one of several methods. If your computer can boot from the CD-ROM, you can start the installation directly from the CD-ROM. Just place the Red Hat CD-ROM in the CD-ROM drive before you start your computer. If you have a DOS system installed on your hard drive, you can start up DOS and then use the **autoboot.bat** command in the **dosutils** directory to start the installation, as shown here. You have to execute this command from a DOS system, not the Windows DOS window. Only DOS can be running for this command to work.

```
e:\dosutils\autoboot.bat
```

If neither of these options is feasible for you, you can use the install floppy disk (see the previous section on creating a boot disk). This is perhaps the most fail-safe method of installing Linux. Insert the Linux install disk into your floppy drive and reboot your computer. Performing a cold boot is best: turn off the computer completely and then turn it on again with the install disk in the floppy drive.

The installation program will start, presenting you with an Introduction screen. After a moment, the following prompt will appear at the bottom of your screen:

```
boot:
```

Press ENTER. (If necessary, you can enter boot parameters as described in the Red Hat manual.) Configuration information will fill your screen as the installation program attempts to detect your hardware components automatically.

Your system then detects the type of CD-ROM you have. If it cannot do so, your system will ask you to select yours from a list. If you have an IDE CD-ROM and the system fails to detect it, this may be because it is not connected on the default HDC device interface. You must restart the installation, providing the CD-ROM device name at the boot prompt.

```
Boot: linux hdx=cdrom
```

Replace the x with one of the following letters, depending on the interface the unit is connected to, and whether it is configured as master or a slave:

a First IDE controller master

b First IDE controller slave

c Second IDE controller master

d Second IDE controller slave

As an alternative to the CD-ROM installation, you can copy the entire CD-ROM to a Windows partition (one large enough), and then install using that partition instead of the CD-ROM. You need to know the device name of the partition and the directory to which you should copy the CD-ROM files. When asked to choose the installation method, you can select hard disk. You then have to specify the partition name and the directory.

Red Hat Installation

The first screen asks you to select the language you want to use. Click the language you want and then click the Next button. On the following screen, you will configure your keyboard. The screen displays lists for selecting your keyboard model, layout, and options. A generic model works in most cases.

On the next screen, you configure your mouse (see Figure 2-1). The screen lists the different mouse brands along with specific models. Click a + symbol to expand a model list. Select your mouse. You can also check a button at the bottom of the screen to have a two-button mouse emulate a three-button mouse. A generic two-button PS/2 or serial mouse will work if your model is not listed. If you select a serial mouse, you also must select the port and device to which it is connected.

Now that the keyboard and mouse are configured, you can begin the installation process. The next screen displays a Welcome to Red Hat message. Click the Next button to continue.

On the following screen, labeled Install Type, you select whether you want to install a new system or upgrade a previous one. On the panel labeled Install Type, click the button for either Install or Upgrade. You use the Upgrade option to upgrade a version of Red Hat (2.0 or higher) that is already on your system. All your current configuration files are preserved in files with a **.rpmsave** extension. You can use them to restore your system configuration. With new software versions, configuration files sometimes change format, so be sure to check for any changes.

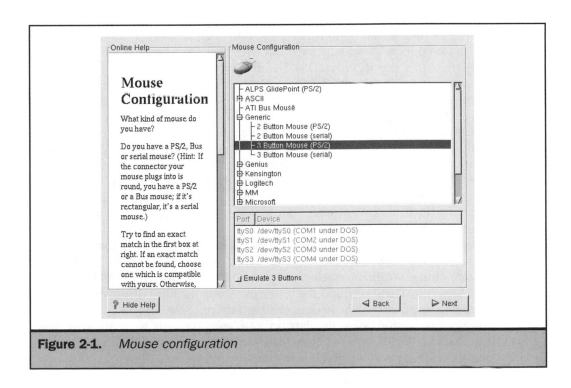

Figure 2-1.   *Mouse configuration*

Should you select the Install option, you can then specify a different class of installation. You can select a workstation installation, a server installation, or a custom installation. Most first-time users will want to use a custom installation. The other classes of installation also perform automatic formatting of your partitions, erasing all current data on them. Use them only if you are sure of what you are doing. Workstation installations automatically erase any and all Linux partitions on your computer and use them to install Red Hat Linux. Be very careful with the Server installation. The Server installation will erase all partitions on your computer hard drives, including Windows and OS/2 partitions. The Server installation is intended for computers that will operate as dedicated servers, performing only network server tasks. Should you be using Windows on the same computer that you want to use Linux on, do *not* select the Server option.

The workstation installations will install all the needed applications for a Linux workstation with either the Gnome or KDE desktop as your default desktop. Server installation will install server programs to enable your Linux system to operate as a network server. The custom installation enables you to choose what software packages you want installed on your system.

Partitions

If you chose the Custom install option, then an Automatic Partitioning screen is displayed with two options, Manually partition with Disk Druid and Manually partition with fdisk [for experts only]. Disk Druid is an easy-to-use partition manager that employs a graphical interface. fdisk is the Linux fdisk utility that uses a simple command line interface. Use fdisk only if you are familiar with it already.

If you chose the Workstation or Server options, then an Automatic Partitioning screen is displayed with three options, Manually partition with Disk Druid, Manually partition with fdisk, and Automatically partition and Remove data. If you choose either manual partition entry, then you can control and select the partitions you want set up and formatted. If you choose the Remove data entry, then the Workstation install will erase any current Linux partition on your system, whereas the Server install will erase all your partitions (including Windows). Should you want to back out to select a custom installation, you can just click the Back button.

If you choose a Custom installation or the Manual partition in the Automatic Partitioning screen, the Partitions screen is displayed (see Figure 2-2). Here, you can manually create Linux partitions or select the one where you want to install Red Hat. The top pane lists your Partitions, and the lower pane lists the hard drives on your computer (many computers will have only one hard drive). Selecting a hard drive will list its partitions. The button below the Partitions pane enables you to create, edit, and delete partitions. The Partitions screen is actually an interface for the Red Hat Disk Druid program, used in previous Red Hat installation programs.

Figure 2-2.   *Partitions*

You are advised to set up at least two Linux partitions, a swap partition and a root partition. The *root partition* is where the Linux system and application files are installed. If you have a large hard drive, one over 8.4GB, you should set up another partition to be used to boot your Linux system. This "boot" partition will hold the Linux kernel and other files needed to start up Linux. Application and other files will be installed on the root partition. If you are sharing a large hard drive with other systems like Windows, be sure to install the Linux boot partition within the first 8.4GB of the hard drive. Boot loaders like LILO can only boot systems that are located within the first 8.4GB. The root and swap partitions, however, can be located anywhere on the hard drive, even past the first 8.4GB.

Except for the swap partition, when setting up a Linux partition you must specify a mount point. A *mount point* is a directory where the files on that partition are connected to the overall Linux file structure for your system. The mount point for your root partition is the root directory, represented by a single slash, /. The mount point for your boot partition is the path **/boot**.

When creating a new partition, you must specify its size. Be sure enough space is available for it on your hard drive. If not, you will receive a Unallocated Requested

Partition message. You can free space by deleted unwanted partitions already set up or edit the new partition's entry and change its requested size. Check the entry for your hard drive in the Drive summaries pane to find out how much free space is available on your hard drive.

To create the new partition, click the Add button to display a dialog box where you can enter the mount point, the size (in megabytes), the partition type, and the hard disk on which you want to create the partition. For the size, you can select a "Grow to fill disk" option to have the partition automatically expand to the size of the remaining free space on the disk. You can have this option selected for more than one partition. In that case, the partition size will be taken as a required minimum and the remaining free space will be shared equally among the partitions. For partition type, select Linux native for standard Linux partitions and select the Linux swap type for your swap partition. You can even use Disk Druid to create DOS partitions. To make any changes later, you can Edit a partition by selecting it and clicking the Edit button.

If you want to change the size of partition that has already been created, you must first delete it and then create a new one. Remember, deleting a partition erases all data on it. To delete a partition, select it and click the Delete button.

Once you create your partitions, you can format them. The next screen is the Choose Partitions to Format screen, which lists the Linux partitions on your system. Click the ones you want to format. You should format all new Linux partitions and any old ones you may have that you no longer need. However, if you already have a Linux system and have installed Red Hat on it, then you will most likely have several Linux partitions already. Some of these may be used for just the system software, such as the boot and root partitions. These should be formatted. Others may have extensive user files, such as a /home partition that normally holds user home directories and all the files they have created. You should *not* format such partitions.

LILO

Once your partitions are prepared, you install LInux LOader (LILO). You use LILO to start Red Hat Linux from your hard drive. You can also use it to start any other operating system you may have installed on your computer, such as Windows. You have two choices for where to install LILO: the Master Boot Record (MBR) or the root partition. The recommended place is the MBR.

The LILO Configuration screen lists various LILO options (see Figure 2-3). Here you can select where to install LILO (MBR or root partition), specify a label for the Linux system (usually linux), decide whether it is to be the default system (if you have more than one operating system), and specify any kernel parameters your system may require for Linux. At the top of the screen are options for creating a boot disk and *not* to install LILO. The boot disk option is automatically selected for you. You can use the boot disk to start your Linux system should there ever be a problem starting from your hard drive (for example, if you reinstall Windows on your hard drive, LILO is removed and you will need to use the boot disk to start Linux so that you can reinstall LILO).

Figure 2-3. *LILO Configuration*

The bottom of the screen displays a list of bootable partitions. Selecting one enables you to enter specific information for the partition in the top pane, such as the label you want to give to this partition and any kernel parameters required. The root or boot Linux partition is usually given the label "linux"; a Window partition could be given a label like "win."

Network Configuration

The Network Configuration screen displays tabbed panes in the top half for the different network devices on your computer (see Figure 2-4). Click the tab for the device you want to configure. For computers already connected to a network with an Ethernet card, the tab is usually labeled eth0. Such a tab displays a pane with boxes for entering the various IP addresses for the network accessible through this device. These include the device's IP address (usually your computer's IP address), the network's address, and the broadcast address, along with the netmask. You could have a computer with several Ethernet devices, each connected to a different (or the same) network. If your network supports DHCP, then you can click the DHCP button instead of manually entering these addresses. DHCP automatically provides your computer with the needed IP addresses. You can also choose to have the device activated when your system boots or not.

Figure 2-4. *Network Configuration*

The bottom pane holds boxes for entering the IP addresses for your network's Domain Name Servers (DNS) and Gateway computer, as well as the host name you want to give to your system. In the Hostname box, enter the fully qualified domain name for your computer.

On the Time Zone Configuration screen, you have the option of setting the time by using a map to specify your location or by using Universal Coordinated Time (UTC) entries.

On the Account Configuration screen, as shown in Figure 2-5, you can set the root password for the root account on our system. This is the account used for system administration operations, such as installing software and managing users. On this same screen, you can also add ordinary user accounts. In the boxes for the Account name, password, and Full name, enter the username, the password for that account, and the user's full name. Then click the Add button to create the account. You will see it displayed in the following list. To add another user, first click the New button, enter the new user's information, and then click the Add button. You can add as many users as you wish. You can also add users at any time after you install your system.

Figure 2-5. *Account Configuration*

On the Authentication Configuration screen, you can add further levels of security for passwords. MD5 allows for long passwords up to 256 characters and shadow passwords that will save password information in a secure file on your system. Also, if your network supports the Network Information Service (NIS), you can enable the service and enter its domain name and server address.

For Custom installations, you are presented with a Package Group Selection screen. Here you can choose to install whole sets of packages for different categories. For example, you can install all the packages you would need for the Gnome desktop or the X Window System. To install all packages, select the Everything entry at the end of the list.

If you want to select individual software packages, click the Select individual packages check box. This will display a new screen with two panes, the left showing an expandable tree of software categories and the right displaying icons for the individual software packages. To select a package for installation, double-click it. You can also single-click, and then click the "Select package for installation" check box below. Whenever you single-click any icon, a description of the package is displayed on the bottom pane. Many software packages require that other software packages also be installed. Should you not have these already selected for installation, then an Unresolved dependencies screen is displayed showing the packages you need to install. You can then select them for installation.

X Window System Configuration

The X Configuration screen then configures the X Window System. This enables GUI interfaces, such as Gnome and KDE. X configuration uses the Xconfigurator utility to detect your video card and monitor automatically.

On the Monitor Configuration screen, you select your monitor (see Figure 2-6). Initially, Xconfigurator will automatically probe your monitor and select a make and model from those listed on the screen. Check to see that the correct monitor is selected. If not, find its entry and click it. Monitor entries are organized by company in a expanding tree. If you have a Hewlett-Packard monitor, click the + symbol next to the HP entry to list all the monitors that Hewlett-Packard makes. Then click your model. When you select a monitor, the horizontal and vertical boxes at the bottom of the screen will display your monitor's horizontal sync range and vertical sync range (these values are generally available in the documentation that accompanies your monitor or from your monitor's vendor or manufacturer).

Figure 2-6. Monitor Configuration

If your monitor does not appears on the list, then select a Generic entry (usually Generic multisync). Xconfigurator will then supply horizontal and vertical frequency values in the labeled boxes at the bottom of the screen. Check that the correct horizontal and vertical frequencies are entered. If you enter values that are too high, you could overclock your monitor and possibly damage or destroy it. Do not select a monitor "similar" to your monitor unless you are certain the monitor you are selecting does not exceed the capabilities of your monitor.

On the X Configuration screen, you complete your X Window System configuration by selecting your video card, resolution, default desktop, and login preference (see Figure 2-7). Xconfigurator will initially probe your card and select it from a list of video cards shown on the screen. Check to see if your card is selected. If not, locate your card in the list and click it. You will need to know the brand and model number for your card. If your video card does not appear on the list, XFree86 may not support it. If you have technical knowledge about your card, however, you may choose Unlisted Card and attempt to configure it by matching your card's video chipset with one of the available X servers. If the video card you select has a video clock chip, Xconfigurator presents a list of clock chips. The recommended choice is No Clockchip Setting because, in most cases, XFree86 can automatically detect the proper clock chip.

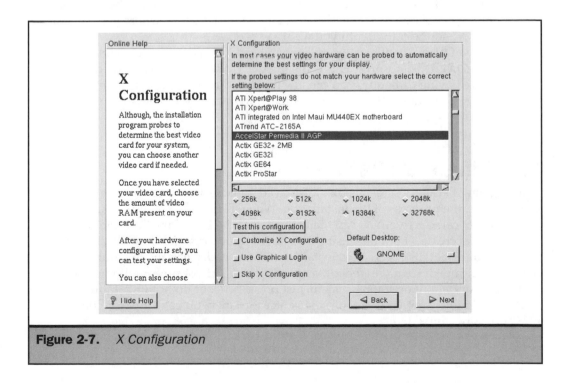

Figure 2-7.   *X Configuration*

If you know how much video memory is on your video card, you can check the appropriate check box for that amount located below the list of video cards. If an incorrect amount is selected, you can select the appropriate one.

Then click the Test this configuration setting to run your X Window System. If all goes well, a screen will appear with a button to click if it is running properly. You will then return to the X Configuration screen.

You can choose to use a graphical login instead of the command line login. Click the graphical login check box. If you choose this option, when you start, the Gnome Desktop Manager (GDM) will start and display a login screen where you can enter the username and password. A Sessions submenu in the Options menu enables you to choose whether to start KDE, Gnome, or the AnotherLevel window manager. When you log in, your desktop automatically starts up. When you log out of your desktop, the GDM login window is redisplayed. Select Shutdown from the Options menu to shut down Linux. To set your default desktop, select either Gnome or KDE from the Default Desktop pop-up menu.

If you do not choose this option, you will start up with the command line interface. Enter the username at the login prompt and the password at the password prompt to log in. Use **startx** to start Gnome and **switchdesk** to switch to KDE or AnotherLevel. The **logout** command logs out, and CTRL-ALT-DEL will shut down Linux. While you are logged in, you can also enter the **halt** command to shutdown Linux.

You can specify your card's resolution and color depth by clicking the Customize X Configuration check box. A screen appears, after you click Next, where you can enter the resolution and the color depth you want.

When you finish, Xconfigurator will generate an X Window System configuration file called **/etc/X11/XF86Config**. This is the file the X Window System uses to start up.

If you are having difficulty, you can always click the Skip X Configuration check box to skip the X Window System configuration and perform it later, after you have installed your system.

Finishing Installation

The Installing Packages screen is then displayed, which shows each package as it is installed and the progress of the installation. When the installation finishes, the Next button will become active. You can then move on to the Boot Disk Creation screen. Here, you can create a boot disk using a standard floppy disk (or you can elect to skip it). Once your Boot disk is created, installation is finished. Click the Exit button of the final screen. Your system will reboot, displaying a LILO boot prompt. If you set up Linux as your default operating system, just press ENTER or do nothing. Linux will then start up. If Linux is not your default, then enter the label you gave it when configuring LILO (usually "linux").

When your system restarts, the login prompt or the GDM login screen will appear, depending upon whether you chose to have the X Window System start up automatically. You can then log into your Linux system using a login name and a password for any of the users you have set up. If you log in as the root user, you can perform administrative operations, such as installing new software or creating more users. To log in as the root user, enter **root** at the login prompt and the root user password at the password prompt.

If you are upgrading from a previously installed Red Hat Linux system and used the upgrade options, you can restore your previous configuration files, which are currently saved on your new system with the **.rpmsave** extension to their filenames. If you are upgrading from a another Linux system and have manually saved configuration files, you can restore them now. Mount the floppy disk on which you saved these files and copy the configuration files to your new system. You can also restore any **tar** archived files and packages with the **tar xvMf/dev/fd0** command.

When you finish, log out of your account using the command **logout**. You then need to shut down the entire system. From the GDM login window, select Shutdown from the Options menu. From the command line interface, either hold down the CTRL and ALT keys and press DEL (CTRL-ALT-DEL) or enter the **halt** command. Remember, you must always use CTRL-ALT-DEL to shut down the system. Never turn it off as you do with DOS.

Should your Linux system fail to boot at any time, you can use the boot disk you created to perform an emergency boot. You can also use the install disk and, at the boot prompt, enter: **boot rw root=** with the device name of the root Linux partition. For example, if your root Linux partition is **/dev/hda4**, then you would enter **boot rw root=/dev/hda4** as shown here:

```
boot> boot rw root=/dev/hda4
```

The
Complete
Reference

Chapter 3

Installing OpenLinux

This chapter describes the installation procedure for the OpenLinux CD-ROM provided with this book. The installation includes the Linux operating system, a great many Linux applications, and a complete set of Internet servers. Different Linux distributions usually have their own installation programs. The Caldera OpenLinux installation program is designed to be efficient and brief while installing as many features as possible.

OpenLinux provides a very detailed installation manual both on the CD-ROM provided with this book and at its Web site, along with extensive documentation. The manual consists of Web pages that you can view using any browser. They include detailed figures and step-by-step descriptions. It is advisable for you to check this manual before you install. This chapter presents all the steps in the installation process but is not as detailed as the OpenLinux manual.

You can easily view the documentation and installation guide located on your OpenLinux CD-ROM using any Windows system. Start Windows and then place the CD-ROM in the CD-ROM drive. This automatically starts the Caldera Systems OpenLinux tools window with several choices. Select the Browse This CD-ROM entry. This then opens your Web browser and displays a Welcome page with options for Online Docs, Frequent Questions, and Special Offers. Select Online Docs. This will actually access the documentation on your CD-ROM. You do not have to be connected to the Internet. The Online Docs page lists the entries for documentation. For the OpenLinux installation guide, select the first entry. This will give you detailed instructions on preparing for installation, a step-by-step description of the process, and initial configuration information.

OpenLinux 2.4 Getting Started Guide

Bear in mind that the chapters referring to PartitionMagic do not apply to the version of OpenLinux provided by this book. This CD-ROM does not include PartitionMagic or BootMagic. You have to use the **defrag** and **fips** utilities described in the previous chapter to set up partitions for hard disks that will share both Windows and Linux.

On the Caldera Web site at **www.calderasystems.com**, click Support and click Links to Resources. This displays a list of online resources. Click Caldera Systems Online Manuals & Documentation to display a list of online documentation, including the eDesktop 2.4 Users Guide.

Installing Linux involves several steps. First, you need to determine whether your computer meets the basic hardware and software requirements. These days, most Intel-based PC computers do. Then you will need certain technical specifications about the hardware you use, such as your monitor type and the type of chips used in your video card. This kind of information is available in the manuals that came with the hardware. If you are connected to a local area network with an network card like Ethernet, you will have to know whether automatic network configuration is provided by DHCP or BOOTP, or know the network IP addresses and domain names for your computer and network.

If you want to have your Linux system share a hard drive with another operating system, you may need to resize your hard disk partitions. For a hard disk with existing Windows partitions, you use the Windows **defrag** utility to reorganize your file space and then use **fips** in the **col\tools\fips** directory on your OpenLinux CD-ROM to resize your partitions, freeing up space for Linux. See Chapter 2 for a discussion on preparing Windows partitions to share a hard disk with Linux.

You then need to prepare a boot disk with which you will start the installation program. Once the installation program begins, you simply follow the instructions, screen by screen. There are two installation programs that you can use, Lizard and LISA. Lizard is a new program with a much better interface, whereas LISA is an older program. The only disadvantage to using Lizard exists for those who want to have both Windows and Linux on the same hard disk. Unlike LISA, Lizard does not install LILO, the boot loader that lets you select which system to use, Linux or Windows. However, this is very easily remedied by running LISA after you install Linux, and having it just set up and install LILO. The Lizard install process is so much better than LISA that you will find it easier to use Lizard and just install LILO later.

The installation program progresses through several phases. First you create Linux partitions on your hard drive, and then you install the software packages. After that you can configure your network connection and then your X Windows server for graphical user interface support. Both X Windows and network configurations can be performed independently at a later time.

You have the option of installing just the operating system, the system with a standard set of applications, or all the software available on the CD-ROM. If you choose a standard installation, you can add the uninstalled software packages later. Chapter 4 describes how you can use the COAS utility or the Red Hat Package Manager to install, or even uninstall, the software packages.

Creating the OpenLinux Install Disks from Windows

The OpenLinux CD-ROM provided with this book is based on an enhanced version designed to install from a Windows system. This CD-ROM cannot do that. You need to create an install disk and boot the install disk to start the installation process. However, you can easily create the install disks using the Windows OpenLinux installation window. Start Windows, and then put your OpenLinux CD-ROM into your CD-ROM drive. Windows should automatically detect the CD-ROM and launches the Caldera Systems OpenLinux tools. This displays a window listing several options, including Browse The CD, View Our Web Site, and Install Products. Select Install Products. Of the options listed on this window, you can only choose one:

```
Create Floppy Install Disks
```

This window then displays four entries, two for Lizard installation disks and two for LISA. In each case, you will have to create two floppy disks, an install disk and a modules disk. The modules disk is for any kernel modules that may be needed for specialized hardware such as some SCSI adapters. For most systems, you will not need to use it. It is preferable to use the Lizard install process. For this, just click Create Lizard Install Disk to create your Lizard install disk, and for the Lizard modules disk, click Create Lizard Modules Disk. If you want to use LISA instead, you use the LISA entries to create LISA install and modules disks.

When you click a create disk entry, a DOS window opens up labeled rawrite. The window displays a prompt at which you enter your destination drive. On most systems, your floppy drive is your A drive. First place an empty formatted DOS disk in your floppy drive. Then enter the drive letter for your floppy drive and press ENTER. The install disk image for Lizard is then copied to the floppy disk. Do the same for the modules disk. As a precaution, you might also want to create the LISA disk, should you have trouble with Lizard.

Creating the OpenLinux Install Disks from DOS

If you do not have Windows, then you can use a DOS system to create your install disks. You create the Install disk using the MS-DOS program **rawrite** and an install disk image. On the OpenLinux CD-ROM, the LISA install disk images are in the **col\launch\ lisa\floppy** directory with **install.144** being the install image and **modules.144** the modules image. You can use the **rawrite** command in this directory in DOS to create the disk images. The Lizard install disks are located in **col\launch\floppy** and have the same filenames. You can also use the **rawrite** command to create the disks. Insert the OpenLinux CD-ROM into your CD-ROM drive. At your DOS prompt, change to your CD-ROM drive, using whatever the letter for that drive may be. For example, if your CD-ROM drive is the E drive, just type **e:** and press ENTER. Once you have changed to the CD-ROM drive, you then need to change to the **\col\launch\floppy** directory to create Lizard install disks. For LISA install disks, you change to the **\col\launch\lisa\ floppy** directory. The Install disk images are there, as well as the **rawrite** command you use to create the disks. Several install image files are designed for different types of floppy disks. Most PCs support 1.44MB floppy disks. For these, you use the **install.144** image file.

To create the install disk, insert a blank floppy disk into your floppy drive. Now start the **rawrite** command, which will actually write the disk image to your floppy disk. The **rawrite** command will first prompt you for the name of the disk image file you want to copy. Enter the full name of the install image file (in this example, **INSTALL.144**). The program will then ask you to enter the letter of the floppy drive where you put your floppy disk. On many systems this will be the A drive.

```
E:\> cd col\launch\floppy
E:\col\launch\floppy > rawrite
```

```
Enter source file name: INSTALL.144
Enter destination drive (A or B) and press enter: A
```

Press ENTER to confirm that you have a blank floppy disk in the drive. The **rawrite** command will then copy the image file to your disk, creating your install disk. When it finishes, remove your disk from the floppy drive. This is the disk that the installation procedure described later refers to as the Install disk.

You should also create a modules disk. This disk contains kernel modules that support certain hardware components. Most systems will not need to use the modules disk. But some, particularly those with SCSI components, may need to use it. Repeat the same process to make a modules disk. For example, for a 1.44MB floppy disk you would use the **modules.144** disk image.

Installing Linux with Lizard

Installing Linux involves several processes, beginning with creating Linux partitions, then loading the Linux software, configuring your X Windows interface, installing the Linux Loader (LILO) that will boot your system, and creating new user accounts. The Lizard and LISA install procedures perform the same tasks but use radically different interfaces. Both are described in this chapter, beginning with Lizard (Linux Installation Wizard).

Lizard provides a full-screen interface with mouse support that lets you easily select entries and move to the next screen much as you would using a Windows install wizard. Each screen has a right pane that describes in detail the actions to be take in that screen. For each screen there is also a Help button that will display detailed context help about the task performed by a particular screen. When you are finished with a screen, click its Next button to move to the next one. Much of the installation process is automatic, such as detecting your hardware components and X Window System configuration. There are very few entries that you actually have to make.

If you are installing Linux on a hard disk that will shared with another system such as Windows, then be sure you have already freed up space on the disk. See the previous chapter on preparing the hard disk.

Insert the Linux boot disk into your floppy drive, reboot your computer, and then CD-ROM into the CD-ROM drive. When the installation begins, OpenLinux opens a graphical display. Configuration information will fill your screen as the installation program attempts to detect your hardware components automatically. Should Linux have a problem identifying one of your components, that fact will be listed here. For example, OpenLinux will automatically detect your CD-ROM and know that you are using it to install OpenLinux. After the hardware detection is complete, the Caldera logo appears.

You are then provided with several Installation modes. The Standard install is recommended.

Standard Install Mode (recommended)	By default, the installation program (Lizard) automatically probes your computer's hardware to make the process more automatic.
Cautious Install Mode	Cautious mode reduces the level of hardware probing, asking you to confirm the graphics card, monitor, and video mode selection, and makes no attempt to configure your X server.
Expert Install Mode	Expert mode automatically probes all hardware, but then allows you to change all settings before actual installation.
Unattended Install Mode	This mode automates the process of installing OpenLinux from an Install Server.
VESA Install Mode	This mode forces Lizard to perform the installation in a very simple graphics mode.
Non-Graphic Install Mode	This mode installs OpenLinux using an older, text-only installation program called LISA.

The next screen displays a list of languages to choose from. If your mouse is not working at this point, use the TAB and arrow keys to make your selection, though on most systems you can use your mouse.

The next screen configures your mouse so that you can use it to make selections in the following screen (see Figure 3-1). First, move your mouse. Then select the type of port your mouse is connected to, PS/2 or Serial (most Pentium II systems have PS/2 mice). If you have a serial mouse, then select the serial port it is connected to, usually the first serial port, **/dev/ttyS0** (COM1). Then, from the drop-down menu, select the entry that best describes your mouse. You can even check your mouse by clicking the keys on the keypad. Click Next when you are finished to go to the next screen.

On the Select keyboard type screen, you select your keyboard type and language.

On the Select video mode screen, you select the video resolution, refresh rate, color depth combination that you want for your monitor and video card (see Figure 3-2). Caldera automatically detects your monitor and video card. Click the Test this resolution button to make sure your selection will work. If you cannot find a resolution you want or cannot get it to work, pick the most basic one for now. You can later configure your X Window System with more precision using lizardx or XF86Setup after the installation.

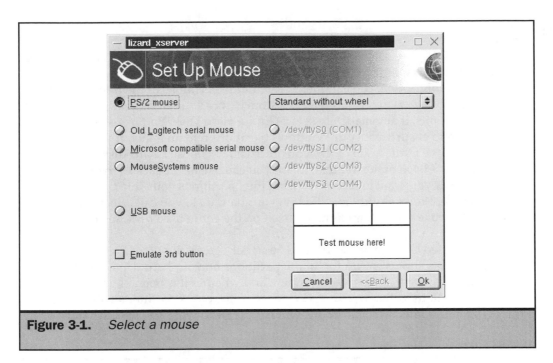

Figure 3-1. *Select a mouse*

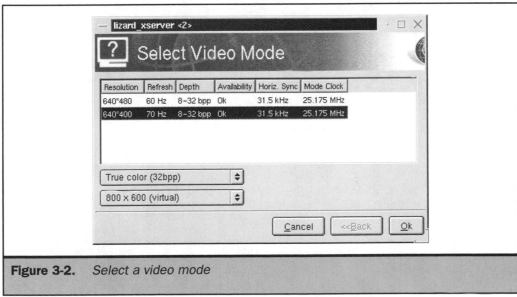

Figure 3-2. *Select a video mode*

Partitions

On the Select Target screen, you select the kind of partitions you want to install Linux on. If you are sharing the hard disk between Linux and Windows, always select Custom. With this option, you can then create Linux partitions in the free space on your hard disk. Be very careful to select Custom before you select Next. If Lizard finds no Linux partitions, it automatically selects Entire Hard Disk. You have to manually select Custom to ensure that your Windows partitions remain intact. If you accidentally move to the next screen, you are asked to choose a hard disk to prepare for Linux. There is a Back button on this screen you can use to get back to the Installation Target screen. If you want to just overwrite Linux partitions you already set up for a older version of Linux already installed on your hard disk, you can select Prepared Partitions. If you are installing Linux by itself on the entire hard disk, select Entire Hard Disk.

If you selected Custom, the Partition Hard Disk screen shown in Figure 3-3 is displayed. This shows entries for all the partitions on your hard drive. There are fields for the size, system type, mount point, and whether it is bootable or not. Your Windows partitions will have a DOS/Windows type. Linux partitions will have a Linux type, and Linux swap partitions will have a Swap type. The first IDE hard drive

Figure 3-3. *The Lizard Partition Hard Disk screen*

will have a device name of **hda**, and the first SCSI hard drive will have a device name of **sda**. Partition numbers are attached to the device name. The first partition in the IDE hard drive is **hda1**, the second is **hda2**, the third, **hda3**, and so on. The first partition in a SCSI disk is **sda1**, the second, **sda2**, and so on.

You will see entries for the swap and Linux partitions, but you still have to define them and set their sizes. Double-click an entry to display a window where you can enter the size and the mount point. A top section labeled Partition Boundaries will have two boxes, the left one labeled Start and the right one labeled End. To set the size, you will use these two boxes, one for the starting cylinder and the second for the ending cylinder (a cylinder is a segment of space on your hard disk). You specify the size of a partition by selecting its start and ending cylinders.

You should leave the Start value untouched, as this is determined automatically for you; it is the hard disk's first empty cylinder. The End cylinder can have any number larger than the first cylinder. As you enter a number for the end cylinder, you will see the size in megabytes displayed next to it. The partition should be from 300MB for the smallest installation to at least 2GB for the largest installation. The smallest OpenLinux installation is 160MB, and the largest, 1.4GB. Be sure to specify the mount point. If you want to use more than one Linux partition, you can add them here. When you are finished, click Next.

You then select the System Type. This can be linux, dos, or swap. For a Linux partition, select the linux type, and swap for your Swap partition. For a Mount Point, you would usually select /.

If you have trouble setting up your partition, you can always use LISA to create them with the Linux fdisk utility.

1. Start the installation process with the LISA floppy disk and follow the instructions in the next section up to and including the point of creating your Linux partitions (see Chapter 2 for instructions on using fdisk).

2. You will then have to restart your system, but you can then use Lizard. Take out the LISA disk and put the Lizard one back in.

3. When you get to the Installation Target screen, you can then skip the Custom Partitions screen and select the Prepared Partitions entry instead.

4. If the Prepared Partitions entry will not let you select it, then your partitions were not set up. Redo the process and make sure you write the partition configuration in fdisk.

The Select Root Partition screen will list your Native and Swap Linux partitions. If you have only one Linux partition, it will be shown and selected. If you have several, you can choose on which to install your Linux system.

The Partition Information screen is used to format your Linux partitions. The screen shows the Linux partitions you set up on your hard drive. To format them, click the Format Chosen Partitions button at the bottom of the screen.

Package Installation

You are now ready to install OpenLinux. The Select Software screen lets you choose a minimal (160MB), recommended (500MB), or full (1.4GB) installation. Click the one you want. Recommended is selected by default. When you click Next, the installation process will begin as packages are copied over to your Linux partitions. As packages are copied, you can continue with the remainder of the installation process. You will see a progress bar at the bottom of the screen showing the current percentage installed. Once the installation of the packages begins, you will notice that the install procedure for the next step may become sluggish. This is nothing to be concerned about. Just wait for a response.

The Set Root Password screen shows two prompts for entering the password for the root user, the user that performs system administration functions.

The Set Login Names screen then lets you define users for your system. (You can always define them later when you have your system running.) At the boxes provided, enter the user's real name, login name, password, and login shell. Then click Add User to add the user. You can add as many users as you want.

Networking

The Set Up Networking screen shown in Figure 3-4 then lets you enter network information for a local area network (LAN) connected through an Ethernet card. If you

Figure 3-4.   *The Lizard Set Up Networking dialog box*

use a modem to dial in instead, click the No Ethernet entry. First enter a fully qualified host name for your computer in the Hostname box in the lower half of the screen. Include the host and domain names as in **turtle.mytrek.com**.

At the top of the screen are boxes for network addresses needed if you are connected to a local area network with an Ethernet card. If you use a dial-up ISP, you can skip this part. If your network provides network configuration with DHCP, select its entry at the top of the window. If you have to enter the network information yourself, select Ethernet Configured Statically. Then enter the IP address, name server, gateways, and netmask addresses.

- In the Setup Modem screen, you can select your modem type, device, speed, and options. This screen appears if you checked No Ethernet in the previous screen. In the Setup Internet Provider screen, you can select your Internet provider from a list and then enter your login, password, and connection information (see Figure 3-5).

- The Setup Printer screen will then detect your printer. Be sure it is turned on and connected. Check the model type and the paper size. Then click the Add button. Click Test to check that the printer connection is working.

- In the Choose Time Zone screen, select your time zone from the drop-down list and whether your hardware clock is local or GMT.

Figure 3-5.   *Set up an Internet provider*

- The next screen provides entertainment as you wait for your packages to finish installing. When the progress bar at the bottom reaches 100 percent, click Finish.

- The installation is finished; your system will reboot with Linux.

If you use Lizard for the installation , the K Display Manager (KDM) is automatically installed. Whenever Linux starts, it will display a login window with boxes for the login name and password. To log in as the root user, enter **root** and the root password you specified during installation. This will start the K desktop automatically. When you log out of the K desktop, you return to the KDM window. Click the Shutdown button to shut down the system.

If you have installed both Linux and Windows on your system, either on the same hard disk or on different ones if you have more than one, you will now have to install the LILO boot loader that will let you select the system you want to use by default whenever you boot your system. Follow the instructions in the following section to install LILO.

Installing LILO with LISA

If you had difficulty installing LILO, you can use the Linux Installation and System Administration (LISA) program to install it if Linux is sharing your hard disks with another system like Windows. First log in as the root user. This will start up the K Desktop. LISA is a screen-based utility that you run from the command line interface. You can either click the terminal icon in the KDE panel to start a terminal window and then run LISA there, or you can switch to the command line interface with the CTRL-ALT-F1 keys. This provides a much larger screen. Use CTRL-ALT-F7 to return to Gnome.

LISA is a simple menu-driven tool that you start from the command line or a terminal window by entering the command **lisa**.

```
# lisa
```

The UP ARROW and DOWN ARROW keys move from one menu entry to another. Use the TAB key to move from one button to another. RIGHT ARROW and LEFT ARROW let you select either the Call or Continue button. You know you've selected a button if its letters are white. To select a menu entry, move to the entry you want, make sure the Call button is selected, and then press ENTER. The Continue button will move back to the previous menu.

The System Configuration entry in the LISA main menu brings you into other menus for adding to or changing features of your system configuration.

1. Select the Configure boot manager entry. This will start the LILO configuration. You will be first asked what partition you want to install LILO on. A screen is

displayed showing partitions where you can install LILO. You should always choose the Master Boot Record, unless you are already using a boot loader for another system like OS/2. In that case, choose the first Linux partition.

2. The next screen then shows your bootable partitions and asks you to choose the system you want to start as a default. This is usually Linux or DOS. The Linux system is identified as **/boot/vmlinuz** (Linux kernel image). Your DOS or Windows 95/98 system will include the term DOS with Windows in it.

3. You are then asked to enter a label for that system. A default term will be displayed for you, DOS for DOS/Windows 95 and Linux for Linux. To use the default label, choose OK by pressing ENTER. You can backspace and type in another name if you wish.

4. If you choose the Linux system, then any special hardware boot parameters that you had to specify are displayed. If you had no special hardware configuration problems, this entry will be blank. Choose OK to continue.

5. You can now make additional entries for other operating systems. The screen will list all the systems on your hard drives, DOS as well as Linux. If you have both DOS and Linux on your system, you now need to choose the other operating system. For example, if you chose DOS for your default system, you would now have to choose your Linux system, and vice versa (the Linux system is labeled /boot/**vmlinuz**).

6. Choose the other operating system, DOS or Linux. You are then prompted to enter a name for this other operating system. If you are now choosing Linux, the term Linux will be displayed for you and you can just choose OK. Otherwise, enter the label you want to give this other operating system. You can repeat the steps for adding new labels for as many operating systems as you have. Most people would have no more than two, DOS and Linux. If, however, you should have a third operating system on your hard disk, choose its partition and repeat the previous steps.

7. Once you have finished making entries, choose the entry No further entries to add to LILO, and then press ENTER.

8. Your **lilo.conf** file will then be displayed. This is the file that actually configures LILO. You will see entries for Linux and other operating systems that you entered, such as DOS. Press ENTER to confirm installation of LILO.

9. You are then asked to install LILO as configured. Press Y or ENTER to do so.

10. When LILO finishes its installation, press ENTER to continue.

11. You may then be asked to mark the LILO partition as active. Press ENTER to do so.

12. You can then select the Continue button to return to the main menu. You can now log out and shut down. When you restart, you will be prompted by LILO with a boot prompt. Enter the label of the system you want to start.

Once LILO is installed, you will first be presented with a boot prompt whenever you start your computer. At the prompt, enter the label for the system you want, such as Linux or DOS. These are labels that were assigned in the LILO install process. If you enter nothing, then after a few moments, the default system starts.

```
boot: linux
```

Configuring the X Window System with lizardx

If you are dissatisfied with Caldera's automatic X Window System configuration, you can re-install and configure it yourself. You can do this with Xconfigurator, XF86Setup, lizardx, xf86cfg, or xf86config. xf86config is a simple line-based configuration utility. lizardx is a Caldera utility that provides a full-screen interface for configuring X. This is the interface described here. If you have trouble with it, try the other utilities. Before you start a configuration tool like lizardx, Xconfigurator, or XF86Setup, check your monitor hardware documentation for the vertical and horizontal frequencies of your monitor. The frequencies could be single numbers or ranges. For example, the synchronization frequencies for an NEC 3V are 31–50 for horizontal and 55–90 for vertical.

 Before you choose a monitor frequency (Hz), check your hardware documentation. If you set the frequency higher than your monitor supports, you can cause serious damage.

To configure your X Window System interface with lizardx, you enter the command **lizardx** at the shell prompt.

```
$ lizardx
```

On the first two screens, you select the type of mouse and the keyboard you use and its language (see Figure 3-6).

The lizardx utility then automatically determines the type of video card you have and, in the Select Video Card screen shown in Figure 3-7, displays it along with minimum configuration specifications. The Card Type drop-down menu will hold the make and model of your video card. The Video RAM box will indicate the video RAM on the card.

1. If your card is not already selected, click the Probe button to have Lizard detect your card.

2. A message box will warn you that the screen will go blank for a few seconds as your card is probed. Choose Probe in the message box to continue.

3. When probing is finished, another message box tells you probing was successful. If the video RAM on your card is more than what is selected on the panel, you can select the correct size. If lizardx is unable to detect your card or

INTRODUCTION

Figure 3-6.   *The lizardx keyboard*

detects the wrong card, you can select a generic card with similar capabilities. Click OK to return to the Video Card screen.

4. Click Next to continue.

On the Select Monitor screen, you select the type of monitor you have (see Figure 3-8). The screen displays an extensive list of monitor brand names.

1. Scroll through the list until you find the brand name for your monitor, such as NEC or Iiyama.

2. Then click the + check box to the left of the brand name. This expands to a list of all monitor models for that brand.

3. Select the one for your monitor. When you select a monitor, the hardware specification boxes at the bottom of the screen are automatically filled.

If your monitor is not on the list, then enter its hardware specification in the boxes at the bottom of the screen. You need to enter the horizontal and vertical

Figure 3-7. The Lizard Select Video Card screen

Figure 3-8. The lizardx monitor screen

Figure 3-9.   *The lizardx video mode*

sync ranges. Be sure these do not exceed the actual ranges of your monitor, or you could damage it.

The next screen (Figure 3-9) lets you select your video mode. Here you can choose from all the possible modes that your card supports. Fields specify the resolution, color depth, refresh rate, and horizontal sync. A standard 15-inch monitor usually uses an 800 × 600 resolution and a 24-bit color depth, whereas 17- and 19-inch monitors use a 1024 × 768 resolution and a 24-bit color depth. Newer cards support a 32-bit color depth. Newer monitors can easily support 85 Hz refresh rates, whereas older ones may only go as high as 60 Hz. Once you select your mode, choose the color depth from the button at the bottom of the screen. You can click Test to see how the mode will be displayed on your monitor.

INTRODUCTION

The Complete Reference

Chapter 4

Interface Basics

To start using Linux, you must know how to access your Linux system and, once you are on the system, how to execute commands and run applications. Accessing Linux involves more than just turning on your computer. Once Linux is running, you have to log in to the system using a predetermined login name and password. Once on the system, you can start executing commands and running applications. You can then interact with your Linux system using either a command line interface or a *graphical user interface* (*GUI*). The Linux systems use desktops to provide a fully functional GUI with which you can use windows, menus, and icons to interact with your system.

Obtaining information quickly about Linux commands and utilities while logged in to the system is easy. Linux has several online utilities that provide information and help. You can access an online manual that describes each command or obtain help that provides more detailed explanations of different Linux features. A complete set of manuals provided by the Linux Documentation Project is on your system and available for you to browse through or print.

Note *To make effective use of your Linux system, you must know how to configure certain features. Administrative operations such as adding users, specifying network settings, accessing CD-ROM drives, and installing software can now be performed with user-friendly system tools.*

This chapter discusses how to access your Linux system, including logging in and out of user accounts, as well as starting the system and shutting it down. Linux commands and utilities are also covered, along with basic operations of the Gnome and KDE desktops. The chapter ends with an explanation of basic system administration operations, such as creating new user accounts and installing software packages.

User Accounts

You never directly access a Linux system. Instead, Linux sets up an interface called a *shell* through which you can interact. A Linux system can actually set up and operate several user shells at once, accommodating several users simultaneously. In fact, you can have many users working off the same computer running a Linux system. Each particular user appears to be the only one working on the system, as if Linux can set up several virtual computers and each user can then work on his or her own virtual computer. Such virtual computers are actually individually managed interfaces whereby each user interacts with the Linux system.

These user shells are frequently referred to as *accounts*. UNIX, which Linux is based on, was first used on large minicomputers and mainframes that could accommodate hundreds of users at the same time. Using one of many terminals connected to the computer, users could log in to the UNIX system using their login names and passwords. All of this activity was managed by system administrators. To gain access to the system, you needed to have a user account set up for you. This was commonly known as "opening an account." A system administrator created the account on the UNIX system, assigning a login name and password for it. You then used your account to log in and use the system.

Each account is identified by a login name with access protected by a password. Of course, you can access any account if you know its login name and password. On your Linux system, you can create several accounts, logging into different ones as you choose. Other people can access your Linux system, making use of login names and passwords you provide for them. They have their own accounts on your system. Recall that in the previous chapter on installing Linux, you created a login name and password for yourself. These are what you use to access Linux regularly. When you created the login name and password, you were actually creating a new user account for yourself.

Note   *You can, in fact, create other new user accounts using special system administration tools. These tools become available to you when you log in as the root user. The root user is a special user account reserved for system administration tasks, such as creating users and installing new software. Basic system administration operations are discussed briefly in Chapter 5, but they are discussed in detail in Chapters 29 through 39. For now, you only need your regular login name and password.*

Accessing Your Linux System

To access and use your Linux system, you must carefully follow required startup and shutdown procedures. You do not simply turn off and turn on your computer. If you have installed the Linux Loader, LILO, when you turn on or reset your computer, LILO first decides what operating system to load and run. You see the following prompt: enter **linux** to start up the Linux operating system:

```
LILO: linux
```

If, instead, you wait a moment or press the ENTER key, LILO loads the default operating system. (Recall that earlier you designated a default operating system.) If you want to run Windows instead, LILO gives you a moment at the prompt to type in the name you gave for Windows, such as dos or win.

You can think of your Linux operating system as operating on two different levels, one running on top of the other. The first level is when you start your Linux system, and the system loads and runs. It has control of your computer and all its peripherals. You still are not able to interact with it, however. After Linux starts, it displays a login prompt, waiting for a user to come along and log in to the system to start using it. To gain access to Linux, you have to log in first.

You can think of logging in and using Linux as the next level. Now you can issue commands instructing Linux to perform tasks. You can use utilities and programs, such as editors or compilers, or even games. Depending on a choice you made during installation, however, you may either be interacting with the system using a simple command line interface or using the desktop directly. There are both command line login prompts and graphical login windows. In the case of most Linux distributions such as Red Hat and Caldera, if you choose to use a graphical interface at the end of the installation, you are presented with a graphical login window at which you enter your login and password. If you choose not to use the graphical interface, you are presented with a simple command line prompt to enter your login name.

On the command line interface, you are presented with a simple prompt, such as a $ or # symbol. You type in a command and press ENTER to have the system perform actions. You can start up the GUI desktop from the command line interface, if you want. In Linux, the command **startx** starts the X Window System along with a GUI, which then enables you to interact with the system using windows, menus, and icons. On Red Hat, the **startx** command starts the Gnome desktop by default, though you can configure it to start up another desktop such as KDE or even a window manager. On Caldera, you use the kde command to start the KDE desktop. Once you shut down the GUI interface, you will return to your command line interface, still logged in.

Shutting down from a command line interface involves several steps. If you are using the GUI started from the command line interface, you first need to exit the GUI, returning to the command line interface. While still logged into your account, you can issue the halt command to shut down the system.

$ **halt**

Alternatively, you can use the shutdown command with the **-h** option. With the **-r** option, it shuts down the system and then reboots it. In the next example, the system is shut down after five minutes. To shut down the system immediately, you can use **+0** or the word **now** (see Chapter 29 for more details).

shutdown -h now

Shutting down involves a series of important actions, such as unmounting file systems and shutting down any servers (never simply turn off the computer).

You can also reboot your system from the login prompt. Logging out does *not* shut down the system: it is still running and has control of your machine. To shut down and reboot your system, hold down the CTRL and ALT keys, and then press the DEL key (CTRL-ALT-DEL). You system will go through the standard shutdown procedure and then reboot your computer. At this point it is safe to turn off your computer if you wish, or just let the system restart.

With the graphical login, your X Window System starts up immediately and displays a login window with boxes for a user login name and a password. When you enter your login name and password, and then click the OK or GO button, your default GUI starts up. On Red Hat, this is usually Gnome, and on Caldera this is KDE. On Red Hat, you can easily change this to KDE or another window manager. When you quit your GUI, you are also logging out of your account. The login window is then redisplayed. To shut down, you simply select the Shutdown entry in the Options menu or click Shutdown.

For Red Hat, graphical logins are handled by the *Gnome Display Manager* (*GDM*). The GDM manages the login interface along with authenticating a user password and login name, and then starting up a selected desktop. For Caldera and SuSE, graphical logins are handled by the KDE Display Manager (KDM). It operates much like GDM.

If problems ever occur using the X Window System display of the GUI interface, you can force a shutdown of the X Window System and the GUI with the CTRL-ALT-BACKSPACE keys. For GUI logins, it will restart the X Window System returning you to the login screen. Also, from the GDM and KDM, you can shift to the command line interface with the CTRL-ALT-F1 keys, and then shift back to the X Window System with the CTRL-ALT-F7 keys.

Gnome Display Manager: GDM

When the GDM starts up, it shows a login window with a box for login, as shown in Figure 4-1. Three menus are at the top of the window, labeled Session, Language, and System. To log in, enter your login name in the Login box and press ENTER. Then you are prompted to enter your password. Do so, and then press ENTER. By default, the Gnome desktop is then started up. When you log out from the desktop, you return to the GDM login window. To shut down your Linux system, click the System menu to display the entries Reboot or Halt. Select Halt to shut down your system.

Figure 4-1.   *The Gnome Display Manager*

INTRODUCTION

From the Session menu, you can select the desktop or window manager you want to start up. The following illustration shows the default entries for Red Hat's GDM Session menu. Here you can select KDE to start up the K Desktop instead of Gnome, among others. The Language menu lists a variety of different languages Red Hat Linux supports. Choose one to change the language interface.

KDE Display Manager: KDM

On systems that use the KDE Display Manager, the login window also shows boxes for Login and Password. To log in, enter your login name and password and then click Go. Your GUI starts up. When you log out of your GUI, you return to the KDM login screen. To shut down the system, click Shutdown to display a Shutdown dialog box from which you can choose to shut down, restart the X server, or shift to the console mode (command line interface).

You can use the Sessions drop-down menu to select the GUI to use. On OpenLinux, there is only an entry for the KDE. KDM also displays icons for different users defined on the system at the top of its login window. You can click a user's icon to have that user's name automatically entered in the login box. The root user has the image of a conductor. To log in as root, just click it and you will see the word "root" appear in the login box. Then enter the root user password in the Password box.

If you log in as the root user to the KDE desktop, you can then use the KDM Configuration Manager to configure the KDM interface. Select KDM Login Manager from the Applications menu in the Settings menu. Here you can select what background picture to use, the color of the login window, the icons to use for particular users, and the logo you want displayed. The Sessions panel lets you select what GUIs you want to access, provided they are installed on your system.

Command Line Interface

For the command line interface, you are initially given a login prompt. The system is now running and waiting for a user to log in and use it. You can enter your user name and password to use the system. The login prompt is preceded by the hostname you gave your system. In this example, the hostname is **turtle**. When you finish using Linux, you first log out. Linux then displays exactly the same login prompt, waiting for you or another user to log in again. This is the equivalent of the login window provided by the GDM. You can then log into another account.

```
Red hat Linux release 7.0 (Guinness)
Kernel 2.2.16-22 on i686

turtle login:
```

If you want to turn off your computer, you must first shut down Linux. If you don't shut down Linux, you could require Linux to perform a lengthy systems check when it starts up again. You shut down your system either of two ways. First, login to an account and then enter the **halt** command. This command will log you out and shut down the system (you can also use the **shutdown** command with the **-h** option, or the **-r** option to reboot).

```
$ halt
```

Alternatively you can reboot your system at the login prompt by holding down both the CTRL and ALT keys, and then pressing the DEL key, CTRL-ALT-DEL.

When you shut down, you will see several messages as Linux shuts itself down. It is not finished until you see the "System is halted" message. If you are rebooting, Linux will shut down and then reboot your system, at which time you can turn it off if you wish. The following steps include all the startup and shutdown procedures for the command line interface:

1. Boot your computer.

2. At the LILO prompt, type **linux** and press ENTER. (Or, press ENTER if Linux is your default.)

3. After a few messages, the login prompt appears, and then you can log in to the system and use it.

4. When you finish working in an account, you can log out. The login prompt then reappears, and you can login to another account.

5. If you are finished working on Linux and want to shut it down, enter the **halt** command while still logged into your account (**shutdown -r** will reboot).

6. At the login prompt, you can also shut down and reboot the system with CTRL-ALT-DEL. The system first shuts down and then restarts, at which time you can turn off your computer or just let the system start up again.

Once you log in to an account, you can enter and execute commands. Logging in to your Linux account involves two steps: entering your user name, and then your password. You already know what the login prompt looks like. Type in the login name for your user account. If you make a mistake, you can erase characters with the

BACKSPACE key. In the next example, the user enters the user name richlp and is then prompted to enter the password:

```
Red hat Linux release 7.0 (Guinness)
Kernel 2.2.16-22 on i686

turtle login: richlp
Password:
```

When you type in your password, it does not appear on the screen. This is to protect your password from being seen by others. If you enter either the login or password incorrectly, the system will respond with the error message "Login incorrect" and will ask for your login name again, starting the login process over. You can then reenter your login name and password.

Once you enter your user name and password correctly, you are logged in to the system. Your command line prompt is displayed, waiting for you to enter a command. Notice the command line prompt is a dollar sign (**$**), not a sharp sign (**#**). The **$** is the prompt for regular users, whereas the **#** is the prompt solely for the root user. In this version of Linux, your prompt is preceded by the hostname and the directory you are in. Both are bounded by a set of brackets.

```
[turtle /home/richlp]$
```

To end your session, issue the **logout** or exit commands. This returns you to the login prompt, and Linux waits for another user to log in.

```
$ logout
```

Once logged into the system, you have the option of starting an X Window System GUI, such as Gnome or KDE, and using it to interact with your Linux system. You start the X GUI by entering **startx** on the command line (on OpenLinux you enter **kde**). On Red Hat, you can use the **switchdesk** command, while in your desktop, to switch between Gnome, KDE, or the FVWM window manager. You make your selection and then quit the desktop to return to the command line interface. When you start up the GUI again, the desktop you selected is used.

Gnome Desktop

The Gnome desktop display shown in Figure 4-2 initially displays a panel at the bottom of the screen, as well as any icons for folders and Web pages initially set up by your distribution. For Red Hat, you see several Web page icons and a folder for your home directory. The panel at the bottom of the screen contains icons for starting applications, such as Netscape (the Netscape logo) and the Help system (the question mark logo). You can start applications using the main menu, which you display by clicking the Gnome icon (the image of a bare footprint), located on the left side of the panel.

When you click the folder for your home directory on your desktop or select the File Manager entry on the main menu, a file manager window opens showing your home directory. You can display files in your home directory and use the UP ARROW button to move to the parent directory. Back and Forward buttons move through previously displayed directories. In the location window you can enter the pathname for a directory to move directly to it. The file manager is also Internet-aware. You can use it to access remote FTP directories and to display or download their files (though it cannot display Web pages).

Figure 4-2.   *Gnome*

To move a window, click and drag its title bar or right-click its other borders. Each window supports Maximize, Minimize, and Close buttons, as well as a Stick Pin button. Double-clicking the title bar reduces the window to only its title bar; you can redisplay the window with another double-click. The desktop supports full drag-and-drop capabilities. You can drag folders, icons, and applications to the desktop or other file manager windows open to other folders. The move operation is the default drag operation. CTRL-click to copy files and middle-click to create links (a middle-click on a two-button mouse is holding down both buttons at the same time). In most cases, you would use links for desktop icons.

The panel also contains a pager for desktop areas, which appears as four squares. Clicking a square moves you to that area. You can think of the desktop work area as being four times larger than your monitor screen, and you can use the pager to display different parts. You can configure your Gnome interface, setting features such as the background by using the Gnome Control panel. Click the image of a toolbox on the panel. To execute a command using the command line interface, open a terminal window and click the image of a monitor on the panel. In that window, at the $ prompt, type in your command.

To quit the Gnome desktop, select the logout entry at the bottom of the main menu. If you entered from a login window, you are then logged out of your account and returned to the login window. If you started Gnome from the command line, you are returned to the command line prompt, still logged into your account.

Although Gnome is the default desktop for Red Hat, you can easily switch to the KDE desktop. Red Hat installs the complete KDE desktop as part of its distribution. If you are performing a graphical login using the Gnome Desktop Manager, you can use the Session menu on the Options button to select KDE as the desktop you want to run. If you are logging in to Linux using the command line interface, and then starting the desktop with the **startx** command, you can start the Gnome desktop and then use the Desktop Switcher located in the System directory to select KDE. When you quit Gnome and restart with the **startx** command, KDE is used as your desktop instead of Gnome. On KDE, you can then use the Desktop Switcher located in the Red Hat System menu to switch back to Gnome (see Figure 4-3).

The K Desktop

The KDE Desktop display, shown in Figure 4-4, initially displays a panel at the bottom of the screen, as well as any icons for folders and Web pages initially set up by your distribution. In the upper-left corner, you can see folder icons labeled Autostart, Trash, and Templates. When a user starts KDE for the first time, the KDE Setup Wizard is run, displaying a series of four windows advising you to set up icons for KDE Web pages, as well as CD-ROM and printer icons. Initially, the KDE Wizard enables you to choose a theme, such as a Windows, KDE standard, or Mac theme. You can change this later if you want. The next windows ask if you want to add icons for your CD-ROM and printer, and links to certain Web sites, such as the KDE Web site.

Figure 4-3. *Desktop Switcher*

Figure 4-4. *The K Desktop (KDE 2.0)*

You can start applications using the main menu, which you display by clicking the button in the panel with the large *K* on a cogwheel. This button is located on the left side of the panel. When you click the folder for your home directory on your panel (the icon of a folder with a house on it) or select the File Manager entry on the main menu, a file manager window opens, showing your home directory. You can display files in your home directory and use the UP ARROW button to move to the parent directory. Back and Forward buttons move through previously displayed directories. In the location window, you can enter the pathname for a directory to move directly to it. The file manager is also Internet-aware and a fully functional Web browser. You can use it to access remote Web and FTP sites, displaying Web pages or downloading files from an FTP site.

To move a window, click and drag its title bar or click and drag its other borders. Each window supports Stick pin, Maximize, Minimize, and Close buttons. Double-clicking the title bar reduces the window to only its title bar, which you can redisplay with another double-click. The desktop supports full drag-and-drop capabilities. You can drag folders, icons, and applications to the desktop or to another file manager window open to other folders. Clicking the cogwheel in the right corner of a file manager window opens a duplicate window.

Selection of an icon in a file manager window is different than in other GUIs. To select an item, CTRL-click, instead of making a single left-click. The single left-click is the same as a double-click on other GUIs, executing the item or opening it with its associated application. So, if you single-click on a folder icon, you open the folder (as opposed simply to selecting it). If you single-click a file, you start up the application using that file. To select items, be sure to CTRL-click them. To unselect a selected item, be sure to CTRL-click again. When you click and drag a file to the desktop or another file manager window, a pop-up menu appears, which then enables you to choose whether you want to move, copy, or create a link for the item.

The panel also contains a pager for virtual desktops. This appears as four squares. Clicking a square moves you to that desktop. You can think of the virtual desktops as separate desktops, and you can use the pager to move to the different ones. To execute a command using the command line interface, open a console window. Click the image of a monitor on the panel. In that window, at the $ prompt, type in your command. You can modify your KDE interface at any time using the KDE Control Center. Click the image of a monitor with a circuit board on the panel or select the KDE Control Center from the main menu.

To quit the KDE desktop, select the Logout entry at the bottom of the main menu. If you entered from a login window, you are logged out of your account and returned to the login window. If you started KDE from the command line, you are returned to the command line prompt, still logged in to your account.

An earlier version of KDE is still in use on many systems. Its interface is slightly different from KDE 2.0 as shown in Figure 4-5.

INTRODUCTION

Figure 4-5.   *KDE 1.1*

Command Line Interface

When using the command line interface, you are given a simple prompt at which you type in your command. Even with a GUI, you sometimes need to execute commands on a command line. Linux commands make extensive use of options and arguments. Be careful to place your arguments and options in their correct order on the command line. The format for a Linux command is the command name followed by options, and then by arguments, as shown here:

```
$ command-name  options  arguments
```

An *option* is a one-letter code preceded by a dash, which modifies the type of action the command takes. Options and arguments may or may not be optional, depending on the command. For example, the **ls** command can take an option, **-s.** The **ls** command displays a listing of files in your directory, and the **-s** option adds the size of each file in blocks. You enter the command and its option on the command line as follows:

```
$ ls -s
```

An *argument* is data the command may need to execute its task. In many cases, this is a filename. An argument is entered as a word on the command line after any options. For example, to display the contents of a file, you can use the **more** command with the file's name as its argument. The **more** command used with the filename **mydata** would be entered on the command line as follows:

```
$ more mydata
```

The command line is actually a buffer of text you can edit. Before you press ENTER, you can perform editing commands on the existing text. The editing capabilities provide a way to correct mistakes you may make when typing in a command and its options. The BACKSPACE and DEL keys enable you to erase the character you just typed in. With this character-erasing capability, you can BACKSPACE over the entire line if you want, erasing what you entered. CTRL-U erases the whole line and enables you to start over again at the prompt.

You can use the UP ARROW *to redisplay your previously executed command. You can then reexecute that command, or you can edit it and execute the modified command. This is helpful when you have to repeat certain operations over and over, such as editing the same file. This is also helpful when you've already executed a command you entered incorrectly.*

Help

A great deal of help is already installed on your system, as well as accessible from online sources. Both the Gnome and KDE desktops feature Help systems that use a browser-like interface to display help files. To start KDE Help, click the Book icon in the panel. Here, you can select from the KDE manual, the Linux Man pages, or the GNU info pages. KDE Help features browser capabilities, including bookmarks and history lists for documents you view.

To start the Gnome Help browser, click the icon with the question mark (?) in the panel. You can then choose from the Gnome user guide, Man pages, and info pages (see Figure 4-6). The Gnome Help browser and KDE Help Center also feature bookmarks and history lists.

Both Gnome and KDE, along with other applications, such as Linuxconf, also provide context-sensitive help. Each KDE and Gnome application features detailed manuals that are displayed using their respective Help browsers. Also, applications like Linuxconf feature detailed context-sensitive help. Most panels on Linuxconf have Help buttons that display detailed explanations for the operations on that panel.

Note   *In addition, extensive help is provided online. The Red Hat and Caldera desktops display Web page icons for support pages, including online manuals and tutorials.*

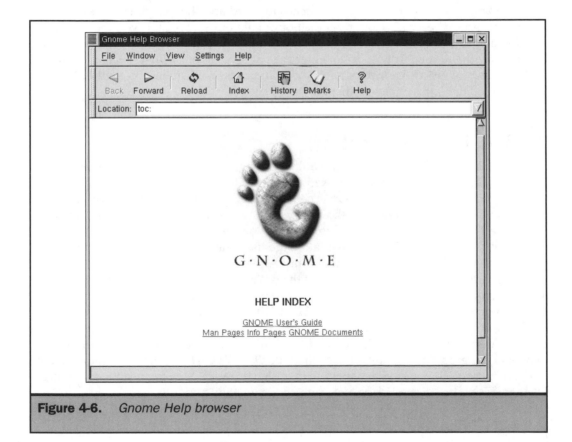

Figure 4-6.   *Gnome Help browser*

On your system, the **/usr/share/doc** directory contains documentation files installed by each application. Within this directory, you can also find a **HOWTO** directory that lists all the Linux HOW-TO documents. The **HTML** directory holds these same documents in Web page form. You can view them with your Web browser.

You can also access the online manual for Linux commands from the command line interface using the **man** command. Enter **man** with the command on which you want information.

```
$ man ls
```

Pressing either the SPACEBAR or the F key advances you to the next page. Pressing the B key moves you back a page. When you finish, press the Q key to quit the **man** utility and to return to the command line. You activate a search by pressing either the slash (/) or question mark (**?**). The / searches forward and the ? searches backward. When you press the /, a line opens at the bottom of your screen, and you then enter a word to search for. Press ENTER to activate the search. You can repeat the same search by pressing the N key. You needn't reenter the pattern. Other utilities, such as **Xman** and **Tkman** provide a GUI front end for the Man pages. You can also use either the Gnome or KDE Help systems to display Man pages.

Online Documentation

When you start up your browser, a default Web page lists links for documentation both on your own system and at the Red Hat Web site. To use the Red Hat Web site, you first must be connected to the Internet. However, your CD-ROM and your system contain extensive documentation showing you how to use the desktop and take you through a detailed explanation of Linux applications, including the Vi editor and shell operations. The links to this documentation are listed here. Other documentation provides detailed tutorials on different Linux topics.

The **/usr/share/doc** directory contains the online documentation for many Linux applications, including subdirectories with the names of installed Linux applications that contain documentation, such as README files. You can access the complete set of HOW-TO text files in the **/usr/share/doc/HOWTO** directory. The HOW-TO series contains detailed documentation on all Linux topics from hardware installation to network configuration. In addition, **/usr/share/doc/HOWTO/HTML** holds documentation in the form of Web pages you display with a Web browser. You can use the following URL on a Web browser, such as Netscape, to view the documents.

```
file:/usr/share/doc/HOWTO/HTML
```

Online documentation for GNU applications, such as the gcc compiler and the Emacs editor, also exists. You can access this documentation by entering the command **info.** This brings up a special screen listing different GNU applications. The info interface has its own set of commands. You can learn more about it by entering **info info**. Typing **m** opens a line at the bottom of the screen where you can enter the first few letters of the application. Pressing ENTER brings up the info file on that application.

Note *You can also display **info** documents using either the Gnome or KDE Help browsers.*

The Complete Reference

Linux

Chapter 5

System Configuration

To make effective use of your Linux system, you must know how to configure certain features. Administrative operations such as adding users, accessing CD-ROM drives, and installing software can now be performed with user-friendly system tools. This chapter discusses basic system administration operations that you need to get your system up and running, as well as to perform basic maintenance such as adding new users or devices.

The chapter is geared toward administering the Red Hat and Caldera OpenLinux Linux distributions provided on the CD-ROMs included with this book. On Red Hat the primary administrative tool is Linuxconf, which can also be used on other distributions such as SuSE and Mandrake. In addition Red Hat also provides a set of older administrative tools tailored to older versions of Red Hat that are still in wide use. Caldera's OpenLinux provides two administration tools, COAS and Webmin. COAS is an older tool found primarily on Caldera systems, whereas Webmin is a newer tool that, like Linuxconf, can be used with several Linux distributions.

Configuring Red Hat

The official Red Hat configuration tool is Linuxconf. Linuxconf supports three interfaces: an X Window System interface, a cursor-based interface, and a Web interface. You use the cursor-based interface from a Linux command line, and you needn't be running a GUI. The interface presents a full-screen display on which you can use arrow keys, the TAB key, the SPACEBAR, and the ENTER key to make selections. With the Web-based interface, you use your Web browser to make selections (though this is meant for use on local networks). Use the URL for your system with a **:90** attached, as in **turtle.mytrek.com:90**.

Linuxconf provides an extensive set of configuration options, enabling you to configure features, such as user accounts and file systems, as well as your Internet servers, dial-up connections, and LILO. You can access the main Linuxconf interface with its entire set of configuration options or use specialized commands that display entries for a particular task, such as configuring user's accounts or entering your network settings. The specialized commands include **userconf** for user accounts, **fsconf** for file systems, and **netconf** for networks (see Chapter 6). In all cases, you need to log in as the root user. Configuration tools are only accessible by the root user.

Users: userconf

To add users on Red Hat, use the **userconf** command. If you are using Gnome or KDE, open a terminal window and enter the command **userconf** and then press ENTER. You see a window displayed showing buttons for users and groups, as shown in Figure 5-1. Clicking User accounts displays a window listing all the users on your system. Click Add here to add a new user. This opens another window where you can enter the user login, home directory, and login shell, though you can use defaults for the login shell. You can use the other panels in this window to add mail aliases or set

Figure 5-1.   *User account configuration*

privileges, such as allowing the user to mount a CD-ROM. When you finish, another window opens that prompts you to specify a password for the user.

To change any settings for a user, double-click its entry in the User Accounts window. This displays the User Information for this user. Click Passwd to change the password, if you want.

Any user can change their password using the **passwd** *command. Enter the command passwd at a shell prompt and you will be prompted for a new password, twice.*

File Systems

Files and directories contained on different hardware devices such as floppy disks, CD-ROMs, and hard disk partitions are called *file systems*. The Linux partition you used to install your Linux system on is called the *root partition*. This is where you mounted the root file system, the root directory indicated with a single slash, /. The root partition contains the main file system with a directory tree, starting from the root and spreading out to different system and user subdirectories. To access files on another file system, say, a CD-ROM disc, you need to attach that file system to your main system. Attaching a file system is called *mounting the file system*. You first set up an empty directory to which you want to mount the file system.

Note   *On most distributions including Red Hat and Caldera, the **/mnt/cdrom** directory is already reserved for mounting CD-ROMs and the **/mnt/floppy** directory is reserved for floppy disks.*

Although you can mount a CD-ROM using Linuxconf, the Red Hat Gnome interface also provides a simple method for mounting and unmounting a CD-ROM. Simply insert the CD-ROM into your CD-ROM drive; you then see an icon labeled CD-ROM appear on the Gnome desktop. A CD-ROM is automatically mounted. A Gnome file manager window also automatically appears, which displays the contents of the CD-ROM. You can also mount and unmount the CD-ROM using a pop-up menu on the CD-ROM icon. Right-click it to display a pop-up menu with options to mount, unmount, or eject the CD-ROM (see the following illustration). You can access the CD-ROM you placed in your CD drive by double-clicking the CD-ROM icon. Your CD-ROM drive remains locked until you select the Unmount entry that is now displayed on the pop-up menu. If you do not see an icon for your CD-ROM, you must first make it user-mountable. Use **fsconf** or Linuxconf to select the local drive and double-click the cdrom entry in the Local volume window. Then, on the Options panel select the user mountable option. Click Act/Changes to register the change. Then right-click the desktop and select Rescan Desktop Shortcuts from the pop-up menu.

To mount a file system, you first start up Linuxconf with the **fsconf** command. This displays a Filesystem Configurator window with a button for the local drive. Click this button to display the local volume window. This lists the entries for all the file systems currently accessible on your system. To mount your CD-ROM, double-click the **/mnt/cdrom** entry to open a Volume specification window, and then click the Mount button. Now you can access the contents of the CD-ROM at the **/mnt/cdrom** directory on your system. The CD-ROM remains locked until you click Umount.

You can also use the Local Volume window to add new entries for mounting any Windows partitions that may be on your system's hard drives. Figure 5-2 shows the entries for a Windows partition (type vfat) to be mounted at the **/dos** directory. If you have another CD-ROM drive on your system, you can add another entry for it (use the iso9660 type).

Printer Configuration

As part of the installation procedure for Red Hat Linux, you configured a printer connected to your computer. To change configurations or to add a new printer later, you can use the Red Hat Linux Print Manager, also known as *PrintTool*. You can access PrintTool through the Control panel on the Gnome System menu or from the Another Level menu and the System submenu. The Red Hat Print Manager enables you to select

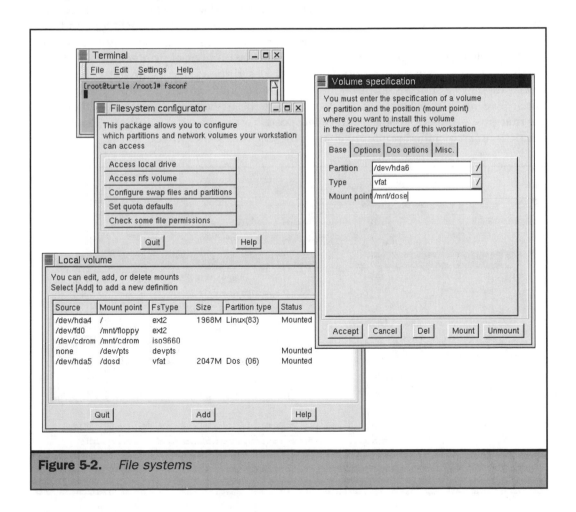

Figure 5-2.   *File systems*

the appropriate driver for your printer, as well as to set print options such as paper size and print resolutions. You can use the Red Hat Print Manager to access a printer connected directly to your local computer or to a printer on a remote system on your network (see Chapter 33).

When you start up the Red Hat Print Manager, you are presented with a window that lists your installed printers (see Figure 5-3). To add a new printer, click the Add button. To edit an installed printer, double-click its entry. For a new printer, you are first asked to specify whether the printer is local or remotely connected through a UNIX, Windows (SMB), or NetWare network. Then a window opens with entries for the printer device, spool directory, and input filter (see Figure 5-3). Default settings are entered for each.

The name can be any name you choose to give your printer. The device is the port to which the printer is connected. For the first three parallel ports, these are **lp0**, **lp1**, **lp2**; for serial ports, these are **ttyS0**, **ttyS1**, and **ttyS2**; and so on. The input filter entry is your print driver. Click the Input Filter button to open a Configure Printer window where you can select your printer and configure the print settings (see Figure 5-4). The Printer Type panel on this window lists an extensive number of printers. Choose the one for the printer you are adding. The Driver Description pane in the upper-right corner displays a short description of the selected printer driver. Use the Resolution, Paper Size, and Color Depth panels to configure these features. You can also choose the margins, number of copies, and print speed. You can use the Configure Printer window on an installed printer to change these features later, if you want.

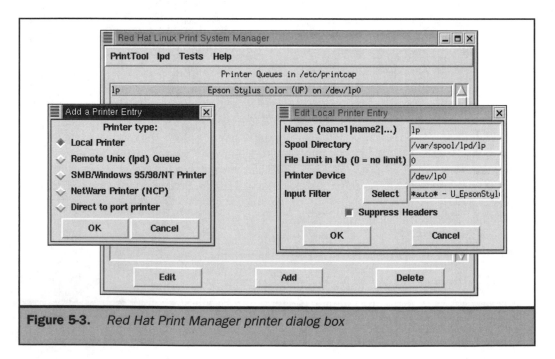

Figure 5-3.   *Red Hat Print Manager printer dialog box*

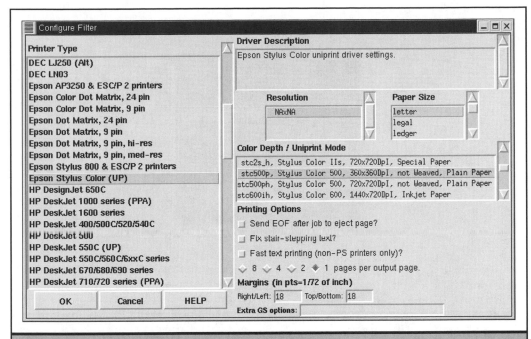

Figure 5-4. *Red Hat Print Manager filter configuration*

Configuration Using Red Hat Setup

Red Hat also provides a setup utility with which you can configure different devices and system settings, such as your keyboard, mouse, and time zone. The **setup** utility is useful if you have changed any of your devices—say, installed a new mouse, keyboard, or sound card. Setup is designed to be run from the command line interface and several of its components, such as **kbdconfig** and **mouseconfig**, only work from that interface. You start the utility with the command **setup**, which you enter at a shell command line. Setup provides a full-screen, cursor-based interface where you can use arrow, TAB, and ENTER keys to make your selections. Initially, Setup displays a menu of configuration tools from which you can choose. Use the arrow keys to select one, and then press the TAB key to move to the Run Tool and Quit buttons. Figure 5-5 shows the initial Setup menu.

Setup is actually an interface for running several configuration tools (see Table 5-1). You can call any of these tools separately using their commands. For example, the **kbdconfig** command starts the keyboard configuration utility that enables you to select the type of keyboard, while the **mouseconfig** command enables you to select the type of mouse.

```
Text Mode Setup Utility 1.2                (C) 1999 Red Hat Software

                    ┤ Pick a Tool ├
            Authentication configuration
            Keyboard configuration
            Mouse configuration
            System services
            Sound card configuration
            Timezone configuration
            X configuration


                  Run Tool      Quit



     <Tab>/<Alt-Tab> between elements  |   Use <Enter> to edit a selection
```

Figure 5-5. *Red Hat Setup*

Tools	Description
setup	Red Hat setup interface listing configuration tools for system and device settings
authconfig	Authentication options, such as enabling NIS, shadow passwords, and MD5 passwords
kbdconfig	Selects the keyboard type
mouseconfig	Selects the mouse type
ntsysv	Selects servers and daemons to start up at boot time
sndconfig	Detects and configures your sound card
timeconfig	Selects the time zone
Xconfigurator	Configures your X Window System for your video card and monitor

Table 5-1. *Setup Tools*

With **kbdconfig**, you can select the type of keyboard you are using. A text-based dialog box appears with a list of different keyboard types, which should be run from the command line interface, not a desktop.

With **mouseconfig**, you can select the type of mouse you are using. A cursor-based dialog box appears with a list of different mouse device types. Your system is automatically probed for the type of the mouse connected to your system and the cursor is positioned at that entry. If you have a two-button mouse, you can select the three-button emulation option to let a simultaneous click on both the left and right mouse buttons emulate a third mouse button. This should be run from the command line interface, not from a desktop.

The **ntsysv** utility is a simple utility for specifying which servers and services should be automatically started at boot time (see Chapter 15). The dialog box lists the possible servers and services from which to choose. Move to the entry you want and use the SPACEBAR to toggle it on or off. An entry with an asterisk next to it is selected and is started automatically the next time you boot your system.

The **sndconfig** utility enables you to select and configure your sound card. It should be run from the command line interface, not from a desktop. Initially, the **sndconfig** utility tries to detect your sound card automatically. If the automatic detection fails, a dialog box appears with a listing of different sound cards. Select the one on your system. Another dialog box appears where you need to enter the setting for your sound card. **sndconfig** then tries to play sample sound and MIDI files to test the card. As an alternative to **sndconfig**, you can obtain, load, and configure sound drivers yourself (see Chapter 25).

Xconfigurator

One important utility is Xconfigurator, the X Window System configuration program. If you have trouble with your X Window System configuration, you can use this utility to configure it again. Xconfigurator is also helpful for updating X Windows if you change your video card. Simply run Xconfigurator again and select the card. You can run Xconfigurator by entering the **Xconfigurator** command on the command line, or by selecting the X configuration entry in the Setup utility's menu.

Xconfigurator first probes your system in an attempt to determine what type of video card you have. Failing that, Xconfigurator presents a list of video cards. Select your video card from the list and press ENTER. If your video card does not appear on the list, XFree86 may not support it. If you have technical knowledge about your card, however, you may choose Unlisted Card and attempt to configure it by matching your card's video chipset with one of the available X servers.

Once you select your video card, the installation program installs the appropriate XFree86 server, and Xconfigurator presents a list of monitors, as shown in Figure 5-6. If your monitor appears on the list, select it and press ENTER. If it is not on the list, select Custom. This displays a screen where you enter the horizontal sync range and vertical sync range of your monitor (these values are generally available in the documentation

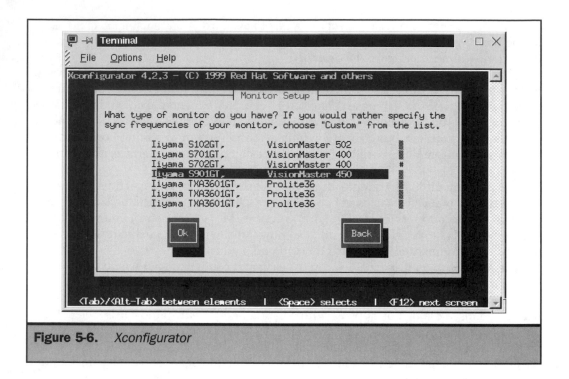

Figure 5-6. *Xconfigurator*

that accompanies your monitor or from your monitor's vendor or manufacturer). Be careful to enter the correct horizontal and vertical frequencies. If you enter values that are too high, you may overclock your monitor, and damage or destroy it. Do not select a monitor similar to your monitor unless you are certain the monitor you are selecting does not exceed the capabilities of your monitor.

The next screen prompts you for the amount of video memory installed on your video card. If you are not sure, please consult the documentation accompanying your video card. Choosing more memory than is available does not damage your video card, but the XFree86 server may not start correctly if you do.

If the video card you selected has a video clock chip, Xconfigurator presents a list of clock chips. The recommended choice is No Clockchip Setting because, in most cases, XFree86 can automatically detect the proper clock chip.

In the next screen, Xconfigurator prompts you to select the video modes you want to use. These are screen resolutions you may want to use. You can select one or more by moving to it and pressing the SPACEBAR. Xconfigurator then starts the X Window System and displays a dialog box asking if you can see it.

Note   *Xconfigurator then generates an X Window System configuration file called /etc/X11/XF86Config. This is the file the X Window System uses to start up.*

OpenLinux Configuration

On OpenLinux, you configure your system using either the Caldera Open Administration System (COAS) or Webmin. You will find an entry for COAS and Webmin in the root user KDE main menu and on the KDE Panel. COAS also supports a cursor-base interface that you can run from the command line by entering the command **coastool**. Use the arrow keys, TAB, and ENTER to make selections. Webmin is a Web page–based interface that you can run on any Web browser by accessing port 1000. The initial Webmin page will show panels for different kinds of configuration tasks such as system, hardware, and servers. For basic administration tasks, click the System panel to show icons for different system administration tasks such as managing users and mounting file systems. With Webmin, you can perform all the tasks that COAS can perform. To configure your X Window System, you can use **lizardx**, as described in Chapter 3.

Users

Under System Administration, select Account Administration. This displays a window showing your user accounts. To add a new user, select Add from the Actions menu. This opens an Edit User window where you can enter the user login name, the home directory, and the password. To edit a current user, double-click its entry to display its Edit User window (see Chapter 30 for more details).

For Webmin, you can manage users with the Users and Groups page selected from the System page. Here you can add new users, entering their user names and passwords. Current users are each listed with the user name as a link you can use to display a page for editing a user's account.

File Systems

To mount file systems, select File System from the System Administration menu. This displays a File System window showing mountable devices on the left and the directories for mounted file systems on the right. To mount a file system, such as a CD-ROM, select its device in the left list and click Mount. An IDE CD-ROM will often have a device name like **hdc** or **hdd**. To check what a device is used for, click it and then click Info. When you mount a file system, a window opens showing the device name, the directory it will be mounted on, and the file system type (see Figure 5-7). For a new device, you will have to enter a directory and a type. CD-ROMs have the type iso9660, and Linux floppy disks use ext2. Windows partitions have a type of vfat. You can further set options such as read only or user mountable. You can also elect to have the device added to the **fstab** file, which then makes it a permanent entry and easier to mount again later.

On Webmin, you can manage your file systems using the Disk and Network Filesystem page accessible from the System page. Here you can add a new file system or edit one previously mounted. To mount or unmount a system, click its entry in the

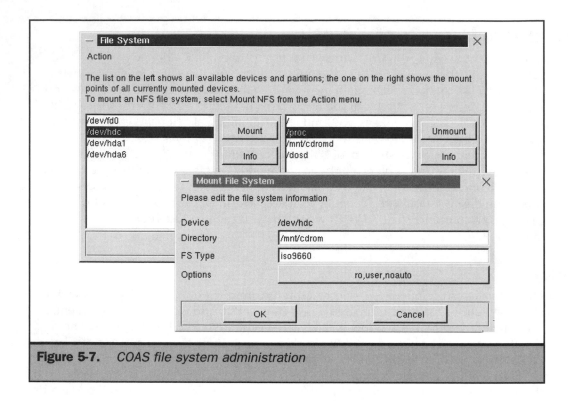

Figure 5-7. COAS file system administration

Mounted As column. This opens an Edit Mount page for that file system. Click the Mount or Unmount check box on this page positioned next to the Mount Now? label.

Printer

To configure a printer in OpenLinux, select the Printer entry in the Peripherals entry in the main COAS menu. The Printer configuration window will display a list of installed printers. To add a new one, click the Add entry in the Printer menu located on this window. This opens up a Printer attributes window where you can enter features such as the printer name, the resolution, the paper size, the device name, and the printer type. The Type entry supports a lengthy drop-down menu listing numerous printer types. Here is where you select the printer driver for your printer.

On Webmin, select the Printer Administration page accessible from the Hardware page. Click the Add a new printer link to open a Create Printer page. Here you can enter Printer configuration information such as the device used and the printer name. You can further select whether this printer is a remote printer or local printer. For a remote printer, you can enter its host name along with that printer's name on the remote system. You can then choose a printer driver for the kind of printer you have.

SuSE Configuration

On SuSE you configure your system using the Yet Another System Tool (YaST). You start YaST by entering the command **yast** on the command line. Use the arrow keys, TAB, and ENTER to make selections. On the main menu choose System Administration and press ENTER. This will display a submenu for different configuration options. For example, to set up your X Window System, select Configure XFree86 and press ENTER. You can then choose from several X Window System configuration tools, including SaX2, the SuSE XFree86 configuration tool. SaX provides a simple and easy-to-use interface for configuring your mouse, keyboard, video card, and monitor. You can use susewm to select the window manager you want to use. Select Settings of susewm from the System Administration menu to list a window with the different window managers available.

To add or edit users, select User Administration from the System Administration window and press ENTER. This displays a User administration window where you can edit or add new users. Press F3 to add a new user or select a current one. You can then make entries in the displayed fields. Use the Group Administration entry to add or change groups.

> **Note** *SuSE also provides a GUI version of YaST called YaST2. It must run from an X Window System interface such as KDE.*

File system management is currently performed by manually editing the **/etc/fstab** file and using the **mount** command to mount and unmount file systems.

To choose whether you want to start the system with the command line or the display manager (KDM), select Login configuration and make your choice.

You can also download Linuxconf, install it, and use it to configure your system.

Command Line Configuration

When logged in as the root user, you can also perform certain configuration operations from the command line. You can manually access system configuration files, editing them and making entries yourself. For example, the domain name server entries are kept in the **/etc/resolv.conf** file. You can edit this file and type in the addresses.

You can use the **useradd** command to add user accounts and the **userdel** command to remove them. One common operation performed from the command line is to change a password. Any user can change his own password with the **passwd** command. The command prompts you for your current password. After entering your current password and pressing ENTER, you are then prompted for your new password. After entering the new password, you are asked to reenter it. This is to make sure you actually entered the password you intended to enter. Because password characters are not displayed when you type them, it is easy to make a mistake and to press a wrong key.

```
$ passwd
Old password:
New password:
Retype new password:
$
```

File Systems

You can easily mount and unmount file systems with the **mount** and **unmount** commands. To mount your CD-ROM, you only have to enter the command mount and the directory **/mnt/cdrom**. You can then access the contents of the CD-ROM at the **/mnt/cdrom** directory.

```
$ mount /mnt/cdrom
```

When you finish, unmount the CD-ROM with the **umount** command.

```
$ umount /mnt/cdrom
```

 You can also manually mount and unmount floppy disks and hard disk partitions. See Chapter 32 for a detailed discussion.

 # Installing Software Packages

Now that you know how to start Linux and access the root user, you can install any other software packages you may want. Installing software is an administrative function performed by the root user. Unless you chose to install all your packages during your installation, only some of the many applications and utilities available for users on Linux were installed on your system. Red Hat uses the *Red Hat Package Manager (RPM)* to organize Linux software into packages you can automatically install or remove. An RPM software package operates like its own installation program for a software application. A Linux software application often consists of several files that must be installed in different directories. The program itself is most likely placed in a directory called **/usr/bin**, online manual files go in another directory, and library files, in yet another directory. In addition, the installation may require modification of certain configuration files on your system. The RPM software packages on your Red Hat CD-ROM performs all these tasks for you. Also, if you later decide you don't want a specific application, you can uninstall packages to remove all the files and configuration information from your system (see Chapter 19 or more details).

The easiest way to install an RPM package is to use the Gnome desktop. Simply locate the RPM file using a Gnome file manager window, then double-click it. The package is automatically installed.

The RPM packages on your CD-ROMs represent only a small portion of the software packages available for Linux. You can download additional software in the form of RPM packages from distribution sites, such as **ftp.redhat.com** for Red Hat packages. In addition, these packages are organized into **lib5** and **lib6** directories: **lib5** refers to the packages using the older libraries, whereas **lib6** refers to those using the new GNU 2.*x* libraries. For Red Hat 7.0, you should use the **lib6** versions, though **lib5** versions also work. An extensive repository for RPM packages is located at **http://rpmfind.net**/. Packages here are indexed according to distribution, group, and name. This includes packages for every distribution, including previous versions of those distributions. You can also locate many of the newest Linux applications from **http://freshmeat.net** or **www.linuxapps.com**. Here, you can link to the original development sites for these applications and download documentation and the recent versions. Table 5-2 lists several Linux software sites.

Installing Packages on Red Hat

The easiest way to install an RPM package on Red Hat is to use the Gnome file manager. Use the file manager window to access the directory with your package. For your Red Hat

Internet sites	Description
www.linuxapps.com	Linux Software Repository
freshmeat.net	New Linux software
rpmfind.net	RPM package repository
metalab.unc.edu	Mirror site for Linux software and distributions
ftp.redhat.com	Red Hat Linux and Updates
ftp.caldera.com	OpenLinux (Caldera)
sourceforge.net	Source Forge Opensource Software repository and development site
apps.kde.com	KDE software repository
www.gnome.org	Gnome Applications

Table 5-2. *Linux Software Sites*

CD-ROM, first be sure to mount the CD-ROM, and then use the Gnome file manager to access the **/mnt/cdrom/RedHat/RPMS** directory, where you will find your packages listed. Then simply double-click the RPM package filename. Gnome will recognize that it is an RPM package and that you want to install it. A window will open up showing the install progress, disappearing when the package has finished installing (see Figure 5-8). That is all there is to it. You can also right-click the package name or icon. In the pop-up menu, you can select the Install option to install the package.

Problems can occurs if the package requires that another package be installed or updated first. This is often the case where an application may need an updated version of a shared library. In this case, you will be notified of the problem and asked if you want to proceed. You can cancel at that time by clicking No, and then locate and install any packages that are required first.

Figure 5-8. *Installing a software package on Gnome*

You can use this same method for FTP sites. The Gnome file manager is Internet-aware. You can enter a URL for an FTP site in its location box to access the site. When you locate the package, right-click it and select Install or Update. The file is downloaded and then automatically installed on your system.

Instead of the Gnome file manager, you can use GnomeRPM to install RPM packages. Select the GnomeRPM entry in the Gnome main menu under Systems. With GnomeRPM, you can locate packages on your file system. Choose the packages you want to install. GnomeRPM lists packages already installed. You can select them to view their details and file list.

Updating Red Hat

New versions of distributions are often released every 6 to 12 months. In the meantime, new updates are continually being prepared for particular software packages. These are posted as updates you can download from a distribution's FTP site and install on your system. These include new versions of applications, servers, and even the kernel. Downloading and installing updates is a fairly straightforward process, made even easier with the Gnome and KDE desktops.

In the period between major releases, Red Hat posts RPM package updates for software installed from your CD-ROM in its **update** directory at its FTP site at **ftp.redhat.com**. Such updates may range from single software packages to whole components, for instance, all the core, applications, and development packages issued when a new release of Gnome, KDE, or XFree86 is made available.

With version 7.0, Red Hat now provides an Update Agent that automatically locates, downloads, and installs any updates for your Red Hat System. To use Update Agent, however, you first must register your copy of Red Hat at the Red Hat Web site at **www.redhat.com**. You are then provided with a user name and password with which you can configure Update Agent to access Red Hat's special secure server at **priority.redhat.com.** To start Update Agent, select its entry in the System menu in the Gnome main menu. On starting Update Agent, you are asked for your root user password as an added precaution.

The first time you use Update Agent, you will have to configure it, providing information about your system. Click the Configure button to display the Configuration dialog box with three tabbed panels: one each for user, retrieval, and exceptions. The User panel holds your registration information and your e-mail address. The Retrieval panel is where you enter in the server you want to use (for example, priority.redhat.com) as well as download instructions and the download directory you want to use. The Exception panel holds the names of any packages you do not want to automatically update.

To use Update Agent, click the Connect button. Update Agent connects to the FTP server, opens your Web browser (such as Netscape), and displays a Web page listing the possible updates it found. You can select individual packages by clicking the check boxes next to them, and then click the Request Selected packages button. To select all packages, click the Request ALL packages button. Once you select your packages, you can click the Request Packages button. The browser then closes and the Update Agent begins downloading the selected packages. The packages are listed with a Status icon. The packages are first downloaded, during which time the Status icon is a button, and then they are installed, which is indicated by a red arrow. When finished, the status icon becomes a check mark.

Alternatively, you can upgrade manually by first downloading all the packages and installing them yourself. For example, to install new releases of the K Desktop, you can download distribution versions of their packages from the KDE FTP site at **ftp.kde.org** or from distribution FTP sites. You can use an FTP client, such as **ncftp**, to download them all at once, including any subdirectories (see Chapter 16). Then change to that directory and use the **rpm -Uvh** command to install the packages.

RPM update packages are kept in the Red Hat update site at **ftp.redhat.com** and its mirror sites. You can access the site, locate the updates for your distribution version, and then download them to your system. Then you can install them using an RPM utility, such as GnomeRPM, or the **rpm** command using the update option, **-U**. Perhaps the easiest way to do this is to use the Gnome file manager to download the files first (see Figure 5-9). First, open a file manager window and enter the URL for the Red Hat update site in its location box. Then access the update site. Within that directory, move to the **current** directory, where you can see a list of all the updates. Download any new updates or all of them if this is the first update for your version. To download, open another file manager window and create a new directory to hold your update. Now open that directory. Then select and drag the update files from the file manager window for the update site to that new directory. You may not need all the files. In the case of kernel updates, you only need the kernel file for your processor: i386, i586 (Pentium), or i686 (Pentium II). As files are downloaded, a dialog box displays the filename and the percentage downloaded.

Once the update is downloaded, you can open a Terminal window and change to that new directory. You open a Terminal window by clicking the Monitor icon in the panel. Then use the **cd** command to change to that directory. If the directory name is **redup**, you would enter

```
# cd redup
```

Then issue the **rpm** command with the Uvh options. U will update a previously installed package, v specifies a verbose install, and h will display hatch symbols across the screen to show the install progress. You should install any libraries or kernel updates first, paying attention to any dependency warnings. The ***** is a special operator that will match on filenames. For example, ***rpm** will match on all files ending with "rpm." You can use this to install selected groups of packages. The following example installs all KDE packages.

```
$ rpm -Uvh  kde*rpm
```

Figure 5-9.   *Downloading updates on the Gnome desktop*

You can also open the GnomeRPM utility, and then open the dialog box for installing packages. From the file manager window displaying the packages, you can drag and drop the files to the GnomeRPM install dialog box. You may receive error messages noting dependency requirements. You usually can safely ignore these messages. If you also receive install conflicts, you may be trying to install two versions of the same package. In that case, you must install one or the other.

Installing Packages on Caldera OpenLinux

To install packages from the OpenLinux CD-ROM, select Software Management from the COAS menu. This opens a window, as shown in Figure 5-10, that lists software packages by category. Packages are listed in the right-most column, with specific to general categories listed from right to left. Selecting different categories displays the packages in them.

Figure 5-10. COAS software selection

On Webmin, use the Software Packages page accessible from the System page. This page will display a list of folder entries for different software groups like Administration or Server. Click an entry to expand it to subcategories, and then select a subcategory to see the packages installed for it. Clicking a package displays an Edit Package page that lists information about the package, including its list files. On this page, you can click an Uninstall button to uninstall the package.

Note *The easiest way to install an RPM package on Caldera/OpenLinux is to use the KDE desktop. Simply locate the RPM file using a KDE file manager window, then single-click it. The kpackage program is automatically started up showing that package. Click the Install button to install the package.*

Alternatively, on the KDE desktop, you can also use kpackage to install packages. Select the Open entry in the File menu and move to the CD-ROM. It will be located in the **/mnt/cdrom** directory, and the RPM packages will be listed in the **Packages** directory.

On the KDE desktop, you can install an RPM package simply by locating its RPM file on your system using the file manager and then single-clicking its icon or name. This will automatically open kpackage with the RPM package loaded. It will be displayed on a window with panels for the package information and the list of files in it. At the bottom of the panels is an Install button. Click it to install the package.

As the KDE file manager is Internet aware, you can use this same method to both download and install RPM packages from FTP sites. Locate the FTP site with the file manager (enter its URL in the location box), and then locate your package. Once it is listed in the file manager window, just click it. It will be automatically downloaded, and then kpackage will start up showing the package. Just click Install to install it.

Updating OpenLinux

To update OpenLinux, you can perform much the same kind of operation. Use the KDE file manager window to access the OpenLinux update directory located at the Caldera FTP site at **ftp.caldera.com**. Be sure to view any README files for any special instructions on installing the updates. Then open another file manager window to a new directory where you want to store your update files. Select all the files and then drag and drop them to that new file manager window. A dialog box will appear as each file is downloaded, showing the percentage of the download. Once download is complete, you individually install packages with kpackage, or use the **rpm** command. If there are many files, you may want to use the **rpm** command. Open a Terminal window by clicking the Monitor icon in the panel. Then use the **cd** command to change to that directory. If the directory name is **caldup**, you would enter:

```
# cd caldup
```

Then use the **rpm** command with the –Uvh options and ***rpm** to select all the RPM packages at once. You can refine the install using more refined filename matching.

```
# rpm –Uvh --nodeps   *rpm
```

Command Line Installation

If you do not have access to the desktop or you prefer to work from the command line interface, you can use the **rpm** command to manage and install software packages. The command name stands for the Red Hat Package Manager. This is the command that actually performs installation, removal, and verification of software packages. Each software package is actually an RPM package, consisting of an archive of software files and information about how to install those files. Each archive resides as a single file with a name that ends with **.rpm**, indicating it is a software package that can be installed by the Red Hat Package Manager.

You can use the **rpm** command either to install or uninstall a package. The **rpm** command uses a set of options to determine what action to take. Table 5-3 lists the set of **rpm** options. The **–i** option installs the specified software package, and the **–U** option updates a package. With an **–e** option, **rpm** uninstalls the package. A *q* placed before an *i* (**-qi**) queries the system to see if a software package is already installed and displays information about the software (**-qpi** queries an uninstalled package file). The **--h** option provides a complete list of **rpm** options. A helpful option is the **--nodeps** option, which installs without performing dependency checks . The syntax for the **rpm** command is as follows (*rpm-package-name* is the name of the software package you want to install):

```
rpm options rpm-package-name
```

The software package name is usually quite lengthy, including information about version and release date in its name. All end with **.rpm**. In the next example, the user installs the linuxconf package using the **rpm** command. Notice that the full filename is entered. To list the full name, you can use the **ls** command with the first few characters and an asterisk, **ls linuxconf***. You can also use the ***** to match the remainder of the name, as in **linuxconf-1.16*.rpm**. In most cases, you are installing packages with the **–U** option, update. Even if the package is not already installed, **–U** still installs it.

```
$ rpm   -Uvh linuxconf-1.21r6-1.i386.rpm
```

When RPM performs an installation, it first checks for any dependent packages. These are other software packages with programs the application you are installing needs to use. If other dependent packages must be installed first, RPM cancels the installation and lists those packages. You can install those packages, and then repeat the installation of the application. In a few situations, such as a major distribution

Option	Action
-U	Update package
-i	Install package
-e	Remove package
-qi	Display information for an installed package
-ql	Display file list for installed package
-qpi	Display information from an RPM package file (used for uninstalled packages)
-qpl	Display file list from an RPM package file (used for uninstalled packages)

Table 5-3. *RPM Options*

update where packages may be installed out of order, installing without dependency checks is all right. For this, you use the **--nodeps** option. This assumes all the needed packages are being installed, though.

To determine if a package is already installed, use the **-qi** option with **rpm**. The **-q** stands for query. To obtain a list of all the files the package has installed, as well as the directories it installed to, use the **-ql** option.

To query package files, add the **p** option. The **-qpi** option displays information about a package, and **-qpl** lists the files in it. The following example lists all the files in the Linuxconf package.

```
$ rpm -qpl linuxconf-1.21r6-1.i386.rpm
```

To remove a software package from your system, first use **rpm -qi** to make sure it is actually installed, and then use the **-e** option to uninstall it. As with the **-qi** option, you needn't use the full name of the installed file. You only need the name of the application. In the next example, the user removes the xtetris game from the system:

```
$ rpm  -e  xtetris
```

An important update you may need to perform is to update the Xfree86 packages. If you install a new video card or a monitor, and the current Xfree86 package does not support it, chances are the new one should. Simply download those packages from the distribution update sites and install them with the RPM update operation, as shown here.

```
$ rpm -Uvh  --nodeps  XFree86*rpm
```

Chapter 6

Network Configuration

This chapter discusses the network configuration tools available for easily configuring network connections on Red Hat and Caldera Linux. Network configuration differs depending on whether you are connected to a *local area network* (*LAN*) with an Ethernet card or you use a dial-up ISP connection. You had the opportunity to enter your LAN network settings during the installation process. For a dial-up ISP using a modem, you will have to configure your network connection using a PPP configuration utility such as the Red Hat PPP Dialer or KDE's Kppp.

Red Hat Network Configuration

On Red Hat Linux, you can configure both LAN and PPP connections by accessing Linuxconf with the **netconf** command. This displays the Network Configurator window that lists buttons for different network settings. (As an alternative to Linuxconf, you can use **netcfg** in the Control panel or Kppp, as described in Chapter 36). For PPP connections, you can use RP3, the Red Hat PPP Dialer, as well as **netconf**, Kppp, or **netcfg**. The Red Hat PPP Dialer utility provides an easy-to-use interface with panels for login information, modem configuration, and dial-up connections.

LAN

To configure a LAN connection in Linuxconf, click the Basic Host Information button to display the host configuration window. In the first Adapter panel, you can enter the IP address, network device (usually eth0), and the kernel module to use (the drivers for your Ethernet card) along with other data like the hostname and netmask. Then, in the Network Configurator window, click the Name Server Specification button to display the Resolver Configuration window, where you can enter the IP addresses for the domain name servers on your network (see Figure 6-1). Click on the Routers and Gateway button to enter the IP address for the gateway computer. See Chapter 2 about detailed descriptions for the information you will need for your LAN configuration, and Chapter 36 for a detailed description of using Linuxconf to configure your LAN.

If you are on a network, you can obtain most of your network information from your network administrator or from your ISP (Internet service provider). You will need the following information.

- **The device name for your network interface connection card (NIC)**   This is usually an Ethernet card and has the name eth0 or eth1.

- **Hostname**   Your computer will be identified by this name on the Internet. Do not use "localhost"; that name is reserved for special use by your system. The hostname should be a simple alphabetic word, which can include numbers but not punctuation such as periods and backslashes.

- **Domain name**   This is the name of your network.

INTRODUCTION

Figure 6-1.   *An example of netconf for LAN network settings*

■ **The Internet Protocol (IP) address assigned to your machine**   Every host on the Internet is assigned an IP address. This address is a set of four numbers, separated by periods, which uniquely identifies a single location on the Internet, allowing information from other locations to reach that computer.

■ **Your network IP address**   This address is usually the similar to the IP address, but with one or more zeros at the end.

■ **The netmask**   This is usually 255.255.255.0 for most networks. If, however, you are part of a large network, check with your network administrator or ISP.

■ **The broadcast address for your network, if available (optional)**   Usually, your broadcast address is the same as your IP address with the number 255 added at the end.

■ **The IP address of your network's gateway computer**   This is the computer that connect your local network to a larger one like the Internet.

■ **Nameservers**   The IP address of the name servers your network uses. These enable the use of URLs.

■ **NIS domain and IP address for an NIS server**   Necessary if your network uses an NIS server (optional).

The Red Hat PPP Dialer

If you have a dial-up connection to a *Internet service provider* (*ISP*), you need to configure a PPP interface. Almost all ISPs currently use PPP connections. You can easily set up a PPP connection using the Red Hat PPP Dialer (rp3). Select its entry in the Internet submenu on the Gnome desktop. If you do not have any Internet connections set up already, the Add New Internet Connection dialog box starts up (to add a new connection, you can click the New button on the Red Hat Dialup Configuration Tool window, opened from its entry on the Gnome Internet menu). If you have not yet configured your modem, the Dialer automatically attempts to detect your modem and to provide information, such as the speed and serial device it uses. You see a screen displaying this information, along with the sound level, which you can adjust (see Figure 6-2).

Next, you are asked to enter the name you want to use to identify this connection on your system, the account name (see Figure 6-3). You also enter the phone number used to dial your ISP.

Figure 6-2.   *Red Hat PPP Dialer modem configuration*

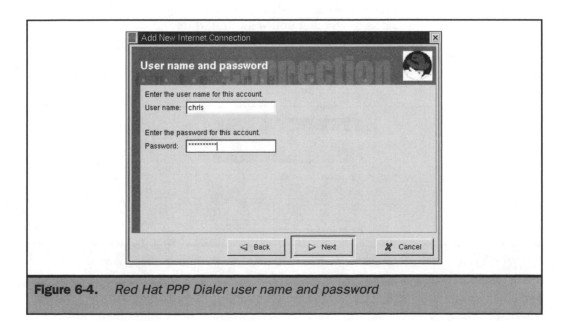

Figure 6-3.   *Red Hat PPP Dialer name and phone number*

You then enter the user name for your ISP account, along with its password (see Figure 6-4).

When you finish, the final screen appears listing the account name, user name, and phone number, as shown in Figure 6-5.

Figure 6-4.   *Red Hat PPP Dialer user name and password*

Figure 6-5. *Red Hat PPP Dialer final setup screen*

Each time you want to connect, select the Red Hat PPP Dialer entry from the Gnome Internet menu. This displays a Choose window listing all your network connections, including any you created with the Red Hat PPP Dialer (see Figure 6-6). Double-click the account name you set up for your PPP connection. In Figure 6-6, the account name used for the PPP connection is **myisp**, which also shows an Ethernet connection (eth0) and the localhost connection.

You are then prompted as to whether you want to start up the connection. Click the Yes button. A window appears that monitors the connection, showing a graph indicating the current activity on it (see the following illustration). You can minimize the monitor, docking it to the Gnome panel. Right-clicking the Monitor icon displays

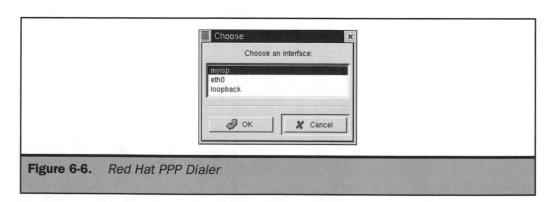

Figure 6-6. *Red Hat PPP Dialer*

a menu with entries for starting, stopping, and configuring the connections, along with the connection properties. The Properties dialog box enables you to set such features as calculating the time and the cost of a connected session. The monitor is actually part of the Red Hat Network Monitor tool. You can select this tool independently on the Gnome Internet menu and display monitors for all your network connections.

You can also place the network monitor for your PPP connection on the Gnome panel. Here it is displayed in a smaller size as a Gnome applet. To start your PPP connection, you only need to double-click the PPP network monitor. Right-clicking the monitor image displays a menu with options for starting and configuring your connection. To add a monitor to the Gnome panel, use the Panel menu on the Gnome Main menu. In the Panel menu, select Add Applet, and then the Network submenu, and, from there, select the RH PPP Dialer entry. This displays a list of all the network connections on your system. Select the one you want placed on the panel. The monitor bears the name you have to the PPP connection. In Figure 6-7, the PPP network monitor has the name myisp. You can place any of your network monitors on the Gnome panel. Figure 6-7 shows a monitor for both the Ethernet and PPP connections.

To change your setting or to add a new connection, use the Red Hat PPP Dialer Configuration tool. On the Gnome Internet menu, select the Dialup Configuration Tool entry to start up the Configuration tool. It then displays a window with two tabbed panels: one listing your accounts and the other for your modem configuration. Buttons on the right side of the Accounts panel enable you to add new connections or to edit current ones (see Figure 6-8).

Figure 6-7. *Red Hat network monitors on the panel*

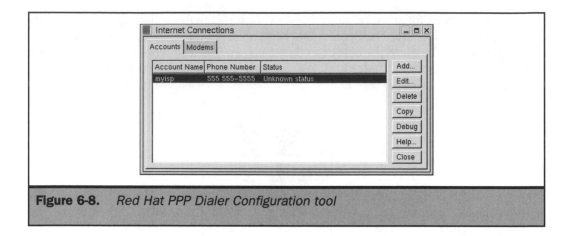

Figure 6-8. *Red Hat PPP Dialer Configuration tool*

The Edit button opens a window with panels for modifying connection and modem information (see Figure 6-9). On the Account Info panel, you can change your login name (user name), password, and phone number for your ISP. On the Advanced panel, you can enter information such as the IP address of your ISP's domain name servers.

The Red Hat PPP Dialer uses **wvdial** utility to perform the connection operations. You can find the configuration information for your connections in the **/etc/wvdial.conf** file. You can, if you choose, edit this file directly to configure your PPP connections.

Linuxconf PPP Configuration

To use netconf to configure PPP connections, click the PPP/SLIP/PLIP button on the Network Configurator window. A window then opens that asks you to choose the type

Figure 6-9. *Editing a PPP connection*

of interface you want. Select PPP. Then a small window opens displaying a ppp0 entry. Double-click it to display the PPP interface window with panels for setting your modem connections, the phone number to dial, and the Expect and Send entries for your login name and password. To activate a connection, click Connect. You can also use dial-up managers like Kppp, xisp, and gnomeppp to set up and manage your PPP connections.

Caldera OpenLinux Network Configuration

On Caldera OpenLinux, you can choose from either COAS or Webmin to configure your LAN connection. For PPP connections you will need to use Kppp. All have an easy to use graphical interface.

LAN Networks

To configure a LAN connection, you select Network Administration from the COAS menu. You can then further select Ethernet Interfaces to enter your network settings. This displays a window where you can enter your IP, gateway, and broadcast addresses, and the netmask, as well as the name of your Ethernet device (see Figure 6-10). When finished, you can then select the Hostname Resolution entry in the Network Administration menu to open a window where you can enter your domain name server addresses (see the previous section on Red Hat LAN networks).

With Webmin, select the Network Configuration page on the Hardware page. From the Network Configuration page, select the Network Interfaces page to configure your Ethernet device, entering information like the IP address, the netmask, and the device

Figure 6-10.   *OpenLinux LAN Configuration screen*

name. On the Routing and Gateways page, you enter the IP address of your network's gateway, and on the DNS page you enter your name server addresses. On the Host Address page, you enter the hostname and IP address for your system along with any others you want.

PPP Dial-Up Connections

If you use a dial-up PPP connection to an ISP, you will need to use a PPP connection utility. OpenLinux provides Kppp, which you can access in the Utilities menu on your KDE main menu. The Kppp utility is described in detail in Chapter 36. Click Setup on the Kppp window to display a configuration window with tabbed panels for accounts, device, and modem settings. Then click New in the Accounts panel to display a window of tabbed panels for entering your account connection information. The login script panel is where you enter your Expect/Send login and password strings.

SuSE Network Configuration

To add or change your network configuration, start YaST. Then select Network Configuration from the System Administration menu, and then Basic Network Configuration. For an Ethernet connection, press F5, then F6, and enter your IP address, netmask, and gateway. Press F4 to activate the network, and F10 to save the configuration. You then select Configure Nameserver to enter your name server addresses, and then Configure Network Services to specify the network service you want, such as inetd and NFS. For PPP, use Kppp on the KDE desktop or the command line form of pppd as shown in the next section.

Command Line PPP Access: wvdial and pppd

If, for some reason, you have been unable to set up your X Window System, you may have to set up such a network connection from the command line interface instead of a desktop. The following discussion shows how to make such a connection. You can use either the wvdial dialer or pppd. wvdial is the standard dialer used on Red Hat systems, though most systems use pppd.

For a dial-up PPP connection you can use the wvdial dialer, the same dialer used for the Red Hat PPP Dialer. wvdial is an intelligent dialer, which not only dials up an ISP service but also performs login operations, supplying your user name and password. wvdial first loads its configuration from the **/etc/wvdial.conf** file. In here, you can place modem and account information, including modem speed and serial device, as well as ISP phone number, user name, and password. The **wvdial.conf** file is organized into sections, beginning with a section label enclosed in brackets. A section holds variables for different parameters that are assigned values, such as username = chris. The default section holds default values inherited by other sections, so you needn't repeat them. Table 6-1 lists the wvdial variables.

Variable	Description
Inherits	Explicitly inherit from the specified section. By default, sections inherit from the [Dialer Defaults] section.
Modem	The device wvdial should use as your modem. The default is **/dev/modem**.
Baud	The speed at which wvdial communicates with your modem. The default is 57,600 baud.
Init1 ... Init9	Specifies the initialization strings to be used by your modem. wvdial can use up to 9. The default is "ATZ" for Init1.
Phone	The phone number you want wvdial to dial.
Area Code	Specifies the area code, if any.
Dial Prefix	Specifies any needed dialing prefix—for example, 70 to disable call waiting or 9 for an outside line.
Dial Command	Specifies the dial operation. The default is "ATDT".
Login	Specifies the user name you use at your ISP.
Login Prompt	If your ISP has an unusual login prompt, you can specify it here.
Password	Specifies the password you use at your ISP.
Password Prompt	If your ISP has an unusual password prompt, you can specify it here.
PPPD PATH	If pppd is installed on your Linux system somewhere other than **/usr/sbin/pppd**, you need to specify its location with this option.
Force Address	Specifies a static IP address to use (for ISPs that provide static IP addresses to users).
Remote Name	For PAP or CHAP authentication, you may have to change this to your ISP's authentication name. The default value is *.
Carrier Check	Setting this option to No disables the carrier check by your modem. Used for a modem that reports its carrier line is always down.

Table 6-1. *wvdial Variables*

Variable	Description
Stupid Mode	In Stupid Mode, wvduak does not attempt to interpret any prompts from the terminal server and starts pppd after the modem connects.
New PPPD	Enable this option for use with pppd version 2.3.0 or newer. Instructs pppd to look for a required file **/etc/ppp/peers/wvdial**.
Default Reply	Specifies the default response for prompts that wvdial does not recognize. The default is **ppp**.
Auto Reconnect	If enabled, wvdial attempts to reestablish a connection automatically if you are randomly disconnected by the other side. This option is **on** by default.

Table 6-1.   *wvdial Variables* (continued)

The following example shows the **/etc/wvdial.conf** file:

/etc/wvdial.conf

```
[Modem0]
Modem = /dev/ttyS0
Baud = 57600
Init1 = ATZ
SetVolume = 0
Dial Command = ATDT

[Dialer Defaults]
Modem = /dev/ttyS0
Baud = 57600
Init1 = ATZ
SetVolume = 0
Dial Command = ATDT

[Dialer myisp]
Username = chris
Password = mypassword
Modem = /dev/ttyS0
Phone = 555-5555
Area Code = 555
Baud = 57600
Stupid mode = 0
```

To start wvdial, enter the command **wvdial**, which then reads the connection configuration information from the **/etc/wvdial.coonf** file. **wvdial** then dials the ISP and initiates the PPP connection, providing your user name and password when requested.

```
$ wvdial
```

You can set up connection configurations for any number of connections in the **/etc/wvdial.conf** file. To select one, enter its label as an argument to the **wvdial** command, as shown here:

```
$ wvdial myisp
```

As an alternative to using **wvdial**, you can use the **pppd** command directly. The **connect** option instructs to make a connection. The **pppd** command takes as its argument a Linux command that will actually make the connection—usually the **chat** command. You enter **pppd**, followed by the **connect** option and the **chat** command with its expect-reply pairs. The entire **chat** operation is encased in single quotes. In the next example, the user invokes **pppd** with the **chat** operation. The modem is connected to port 2, **/dev/ttyS0**, and the speed is 57,600 baud. Notice the single quotes around the entire **chat** operation with its expect-reply pairs.

```
# pppd connect   'chat -v "" ATDT5556666 ogin: mylogin   word: mypass'
   /dev/ttyS0   57600
```

Modem Setup

If you have a modem connected to your PC, it is connected to one of four communications ports. The PC names for these ports are COM1, COM2, COM3, and COM4. These ports can also be used for other serial devices, such as a serial mouse (though not for PS/2 mice). Usually, a serial mouse is connected to COM1 and a modem is connected to COM2, though in many cases your modem may be connected to COM4. Find out which ports your modem and mouse are connected to, because you must know this to access your modem. On the PC, COM1 and COM3 share the same access point to your computer; the same is true of COM2 and COM4. For this reason, if you have a serial mouse connected to COM1, you should not have your modem on COM3. You could find your mouse cutting out whenever you use your modem. If your mouse is on COM1, then your modem should either be on COM2 or COM4.

In Linux, you use the serial communication ports for your modem. Serial ports begin with the name **/dev/ttyS**, with an attached number from 0 to 3. (Notice the numbering begins from 0, not 1.) The first port, COM1, is **/dev/ttyS0**, and **/dev/ttyS1** is the second port. The third and fourth ports are **/dev/ttyS2** and **/dev/ttyS3**. In many Linux communication programs, you need to know the port for your modem, which is either **/dev/ttyS1** for COM2 or **/dev/ttyS3** for COM4.

Some communication programs try to access the modem port using only the name **/dev/modem**. This is meant to be an alias, another name, for whatever your modem port actually is. If your system has not already set up this alias, you can easily create this alias using the **ln -s** command or the **modemtool** utility on Red Hat. **modemtool** has a GUI interface and is run on an X Window System desktop, such as Gnome or KDE. It displays four entries, one for each serial port. Click the one that applies to your system.

You can also create an alias on the command line using the **ln** command. The following example creates an alias called **modem** for the COM2 port, **/dev/ttyS1**. If your modem port is **/dev/ttyS3**, use that instead. (You must be logged in as a root user to execute this command.) The following example sets up the **/dev/modem** alias for the second serial port, **/dev/ ttyS1**.

```
# ln -s /dev/ttyS1  /dev/modem
```

Your **/dev/mouse** alias should already be set up for the port it uses. For a serial mouse, this is usually the COM1 port, **/dev/ ttyS0**. If the alias is not set up or if you need to change it, you can use the **ln -s** command. The following example sets up the **/dev/mouse** alias for the first serial port, **/dev/ ttyS0**.

```
# ln -s /dev/ttyS0  /dev/mouse
```

The Complete Reference

Chapter 7

Security Configuration

Once you have installed your Linux system, you should carry out some basic security measures to protect your system from outside attacks. Systems connected to the Internet are open to attempts by outside users to gain unauthorized access. This usually takes the form of either trying to break into the system, or attempting to intercept communications from remote users connected to that system. Firewalls and encryption are ways of protecting against such attacks (see Chapter 39). A firewall prevents any direct unauthorized attempts at access, and encryption protects transmissions from authorized remote users.

A good foundation for your network security is to set up a Linux system to operate as a firewall for your network, protecting it from unauthorized access. You can use a firewall to implement either packet filtering or proxies. *Packet filtering* is simply the process of deciding whether a packet received by the firewall host should be passed on into the local network. It checks the address of the packet and sends the packet on, if it's allowed. There are two firewall packages currently in use, *ipchains* for kernel 2.2 and its replacement, *Netfilter* (iptables) for kernel 2.4. To implement a firewall, you simply provide a series of rules to govern what kind of access you want to allow on your system. If that system is also a gateway for a private network, then the system's firewall capability can effectively protect the network from outside attacks.

To protect remote communications, transmission can be simply encrypted. For Linux systems, you can use the *Secure Shell* (*SSH*) suite of programs to encrypt any transmissions, preventing them from being read by anyone else. If you don't use SSH, it is best to avoid the standard remote communications tools such as **telnet** and **rcp** (see Chapter 18) for remote access over an unprotected networks like the Internet. Outside users may also try to gain unauthorized access through any Internet services you may be hosting, such as a Web site. In such a case, you can set up a proxy to protect your site from attack. For Linux systems, use Squid proxy software to set up a proxy to protect your Web server (see Chapter 28).

This chapter will show you some simple steps you can take to provide a basic level of security. Netfilter, Squid, and SSH are covered briefly. See Chapters 28 and 39 for a more detailed analysis of these applications.

Setting Up a Simple Firewall with Linuxconf

The process of setting up and maintaining firewall chains can be complex. To simplify the process, you can use a GUI-based firewall configuration tool, such as Linuxconf. Linuxconf provides a configuration interface for maintaining simple chain rules. Currently Linuxconf implements ipchains rules (iptables is not yet supported). To use Linuxconf Firewalling, select Firewalling under Networking, and then choose the panel for the kind of chain rules you want to configure: Input, Forward, and Output.

These rules are explained in detail in the next section. Figure 7-1 shows a simple configuration similar to that implemented in the following sections. The panel for an Input rule is shown. New connections are refused from the outside by leaving the checkbox to Accept TCP Syn packet unchecked. The policy for the chain is set to accept, making the default rule to accept all packets. Alternatively you could make the default rule to deny or reject packets. You can further specify the network interface, port, or the source or destination hosts (From and To panels). Linuxconf simply generates a list of **ipchain** commands saved to the **/var/run/ipchain.sh** script file. It is these commands that actually implement the ipchain rules for your firewall. This file is run when your system starts. You can check it to find out what **ipchain** commands the Linuxconf Firewalling has actually generated.

Tip   *If Linuxconf Firewalling does not appear on Linuxconf, you may have to first load the Linuxconf's own firewall module (check Configure Linuxconf modules in the Linuxconf Control panel).*

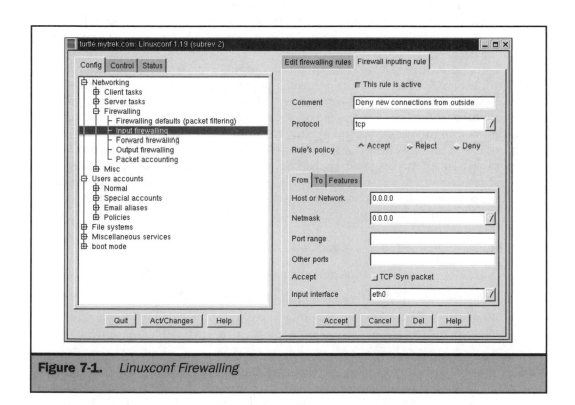

Figure 7-1.   *Linuxconf Firewalling*

Setting Up a Simple Firewall with IP Chains (kernel 2.2)

The tool used to implement packet-filtering on firewalls for the Linux 2.2 kernel is ipchains. With the **ipchains** command you can enter chain rules with which you can control access to your system. The Linux Web site for ipchains is currently **netfilter.kernelnotes.org/ipchains/**. The *ipchains* program is the successor to ipfwadm, used on older versions of Linux.

IP Chains Rules

The kernel uses chains to manage packets it receives. A *chain* is simply a checklist of rules. These rules specify what action to take for packets containing certain headers. The rules operate with an if-then-else structure. If a packet does not match the first rule, the next rule is then checked, and so on. If the packet does not match any rules, then the kernel consults chain policy. The default policy is to accept the packet (ACCEPT), and that value is assumed in the examples used in this chapter. For more restrictive chains, this policy often set to DENY (see Chapter 39). On the other hand, if the packet does match a rule, it is passed to its target, which determines what to do with the packet.

The kernel uses three firewall chains: input, output, and forward (you can create your own). When a packet is received through an interface, the input chain is used to determine what to do with it. The kernel then uses its routing information to decide where to send it. If the kernel sends the packet to another host, then the forward chain is checked. Before the packet is actually sent, the output chain is also checked.

You add and modify chain rules using the **ipchains** commands. An **ipchains** command consists of the keyword **ipchains**, followed by an argument denoting the command to execute; for instance, **ipchains -A** is the command to add a new rule, whereas **ipchains -L** is the command to list all active rules. The **ipchains** commands you will need to implement a simple firewall are listed in the following table.

Rule	Function
-A *chain*	Append a rule to a chain.
-L [*chain*]	List the rules in *chain* or all chains.
-F [*chain*]	Delete (flush) all rules in *chain* or all chains.

Following the command, list the chain to which the rule applies, such as the input, output, or forward chain, or else a user-defined chain. Next, list different options that specify the actions you want taken. Options exist to specify the address a rule is to match on (**-s, -d**) and to specify the target the rule is to execute (**-j**). Table 7-1 lists several basic options. In the following example, the user adds a rule to the input chain to accept all packets with the address 192.168.1.55. The **-s** option specifies the address

Option	Function
-p [**!**] *protocol*	Specify a protocol, such as TCP, UDP, ICMP, or ALL.
-s [**!**] *address* [*port*]	Source address to match. With the *port* argument, you can specify the port.
-d [**!**] *address* [*port*]	Destination address to match. With the *port* argument, you can specify the port.
-i [**!**] *name*	Specify a network interface using its name (for example, eth0).
-j *target* [**port**]	Specify the target for a rule (specify [**port**] for REDIRECT *target*).
-l	Turn on kernel logging for matching packets, logging them in the syslog.
[**!**] **-y**	Match SYN TCP packets only (TCP packets requesting connections). A **!** placed before **-y** specifies all packets except SYN TCP packets.
!	Negate an option or address.

Table 7-1. *ipchains Options*

attached to the packet, while the **-j** option specifies the target. The standard targets used for a simple firewall are ACCEPT and DENY. The ACCEPT target will allow a packet to pass, whereas a DENY target will reject it. Any packets that are received (input) whose source address (**-s**) matches 192.168.1.55 are accepted and passed through.

```
ipchains -A input -s 192.168.1.55 -j ACCEPT
```

To deny access from a particular site, simply specify the DENY target (in iptables this was changed to DROP). In the following example, any packet received from **www.myjunk.com** is rejected.

```
ipchains -A input -s www.myjunk.com -j DENY
```

With the **!** operator, you can change the effect of a rule to its inverse. The **!** operator works like a "not" logical operator in programming languages. Placing a **!**

operator before a **-s** entry matches any address that is not the specified address. For example, **! -s 192.168.1.66** matches any packet whose address is not 192.168.1.66. The operator is helpful if you want to restrict access to your system by only a few selected sites. The following example allows access by 192.168.1.66, denying access to all others.

```
ipchains -A input ! -s 192.168.1.66 -j DENY
```

The inverse can apply also to ports, protocols, and devices. For example, to allow access to any device except the Ethernet device eth2, you would use

```
ipchains -A input ! -i eth2 -j ACCEPT
```

A method of basic security protection is to deny access by a particular kind of packet used to initiate a connection. The idea is that an attacker must initiate a connection from the outside. The headers of these kinds of packets have their SYN bit set on and their FIN and ACK bits empty. The **ipchains -y** option matches on any such SYN packet. By specifying a DENY target for such packets, you deny access by any packet that is part of an attempt to make a connection with your system. Anyone trying to connect to your system from the outside is unable to do so. Users on your local system who have initiated connections with outside hosts can still communicate with them.

```
ipchains -A input -y -j DENY
```

IP Chains Scripts

You can enter **ipchains** commands from the shell command line. When you shut down your system, however, these commands will be lost. To save your commands, you can use the **ipchains-save** script to save them to a file. The recommended file to use is **/etc/ipchains.rules**. The **ipchains-save** command outputs rules to the standard output. To save them in a file, you must redirect the output to a file with the redirection operator, **>**, as shown here.

```
ipchains-save > /etc/ipchains.rules
```

Then, to restore the rules, use the **ipchains-restore** script to read the ipchains commands from that saved file.

```
ipchains-restore < /etc/ipchains.rules
```

An example of the output from the **ipchains-save** script is shown here.

/etc/ipchains.rules

```
:input ACCEPT
:forward ACCEPT
:output ACCEPT
-A input -s 192.168.1.1/255.255.255.255 -d 0.0.0.0/0.0.0.0 -i eth0 -j
DENY -l
-A input -s 127.0.0.0/255.0.0.0 -d 0.0.0.0/0.0.0.0 -i ! lo -j DENY -l
-A input -s 0.0.0.0/0.0.0.0 -d 0.0.0.0/0.0.0.0 -i eth0 -p 6 -j DENY -y
```

The following example shows a simple ipchains script called **mychains**. It configures a simple firewall for a single system connected to the Internet. This configuration initiates two forms of protection, defending against IP spoofing and from any attempt from outside users to initiate connections. Controls are placed on both the input and forward chains. Access from the system to the outside is unrestricted.

Note *Notice that in these scripts, the ! is escaped with a backslash, \, (\ !). ! is also a shell operator and, as part of the shell script, needs to be quoted with a \ to prevent the shell from executing it instead of ipchains or iptables.*

mychains

```
#Computer address is 192.168.1.1 using Ethernet device eth0
# turn off IP forwarding
 echo 0 > /proc/sys/net/ipv4/ip_forward

# Flush chain rules
ipchains -F input
# Set default Input chain rule (policy)
ipchains -P input ACCEPT

# IP spoofing, deny any outside packets with your own address
 ipchains -A input -j DENY  -i eth0  -s 192.168.1.1 -l
# IP spoofing, deny any outside packets with localhost address
ipchains -A input -j DENY  -i \! lo  -s  127.0.0.0/255.0.0.0 -l

# prevent outside initiated connections, allow established ones
 ipchains -A input -j DENY -p tcp -i eth0  -y

# Turn on IP Forwarding
 echo 1 > /proc/sys/net/ipv4/ip_forward
```

Tip *When re-executing as ipchains or iptables script, be sure to flush the chains, deleting your prevous chain rules (-F command). Otherwise the rules implemented by your script will just be added to the ones set up when you previously ran your script, generating many duplicate rules.*

Initially, in the script you would clear your current ipchains with the flush command (**-F**) and then set the policies (default targets) for the non-user-defined rules. IP forwarding should also be turned off while the chain rules are being set.

```
echo 0 > /proc/sys/net/ipv4/ip_forward
```

One way to protect the private network from IP spoofing of any packets is to check for any outside addresses on the Ethernet device claiming your computer as a source. In this example, any incoming packet on device eth0, the Ethernet connection to the Internet (ppp0 for PPP connections) whose source address claims to be that of the computer's (**-s 192.168.1.1**) is denied. The same strategy can be applied to the local host. Any packet on the localhost interface that did originate from the localhost is denied. This prevents access by an outsider pretending to be your localhost. The **-l** option will log all denied attempts.

```
# IP spoofing, deny any outside packets with your own address
ipchains -A input -j DENY  -i eth0 -s 192.168.1.1 -l
# IP spoofing, deny any outside packets with localhost address
ipchains -A input -j DENY  -i \! lo  -s  127.0.0.0/255.0.0.0 -l
```

To prevent outsiders from initiating any access to your system, create a rule to block access by SYN packets from the outside. Syn packets are referenced with the –y option. In the following example a rule is added to the input chain to deny access by any SYN packet.

```
ipchains -A input -j DENY -i eth0 -p tcp  -y
```

At the end, IP forwarding is turned on again:

```
echo 1 > /proc/sys/net/ipv4/ip_forward
```

The following example lists the chain rules for the **mychains** script (the ifname entry has been manually added for this example to show the network interfaces). Adding the **--verbose** option will give you a more detailed listing.

```
# ipchains -L
Chain input (policy ACCEPT):
target  prot opt     ifname source            destination ports
DENY    all  ----l- eth0   turtle.mytrek.com anywhere    n/a
DENY    all  ----l- !lo    127.0.0.0/8       anywhere    n/a
DENY    tcp  -y---- eth0   anywhere          anywhere    any->any
Chain forward (policy ACCEPT):
Chain output (policy ACCEPT):
```

Setting Up a Simple Firewall with IP Tables (kernel 2.4)

In the 2.4 kernel, ipchains has been superseded by iptables. Like ipchains, iptables uses a chain of rules to manage packets it receives. iptables has been developed by the Netfilter Project at **netfilter.kernelnotes.org**. iptables is very similar to ipchains, using many of the same principles, with several syntax changes for certain commands, as well as new commands. You can still use ipchains and the earlier ipfwadm commands by loading the ipchains.o or ipfwadm.o modules provided with the Netfilter software.

IP Tables Rules

With iptables, the kernel still uses three firewall chains: INPUT, OUTPUT, and FORWARD. When a packet is received through an interface, the INPUT chain is used to determine what to do with it. The kernel then uses its routing information to decide where to send it. If the kernel sends the packet to another host, then the FORWARD chain is checked. Before the packet is actually sent, the output chain is also checked. The rules in a chain operate in an if-then-else structure as they do in ipchains. If none of the rules match, then the default policy is used. The default policy for a chain is to accept the packet, as is assumed in these examples. More restrictive chains will set the default policy to drop the packet (see Chapter 39).

> **Note** In **iptables** commands, chain names have to be entered in uppercase. This means that the chain names INPUT, OUTPUT, and FORWARD have to be written using uppercase letters, exactly as the appear here.

Rule	Function
-A *chain*	Append a rule to a chain.
-L [*chain*]	List the rules in a chain or all chains.
-F [*chain*]	Delete (flush) all rules in chain or all chains.

Following the command, list the chain to which the rule applies, such as the INPUT, OUTPUT, or FORWARD chain, or else a user-defined chain. Next, list different options that specify the actions you want taken. Options exist to specify the address a rule is to match on (**-s**, **-d**) and to specify the target the rule is to execute (**-j**). Table 7-2 lists several basic options. Many are similar to the ipchains options, but some, like **-i**, are different and others are missing (like **-y**). In the following example, the user adds a rule to the input chain to accept all packets originating from the address 192.168.1.55. The **-s** option specifies the address attached to the packet, while the **-j** option specifies the target. The standard targets used for a simple firewall are ACCEPT and DROP. The ACCEPT target will allow a packet to pass, whereas a DROP target

Option	Function
-p **[!]** *protocol*	Specify a protocol, such as TCP, UDP, ICMP, or ALL.
-s **[!]** *address* **[***port***]**	Source address to match. With the *port* argument, you can specify the port.
-d **[!]** *address* **[***port***]**	Destination address to match. With the *port* argument, you can specify the port.
-i **[!]** *name*	Specify an input network interface using its name (for example, eth0).
-j *target* **[***port***]**	Specify the target for a rule (specify **[***port***]** for REDIRECT *target*).
-o **[!]** *name*	Specify an output network interface using its name (for example, eth0).
!	Negate an option or address.
-m	Specify a module to use, such as state.
--state	Specify options for the state module such as NEW, INVALID, RELATED, and ESTABLISHED. Used to detect packets state.

Table 7-2. *iptables Options*

will refuse access (DROP is the same as DENY in ipchains). Any packets received (input) whose source address (**-s**) matches 192.168.1.55 are accepted and passed through.

```
iptables -A INPUT -s 192.168.1.1 -j ACCEPT
```

To deny access from a particular site, simply specify the DROP target. In the following example, any packet received from **www.myjunk.com** is rejected.

```
ipchains -A INPUT -s www.myjunk.com -j DROP
```

The iptables rules are usually applied to a specific network interface such as the Ethernet interface used to connect to the Internet. For a single system connected to the Internet, you will have two interfaces, your Internet connection and a localhost interface (lo) for internal connections between users on your system. The network interface for the Internet is referenced using the device name for the interface. For example, an Ethernet card with the device name **/dev/eth0** would be referenced by the name eth0. A modem using PPP protocols with the device name **/dev/ppp0** would have the name ppp0. In iptables rules, you use **-i** option to indicate the input device; this option can only be used with the input and forward chains. The **-o** option indicates the output device and can only be used for output and forward chains. Rules can then be applied to packets arriving and leaving on particular network devices. In the following examples, the first rule references the Ethernet device, eth0, and the second, the localhost.

```
iptables -A INPUT -j DROP -i eth0 -s 192.168.44.87
iptables -A INPUT -j ACCEPT  -i lo
```

The iptables program is designed to be extensible, and a number of options with selection criteria can be included with iptables. One of the more useful extensions is the state extension, which can easily detect tracking information for a packet. You need to specify the state module first with **-m state**. Then you can use the **--state** option. Here you can specify any of the following criteria:

Option	Function
NEW	A packet that creates a new connection
ESTABLISHED	A packet that belongs to an existing connection
RELATED	A packet that is related to, but not part of, an existing connection, such as an ICMP error or a packet establishing an FTP data connection

The following example will drop any packets trying to create a new connection on the eth0 interface.

```
iptables -A input -m state --state NEW -i eth0 -j DROP
```

IP Tables Scripts

You can enter **iptables** commands from the shell command line. When you shut down your system, however, these commands will be lost. To save your commands, you can place them in a script (the **iptables-save** and **iptables.restore** commands are currently under development). You can create a script called **/etc/iptables.rules** and place your **iptables** commands in it.. The **iptables-save** command outputs rules to the standard output.

You now have enough information to create a simple iptables script that will provide basic protection for a single system connected to the Internet. The following script provides a simple IP Tables filtering process to protect a single system from outside attacks. First a DROP policy is set up for input and forward built-in IP chains. This means that if a packet does not meet a criterion in any of the rules to let it pass, it will be dropped. Then both IP spoofing attacks and any attempt from the outside to initiate connections (SYN packets) are rejected. Outside connection attempts are also logged. This is a very basic configuration that can easily be refined to your own needs by adding IP Tables rules.

myfilter

```
# IP address is 192.168.1.1 using Ethernet device eth0
# turn off IP forwarding
echo 0 > /proc/sys/net/ipv4/ip_forward

# Flush chain rules
iptables -F INPUT
# Set default INPUT rule (policy)
iptables -P INPUT ACCEPT

# IP spoofing, deny any outside packets with internal address
iptables -A INPUT -j DROP -i eth0 -s 192.168.1.1
# IP spoofing, deny any outside packets with localhost address
iptables -A INPUT -j DROP -i eth0 -s  127.0.0.0/255.0.0.0
iptables -A INPUT -m state —state NEW  -j DROP  -i eth0  -p tcp

# prevent outside initiated connections, allow established ones
#iptables -A INPUT -m state —state NEW -i eth0 -j DROP
# Turn on IP Forwarding
echo 1 > /proc/sys/net/ipv4/ip_forward
```

Initially, in the script you would clear your current iptables with the flush command (**-F**). IP forwarding should also be turned off while the chain rules are being set.

```
echo 0 > /proc/sys/net/ipv4/ip_forward
```

Flush any previous rules for the INPUT chain and then set the default rule to ACCEPT. The **-P** option will set a chain's policy. The rule specified here will be executed if no other rules match a packet. In this example, the policy for the INPUT chain is the ACCEPT rule. Any packets not matching any other rules in the INPUT chain will be accepted and passed into the system.

```
# Flush chain rules
iptables -F INPUT
# Set default INPUT rule (policy)
iptables -P INPUT ACCEPT
```

One way to protect your system from IP spoofing any packets is to check for any outside addresses pretending to be the IP address of your own system. In this example, any packet whose source address is your own system is denied. The same strategy can be applied to the local host. Any packet with a localhost source address that arrives from the outside on the eth0 interface is denied. This is an outsider pretending to be your localhost.

```
# IP spoofing, deny any outside packets with internal address
iptables -A INPUT -j DROP -i eth0 -s 192.168.1.1
# IP spoofing, deny any outside packets with localhost address
iptables -A INPUT -j DROP -i eth0 -s  127.0.0.0/255.0.0.0
```

To prevent outsiders from initiating any access to your system, create a rule to block access by SYN packets (new connections) from the outside using the **state** option with **NEW**. Deny any new connections on the eth0 connection (assumes only eth0 is connected to the Internet or outside network).

```
iptables -A INPUT -m state --state NEW  -j DROP  -i eth0  -p tcp
```

At the end, IP forwarding is turned on again:

```
echo 1 > /proc/sys/net/ipv4/ip_forward
```

You can list the rules held by iptables using the **-L** option. Adding the **--verbose** option will display a detailed listing. The following example lists the rules that where set up by the **myfilter** script shown previously.

```
# iptables -L
Chain INPUT (policy ACCEPT 2 packets, 206 bytes)
target prot opt in    out   source             destination
DROP   all  --  eth0 any  turtle.mytrek.com  anywhere
DROP   all  --  eth0 any  127.0.0.0/8        anywhere
DROP   tcp  --  eth0 any  anywhere           anywhere    state NEW

Chain FORWARD (policy ACCEPT 773 packets, 318322 bytes)
target  prot opt in    out     source    destination

Chain OUTPUT (policy ACCEPT 88 packets, 11508 bytes)
target  prot opt in     out     source    destination
```

Proxies (Squid)

Squid is a proxy-caching server for Web clients, designed to speed Internet access. It implements a proxy-caching service for Web clients that caches Web pages as users make requests and provides security controls for Web site access. Squid is supported and distributed under a GNU public license by the *National Laboratory for Applied Network Research* (*NLANR*) at the University of California, San Diego. The work is based on the Harvest Project. You can obtain current source code versions and online documentation from the Squid homepage at **http://squid.nlanr.net** and the Squid FTP site at **ftp.nlanr.net**.

Tip   *You can also configure Squid using Linuxconf or Webmin. In Webmin select the Squid Proxy Server from the Servers page.*

To configure Squid to provide security to your Web server, you first define access control lists (ACL) using the **acl** command, in which you create a label for the systems on which you are setting controls. You then use commands such as **http_access** to define these controls. You can define a system, or a group of systems, according to several **acl** options, such as the source IP address, the domain name, or even the time and date (see Table 7-3). For example, the **src** option is used to define a system or group of systems with a certain source address. To define a **mylan acl** entry for systems in a local network with the addresses 192.168.1.0 through 192.168.1.255, use the following ACL definition.

```
acl mylan src 192.168.1.0/255.255.255.0
```

Once these are defined, you can use an ACL definition in a **Squid** option to specify a control you want to place on those systems. For example, to allow access by the mylan group of local systems to the Web through the proxy, use a **http_access** option with the **allow** action specifying **mylan** as the **acl** definition to use, as shown here.

```
http_access allow mylan
```

By defining ACLs and using them in **Squid** options, you can tailor your Web site with the kind of security you want. See Chapter 18 for a more detailed discussion of Squid.

Secure Shell (SSH)

Although a firewall can protect a network from attempts to break in to it from the outside, the problem of securing legitimate communications to the network from outside sources still exists. A particular problem is one of users who want to connect to your network remotely. Such connections could be monitored, and information such as passwords and user IDs used when the user logs into your network could be copied and used later to break in. One solution is to use SSH for remote logins and other kinds of remote connections such as FTP transfers. SSH encrypts any communications between the remote user and a system on your network.

SSH was originally designed to replace remote access operations, such as rlogin, rcp, and telnet (see Chapter 18). The ssh-clients package contains corresponding SSH clients to replace these applications. With slogin or ssh, you can log in from a remote host to execute commands and run applications, much as you can with rlogin and rsh. With scp, you can copy files between the remote host and a network host, just as with rcp.

Each user who intends to use SSH applications first needs to create the public and private keys to use for the encryption process. You do this using the **ssh-keygen** command. The **ssh-keygen** command prompts you for a pass-phrase, which it will use as a kind of password to protect your private key. The pass-phrase should be several words long. The **ssh-keygen** command generates the public key and places it in your **.ssh/identity.pub** file; it places the private key in the **.ssh/identity** file. If you need to change your pass-phrase, you can do so with the **ssh-keygen** command and the **-p** option. Each user will have her own SSH configuration directory, called **.ssh**, located in her own home directory. The public and private keys, as well as SSH configuration files, are placed here.

A public key is used to identify a user and its host. You use the public key on a remote system to allow that user access. The public key is placed in the remote user account's **.ssh/authorized_keys** file. Recall that the public key is held in the **.ssh/identiy.pub** file. If a user wants to log in remotely from a local account to an account on a remote system, he would first place his public key in the **.ssh/authorized_keys** file in the account on the remote system he wants to access. If the user larisa on **turtle.mytrek.com** wants to access the aleina account on **rabbit.mytrek.com,** larisa's public key from **/home/larisa/.ssh/identity.pub** first must be placed in aleina's **authorized_keys** file, **/home/aleina/.ssh/authorized_keys**.

With **ssh**, you can log in from a local site to a remote host on your network and then send commands to be executed on that host. **ssh** is also capable of supporting X Window System connections. This feature is automatically enabled if you make an **ssh** connection from an X Window System environment, such as Gnome or KDE. A connection is set up for you between the local X server and the remote X server. The remote host sets up a dummy X server and sends any X Window System data through it to your local system to be processed by your own local X server.

To login with ssh, you enter the **ssh** command with the address of the remote host, followed by an **-l** option and the login name (user name) of the remote account you are logging into. The following example logs into the aleina user account on the **rabbit.mytrek.com** host.

```
ssh rabbit.mytrek.com -l aleina
```

You use scp to copy files from one host to another on a network. Designed to replace rcp, scp actually uses ssh to transfer data and employs the same authentication and encryption. If authentication requires it, scp requests a password or pass-phrase. Directories and files on remote hosts are specified using the user name and the host address before the filename or directory. The user name specifies the remote user account that scp is accessing, and the host is the remote system where that account is located. You separate the user from the host address with an at sign (@), and you separate the host address from the file or directory name with a colon (:). The following example copies the file **party** from a user current directory to the user **aleina**'s **birthday** directory, located on the **rabbit.mytrek.com** host.

```
scp party aleina@rabbit.mytrek.com:/birthday/party
```

Of particular interest is the **-r** option, which enables you to copy whole directories. In the next example, the user copies the entire **reports** directory to the **projects** directory of the user **justin**.

```
scp -r reports justin@rabbit.mytrek.com:/projects
```

The Complete Reference

Part II

Environments

The
Complete
Reference

## Chapter 8

The K Desktop
Environment: KDE

The *K Desktop Environment* (*KDE*) is a network transparent desktop that includes the standard desktop features, such as a window manager and a file manager, as well as an extensive set of applications that cover most Linux tasks. KDE is an Internet- aware system that includes a full set of integrated network/Internet applications, including a mailer, a newsreader, and a Web browser. The file manager doubles as a Web and FTP client, enabling you to access Internet sites directly from your desktop. KDE aims to provide a level of desktop functionality and ease of use found in MAC/OS and Windows systems, combined with the power and flexibility of the Unix operating system.

KDE version 2.0, also known as Kopernicus, has currently superseded the earlier 1.1 version of KDE. This chapter describes version 2.0. There are many similarities with version 1.1; however, users familiar with the old KDE will find some important changes. KDE 2.0 features a new file manager and control center. It includes a new multimedia architecture based on ARTS (Analog Realtime Synthesizer) for both sound and video applications. One of the more dramatic changes is KOffice suite of office applications. The suite is part of the standard KDE 2.0 software package and includes a professional-level publishing program, an illustrator, and a spreadsheet, among other applications (see Chapter 20).

The KDE desktop is developed and distributed by the KDE project, which is a large open group of hundreds of programmers around the world. KDE is entirely free and open software provided under a GNU public license and is available free of charge along with its source code. KDE development is managed by a core group: the KDE Core Team. Anyone can apply, though membership is based on merit.

KDE applications are developed using several supporting KDE technologies. These include KIO, which offers seamless and modular access of files and directories across a network. For interprocess communication, KDE uses the Desktop Communications Protocol (DCOP). KParts is the KDE component object model used to embed an application within another, such as a spreadsheet within a word processor. The XML GUI uses XML to generate and place GUI objects such as menus and toolbars. KHTML is a rendering and drawing engine that supports a range of Internet technologies such as Java, Netscape plug-ins, and the Secure Sockets Layer (SSL).

Numerous applications written specifically for KDE are easily accessible from the desktop. These include editors, photo and paint image applications, spreadsheets, and office applications. Such applications usually have the letter *k* as part of their name— for example, KWord or KMail. Provided with the KDE desktop are a variety of tools. These include calculators, console windows, notepads, and even software package managers. On a system administration level, KDE provides several tools for configuring your system. With KUser, you can manage user accounts, adding new ones or removing old ones. Kppp enables you to connect easily to remote networks with *Point-to-Point Protocol* (*PPP*) protocols using a modem. Practically all your Linux tasks can be performed from the KDE desktop. KDE applications also feature a built-in Help application. Choosing the Contents entry in the Help menu starts the KDE Help viewer, which provides a Web page–like interface with links for navigating through the Help documents. KDE version 2.0 includes an office application suite called *KOffice,* based on KDE's KOM/OpenParts technology.

KOffice includes a presentation application, a spreadsheet, an illustrator, and a word processor, among other components (see Chapter 20 for more details). In addition, an *Interactive Development Environment* (*IDE*), called *KDevelop,* is also available to help programmers create KDE-based software.

KDE was initiated by Matthias Ettrich in October 1996, and it has an extensive list of sponsors, including SuSE, Caldera, Red Hat, O'Reilly, DLD, Delix, Live, Linux Verband, and others. KDE is designed to run on any Unix implementation, including Linux, Solaris, HP-UX, and FreeBSD. The official KDE Web site is **www.kde.org**, which provides news updates, download links, and documentation. KDE software packages can be downloaded from the KDE FTP site at **ftp.kde.org** and its mirror sites. Several KDE mailing lists are available for users and developers, including announcements, administration, and other topics. See the KDE Web site to subscribe. A great many software applications are currently available for KDE at **apps.kde.com**. Development support and documentation can be obtained at **developer.kde.org**. Various KDE Web sites are listed in Table 8-1.

Qt and Harmony

KDE uses as its library of GUI tools the Qt library, developed and supported by Troll Tech (**www.trolltech.com**). *Qt* is considered one of the best GUI libraries available for Unix/Linux systems. Using Qt has the advantage of relying on a commercially developed and supported GUI library. Also, using the Qt libraries drastically reduced the development time for KDE. Troll Tech provides the Qt libraries as open source

Web Site	Description
www.kde.org	KDE Web site
ftp.kde.org	KDE FTP site
apps.kde.com	KDE software repository
developer.kde.org	KDE developer site
www.trolltech.com	Site for Qt Libraries
koffice.kde.org	KOffice Office Suite
kde.themes.org	KDE desktop themes
lists.kde.org	KDE mailing lists

Table 8-1.   *KDE Web Sites*

software that is freely distributable. Certain restrictions exist, however: Qt-based (KDE) applications must be free and open sourced, with no modifications made to the Qt libraries. If you develop an application with the Qt libraries and want to sell it, then you have to buy a license from Troll Tech. In other words, the Qt library is free for free applications, but not for commercial ones.

The Harmony Project is currently developing a free alternative to the Qt libraries. Harmony will include all Qt functionality, as well as added features, such as multi-threading and theming. It will be entirely compatible with any KDE applications developed using Qt libraries. Harmony will be provided under the *GNU library public license* (*LGPL*). See **www.gnu.org/software/harmony** for more information.

KDE Desktop

One of KDE's aims is to provide users with a consistent integrated desktop, where all applications use GUI interfaces (see Figure 8-1). To this end, KDE provides its own window manager (kwm), file manager (Konqueror), program manager, and desktop

Figure 8-1. *The KDE desktop*

panel. You can run any other X Window System–compliant application, such as Netscape, in KDE, as well as any Gnome application. In turn, you can also run any KDE application, including the Konqueror file manager, with any other Linux window manager, including Blackbox, Afterstep, and even Enlightenment. You can even run KDE applications in Gnome.

When you first start KDE, the initial file manager window is displayed on your screen showing your current working directory. At the bottom of the screen is the KDE panel. Located on the panel are icons for menus and programs, as well as buttons for different desktop screens. The icon for the Applications Starter shows a large K on a cog wheel with a small arrow at the top indicating it is a menu. Click this icon to display the menu listing all the applications you can run. The Applications Starter operates somewhat like the Start menu in Windows. The standard KDE applications installed with the KDE can be accessed through this menu. You can find entries for different categories such as Internet, Systems, Multimedia, and Utilities. These submenus list KDE applications you can use. For example, to start the KDE mailer, select the Mail Client entry in the Internet submenu. To quit KDE, you can select the Logout entry in the Applications Starter menu. You can also right-click anywhere on the desktop and select the Logout entry from the pop-up menu. If you leave any KDE or X11 applications or windows open when you quit, they are automatically restored when you start up again.

Across the top of the desktop is a menu for desktop operations such as creating new shortcuts called desktop files for applications and devices (known as kdelink files in previous versions), as well as accessing open windows or changing to different virtual desktops. You can bring up the same set of menus by right-clicking anywhere on the desktop background.

Two icons are initially displayed in the upper-left corner of the desktop, a directory folder icon labeled Home and the Trash icon. The Home directory folder is a link to your home directory. Click on it to open the file manager to display the files in your home directory. The Trash icon operates like the Recycle Bin in Windows or the trash can on the Mac. Drag items to it to hold them for deletion. The panel initially shows small icons for the Applications Starter, the window list, your home directory, a terminal window, and buttons for virtual desktops, among others. The Window List icon looks like several grouped windows. It displays a list of all open windows and the desktop they are on. The Home Directory icon shows a folder with a house. Click it to open a file manager window showing your home directory. The Help Viewer icon is an image of a book. The Terminal Window icon is a picture of a two computer monitors. Click this to open a terminal window where you can enter Linux shell commands.

The desktop supports drag-and-drop operations. For example, to print a document, drag it to the Printer icon. You can place any directories on the desktop by simply dragging them from a file manager window to the desktop. With KDE 2.0, the desktop also supports copy-and-paste operations, holding text you copied from one application in a desktop clipboard that you can then use to paste to another application. For example, you can copy a Web address from a Web page and then past it into an e-mail message or a word processing document. This feature is supported by the Klipper utility located on the Panel.

You can create new directories on the desktop by right-clicking anywhere on the desktop and selecting New and then Directory from the pop-up menu. All items that appear on the desktop are located in the **Desktop** directory in your home directory. There you can find the **Trash** and **Home** directories, along with any others you place on the desktop. Home is a link to your user home directory. To configure your desktop, either click the Desktop icon located on the right of your panel, or right-click the desktop and select the Display Properties entry. This displays a window with several tabbed panels for different desktop settings, such as the background or style.

Desktop Files

On the KDE 2.0 desktop, special files called *desktop* files are used to manage a variety of tasks, including device management, Internet connections, program management, and document types. (These were known as *kdelink* files in previous versions of KDE.) You create a desktop file by right-clicking the desktop and then selecting New. From this menu, you choose the type of desktop file you want to create (see Figure 8-2). Application is for launching applications. The CD-ROM and Floppy Device entries each create a desktop file that can mount CD-ROMs or floppy disks on your system. The Text File and HTML File entries are used to reference text files and Web pages on your system. The Internet Address entry holds a URL address that you can use to access a Web or FTP site. The Application and Device entries are covered in later sections.

Given a desktop file that holds an Internet URL address, you can access that site directly by simply clicking the desktop icon on the desktop. You can also place the desktop file on your desktop or put it in your panel, where it is easily accessible. You can configure the file to display any icon you choose. In effect, you can have an icon on your desktop you can click to immediately access a Web site. When you click the URL desktop file, the file manager starts up in its Web browser mode and will access that address, displaying the Web page. For FTP sites, it performs an anonymous login and displays the remote directory.

Figure 8-2. *The desktop (New) menu*

To create a URL desktop file, right-click the desktop and select the New menu. A window appears that displays a box that prompts you to enter the URL address. A desktop dialog box for URL access is then displayed. This dialog box has three tabbed panels: General, Permissions, and URL (See Figure 8-3). On the General panel is the name of your desktop file. It will have as its name the URL address that you entered. You can change this to a more descriptive name if you wish, adding the suffix **.desktop**. Go to the URL panel. There, you see a box labeled URL with a URL you entered already in it. You can change it if you want. For example, for KDE themes the URL would be **http://kde.themes.org**. Be sure to include the protocol, such as **http://** or **ftp://**. An Icon button on this panel shows the icon that will be displayed for this desktop file on your desktop. The default is a Web World icon. You can change it if you want by clicking the Icon button to open a window that lists icons you can choose from. Click OK when you are finished. The desktop file then appears on your desktop with that icon. Click it to access the Web site. An alternative and easier way to create a URL desktop file is simply to drag a URL from a Web page displayed on the file manager to your desktop. A desktop file is automatically generated with that URL. To change the default icon used, you can

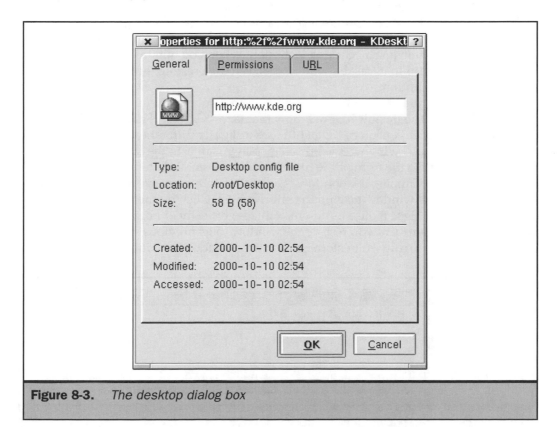

Figure 8-3.   *The desktop dialog box*

right-click the file and choose Properties to display the desktop dialog box. Click the Icon button to choose a new icon.

KDE Windows

A KDE window has the same functionality you find in other window managers and desktops. You can resize the window by clicking and dragging any of its corners or sides. A click-and-drag operation on a side extends the window in that dimension, whereas a corner extends both height and width at the same time. Notice that the corners are slightly enhanced. The top of the window has a title bar showing the name of the window, the program name in the case of applications and the current directory name for the file manager windows. The active window has the title bar highlighted. To move the window, click this title bar and drag it where you want. Right-clicking the window title bar displays a drop-down menu with entries for window operations, such as closing or resizing the window. Within the window, menus, icons, and toolbars for the particular application are displayed. Figure 8-4 shows an example of a KDE window.

Opened windows are also shown as buttons on the KDE taskbar located on the panel. The taskbar shows the different programs you are running or windows you have open. This is essentially a docking mechanism that enables you to change to a window or application just by clicking its button. When you minimize (iconify) a window, it is reduced to its taskbar button. You can then restore the window by clicking its taskbar button.

KDE supports numerous different themes, each displaying window elements in different ways. The default KDE window theme for KDE 2.0 is shown in these examples. The earlier version of KDE (1.0) uses a slightly different window theme. In the default KDE 2.0 window, the button displaying an X to the left of the title will close the window. To the right of the title bar are three small buttons for sticking, minimizing, or maximizing the window. The button with a up arrow maximizes the window, letting the window take up the entire screen. Clicking the Maximize button with the middle or right mouse button maximizes vertically or horizontally. Click the button with the down arrow to restore the window to its previous size. The button showing the down arrow will restore a maximized window or minimize a standard

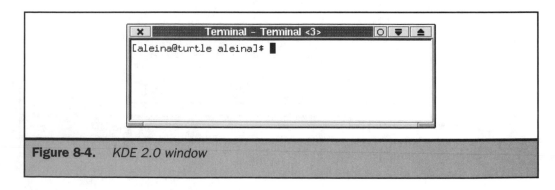

Figure 8-4.   *KDE 2.0 window*

window. On KDE, when you minimize a window, it is no longer displayed on the desktop, but its button entry remains in the taskbar on the Panel (shown next). Click that button to redisplay the window. You can also reduce a window to its title bar by double-clicking the title bar. To restore the window, double-click the title bar again.

The button with an *O* image in it is a Stick Pin button. The Stick Pin button it is used to have a window appear on all your virtual desktops, no matter to which one you change. In effect, the window sticks on the screen when you change to another virtual desktop. When active, it appears as an *O* with a period inside. When inactive, it shows just an empty *O* symbol. Application windows may also display a help notes button, shown next to the Stick Pin button and displaying a question mark. Clicking this button changes your cursor to a question mark. You can then move the cursor to an item such as an icon on a toolbar, then click it to display a small help note explaining what the item does. Clicking a forward button in the file manager taskbar will show a note explaining that this button performs a browser forward operation.

Tip   *When a window is not active, its contrast is reduced to make it easier for you to notice the active window.*

As a multitasking operating system, Linux enables you to run several applications at the same time. This means you can have several applications open and running on your desktop, each with its own window. You can switch between them by moving from one window to another. When an application is open, a button for it is placed in the taskbar at the top of the desktop. You can switch to that application at any time by clicking its Taskbar button. From the keyboard, you can use the ALT-TAB key combination to display a list of current applications. Holding down the ALT key and sequentially pressing TAB moves you through the list. You can hide an application at any time by clicking its window's Minimize button. The Taskbar button entry for it remains. Click this to restore the application. Table 8-2 shows the KDE keyboard shortcuts.

Virtual Desktops: The KDE Desktop Pager

KDE, like most Linux window managers, supports virtual desktops. In effect, this extends the desktop area on which you can work. You could have Netscape running on one desktop and be using a text editor in another. KDE can support up to 16 virtual desktops, though the default is four. Your virtual desktops can be displayed and accessed using the KDE Desktop Pager located on the Panel. The KDE Desktop Pager represents your virtual desktops as miniature screens showing small squares for each desktop.

Keys	Effect
ALT-ESC or CTRL-ESC	Current Session manager with Logout button
ALT-TAB and ALT-SHIFT-TAB	Traverse the windows of the current desktop
CTRL-TAB and CTRL-SHIFT-TAB	Traverse the virtual desktops
ALT-F2	Open small command line window
ALT-F3	Window operation menu
ALT-F4	Close window
CTRL-F[1..8]	Switch to a particular virtual desktop
CTRL-ALT-ESC	Force shutdown of X Windows

Table 8-2.   *KDE Keyboard Shortcuts*

By default there are four squares, numbered 1, 2, 3, and 4. You can have up to 16.
To move from one desktop to another, click the square for the destination desktop.
Clicking 3 displays the third desktop, and clicking 1 moves you back to the first desktop.

Normally, when you open an application on a particular desktop, it appears only
in that desktop. When you move to another desktop, the application disappears from
your screen. Moving back again shows the application. For example, if you open KMail
on the third desktop and then move to the second desktop, KMail disappears from
your screen. Moving back to the third desktop causes KMail to appear again. Selecting
the Taskbar button for an application also switches you to the desktop on which the
application is open. In the example, clicking the KMail Taskbar button switches to the
third desktop. You can also use the Window list menu in the panel to display a listing
of all open windows in each desktop. Selecting a window entry moves to that desktop.
If you want an application to appear on all desktops, no matter which one you move
to, click its window's Stick Pin button.

If you want to move a window to a different desktop, first open the window's menu
by right-clicking the window's title bar. Then, select the To Desktop entry, which lists

the available desktops. Choose the one you want. You can also right-click the window's title bar to display the window's menu.

You can also configure KDE so that, if you move the mouse over the edge of a desktop screen, it automatically moves to the adjoining desktop. You need to imagine the desktops arranged in a four-square configuration, with two top desktops next to each other and two desktops below them. You enable this feature by selecting the Active Desktop Borders entry in the Desktop panel in the KDE Control Center.

To change the number of virtual desktops, you use the KPanel configuration window. From the Applications Starter menu, select Panel and then Configure. On the KPanel configuration window, select the Desktop panel. You then see entries for the current desktops. The visible bar controls the number of desktops. Slide this to the right to add more and to the left to reduce the number. The width bar controls the width of the desktop buttons on the panel. You can change any of the desktop names by clicking a name and entering a new one.

You can also configure desktop features, such as color background, for each virtual desktop. In the Applications Starter menu, select Settings and then Desktop. From this menu, you can choose various features to change. Selecting Background displays a Display Settings window. A list of virtual desktops is then shown. Select the one whose background you want to change, and then you can choose from colors and wallpaper. You can select wallpaper from a preselected list or choose your own.

KDE Panel and Applications Starter

The KDE panel is located at the bottom of the screen (shown next). Through it, you can access most KDE functions. The panel includes icons for menus, directory windows, specific programs, and virtual desktops. At the left end of the panel is an icon with a large *K* on a cog wheel. This is the icon for the KDE Application Starter. Click this icon to display the menu of applications you run. From the KDE menu, you can access numerous submenus for different kinds of applications. You can also open the Application Starter with the ALT-F1 key.

To add an application to the panel, select the Add application entry in the panel submenu located in the Applications Starter. This menu displays all installed KDE applications. To add a button for an application to the panel, click the application entry. You can also drag applications from a File Manager window to the panel directly and have them automatically placed in the panel. The panel only displays desktop files. When you drag-and-drop a file to the panel, a desktop file for it is automatically generated.

To configure the panel position and behavior, right-click the panel and select the configure entry. This displays a panel configuration dialog box with several tabbed panels. The Positions panel enables you to specify the edges of the screen where you want your panel and taskbar displayed. You can also enlarge or reduce it in size. On the Options panel, you can set auto-hide options for the panel and taskbar. The Desktops panel is used for configuring your virtual desktops, enabling you to add more desktops and rename the current ones.

You can add or remove menu items in your Applications Starter menu using the Edit Menus program. Right-click its *K* icon and select Configure. This launches the Edit Menus window, displaying the Applications Starter menu to the right and a menu button to the left, labeled Empty. To add a new item, drag this button to the Launcher menu. You can even place it in a submenu. To enter a label and an application for it to start, you right-click the button. This displays a dialog box with fields for the application program, the menu item name, and the MIME types to be associated with the program. You can also specify if you want the program opened in a terminal window. For example, to create a menu entry for the notorious Vi editor, drag the Empty button to the Launcher menu. Right-click it and enter **vi** as the command and **The Vi Editor** as the name. Click the check box for Open in terminal window because Vi is a shell-based program. Before you quit, be sure to select Save from the File menu. You then see an entry for the Vi editor in the Applications Starter menu. You can also delete entries using Edit Menus.

KDE Themes

For your desktop, you can select a variety of different themes. A *theme* changes the look and feel of your desktop, affecting the appearance of GUI elements, such as scrollbars, buttons, and icons. For example, you use the Mac OS theme to make your K desktop look like a Macintosh. Themes for the K desktop can be downloaded from the **kde. themes.org** Web site. Information and links for themes for different window managers can be found at **www.themes.org**. You can use the KthemeMgr program to install and change your themes.

The KDE Help System

The KDE Help viewer provides a browser-like interface for accessing and displaying both KDE Help files and Linux man and info files. You can start the Help system either by selecting its entry in the Applications Starter menu or by right-clicking the desktop and selecting the Help entry (see Figure 8-5). The Help window is divided into two frames. The left frame of the help screen holds two tabbed panels, one listing contents and the other providing a search engine. The left frame displays currently selected documents. A help tree on the content's panel lets you choose the kind of help documents you want to access. Here you can choose manuals, man pages, or info documents. The help center includes a detailed user manual, a FAQ, and KDE Web site access.

You can also use a URL format to access man and info pages, info: and man:. For example, **man:cp** displays the man page for the **cp** command. A navigation toolbar enables you to move through previously viewed documents. KDE Help documents use

Figure 8-5.   *The KDE Help System*

an HTML format with links you can click to access other documents. The Back and Forward commands move you through the list of previously viewed documents. The KDE Help system provides an effective search tool for searching for patterns in Help documents, including man and info pages. Select the Search entry to display a page where you can enter your pattern. You can also click the small icon in the toolbar of a page with a spyglass.

Applications

You can start an application in KDE in several ways. If an entry for it is in the Applications Starter menu, you can select that entry to start the application. Some applications also have buttons on the KDE panel you can click to start them. The panel already holds several of the commonly used programs, such as the KMail and Kalendar. You can also use the file manager to locate a file using that application or the application program itself. Clicking its icon starts the application. Or, you can open a shell window and enter the name of the application at the shell prompt and press ENTER to start an application. You can also use the ALT-F2 key to open a small window consisting of a box to enter a single command. You can use the UP ARROW and DOWN ARROW keys to display previous commands, and the RIGHT ARROW and LEFT ARROW keys or the BACKSPACE key to edit any of them. Press ENTER to execute a command.

> **Note** *You can create a desktop file on your desktop for any application already on your KDE menu by simply clicking and dragging its menu entry to the desktop. Select copy, and a desktop file for that application is created for you on your desktop, showing its icon.*

You can also access applications directly from your desktop. To access an application from the desktop, either create a desktop file or a standard link file that can link to the original application program. With a desktop file, you can choose your own icon and specify a tooltip comment. You can also use a desktop file to start a shell-based application running in its own terminal window. A standard link, on the other hand, is a simple reference to the original program file. Using a link starts the program up directly with no arguments. To create a standard link file, locate the application on your file system, usually in the **/opt/kde2/bin** directory. Then, click and drag the application icon to your desktop. In the pop-up menu, select Link. The link has the same icon as the original application. Whenever you then click that icon, you can select Start from the pop-up menu to start the application.

To create a new desktop file for an Application, you right-click anywhere on the empty desktop, select New from the pop-up menu, and then choose Application. Enter the name for the program and a desktop file for it appears on the desktop with that name. A properties dialog box then opens with four panels: General, Permissions, Execute, and Application. The General panel displays the name of the link. To specify the application the desktop file runs, go to the Execute panel and either enter the application's program name in the Execute box or click Browse to select it (see Figure 8-6). If this is a shell program, you can elect to run it from within a terminal window. To select an icon image for the desktop file, click the Cog icon. The Select icon window is displayed, listing icons from which you can choose. To run a shell-based program such as Vi or Pine, click the Run in terminal check box and specify any terminal options. Certain KDE programs can minimize to a small icon, which can be displayed in the panel while they are running. This is referred to as *swallowing on the panel.* Enter the name of the program in that Execute box.

On the Permissions panel, be sure to set execute permissions so that the program can be run. In the Application panel, you can specify the type of documents to be associated with this application. The bottom of the panel shows two lists. The left

Figure 8-6.   *KDE Application desktop dialog*

list is for MIME types you want associated with this program, and the right list is the
listing of available MIME types from which to choose (see Figure 8-7). To add a MIME
type, select an entry in the right list and click the Left Arrow button. Use the Right
Arrow button to remove a MIME type. On the panel you also specify the comment,
the file manager program name, and the name in your language. The comment is the
Help note that appears when you pass your mouse over the icon. For the file manager
program name, enter the name followed by a semicolon. This is the name used for
the link, if you use the file manager to display it. Desktop files needn't reside on the
desktop. You can place them in any directory and access them through the file manager.
You can later make changes to a desktop file by right-clicking its icon and selecting
Properties from the pop-up menu. This again displays the dialog box for this file. You
can change its icon and even the application it runs. You can download other icons
from **icons.themes.org**.

You can have KDE automatically display selected directories or start certain
applications whenever it starts up. To do so, place links for these windows and
applications in the **AutoStart** directory. Currently, the AutoStart folder is located
in your **.kde2** directory. To place a link for a directory in the AutoStart folder, first
locate the Directory icon using the file manager. Then, click and drag the icon to the

Figure 8-7. *KDE Application desktop MIME type entries*

AutoStart folder. From the pop-up menu that appears, select Link (do not select Copy or Move). Whenever you start KDE, that directory is displayed in a file manager window. You can do the same for applications and files. Locate the application with the file manager and click and drag it to the AutoStart folder, selecting Link. For a file, do the same. Whenever KDE starts, those applications automatically start. For files, the application associated with a file starts using that file. For example, to start KMail automatically, click and drag its icon to the AutoStart folder, selecting Link.

Mounting CD-ROMs and Floppy Disks from the Desktop

With KDE, you can create icons on your desktop that you can use to access a CD-ROM or floppy disk easily with these icons. The icons are *desktop files*, which are special files that can perform a variety of tasks, including accessing devices such as CD-ROMs. Once you set up a desktop file for your CD-ROM, to access a CD-ROM disk, place the CD-ROM disk in your CD-ROM drive and click the CD-ROM icon. The file manager window then opens, displaying the contents of the CD-ROM's top-level directory. You can also right-click the icon to display a pop-up menu with an entry to mount or unmount the disk. When the

CD-ROM holds a mounted CD disk, the CD-ROM icon displays a small red rectangle on its image. Unlike on Windows systems, the CD-ROM disk remains locked in the CD-ROM drive until you unlock it. To unmount the CD, right-click the CD-ROM's icon and select Unmount from the pop-up menu. You can then open the CD-ROM drive and remove the CD.

To access a floppy disk, you can perform a similar operation using the Floppy Disk icon. Place the floppy disk in the disk drive and click the Floppy Disk icon. This displays a file manager window with the contents for floppy disk. Or, you can right-click the icon to display a pop-up menu with an entry to mount the disk. Once it is mounted, you can access it, copying files to and from the disk. Be careful not to remove the disk unless you first unmount it. To unmount the disk, right-click its icon and select Unmount from the icon's pop-up menu. You can perform one added operation with floppy disks. If you put in a blank disk, you can format it. You can choose from several file system formats, including MS-DOS. To format a standard Linux file system, select the ext2 entry.

A desktop you use for your CD-ROM is a special kind of desktop file designed for file system devices. Should you add a new CD-ROM or Floppy drive, you can create a new desktop file for it to enable you to access the drive from your desktop. To create one, first right-click anywhere on the desktop, select New, and then select either CD-ROM Device for a CD-ROM drive or Floppy Device for a floppy drive. This opens a properties window with tabs for General, Permissions, and Device. In the General tab you can set the name for the device icon that will appear on the desktop, as well as choose the icon you want to show a mounted CD-ROM or Floppy disk (a default is already provided). On the Device panel, you select the actual device, its mount point on your file system, and the type of file system it will mount, as well as the icon used to indicate when it is unmounted (see Figure 8-8). On the permissions panel, you can also indicate the permissions that have been set to allow access to the device. See the chapter on file administration, Chapter 32, for a discussion on devices and file systems. The desktop file does not perform the necessary system administration operations that enable access to the CD-ROM by ordinary users. Normally, only the systems administrator (root user) can mount or unmount CD-ROMs and floppy disks. You also must make sure an entry is in the **/etc/fstab** file for the CD-ROM or floppy drive. If not, you have to add one. Such operations are fairly easy to perform using the file system management tools provided by Linuxconf and fsconf. Check Chapter 4 and Chapter 32 for the procedures to use.

KDE File Manager and Internet Client: Konqueror

The *KDE file manager* is a multifunctional utility with which you can manage files, start programs, browse the Web, and download files from remote sites (see Figure 8-9). Traditionally, the term "file manager" was used to refer to managing files on a local hard disk. The KDE file manager extends its functionality well beyond this traditional

Figure 8-8. *The desktop dialog box for CD-ROM devices*

Figure 8-9. *The KDE file manager*

function because it is Internet capable, seamlessly displaying remote file systems as if they were your own, as well as viewing Web pages with browser capabilities. With KDE 2.0, the original KDE file manager, kfm, was replaced by a new file manager called Konqueror.

A KDE file manager window consists of a menu bar, a navigation toolbar, a location field, a status bar, and a pane of file and directory icons for the current working directory. When you first display the file manager window, it displays the file and subdirectory icons for your **home** directory. The files listed in a directory can be viewed in several different ways. You can view files and directories as icons, small icons, or in a detailed listing. The detailed listing provides permissions, owner, group, and size information. Permissions are the permissions controlling access to this file (see Chapter 12). Configuration files are not usually displayed. These are files beginning with a period and are often referred to as *dot files.* To have the file manager display these files, select Show Dot Files from the View menu.

To search for files, select the Find entry in the Tools menu. This opens a dialog box with which you can search for filenames using wildcard matching symbols, such as *****. Click the small image of a looking glass in the toolbar to run the search and on the stoplight to stop it (see Figure 8-10). The search results are displayed in a pane in the lower half of the search window. You can click a file and have it open with its appropriate application. Text files are displayed by the KWrite text editor, and images are displayed

Figure 8-10.   *The KDE Search tool*

by KView. Applications are run. The search program also enables you to save your search results for later reference. You can even select files from the search and add them to an archive.

You can open a file either by clicking it or by selecting it, and then choosing the Open entry in the File menu. A single-click, not a double-click, opens the file. If you want to select the file or directory, you need to hold down the CTRL key while you click it. A selection is performed with a CTRL-click. If the file is a program, that program starts up. If it is a data file, such as text file, then the associated application is run using that data file. For example, if you click a text file, then the KWrite application starts displaying that file. If Konqueror cannot determine the application to use, it opens a dialog box prompting you to enter the application name. You can click the Browse button on this box to use a directory tree to locate the application program you want.

The file manager can also extract tar archives and install RPM packages. An *archive* is a file ending in **.tar.gz**, **.tar**, or **.tgz**. Clicking the archive lists the files in it. You can extract a particular file simply by dragging it out the window. Clicking a text file displays it with KWrite, while clicking an image file displays it with KView. Selecting an RPM package opens it with the kpackage utility, which you can then use to install the package.

Moving Through the File System

A single-click on a Directory icon moves to that directory and displays its file and Subdirectory icons. Unlike other interfaces, KDE does not use double-clicking to open a directory. To move back up to the parent directory, you click the Up Arrow button located on the left end of the navigation toolbar. A single-click on a Directory icon moves you down the directory tree, one directory at a time. By clicking the Up Arrow button, you move up the tree. To move directly to a specific directory, you can enter its pathname in the location box located just above the pane that displays the File and Directory icons. Figure 8-9 shows the KDE file manager window displaying the current directory. You can also use several keyboard shortcuts to perform such operations, as listed in Table 8-3.

Like a Web browser, the file manager remembers the previous directories it has displayed. You can use the Back and Forward Arrow buttons to move through this list of prior directories. For example, a user could use the Location field to move to the **~/birthday** directory and use it again to move to the **~/reports** directory. Clicking the Back Arrow button displays the **~/birthday** directory (the ~ represents the user's home directory). Then, clicking the Forward Arrow button moves it back to the **~/reports** directory. You can move directly to your **home** directory by clicking the Home button. This has the same effect as the **cd** command in the shell. If you know you want to access particular directories again, you can bookmark them, much as you do a Web page. Just open the directory and select the Add Bookmarks entry in the Bookmarks menu. An entry for that directory is then placed in the file manager's Bookmark menu. To move to the directory again, select its entry in the Bookmark

Keys	Description
ALT-LEFT ARROW	Back in History
ALT-RIGHT ARROW	Forward in History
ALT-UP ARROW	One directory up
ENTER	Open a file/directory
ESC	Open a pop-up menu for the current file
LEFT/RIGHT/UP/DOWN ARROWS	Move among the icons
SPACEBAR	Select/unselect file
PAGE UP	Scroll up fast
PAGE DOWN	Scroll down fast
RIGHT ARROW	Scroll right (on Web pages)
LEFT ARROW	Scroll left (on Web pages)
UP ARROW	Scroll up (on Web pages)
DOWN ARROW	Scroll down (on Web pages)
CTRL-C	Copy selected file to Clipboard
CTRL-V	Paste files from Clipboard to current directory
CTRL-S	Select files by pattern
CTRL-T	Open a terminal in the current directory
CTRL-L	Open new location
CTRL-F	Find files
CTRL-W	Close window

Table 8-3. *KDE File Manager Keyboard Shortcuts*

menu. This is helpful for directories you might use frequently or for directories you must access with lengthy or complex pathnames. Bookmarks also apply to individual files and applications. You can even bookmark desktop icons. To bookmark a file, first select a file, and then choose the Add Bookmarks entry in the Bookmark menu. Later, selecting that bookmark opens that file. You can do the same thing with applications, where selecting the application's bookmark starts the application. Each bookmark is a file placed in your **.kde2/share/apps/konqueror/bookmarks** directory (kfm instead of Konqueror if you are upgrading from KDE 1.0). You can go to this directory and change the names of any of the files and they then appear as changed on your Bookmark menu. To change their names, right-click the file and select Properties from the pop-up menu. In the dialog box displayed, you see the filename is the full pathname on a panel tabbed General. You can replace the pathname with one of your own choosing. This bookmark would then appear as **myreport**. The pathname used to access the file is actually on the URL panel.

To help you navigate from one directory to another, you can use the Location field or the directory tree. In the Location field, you can enter the pathname of a directory, if you know it, and press ENTER. The file manager then displays that directory. The directory tree provides a tree listing all directories on your system and in your **home** directory. You can activate the directory tree by selecting Show Tree entry in the View menu. The directory tree has three main entries: Root, My Home, and Desktop. The Root entry displays the directories starting from the system root directory, the My Home entry displays directories starting from your **home** directory, and the Desktop entry displays the files and links on your desktop. Click a side triangle to expand a directory entry, and click a down triangle of an expanded directory entry to hide it.

Internet Access

The KDE file manager doubles as a Web browser and an FTP client. It includes a box for entering either a pathname for a local file, or a URL for a Web page on the Internet or your intranet. A navigation toolbar can be used to display previous Web pages or previous directories. When accessing a Web page, the page is displayed as on any Web browser. With the navigation toolbar, you can move back and forth through the list of previously displayed pages in that session. This feature is particularly convenient for displaying local Web pages, such as documentation in HTML format. Most Linux distributions provide extensive documentation in the form of Web pages you can easily access and display using a KDE file manager window. Figure 8-11 shows the KDE file manager window, operating as a Web browser, displaying a Web page.

The KDE file manager also operates as an FTP client. When you access an FTP site, you navigate the remote directories as you would your own. The operations to download a file are the same as copying a file on your local system. Just select the file's icon or entry in the file manager window and drag it to a window showing the local directory to which you want it downloaded. Then, select the Copy entry from the pop-up menu that appears.

By default, KDE attempts an anonymous login. If you want to perform a non-anonymous login as a particular user, add the username with an **@** symbol before the FTP address. You are then prompted for the user password. For example, the following entry logs in to the **ftp.mygames.com** server as the chris user:

```
ftp://chris@ftp.mygames.com
```

Figure 8-11.   *File manager as Web browser*

Copy, Move, Delete, and Archive Operations

To perform an operation on a file or directory, you first have to select it. In KDE, to select a file or directory, you hold the CTRL key down while clicking the file's icon or listing. To select more than one file, continually hold the CTRL key down while you click the files you want. You can also use the keyboard arrow keys to move from one file icon to another and then use the SPACEBAR to select the file you want.

To copy and move files, you can use the standard drag-and-drop method with your mouse. To copy a file, you locate it by using the file manager. Open another file manager window to the directory to which you want the file copied. Then, click and drag the File icon to that window (be sure to keep holding down the mouse button). A pop-up menu appears with selections for Move, Copy, or Link. Choose Copy. To move a file to another directory, follow the same procedure, but select Move from the pop-up menu. To copy or move a directory, use the same procedure as for files. All the directory's files and subdirectories are also copied or moved.

You can also move or copy files using the Copy and Paste commands. First, use a CTRL-click to select a file or directory (hold the CTRL key down while clicking the File icon). Either select the Copy entry from the Edit menu or click the Copy button in the navigation bar. Change to the directory to which you want to copy the selected file. Then, either select Paste from the Edit menu or click the Paste button. Follow the same procedure for moving files, using the Move entry from the Edit menu or the Move button in the navigation toolbar. Most of the basic file manager operations can be selected from a pop-up menu displayed whenever you right-click a file or directory. Here, you can find entries for copying, moving, and deleting the file, as well as navigating to a different directory.

Distinguishing between a copy of a file or directory and a link is important. A *copy* creates a duplicate, whereas a *link* is just another name for the same item. Links are used extensively as ways of providing different access points to the same document. If you want to access a file using an icon on your desktop, creating a link on the desktop, rather than a copy, is best. With a copy, you have two different documents, whereas with a link, you are accessing and changing the same document. To create a link on your desktop, click and drag the File icon from the directory window to the desktop and select Link from the pop-up menu. Clicking the link brings up the original document. Deleting the link only removes the link, not the original document. You can create links for directories or applications using the same procedure. You can also place links in a directory: click and drag the files to which you want to link in to that directory and select Link from the pop-up menu.

You delete a file by removing it immediately or placing it in a Trash folder to delete later. To delete a file, select it and then choose the Delete entry in the Edit menu. You can also right-click the icon and select Delete. To place a file in the Trash folder, click and drag it to the Trash icon on your desktop or select Move to Trash from the Edit menu. You can later open the Trash folder and delete the files. To delete all the files in the Trash folder, right-click the Trash icon and select Empty Trash Bin from the pop-up menu. To restore any files in the Trash bin, open the Trash bin and drag them out of the Trash folder.

Each file or directory has properties associated with it that include permissions, the filename, and its directory. To display the properties window for a given file, right-click the file's icon and select the Properties entry. On the General panel, you see the name of the file displayed. To change the file's name, replace the name there with a new one. Permissions are set on the Permissions panel. Here, you can set read, write, and execute permissions for user, group, or other access to the file. See Chapter 8 for a discussion of permissions. The group entry enables you to change the group for a file.

.directory

KDE automatically searches for and reads an existing **.directory** file located in a directory. A **.directory** file holds KDE configuration information used to determine how the directory is displayed. You can create such a file in a directory and place a setting in it to set display features, such as the icon to use to display the directory folder.

KDE Configuration: KDE Control Center

With the KDE Control Center, you can configure your desktop and system, changing the way it is displayed and the features it supports (see Figure 8-12). You can open the Control Center directly to a selected component by selecting its entry in the Applications Starter Settings menu. The Settings menu displays a submenu listing the configuration categories. Select a category, and then select the component you want. For example, to configure your screen saver, select the screen saver config entry in the Desktop menu located in the Settings menu. The Control Center can be directly started by either clicking the Control Center icon in the panel or selecting Control Center from the Applications Starter menu.

The Control Center window is divided into two panes. The left pane shows a tree view of all the components you can configure and the right pane displays the dialog windows for a selected component. On the left pane, components are arranged into categories whose titles you can expand or shrink. The Applications heading holds

Figure 8-12.   *KDE Control Center*

entries for configuring the KDE file manager's Web browser features, as well as its file management operations. Under Desktop, you can set different features for displaying and controlling your desktop. For example, the Background entry enables you to select a different background color or image for each one of your virtual desktops. Other desktop entries enable you to configure components such as the screen saver, the language used, and the window style. Some entries enable you to configure your mouse, key mappings, network connections, sound events, and window components. You can change key bindings for any of the window operations or standard operations, such as cut-and-paste. You can also change any of the specialize key mappings, such as the ALT-TAB key, which moves through your open applications, CTRL-TAB, which moves through your virtual desktops, or ALT-F2, which displays a dialog box for executing commands. Configuration components are actually modules. In future releases, more modules will be included as more applications and tools are added to the K desktop. See the Help viewer for a current listing of K desktop configuration modules.

.kde2/share/config

Your **.kde2** directories holds files and directories used to maintain your KDE desktop. The **.desktops** directory holds KDE desktop files whose icons are displayed on the desktop. Configuration files are located in the **.kde2/share/config** directory (.kde/share/config for KDE 1.1). Here, you can find the general KDE configuration file **kfmrc,** as well as configuration files for different KDE components. **krootwmrc** holds configuration commands for your root window, **kwmrc** for the window manager, **ksoundrc** for sound, and **kcmpanelrc** for your panel. You can place configuration directives directly in any of these files—for example, to have the left mouse button display the Applications Starter menu on the desktop, place the following lines in your **krootwmrc** file:

```
[MouseButtons]
 Left=Menu
```

MIME Types and Associated Applications

As you install new kinds of programs, they may use files of a certain type. In that case, you will need to register the type with KDE, so that it can be associated with a given application or group of applications. For example, the MIME type for Gif images is **image/gif**, which is associated with image-viewing programs. You use the KDE Control Center to set up a new MIME type or to change MIME type associations with applications. Select the File Association entry under File Browsing. This will list MIME types and their associated filename extensions. Select an entry to edit it, where you can change the applications associated with it. KDE saves its MIME type information in a separate file called **mimelnk** in the KDE configuration directory.

To change the associated application for a particular file, find the application with the file manager and then right-click it and select Edit File Type. This displays a window with two panels, General and Embedded. On the General menu, you can add an extension by clicking the Add button and entering the extension for the file type, using a * to match the prefix. For example, ***.gif; *.gif** would match any file ending with **.gif**. In the Application Preference Order section, use the Add button to select the application you want associated with the file. You can have several applications for a single file, changing the preference order for them as you wish. Click the Apply button to save your changes.

KDE Directories and Files

For many distributions, KDE 2.0 may be installed in the **/opt/kde2** directory (**/opt/kde** is used for the older KDE 1.1). On some systems, including Red Hat, KDE may be installed in the standard system directories, such as **/usr/bin**, **/usr/lib**.

The directories located in **/opt/kde2/share** contain files used to configure your KDE environment. The **/opt/kde2/share/applnk** directory maps its files to the Applications Launcher menu. Its directories and subdirectories appear as menu items and submenus on the main menu. Their contents consist of desktop files having the extension **.desktop**, one for each menu entry. The **/opt/kde2/share/apps** file contains files and directories set up by KDE applications. **/opt/kde2/share/mimelnk** holds MIME type definitions. **/opt/kde2/share/config** contains the configuration files for particular KDE applications. For example, **kfmrc** holds configuration entries for displaying and using the Konqueror file manager. These are the system-wide defaults that can be overridden by users' own configurations in their own **.kde2/share/config** directories. **/opt/kde2/share/icons** holds the default icons used on your KDE desktop and by KDE applications. The **/opt/kde2/share** directory also holds files for other configuration elements such as wallpaper, toolbars, and languages.

In the user's home directory, the **.kde2** directory holds a user's own KDE configuration for the desktop and its applications. The **.kde2/share** directory holds user versions of the **/opt/kde2//share** directories, specifying user configurations for menus, icons, MIME types, sounds, and applications. **.kde2/share/config** holds configuration files with users' own configuration specifications for their use of KDE applications. For example, **kmailrc** holds display configurations the user set up for KMail. **.kde2/share/icons** holds the icons for a user's particular themes, and **/.kde2/share/sounds** holds sound files. **.kde2/share/applnk** holds the desktop files for the menu entries in the Personal section of the Applications Launcher menu added by the user. In a user's **home** directory, the **.kderc** file contains current desktop configuration directives for resources such as key bindings, colors, and window styles.

Each user has a **Desktop** directory that holds KDE link files for all icons and folders on the user's desktop (see Table 8-4). These include the AutoStart, Trash, and Template folders. The AutoStart folder holds links to applications that are automatically started up whenever KDE starts. The Trash folder holds files you want to delete, and the Templates folder holds default kdelink files you can use as a basis for creating particular kdelink files.

System KDE Directories	Description
/opt/kde2/bin	KDE programs
/opt/kde2/lib	KDE libraries
/opt/kde2/include	Header files for use in compiling and developing KDE applications
/opt/kde2/share/config	KDE desktop and application configuration files
/opt/kde2/share/applnk	Desktop files used to build the main menu
/opt/kde2/share/apps	Files used by KDE applications
/opt/kde2/share/icons	Icons used in KDE desktop and applications
/opt/kde2/share/sounds	Sounds used in KDE desktop and applications
/opt/kde2/share/doc	KDE Help system
KDEDIR	System variable that holds KDE directory for other distributions, **KDEDIR=/opt/kde**

User KDE Directories	Description
.kde2/AutoStart	Applications automatically started up with KDE
.kde2/share/config	User KDE desktop and application configuration files for user-specified features
.kde2/share/applnk	Desktop files used to build the user's personal menu entries on the KDE main menu
.kde2/share/apps	Directories and files used by KDE applications
.kde2/share/icons	Icons used in the user's KDE desktop and applications, such as the ones for the user-specified theme
.kde2/share/sounds	Sounds used in KDE desktop and applications
.kderc	User configurations directives for desktop resources
Desktop	Holds desktop files for icons and folders displayed on the user's KDE desktop
Desktop/Trash	Trash folder for files marked for deletion

Table 8-4.   *KDE Installation Directories*

System Configuration Using KDE

KDE provides some system administration tools, though for most tasks, using Linuxconf is preferable. You can access the KDE system administration tools through the root desktop. Log in as the root user and start KDE. You then find system tools in both the System and Utilities menus in the Applications Starter menu. **kuser** provides a KDE interface for managing users on your system. You can add or remove users, or set permissions for current ones. The K desktop provides two utilities for viewing and managing your processes: the KDE Task Manager (KTop) and the KDE Process Manager (**kpm**). The SysV Init Editor is a version of the System V Init Manager (see Chapter 23). You can use the SysV Init Editor to start and stop servers and to determine at what runlevel they will start. See the chapters on system administration, Chapters 29-35, for a more detailed discussion on administration tasks. With **kppp**, you can connect to the Internet using a modem. Use **kppp** to connect to an *Internet service provider (ISP)* that supports the PPP protocols. **kppp** is discussed in more detail in the chapter on network administration, Chapter 36. **kpackage** enables you to manage the RPM packages you have installed. You can use it to install new packages, see the ones that are installed, and easily display information about each package. With **kpackage**, you can list the files in a particular package and display the release information. You can even display text files, such as Readme and configuration files. This is an easy way to find out exactly where an application's program and configuration files are installed on your system.

Updating KDE

Currently, new versions of KDE are being released frequently, sometimes every few months. KDE releases are designed to enable users to upgrade their older versions easily. Be sure to obtain the release for your particular distributions (though you can install from the source code if you want). Packages tailored for various distributions can be downloaded through the KDE Web site at **www.kde.org** or directly from the KDE FTP site at **ftp.kde.org** and its mirror sites in the **stable** directory. RPM packages for a particular distribution can be obtained from the distribution's FTP site such as **ftp.redhat.com**, **ftp.suse.com**, or **ftp.caldera.com**.

First, log in as the root user, and then create a directory to hold the KDE files. Then connect to an FTP site. You can use a Web browser such as Netscape, but using an FTP client such as ftp, NcFTP, or even the KDE file manager is preferable. Download the files for the new version to your new directory. For Red Hat and Caldera, these are a series of RPM package files. To download using ftp, be sure to turn off prompts with the `prompt` command and use `mget *` to download all the files at once. With the KDE file manager, select the files and drag them to a window open to the local directory and select Copy from the pop-up menu. Install QT, the KDE libraries and support packages, and then the KDE base packages followed by the remaining packages. Use the option `-Uvh` to upgrade the packages as shown on the next page.

```
rpm -Uvh  kdebase-2.0-4.i386.rpm
```

To install a particular KDE RPM package manually, you use the **rpm** command with the **-Uvh** options. This example installs the kdenetwork package:

```
rpm -Uvh  kdenetwork-2.0-4.i386.rpm
```

Chapter 9

Gnome

The *GNU Network Object Model Environment*, also known as *Gnome*, is a powerful and easy-to-use environment consisting primarily of a panel, a desktop, and a set of GUI tools with which program interfaces can be constructed. Gnome is designed to provide a flexible platform for the development of powerful applications. Currently, Gnome is strongly supported by Red Hat and is its primary GUI interface, though Gnome is also provided by most other distributions. Gnome is completely free under the GNU Public License. You can obtain the source directly, as well as documentation and other Gnome software from the Gnome Web site, at **www.gnome.org**. Recently, several companies have joined together to form the Gnome Foundation, an organization dedicated to coordinating the development of Gnome and Gnome software applications. These include such companies as Sun, IBM, and Hewlett-Packard, as well as Linux distributors like Red Hat, VA Linux, and TurboLinux, along with Gnome developers such as Helix Code and Eazel. Modeled on the Apache Foundation, which developed the Apache Web server, the Gnome Foundation will provide direction to Gnome development, as well as organization, financial, and legal support.

The core components of the Gnome desktop consist of a panel for starting programs and desktop functionality. Other components normally found in a desktop, such as a file manager, Web browser, and window manager are provided by Gnome-compliant applications. Gnome provides libraries of Gnome GUI tools that developers can use to create Gnome applications. Programs that use buttons, menus, and windows that adhere to a Gnome standard can be said to be Gnome-compliant. For a file manager, the Gnome desktop currently uses a Gnome version of Midnight Commander and will soon replace it with Nautilus. The Gnome desktop does not have its own window manager as KDE does. The Gnome desktop uses any Gnome-compliant window manager. Currently, the Sawfish window manager is the one bundled with the Gnome distributions.

Integrated into Gnome is support for component model interfaces, allowing software components to interconnect regardless of the computer language in which they are implemented or the kind of machine on which they are running. The standard used in Gnome for such interfaces is the *Common Object Request Broker Architecture* (*CORBA*), developed by the Object Model Group for use on UNIX systems. Gnome uses the ORBit implementation of CORBA. With such a framework, Gnome applications and clients can directly communicate with each other, enabling you to use components of one application in another.

You can find out more about Gnome at its Web site at **www.gnome.org**. This site not only provides a detailed software map of current Gnome projects with links to their development sites, it also maintains extensive mailing lists for Gnome projects to which you can subscribe. The Web site provides online documentation, such as the Gnome User's Guide and FAQs. If you want to develop Gnome programs, check the Gnome developer's Web site at **developer.gnome.org**. The site provides tutorials, programming guides, and development tools. Here you can find the complete API reference manual online, as well as extensive support tools such as tutorials and *Interactive Development Environments* (*IDE*). The site also includes detailed online documentation for the GTK+ library, Gnome widgets, and the Gnome desktop.

GTK+

GTK+ is the widget set used for Gnome applications. Its look and feel was originally derived from Motif. The widget set is designed from the ground up for power and flexibility. For example, buttons can have labels, images, or any combination thereof. Objects can be dynamically queried and modified at runtime. It also includes a theme engine that enables users to change the look and feel of applications using these widgets. At the same time, the GTK+ widget set remains small and efficient.

The GTK+ widget set is entirely free under the *Library General Public License* (*LGPL*). The LGPL enables developers to use the widget set with proprietary, as well as free, software (GPL would restrict it to just free software). The widget set also features an extensive set of programming language bindings, including C++, Perl, Python, Pascal, Objective C, Guile, and Ada. Internalization is fully supported, permitting GTK+-based applications to be used with other character sets, such as those in Asian languages. The drag-and-drop functionality supports both Xdnd and Motif protocols, allowing drag-and-drop operations with other widget sets that support these protocols, such as Qt and Motif.

The Gnome Enhancements: Helix Code and Eazel

Currently two organizations are developing software for Gnome: Helix Code and Eazel. The software they are developing is distributed under the GNU license, making it available to everyone free of charge. Both are active members of the Gnome Foundation.

Helix Code is working to make the Gnome an effective and user-friendly desktop, adding enhancements such as improved desktop utilities and office applications. They currently provide an improved version of Gnome known as Helix Gnome and are planning to offer a full suite of office applications. Currently, they offer a full-featured mail client called Evolution and a spreadsheet called Gnumeric. Evolution is a fully loaded communications application that includes a mail client, address book, calendar, and contact manager. Their next project is a full-featured word processor. You can obtain more information about Helix Code from its Web site at **www.helixcode.com**.

Helix Gnome is an enhancement of Gnome that is fully compatible with all Gnome software. You first need to have Gnome installed on your system, and then you can download and install Helix Gnome. Some applications, such as Helix Code's Evolution, require that you first install Helix Code Gnome. You can download Helix Gnome from its Web site at **www.helixcode.com**, selecting the version for your particular Linux distribution.

Eazel is a Gnome development organization that is currently working on a new file manager for the Gnome desktop, called Nautilus. Nautilus will officially replace the GNU Midnight Commander file manager now used on Gnome desktop. Nautilus is designed to operate as a desktop shell that can support numerous components, letting you operate a Web browser within it or decompress files. You can find out more about Eazel at **www.eazel.com**, and download the newest release of Nautilus from **nautilus.eazel.com**.

The Gnome Interface

The Gnome interface consists of the panel and a desktop, as shown in Figure 9-1. The panel appears as a long bar across the bottom of the screen. It holds menus, programs, and applets. An *applet* is a small program designed to be run within the panel. On the panel is a button with a large bare foot imprint on it. This is the Gnome applications menu, the main menu. The menu operates like the Start menu in Windows, listing entries for applications you can run on your desktop. You can display panels horizontally or vertically, and have them automatically hide to show you a full screen.

The remainder of the screen is the desktop. Here, you can place directories, files, or programs. You can create them on the desktop directly or drag them from a file manager window. A click-and-drag operation with the middle mouse button enables you to create links on the desktop to installed programs. Initially, the desktop only holds an icon for your home directory. Clicking it opens a file manager window to that directory.

From a user's point of view, you can think of the Gnome interface as having four components: the desktop, the panel, the main menu, and the file manager. In its standard default configuration, the Gnome desktop displays a Folder icon for your home

Figure 9-1. *Gnome*

directory in the upper-left corner. Some distributions may include other icons, such as links to the Gnome Web site or to the Linux Documentation site. Initially, a file manager window opens on the desktop, displaying your home directory. The panel has several default icons: The main menu (Bare Foot), the terminal program (Monitor), the Gnome Help System (Question Mark), the Gnome Control Center (Toolbox), the Gnome pager (Squares), and a clock. Red Hat also includes the Netscape Web browser.

To start a program, you can select its entry in the main menu, click its application launcher button in the panel (if there is one), double-click its icon in either the desktop or the file manager window, drag a data file to its icon, or select the Run Program entry in the main menu. This opens a small window where you can type in the program name.

To quit Gnome, you select the Logout entry in the main menu. You can also add a Logout button to the panel, which you could use instead. To add the Logout button, right-click the panel and select the Add Logout Button entry. A Logout button then appears in the panel. When you log out, the Logout dialog box is displayed. You have three options. The first option, Logout, quits Gnome, returning you to your command line shell still logged in to your Linux account. The second option, Halt, not only quits Gnome, but also shuts down your entire system. The third option, the Reboot entry, shuts down and reboots your system. The Logout entry is selected by default. Halt and Reboot are only available to the root user. If normal users execute them, they are prompted to enter the root user password to shut down. You can also elect to retain your desktop by clicking the "Save current setup" check box. This reopens any programs or directories still open when you logged out. Gnome-compliant window managers also quit when you log out of Gnome. You then must separately quit a window manager that is not Gnome-compliant after logging out of Gnome.

The Gnome Help system, shown in Figure 9-2, provides a browser-like interface for displaying the Gnome user's manual, Man pages, and info documents. It features a toolbar that enables you to move through the list of previously viewed documents. You can even bookmark specific items. A Web page interface enables you to use links to connect to different documents. You can easily move the manual or the list of Man pages and info documents. You can place entries in the location box to access specific documents directly. Special URL-like protocols are supported for the different types of documents: ghelp: for Gnome help, man: for man pages, and info: for the info documents.

The Gnome Desktop

The Gnome desktop provides you with all the capabilities of GUI-based operating systems (see Figure 9-3). You can drag files, applications, and directories to the desktop and then back to Gnome-compliant applications. If the desktop stops functioning, you can restart it by starting the Gnome file manager. The desktop is actually a backend process in the Gnome file manager, but you needn't have the file manager open to use the desktop.

Although the Gnome desktop supports drag-and-drop operations, these work only for applications that are Gnome compliant. You can drag any items from a Gnome-compliant application to your desktop, and vice versa. Any icon for an item that you

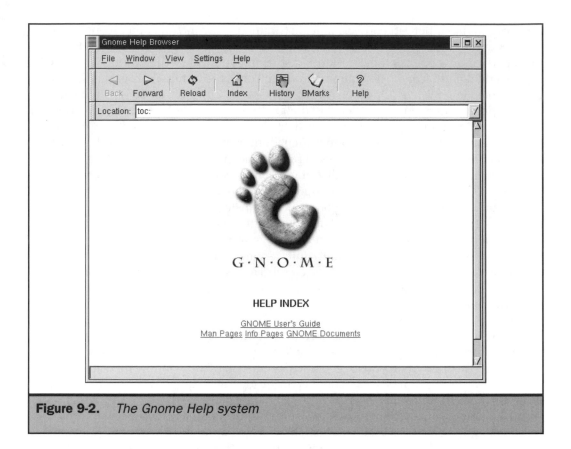

Figure 9-2. *The Gnome Help system*

drag from a file manager window to the desktop also appears on the desktop. However, the default drag-and-drop operation is a move operation. If you select a file in your file manager window and drag it to the desktop, you are actually moving the file from its current directory to the **.gnome-desktop** directory, which is located in your home directory and holds all items on the desktop (notice this is a dot file). In the case of dragging directory folders to the desktop, the entire directory and its subdirectories would be copied to the **.gnome-desktop** directory.

In most cases, you only want to create on the desktop another way to access a file without moving it from its original directory. You can do this by creating a link or a program launcher instead of moving the file. To create a link, drag the file while holding down the middle mouse button. When you release the mouse button, a pop-up menu appears with entries for copy, move, or link. Select the link entry. A copy of the icon then appears with a small arrow in the right corner indicating it is a link. You can then click this link to start the program, open the file, or open the directory, depending on what kind of file you linked to. To create a program launcher, right-click anywhere on the desktop and choose the Create Launcher applet entry. This opens a dialog box where you can enter the program name, select an icon for it, and set its permissions.

Figure 9-3.   *The Gnome desktop*

You can then use that icon to access the item directly. This is often used for starting common programs. For example, you can middle-click and drag the Netscape icon to the desktop and select Link from the pop-up menu to create a Link icon for Netscape. Double-clicking the icon starts Netscape. You can do the same with files. In this case, their respective program is started. If the item is a directory, then the file manager starts up, opened to that directory. If you want to have an application placed on your desktop that is not Gnome-compliant, you can manually place a link in your home directory's **.gnome-desktop** directory.

As an alternative to the desktop, you can drag any program, file, or directory to the panel; a launcher applet is then automatically created for it on the panel. The item is not moved or copied. You can also right-click anywhere on the empty desktop to display a menu, some of whose entries will start applications. The entries for this menu are listed in Table 9-1. You will notice entries for a new directory. Remember, this entry creates a new directory on your desktop, specifically in the your **.gnome-desktop** directory.

ENVIRONMENTS

Menu Item	Description
New | Terminal	Launches a new Gnome terminal window that navigates to the **~/.gnome-desktop** directory.
New | Directory	Creates a new directory on your desktop.
New | Launcher	Places a new application launcher on the desktop. Uses the Application Launcher dialog box to have you specify the application and its properties.
New | [*application*]	Some Gnome applications place entries in the New menu that enable you to start new sessions easily for those applications.
Arrange Icons	Arranges your desktop icons.
Create New Window	Launches a new Gnome file manager window showing your home directory.
Rescan Devices	Rescans the mountable devices on your machine and displays an icon for any new devices.
Rescan Desktop	Rescans the files in your **~/.gnome-desktop** directory.

Table 9-1.   *The Gnome Desktop Menu*

The desktop also displays icons for any drives you have access to, such as a CD-ROM or floppy drive, provided they are user mountable. You can easily do this with Linuxconf. Select the Access Local Drive entry, and then select the drive and the Options panel for that drive. On this panel, select the User Mountable option. If you do not have Linuxconf, you must make the appropriate entry in the **fstab** file, adding "user" to the options field for that device.

Note   *If you insert a new CD-ROM, then Gnome will automatically mount the CD-ROM and open a file manager window displaying its contents.*

You can mount file systems on these devices by right-clicking their icons and choosing the Mount entry. For example, to mount a CD-ROM disk, right-click the CD-ROM icon and select the Mount Device entry. You can then access the disk in the

CD-ROM drive either by double-clicking it or right-clicking and selecting the Open entry. A file manager window opens to display the contents of the CD-ROM disk. To unmount a CD-ROM, right-click the CD-ROM icon, and select the Unmount entry. You can then safely remove the CD-ROM disk. You can use the Eject entry to open your CD-ROM tray. The same procedure works for floppy disks, using the Floppy Disk icon. Be sure you don't remove a mounted floppy disk until you have first unmounted it, selecting the Unmount entry in the pop-up menu. If, for some reason, not all your devices are showing up, you can have Gnome rescan your system for them. Right-click anywhere on the empty desktop to display a pop-up menu. From the menu, select Rescan Devices.

Usually a window manager extends a desktop into several areas that appear as different screens. Gnome's drag-and-drop operation works on desktop areas provided by a Gnome-compliant window manager. Gnome does not directly manage desktop areas, though you can use the Gnome pager to move to them. You use the window manager configuration tool to configure them. In addition, most window managers also support virtual desktops. Instead of being extensions of the same desktop area, virtual desktops are separate entities. Gnome does not support its drag-and-drop capabilities on virtual desktops. It is aware of only a single desktop with multiple areas. An *area* is an extension of a desktop, making it larger than the screen, whereas virtual desktops are entirely separate entities. KDE implements virtual desktops, whereas Gnome supports desktop operations only on desktop areas. The Gnome pager, however, does support virtual desktops, creating icons for each in the panel, along with task buttons for any applications open on them. You can use the Gnome pager to move to different virtual desktops and their areas.

Window Managers

Gnome works with any window manager. However, desktop functionality, such as drag-and-drop capabilities and the Gnome pager, only work with window managers that are Gnome-compliant. The current release of Gnome uses the Sawfish window manager. Its is completely Gnome-compliant and is designed to integrate with the Gnome desktop without any duplication of functionality. However, other window managers such as Enlightenment, FVWM, IceWin, and Window Maker can also be used. Check a window manager's documentation to see if it is Gnome-compliant.

Sawfish employs much the same window operations as used on other window managers. You can resize a window by clicking any of its sides or corners and dragging. You can move the window with a click-and-drag operation on its title bar. You can also right-click and drag any border to move the window, as well as ALT-click anywhere on the window. The upper-right corner lists the Maximize, Minimize, and Close buttons. If the Gnome pager is running in your panel, then Minimize creates a button for the window in the panel that you can click to restore it. If the Gnome pager is not present, then the window will iconify, minimizing to an icon on the desktop. You can right-click on the title bar of a window to display a window menu with entries for window operations. These include a desktop entry to move the window to another desktop area and the Stick option, which displays the window no matter to what desktop area you move.

You can also access the Sawfish desktop menu. To display the menu, middle-click anywhere on the desktop (hold both mouse buttons down at the same time for a two-button mouse). A pop-up menu then appears with submenus for Gnome, user, and other applications, as well as the Desktop, Themes, and Sawfish configurations. You can use this menu to start any application, if you want. With the desktop menus, you move to different desktop areas and virtual desktops. The Themes menu enables you to choose different Sawfish themes (these are separate from KDE themes). Sawfish also has extensive configuration options, discussed in a later section.

If you have several window managers installed on your system, you can change from one to the other using the Window Manager capplet in the Gnome Control Center. *capplet* is the term used for a *control applet*, a module used to configure your desktop. Select the Control Center entry in the main menu to start the Control Center. In the Control Center window, select Window Manager, listed under Desktop in the tree on the left. A panel is displayed listing your window managers. Initially, only Enlightenment is listed. To add others to the list, click the Add button on the right side of the panel. This opens a window that prompts you to enter an identifying name for the window manager, the command that starts the window manager, and any configuration tool it may use. If the window manager is Gnome-compliant, you can click the button Window Manager Is Session Managed. Once you finish making your entries and click OK, the new window manager appears in the list on the Control Center panel. Select it and click Try to run that window manager. If you want to run the window manager's configuration tool, click the Run Configuration Tool button.

The Gnome File Managers: GMC and Nautilus

The current version of Gnome uses *GNU Midnight Commander* (*GMC*, shown in Figure 9-4) for its file manager. Later versions will use Nautilus by Eazel. GMC is the Midnight Commander file manager with a Gnome front end. The GMC window consists of a menu bar, a toolbar, a location box, and two panes. The left pane displays a directory tree from which you can directly select directories. The right pane is the Directory view, which displays the files and subdirectories for the currently selected directory. The directory tree maps all the directories on your system, starting from the root directory. You can expand or shrink any directory by clicking the + or – symbol before its name. Select a directory by clicking the directory name. The contents of that directory are then displayed in the right-hand pane, the Directory view.

The Directory view has several viewing options. You can view a directory's contents as icons, a brief list, a detailed list, or a custom view. You select the different options from the Layout menu or by clicking their respective buttons in the toolbar.

Figure 9-4.   *Gnome file manager*

The brief list simply provides the name, whereas the detailed list provides the name, permissions, size, date, owner, and group. For a custom view, you can select the informational fields you want displayed for your files. In all the list views, buttons are displayed for each field across the top of the Directory View pane. You can use these buttons to sort the lists according to that field. For example, to sort the files by date, click the Date button; to sort by size, click the Size button. You can also select a field from the Sort By entry in the Layout menu.

The GMC file manager operates similarly to a Web browser. It maintains a list of previously viewed directories; you can move back and forth through that list using the toolbar buttons. The LEFT ARROW button moves you to the previously displayed directory, and the RIGHT ARROW button moves you to the next displayed directory. The UP ARROW button moves you to the parent directory, and the Home button moves you to your home directory. To use a pathname to go directly to a given directory, you can type the pathname in the Location box and press ENTER. GMC is also Internet-aware. You can use the Location box to access an FTP site and display the directories on that remote site, and then drag and drop files to another file manager window to download them to your system. Be sure to include the FTP protocol specification, **ftp://**.

To open a subdirectory, you can double-click its icon, or single-click the icon and select Open from the File menu. If you want to open a separate GMC window for that directory, click the middle mouse button on the directory's icon (for two-button mice, click the right and left buttons at the same time).

As a Gnome-compliant file manager, Midnight Commander supports GUI drag-and-drop operations for copying and moving files. To move a file or directory, click and drag from one directory to another, as you would on Windows or Mac interfaces. The move operation is the default drag-and-drop operation in Gnome. To copy a file, hold the CTRL key down while you click the item and drag it.

If you click and drag a file with the middle mouse button, when you reach the destination and lift up on the mouse button, a pop-up menu appears listing several options: Copy, Move, Link, or Cancel Drag. This is a convenient way to create a link to a file, such as an application. Just click and drag with the middle mouse button, and then choose Link from the pop-up menu.

You can also perform file operations on a file by right-clicking its icon and selecting the action you want from the pop-up menu that appears (see Table 9-2). For example, to delete an item, right-click it and select the Delete entry from the pop-up menu. To move a file, select the Move entry. This displays a dialog box where you can change the pathname of the file you want to rename. A Browse button enables you to use a directory tree to select a new directory location. The Advanced Options panel in this dialog box enables you to select a Preserve Symlinks option. With this option, any symbolic links to this file are changed to point to the new location. To copy a file, you can select Copy from the pop-up menu and use the dialog box to select the new location for the copy and a new name if you want. The destination directory displayed in the Move, Copy, or Links menu is that of the currently active file manger window. To move a file from one directory to another, open a file manger window to that new directory, click it, and then, in your source window, right-click directly on the File icon for the file you are moving. The Location box in the Move window shows the pathname for the directory whose file manager window you just selected. The same process works for Copy and Link operations. For example, to create a link in the **presents** directory to the **party** file in the **birthday** directory, you open a file manager window for both the **birthday** and **presents** directories, click the **presents** directory, and then right-click the **party** file in the **birthday** directory and select the Link entry. You see the Location box in the Link window showing the pathname for the **birthday** directory. Add in the name you want to give to the link file.

Menu Item	Description
Open	Open the file with its associated application.
Open With	Select an application with which to open this file.
View	View the file with a basic text viewer.
Edit	Use an editor to edit the file.

Table 9-2. *The File Pop-Up Menu*

Menu Item	Description
Copy	Copy the file to the clipboard so it can be pasted elsewhere.
Delete	Delete the file.
Move	Display the Move dialog box, with which you can move the file.
Properties	Display the Properties dialog box for this file. There are three panels: Statistics, Options, and Permissions.

Table 9-2.   *The File Pop-Up Menu* (continued)

You can use this same procedure to rename a file. Right-click and select the Move entry from the pop-up menu. In the dialog box, enter a new name for the file. You can also rename a file either by entering a new name in its Properties dialog box or by slowly clicking the name displayed under the icon. Use a right-click and select Properties from the pop-up menu to display the Properties dialog box.

File operations can be performed on a selected group of files and directories. You can select a group of items in several ways. You can click the first item and then hold down the SHIFT key while clicking the last item. You can also click and drag the mouse across items you want to select. To select separated items, hold the CTRL key down as you click the individual icons. If you want to select all the items in the directory, choose the Select All entry in the Edit menu. You can also select files based on pattern matches on the filenames. Choose the Select Files entry in the Edit menu. You can then enter a pattern using Linux file-matching wildcard symbols such as * (see Chapter 11). For example, the pattern *.c would select all C source code files (those ending with the extension .c). You can then click and drag a set of items at once. This enables you to copy, move, or even delete several files at once. To move files between directories, open two file manager windows to the respective directories. Then click and drag the items from one window to the other.

You can start any application in the file manager by double-clicking either the application itself or a data file used for that application. If a file does not have an associated application, you can right-click the file and select the Open With entry. A dialog box is then displayed where you can choose the application with which you want to open this file. Drag-and-drop operations are also supported for applications. You can drag a data file to its associated application icon (say, one on the desktop); the application then starts up using that data file.

With the Properties dialog box, you can view detailed information on a file and set options and permissions. A Properties box has three panels: Statistics, Options, and Permissions. The *Statistics panel* shows detailed information such as size, date, and ownership. The *Options panel* enables you set the open, view, and edit operations for this file. You can choose what application to open it with, which one to use to view it, and which one to use to edit it. The *Permissions panel* shows the read, write, and execute permissions for user, group, and other, as set for this file. You can change any of the permissions here, provided the file belongs to you.

You can set preferences for your GMC file manager in the Preferences dialog box. Access this dialog box by selecting the Preferences item in the Edit menu. The Preferences dialog box has five panels: File Display, Confirmation, Custom View, Caching, and VFS. On the File Display panel, you can select such features as hiding or showing hidden (dot) files. The Confirmation panel is where confirmation checks are specified for deleting and overwriting files. The Virtual File System (VFS) panel enables you to set options for accessing remote file systems, such as FTP sites. You can specify an anonymous FTP password, a timeout period, and whether you have to use an FTP proxy server. The Caching panel enables you to specify caching options for directory and FTP information. GMC keeps a copy of displayed directories for a given amount of time per session, which allows fast reload of previously displayed directories. You use the Custom View panel to select the fields you want displayed in your custom view of a directory listing. These are such fields as date, time, and permissions. You have two panes: one listing possible fields (Possible Columns) and the other listing the fields you have chosen (Displayed Columns). Use the Add button to add a field to your list; use the Remove button to remove one. You can drag entries up or down in the Displayed Columns pane to reorder them.

Nautilus is a file manager designed as a desktop shell in which different components can be employed to add functionality. For example, within Nautilus, a Web browser can be executed to provide Web browser capabilities within a Nautilus file manager window. Nautilus is not only a file manager, but also a desktop shell based on a component architecture. Different components, such as a Web browser, compression commands, or an image viewer, can be used to add capabilities to this desktop shell. These capabilities are not built in to Nautilus, but must be added by the different components.

As a file manager, Nautilus supports the standard features for copying, removing, and deleting items, as well as setting permissions and displaying items just as GMC does. Nautilus also provides enhancements such as zooming capabilities, user levels, and theme support. You can enlarge or reduce the size of your file icons, select from novice, intermediate, or expert levels of use, and customize the look and feel of Nautilus with different themes. Nautilus also lets you set up customized views of file listings, enabling you to display images for directory icons and run component applications within the file manager window. For example, a directory of mp3 files could have an album cover for its directory icon and run a component mp3 player within the file manager window to play a file.

The standard Nautilus window displays a menu bar of file manager commands and a Location box at the top. The rest of the window is divided into two panes, the left for an icon showing the current working directory and the right for the list of files and subdirectories in it. Next to the Location box is an element for zooming in and out the view of the files. Click the + button to zoom in and the – button to zoom out. Next to the zoom element is a drop-down menu for selecting the different views for your files such as icons, small icons, or details.

The Gnome Panel

The *panel* is the center of the Gnome interface, shown in the following illustration. Through it you can start your applications, run applets, and access desktop areas. You can think of the Gnome panel as a type of tool you can use on your desktop. You can have several Gnome panels displayed on your desktop, each with applets and menus you have placed in them. In this respect, Gnome is flexible, enabling you to configure your panels any way you want. You can customize a panel to fit your own needs, holding applets and menus of your own selection. You may add new panels, add applications to the panel, and add various applets.

You can hide the panel at any time by clicking either of the Hide buttons located on each end of the panel. The Hide buttons are thin buttons showing a small arrow. This is the direction in which the panel will hide. To redisplay the panel, move your mouse off the screen in that direction at the bottom of the screen. If you want the panel to automatically hide when you are not using it, select the Autohide option in the panel configuration window. Moving the mouse to the bottom of the screen redisplays the panel. You can also move the panel to another edge of the screen by clicking and dragging on either end of the panel with your middle mouse button (both buttons simultaneously for two-button mice).

To add a new panel, select the Create Panel entry in the Panel menu. You can then select the panel type, choosing from a menu, edge, floating, sliding, or aligned panel. The default is an edge panel. An *edge panel* is displayed across one of the edges of the screen. Your original panel is an edge panel. A menu panel is a panel implemented as a menu bar across the top of the desktop with menus for Programs, Favorites, Settings, and Desktop. It can hold any objects that a standard panel can hold. A floating panel is a one that you can position anywhere on the desktop. A *sliding panel* is sized to the number of items in the panel and can be placed anywhere on the edge of the desktop. An aligned panel is a smaller panel also sized to the number of items on it and is positioned in the center of the edge of a desktop. You can change a panel's type at any time by right-clicking the panel and selecting the alternate configuration. Figure 9-5 shows examples for the different types of Gnome panels.

ENVIRONMENTS

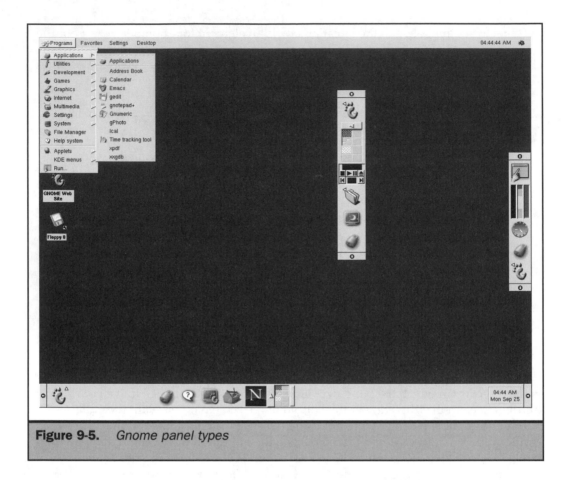

Figure 9-5. *Gnome panel types*

Adding Applications and Applets

Adding applications to a panel is easy. For an application already in the main menu, you only need to go to its entry and right-click it. Then select the Add This Launcher To Panel entry. An application launcher for that application is then automatically added to the panel. Suppose you use gEdit frequently and want to add its icon to the panel, instead of having to go through the main menu all the time. Right-click the gEdit menu entry and select the Add This Launcher To Panel option. The gEdit icon now appears in your panel.

To add an application icon not in the Mail menu, first right-click the panel to display the pop-up menu and select the Add New Launcher entry. This opens the Create Launcher Applet window for entering properties for the applications launcher. You are prompted for the application name, the command that invokes it, and its type. To select an icon for your launcher, click the Icon button. This opens the Icon Picker window, listing icons from which you can choose.

You can also group applications under a Drawer icon. Clicking the Drawer icon displays a list of the different application icons you can then select. To add a drawer to your panel, right-click the panel and select the Add Drawer entry. If you want to add a whole menu of applications on the main menu to your panel, right-click the menu title displayed at the top of the menu and select the Add This As Drawer To Panel entry. The entire menu appears as a drawer on your panel, holding icons instead of menu entries (see Figure 9-6). For example, suppose you want to place the Internet applications menu on your panel. Right-click the Internet item and select Add This As Drawer To Panel. A drawer appears on your panel labeled Internet, and clicking it displays a pop-up list of icons for all the Internet applications.

A menu differs from a drawer in that a *drawer* holds application icons instead of menu entries. You can add menus to your panel, much as you add drawers. To add a submenu in the main menu to your panel, right-click the menu title and select the Add This As Menu To Panel entry. The menu title appears in the panel; you can click it to display the menu entries.

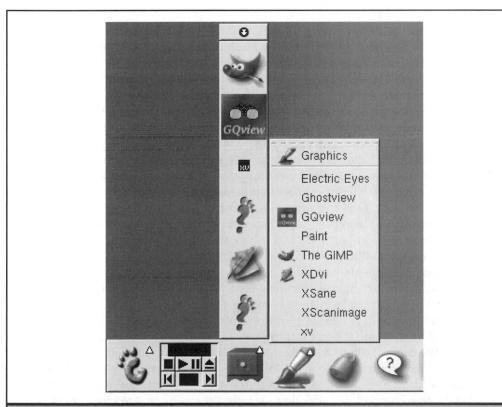

Figure 9-6.   *Gnome panel drawers and menus*

ENVIRONMENTS

You can also add directory folders to a panel. Click and drag the Folder icon from the file manager window to your panel. Whenever you click this Folder button, a file manager window opens, displaying that directory. You already have a Folder button for your home directory. You can add directory folders to any drawer on your panel.

Moving and Removing Panel Objects

To move any object on the panel, even the Menu icon, just drag it with the middle mouse button. You can also right-click on it and choose Move Applet to let you move the applet. You can move it either to a different place on the same panel or to a different panel. When moving objects, you can have them either push over, switch with, or jump over other objects that they run into on the panel. To push over an object, you hold the SHIFT key down while moving the object. To switch with an object, you hold down the CTRL key; and to jump over an object, you hold down the ALT key.

To remove an object from the panel, right-click it to display a pop-up menu for it and then and choose the Remove From Panel entry.

Main Menu

You open the main menu by clicking its button on the panel. The Main Menu button is a stylized picture of a bare foot. It is initially located on the left side of your panel, the lower left-hand corner of your screen. You only need to single-click the Main Menu button. You needn't keep holding your mouse button down. The menu pops up much like the Start menu in Windows.

You can configure menus using the Menu Properties dialog box. To change the properties for a menu on the panel, including the main menu, right-click its icon in the panel and select the Properties entry. This displays the Menu Properties dialog box, which has two sections: Menu Type and Main Menu. In the Main Menu section, you can set properties for that main menu. Several possible submenus can be displayed on the main menu, either directly or in other submenus. You can choose from the System, User, Red Hat, KDE, and Debian menus. Red Hat and Debian menus are those used for specific Red Hat or Debian programs installed by those distributions that are not specifically Gnome applications. KDE is used for KDE applications, if the KDE desktop is also installed on your system.

You can customize the main menu, adding your own entries, with the Menu Editor. The main menu is divided into two sections: the Systems menu and the User menu. The *Systems menu,* which can be changed only by the system administrator—the root user—contains the default Gnome applications installed with Gnome. The *User menu* can be changed by individual users, adding entries for applications a user frequently runs. To start the Menu Editor, select the Menu Editor entry in the Setting submenu located in the main menu. The Menu Editor is divided into two panes, the left being a tree view of the main menu. You can expand or shrink any of the submenus. The right pane holds configuration information for a selected entry. There are two panels: basic and advanced. The basic panel displays the name, command, and application type, as well as the icon. You can click the icon to change it. You can also change the Name, Command, or Type fields.

To add a new application, click the New Item button on the toolbar. The new item is placed in the currently selected menu. Enter the name, command, and type information, and then select an icon. Then click the Save button to add the entry to the menu. You can move the menu item in the menu by clicking the UP or DOWN ARROW button in the toolbar, or by dragging it with the mouse. If you are a user, remember you can only add entries to the User menu, not to the Systems menu.

An easier way to add an application is to use the drag-and-drop method. Locate the application you want to add with the file manager, and then drag and drop its icon to the appropriate menu in the Menu Editor. The entry is made automatically, using configuration information provided for that application by the file manager.

Panel Configuration

You use the Global Panel Configuration dialog box to configure properties for all Gnome panels. Either right-click the panel and select Global Properties or select Global Properties in the Panel submenu in the main menu to display this dialog window. The Global Panel Configuration dialog box has six tabbed panels: Animation, Launcher Icon, Drawer Icon, Menu Icon, Logout Icon, and Miscellaneous. With the Animation panel, you can enable panel animations, setting various options for them. The various icon panels enable you to select the images you want to use to denote active or inactive elements, among other features, such as border and depth. On the Miscellaneous panel, you set certain options such as allowing pop-up menus on the desktop, prompting before logout, or keeping panels below windows.

To configure individual panels, you use the Panel Properties dialog box. To display this dialog box, you right-click the particular panel and select the This Panel Properties entry in the pop-up menu, or select This Panel Properties in the main menu's Panel menu. For individual panels, you can set features for edge panel configuration and the background. The Panel Properties dialog box includes a tabbed panel for each. On the Edge panel, you can choose options for positioning an edge panel and for minimizing it, including the Autohide feature. The Hide Buttons feature enables you to hide the panel yourself.

On the Background panel, you can change the background image used for the panel. You can select an image, have it scaled to fit the panel, and select a background color. For an image, you can also drag and drop an image file from the file manager to the panel, and that image then becomes the background image for the panel.

Gnome Applets

As previously stated, applets are small programs that perform tasks within the panel. To add an applet, right-click the panel and select Add New Applet from the pop-up menu. This, in turn, displays other pop-up menus listing categories of applets with further listings of available applets. Select the one you want. For example, to add the clock to your panel, select Clock from the Utility menu. To remove an applet, right-click it and select the Remove From Panel entry.

Gnome features a number of helpful applets, such as a CPU monitor and a mail checker. Some applets monitor your system, such as the Battery Monitor, which checks the battery in laptops; and CPU/MEM Usage, which shows a graph indicating your current CPU and memory use; as well as separate applets for CPU and memory load: CPULoad and MemLoad. The Mixer applet displays a small scroll bar for adjusting sound levels. The CD player displays a small CD interface for playing music CDs.

For network tasks, there are MailCheck, Modem Lights, and Web Control applets. MailCheck checks for received mail. To configure MailCheck, right-click it and select the Properties entry. You can set the frequency of checks, as well as specify a more sophisticated mail checker to run, such as `fetchmail`. The Modem Lights feature monitors you modem connection. You can configure it to monitor a PPP connection to an ISP over a modem. Web Control enables you to start your Web browser with a specified URL.

Several helpful utility applets provide added functionality to your desktop. The Clock applet can display time in a 12- or 24-hour format. Right-click the Clock applet and select the Properties entry to change its setup. You use the Printer applet to print your files. To print a file, drag its icon to the Printer applet. To configure the Printer applet, right-click it and select Properties. Here, you can specify the printer name and the printer command to use, helpful if you have more than one printer. The Drive Mount applet enables you to mount a drive using a single click. You can create a Drive Mount applet for each device you have, such as a floppy drive and a CD-ROM. To mount a file system, all you have to do is click the appropriate Drive Mount icon in the panel. To specify the file systems to mount, use the applet's Drive Mount Settings dialog box.

Gnome Desk Guide

The *Gnome Desk Guide*, shown in the following illustration, appears in the panel and shows a view of your virtual desktops, along with their desktop areas. Virtual desktops and their desktop areas are defined in the window manager. Desk Guide lets you easily move from one to another with the click of a mouse. The Gnome Desk Guide is a panel applet that works only in the panel.

<table>
<tr><td>**Note**</td><td>*If the Desk Guide is not already active, you can activate the Gnome Desk Guide by right-clicking the panel and selecting Add New Applet from the pop-up menu. This, in turn, displays other pop-up menus listing categories of applets and their listings of available applets. Select the Utility category and, in that menu, select Desk Guide.*</td></tr>
</table>

Desk Guide shows your entire virtual desktop as separate rectangles within a box. Each rectangle in turn is cut into small adjoining squares to show the desktop areas for each virtual desktop. Open windows show up as small colored rectangles in these squares. You can move any window from one virtual desktop or area to another by clicking and dragging its image in the Desk Guide with your middle mouse button. If you click the small arrow to the right of the Desktop view, the task list window opens, listing all the tasks (windows) currently open and running. You can select a task to move to its window and the desktop it is currently positioned in. The previous illustration shows a simple Desk View applet displaying two virtual desktops, each with four desktop areas. The next illustration shows a more complex Desktop view with four virtual desktops each with four desktop areas.

Note	*Various window managers use different terms to describe virtual desktops and their desktop areas. Enlightenment uses the terms "desktops" and "screens," whereas Sawfish uses "workspaces" that are then divided into "columns" and "rows." "Desk Guide officially calls them "desktops" and "viewports."*

To configure the Desk Guide, right-click it and select Properties to display the Properties dialog box. Here, you can choose from panels to configure the display, tasks, geometry, and advanced features like window manager options. You can set the size of the Desk Guide to extend beyond the height of the panel, elect to display any virtual desktop names, or even show hidden tasks. Remember, the window manager you are using may also have a pager you can use that may operate much like the Desk Guide. Check your window manager documentation on how to activate it.

Gnome Tasklist

The *Tasklist* shows currently opened application. The Tasklist arranges task currently running in a series of buttons, one for each window. A task can be any open application, usually denoted by a window displayed on the screen. These can include applications such as a Web browser or a file manager window displaying a directory. You can move from one task to another by clicking on its button, in effect moving from one window to another. When you minimize a window, you can later restore it by clicking on its entry in the Tasklist. The following illustration shows a Tasklist displaying buttons for several different kinds of windowed applications.

A right-click on a window's Tasklist entry opens a menu that lets you iconify or restore, shade, stick, or close the window. The iconify operation will reduce the window to its Tasklist entry. A right-click on the entry will display the menu with a Restore option instead of an iconify one, which you can then use to redisplay the window. The Shade entry will reduce the window to its title bar, and the Stick entry will display the window in any desktop you move to. The Kill entry will close the window, ending its application.

To configure the Tasklist, you right-click on it and select the Properties entry. Here, you can set features such as the size of the task list, the number of rows, whether to display mini-icons, and the tasks to show.

Quicklaunch

You can use the Quicklaunch applet in the panel to start programs. The *Quicklaunch applet* holds a collection of small icons for application launchers. Click them to launch your application. The Quicklaunch applet can use only launchers that are already set up either on the main menu or on your desktop. To add a launcher to Quicklaunch, drag and drop the launcher to the Quicklaunch applet in the panel. A small icon is then created for it in the Quicklaunch applet. For main menu items, click an item and drag it to the Quicklaunch applet. Right-click a particular application's icon and select Properties to configure that launcher.

Gnome Configuration: Control Center

With the Gnome Control Center, shown in Figure 9-7, you can configure different parts of your system using tools called *capplets*. Think of capplets as modules or plug-ins that can be added to the Control Center to enable you to configure various applications. Capplets exist for the core set of Gnome applications, as well as for other applications for which developers may have written capplets. You can either start the Control Center directly or start up a particular capplet that starts the Control Center, open to that capplet. To start the Control Center directly, select the Control Center entry in the System menu located in the main menu or on its applet in the panel (icon of a toolbox). The Control Center menu also lists the capplets currently available on your system. To start using a capplet, select the particular application capplet you want from the Control Center menu.

The Control Center window is divided into two panes. The left one is a tree view of the capplets available on your system, which are arranged into categories you can expand or shrink. The left pane displays the panel for configuring that particular application. Click the entry in the view tree for the application you want to configure, and its configuration panel then appears to the left.

Your Gnome system provides several desktop capplets you can use to configure your desktop: Background, Screensaver, Theme Selector, and Window Manager. You use the Background capplet to select a background color or image, the Screensaver capplet to select the screensaver images and wait time, the Theme selector to choose a theme, and the Window Manager capplet to choose the window manager you want to use.

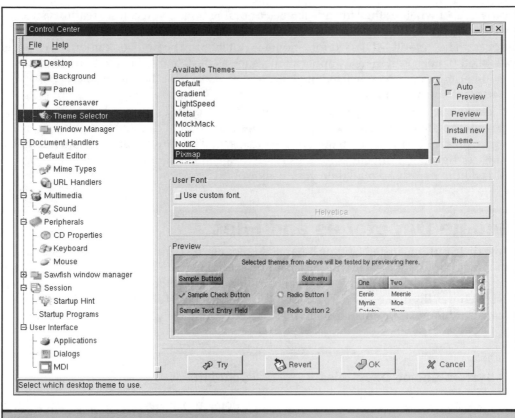

Figure 9-7. *The Gnome Control Center*

Gnome Default Editor entry enables you to choose an editor as your default editor for Gnome, the editor the Gnome file manager uses to open text files. The Gnome MIME Types capplet enables you to specify *Multipurpose Internet Mail Extensions* (*MIME*) type entries for your system, associating given MIME types with certain applications. Notice basic MIME type entries are already present. You can edit an entry and change its associated application. Also listed are Multimedia and Peripheral capplets. For the sound configuration, you can select sound files to play for events in different Gnome applications. For your keyboard, you can set the repeat sensitivity and click sound. You can configure mouse buttons for your right or left hand, and adjust the mouse motion. With the Session Manager capplet, you can configure certain Gnome session features, specifying non-Gnome programs to start up and whether you want a logout prompt.

Several User Interface capplets enable you to configure different interface components, such as menus, toolbars, and status bars. There are capplets for setting these features for applications, dialog boxes, and the *Multiple Document Interface* (*MDI*). You can specify whether toolbars and menus can be detached, whether they have relief borders, and whether they include icons. For dialog boxes, you can set features such as the arrangement of buttons or the position of the dialog box on the screen when it appears. The default MDI used for Gnome is notebook. The notebook interface consists of tabbed panels used in many applications, such as the Control Center. You can choose two other interfaces: toplevel and modal. You can also adjust the way the notebook interface displays its tabs.

Gnome sets up several configuration files and directories in your home directory. The **.gnome** directory holds configuration files for different desktop components, such as **gmc** for the file manager, **panel** for the panels, and **gmenu** for the main menu. **.gtkrc** holds configuration directives for the GTK+ widgets. The **.gnome-desktop** directory holds all the items you placed on your desktop.

Gnome Directories and Files

Most distributions install Gnome binaries in the **/usr/bin** directory on your system. Gnome libraries are located in the **/usr/lib** directory. Gnome also has its own **include** directories with header files for use in compiling and developing Gnome applications, **/usr/include/libgnome** and **/usr/include/libgnomeui** (see Table 9-3). The directories located in **/usr/share/gnome** contain files used to configure your Gnome environment.

System Gnome Directories	Contents
/usr/bin	Gnome programs
/usr/lib	Gnome libraries
/usr/include/libgnome	Header files for use in compiling and developing Gnome applications
/usr/include/libgnomeui	Header files for use in compiling and developing Gnome user interface components
/usr/share/gnome/apps	Files used by Gnome applications
/usr/share/gnome/help	Files used by Gnome Help System
/usr/share/doc/gnome*	Documentation for various Gnome packages, including libraries
/etc/X11/gdm/gnomerc	Gnome configuration file invoked with the Gnome Display Manager (GDM)

Table 9-3. *Gnome Configuration Directories*

User Gnome Directories	Contents
.gnome	Holds configuration files for the user's Gnome desktop and Gnome applications. Includes configuration files for the panel, Control Center, background, GnomeRPM, MIME types, and sessions
.gnome-desktop	Directory where files, directories, and links you place on the desktop will reside
.gnome-help-browser	Contains Gnome Help System configuration files, including history and bookmark files set up by the user
.gnome_private	The user private Gnome directory
.gtkrc	GTK+ configuration file
.mc	Configuration files for the Midnight Commander file manager

Table 9-3. *Gnome Configuration Directories* (continued)

ENVIRONMENTS

Gnome sets up several hidden directories for each user in their home directory that begin with ".gnome" and include a preceding period in the name. **.gnome** holds files used to configure a user's Gnome desktop and applications. Configuration files for the panel, Control Center, GnomeRPM, MIME types, and sessions, among others, are located here. The files **Gnome**, **GnomeHelp**, **Background**, and **Terminal** all hold Gnome configuration commands for how to display and use these components. For example, **Gnome** holds general display features for the desktop, while **GnomeHelp** specifies the history and bookmark files for the help system. Configuration files for particular Gnome applications are kept in the subdirectory **apps**. On Red Hat, the **redhat-apps** directory holds **.desktop** files containing Gnome instructions on how to handle different Red Hat utilities, such as **netcfg**. **.gnome-desktop** holds any files, folders, or links the user has dragged to the desktop. **.gnome-help-browser** holds the bookmark and history files for the Gnome Help System. These are the bookmarks and the list of previous documents the user consulted with the Gnome Help browser. **.gtckrc** is the user configuration file for the GTK+ libraries, which contains current desktop configuration directives for resources such as key bindings, colors, and window styles.

Sawfish Window Manager

Sawfish is a fully Gnome-compliant window manager. It is designed to perform window managing tasks only and does not include features like application docks found on other window managers like Afterstep. This minimal approach to window management means that Sawfish does not duplicate Gnome desktop features as other window managers do (such as Enlightenment). At the same time, Sawfish is designed to be extensible, providing a Lisp-based set of commands you can use to fully configure all aspects of window management. Sawfish can be fully configured within Gnome using the Gnome Control Center. First select Sawfish in the Control Center's Window Manager panel, and then select Run Configuration Tool For Sawfish. This runs the Sawfish configuration program, displaying the Sawfish configuration window shown in Figure 9-8. You can find out more about Sawfish and obtain current versions from its Web site at **sawmill.sourceforge.net**. Sawfish was originally named sawmill, so many of its Internet sites still bear that name. The site also provides detailed documentation of Sawfish commands and features. If you download the source code and want to compile it for use on Gnome be sure to include the **--enable-capplet** option to add it in the Gnome Control Center.

Figure 9-8.   *Sawfish configuration*

The Sawfish Configuration window displays a list of configuration topics on the left and the panel for the selected topic on the right. Basic options set window displays, enabling you to select resize and move methods. With the Desktops option, you can create virtual desktops and specify the number of desktop areas for each one. On the panel are two configuration tools. The left one, labeled Size Of Virtual Screen, is used to determine the number of desktop areas. The right one, labeled Separate Desktops, is used to specify the number of virtual desktops. Recall, however, that the Gnome desktop is only supported on the first virtual desktop, not on any others. This means drag-and-drop operations do not work on the other virtual desktops. They do, however, work on any of the desktop areas on that first virtual desktop. The Gnome pager supports all the virtual desktop, displaying rectangles for each in the panel. Other topics cover features such as sounds, special effects, window focus, keyboard shortcuts, and backgrounds. You can set different backgrounds for each virtual desktop.

The Themes panel enables you to use a Sawfish theme, from which there are many to choose. Enlightenment is known for its magnificent themes. See **sawmill.themes.org** for themes you can download. To make a theme available, place it in your home directory's **.sawfish/themes** directory. Make sure that file has an **.sawfishtheme** extension. Sawfish maintains its own configuration directory, called **.sawfish**, in your home directory. It contains subdirectories for themes, backgrounds, and windows.

Gnome Themes

You can display your Gnome desktop using different themes that change the appearance of desktop objects such as windows, buttons, and scrollbars. Gnome functionality is not affected in any way. You can choose from a variety of themes. Many are posted on the Internet at **gtk.themes.org**. Technically, these are referred to as *GTK themes,* which allow the GTK widget set to change their look and feel.

To select a theme, use the Gnome Control Center and select Themes in the Desktop listing. You can select a theme from the Available Themes list on the Configuration panel. The Auto Preview button enables you to see an example of the theme. To use the theme, click Try. To install a theme you have downloaded from the Internet, click the Install New Theme button and locate the theme file. The theme is then installed on your system, and an entry for it appears in the Available Themes list.

Updating Gnome

Currently, new versions of Gnome are being released frequently, sometimes every few months. Gnome releases are designed to enable users to upgrade their older versions easily. Be sure to obtain the release for your particular distributions (though you can install from the source code if you want). Packages tailored for various distributions can be downloaded through the Gnome Web site at **www.gnome.org** or directly from the Gnome FTP site at **ftp.gnome.org** (and its mirror sites). RPM packages can also be obtained from the **updates** directory for the current distributions located on the distribution FTP sites such as **ftp.redhat.com**. For Red Hat, you can use the Red Hat update agent to update any Gnome updates located on the Red Hat FTP site automatically.

Or, you can manually download the update files and install them yourself. First, log in as the root user and then create a directory to hold the Gnome files. Then connect to an FTP site. You can use a Web browser, such as Netscape, but using an FTP client such as **nctp**, gFTP, or even the Gnome file manager is preferable. Download the files for the new version to your new directory. For Red Hat and Caldera, these are a series of RPM package files. To download using the Gnome file manager, enter the FTP URL in a file manager window's Location box to access the site. Move to the directory holding the Gnome files. Then select the files and drag and drop them to another file manager window that is open to the local directory in which you want them placed. The files are downloaded for you. To download using FTP, be sure to turn off prompts with the **prompt** command and use **mget *** to download all the files at once. Once they are downloaded, you can use the **rpm** command with the **-Uvh** option to install them or the GnomeRPM utility. Be sure to read any installation instructions first. These can be found in **readme** or **install** files. You may have to install some packages before others. The GnomeRPM utility will tell you if a certain package requires that other packages be installed first. It will list these other packages as dependencies, meaning that the package you want to install is dependent on them and needs to have these other packages already installed.

To install a particular Gnome RPM package manually, use the **rpm** command with the **-Uvh** options or an RPM package utility like GnomeRPM (see Chapters 4 and Chapter 19). This example installs the games package:

```
rpm -Uvh gnome-games-1.2.0-93.i386.rpm
```

Many of the most recent updates are provided in the form of source files that you can download and compile. These are usually packages in compressed archives with **.tar.gz** extensions. At **ftp.gnome.org**, these are currently located in **pub/Gnome/sources**. Check the Gnome Web site for announcements. For example, a new version of the Gnome core programs could be

```
ftp.gnome.org/pub/GNOME/sources/gnome-core/gnome-core-1.2.1-33.tar.gz
```

Once you download the archive, use the **tar** command with the **xvzf** options to decompress and extract it. In the directory generated, use the ./**configure**, **make**, and **make install** commands to configure, create, and install the programs.

```
tar xvzf gnome-core-1.2.1-33.tar.gz
```

The
Complete
Reference

Linux

Chapter 10

Window Managers

Instead of the command line interface, you can use an X Window System (X) GUI to interact with your Linux system. With such an interface, you can use icons, windows, and menus to issue commands and run applications. Unlike PC-based GUIs such as Windows or the Mac OS, Linux and Unix systems divide the GUI into three separate components: the X Window System, window managers, and program/file managers. The X Window System, also known as X and X11, is an underlying standardized graphic utility that provides basic graphic operations such as opening windows or displaying images. A window manager handles windowing operations such as resizing and moving windows. Window managers vary in the way windows are displayed, using different borders and window menus. All, however, use the same underlying X graphic utility. A file manager handles file operations using icons and menus, and a program manager runs programs, often allowing you to select commonly used ones from a taskbar. Unlike window managers, file and program managers can vary greatly in their capabilities. In most cases, different file and program managers can run on the same window manager.

All Linux and Unix systems use the same standard underlying X graphics utility. This means, in most cases, that an X Window System–based program can run on any of the window managers and desktops. X Window System–based software is often found at Linux or Unix FTP sites in directories labeled **X11**. You can download these packages and run them on any window manager running on your Linux system. Some may already be in the form of Linux binaries that you can download, install, and run directly. Netscape is an example. Others will be in the form of source code that can easily be configured, compiled, and installed on your system with a few simple commands. Some applications, such as Motif applications, may require special libraries.

With a window manager, you can think of a window as taking the place of a command line. Operations you perform through the window are interpreted and sent to the Linux system for execution. Window managers operate off the underlying X Window System, which actually provides the basic window operations that allow you to open, move, and close windows, as well as display menus and select icons. FVWM2 and AfterStep manage these operations, each in its own way, providing their own unique interfaces. The advantage of such a design is that different window managers can operate on the same Linux system. In this sense, Linux is not tied to one type of graphical user interface (GUI). On the same Linux system, one user may be using the FVWM2 window manager, another may be using the Xview window manager, and still another, the Enlightenment window manager, all at the same time. You can find out detailed information about different window managers available for Linux from the X11 Web site at **www.X11.org**. The site provides reviews, screenshots, and links to home sites, as well as a comparison table listing the features available for the different window managers.

Window, File, and Program Managers

With a window manager, you can use your mouse to perform windowing operations such as opening, closing, resizing, and moving windows. Several window managers are available for Linux (see Table 10-1). Some of the more popular ones are Sawfish , Enlightenment , Window Maker , AfterStep, and the Free Virtual Window Manager 2.0 (FVWM2). FVWM2 is traditionally used as the default backup window manager on most Linux systems. Window Maker and AfterStep are originally based on the NeXTSTEP interface used for the NeXT operating system. Enlightenment and Sawfish are the default window managers for Gnome by several distributions. Red Hat provides its own configuration of FVWM2 called AnotherLevel. Most distributions currently include Enlightenment, Window Maker, AfterStep, Sawfish, and AnotherLevel (FVWM2). On Red Hat systems, Sawfish is used as the default window manager for Gnome and AnotherLevel for a standard X Window System environment.

Window managers operate through the underlying X graphics utility. The X Window System actually provides the basic operations that allow you to open, move, and close windows, as well as display menus and select icons. Window managers manage these operations each in their own way, providing different interfaces from which to choose. All window managers, no matter how different they may appear, use X Window System tools. In this sense, Linux is not tied to one type of graphical user interface. On the same Linux system, one user may be using the FVWM2 window manager on their terminal, another may be using Enlightenment on another terminal connected to the system, and yet another, Window Maker. You can find out more about the X Window System at **www.x.org**.

Window managers originally provided only very basic window management operations such as opening, closing, and resizing of windows. Their features have been enhanced in the more sophisticated window managers such as Window Maker and Enlightenment to include support for virtual desktops, docking panels, and themes that let users change the look and feel of their desktop. However, to work with files and customize applications, you need to use file and program managers. With a file manager, you can copy, move, or erase files within different directory windows. With a program manager, you can execute commands and run programs using taskbars and program icons. A desktop program will combine the capabilities of window, file, and program managers, providing a desktop metaphor with icons and menus to run programs and access files. Gnome and the K Desktop are two such desktop programs.

Several window managers have been enhanced to include many of the features of a desktop. The window managers included with many Linux distributions have program management capabilities, in addition to window handling. FVWM2 and AfterStep have a taskbar and a workplace menu that you can use to access all your X programs. With either the menu or the taskbar, you can run any X program directly from FVWM2. Window Maker provides a NeXTSTEP interface that features a docking panel for your applications with drag-and-drop support. You can drag a file to the application icon to start it with that file.

Using just a window manager, you can run any X program. Window managers have their own workspace menu and taskbar. You can also run any X program from an Xterm terminal window. There you can type the name of an X application; when you press ENTER, the X application will start up with its own window. It is best to invoke an X application as a background process by adding an ampersand after the command. A separate window will open for the X application that you can work in.

Window Managers

Instead of the command line interface, you can use an X window manager and file manager, which will allow you to interact with your Linux system using windows, buttons, and menus. Window managers provide basic window management operations such as opening, closing, and resizing windows, and file managers allow you to manage and run programs using icons and menus. The X Window System supports a variety of window managers. See Table 10-1 for a listing of window managers and desktops, along with their Web sites where you can obtain more information. You can also download current versions from these Web sites.

Window Manager	Command	Description	Internet Sites
AfterStep	**afterstep**	Based on the NeXTSTEP interface	**www.afterstep.org ftp.afterstep.org afterstep.themes.org**
Blackbox	**blackbox**	Simple and fast window manager	**blackbox.alug.org blackbox.themes.org**
Enlightenment	**enlightenment**	Window manager supporting themes	**www.enlightenment.org e.themes.org**
eXode		Enhanced X Open Desktop	**www.simplicity.net/exode/**
FVWM2	**fvwm2**	The free virtual window manager (v. 1.24)	**www.fvwm.org fvwm.themes.org**
FVWM95	**fvwm95**	Windows 95 interface	**mitac11.uia.ac.be/html-test/ fvwm95.html**

Table 10-1. *Window Managers*

Window Manager	Command	Description	Internet Sites
Gnome	`gnome-session`	GNU Network Object ModelEnvironment	www.gnome.org ftp.gnome.org gnome.themes.org
IceWM	`icewm`	Ice window manager	icewm.sourceforge.net
The K desktop	`startkde`	The K Desktop Environment	www.kde.org ftp.kde.org kde.themes.org
LessTif	`mwm`	A clone of Motif	www.lesstif.org
Macintosh-like Virtual Window Manager	`mlvwm`	A clone of the Macintosh interface	www2u.biglobe.ne.jp/~y-m iyata/mlvwm.html
Motif	`mwm`	Motif window manager	
Sawfish	`sawfish`	Extensible windows	sawmill.sourceforge.net sawmill.ethemes.org
TWM and VTWM	`twm`	Tom's window manager	
Window Maker	`wmaker`	Originally based on NeXTSTEP	www.windowmaker.org ftp.windowmaker.org wm.themes.org
Xview	`olwm` `olvwm`	The Xview window manager (OpenLook)	metalab.unc.edu/pub/ Linux/libs/X/xview
X11.ORG	X Window System Web site	Detailed window manager and desktop information	www.x11.org
Themes.org	Themes Web site	Window manager themes and links	themes.org

Table 10-1.   *Window Managers* (continued)

ENVIRONMENTS

Windows and Icons

You run applications, display information, or list files in windows. A *window* is made up of several basic components. The *outer border* contains resize controls. Also, various buttons enable you to control the size of a window or close the window. Inside the outer border are the main components of the window: the *title bar,* which displays the name of the window; the *menu*, through which you can issue commands; and the *window pane,* which displays the contents of a window. You can change a window's size and shape using buttons and resize areas. The resize areas are the corner borders of the window. Click and hold a resize area and move the mouse to make the window larger or smaller in both height and width. You can make the window fill the whole screen using a maximize operation. Most windows managers include a small button in the upper-right corner that you can click to maximize the window. To reduce the window to its original size, just click the Maximize button again. If you want to reduce the window to an icon, click the Minimize button. It's the small square with a dot in the center next to the Maximize button. Once you have reduced the window to an icon, you can reopen it later by double-clicking that icon (see Figure 10-4).

You can move any window around the desktop by selecting either its title bar or its border (not a corner). Move your mouse pointer to the window's title bar; then click and hold it while you move your mouse pointer. You will see the window move. When you have reached the position you want, release the mouse button. Just clicking the title bar will move the window to the front of any overlapping windows. The same process holds true for borders. Move the mouse pointer to the edge of the window until you see the pointer transform into a small straight line. Then click and hold that edge, and move the mouse pointer. You will see the entire window move.

Applications that have been designed as X programs will have their own menus, buttons, and even icons within their windows. You execute commands in such X applications using menus and icons. If you are running an application such as an editor, the contents of the window will be data that the menus operate on. If you are using the file manager, the contents will be icons representing files and directories. Some windows, such as terminal windows, may not have menus.

You can have several windows open at the same time. However, only one of those windows will be active. The active window will have dark borders, and the inactive windows will have light borders. On some window managers, just moving your mouse pointer to a particular window makes it the active window, rendering all others inactive. You will need to click the title bars of others. Most window managers let the user configure the method for making the window active.

Themes

Many window managers, such as Enlightenment, Sawfish, Window Maker, AfterStep, and FVWM2, support themes. Themes change the look and feel for widgets on your desktop, providing different background images, animation, and sound events. With themes, users with the same window manager may have desktops that appear radically different. The underlying functionality of the window manager does not change. You can easily download themes from Web sites and install them on your window manager. New ones are constantly being added. Information and links to window manager theme sites can be found at **themes.org**.

Workspace Menu

Most window managers provide a menu through which you can start applications, perform window configurations, and exit the window manager. Window managers give this menu different names. Enlightenment calls it the applications menu, Window Maker refers to it as the root-window menu, and FVWM2 calls it the workplace menu. In this chapter, it is referred to as the *workspace menu*. This menu is usually a pop-up menu that you can display by clicking anywhere on the desktop. The mouse button you use differs with window managers. Enlightenment and Sawfish use a middle-click, whereas Window Maker uses a right-click, and FVWM2 uses a left-click. Many of the entries on this workspace menu lead to submenus that in turn may have their own submenus. For example, applications will bring up a submenu listing categories for all your X programs. Selecting the graphics item will bring up a list of all the X graphic programs on your system. If you choose Xpaint, the Xpaint program will then start up. On some window managers you will find entries for window configuration and themes. Here will be items and submenus for configuring your window manager. For example, both AfterStep and Enlightenment have menus for changing your theme (see Figures 10-3 and 10-4 later in this chapter for examples of workspace menus).

Desktop Areas and Virtual Desktops

Initially, you may find desktop areas disconcerting—they provide a kind of built-in enlargement feature. You will discover that the area displayed on your screen may be only part of the desktop. Moving your mouse pointer to the edge of your screen moves the screen over the hidden portions of the desktop. You will also notice a small square located on your desktop or in your window manager's icon bar, taskbar, or panel. This is called the *pager,* and you use it to view different areas of your virtual desktop. The pager will display a rectangle for every active virtual desktop. Some window managers such as FVWM2 will display only two, others such as AfterStep will have four, and others such as FVWM will start out with only one.

Each desktop rectangle will be divided into smaller squares called *desktop areas.* You can think of each desktop area as a separate extension of your desktop. It's as if you have a very large desk, only part of which is shown on the screen. The active part of the desktop is shown in the pager as a highlighted square, usually in white. This is the area of the desktop currently displayed by your screen. A desktop can have as many as 25 squares, though the default is usually 4. You can click one of the squares in the rectangle to move to that part of your desk. You could place different windows in different parts of your desk and then move to each part when you want to use its windows.

In this way, everything you want on your desktop does not have to be displayed on your screen at once, cluttering it up. If you are working on the desktop and everything suddenly disappears, it may be that you accidentally clicked one of the other squares. Certain items will always be displayed on your screen, no matter what part of the virtual desktop you display. These are called "sticky" items. The pager is one, along with taskbars or panels. For example, the taskbars, iconbars, and pager will always show up on your screen no matter what part of the virtual desktop you are viewing. Windows by default are not sticky, though you can make them sticky.

Most window managers also support virtual desktops. A desktop includes all the desktop areas, along with the items displayed on them such as icons, menus, and windows. Window managers such as Enlightenment, Sawfish, AfterStep, and FVWM2 allow you to use several virtual desktops. Unlike desktop areas, which just extend a desktop, virtual desktops are separate entities. Most pagers will display the different virtual desktops as separate rectangles, each subdivided into its respective desktop areas. To move to a virtual desktop, you click its rectangle. In some window managers, such as Window Maker, you select the desktop from a list. Window managers will provide entries on their main menus for selecting virtual desktops and even moving windows from one desktop to another. Use a window manager's configuration program or configuration files to specify the number of virtual desktops you want. For example, on Sawfish you can choose the number of virtual desktops and then add as many virtual areas as you want to each, extending the area as rows and columns. Only one virtual desktop can be active at any one time.

Panels, Buttonbars, Taskbars, and Window Lists

A *panel* displays buttons for frequently used X Window System commands. Popular panels include Wharf and Zharf for AfterStep and FVWM2, the Clip on Window Maker, and GoodStuff for FVWM. Each icon on the panel will display an image and the name of a program. Just click the button to start that program. For example, to open an Xterm window, just click the icon labeled Xterm.

Each window manager has different ways to add applications to the panel. Adding an entry in Window Maker is as simple as dragging an application's icon to the docking panel. In most cases, you can just edit the panel entries in the window manager configuration files. For example, the entries beginning with the keyword ***GoodStuff** will configure the GoodStuff panel in FVWM2 configuration files. In addition, some window managers support button bars with small icons for applications. A taskbar shows tasks that are running and can hold menu buttons for displaying menus. The FVWM2 taskbar features a Start menu for applications and lists buttons for current tasks. Windows can be minimized to the taskbar, much like minimizing windows in Windows 98. Open windows will also be listed in the taskbar. Most window managers also provide a window list. Window lists are handy if you have work spread across different desktop areas and virtual desktops. Selecting a window entry in the window list will move you directly to that window and its virtual desktop/area.

The Terminal Window: Xterm

From within a Linux window manager, you can open a special window called a *terminal* window, which will provide you with a standard command line interface. You can then enter commands on a command line with options and arguments at the prompt displayed in this window. You can use any of several programs to create a terminal window, the most commonly used one being a program called Xterm. Rxvt is an alternative terminal window program that is a stripped-down version of Xterm, lacking some configuration and emulation features, but smaller and faster. Most window manager workspace menus and panels have entries for starting a terminal window with either Xterm or Rxvt. An entry may be labeled with one of those names or an icon of a monitor.

Once opened, the window will display a shell prompt, usually the **$**, where you can enter Linux commands just as you would on the command line. You will see any results of your commands displayed within the terminal window, followed by a shell prompt indicating the beginning of the command line. An Xterm window supports several text-handling features. To the left of the window is a scroll bar that you can use to scroll back to view previously displayed text. As text moves off the top of the screen, you can scroll back to see it. This is particularly helpful if you are displaying directories with a large number of files that will not fit on one screen. Xterm also lets you copy text and paste it to the command line. You use the left mouse button to copy text and the second mouse button to paste it. You can copy any of the text previously displayed, such as previous commands or output from those commands. To copy text, click and hold down the left mouse button while dragging across the text you want to copy, letting up when you reach the end. Also, double-clicking will select a word, and a triple-click will select a line. If you want to extend the selected text, use the third mouse button. Once you have selected text, click the second mouse button. This automatically pastes the text to the end of the command line. Repeating clicks repeats the paste. The copy-and-paste operation is particularly helpful for constructing a complex command from previous ones. You can also copy and paste across different terminal windows.

The terminal window has the special capability of being able to run any X program from its command line. The terminal window operates within the X Window System environment. To run any X program, just open an Xterm window and enter the command, terminating it by pressing ENTER. The X program will then start up in its own window. For example, to run Netscape, you could open a terminal window and type the command **netscape**. A new window will open up running Netscape. You can open as many terminal windows as you want and then start an X program from each. However, closing a terminal window will also close the program started from it.

You will notice that the terminal window in which you entered the X command appears to suspend itself. There is no following prompt after you press ENTER to run the program. That is because the terminal window is currently busy running the X program you just executed. You can free the terminal window to execute other commands while that program is running by invoking the program with an ampersand (&). Technically, this places it in the background as far as the terminal window is concerned. But you are free to move to that X program's window and run it there. The following example would run Netscape, freeing the terminal window to run other commands. Notice the prompt:

```
$ netscape  &
```

When you are finished using the terminal window, close it by typing the command **exit** on the command line. Each terminal window is its own shell, and **exit** is the command to end a shell. (Shells are discussed in detail in Chapter 11.) Figure 10-1 shows the terminal window. The user has entered several commands, and the output is displayed in the window. As you reach the bottom of the window, the text displayed

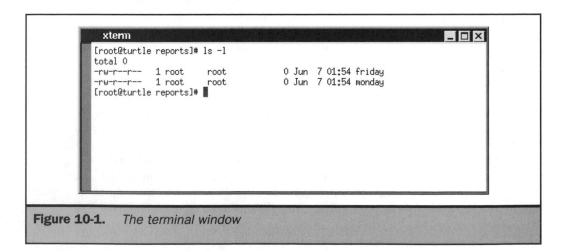

Figure 10-1. *The terminal window*

will scroll up, line by line, just as a normal terminal screen would. You can, of course, use the window controls to make the terminal window larger or smaller. You can even minimize it to an icon and later reopen it.

Note *The terminal window is actually a parent of the application you are running. Closing the terminal window in which you issued the application command will also close that application. For example, closing a terminal window in which you started up Netscape with the **netscape &** command will also close the Netscape window and any windows you opened up from Netscape.*

An Xterm window has four menus: the main menu, a VT options menu, a VT font menu, and a Tektronix window options menu. To bring up the main menu, hold down the CTRL key and click the left mouse button. For the VT options menu, hold down the CTRL key and click the second (right or middle) mouse button. To bring up the font menu, use the CTRL key and the third mouse button. You can then set the font and size of characters displayed.

Tip *The terms second mouse button and third mouse button can be confusing. On a two-button mouse, the second button is the right button, and the third button is the left and right buttons held down at the same time. On a three-button mouse, the second button is the middle button, and the third button is the rightmost button.*

X Window System Multitasking

One of the most useful features of your Linux X Window System interface is its capability to open several operations at the same time, each with its own window. Notice that in the command line interface you can only work on one task at a time (Chapter 11 describes an exception, in the case of what are called *background processes*). You issue a command and after it executes, you can execute another. In the X Window System, you can have several different applications running at once. Moving your mouse pointer from one window to another effectively moves you from one application to another. This feature of the X Window System illustrates one of the most useful capabilities of Linux: concurrency, the capability to have several processes operating at the same time. In your X Window System interface, you can have several applications running at the same time, each with its own window.

This feature can be easily illustrated using terminal windows. You can have several terminal windows open at the same time, each with its own command line. From the window manager's Main menu, you can open terminal windows. Each terminal window will have its own command line, and moving your mouse pointer from one window to another moves you from one command line to another. You can type a command in the active window and execute it. You can then move to another terminal window and type in another command. Each terminal window operates independently of the other.

ENVIRONMENTS

If you issue a command that takes a while to execute, and you move to another window, you will notice that the command in the window you just left is still executing.

File Managers

A file manager uses directory windows that allow you to use menus, icons, and windows to manage files and directories. A directory is displayed as a window, with files displayed as icons. Directories are usually represented by icons that look like folders. You open a directory and examine the files in it, just as you would open a folder and examine its contents. A directory window has menus for performing standard file and directory operations such as opening or deleting a file. Most file managers can also display files as lists providing details like the sizes and dates. Desktop file managers such as Gnome Midnight Commander (gmc) in Gnome and konqueror in KDE support drag-and-drop operations where you can copy or move files with a click-and-drag operation from one file manager window to another. You can also use gmc and konqueror without their desktop interface, running on any window manager, though Gnome and KDE still have to be installed on your system. Xfm is another popular file manager that provides basic directory and file operations.

Desktops

A *desktop* is an integrated program and file manager, providing you with menus and icons with which you can manage your files, run programs, and configure your system. Two desktops currently included in most Linux distributions are the K Desktop Environment (KDE) and the Gnome. They provide easy access to Internet tools, as well as the many Linux programs written for them or for the X Window System. You will be able to take full advantage of all desktop features, such as toolbars, configuration utilities, file management windows, and automatic history lists. KDE includes its own window manager with its desktop, though you can use any window manager. Gnome uses a separate window manager, though it should be Gnome compliant like Enlightenment. Most distributions provide both KDE and Gnome. On Red Hat, you can switch between the two using the desktop switching tool, **switchdesk**. The interfaces vary, but both include certain basic features. Desktop drag-and-drop operations are supported. A panel holds an application's starter menu, small utility programs, and icons for starting programs. The desktops also include an Internet-aware file manager that can access FTP sites and, in the case of KDE, operate as a Web browser. For each directory, you can open a window that shows all the files in that directory, displayed as icons. You can then run applications by double-clicking their icons (for KDE you single-click), or you can move the icons out of the file manager window and onto the desktop for easier access. By selecting different windows, menus, and icons on your screen using a mouse, you can run the application associated with the icon, opening a new window for it.

Starting Window Managers

As noted in Chapter 4, the X Window System is started either automatically using a display manager with a login window, or from the command line by entering the **startx** command. Your X Window System server will then load, followed immediately by the window manager. You exit the window manager by choosing an exit or quit entry in the desktop workspace menu. The display manager and some window managers, like FVWM2 and Window Maker, will give you the option of starting other window managers. If you get into trouble and the window manager hangs, you can forcibly exit the X Window System with the keys CTRL-ALT-BACKSPACE. You can change your resolution using CTRL-ALT-+, access a command line interface with CTRL-ALT-F1, and return to the window manager with CTRL-ALT-F7. These are the keystrokes available to you at the window manager level.

- CTRL-ALT-BACKSPACE Forcibly exit the window manager and return to the command line or graphical login
- CTRL-ALT-+ Change to the next highest resolution for your screen
- CTRL-ALT-- Change to the next lowest resolution for your screen
- CTRL-ALT-F1 Access the command line interface
- CTRL-ALT-F7 Return from the command line interface to the window manager

The window manager that you will start is the default one set up by your Linux distribution when you installed your system. Many distributions now use as their default either Gnome or KDE. For Gnome and the K Desktop different window managers are used, kwm for the K Desktop and Enlightenment or Sawfish for Gnome. You can run Gnome or KDE applications on most window managers. To have Gnome use a particular window manager, you need to select it using the Gnome Control Center. It is possible to use a window manager in place of kwm for KDE. Check the window manager's Web site for current information on Gnome and KDE compatibility. Currently, Enlightenment and Sawfish are fully Gnome compliant, and AfterStep and Window Maker are nearly so.

To use a different window manager, first install it. RPM packages will install with a default configuration for the window manager. If you are installing from source code you compiled, follow the included installation instructions. You can then configure Gnome or KDE to use that window manager, provided it is compliant with them. Alternatively, you can configure your system to start a particular window manager without either desktop. To do this, you have to place an entry for your window manager in an X Window System startup file. There are different startup files for the display manager and the **startx** command. The startup file for the display manager is called **/etc/X11/xdm/Xsession**, and the one for the **startx** command is called **/etc/X11/xinit/Xclients**. For **startx**, users can also set up their own **.Xclients** files in their home directories. The **startx** command first checks the user's home directory for the existence of an **.Xclients** file and, if it finds one, will execute that instead of the

ENVIRONMENTS

system's **/etc/X11/xinit/Xclients** file. Modifying these files can be complex process. The procedure is described in detail in Chapter 35.

Window managers will provide default configuration files and include utilities for changing your configuration. Both AfterStep and Window Maker use the GNUstep configuration standard, placing configuration files in a directory named **GNUstep** in a user's home directory. Sawfish places its configuration files in the user's **.sawfish** directory. Red Hat features a customized configuration of FVWM2 called AnotherLevel. Some distributions support the use of the **wmconfig** program to generate workspace menu entries for different window managers. On Red Hat, both AfterStep and FVWM2 are currently supported.

Window Managers for Linux

Several of the more popular Linux window managers are the Free Virtual Window Manager 2.0 (FVWM2), Sawfish (**sawfish**), Enlightenment (**enlightenment**), Window Maker (**wmaker**), Blackbox (**blackbox**), ICEWin, Xview (**olwm**), TWM (**twm**), LessTif (**mwm**), AfterStep (**afterstep**), and Motif (**mwm**). All except Motif are free. Most are easily configurable and provide theme support. Enlightenment and Sawfish are currently the default window managers for Gnome on different distributions. AfterStep and Window Maker are based on the NeXTSTEP interface. Xview is the Linux version of the Sun System's OpenLook interface. FVWM2 is the replacement for the original FVWM window manager, which was until recently the standard window manager used by most Linux distributions. LessTif is a free Motif clone that provides a Motif interface and will run many Motif applications. TWM is an older window manager that provides basic windowing capabilities and TVWM is a more recent version that supports virtual desktops. AfterStep, Window Maker, FVWM2, twm, Sawfish, and Enlightenment are included with most major distributions such as Red Hat and Caldera. You can download the other window managers from their Web sites. You can download and install recent versions of any window manager as they become available. These window managers are GNU public-licensed software—they are yours free of cost.

Sawfish

Sawfish is an extensible window manager designed for flexibility in the basic tasks of managing windows. You can easily configure window elements using simple Emacs-Lisp like commands. Sawfish aims only to manage windows and lacks other features such as docks and panels as found in AfterStep and Window Manager. Should you run Sawfish directly, noting is displayed except the bare X Window System gray background. The Workspace menu is accessed using a middle click on the mouse. Currently Sawfish is the default window manager for Red Hat, replacing Enlightenment. You can find out more about Sawfish at **sawmill.sourceforge.net**. Also check Chapter 9 for a detailed discussion on configuring Sawfish.

Enlightenment

Enlightenment aims to provide a highly configurable graphical shell for a user's work environment. It is still undergoing development, though releases are very stable. It is currently the default window manager distributed with Gnome. You can download new releases from the Enlightenment Web site at **www.enlightenment.org**, which also includes documentation. RPM packages for Red Hat and Caldera are available on their respective FTP sites. Enlightenment has the same window operations as used on other window managers, as shown in Figure 10-2. You can resize a window by clicking and dragging any of its sides or corners. You can move the window with a click-and-drag operation on its title bar. You can also right-click and drag any border to move the window. The upper-right corner lists the Maximize, Minimize, and Close buttons. The Minimize button will minimize to an icon on the desktop. You can click the upper-left corner of a window to display a window menu with entries for window operations. These include a Desktop entry to move the window to another desktop area and the Stick option, which displays the window no matter what desktop area you move to.

Figure 10-2. *The Enlightenment window manager*

To access the Enlightenment workspace menu, middle-click anywhere on the desktop (hold both mouse buttons down at the same time for a two-button mouse). There will be entries for applications as well as the desktop, themes, and Enlightenment configuration. With the desktop menus, you move to different desktop areas and virtual desktops. The themes menu lets you choose different Enlightenment themes.

To configure Enlightenment, use its GUI configuration tool. The Enlightenment Configuration window displays a list of configuration topics on the left and the panel for the selected topic on the right. Basic options set window displays, letting you select resize and move methods. With the Desktops option, you can create virtual desktops and specify the number of desktop areas for each one. Other topics cover features such as sounds, special effects, window focus, keyboard shortcuts, and backgrounds. You can set different backgrounds for each virtual desktop. The Themes panel lets you use an Enlightenment theme, of which there are many to choose from. Enlightenment is known for its impressive themes. See **e.themes.org** for ones that you can download. To make a theme available, place it in your home directory's **.enlightenment/themes** directory. Make sure that file has a **.etheme** extension. Enlightenment maintains its own configuration directory in your home directory called **.enlightenment**. It contains subdirectories for themes, backgrounds, and windows.

AfterStep

Originally based on the NeXTSTEP interface used on the NeXT operating system, AfterStep has evolved into a window manager in its own right. It includes the advantages of the NeXTSTEP interface, while adding features of its own. AfterStep began as a continuation of the BowMan window manager, which, in turn, was based on FVWM. It is available for free under the GNU Public License. You can download AfterStep from the AfterStep Web site (**www.afterstep.org**) or obtain the RPM version from the distribution FTP site.

Windows, menus, and icons are intentionally similar to those for NeXTSTEP. Clicking anywhere on the desktop will display the workspace menu. Clicking and dragging a menu title will tear it off from the menu and let it stick to the desktop, as shown in Figure 10-3. To start applications, you can also access features from an icon bar called Wharf. It is initially displayed on the left side, though it can be placed on any edge. Double-click an application's icon to start it. Wharf can contain folders that themselves expand to rows of application icons. There is also a Windows list that maintains a list of all open windows. The pager will initially display pages for four virtual desktops, each with four desktop areas. These will appear above Wharf. Click a desktop or a desktop area to move to it.

AfterStep includes an extensive set of modules and support themes. You can download themes from the **as.themes.org** Web site. The AfterStep Web site contains documentation, themes, and current releases. It also maintains links to sites that provide added material such as the AfterStep configuration guide, applets, and themes. AfterStep is ICCCM (Inter-Client Communications Conventions Manual), Gnome, and KDE compliant. To start AfterStep, use the command **afterstep** where your X Window System configuration files start your window manager (usually **.xinitrc** or **.Xclients**). The AfterStep configuration files are located in the directory **GNUstep/Library/AfterStep**

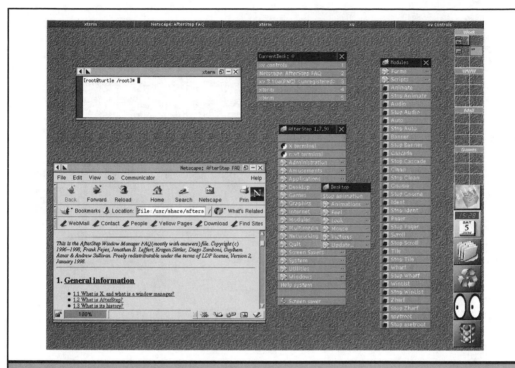

Figure 10-3.   *The AfterStep window manager*

ENVIRONMENTS

in a user's home directory. Configuration follows the GNUstep/Library standard. Separate configuration files are used for different components such as Wharf, Pager, and other modules and applications. A standard configuration is included with the installation, and you can download others from AfterStep sites. Most AfterStep material, including the current release, can be downloaded from the AfterStep FTP site at **ftp.afterstep.org**.

Window Maker

Window Maker, as shown in Figure 10-4, is a window manager designed to closely emulate NeXTSTEP. It includes additional support for GNUstep applications. GNUstep is an attempt to develop a GNU version of Next's OpenStep API. Window Maker plans to be Gnome and KDE compliant (see the Web site for current status). The Window Maker Web site at **www.windowmaker.org** provides online documentation, links, screenshots, and new releases. You can download the newest version directly from **ftp.windowmaker.org**.

A right-click will display the root-window menu (workspace). A middle-click will display a window list of currently opened windows. You can make frequently used menus "stick" to the desktop by dragging the title bar of the menu. This will make a Close button appear in the menu title bar. If you want to close the menu, just click that

Figure 10-4. *The Window Maker window manager*

button. Docked icons are listed in a icons bar. Initially this is shrunk to the GNUstep logo. Click and drag the logo to display the dock. To start an application, just double-click its icon. Whenever you start an application, a small icon for it, known as an appicon, is placed on the desktop. To add that application to the dock, just drag this icon to it. The dock icons support drag-and-drop operations. Just drag a file to an application's icon to start the application with that file. Window Maker supports multiple desktops, which it calls workspaces. You use the Workspaces menu to create new workspaces and change to current ones. There is also a workspace-dependent dock called the Clip, where you can have different clips of programs for each workspace.

You resize windows using a resize bar at the bottom of a window. You can move a window by dragging the title bar. To the left of the title bar is a miniaturizing window that reduces the window to a miniature window with its own title bar. To restore the window, double-click its miniature. To maximize the window, hold the CTRL key down while you double-click the title bar. Do the same to restore it.

Window Maker also supports themes. You can download Window Maker themes from **wm.themes.org**. To install a theme, extract its archive in your **GNUstep/Library/**

WindowMaker/Themes directory. Then from the root-window menu, select Themes and choose the theme from the list. Window Maker also features an extensive number of dock applications specifically designed to run within the dock (like Gnome applets in the panel). For example you can run a miniature network interface monitor, a POP3 mail checker, or, of course, a CD player.

Window Maker is configured using a GUI configuration utility, WPrefs. There is also a Wmakerconf utility that automatically generates the configuration files. Configuration files are kept in your **GNUstep/WindowMaker** directory. Attributes for different applications are kept in the **GNUstep/Defaults** directory. For example, the entries for the application's menu are kept in the **GNUstep/Defaults/WMRootMenu** file.

Blackbox

The Blackbox window manager is designed to be simple and fast. It provides multiple workspaces and small menus. Its source code can be compiled using just a C++ compiler and the X11 development libraries. It uses no special graphic libraries. It is nearly compliant with the Inter-Client Communications Conventions Manual (ICCCM). Though it has an interface similar to Window Maker, it is an entirely original program written in C++ sharing no common code with any other window manager. Blackbox was written by Brad Hughes, who currently maintains it. Blackbox provides support for KDE and Motif, but not Gnome. Blackbox also supports themes. You can download Blackbox themes from **blackbox.themes.org**. You can find out more about Blackbox from its Web site, **blackbox.alug.org**. Blackbox comes with a standard configuration, though you can set up your own in a **.blackboxrc** configuration file.

IceWM

The IceWM window manager supports many of the same features as FVWM, including themes. You can obtain recent releases, screenshots, and themes from the IceWM Web page currently at **icewm.sourceforge.net**. IceWM features a taskbar where open windows and running applications are docked. A sequence of labeled buttons represents different desktops. Click one to move to that desktop. To the left is a Linux button that you can click to display the Workspace menu. Next to the Linux button is a Window List button to display your open windows. Windows have Minimize, Maximize, and Close buttons in the upper-right corner. Resize borders are on every corner of a window. Clicking anywhere on the desktop will display the workspace menu. Configuration can be performed using the IcePref configuration tool.

FVWM2 and AnotherLevel

FVWM2 supports features such as the taskbar, workplace menu, modules, and themes (see Figure 10-5). Modules are small programs that can be loaded and run dynamically. FVWM2 replaces FVWM, which is no longer under development. You can obtain

Figure 10-5. *The FVWM2 window manager*

newer versions of FVWM2 as they come out, from the FVWM2 Web page, currently located at **www.fvwm.org**. RPM packages of the new FVWM2 versions are also available at the distribution FTP sites. You can download FVWM2 themes from **fvwm.themes.org**.

FVWM2 is usually the default window manager for most distributions, used when you have not specified a window manager (Gnome or KDE specify their own window managers). FVWM2 extends the capabilities of FVWM to provide better configuration files, allows customization of individual windows, and provides better module support. There are modules for a taskbar that adds Windows 95–like docking and Start menu capabilities. FVWM2 supports virtual desktops and desktop areas. FVWM2 also supports the Wharf icon bar. A pager display lets you move from one desktop to another. Clicking anywhere on the desktop will display a workplace menu. To quit FVWM2, select the Quit entry from this menu.

When the FVWM window manager starts up, it will execute its own configuration file, performing tasks such as displaying buttons on the FVWM taskbar, setting up entries in the workplace menu, and determining what programs to initially start up, if any. The default configuration file is **/etc/X11/fvwm2/system.fvwm2rc**. The configuration file for the older FVWM window manager is **/etc/X11/fvwm/system.fvwmrc**. You can modify any of these files to configure your FVWM window manager as you wish. For example, if you want to set the number of virtual desktops, you can modify the DeskTopNum entry in this file. Changes to this file are global for all users. Individual users can create their own **.fvwm2rc** files in their home directories and edit entries to customize their window managers. To start, users can copy the **system.fvwm2rc** file to their home directories as their **.fvwm2rc** file to use as a basis for their own configurations. The following entry determines the number of desktop areas to support in a virtual desktop. It is measured by the number of squares on the length and width, so 3 × 3 would be nine desktop areas.

```
DeskTopSize 2x2
```

Red Hat uses the AnotherLevel configuration for FVWM2 to create a custom FVWM2 desktop with Red Hat icons and menus. AnotherLevel uses a set of M4 macro files located in the **/etc/X11/AnotherLevel** directory. Different configuration features are organized into separate files such as **fvwm2rc.keys.m4** for key bindings and **fvwm2rc.modules.m4** for modules used. The **fvwm2rc.defines.m4** file holds definitions for many configuration values, including the number of virtual desktops and the number of areas set up for them. Values are defined using macros:

```
# NUM_DESKTOPS is number of desktops -- each desktop is DESKTOP_SIZE panes
define(`NUM_DESKTOPS',2)

# DESKTOP_SIZE is a geometry specifying horizontal desktop x vertical
desktops
# So 3x3 gives 9 panes per desktop
define(`DESKTOP_SIZE',2x2)
```

Xview: olwm and olvwm

Xview is the implementation of Sun System's OpenLook interface. Those familiar with OpenLook will find that the Linux version runs in much the same way. You can download Xview from ftp.**metalab.unc.edu** FTP site. The Xview archive files are located in the **/pub/Linux/libs/X/xview** directory, currently **xview-3.2p1.4. bin.tar.gz**. This Xview package includes both the olwm and olvwm window managers, as well as several utilities such as a clock and a text editor. The olvwm version of Xview supports a virtual desktop.

The Xview package many distributions provide contains a set of shared libraries that provide OpenLook menus, buttons, and other widgets. These are used in many Linux applications. Though applications that use these Xview widgets do not have to use the Xview window manager, they do use the Xview libraries. So, you can run applications like the textedit Xview editor in the FVWM window manager. The buttons and menus that textedit uses are Xview widgets, though it can operate in an FVWM window. Such an Xview package is not the full Xview window manager. It is a subset of libraries with a few popular applications.

To install the full Xview window manager, first download its tar archive from **ftp.metalab.unc.edu**. If your distribution previously installed the Xview package, you will need to remove the **/usr/openwin** directory. Then unpack the Xview package you downloaded with the **tar xvf** command. This creates a subdirectory named **usr** in your current directory. In this **usr** directory is a subdirectory named **openwin**, which you move into the **/usr** directory (notice the forward slash).

```
# mv usr/openwin  /usr
```

Then run the **ldconfig** command on the **/usr/openwin/lib** directory. This sets up the Xview libraries.

```
# ldconfig /usr/openwin/lib
```

Make sure a **/usr/openwin/lib** entry is in the **/etc/ld.so.config** file (see Chapter 19). Because the Xview archive is not an RPM package, you have to perform the installation tasks yourself, such as moving files to the right directory and running **ldconfig**. Other window managers can be obtained in RPM format that will automatically install and configure their files for you. You then place an entry to start **olvwm** in either the **.xinitrc** file or the **.xsessions** file.

When you first bring up the olvwm window manager, you will be presented with a blank screen and a pager with six squares displayed in the upper-left corner. Double-click any square to move to that screen. To bring up the Xview workspace menu, click anywhere on the screen with the right mouse button. The workspace menu is a pinnable menu. You will see a picture of a push-pin at the top. If you click it, the workplace menu will remain displayed at that place on the screen. Click the pin again to be able to remove the workplace menu. The "X11 Progs" entry in the workspace menu automatically lists installed X11 programs, and the "Xview Progs" entry lists all Xview programs (those installed in **/usr/openwin/bin**).

Window components are slightly different from other window managers, though they serve much the same function. Menus are displayed with the right mouse button. On the workspace menu, you bring up submenus by right-clicking the small triangle to the right of a menu item. To move windows and pinned menus, you click and drag with the left mouse button on the very edge of the window.

Xview components are installed in the **/usr/openwin** directory. Here you will find subdirectories such as **/usr/openwin/bin** that hold Xview programs and others such as **/usr/openwin/lib** that hold Xview libraries. When the X Window System starts up, it has to have a shell variable called OPENWINHOME set to the Xview directory, **/usr/openwin**. Such assignments should also be placed in the respective X startup files like **.xinitrc** or **.xessions**.

The **/usr/openwin/lib** directory contains the menu files used to display the Xview workspace menu and its submenus. You can add entries to these menus if you wish. An entry consists of the label to be displayed followed by the action to take. For example, to add an entry to the workspace menu for Netscape, you would place the following entry in the **openwin-menu** file. The **Xview** man pages have a detailed explanation of Xview menus and the kinds of entries you can make.

```
"Netscape"      exec /usr/bin/netscape
```

LessTif: mwm

LessTif is an Motif clone designed to run any Motif program. It describes itself as the Hungry Programmers' version of OSF/Motif. It is currently source compatible with OSF/Motif® 1.2; that is, the same source code will compile with either LessTif or Motif. LessTif is provided free under the GNU Library General Public License (LGPL). You can download it from the LessTif Web site at **www.lesstif.org**. You can also download RPM versions from the Red Hat contrib site, **contrib.redhat.com**. The LessTif site also provides documentation and a listing of applications that currently work under LessTif. You invoke LessTif with the command **mwm**. It uses a global configuration file, **/etc/X11/mwm/system.mwmrc**, and a user configuration file, **.mwmrc**. Currently, LessTif does not run all Motif programs. The project is still under development, but it provides the same window management look and feel as that of Motif. Plans are to provide compatibility first with Motif 1.2 and then with version 2.0.

Motif

Motif is proprietary software that you have to purchase from a vendor for about $150. Motif and Xview were the two major competing window interfaces provided for Unix, representing two different window standards. These two standards have been recently integrated into a new GUI standard for Unix called the Common Desktop Environment (CDE).

The Common Desktop Environment (CDE)

The Common Desktop Environment (CDE) provides a common set of desktop interface standards that were proposed by Hewlett-Packard, Novel, IBM, and Sun in 1995. It was designed to merge OpenLook and Motif into one standard interface that could be used on all versions of Unix. Commercial versions of CDE such as TriTeal CDE are available for Linux (**www.triteal.com**). The CDE desktop provides an interface somewhat similar to Gnome and KDE. Along with window and desktop support it provides a panel for launching applications. Most CDE desktops include a set of CDE applications such as a file manager, a mail client, and a text editor. Like other desktops and window managers, CDE supports virtual desktops. Help is context sensitive, letting you displaying information about a component by clicking a help entry in its pop-up menu.

Chapter 11

The Shell

The *shell* is a command interpreter that provides a line-oriented interactive interface between the user and the operating system. You enter commands on a command line, they are interpreted by the shell, and then sent as instructions to the operating system. This interpretive capability of the shell provides for many sophisticated features. For example, the shell has a set of wildcard characters that can generate file names. The shell can redirect input and output, as well as run operations in the background, freeing you to perform other tasks.

Several different types of shells have been developed for Linux: the *Bourne Again shell (BASH), the Public Domain Korn shell (PDKSH)*, the TCSH shell, and the Z-shell. All shells are available for your use, although the BASH shell is the default. You only need one type of shell to do your work. Red Hat Linux includes all the major shells, although it installs and uses the BASH shell as the default. If you use the Red Hat Linux command line shell, you will be using the BASH shell unless you specify another. This chapter discusses the BASH shell that shares many of the same features as other shells.

*You can find out more about the BASH shell at www.gnu.org/software/bash. A detailed online manual is available on your Linux system using the **man** command with the **bash** keyword.*

The Command Line

The Linux command line interface consists of a single line into which you enter commands with any of their options and arguments. Red Hat Linux installs with the BASH shell. By default, The BASH shell has a dollar (**$**) sign prompt, but Linux has several other types of shells, each with its own prompt. A shell *prompt*, such as the one shown here, marks the beginning of the command line:

```
$
```

The prompt designates the beginning of the command line. You are now ready to enter a command and its arguments at the prompt. In the next example, the user enters the **date** command, which displays the date. The user types the command on the first line, and then presses ENTER to execute the command.

```
$ date
Sun July 8 10:30:21 PST 2000
```

The *command line interface* is the primary interface for the shell, which interprets the commands you enter and sends them to the system. The shell follows a special syntax for interpreting the command line. The first word entered on a command line must be the name of a command. The next words are options and arguments for the command.

Each word on the command line must be separated from the others by one or more spaces or tabs.

```
$ Command      Options      Arguments
```

An *option* is a one-letter code preceded by a dash that modifies the type of action the command takes. One example of a command that has options is the **ls** command. The **ls** *command*, with no options, displays a list of all the files in your current directory. It merely lists the name of each file with no other information.

With a **-l** option, the **ls** command modifies its task by displaying a line of information about each file, listing such data as its size, and the date and time it was last modified. In the next example, the user enters the **ls** command followed by a **-l** option. The dash before the **-l** option is required. Linux uses it to distinguish an option from an argument.

```
$ ls -l
```

Another option, **-a**, lists all the files in your directory, including what are known as hidden files. *Hidden files* are often configuration files and they always have names beginning with a period. For this reason, hidden files are often referred to as *dot files*. In most cases, you can also combine options. You do so by preceding the options with an initial dash and then listing the options you want. The options **-al**, for example, list information about all the files in your directory, including any hidden files.

Tip *Another option for the **ls** command is **-F**. With this option, the **ls** command displays directory names with a preceding slash, so you can easily identify them.*

```
$ ls -al
```

Most commands are designed to take arguments. An *argument* is a word you type in on the command line after any options. Many file management commands take file names as their arguments. For example, if you only wanted the information displayed for a particular file, you could add that file's name after the **-l** option:

```
$ ls -l mydata
```

The shell you will start working in is the BASH shell, your default shell. This shell has special command line editing capabilities that you may find helpful as you learn Linux. You can easily modify commands you have entered before executing them, moving anywhere on the command line and inserting or deleting characters. This is particularly helpful for complex commands. You can use the CTRL-F or RIGHT ARROW key to move forward a character, or the CTRL-B or LEFT ARROW key to move back a

ENVIRONMENTS

character. CTRL-D or DEL deletes the character the cursor is on, and CTRL-H or BACKSPACE deletes the character before the cursor. To add text, you use the arrow keys to move the cursor to where you want to insert text and type in the new characters. At any time, you can press ENTER to execute the command. For example, if you make a spelling mistake when entering a command, rather than reentering the entire command, you can use the editing operations to correct the mistake.

You can also use the UP ARROW key to redisplay your previously executed command. You can then reexecute that command or edit it and execute the modified command. You'll find this capability helpful when you have to repeat certain operations over and over, such as editing the same file.

> **Tip**   *The capability to redisplay a previous command is helpful when you've already executed a command you had entered incorrectly. In this case, you would be presented with an error message and a new, empty command line. By pressing the UP ARROW key, you can redisplay your previous command, make corrections to it, and then execute it again. This way, you would not have to enter the whole command again.*

The BASH shell keeps a list, called a *history list*, of your previously entered commands. You can display each command, in turn, on your command line by pressing the UP ARROW key. The DOWN ARROW key moves you down the list. You can modify and execute any of these previous commands when you display them on your command line. This history feature is discussed in more detail in Chapter 15.

> **Tip**   *Some commands can be complex and take some time to execute. When you mistakenly execute the wrong command, you can interrupt and stop such commands with the interrupt keys—CTRL-C or DEL.*

You can enter a command on several lines by typing a backslash just before you press ENTER. The backslash "escapes" the ENTER key, effectively continuing the same command line to the next line. In the next example, the **cp** command is entered on three lines. The first two lines end in a backslash, effectively making all three lines one command line.

```
$ cp -i \
mydata \
newdata
```

Wildcards and Filename Arguments: *, ?, [ ]

Filenames are the most common arguments used in a command. Often you may know only part of the file name, or you may want to reference several file names that have the same extension or begin with the same characters. The shell provides a set of special characters called *wildcards* that search out, match, and generate a list of file names. The *wildcard characters* are the asterisk, the question mark, and brackets (*****, **?**, **[]**). Given a partial file name, the shell uses these matching operators to search for files and generate a list of file names found. The shell replaces the partial file name argument with the list of matched file names. This list of file names can then become the arguments for commands such as **ls**, which can operate on many files. Table 11-1 lists the shell's wildcard characters.

ENVIRONMENTS

Common Shell Symbols	Execution
ENTER	Execute a command line.
;	Separate commands on the same command line.
\`command\`	Execute a command.
[]	Match on a class of possible characters in file names.
\	Quote the following character. Used to quote special characters.
|	Pipe the standard output of one command as input for another command.
&	Execute a command in the background.
!	History command.
Wildcard Symbols	**Execution**
*	Match on any set of characters in file names.
?	Match on any single character in file names.
Redirection Symbols	**Execution**
>	Redirect the standard output to a file or device, creating the file if it does not exist and overwriting the file if it does exist.

Table 11-1. *Shell Symbols*

Redirection Symbols	Execution
>!	The exclamation point forces the overwriting of a file if it already exists. This overrides the noclobber option.
<	Redirect the standard input from a file or device to a program.
>>	Redirect the standard output to a file or device, appending the output to the end of the file.

Standard Error Redirection Symbols	Execution
2>	Redirect the standard error to a file or device.
2>>	Redirect and append the standard error to a file or device.
2>&1	Redirect the standard error to the standard output.
>&	Redirect the standard error to a file or device.
|&	Pipe the standard error as input to another command.

Table 11-1.   *Shell Symbols* (continued)

The *asterisk,* *****, references files beginning or ending with a specific set of characters. You place the asterisk before or after a set of characters that form a pattern to be searched for in file names. If the asterisk is placed before the pattern, file names that end in that pattern are searched for. If the asterisk is placed after the pattern, file names that begin with that pattern are searched for. Any matching file name is copied into a list of file names generated by this operation. In the next example, all file names beginning with the pattern "doc" are searched for and a list generated. Then all file names ending with the pattern "day" are searched for and a list is generated. The last example shows how the * can be used in any combination of characters.

```
$ ls
doc1 doc2 document docs mydoc monday tuesday
$ ls doc*
doc1 doc2 document docs
$ ls *day
monday tuesday
$ ls m*d*
monday tuesday
$
```

File names often include an extension specified with a period and followed by a string denoting the file type such as **.c** for C files, **.cpp** for C++ files, or even **.jpg** for JPEG image files. The extension has no special status and is only part of the characters making up the file name. Using the asterisk makes it easy to select files with a given extension. In the next example, the asterisk is used to list only those files with a **.c** extension. The asterisk placed before the **.c** constitutes the argument for **ls**.

```
$ ls *.c
calc.c main.c
```

You can use * with the **rm** command to erase several files at once. The asterisk first selects a list of files with a given extension, or beginning or ending with a given set of characters, and then it presents this list of files to the **rm** command to be erased. In the next example, the **rm** command erases all files beginning with the pattern "doc":

```
$ rm doc*
```

The asterisk by itself matches all files. If you use a single asterisk as the argument for an **rm** command, all your files will be erased. In the next example, the **ls *** command lists all files, and the **rm *** command erases all files:

```
$ ls *
doc1 doc2 document docs mydoc myletter yourletter
$ rm *
$ ls
$
```

ENVIRONMENTS

Use the * wildcard character carefully and sparingly with the **rm** command. The combination can be dangerous. A misplaced * in an **rm** command without the **-i** option could easily erase all your files. The first command in the next example erases only those files with a **.c** extension. The second command, however, erases all files. Notice the space between the asterisk and the period in the second command. A space in a command line functions as a *delimiter*, separating arguments. The asterisk is considered one argument, and the **.c**, another argument. The asterisk by itself matches all files and, when used as an argument with the **rm** command, instructs **rm** to erase all your files.

```
$ rm *.c
$ rm * .c
```

The *question mark*, **?**, matches only a single incomplete character in file names. Suppose you want to match the files **doc1** and **docA**, but not **document**. Whereas the asterisk will match file names of any length, the question mark limits the match to just one extra character. The next example matches files that begin with the word "doc" followed by a single differing letter:

```
$ ls
doc1 docA document
$ ls doc?
doc1 docA
```

Whereas the * and **?** wildcard characters specify incomplete portions of a file name, the *brackets*, **[ ]**, enable you to specify a set of valid characters to search for. Any character placed within the brackets will be matched in the file name. Suppose you want to list files beginning with "doc", but only ending in *1* or *A*. You are not interested in file names ending in *2* or *B*, or any other character. Here is how it's done:

```
$ ls
doc1 doc2 doc3 docA docB docD document
$ ls doc[1A]
doc1 docA
```

You can also specify a set of characters as a range, rather than listing them one by one. A dash placed between the upper and lower bounds of a set of characters selects all characters within that range. The range is usually determined by the character set in use. In an ASCII character set, the range "a–g" will select all lowercase alphabetic characters from *a* through *g*, inclusive. In the next example, files beginning with the pattern "doc" and ending in characters *1* through *3* are selected. Then, those ending in characters *B* through *E* are matched.

```
$ ls doc[1-3]
doc1 doc2 doc3
$ ls doc[B-E]
docB docD
```

You can combine the brackets with other wildcard characters to form flexible matching operators. Suppose you only want to list file names ending in either a **.c** or **.o** extension, but no other extension. You can use a combination of the asterisk and brackets: ***[co]**. The asterisk matches all file names, and the brackets match only file names with extension **.c** or **.o**.

```
$ ls *.[co]
main.c   main.o   calc.c
```

At times, a wildcard character is actually part of a file name. In these cases, you need to quote the character by preceding it with a backslash to reference the file. In the next example, the user needs to reference a file that ends with the **?** character, **answers?**. The **?** is, however, a wildcard character and would match any file name beginning with "answers" that has one or more characters. In this case, the user quotes the **?** with a preceding backslash to reference the file name.

```
$ ls answers\?
answers?
```

Standard Input/Output and Redirection

When UNIX was designed, a decision was made to distinguish between the physical implementation and the logical organization of a file. Physically, UNIX files are accessed in randomly arranged blocks. Logically, all files are organized as a continuous stream of bytes. Linux, as a version of UNIX, has this same organization. Aside from special system calls, the user never references the physical structure of a file. To the user, all files have the same organization—a byte stream. Any file can be easily copied or appended to another because all files are organized in the same way. In this sense, only one standard type of file exists in Linux, the *byte-stream file*. Linux makes no implementational distinction between a character file and a record file, or a text file and a binary file.

This logical file organization extends to input and output operations. The data in input and output operations is organized like a file. Data input at the keyboard is placed in a data stream arranged as a continuous set of bytes. Data output from a command or program is also placed in a data stream and arranged as a continuous set of bytes. This input data stream is referred to in Linux as the *standard input*, while the output data stream is called the *standard output*. There is also a separate output data stream reserved solely for error messages called the standard error (see section on the standard error later in this chapter).

Because the standard input and standard output have the same organization as that of a file, they can easily interact with files. Linux has a redirection capability that lets you easily move data in and out of files. You can redirect the standard output so that, instead of displaying the output on a screen, you can save it in a file. You can also redirect the standard input away from the keyboard to a file, so that input is read from a file instead of from your keyboard.

When a Linux command is executed that produces output, this output is placed in the standard output data stream. The default destination for the standard output data stream is a device—in this case, the screen. *Devices*, such as the keyboard and screen, are treated as files. They receive and send out streams of bytes with the same organization as that of a byte-stream file. The screen is a device that displays a continuous stream of bytes. By default, the standard output will send its data to the screen device, which will then display the data.

For example, the **ls** command generates a list of all file names and outputs this list to the standard output. Next, this stream of bytes in the standard output is directed to the screen device. The list of file names is then printed on the screen. The **cat** command also sends output to the standard output. The contents of a file are copied to the standard output whose default destination is the screen. The contents of the file are then displayed on the screen.

Redirecting the Standard Output: > and >>

Suppose that instead of displaying a list of files on the screen, you would like to save this list in a file. In other words, you would like to direct the standard output to a file rather than the screen. To do this, you place the *output redirection operator*, **>** (greater-than sign), and the name of a file on the command line after the Linux command. Table 11-2 lists the different ways you can use the redirection operators. In the next example, the output of the **cat** command is redirected from the screen device to a file:

```
$ cat myletter > newletter
```

The redirection operation creates the new destination file. If the file already exists, it will be overwritten with the data in the standard output. You can set the **noclobber** feature to prevent overwriting an existing file with the redirection operation. In this case, the redirection operation on an existing file will fail. You can overcome the **noclobber** feature by placing an exclamation point after the redirection operator. You can place the **noclobber** command in a shell configuration file to make it an automatic default operation (see Chapter 13). The next example sets the **noclobber**

Command	Execution
ENTER	Execute a command line.
;	Separate commands on the same command line.
command\ *opts args*	Enter backslash before carriage return to continue entering a command on the next line.
`command`	Execute a command.
BACKSPACE CTRL-H	Erase the previous character.
CTRL-U	Erase the command line and start over.
CTRL-C	Interrupt and stop a command execution.

Special Characters for File Name Generation	Execution
*	Match on any set of characters.
?	Match on any single characters.
[]	Match on a class of possible characters.
\	Quote the following character. Used to quote special characters.

Redirection	Execution
command > *filename*	Redirect the standard output to a file or device, creating the file if it does not exist and overwriting the file if it does exist.
command < *filename*	Redirect the standard input from a file or device to a program.
command >> *filename*	Redirect the standard output to a file or device, appending the output to the end of the file.
command >! *filename*	In the C-shell and the Korn shell, the exclamation point forces the overwriting of a file if it already exists. This overrides the noclobber option.
command 2> *filename*	Redirect the standard error to a file or device in the Bourne shell.

Table 11-2.   *The Shell Operations*

Redirection	Execution
command **2>>** *filename*	Redirect and append the standard error to a file or device in the Bourne shell.
command **2>&1**	Redirect the standard error to the standard output in the Bourne shell.
command **>&** *filename*	Redirect the standard error to a file or device in the C-shell.
Pipes	**Execution**
command **|** *command*	Pipe the standard output of one command as input for another command.
command **|&** *command*	Pipe the standard error as input to another command in the C-shell.
Background Jobs	**Execution**
&	Execute a command in the background.
fg *%jobnum*	Bring a command in the background to the foreground or resume an interrupted program.
bg	Place a command in the foreground into the background.
CTRL-Z	Interrupt and stop the currently running program. The program remains stopped and waiting in the background for you resume it.
notify *%jobnum*	Notify you when a job ends.
kill *%jobnum* **kill** *proccessnum*	Cancel and end a job running in the background.
jobs	List all background jobs. The **jobs** command is not available in the Bourne shell, unless it is using the jsh shell.
ps	List all currently running processes including background jobs.
at *time date*	Execute commands at a specified time and date. The time can be entered with hours and minutes and qualified as A.M. or P.M.

Table 11-2. *The Shell Operations* (continued)

feature for the BASH shell and then forces the overwriting of the **oldletter** file if it already exists:

```
$ set -o noclobber
$ cat myletter >! oldletter
```

Although the redirection operator and the file name are placed after the command, the redirection operation is not executed after the command. In fact, it is executed before the command. The redirection operation creates the file and sets up the redirection before it receives any data from the standard output. If the file already exists, it will be destroyed and replaced by a file of the same name. In effect, the command generating the output is executed only after the redirected file has been created.

In the next example, the output of the **ls** command is redirected from the screen device to a file. First the **ls** command lists files and, in the next command, **ls** redirects its file list to the **listf** file. Then the **cat** command displays the list of files saved in **listf**. Notice the list of files in **listf** includes the **listf** file name. The list of file names generated by the **ls** command include the name of the file created by the redirection operation—in this case, **listf**. The **listf** file is first created by the redirection operation, and then the **ls** command lists it along with other files. This file list output by **ls** is then redirected to the **listf** file, instead of being printed on the screen.

```
$ ls
mydata intro preface
$ ls > listf
$ cat listf
mydata intro listf preface
```

Errors occur when you try to use the same file name for both an input file for the command and the redirected destination file. In this case, because the redirection operation is executed first, the input file, because it exists, is destroyed and replaced by a file of the same name. When the command is executed, it finds an input file that is empty.

In the **cat** command shown next, the file **myletter** is the name for both the destination file for redirected output and the input file for the **cat** operation. As shown in the next example, the redirection operation is executed first, destroying the **myletter** file and replacing it with a new and empty **myletter** file. Then the **cat** operation is executed and attempts to read all the data in the **myletter** file. However, nothing new is now in the **myletter** file.

```
$ cat myletter > myletter
```

ENVIRONMENTS

You can also append the standard output to an existing file using the **>>** redirection operator. Instead of overwriting the file, the data in the standard output is added at the end of the file. In the next example, the **myletter** and **oldletter** files are appended to the **alletters** file. The **alletters** file will then contain the contents of both **myletter** and **oldletter**.

```
$ cat myletter >> alletters
$ cat oldletter >> alletters
```

The Standard Input

Many Linux commands can receive data from the standard input. The standard input itself receives data from a device or a file. The default device for the standard input is the keyboard. Characters typed into the keyboard are placed in the standard input, which is then directed to the Linux command. The **cat** command without a file name argument reads data from standard input. When you type in data on the keyboard, each character will be placed in the standard input and directed to the **cat** command. The **cat** command then sends the character to the standard output—the screen device—which displays the character on the screen.

If you combine the **cat** command with redirection, you have an easy way of saving what you have typed to a file. As shown in the next example, the output of the **cat** operation is redirected to the **mydat** file. The **mydat** file will now contain all the data typed in at the keyboard. The **cat** command, in this case, still has no file arguments. It will receive its data from the standard input, the keyboard device. The redirection operator redirects the output of the **cat** command to the file **mydat**. The **cat** command has no direct contact with any files; it is simply receiving input from the standard input and sending output to the standard output.

```
$ cat > mydat
This is a new line
for the cat
command
^D
$
```

Just as with the standard output, you can also redirect the standard input. The standard input may be received from a file rather than the keyboard. The operator for redirecting the standard input is the less-than sign, **<**. In the next example, the standard input is redirected to receive input from the **myletter** file, rather than the keyboard device. The contents of **myletter** are read into the standard input by the redirection operation. Then the **cat** command reads the standard input and displays the contents of **myletter**.

```
$ cat < myletter
hello Christopher
How are you today
$
```

You can combine the redirection operations for both standard input and standard output. In the next example, the **cat** command has no file name arguments. Without file name arguments, the **cat** command receives input from the standard input and sends output to the standard output. However, the standard input has been redirected to receive its data from a file, while the standard output has been redirected to place its data in a file.

```
$ cat < myletter > newletter
```

Pipes: |

You may find yourself in situations in which you need to send data from one command to another. In other words, you may want to send the standard output of a command to another command, not to a destination file. Suppose you want to send a list of your file names to the printer to be printed. You need two commands to do this: the **ls** command to generate a list of file names and the **lpr** command to send the list to the printer. In effect, you need to take the output of the **ls** command and use it as input for the **lpr** command. You can think of the data as flowing from one command to another. To form such a connection in Linux, you use what is called a *pipe*. The *pipe operator*, | (vertical bar character), placed between two commands forms a connection between them. The standard output of one command becomes the standard input for the other. The pipe operation receives output from the command placed before the pipe and sends this data as input to the command placed after the pipe. As shown in the next example, you can connect the **ls** command and the **lpr** command with a pipe. The list of file names output by the **ls** command is piped into the **lpr** command.

```
$ ls | lpr
```

You can combine the pipe operation with other shell features, such as wildcard characters, to perform specialized operations. The next example prints only files with a **.c** extension. The **ls** command is used with the asterisk and ".c" to generate a list of file names with the .c extension. Then this list is piped to the **lpr** command.

```
$ ls *.c | lpr
```

ENVIRONMENTS

In the previous example, a list of file names was used as input, but what is important to note is pipes operate on the standard output of a command, whatever that might be. The contents of whole files or even several files can be piped from one command to another. In the next example, the **cat** command reads and outputs the contents of the **mydata** file, which are then piped to the **lpr** command:

```
$ cat mydata | lpr
```

Linux has many commands that generate modified output. For example, the **sort** command takes the contents of a file and generates a version with each line sorted in alphabetic order. The **sort** command works best with files that are lists of items. Commands such as **sort** that output a modified version of its input are referred to as *filters*. Filters are often used with pipes. In the next example, a sorted version of **mylist** is generated and piped into the **more** command for display on the screen. Note that the original file, **mylist**, has not been changed and is not itself sorted. Only the output of **sort** in the standard output is sorted.

```
$ sort mylist | more
```

You can, of course, combine several commands, connecting each pair with a pipe. The output of one command can be piped into another command, which, in turn, can pipe its output into still another command. Suppose you have a file with a list of items you want to print both numbered and in alphabetical order. To print the numbered and sorted list, you can first generate a sorted version with the **sort** command and then pipe that output to the **cat** command. The **cat** command with the **-n** option then takes as its input the sorted list and generates as its output a numbered, sorted list. The numbered, sorted list can then be piped to the **lpr** command for printing. The next example shows the command:

```
$ sort mylist | cat -n | lpr
```

The standard input piped into a command can be more carefully controlled with the standard input argument, **-**. When you use the dash as an argument for a command, it represents the standard input. Suppose you want to print a file with the name of its directory at the top. The **pwd** command outputs a directory name, and the **cat** command outputs the contents of a file. In this case, the **cat** command needs to take as its input both the file and the standard input piped in from the **pwd** command. The **cat** command will have two arguments: the standard input as represented by the dash and the file name of the file to be printed.

In the next example, the **pwd** command generates the directory name and pipes it into the **cat** command. For the **cat** command, this piped-in standard input now contains the directory name. As represented by the dash, the standard input is the first argument to the **cat** command. The **cat** command copies the directory name and the contents of the **mylist** file to the standard output, which is then piped to the **lpr** command for printing. If you want to print the directory name at the end of the file instead, simply make the dash the last argument and the file name the first argument, as in **cat mylist -**.

```
$ pwd | cat - mylist | lpr
```

Redirecting and Piping the Standard Error: >&, 2>

When you execute commands, an error could possibly occur. You may give the wrong number of arguments, or some kind of system error could take place. When an error occurs, the system issues an error message. Usually such error messages are displayed on the screen, along with the standard output. Linux distinguishes between standard output and error messages, however. Error messages are placed in yet another standard byte stream called the *standard error*. In the next example, the **cat** command is given as its argument the name of a file that does not exist, **myintro**. In this case, the **cat** command simply issues an error:

```
$ cat myintro
cat : myintro not found
$
```

Because error messages are in a separate data stream from the standard output, error messages still appear on the screen for you to see even if you have redirected the standard output to a file. In the next example, the standard output of the **cat** command is redirected to the file **mydata**. However, the standard error, containing the error messages, is still directed to the screen.

```
$ cat myintro > mydata
cat : myintro not found
$
```

You can redirect the standard error as you can the standard output. This means you can save your error messages in a file for future reference. This is helpful if you need a record of the error messages. Like the standard output, the standard error has the screen device for its default destination. However, you can redirect the standard error to any file or device you choose using special redirection operators. In this case, the error messages will not be displayed on the screen.

Redirection of the standard error relies on a special feature of shell redirection. You can reference all the standard byte streams in redirection operations with numbers. The numbers 0, 1, and 2 reference the standard input, standard output, and standard error, respectively. By default, an output redirection, **>**, operates on the standard output, 1. You can modify the output redirection to operate on the standard error, however, by preceding the output redirection operator with the number 2. In the next example, the **cat** command again will generate an error. The error message is redirected to the standard byte stream represented by the number 2, the standard error.

```
$ cat nodata 2> myerrors
$ cat myerrors
cat : nodata not found
$
```

You can also append the standard error to a file by using the number 2 and the redirection append operator, **>>**. In the next example, the user appends the standard error to the **myerrors** file, which then functions as a log of errors:

```
$ cat nodata 2>> myerrors
```

Shell Variables

You define variables within a shell, and such variables are known—logically enough—as *shell variables*. Many different shells exist. Some utilities, such as the *mailx utility*, have their own shells with their own shell variables. You can also create your own shell using what are called *shell scripts*. You have a user shell that becomes active as soon as you log in. This is often referred to as the *login shell*. Special system variables are defined within this login shell. Shell variables can also be used to define a shell's environment as described in Chapter 13.

 Shell variables exist as long as your shell is active—that is, until you exit the shell. For example, logging out will exit the login shell. When you log in again, any variables you may need in your login shell must be defined once again.

Definition and Evaluation of Variables: =, $, set, unset

You define a variable in a shell when you first use the variable's name. A variable's name may be any set of alphabetic characters, including the underscore. The name may also include a number, but the number cannot be the first character in the name. A name may not have any other type of character, such as an exclamation point, an ampersand, or even a space. Such symbols are reserved by the shell for its own use. Also, a name may not include more than one word. The shell uses spaces on the command line to distinguish different components of a command such as options, arguments, and the name of the command.

You assign a value to a variable with the assignment operator, **=**. You type in the variable name, the assignment operator, and then the value assigned. Do not place any spaces around the assignment operator. The assignment operation **poet = Virgil**, for example, will fail. (The C-shell has a slightly different type of assignment operation that is described in the section on C-shell variables later in this chapter.) You can assign any set of characters to a variable. In the next example, the variable **poet** is assigned the string **Virgil**:

```
$ poet=Virgil
```

Once you have assigned a value to a variable, you can then use the variable name to reference the value. Often you use the values of variables as arguments for a command. You can reference the value of a variable using the variable name preceded by the **$** operator. The dollar sign is a special operator that uses the variable name to reference a variable's value, in effect, evaluating the variable. Evaluation retrieves a variable's value, usually a set of characters. This set of characters then replaces the variable name on the command line. Wherever a **$** is placed before the variable name, the variable name is replaced with the value of the variable. In the next example, the shell variable **poet** is evaluated and its contents, **Virgil**, are then used as the argument for an **echo** command. The **echo** command simply echoes or prints a set of characters to the screen.

```
$ echo $poet
Virgil
```

You must be careful to distinguish between the evaluation of a variable and its name alone. If you leave out the **$** operator before the variable name, all you have is the variable name itself. In the next example, the **$** operator is absent from the variable name. In this case, the **echo** command has as its argument the word "poet", and so prints out "poet":

```
$ echo poet
poet
```

The contents of a variable are often used as command arguments. A common command argument is a directory path name. It can be tedious to retype a directory path that is being used over and over again. If you assign the directory path name to a variable, you can simply use the evaluated variable in its place. The directory path you assign to the variable is retrieved when the variable is evaluated with the **$** operator. The next example assigns a directory path name to a variable and then uses the evaluated variable in a copy command. The evaluation of **ldir** (which is **$ldir**) results in the path name **/home/chris/letters**. The copy command evaluates to **cp myletter /home/chris/letters**.

```
$ ldir=/home/chris/letters
$ cp myletter $ldir
```

You can obtain a list of all the defined variables with the **set** command. The next example uses the **set** command to display a list of all defined variables and their values:

```
$ set
poet   Virgil
ldir   /home/chris/letters/old
$
```

If you decide you do not want a certain variable, you can remove it with the **unset** command. The **unset** command undefines a variable. The next example undefines the variable **poet**. Then the user executes the **set** command to list all defined variables. Notice that **poet** is missing.

```
$ unset poet
$ set
ldir   /home/chris/letters/old
$
```

Shell Scripts: User-Defined Commands

You can place shell commands within a file and then have the shell read and execute the commands in the file. In this sense, the file functions as a shell program, executing shell commands as if they were statements in a program. A file that contains shell commands is called a *shell script*.

You enter shell commands into a script file using a standard text editor such as the Vi editor. The **sh** or **.** command used with the script's file name will read the script file and execute the commands. In the next example, the text file called **lsc** contains an **ls** command that displays only files with the extension .c:

lsc

```
ls *.c
```

```
$ sh lsc
main.c calc.c
```

```
$ . lsc
main.c calc.c
```

You can dispense with the **sh** and **.** commands by setting the executable permission of a script file. When the script file is first created by your text editor, it is only given read and write permission. The **chmod** command with the **+x** option will give the script file executable permission. (Permissions are discussed in Chapter 13.) Once it is executable, entering the name of the script file at the shell prompt and pressing ENTER will execute the script file and the shell commands in it. In effect, the script's file name becomes a new shell command. In this way, you can use shell scripts to design and create your own Linux commands. You only need to set the permission once. In the next example, the **lsc** file's executable permission for the owner is set to on. Then the **lsc** shell script is directly executed like any Linux command.

```
$ chmod u+x lsc
$ lsc
main.c calc.c
```

You may have to specify that the script you are using is in your current working directory. You do this by prefixing the script name with a period and slash combination, ./, as in ./lsc. The period is a special character representing the name of your current working directory. The slash is a directory path name separator, as explained more fully in Chapter 12. The following example would show how you would execute the hello script:

```
$ ./lsc
main.c calc.c
```

Just as any Linux command can take arguments, so also can a shell script. Arguments on the command line are referenced sequentially starting with **1**. An argument is referenced using the **$** operator and the number of its position. The first argument is referenced with **$1**, the second, with **$2**, and so on. In the next example, the **lsext** script prints out files with a specified extension. The first argument is the extension. The script is then executed with the argument **c** (of course, the executable permission must have been set).

lsext
```
ls *.$1
```

```
$ lsext c
main.c calc.c
```

In the next example, the commands to print out a file with line numbers have been placed in an executable file called **lpnum**, which takes a file name as its argument. The **cat** command with the **-n** option first outputs the contents of the file with line numbers. Then this output is piped into the **lp** command, which prints it. The command to print out the line numbers is executed in the background.

lpnum

```
cat -n $1 | lp &
```

 $ **lpnum mydata**

You may need to reference more than one argument at a time. The number of arguments used may vary. In **lpnum,** you may want to print out three files at one time and five files at some other time. The **$** operator with the asterisk, **$***, references all the arguments on the command line. Using **$*** enables you to create scripts that take a varying number of arguments. In the next example, **lpnum** is rewritten using **$*** so it can take a different number of arguments each time you use it:

lpnum

```
cat -n $* | lp &
```

 $ **lpnum mydata preface**

Jobs: Background, Kills, and Interruptions

In Linux, you not only have control over a command's input and output, but also over its execution. You can run a job in the background while you execute other commands. You can also cancel commands before they have finished executing. You can even interrupt a command, starting it again later from where you left off. Background operations are particularly useful for long jobs. Instead of waiting at the terminal until a command has finished execution, you can place it in the background. You can then continue executing other Linux commands. You can, for example, edit a file while other files are printing.

Canceling a background command can often save you a lot of unnecessary expense. If, say, you execute a command to print all your files and then realize you have some large files you do not want to print, you can reference that execution of the print command and cancel it. Interrupting commands is rarely used, and sometimes it is unintentionally executed. You can, if you want, interrupt an editing session to send mail and then return to your editing session, continuing from where you left off. The background commands, as well as commands to cancel and interrupt jobs, are listed in Table 11-2.

In Linux, a command is considered a *process*—a task to be performed. A Linux system can execute several processes at the same time, just as Linux can handle several users at the same time. Commands to examine and control processes exist, though they are often reserved for system administration operations. Processes actually include not only the commands a user executes, but also all the tasks the system must perform to keep Linux running.

The commands that users execute are often called *jobs* to distinguish them from system processes. When the user executes a command, it becomes a job to be performed by the system. The shell provides a set of job control operations that enable the user to control the execution of these jobs. You can place a job in the background, cancel a job, or interrupt one.

You execute a command in the background by placing an ampersand on the command line at the end of the command. When you do so, a user job number and a system process number are displayed. The user job number, placed in brackets, is the number by which the user references the job. The system process number is the number by which the system identifies the job. In the next example, the command to print the file **mydata** is placed in the background:

```
$ lpr mydata &
[1]  534
$
```

You can place more than one command in the background. Each is classified as a job and given a name and a job number. The command **jobs** lists the jobs being run in the background. Each entry in the list consists of the job number in brackets, whether it is stopped or running, and the name of the job. The **+** sign indicates the job currently being processed, and the **–** sign indicates the next job to be executed. In the next example, two commands have been placed in the background. The **jobs** command then lists those jobs, showing which one is currently being executed.

```
$ lpr intro &
[1]  547
$ cat *.c > myprogs &
[2]  548
$ jobs
[1]  +  Running  lpr intro
[2]  -  Running  cat *.c > myprogs
$
```

If you wish, you can place several commands at once in the background by entering the commands on the command line, separated by an ampersand, **&**. In this case, the **&** both separates commands on the command line and executes them in the background.

In the next example, the first command, to **sort** and redirect all files with a **.l** extension, is placed in the background. On the same command line, the second command, to print all files with a **.c** extension, is also placed in the background. Notice the two commands each end with **&**. The **jobs** command then lists the **sort** and **lpr** commands as separate operations.

```
$ sort *.l > ldocs &; lpr *.c &
[1]   534

[2]   567
$ jobs
[1]   +   Running   sort *.l > ldocs
[2]   -   Running   lpr
$
```

After you execute any command in Linux, the system tells you what background jobs, if you have any running, have been completed so far. The system does not interrupt any operation, such as editing, to notify you about a completed job. If you want to be notified immediately when a certain job ends, no matter what you are doing on the system, you can use the **notify** command to instruct the system to tell you. The **notify** command takes a job number as its argument. When that job is finished, the system interrupts what you are doing to notify you the job has ended. The next example tells the system to notify the user when job 2 has finished:

```
$ notify %2
```

You can bring a job out of the background with the foreground command, **fg**. If only one job is in the background, the **fg** command alone will bring it to the foreground. If more than one job is in the background, you must use the job's number with the command. You place the job number after the **fg** command, preceded with a percent sign. A **bg** command also places a job in the background. This command is usually used for interrupted jobs. In the next example, the second job is brought back into the foreground. You may not immediately receive a prompt again because the second command is now in the foreground and executing. When the command is finished executing, the prompt appears, and you can execute another command.

```
$ fg %2
cat *.c > myprogs
$
```

If you want to stop a job running in the background, you can force it to end with the **kill** command. The *kill command* takes as its argument either the user job number or the system process number. The user job number must be preceded by a percent sign, **%**. You can find out the job number from the **jobs** command. In the next example, the **jobs** command lists the background jobs; then job 2 is canceled:

```
$ jobs
[1]  +  Running  lpr intro
[2]  -  Running  cat *.c > myprogs
$ kill %2
$
```

You can also cancel a job using the system process number, which you can obtain with the **ps** command. The **ps** command displays a great deal more information than the **jobs** command does. It is discussed in detail in Chapter 29 on systems administration. The next example lists the processes a user is running. The *PID* is the *system process number*, also known as the *process ID*. TTY is the terminal identifier. The time is how long the process has taken so far. COMMAND is the name of the process.

```
$ ps
PID      TTY        TIME      COMMAND
523      tty24      0:05      sh
567      tty24      0:01      lpr
570      tty24      0:00      ps
```

You can then reference the system process number in a **kill** command. Use the process number without any preceding percent sign. The next example kills process 567:

```
$ kill 567
```

You can suspend a job and stop it with the CTRL-Z keys. This places the job to the side until it is restarted. The job is not ended; it merely remains suspended until you want to continue. When you're ready, you can continue with the job in either the foreground or the background using the **fg** or **bg** command. The **fg** command restarts a suspended job in the foreground. The **bg** command places the suspended job in the background.

At times, you may need to place a currently running job in the foreground into the background. However, you cannot move a currently running job directly into the background. You first need to suspend it with CTRL-Z, and then place it in the background with the **bg** command. In the next example, the current command to list and redirect **.c** files is first suspended with a CTRL-Z. Then that job is placed in the background.

```
$ cat *.c > myprogs
^Z
$ bg
```

Filters and Regular Expressions

Filters are commands that read data, perform operations on that data, and then send the results to the standard output. Filters generate different kinds of output, depending on their task. Some filters only generate information about the input, other filters output selected parts of the input, and still other filters output an entire version of the input, but in a modified way. Some filters are limited to one of these, while others have options that specify one or the other. You can think of a filter as operating on a stream of data—receiving data and generating modified output. As data is passed through the filter, it is analyzed, screened, or modified.

The data stream input to a filter consists of a sequence of bytes that can be received from files, devices, or the output of other commands or filters. The filter operates on the data stream, but it does not modify the source of the data. If a filter receives input from a file, the file itself is not modified. Only its data is read and fed into the filter.

The output of a filter is usually sent to the standard output. It can then be redirected to another file or device, or piped as input to another utility or filter. All the features of redirection and pipes apply to filters. Often data is read by one filter and its modified output piped into another filter.

Data could easily undergo several modifications as it is passed from one filter to another. However, it is always important to realize the original source of the data is never changed.

Many utilities and filters use patterns to locate and select specific text in your file. Sometimes, you may need to use patterns in a more flexible and powerful way, searching for several different variations on a given pattern. You can include a set of special characters in your pattern to enable a flexible search. A pattern that contains such special characters is called a *regular expression*. Regular expressions can be used in most filters and utilities that employ pattern searches such as Ed, **sed**, **awk**, **grep**, and **egrep**.

Although many of the special characters used for regular expressions are similar to the shell wildcard characters, they are used in a different way. Shell wildcard characters operate on file names. Regular expressions search text.

In Linux, as in UNIX, text files are organized into a series of lines. For this reason, many editors and filters are designed to operate on a text file line by line. The first UNIX editor, *Ed*, is a line editor whose commands reference and operate on a text file one line at a time. Other editing utilities and filters operate on text much the same way as the Ed line editor. In fact, the Ed editor and other editing filters use the same set of core line editing commands. The editing filters such as **sed** and **diff** use those same line editing commands to edit filter input. An edit filter receives lines of text as its input and performs line editing operations on them, outputting a modified version of the text. Three major edit filters exist: **tr**, which translates characters; **diff**, which outputs editing information about two files; and **sed**, which performs line editing operations on the input. Table 11-4 lists the different editing filters.

Using Redirection and Pipes with Filters

Filters send their output to the standard output and so, by default, display their output on the screen. The simplest filters merely output the contents of files. You have already seen the **cat** commands. What you may not have realized is that **cat** is a filter. It receives lines of data and outputs a version of that data. The **cat** filter receives input and copies it out to the standard output, which, by default, is displayed on the screen. Commonly used filters are listed in Tables 11-3 and 11-4.

You can save the output of a filter in a file or send it to a printer. To do so, you need to use redirection or pipes. To save the output of a filter to a file, you redirect it to a file using the redirection operation, **>**. To send output to the printer, you pipe the output to the **lpr** utility, which then prints it. In the next command, the **cat** command pipes its output to the **lpr** command, which then prints it.

```
$ cat complist | lpr
```

Other commands for displaying files, such as **more**, may seem to operate like a filter, but they are not filters. You need to distinguish between filters and device-oriented utilities, such as **lpr** and **more**. Filters send their output to the standard output. A device-oriented utility such as **lpr**, though it receives input from the standard input, sends its output to a device. In the case of **lpr**, the device is a printer; for **more**, the device is the terminal. Such device-oriented utilities may receive their input from a filter, but they can only output to their device.

All filters accept input from the standard input. In fact, the output of one filter can be piped as the input for another filter. Many filters also accept input directly from files, however. Such filters can take file names as their arguments and read data directly from those files. The **cat** and **sort** filters operate in this way. They can receive input from the standard input or use file name arguments to read data directly from files.

One of the more powerful features of **cat** is it can combine the contents of several files into one output stream. This output can then be piped into a utility or even another filter, allowing the utility or filter to operate on the combined contents of files as one data stream. For example, if you want to view the contents of several files at once, screen by screen, you must first combine them with the **cat** filter and then pipe the combined data into the **more** filter. The **more** command is, then, receiving its input from the standard input. In the following set of examples, the **cat** filter copies the contents of **preface** and **intro** into a combined output. In the first example, this output is piped into the **more** command. The **more** filter then enables you to view the combined text, screen by screen. In the second, the output is piped to the printer using the **lpr** command and, in the third, the output is redirected to a file called **frontdata**.

```
$ cat preface intro | more
$ cat preface intro | lpr
$ cat preface intro > frontdata
```

Types of Filter Output: wc, spell, and sort

The output of a filter may be a modified copy of the input, selected parts of the input, or simply some information about the input. Some filters are limited to one of these, while others have options that specify one or the other. The **wc**, **spell**, and **sort** filters illustrate all three kinds of output. The **wc** filter merely prints counts of the number of lines, words, and characters in a file. The **spell** filter selects misspelled words and outputs only those words. The **sort** filter outputs a complete version of the input, but in sorted order. These three filters are listed in Table 11-3, along with their more commonly used options.

The *wc filter* takes as its input a data stream, which is usually data read from a file. It then counts the number of lines, words, and characters (including the newline character, found at the end of a line) in the file and simply outputs these counts. In the next example, the **wc** command is used to find the number of lines, words, and characters in the **preface** file.

```
$ wc preface
6       27      142     preface
```

The *spell filter* checks the spelling of words in its input and outputs only the misspelled.

```
$ spell foodlistsp
soop
vegetebels
```

Using redirection, you can save those words in a file. With a pipe, you can print them. In the next example, the user saves the misspelled words to a file called **misspell**:

```
$ spell foodlistsp > misspell
```

You can pipe the output of one filter into another filter, in effect, applying the capabilities of several filters to your data. For example, suppose you only want to know how many words are misspelled. You could pipe the output of the **spell** filter into the **wc** filter, which would count the number of misspelled words. In the next example, the words in the **foodlistsp** file are spell-checked, and the list of misspelled words is piped to the **wc** filter. The **wc** filter, with its **-w** option, then counts those words and outputs the count.

```
$ spell preface | wc -w
2
```

The **sort** *filter* outputs a sorted version of a file. **sort** is a useful utility with many different sorting options. These options are primarily designed to operate on files arranged in a database format. In fact, **sort** can be thought of as a powerful data manipulation tool, arranging records in a database-like file. This chapter examines how **sort** can be used to alphabetize a simple list of words. The **sort** filter sorts, character by character, on a line. If the first character in two lines is the same, then **sort** will sort on the next character in each line. You can, of course, save the sorted version in a file or send it to the printer. In the next example, the user saves the sorted output in a file called **slist**:

```
$ sort foodlist > slist
```

Command	Execution
cat *filenames*	Displays a file. It can take file names for its arguments. It outputs the contents of those files directly to the standard output, which, by default, is the screen.
tee *filename*	Copies the standard input to a file while sending it on to the standard output. It is usually used with another filter and enables you to save output to a file while sending the output on to another filter or utility.

Table 11-3.   *Filters*

Command	Execution
head *filename*	Displays the first few lines of a file. The default is ten lines, but you can specify the number of lines.
tail *filename*	Displays the last lines in a file. The default is ten lines, but you can specify the number of lines **$ tail** *filenames.*
wc *filename*	Counts the number of lines, words, and characters in a file and outputs only that number.
	c Counts the number of characters in a file.
	l Counts the number of lines in a file.
	w Counts the number of words in a file.
spell *filename*	Checks the spelling of each word in a file and outputs only the misspelled words.
sort *filename*	Outputs a sorted version of a file.
cmp *filename filename*	Compares two files, character by character, checking for differences. Stops at the first difference it finds and outputs the character position and line number.
comm. *filename filename*	Compares two files, line by line, and outputs both files according to lines that are similar and different for each.
grep *pattern filenames*	Searches files for a pattern and lists any matched lines.
	i Ignores uppercase and lowercase differences.
	c Only outputs a number—the count of the lines with the pattern.

Table 11-3. *Filters* (continued)

Command	Execution
grep *pattern filenames* (continued)	
	l Displays the names of the files that contain the matching pattern.
	n Outputs the line number along with the text of those lines with the matching pattern.
	v Outputs all those lines that do not contain the matching pattern.
fgrep *patterns file-list*	Searches files in the file list for several patterns at the same time. Executes much faster than either **grep** or **egrep**; however, **fgrep** cannot interpret special characters and cannot search for regular expressions.
egrep *pattern file-list*	Searches files in the file list for the occurrence of a pattern. Like **fgrep**, it can read patterns from a file. Like **grep**, it can use regular expressions, interpreting special characters. However, unlike **grep**, it can also interpret extended special characters such as **?**, **|**, and **+**.
Pr	Outputs a paginated version of the input, adding headers, page numbers, and any other specified format.
cpio *generated-filenames* | **cpio -o >** *archive-file* **cpio -i** *filenames* **<** *archive-file*	Copies files to an archive and extracts files from an archive. Has two modes of operation: one using the **–o** option to copy files to an archive and the other using the **–i** option to extract files from an archive. When copying files to an archive, you need first to generate the list of file names using a command such as **ls** or **find**.

Table 11-3. *Filters* (continued)

Command	Execution
sed *editing-command file-list*	Outputs an edited form of its input. **sed** takes as an argument an editing command and a file list. The editing command is executed on input read from files in the file list. **sed** then outputs an edited version of the files. The editing commands are line editing commands similar to those used for the Ed line editor.
n	With this option, **sed** does not output lines automatically. This option is usually used with the **p** command to output only selected lines.
f *filename*	With this option, **sed** reads editing commands *filename*.
	(You need to quote any new line characters if you are entering more than one line)
Sed Line Commands	
a	Appends text after a line.
i	Inserts text before a line.
c	Changes text.
d	Deletes lines.
p	Prints lines.
w	Writes lines to a file.
r	Reads lines from a file.
q	Quits the **sed** editor before all lines are processed.
n	Skips processing to next line.
s/*pattern*/*replacement*/	Substitutes matched pattern with replacement text.
g **s**/*pat*/*rep*/**g**	Global substitution on a line.

Table 11-4. *Edit Filters*

Sed Line Commands

p	**s**/*pat*/*rep*/**p**	Outputs the modified line.
w	**s**/*pat*/*rep*/**w** *fname*	Writes the modified line to a file.
	/*pattern*/	A line can be located and referenced by a pattern.
diff *filename filename*		Compares two files and outputs the lines that are different as well as the editing changes needed to make the first file the same as the second file.
f1-linenum **a** *f2-line1, f2-line2*		Appends lines from file2 to after *f1-linenum* in file1.
f1-line1, f1-line2 **d** *f1-linenum*		Deletes the lines in file1.
f1-line1, f1-line2 **c** *f2-line1, f2-line2*		Replaces lines in file1 with lines in file2.
b		Ignores any trailing or duplicate blank.
c		Outputs a context for differing lines. Three lines above and below are displayed.
e		Outputs a list of Ed editing commands that, when executed, change the first file into an exact copy of the second file.
tr *first-character-list second-character-list*		Outputs a version of the input in which characters in the first character list that occur in the input are replaced in the output by corresponding characters in the second character list.

Table 11-4. *Edit Filters* (continued)

Searching Files: grep and fgrep

The **grep** and **fgrep** *filters* search the contents of files for a pattern. They then inform you of what file the pattern was found in and print the lines in which it occurred in each file. Preceding each line is the name of the file in which the line is located. **grep** can search for only one pattern, whereas **fgrep** can search for more than one pattern at a time. The **grep** and **fgrep** filters, along with their options, are described in Table 11-3.

The **grep** filter takes two types of arguments. The first argument is the pattern to be searched for; the second argument is a list of file names, which are the files to be searched. You enter the file names on the command line after the pattern. You can also use special characters, such as the asterisk, to generate a file list.

```
$ grep pattern filenames-list
```

In the next example, the **grep** command searches the lines in the **preface** file for the pattern "stream":

```
$ cat preface
A text file in Unix
consists of a stream of
characters.  An editor can
be used to create such
text files, changing or
adding to the character
data in the file.
$ grep stream preface
 consists of a stream of
```

If you want to include more than one word in the pattern search, you enclose the words within single quotation marks. This is to quote the spaces between the words in the pattern. Otherwise, the shell would interpret the space as a delimiter or argument on the command line, and **grep** would try to interpret words in the pattern as part of the file list. In the next example, **grep** searches for the pattern "text file":

```
$ grep 'text file' preface
A text file in Unix
text files, changing or
```

If you use more than one file in the file list, **grep** will output the name of the file before the matching line. In the next example, two files, **preface** and **intro**, are searched for the pattern "data". Before each occurrence, the file name is output.

```
$ grep data preface intro
 preface: data in the file.
 intro: new data
```

As mentioned earlier, you can also use shell wildcard characters to generate a list of files to be searched. In the next example, the asterisk wildcard character is used to generate a list of all files in your directory. This is a simple way of searching all of a directory's files for a pattern.

```
$ grep data *
```

The special characters are often useful for searching a selected set of files. For example, if you want to search all your C program source code files for a particular pattern, you can specify the set of source code files with ***.c**. Suppose you have an unintended infinite loop in your program and you need to locate all instances of iterations. The next example searches only those files with a .c extension for the pattern "while" and displays the lines of code that perform iterations:

```
$ grep while *.c
```

Regular Expressions

Regular expressions enable you to match possible variations on a pattern, as well as patterns located at different points in the text. You can search for patterns in your text that have different ending or beginning letters, or you can match text at the beginning or end of a line. The regular expression special characters are the circumflex, dollar sign, asterisk, period, and brackets: **^, $, *, ., []**. The circumflex and dollar sign match on the beginning and end of a line. The asterisk matches repeated characters, the period matches single characters, and the brackets match on classes of characters. See Table 11-5 for a listing of the regular expression special characters.

Note   *Regular expressions are used extensively in many Linux filters and applications to perform searches and matching operations. The Vi and Emacs editors and the **sed**, **diff**, **grep**, and **gawk** filters all use regular expressions.*

To match on patterns at the beginning of a line, you enter the ^ followed immediately by a pattern. The ^ special character makes the beginning of the line an actual part of the pattern to be searched. In the next example, **^consists** matches on the line beginning with the pattern "consists":

```
^consists
consists of a stream of
```

ENVIRONMENTS

The next example uses the **$** special character to match patterns at the end of a line:

```
such$
 be used to create such
```

The *period* is a special character that matches any one character. Any character will match a period in your pattern. The pattern **b.d** will find a pattern consisting of three letters. The first letter will be *b*, the third letter will be *d*, and the second letter can be any character. It will match on "bid", "bad", "bed", "b+d", or "b d", for example. Notice the space is a valid character (so is a tab).

For the period special character to have much effect, you should provide it with a context—a beginning and ending pattern. The pattern **b.d** provides a context consisting of the preceding *b* and the following *d*. If you specified **b.** without a *d*, then any pattern beginning with *b* and having at least one more character would match. The pattern would match on "bid", "bath", "bedroom", and "bump", as well as "submit", "habit", and "harbor".

The asterisk special character, *****, matches on zero or more consecutive instances of a character. The character matched is the one placed before the asterisk in the pattern. You can think of the asterisk as an operator that takes the preceding character as its operand. The asterisk will search for any repeated instances of this character. Here is the syntax of the asterisk special character:

```
c*    matches on zero or more repeated occurrences of whatever
      the character c is:
c cc ccc cccc  and so on.
```

The asterisk comes in handy when you need to replace several consecutive instances of the same character. The next example matches on a pattern beginning with *b* and followed by consecutive instances of the character *o*. This regular expression will match on "boooo", "bo", "boo", and "b".

```
bo*
    book
    born
    booom
    zoom    no match
```

The **.*** pattern used by itself will match on any character in the line; in fact, it selects the entire line. If you have a context for **.***, you can match different segments of the line. A pattern placed before the **.*** special characters will match the remainder of the line from the occurrence of the pattern. A pattern placed after the `.*` will match the beginning of the line up until the pattern. The `.*` placed between patterns will match any intervening text between those patterns on the line. In the next example, the pattern `.*and` matches everything in the line from the beginning up to and including the letters "and". Then the pattern `and.*` matches everything in the line from and including the letters "and" to the end of the line. Finally, the pattern `/o.*F/` matches all the text between and including the letters *o* and *F*.

    .*and   **Hello to you and** to them Farewell

    and.*   Hello to you **and to them Farewell**

    o.*F   Hell**o to you and to them F**arewell

 Tip   *Because the ***** special character matches zero or more instances of the character, you can provide a context with zero intervening characters. For example, the pattern **I.*t** matches on "It" as well as "Intelligent".*

Suppose instead of matching on a specific character or allowing a match on any character, you need to match only on a selected set of characters. For example, you might want to match on words ending with an *A* or *H*, as in "seriesA" and "seriesH", but not "seriesB" or "seriesK". If you used a period, you would match on all instances. Instead, you need to specify that *A* and *H* are the only possible matches. You can do so with the brackets special characters.

You use the brackets special characters to match on a set of possible characters. The characters in the set are placed within brackets and listed next to each other. Their order of listing does not matter. You can think of this set of possible characters as defining a class of characters, and characters that fall into this class are matched. You may notice the brackets operate much like the shell brackets. In the next example, the user searches for a pattern beginning with "doc" and ending with either the letters *a*, *g*, or *N*. It will match on "doca", "docg", or "docN", but not on "docP".

    doc[agN]
        List of documents
        doca docb
        docg docN docP

The brackets special characters are particularly useful for matching on various suffixes or prefixes for a pattern. For example, suppose you need to match on file names that begin with the pattern "week" and have several different suffixes, as in **week1, week2**, and so on. To match on just those files with suffixes 2, 4, and 5, you

enclose those characters within brackets. In the next example, notice the pattern
week[245] matches on **week2** and **week4**, but not on **week1**:

```
week[245]
    week2 weather
    reports on week4
    week1 reports          no match
```

The brackets special characters are also useful for matching on a pattern that
begins in either uppercase or lowercase. Linux distinguishes between uppercase
and lowercase characters. The pattern "computer" is different from the pattern
"Computer"; "computer" would not match on the version beginning with an uppercase
C. To match on both patterns, you need to use the brackets special characters to specify
both *c* and *C* as possible first characters in the pattern. Place the uppercase and
lowercase versions of the same character within brackets at the beginning of the
pattern. For example, the pattern **[Cc]omputer** searches for the pattern "computer"
beginning with either an uppercase *C* or a lowercase *c*.

You can specify a range of characters within the brackets with the dash. Characters
are ranged according to the character set being used. In the ASCII character set,
lowercase letters are grouped together. Specifying a range with **[a-z]** selects all the
lowercase letters. In the first example, shown next, any lowercase letter will match the
pattern. More than one range can be specified by separating the ranges with a comma.
The ranges **[A-Za-z]** select all alphabetic letters, both uppercase and lowercase.

```
doc[a-z]          doca docg docN docP
doc[A-Za-z]       doca docg docN docP
```

Although shell file matching characters enable you to match on file names, regular
expressions enable you to match on data within files. Using **grep** with regular
expressions, you can locate files and the lines in them that match a specified pattern.
You can use special characters in a **grep** pattern, making the pattern a regular
expression. **grep** regular expressions use the *****, **.**, and **[]** special characters, as well
as the **^** and **$** special characters.

Suppose you want to use the long form output of **ls** to display just your
directories. One way to do this is to generate a list of all directories in the long form
and pipe this list to **grep**, which can then pick out the directory entries. You can do
this by using the **^** special character to specify the beginning of a line. Remember, in
the long-form output of **ls**, the first character indicates the file type. A **d** represents a
directory, a **l** represents a symbolic link, and an **a** represents a regular file. Using the
pattern '**^d**', **grep** will match only on those lines beginning with a *d*.

Character	Match	Operation
^	Start of a line	References the beginning of a line
$	End of a line	References the end of a line
.	Any character	Matches on any one possible character in a pattern
*	Repeated characters	Matches on repeated characters in a pattern
[]	Classes	Matches on classes of characters (a set of characters) in the pattern

Table 11-5. *Regular Expression Special Characters*

```
$ ls -l | grep '^d'
drwxr-x---  2  chris 512 Feb 10 04:30   reports
drwxr-x---  2  chris 512 Jan 6  01:20   letters
```

If you only want to list those files that have symbolic links, you can use the pattern ^1:

```
$ ls -l | grep '^1'
lrw-rw-r-- 1  chris  group 4    Feb 14   10:30  lunch
```

Be sure to distinguish between the shell wildcard character and special characters used in the pattern. When you include special characters in your **grep** pattern, you need to quote the pattern. Notice regular-expression special characters and shell wildcard characters use the same symbols: the asterisk, period, and brackets. If you do not, then any special characters in the pattern will be interpreted by the shell as shell wildcard characters. Without quotes, an asterisk would be used to generate file names rather than being evaluated by **grep** to search for repeated characters. Quoting the pattern guarantees that **grep** will evaluate the special characters as part of a regular expression. In the next example, the asterisk special character is used in the pattern as a regular expression and in the file name list as a shell wildcard character to generate file names. In this case, all files in the current directory will be searched for patterns with zero or more *s*'s after "report":

```
$ grep 'reports*' *
mydata: The report was sitting on his desk.
weather: The weather reports were totally accurate.
```

The brackets match on either a set of characters, a range of characters, or a nonmatch of those characters. For example, the pattern **doc[abc]** matches on the patterns "doca", "docb", and "docc", but not on "docd". The same pattern can be specified with a range: **doc[a-c]**. However, the pattern **doc[^ab]** will match on any pattern beginning with "doc", but not ending in *a* or *b*. Thus, "docc" will be retrieved, but not "doca" or "docb". In the next example, the user finds all lines that reference "doca", "docb", or "docc":

```
$ grep 'doc[abc]' myletter
File letter doca and docb.
We need to redo docc.
```

Certain Linux utilities, such as **egrep** and **awk**, can make use of an extended set of special characters in their patterns. These special characters are **|**, **( )**, **+**, and **?**, and are listed in Table 11-6.

Character	Execution
*pattern	pattern*	Logical OR for searching for alternative patterns
(pattern)	Parentheses for grouping patterns
char+	Searches for one or more repetitions of the previous character
char?	Searches for zero or one instance of the previous character

Table 11-6. *Full Regular Expression Special Characters*

The **+** and **?** are variations on the ***** special character, whereas **|** and **( )** provide new capabilities. Patterns that can use such special characters are referred to as full regular expressions. The Ed and Ex standard line editors do not have these extended special characters. Only **egrep**, which is discussed here, and awk have extended special characters.

The **+** sign matches one or more instances of a character. For example, **t+** matches at least one or more *t*'s, just as **tt*** does. **t+** matches on "sitting" or "biting", but not "ziing". The **?** matches zero or one instance of a character. For example, **t?** matches on one *t* or no *t*'s, but not "tt". The expression **it?i** matches on "ziing" and "biting", but not "sitting". With the **+** special character, the regular expression **an+e** matches on one or more instances of *n* preceded by *a* and followed by *e*. The "ane" is matched in "anew", and "anne" is matched on "canned".

The **|** and **( )** special characters operate on pattern segments, rather than just characters. The **|** is a logical OR special character that specifies alternative search patterns within a single regular expression. Although part of the same regular expression, the patterns are searched for as separate patterns. The search pattern **create|stream** searches for either the pattern "create" or "stream".

```
create|stream
 consists of a stream of
 be used to create such
```

The **egrep** command combines the capabilities of **grep** and **fgrep**. Like **fgrep**, it can search for several patterns at the same time. Like **grep**, it can evaluate special characters in its patterns and search for regular expressions. Unlike **grep**, however, it can evaluate extended special characters, such as the logical OR operator, **|**. In this respect, **egrep** is the most powerful of the three search filters.

To search for several patterns at once, you can either enter them on the command line separated by a newline character as **fgrep** does, or you can use the logical OR special character in a pattern to specify alternative patterns to be searched for in a file. The patterns are actually part of the same regular expression, but they are searched for as separate patterns. The pattern **create|stream egrep** will search for either the pattern "create" or the pattern "stream".

```
$ egrep 'create|stream' preface
consists of a stream of
 be used to create such
```

The
Complete
Reference

Chapter 12

The Linux File Structure

In Linux, all files are organized into directories that, in turn, are hierarchically connected to each other in one overall file structure. A file is referenced not just according to its name, but also according to its place in this file structure. You can create as many new directories as you want, adding more directories to the file structure. The Linux file commands can perform sophisticated operations, such as moving or copying whole directories along with their subdirectories. You can use file operations such as **find**, **cp**, **mv**, and **ln** to locate files and copy, move, or link them from one directory to another. Desktop file managers, such as Konqueror and Midnight Commander used on the KDE and Gnome desktops, provide a graphical user interface to perform the same operations using icons, windows, and menus.

Together, these features make up the Linux file structure. This chapter first examines different types of files, as well as file classes. Then, the chapter examines the overall Linux file structure and how directories and files can be referenced using pathnames and the working directory. The last part of the chapter discusses the different file operations such as copying, moving, and linking files, as well as file permissions. The organization of the Linux file structure into its various system and network administration directories is discussed in detail in Chapter 32.

Linux Files

You can name a file using any alphabetic characters, underscores, and numbers. You can also include periods and commas. Except in certain special cases, you should never begin a filename with a period. Other characters, such as slashes, question marks, or asterisks, are reserved for use as special characters by the system and cannot be part of a filename. Filenames can be as long as 256 characters.

You can include an extension as part of a filename. A period is used to distinguish the filename proper from the extension. Extensions can be useful for categorizing your files. You are probably familiar with certain standard extensions that have been adopted by convention. For example, C source code files always have an extension of **.c**. Files that contain compiled object code have a **.o** extension. You can, of course, make up your own file extensions. The following examples are all valid Linux filenames:

```
preface
chapter2
9700info
New_Revisions
calc.c
intro.bk1
```

Special initialization files are also used to hold shell configuration commands. These are the hidden, or dot files, referred to in Chapter 5 that begin with a period. Dot files used by commands and applications have predetermined names. Recall that when you use **ls** to display your filenames, the dot files will not be displayed. To include the dot files, you need to use **ls** with the **-a** option. Dot files are discussed in more detail in the chapter on shell configuration, Chapter 13.

As shown in Figure 12-1, the **ls -l** command displays detailed information about a file. First the permissions are displayed, followed by the number of links, the owner of the file, the name of the group the user belongs to, the file size in bytes, the date and time the file was last modified, and the name of the file. Permissions indicate who can access the file: the user, members of a group, or all other user. Permissions are discussed in detail in Chapter 9. The group name indicates the group permitted to access the file object. In Figure 12-1, the file type for **mydata** is that of an ordinary file. Only one link exists, indicating the file has no other names and no other links. The owner's name is **chris**, the same as the login name, and the group name is **weather**. Other users probably also belong to the **weather** group. The size of the file is 207 bytes and it was last modified on February 20, at 11:55 A.M. The name of the file is **mydata**.

If you want to display this detailed information for all the files in a directory, simply use the **ls -l** command without an argument.

```
$ ls -l
-rw-r--r--   1   chris  weather 207   Feb 20   11:55   mydata
-rw-rw-r--   1   chris  weather 568   Feb 14   10:30   today
-rw-rw-r--   1   chris  weather 308   Feb 17   12:40   monday
```

All files in Linux have one physical format—a byte stream. A *byte stream* is just a sequence of bytes. This allows Linux to apply the file concept to every data component in the system. Directories are classified as files, as are devices. Treating everything as a file allows Linux to organize and exchange data more easily. The data in a file can be sent directly to a device such as a screen because a device interfaces with the system using the same byte-stream file format as regular files.

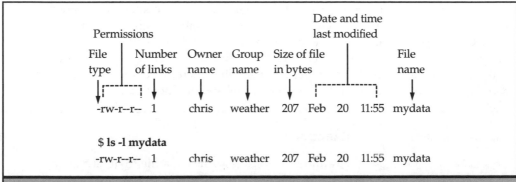

Figure 12-1.   *File information displayed using the -l option for the ls command*

This same file format is used to implement other operating system components. The interface to a device, such as the screen or keyboard, is designated as a file. Other components, such as directories, are themselves byte-stream files, but they have a special internal organization. A directory file contains information about a directory, organized in a special directory format. Because these different components are treated as files, they can be said to constitute different *file types.* A character device is one file type. A directory is another file type. The number of these file types may vary according to your specific implementation of Linux. Five common types of files exist, however: ordinary files, directory files, first-in first-out pipes, character device files, and block device files. Although you may rarely reference a file's type, it can be useful when searching for directories or devices. Later in the chapter, you see how to use the file type in a search criterion with the **find** command to search specifically for directory or device names.

Although all ordinary files have a byte-stream format, they may be used in different ways. The most significant difference is between binary and text files. Compiled programs are examples of binary files. However, even text files can be classified according to their different uses. You can have files that contain C programming source code or shell commands, or even a file that is empty. The file could be an executable program or a directory file. The Linux **file** command helps you determine for what a file is used. It examines the first few lines of a file and tries to determine a classification for it. The **file** command looks for special keywords or special numbers in those first few lines, but it is not always accurate. In the next example, the **file** command examines the contents of two files and determines a classification for them:

```
$ file monday reports
monday:     text
reports:    directory
```

If you need to examine the entire file byte by byte, you can do so with the **od** (octal dump) command. The **od** command performs a dump of a file. By default, it prints every byte in its octal representation. However, you can also specify a character, decimal, or hexadecimal representation. The **od** command is helpful when you need to detect any special character in your file, or if you want to display a binary file. If you perform a character dump, then certain nonprinting characters will be represented in a character notation. For example, the carriage return is represented by a \n. Both the **file** and **od** commands, with their options, are listed in Table 12-1.

Commands	Execution
file	Examines the first few lines of a file to determine a classification

Table 12-1. Common *file* and *od* Options

Commands Options	Execution
-f *filename*	Reads the list of filenames to be examined from a file
od	Prints the contents of a file byte by byte in either octal, character, decimal, or hexadecimal; octal is the default
Options	
-c	Outputs character form of byte values; nonprinting characters have a corresponding character representation
-d	Outputs decimal form of byte values
-x	Outputs hexadecimal form of byte values
-o	Outputs octal form of byte values

Table 12-1. *Common `file` and `od` Options* (continued)

The File Structure

Linux organizes files into a hierarchically connected set of directories. Each directory may contain either files or other directories. In this respect, directories perform two important functions. A *directory* holds files, much like files held in a file drawer, and a directory connects to other directories, much like a branch in a tree is connected to other branches. With respect to files, directories appear to operate like file drawers, with each drawer holding several files. To access files, you open a file drawer. Unlike file drawers, however, directories can contain not only files, but other directories, as well. In this way, a directory can connect to another directory.

Because of the similarities to a tree, such a structure is often referred to as a *tree structure*. This structure could more accurately be thought of as an upside-down bush rather than a tree, however, because no trunk exists. The tree is represented upside down, with the root at the top. Extending down from the root are the branches. Each branch grows out of only one branch, but it can have many lower branches. In this respect, it can be said to have a *parent-child structure*. In the same way, each directory is itself a subdirectory of one other directory. Each directory may contain many subdirectories, but is itself the child of only one parent directory.

The Linux file structure branches into several directories beginning with a root directory, /. Within the root directory several system directories contain files and programs that are features of the Linux system. The root directory also contains a directory called **home** that contains the home directories of all the users in the system.

Each user's home directory, in turn, contains the directories the user has made for his or her use. Each of these could also contain directories. Such nested directories would branch out from the user's home directory, as shown in Figure 12-2.

> **Note** *The user's home directory can be any directory, though it is usually the directory that bears the user's login name. This directory is located in the directory named /home on your Linux system. For example, a user named **dylan** will have a home directory called **dylan** located in the system's /home directory. The user's home directory is a subdirectory of the directory called /home on your system.*

Home Directories

When you log in to the system, you are placed within your home directory. The name given to this directory by the system is the same as your login name. Any files you create when you first log in are organized within your home directory. Within your home directory, however, you can create more directories. You can then change to these directories and store files in them. The same is true for other users on the system. Each user has his or her own home directory, identified by the appropriate login name. Users, in turn, can create their own directories.

You can access a directory either through its name or by making it the default directory. Each directory is given a name when it is created. You can use this name in file operations to access files in that directory. You can also make the directory your default directory. If you do not use any directory names in a file operation, then the default directory will be accessed. The default directory is referred to as the *working directory*. In this sense, the working directory is the one from which you are currently working.

When you log in, the working directory is your home directory, usually having the same name as your login name. You can change the working directory by using the **cd** command to designate another directory as the working directory. As the working directory is changed, you can move from one directory to another. Another way to

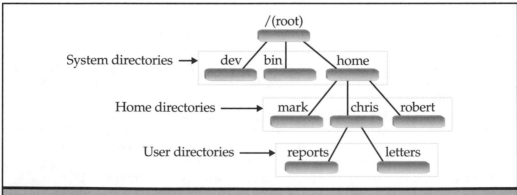

Figure 12-2. *The Linux file structure beginning at the root directory*

think of a directory is as a corridor. In such a corridor, there are doors with names on them. Some doors lead to rooms; others lead to other corridors. The doors that open to rooms are like files in a directory. The doors that lead to other corridors are like other directories. Moving from one corridor to the next corridor is like changing the working directory. Moving through several corridors is like moving through several directories.

Pathnames

The name you give to a directory or file when you create it is not its full name. The full name of a directory is its *pathname*. The hierarchically nested relationship among directories forms paths, and these paths can be used to identify and reference any directory or file unambiguously. In Figure 12-3, a path exists from the root directory, /, through the **home** directory to the **robert** directory. Another path exists from the root directory through the **home** and **chris** directories to the **reports** directory. Although parts of each path may at first be shared, at some point they differ. Both the directories **robert** and **reports** share the two directories, **root** and **home**. Then they differ. In the **home** directory, **robert** ends with **robert**, but the directory **chris** then leads to **reports**. In this way, each directory in the file structure can be said to have its own unique path. The actual name by which the system identifies a directory always begins with the root directory and consists of all directories nested above that directory.

In Linux, you write a pathname by listing each directory in the path separated by a forward slash. A slash preceding the first directory in the path represents the root. The pathname for the **robert** directory is **/home/robert**. The pathname for the **reports** directory is **/home/chris/reports**. Pathnames also apply to files. When you create a file within a directory, you give the file a name. The actual name by which the system identifies the file, however, is the filename combined with the path of directories from the root to the file's directory. In Figure 12-4, the path for the **weather** file consists of the root, **home**, and **chris** directories and the filename **weather**. The pathname for **weather** is **/home/chris /weather** (the root directory is represented by the first slash).

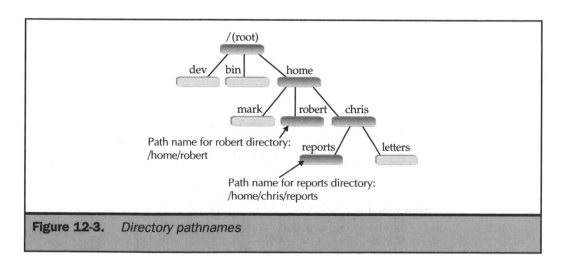

Figure 12-3.   *Directory pathnames*

ENVIRONMENTS

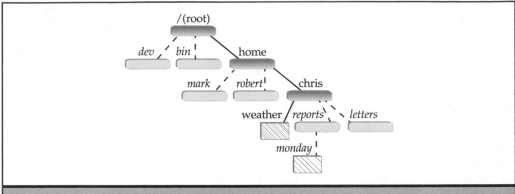

Figure 12-4.   *Pathname for weather:* /home/chris/weather

Pathnames may be absolute or relative. An *absolute pathname* is the complete pathname of a file or directory beginning with the root directory. A *relative pathname* begins from your working directory; it is the path of a file relative to your working directory. The working directory is the one you are currently operating in. Using the directory structure described in Figure 12-4, if **chris** is your working directory, the relative pathname for the file **monday** is **/reports/monday**. The absolute pathname for **monday** is **/home/chris/reports/monday**.

The absolute pathname from the root to your home directory could be especially complex and, at times, even subject to change by the system administrator. To make it easier to reference, you can use a special character, the tilde ~, which represents the absolute pathname of your home directory. In the next example, from the **thankyou** directory, the user references the **weather** file in the home directory by placing a tilde and slash before **weather**:

```
$ pwd
/home/chris/letters/thankyou
$ cat ~/weather
raining and warm
$
```

You must specify the rest of the path from your home directory. In the next example, the user references the **monday** file in the **reports** directory. The tilde represents the path to the user's home directory, **/home/chris**, and then the rest of the path to the **monday** file is specified.

```
$ cat ~/reports/monday
```

System Directories

The root directory that begins the Linux file structure contains several system directories. The system directories contain files and programs used to run and maintain the system. Many contain other subdirectories with programs for executing specific features of Linux. For example, the directory **/usr/bin** contains the various Linux commands that users execute, such as **cp** and **mv**. The directory **/bin** holds interfaces with different system devices, such as the printer or the terminal. Table 12-2 lists the basic system directories.

Note *The overall organization of the Linux file structure for system directories and other useful directories such as those used for the kernel and X Window System are discussed in detail in Chapter 32.*

Directory	Function
/	Begins the file system structure, called the *root*
/home	Contains users' home directories
/bin	Holds all the standard commands and utility programs
/usr	Holds those files and commands used by the system; this directory breaks down into several subdirectories
/usr/bin	Holds user-oriented commands and utility programs
/usr/sbin	Holds system administration commands
/usr/lib	Holds libraries for programming languages
/usr/doc	Holds Linux documentation
/usr/man	Holds the online manual Man files
/usr/spool	Holds spooled files, such as those generated for printing jobs and network transfers
/sbin	Holds system administration commands for booting the system
/var	Holds files that vary, such as mailbox files
/dev	Holds file interfaces for devices such as the terminals and printers
/etc	Holds system configuration files and any other system files

Table 12-2. *Standard System Directories in Linux*

ENVIRONMENTS

Listing, Displaying, and Printing Files: ls, cat, more, and lpr

One of the primary functions of an operating system is the management of files. You may need to perform certain basic output operations on your files, such as displaying them on your screen or printing them. The Linux system provides a set of commands that perform basic file-management operations, such as listing, displaying, and printing files, as well as copying, renaming, and erasing files. These commands are usually made up of abbreviated versions of words. For example, the **ls** command is a shortened form of "list" and lists the files in your directory. The **lpr** command is an abbreviated form of "line print" and will print a file. The **cat** and **more** commands display the contents of a file on the screen. Table 12-3 lists these commands with their different options. When you log in to your Linux system, you may want a list of the files in your home directory. The **ls** command, which outputs a list of your file and directory names, is useful for this. The **ls** command has many possible options for displaying filenames according to specific features. These are discussed in more detail at the end of the chapter.

Command or Option	Execution
ls	This command lists file and directory names: $ **ls** *filenames*
cat	This filter can be used to display a file. It can take filenames for its arguments. It outputs the contents of those files directly to the standard output, which, by default, is directed to the screen: $ **cat** *filenames*

Table 12-3.   *Listing, Displaying, and Printing Files*

Command or Option	Execution

more	This utility displays a file screen by screen. It can take filenames for its arguments. It outputs the contents of those files to the screen, one screen at a time:
	$ more *filenames*
	   Options
	      +*num* Begins displaying the file at page *num*
	   Commands
	      *num***f** Skips forward *num* number of screens
	      *num***b** Skips backward *num* number of screens
	      d Displays half a screen
	      h Lists all **more** commands
	      q Quits **more** utility

lpr	Sends a file to the line printer to be printed; a list of files may be used as arguments
	$ lpr *filenames*
	   Options
	      -P *printer-name* Selects a specific printer

lpq	Lists the print queue for printing jobs
lprm	Removes a printing job from the printing queue

Table 12-3.   *Listing, Displaying, and Printing Files* (continued)

Displaying Files: cat and more

You may also need to look at the contents of a file. The **cat** and **more** commands display the contents of a file on the screen. The command **cat** stands for *concatenate*.

It is complex and versatile, as described in Chapter 7. Here it is used in a limited way, displaying the text of a file on the screen:

```
$ cat mydata
computers
```

The **cat** command outputs the entire text of a file to the screen at once. This presents a problem when the file is large because its text quickly speeds past on the screen. The **more** command is designed to overcome this limitation by displaying one screen of text at a time. You can then move forward or backward in the text at your leisure. You invoke the **more** command by entering the command name followed by the name of the file you want to view.

```
$ more mydata
```

When **more** invokes a file, the first screen of text is displayed. To continue to the next screen, you press the F key or the SPACEBAR. To move back in the text, you press the B key. You can quit at any time by pressing the Q key.

Printing Files: lpr, lpq, and lprm

With the printer commands like **lpr** and **lprm,** you can perform printing operations like printing files or canceling print jobs (see Table 12-3). When you need to print files, use the **lpr** command to send files to the printer connected to your system. In the next example, the user prints the **mydata** file:

```
$ lpr mydata
```

If you want to print several files at once, you can specify more than one file on the command line after the **lpr** command. In the next example, the user prints out both the **mydata** and **preface** files:

```
$ lpr mydata preface
```

Printing jobs are placed in a queue and printed one, at a time, in the background. You can continue with other work as your files print. You can see the position of a particular printing job at any given time with the **lpq** command. **lpq** gives the owner of the printing job (the login name of the user who sent the job), the print job ID, the size in bytes, and the temporary file in which it is currently held. In this example, the owner is **chris** and the print ID is **00015**:

```
$ lpq
Owner      ID      Chars      Filename
chris      00015   360        /usr/lpd/cfa00015
```

If you need to cancel an unwanted printing job, you can do so with the **lprm** command. **lprm** takes as its argument either the ID number of the printing job or the owner's name. **lprm** then removes the print job from the print queue. For this task, **lpq** is helpful, for it provides you with the ID number and owner of the printing job you need to use with **lprm**. In the next example, the print job 15 is canceled:

```
$ lprm  00015
```

You can have several printers connected to your Linux system. One of these will be designated the default printer, and **lpr** prints to this printer unless another printer is specified. With **lpr**, you can specify the particular printer on which you want your file printed. Each printer on your system will have its own name. You can specify which printer to use with the **-P** option followed by that printer's name. In the next example, the file **mydata** is printed on the evans1 printer:

```
$ lpr -Pevans1 mydata
```

Managing Directories:
mkdir, rmdir, ls, cd, and pwd

You can create and remove your own directories, as well as change your working directory, with the **mkdir**, **rmdir**, and **cd** commands. Each of these commands can take as its argument the pathname for a directory. The **pwd** command displays the absolute pathname of your working directory. In addition to these commands, the special characters represented by a single dot, a double dot, and a tilde can be used to reference the working directory, the parent of the working directory, and the home directory, respectively. Taken together, these commands enable you to manage your directories. You can create nested directories, move from one directory to another, and use pathnames to reference any of your directories. Those commands commonly used to manage directories are listed in Table 12-4.

Command	Execution
mkdir	Creates a directory: `$ mkdir reports`

Table 12-4.   *Directory Commands*

Command	Execution
rmdir	Erases a directory: `$ rmdir letters`

ls -F	Lists directory name with a preceding slash:
	`$ ls -F`
	`today /reports /letters`

ls -R	Lists working directory as well as all subdirectories

cd *directory name*	Changes to the specified directory, making it the working directory. **cd** without a directory name changes back to the home directory:
	`$ cd reports`
	`$ cd`

pwd	Displays the pathname of the working directory:
	`$ pwd`
	`/home/chris/reports`

directory name/`filename`	A slash is used in pathnames to separate each directory name. In the case of pathnames for files, a slash separates the preceding directory names from the filename:
	`$ cd /home/chris/reports`
	`$ cat /home/chris/reports/mydata`

..	References the parent directory. You can use it as an argument or as part of a pathname:
	`$ cd ..`
	`$ mv ../larisa oldletters`

.	References the working directory. You can use it as an argument or as part of a pathname:
	`$ ls .`
	`$ mv ../aleina .`

~/*pathname*	The tilde is a special character that represents the pathname for the **home** directory. It is useful when you need to use an absolute pathname for a file or directory:
	`$ cp monday ~/today`
	`$ mv tuesday ~/weather`

Table 12-4. *Directory Commands* (continued)

You create and remove directories with the **mkdir** and **rmdir** commands. In either case, you can also use pathnames for the directories. In the next example, the user creates the directory **reports**. Then, the user creates the directory **letters** using a pathname.

```
$ mkdir reports
$ mkdir /home/chris/letters
```

You can remove a directory with the **rmdir** command followed by the directory name. In the next example, the user removes the directory **reports** with the **rmdir** command. Then, the directory **letters** is removed using its pathname.

```
$ rmdir reports
$ rmdir /home/chris/letters
```

You have seen how to use the **ls** command to list the files and directories within your working directory. To distinguish between file and directory names, however, you need to use the **ls** command with the **-F** option. A slash is then placed after each directory name in the list.

```
$ ls
weather reports letters
$ ls -F
weather reports/ letters/
```

The **ls** command also takes as an argument any directory name or directory pathname. This enables you to list the files in any directory without first having to change to that directory. In the next example, the **ls** command takes as its argument the name of a directory, **reports**. Then the **ls** command is executed again, only this time the absolute pathname of **reports** is used.

```
$ ls reports
monday tuesday
$ ls /home/chris/reports
monday tuesday
$
```

Within each directory, you can create still other directories; in effect, nesting directories. Using the **cd** command, you can change from one directory to another. No indicator tells you what directory you are currently in, however. To find out what directory you have changed to, use the **pwd** command to display the name of your current working directory. The **pwd** command displays more than just the name of the directory—it displays the full pathname, as shown in the next example. The pathname displayed here consists of the user's home directory, **dylan**, and the directory it is a part of, the directory called **home**, and directory that **home** is part of, **/**, the root directory. Each directory name is separated by a slash. The root directory is represented by a beginning slash.

```
$ pwd
/home/dylan
```

As you already know, you can change directories with the **cd** command. Changing to a directory makes that directory the working directory, which is your default directory.

 *File commands, such as **ls** and **cp**, unless specifically told otherwise, operate on files in your working directory.*

When you log in to the system, your working directory is your home directory. When a user account is created, the system also creates a home directory for that user. When you log in, you are always placed in your home directory. The **cd** command enables you to make another directory the working directory. In a sense, you can move from your home directory into another directory. This other directory then becomes the default directory for any commands and any new files created. For example, the **ls** command now lists files in this new working directory.

The **cd** command takes as its argument the name of the directory to which you want to change. The name of the directory can be the name of a subdirectory in your working directory or the full pathname of any directory on the system. If you want to change back to your home directory, you only need to enter the **cd** command by itself, without a filename argument.

```
$ pwd
/home/dylan
$ cd props
$ pwd
/home/dylan/props
$ cd /home/chris/letters
$ pwd
/home/chris/letters
$
```

You can use a double dots "**..**", to represent a directory's parent. This literally represents the pathname of the parent directory. You can use the double dot symbol with the **cd** command to move back up to the parent directory, making the parent directory the current directory. In the next example, the user moves to the **letters** directory and then changes back to the home directory:

```
$ cd letters
$ pwd
/home/chris/letters
$ cd ..
$ pwd
/home/chris
```

A directory always has a parent (except, of course, for the root). For example, in the previous listing, the parent for **thankyou** is the **letters** directory. When a directory is created, two entries are made: one represented with a dot, **.**, and the other represented by a double dot, **..** . The dot represents the pathnames of the directory, and the double dot represents the pathname of its parent directory. The double dot, used as an argument in a command, references a parent directory. The single dot references the directory itself. In the next example, the user changes to the **letters** directory. The **ls** command is used with the **.** argument to list the files in the **letters** directory. Then, the **ls** command is used with the **..** argument to list the files in the parent directory of **letters**, the **chris** directory.

```
$ cd letters
$ ls .
thankyou
$ ls ..
weather letters
$
```

You can use the single dot to reference your working directory, instead of using its pathname. For example, to copy a file to the working directory retaining the same name, the dot can be used in place of the working directory's pathname. In this sense, the dot is another name for the working directory. In the next example, the user copies the **weather** file from the **chris** directory to the **reports** directory. The **reports** directory is the working directory and can be represented with the single dot.

```
$ cd reports
$ cp /home/chris/weather   .
```

The **..** symbol is often used to reference files in the parent directory. In the next example, the **cat** command displays the **weather** file in the parent directory. The pathname for the file is the **..** symbol followed by a slash and the filename.

```
$ cat ../weather
raining and warm
```

*You can use the **cd** command with the **. .** symbol to step back through successive parent directories of the directory tree from a lower directory.*

File and Directory Operations: find, cp, mv, rm, and ln

As you create more and more files, you may want to back them up, change their names, erase some of them, or even give them added names. Linux provides you with several file commands that enable you to search for files, copy files, rename files, or remove files (see Tables 12-5 and 12-6). If you have a large number of files, you can also search them to locate a specific one. The commands are shortened forms of full words, consisting of only two characters. The **cp** command stands for "copy" and copies a file, **mv** stands for "move" and renames or moves a file, **rm** stands for "remove" and erases a file, and **ln** stands for "link" and adds another name for a file. One exception to this rule is the **find** command, which performs searches of your filenames to find a file.

Searching Directories: find

Once you have a large number of files in many different directories, you may need to search them to locate a specific file, or files, of a certain type. The **find** command enables you to perform such a search. The **find** command takes as its arguments directory names followed by several possible options that specify the type of search and the criteria for the search. **find** then searches within the directories listed and their subdirectories for files that meet these criteria. The **find** command can search for a file based on its name, type, owner, and even the time of the last update.

```
$ find directory-list -option  criteria
```

The **-name** option has as its criteria a pattern and instructs **find** to search for the filename that matches that pattern. To search for a file by name, you use the **find** command with the directory name followed by the **-name** option and the name of the file.

```
$ find directory-list -name filename
```

The **find** command also has options that merely perform actions, such as outputting the results of a search. If you want **find** to display the filenames it has found, you simply include the **-print** option on the command line along with any other options. The **-print** option instructs **find** to output to the standard output the names of all the files it locates. In the next example, the user searches for all the files in the **reports** directory with the name **monday**. Once located, the file, with its relative pathname, is printed.

```
$ find reports -name monday -print
reports/monday
```

The **find** command prints out the filenames using the directory name specified in the directory list. If you specify an absolute pathname, the absolute path of the found directories will be output. If you specify a relative pathname, only the relative pathname is output. In the previous example, the user specified a relative pathname, **reports**, in the directory list. Located filenames were output beginning with this relative pathname. In the next example, the user specifies an absolute pathname in the directory list. Located filenames are then output using this absolute pathname.

```
$ find /home/chris -name monday -print
/home/chris/reports/monday
```

If you want to search your working directory, you can use the dot in the directory pathname to represent your working directory. The double dot would represent the parent directory. The next example searches all files and subdirectories in the working directory, using the dot to represent the working directory. If you are located in your **home** directory, this is a convenient way to search through all your own directories. Notice the located filenames are output beginning with a dot.

```
$ find . -name weather -print
./weather
```

You can use shell wildcard characters as part of the pattern criteria for searching files. The special character must be quoted, however, to avoid evaluation by the shell. In the next example, all files with the **.c** extension in the **programs** directory are searched for:

```
$ find programs -name '*.c' -print
```

You can also use the **find** command to locate other directories. In Linux, a directory is officially classified as a special type of file. Although all files have a byte-stream format, some files, such as directories, are used in special ways. In this sense, a file can be said to have a file type. The **find** command has an option called **-type** that searches for a file of a given type. The **-type** option takes a one-character modifier that represents the file type. The modifier that represents a directory is a **d**. In the next example, both the directory name and the directory file type are used to search for the directory called **thankyou**:

```
$ find /home/chris -name thankyou -type d -print
/home/chris/letters/thankyou
$
```

File types are not so much different types of files as they are the file format applied to other components of the operating system, such as devices. In this sense, a device is treated as a type of file, and you can use **find** to search for devices and directories, as well as ordinary files. Table 12-5 lists the different types available for the **find** command's **-type** option.

Command or Option	Execution
find	Searches directories for files based on search criteria. This command has several options that specify the type of criteria and actions to be taken.
Options	
-name *pattern*	Searches for files with the *pattern* in the name.
-group *name*	Searches for files belonging to this group *name*.
-size *numc*	Searches for files with the size *num* in blocks. If **c** is added after *num*, then the size in bytes (characters) is searched for.
-mtime *num*	Searches for files last modified *num* days ago.
-newer *pattern*	Searches for files modified after the one matched by *pattern*.
-print	Outputs the result of the search to the standard output. The result is usually a list of filenames, including their full pathnames.
-type *filetype*	Searches for files with the specified file type. **file types** **b** Block device file. **c** Character device file. **d** Directory file. **f** Ordinary (regular) file. **p** Named pipes (fifo). **l** Symbolic links.

Table 12-5. *The* find *Command*

Moving and Copying Files

To make a copy of a file, you simply give **cp** two filenames as its arguments (see Table 12-6). The first filename is the name of the file to be copied—the one that already exists. This is often referred to as the *source file*. The second filename is the name you want for the copy. This will be a new file containing a copy of all the data in the source file. This second argument is often referred to as the *destination file*. The syntax for the **cp** command follows:

```
$ cp source-file destination-file
```

In the next example, the user copies a file called **proposal** to a new file called **oldprop**:

```
$ cp proposal oldprop
```

When the user lists the files in that directory, the new copy will be among them.

```
$ ls
proposal  oldprop
```

You could unintentionally destroy another file with the **cp** command. The **cp** command generates a copy by first creating a file and then copying data into it. If another file has the same name as the destination file, then that file is destroyed and a new file with that name is created. In a sense, the original file is overwritten with the new copy. In the next example, the **proposal** file is overwritten by the **newprop** file. The **proposal** file already exists.

```
$ cp newprop  proposal
```

Most Linux distributions configure your system to detect this overwrite condition. If not, you can use the **cp** command with the **-i** (for interactive) option to detect it. With this option, **cp** first checks to see if the file already exists. If it does, you are then asked if you want to overwrite the existing file. If you enter **y**, the existing file is destroyed and a new one created as the copy. If you enter anything else, this is taken as a negative answer and the **cp** command is interrupted, preserving the original file.

```
$ cp -i  newprop  proposal
Overwrite proposal?  n
$
```

To copy a file from your working directory to another directory, you only need to use that directory name as the second argument in the **cp** command. The name of the new copy will be the same as the original, but the copy will be placed in a different directory. Files in different directories can have the same names. Because files are in different directories, they are registered as different files.

```
$ cp filenames directory-name
```

The **cp** command can take a list of several filenames for its arguments, so you can copy more than one file at a time to a directory. Simply specify the filenames on the command line, entering the directory name as the last argument. All the files are then copied to the specified directory. In the next example, the user copies both the files **preface** and **doc1** to the **props** directory. Notice **props** is the last argument.

```
$ cp preface doc1 props
```

You can use any of the wildcard characters to generate a list of filenames to use with **cp** or **mv**. For example, suppose you need to copy all your C source code files to a given directory. Instead of listing each one individually on the command line, you could use a ***** character with the **.c** extension to match on and generate a list of C source code files (all files with a **.c** extension). In the next example, the user copies all source code files in the current directory to the **sourcebks** directory:

```
$ cp *.c sourcebks
```

If you want to copy all the files in a given directory to another directory, you could use ***** to match on and generate a list of all those files in a **cp** command. In the next example, the user copies all the files in the **props** directory to the **oldprop** directory. Notice the use of a **props** pathname preceding the ***** special characters. In this context, **props** is a pathname that will be appended before each file in the list that ***** generates.

```
$ cp props/* oldprop
```

You can, of course, use any of the other special characters, such as **.**, **?**, or **[ ]**. In the next example, the user copies both source code and object code files (**.c** and **.o**) to the **projbk** directory:

```
$ cp *.[oc] projbk
```

When you copy a file, you may want to give the copy a different name than the original. To do so, place the new filename after the directory name, separated by a slash.

```
$ cp filename directory-name/new-filename
```

In the next example, the file **newprop** is copied to the directory **props** and the copy is given the name **version1**. The user then changes to the **props** directory and lists the files. Only one file exists, which is called **version1**.

```
$ cp newprop props/version1
$ cd props
$ ls
version1
```

You can use the **mv** command either to rename a file or to move a file from one directory to another. When using **mv** to rename a file, you simply use the new filename as the second argument. The first argument is the current name of the file you are renaming.

```
$ mv original-filename   new-filename
```

In the next example, the **proposal** file is renamed with the name **version1**:

```
$ mv proposal version1
```

As with **cp**, it is easy for **mv** to erase a file accidentally. When renaming a file, you might accidentally choose a filename already used by another file. In this case, that other file will be erased. The **mv** command also has an **-i** option that checks first to see if a file by that name already exists. If it does, then you are asked first if you want to overwrite it. In the next example, a file already exists with the name **version1**. The overwrite condition is detected and you are asked whether you want to overwrite that file.

```
$ ls
proposal version1
$ mv -i  version1  proposal
Overwrite proposal?  n
$
```

You can move a file from one directory to another by using the directory name as the second argument in the **mv** command. In this case, you can think of the **mv** command as simply moving a file from one directory to another, rather than renaming the file. After you move the file, it will have the same name as it had in its original directory unless you specify otherwise.

```
$ mv filename directory-name
```

If you want to rename a file when you move it, you can specify the new name of the file after the directory name. The directory name and the new filename are separated by a forward slash. In the next example, the file **newprop** is moved to the directory **props** and renamed as **version1**:

```
$ mv newprops props/version1
$ cd props
$ ls
version1
```

You can also use any of the special characters described in Chapter 5 to generate a list of filenames to use with **mv**. In the next example, the user moves all source code files in the current directory to the **newproj** directory:

```
$ mv *.c newproj
```

If you want to move all the files in a given directory to another directory, you can use ***** to match on and generate a list of all those files. In the next example, the user moves all the files in the **reports** directory to the **repbks** directory:

```
$ mv reports/*  repbks
```

Moving and Copying Directories

You can also copy or move whole directories at once. Both **cp** and **mv** can take as their first argument a directory name, enabling you to copy or move subdirectories from one directory into another (see Table 12-6). The first argument is the name of the directory to be moved or copied, while the second argument is the name of the directory within which it is to be placed. The same pathname structure used for files applies to moving or copying directories.

Command	Execution
cp *filename filename*	Copies a file. **cp** takes two arguments: the original file and the name of the new copy. You can use pathnames for the files to copy across directories: `$ cp today reports/monday`

Table 12-6. *File Operations*

Command	Execution
cp -r *dirname dirname*	Copies a subdirectory from one directory to another. The copied directory includes all its own subdirectories: **$ cp -r letters/thankyou oldletters**
mv *filename filename*	Moves (renames) a file. **mv** takes two arguments: the first is the file to be moved. The second argument can be the new filename or the pathname of a directory. If it is the name of a directory, then the file is literally moved to that directory, changing the file's pathname: **$ mv today /home/chris/reports**
mv *dirname dirname*	Moves directories. In this case, the first and last arguments are directories: **$ mv letters/thankyou oldletters**
ln *filename filename*	Creates added names for files referred to as links. A link can be created in one directory that references a file in another directory: **$ ln today reports/monday**
rm *filenames*	Removes (erases) a file. Can take any number of filenames as its arguments. Literally removes links to a file. If a file has more than one link, you need to remove all of them to erase a file: **$rm today weather weekend**

Table 12-6.   *File Operations* (continued)

You can just as easily copy subdirectories from one directory to another. To copy a directory, the **cp** command requires you to use the **-r** option. The **-r** option stands for "recursive." It directs the **cp** command to copy a directory, as well as any subdirectories it may contain. In other words, the entire directory subtree, from that directory on, will be copied. In the next example, the **thankyou** directory is copied to the **oldletters** directory. Now two **thankyou** subdirectories exist, one in **letters** and one in **oldletters**.

```
$ cp -r letters/thankyou oldletters
$ ls -F letters
/thankyou
$ ls -F oldletters
/thankyou
```

Erasing a File: the rm Command

As you use Linux, you will find the number of files you use increases rapidly. Generating files in Linux is easy. Applications such as editors, and commands such as **cp**, easily create files. Eventually, many of these files may become outdated and useless. You can then remove them with the **rm** command. In the next example, the user erases the file **oldprop**:

```
$ rm oldprop
```

The **rm** command can take any number of arguments, enabling you to list several filenames and erase them all at the same time. You just list them on the command line after you type **rm**.

```
$ rm proposal version1 version2
```

Be careful when using the **rm** command because it is irrevocable. Once a file is removed, it cannot be restored (there is no undo). Suppose, for example, you enter the **rm** command by accident while meaning to enter some other command, such as **cp** or **mv**. By the time you press ENTER and realize your mistake, it is too late. The files are gone. To protect against this kind of situation, you can use the **rm** command's **-i** option to confirm you want to erase a file. With the **-i** option, you are prompted separately for each file and asked whether to remove it. If you enter **y**, the file will be removed. If you enter anything else, the file is not removed. In the next example, the **rm** command is instructed to erase the files **proposal** and **oldprop**. The **rm** command then asks for confirmation for each file. The user decides to remove **oldprop,** but not **proposal**.

```
$ rm -i proposal oldprop
Remove proposal? n
Remove oldprop? y
$
```

To remove a directory and all its subdirectories you use the **rm** command with the **-r** option. This is a very powerful command and could easily be used to erase all your files. The following example deletes the **reports** directory and all its subdirectories:

```
$ rm -r reports
```

Be careful of using the asterisk matching character as described Chapter 11. The following command will erase every file in your current working directory.

```
$ rm *
```

> **Note**   *This is a very powerful operation, capable of erasing large segments of your file systems. Use with caution.*

Links: the ln Command

You can give a file more than one name using the **ln** command. You might want to reference a file using different filenames to access it from different directories. The added names are often referred to as *links*.

The **ln** command takes two arguments: the name of the original file and the new, added filename. The **ls** operation lists both filenames, but only one physical file will exist.

```
$ ln original-file-name added-file-name
```

In the next example, the **today** file is given the additional name **weather**. It is just another name for the **today** file.

```
$ ls
today
$ ln today weather
$ ls
today weather
```

You can give the same file several names by using the **ln** command on the same file many times. In the next example, the file **today** is given both the name **weather** and **weekend**:

```
$ ln today weather
$ ln today weekend
$ ls
today weather weekend
```

You can use the **ls** command with the **-l** option to find if a file has several links. **ls** with **-l** lists several pieces of information, such as permissions, the number of links a file has, its size, and the date it was last modified. In this line of information, the first number, which precedes the user's login name, specifies the number of links a file has. The number before the date is the size of the file. The date is the last time a file was modified. In the next example, the user lists the full information for both **today** and **weather**. Notice the number of links in both files is two. Furthermore, the size and date are the same. This suggests both files are actually different names for the same file.

```
$ ls -l today weather
-rw-rw-r-- 2  chris   group 563   Feb  14   10:30  today
-rw-rw-r-- 2  chris   group 563   Feb  14   10:30  weather
```

This still does not tell you specifically what filenames are linked. You can be somewhat sure if two files have exactly the same number of links, sizes, and modification dates, as in the case of the files **today** and **weather**. To be certain, however, you can use the **ls** command with the **-i** option. With the **-i** option, the **ls** command lists the filename and its inode number. An *inode* number is a unique number used by the system to identify a specific file. If two filenames have the same inode number, they reference exactly the same file. They are two names for the same file. In the next example, the user lists **today**, **weather**, and **larisa**. Notice that **today** and **weather** have the same inode number.

```
$ ls -i today weather larisa
1234 today    1234 weather    3976 larisa
```

The added names, or links, created with **ln** are often used to reference the same file from different directories. A file in one directory can be linked to and accessed from another directory. Suppose you need to reference a file in the home directory from within another directory. You can set up a link from that directory to the file in the home directory. This link is actually another name for the file. Because the link is in another directory, it can have the same name as the original file.

To link a file in the home directory to another directory, use the name of that directory as the second argument in the **ln** command.

```
$ ln filename directory-name
```

In the next example, the file **today** in the **chris** directory is linked to the **reports** directory. The **ls** command lists the **today** file in both the **chris** directory and the **reports** directory. In fact, only one copy of the **today** file exists, the original file in the home directory.

```
$ ln today reports
$ ls
today reports
$ ls reports
today
$
```

Just as with the **cp** and **mv** commands, you can give another name to the link. Simply place the new name after the directory name, separated by a slash. In the next example, the file **today** is linked to the **reports** directory with the name **wednesday**. Only one actual file still exists, the original file called **today** in the **chris** directory. However, **today** is now linked to the directory **reports** with the name **wednesday**. In this sense, **today** has been given another name. In the **reports** directory, the **today** file goes by the name **wednesday**.

```
$ ln today reports/wednesday
$ ls
today reports
$ ls reports
wednesday
$
```

You can easily link a file in any directory to a file in another directory by referencing the files with their pathnames. In the next example, the file **monday** in the **reports** directory is linked to the directory, **chris**. Notice the second argument is an absolute pathname.

```
$ ln monday /home/chris
```

To erase a file, you need to remove all its links. The name of a file is actually considered a link to that file. Hence the command **rm** that removes the link to the file. If you have several links to the file and remove only one of them, the others stay in place and you can reference the file through them. The same is true even if you remove the original link—the original name of the file. Any added links will work just as well. In the next example, the **today** file is removed with the **rm** command. However, a link to that same file exists, called **weather**. The file can then be referenced under the name **weather**.

```
$ ln today weather
$ rm today
$ cat weather
The storm broke today
and the sun came out.
$
```

Symbolic Links and Hard Links

Linux supports what are known as symbolic links. Links, as they have been described so far, are called *hard links*. Although hard links will suffice for most of your needs, they suffer from one major limitation. A hard link may in some situations fail when you try to link to a file on some other user's directory. This is because the Linux file structure can be physically segmented into what are called file systems. A *file system* can be made up of any physical memory device or devices, from a floppy disk to a bank of hard disks. Although the files and directories in all file systems are attached to the same overall directory tree, each file system physically manages its own files and directories. This means a file in one file system cannot be linked by a hard link to a file in another file system. If you try to link to a file on another user's directory that is located on another file system, your hard link will fail.

To overcome this restriction, you use symbolic links. A *symbolic link* holds the pathname of the file to which it is linking. It is not a direct hard link but, rather, information on how to locate a specific file. Instead of registering another name for the same file as a hard link does, a symbolic link can be thought of as another symbol that represents the file's pathname. A symbolic link is another way of writing the file's pathname.

You create a symbolic link using the **ln** command with the **-s** option. In the next example, the user creates a link called **lunch** to the file **/home/george/veglist**:

```
$ ln -s lunch /home/george/veglist
```

If you list the full information about a symbolic link and its file, you will find the information displayed is different. In the next example, the user lists the full information for both **lunch** and **/home/george/veglist** using the **ls** command with the **-l** option. The first character in the line specifies the file type. Symbolic links have their own file type represented by a l. The file type for **lunch** is l, indicating it is a symbolic link, not an ordinary file. The number after the term "group" is the size of the file. Notice the sizes differ. The size of the **lunch** file is only 4 bytes. This is because **lunch** is only a symbolic link—a file that holds the pathname of another file—and a pathname takes up only a few bytes. It is not a direct hard link to the **veglist** file.

```
$ ls lunch /home/george/veglist
lrw-rw-r-- 1  chris   group 4    Feb  14   10:30  lunch
-rw-rw-r-- 1  george  group 793  Feb  14   10:30  veglist
```

To erase a file, you need to remove only its hard links. If any symbolic links are left over, they will be unable to access the file. In this case, a symbolic link would hold the pathname of a file that no longer exists.

Unlike hard links, you can use symbolic links to create links to directories. In effect, you can create another name with which you can reference a directory. If you use a symbolic link for a directory name, however, remember the **pwd** command always displays the actual directory name, not the symbolic name. In the next example, the user links the directory **thankyou** with the symbolic link **gifts**. When the user uses **gifts** in the **cd** command, the user is actually changed to the **thankyou** directory. **pwd** displays the pathname for the **thankyou** directory.

```
$ ln -s /home/chris/letters/thankyou  gifts
$ cd gifts
$ pwd
/home/chris/letters/thankyou
$
```

If you want to display the name of the symbolic link, you can access it in the **cwd** variable. The **cwd** *variable* is a special system variable that holds the name of a directory's symbolic link, if one exists. Variables such as **cwd** are discussed in Chapter 15. You display the contents of **cwd** with the command **echo $cwd**.

```
$ pwd
/home/chris/letters/thankyou
$ echo $cwd
/home/chris/gifts
```

File and Directory Permissions: chmod

Each file and directory in Linux contains a set of permissions that determines who can access them and how. You set these permissions to limit access in one of three ways: You can restrict access to yourself alone, you can allow users in a predesignated group to have access, or you can permit anyone on your system to have access; and, you can control how a given file or directory is accessed. A file and directory may have read, write, and execute permission. When a file is created, it is automatically given read and write permissions for the owner, enabling you to display and modify the file. You may change these permissions to any combination you want. A file could have read-only permission, preventing any modifications. A file could also have execute permission, allowing it to be executed as a program.

Three different categories of users can have access to a file or directory: the owner, the group, or others. The owner is the user who created the file. Any file you create, you own. You can also permit your group to have access to a file. Often, users are collected into groups. For example, all the users for a given class or project could be formed into a group by the system administrator. A user can give access to a file to other members of the group. Finally, you can also open up access to a file to all other users on the system. In this case, every user on your system could have access to one of your files or directories. In this sense, every other user on the system makes up the "others" category.

Each category has its own set of read, write, and execute permissions. The first set controls the user's own access to his or her files—the owner access. The second set controls the access of the group to a user's files. The third set controls the access of all other users to the user's files. The three sets of read, write, and execute permissions for the three categories—owner, group, and other—make a total of nine types of permissions.

As you saw in the previous section, the **ls** command with the **–l** option displays detailed information about the file, including the permissions. In the next example, the first set of characters on the left is a list of the permissions set for the **mydata** file:

```
$ ls -l mydata
-rw-r--r--  1  chris weather 207 Feb  20  11:55   mydata
```

An empty permission is represented by a dash, **-**. The read permission is represented by *r*, write by *w*, and execute by *x*. Notice there are ten positions. The first character indicates the file type. In a general sense, a directory can be considered a type of file. If the first character is a dash, a file is being listed. If it is *d*, information about a directory is being displayed.

The next nine characters are arranged according to the different user categories. The first set of three characters is the owner's set of permissions for the file. The second set of three characters is the group's set of permissions for the file. The last set of three characters is the other users' set of permissions for the file. In Figure 12-5, the **mydata** file has the read and write permissions set for the owner category, the read permission only set for the group category, and the read permission set for the other users category. This means, although anyone in the group or any other user on the system can read the file, only the owner can modify it.

You use the **chmod** command to change different permission configurations. **chmod** takes two lists as its arguments: permission changes and filenames. You can specify the list of permissions in two different ways. One way uses permission symbols and is referred to as the *symbolic method*. The other uses what is known as a "binary mask" and is referred to as either the *absolute* or the *relative method*. Of the two, the symbolic method is the more intuitive and will be presented first. Table 12-7 lists options for the **chmod** command.

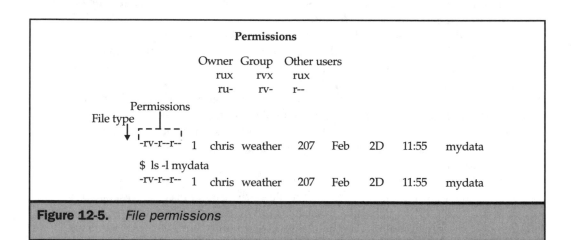

Figure 12-5.   *File permissions*

ENVIRONMENTS

Command or Option	Execution
`chmod`	Changes the permission of a file or directory.
Options	
+	Adds a permission.
–	Removes a permission.
=	Assigns entire set of permissions.
r	Sets read permission for a file or directory. A file can be displayed or printed. A directory can have the list of its files displayed.
w	Sets write permission for a file or directory. A file can be edited or erased. A directory can be removed.
x	Sets execute permission for a file or directory. If the file is a shell script, it can be executed as a program. A directory can be changed to and entered.
u	Sets permissions for the user who created and owns the file or directory.
g	Sets permissions for group access to a file or directory.
o	Sets permissions for access to a file or directory by all other users on the system.
a	Sets permissions for access by the user, group, and all other users.
s	Set User ID and Group ID permission; program owned by owner and group.
t	Set sticky bit permission; program remains in memory.

Table 12-7. *File and Directory Permission Operations*

Command or Option	Execution
chgrp *groupname filenames*	Changes the group for a file or files.
chown *user-name filenames*	Changes the owner of a file or files
ls -l *filename*	Lists a filename with its permissions displayed.
ls -ld *directory*	Lists a directory name with its permissions displayed.
ls -l	Lists all files in a directory with its permissions displayed.

Table 12-7. *File and Directory Permission Operations* (continued)

Setting Permissions: Permission Symbols

As you might have guessed, the symbolic method of setting permissions uses the characters *r, w,* and *x* for read, write, and execute, respectively. Any of these permissions can be added or removed. The symbol to add a permission is the plus sign, **+**. The symbol to remove a permission is the minus sign, **-**. In the next example, the **chmod** command adds the execute permission and removes the write permission for the **mydata** file. The read permission is not changed.

```
$ chmod +x-w mydata
```

Permission symbols also specify each user category. The owner, group, and others categories are represented by the *u, g,* and *o* characters, respectively. Notice the owner category is represented by a *u* and can be thought of as the user. The symbol for a category is placed before the read, write, and execute permissions. If no category symbol is used, all categories are assumed, and the permissions specified are set for the user, group, and others. In the next example, the first **chmod** command sets the permissions for the group to read and write. The second **chmod** command sets permissions for other users to read. Notice no spaces are between the permission specifications and the category. The permissions list is simply one long phrase, with no spaces.

```
$ chmod g+rw mydata
$ chmod o+r mydata
```

A user may remove permissions as well as add them. In the next example, the read permission is set for other users, but the write and execute permissions are removed:

```
$ chmod o+r-wx mydata
```

Another permission symbol exists, **a**, which represents all the categories. The *a* symbol is the default. In the next example, both commands are equivalent. The read permission is explicitly set with the *a* symbol denoting all types of users: other, group, and user.

```
$ chmod a+r mydata
$ chmod +r mydata
```

One of the most common permission operations is setting a file's executable permission. This is often done in the case of shell program files, which are discussed in Chapters 12 and 16. The executable permission indicates a file contains executable instructions and can be directly run by the system. In the next example, the file **lsc** has its executable permission set and then executed:

```
$ chmod u+x lsc
$ lsc
main.c lib.c
$
```

In addition to the read/write/execute permissions, you can also set ownership permissions for executable programs. Normally, the user who runs a program owns it while it is running, even though the program file itself may be owned by another user. The Set User ID permission allows the original owner of the program to own it always, even while another user is running the program. For example, most software on the system is owned by the root user, but is run by ordinary users. Some such software may have to modify files owned by the root. In this case, the ordinary user would need to run that program with the root retaining ownership so the program could have the permissions to change those root-owned files. The Group ID permission works the same way, except for groups. Programs owned by a group retain ownership, even when run by users from another group. The program can then change the owner group's files.

To add both the User ID and Group ID permissions to a file, you use the **s** option. The following example adds the User ID permission to the **pppd** program, which is owned by the root user. When an ordinary user runs **pppd**, the root user retains ownership, allowing the **pppd** program to change root-owned files.

```
#   chmod +s /usr/sbin/pppd
```

The Set User ID and Set Group ID permissions show up as an *s* in the execute position of the owner and group segments. Set User ID and Group ID are essentially variations of the execute permission, *x*. Read, write, and User ID permission would be *rws* instead of just *rwx*.

```
# ls -l /usr/sbin/pppd
-rwsr-sr-x  1 root root  84604 Aug 14  1996 /usr/sbin/pppd
```

One other special permission provides efficient use of programs. The sticky bit instructs the system to keep a program in memory (on swap device) after it finishes execution. This is useful for small programs used frequently by many users. The sticky bit permission is *t*. The sticky bit shows up as a *t* in the execute position of the other permissions. A program with read and execute permission with the sticky bit would have its permissions displayed as *r-t*.

```
# chmod +t  /usr/X11R6/bin/xtetris
# ls -l /usr/X11R6/bin/xtetris
-rwxr-xr-t  1 root   root   27428 Nov 19  1996
/usr/X11R6/bin/xtetris
```

Absolute Permissions: Binary Masks

Instead of permission symbols, many users find it more convenient to use the absolute method. The *absolute method* changes all the permissions at once, instead of specifying one or the other. It uses a binary mask that references all the permissions in each category. The three categories, each with three permissions, conform to an octal binary format. Octal numbers have a base eight structure. When translated into a binary number, each octal digit becomes three binary digits. A binary number is a set of 1 and 0 digits. Three octal digits in a number translate into three sets of three binary digits, which is nine altogether—and the exact number of permissions for a file.

You can use the octal digits as a mask to set the different file permissions. Each octal digit applies to one of the user categories. You can think of the digits matching up with the permission categories from left to right, beginning with the owner category. The first octal digit applies to the owner category, the second to the group, and the third to the others category.

The actual octal digit you choose determines the read, write, and execute permissions for each category. At this point, you need to know how octal digits translate into their binary equivalents. The following table shows how the different octal digits, 0 through 7, translate into their three-digit binary equivalents. You can think of the octal digit first being translated into its binary form, and then each of those three binary digits being used to set the read, write, and execute permissions. Each binary digit is then matched up with a corresponding permission, again moving from left to right. If a binary digit is 0, the permission is turned off. If the binary digit is 1, the permission is turned on. The first binary digit sets the read permission on or off, the second sets the write permission, and

ENVIRONMENTS

the third sets the execute permission. For example, an octal digit 6 translates into the binary digits 110. This would set the read and write permission on, but set the execute permission off.

Octal	Binary
0	000
1	001
2	010
3	011
4	100
5	101
6	110
7	111

When dealing with a binary mask, you need to specify three digits for all three categories, as well as their permissions. This makes a binary mask less versatile than the permission symbols. To set the owner execute permission on and the write permission off for the **mydata** file, as well as retain the read permission, you need to use the octal digit 5 (101). At the same time, you need to specify the digits for group and other users access. If these categories are to retain read access, you need the octal number 4 for each (100). This gives you three octal digits, 544, which translate into the binary digits 101 100 100.

```
$ chmod 544 mydata
```

One of the most common uses of the binary mask is to set the execute permission. As you learned in Chapter 11, you can create files that contain Linux commands, and these files are called shell scripts. To have the commands in a shell script executed, you must first indicate the file is executable—that it contains commands the system can execute. You can do this in several ways, one of which is to set the executable permission on the shell script file. Suppose you just completed a shell script file and you need to give it executable permission to run it. You also want to retain read and write permission, but deny any access by the group or other users. The octal digit 7 (111) will set all three permissions, including execute (you can also add 4-read, 2-write, and 1-execute to get 7). Using 0 for the group and other users denies them access. This gives you the digits 700, which are equivalent to the binary digits 111 000 000. In the next example, the owner permission for the **myprog** file is set to include execute permission:

```
$ chmod 700 myprog
```

If you want others to be able to execute and read the file, but not change it, you can set the read and execute permissions and turn off the write permission with the digit 5 (101). In this case, you would use the octal digits 755, having the binary equivalent of 111 101 101.

```
$ chmod 755 myprog
```

A simple way to calculate the octal number makes use of the fact that any number used for permissions will be a combination derived from adding in decimal terms the numbers 4, 2, and 1. Use 4 for read permission, 2 for write, and 1 for execute. The read, write, execute permission is simply the addition of 4 + 2 + 1 to get 7. The read and execute permission adds 4 and 1, to get 5. You can use this method to calculate the octal number for each category. To get 755, you would add 4 + 2 + 1 for the user read, write, and execute permission, 4 + 1 for the group read and execute permission, and 4 + 1 again for the other read and execute permission.

For the ownership and sticky bit permissions, you add another octal number to the beginning of the octal digits. The octal digit for User ID permission is 4 (100); for Group ID, it is 2 (010); and for the sticky bit, it is 1 (001). The following example sets the User ID permission to the **pppd** program, along with read and execute permissions for the owner, group, and others:

```
#   chmod 4555 /usr/sbin/pppd
```

The following example sets the sticky bit for the xtetris program:

```
# chmod 1755  /usr/X11R6/bin/xtetris
```

The next example would set both the sticky bit and the User ID permission on the **xman** program. The permission 5755 has the binary equivalent of 101 111 101 101.

```
# chmod 5755 /usr/X11R6/bin/xman
# ls -l /usr/X11R6/bin/xman
-rwsr-xr-t   1 root      root           44364 Mar 26 04:28
/usr/X11R6/bin/xman
```

Directory Permissions

You can also set permissions on directories. The read permission set on a directory allows the list of files in a directory to be displayed. The execute permission enables a user to change to that directory. The write permission enables a user to create and remove his or her files in that directory. If you allow other users to have write permission on a directory, they can add their own files to it. When you create a directory, it is automatically given read, write, and execute permission for the owner. You may list the files in that directory, change to it, and create files in it.

Like files, directories have sets of permissions for the owner, the group, and all other users. Often, you may want to allow other users to change to and list the files in one of your directories, but not let them add their own files to it. In this case, you would set read and execute permissions on the directory, but not write permission. This would allow other users to change to the directory and list the files in it, but not to create new files or to copy any of their files into it. The next example sets read and execute permission for the group for the **thankyou** directory, but removes the write permission. Members of the group may enter the **thankyou** directory and list the files there, but they may not create new ones.

```
$ chmod g+rx-w letters/thankyou
```

Just as with files, you can also use octal digits to set a directory permission. To set the same permissions as in the previous example, you would use the octal digits 750, which have the binary equivalents of 111 101 000.

```
$ chmod 750 letters/thankyou
```

As you know, the **ls** command with the **-1** option will list all files in a directory. To list only the information about the directory itself, add a **d** modifier. In the next example, **ls -ld** displays information about the **thankyou** directory. Notice the first character in the permissions list is *d*, indicating it is a directory.

```
$ ls -ld thankyou
drwxr-x---  2  chris 512 Feb 10 04:30  thankyou
```

If you have files you want other users to have access to, you not only need to set permissions for that file, you also must make sure the permissions are set for the directory in which the file is located. Another user, in order to access your file, must first access the file's directory. The same applies to parents of directories. Although a directory may give permission to others to access it, if its parent directory denies access, the directory cannot be reached. In this respect, you must pay close attention to your directory tree. To provide access to a directory, all other directories above it in the directory tree must also be accessible to other users.

Changing a File's Owner or Group: chown and chgrp

Although other users may be able to access a file, only the owner can change its permissions. If, however, you want to give some other user control over one of your file's permissions, you can change the owner of the file from yourself to the other user. The **chown** command transfers control over a file to another user. This command takes as its first argument the name of the other user. Following the user name, you can list the files you are giving up. In the next example, the user gives control of the **mydata** file to Robert:

```
$ chown robert mydata
$ ls -l mydata
-rw-r--r--  1  robert weather 207  Feb  20 11:55  mydata
```

You can also, if you wish, change the group for a file, using the **chgrp** command. **chgrp** takes as its first argument the name of the new group for a file or files. Following the new group name, you list the files you want changed to that group. In the next example, the user changes the group name for **today** and **weekend** to the **forecast** group. The **ls -l** command then reflects the group change.

```
$ chgrp forecast today weekend
$ ls -l
-rw-r--r--  1  chris weather 207  Feb  20 11:55  mydata
-rw-rw-r--  1  chris forecast 568  Feb  14 10:30  today
-rw-rw-r--  1  chris forecast 308  Feb  17 12:40  weekend
```

You can combine the **chgrp** operation in the **chown** command by attaching a group to the new owner with a colon, as shown here:

```
$ chown larisa:storm today
$ ls -l
-rw-r--r-- 1 larisa storm 568 Feb 14 10:30 today
```

The Complete Reference

Linux

Chapter 13

Shell Configuration

Four different major shells are commonly used on Linux systems: the Bourne Again shell (BASH), the Public Domain Korn shell (PDKSH), the TCSH shell, and the Z-shell. The BASH shell is an advanced version of the Bourne shell, which includes most of the advanced features developed for the Korn shell and the C-shell. TCSH is an enhanced version of the C-shell, originally developed for BSD versions of UNIX. PDKSH is a subset of the UNIX Korn shell, whereas the Z-shell is an enhanced version of the Korn shell. Although their UNIX counterparts differ greatly, the Linux shells share many of the same features. In UNIX, the Bourne shell lacks many capabilities found in the other UNIX shells. In Linux, however, the BASH shell incorporates all the advanced features of the Korn shell and C-shell, as well as the TCSH shell. All four shells are available for your use, though the BASH shell is the default.

So far, all examples in this book have used the BASH shell. You log into your default shell, but you can change to another shell by entering its name. **tcsh** invokes the TCSH shell, **bash** the BASH shell, **ksh** the PDKSH shell, and **zsh** the Zshell. You can leave a shell with the CTRL-D or **exit** command. You only need one type of shell to do your work. This chapter describes common features of the BASH shell, such as history and aliases, as well as how to configure the shell to your own needs using shell variables and initialization files. The other shells share many of the same features, and use similar variables and initialization files.

Command and Filename Completion

The BASH command line has a built-in feature that performs command and filename completion. If you enter an incomplete pattern as a command or filename argument, you can then press the TAB key to activate the command and filename completion feature, which completes the pattern. If more than one command or file has the same prefix, the shell simply beeps and waits for you to add enough characters to select a unique command or filename. In the next example, the user issues a **cat** command with an incomplete filename. Upon pressing the TAB key, the system searches for a match and, when it finds one, fills in the filename. The user can then press ENTER to execute the command.

```
$ cat pre tab
$ cat preface
```

The shell can also perform filename completion to list the partially matching files in your current directory. If you press ESC followed by a question mark, ESC-?, the shell lists all filenames matching the incomplete pattern. In the next example, the ESC-? after the incomplete filename generates a list of possible filenames. The shell then redraws the command line, and you can type in the complete name of the file you want, or type in distinguishing characters and press the TAB key to have the filename completed.

```
$ ls
document docudrama
$ cat doc escape ?
document
docudrama
$ cat docudrama
```

Command Line Editing

The BASH shell has built-in command line editing capabilities that enable you to easily modify commands you have entered before executing them. If you make a spelling mistake when entering a command, rather than reentering the entire command, you can use the editing operations to correct the mistake before executing the command. This is most helpful for commands that use arguments with lengthy pathnames. The command line editing operations are a subset of the Emacs editing commands (see Table 13-1). You can use CTRL-F or the RIGHT ARROW key to move forward a character, and the CTRL-B or the LEFT ARROW key to move back a character. CTRL-D or DEL deletes the character the cursor is on. To add text, you move the cursor to where you want to insert text and type in the new characters. At any time, you can press ENTER to execute the command.

Note   *As described in the next section, you can also use the command line editing operations to modify history events—previous commands you have entered.*

Command-Line Editing	
CTRL-B or LEFT ARROW	Moves left one character (backward to the previous character)
CTRL-F or RIGHT ARROW	Moves right one character (forward to the next character)
CTRL-A	Moves to the beginning of a line
CTRL-A	Moves to the end of a line

Table 13-1.   *Command Line Editing, History Commands, and History Event References*

Command-Line Editing

ESC-F	Moves forward one word
ESC-B	Moves backward one word
DEL	Deletes the character the cursor is on
BACKSPACE or CTRL-H	Deletes the character before the cursor
CTRL-D	Deletes the character after the cursor
CTRL-K	Removes (kills) the remainder of a line

History Commands

CTRL-N or DOWN ARROW	Moves down to the next event in the history list
CTRL-P or UP ARROW	Moves up to the previous event in the history list
ESC-<	Moves to the beginning of the history event list
ESC->	Moves to the end of the history event list
ESC-TAB	History of event matching and completion
fc *event-reference*	Edits an event with the standard editor and then executes it

    options

-l	List recent history events; same as **history** command
-e *editor event-reference*	Invokes a specified editor to edit a specific event

History Event References

! *event num*	References an event with an event number
! *characters*	References an event with beginning characters
!? *pattern* **?**	References an event with a pattern in the event
! *-event num*	References an event with an offset from the first event
! *num-num*	References a range of events

Table 13-1. *Command Line Editing, History Commands, and History Event References* (continued)

History

In the BASH shell, the *history utility* keeps a record of the most recent commands you have executed. The commands are numbered starting at 1 and a limit exists to the number of commands remembered—the default is 500. The history utility is a kind of short-term memory, keeping track of the most recent commands you have executed. To see the set of your most recent commands, type **history** on the command line and press ENTER. A list of your most recent commands is then displayed, preceded by a number.

```
$ history
1 cp mydata today
2 vi mydata
3 mv mydata reports
4 cd reports
5 ls
```

Each of these commands is technically referred to as an "event." An *event* describes an action that has been taken—a command that has been executed. The events are numbered according to their sequence of execution. The most recent event has the highest number. Each of these events can be identified by its number or beginning characters in the command.

The history utility enables you to reference a former event, placing it on your command line and enabling you to execute it. The easiest way to do this is to use the UP ARROW and DOWN ARROW keys to place history events on your command line, one at a time. You needn't display the list first with **history**. Pressing the UP ARROW key once places the last history event on your command line. Pressing it again places the next history event on your command line. Pressing the DOWN ARRROW key places the previous event on the command line.

The BASH shell also has a history event completion operation invoked by the ESC-TAB command. Much like standard command line completion, you enter part of the history event you want. Then you press ESC, followed by TAB. The event that matches the text you have entered is then located and used to complete your command line entry.

Note *If more than one history event matches what you have entered, you will hear a beep, and you can then enter more characters to help uniquely identify the event you want.*

You can edit the event displayed on your command line using the command line editing operations. The LEFT ARROW and RIGHT ARROW keys move you along the command line. You can insert text wherever you stop your cursor. With BACKSPACE and DEL, you can delete characters. Once the event is displayed on your command line, you can press ENTER to execute it.

You can also reference and execute history events using the ! history command. The ! is followed by a reference that identifies the command. The reference can be either the number of the event or a beginning set of characters in the event. In the next example, the third command in the history list is referenced first by number and then by the beginning characters:

```
$ !3
mv mydata reports
$ !mv
mv mydata reports
```

You can also reference an event using an offset from the end of the list. A negative number will offset from the end of the list to that event, thereby referencing it. In the next example, the fourth command, **cd mydata**, is referenced using a negative offset, and then executed. Remember that you are offsetting from the end of the list—in this case, event 5, up toward the beginning of the list, event 1. An offset of 4 beginning from event 5 places you at event 2.

```
$ !-4
vi mydata
```

If no event reference is used, then the last event is assumed. In the next example, the command ! by itself executes the last command the user executed—in this case, **ls**:

```
$ !
ls
mydata today reports
```

History Event Editing

You can also edit any event in the history list before you execute it. In the BASH shell, you can do this two ways. You can use the command line editor capability to reference and edit any event in the history list. You can also use a history **fc** command option to reference an event and edit it with the full Vi editor. Each approach involves two different editing capabilities. The first is limited to the commands in the command line editor, which edits only a single line with a subset of Emacs commands. At the same time, however, it enables you to reference events easily in the history list. The second approach invokes the standard Vi editor with all its features, but only for a specified history event.

With the command line editor, not only can you edit the current command, but you can also move to a previous event in the history list to edit and execute it. The CTRL-P command then moves you up to the prior event in the list. The CTRL-N command moves you down the list. The ESC-< command moves you to the top of the list, and the ESC-> command moves you to the bottom. You can even use a pattern to search for a given event. The slash followed by a pattern searches backward in the list, and the question mark followed by a pattern searches forward in the list. The **n** command repeats the search.

Once you locate the event you want to edit, you use the Emacs command line editing commands to edit the line. CTRL-D deletes a character. CTRL-F or the RIGHT ARROW moves you forward a character, and CTRL-B or the LEFT ARROW moves you back a character. To add text, you position your cursor and type in the characters you want. Table 13-1 lists the different commands for referencing the history list.

If you want to edit an event using a standard editor instead, you need to reference the event using the **fc** command and a specific event reference, such as an event number. The editor used is the one specified by the shell in the **EDITOR** variable. This serves as the default editor for the **fc** command. You can assign to the **EDITOR** variable a different editor if you wish, such as **emacs** instead of **vi**. The next example will edit the fourth event, **cd reports**, with the standard editor and then execute the edited event:

```
$ fc 4
```

You can select more than one command at a time to be edited and executed by referencing a range of commands. You select a range of commands by indicating an identifier for the first command followed by an identifier for the last command in the range. An identifier can be the command number or the beginning characters in the command. In the next example, the range of commands 2 through 4 are edited and executed, first using event numbers and then using beginning characters in those events:

```
$ fc 2 4
$ fc vi c
```

fc uses the default editor specified in the **FCEDIT** special variable. Usually, this is the Vi editor. If you want to use the Emacs editor instead, you use the **-e** option and the term **emacs** when you invoke **fc**. The next example will edit the fourth event, **cd reports**, with the Emacs editor and then execute the edited event:

```
$ fc -e emacs 4
```

Configuring History: HISTFILE and HISTSAVE

The number of events saved by your system is kept in a special system variable called **HISTSIZE**. By default, this is usually set to 500. You can change this to another number by simply assigning a new value to **HISTSIZE**. In the next example, the user changes the number of history events saved to 10 by resetting the **HISTSIZE** variable:

```
$ HISTSIZE=10
```

The actual history events are saved in a file whose name is held in a special variable called **HISTFILE**. By default, this file is the **.bash_history** file. You can change the file in which history events are saved, however, by assigning its name to the **HISTFILE** variable. In the next example, the value of **HISTFILE** is displayed. Then a new filename is assigned to it, **newhist**. History events are then saved in the **newhist** file.

```
$ echo $HISTFILE
.bash_history
$ HISTFILE="newhist"
$ echo $HISTFILE
newhist
```

Aliases

You use the **alias** command to create another name for a command. The **alias** command operates like a macro that expands to the command it represents. The alias does not literally replace the name of the command; it simply gives another name to that command. An **alias** command begins with the keyword **alias** and the new name for the command, followed by an equal sign and the command the alias will reference.

Note *No spaces can be around the equal sign used in the alias command.*

In the next example, **list** becomes another name for the **ls** command:

```
$ alias list=ls
$ ls
mydata today
$ list
mydata today
$
```

You can also use an alias to substitute for a command and its option, but you need to enclose both the command and the option within single quotes. Any command you alias that contains spaces must be enclosed in single quotes. In the next example, the alias **lss** references the **ls** command with its **-s** option, and the alias **lsa** references the **ls** command with the **-F** option. **ls** with the **-s** option lists files and their sizes in blocks, and the **ls** with the **-F** option places a slash before directory names. Notice single quotes enclose the command and its option.

```
$ alias lss='ls -s'
$ lss

mydata 14    today  6    reports  1
$ alias lsa='ls -F'
$ lsa
mydata today /reports
$
```

You may often use an alias to include a command name with an argument. If you execute a command that has an argument with a complex combination of special characters on a regular basis, you may want to alias it. For example, suppose you often list just your source code and object code files—those files ending in either a **.c** or **.o**. You would need to use as an argument for **ls** a combination of special characters such as ***.[co]**. Instead, you could alias **ls** with the ***.[co]** argument, giving it a simple name. In the next example, the user creates an alias called **lsc** for the command **ls*.[co]**:

```
$ alias lsc='ls *.[co]'
$ lsc
main.c main.o lib.c lib.o
```

You can also use the name of a command as an alias. This can be helpful in cases where you should only use a command with a specific option. In the case of the **rm**, **cp**, and **mv** commands, the **-i** option should always be used to ensure an existing file is not overwritten. Instead of constantly being careful to use the **-i** option each time you use one of these commands, the command name can be aliased to include the option. In the next example, the **rm**, **cp**, and **mv** commands have been aliased to include the **-i** option:

```
$ alias rm='rm -i'
$ alias mv='mv -i'
$ alias cp='cp -i'
```

The **alias** command by itself provides a list of all aliases that have been defined, showing the commands they represent. You can remove an alias by using the **unalias** command. In the next example, the user lists the current aliases and then removes the **lsa** alias:

```
$ alias
lsa=ls -F
list=ls
rm=rm -i
$ unalias lsa
```

Controlling Shell Operations

The BASH shell has several features that enable you to control the way different shell operations work. For example, setting the **noclobber** feature prevents redirection from overwriting files. You can turn these features on and off like a toggle, using the **set** command. The **set** command takes two arguments: an option specifying on or off and the name of the feature. To set a feature on, you use the **-o** option, and to set it off, you use the **+o** option. Here is the basic form:

```
$ set -o feature      turn the feature on
$ set +o feature      turn the feature off
```

Three of the most common features are described here: **ignoreeof**, **noclobber**, and **noglob**. Table 13-2 lists these different features, as well as the **set** command. Setting **ignoreeof** enables a feature that prevents you from logging out of the user shell with a CTRL-D. CTRL-D is not only used to log out of the user shell, but also to end user input entered directly into the standard input. CTRL-D is used often for the Mailx program or for utilities such as **cat**. You could easily enter an extra CTRL-D in such circumstances and accidentally log yourself out. The **ignoreeof** feature prevents such accidental logouts. In the next example, the **ignoreeof** feature is turned on using the **set** command with the **-o** option. The user can now only log out by entering the **logout** command.

```
$ set -o ignoreeof
$ ctrl-d
Use exit to logout
$
```

Setting **noclobber** enables a feature that safeguards existing files from redirected output. With the **noclobber** feature, if you redirect output to a file that already exists, the file will not be overwritten with the standard output. The original file is preserved.

BASH Shell Features

`$ set -+o` *feature*	Korn shell features are turned on and off with the **set** command; **-o** sets a feature on and **+o** turns it off: `$ set -o noclobber` *set noclobber on* `$ set +o noclobber` *set noclobber off*
`ignoreeof`	Disabled CTRL-D logout
`noclobber`	Does not overwrite files through redirection
`noglob`	Disables special characters used for filename expansion: *****, **?**, **~**, and **[ ]**

Table 13-2. *BASH Shell Special Features*

ENVIRONMENTS

Situations may occur in which you use, as the name for a file to hold the redirected output, a name you have already given to an existing file. The **noclobber** feature prevents you from accidentally overwriting your original file. In the next example, the user sets the **noclobber** feature on and then tries to overwrite an existing file, **myfile**, using redirection. The system returns an error message.

```
$ set -o noclobber
$ cat preface > myfile
myfile: file exists
$
```

At times, you may want to overwrite a file with redirected output. In this case, you can place an exclamation point after the redirection operator. This will override the **noclobber** feature, replacing the contents of the file with the standard output.

```
$ cat preface >! myfile
```

Setting **noglob** enables a feature that disables special characters in the user shell. The characters *****, **?**, **[ ]**, and **~** will no longer expand to matched filenames. This feature is helpful if you have special characters as part of the name of a file. In the next example, the user needs to reference a file that ends with the **?** character, **answers?**. First, the user turns off special characters using the **noglob** feature. Now the question mark on the command line is taken as part of the filename, not as a special character, and the user can reference the **answers?** file.

```
$ set -o noglob
$ ls answers?
answers?
```

Environment Variables and Subshells: export

When you log in to your account, Linux generates your user shell. Within this shell, you can issue commands and declare variables. You can also create and execute shell scripts. When you execute a shell script, however, the system generates a subshell. You then have two shells, the one you logged into and the one generated for the script. Within the script shell, you could execute another shell script, which would have its own shell. When a script has finished execution, its shell terminates and you return to the shell from which it was executed. In this sense, you can have many shells, each nested within the other. Variables you define within a shell are local to it. If you define a variable in a shell script, then, when the script is run, the variable is defined with that script's shell and is local to it. No other shell can reference that variable. In a sense, the variable is hidden within its shell.

You can define environment variables in all types of shells including the BASH, Z-shell, and TCSH shells. The strategy used to implement environment variables in the BASH shell, however, is different from that of the TCSH shell. In the BASH shell, environment variables are exported. That is to say, a copy of an environment variable is made in each subshell. For example, if the **EDITOR** variable is exported, a copy is automatically defined in each subshell for you. In the TCSH shell, on the other hand, an environment variable is defined only once and can be directly referenced by any subshell.

In the BASH shell, an environment variable can be thought of as a regular variable with added capabilities. To make an environment variable, you apply the **export** command to a variable you have already defined. The **export** command instructs the system to define a copy of that variable for each new shell generated. Each new shell will have its own copy of the environment variable. This process is called *exporting variables*. Thinking of exported environment variables as global variables is a mistake. A new shell can never reference a variable outside of itself. Instead, a copy of the variable with its value is generated for the new shell.

Note *You can think of exported variables as exporting their values to a shell, not to themselves. For those familiar with programming structures, exported variables can be thought of as a form of "call by value."*

Configuring Your Shell with Special Shell Variables

When you log in to your account, the system generates a shell for you. This shell is referred to as either your login shell or your user shell. When you execute scripts, you are generating subshells of your user shell. You can define variables within your user shell, and you can also define environment variables that can be referenced by any subshells you generate. Linux sets up special shell variables you can use to configure your user shell. Many of these special shell variables are defined by the system when you log in, but you define others yourself. See Table 13-3 for a list of the commonly used ones.

A reserved set of keywords is used for the names of these special variables. You should not use these keywords as the names of any of your own variable names. The special shell variables are all specified in uppercase letters, making them easy to identify. Shell feature variables are in lowercase letters. For example, the keyword **HOME** is used by the system to define the **HOME** variable. **HOME** is a special environment variable that holds the pathname of the user's **home** directory. On the other hand, the keyword **noclobber**, covered earlier in the chapter, is used to set the **noclobber** feature on or off.

Common Special Variables

Many of the special variables automatically defined and assigned initial values by the system when you log in can be changed, if you wish. Some special variables exist whose values should not be changed, however. For example, the **HOME** variable holds the pathname for your **home** directory. Commands, such as **cd,** reference the pathname in the **HOME** special variable to locate your **home** directory. Some of the more common of these special variables are described in this section. Other special variables are defined by the system and given an initial value that you are free to change. To do this, you redefine them and assign a new value. For example, the **PATH** variable is defined by the system and given an initial value; it contains the pathnames of directories where commands are located. Whenever you execute a command, the shell searches for it in these directories. You can add a new directory to be searched by redefining the **PATH** variable yourself, so it will include the new directory's pathname. Still other special variables exist that the system does not define. These are usually optional features, such as the **EXINIT** variable that enables you to set options for the Vi editor. Each time you log in, you must define and assign a value to such variables.

> **Note** *You can obtain a listing of the currently defined special variables using the **env** command. The **env** command operates like the **set** command, but it only lists special variables.*

You can automatically define special variables using special shell scripts called "initialization files." An *initialization file* is a specially named shell script executed

BASH Shell Special Variables	Description
HOME	Pathname for user's home directory
LOGNAME	Login name
USER	Login name
NNTPSERVER	NNTP News Server
SHELL	Pathname of program for type of shell you are using
PATH	List of pathnames for directories searched for executable commands
PS1	Primary shell prompt
PS2	Secondary shell prompt
IFS	Interfield delimiter symbol
MAIL	Name of mail file checked by mail utility for received messages
MAILCHECK	Interval for checking for received mail
MAILPATH	List of mail files to be check by mail for received messages
TERM	Terminal name
CDPATH	Pathnames for directories searched by **cd** command for subdirectories
EXINIT	Initialization commands for Ex/Vi editor

Table 13-3. *BASH Shell Special Variables*

whenever you enter a certain shell. You can edit the initialization file and place in it definitions and assignments for special variables. When you enter the shell, the initialization file will execute these definitions and assignments, effectively initializing special variables with your own values. For example, the BASH shell's **.bash_profile** file is an initialization file executed every time you log in. It contains definitions and assignments of special variables. However, the **.bash_profile** file is basically only a shell script, which you can edit with any text editor such as the Vi editor—changing, if you wish, the values assigned to special variables. Instead of the name **.bash_profile**, the BASH shell initialization file may be called **.profile**, as it is in OpenLinux.

In the BASH shell, all the special variables are designed to be environment variables. When you define or redefine a special variable, you also need to export it to make it an environment variable. This means any change you make to a special variable must be accompanied by an **export** command. You shall see that at the end of the login initialization file, **.bash_profile**, there is usually an **export** command for all the special variables defined in it.

The **HOME** variable contains the pathname of your **home** directory. Your **home** directory is determined by the system administrator when your account is created. The pathname for your **home** directory is automatically read into your **HOME** variable when you log in. In the next example, the **echo** command displays the contents of the **HOME** variable:

```
$ echo $HOME
/home/chris
```

The **HOME** variable is often used when you need to specify the absolute pathname of your **home** directory. In the next example, the absolute pathname of **reports** is specified using **HOME** for the **home** directory's path:

```
$ ls $HOME/reports
```

Some of the more common special variables are **SHELL**, **PATH**, **PS1**, **PS2**, and **MAIL**. The **SHELL** variable holds the pathname of the program for the type of shell you log in to. The **PATH** variable lists the different directories to be searched for a Linux command. The **PS1** and **PS2** variables hold the prompt symbols. The **MAIL** variable holds the pathname of your mailbox file. You can modify the values for any of them to customize your shell.

The **PATH** variable contains a series of directory paths separated by colons. Each time a command is executed, the paths listed in the **PATH** variable are searched one by one for that command. For example, the **cp** command resides on the system in the directory **/usr/bin**. This directory path is one of the directories listed in the **PATH** variable. Each time you execute the **cp** command, this path is searched and the **cp** command located. The system defines and assigns **PATH** an initial set of pathnames. In Linux, the initial pathnames are **/usr/bin** and **usr/sbin**.

The shell can execute any executable file, including programs and scripts you have created. For this reason, the **PATH** variable can also reference your working directory, so if you want to execute one of your own scripts or programs in your working directory, the shell can locate it. No spaces can be between the pathnames in the string. A colon with no pathname specified references your working directory. Usually, a single colon is placed at the end of the pathnames as an empty entry specifying your working directory. For example, the pathname **/usr/bin:/usr/sbin:** references three directories: **/usr/bin**, **/usr/sbin**, and your current working directory.

```
$ echo $PATH
/usr/bin:/usr/sbin:
```

You can add any new directory path you want to the **PATH** variable. This can be useful if you have created several of your own Linux commands using shell scripts. You could place these new shell script commands in a directory you created and then add that directory to the **PATH** list. Then, no matter what directory you are in, you can execute one of your shell scripts. The **PATH** variable will contain the directory for that script, so that directory will be searched each time you issue a command.

You add a directory to the **PATH** variable with a variable assignment. You can execute this assignment directly in your shell. In the next example, the user **chris** adds a new directory, called **mybin,** to the **PATH**. Although you could carefully type in the complete pathnames listed in **PATH** for the assignment, you can also use an evaluation of **PATH**, **$PATH**, in their place. In this example, an evaluation of **HOME** is also used to designate the user's **home** directory in the new directory's pathname. Notice the empty entry between two colons, which specifies the working directory.

```
$ PATH=$PATH:$HOME/mybin:
$ export PATH
$ echo $PATH
/usr/bin:/usr/sbin::/home/chris/mybin
```

If you add a directory to **PATH** yourself while you are logged in, the directory would be added only for the duration of your login session. When you log back in, the login initialization file, **.bash_profile**, would again initialize your **PATH** with its original set of directories. The **.bash_profile** file is described in detail a bit later in this chapter. To add a new directory to your **PATH** permanently, you need to edit your **.bash_profile** file and find the assignment for the **PATH** variable. Then, you simply insert the directory, preceded by a colon, into the set of pathnames assigned to **PATH**.

The **PS1** and **PS2** variables contain the primary and secondary prompt symbols, respectively. The primary prompt symbol for the BASH shell is a dollar sign, **$**. You can change the prompt symbol by assigning a new set of characters to the **PS1** variable. In the next example, the shell prompt is changed to the **->** symbol:

```
$ PS1="->"
-> export PS1
->
```

You can change the prompt to be any set of characters, including a string, as shown in the next example:

```
$ PS1="Please enter a command: "
Please enter a command: export PS1
Please enter a command: ls
mydata /reports
Please enter a command:
```

The **PS2** variable holds the secondary prompt symbol, which is used for commands that take several lines to complete. The default secondary prompt is **>**. The added command lines begin with the secondary prompt instead of the primary prompt. You can change the secondary prompt just as easily as the primary prompt, as shown here:

```
$ PS2="@"
```

Like the TCSH shell, the BASH shell provides you with a predefined set of codes you can use to configure your prompt. With them you can make the time, your user name, or your directory pathname a part of your prompt. You can even have your prompt display the history event number of the current command you are about to enter. Each code is preceded by a \ symbol. **\w** represents the current working directory, **\t** the time, and **\u** your user name. **\!** will display the next history event number. In the next example, the user adds the current working directory to the prompt:

```
$ PS1="\w $"
/home/dylan $
```

The codes must be included within a quoted string. If no quotes exist, the code characters are not evaluated and are themselves used as the prompt. **PS1=\w** sets the prompt to the characters **\w**, not the working directory. The next example incorporates both the time and the history event number with a new prompt:

```
$ PS1="\t \! ->"
```

The following table lists the codes for configuring your prompt.

Prompt Codes	Description
\!	Current history number.
\$	Use **$** as prompt for all users except the root user, which has the **#** as its prompt.
\d	Current date.
\s	Shell currently active.
\t	Time of day.
\u	User name.
\w	Current working directory.

If **CDPATH** is undefined, then when the **cd** command is given a directory name as its argument, it searches only the current working directory for that name. If **CDPATH** is defined, however, **cd** also searches the directories listed in **CDPATH** for that directory name. If the directory name is found, **cd** changes to that directory. This is helpful if you are working on a project in which you constantly must change to directories in another part of the file system. To change to a directory that has a pathname very different from the one you are in, you would need to know the full pathname of that directory. Instead, you could simply place the pathname of that directory's parent in **CDPATH**. Then, **cd** automatically searches the parent directory, finding the name of the directory you want.

Note — *Notice that you assign to **CDPATH** the pathname of the parent of the directory you want to change to, not the pathname of the directory itself.*

Using the **HOME** variable to specify the user's home directory part of the path in any new pathname added to **CDPATH** is advisable. This is because the pathname for your home directory could possibly be changed by the system administrator during a reorganization of the file system. **HOME** will always hold the current pathname of the user's home directory. In the next example, the pathname **/home/chris/letters** is specified with **$HOME/letters**:

$ CDPATH=$CDPATH:$HOME/letters
$ export CDPATH
$ echo $CDPATH
:/home/chris/letters

Several shell special variables are used to set values used by network applications, such as Web browsers or newsreaders. **NNTPSERVER** is used to set the value of a remote news server accessible on your network. If you are using an ISP, the ISP usually provides a news server you can access with your newsreader applications. However, you first have to provide your newsreaders with the Internet address of the news server. This is the role of the **NNTPSERVER**. News servers on the Internet usually use the NNTP protocol. **NNTPSERVER** should hold the address of such a news server. For many ISPs, the news server address is a domain name that begins with **nntp**. The following example assigns the news server address **nntp.myservice.com** to the **NNTPSERVER** special variables. Newsreader applications automatically obtain the news server address from **NNTPSERVER**. Usually, this assignment is placed in the shell initialization file, **.bash_profile**, so it is automatically set each time a user logs in.

```
NNTPSERVER=nntp.myservice.com
export NNTPSERVER
```

Other special variables are used for specific applications. The **KDEDIR** variable holds the pathname for the KDE Desktop program files. This is usually **/opt/kde** but, at the time of installation, you can choose to install KDE in a different directory and then change the value of **KDEDIR** accordingly.

```
export KDEDIR=/opt/kde
```

Configuring Your Login Shell: .bash_profile

The **.bash_profile** file is the BASH shell's login initialization file, which can also be named **.profile**. It is a script file that is automatically executed whenever a user logs in. The file contains shell commands that define special environment variables used to manage your shell. They may be either redefinitions of system-defined special variables or definitions of user-defined special variables. For example, when you log in, your user shell needs to know what directories hold Linux commands. It will reference the **PATH** variable to find the pathnames for these directories. However, first, the **PATH** variable must be assigned those pathnames. In the **.bash_profile** file, an assignment operation does just this. Because it is in the **.bash_profile** file, the assignment is executed automatically when the user logs in.

Special variables also need to be exported, using the **export** command, to make them accessible to any subshells you may enter. You can export several variables in one **export** command by listing them as arguments. Usually, at the end of the **.bash_profile** file is an **export** command with a list of all the variables defined in the file. If a variable is missing from this list, you may be unable to access it. Notice the **export** command at the end of the **.profile** file in the example described next. You can also combine the assignment and **export** command in to one operation as show here for **NNTPSEVER**:

```
export NNTPSERVER=nntp.myservice.com
```

A copy of the standard **.bash_profile** file provided for you when your account is created is listed in the next example. Notice how **PATH** is assigned, as is the value of **$HOME**. Both **PATH** and **HOME** are system special variables the system has already defined. **PATH** holds the pathnames of directories searched for any command you enter, and **HOME** holds the pathname of your **home** directory. The assignment **PATH=$PATH:$HOME/bin** has the effect of redefining **PATH** to include your **bin** directory within your **home** directory. So, your **bin** directory will also be searched for any commands, including ones you create yourself, such as scripts or programs. Notice **PATH** is then exported, so it can be accessed by any subshells. Should you want to have your **home** directory searched also, you can use any text editor to modify this line in your **.bash_profile** file to **PATH=$PATH:$HOME\bin:$HOME**, adding **:$HOME** at the end. In fact, you can change this entry to add as many directories as you want searched.

.bash_profile

```
# .bash_profile

# Get the aliases and functions
if [ -f ~/.bashrc ]; then
      . ~/.bashrc
fi

# User specific environment and startup programs

PATH=$PATH:$HOME/bin
BASH_ENV=$HOME/.bashrc
USERNAME=""

export USERNAME BASH_ENV PATH
```

Your Linux system also has its own profile file that it executes whenever any user logs in. This system initialization file is simply called **profile** and is found in the **/etc** directory, **/etc/profile**. This file contains special variable definitions the system needs to provide for each user. A copy of the system's **.profile** file follows. Notice how **PATH** is redefined to include the **/usr/X11R6/bin** directory. This is the directory that holds the X-Windows commands you execute when using the desktop. Also, **PATH** includes the pathname for the KDE Desktop programs, **/opt/kde/bin**. **HISTFILE** is also redefined to include a larger number of history events. An entry has been added here for the **NNTPSERVER** variable. Normally, a news server address is a value that needs to be set for all users. Such assignments should be made in the system's **/etc/profile** file by the system administrator, rather than in each individual user's own **.bash_profile** file. The **/etc/profile** file also executes any scripts in the directory **/etc/profile.d**. This design allows for a more modular structure. Rather than make entries by editing the **/etc/profile** file, you can just add a script to the **profile.d** directory. The scripts for the BASH shell have the extension **.sh**. For example, the **kde.sh** script in the **profile.d** directory checks for a definition of the **KDEDIR** variable and makes one if none is in effect.

/etc/profile

```
# /etc/profile

# System wide environment and startup programs
# Functions and aliases go in /etc/bashrc

PATH="$PATH:/usr/X11R6/bin:/opt/kde/bin:"
PS1="[\u@\h \W]\\$ "

ulimit -c 1000000
```

```
if [ `id -gn` = `id -un` -a `id -u` -gt 14 ]; then
    umask 002
else
    umask 022
fi

USER=`id -un`
LOGNAME=$USER
MAIL="/var/spool/mail/$USER"

HOSTNAME=`/bin/hostname`
HISTSIZE=1000
HISTFILESIZE=1000
NNTPSERVER=nntp.myservice.com
export PATH PS1 HOSTNAME HISTSIZE HISTFILESIZE MAIL NNTPSERVER

for i in /etc/profile.d/*.sh ; do
  if [ -x $i ]; then
      . $i
  fi
done

unset i
```

Your **.bash_profile** initialization file is a text file that can be edited by a text editor, like any other text file. You can easily add new directories to your **PATH** by editing .bash_profile and using editing commands to insert a new directory pathname in the list of directory pathnames assigned to the **PATH** variable. You can even add new variable definitions. If you do so, however, be sure to include the new variable's name in the **export** command's argument list. For example, if your **.bash_profile** file does not have any definition of the **EXINIT** variable, you can edit the file and add a new line that assigns a value to **EXINIT**. The definition **EXINIT='set nu ai'** will configure the Vi editor with line numbering and indentation. You then need to add **EXINIT** to the **export** command's argument list. When the **.bash_profile** file executes again, the **EXINIT** variable will be set to the command **set nu ai**. When the Vi editor is invoked, the command in the **EXINIT** variable will be executed, setting the line number and auto-indent options automatically.

In the following example, the user's **.bash_profile** has been modified to include definitions of **EXINIT** and redefinitions of **PATH**, **CDPATH**, **PS1**, and **HISTSIZE**. The **PATH** variable has **$HOME:** added to its value. **$HOME** is a variable that evaluates to the user's **home** directory and the ending colon specifies the current working directory, enabling you to execute commands that may be located in either the **home** directory or the working directory. The redefinition of **HISTSIZE** reduces the number of history events saved, from 1,000 defined in the system's **.profile** file, to 30. The redefinition of the **PS1** special variable changes the prompt to include the pathname of the current working directory. Any changes you make to special variables within your

.bash_profile file override those made earlier by the system's **.profile** file. All these special variables are then exported with the **export** command.

.bash_profile

```
# .bash_profile

# Get the aliases and functions
if [ -f ~/.bashrc ];
 then
    . ~/.bashrc
fi
# User-specific environment and startup programs
PATH=$PATH:$HOME/bin:$HOME:
ENV=$HOME/.bashrc
USERNAME=""
CDPATH=$CDPATH:$HOME/bin:$HOME
HISTSIZE=30
NNTPSERVER=nntp.myserver.com
EXINIT='set nu ai'
PS1="\w \$"
export USERNAME ENV PATH CDPATH HISTSIZE EXINIT PS1
```

Although **.profile** is executed each time you log in, it is not automatically reexecuted after you make changes to it. The **.profile** file is an initialization file that is *only* executed whenever you log in. If you want to take advantage of any changes you make to it without having to log out and log in again, you can reexecute **.profile** with the dot (.) command. **.profile** is a shell script and, like any shell script, can be executed with the **.** command.

 $ **.bash_profile**

Configuring the BASH Shell: .bashrc

The **.bashrc** file is a configuration file executed each time you enter the BASH shell or generate any subshells. If the BASH shell is your login shell, **.bashrc** is executed along with your **.bash_login** file when you log in. If you enter the BASH shell from another shell, the **.bashrc** file is automatically executed, and the variable and alias definitions it contains will be defined. If you enter a different type of shell, then the configuration file for that shell will be executed instead. For example, if you were to enter the TCSH shell with the **tcsh** command, then the **.tcshrc** configuration file is executed instead of **.bashrc**.

The **.bashrc** shell configuration file is actually executed each time you generate a BASH shell, such as when you run a shell script. In other words, each time a subshell is created, the **.bashrc** file is executed. This has the effect of exporting any local variables or aliases you have defined in the **.bashrc** shell initialization file. The **.bashrc** file usually contains the definition of aliases and any feature variables used to turn on

shell features. Aliases and feature variables are locally defined within the shell. But the
.bashrc file defines them in every shell. For this reason, the **.bashrc** file usually holds
such aliases as those defined for the **rm**, **cp**, and **mv** commands. The next example is a
.bashrc file with many of the standard definitions:

.bashrc

```
# Source global definitions
if [ -f /etc/bashrc ];
 then
      . /etc/bashrc
fi
set  -o ignoreeof
set  -o noclobber
alias rm 'rm -i'
alias mv 'mv -i'
alias cp 'cp -i'
```

Linux systems usually contain a system **.bashrc** file executed for all users. This may
contain certain global aliases and features needed by all users whenever they enter a
BASH shell. This is located in the **/etc** directory, **/etc/.bashrc**. A user's own **.bashrc** file,
located in the **home** directory, contains commands to execute this system **.bashrc** file.
The **./etc/bashrc** command in the previous example of **.bashrc** does just that. You
can add any commands or definitions of your own to your **.bashrc** file. If you have
made changes to **.bashrc** and you want them to take effect during your current login
session, you need to reexecute the file with either the **.** or the **source** command.

```
$ . .bashrc
```

The BASH Shell Logout File: .bash_logout

The **.bash_logout** file is also a configuration file, which is executed when the user logs
out. It is designed to perform any operations you want done whenever you log out.
Instead of variable definitions, the **.bash_logout** file usually contains shell commands
that form a kind of shutdown procedure—actions you always want taken before you
log out. One common logout command is to clear the screen and then issue a farewell
message.

As with **.bash_profile**, you can add your own shell commands to **.bash_logout**. In
fact, the **.bash_logout** file is not automatically set up for you when your account is first
created. You need to create it yourself, using the Vi or Emacs editor. You could then
add a farewell message or other operations. In the next example, the user has a **clear**
and an **echo** command in the **.bash_logout** file. When the user logs out, the **clear**
command clears the screen, and then the **echo** command displays the message
"Good-bye for now."

.bash_logout

```
clear
echo "Good-bye for now"
```

Other Initialization and Configuration Files

Each type of shell has is its own set of initialization and configuration files. The TCSH shell used **.login**, **.tcshrc**, and **.logout** files in place of **.bash_profile**, **.bashrc**, and **.bash_logout**. The Z-shell has several initialization files: **.zshenv**, **.zlogin**, **.zprofile**, **.zschrc**, and **.zlogout**. See Table 13-4 for a listing. Check the Man pages for each shell to see how they are usually configured. When you install a shell, default versions of these files are automatically placed in the users' home directories. Except for the TCSH shell, all shells use much the same syntax for variable definitions and assigning values (TCSH uses a slightly different syntax, described in its Man pages).

BASH Shell	Function
.bash_profile	Login initialization file
.bashrc	BASH shell configuration file
.bash_logout	Logout name
TCSH Shell	
.login	Login initialization file
.tcshrc	TCSH shell configuration file
.logout	Logout file
Z-shell	
.zshenv	Shell login file (first read)
.zprofile	Login initialization file
.zlogin	Shell login file
.zshrc	Z-shell shell configuration file
.zlogout	Logout file
PDKSH Shell	
.profile	Login initialization file
.kshrc	PDKSH shell configuration file

Table 13-4. *Shell Configuration Files*

Configuration Directories and Files

Applications often install configuration files in a user's **home** directory that contain specific configuration information, which tailors the application to the needs of that particular user. This may take the form of a single configuration file that begins with a period, or a directory that contains several configuration files. The directory name will also begin with a period. For example, Netscape installs a directory called **.netscape** in the user's **home** directory that contains configuration files. On the other hand, the mailx application use a single file called **.mailrc** to hold alias and feature settings set up by the user. Most single configuration files end in the letters **rc**. **ftp** uses a file called **.netrc**. Most newsreaders use a file called **.newsrc**. Entries in configuration files are usually set by the application, though you can usually make entries directly by editing the file. Applications have their own set of special variables to which you can define and assign values. Of particular interest is the **.wm_style** file that holds the name of the Window manager the user wants to use. You can edit and change the name there to that of another window manager to start up a new one. You can list the configuration files in your **home** directory with the **ls -a** command.

ENVIRONMENTS

The Complete Reference

Linux

Part III

Internet

The Complete Reference

Chapter 14

Mail Clients

Your Linux system has electronic mail clients that enable you to send messages to other users on your system or other systems, such as those on the Internet. You can send and receive messages in a variety of ways, depending on the type of mail client you use. Although all electronic mail utilities perform the same basic tasks of receiving and sending messages, they tend to have different interfaces. Some mail clients operate on a desktop, such as KDE or Gnome. Others run on any X Windows window managers. Several popular mail clients were designed to use a screen-based interface and can run from only the command line. Other traditional mail clients were developed for just the command line interface, which requires you to type your commands. Most mail clients described here are included in standard Linux distributions and come in a standard RPM package for easy installation. For Web-based Internet mail services, such as Hotmail, Lycos, and Yahoo, you use a Web browser instead of a mail client to access mail accounts provided by those services. Table 14-1 lists several popular Linux mail clients.

Mail is transported to and from destinations using mail transport agents. sendmail and smail send and receive mail from destinations on the Internet or at other sites on a network (see Chapter 27). To send mail over the Internet, they use the Simple Mail Transport Protocol (SMTP). Most Linux distributions, such as Red Hat and OpenLinux, automatically install and configure sendmail for you. On starting up your system, you can send and receive messages over the Internet.

Mail Client	Description
KMail	The K Desktop mail client
Balsa, Gmail, GNOMail, Evolution, etc.	Gnome mail clients (see Table 14-2)
Netscape	Web browser–based mail client
exmh	X Windows Mail Handler mail client
GNUEmacs and XEmacs	Emacs mail clients
Pine	Mail client and newsreader
Mutt	Screen-based mail client
Elm	Screen-based mail client
Mail	Original Unix-based command line mail client
MH	Mail Handler command line mail client

Table 14-1. *Linux Mail Clients*

Local and Internet Addresses

Each user on a Linux system has a mail address, and whenever you send mail, you are required to provide the address of the user to whom you are sending the message. For users on your local Linux system, addresses can consist of only the user's login name. When sending messages to users on other systems, however, you need to know not only the login name, but also the address of the system they are on. Internet addresses require the system address to be uniquely identified.

Most systems have Internet addresses you can use to send mail. Internet addresses use a form of addressing called *domain addressing.* A system is assigned a domain name, which when combined with the system name, gives the system a unique address. This domain name is separated from the system name by a period and may be further qualified by additional domain names. Here is the syntax for domain addresses:

```
login-name@system-name.domain-name
```

Systems that are part of a local network are often given the same domain name. The domain name for both the **garnet** and **violet** systems at U.C. Berkeley is **berkeley.edu**. To send a message to **chris** on the **garnet** system, you simply include the domain name:

```
chris@garnet.berkeley.edu.
```

In the next example, a message is sent to **chris,** located on the garnet system, using domain addressing:

```
$ mail chris@garnet.berkeley.edu < mydata
```

Early domain names reflect that the Internet was first developed in the United States. They qualify Internet addresses by category, such as commercial, military, or educational systems. The domain name *.com* indicates a commercial organization, whereas *.edu* is used for educational institutions. As the Internet developed into a global network, a set of international domain names was established. These domain names indicate the country in which a system is located—for example, *.fr* represents France, *.jp* represents Japan, and *.us* represents the United States.

Signature Files: .signature

You can end your e-mail message with the same standard signature information, such as your name, Internet address or addresses, or farewell phrase. Having your signature information automatically added to your messages is helpful. To do so, you need to create a signature file in your **home** directory and enter your signature information in it. A *signature file* is a standard text file you can edit using any text editor. Mail clients such as KMail enable you to specify a file to function as your signature file. Others, such as Mail, expect the signature file to be named **.signature**.

MIME

MIME (the term stands for Multipurpose Internet Mail Extensions) is used to enable mail clients to send and receive multimedia files and files using different characters sets such as those for different languages. Multimedia files can be images, sound, or even video. Mail clients that support MIME can send binary files automatically as attachments to messages. MIME-capable mail clients maintain a file called **mailcap** that maps different types of MIME messages to applications on your system that can view or display them. For example, an image file will be mapped to an application that can display images. Your mail clients can then run that program to display the image message. A sound file will be mapped to an application that can play sound files on your speakers. Most mail clients have MIME capabilities built in and use their own version of the **mailcap** file. Others, like Elm, use a program called metamail that adds Pine support. MIME is not only used in mail clients. As noted in Chapters 8 and 9, both the KDE and Gnome file managers use MIME to map a file to a particular application so that you can launch the application directly from the file.

Applications are associated with binary files by means of the **mailcap** and **mime.types** files. The **mime.types** file defines different MIME types, associating a MIME type with a certain application. The **mailcap** file then associates each MIME type with a specified application. Your system maintains its own MIME types file, usually **/etc/mime.types**.

Entries in the MIME types file associate a MIME type and possible subtype of an application with a set of possible file extensions used for files that run on a given kind of application. The MIME type is usually further qualified by a subtype, separated from the major type by a slash. For example, a MIME type image can have several subtypes such as jpeg, gif, or tiff. A sample MIME type entry defining a MIME type for JPEG files is shown here. The MIME type is image/jpeg, and the list of possible file extensions is "jpeg jpg jpe."

```
image/jpeg      jpeg jpg jpe
```

The applications specified will depend on those available on your particular system. The MIME type is separated from the application with a semicolon. In many cases X Window System–based programs are specified. Comments are indicated with a #. An * used in a MIME subtype references all subtypes. The entry image/* would be used for an application that can run all types of image files. A formatting code, %s, is used to reference the attachment file that will be run on this application. Sample **mailcap** entries are shown here. The first associates all **image** files with the xv image viewer. The next two associate video and video MPEG files with the xanim application.

```
image/*; xv %s
video/*; xanim %s
video/mpeg; xanim %s
```

You can also create and edit MIME types on the Gnome and KDE desktops. For Gnome, use the Gnome Control Center's MIME types capplet. This capplet will list the MIME types defined for your system along with their associated filename extensions. Edit an entry to change the application and icon associated with that MIME type, that type of file. On KDE, use the KDE Control Center's File Association entry under File Browsing. This will list MIME types and their associated filename extensions. Select an entry to edit it and change the applications associated with it. KDE saves its MIME type information in a separate file called **mimelnk** in the KDE configuration directory.

Though you can create your own MIME types, a standard set already is in use. The types text, image, audio, video, application, multipart, and message, along with their subtypes, have already been defined for your system. You will find that commonly used file extensions such as **.tif** and **.jpg** for TIFF and JPEG image files are already associated with a MIME type and an application. Though you can easily change the associated application, it is best to keep the MIME types already installed. The current official MIME types are listed at the IANA Web site (**www.iana.org**) under the name Media Types, provided as part of their Assignment Services. You can access the media-types file directly on their FTP site at:

```
ftp.iana.org/in-notes/iana/assignments/media-types/
```

The K Desktop Mail Client: KMail

The K Desktop mail client, *KMail*, provides a full-featured GUI interface for composing, sending, and receiving mail messages. The KMail window displays three panes for folders, headers, and messages, as shown in Figure 14-1. The upper-left pane displays your mail folders. You have an inbox folder for received mail, an outbox folder for mail you have composed but have not sent yet, and a sent-mail folder for messages you have previously sent. You can create your own mail folders and save selected messages in them, if you wish. The top-right pane displays mail headers for the currently selected mail folder. You can use the scroll bar to the right to move through the list of headers. The headers are segmented according to fields, beginning with sender and subject. A color code is used to indicate read and unread messages. New messages are listed in red. Read messages are in green. A bullet symbol also appears at the beginning of unread message headers. To display a message, click its header. The message is then displayed in the large pane below the header list. You can also send and receive attachments, including binary files. Pictures and movies that are received are displayed using the appropriate K Desktop utility. If you right-click the message, a pop-up menu displays options for actions you may want to perform on it. You can move or copy it to another folder, or simply delete it. You can also compose a reply or forward the message.

Figure 14-1. *The K Desktop mail program*

The menus in the menu bar at the top of the window contain the commands and options you can use for managing your mail. An icon bar for commonly used mail commands is displayed below the menu bar. To get new mail, click the icon showing a page with a question mark (?). To print a message, click the Printer icon. To save a message, click the Disk icon. To check your mail, click the Check Mail icon. If you hold the mouse over an icon, a short description of its function is displayed. The icon of an open book opens the KMail address book. Here, you can enter a list of e-mail addresses. Also, right-clicking a displayed message gives you the option of automatically adding its e-mail address to your address book. You can use the Help button or the Help menu to obtain more detailed descriptions of the different KMail features. The Help button opens the KMail Handbook, which provides easy reference to different operations.

You click the Blank Page icon to compose and send a new message. If you want to compose a reply, select the header of the message you want to reply to, and then click the icon showing a page with a single curved arrow. A message window opens with the To entry already filled with the sender's address, the From entry with your address, and the Subject line with the sender's subject with a preceding RE:. To forward a message, select the message's header and click the icon showing a page with two curved arrows.

When you compose a message, a new window opens with entries for the e-mail address, Carbon-copy (CC), and Subject. A button with three dots is placed next to address entries like From and CC. Clicking one of these buttons invokes your K address book, from which you can select an e-mail address. You enter the message in the body of the window. You can use any of the standard mouse-based editing capabilities to cut, copy, paste, and select text. All commands available to you for composing messages are listed in the menus in the menu bar at the top of the window. A button bar of commonly used functions is displayed just below the menu bar. To send the message, click the Envelope button. To attach a file, you can select the Attach entry in the Attach menu or click the Paper Clip button. This menu also has entries for inserting the text of files into the message or appending a signature file. Other composition features, such as the spell-checker and encryption, are also supported. The standard message window does not display all the header entries unless you select All from the View menu. You can also individually select the fields you want displayed. The Options menu enables you to mark a message as urgent or request a delivery confirmation.

To set up KMail for use with your mail accounts, you must enter account information. Select the Configure entry in the Settings menu. Several panels are available on the Settings window, which you can display by clicking their icons in the left column (see Figure 14-2). For accounts, you select the Network panel. Two sections are on this panel: one for sending mail and one for receiving mail. In the sending-mail section, enter the SMTP server you use. If you have an ISP or you are on a LAN, enter the server name for your network. The default is the sendmail utility on your own Linux system. In the receiving mail section, you can add any mail accounts you may have. You may have more than one mail account on mail servers maintained by your ISP or LAN. A configure window is displayed where you can enter login, password, and host information. The *host* is the name of the POP or IMAP server this particular account uses.

Gnome Mail Clients: Balsa, Gmail, Mahogany, and Others

Currently, several Gnome-based mail clients are under development, many of which you can currently use (see Table 14-2). These include Balsa, Mahogany, Gmail, GnoMail, Eucalyptus, Glacier, Pygmy, Spruce, and N-tool (both Balsa and Mahogany are discussed further). Check the Gnome Web site for more mail clients as they come out. Many are based on the gnome-mail client libraries (camel) currently under development, which provide support for standard mail operations. *Balsa* is a Gnome mail client with extensive features, though it can operate under any window manager, including KDE, as long as Gnome is installed on your system. The *Mahogany* mail client is a Gnome mail client that also has versions for other platforms. *Gmail* is meant to be a light and fast e-mail client, supporting basic mail operations, such as forwarding, replies, and

Figure 14-2. KMail configuration

mailboxes. GnoMail is yet another Gnome mail client that also uses the gnome-mailer libraries. Glacier is a GNU mail client with extensive MIME support. Eucalyptus is a MIME-compliant mail client that supports unlimited folders, addresses, filters, and multiple POP servers. Eucalyptus was previously implemented on the Amiga. Pygmy is a simple GNOME mail client written in the Python programming language that supports attachments and MIME message. The N-tool is a Gnome mail client with Japanese language support, providing standard features, including mailboxes and full MIME support. Spruce is a Gnome e-mail client with support for multiple accounts. LinPopUp is a port of WinPopUp that operates on Samba-connected networks and can send messages to users on Windows machines running WinPopUp. Evolution is an integrated mail client, calendar, and contact manager from Helix Code.

Balsa provides a full-featured GUI interface for composing, sending, and receiving mail messages. The Balsa window displays three panes for folders, headers, and messages, as shown in Figure 14-3. The left-side pane displays your mail folders. You initially have three folders: an inbox folder for received mail, an outbox folder for mail

Application	Description
Balsa	Balsa is an e-mail client for GNOME that supports POP3, IMAP, local folders, and multithreading.
Evolution	Evolution is a Helix Code integrated mail client, calendar, and contact manager.
Eucalyptus	Eucalyptus is an advanced MIME-compliant e-mail application.
Glacier	Glacier is an e-mail client for Gnome that supports MIME parsing.
Gmail	Gmail is an experimental folder-based e-mail system (using mysql).
GnoMail	GnoMail is a mail user agent that uses the gnome-mailer interface.
LinPopUp	LinPopUp is an X Window graphical port of Winpopup, running over Samba.
Mahogany	Mahogany is a cross-platform e-mail application.
N-tool	N-tool is a GUI Mail tool that supports the Japanese language (ISO-2022-JP).
Pygmy	Pygmy is a Gnome mail client written in the Python programming language.
Spruce	Spruce is an e-mail client with support for multiple accounts
Grin	Grin is a mail client with news reading features.
MMC	MMC is a Gnome mail client.
CSC Mail	CSC Mail is a mail client with support for multiple POP3 accounts and messaging.
Sonicmail	Sonicmail is a Gnome POP3 mail notifier applet.

Table 14-2.   *Gnome Mail Clients*

you have composed but have not sent yet, and a trash folder for messages you have deleted. You can also create your own mail folders in which you can store particular messages. To place a message in a folder you have created, click and drag the message header for that message to the folder.

The right side of the Balsa window consists of two panes. The top-right pane lists the message headers for the currently selected folder. Message headers are displayed showing the subject, sender, and date. An Envelope icon indicates an unread message, and a Trash Can icon indicates a message to be deleted. Headers are segmented into fields with buttons for the fields shown at the top of the pane. You can click these buttons to sort headers by different fields, such as subject or sender. To display a message, you click it. It is then displayed in the pane below the message headers. You can click the Right and Left Arrow icons in the icon bar to move through the header list.

To display message headers for a particular folder, you first must open that folder. Double-clicking the folder's icon both opens the folder and selects it, with its headers displayed. You can also single-click the folder's icon and select Open from the Mailbox menu. This opens the folder and displays a button for it in the bar separating the folder pane from the right-side panes. You can open several folders at once. Each will have its own button in the bar. To have an open folder's message header display, you can click its button in this middle bar. To close a folder, select it and then choose the Close entry on the Mailbox menu.

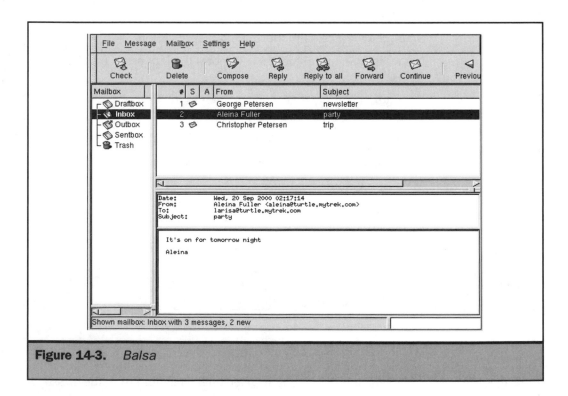

Figure 14-3. *Balsa*

You can access commands for managing your mail through the menus on the menu bar located at the top the Balsa window. An icon bar for commonly used mail commands is displayed below the menu bar. To retrieve new messages, click the Check icon or select the Get New Mail item in the File menu. To print a message, click its header and then the Printer icon. To delete a message, select its header and click the Delete icon. The icons featuring envelopes are different forms of message composition: one for new messages, one for replies, and one for forwarding messages. Balsa also supports filters for automatically performing operations on received mail. You can create a filter that matches a specified string in a header field and then automatically perform an operation on that message. For example, you could have any message from a certain person automatically deleted or messages on a certain subject automatically printed.

To compose a message, click the Compose icon or select the New item on the Message menu. A new message window opens with entries for the To, From, Subject, and Carbon copy header fields. If you select the Reply or Forward icons, the To, From, and Subject fields are already filled in with your address and the sender's address, and the sender's subject with a preceding Re: for replies and Fwd: for forwards. Fields that use addresses have a small Address Book button at the end of their fields. You can click this button to use the address book to enter an address for a field. Enter the message in the body of the window. The standard GUI editing operations are supported, enabling you to use your mouse to select, cut, copy, and move text. To send the message, click the Send icon in the icon bar or select the Send entry in the File menu. Icons also exist for operations such as selecting attachments or printing the message. Attachments added to a message are displayed in a pane just below the icon bar.

You can configure Balsa to access any number of mail accounts. Select the Preferences entry to bring up a window with panels for configuring Balsa. The Mail Servers panel shows three sections: one for remote mailbox servers, another for local mail, and the last for outgoing mail. In the remote mailbox servers section, you can add the server information for your network. Clicking the Add button opens a mailbox configurator window where you can enter your account's username and password, as well as the server name for that mailbox server. The mailbox name is any name you want to use to identify this mail service.

The Mahogany mail client window uses a format similar to Balsa. Three panes are there: a left pane for listing folders, and two other panes on the right side for headers and message text. The headers pane has buttons for sorting headers by different fields, such as subject or sender. Mail operations can be performed using the menus or the button bar at the top of the window. To compose a message, you can click the Envelope button. This opens a window with entries for From, To, and Subject header fields. Mouse-based editing operations, such as cut-and-paste, are currently not supported, though you can invoke an external editor. A menu bar and an icon bar at the top of the window list the different message operations you can perform, such as the spell-checking and printing.

X Window Mail Clients: Netscape and exmh

Although many of the newer mail clients are being designed for either Gnome or the K Desktop, several mail clients were developed for use on X Windows and operate under any window manager or desktop. They do not require either Gnome or the K Desktop. Netscape Messenger and exmh are two of the more popular mail clients. The Emacs mail clients are integrated into the Emacs environment, of which the Emacs editor is the primary application. They are, however, fully functional mail clients. The GNU Emacs mail client can operate either with X Windows capabilities or with a screen-based interface like Pine. The XEmacs mail client operates solely as an X Windows application.

Netscape Messenger

Netscape Communicator includes a mail client called Messenger. To use the mail client, you have to select the mail window item in Navigator's window menu or select the Messenger icon in the Communicator window. Account information, such as your mail server, username, and password, must be entered in the Mail panel in the Preferences window, accessible from the Edit menu. Received messages are displayed in the Messenger window. The window is divided into two panes, the upper one listing headers of received messages and the lower one for displaying messages. To display a message, click its header. The icon bar displays icons for several common mail operations, such as sending, deleting, or forwarding messages.

To send a message, click the New Message icon. This opens a window that displays three sections. The middle section is for entering the subject line, and the bottom section is for entering the text of your message. The top section switches among three alternate panes: address, attachments, and options. You can use the small buttons on the left side of the section to switch between panes. The address pane features a drop-down menu for selecting which address field you want to fill. Entries exist for the To, From, Cc, and Bcc fields. The attachments pane lists files attached to this message. Use the Attachments icon in the icon bar to add attachments. The options pane lists several options, such as priority, encryption, and receipts. For the text section, Messenger supports a wide range of composition features, such as HTML addresses, fonts, formatting, and spell-checker. It supports standard GUI editing operations including cut-and-paste, though you use the ALT key instead of the CTRL key for keyboard equivalents.

exmh

The *exmh* program is an X Windows version of the MH mail client, described later in this chapter. It displays a window with two panes (see Figure 14-4). The upper pane lists the headers for received mail, and the lower pane displays a selected message. Above each pane is a button bar for various MH commands (these are the same as the commands for the MH mail client). To check for new mail, you press the Inc button on the top pane. Headers for unread messages are colored blue, and the selected header is displayed in red. You can add new mailbox folders by pressing the New button.

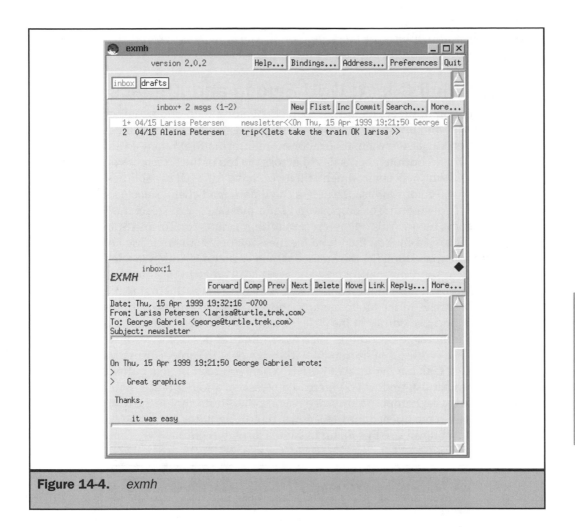

Figure 14-4. *exmh*

To read a message, click its header, which is displayed in the lower pane. Buttons for managing a message are listed across the top of that pane. Long messages are displayed screen by screen, and you can see the next screen by clicking the More button. The Next and Previous buttons move you directly to the next or previous message. Comp, Reply, and Forward all open a new message window for composing and sending a message. Comp is for new messages, and Reply and Forward include your address, the sender's, and the current message's subject.

To compose a new message, click the Comp button in the lower pane. Header fields and their titles are listed from the top. Click next to a header title and enter its value. For example, to enter a value for the To field, click after "To" and type the address you want. A line below the header separates the header from the text of the message. Click below this line and enter your message. You can change any of the header fields and the text of your message at any time. Click the Send button to send the message.

The Emacs Mail Client: GNU Emacs and XEmacs

The GNU version of Emacs includes a mail client along with other components, such as a newsreader and editor. GNU Emacs is included on Red Hat distributions. Check the Emacs Web site at **www.emacs.org** for more information. When you start up GNU Emacs, menu buttons are displayed across the top of the screen. If you are running Emacs in an X Windows environment, then you have full GUI capabilities and can select menus using your mouse. To access the Emacs mail client, select from the mail entries in the Tools menu. To compose and send messages, just select the Send Mail item in the Tools menu. This opens a screen with prompts for To: and Subject: header entries (see Figure 14-5). You then type the message below them, using any of the Emacs editing capabilities. On the menu bar, a new menu is added labeled Mail. When you are ready to send the mail, choose the Send Mail entry in this menu. To read mail, select the Read Mail item in the Tools menu, which displays the first mail message received. Use entries in the Move menu to move to the next message or back to a previous one, and use entries in the Delete menu to remove a message. The Mail menu lists entries for message operations, such as sending replies or forwarding the message. GNU Emacs is a working environment within which you can perform a variety of tasks, with each task having its own buffer. When you read mail, a buffer is opened to hold the header list, and when you read a message, another buffer will hold the contents. When you compose a message, yet another buffer holds the text you wrote. The buffers you have opened for mail, news, or editing notes or files are listed in the Buffers menu. You can use this menu to switch among them.

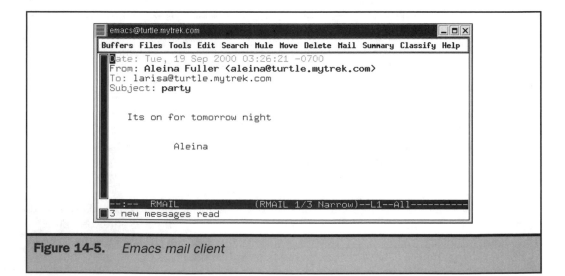

Figure 14-5. Emacs mail client

XEmacs is another version of Emacs designed to operate solely with a GUI interface. The Internet applications, which you can easily access from the main XEmacs button bar, include a Web browser, a mail utility, and a newsreader. Currently, XEmacs is distributed on OpenLinux. Clicking the Mail button brings up another window that lists received messages and also enables you to compose new ones. You can compose, reply, or print messages using buttons on the side of the window. To display a message, click its header and press the SPACEBAR. You can display the headers by choosing the Display item in the Folder menu. When composing a message, you have full use of the Emacs editor with all its features, including the spell-checker and search/replace. A new window is opened that prompts you for the address and subject. When you finish editing your message, choose Send and Exit in the Mail menu located at the end of the menu bar.

Screen-Based Mail Clients

You can invoke several powerful mail clients on the command line that provide a full-screen, cursor-based interface. Menus are displayed on the screen whose entries you can select using your keyboard. Basic cursor movement is supported with arrow keys. Pine, Elm, and Mutt are all mail clients that provide a screen-based interface. Although screen-based, the mail clients are very powerful. Pine, in particular, has an extensive set of features and options.

Pine

Pine stands for *Program for Internet News and E-mail*. It features full MIME support, enabling you to send messages, documents, and pictures easily. Pine has an extensive list of options, and it has flexible Internet connection capabilities, letting you receive both mail and Usenet news. Pine also enables you to maintain an address book where you can place frequently used e-mail addresses. You can find more information about Pine, including documentation and recent versions, from the Pine Information Center Web site at **www.washington.edu/pine**. The Pine newsgroup is **comp.mail.pine,** where you can post questions.

Pine runs from the command line using a simple cursor-based interface. Enter the **pine** command to start Pine. Pine supports full-screen cursor controls. It displays a menu whose items you can select by moving the cursor with the arrow keys to the entry of your choice and pressing ENTER. Each item is labeled with a capital letter, which you use to select it. The **O** command brings up a list of other Pine commands you can use.

To send a message, select the Compose Message item. This brings up a screen where you can enter your message. You are first taken through the different entries for the header, which prompts you for an e-mail address and subject. You can even attach files. Then, you type in the text of the message. A set of commands listed at the bottom of the screen specify different tasks. You can read a file with CTRL-R and cancel the message with CTRL-C. Use CTRL-X to send the message, as shown in Figure 14-6.

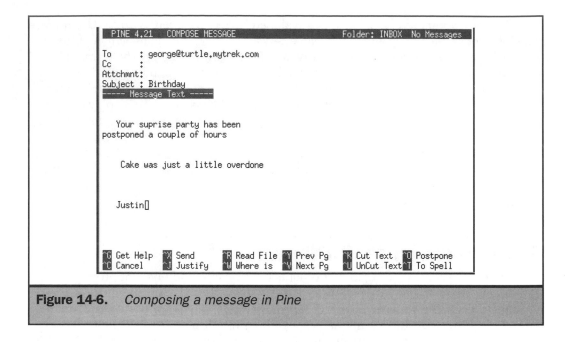

Figure 14-6. *Composing a message in Pine*

Pine organizes both sent and received messages into folders that you select using the Folder List entry on the main menu. The different available folders are listed from left to right. Three folders are automatically set up for you: INBOX, sent-mail, and saved-messages. The INBOX folder holds mail you have received but have not yet read. Sent-mail is for messages you have sent to others, while saved-messages are messages you have read and want to keep. Use the LEFT and RIGHT ARROW keys to select the one you want and then press ENTER. Selecting the INBOX folder will list the messages you have received. Headers for received messages are then displayed, and you can choose a specific header to view your message. The folder you select becomes your default folder. You can return to it by selecting the Folder Index entry in the main menu.

Mutt

Mutt incorporates many of the features of both Elm and Pine. It has an easy-to-use screen-based interface similar to Elm. Like Pine, Mutt has an extensive set of features, such as MIME support. You can find more information about Mutt from the Mutt Web page at **www.mutt.org**. Here, you can download recent versions of Mutt and access online manuals and help resources. On most distributions, the Mutt manual is located in the **/usr/doc** directory under Mutt. The Mutt newsgroup is **comp.mail.mutt**, where you can post queries and discuss recent Mutt developments.

Mutt screens have both an index mode and a pager mode. The *index mode* is used to display and manage message header lists, while the *pager mode* is used to display and compose messages. Mutt screens support ANSI escape sequences for color coding, displaying commands, prompts, and selected entries in different colors. You invoke Mutt with the command **mutt** entered on a Linux shell command line. Mutt displays a list of common commands across the top of the screen. Pressing the single key listed before the command executes that command. For example, pressing **q** quits Mutt, **s** saves the current message, and **r** enables you to send a reply to a message. Press the **?** key to obtain a complete listing of Mutt commands.

To compose a new message, press **m**. On the bottom line, you are then sequentially prompted to enter the address of the person to whom you are sending a message, the subject line, and a carbon copy list. Then you are placed in the standard editor, usually Vi or Emacs, and you can use the editor to enter your message. If you are using Vi, you first have to press the **a** or **i** command before you can enter text (see Chapter 22). After entering your text, you press ESC to return to the Vi command mode. When you finish entering your message, you save and exit Vi with the **ZZ** command. After editing the message, Mutt displays the header and a list of possible commands at the top of the screen. You can then edit the message or any of the header fields again. With the **a** command, you can add attachments to the message, and with the **q** command you can cancel the message. Press the **y** command to send the message.

Headers listing received messages are shown in the main screen upon starting Mutt. You can use the arrow keys to move from one to the next. The selected header is highlighted. Press the ENTER key to display the contents of the message, as shown in Figure 14-7. This opens another screen showing the header fields and the text of the

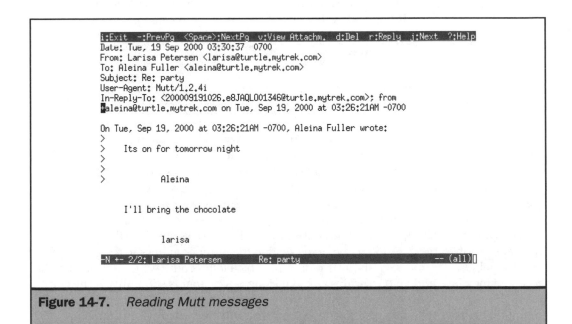

Figure 14-7.   *Reading Mutt messages*

INTERNET

message. Long messages are displayed screen by screen. You can use the PAGE UP or SPACEBAR key to move to the next screen, and the PAGE DOWN or − key to move back to the previous screen. The commands for operations you can perform on the message are listed across the top of the screen. With the **r** command, you can compose and send a reply to the message, while the **d** command deletes the message. Once you examine your message, you can use the **i** command to return to the main screen.

Elm

Elm has a screen-oriented, user-friendly interface that makes mail tasks easy to execute. Messages are displayed one screen at a time, and you can move back and forth through the message screen by screen. The Elm newsgroup is **comp.mail.elm,** where you can post queries for problems you may encounter. To send a message using Elm, you type **elm** along with the address of the person to whom you are sending the message. When you press ENTER, Elm displays the name of the person to whom you are sending the message and then prompts you for the subject. Elm displays the actual name of the person, not the address. At the subject prompt, you enter a subject. Then Elm prompts you for a carbon copy list. You can then enter the addresses of other users whom you want to have a copy of the message, or you can simply press ENTER if you do not want any carbon copies sent. Upon pressing ENTER at this point, you are placed in the standard editor, either Vi or Emacs, and you can use the editor to enter your message. After editing the message, Elm prompts you for an action, at which time you can send it, quit without sending, edit the message again, or edit its headers, as shown here. Each option is listed with a single-letter command. The **h** option displayed in the Elm message menu is for editing the header. With this option, you can change any of the entries in your message header, and you can enter other header values, such as addresses for blind carbon copies.

```
Please choose one of the following options by parenthesized letter:
e)dit message, edit h)eaders, s)end it, or f)orget it
```

To receive mail using Elm, you enter **elm** by itself on the command line. Elm then displays a list of message headers representing messages you have received. The headers are displayed from the top of the screen. At the bottom of the screen is an information menu listing the different commands you can perform on the screen of message headers (see Figure 14-8). This list of headers is referred to in Elm as the *index.* If you have more than one screen of message headers, you can move to the next screen with the + key. You can also move back a screen with the − key. An Elm header displays the status, the message number, the date, the name of the sender, the number of lines in the message, and the subject. The message status is represented by a letter code. An **N** indicates a newly received message, and an **O** indicates an old message—one that is still unread. The current header is either preceded by an arrow, **->**, or highlighted by the background. The arrow or highlight moves as you use arrow keys to move to the next or previous message header. To display the current message, press ENTER. A new screen appears in which the message is displayed. If the message is larger than a screen, you can move through it, screen by screen, using the same commands as those in the **more** utility. Pressing the SPACEBAR moves you to the next screen, and pressing **b** moves you back a screen. You can even search for particular patterns in the message. Once you examine your message, you can use the **i** command to return to the header screen. The **i** stands for *index*, which is the term Elm uses to refer to the list of headers. You quit Elm by pressing the **q** key.

With Elm, you create any number of different mailbox files in which you can save your messages. The **c** command prompts you for the name of a mailbox file. Simply press the **c** key and the prompt appears. The prompt displays the name of the mailbox file used to hold received messages from the sender in the current message header. You can specify your own mailbox file by entering the name of the file preceded by a **=** sign; for instance, **=birthdays** specifies the **birthdays** mailbox file. Once you change to the other folder, the headers for all the messages in this mailbox file are displayed and you can display the messages, delete them from the file, or send replies. The folder's name is displayed at the top of the screen.

Elm maintains an **.elm** directory in your home directory with which it configures your use of Elm. Each time you invoke Elm, it generates a shell for your own use, within which you can define your own aliases and configuration variables. The **.elm** directory contains special configuration files in which you can place alias or variable definitions. You can set options either by entering assignments to the **.elmrc** file in your **.elm** directory or by using the Options menu within Elm (command **o** displays the

```
          Mailbox is '/var/spool/mail/larisa' with 3 messages [ELM 2.5 PL3]


     N   1    Sep 19   Gabriel Matoza     (16)   Budget
     N   2    Sep 19   George Petersen    (16)   homework
     N   3    Sep 19   Aleina Fuller      (17)   party










     You can use any of the following commands by pressing the first character;
  d)elete or u)ndelete mail,  m)ail a message,  r)eply or f)orward mail,  q)uit
       To read a message, press <return>.  j = move down, k = move up, ? = help

 Command: █
```

Figure 14-8.   *Elm header list*

INTERNET

options menu). Elm also enables you to create mail aliases. You can create aliases either by using the Alias menu within the utility or by entering aliases in the **aliases.text** file in the **.elm** directory.

Command Line Mail Clients

Several mail clients use a simple command line interface. They can be run without any other kind of support, such as X Windows, desktops, or cursor support. They are simple and easy to use but include an extensive set of features and options. Two of the more widely used mail clients of this type are Mail and Mail Handler (MH). Mail is the mailx mail client that was developed for the Unix system. It is considered a kind of default mail client that can be found on all Unix and Linux systems.

You can also use the Emacs mail client from the command line, as described in the previous section.

Mail

What is known now as the mail utility was originally created for BSD Unix and called, simply, mail. Later versions of Unix System V adopted the BSD mail utility and renamed it *mailx*. Now, it is simply referred to as *Mail*. Mail functions as a de facto default mail client on Unix and Linux systems. All systems have the mail client called Mail, whereas they may not have other mail clients.

To send a message with Mail, type **mail** along with the address of the person to whom you are sending the message. Press ENTER and you are prompted for a subject. Enter the subject of the message and press ENTER again. At this point, you are placed in input mode. Anything typed in is taken as the contents of the message. Pressing ENTER adds a new line to the text. When you finish typing your message, press CTRL-D on a line of its own to end the message and send it. You see *EOT* (*end-of-transmission*) displayed after you press CTRL-D. In the next example, the user sends a message to another user whose address is **robert**. The subject of the message is Birthday. After typing in the text of the message, the user presses CTRL-D.

```
$ mail robert
Subject: Birthday
    Your present is in the mail
    really.

^D
EOT
$
```

The Mail utility receives input from the standard input. By default, the standard input is taken from what the user enters on the keyboard. With redirection, however, you can use the contents of a file as the message for the Mail program. In the next example, the file **mydata** is redirected as input for the Mail utility and sent to **robert**.

```
$ mail robert < mydata
```

You can send a message to several users at the same time by listing those users' addresses as arguments on the command line following the **mail** command. In the next example, the user sends the same message to both **chris** and **aleina**.

```
$ mail chris aleina
```

You may also want to save a copy of the message you are sending for yourself. You can copy a mail message to a file in your account by specifying a filename on the command line after the addresses. The filename must be a relative or full pathname, containing a slash. A pathname identifies an argument as a filename to which Mail saves a copy of the message being sent. In the next example, the user saves a copy of the message to a file called **birthnote**. A relative pathname is used, with the period denoting the current working directory: **./birthnote**.

```
$ mail robert ./birthnote
```

To receive mail, you enter only the **mail** command and press ENTER. This invokes a Mail shell with its own prompt and mail commands. A list of message headers is displayed. Header information is arranged into fields beginning with the status of the message and the message number. The status of a message is indicated by a single uppercase letter, usually **N**, for *new,* or **U**, for *unread.* A message number, used for easy reference to your messages, follows the status field. The next field is the address of the sender, followed by the date and time the message was received, and then the number of lines and characters in the message. The last field contains the subject the sender gave for the message. After the headers, the Mail shell displays its prompt, a question mark, **?**. At the Mail prompt, you enter commands that operate on the messages. The commonly used Mail commands are listed in Table 14-3. An example of a Mail headers and prompt follows:

```
$ mail
Mail version 5.5-kw 5/30/00. Type ? for help.
"/var/spool/mail/chris": 3 messages 3 new
>N  1 valerie    Tue Feb 11 10:14:32 5/44    "Budget"
 N  2 aleina     Wed Feb 12 12:30:17 28/537 "Birthday"
```

```
 N 3 robert      Fri Feb 14  8:15:24 16/293 "Homework"
?
```

Mail references messages either through a message list or through the current message marker (**>**). The greater-than sign (>) is placed before a message considered the current message. The current message is referenced by default when no message number is included with a Mail command. You can also reference messages using a message list consisting of several message numbers. Given the messages in the previous example, you can reference all three messages with **1-3**. The **^** references the first message; for example, **^-3** specifies the range of messages from the first message to the third message. The **$** references the last message. The period, **.**, references the current message. And the asterisk, *****, references all messages. Simply entering the number of the message by itself will display that message. The message is then output screen by screen. Press the SPACEBAR or the ENTER key to continue to the next screen.

You use the **R** and **r** commands to reply to a message you have received. The **R** command entered with a message number generates a header for sending a message and then places you into the input mode to type in the message. The **q** command quits Mail. When you quit, messages you have already read are placed in a file called **mbox** in your **home** directory. Instead of saving messages in the **mbox** file, you can use the **s** command to save a message explicitly to a file of your choice. The **s** command, however, saves a message with its header, in effect, creating another mailbox file. You can then later access a mailbox file either by invoking the Mail utility with the **-f** option and the mailbox filename or, if you are already using Mail, by executing the **folder** command that switches to a specified mailbox file. For example, the command **mail -f family_msgs** accesses the mailbox file **family_msgs**. Each message in the **family_msgs** mailbox file is then displayed in a message list.

Mail has its own initialization file, called **.mailrc**, that is executed each time Mail is invoked, for either sending or receiving messages. Within it, you can define Mail options and create Mail aliases. You can set options that add different features to mail, such as changing the prompt or saving copies of messages you send. To define an alias, you enter the keyword **alias**, followed by the alias you have chosen and then the list of addresses it represents. In the next example, the alias **myclass** is defined in the **.mailrc** file.

.mailrc

```
alias myclass chris dylan aleina justin larisa
```

In the next example, the contents of the file **homework** are sent to all the users whose addresses are aliased by **myclass**.

```
$ mail myclass < homework
```

INTERNET

Status Codes	Description
N	Newly received messages
U	Previously unread messages
R	Reads messages in the current session
P	Preserved messages, read in the previous session and kept in incoming mailbox
D	Deleted messages; messages marked for deletion
O	Old messages
*	Messages you saved to another mailbox file

Display Messages	Description
h	Redisplay the message headers
z+ z-	If header list takes up more than one screen, scrolls header list forward and backward
t *message-list*	Displays a message referenced by the message list; if no message list is used, the current message is displayed
p *message-list*	Displays a message referenced by the message list; if no message list is used, the current message is displayed
n or +	Displays next message
-	Displays previous message
top *message-list*	Displays the top few lines of a message referenced by the message list; if no message list is used, the current message is displayed

Message Lists	Description
message-number	References message with message number
num1-num2	References a range of messages beginning with *num1* and ending with *num2*
.	Current message
^	First message

Table 14-3.   *Mail Commands*

Message Lists	Description
$	Last message
*	All the messages waiting in the mailbox
/pattern	All messages with *pattern* in the subject field
Address	All messages sent from the user with *address*
:c	All messages of the type indicated by *c*; message types are as follows:

	n	newly received messages
	o	old messages previously received
	r	read messages
	u	unread messages
	d	deleted messages

Deleting and Restoring Messages	Description
d *message-list*	Deletes a message referenced by the indicated message list from your mailbox
u *message-list*	Undeletes a message referenced by the indicated message list that has been previously deleted
q	Quits the Mail utility and saves any read messages in the **mbox** file
x	Quits the Mail utility and does *not* erase any messages you deleted; this is equivalent to executing a **u** command on all deleted messages before quitting
pre *message-list*	Preserves messages in your waiting mailbox even if you have already read them

Sending and Editing Messages	Description
r	Sends a reply to all persons who received a message
R	Sends a reply to the person who sent you a message
m *address*	Sends a message to someone while in the Mail utility
v *message-list*	Edits a message with the Vi editor

Table 14-3.   *Mail Commands* (continued)

Saving Messages	Description
s *message-list filename*	Saves a message referenced by the message list in a file, including the header of the message
S *message-list*	Saves a message referenced by the message list in a file named for the sender of the message
Saving Messages	**Description**
w *message-list filename*	Saves a message referenced by the message list in a file without the header; only the text of the message is saved
folder *mailbox-filename*	Switches to another mailbox file
%	Represents the name of incoming mailbox file: **folder %** switches to incoming mailbox file
#	Represents name of previously accessed mailbox file: **folder #** switches to previous mailbox file
&	Represents name of mailbox file used to save your read messages automatically; usually called **mbox**: **folder &** switches to **mbox** file
General Commands	**Description**
?	Displays a list of all the Mail commands
! *command*	Executes a user shell command from within the Mail shell

Table 14-3.   *Mail Commands* (continued)

The Mail Handler Utility: MH

The Mail Handler mail client, commonly known as MH, takes a different approach to managing mail than most other mail clients. MH consists of a set of commands you execute within your user shell, just as you would execute any other Unix command. No special mail shell exists, as there is for Mail. One MH command sends a message, another displays your incoming messages, and still another saves a message. The MH commands and their options are listed in Table 14-4. A set of environment variables provides a context for the MH commands you execute, such as keeping track of the current messages or mail folders.

Note *Instead of working from a command line interface, you can use xmh or ezmh, which provides an X Windows interface for accessing MH messages.*

To send a message using MH, you first need to compose the message using the **comp** command, and then send the message with the **send** command. To compose a message, type in the word **comp** on the command line by itself and press RETURN. Then you are prompted for each header component, beginning with the address of the user to whom you are sending the message. After entering a subject, you are placed in an input mode for the default editor used for MH (usually the Vi editor). Next, you type the contents of the message, and then save and quit the editor as you normally would (ESC-SHIFT-**ZZ** for Vi). At the **What now?** prompt, you can send the message, edit it, save it to a file, display it again, or quit without sending the message. The send command sends the message. Pressing ENTER at the **What now?** prompt displays a list of commands you can enter. In the next example, the user composes a message for another user whose address is **robert**.

```
$ comp
To: robert
cc:
Subject: Birthday
------------------
Your present is in the mail
really.

What now? send
$
```

To read your mail with MH, you first need to store newly received mail into a designated MH mailbox file with the **inc** command. The **inc** command displays a list of headers for each mail message in your incoming mailbox. A MH message header consists only of the message number, the month and year, the address of the sender, and the beginning of the message text.

```
$ inc
1+  02/97  To:valerie    budget <<You are way under
2   02/97  To:aleina     birthday <<Yes, I did remember
$
```

If you want to redisplay the headers, you need to use another MH command called **scan**.

```
$ scan
1+  02/97  To:valerie    budget <<You are way under
2   02/97  To:aleina     birthday <<Yes, I did remember
$
```

You use the **show, next**, and **prev** commands to display a message. The **show** command displays the current message, the **next** command displays the message after the current one, and the **prev** command displays the message before the current one. Initially, the current message is the first of the newly received messages. If you want to display a particular message, you can use the **show** command with the number of the message. **show 2** displays message 2. You can also reference several messages at once by listing their message numbers. The command **show 1 3** displays messages 1 and 3. You can also designate a range of messages by specifying the first message number in the range, and the last number, separated by a minus sign. **show 1-3** displays messages 1, 2, and 3.

```
$ show
$ next
```

To print a message, you first output it with **show,** and then pipe the output to a printer. You save a message to a text file in much the same way. First you output the message using the **show** command, and then you redirect that output to a file.

```
$ show | lpr
$ show > myfile
```

You reply to the current message using the **repl** command. You need to know either the message number or the address and subject of the message to reply to it. You delete the current message using the **rmm** command. To delete a specific message, use the message number with **rmm. rmm 2** deletes the second message. You can create your own mailbox files for MH using the **folder** command. MH mailbox files are commonly referred to as *folders*. To create a new folder, enter in the **folder** command followed by the name of your folder preceded by a **+** sign. The **+** sign identifies an argument as a folder name.

```
$ repl 2
$ rmm 2
$ folder +mybox
```

Commands	Descriptions
inc	Places received mail in your incoming mailbox and displays message headers
show *num*	Displays current message or specified messages
prev	Displays the previous message
next	Displays the next message
scan	Redisplays message headers
mhl	Displays formatted listing of messages
folders	Lists all mail folders
forw	Forwards a message
repl	Replies to a message
send	Resends a message or sends a file as a message
pick	Selects messages by specified criteria and assigns them a sequence
folder	Changes to another mailbox file (folder)

Table 14-4. *MH Commands*

Notifications of Received Mail: From and biff

As your mail messages are received, they are automatically placed in your mailbox file, but you are not automatically notified when you receive a message. To find out if you have any messages waiting, you can either use a mail client to retrieve messages or you can use the From and biff utilities to tell you if you have any mail waiting (some mail clients like Elm will also notify you of received mail when they are open).

The From utility tells what messages you have received and are waiting to be read. For each waiting message, it lists the senders' addresses and times each message was received. To use From, you enter the keyword **from** and press ENTER.

```
$ from
1 From valerie Sun Feb 11 10:14:32 1996
  Subject: Budget
2 From aleina Mon Feb 12 12:30:17 1996
  Subject: Birthday
```

```
3 From robert Wed Feb 14  8:15:24 1996
  Subject: Homework
$
```

The biff utility notifies you immediately when a message is received. This is helpful when you are expecting a message and want to know as soon as it arrives. biff automatically displays the header and beginning lines of messages as they are received. To turn on biff, you enter **biff y** on the command line. To turn it off, you enter **biff n**. To find out if biff is turned on, enter **biff** alone. biff displays a message notification whenever a message arrives, no matter what you may be doing at the time. You could be in the middle of an editing session; biff will interrupt it to display the notification on your screen. You can then return to your editing session. In the next example, the user first sets biff on. Then biff notifies the user that a message has been received. The user then checks to see if biff is still on.

```
$ biff y
$
New mail for chris has arrived:
--Date: Sun Feb 11 12:30:21
From: dylan
To: chris
Subject: Food
    Chris,
        Have you tried the chocolate
...more...

$
$ biff
is y
$
```

You can temporarily block biff by using the **mesg n** command to prevent any message displays on your screen. Not only does **mesg n** stop any Write and Talk messages, it also stops biff and Notify messages. Later, you can unblock biff with a **mesg y** command. A **mesg n** command comes in handy if you don't want to be disturbed while working on some project.

If you are running a window manager, such as fvwm or AfterStep, you can use the xbiff utility to perform the same function. xbiff displays an icon of a mailbox, which has a flag on it, on your desktop. When mail arrives, the flag goes up. xbiff can also beep or produce some other sound, if you prefer.

The K Desktop has a biff utility called *Kbiff* that works in much the same way. With Kbiff, you can set numerous options. Kbiff can show an empty inbox tray when there is

INTERNET

no mail and a tray with slanted letters in it when mail arrives. If old mail is still in your mailbox, letters are displayed in a neat square. You can set these icons as any image you want. You can also specify the mail client to use and the polling interval for checking for new mail. If you have several mail accounts, you can set up a Kbiff profile for each one. Different icons can appear for each account telling you when mail arrives in one of them.

There are also a number of mail monitors available for use on Gnome. Many operate as applets on the Gnome panel. For example, Sonicmail will notifiy you of any POP3 mail arrivals. PyBiff performs much the same kind of mail monitoring as biff and Kbiff. gbox_applet will monitor mailboxes, assigning priorities to each. GMailWatch is a mail monitor applet that will display a summary of incoming mail.

Accessing Mail on Remote POP Mail Servers

Most newer mail clients are equipped to access mail accounts on remote servers. For such mail clients, you can specify a separate mail account with its own mailbox. For example, if you are using an ISP, most likely you will use that ISP's mail server to receive mail. You will have set up a mail account with a username and password for accessing your mail. Your e-mail address is usually your username and the ISP's domain name. For example, a username of larisa for an ISP domain named **mynet.com** would have the address **larisa@mynet.com**. The username would be larisa. The address of the actual mail server could be something like **mail.mynet.com**. The user larisa would log into the **mail.mynet.com** server using the username larisa and password to access mail sent to the address **larisa@mynet.com**. Newer mail clients. such as KMail, Balsa, and Netscape, enable you to set up a mailbox for such an account and access your ISP's mail server to check for and download received mail. You must specify what protocol a mail server uses. This is usually the *Post Office Protocol* (*POP*). This procedure is used for any remote mail server. Using a mail server address, you can access your account with your username and password.

Instead of creating separate mailboxes in different mail clients, you can arrange to have mail from different accounts sent directly to the inbox maintained by your Linux system for your Linux account. All your mail, whether from other users on your Linux system or from ISP mail servers, will appear in your local inbox. Such a feature is helpful if you are using a mail client, such as Elm or Mail, that does not have the capability to access mail on your ISP's mail server. You can implement such a feature with Fetchmail. *Fetchmail* checks for mail on remote mail servers and downloads it to your local inbox, where it appears as newly received mail.

To use Fetchmail, you have to know a remote mail server's Internet address and mail protocol. Most remote mail servers use the POP3 protocol, but others may use the IMAP, ETRM, or POP2 protocols. Enter **fetchmail** on the command line with the mail server address and any needed options. The mail protocol is indicated with the **-p** option and the mail server type, usually POP3. If your e-mail username is different from your Linux login name, then you use the **-u** option and the e-mail name. Once you execute the **fetchmail** command, you are prompted for a password. The syntax for the **fetchmail** command for a POP3 mail server follows:

```
fetchmail -p POP3 -u username mail-server
```

To use Fetchmail, connect to your ISP, and then enter the **fetchmail** commands with the options and the POP server name on the command line. You will see messages telling you if mail is there and, if so, how many messages are being downloaded. You can then use a mail client to read the messages from your inbox. You can run Fetchmail in daemon mode to have it automatically check for mail. You have to include an option specifying the interval in seconds for checking mail.

```
fetchmail -d  1200
```

You can specify options such as the server type, username, and password in a **.fetchmailrc** file in your **home** directory. You can also have entries for other mail servers and accounts you may have. Instead of entering options directly into the **.fetchmailrc** file, you can use the **fetchmailconf** program. **fetchmailconf** provides a GUI interface for selecting Fetchmail options and entering mail account information. **fetchmailconf** runs only under X Windows and requires that python and Tk be installed (most distributions automatically install these during installation). It displays windows for adding news servers, configuring a mail server, and configuring a user account on a particular mail server. The expert version displays the same kind of windows, but with many more options. Initially, **fetchmailconf** displays a window with buttons for choosing a novice or expert version (see Figure 14-9). Choosing the novice version displays a window with an entry labeled "New Server." Type the address of your mail server in the adjoining box and press ENTER. The server address then appears in a list below. To configure that server, click the server name and then the Edit button at the bottom of the window. A new window opens with entries such as user accounts and server protocols. You can add as many user accounts as you may have on that server. You can then further configure an individual account by selecting the username and clicking the Edit button. This opens another window for user account options. You can specify a password and specify any corresponding local users for which you want mail for this account downloaded.

Once it is configured, you can enter **fetchmail** with no arguments; it will read entries from your **.fetchmailrc** file. Accounts you have specified are checked and any new mail is placed in your inbox. If you want Fetchmail to check automatically for new

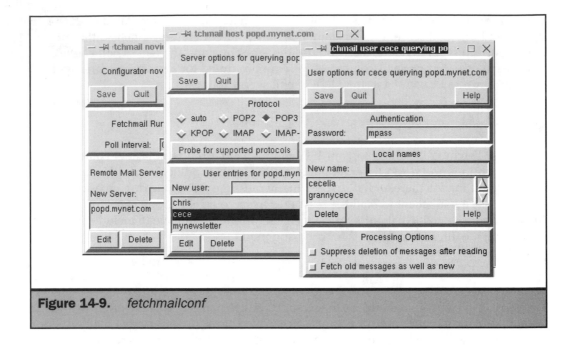

Figure 14-9. *fetchmailconf*

mail periodically, you can activate its daemon mode. To do so, place a daemon entry in the **.fetchmailrc** file. The following entry activates the Fetchmail daemon mode, checking for mail every 1,200 seconds:

```
Set daemon  1200
```

You can also make entries directly in the **.fetchmailrc** file. An entry in the **.fetchmailrc** file for a particular mail account consists of several fields and their values: poll, protocol, username, and password. *Poll* is used to specify the mail server name, and *protocol,* the type of protocol used. Notice you can also specify your password, instead of having to enter it each time Fetchmail accesses the mail server. The syntax for an entry follows:

```
poll SERVERNAME protocol PROTOCOL username NAME password PASSWORD
```

You can use abbreviations for certain field names if you want: *proto* for protocol, *user* for username, and *pass* for password. An example follows for a POP3 server and an account with the username chris and the password mypass:

```
poll popd.mynet.com proto pop3 user chris password mypass
```

You can specify a default entry for any of these fields and not have to repeat them for each account entry. The default must be placed before the mail server entries. The following example sets the default protocol to POP3 and the username to chris:

```
defaults protocol pop3 user chris
```

This next example would reference the chris account with the password newpass on the **popd.train.com** mail server using the POP3 protocol. The missing fields are filled in by default.

```
poll popd.train.com password newpass
```

Fetchmail enables you to download messages to a specific user on your local system. In fact, you can access several accounts on the remote system and have them downloaded to specific users on the your local system. This is useful when running Fetchmail in daemon mode. Essentially, Fetchmail is transferring mail from one set of remote accounts to corresponding ones on your local system. You could even have Fetchmail download from one remote account to several local ones, sending copies of the same mail to each. This is helpful if you are using several accounts on your Linux system, or if a group of users is using an account on the remote server for group mail. Local users are specified with the keyword **is** or **to** followed by the usernames, terminating with the keyword **here**. The following examples show different ways of specifying local users. The last entry will send all mail retrieved from the mynewsletter account to the users larisa, aleina, and dylan.

```
poll popd.mynet.com proto pop3 user chris password mypass is chris here
poll popd.othernet.com proto pop3 user neil password mypass is chris here
poll popd.mynet.com proto pop3 user cece password mypass to cecelia grannycece here
poll popd.mynet.com proto pop3 user mynewsletter password mypass to larisa aleina dylan here
```

 Fetchmail also supports a multidrop mailbox feature. You can have several users' mail sent to one mailbox on the mail server, and then download it from there to the inboxes for their Linux accounts.

The Complete Reference

Chapter 15

Usenet
and Newsreaders

senet is an open mail system on which users post news and opinions. It operates like a system-wide mailbox that any user on your Linux system can read or send messages to. Users' messages are incorporated into Usenet files, which are distributed to any system signed up to receive them. Each system that receives Usenet files is referred to as a *site*. Certain sites perform organizational and distribution operations for Usenet, receiving messages from other sites and organizing them into Usenet files, which are then broadcast to many other sites. Such sites are called *backbone sites* and they operate like publishers, receiving articles and organizing them into different groups.

To access Usenet news, you need access to a news server. A news server receives the daily Usenet newsfeeds and makes them accessible to other systems. Your network may have a system that operates as a news server. If you are using an Internet service provider (ISP), a news server is probably maintained for your use. To read Usenet articles, you use a *newsreader*—a client program that connects to a news server and accesses the articles. On the Internet and in TCP/IP networks, news servers communicate with newsreaders using the *Network News Transfer Protocol* (*NNTP*) and are often referred to as NNTP news servers. Or, you could also create your own news server on your Linux system to run a local Usenet news service or to download and maintain the full set of Usenet articles. Several Linux programs, called *news transport agents,* can be used to create such a server. This chapter focuses on the variety of news readers available for the Linux platform. The configuration administration and architecture of the NNTP server are covered in Chapter 28.

Usenet News

Usenet files were originally designed to function like journals. Messages contained in the files are referred to as *articles*. A user could write an article, post it in Usenet, and have it immediately distributed to other systems around the world. Someone could then read the article on Usenet, instead of waiting for a journal publication. Usenet files themselves were organized as journal publications. Because journals are designed to address specific groups, Usenet files were organized according to groups called *newsgroups*. When a user posts an article, it is assigned to a specific newsgroup. If another user wants to read that article, he or she looks at the articles in that newsgroup. You can think of each newsgroup as a constantly updated magazine. For example, to read articles on computer science, you would access the Usenet newsgroup on computer science. More recently, Usenet files have also been used as bulletin boards on which people carry on debates. Again, such files are classified into newsgroups, though their articles read more like conversations than journal articles. You can also create articles of your own, which you can then add to a newsgroup for others to read. Adding an article to a newsgroup is called *posting* the article.

Each newsgroup has its own name, which is often segmented to classify newsgroups. Usually, the names are divided into three segments: a general topic, a subtopic, and a specific topic. The segments are delimited by periods. For example, you may have several newsgroups dealing with the general topic *rec,* which stands for recreation. Of those, some newsgroups may deal with only the subtopic food. Again, of those, a group may only discuss a specific topic, such as recipes. In this case, the newsgroup name would be **rec.food.recipes**.

Many of the bulletin board groups are designed for discussion only, lacking any journal-like articles. A good number of these begin with either alt or talk as their general topic. For example, **talk.food.chocolate** may contain conversations about how wonderful or awful chocolate is perceived, while **alt.food.chocolate** may contain informal speculations about the importance of chocolate to the basic structure of civilization as we know it. Here are some examples of Usenet newsgroup names:

```
comp.ai.neural-nets
comp.lang.pascal
sci.physics.fusion
rec.arts.movies
rec.food.recipes
talk.politics.theory
```

Linux has newsgroups on various topics. Some are for discussion, and others are sources of information about recent developments. On some, you can ask for help for specific problems. A selection of some of the popular Linux newsgroups is provided here:

Newsgroup	Topic
comp.os.linux.announce	Announcements of Linux developments
comp.os.linux.admin	System administration questions
comp.os.linux.misc	Special questions and issues
comp.os.linux.setup	Installation problems
comp.os.linux.help	Questions and answers for particular problems

You read Usenet articles with a newsreader, such as KNode, Pan, Pine, Netscape, trn, or **tin**, which enables you first to select a specific newsgroup and then read the articles in it. A newsreader operates like a user interface, enabling you to browse through and select available articles for reading, saving, or printing. Most newsreaders employ a sophisticated retrieval feature called *threads* that pulls together articles on the same discussion or topic. Newsreaders are designed to operate using certain kinds of interfaces. For example, KNode is a KDE newsreader that has a KDE interface and is designed for the KDE desktop. Pan has a Gnome interface and is designed to operate on the Gnome desktop. Pine is a cursor-based newsreader, meaning that it provides a full-screen interface that you can work with using a simple screen-based cursor that you can move with arrow keys. It does not support a mouse or any other GUI feature. trn uses a simple

INTERNET

command line interface with limited cursor support. Most commands you type in and press ENTER to execute. Several popular newsreaders are listed in Table 15-1.

> **Note** *Numerous newsreaders currently are under development for both Gnome and KDE. You can check for KDE newsreaders on the software list on the K Desktop Web site at **apps.kde.com**. For Gnome newsreaders, check Internet tools on the software map on the Gnome Web site at **www.gnome.org**.*

Most newsreaders can read Usenet news provided on remote news servers that use the NNTP. Many such remote news servers are available through the Internet. Desktop newsreaders, such as KNode and Pan, have you specify the Internet address for the remote news server in their own configuration settings. Several shell-based newsreaders, however, such as trn, tin, and Pine, obtain the news server's Internet address from the **NNTPSERVER** shell variable (see Table 15-1). Before you can connect to a remote news server with such newsreaders, you first have to assign the Internet address of the news server to the **NNTPSERVER** shell variable, and then export that variable. You can place the assignment and export of **NNTPSERVER** in a login initialization file, such as **.bash_profile**, so it is performed automatically whenever you log in.

```
$ NNTPSERVER=news.mydomain.com
$ export NNTPSERVER
```

Newsreader	Description
Pan	Gnome Desktop newsreader
KNode	KDE Desktop newsreader
Netscape	Web utility with newsreader capabilities. (X Windows–based)
Pine	Mail client with newsreader capabilities (cursor based)
slrn	Newsreader (cursor based)
Emacs	Emacs editor, mail client, and newsreader. (cursor based)
trn	Newsreader (command line interface)
tin	Newsreader (command line interface)

Table 15-1. *Linux Newsreaders*

News Transport Agents

Usenet news is provided over the Internet as a daily newsfeed of articles for thousands of newsgroups. This newsfeed is sent to sites that can then provide access to the news for other systems through newsreaders. These sites operate as news servers; the newsreaders used to access them are their clients. The news server software, called *news transport agents,* is what provides newsreaders with news, enabling you to read newsgroups and post articles. For Linux, three of the popular news transport agents are INN, Leafnode, and Cnews. Both Cnews and Leafnode are smaller and simpler, and useful for small networks. INN is more powerful and complex, designed with large systems in mind (see **www.isc.org** for more details).

Daily newsfeeds on Usenet are often large and consume much of a news server's resources in both time and memory. For this reason, you may not want to set up your own Linux system to receive such newsfeeds. If you are operating in a network of Linux systems, you can designate one of them as the news server and install the news transport agent on it to receive and manage the Usenet newsfeeds. Users on other systems on your network can then access that news server with their own newsreaders.

If your network already has a news server, you needn't install a news transport agent at all. You only have to use your newsreaders to remotely access that server (see **NNTPSERVER** in the previous section). In the case of an ISP, such providers often operate their own news servers, which you can also remotely access using your own newsreaders, such as trn and tin. Remember, though, trn and tin must take the time to download all the articles for selected newsgroups, as well as updated information on all the newsgroups.

You can also use news transport agents to run local versions of news for only the users on your system or your local network. To do this, install INN, Leafnode, or Cnews and configure them just to manage local newsgroups. Users on your system could then post articles and read local news.

Mailing Lists

As an alternative to newsgroups, you can subscribe to mailing lists. Users on mailing lists automatically receive messages and articles sent to the lists. Mailing lists work much like a mail alias, broadcasting messages to all users on the list. Mailing lists were designed to serve small, specialized groups of people. Instead of posting articles for anyone to see, only those who subscribe receive them. Numerous mailing lists, as well as other subjects, are available for Linux. For example, at the **www.gnome.org** site, you can subscribe to any of several mailing lists on Gnome topics, such as **gnome-themes-list@gnome.org**, which deals with Gnome desktop themes. You can do the same at **lists.kde.org** for KDE topics. At **www.liszt.com,** you can search for mailing lists on various topics. By convention, to subscribe to a list, you send a request to the mailing list address with a **–request** term added to its user name. For example, to subscribe to **gnome-themes-list@gnome.org,** you send a request to **gnome-themes-list-request@gnome.org.** At **www.linux.org,** you can link to sites that support Linux-oriented mailing lists, such as Majordomo and the Linux Mailing Lists Web site. Lists exist for such topics as the Linux kernel, administration, and different distributions.

Gnome Newsreaders

Several Gnome newsreaders are under development, including Pan, Elknews, Gnews, GNONews, and Gone (see Table 15-2). Check the Internet tool section on the Gnome software map at **www.gnome.org** for current versions and updates. *Pan* is a newsreader modeled after the Windows program, Agent, featuring decoding of binaries and automatic grouping of multipart posts. You can download RPM versions from the Pan Web site, accessible through the Gnome Web site. *Elknews* is a simple newsreader featuring threading, sorting, posting, group listing, and custom port connections. *GNews* is a newsreader that supports multithreading with pthreads. *GNONews* newsreader plans to implement Agent-like features to Gnome. *Gone,* which stands for *Gnome's Other News Editor,* is a GNU newsreader that features MIME support, drag-and-drop attachments, inline image viewing, and plug-in filter support. Grn is another Gnome newsreader that is Perl extensible and includes full MIME support. If you just want to download and decode binaries attached to articles, you can use Glitter to detect, download, combine, and decode binary applications posted as several encoded news articles.

Pan is a powerful newsreader letting you sort articles, decode binaries, and set up rules for selecting articles. Pan features both a pane and a notebook display. Initially newsgroups, article headers, and article contents are displayed in three panes (see Figure 15-1). You can switch to a notebook display that will show each pane as a tabbed panel covering the entire window. In the newsgroup pane, a drop-down menu lets you choose whether to display all newsgroups or only subscribed ones. You can also search for particular newsgroups. For the article headers, an icon bar lets you display read or unread articles, as well as save and search articles. A selected article is displayed in the pane below the headers.

Figure 15-1.   *The Pan Gnome newsreader*

Newsreader	Description
Pan	Agent-like Gnome newsreader
Elknews	A simple Gnome newsreader
Gnews	Gnome newsreader (in development)
GNONews	Gnome newsreader (in development)
Gone	Gnome's Other News Editor
Grn	Gnome Read News Perl extensible newsreader
Glitter	Newsreader to extract and decode binaries

Table 15-2.   *Gnome Newsreaders*

INTERNET

The K Desktop Newsreaders: KNode and Krn

The K Desktop features several newsreaders including KNode, Krn, and Kexpress (see Table 15-3). KNode is currently the standard newsreader distributed with KDE 2.0 and Krn was included with previous versions of KDE. Updated versions are available from **apps.kde.com, sourceforge.net**, or **freshmeat.net**. If you just want to download binaries attached to articles you can use Kng.

The KNode newsreader includes standard features such as follow-ups, saving and printing articles, article and newsgroup searches, and thread displays. It also supports more powerful features such as binary encoding and decoding, displaying attached image files, and separate window displays for articles. In addition, it supports multiple accounts, and customized configuration for features such as colors, fonts, window displays, and article search filters. You can find out more about KNode at **knode.sourceforge.net**.

The main KNode window will show three panes, a left one for newsgroups, one for article headers in the selected newsgroup, and one for displaying a selected article (see Figure 15-2). KNode commands are accessible through menus on the menu bar at the top of the window. There are menus for File, Edit, and configuration (Settings) operations, as well as for managing newsgroups, accessing articles, and getting help. An icon bar just below the menus lists several common newsgroup operations. Initially, you will have to configure KNode to access your news server. Select the Preferences entry in the Settings menu. This opens a dialog window that includes entries for Mail and News accounts. Select the News entry and enter the information for your news server, giving it a name you want to identify it with for KNode. If you have access to several news servers, you can create an entry for each. Your news servers will appear on the main window in the left pane. These appear in the form of an expandable tree. Clicking on a news server entry expands to list your subscribed

Newsreader	Description
KNode	KDE newsreader for KDE 2.0 designed for local news servers: **knode.sourceforge.net**
Krn	KDE newsreader will a full compliment of features: **krn.sourceforge.net**
Kexpress	KDE newsreader designed for speed
Kng	KDE news grabber for downloading and decoding binaries.

Table 15-3. *KDE Newsreaders*

Figure 15-2.   *KNode KDE mail client and newsreader*

INTERNET

newsgroups for that news server. Clicking on the newsgroup will display the article headers for it on the upper-right pane. Buttons appear at the top of the header pane for each of the header fields. Fields for subject, sender, and date exist. Clicking a button sorts the headers by that field. For example, clicking the Date field sorts all headers by date. Clicking on the article header will display the article.

Krn is another newsreader for the K Desktop included with previous versions of KDE. You can find out more about Krn at **krn.sourceforge.net**. The Krn newsreader window displays two folders: one for subscribed newsgroups and one for all newsgroups. You can expand or contract either by clicking their Folder icon. A menu bar is at the top of the window for newsgroup and configuration operations. An icon bar just below the menus lists several common newsgroup operations. To connect to your news server, click the first icon on this list. The second icon then disconnects. The icon with several lines downloads a current, complete list of newsgroups. The Curved Arrow icon checks to see if new articles have been posted for your newsgroups. The icon of a sheet of paper with a small, blue line partway through its left side is used to subscribe or unsubscribe to a newsgroup. To subscribe to a newsgroup, you first select it from the list of All Newsgroups. Then, click the Subscribe icon on the icon bar. It automatically appears in your list of subscribed-to newsgroups.

To display articles in a newsgroup, double-click the newsgroup entry. A window opens up consisting of two panes. The top pane lists the headers for articles in the newsgroup. You can scroll through the list using the scroll bar to the right. Articles you have read appear in blue type. If you right-click an article header, a pop-up menu displays options for moving or copying it to another folder, or deleting it. Buttons appear at the top of the header pane for each of the header fields. Fields for subject, sender, and date exist. Clicking a button sorts the headers by that field. For example, clicking the Date field sorts all headers by date. Another field is named *Score*. This is for score rules you can set up for the newsgroup. A score rule searches for keywords in certain fields and gives a score you specified to the articles if the keywords are found.

To read an article, click its header. The text of the article appears in the pane below (see Figure 15-3). A menu bar at the top of the window holds commands for accessing articles. Two icon bars below enable you to execute commonly used commands. In the top icon bar, the arrows move through the list of articles. The icon with a looking glass opens a find window for searching articles by subject, sender, text, or other fields. The blank page posts a new article and the icon with lines in it downloads a current list of articles for the group. To the left is a box for adjusting the number of articles you want displayed.

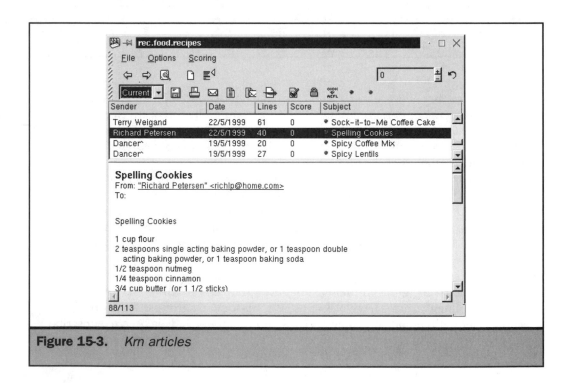

Figure 15-3. *Krn articles*

Netscape Newsreader

The Netscape newsreader is part of the Netscape Communicator package. You can configure the newsreader function by editing the Netscape Preferences for news. From the Edit menu in Netscape Navigator, select the Preferences entry. Then, select News from the list on the left. This displays a pane that includes an entry for your news server. Here, you enter the address of your news server. You can set other options here also, such as the number of articles to display at a time for a newsgroup. Figure 15-4 shows the Netscape news window.

To access a newsgroup, select the Newsgroups entry from the Communicator menu. This opens a Netscape Messenger window with the mailbox folders listed to the left. Below the mailbox folders is the list of news servers. Most likely, you have only one. Click this entry to expand to a list of newsgroups to which you have subscribed. Then, double-click the newsgroup name to see its articles.

When you select a newsgroup, a new window opens with two panes. The pane on top lists the headers for articles in the newsgroup. Use the scroll bar to the right to

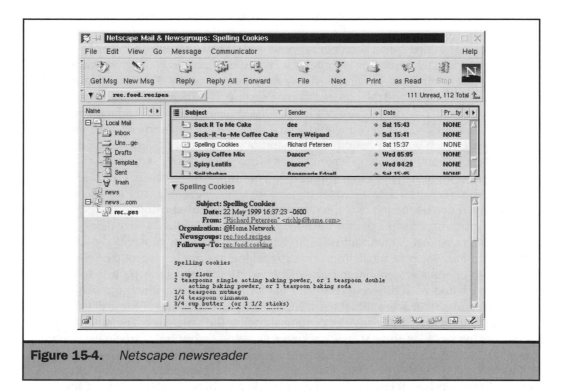

Figure 15-4. *Netscape newsreader*

move through the list. To display the contents of the article, click it and it is displayed in the large pane in the lower half of the window. Header information is shown first. If the article is a picture file, the picture is automatically decoded and displayed in the pane. If the article is a video file, the appropriate program for running video starts up and runs it. You can search for articles by subject or sender by selecting the Search Messages entry in the Edit menu. The icons in the icon bar at the top can be used to post new articles or follow-ups to the current newsgroup. A new window opens that appears much like a Netscape Mail message window.

You can subscribe to newsgroups by selecting the Subscribe entry in the File menu. This opens a window that shows a list of all available newsgroups. The list is compressed, with beginning strings that can be expanded by clicking the **+** signs next to them. Select the one you want and click the Join button in the upper-right corner. When you close the window, the newsgroup appears under your newsgroup server name.

Pine and slrn

Pine is designed to work with the Internet and is capable of reading Internet newsgroups. The Config entry listed on the Setup screen opens an options list in which you can place entries for your Internet mail server or news server. If you are using an ISP or LAN, you can enter the domain names for your news server or mail server. Newsgroups are treated by Pine as just another mail folder. To list a newsgroup, select the Folder List entry and use the **A** command to add the name of the newsgroup. It is then listed as another folder. When you select it, the newsgroup headers are listed instead of mail headers. You can also post news using Pine, just as you would send a message. Pine has an extensive list of options with which you can customize its operations. These options are accessed through the Config selection in the Setup screen, which is accessible from the main menu. The options you change are saved in a **.pinrc** file in your **home** directory.

Slrn is a screen-based newsreader that has an interface similar to Pine's. Commands are displayed across the top of the screen and can be executed using the listed keys. Different types of screens exist for the newsgroup list, article list, and article content, each with its own set of commands. An initial screen lists your subscribed newsgroups with commands for posting, listing, and subscribing to your newsgroups. Selecting a newsgroup opens a screen that initially displays only the newsgroup's articles. Article headers are listed with different colors for the article number, author, and subject fields. Selecting an article splits the screen, showing the contents of the article in a larger portion below, and a smaller portion showing the article list. The ARROW keys as well as the PAGE UP and PAGE DOWN keys move you through the article list, whereas the SPACEBAR and **b** keys move you forward and backward through the currently displayed article text. Selecting a new article displays it in the lower section of the screen. Commands you can perform on an article are shown at the bottom of the screen. They include commands for posting follow-ups and paging operations.

Emacs News

The GNU version of Emacs also includes a newsreader along with other components, such as a mailer and an editor. GNU Emacs is included on Red Hat distributions. Check the Emacs Web site at **www.emacs.org** for more information. When you start up GNU Emacs, menu buttons are displayed across the top of the screen. If you are running Emacs in an X Windows environment, you have full GUI capabilities and can select menus using your mouse. Be sure the **NNTPSERVER** variable is set to your news server address in your **.bash_profile** file and it is exported.

To access the Emacs newsreader, select from the Read Net News entry in the Tools menu. A listing of newsgroups is displayed. The menus across the top of the screen change, adding Misc, Groups, and Groups menu. The Groups menu holds entries for managing newsgroups, such as sorting and searching for groups, as well as subscribing to new ones or listing only subscribed or unsubscribed groups. To select a group, click it or move to it with the ARROW keys, and then press the SPACEBAR.

When you select a newsgroup, a split screen is displayed where the headers for the newsgroup articles are listed in the top screen, while the contents of the currently selected article are shown in the bottom screen. Use the TAB key or the mouse to select the screen you want. When you select the header screen, the menus change, listing Search, Misc, Post, Threads, and Article menus. These hold commands for managing the headers. For example, you can post a follow-up by selecting the article and choosing the Followup entry in the Post menu. In the Article menu, you can move to the bottom of the header list or the top, highlight selected headers, and save articles. In the Thread menu, you can move to the header for the next thread or toggle threads on or off. From the Search menu, you can search for headers using patterns and regular expressions. When you finish with a newsgroup, choose Exit from the Misc menu.

On the bottom screen, an article is displayed. When you select this screen, the menus change to Search, Misc, Post, Treatment, and Article. Here, the Article menu enables you to page forward and backward through the article. The Treatment menu has entries for hiding or showing headers and signatures. From the Post menu, you can post follow-ups and replies for this particular article. The Search menu now performs searches on the article text.

GNU Emacs is a working environment in which each task has its own buffer. When you read news, a buffer is opened to hold the newsgroup and article headers, and when you read an article, another buffer holds the contents. When you compose an article, yet another buffer holds the text you wrote. The buffers you opened for mail, news, or editing notes or files are listed in the Buffers menu. You can use this menu to switch among them.

XEmacs is the complete Emacs editor with a graphical user interface and Internet applications. The Internet applications, which you can easily access from the main XEmacs button bar, include a Web browser, a mail utility, and a newsreader. Clicking the News button brings up another window that displays the newsreader, listing your

INTERNET

Usenet newsgroups. If you are using an ISP, it uses the name of the news server in the **NNTPSERVER** variable. You can then access newsgroups, displaying articles.

trn

With the trn newsreader, you can display and search articles by subject, article, or threads. To use trn to access remote news servers, be sure the **NNTPSERVER** variable is set in your **.bash_profile** file. The trn interface has several powerful features, such as pattern searches for groups of articles. The *t* in trn stands for *threaded*. A *thread* is any connection between articles, such as articles that share the same subject or follow-up articles to a previously posted article. The special interface of trn, called a *selector*, enables you to move through a threaded set of articles. For example, if you are reading an article on a particular subject and you give an **n** command to go to the next article, you go to the next article on that subject (in the thread), not to the next sequentially posted article, as you would normally do. Instead of moving through a newsgroup's articles according to their posted order, you can move through them using different threads, examining articles according to different subjects. The same is true for an article and its follow-up articles. An article and its follow-ups are threaded, so upon reading an article, pressing the **n** command moves you to the first follow-up to that article, not to the next sequentially posted article. Using threads, you can use the **n** command to read an article with all of its follow-ups, instead of searching separately for each one. The trn newsreader commands are listed in Table 15-4.

Trn operates on two levels: the newsgroup list and the article list. When you first execute trn, you select a newsgroup from a list of newsgroups. Commands move you from one newsgroup to another in the list. Once you find the one you want, you can then select articles to read in that newsgroup. When you finish reading, you can leave that newsgroup and select another in the newsgroup list. You use the trn selector to display, organize, and move through the article list, though you can also use the standard **rn** commands to manage the article list.

You enter the trn newsreader by typing the command **trn** at your Linux prompt. The **trn** command initially displays a short list of newsgroup headers. Before doing so, however, the **trn** command first checks an official list of new newsgroups with those listed in your **.newsrc** file. If any new newsgroups are not yet listed in your **.newsrc** file, then trn asks, one by one, if you want to subscribe to them. At each prompt, you can enter **y** to add the newsgroup and **n** not to add it. With **-q,** trn goes directly to displaying the newsgroup headers, skipping any new newsgroup queries.

```
$ trn -q
```

After the subscription phase, trn checks to see if any newsgroups are listed in your **.newsrc** file that have unread news in them. If so, the newsgroup headers for the first few of these are displayed. Each newsgroup header tells how many unread articles remain in a given newsgroup. trn then prompts you as to whether you want to read articles in the first newsgroup. If not, you can enter the **n** command to move to the next newsgroup. The **p** command moves you back to the previous newsgroup.

To list articles in a newsgroup, you enter **+** at the prompt. This displays the trn selector from which you can select the article you want to display. If you enter **y,** you skip the list of articles and display the first article in the newsgroup. You are then prompted to read the next article or quit and return to the newsgroup list. You can leave the newsgroup and return to the newsgroup list by entering **q** at the prompt.

trn has a variety of commands for moving through the list of newsgroups. You can move to the first or last newsgroup, the next or previous newsgroup, or the newsgroup whose name has a specific pattern. For example, a **$** places you at the end of the newsgroup list. Many commands are designed to distinguish between read and unread newsgroups. The **^** places you at the first newsgroup with unread news, whereas the number **1** places you at the first newsgroup in the list, whether or not it is read. The lowercase **n** and **p** commands place you at the next and previous unread newsgroups, respectively. To move to the next or previous newsgroup, regardless of whether it is read, use the uppercase **N** and **P** commands. The pattern searching commands give trn great versatility in locating newsgroups. To perform a pattern search for a newsgroup, at the prompt, enter a **/** followed by the pattern. The **/** performs a forward search through the list of newsgroups. The **?** performs a backward search.

As mentioned earlier, typing **+** at the trn prompt enters the selector, which enables you to use threads. The selector consists of a screen that lists each article's author, thread count, and subject. Any follow-up articles are preceded by a **>** symbol. Articles are grouped according to the threads to which they belong. The first article in each thread is preceded by an ID, consisting of a lowercase alphabetic character or a single digit, starting from *a*.

The selector has three display modes—article, subject, and thread—which correspond to how the selector displays articles. You can easily choose the mode you want by pressing the **S** command and entering **a** for article, **s** for subject, or **t** for thread. You can also switch back and forth between the different modes by pressing the **=** key. A subject is whatever a user enters into the Subject field of an article's header. Articles with the same subject entry are threaded together. When using the thread mode, articles are grouped with any posted follow-ups, as well as with articles of the same subject. The follow-up articles are preceded by a **>** symbol. The article mode does not display threads. Articles are listed individually, each preceded by its own ID, in posted sequence.

When you display an article in a thread, a thread tree appears in the upper-right corner of the screen. A thread tree represents the connections between articles in a thread. Each unread article is represented by a number, starting from 1, with each enclosed in brackets. Lines connect the different article numbers. The number representing the article you are currently displaying is highlighted in the thread tree. Once you read an article and move on to another, the read article's number is enclosed in parentheses and the next article's number is highlighted.

Although most newsreaders let you post news, some such as trn, do not. You can post articles directly using Pnews. *Pnews* prompts you for certain header information, places you in an editor in which you can type in your article, and then prompts you either to send, edit, save, or quit the article. Pnews operates directly from the command line, providing you with a full-screen interface, much like other screen-based applications such as Pine, mutt, and **tin**. To begin, enter the **Pnews** command at your Linux shell prompt. You are then prompted to enter the newsgroup for the article. To see the full list of newsgroups, enter a **?** at the newsgroups prompt. (A good idea is, in advance, to decide on what newsgroups you want.) You can obtain a listing of newsgroups at any time from the newsgroup file located in the **news** directory on your system.

You usually end an article with the same standard signature information, such as your name, Internet address or addresses, and a polite sign-off. As you write more articles, having your signature information automatically added to your articles is helpful. To do so, you need to create a file called **.signature** in your home directory and enter your signature information in it. Pnews then reads the contents of the **.signature** file and places them at the end of your article. You can use any standard editor to create your **.signature** file.

Command	Description
N	Moves to the next newsgroup
p	Moves to the previous newsgroup with unread articles
P	Moves to the previous newsgroup
-	Moves to the previously selected newsgroup
^	Moves to the first newsgroup with unread articles
num	Moves to newsgroup with that number
$	Moves to the last newsgroup
g*newsgroup-name*	Moves to newsgroup with that name
/*pattern*	Searches forward to the newsgroup with that pattern
?*pattern*	Searches backward to the newsgroup with that pattern
L	Lists subscribed newsgroups
l*pattern*	Lists unsubscribed newsgroups
u *newsgroup-name*	Unsubscribed newsgroups

Table 15-4.   *trn Newsreader*

Command	Description
a *newsgroup-name*	Subscribed to a newsgroup
c	Marks articles in a newsgroup as read
Displaying Selector	
+	Enters the selector from the trn line prompt, or leaves the selector and returns to the trn line prompt
s	Selects selector mode: subject, thread, or article
=	Switches between article and subject/thread selector
o	Sorts selector items by date, author, thread count, or subject. User is prompted to enter **d**, **a**, **n**, or **s**.
U	Displays unread articles
Moving Through Selector	
SPACEBAR	Displays the next screen of articles
>	Displays the next screen of threads
<	Displays the previous screen of articles
$	Displays the last screen of articles
^	Displays the first screen of articles
Selecting Articles in the Selector	
id	Selects/deselects an article thread
*id**	Selects/deselects articles with the same subject as ID
n	Moves to the next thread ID
p	Moves to the previous thread ID
/*pattern*	Searches forward to the article with that pattern in each article's Subject field
?*pattern?*	Searches backward to the article with that pattern in each article's Subject field

Table 15-4.   *trn Newsreader* (continued)

INTERNET

Command	Description
Displaying Articles	
SPACEBAR	Displays the next screen of the article
ENTER	Scrolls to the next line of the article
b	Displays the previous screen of the article
g *pattern*	Searches for pattern in the text
G	Repeats pattern search in the text
Replying to Articles	
r	Replies to current article
R	Replies to current article and includes article text in the reply
f	Posts a follow-up to the current article
F	Posts a follow-up including the text of the current article

Table 15-4.   *trn Newsreader* (continued)

tin

The tin newsreader operates using a selector much like the one used in the trn
newsreader. However, tin has a screen selector for both newsgroups and articles. When
you enter **tin**, the selector displays the screen listing your newsgroups. You can then
select the newsgroup you want and display a screen for its articles. One set of screen
movement commands is used for all screens, whether for newsgroups, article lists, or
article text. CTRL-D, CTRL-F, and SPACEBAR all move you forward to the next screen.
CTRL-U, CTRL-B, and **b** all move you backward to the previous screen. The UP ARROW
and the **k** key move you up one line on the screen, while the DOWN ARROW and **j** key
move you down one line. The **q** command moves you back from one selector to
another. For example, if you are in the article selector, pressing **q** moves you back
to the newsgroup selector. **Q** quits the tin newsreader entirely.

Tin also has a set of editing and history commands you can use to edit any
commands you enter. ESC always erases a command you have entered and lets you
start over. The editing commands are a subset of the Emacs commands. CTRL-D deletes
a character, CTRL-F and the RIGHT ARROW key move right one character. CTRL-B and the

LEFT ARROW key move back one character. To insert new text, move your cursor to the position you want and start typing. Tin also keeps a history of the commands you enter. You can recall the previous commands with CTRL-P, moving back, one by one, through a list of your previously entered commands. CTRL-N moves you forward through the list. You can find a complete listing of all tin commands in the tin manual pages, which you can invoke by typing **man tin**. The tin newsreader commands are listed in Table 15-5.

When you start **tin**, it first displays a screen of newsgroups. The term "Group Selection" is shown at the top of the screen. To its right is "h=help." Pressing the **h** key brings up a Help menu. The newsgroups are listed with a selection number that identifies the newsgroup, followed by the number of unread articles, and then by the name of the newsgroup. To select a newsgroup, you must first move to it. You can do this in a variety of ways. If you see your newsgroup displayed on the screen, you can use your UP ARRROW and DOWN ARROW keys to move to it. CTRL-D moves you to the next screen; CTRL-U moves you back. Instead of using the ARROW keys, you can move directly to a newsgroup by entering its index number. You can also locate a newsgroup by using pattern searches. You enter the **/** followed by a pattern. **?** performs a backward search.

Once you locate the newsgroup you want, press ENTER to display a list of its articles. A list of commonly used commands is displayed at the bottom of the screen. The **s** command subscribes to a new newsgroup and the **u** command unsubscribes.

The **tin** newsreader displays the subject and author of each article in the newsgroup, preceded by an index number and, if unread, a **+**. The **+** sign indicates all unread articles. Working from the selector, you can choose articles you want to display. You select an article by moving the cursor to that article and pressing ENTER. Both the newsgroup and article selector screens use many of the same commands. The UP ARROW and DOWN ARROW keys move you from one article to the next. If more than one screen of articles exists, you can move back and forth through them using CTRL-U or CTRL-D. You can also move to an article by typing its index number. An example of the **tin** article selector screen follows:

```
rec.food.recipes (119T 124A 0K 0H R)          h=help

65    +    Fruit Salad                  Dylan Chris
66    +    Fudge Cake                   Cecelia Petersen
67    +    Chocolate News               Richard Leland
68    +    Chocolate News               Larisa@atlash
69    +    Apple Muffins                George Petersen
70    +    REQUEST: romantic dinners    Marylou Carrion
71    +    REQUEST: Dehydrated Goodies  Valerie Fuller
72    +    REQUEST: Devonshire Cream    Carolyn Blacklock
73    +    Sauces                       Bonnie Matoza
74    +    Passion Fruit                Gabriel Matoza
75    +    REQUEST: blackened (red)fish Ken Blacklock
76    +    REQUEST: Cheese Toast        dylan@sf
```

INTERNET

```
77    +      REQUEST: Sausage Recipes        Penny Bode
78    +      Biscuit Recipe                  gloria@stlake
79    +      >blackened (red)fish            augie@napa
80    +      Oatmeal Cookies                 John Gunther
81    +      REQUEST: Potato Salad           Margaret
82    +      REQUEST: Sesame Chicken         Frank Moitoza
83    +      >Summer desserts                maryann@sebast

    <n>=set current to n, TAB=next unread, /=search pattern, ^K)ill/select,
 a)uthor search, c)atchup, j=line down, k=line up, K=mark read, l)ist thread,
  |=pipe, m)ail, o=print, q)uit, r=toggle all/unread, s)ave, t)ag, w=post
```

The commonly used commands for accessing articles are displayed at the bottom of the screen. You can search articles for a specified pattern with the **/** command. The **a** command enables you to search for articles by a specified author. The **s** command saves an article. You can post an article of your own to the newsgroup by pressing the **w** command. You are prompted for header information, and then you enter the text of your message. Once you select an article, it is displayed. If the article takes up more than one screen, you can move forward by pressing the SPACEBAR and backward by pressing the **b** key. With the **B** command, you can search the article for a specified pattern, and with the **s** command you can save it. With the **f** command, you can post a follow-up to the article, while with the **r** command, you can send a message to the author.

tin supports an extensive set of options, features, attributes, and variables. Configuration files are placed in the **.tin** directory maintained in your **home** directory. Options can be set using the **tin** Global Options menu or by entering them directly in the **tinrc** file in the **.tin** directory. Attributes for particular newsgroups can be set in the **.tin** attributes file. For accessing remote news servers, be sure the **NNTPSERVER** variable is set in your **.bash_profile** file.

Screen Movement Commands	Effect/Description
DOWN ARROW, **j**	Moves down a line
UP ARROW, **k**	Moves up a line
$	Goes to last line
CTRL-**U**, CTRL-**B**, **b**, PAGE UP	Goes to previous screen

Table 15-5.   *tin Newsreader*

Screen Movement Commands	Effect/Description
CTRL-**D**, CTRL-**F**, SPACEBAR, PAGE DOWN	Goes to next screen
Q	Quits tin
Newsgroup Selector	
num	Goes to newsgroup with that index number
ENTER	Selects current newsgroup
/	Searches forward
?	Searches backward
l	Lists articles within current thread
s	Subscribes to a newsgroup
u	Unsubscribes to a newsgroup
h	Help command
Article Selector	
num	Goes to article with that index number
$	Goes to last article
ENTER	Selects current article
TAB	Goes to next unread article
/	Subject forward search
?	Subject backward search
Article Selector	**Effect/Description**
n	Goes to next group
p	Goes to previous group
N	Goes to next unread article
P	Goes to previous unread article
z	Marks article as unread

Table 15-5.   *tin Newsreader* (continued)

INTERNET

Screen Movement Commands	Effect/Description
Displaying Article	
b	Moves back a page
SPACEBAR	Moves forward a page
B	Article body search
s	Saves article/thread/hot/pattern/tagged articles to file
m	Mails article/thread/hot/pattern/tagged articles to someone
o	Outputs article/thread/hot/pattern/tagged articles to printer
w	Posts an article to current group
f	Posts follow-up for current article
r	Sends reply to author of article

Table 15-5. *tin Newsreader* (continued)

The Complete Reference

Linux

Chapter 16

FTP Clients

The *Internet* is a network of computers around the world you can access with an Internet address and a set of Internet tools. Many computers on the Internet are configured to operate as servers, providing information to anyone who requests it. The information is contained in files you can access and copy. Each server, often referred to as a *site,* has its own Internet address by which it can be located. Linux provides a set of Internet tools you can use to access sites on the Internet, and then locate and download information from them. These tools are known as *clients.* A client application, such as an FTP or a Web client, can communicate with a corresponding server application running on a remote system. An FTP client can communicate with an FTP server program on another system. The server lets the client access certain specified resources on its system and lets an FTP client transfer certain files. Several popular FTP clients are shown in Table 16-1.

To access Internet sites, your computer must be connected to the Internet. You may be part of a network already connected to the Internet. If you have a standalone computer, such as a personal computer, you can obtain an Internet connection from an *Internet service provider* (*ISP*). Once you have an Internet address of your own, you can configure your Linux system to connect to the Internet and use various Internet tools to access different sites. Chapter 36 describes how to configure your Linux system to make such a connection.

The primary tools for accessing Internet sites are FTP clients and Web browsers. With FTP clients, you can connect to a corresponding FTP site and download files from it. FTP clients are commonly used to download software from FTP sites that operate as software repositories. Most Linux software applications can be downloaded to your Linux system from such sites. A distribution site like **ftp.redhat.com** is an example of one such FTP site, holding an extensive set of packaged Linux applications you can download using an FTP client and then easily install on your system. In the last few years, the Web browsers have become the primary tool for accessing information on

FTP Clients	Description
Konquerer and kfm	The K Desktop file managers
GNU Midnight Commander	The Gnome file manager
gFTP	Gnome FTP client
IglooFTP	Gnome FTP client
NcFTP	Screen based FTP client
ftp	Command line FTP client

Table 16-1. *Linux FTP clients*

the Internet. Most of the tasks you perform on the Internet may be done easily with a Web browser. You only need to use an FTP client to download or upload files from or to a specific FTP site.

Other Internet tools are also available for your use, such as Gopher, telnet, and IRC clients. *Gopher* is as a kind of hybrid of FTP and Web clients. It provides you with a series of menus listing different topics. You move from one menu to the other, narrowing your topic until you find the information you want. Often, this is in the form of a file that you download by selecting its menu entry. The *telnet* protocol enables you to log into an account directly on another system. *IRC clients* set up chat rooms through which you can communicate with other users over the Internet. Web clients are discussed in the next chapter, and telnet and IRC clients are discussed in Chapter 18.

Internet Addresses

The Internet uses a set of network protocols called *TCP/IP*, which stands for *Transmission Control Protocol/Internet Protocol*. In a TCP/IP network, messages are broken into small components called *datagrams*, which are then transmitted through various interlocking routes and delivered to their destination computers. Once received, the datagrams are reassembled into the original message. Datagrams are also referred to as *packets*. Sending messages as small components has proved far more reliable and faster than sending them as one large bulky transmission. With small components, if one is lost or damaged, only that component has to be resent, whereas if any part of a large transmission is corrupted or lost, the entire message must be resent.

On a TCP/IP network such as the Internet, each computer is given a unique address called an *IP address.* The IP address is used to identify and locate a particular host—a computer connected to the network. IP addressing is described in detail in Chapter 38. A brief description is provided here to give an idea of what an IP address is and how it operates. An IP address is written as a set of four segments, each pair separated by a period. The segments consist of numbers that range from 0 to 255, with certain values reserved for special use. However, it is important to realize that these segments denote a single number and that number taken as a whole is the IP address. The IP address is divided into two parts: one part identifies the network, and the other part identifies a particular host. The size of each part is determined by the network mask. The network mask can be used to retrieve just the network or host part of the IP address. This method of determining the network and host segments is called Classless Interdomain Routing (CIDR), which replaced the traditional method based on network classes (see Chapter 38). Many IP addresses still fall into a class-based organization that can be helpful in understanding how an IP address works. In class-based IP addressing, networks are organized into three classes depending on their size—classes A, B, and C. A class A network uses only the first segment for the IP address and the remaining three for the host, allowing a great many computers to be connected to the same network. Most IP addresses reference smaller, class C, networks. For a class C network, the first three segments are used to identify the network and only the last segment identifies the host. The syntax looks like this:

```
net.net.net.host
```

For example, the Internet address 192.168.187.4 references the fourth computer connected to the network identified by the number **192.168.187**.

192.168.187.4	IP address
192.168.187	Network identification
4	Host identification

A special set of numbers is reserved for use on non-Internet local area networks. These are numbers that begin with the special network number 192.168., as used in these examples. If you are setting up a local area network, such as a small business or home network, you are free to use these numbers for your local machines. You can set up an intranet using network cards such as Ethernet cards and Ethernet hubs, and then configure your machines with IP addresses starting from 192.168.1.1. The host segment can go up to 256. If you have three machines on your home network, you could give them the addresses 192.168.1.1, 192.168.1.2, 192.168.1.3. You can implement "Internet" services, such as FTP, Web, and mail services, on your local machines, and use any of the "Internet" tools to make use of those services. They all use the same TCP/IP protocols as used on the Internet. For example, with FTP tools you can transfer files between the machines on your network, with mail tools you can send messages from one machine to the other, and with a Web browser you can access local "Web" sites that may be installed on a machine running its own "Web" servers. If you want to have one of your machines connected to the Internet or some other network, you can set it up to be a gateway machine. By conventions, the gateway machine is usually given the address 192.168.1.1. With a method called *IP masquerading*, you can have any of the non-Internet machines use a gateway to connect to the Internet.

All hosts on the Internet are identified by their IP addresses. When you send a message to a host on the Internet, you must provide its IP address. Using a sequence of four numbers of an IP address, however, can be difficult. They are hard to remember, and it's easy to make mistakes when typing them. To make identifying a computer on the Internet easier, the *Domain Name Service* (*DNS*) was implemented. The DNS establishes a domain name address for each IP address. The domain name address is a series of names separated by periods. Whenever you use a domain name address, it is automatically converted to an IP address, which is then used to identify that Internet host. The domain name address is far easier to use than its corresponding IP address.

A domain name address needs to be registered with the NIC so that each computer on the Internet can have a unique name. Creating a name follows specified naming conventions, as discussed earlier, in Chapter 26. The domain name address consists of the hostname, the name you gave to your computer; a domain name, the name that identifies your network; and an extension that identifies the type of network you are on. Here is the syntax for domain addresses:

```
host-name.domain-name.extension
```

In the following example, the domain address references a computer called *metalab* on a network referred to as *unc*. It is part of an educational institution, as indicated by the extension *edu*.

```
metalab.unc.edu
```

The conversion of domain addresses to IP addresses used to be performed by each individual host. And, for a few frequently used addresses for which you know the IP address, this can still be done. So many computers are now connected to the Internet, however, that domain name conversion has to be performed by special servers known as *Domain Name Servers* or simply name servers. A *name server* holds a database of domain name addresses and their IP addresses. Local networks sometimes have their own name servers. If a name server does not have the address, then it may call on other name servers to perform the conversion. A program on your computer called a *resolver* obtains the IP address from a name server and then uses it in the application where you specified the domain name address.

With the **whois** and **nslookup** commands, you can obtain information for domain name servers about different networks and hosts connected to the Internet. Enter **whois** and the domain name address of the host or network, and **whois** displays information about the host, such as the street address and phone number, as well as contact persons.

```
$ whois   domain-address
```

The nslookup command takes a domain address and finds its corresponding IP address.

```
$ nslookup   domain-address
```

The **nslookup** command has an interactive mode you enter by not specifying any domain name. You can then use **nslookup** to search for other kinds of information about a host. For example, the HINFO option finds out what type of operating system a host uses. The nslookup man page specifies a list of different options and how to use them.

Network File Transfer: FTP

You can use *File Transfer Protocol* (*FTP*) clients to transfer extremely large files directly from one site to another. FTP can handle both text and binary files. This is one of the TCP/IP protocols, and it operates on systems connected to networks that use the TCP/IP protocols, such as the Internet. FTP performs a remote login to another account on another system connected to you on a network, such as the Internet. Once logged into that other system, you can transfer files to and from it. To log in, you need to know the login name and password for the account on the remote system. For example, if you have accounts at two different sites on the Internet, you can use FTP to transfer files from one to the other. Many sites on the Internet allow public access using FTP, however. Many sites serve as depositories for large files anyone can access and download. Such sites are often referred to as *FTP sites,* and in many cases, their Internet address begins with the word *ftp,* such as **ftp.caldera.com** or **ftp.redhat.com**. Others begin with other names, such as **metalab.unc.edu**. These public sites allow anonymous FTP login from any user. For the login name, you use the word "anonymous," and for the password you use your Internet address. You can then transfer files from that site to your own system.

You can perform FTP operations using any one of a number of FTP client programs. For Linux systems, you can choose from several FTP clients. Many now operate using GUI interfaces such as Gnome. Some, such as Netscape, have limited capabilities, whereas others, such as NcFTP, include an extensive set of enhancements. The original FTP client is just as effective, though not as easy to use. It operates using a simple command line interface and requires no GUI or cursor support, as do other clients.

Web Browser–Based FTP: Netscape

You access an FTP site and download files from it with any Web browser. A Web browser is effective for checking out an FTP site to see what files are listed there. When you access an FTP site with a Web browser, the entire list of files in a directory is listed as a Web page. You can move to a subdirectory by clicking its entry. Click the .. entry at the top of the page to move back up to the parent directory. With Netscape Navigator, you can easily browse through an FTP site to download files. To download a file, you left-click (not right-click) its entry. If the file is simply displayed on a Web page, go back and hold down the SHIFT key when you click the file. This will start the transfer operation. This opens a box for selecting your local directory and the name for the file (see Figure 16-1). The default name is the same as on the remote system. Netscape Navigator has some important limitations. You cannot upload a file, and you cannot

Figure 16-1. *Netscape Navigator FTP file transfer*

download more than one file at a time. Navigator is useful for locating individual files, though not for downloading a large set of files, as is usually required for a system update.

The K Desktop File Manager: Konqueror and kfm

On the K Desktop, the desktop file manager (Konqueror for KDE 2.0 and kfm for previous versions) has a built-in FTP capability, as shown in Figure 16-2. The FTP operation has been seamlessly integrated into standard desktop file operations. Downloading files from an FTP site is as simple as copying files by dragging them

Figure 16-2. *The K Desktop file manager (Konqueror) performing FTP operations*

from one directory window to another, but one of the directories happens to be located on a remote FTP site. On the K Desktop, you can use a file manager window to access a remote FTP site. Files in the remote directory are listed just as your local files are. To download files from an FTP site, you open a window to access that site, entering the URL for the FTP site in the window's location box. Open the directory you want, and then open another window for the local directory to which you want the remote files copied. In the window showing the FTP files, select the ones you want to download. Then, simply click-and-drag those files to the window for the local directory. A pop-up menu appears with choices for copy or move. Select move. The selected files are then downloaded. Another window then opens, showing the download progress and displaying the name of each file in turn, and a bar indicating the percentage downloaded so far.

Gnome FTP: GNU Midnight Commander, gFTP, and IglooFTP

The easiest way to download files is to use the built-in FTP capabilities of the Gnome file manager, Midnight Commander. You can also use several Gnome-based FTP clients that offer more features, including gFTP and IglooFTP. Check the Gnome Web site at **www.gnome.org** for more. gFTP is included with the current Gnome release. IglooFTP is a commercial product that can be downloaded from its Web site at **www.littleigloo.org**.

Gnome File Manager

On Gnome, the desktop file manager—*GNU Midnight Commander*—has a built-in FTP capability much like the KDE file manager. The FTP operation has been seamlessly integrated into standard desktop file operations. Downloading files from an FTP site is as simple as dragging files from one directory window to another, where one of the directories happens to be located on a remote FTP site. Use the Gnome file manager to access a remote FTP site, listing files in the remote directory, just as local files are. Just enter the ftp URL following the prefix **ftp://** and press ENTER. The top directory of the remote FTP site will be displayed. Simply use the file manager to progress through the remote FTP site's directory tree until you find the file you want. Then open another window for the local directory to which you want the remote files copied. In the window showing the FTP files, select those you want to download. Then use a CTRL-click and drag those files to the window for the local directory. A CTRL-click performs a copy operation, not a move. As files are downloaded, a dialog window appears showing the progress (see Figure 16-3).

gFTP

The *gFTP* program is a simpler Gnome FTP client designed to let you make standard FTP file transfers. It has an interface similar to WS_FTP used on Windows (see Figure 16-4). The gFTP window consists of several panes. The top-left pane lists files in your local directory, and the top-right pane lists your remote directory. Subdirectories have folder icons preceding their names. The parent directory can be referenced by a .. entry with an up-arrow at the top of each list. Double-click a directory entry to access it. The pathnames for all directories are displayed in boxes above each pane. You can enter a new pathname for a different directory to change to it, if you want.

Figure 16-3. *The Gnome GNU Midnight Commander file manager performing FTP transfers*

Two buttons between the panes are used for transferring files. The left arrow, <-, button downloads selected files in the remote directory, and the right arrow, ->, button uploads files from the local directory. To download a file, click it in the right-side pane and then click the left arrow button, <-. When the file is downloaded, its name appears in the left-side pane, your local directory. Menus across the top of the window can be used to manage your transfers. A connection manager enables you to enter login information about a specific site. You can specify whether to perform an anonymous

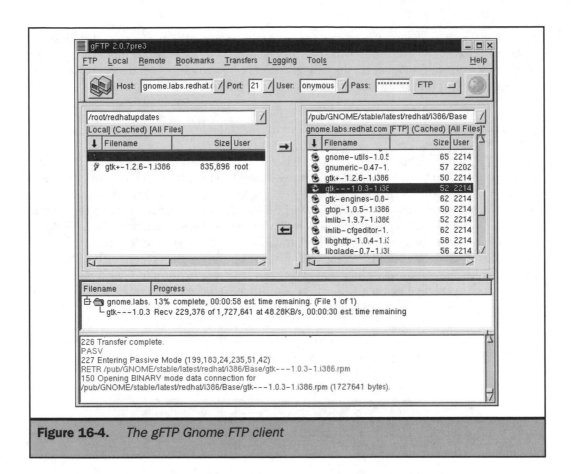

Figure 16-4.   *The gFTP Gnome FTP client*

login or to provide a user name and password. Click the Connect button to connect to that site. A drop-down menu for sites enables you to choose the site you want.

IglooFTP

IglooFTP is a commercial product designed to be a Linux version of Bullet-proof FTP, used on Windows systems (**www.littleigloo.com**). It has an extensive set of features with an easy-to-use interface. You can perform FTP operations graphically, selecting files with your mouse and clicking a button or menu for a specified task. IglooFTP download features include recursive downloading, queue transfers, and firewall support. You can download a directory with all its subdirectories with only one operation, as well as download from different sites at the same time. Queue transfers feature auto-resume support in case of interruptions. IglooFTP provides operations

INTERNET

managing files and directories on your remote site, provided you have the permission to do so. It features a graphical directory browser for both local and remote file systems to locate directories and files easily. The graphical directory browser displays files and directory in a tree-like structure whose directories (folders) can be shrunk or expanded.

NcFTP

The *NcFTP program*, shown in Figure 16-5, has a screen-based interface that can be run from any shell command line. It does not use a desktop interface. FTP operations are executed using commands you enter at a prompt. Options and bookmarks can be selected using cursor-based menus. To start up NcFTP, you enter the **ncftp** command on the command line. If you are working in a window manager, such as KDE, GNOME, or FVWM, open a shell terminal window and enter the command at its prompt. The main NcFTP screen consists of an input line at the bottom of the screen with a status line above it. The remainder of the screen is used to display commands and responses from remote systems. For example, when you download files, a message specifying the files to be downloaded is displayed in the status line. NcFTP lets you set preferences for different features, such as anonymous login, progress meters, or a download directory. Enter the **pref** command to open the preferences screen. From there, you can select and modify the listed preferences.

Figure 16-5. *NcFTP*

To connect to an FTP site, you enter the **open** command on the input line, followed by the site's address. The address can be either an IP address or a domain name, such as **ftp.gnome.org**. If you don't supply an address, then a list of your bookmarked sites is displayed, and you can choose one from there. By default, NcFTP attempts an anonymous login, using the term "anonymous" as your user name and your e-mail address as the password. When you successfully connect, the status bar displays the remote site's name on the left and the remote directory name on the right.

```
open ftp.gnome.org
```

If you want to log into a specific account on a remote site, have yourself prompted for the user name and password by using the **-u** option with the **open** command. The **open** command remembers the last kind of login you performed for a specific site and repeats it. If you want to change back to an anonymous login from a user login, you use the **-a** option with the **open** command. For busy sites, you may be unable to connect on the first try and you must repeat the open process. NcFTP has a redial capability you turn on with the **-r** option. The **-d** option sets the delay for the next attempt, and the **-g** option sets the maximum number of connection attempts. With the lookup command, you can obtain the IP and domain name addresses for an FTP site. The lookup command takes as an argument either the IP or domain name address and then displays both. This is useful for finding a site's IP address. With the **-v** option, more information, such as aliases, is retrieved. The NcFTP open options are shown in Table 16-2.

Once connected, you enter commands on the input line to perform FTP operations such as displaying file lists, changing directories, or downloading files. With the **ls** command, you can list the contents of the current remote directory. Use the **cd** command to change to another remote directory. The **dir** command displays a detailed listing of

Option	Description
-a	Connect anonymously
-u	Connect with user name and password prompts
-p *num*	Use specified port number when connecting
-r	Redial until connected
-d *num*	Set delay (*num*) in number of seconds for redial option
-g *num*	Specify the maximum number of redials

Table 16-2. *NcFTP Open Options*

files. With the **page** command, you view the contents of a remote file, a screen at a time. To download files, you use the **get** command, and to upload files, you use the **put** command. During a download, a progress meter above the status bar displays how much of the file has been downloaded so far. The **get** command has several features described in more detail in the following section. When you finish, you can disconnect from the site with the **close** command. You can then use **open** to connect to another site, or quit the NcFTP program with the **quit** command. The **help** command lists all NcFTP commands. You can use the **help** command, followed by the name of a command to display specific information on it.

The NcFTP program supports several commands that operate on your local system. These are usually standard FTP command names preceded by an *l*. **lcd** changes your local working directory, **lls** lists the contents of your local directory, **lpage** displays the contents of a local file a screen at a time, and **lpwd** displays the local directory's full pathname. For any other local commands or scripts you need to execute, use the shell escape command, !. Simply precede the shell command or script with a !.

The NcFTP program also provides commands for managing files and directories on your remote site, provided you have the permission to do so. You can use **mkdir** to create a remote directory, and **rmdir** to remove one. Use the **rm** command to erase remote files. With the **rename** command, you can change their names. The NcFTP commands are listed in Table 16-3.

The NcFTP program also has a colon mode of operation that enables you to issue a single **ncftp** command to download a file. Enter the **ncftp** command, followed by a URL, for the file you want. You can enter the command on the shell command line or place it within a script. For example, the following command downloads the README file on the Red Hat FTP site.

```
$ ncftp ftp.redhat.com/pub/README
```

In the colon mode, the **-c** option sends the file to the standard output and the **-m** option pipes it to your pager, usually the more program.

```
$ ncftp -c ftp.redhat.com/pub/README > ~/redhatinfo/readme
$ ncftp -m ftp.redhat.com/pub/README
```

NcFTP Download Features

The NcFTP **get** command differs significantly from the original FTP client's **get** command. Whereas the original FTP client uses two commands, **get** and **mget**, to perform download operations, NcFTP uses only the **get** command. However, the NcFTP get command combines the capabilities of both **mget** and **get** into the **get** command, as well as adding several new features. Table 13-4 lists the various **get** command options. By default, the NcFTP **get** command performs wildcard matching

Command	Description
help [*command*]	Lists names of NcFTP commands
cd [*directory*]	Changes the working directory on the remote host
create [*filename*]	Creates an empty file on the remote host, enabling you to use the filename as a message
debug	Turns debugging on or off
version	Displays version information
dir	Displays a detailed directory listing
echo	Displays a string, useful for macros
get	Downloads files from a remote host to your working directory
lcd [*directory*]	Changes the local working directory
lls	Lists files in your local working directory
lookup *host*	Looks up entries for remote hosts
lpage *filename*	Displays contents of local file, a page at time
lpwd	Displays the local current working directory
mkdir *directory name*	Creates a directory on the remote host
mode *mode*	Specifies transfer mode (*b* for block mode, *s* for stream mode)
open [*option*] *hostname*	Connects to a remote host. If no hostname is specified, then the bookmark editor displays a host list from which you can choose one (-a forces anonymous login, -u forces user login, -r redials automatically, -d specifies time delay before redial—used with -r, and -g specifies the maximum number of redials—used with -r)
page *filename*	Displays the contents of a remote file
pdir	Same as dir, but outputs to your pager, enabling you to display a remote file list a page at a time. Used for command line interface

Table 16-3.   *NcFTP Commands*

INTERNET

Command	Description
pls	Same as ls, but outputs to your pager; used for command line interface
redir	Redisplays the last directory listing
predir	Redisplays the last directory listing and outputs to pager if working in command line interface
put *filename*	Uploads a file to a remote host
pwd	Displays the remote current working directory
rename *orig-name new-name*	Changes the name of a remote file
quit	Quits NcFTP
quote	Sends an FTP protocol command to the remote server
rhelp [*command*]	Sends a help request to the remote host
rm *filenames*	Erases remote files
rmdir *directories*	Removes remote directories
site *command*	Executes site-specific commands
type *type*	Changes transfer type (ASCII, binary, image)
! *command*	Escapes to the shell and executes the following shell command or script

Table 16-3.   *NcFTP Commands* (continued*)*

for filenames. If you enter only part of a filename, the **get** command tries to download all files beginning with that name. You can turn off wildcard matching with the **-G** option, in which case you must enter the full names of the files you want. The following example downloads all files with names beginning with "Xfree86" and is similar to using mget Xfree86* in the original FTP.

```
get Xfree86
```

The **get** command checks to see if you already have a file you are trying to download. If so, it skips the download. The **get** command also checks if the file you already have is a newer version, in which case it also skips the download. This is a helpful feature for easily maintaining upgrade files. You can simply access the update directory on the remote site, and then use the **get** command with the ***** to download to the directory you are using to keep your upgrade file. Only newer versions or newly added upgrade files are download, instead of the entire set. If you want to download a file, even though you have it already, you can force the download with the **-f** option. For example, to download upgrades for Red Hat manually, you can connect to the Red Hat upgrade directory in the Red Hat FTP site and then issue the following **get** command:

```
get *
```

Tip *If you were interrupted during a download, you can restart the download from where you left off. This feature is built into NcFTP. (On other FTP programs, it can be invoked with the **reget** command.) NcFTP checks to see if you have already started to download a file and then continues from where you left off.*

Certain features require you to enter an option on the command line after the get command. For example, adding the **-R** command specifies a recursive capability, enabling you to download and create subdirectories and their files. This command is particularly helpful in downloading upgrade directories, such as Red Hat's, which contain several subdirectories. The following example downloads the **i386** directory and all its subdirectories.

```
get -R i386
```

If you want to give a file a different name on your local system, use the **-z** option. Enter the local filename you want after the remote filename. The following example downloads the **readme** file and renames it **calinfo**. If you did not use the **-z** option, then both names would be taken as files to be downloaded, instead of only the first.

```
get -z readme calinfo
```

To obtain recent files only, you can use the **-n** option, which takes as its argument a number of days. Files older than the specified number of days are not retrieved. The following example downloads files posted within the last 30 days.

```
get -n 30 *
```

INTERNET

Command	Description
-G	Turn wildcard matching for filenames on or off
-R *directory*	Download a directory and all its subdirectories (recursive)
-f *filenames*	Force the download of all specified files, even if older or the same as local ones
-C	Force resumption of a download from where it was interrupted
-z *remote-file local-file*	Rename a remote file on your local system
-n *num*	Download files no older than the specified number of days

Table 16-4. *NcFTP* **get** *Options*

Bookmarks and Macros

When you disconnect (close) from a site, NcFTP automatically saves information about it. This includes the site address, the directory you were in, and the login information. This information is placed in a file called **bookmarks** in your **.ncftp** directory. The site information is given a bookmark name you can use to access the site easily again. The bookmark name is usually the key name in the site's address. You can use this name to connect to the site. For example, **ftp.redhat.com** could be named redhat. You could then connect to it with the command

```
open redhat
```

You can edit your bookmark entries using the bookmark editor. Enter the command bookmarks to bring up the editor. Remote systems you have accessed are listed on the right side of the screen. Bookmark commands are listed on the left. You can change the bookmark name or edit login information, such as the user name or password, the remote directory, or the transfer mode.

The NcFTP program supports macros for simple operations. You create macros by entering macro definitions in the macros file located in your **.ncftp** directory. Initially, no such file will exist, so you have to create one using any text editor. The macros file is a simple text file you can edit with any text editor. The syntax for a macro definition is as follows:

```
macro macro-name
    ftp-commands
end
```

A macro executes NcFTP commands. Remember, however, the ! is an NcFTP command that enables you to execute any Linux command or script. With a preceding ! you can define an NcFTP macro that executes any shell command or any script you have written. A simple example of a macro is

```
macro ascii
    type ascii
end
```

Macros support parameters similar to those used by shell programs. Arguments entered after a macro name can be referenced in the macro using a $ sign and the number of the argument in the argument list. $1 references the first argument, $2 the second, and so on. $* is a special parameter that references all arguments, and $@ references all arguments, encasing each in double quotes.

```
macro cdls
  cd $1
  ls
end
```

The NcFTP program also supports a limited numbers of event macros. These are macros executed when a certain event is detected, such as when the program starts or shuts down. For example, a macro defined with the name **.start.ncftp** has its commands executed every time you start NcFTP; **.quit.ncftp** executes its commands when you quit. Site-specific macros also execute whenever it is necessary to access or disconnect from certain sites. These macros begin with either the open or close event, followed by the site's bookmark. For example, a macro defined with the name **.open.redhat** would execute its commands whenever you connected to the Red Hat site. A macro named **.open.any** has its commands executed whenever you connect to any site, and one named **.close.any** executes whenever you disconnect from a site.

ftp

The name **ftp** designates the original FTP client used on Unix and Linux systems. **Ftp** uses a command line interface, and it has an extensive set of commands and options you can use to manage your FTP transfers. You start the **ftp** client by entering the command **ftp** at a shell prompt. If you have a specific site you want to connect to, you can include the name of that site on the command line after the **ftp** keyword.

Otherwise, you need to connect to the remote system with the **ftp** command **open**. You are then prompted for the name of the remote system with the prompt (to). Upon entering the remote system name, **ftp** connects you to the system and then prompts you for a login name. The prompt for the login name consists of the word "Name" and, in parentheses, the system name and your local login name. Sometimes the login name on the remote system is the same as the login name on your own system. If the names are the same, press ENTER at the prompt. If they are different, enter the remote system's login name. After entering the login name, you are prompted for the password. In the next example, the user connects to the remote system **garnet** and logs into the **robert** account.

```
$ ftp
ftp> open
(to) garnet
Connected to garnet.berkeley.edu.
220 garnet.berkeley.edu FTP server (ULTRIX Version 4.1 Sun May 16 10:23:46 EDT
1996) ready.
Name (garnet.berkeley.edu:root): robert
password required
Password:
user robert logged in
ftp>
```

Once logged in, you can execute Linux commands on either the remote system or your local system. You execute a command on your local system in **ftp** by preceding the command with an exclamation point. Any Linux commands without an exclamation point are executed on the remote system. One exception exists to this rule. Whereas you can change directories on the remote system with the **cd** command, to change directories on your local system, you need to use a special **ftp** command called **lcd** (local **cd**). In the next example, the first command lists files in the remote system, while the second command lists files in the local system.

```
ftp> ls
ftp> !ls
```

The **ftp** program provides a basic set of commands for managing files and directories on your remote site, provided you have the permission to do so. You can use **mkdir** to create a remote directory, and **rmdir** to remove one. Use the **delete** command to erase a remote file. With the **rename** command, you can change the names of files. You close your connection to a system with the **close** command. You can then open another connection if you want. To end the **ftp** session, use the **quit** or **bye** command.

```
ftp> close
ftp> bye
Good-bye
$
```

File Transfer

To transfer files to and from the remote system, use the **get** and **put** commands. The **get** command receives files from the remote system to your local system, and the **put** command sends files from your local system to the remote system. In a sense, your local system gets files *from* the remote and puts files *to* the remote. In the next example, the file **weather** is sent from the local system to the remote system using the **put** command.

```
ftp> put weather
PORT command successful.
ASCII data connection
ASCII Transfer complete.
ftp>
```

If a download is ever interrupted, you can resume the download with **reget**. This is helpful for an extremely large file. The download resumes from where it left off, so the whole file needn't be downloaded again. Also, be sure to download binary files in binary mode. For most FTP sites, the binary mode is the default, but some sites might have ASCII (text) as the default. The command **ascii** sets the character mode, and the command **binary** sets the binary mode. Most software packages available at Internet sites are archived and compressed files, which are binary files. In the next example, the transfer mode is set to binary, and the archived software package **mydata.tar.gz** is sent from the remote system to your local system using the **get** command.

```
ftp> binary
ftp> get mydata.tar.gz
PORT command successful.
Binary data connection
Binary Transfer complete.
ftp>
```

You may often want to send several files, specifying their names with wildcard characters. The **put** and **get** commands, however, operate only on a single file and do not work with special characters. To transfer several files at a time, you have to use two other commands, **mput** and **mget**. When you use **mput** or **mget**, you are prompted for a file list. You can then either enter the list of files or a file-list specification using special characters. For example, ***.c** specifies all the files with a **.c** extension, and ***** specifies all files in the current directory. In the case of **mget**, each file is sent, one by one, from the remote system to your local system. Each time, you are prompted with the name of the file being sent. You can type **y** to send the file or **n** to cancel the transmission. You are then prompted for the next file. The **mput** command works in the same way, but it sends files from your local system to the remote system. In the next example, all files with a **.c** extension are sent to your local system using **mget**.

```
ftp> mget
(remote-files) *.c
mget calc.c? y
PORT command successful
ASCII data connection
ASCII transfer complete
mget main.c? y
PORT command successful
ASCII data connection
ASCII transfer complete
ftp>
```

Answering the prompt for each file can be a tedious prospect if you plan to download a large number of files, such as those for a system update. In this case, you can turn off the prompt with the **prompt** command, which toggles the interactive mode on and off. The **mget** operation then downloads all files it matches, one after the other.

```
ftp> prompt
Interactive mode off.
ftp> mget
(remote-files) *.c
 PORT command successful
ASCII data connection
ASCII transfer complete
PORT command successful
ASCII data connection
ASCII transfer complete
ftp>
```

Note   *To access a public FTP site, you have to perform an anonymous login. Instead of a login name, you enter the keyword "anonymous" (or "ftp"). Then, for the password, you enter your Internet address. Once the **ftp** prompt is displayed, you are ready to transfer files. You may need to change to the appropriate directory first or set the transfer mode to binary.*

Command	Effect
ftp	Invokes **ftp** program.
open *site-address*	Opens a connection to another system.
close	Closes connection to a system.
quit or **bye**	Ends **ftp** session.
ls	Lists the contents of a directory.
dir	Lists the contents of a directory in long form.
get *filename*	Sends file from remote system to local system.
put *filename*	Sends file from local system to remote system.
mget *regular-expression*	Enables you to download several files at once from a remote system; you can use special characters to specify the files; you are prompted one-by-one, in turn, for each file transfer.
mput *regular-expression*	Enables you to send several files at once to a remote system; you can use special characters to specify the files; you are prompted one-by-one for each file to be transferred.
runique	Toggles storing of files with unique filenames. If a file already exists with the same filename on the local system, a new filename is generated.
reget *filename*	Resumes transfer of an interrupted file from where you left off.
binary	Transfers files in binary mode.
ascii	Transfers files in ASCII mode.
cd *directory*	Changes directories on the remote system.
lcd *directory*	Changes directories on the local system.
help or **?**	Lists **ftp** commands.
mkdir *directory*	Creates a directory on the remote system.
rmdir	Deletes a remote directory.

Table 16-5.   *ftp* Client Commands

INTERNET

Command	Effect
delete *file name*	Deletes a file on the remote system.
mdelete *file-list*	Deletes several remote files at once.
rename	Renames a file on a remote system.
hash	Displays progressive hash signs during download.
status	Displays current status of **ftp**.

Table 16-5. *ftp* Client Commands (continued)

Automatic Login and Macros: .netrc

The **ftp** client has an automatic login capability and support for macros. Both are entered in a user's **ftp** configuration file called **.netrc**. Each time you connect to a site, the **.netrc** file is checked for connection information, such as a login name and password. In this way, you needn't enter a login name and password each time you connect to a site. This feature is particularly useful for anonymous logins. Instead of your having to enter the user name "anonymous" and your e-mail address as your password, they can be automatically read from the **.netrc** file. You can even make anonymous login information your default so that, unless otherwise specified, an anonymous login is attempted for any FTP site to which you try to connect. If you have sites you must log into, you can specify them in the **.netrc** file and, when you connect, either automatically log in with your user name and password for that site or be prompted for them.

Entries in the **.netrc** file have the following syntax. An entry for a site begins with the term "machine," followed by the network or Internet address, and then the login and password information.

```
machine system-address  login  remote-login-name  password  password
```

The following example shows an entry for logging into the **dylan** account on the **turtle.trek.com** system.

```
machine golf.mygames.com login  dylan password legogolf
```

For a site you would anonymously log into, you enter the word "anonymous" for the login name and your e-mail address for the password.

```
machine  ftp.redhat.com  login anonymous  password dylan@turtle.trek.com
```

In most cases, you are using **ftp** to access anonymous FTP sites. Instead of trying to make an entry for each one, you can make a default entry for anonymous FTP login. When you connect to a site, **ftp** looks for a machine entry for it in the **.netrc** file. If none exists, then **ftp** looks for a default entry and uses that. A default entry begins with the term "default" with no network address. To make anonymous logins your default, enter "anonymous" and your e-mail address as your login and password.

```
    default  login anonymous  password dylan@turtle.trek.com
```

.netrc

```
machine golf.mygames.com  login   dylan  password  legogolf
default   login anonymous  password dylan@turtle.trek.com
```

You can also define macros in your **.netrc** file. With a macro, you can execute several **ftp** operations at once using only the macro name. Macros remain in effect during a connection. When you close a connection, the macros are undefined. Although a macro can be defined on your **ftp** command line, defining them in **.netrc** entries makes more sense. This way, you needn't redefine them again. They are read automatically from the **.netrc** file and defined for you. You can place macro definitions within a particular machine entry in the **.netrc** file or in the default entry. Macros defined in machine entries are defined only when you connect to that site. Macros in the default entry are defined whenever you make a connection to any site.

The syntax for a macro definition follows. It begins with the keyword **macdef**, followed by the macro name you want to give it, and ends with an empty line. **ftp** macros can take arguments, referenced within the macro with $n, where $1 references the first argument, and $2 the second, and so on. If you need to use a $ character in a macro, you have to quote it using the backslash, \$.

```
macdef  macro-name
ftp commands
empty-line
```

The **redupd** macro, defined next, changes to a directory where it then downloads Red Hat updates for the current release. It also changes to a local directory where the update files are to be placed. The **prompt** command turns off the download prompts for each file. The **mget** command then downloads the files. The macro assumes you are connected to the Red Hat FTP site.

```
defmac redupd
cd pub/redhat/current
lcd /root/redupdate
prompt
mget *
```

A sample **.netrc** file follows with macros defined for both specific and default entries. An empty line is placed after each macro definition. You can define several macros for a machine or the default entry. The macro definitions following a machine entry up to the next machine entry are automatically defined for that machine connection.

.netrc

```
machine updates.redhat.com  login   anonymous  password
dylan@turtle.trek.com
# define a macro for downloading updated from the Red Hat site
defmac redupd
     cd pub/redhat/current
     lcd /root/redupdate
     prompt
     mget *

default login anonymous password dylan@turtle.trek.com
defmac lls
!ls
```

Online FTP Resources

The Internet has a great many sites open to public access. They contain files anyone can obtain using file transfer programs, such as **ftp**. Unless you already know where a file is located, however, finding it can be difficult. To search for files on FTP sites, you can use search engines provided by Web sites, such as Yahoo!, Excite, Alta Vista, Google, or Lycos. For Linux software, you can check sites such as **freshmeat.net, sourceforge.net**, **rpmfind.net**, **apps.kde.com**, and **www.linuxapps.com**. These sites usually search for both Web pages and FTP files. Normally, you must use a Web browser to access such sites and perform searches. However, Linux utilities are being developed that can access sites directly and list the results. *Ganesha* is one such utility, which is a Gnome-based application that accesses the Lycos FTP search service at **ftpsearch.lycos.com**, performs a search, and displays the results, as shown in Figure 16-6. You enter the search string and press ENTER. Results are listed showing round-trip

Figure 16-6. A Ganesha FTP search

times, number of hops, the FTP site, and the full pathname of the file. You can then select items and save them to your disk. The number of hops to a location indicates how far away the site is. You can also drag Netscape URLs into the Ganesha window to check the round-trip times and number of hops to a Web site.

Another utility you can use for locating files is *Archie. Xarchie* is an X Windows version, and karchie is the KDE version. *Xarchie* enables you to use menus and list boxes to perform an Archie search and to display its results. You can even use Xarchie to perform an FTP operation for a file you select, downloading it to your system. Xarchie has three menus, File, Settings, and Query. Xarchie operates by accessing an Archie server to perform a search and then displays the results. The list of Archie servers is displayed by selecting the Archie Host item in the Settings menu. To perform a search, enter the search term in the box labeled Search Term, and then select the Item entry in the Query menu. The display window is separated into several list boxes, the first of which lists the Internet sites found. When you click a particular site, the pathname for the file you are looking for is displayed in the second list box (there can be more than one list box). The third list box shows the item found, which can be either a file or a directory.

INTERNET

The
Complete
Reference

Chapter 17

The World Wide Web

The World Wide Web (*WWW* or the *Web*) is a hypertext database of different types of information, distributed across many different sites on the Internet. A *hypertext database* consists of items linked to other items, which, in turn, may be linked to yet other items, and so on. Upon retrieving an item, you can use that item to retrieve any related items. For example, you could retrieve an article on the Amazon rain forest and then use it to retrieve a map or a picture of the rain forest. In this respect, a hypertext database is like a web of interconnected data you can trace from one data item to another. Information is displayed in pages known as *Web pages*. On a Web page, certain keywords are highlighted that form links to other Web pages or to items, such as pictures, articles, or files.

The Web links data across different sites on the Internet throughout the world. The Web originated in Europe at CERN research laboratories, and CERN remains the original Web server. An Internet site that operates as a Web server is known as a *Web site*. Such Web sites are often dedicated to specialized topics or institutions—for example, the Smithsonian Web site or the NASA Web site. These Web sites usually have an Internet address that begins with www, as in **www.redhat.com**, the Web site for Red Hat, Inc. Once connected to a Web site, you can use hypertext links to move from one Web page to another.

To access the Web, you use a client program called a *browser*. You can choose from many different Web browsers. Browsers are available for use on UNIX, Windows, the Mac, and Linux. Certain browsers, such as Netscape and Mosaic, have versions that operate on all such systems. On your Linux system, you can choose from several Web browsers, including Netscape Navigator. Navigator is available as part of all Linux distributions. Netscape and Mosaic are X Windows–based browsers that provide full picture, sound, and video display capabilities. Most distributions also include the Lynx browser, a line-mode browser that displays only lines of text. The K Desktop incorporates Web browser capabilities into its file manager, letting a directory window operate as a Web browser. Gnome-based browsers, such as Express and Mnemonic, are also designed to be easily enhanced.

URL Addresses

An Internet resource is accessed using a *Universal Resource Locator* (*URL*). A URL is composed of three elements: the transfer protocol, the hostname, and the pathname. The transfer protocol and the hostname are separated by a colon and two slashes, **://**. The *pathname* always begins with a single slash.

```
transfer-protocol://host-name/path-name
```

The *transfer protocol* is usually HTTP (Hypertext Transfer Protocol), indicating a Web page. Other possible values for transfer protocols are gopher, ftp, and file. As their names suggest, gopher and ftp initiate Gopher and FTP sessions, whereas file displays a local file on your own system, such as a text or an HTML file. Table 17-1 lists the various transfer protocols.

The *hostname* is the computer on which a particular Web site is located. You can think of this as the address of the Web site. By convention, most hostnames begin with www. In the next example, the URL locates a Web page called guides.html on the **www.kernel.org** Web site in the LDP directory:

```
http://www.kernel.org/LDP/guides.html
```

If you do not want to access a particular Web page, you can leave the file reference out, and then you automatically access the Web site's home page. To access a Web site directly, use its hostname. The default name for a Web site's home page is **index.html**, located in the site's top directory. A Web site can override the default and specify a particular file as the home page. If no file is specified, however, the **index.html** file is taken as the home page. In the next example, the user brings up the Red Hat home page:

```
http://www.redhat.com/
```

Protocol	Description
http	Hypertext Transfer Protocol for Web site access
gopher	Access Gopher site
ftp	File Transfer Protocol for anonymous FTP connections
telnet	Makes a telnet connection
wais	Access WAIS site
news	Reading Usenet news; uses Net News Transfer Protocol (NNTP)

Table 17-1.   *Web Protocols*

The pathname specifies the directory where the resource can be found on the host system, as well as the name of the resource's file. For example, **/pub/Linux/newdat.html** references an HTML document called newdat located in the **/pub/Linux** directory. As you move to other Web pages on a site, you may move more deeply into the directory tree. In the following example, the user accesses the FAQ.html document in the directory **support/docs/howto/installing_linux.html**:

```
http://www.redhat.com/support/docs/howto/installing_linux.html
```

As just explained, if you specify a directory pathname without a particular Web page file, the Web site looks for a file called **index.html** in that directory. An **index.html** file in a directory operates as the default Web page for that directory. In the next example, the index.html Web page in the **/apps/support** directory is displayed:

```
http://www.redhat.com/apps/support/index.html
```

You can use this technique to access local Web pages on your system. For example, once installed, the demo Web pages for Java are located in **/usr/local/java/**. Because this is on your local system, you needn't include a hostname. An index.html page in the **/usr/local/java/** directory is automatically displayed when you specify the directory path. You can do the same for your system documentation, which, on most distributions, is in Web-page format located in the **/usr/doc/HTML/ldp** directory.

```
file:/usr/local/java
file:/usr/doc/HTML/ldp
```

If you reference a directory that has no **index.html** file, the Web server creates one for you, and your browser then displays it (see Chapter 25). This index simply lists the different files and directories in that directory. You can click an entry to display a file or to move to another directory. The first entry is a special entry for the parent directory.

The resource file's extension indicates the type of action to be taken on it. A picture has a **.gif** or **.jpeg** extension and is converted for display. A sound file has a **.au** or **.wav** extension and is played. The following URL references a **.gif** file. Instead of displaying a Web page, your browser invokes a graphics viewer to display the picture. Table 17-2 provides a list of the different file extensions.

```
http://www.train.com/engine/engine1.gif
```

File Type	Description
.html	Web page document formatted using HTML, the Hypertext Markup Language
Graphics Files	
.gif	Graphics, using GIF compression
.jpeg	Graphics, using JPEG compression
Sound Files	
.au	Sun (UNIX) sound file
.wav	Microsoft Windows sound file
.aiff	Macintosh sound file
Video Files	
.QT	QuickTime video file, multiplatform
.mpeg	Video file
.avi	Microsoft Windows video file

Table 17-2.   *Web File Types*

Web Pages

A *Web page* is a specially formatted document that can be displayed by any Web browser. You can think of a Web page as a word processing document that can display both text and graphics. Within the Web page, links can be embedded that call up other Internet resources. An Internet resource can be a graphic, a file, a telnet connection, or even another Web page. The Web page acts as an interface for accessing different Internet tools, such as FTP to download files or telnet to connect to an online catalog or other remote service.

Web pages display both text and graphics. Text is formatted with paragraphs and can be organized with different headings. Graphics of various sizes may be placed anywhere in the page. Throughout the page there are usually anchor points you can use to call up other Internet resources. Each *anchor point* is associated with a particular Internet resource. One anchor point may reference a picture; another, a file. Others may reference other Web pages or even other Web sites. These anchor points are specially highlighted text or graphics that usually appear in a different color from the rest of the text. Whereas ordinary text may be black, text used for anchor points might be green, blue, or red. You select a particular anchor point by moving your mouse pointer to that text or picture, and then clicking it. The Internet resource associated with that anchor point is then called up. If the resource is a picture, the picture is displayed. If it is another Web page, that Web page is displayed. If the Internet resource is on another Web site, that site is accessed. The color of an anchor point indicates its status and the particular Web browser you are using. Both Mosaic and Netscape browsers by default use blue for anchors you have not yet accessed. Netscape uses the color purple for anchors you have already accessed, and Mosaic uses red. All these colors can be overridden by a particular Web page.

Your Web browser keeps a list of the different Web pages you access for each session. You can move back and forth easily in that list. Having called up another Web page, you can use your browser to move back to the previous one. Web browsers construct their lists according to the sequence in which you displayed your Web pages. They keep track of the Web pages you are accessing, whatever they may be. On many Web sites, however, several Web pages are meant to be connected in a particular order, like chapters in a book. Such pages usually have buttons displayed at the bottom of the page that reference the next and previous pages in the sequence. Clicking Next displays the next Web page for this site. The Home button returns you to the first page for this sequence.

Web Browsers

Most *Web browsers* are designed to access several different kinds of information. Web browsers can access a Web page on a remote Web site or a file on your own system. Some browsers can also access a remote news server or an FTP site. The type of information for a site is specified by the keyword **http** for Web sites, **nntp** for news servers, **ftp** for FTP sites, and **file** for files on your own system.

To access a Web site, you enter **http://** followed by the Internet address of the Web site. If you know a particular Web page you want to access on that Web site, you can add the pathname for that page, attaching it to the Internet address. Then simply press ENTER. The browser connects you to that Web site and display its home page or the page you specified.

You can just as easily use a Web browser to display Web pages on your own system by entering the term **file** followed by a colon, **file:**, with the pathname of the Web page you want to display. You do not specify an Internet site. Remember, all Web pages have the extension **.html.** Links within a Web page on your own system can connect you to other Web pages on your system or to Web pages on remote systems. When you first start a Web browser, your browser displays a local Web page on your own system. The default page is usually a page for your particular distribution, such as OpenLinux or Red Hat. Such pages have links to a distribution's Web site where you can obtain online support. If you want, you can create your own Web pages, with their own links, and make one of them your default Web page.

Web pages on a Web site often contain links to other Web pages, some on the same site and others at other Web sites. Through these links, you can move from one page to another. As you move from Web page to Web page using the anchor points or buttons, your browser displays the URL for the current page. Your browser keeps a list of the different Web pages you have accessed in a given session. Most browsers have buttons that enable you to move back and forth through this list. You can move to the Web page you displayed before the current one and then move back further to the previous one. You can move forward again to the next page, and so on.

To get to a particular page, you may have moved through a series of pages, using links in each finally to reach the Web page you want. To access any Web page, all you need is its URL address. If you want to access a particular page again, you can enter its URL address and move directly to it, without moving through the intervening pages as you did the first time. Instead of writing down the URL addresses and entering them yourself, most Web browsers can keep *bookmarks*—a list of favorite Web pages you want to access directly. When you are displaying a Web page you want to access later, instruct your browser to place it on the Bookmarks list. The Web page is usually listed in the Bookmarks list by its title, not its URL. To access that Web page later, select the entry in the Bookmark list.

Most Web browsers can also access FTP and Gopher sites. You may find using a Web browser to access an FTP site with anonymous access is easier than using an FTP client. Directories and files are automatically listed, and selecting a file or directory is only a matter of clicking its name. First enter **ftp://** and then the Internet address of the FTP site. The contents of a directory are then displayed, listing files and subdirectories. To move to another directory, just click it. To download a file, click its name. You see an entry listed as **. .**, representing the parent directory. You can move down the file structure from one subdirectory to another and move back up one directory at a time by selecting **..**. To leave the FTP site, return to your own home page. You can also use your browser to access Gopher sites. Enter **gopher://** followed by the Internet address of the Gopher site. Your Web browser then displays the main Gopher menu for that site, and you can move from one Gopher menu to the next.

Most browsers can connect to your news server to access specified newsgroups or articles. This is a local operation, accessing the news server to which you are already connected. You enter **nntp** followed by a colon and the newsgroup or news article. Some browsers, such as Netscape, have an added newsreader browser that allows them to access any remote news servers.

As noted previously, several popular browsers are available for Linux. Three distinctive ones are described here: Netscape Navigator, Konqueror, and Lynx. Netscape is an X Windows–based Web browser capable of displaying graphics, video, and sound, as well as operating as a newsreader and mailer. Konqueror is the K Desktop file manager. KDE has integrated full Web-browsing capability into the Konqueror file manager, letting you seamlessly access the Web and your file system with the same application. Lynx is a command line–based browser with no graphics capabilities, but in every other respect it is a fully functional Web browser.

Netscape Navigator and Mozilla

Hypertext databases are designed to access any kind of data, whether it is text, graphics, sound, or even video. Whether you can actually access such data depends to a large extent on the type of browser you use. One of the more popular Web browsers is Netscape Navigator. Versions of Netscape operate on different graphical user interfaces such as X Windows, Microsoft Windows, and the Macintosh. Using X Windows, the Netscape browser can display graphics, sound, video, and Java-based programs (you learn about Java a little later in the chapter). You can obtain more information about Netscape on its Web site: **www.netscape.com**.

Netscape Navigator is now included on most Linux distributions. For more recent versions as they come out, you can access a distribution FTP site such as **ftp.redhat.com**. You can also obtain compressed archive versions (**.tar.gz**) from the Netscape FTP site at **ftp.netscape.com**. A compressed archive version has to be decompressed and unpacked with the **gunzip** and **tar xvf** commands, once the archive has been placed in an install directory such as **/usr/local**.

Netscape Navigator is an X Windows application you operate from your desktop. Many distributions have a desktop icon for Netscape or an entry for it in the desktop's menu. Netscape Navigator displays an area at the top of the screen for entering a URL address and a series of buttons for various Web page operations. Drop-down menus provide access to Netscape features. To access a Web site, you enter its address in the URL area and press ENTER. The icon bar across the top of the browser holds buttons for moving from one page to another and performing other operations (see Figure 17-1).

Netscape refers to the URLs of Web pages you want to keep in a hotlist as *bookmarks*, marking pages you want to access directly. The Bookmarks menu enables you to add your favorite Web pages to a hotlist. You can then view your bookmarks and select one to view. Items in the Windows menu enhance your Web browser operations. In the address book, you can keep a list of Web site URLs. The Bookmark item enables you to edit your list of bookmarks, adding new ones or removing old ones. The History item is a list of previous URLs you have accessed. If you want to return to a Web page you did not save as a bookmark, you can find it in the History list. Additionally, you can use Netscape to receive and send mail, as well as to access Usenet newsgroups.

The Options menu in the Netscape Navigator enables you to set several different kinds of preferences for your browser. You can set preferences for mail and news, the network, and security, as well as general preferences. In general preferences, you can

Figure 17-1.   *Netscape Navigator Web browser*

determine your home page and how you want the toolbar displayed. For mail and news, you can enter the mail and news servers you use on the Internet. Netscape can be set to access any number of news servers you subscribe to and that use the NNTP transfer protocols. You can switch from one news server to another if you want.

If you are on a network that connects to the Internet through a firewall, you must use the Proxies screen to enter the address of your network's firewall gateway computer. A *firewall* is a computer that operates as a controlled gateway to the Internet for your network. Several types of firewalls exist. One of the most restrictive uses programs called *proxies*, which receive Internet requests from users and then make those requests on their behalf. There is no direct connection to the Internet. From the Options menu, select Network and then choose the Proxies screen. Here, enter the IP address of your network's firewall gateway computer.

Through the Mail item in the Windows menu, you can open a fully functional mail client with which you can send and receive messages over the Internet. The News item, also in the Windows menu, opens a fully functional newsreader with which you can read and post articles in Usenet newsgroups. In this respect, your Netscape Navigator is more than just a Web browser. It is also a mail program and a newsreader.

Mozilla is a browser based on the Netscape core source code known as mozilla. In 1998, Netscape made this source code freely available under the Netscape Public License (NPL). The Mozilla Project based at **www.mozilla.org** is developing a commercial-level browser based on mozilla source code. Mozilla is developed on an open source model much like Linux, KDE, and Gnome. Developers can submit modifications and additions over the Internet to the mozilla Web site. Mozilla releases are referred to as Milestones, the current one being M18. Mozilla is currently released under both the NPL license for modifications of mozilla code and the MPL license (Mozilla Public License) for new additions.

K Desktop File Manager: Konqueror

If you are using the K Desktop, then you can use a file manager window as a Web browser, as shown in Figure 17-2. The K Desktop's file manager is automatically

Figure 17-2. *The K Desktop file manager as a Web browser*

configured to act as a Web browser. It can display Web pages, including graphics and links. The K Desktop's file manager supports standard Web page operation, such as moving forward and backward through accessed pages. Clicking a link accesses and displays the Web page referenced. In this respect, the Web becomes seamlessly integrated into the K Desktop.

Gnome Web Browsers: Galeon, Express, and Mnemonic

Unlike the K Desktop, the Gnome file manager does not support Web access. You use a Web browser such as Netscape, Galeon, or Mnemonic. Galeon, Express, and Mnemonic are Gnome-based Web browsers that support standard Web operations. Galeon is a GNOME Web browser designed to be fast with a very light interface (see Figure 17-3). It supports drag-and-drop operations, multiple selections, and bookmark imports. It is based on Gecko (the mozilla rendering engine). You can find out more about Galeon at **galeon.sourceforge.net**.

Express is designed to rely on plug-ins for Web features. This way, the browser can be made as complex or simple as you want. All major operations, such as viewers and protocols, are handled as plug-ins. This design allows new features to be easily added

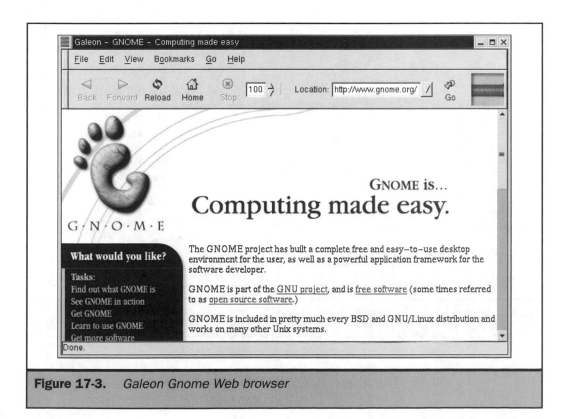

Figure 17-3. *Galeon Gnome Web browser*

in this way. Mnemonic is an extensible and modular Web browser that integrates a set of *Object Implementation Libraries* (*OILs*) into a Web browser with a Gnome interface. Encompass is designed to be a small fast browser that will operate within Gnome, able to share cookies with other apps and handle all special URLs and MIME types.

Lynx: Line-Mode Browser

Lynx is a line-mode browser you can use without X Windows. A Web page is displayed as text only (see Figure 17-4). A text page can contain links to other Internet resources, but does not display any graphics, video, or sound. Except for the display limitations, Lynx is a fully functional Web browser. You can use Lynx to download files or to make telnet connections. All information on the Web is still accessible to you. Because it does not require much of the overhead graphics-based browsers need, Lynx can operate much faster, quickly displaying Web page text. To start the Lynx browser, you enter **lynx** on the command line and press ENTER.

```
                                    The Linux Kernel Archives (p1 of 7)

                    The Linux Kernel Archives

    Welcome to the Linux Kernel Archives. This is the primary site for the
    Linux kernel source, but it has much more than just kernels.

    Protocol Location
    HTTP http://www.kernel.org/pub/
    FTP ftp://ftp.kernel.org/pub/
    RSYNC rsync://rsync.kernel.org/pub/

    Unfortunately, all our mirror services (our mirroring other sites)
    except the Linux Documentation Project (LDP) are currently
    unavailable. This includes all distributions and ISO images. We cannot
    give any kind of information about when they may become available
    again at this time. The Linux Kernel Archives Mirror System is fully
    operational.
    This site is now connected via a dedicated 100 Mbit/s connection
    graciously provided by Globix. A new VArServer 700 with a 100 GB RAID
    provided by VA Linux Systems is powering this connection. We hope that
  — press space for next page —
    Arrow keys: Up and Down to move.  Right to follow a link; Left to go back.
    H)elp O)ptions P)rint G)o M)ain screen Q)uit /=search [delete]=history list
```

Figure 17-4. *Lynx Web browser*

The links are displayed in bold and dispersed throughout the text of the Web page. A selected link is highlighted in reverse video with a shaded rectangle around the link text. The first link is automatically selected. You can then move sequentially from one link to the next on a page by pressing the DOWN ARROW key. The UP ARROW key moves you back to a previous link. To choose a link, first highlight it and then press either ENTER or the RIGHT ARROW key. If you want to go to a specific site, press G. This opens a line at the bottom of the screen with the prompt **URL to open:**. There, you can enter the URL for the site you want. Pressing M returns you to your home page. The text of a Web page is displayed one screen at a time. To move to the next screen of text, you can either press SPACEBAR or PAGE DOWN. PAGE UP displays the previous screen of text. Pressing DOWN ARROW and UP ARROW moves to the next or previous links in the text, displaying the full screen of text around the link. To display a description of the current Web page with its URL, press the = key.

Lynx uses a set of one-letter commands to perform various browser functions. By pressing the **?** key at any time, you can display a list of these commands. For example, pressing the D key downloads a file. The H key brings up a help menu. To search the text of your current Web page, press the **/** key. This opens a line at the bottom of the screen where you enter your search pattern. Lynx then highlights the next instance of that pattern in the text. If you press N, Lynx displays the next instance. The **** key toggles you between a source and rendered version of the current Web page, showing you the HTML tags or the formatted text.

JAVA for Linux: Blackdown

To develop Java applications, use Java tools, and run many Java products, you must install the Java Development Kit and the Java Runtime Environment on your system. Sun does not support or develop Linux versions of these products. They have been ported to Linux by the Blackdown project, however, and you can download the Blackdown ports of the JDK and JRE and install them on your system. More information and documentation are available at the Blackdown Web site at **www.blackdown.org**.

Numerous Java-based products and tools are currently adaptable for Linux. Linux versions of the HotJava browser and the Java Web server exist. Tools include IDE development environments, *Just In Time* compilers (*JIT*), and Java virtual machines. Most of the products and some of the tools are free. You can download most of the products and tools through links in the Blackdown Web page located at **www.blackdown.org**. Select the JavaSoft Products entry for a list of links to available Java products; select Java Tools for Linux for a list of tools. Many of the products run directly as provided by Sun. You can download several directly from the Sun Java Web site at **java.sun.com**. A few of the currently available products are listed in Table 17-3.

Application	Description
Java Development Kit (JDK) and Java Runtime Environment (JRE)	A Java development environment with a compiler, interpreters, debugger, and more. Download the Linux port from your distribution's update through **www.blackdown.org**.
HotJava browser	Sun's HTML 3.2– and JDK 1.1–compliant Web browser. Download the Linux version from **java.sun.com**.
Java Foundation Classes (Swing Set)	Swing is a new set of GUI components being developed by JavaSoft.
The Java Servlet Development Kit	Provides resources for running, testing, and operating servlets with Netscape, Microsoft, and Apache Web servers.
Java Web Server	A Web server implemented with Java. Available at Java Web site at **java.sun.com**.
The JDBC Database Access API	A SQL database access interface for Java.

Table 17-3. *Java Applications*

The Java Development Kit: JDK and JRE

The *Java Development Kit* (*JDK*) provides tools for creating and debugging your own Java applets and provides support for Java applications, such as the HotJava browser. The kit includes demonstration applets with source code. You can obtain detailed documentation about the JDK from the Sun Web site at **java.sun.com**. Three major releases of the JDK are currently available—1.0, 1.1.*x*, and 1.2—with corresponding versions for the *Java Runtime Environment* (*JRE*) for 1.1 and 1.2. JDK 1.0 is an earlier version of the JDK that is compatible with older browsers. JDK 1.1.*x* includes standard features such as JavaBeans and database connectivity. The current version of JDK 1.1.*x* is 1.1.7. JAVA 2 adds capabilities for security, Swing, and running Java enhancements, such as Java3D and Java Sound. JDK 1.2 is also known as JAVA 2 (SDK). All JDK and JRE releases are available for Linux. You can download them from a Java-Linux mirror site that you can link to through the Blackdown Web page (**www.blackdown.org**) mentioned earlier. JDK and JRE 1.2 are usually included on current Linux distribution CD-ROMs such as Red Hat and Caldera. You can also download RPM versions from the Red Hat and Caldera sites. You can also download JKD and JRE 1.2 through **www.blackdown.org** as a compressed archive, **.tar.gz** file.

JDK 1.1 includes features such as for internationalization, signed applets, JAR file format, AWT (window toolkit) enhancements, JavaBeans component model, networking enhancements, a math package for large numbers, *database connectivity* (*JDBC*), object serialization, and inner classes. Detailed descriptions of these features can be found in the JDK documentation. The JDK package installs the Java applications, libraries, and demos in the specified directory. Java applications include a Java compiler, javac, a Java debugger, jdb, and an applet viewer, **appletviewer**.

JAVA 2 offers numerous capabilities over JDK 1.1, such as integrated Swing, Java 2d, the new security model, the Collections framework, CORBA, and JDBC 2.0. The Blackdown port of Java 2 has support for both native threads and green threads, and it includes a Just In Time dynamic bytecode compiler. With JAVA 2, you can run the Blackdown port of Java 3D, Java Advanced Imaging, Java Media Framework, and Java Sound. Detailed descriptions of these features can be found in the JAVA 2 documentation.

Java Applets

You create a Java applet much as you would create a program using a standard programming language. You first use a text editor to create the source code, which is saved in a file with a **.java** extension. Then you can use the **javac** compiler to compile the source code file, generating a Java applet. This applet file has the extension **.class**. For example, the JDK demo directory includes the Java source code for a Blink applet called **Blink.java.** You can go to that directory and then compile the **Blink.java** file, generating a **Blink.class** file. The **example1.html** file in that directory runs the **Blink.class** applet. Start your browser and access this file to run the Blink applet.

```
# javac Blink.java
```

An applet is called within a Web page using the <applet> HTML tag. This tag can contain several attributes, one of which is required: code. You assign to code the name of the compiled applet. You can use several optional attributes to set features such as the region used to display the applet and its alignment. You can even access applets on a remote Web site. In the following example, the applet called **Blink.class** is displayed in a box on the Web browser that has a height of 140 pixels and a width of 100 pixels, and is aligned in the center.

```
<applet code="Blink.class" width=100 height=140 align=center></applet>
```

To invoke the debugger, use the **appletviewer** command with the **-debug** option and the name of the HTML file that runs the applet.

```
appletviewer -debug mypage.html
```

Numerous *Interface Development Environments* (*IDE*) applications are available for composing Java applets and applications. Although most are commercial, some provide free shareware versions. An IDE provides a GUI interface for constructing Java applets. You can link to and download several IDE applications through the Blackdown Web page.

Web Search Utilities

To search for files on FTP sites, you can use search engines provided by Web sites, such as Yahoo!, Excite, Google, Alta Vista, or Lycos. These usually search for both Web pages and FTP files. To find a particular Web page you want on the Internet, you can use any number of online search sites such as Yahoo!, Excite, Alta Vista, or Lycos. You can use their Web sites or perform searches from any number of Web portals, such as Netscape or Linux online. Web searches have become a standard service of most Web sites. Searches carried out on documents within a Web site may use local search indexes set up and maintained by indexing programs like ht:/Dig and WAIS. Sites using ht:/Dig use a standard Web page search interface, where WAIS provides its own specialized client programs like swais and xwais. WAIS is an older indexing program currently being supplanted by newer search applications like ht:/Dig. You can still obtain a free version of WAIS, called *freeWAIS*, from **ftp.cnidr.org.**

Creating Your Own Web Site

To create your own Web site, you need access to a Web server. Most Linux distributions, such as OpenLinux and Red Hat, automatically install the Apache Web server on their Linux systems. You can also rent Web page space on a remote server—a service many ISPs provide, some free. On Red Hat systems, the directory set up by your Apache Web server for your Web site pages is **/var/httpd/html**. On other systems such as Caldera, it is **/home/httpd/html**. Other servers provide you with a directory for your home page. Place the Web pages you create in that directory. You place your home page here. You can make other subdirectories with their own Web pages to which these can link. Web pages are not difficult to create. Links from one page to another move users through your Web site. You can even create links to Web pages or resources on other sites. Many excellent texts are available on Web page creation and management.

Web Page Composers

Web pages are created using HTML, the Hypertext Markup Language, which is a subset of *Standard Generalized Markup Language* (*SGML*). Creating an HTML document is a matter of inserting HTML tags in a text file. In this respect, creating a Web page is as simple as using a tag-based word processor. You use the HTML tags to format text for display as a Web page. The Web page itself is a text file you can create using any text editor, such as Vi. If you are familiar with tag-based word processing on UNIX systems, you will find it conceptually similar to nroff. Some HTML tags indicate headings, lists, and paragraphs, as well as referencing Web resources.

Instead of manually entering HTML code, you can use Web page composers. A Web page composer provides a graphical interface for constructing Web pages. The Linux version of WordPerfect can automatically generate a Web page from a WordPerfect document. You can create Web pages using all the word processing features of WordPerfect and Star Office. Special Web page creation programs, such as Netscape Composer, also can easily help you create complex Web pages without ever having to type any HTML tags explicitly. Remember, though, no matter what tool you use to create your Web page, the Web page itself will be an HTML document.

Many of the standard editors for the K Desktop and Gnome include Web page construction features. Many enable you to insert links or format headings. The kedit program supports basic text-based Web page components. You can add headings, links, or lines, but not graphics. GXedit can also compose and edit Web pages. You can easily insert HTTP elements, such as links, image references, or headings. GXedit can then access Netscape to preview the page. gnotepad+ is a simple editor for making small text files. It does, however, have a toolbar for Web page composition containing several of the more common HTML elements. You can insert links, headings, and lists, as well as other basic Web page components.

Common Gateway Interfaces

A *Common Gateway Interface* (*CGI*) script is a program a Web server at a Web site can use to interact with Web browsers. When a browser displays a Web page at a particular Web site, the Web page may call up CGI programs to provide you with certain real-time information or to receive information from you. For example, a Web page may execute the server's date command to display the current date whenever the Web page is accessed.

A CGI script can be a Linux shell script, a Perl script, a Tcl/Tk program, or a program developed using a programming language such as C. Two special HTML operations are also considered CGI scripts: query text and forms. Both receive and process interactive responses from particular users. You have seen how a user can use a browser to display Web pages at a given Web site. In effect, the user is receiving information in the form of Web pages from the Web site. A user can also, to a limited extent, send information back to the Web site. This is usually information specifically prompted for in a Web page displayed by your browser. The Web server then receives and processes that information using the CGI programs.

A *form* is a Web page that holds several input fields of various types. These can be input boxes for entering text or check boxes and radio buttons that users simply click. The text boxes can be structured, allowing a certain number of characters to be entered, as in a phone number. They can also be unstructured, enabling users to type in sentences as they would for a comment. Forms are referred to as *form-based queries.* After entering information into a form, the user sends it back to the server by clicking a Submit button. The server receives the form and, along with it, instructions to run a specific CGI program to process the form.

The Complete Reference

Chapter 18

Network Tools

Y ou can use a variety of network tools to perform tasks such as obtaining information about other systems on your network, accessing other systems, and communicating directly with other users. Network information can be obtained using utilities such as **ping**, **finger**, and **host**. Talk, ICQ, and IRC clients enable you to communicate directly with other users on your network. Telnet performs a remote login to an account you may have on another system connected on your network. Each has a corresponding K Desktop or Gnome version. These provide a GUI interface, so you no longer have to use the shell command line to run these tools. In addition, your network may make use of older remote access commands. These are useful for smaller networks and enable you to access remote systems directly to copy files or execute commands.

Network Information: ping, finger, and host

You can use the **ping**, **finger**, **traceroute**, and **host** commands to find out status information about systems and users on your network. **ping** is used to check if a remote system is up and running. You use **finger** to find out information about other users on your network, seeing if they are logged in or if they have received mail. **host** displays address information about a system on your network, giving you a system's IP and domain name addresses. **traceroute** can be used to track the sequence of computer networks and systems your message passed through on its way to you. Table 18-1 lists various network information tools.

On the Gnome desktop, the Gnetutil utility provides a Gnome interface for entering the **ping**, **finger**, and **host** commands. On the K Desktop, you can use the KDE network utilities (knu) to issue **ping** , **finger**, **traceroute**, and **host** commands. Select the appropriate tabbed panel. For the Ping panel, enter the address of the remote system at the box labeled Host and click Go. The results are displayed in the pane below, as shown in Figure 18-1.

ping

The **ping** command detects whether a system is up and running. **ping** takes as its argument the name of the system you want to check. If the system you want to check is down, **ping** issues a timeout message indicating a connection could not be made. The next example checks to see if **www.redhat.com** is up and connected to the network:

```
$ ping www.redhat.com
PING www.portal.redhat.com (206.132.41.231): 56 data bytes
64 bytes from 206.132.41.231: icmp_seq=0 ttl=248 time=24.0 ms
64 bytes from 206.132.41.231: icmp_seq=1 ttl=248 time=124.5 ms
64 bytes from 206.132.41.231: icmp_seq=2 ttl=248 time=77.9 ms
64 bytes from 206.132.41.231: icmp_seq=3 ttl=248 time=220.1 ms
64 bytes from 206.132.41.231: icmp_seq=4 ttl=248 time=14.9 ms

--- www.portal.redhat.com ping statistics ---
6 packets transmitted, 5 packets received, 16% packet loss
round-trip min/avg/max = 14.9/92.2/220.1 ms
```

You can also use **ping** with an IP address instead of a domain name. With an IP address, **ping** can try to detect the remote system directly without having to go through a domain name server to translate the domain name to an IP address. This can be helpful

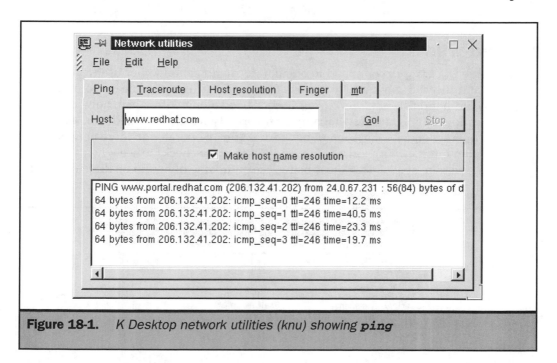

Figure 18-1.   *K Desktop network utilities (knu) showing* `ping`

for situations where your network's domain name server may be temporarily down and you want to check if a particular remote host on your network is connected. In the next example, the user checks the Red Hat site using its IP address.

```
$ ping 206.132.41.231
PING 206.132.41.231 (206.132.41.231): 56 data bytes
64 bytes from 206.132.41.231: icmp_seq=0 ttl=248 time=16.6 ms
64 bytes from 206.132.41.231: icmp_seq=1 ttl=248 time=65.1 ms
64 bytes from 206.132.41.231: icmp_seq=2 ttl=248 time=70.1 ms
64 bytes from 206.132.41.231: icmp_seq=3 ttl=248 time=336.6 ms
64 bytes from 206.132.41.231: icmp_seq=4 ttl=248 time=53.6 ms
64 bytes from 206.132.41.231: icmp_seq=5 ttl=248 time=42.1 ms

--- 206.132.41.231 ping statistics ---
6 packets transmitted, 6 packets received, 0% packet loss
round-trip min/avg/max = 16.6/97.3/336.6 ms
```

finger and who

You can use the **finger** command to obtain information about other users on your network and the **who** command to see what users are currently online on your system. The **who** command lists all users currently connected along with when, how long, and where they logged in. It has several options for specifying the level of detail. **who** is meant to operate on a local system or network. **finger** operates on large networks, including the Internet. As shown in Figure 18-2, **finger** checks to see when a user last logged in, the type of shell that she is using, the pathname of her home directory, and

Figure 18-2. *gfinger Gnome finger utility*

whether any mail has been received. **finger** then checks for a **.plan** file in a user's home directory that may contain information about her. The **.plan** file is a file you create yourself on your own home directory. You can place information you want made publicly available into the **.plan** file. You can enter the command **finger** on the command line with the login name of the user you want to check.

On the K Desktop, you can use the KDE network utilities (knu) to issue finger commands. Click the Finger panel and enter the address of the host you want to check. On the K Desktop, the KFinger tool also provides a GUI for easily sending **finger** queries. It features entries for users and remote servers. You can search for users on specific remote systems. With KFinger, you can also access the K Desktop talk utility to talk with selected users online. You can start KFinger by selecting the User Information entry in the K Desktop's Internet menu.

host

With the **host** command, you can find network address information about a remote system connected to your network. This information usually consists of a system's IP address, domain name address, domain name nicknames, and mail server. This information is obtained from your network's domain name server. For the Internet, this includes all systems you can connect to over the Internet.

The **host** command is an effective way to determine a remote site's IP address or URL. If you have only the IP address of a site, you can use **host** to find out its domain name. For network administration, an IP address can be helpful for making your own domain name entries in your **/etc/host** file. That way, you needn't rely on a remote domain name server (DNS) for locating a site. On the K Desktop, you can use the KDE network utilities for running **host** commands. Click the Host resolution panel and enter the address of the host you want to check. On Gnome, you can use the gHostLookup utility.

```
$ host www.gnome.org
www.gnome.org is a nickname for gnome.labs.redhat.com
gnome.labs.redhat.com has address 199.183.24.235
gnome.labs.redhat.com mail is handled (pri=10) by mail.redhat.com

$ host 199.183.24.235
235.24.183.199.IN-ADDR.ARPA domain name pointer
gnome.labs.redhat.com
```

The *Gwhois* program is a Gnome-based client that displays information about hosts obtained from NIC network services. Gwhois provides an X Windows interface with a list of NIC servers from which to choose. gHostLookup is a simple Gnome application that returns a machine's IP address when you give it the hostname.

Network Information Tools	Description
ping	Detects whether a system is connected to the network
finger	Obtains information about users on the network
who	Checks what users are currently online
host	Obtains network address information about a remote host
traceroute	Tracks the sequence of computer networks and hosts your message passes through
knu	The KDE Network utilities featuring **finger**, **ping**, **traceroute**, and **host**
Gnetutil	The Gnome Network utilities featuring **finger**, **ping**, **traceroute**, and **host**
gfinger	Gnome finger client
KFinger	Kde **finger** utility
gHostLookup	Gnome utility to find IP addresses for host names
Gwhois	Obtains information about networks, hosts, and users

Table 18-1.   *Network Tools*

Network Talk Clients

You may, at times, want to communicate directly with other users on your network. You can do so with talk and IRC utilities, provided the other user is also logged into a connected system at the same time. The **talk** utility operates like a telephone, enabling you to have a direct two-way conversation with another user. **talk** is designed for users on the same system or connected on a local network. *ICQ* (*I Seek You*) is an Internet tool that notifies you when other users are online and enables you to communicate with them. ICQ works much like an instant messenger. With an *Internet Relay Chat utility* (*IRC*), you can connect to a remote server where other users are also connected and talk with them.

Talk

You can use the **talk** utility to set up an interactive two-way communication between you and another user. **talk** operates more like a phone call—both you and the other user can type in messages simultaneously—where two people are constantly talking back and forth to each other. You initiate the communication by entering the **talk** command followed by the other user's address, usually the login name. This displays a message on the other user's screen asking if she or he wants to talk and giving your address. The user then responds with a **talk** command of her or his own, using your address. Both your screen and the other user's screen then split into two segments. The top segment displays what you type and the bottom segment displays what the other user types. Either user can end the session with an interrupt character, usually CTRL-C.

A K Desktop version of **talk** called KTalk displays user screens as panes in a K Desktop window. **ktalk** includes an address book and supports word-wrap and file transfer features. **ktalkd** is a KDE-aware Talk daemon with answering machine features and forwarding capabilities. *GNU Talk* is a Gnome version of Talk that supports multiple clients, file transfers, encryption, shared applications, autoanswer, and call-forwarding. GNU Talk includes both clients and a daemon. The client can operate using different front ends such as Emacs, *screen-based cursors* (*curses*), X Window System, Motif, and Gnome. Among applications included with GNU Talk is one that enables you to draw pictures with another user.

ICQ clients

The ICQ protocol enables you to communicate directly with other users online, but like an instant messenger utility. Using an ICQ client, you can send users messages, chat with them, or send files. You can set up a contact list of users who you may want to contact when they are online. You are then notified in real time when they connect, and you can communicate with them if you wish. Several modes of communication are supported. These include chat, message, e-mail, file transfer, or games. To use ICQ, you register with an ICQ server that provides you with an ICQ number, also known as a Universal Internet Number (UIN). You can find out more about the ICQ protocol at **www.mirabilis.com**.

Several Gnome-based ICQ clients are available for your use. Check the Gnome software map at **www.gnome.org** for new versions and recent updates. *GnomeICU* (formerly GtkICQ) is an ICQ client that can communicate with other ICQ users on any platform, whether Linux, Windows, or the Mac. You can find out more about GnomeICU at **gnomeicu.gdev.net**. Currently, GnomeICU features include message history for individual users, chat, messages, and sound events. File transfers will be supported in future updates. *Gicq* is a Gnome ICQ instant messenger client. You can currently use it to send and receive messages and to search for users to add to your client list. *kicq* and *KXicq* are K Desktop ICQ clients currently under development. They will support instant messaging, client lists, and other ICQ features.

Internet Relay Chat

Internet Relay Chat (IRC) operates like a chat room, where you can enter channels and talk to other users already there. First, you select an IRC server to connect to. Various servers are available for different locales and topics. Once connected to a server, you can choose from a list of channels to enter. The interface works much like a chat room. When you connect to the server, you can choose a nickname by which you will be referred. Several Internet Relay Chat clients are available for use on Linux systems. Most operate on either X Windows, KDE, or Gnome platforms. Irssi, X Chat, and yaggIRC are Gnome IRC clients, though there are versions for other platforms. All have support for multiple concurrent server connections, multiple windows, DCC (Send Chat Voice and Resume), and Perl scripts. X Chat has a plug-in interface for adding new features (see **xchat.linuxpower.org** for more details). Irssi has an easy-to-use interface with support for the Gnome panel. kvirc and kSirc are K Desktop IRC clients. Kvirc features an alias and events editor, DCC, and scripting. Xirc is an X Windows client.

Telnet

You use the **telnet** command to log in remotely to another system on your network. The system can be on your local area network or available through an Internet connection. Telnet operates as if you were logging into another system from a remote terminal. You will be asked for a login name and, in some cases, a password. In effect, you are logging into another account on another system. In fact, if you have an account on another system, you could use telnet to log into it. You invoke the **telnet** utility with the keyword **telnet**. If you know the name of the site you want to connect with, you can enter **telnet** and the name of the site on the Linux command line. As an alternative, you can use the K Desktop KTelnet utility. This provides a GUI interface to connecting and logging into remote systems.

```
$ telnet garnet.berkeley.edu
Connected to garnet
login:
```

The telnet program also has a command mode with a series of commands you can use to configure your connection. You can enter the telnet command mode either by invoking telnet with the keyword **telnet** or by pressing CTRL-] during a session. The telnet **help** command lists all the telnet commands you can use. A comprehensive list is available on the Man pages (**man telnet**). In the next example, the user first invokes the **telnet** utility. A prompt is displayed next, indicating the command mode, **telnet>**. The telnet command **open** then connects to another system.

```
$ telnet
telnet> open garnet.berkeley.edu
Connected to garnet.berkeley.edu
login:
```

Once connected, you follow the login procedure for that system. If you are logging into a regular system, you must provide a login name and password. Once logged in, you are provided with the operating system prompt that, in the case of Linux or UNIX, will either be **$** or **%**. You are then directly connected to an account on that system and can issue any commands you want. When you finish your work, you log out. This breaks the connection and returns you to the telnet prompt on your own system. You can then quit telnet with the **quit** command.

```
telnet> quit
```

When using telnet to connect to a site that provides public access, you needn't provide a login name or password. Access is usually controlled by a series of menus that restricts what you can do on that system.

If you are logging into a specific account on another system, you can use the **-1** option to specify the login name of that account. This enables you to skip the login prompt. You can use the **-1** option either with the telnet invocation on the command line or with the **open** command, as shown in the next examples. Here, the user is logging into a specific account called **dylan** on the **rose.berkeley.edu** system:

```
$ telnet rose.berkeley.edu -1 dylan
telnet> open rose.berkeley.edu -1 dylan
```

Note   *You can also use telnet to connect to different Internet-based services like FTP.*

Remote Access Commands: rwho, rlogin, rcp, and rsh

The remote access commands were designed for smaller networks, such as intranets. They enable you to log in remotely to another account on another system and to copy files from one system to another. You can also obtain information about another system, such as who is logged on currently (see Table 18-2). Many of the remote commands have comparable network communication utilities used for the Internet. For example, **rlogin**, which remotely logs into a system, is similar to **telnet**. The **rcp** command, which remotely copies files, performs much the same function as **ftp**. In place of these commands, secure versions provided by the Secure SHell (SSH) are now commonly used (see Chapter 39).

You can use several commands to obtain information about different systems on your network. You can find out who is logged in, get information about a user on another system, or find out if a system is up and running. For example, the **rwho** command functions in the same way as the **who** command. It displays all the users currently logged into each system in your network.

```
$ rwho
violet      robert:tty1      Sept 10 10:34
garnet      chris:tty2       Sept 10 09:22
```

The **ruptime** command displays information about each system on your network. The information shows how each system has been performing. **ruptime** shows whether a system is up or down, how long it has been up or down, the number of users on the system, and the average load on the system for the last five, ten, and fifteen minutes.

```
$ ruptime
violet      up      11+04:10,      8 users,  load 1.20 1.10      1.00
garnet      up      11+04:10,     20 users,  load 1.50 1.40      1.30
```

Remote Access Permission: .rhosts

You use an **.rhosts** file to control access to your account by users using TCP/IP commands. Users create the **.rhosts** file on their own accounts using a standard editor such as Vi. It must be located in the user's **home** directory. In the next example, the user displays the contents of a **.rhosts** file:

```
$ cat .rhosts
garnet chris
violet robert
```

The **.rhosts** file is a simple way to allow other people access to your account without giving out your password. To deny access to a user, simply delete the system's name and the user's login name from your **.rhosts** file. If a user's login name and system are in a **.rhosts** file, then that user can directly access that account without knowing the password (in place of using **.rhosts**, you could use a password instead); the **.rhosts** file is required for other remote commands, such as remotely copying files or remotely executing Linux commands. If you want to execute such commands on an account in a remote system, that account must have your login name and system name in its **.rhosts** file.

The type of access **.rhosts** provides enables you to use TCP/IP commands to access other accounts directly that you might have on other systems. You do not have to log into them first. In effect, you can treat your accounts on other systems as extensions of the one you are currently logged into. Using the **rcp** command, you can copy any files from one directory to another no matter what account they are on. With the **rsh** command, you can execute any Linux command you want on any of your other accounts.

rlogin, rcp, and rsh

You may have accounts on different systems in your network, or you may be permitted to access someone else's account on another system. You could access an account on another system by first logging into your own and then remotely logging in across your network to the account on the other system. You can perform such a remote login using the **rlogin** command, which takes as its argument a system name. The command connects you to the other system and begins login procedures.

Login procedures using **rlogin** differ from regular login procedures in that the user is not prompted for a login name. **rlogin** assumes the login name on your local system is the same as the login name on the remote system. Upon executing the **rlogin** command, you are immediately prompted for a password. After entering the password, you are logged into the account on the remote system. Once logged into a remote system, you can execute any command you want. You can end the connection with **exit**, CTRL-D, **~.**, or **logout** (TCSH or C shell). **rlogin** assumes the login name on the remote system is the same as the one on the local system because most people use **rlogin** to access accounts they have on other systems with their own login name. When the login name on the remote system is different from the one on the local system, however, the **-l** option enables you to enter it. The syntax is shown here:

```
$ rlogin system-name -l login-name
```

You can use the **rcp** command to copy files to and from remote and local systems. **rcp** is a file transfer utility that operates like the **cp** command, but across a network connection to a remote system. The **rcp** command requires the remote system to have your local system and login name in its **.rhosts** file. The **rcp** command begins with the keyword **rcp** and has as its arguments the source file and copy filenames. To specify the file on the remote system, you need to place the remote system name before the filename, separated by a colon. When you are copying a file on the remote system to your own, the source file is a remote file and requires the remote system's name. The copy file is a file on your own system and does not require a system name:

```
$ rcp remote-system-name:source-file   copy-file
```

In the next example, the user copies the file **wednesday** from the remote system **violet** to her own system and renames the file **today**.

```
$ rcp violet:wednesday today
```

You can also use **rcp** to copy whole directories to or from a remote system. The **rcp** command with the **-r** option copies a directory and all its subdirectories from one system to another. Like the **cp** command, **rcp** requires source and copy directories. The directory on the remote system requires the system name and colon be placed before the directory name. When you copy a directory from your own system to a remote system, the copy directory is on the remote system and requires the remote system's name. In the next example, the user copies the directory **letters** to the directory **oldnotes** on the remote system **violet**:

```
$ rcp -r letters violet:oldnotes
```

At times, you may need to execute a single command on a remote system. The **rsh** command executes a Linux command on another system and displays the results on your own. Your system name and login name must, of course, be in the remote system's **.rhosts** file. The **rsh** command takes two general arguments: a system name and a Linux command. The syntax is as follows:

```
$ rsh remote-system-name  Linux-command
```

In the next example, the **rsh** command executes an **ls** command on the remote system **violet** to list the files in the **/home/robert** directory on **violet**.

```
$ rsh violet ls /home/robert
```

Special characters are evaluated by the local system unless quoted. This is particularly true of special characters that control the standard output, such as redirection operators or pipes. The next example lists the files on the remote system and sends them to the standard output on the local system. The redirection operator is evaluated by the local system and redirects the output to **myfiles**, which is a file on the local system.

```
$ rsh violet ls /home/robert > myfiles
```

If you quote a special character, it becomes part of the Linux command evaluated on the remote system. Quoting redirection operators enables you to perform redirection operations on the remote system. In the next example, the redirection operator is quoted. It becomes part of the Linux command, including its argument, the file name **myfiles**. The **ls** command then generates a list of filenames that is redirected on the remote system to a file called **myfiles**, also located on the remote system.

```
$ rsh violet ls /home/robert '>' myfiles
```

The same is true for pipes. The first command (shown next) prints the list of files on the local system's printer. The standard output is piped to your own line printer. In the second command, the list of files is printed on the remote system's printer. The pipe is quoted and evaluated by the remote system, piping the standard output to the printer on the remote system.

```
$ rsh violet ls /home/robert | lpr
$ rsh violet ls /home/robert '|' lpr
```

Remote Commands	Effect
rwho	Displays all users logged into systems in your network
ruptime	Displays information about each system on your network
rlogin *system-name*	Allows you to log in remotely to an account on another system 　**$ rlogin violet**
-l	Allows you to specify the login name of the account 　**$ rlogin violet -l robert**
rcp *sys-name:file1* *sys-name:file2*	Allows you to copy a file from an account on one system to an account on another system; if no system name is given, the current system is assumed 　**$ rcp mydata violet:newdata**
-r	With the **-r** option, allows you to copy directories instead of just files 　**$ rcp -r newdocs violet:edition**
-p	Preserves the modification times and modes of source files

Table 18-2.   *Remote Access Commands*

INTERNET

Remote Commands	Effect
rsh *sys-name Linux-command*	Allows you to remotely execute a command on another system $ **rsh violet ls**
-l	Allows you to specify the login name $ **rsh -l ls**
-n	Redirects input from the null special device, **/dev/null**

Table 18-2. *Remote Access Commands* (continued)

UNIX to UNIX CoPy: UUCP

The UUCP protocols are an alternative set of protocols to those of the Internet (TCP/IP) that provide network communication between Linux and UNIX systems. However, UUCP is an older protocol designed to operate between systems not already connected on a network. With UUCP, one system can connect to another across phone lines at a predetermined time, sending a batched set of communications all at once. UUCP is helpful for making a direct connection to a particular system, transferring data, and then cutting the connection. UUCP enables you to set up direct modem-to-modem communication with another system.

UUCP has its own set of remote access commands: **uuto**, **uupick**, **uucp**, and **uux**. The **uuto** command mails files to other systems, while **uupick** receives those files. These commands are used for sending and receiving large files. The **uucp** command copies files from one system to another. The **uux** command remotely executes a Linux command on another system. Many of the UUCP commands correspond to the TCP/IP remote access commands. **uucp** operates much like **rcp** and **uux** like **rsh**. UUCP commands are subject to the same permission restrictions as your own local commands. Protected files and directories cannot be accessed; only files and directories with the other user permissions set can be accessed.

You can think of UUCP commands as referencing files on other Linux systems through a mail system. These commands are designed to operate using point-to-point communication. This is as if you were using the mail capabilities of different systems to implement a network. When you issue a UUCP command for a given system, the command is queued and collected with other commands for that same system. The commands are then mailed to that system for execution. Once that system receives the commands and executes them, it mails back any results. Several systems can arrange to receive and send commands to each other, forming a UUCP network. The entire process then depends on each system in the network sending and receiving commands to and from other systems. In this respect, the network is only as strong as its weakest link. On the other hand, it requires no special structure, only the sending and receiving of what are essentially messages.

INTERNET

The
Complete
Reference

Linux

Part IV

Applications

The
Complete
Reference

Chapter 19

Software Management

Installing or updating software packages has always been a simple process in Linux due to the widespread use of the Red Hat Package Manager. Instead of using a standard **tar** archive, software is packaged in a special archive for use with the Red Hat Package Manager. These archives have become known as RPMs, where *RPM* stands for *Red Hat Package Manager.* An RPM archive contains all the program files, configuration files, data files, and even documentation that constitute a software application. With one simple operation, the Red Hat Package Manager installs all these for you from an RPM software package. You can even create your own RPM packages. You can use any of several RPM window-based utilities to manage your RPM packages, installing new ones or uninstalling ones you have. These utilities provide an easy-to-use interface for managing your packages, enabling you to obtain detailed information on a package easily, including a complete listing of the files it installs. Also, as part of their administration tools, distributions like Red Hat also provide software management for packages on their CD-ROMs.

You can also download source code versions of applications, and then compile and install them on your system. Where this process once was complex, it has been significantly streamlined with the addition of configure scripts. Most current source code, including GNU software, is distributed with a configure script. The *configure script* automatically detects your system configuration and generates a **Makefile** with which a binary file is created compatible to your system, is created. With three simple commands, you can compile and install complex source code on any system.

Extensive online sources exist for downloading Linux software. Sites are available for particular kinds of applications, such as Gnome and KDE, as well as for particular distributions, such as Red Hat and Caldera. Some are repositories for RPM packages, such as **rpmfind.net,** while others like **freshmeat.net** refer you to original development sites where you can download software packages. The **freshmeat.net** and **www.linuxapps.com** sites are useful for finding out about new available software. Many of the open source Linux projects can now be found at **sourceforge.net**. Here you will find detailed documentation and recent versions of software packages. For particular database and office applications, you can download software packages directly from the company's Web site, such as **www.sun.com** for the StarOffice office suite and **www.oracle.com** for the Oracle database (see Chapters 22 and 23). For RPM packages , which are not part of a distribution, you can check the **contrib** directory on the distribution FTP site, such as the **ftp.redhat.com** site. Here, you can find Red Hat RPM packages for applications, such as ProFTPD and htDig. Table 19-1 lists several popular Linux software sites.

Red Hat Package Manager (RPM)

Several Linux distributions, including Red Hat, OpenLinux, and SuSE, use RPM to organize Linux software into packages you can automatically install or remove. An RPM software package operates as its own installation program for a software

FTP and Web sites	Applications
ftp.redhat.com	Software packaged in RPM packages for Red Hat. Check the **contrib** directory for contributed software.
freshmeat.net	Linux software, includes RPMs.
linuxapps.com	Linux software, includes RPMs.
rpmfind.net	RPM package repository.
www.sourceforge.net	Linux open source software projects.
www.gnome.org	Gnome software.
apps.kde.com	KDE software.
http://www.xnet.com/~blatura/linapps.shtml	Linux applications and utilities page.
www.filewatcher.org	Linux FTP site watcher.
www.gnu.org	GNU archive.
www.helixcode.com	Helix Code, office applications for Gnome.
koffice.kde.com	The KDE KOffice suite of office applications.
www.xdt.com/ar/linux-snd	Linux MIDI and sound pages.
www.linuxvideo.org	The Linux Video and DVD Project, LiViD.
www.opensound.com	Open Sound System drivers.
metalab.unc.edu	Extensive Linux archive (formerly **sunsite.unc.edu**).
happypenquin.org	Linux Game Tome.
www.linuxgames.org	Linux games.
www.linuxquake.com	Quake.

Table 19-1.   *Linux Software Sites*

APPLICATIONS

application. A Linux software application often consists of several files that need to be installed in different directories. The program itself is most likely placed in a directory called **/usr/bin**, online manual files go in another directory, and library files in yet another directory. In addition, the installation may require modification of certain configuration files on your system. The RPM software packages performs all these tasks for you. Also, if you later decide you don't want a specific application, you can uninstall packages to remove all the files and configuration information from your system. RPM works similarly to the Windows Install Wizard, automatically installing software, including configuration, documentation, image, sample, and program files, along with any other files an application may use. All are installed in their appropriate directories on your system. RPM maintains a database of installed software, keeping track of all the files installed. This enables you to use RPM also to uninstall software, automatically removing all files that are part of the application.

To install and uninstall RPM packages, you can use the **rpm** command on a shell command line or any available RPM window-based program, such as Kpackage or GnomeRPM. Also, distribution install and management utilities, such as COAS, Lisa, and YaST, enable you to install or uninstall your distribution software packages. These are usually the RPM packages on your CD-ROM. Although you should download RPM packages from your particular distribution, numerous RPM software packages are designed to run on any Linux system. Many of these are located at distribution contrib directories . You can learn more about RPM at its Web site at **www.rpm.org**. The site contains up-to-date versions for RPM, documentation, and RPM support programs, such as **rpm2html** and **rpm2cpio**. **rpm2html** takes a directory containing RPM packages and generates Web pages listing those packages as links that can be used to download them. **rpm2cpio** is Perl script to extract RPMs. You can obtain further documentation from the RPM Documentation Project site at **www.rpmdp.org**.

The RPM packages on your CD-ROMs only represent a small portion of the software packages available for Linux. You can download additional software in the form of RPM packages from distribution contribution locations, such as the **contrib** directory in the Red Hat FTP site at **ftp.redhat.com**. In addition, these packages are organized into **lib5** and **lib6** directories. **lib5** refers to the packages using the older libraries, whereas **lib6** refers to those using the new GNU 2.*x* libraries. For Red Hat 6.0 and later, you should use the **lib6** versions, though many packages still use the **lib5** versions which also work.

An extensive repository for RPM packages is also located at **http://rpmfind.net/linux/RPM**. Packages here are indexed according to distribution, group, and name. It includes packages for every distribution, including previous versions of those distributions. From **http://rpmfind.net,** you can download the **rpmfind** command that enables you to search for RPM packages, either on your local system or on the RPM repository at **rpmfind.net**. You can even use **rpmfind** to download and update packages. **rpmfind** detects your system's distribution and lists RPM packages for it. Search results also tell you on what other packages a given RPM can depend. With the **--appropos** option, you can use more general terms to locate a package, instead of filename patterns. With the **--upgrade** option, you can download and install newer versions of installed packages. The **rpmfind** command also sets up a **.rpmfind** configuration file, where you can specify such features as a download directory, the remote servers to search, and the location of local RPM packages on your system.

Your distribution CD-ROMs like the Caldera and RedHat ones included with this book, will contain an extensive set of applications located in an **RPMS** directory on the CD-ROM. On RedHat this is at **RedHat/RPMS**, and on Caldera it is at **/col/install/RPMS**. You can install or uninstall any of these packages using an **rpm** command, a GUI RPM utility, or the software manager screen on your distribution administration tool. To install a software package from your CD-ROM using the **rpm** command, it is easier to move first to the **RPMS** directory and then install the package you want. Be sure to mount the CD-ROM first before you try to access it.

You have to download additional RPM packages not located on your CD-ROM from distribution sites, such as **ftp.redhat.com** and **ftp.caldera.com**. Web sites for the particular software you want may also have RPM packages already set up for you for your distribution. For example, you can obtain the ProFTPD RPM package for Red Hat from **ftp.redhat.com**, and the current Red Hat or Linuxconf RPM packages from the Linuxconf Web site (see Chapter 30). You could place these packages in a directory on your system and then use either **rpm** or a **GUI RPM** utility, such as GnomeRPM to install it. Normally, you should always try to use the version of the RPM package set up for your distribution. In many cases, attempting to install an RPM package meant for a different distribution may fail. Popular RPM package managers are listed here:

Kpackage	K Desktop RPM package manager
GnomeRPM	Gnome RPM package manager
rpm	The shell command to manage RPM packages
xrpm	X Window System RPM package manager
Glint	Older X Window System RPM package manager

The K Desktop Package Manager: Kpackage

The KDE desktop provides a powerful and easy-to-use RPM package manager called *Kpackage* (see Figure 19-1). You run Kpackage under any window manager or desktop (including Gnome), as long as you have installed the K Desktop on your system. You can start Kpackage by selecting its entry in the K menu Utility menu or by entering the **kpackage** command in a terminal window.

The right side of Kpackage contains two tabbed panels: one for Properties and the other for the File List. The Properties panel displays information about the software in the currently selected RPM package, including the version number and the authors. The File List lists all the files contained in the software package, including **readme** files. If you are using Kpackage on the K Desktop, you can click any text file in the File List,

APPLICATIONS

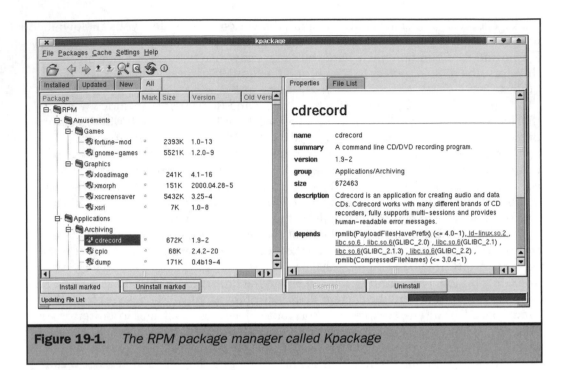

Figure 19-1. *The RPM package manager called Kpackage*

and it is displayed by the text editor. This is a convenient way to read installation files, such as **readme** or **install** files. To uninstall a package, select it and click Uninstall.

The list of installed packages is often extensive. To locate a particular package, select the Find entry in the File menu. If the Substring check box is selected, you can use a pattern to search for your package instead of a complete name. The Package list in the left pane moves to the first package found, highlighting it. If you use a pattern and more choices exist, you can move to the next one by selecting the Find menu item again. The Kpackage application also enables you to search for a particular file in a package. Select the Find File entry in the File menu and enter the name of the file to locate. You have to use the full pathname for the file. Patterns are not supported.

You can also use Kpackage to install RPM packages. You must know where on the system the packages are located. For example, on Red Hat systems, they are in the **RedHat/RPMS** directory. If you mounted the CD-ROM at **/mnt/cdrom**, the full pathname should be **/mnt/cdrom/RedHat/RPMS**. Packages you download from FTP sites would be in whatever directory you downloaded them to—say, **/root/download**. To install a package, select Open from the File menu. This opens a File Browser dialog box, where you can move to the directory you want and select the RPM package. An Installation dialog box is displayed with options that include updating and testing the package. You select Update for packages that are updated versions of ones already installed. With the **Test** option, you can test an installation without actually having to install it.

GnomeRPM

Although not written by Red Hat, GnomeRPM provides an effective and easy-to-use interface for managing RPM packages on your Gnome desktop. It runs on any window manager, provided Gnome is installed on your system. As Figure 19-2 shows, the GnomeRPM window displays two panes, the left one showing a tree listing categories of different installed RPM packages. Expand a category to display the packages in the right pane. You can query a package by selecting it and clicking the Uninstall icon in the icon bar or by right-clicking it and selecting Uninstall from the pop-up menu. You can use the same method for querying packages and for displaying information and file listings. You can select several packages at once from different categories by CTRL-clicking their icons. A selected package darkens. When you select uninstall, all those packages are uninstalled. CTRL-click the package again to deselect it. Click Unselect to deselect all the packages you selected. The number of selected packages is shown in the lower-left corner of the window. The GnomeRPM package also features a

Figure 19-2.   *The gnomeRPM main window*

APPLICATIONS

find utility, which you can use to locate RPM packages easily. In the find window, you can then query or uninstall the package.

To install new packages with GnomeRPM, click the Install icon. This opens a window that displays the selected packages to install. You then click Add to open a window for locating packages on your system. You can add as many windows as you want to the list. Click Install to install the packages. To upgrade a package that is already installed, click Upgrade and follow the same procedure.

GnomeRPM supports drag-and-drop operations from the desktop and file manager. You can drag one or more RPM packages from a file manager window to the GnomeRPM install dialog window. You can then install or query selected packages. GnomeRPM also enables you to browse through packages available with the rpmfind system. Click the Web Find button. The listing of packages is then downloaded and displayed in the tree menu. Use the tree menu to navigate to the package you want.

KDE and Gnome File Managers

On Gnome, you can install RPM packages directly from the file manager, without using any special utility such as GnomeRPM. Use the file manager window to access the directory with your package, such as your distribution CD-ROM. Then right-click the package name or icon. In the pop-up menu, you can select the **Install** option to install the package. You can also simply just double-click the package. The Gnome file manager automatically detects that it is an RPM package, checks to see if it is installed, and then installs it for you. It will also perform a dependency check to see if there are any conflicts or needed libraries. If there are any problems, it will halt the installation and display any conflict or dependency warnings. You can use this same method for FTP sites. The Gnome file manager is Internet-aware. You can enter a URL for an FTP site in its Location box to access the site. Be sure to include the FTP protocol in the URL, **ftp://**. When you locate the package, right-click it and select Install or Update. The file is downloaded and then automatically installed on your system.

| Tip | *On Gnome, if you just want to find out what a package is, along with a list of files in that package, you can right-click on the package and select the Show Info entry. A window opens up displaying a description of the software and a list of all the files in the package. There are also buttons to let you install or upgrade the software.* |

Problems can arise if the application you want to install is already installed, or if it requires that another application be installed first (Upgrades are considered new software and are not considered a problem). In this case a window titled Installation Problems will appear asking you if you want to ignore problems. The window will display a list of problems encountered (such as, the software is already installed, or it requires other software packages to be installed first). You should cancel the install operation by clicking on the NO button, or, if the NO button is selected, press ENTER. You do NOT want to ignore the problems. Clicking YES instead, will force the installation of the software in a manner that may overwrite previous configuration files or let you try to run the application without required supporting software such as needed libraries.

The KDE file manager also enables you to install RPM packages, though it uses Kpackage to perform the actual installation. Locate an RPM file on your system using the file manager, and then single-click its icon or name. This automatically opens Kpackage with the RPM package loaded, which is then displayed on a window with panels for the package information and the list of files in it. At the bottom of the panels is an Install button. Click it to install the package. Because the KDE file manager is Internet-aware, you can use this same method both to download and install RPM packages from FTP sites. Locate the FTP site with the file manager (enter its URL in the Location box), and then locate your package. Once your package is listed in the file manager window, click it. The package is then automatically downloaded and Kpackage starts up, showing the package. Click the Install button to install it.

Webmin and Linuxconf

With either Webmin or Linuxconf, you can also manage software installations. For Webmin, select the Software Packages icon in the System page. From the Software Packages page, you can then view installed packages or install new ones, as well as search for packages (see Figure 19-3). Clicking on an entry for an installed package will display a page showing package information, as well as a button for uninstalling the package. You can install new packages from your local system or from remote FTP sites.

The recent version of Linuxconf also provides software management modules. On the Control tab open the Package Management (RPM) entry to list several installation tasks (see Figure 19-4). You can install just one package or several packages in a specified directory. You can also browse uninstalled packages, selecting the one you want. You will have to specify the directory in which they are located. Use the Browse Installed Packages entry to list all your install packages by category. Here you can obtain information about a package, as well as uninstall it.

Command Line Installation: rpm

If you do not have access to the desktop or you prefer to work from the command line interface, you can use the **rpm** command to manage and install software packages. **rpm** is the command that actually performs installation, removal, and queries of software packages. In fact, GnomeRPM and Kpackage use the **rpm** command to install and remove packages. An RPM package is an archive of software files that include information about how to install those files. The filenames for RPM packages end with **.rpm**, indicating software packages that can be installed by the Red Hat Package Manager.

With the **rpm** command, you can maintain packages, query them, build your own, and verify the ones you have. Maintaining packages involves installing new ones,

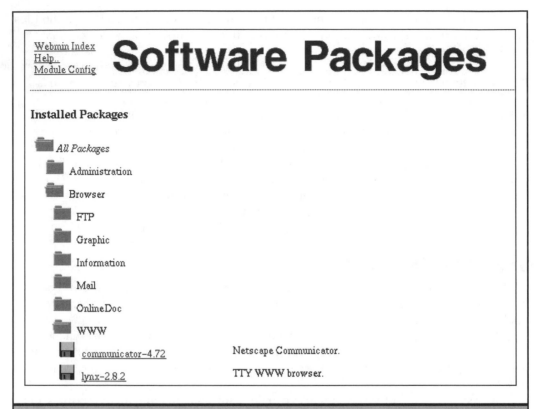

Figure 19-3. Webmin Software Packages page

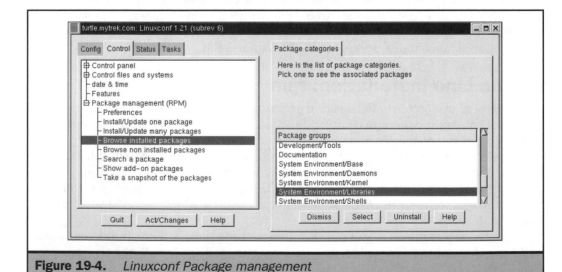

Figure 19-4. Linuxconf Package management

upgrading to new versions, and uninstalling packages. The **rpm** command uses a set of options to determine what action to take. In addition, certain tasks, such as installing or querying packages, have their own options that further qualify the kind of action they take. For example, the **-q** option queries a package, but when combined with the **-l** option it lists all the files in that package. Table 19-2 lists the set of **rpm** options.

Mode of Operation	Effect
rpm -i*options package-file*	Installs a package; the complete name of the package file is required.
rpm -e*options package-name*	Uninstalls (erases) a package; you only need the name of the package, often one word.
rpm -q*options package-name*	Queries a package; an option can be a package name, a further option and package name, or an option applied to all packages.
rpm -U*options package-name*	Upgrade; same as install, but any previous version is removed.
rpm -b*options package-specifications*	Builds your own RPM package.
rpm -F*options package-name*	Upgrade, but only if package is currently installed.
rpm -verify*options*	Verifies a package is correctly installed; uses same options as query; you can use **-V** or **-y** in place of **-verify**.
--nodeps	Installs without doing any dependency checks.
--force	Forces installation despite conflicts.
--percent	Displays percentage of package during installation.
--test	Tests installation; does not install, only checks for conflicts.
-h	Displays **#** symbols as package is installed.
--excludedocs	Excludes documentation files.

Table 19-2.   *Red Hat Package Manager (RPM) Options*

APPLICATIONS

Uninstall Options (to be used with -e)

--test	Tests uninstall; does not remove, only checks for what is to be removed.
--nodeps	Uninstalls without checking for dependencies.
--allmatches	Removes all versions of package.

Query Options (to be used with -q)

package-name	Queries package.
-a	Queries all packages.
-f *filename*	Queries package that owns *filename*.
-R	List packages on which this package depends.
-p *package-name*	Queries an uninstalled package.
-I	Displays all package information.
-l	Lists files in package.
-d	Lists only documentation files in package.
-c	Lists only configuration files in package.
--dump	Lists only files with complete details.

General Options (to be used with any option)

-vv	Debug; displays descriptions of all actions taken.
--quit	Displays only error messages.
--version	Displays **rpm** version number.
--help	Displays detailed use message.
--root*directory*	Uses directory as top-level directory for all operations (instead of root).
--dbpath*directory*	Uses **RPM** database in the specified directory.

Table 19-2. *Red Hat Package Manager (RPM) Options* (continued)

--dbpath *cmd*	Pipes output of RPM to the command *cmd*.
--rebuilddb	Rebuilds the **RPM** database; can use with **-root** and **-dbpath** options.
--initdb	Builds a new **RPM** database; **-root** and **-dbpath** options.
Other Sources of Information	
RPM-HOWTO	More detailed information, particularly on how to build your own RPM packages.
man rpm	Detailed list of options.

Table 19-2.   *Red Hat Package Manager (RPM) Options* (continued)

You use the **-i** option to install a new software package and the **-U** option to update a currently installed package with a newer version. With an **-e** option, **rpm** uninstalls the package. The **-q** option tells you if a package is already installed, and the **-qa** option displays a list of all installed packages. Piping this output to a pager utility, such as **more**, is best.

```
rpm -qa | more
```

In the next example, the user checks to see if xv is already installed on the system. Notice the full filename of the RPM archive is unnecessary. If the package is installed, your system has already registered its name and where it is located.

```
# rpm -q xv
```

 *Keep in mind the distinction between the installed software package name and the package filename. The filename will end in an .rpm extension and can only be queried with a **p** option.*

You can combine the **q** options with the **i** or **l** options to display information about the package. The options **-qi** display information about the software, such as the version number or author (**-qpi** queries an uninstalled package file). The option **-ql** displays a listing of all the files in the software package. The **--h** option provides a complete list of **rpm** options. The syntax for the **rpm** command is as follows (*rpm-package-name* is the name of the software package you want to install):

```
rpm options rpm-package-name
```

The software package filename is usually lengthy, including information about version and release date in its name. All end with **.rpm**.

If you are installing from a CD-ROM, you can change to the CD-ROM's **RedHat/RPMS** directory, which holds the RPM packages. An **ls** command lists all the software packages. If you know how the name of a package begins, you should include that with the **ls** command and an attached *****. The list of packages is extensive and does not all fit on one screen. This is helpful for displaying the detailed name of the package. The following example lists most X Window System packages:

```
# ls x*
```

You use the **-i** option to install new packages and the **-U** option to update currently installed packages with new versions. If you try to use the **-i** option to install a newer version of an installed package, you receive an error saying the package is already installed. In the next example, the user first installs a new package with the **-i** option, and then updates a package with the **-U** option. Including the **-v** and **-h** options is customary. Here, **-v** is the verbose option that displays all files as they are installed, and **-h** displays a cross-hatch symbol periodically to show RPM is still working.

In the following example, the user installs the software package for the mozilla Web browser (see Chapter 17). Notice the full filename is entered. To list the full name, you can use the **ls** command with the first few characters and an asterisk, **ls htdig***. The **h** option displays **#** symbols as the installation takes place. The **rpm** command with the **-q** option is then used to check that the software was installed. For installed packages only, the software name needs to be used, in this case, mozilla-M17.

```
[root@turtle mypackages]# ls mo*
smozilla-M17-3.i386.rpm
[root@turtle mypackages]# rpm -ivh mozilla-M17-3.i386.rpm
mozilla-M17                          #########################################
[root@turtle mypackages]# rpm -q mozilla-M17
mozilla-M17-3
```

To display information about the installed package, use **-qi**, and **-ql** displays a listing of the files a given RPM package contains.

```
# rpm -qi mozilla-M17
# rpm -ql mozilla-M17
```

To display information taken directly from an RPM package, you add the **p** qualifier to the **q** options. The **-qpi** combination displays information about a specific package, and **-qpl** displays a listing of the files a given RPM package contains. In this case, you must specify the entire filename of the RPM package. You can avoid having to enter the entire name simply by entering a unique part of the name and using the * filename matching character to generate the rest.

```
[root@turtle mypackages]# ls proftp*
proftpd-core-1.2.0pre10-1.i386.rpm
[root@turtle mypackages]# rpm -qp proftpd-core-1.2.0pre10-1.i386.rpm
proftpd-1.2.0pre3-2
[root@turtle mypackages]# rpm - qpi proftpd-core-1.2*.rpm
Name        : proftpd                    Relocations: (not relocateable)
Version     : 1.2.0pre10                      Vendor: (none)
................................................
[root@turtle mypackages]# rpm -qpl proftpd*
/etc/logrotate.d/proftpd
/etc/pam.d/ftp
/etc/proftpd.conf
................................................
```

Remember, if you are installing an upgrade, you need to use the **-U** option instead of the **-I** option. If you try to use **-I** to upgrade a package, you receive an error saying the package is already installed. If you receive an error stating dependency conflicts exist, the package may require other packages or their updated versions to be installed first. In some cases, you may have to install with the no dependency check options, **--nodeps** (notice the two dashes before the option). In some rare cases, installation instructions for a particular package may require you to use **--nodeps**. Another risky option is the **--force** option. This forces installation, overwriting any current files. This is a brute-force approach that should be used with care.

To remove a software package from your system, first use **rpm -q** to make sure it is actually installed. Then, use the **-e** option to uninstall it. You needn't use the full name of the installed file. You only need the name of the application. For example, if you decide you do not need Mozilla, you can remove it using the **-e** option and the software name, as shown here:

```
# rpm -e mozilla-M17
```

If direct conflicts occur with another software package, you may have to uninstall the other package first. This is the case with wu-ftpd and ProFTP on many distributions. Man distributions currently install wu-ftpd as the default FTP server. You must first uninstall the wu-ftpd with the **-e** option before you can install ProFTP. However, when you try to do this, you receive a dependency error. You can overcome this error by using the **--nodeps** option. Once wu-ftpd is removed, you can install ProFTP.

```
[root@turtle mypackages]# rpm -e --nodeps wu-ftpd
[root@turtle mypackages]# rpm -ivh proftpd-core-1.2*rpm
proftpd          ###########################################
[root@turtle mypackages]# rpm -q proftpd
proftpd-core-1.2.0pre3-10
```

You can use the verify option (**-V**) to check to see if any problems occurred with the installation. RPM compares the current attributes of installed files with information about them placed in the RPM database when the package was installed. If no discrepancies exist, RPM outputs nothing. Otherwise, RPM outputs a sequence of eight characters, one for each attribute, for each file in the package that fails. Those that do not differ have a period. Those that do differ have a corresponding character code, as shown here:

5	MD5 checksum
S	File size
L	Symbolic link
T	File modification time
D	Device
U	User
G	Group
M	Mode (includes permissions and file types)

The following example verifies the proftpd package:

```
[root@turtle mypackages]# rpm -V proftpd
```

To compare the installed files directly with the files in an RPM package file, you use the **-Vp** option, much like the **-qp** option. To check all packages, use the **-Va** option as shown here:

```
rpm -Va
```

If you want to verify a package, but only know the name of a file in it, you can combine verify with the **-f** option. The following example verifies the RPM package containing the **ftp** command:

```
rpm -Vf   /bin/ftp
```

A complete description of **rpm** and its capabilities is provided in the online manual.

```
# man rpm
```

RPM maintains a record of the packages it has installed in its **RPM** database. You may, at times, have to rebuild this database to ensure RPM has current information on what is installed and what is not. Use the **-rebuilddb** options to rebuild your database file.

```
rpm --rebuilddb
```

To create a new RPM database, use the **-initdb** option. This can be combined with **-dbpath** to specify a location for the new database.

Updating Distributions: Red Hat

In the period between major releases, distributions post RPM package updates for software installed from your CD-ROM. Red Hat posts these packages at their update directory at their FTP site at **ftp.redhat.com**. Such updates may range from single software packages to whole components—for instance, all the core applications and development packages issued when new releases of Gnome, KDE, or XFree86 are made available.

With version 6.1, Red Hat now provides an Update Agent, which automatically locates, downloads, and installs any updates for your Red Hat system. To use the Update Agent, however, you must first register your copy of Red Hat at the Red Hat Web site at **www.redhat.com**. You are then provided with a user name and password with which you can configure the Update Agent to access Red Hat's special secure server at **priority.redhat.com.** To start the Update Agent, select its entry in the System menu in the Gnome main menu. Upon starting the Update Agent, you are asked for your root user password as an added precaution.

The first time you use Update Agent, you must configure it, providing information about your system. Click the Configure button to display the Configuration dialog box with three tabbed panels: User, Retrieval, and Exceptions. The User panel holds your registration information and your e-mail address. The Retrieval panel is where you enter the server you want to use (for example, **priority.redhat.com**), as well as download instructions and the download directory you want to use. The Exceptions panel holds the names of any packages you don't want to update automatically.

To use Update Agent, click the Connect button. The Update Agent connects to the FTP server, and then opens your Web browser (such as Netscape) and displays a Web page listing the possible updates it found. You can then select individual packages by clicking the check boxes next to them. Then click the Request Selected packages button.

To select all packages, click the Request ALL packages button. Once you select your packages, you can click the Request Packages button. The browser closes and the Update Agent begins downloading the selected packages. The packages are listed with a Status icon. They are first downloaded, during which the Status icon is a button, and then they are installed, which is indicated by a red arrow. When finished, the Status icon becomes a check mark.

Or, you can upgrade manually by first downloading all the packages and installing them yourself. For example, to install new releases of the K Desktop, you can download distribution versions of their packages from the KDE FTP site at **ftp.kde.org** or from distribution FTP sites. You can use an FTP client, such as NcFTP, to download them all at once, including any subdirectories (see Chapter 12). Then change to that directory and use the **rpm −Uvh** command to install the packages.

For single packages, you can download them from the distribution FTP site, and then use the **rpm** command with the **−U** option to install them. You could also use an RPM utility such as KPackage. In fact, you can use both KPackageand GnomeRPM to access the distribution FTP sites directly, download the package, and automatically install it on your system. Just enter the FTP URL for the site in the Location box. In the following example, the **rpm** command with the **−Uvh** option installs an upgrade for Linuxconf:

```
$ rpm −Uvh  linuxconf-1.21r6-1.i386.rpm
```

Installing Software from Compressed Archives: .tar.gz

Linux software applications in the form of source code are available at different sites on the Internet. You can download any of this software and install it on your system. You download software using an FTP client as described in Chapter 12. Recent and older software is usually downloaded in the form of a compressed archive file. This is particularly true for the recent versions of Gnome or KDE packages. RPM packages are only intermittently generated. A *compressed archive* is an archive file created with **tar**, and then compressed with **gzip**. To install such a file, you must first decompress it with the **gunzip** utility, and then use **tar** to extract the files and directories making up the software package. Instead of the **gunzip** utility, you could also use **gzip −d**. The next example decompresses the **htdig-3.1.5.tar.gz** file, replacing it with a decompressed version called **htdig-3.1.5.tar**:

```
$ ls
 htdig-3.1.5.tar.gz
$ gunzip htdig-3.1.5.tar.gz
$ ls
htdig-3.1.5.tar.gz
```

First, use **tar** with the **t** option to check the contents of the archive. If the first entry is a directory, then that directory is created and the extracted files are placed in it. If the first entry is not a directory, you should first create one and then copy the archive file to it. Then extract the archive within that directory. If no directory exists as the first entry, files are extracted to the current directory. You must create a directory yourself to hold these files.

```
$ tar tvf htdig-3.1.5.tar
```

Now you are ready to extract the files from the **tar** archive. You use **tar** with the **x** option to extract files, the **v** option to display the pathnames of files as they are extracted, and the **f** option, followed by the name of the archive file:

```
$ tar xvf htdig-3.1.5.tar
```

You can combine the decompressing and unpacking operation into one **tar** command by adding a **z** option to the option list, **xzvf**. The following command both decompresses and unpacks the archive:

```
$ tar xzvf htdig-3.1.5.tar.gz
```

Installation of your software may differ for each package. Instructions are usually provided, along with an installation program.

Downloading Compressed Archives from Online Sites

Many software packages under development or designed for cross-platform implementation may not be in an RPM format. Instead, they may be archived and compressed. The filenames for these files end with the extensions **.tar.gz** or **.tar.Z**. In fact, most software with an RPM format also has a corresponding **.tar.gz** format. After you download such a package, you must first decompress it with **gunzip**, and then unpack it with the **tar** command. Many RPM packages only contain binary versions of software applications. If you want the source code for the application, you must download and unpack the compressed archive for that application.

In the next example, the user uses **ftp** to connect to the **metalab.unc.edu** Linux FTP site. For the login ID, the user enters **anonymous** and for the password, the user enters his or her Internet address. The download mode can be set to binary by entering in the keyword **binary**. With the **cd** command, the user changes to the **pub/Linux/libs/X/ xview** directory, where the Xview window manager software is located (see Chapter 3). The **get** command then downloads the package. The **close** command cuts the connection, and the **quit** command leaves the **ftp** FTP utility.

```
ftp> get xview-3.2p1.4.bin.tar.gz
>local: xview-3.2p1.4.bin.tar.gz remote: xview-3.2p1.4.bin.tar.gz
200 PORT command successful.
150 Opening BINARY mode data connection for xview-3.2p1.4.bin.tar.gz .
226 Transfer complete.
2192197 bytes received in 728 secs (2.9 Kbytes/sec)
ftp>
```

Or, you could use Netscape or another Web browser to access, browse through, and download software without having to bother with all the FTP commands. Be sure to precede an FTP site name with the term **ftp://** instead of the usual **http://**. For Sunsite, you would enter **ftp://sunsite.unc.edu**. Once you have selected the software you want, hold down the SHIFT key and click the software to download it.

Once downloaded, any file that ends with a **.Z** , **bz**, **.zip**, or **.gz** is a compressed file that must be decompressed. Use the **gunzip** command, followed by the name of the file, as follows:

```
# gunzip xview-3.2p1.4.bin.tar.gz
```

If the file then ends with **.tar**, it is an archived file that must be unpacked using the **tar** command. Before you unpack the archive, move it to the directory where you want it. Source code you intend to compile is usually placed in the **/usr/src** directory. Most archives unpack to a subdirectory they create, placing all those files or directories making up the software package into that subdirectory. For example, the file **xview-3.2p1.4.bin.tar** unpacks to a subdirectory called **usr**. To check if an archive unpacks to a directory, use **tar** with the **t** option to list its contents and to see if the names are prefixed by a directory. If so, that directory is created and the extracted files are placed in it. If no directory name exists, create one, and then copy the archive file to it. Then extract the archive within that directory.

```
# tar tf xview-3.2p1.4.bin.tar
```

Now you are ready to extract the files from the **tar** archive. You use **tar** with the **x** option to extract files, the **v** option to display the pathnames of files as they are extracted, and the **f** option, followed by the name of the archive file:

```
# tar xvf xview-3.2p1.4.bin.tar
```

Installation of your software may differ for each package. Instructions are usually provided, along with an installation program. Downloaded software usually includes **README** files or other documentation. Be sure to consult them.

Compiling Software

Some software may be in the form of source code that you need to compile before you can install it. This is particularly true of programs designed for cross-platform implementations. Programs designed to run on various UNIX systems, such as Sun, as well as on Linux, may be distributed as source code that is downloaded and compiled in those different systems. Compiling such software has been greatly simplified in recent years by the use of configuration scripts that automatically detect a given system's configuration and compile the program accordingly. For example, the name of the C compiler on a system could be gcc or cc. Configurations scripts detect which is present and use it to compile the program.

Before you compile software, first read the **README** or **INSTALL** files included with it. These give you detailed instructions on how to compile and install this particular program. If the software used configuration scripts, then compiling and installing usually involves only the following three simple commands:

```
# ./configure
# make
# make install
```

The **./configure** command performs configuration detection. The **make** command performs the actual compiling, using a **Makefile** script generated by the **./configure** operation. The **make install** command installs the program on your system, placing the executable program in a directory, such as **/usr/local/bin,** and any configuration files in **/etc**. Any shared libraries it created may go into **/usr/lib**.

If you are compiling an X-, Gnome-, or KDE-based program, be sure their development libraries have been installed. For X applications, be sure the **xmkmf** program is also installed . If you chose a standard install when you installed your distribution system, these most likely were not installed. For distributions using RPM packages, these come in the form of a set of development RPM packages, usually having the word "development" or "develop" in their name. You need to install them using either RPM, Kpackage, or gnomeRPM. Gnome, in particular, has an extensive set of RPM packages for development libraries. Many X applications may need special shared libraries. For example, some applications may need the xforms library or the qt library. Some of these you need to obtain from online sites.

Some older X applications use xmkmf directly instead of a configure script to generate the needed **Makefile**. In this case, enter the command **xmkmf** in place of **./configure**. Be sure to consult the **INSTALL** and **README** files for the software.

Usually, you only need to issue the following commands within the directory that contains the source code files for the software:

```
xmkmf
make
make install
```

If no configure script exists and the program does not use **xmkmf,** you may have to enter the **make** command, followed by a **make install** operation. Check the **README** or **INSTALL** files for details.

```
make
make install
```

Be sure to check the documentation for such software to see if any changes must be made to the **Makefile**. Only a few changes may be necessary, but more detailed changes require an understanding of C programming and how **make** works with it. If you successfully configure the **Makefile**, you may only have to enter the **make** and **make install** operations. One possible problem is locating the development libraries for C and X Windows. X Windows libraries are in the **/usr/X11R6/lib** directory. Standard C libraries are located in the **/usr/lib** directory. You can set the PATH variable to hold the pathnames for any special libraries as described in the next section.

Command and Program Directories: PATH

Programs and commands are usually installed in several standard system directories, such as **/bin, /usr/bin, /usr/X11R6/bin**, or **/usr/local/bin**. Some packages place their commands in subdirectories, however, which they create within one of these standard directories or in an entirely separate directory. In such cases, you may be unable to run those commands because your system may be unable to locate them in the new subdirectory. Your system maintains a set of directories that searches for commands each time you execute one. This set of directories is kept in a system variable called PATH that is created when you start your system. If a command is in a directory that is not in this list, then your system will be unable to locate and run it. To use such commands, you first need to add the new directory to the set of directories in the PATH variable.

On Red Hat systems, the PATH variable is assigned its set of directories in the **/etc/profile** file, which is a script run when your system starts and is used to configure users' working environments. In this file, you can find a line that begins with PATH, followed by an **=** sign, and then a list of directories, each separated by a colon. These are the directories that contain commands and programs.

To add a directory, carefully edit the **/etc/profile** file using a text editor, such as kedit, gedit, Emacs, or Vi (you may want to make a backup copy first with the **cp** command). At the end of the list of directories, add the new directory with its full pathname before the closing double quote. Be sure a colon separates the new directory from the last one. You should also have a colon at the end. For example, if you install the MH mail utility, the MH commands are installed in a subdirectory called **mh** in the **/usr/bin** directory. The full pathname for this directory is **/usr/bin/mh**. You need to add this directory to the list of directories assigned to PATH in the **/etc/profile** script. (The command **rpm -qpl** *package-name* lists all the directories where commands in an RPM software package are installed.) The following example shows the PATH variable with its list of directories and the **/usr/bin/mh** directory added (shown in boldface):

```
PATH="/bin:/usr/bin:/opt/bin:/usr/X11R6/bin:/usr/openwin/bin:/usr/
local/bin:/usr/bin/mh"
```

The **/etc/profile** script is a system script executed for each user when the user logs in. Individual users can customize their PATH variables by placing a PATH assignment in either their **.bashrc** or **.profile** files. In this way, users can access commands and programs they create or install for their own use in their own user directories (see Chapter 15 for more details). The following entry in the **.profile** file adds a user's **mybin** directory to the PATH variable. Use of $PATH keeps all the directories already listed in the **/etc/profile** script. Notice both the colon placed before the new directory and the use of the $HOME variable to specify the pathname for the user's home directory.

```
PATH=$PATH:$HOME/mybin
```

Packaging Your Software: Autoconf and RPM

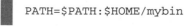

Once you finish developing your software, you may then want to distribute it to others. Ordinarily, you would pack your program into a **tar** archive file. People would then download the file and unpack it. You would have to include detailed instructions on how to install it and where to place any supporting documentation and libraries. If you were distributing the source code, users would have to determine how to adapt the source code to their systems. Any number of variations might stop compilation of a program.

The RPM and Autoconf programs are designed to automate these tasks. The Autoconf program is used to configure the source code for an application automatically to a given system. RPM automatically installs software on a system in the designated directories, along with any documentation, libraries, or support programs. Both have complex and powerful capabilities, and can handle the most complex programs. Simple examples of their use are provided here.

Autoconf

A UNIX system can compile any software written in the C programming language. Different UNIX systems have different configurations, however, some using different compilers or placing programs and libraries in different system directories. Different types of support libraries may be present. In the past, to compile software on different systems, the software had to be configured manually for each system. For example, if your system has the gcc compiler instead of the cc compiler, you would have to set that feature in the software's **Makefile**.

The Autoconf program is designed to automate the configuration process. It automatically detects the configuration of the current UNIX system and generates an appropriate **Makefile** that can then be used to compile that software on this particular system. Much of the current software on the Internet in source form uses Autoconf. A detailed manual on Autoconf can be found in the **/usr/info** directory and is called **autoconf.info.** You can use the **info** command to view it. (You can also view the text with any text editor.) The general operations are described here.

Software that uses Autoconf performs the configuration without any need of the actual Autoconf software. Special shell scripts included with the software detect the different system features the software needs. The **./configure** command usually automatically configures the software for your system. As the configuration is performed, it checks for different features one by one, displaying the result of each check. The operation is entirely automatic and doesn't even require the identity of the system on which it is working.

To create a configuration script for your own software, you use special Autoconf commands. The Autoconf applications package is available on your Red Hat CD-ROM. Generating the configurations involves several stages, using several intermediate configuration files. Autoconf has many options designed to handle the requirements of a complex program. For a simple program, you may only need to follow the basic steps.

The goal is to create a **configure** script. Two phases are in this process, using the **autoscan** and **autoconf** commands. The first phase creates a **configure.scan** file, using the **autoscan** command. The **autoscan** command is applied directly to your source code files. Next, check the **configure.scan** file for any errors with an editor, make any changes or additions you want, and then rename it as the **configure.in** file. This file is used as input for the **autoconf** command, which then generates the **configure** script. The **autoscan** step is an aid in the creation of the **configure.in** file, but **autoscan** and the **configure.scan** file it generates are optional. You can create your own **configure.in** file, entering various Autoconf macros. These are described in detail in the Autoconf info file.

In addition, you need to create a version of the **Makefile** for your program named **makefile.in**. This is essentially your original **Makefile**, with reference to special Autoconf variables. When the software is compiled on another system, the **configure.in** detects the system's features, and then uses this information with the **makefile.in** file to generate a **Makefile** for that particular system. This new **Makefile** is then used to compile the program.

Autoconf is designed to create values for different features, which can then be used with **makefile.in** to create a new **Makefile** containing those features. The feature values are placed in special shell variables called *output* variables. You should place references to these shell variables in the **makefile.in** file wherever you want to use these values. For example, the **CC** variable holds the name of the C compiler on your system (cc or gcc). The **AC_PROG_CC** macro in the **configure** script detects the C compiler in use and places its name in the **CC** variable. A reference to this variable should be placed in the **makefile.in** file wherever you invoke the C compiler. The variable name is bounded by two @ symbols. For example, @CC@ in **makefile.in** references the **CC** variable and its value is substituted in that place.

Once you have the **configure** file, you no longer need the **configure.in** file. You only need **configure**, **makefile.in**, and the source code files, along with any header files. The **configure** file is a shell script designed to execute on its own.

Once another user has received the software package and unpacked all the source code files, you only need to take three steps: configuration, compilation, and installation. The **./configure** command generates a customized **Makefile** for the user's system, the **make** command compiles the program using that **Makefile**, and the **make install** command installs the program on the user's system.

```
./configure
make
make install
```

Creating RPM Packages

The package creation process is designed to take the program through several stages, starting with unpacking it from an archive, compiling its source code, and, finally, generating the RPM package. You can skip any of these stages, up to the last one. If your software is already unpacked, you can start with compiling it. If your software is compiled, you can start with installation. If it is already installed, you can go directly to creating the RPM package.

RPM makes use of three components to build packages: the build tree, the **rpmrc** configuration files, and an **rpm** spec script. The build tree is a set of special instructions used to carry out the different stages of the packaging process. The **rpm** spec script contains instructions for creating the package, as well as the list of files to be placed in it. The **rpmrc** files are used to set configuration features for RPM. The **/usr/lib/rpm/rpmrc** file holds the default options for your system and is always read. You can also set up a **/etc/rpmrc** file for global options you want to set for your system. Entries here will override those in the **/usr/lib/rpm/rpmrc** file. You can also set up a local **.rpmrc** file in your home directory, which will override both of these. To obtain a listing of the **/usr/lib/rpm/rpmrc** file, enter

```
$ rpm --showrc
```

The build tree directories, listed in the following table, are used to hold the different files generated at each stage of the packaging process. The **SOURCES** directory holds the compressed archive. The **BUILD** directory holds the source code unpacked from that archive. The **RPMS** directory is where the RPM package containing the executable binary program is placed, and **SRPMS** is where the RPM package containing the source code is placed. If you are creating a package from software stored in a compressed archive, such as a **tar.gz** file, you first must copy that file to the build tree's **SOURCES** directory.

Directory Name	Description
BUILD	The directory where RPM does all its building
SOURCES	The directory where you should put your original source archive files and your patches
SPECS	The directory where all spec files should go
RPMS	The directory where RPM puts all binary RPMs when built
SRPMS	The directory where all source RPMs are put

The following example copies the compressed archive for the bookrec software to the **SOURCES** directory:

```
# cp bookrec-1.0.tar.gz   /usr/src/redhat/SOURCES
```

The **topdir:** entry in an **rpmrc** file, like **/usr/lib/rpm/rpmrc**, specifies the location of the build tree directories. In this file, you can find an entry for **topdir:**. Currently, the Red Hat system has already set this directory to **/usr/src/redhat**. You can find the **SOURCES**, **BUILD**, **RPMS**, and **SRPMS** directories here. You can specify a different directory for these subdirectories by placing the entry for **topdir:** in the **/etc/rpmrc** file.

```
topdir: /usr/src/redhat
```

A sample of the default values set by **/usr/lib/rpm/rpmrc** is shown here:

```
# Default values, often overridden in /etc/rpmrc
dbpath:       /var/lib/rpm
topdir:       /usr/src/redhat
tmppath:      /var/tmp
cpiobin:      cpio
defaultdocdir:   /usr/doc
```

By default, RPM is designed to work with source code placed in a directory consisting of its name and a release number, separated by a hyphen. For example, a program with the name *bookrec* and *release 1.0* should have its source-code files in a directory called **bookrec-1.0**. If RPM needs to compile the software, it expects to find the source code in that directory within the **BUILD** directory, **BUILD/bookrec-1.0**. The same name and release number also must be specified in the **spec** file.

RPM Spec File

To create a package, first create an **rpm spec** file for it. The **rpm spec** file specifies the files to be included, any actions to build the software, and information about the package. The **spec** file is designed to take the program through several stages, starting with unpacking it from an archive, compiling its source code, and generating the RPM package. In the **spec** file are segments for the different stages and special RPM macros that perform actions at these stages. These are listed here:

File Segment or Macro	Description
%description	A detailed description of the software.
%prep	The prep stage for archives and patches.
%setup	The prep macro for unpacking archives. A **-n** *name* option resets the name of the build directory.
%patch	The prep macro for updating patches.
%build	The build stage for compiling software.
%install	The install stage for installing software.
%files	The files stage that lists the files to be included in the package. A **-f** *filename* option specifies a file that contains a list of files to be included in the package.
%config *file-list*	A file macro that lists configuration files to be placed in the **/etc** directory.

File Segment or Macro	Description
%doc *file-list*	A file macro that lists documentation files to be placed in the **/usr/doc** directory with the subdirectory of the name-version-release.
%dir *directory-list*	The specification of a directory to be included as being owned by a package. (A directory in a file list refers to all files in it, not only the directory).
%pre	A macro to do preinstall scripts.
%preun	A macro to do preuninstall scripts.
%post	A macro to do postinstall scripts.
%postun	A macro to do postuninstall scripts.

A **spec** file is divided into five basic segments: header, prep, build, install, and files. These segments are separated in the file by empty lines. The header segment contains several lines of information, each preceded by a tag and a semicolon. For example, the following tag is used for a short description of the software:

```
Summary: bookrec program to manage book records
```

The name, version, and release tags are used to build the name of the RPM package. The name, version, and release are separated with hyphens. For example, the name *bookrec* with the *version 1.0* and *release 2* has the following name:

```
bookrec-1.0-2
```

The Group entry is a list of categories for the software and is used by the RPM package management utilities like GnomeRPM and Linuxconf to place the software in the correct category folder. The Source entry is the compressed archive where the software is stored on your system. Description is a detailed description of the software.

Following the header are the three stages for creating and installing the software on your system, indicated by the **%prep**, **%build**, and **%install rpm** macros. You can skip any of these stages, say, if the software is already installed. You can also leave any of them out of the **spec** file or comment them out with a preceding **#**. The **spec** file is capable of taking a compressed archive, unpacking it, compiling the source code files, and then installing the program on your system. Then the installed files can be used to create the RPM package.

The **%prep** macro begins the prep segment of the **spec** file. The prep segment's task is to generate the software's source code. This usually means unpacking archives, but it may also have to update the software with patches. The tasks themselves can be performed by shell scripts you write. Special macros can also automatically perform these tasks. The **%setup** macro can decompress and unpack an archive in the **SOURCES** directory, placing the source code files in the **BUILD** directory. The **%patch** macro applies any patches.

The **%build** segment contains the instructions for compiling the software. Usually, this is a simple **make** command, depending on the complexity of your program. The **%install** segment contains the instructions for installing the program. You can use simple shell commands to copy the files or, as in the **bookspec** example that follows, the **install** command that installs files on systems. This could also be the **make install** command, if your **Makefile** has the commands to install your program.

```
%build
make RPM_OPT_FLAGS="$RPM_OPT_FLAGS"

%install
install -s -m 755 -o 0 -g 0 bookrec /usr/bin/bookrec
install -m 644 -o 0 -g 0 bookrec.1 /usr/man/man1
```

The **%files** segment contains the list of files you want placed in the RPM package. Following the **%files** macro, you list the different files, including their full pathnames. The macro **%config** can be used to list configuration files. Any files listed here are placed in the **/etc** directory. The **%doc** macro is used for documentation, such as **README** files. These are placed in the **/usr/doc** directory under a subdirectory consisting of the software's name, version, and release number. In the **bookspec** example shown here, the **README**file is placed in the **/usr/doc/bookrec-1.0-2** directory:

bookspec

```
Summary: bookrec program to manage book records
Name: bookrec
Version: 1.0
Release: 2
Copyright: GPL
Group: Applications/Database
Source: /root/rpmc/bookrec-1.0.tar.gz
%description
This program manages book records by title, providing
price information

%prep
%setup

%build
make RPM_OPT_FLAGS="$RPM_OPT_FLAGS"

%install
```

```
install -s -m 755 -o 0 -g 0 bookrec /usr/bin/bookrec
install -m 644 -o 0 -g 0 bookrec.1 /usr/man/man1

%files
%doc README

/usr/bin/bookrec
/usr/man/man1/bookrec.1
```

RPM Build Operation

To create an RPM software package, you use the **rpm build** options (listed in Table 19-3) with the **rpm** command, followed by the name of a **spec** file. The **-bl** option checks to see if all the files used for the software are present. The **-bb** option builds only the binary package, whereas **-ba** builds both binary and source packages. They expect to find the compressed archive for the software in the build tree's **SOURCES** directory. The **-ba** and **-bb** options execute every stage specified in the **rpm spec** script, starting from the prep stage, to unpacking an archive, compiling the program, followed by installation on the system, and then creation of the package. The completed RPM package for executable binaries is placed in a subdirectory of the build tree's **RPMS** directory. This subdirectory has a name representing the current platform. For a PC, this is **i386**, and the package is placed in the **RPMS/i386** subdirectory. The source-code package is placed directly in the **SRPMS** directory.

The following program generates both a binary and a software package, placing them in the build tree's **RPMS/i386** and **SRPMS** directories. The name of the spec file in this example is **bookspec**.

```
rpm -ba bookspec
```

An executable binary package has a name consisting of the software name, the version number, the release number, the platform name (i386), and the term **rpm**. The name, version, and release are separated by hyphens, whereas the release, platform name, and the **rpm** term are separated by periods. The name of the binary package generated by the previous example, using the **bookspec** spec script, generates the following name:

```
bookrec-1.0-2.i386.rpm
```

The source code package has the same name, but with the term **src** in place of the platform name:

```
bookrec-1.0-2.src.rpm
```

Option	Description
-ba	Create both the executable binary and source code packages. Perform all stages in the spec file: prep, build, install, and create the packages.
-bb	Create only the executable binary package. Perform all stages in the spec file: prep, build, install, and create the package.
-bp	Run only the prep stage from the spec file (**%prep**).
-bl	Do a "list check." The **%files** section from the spec file is macro-expanded, and checks are made to ensure the files exist.
-bc	Do both the prep and build stages, unpacking and compiling the software (**%prep** and **%build**).
-bi	Do the prep, build, and install stages, unpacking, compiling, and installing the software (**%prep**, **%build**, and **%install**).
--short-circuit	Skip to specified stage, not executing any previous stages. Only valid with **-bc** and **-bi**.
--clean	Remove the build tree after the packages are made.
--test	Do not execute any build stages. Used to test spec files.
--recompile *source_package_file*	RPM installs the source code package and performs a prep, compile, and install.
--rebuild *source_package_file*	RPM first installs the named source package and does a prep, compile, and install, and then rebuilds a new binary package.
--showrc	List the configuration variables for the **/usr/lib/rpm/rpmrc** file.

Table 19-3.   *The RPM Build Options*

The Complete Reference

Linux

Chapter 20

Office Applications

A variety of office suites are now available for Linux. These include professional-level word processors, presentation managers, drawing tools, and spreadsheets. The freely available versions are described in this chapter. Currently, you can download personal (noncommercial) versions for both WordPerfect and StarOffice from the Internet for free. KOffice is an entirely free office suite included with KDE 2.0. The Gnome Office is integrating Gnome applications into a productivity suite that will be freely available. Helix Code is developing a professional-level office suite for Gnome. You can also purchase commercial office suites, such as Applixware from Red Hat and Corel Office from Corel. *Applixware* includes a word processor, a spreadsheet, a presentation graphics tool, a drawing tool, an e-mail client, and an object-oriented application builder. Table 20-1 list freely available Linux Office projects.

Accessibility to Microsoft Office

One of the primary concerns for new Linux users is what kind of access they would have to their Microsoft Office files, particularly Word files. The Linux operating system and many applications for it are designed to provide seamless access to MS Office files. The Intel version of Linux can directly mount and access any Windows partition and its files. The major Linux Office suites, including WordPerfect, KOffice, and particularly Star Office, all read and manage any Microsoft Office files. In addition, these office suites are fast approaching the same level of support for office tasks as found in Microsoft Office.

Note   *If you want to use any Windows application on Linux, one important alternative is the VMware virtual platform technology, a commercial package. With Vmware, you can run any Windows application directly on your Linux system. For more information, check the VMware Web site at **www.vmware.com**.*

Web Site	Description
koffice.kde.org	KOffice Suite, for KDE
www.gnome.org/gnome-office	Gnome Office, for Gnome
www.sun.com/products/staroffice	Star Office Suite
www.helixcode.com	Helix Code Gnome desktop and office Applications
linux.corel.com	WordPerfect word processor

Table 20-1.   *Linux Office Projects*

KOffice

KOffice is an integrated office suite for the *KDE* (*K Desktop Environment*) consisting of several office applications, including a word processor, a spreadsheet, and graphic applications. All applications are written for the KOM component model, which allows components from any one application to be used in another. This means you can embed a spreadsheet from KSpread or a drawing from KIllustrator in a KWord document. You can obtain more information about KOffice from the KOffice Web site at **koffice.kde.org**. The first release of KOffice is scheduled as part of KDE version 2.0.

Currently, KOffice includes KSpread, KPresenter, KChart, KImage, KIllustrator, KFormula, KWord, Katabase, KImageShop, and KoHTML (see Table 20-2). KSpread is a spreadsheet, KPresenter is a presentation application, KIllustrator is a vector drawing program, KWord is a Publisher-like word processor, KChart creates charts and diagrams, KFormula is a formula editor, and KImage is a simple image viewer.

Embedded components support real-time updates. For example, if you use KChart to generate a chart in a KWord document using data in a KSpread spreadsheet and then change the selected data in the spreadsheet, the KChart automatically updates the chart in the KWord document. In effect, you are creating a compound document—one made up of several applications. This capability is implemented by the KDE object model known as *K Object Model/OpenParts* (*KOM/OP*). KOM/OP is based on CORBA 2.2, the industry standard for communication between distributed objects. KOM/OP is not dependent on the K Desktop and can be used by any application designed for it on any interface, including Gnome. A Gnome application can be written to use KOM/OP and operate entirely on the Gnome GUI. This feature makes KOffice a possible candidate for a Linux and UNIX standard.

Application	Description
KSpread	Spreadsheet
KPresenter	Presentation program
KIllustrator	Vector drawing program
KWord	Word processor (desktop publisher)
KFormula	Mathematical formula editor
KChart	Tool for drawing charts and diagrams
KImage	A simple image viewer
Katabase	A database not unlike Paradox and Access
KImageShop	An image manipulation program

Table 20-2. *KOffice Applications*

With *KOffice*, you create one kind of document rather than separate ones for different applications. The different applications become views of this document, adding their components to it. KWord sets up the publishing and word processing components, KIllustrator adds drawing components, while KSpread adds spreadsheet components. You use the appropriate application to view the different components in the single document. This means you can have separate windows open at the same time for different components of the document.

KSpread is the spreadsheet application, which incorporates the basic operations found in most spreadsheets, with formulas similar to those used in Excel (see Figure 20-1). You can extend KSpread capabilities with Python scripts. It supports features such as embedded buttons for customized functions; automatic completion for cell contents; and formatting options such as backgrounds, borders, and font styles. To generate a diagram using selected cells, select the Insert Diagram entry from the KSpread menu. This starts up KChart, which you then use to create the diagram—which is then embedded in the spreadsheet. You can also embed pictures or formulas using KImage, KIllustrator, or KFormula.

With *KChart*, you can create different kinds of charts, such as bar graphs, pie charts, and line graphs, as well as create diagrams (see Figure 20-2). To generate a chart, you can use data in KSpread to enter your data.

Figure 20-1.   *KSpread, KOffice spreadsheet*

Figure 20-2. *KChart, KOffice graphs*

With *KPresenter*, you can create presentations consisting of text and graphics modeled using different fonts, orientations, and attributes such as colors (see Figure 20-3). You can add such elements as speech bubbles, arrows, and clip art, as well as embed any KOffice component. KPresenter supports standard editing operations such as shading, rotating, and coloring objects, as well as cut-and-paste and undo/redo capabilities. You can generate templates from a KPresenter document, in effect enabling you to use a document's configuration to create other documents. With KPresenter, you can also create special effects such as simple animation.

KIllustrator is a vector-based graphics program, much like Adobe Illustrator and CorelDRAW (see Figure 20-4). It supports the standard graphic operations such as rotating, scaling, and aligning objects. KIllustrator also includes text formatting capabilities such as alignment to irregular boundaries. You can create complex illustrations using layers, using a layer manager to control the layers. KIllustrator also supports a number of import and export filters for image files of different types like **.jpeg**, **.gif**, and **.eps**.

KWord can best be described as a desktop publisher, with many of the features found in publishing applications like Microsoft Publisher and FrameMaker (see Figure 20-5). Although it is also a fully functional word processor, KWord is not page based like Word or WordPerfect. Instead, text is set up in frames that are placed on the page like objects. Frames, like objects in a drawing program, can be moved, resized, and even reoriented. You can organize frames into a frame set, having text flow from one to the other. Formatting can be applied to a frame set, changing features in all the frames belonging to it at once. The default frame set up for you when you first create

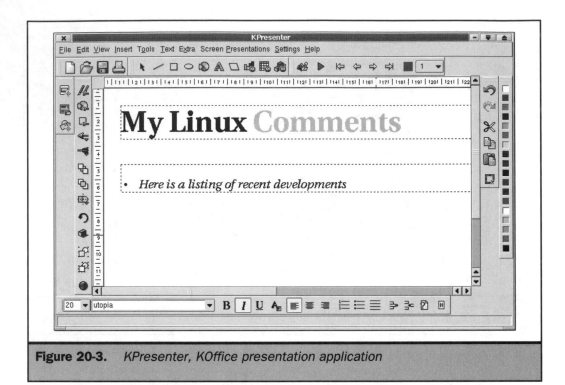

Figure 20-3. KPresenter, KOffice presentation application

Figure 20-4. KIllustrator, KOffice illustration application

a document is the same size as the page. This gives you the effect of a page-based word processor, enabling you to work as if you were using a standard word processor. You can, of course, change the size of your frame and add new ones, if you want.

You can also insert images, illustrations, tables, and other KOffice components such as diagrams and spreadsheets. You can set up a frame to contain an image and place it on top of a text frame, configuring the text frame to flow its text around it.

KWord uses templates to set up a document. You have two different sets of templates from which to choose: one for *desktop publishing* (*DTP*) and the other for standard word processing (*Wordprocessing*). The desktop publishing templates enables you to move frames freely; whereas in the word processing templates, the frames are fixed to the size of the page.

KWord supports the standard word processing features for formatting paragraphs, text, and document elements such as headers and footers, as well as lists and multiple columns. You can also define your own paragraph layouts, specifying features such as indentation, fonts, borders, and alignment. Layouts are the same as styles used in other word processors. Tables are implemented as frames, where each cell is its own frame.

KFormula is a formula editor used to generate mathematical formulas. Although KFormula does not have the power of TeX, you can use it to create fairly complex formulas. It supports standard components like roots, integrals, and fractions, as well as fonts for Greek symbols.

Figure 20-5.   *KWord, KOffice word processor and publisher*

APPLICATIONS

Currently, *KImage* is used only to display images. Later, it will be enhanced with image editing capabilities. For now, you can use it to display images embedded in different KOffice applications. *KImageShop* is an image editor, much like PhotoShop, that is currently under development. *Katabase* is a database application designed to work with KOffice applications (still under development).

WordPerfect

The personal version of Corel's WordPerfect word processor is now available for Linux and is free (it is included with OpenLinux). The personal version is a fully functional word processor. However, it does not currently support TrueType fonts, and it does not allow you to import other objects, such as images. You can download WordPerfect from the Corel Web site at **linux.corel.com**. WordPerfect is more than just a word processor. You can use it to create drawings, spreadsheets, and charts, as well as to edit and publish Web pages.

When you first start WordPerfect, a small window is displayed with the WordPerfect logo and four menus: Program, Preferences, Window, and Help. From the Program menu, you can select WordPerfect. In the Preferences menu, you can open a window with icons for configuring your printer, selecting fonts, choosing colors, and selecting conversion filters. The Window menu moves you to different open windows.

WordPerfect provides many of the standard word processing features, including cut-and-paste operations, font and paragraph styles, and document formatting. The extensive features for WordPerfect are indicated by its set of toolbars. WordPerfect includes such editing features as Grammar-As-You-Go, which checks and highlights suspicious phrases and offers suggestions. With Spell-As-You-Go, words are identified that might be misspelled as you type them. Corel Versions keeps track of document revisions for workgroup collaboration.

WordPerfect includes a chart and drawing tool for creating figures. You can perform drawing operations such as sizing and rotating images, as well as contouring text over image shapes. The drawing tool supports features such as gradients, patterns, and groupings. You can crate a variety of different charts, including 3-D, area, and line charts. WordPerfect supports a number of spreadsheet functions with which you can create tables with spreadsheet cells. You can use such data to generate charts.

You can also use WordPerfect as a Web page editor and publisher, adding or changing HTML components. Use WordPerfect to create your HTML document with hyperlinks and bookmarks, and then place them on your Web site. Any text beginning with an Internet protocol, such as **www**, **ftp**, and **http**, is automatically set up as a hyperlink. You can also save Web pages as WordPerfect documents for easy editing.

 WordPerfect supports an extensive number of file formats, including Microsoft Word 97 files. With WordPerfect, you can effectively edit your Word files.

WordPerfect also has its own file manager. You can use the file manager to locate and open files, but it also performs other operations. You can create directories and modify file permissions, as well as move and copy files.

Gnome Office and Helix Code

Office applications for Gnome have been developed independently, such as the Gnumeric spreadsheet. Currently, Gnome Office is an attempt to integrate the various office applications into a productivity suite. Although most are still under development, some have working stable versions you can download and install. You can find out more from the Gnome Office at **www.gnome.org/gnome-office**. Here, you can link to download pages for current versions and view screen shots. A current listing is shown in Table 20-3. All implement the CORBA model for embedding components, ensuring drag-and-drop capability throughout the Gnome interface. All are based on a set of Gnome technologies, including Bonobo, Gnome-Print, and XML. Bonobo is the Gnome architecture for supporting compound documents and reusable software components. Gnome-Print is the Gnome printing architecture designed to support graphics applications, as well as work easily with any printing resource. XML is used as the native file format to support the easy exchange of data between Gnome applications.

Currently, Gnome Office includes AbiWord, Gnumeric, GIMP, Dia, Eye of Gnome, Gnome-PIM, and Gnome-DB. AbiWord is a word processor, Gnumeric is a spreadsheet, the GIMP is the Gnome image editing application, Dia is a diagram composer, Eye of Gnome is an image viewer, the Gnome Personal Information Manager (Gnome-PIM) is a personal information manager, and Gnome-DB provides database connectivity (see Table 20-3).

Application	Description
AbiWord	Cross-platform word processor
Gnumeric	Spreadsheet
Dia	Diagram and flow chart editor
Eye of Gnome	Image viewer
GIMP	GNU image manipulation program
Gnome-DB	Database interface
Gnome Personal Information Manager	Calendar/organizer and an address book

Table 20-3. *Gnome Office*

The *Gnumeric* is the Gnome spreadsheet, a professional-level program meant to replace commercial spreadsheets (see Figure 20-6). Like Gnome, Gnumeric is freely available under the GNU public license. Gnumeric is included with the Gnome release, and you will find it installed with Gnome on the Red Hat and SuSE distributions. Its development is currently managed by Helix Code. You can download current versions from **www.helixcode.com** or **www.gnome.org/projects/gnumeric**. Gnumeric supports standard GUI spreadsheet features, including autofilling and cell formatting, and it provides an extensive number of formats. It supports drag-and-drop operations, enabling you to select and then move or copy cells to another location. Gnumeric also supports plug-ins, making it possible to extend and customize its capabilities easily.

AbiWord is an open-source word processor that supports such features as unlimited undo operations and Word97 imports. It is part of a set of desktop productivity applications being developed by the AbiSource project (**www.abisource.com**).

The GIMP is the GNU image manipulation program that supports operations such as photo retouching, image composition, and image authoring (see the section on Graphics). You can obtain more information from **www.gimp.org**.

Dia is a drawing program designed to create diagrams (see Figure 20-7). You can select different kinds of diagrams to create, such as database, circuit object, flow chart, and network diagrams. You can easily create elements, along with lines and arcs with different types of endpoints, such as arrows or diamonds. Data can be saved in XML format, making it easily transportable to other applications.

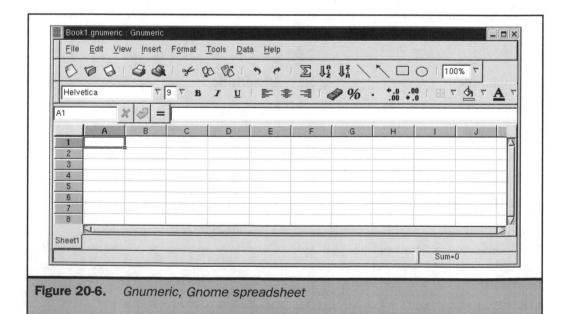

Figure 20-6.   *Gnumeric, Gnome spreadsheet*

Figure 20-7.   *Dia, Gnome diagrams*

APPLICATIONS

The Eye of Gnome (EOG) is an image viewer that can also function as an image cataloging program. It is designed to be both fast and provide high-quality image displays.

Gnome Personal Information Manager (Gnome-PIM) is a personal information manager that currently includes both a calendar (see Figure 20-8) and an address book. Gnome-PIM is included with the current distribution of Gnome. You can obtain updates from **www.gnome.org/gnome-office**.

Gnome-DB is a suite of libraries and applications that allow an easy access to different database systems. It provides an API that databases can plug into. These backend connections are based on CORBA. Through this API, Gnome applications can then access a database. You can find out more about Gnome-DB at **www.gnome.org/gnome-db**.

Helix Code is a Gnome project designed to provide a professional-level desktop for Gnome that will include a full range of office applications. You can find out more about Helix Code at **www.helixcode.com**. Helix Code currently provides an enhanced version of the Gnome desktop called Helix Gnome. It also supports development of

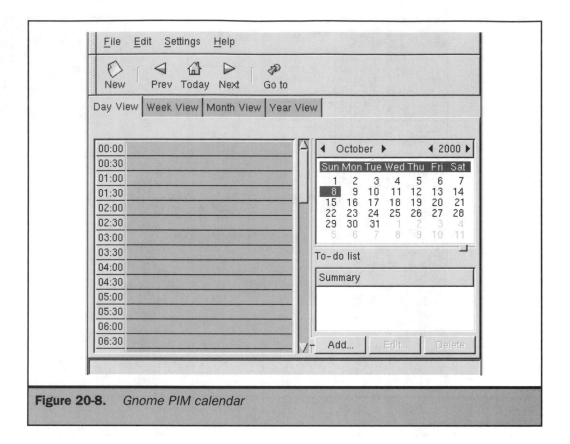

Figure 20-8. *Gnome PIM calendar*

the Gnumeric spreadsheet. Its first office application is a contact, calendar, and mail client application called Evolution. You can download Evolution from the Helix Code Web site, but it requires the Helix Code Gnome desktop to run. Their next project is a word processor.

StarOffice

StarOffice is a fully integrated and Microsoft Office–compatible suite of office applications, developed and supported by Sun Microsystems. It includes Web-enabled word processing, spreadsheet, presentation, e-mail, news, chart, and graphic applications. Versions of StarOffice exist for Linux, Windows, Mac, Solaris, and OS/2. With StarOffice, you can access Microsoft Office (including 2000) files and data to create spreadsheets, presentations, and word processing documents. You can save StarOffice documents in Microsoft formats or as HTML files that you can post on Web sites.

StarOffice is free for all noncommercial, private users, as well as students. You can download a free copy of StarOffice from the Sun Web site at **www.sun.com/ products/staroffice**. The package is about 65 megabytes. The Web site also contains information such as online manuals and FAQs.

StarOffice describes itself as implementing a task-oriented approach to office projects. You can complete an entire project using a variety of different tools in just one place, StarOffice. In addition, StarOffice applications are fully Internet aware, enabling you to connect directly to Web sites and access information from your word processor, spreadsheet, or presenter.

When you start up StarOffice, you are presented with the StarOffice desktop window. From here, you can create documents and access other StarOffice applications. The left pane in this window is the Explorer. This is a tree menu that lists the different resources you can use, such as an address book, a gallery of clip art, and FTP server URLs. The main window of the StarOffice desktop shows icons for applications you can use, your StarOffice documents, and other tools.

To use StarOffice, you create projects. In a particular project, you can place resources such as images, Internet links, e-mail messages, or office documents such as spreadsheets and word processing documents. To create a new document, click the New button in the bottom status bar and select the application you want to use from the pop-up menu. You can create spreadsheets, word processing documents, presentation files, mail messages, charts, images, mathematical formulas, and even Web pages (see Table 20-4). You can also create frame sets for use in Web page frames. Initially, windows are attached (docked) to the desktop window. You can unattach them to their own floating windows by double-clicking the gray area between them.

StarOffice has its own mail and news clients. With StarMail, you can define mail accounts and access your e-mail, as well as compose and send messages. With StarDiscussion, you can access newsgroups, saving articles and posting your own. You can set up icons and entries for mail accounts and newsgroups on your desktop and Explorer window.

The StarWriter word processor supports standard word processing features, such as cut and paste, spell checker, and text formatting, as well as paragraph styles. You can also insert objects in your text, such as images, diagrams, or text frames. Text can be configured to flow around them. A text frame can be further edited to create banner-like text, coloring, blending, and shaping text. The Navigator enables you to move through the document by page or by object, such as from one image to another.

You can open and save documents in the MS Office, WordPerfect, Lotus 1-2-3, and AmiPro formats. This means you can effectively edit MS Word documents with StarOffice. StarWriter also functions as a Web browser—capable of displaying HTML pages—and supports Java, JavaScript, Navigator, and Explorer plug-ins. At the same time, you can edit a Web page, turning StarWriter into a Web page editor.

You can embed objects within documents, such as using StarChart to create a bar chart using data in the spreadsheet. With StarMath, you can create formulas that you can then embed in a text document.

With the presentation manager (StarImpress), you can create images for presentations, such as circles, rectangles, and connecting elements like arrows, as well as vector-based illustrations. StarImpress supports advanced features like morphing objects, grouping objects, and defining gradients. You can also create animation effects and use layers to generate complex images. Any components from other StarOffice applications can be embedded in a presentation document. You can also import Microsoft PowerPoint files and save presentation files as HTML files. An AutoPilot Wizard for StarImpress walks you through the steps for creating a presentation.

StarDraw is a sophisticated drawing tool that includes 3-D modeling tools. You can create simple or complex images, including animation text aligned on curves. You can use it to create buttons and icons for your Web page.

StarSchedule provides scheduling and task management that can be used to coordinate efforts by a group of users. You can use it to track events and to-do lists, connecting automatically to the address book. StarSchedule includes a reminder system to display pop-up alerts and to send e-mail reminders. The StarSchedule server operates independently from StarOffice to provide scheduling services to any client on your network. StarBase is a relational database, somewhat like MS Access, that supports drag-and-drop operations for importing data to your StarOffice applications.

Application	Description
StarDesktop	Main desktop window for StarOffice applications
StarWriter	Word processor
StarImpress	Presentation manager
StarDraw	Drawing tool
StarChart	Chart and graph creator
StarMail	E-mail client
StarDiscussion	Newsgroup client
StarMath	Mathematical formulas
StarImage	Image editor
StarCalc	Spreadsheet
StarSchedule	Schedule manager
StarBase	Relational database

Table 20-4. *StarOffice Applications*

Chapter 21

Database Management Systems, Graphic Tools, and Multimedia

501

A variety of database management systems are now available for Linux. These include high-powered, commercial-level database management systems, such as Oracle, IBM, and Sybase. Most of the database management systems available for Linux are designed to support large relational databases. For small personal databases, you can use the desktop database management systems being developed for KDE and Gnome such as Katabase (see Chapter 20). In addition, some software is available for databases accessed with the xBase database programming language. These are smaller databases using formats originally developed for dBase on the PC. Various database management systems available to run under Linux are listed in Table 21-1.

You can also use a wide range of graphic tools, ranging from simple image viewers like KImage to sophisticated image manipulation programs like the GIMP. You also have newer graphic tools for Gnome and KDE desktops, as well as older X Window System, from which to choose. Graphics tools available for use under Linux are listed in Table 21-2.

Database Management Systems

Database software can be generally organized into three categories: SQL, xBase, and desktop databases. *SQL-based databases* are professional-level relational databases, whose files are managed by a central database server program. Applications that use the database do not access the files directly. Instead, they send requests to the database server, which then performs the actual access. *SQL* is the query language used on these industrial-strength databases.

The *xBase language* is an enhanced version of the dBase programming language used to access database files whose formats were originally developed for dBase on the PC. With xBase, database management systems can directly access the database files. xBase is used mainly for smaller personal databases, with database files often located on a user's own system.

Desktop databases are being developed for both Gnome and KDE. Currently, these are personal databases, designed for individual users. Katabase is meant to be used with a user's KOffice applications, and Gaby, for a user's personal records. Both, however, are designed with a plug-in structure that can easily extend their capabilities.

SQL Databases (RDMS)

SQL databases are *relational database management systems* (*RDMSs*) designed for extensive database management tasks. Many of the major SQL databases now have Linux versions, including Oracle, Informix, Sybase, and IBM (but not, of course, Microsoft). These are commercial and professional database management systems of the highest order. Linux has proved itself capable of supporting complex and demanding database management tasks. In addition, many free SQL databases are available for Linux that offer much the same functionality. Most commercial databases also provide free personal versions, as do Oracle, Adabas D, and MySQL.

PostgreSQL

PostgreSQL is based on the POSTGRES database management system, though it uses SQL as its query language. POSTGRES is a next-generation research prototype developed at the University of California, Berkeley. Linux versions of PostgreSQL are included in Red Hat, Debian, and Slackware distributions. Updates can be obtained from their respective distribution update sites, such as **ftp.redhat.com/updates**. You can also download current versions from the PostgreSQL Web site at **www.postgresql.org**. Development is being managed by a team of developers over the Internet.

PostgresSQL is often used to provide database support for Internet servers such as Web servers. With a few simple commands you can create relational database tables. Use the createuser command to create an PostgresSQL user that you can then log into the server with. You can then create a database with the createdb command and construct relational tables using the create table directive. With an insert command you can add records and then view them with the select command. Access to the server by remote users is controlled by entries in the **pg_hba.conf** file located in the PostgresSQL directory, usually **/var/lib/pgsql**.

Oracle

Oracle offers a fully functional version of its Oracle8 database management system for Linux, as well as the Oracle Application Server. You can download trial versions effective for 30 days from the Oracle Web site at **www.oracle.com**. Oracle8 is a professional database designed for large databases. Expect to use a gigabyte of memory just to install it. The Oracle Application Server provides support for real-time and commerce applications on the Web. As Linux is a fully functional version of Unix, Oracle is particularly effective on it. Oracle was originally designed to operate on Unix, and Linux is a far better platform for it than other PC operating systems.

Oracle offers extensive documentation for its Linux version that you can download from its Documentation page, to which you can link from the Support pages on its Web site. The documentation available includes an installation guide, an administrator's reference, and release notes, as well as the generic documentation. You can find specific information on installing and configuring Oracle for Linux in the Oracle Database HOW-TO.

Informix

Informix offers an entire line of database products for Linux, including its Dynamic Server, Informix SE, Informix 4GL, and C-ISAM. Informix Dynamic Server features Dynamic Scalable Architecture, making it capable of effectively using any hardware setup. Informix SE (special edition) is a user-friendly and reliable database server that requires little database administration, while it provides fast and consistent access supporting SQL. Informix 4GL includes database tools, such as a debugger and compiler. C-ISAM is a library of C functions for indexed sequential access methods. Informix database systems provide flexible indexing, data consistency, integrity constraints, and security. Informix only provides commercial products. No free versions exist, though the company currently provides special promotions for Linux products. You can find out more about Informix at **www.informix.com/linux**.

Informix strongly supports Linux development of its Informix line. It provides developer support through its Informix Developer Network (**www.informix.com/idn**). Informix has a close working relationship with Red Hat and plans to provide joint technical support for their products.

Sybase

Sybase offers a line of database products ported to Linux free. You can download them through the Sybase Web site at **www.sybase.com** or from its FTP site at **ftp.sybase.com/linux**. The free products include the Adaptive Server Enterprise server, the Open Client/C library (unsupported), and SQL Anywhere Studio (evaluation version). You can currently download the Adaptive Server Enterprise server from the Web page **www.sybase.com/products/databaseservers/linux/**, or from the Sybase FTP site at **ftp.sybase.com/linux**. The Sybase Enterprise database features data integration that coordinates all information resources on a network. SQL Anywhere is a database system designed for smaller databases, though with the same level of complexity found in larger databases.

DB2

IBM provides a Linux version of its DB2 Universal Database software. You can download it free from the IBM DB2 Web page for Linux, **www.software.ibm.com/data/db2/linux/**. DB2 Universal Database for Linux includes Internet functionality along with support for Java and Perl. With the Web Control Center, administrators can maintain databases from a Web browser. DB2 features scalability to expand the database easily, support for Binary Large Objects, and cost-based optimization for fast access. DB2 is still very much a mainframe database, though IBM is currently working on refining its Unix/Linux version.

Ingres II

Ingress II is an industrial-strength relational database provided by Computer Associates. You can download a free copy of Ingress II as part of the Computer Associates Open Beta program for Linux. You can find a link for the download at the Computer Associates Web site at **www.cai.com/products/ingres.htm** or at **www.ingres.com**. The Beta version include the complete Ingress II database engine, with features like variable page size, support for Binary Large Objects, interfaces for C, compatibility with IngPerl (database access with the Perl scripting language), and Internet publishing capabilities. A complete set of online documentation is also included.

Adabas D

Adabas D is an intermediate relational database, not quite as powerful or as large as Oracle, which is meant for use on smaller networks of personal databases. It still provides the flexibility and power found in all relational databases. Adabas D provides a personal version for Linux free. For commercial uses, you have to purchase a copy. You can find online documentation, including manuals and FAQs, at the Caldera Web site at **www.calderasystems.com**. You can also check the Adabas D Web site at **www.adabas.com**.

MySQL

MySQL is a true multiuser, multithreaded SQL database server, develop by TcX. MySQL is an open source product available free under the GPL license. You can download a copy from its Web site at **www.mysql.com**. The site also includes detailed documentation including manuals and FAQs. RPM packages are available for Red Hat and OpenLinux at the Red Hat contrib site at **contrib.redhat.com**.

MySQL is structured on a client/server model with a server daemon (mysqld) filling requests from client programs. MySQL is designed for speed, reliability, and ease of use. It is meant to be a fast database management system for large databases and, at the same time, reliable with intensive use.

GNU SQL

GNU SQL is the GNU relational database developed by a group at the Institute for System Programming of the Russian Academy of Sciences and supported by the GNU organization. It is a portable multiuser database management system with a client/server structure that supports SQL. The server processes requests and performs basic administrative operations, such as unloading parts of the database used infrequently. The clients can reside on any computer of a local network. GNU-SQL uses a dialect of SQL based on the SQL-89 standard and designed for use on a Unix-like environment. You can download the database software from the GNU FTP site at **ftp.gnu.org**. For more information, contact the GNU-SQL Web site at **www.ispras.ru/~kml/gss**.

xBase Databases

Databases accessed with *xBase* are smaller in scale, designed for small networks or for personal use. Many are originally PC database programs, such as dBaseIII, Clipper, FoxPro, and Quicksilver. Currently, only Flagship provides an interface for accessing xBase database files, although the Harmony project is currently developing a Clipper clone that may run on Linux systems.

Flagship is a compiler with which you can create interfaces for querying xBase database files. The interfaces support menus and dialog boxes, and they have function calls that execute certain database queries. Flagship can compile dBaseIII+ code and up. It is compatible with dBase and Clipper and can access most xBase file formats, such as **.dbf**, **.dbt**, **.fmt**, and **.frm**. One of Flagship's key features is that its interfaces can be attached to a Web page, enabling users to update databases. Flagship is commercial software, though you can download a free personal version from its Web site at **www.fship.com/free.html**.

Desktop Database

Both Gnome and KDE also have database management applications that take advantage of their respective desktops. KDE's Katabase is part of KOffice and is fully integrated with its other applications. Gnome's Gaby takes advantage of the interface to display and search user databases.

Katabase (KOffice)

Katabase is a database management system that is part of the K Desktop's KOffice suite of programs. It is a desktop database, somewhat like Microsoft Access and Paradox; however, it makes full use of its integration with other Koffice programs by means of KOM/OpenParts. As part of KOffice, any part of Katabase can be embedded into another Koffice application, and Koffice components can be embedded into Katabase. You can find out more about Katabase at **koffice.kde.org**.

The main structure of Katabase is a plug-in framework that operates as a base manager. The database is composed of different parts serviced by a KOM application that plugs into the base manager. *Kdataparse* is where the methods plug in to access different data type. The interface looks the same to the user no matter what method is being used. At Kdataparse, you enter a SQL query. Kforms displays forms, Kreports generates reports, Ktable displays tables, and Kscripts runs scripts. Katabase's modular design allows the addition of other components, expanding its capabilities.

Gaby

Gaby is a small personal database manager using GTK+ and Gnome. It provides access to user databases, such as those for addresses, books, even photos. Gaby's plug-in design makes it easily extensible. You can find out more about Gaby at **gaby.netpedia.net**. Its interface has the same browser-like tools found in most Gnome applications. You can download the current version of Gaby from the Gnome software map at **www.gnome.org**.

Graphic Tools

Gnome, KDE, and the X Window System support an impressive number of graphic tools, including image viewers, window grabbers, image editors, and paint tools. On the KDE and Gnome desktops, these tools can be found under either a Graphics submenu or the Utilities menu.

KDE Graphic Tools

The *kview program* is a simple image viewer for GIF and JPEG image files. The *ksnapshot program* is a simple screen grabber for KDE, which currently supports only a few image formats. The *kfourier program* is an image-processing tool that uses the Fourier transform to apply several filters to an image at once. The *kshow program* is a simple

System	Site
Oracle	Oracle database **www.oracle.com**
Sybase	Sybase database **www.sybase.com**
DB2	IBM database **www.software.ibm.com/data/db2/linux**
Informix	Informix database **www.informix.com/linux**
Ingress II	Computer Associates database **www.cai.com/products/ingres.htm**
Adabas D	Adabas D database **www.adabas.com**
MySQL	MySQL database **www.mysql.com**
GNU SQL	The GNU SQL database **www.ispras.ru/~kml/gss**
PostgreSQL	The PostgreSQL database **www.postgresql.org**
Flagship	Interface for xBase database files **www.fship.com/free.html**
Katabase	KOffice desktop database **koffice.kde.org**
Gaby	Gnome desktop personal database **gaby.netpedia.net**.

Table 21-1.   *Database Management Systems for Linux*

image viewer. The *kuickShow program* is an easy-to-use, comfortable image browser and viewer, based on imlib. The *kpaint program* is a simple paint program with brushes, shapes, and color effects.

Gnome Graphic Tools

ImageShaker is a digital image-processing tool that includes an extensive set of graphic filters, such as alpha blending and median. It uses a stream-like approach that allows batch processing.

Electric Eyes is a simple image viewer. Right-click its window to display a pop-up menu with options. You can load images and also move back and forth through previously viewed ones. You can even make an image your background.

GQview is a simple image viewer supporting features like click file viewing, thumbnail preview, zoom, drag-and-drop, and external editor support, as well as slideshow and full-screen options. Multiple files can be selected for moving, copying, deleting, renaming, or dragging. See **gqview.sourceforge.net** for more information.

The *GIMP* is the *GNU Image Manipulation Program*, a sophisticated image application, much like Adobe Photoshop. You can use GIMP for such tasks as photo retouching, image composition, and image authoring. It supports features like layers, channels, blends, and gradients. GIMP makes particular use of the GTK+ widget set. You can find out more about the GIMP from its Web site at **www.gimp.org**. You can also download the newest versions from here. GIMP is freely distributed under the GNU public license.

The *gPhoto* program is a digital camera tool that can load, select, and edit photos from a digital camera connected to your system. With gPhoto, you can generate thumbnail images to let you select and organize your photos. You can also process photos, changing their orientation.

X Graphic

The *xv program* is a screen capture and image-editing program. After displaying the main screen, right-click it to display its control screen. Use the Grab button to scan a window or a section you select with a drag operation using your middle mouse button. Once you have scanned a window or screen section, you can crop it with a drag operation with your left mouse key and then use crop to reduce it to that selected section. With xv, you can also convert an image file from one format to another. Just load the image and then save it as another file using a different image format.

The *xpaint program* is a painting program, much like MacPaint. You can load paint pictures or photographs, and then create shapes, add text, and add colors. You can use brush tools with various sizes and colors. The xfig program is a drawing program, and xmorph enables you to morph images, changing their shapes.

Multimedia

Many applications are available for both video and sound, including sound editors, mp3 players, and video players (see Table 21-3). Linux sound applications include mixers, digital audio tools, CD audio writers, mp3 players, and network audio support. The Linux Midi and Sound Pages currently at **www.xdt.com/ar/linux-snd** holds links to Web and FTP sites for many of these applications. Many sound applications are currently under development for Gnome, including sound editors, mp3 players, and audio players. Check the software map at **www.gnome.org** for current releases. A variety of applications are available for KDE, including a media player (kmedia), a mixer (kmix), an mp3 player (KJukeBox), and a CD player (kscd). Check **www.kde.org** for recent additions.

Several projects are under way to provide TV, video, and DVD support for Linux (see Table 21-3). The site **linuxtv.org** provides detailed links to DVD, digital TV (DVD), and analog TV Linux projects. The XFree86 version 4.0 with the Xv extensions will include support for video in a window for selected platforms. Several projects

KDE	Description
kview	Simple image viewer for GIF and JPEG image files
ksnapshot	Screen grabber
kfourier	Image processing tool that uses the Fourier transform
kuickShow	Image browser and viewer
kshow	Simple image viewer
kpaint	Paint program
Gnome	
Gqview	Image viewer
ImageShaker	Digital image processing
GIMP	GNU Image Manipulation Program
Electric Eyes	Image viewer
gPhoto	Digital Camera application
X Window System	
xv	Screen grabber and image conversion
xpaint	Paint program
xfig	Drawing program
xmorph	Morphs images
xfractals	Generates fractal images

Table 21-2. *Graphic Tools for Linux*

have already developed applications. The Video 4 Linux project has created the Video4Linux software package, which allows you to play Mpeg1 video sources on Linux. Video4Linux is included with Linux distributions, including Red Hat. Currently under development is Video 4 Linux Two (V4L2). This is a separate project that has established a set of APIs and standards for handling video devices on Linux, providing a common API for video and tuning sources, teletext, and other TV-related VBI data. It includes a suite of related driver specifications for different types of video devices and video-related data. It is intended as a replacement for Video for Linux. Several applications currently support it, including XawTV, Gnomovision, and kTuner.

For KDE, several video applications are available or currently under development, including a video player (action), a TV tuner (kwintv and kTuner), and an mpeg I video player (ZZplayer). Currently available or under development for Gnome are TV tuners (Gnomevision and gnome-tv), a video player (Gnome-Video), an mpeg I video player (gtv), and a video editor (trinity).

For DVD, the Linux Video and DVD Project (LiViD) at **www.linuxvideo.org** supports the development of Mpeg 2 (DVD) software. LiViD DVD and multimedia players are currently under development. LSDVD (**www.csh.rit.edu/projects/lsdvd/**) is currently developing a DVD player that will eventually include fully compliant DVD software decoding. Information about recent efforts to develop Linux DVD can be had at **www.opendvd.org**. The LinuxDVD Project at **linuxdvd.corepower.com** is hosting links and information for the different efforts to develop DVD support on Linux. From here you can access the different DVD and video projects easily.

Projects	Description
Linux MIDI and Sound Pages	Information and links to Linux Sound projects and site: **www.xdt.com/ar/linux-snd**
Advanced Linux Sound Architecture (ALSA)	The Advanced Linux Sound Architecture project (ALSA) is developed on Linux under the GPL: **www.alsa-project.org**
Open Sound System/Free	The standard Linux sound drivers formerly known as USS/Lite, TASD, and Voxware are now called OSS/Free: **www.opensound.com**
linuxtv.org	Links to Video, TV, and DVD sites
video4linux 2	Video for Linux Two
LiViD	The Linux Video and DVD Project **www.linuxvideo.org**
LinuxDVD	The LinuxDVD Project **linuxdvd.corepower.com**
LSDVD	LSDVD Linux Player Project **www.csh.rit.edu/projects/lsdvd/**
GATOS	The Gneral ATI TV and Overlay Software **www.core.binghamton.edu/~insomnia/gatos**

Table 21-3. *Linux Multimedia Projects*

The Complete Reference

Linux

Chapter 22

Editors

Linux distributions include many text editors. These range from simple text editors for simple notes to editors with more complex features, such as spell-checkers, buffers, or pattern matching. All generate character text files and can be used to edit any Linux text files. Text editors are often used to change or add entries in Linux configuration files found in the **/etc** directory or a user's initialization or application dot files located in a user's home directory. You can use any text editor to work on source code files for any of the programming languages or shell program scripts.

Traditionally, most Linux distributions include the cursor-based editors Vim or Emacs. *Vim* is an enhanced version of the Vi text editor used on the Unix system. These editors use simple, cursor-based operations to give you a full-screen format. You can start these editors from the shell command line without any kind of X Window System support. In this mode, their cursor-based operations do not have the ease of use normally found in window-based editors. There are no menus, scroll bars, or mouse-click features. However, the K Desktop and Gnome do support powerful GUI text editors with all these features. These editors operate much more like those found on Mac and Windows systems. They have full mouse support, scroll bars, and menus. You may find them much easier to use than the Vi and Emacs editors. These editors operate from their respective desktops, requiring you first have either KDE or Gnome installed, though the editors can run on either desktop. Vi and Emacs, on the other hand, have powerful editing features that have been refined over the years. Emacs, in particular, is extensible to a full-development environment for programming new applications. Newer versions of Emacs, such as GNU Emacs and XEmacs, provide X Window System support with mouse, menu, and window operations. They can run on any window manager or desktop. In addition, the gvim version of the Vim editor also provides basic window operations. Table 22-1 lists several GUI-based editors for Linux.

K Desktop Editors: KEdit, KWrite, Kjots, and KWord

All the K Desktop editors provide full mouse support, implementing standard GUI operations, such as cut-and-paste to move text, and click-and-drag to select text. The KEdit program is the default editor for the K Desktop. It is a simple text editor meant for editing simple text files, such as configuration files. A toolbar of buttons at the top of the KEdit window enables you to execute common editing commands easily, using just a mouse click. With KEdit, you can also mail files you are editing over a network. The entry for KEdit in the K menu is listed simply as Text Editor. You can start up KEdit by entering the **kedit** command in a terminal window. The KOffice Office Suite also includes a word processor called *KWord*, which is a high-powered word processor you can also use as a simple editor.

A more advanced editor is *KWrite*, with such features as a spell-checker (see Figure 22-1). Formatting options can be set in the options menu and implemented using CTRL-J. Most commands can be selected using menus. A toolbar of icons for common

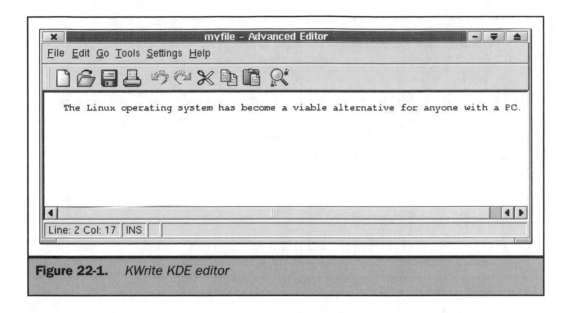

Figure 22-1.   *KWrite KDE editor*

operations is displayed across the top of the KWrite window. A click on the right mouse button displays a pop-up menu with entries for Cut, Copy, and Paste, as well as Open and Save. At the bottom of the KWrite menu is a message box that displays the current operation or any error messages. The entry for KWrite in the K menu is Advanced Editor. You can also start up KWrite by entering the **kwrite** command in a terminal window.

KWrite is designed to be a program editor for editing software programming/ development–related source code files. Although KWrite does not have all the features of Emacs or Vi, it can handle most major tasks. The Highlight entry in the Options menu enables you to set syntax highlighting for different programming languages, such as C, Perl, Java, and HTML. In addition, KWrite has the capability to access and edit files on an FTP or Web site.

The editor *KJots* is designed to enable you to jot down notes in a notebook. It organizes notes you write into notebooks, called simply *books.* You can select the one you want to view or add to from the Books menu. To start KJots, select its entry in the Utilities menu or enter the kjots command in a terminal window.

Gnome Editors: gEdit, gXedit, and gnotepad+

All the Gnome editors provide full mouse support, implementing standard GUI operations, such as cut-and-paste to move text, and click-and-drag to select text. *gEdit* is a basic text editor for the Gnome desktop (see Figure 22-2). You can use gEdit to perform most text editing tasks, such as modifying configuration files. It features a

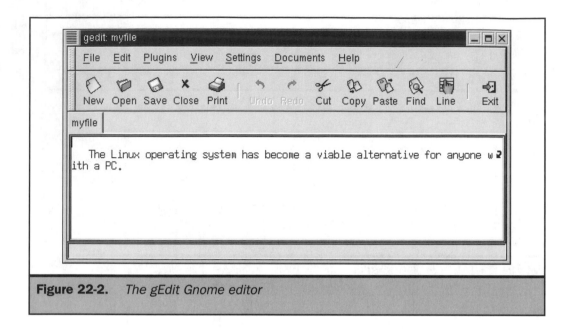

Figure 22-2. *The gEdit Gnome editor*

plug-in menu that provides added functionality, and it includes plug-ins for spell-checking, project management, encryption, and e-mail.

A more powerful editor, *gXedit*, includes standard features such as spell-checking, formatting, autosave, and encryption. Menus contain all the gXedit commands, and a toolbar of icons for commonly used commands is displayed across the top of the gXedit window. The gXedit editor supports a full range of file operations, enabling you to merge, sort, or compare files. You can easily insert the date and the contents of your signature file. You can also use gXedit to compose Man pages, inserting the Man tags for the header, synopsis, description, and options. In addition, gXedit can also compose and edit Web pages. You can easily insert HTTP elements, such as links, image references, or headings, and gXedit can then access Netscape to preview the page. You configure gXedit using the Settings window, which has panels for display, network, macro, and command settings. Settings are saved in the user's **home** directory in the file **.gxedit**.

The editor *gnotepad+* is a simple editor for making small text files. gnotepad+ does, however, have a toolbar for Web page composition containing several of the more common HTML elements. You can insert links, headings, and lists, as well as other basic Web page components.

The K Desktop	Description
KEdit	Text editor, default for K Desktop
KWrite	Text and program editor
KJots	Notebook editor
KWord	Desktop publisher, part of KOffice
Gnome	
gEdit	Text editor
gXedit	Text and HTML editor
gnotepad+	Notebook editor
X Windows	
XEmacs	X Window System version of Emacs editor
GNU Emacs	Emacs editor with X Window System support
gvim	Vim version with X Window System support
WordPerfect	Word processor that can edit text files

Table 22-1.   *Desktop Editors*

The Vi Editor: vim and gvim

The *Vim editor* included with most Linux distributions is an enhanced version of the Vi editor. It includes all the commands and features of the Vi editor. *Vi*, which stands for *visual*, remains one of the most widely used editors in Linux. Keyboard-based editors like Vim and Emacs use a keyboard for two different operations: to specify editing commands and to receive character input. Used for editing commands, certain keys perform deletions, some execute changes, and others perform cursor movement. Used for character input, keys represent characters that can be entered into the file being edited. Usually, these two different functions are divided among different keys on the keyboard. Alphabetic keys are reserved for character input, while function keys and control keys specify editing commands, such as deleting text or moving the cursor. Such editors can rely on the existence of an extended keyboard that includes function and control keys. Editors in Unix, however, were designed to assume a minimal keyboard with alphanumeric characters, and some control characters, as well as the ESC and ENTER keys. Instead of dividing the command and input functions among different keys, the Vi editor has three separate modes of operation for the keyboard: command and input modes, along with a line editing mode. In *command* mode, all the keys on the keyboard become editing commands; in the *input* mode, the keys on the keyboard become input characters. Some of the editing commands, such as **a** or **i**, enter the input mode. On pressing the **i** key, you leave the command mode and enter the input mode. Each key now represents a character to be input to the text. Pressing ESC automatically returns you to the command mode, and the keys once again become editor commands. As you edit text, you are constantly moving from the command mode to the input mode and back again. With Vim, you can use the CTRL-O command to jump quickly to the command mode and enter a command, and then automatically return to the input mode. Table 22-2 lists this basic set of Vi commands you need to get started in Vi.

Although the Vi command mode handles most editing operations, it cannot perform some, such as file saving and global substitutions. For such operations, you need to execute line editing commands. You enter the line editing mode using the Vi colon command, **:**. The colon is a special command that enables you to perform a one-line editing operation. When you press the colon, a line opens up at the bottom of the screen with the cursor placed at the beginning of the line. You are now in the line editing mode. In this mode, you enter an editing command on a line, press ENTER, and the command is executed. Entry into this mode is usually only temporary. Upon pressing ENTER, you are automatically returned to the Vi command mode, and the cursor returns to its previous position on the screen.

Although you can create, save, close, and quit files with the Vi editor, the commands for each are not all that similar. Saving and quitting a file involves the use of special line editing commands, whereas closing a file is a Vi editing command. Creation of a file is usually specified on the same shell command line that invokes the Vi editor. To edit a file, type **vi** or **vim** and the name of a file on the shell command line. If a file by that name does not exist, the system creates it. In effect, giving the name of a file that does not yet exist instructs the Vi editor to create that file. The following command invokes the Vi editor, working on the file **booklist**. If **booklist** does not yet exist, the Vi editor creates it.

```
$ vim booklist
```

After executing the **vim** command, you enter Vi's command mode. Each key becomes a Vi editing command, and the screen becomes a window into the text file. Text is displayed screen by screen. The first screen of text is displayed, and the cursor is positioned in the upper-left corner. With a newly created file, there is no text to display. This fact is indicated by a column of tildes at the left-hand side of the screen. The tildes represent the part of a screen that is not part of the file.

Remember, when you first enter the Vi editor, you are in the command mode. To enter text, you need to enter the input mode. In the command mode, the **a** key is the editor command for appending text. Pressing this key places you in the input mode. Now, the keyboard operates like a typewriter and you can input text to the file. If you press ENTER, you merely start a new line of text. With Vim, you can use the arrow keys to move from one part of the entered text to another and work on different parts of the text. After entering text, you can leave the input mode and return to the command mode by pressing ESC. Once finished with the editing session, you exit Vi by typing two capital Z's, **zz**. Hold down the SHIFT key and press **z** twice. This sequence first saves the file and then exits the Vi editor, returning you to the Linux shell. To save a file while editing, you use the line editing command **w**, which writes a file to the disk. **w** is equivalent to the Save command found in other word processors. You first press the colon key to access the line editing mode, and then type **w** and press ENTER.

You can use the **:q** command to quit an editing session. Unlike the **zz** command, the **:q** command does not perform any save operation before it quits. In this respect, it has one major constraint. If any modifications have been made to your file since the last save operation, then the **:q** command will fail and you will not leave the editor. However, you can override this restriction by placing a **!** qualifier after the **:q** command. The command **:q!** will quit the Vi editor without saving any modifications made to the file in that session since the last save.

To obtain online help, enter the **:help** command. This is a line editing command. Press the colon, enter the word **help** on the line that opens at the bottom of the screen, and then press ENTER. You can add the name of a specific command after the word **help**. The F1 key also brings up online help.

gvim

As an alternative to using Vim in a command-line interface, you can use *gvim*, which provides X Windows–based menus for basic file, editing, and window operations. To use **gvim**, enter the **gvim** command at an X Windows terminal prompt or select it from a Window manager menu. The standard Vi interface is displayed, but with several menu buttons displayed across the top. All the standard Vi commands work just as they are described here. However, you can use your mouse to select items on these menus. You can open and close a file, or open several files using split windows or different windows. The editing menu enables you to cut, copy, and paste text, as well as undo or redo operations. In the editing mode, you can select text with your mouse with a click-and-drag operation, use the Editing menu to cut or copy, and then paste the selected text. Text entry, however, is still performed using the **a**, **i**, or **o** commands to enter the input mode.

Options in Vi: set and .exrc

Vi has a set of options with which to configure your editor. You set an option with the **set** line editing command. You can set options within Vi using the Vi line editing mode. The **set** command followed by the option name sets the option on. If the characters "no" are attached to the beginning of the option name, then the option is set off. For example, the command **set number** sets the **number** option, which numbers your lines; whereas the command **set nonumber** turns off the **number** option. The command **set** by itself provides a list of all options the user has set. If an option is already set, the command **set** followed by that option's name displays the value of the option. The command **set all** displays the settings of all the options.

Vi options can be used to control search operation, text display, and text input. If you set the **ignorecase** option, then searches ignore uppercase or lowercase characters in making matches. A search for **/There** retrieves both "there" and "There." You can abbreviate the **ignorecase** option with **ic**. The commands **set ignorecase** and **set ic** turn the option on, whereas set **noignorecase** and **set noic** turn it off. The **wrapscan** option allows a search to wrap around the file. While in the input mode, you can automatically start a new line at a specified margin (**wrapmargin**), you can automatically indent a new line (**autoindent**), you can check for an opening parenthesis when entering a closing parenthesis, and you can determine the number of spaces you can backtab when in input.

You may want to set certain options for every file you edit. Instead of setting these options manually for each file each time you edit them, you can place these options in your **EXINIT** shell variable or in editor initialization files, and have them automatically set for you. To use the **EXINIT** variable to set your options automatically, you need to assign the **EXINIT** variable a quoted **set** command specifying what options you want set. Whenever you invoke Vi, the **set** command stored in **EXINIT** is automatically executed. In the next example, the user assigns to the **EXINIT** variable the quoted **set** command to set both the **nu** option for numbering lines and the **ic** option for ignoring case in searches:

```
$ EXINIT='set nu ic'
```

Although you can assign the **set** command to the **EXINIT** variable in your shell, you would normally assign it in your login or shell initialization files. Then, whenever you log in, the **EXINIT** variable is automatically assigned its set command. In the next example, the quoted **set** command is assigned to **EXINIT** in the user's **.bash_profile** initialization file. Options set in this way are set for every file you edit. You may need some options for only a selected set of files. For example, you may want to number lines in only your C source code files and word-wrap your lines only in your document files. You can tailor your options for a selected set of files by using an editor initialization file called **.exrc**. The **.exrc** file contains commands to configure your editor. When Vi is invoked, the shell first searches for an **.exrc** file in the current working directory. If one is there, the shell runs it, executing the commands. These usually are **set** commands, setting the options for the editor. If no **.exrc** file is in your working directory, the shell searches your **home** directory for an **.exrc** file. You can have a separate **.exrc** file in as many directories as you want. This enables you to customize the editor according to the files you have in a given directory.

Key	Effect
h	Moves the cursor left one character
l	Moves the cursor right one character
k	Moves the cursor up one line
j	Moves the cursor down one line
w	Moves the cursor forward one word
W	Moves the cursor forward one space-delimited word
b	Moves the cursor back one word
B	Moves the cursor back one space-delimited word
e	Moves the cursor to the end of the next word
E	Moves the cursor to the end of the next space-delimited word
0	Moves the cursor to the beginning of the line
$	Moves the cursor to the end of the line
ENTER	Moves the cursor to beginning of next line
–	Moves the cursor to beginning of previous line
(	Moves the cursor to beginning of sentence
)	Moves the cursor to the end of sentence; successive command moves to beginning of next sentence
{	Moves the cursor to beginning of paragraph
}	Moves the cursor to end of paragraph
CTRL-F	Moves forward by a screen of text; the next screen of text is displayed
CTRL-B	Moves backward by a screen of text; the previous screen of text is displayed

Table 22-2. *Vi Editor Commands*

Key	Effect
CTRL-D	Moves forward by one-half screen of text
CTRL-U	Moves backward by one-half screen of text
G	Moves the cursor to last line in the text
*num*G	Moves the cursor to specific line number: 45G places the cursor on line 45
H	Moves the cursor to line displayed on screen
M	Moves the cursor to middle line displayed on screen
L	Moves the cursor to bottom line displayed on screen
' '	Moves the cursor to its previous location in the text
m*mark*	Places a mark on a line of text; can be any alphabetic character
' *mark*	Moves the cursor to the line with the mark
Input	*(All input commands place the user in input; the user leaves input with* ESC.*)*
a	Enters input after the cursor
A	Enters input at the end of a line
i	Enters input before the cursor
I	Enters input at the beginning of a line
o	Enters input below the line the cursor is on; inserts a new empty line below the one the cursor is currently on
O	Enters input above the line the cursor is on; inserts a new empty line above the one the cursor is currently on
Text Selection (vim)	**Effect**
v	Visual mode; moves the cursor to expand selected text by character. Once selected, press key to execute action: **c** change, **d** delete, **y** copy, **:** line editing command, **J** join lines, **U** uppercase, **u** lowercase.

Table 22-2.   *Vi Editor Commands* (continued)

Text Selection (vim)	Effect
v	Visual mode; moves cursor to expand selected text by line
o	Expands selected text backward
Delete	**Effect**
x	Deletes the character the cursor is on
X	Deletes the character before the character the cursor is on
dw	Deletes the word the cursor is on
dd	Deletes the line the cursor is on
D	Deletes the rest of the line the cursor is on
d0	Deletes text from the cursor to beginning of line
d*c*	Deletes specified component, *c*
J	Joins the line below the cursor to the end of the current line; in effect, deleting the newline character of the line the cursor is on
Change	*(Except for the replace command, **r**, all change commands place the user into input after deleting text.)*
s	Deletes the character the cursor is on and places the user into the input mode
C	Deletes the rest of the line the cursor is on and places the user into input mode
cw	Deletes the word the cursor is on and places the user into the input mode
c0	Changes text from cursor to beginning of line
r	Replaces the character the cursor is on; after pressing **r**, the user enters the replacement character; the change is made without entering input; the user remains in the Vi command mode
R	First places into the input mode, and then overwrites character by character; appears as an overwrite mode on the screen, but actually is in input mode

Table 22-2. *Vi Editor Commands* (continued)

APPLICATIONS

Change	Effect
c*c*	Changes the specified component, *c*
Move	Moves text by first deleting it, moving the cursor to desired place of insertion, and then pressing the p command. (When text is deleted, it is automatically held in a special buffer.)
p	Inserts deleted or copied text after the character or line the cursor is on
P	Inserts deleted or copied text before the character or line the cursor is on
dw p	Deletes a word, and then moves it to the place you indicate with the cursor (Press p to insert the word *after* the word the cursor is on.)
d*c* **p**	Deletes specified component, *c*, then moves it to the place you indicate with the cursor (Press p to insert the word *after* the word the cursor is on.)
yy or **Y**	Copies the line the cursor is on
y*c*	Copies component specified, *c*

Component References	Description
w	Word the cursor is on
b	To beginning of a word
W	Space-delimited word
B	Beginning of a space-delimited word
)	Sentence
}	Paragraph
G	Rest of the file
m	The *m* is a mark
L	To bottom of the screen
yH	To top of the screen

Table 22-2. *Vi Editor Commands* (continued)

Component References	Description
Search	The two search commands open up a line at the bottom of the screen and enable the user to enter a pattern to be searched for; press ENTER after typing in the pattern.
/pattern	Searches forward in the text for a pattern
?*pattern*	Searches backward in the text for a pattern
n	Repeats the previous search, whether it was forward or backward
N	Repeats the previous search in opposite direction
/	Repeats the previous search in forward direction
?	Repeats the previous search in backward direction
Buffers	There are 9 numbered buffers and 26 named buffers; named buffers are named with each lowercase letter in the alphabet, *a–z*. Use the double quote to reference a specific buffer.
"*buf-letter*	Named buffer—references a specific named buffer, a, b, and so forth
"*num*	Numbered buffer—references a numbered buffer with a number 1–9
Help (vim)	**Effect**
:help *command*	Starts help utility; you can specify a command.
F1	Same as :help
Line Editing Commands	**Effect**
w	Saves file
r *filename*	Inserts file text
q	Quits editor, **q!** quits without saving
d	Deletes a line or set of lines
m *Num*	Moves a line or set of lines by deleting them and then inserting them after line *Num*

Table 22-2. *Vi Editor Commands* (continued)

APPLICATIONS

Line Editing Commands	Effect
co_Num_	Copies a line or set of lines by copying them, and then inserting the copied text after line _Num_

Line Reference	Description
Num	A number references that line number.
Num, _Num_	Two numbers separated by a comma references a set of lines.
Num–Num	Two numbers separated by a dash references a range of lines.
–Num	The minus sign (–) preceding a number offsets to a line before the current line.
+Num	The plus sign (+) preceding a number offsets to a line after the current line.
$	The dollar sign symbol ($) references the last line in the file.
/_Pattern_**/**	A line can be located and referenced by a pattern; the slash searches forward.
?_Pattern_**?**	A line can be located and referenced by a pattern; the question mark (?) searches backward.
g/_Pattern_**/**	A set of lines can be located and referenced by a repeated pattern reference; all lines with a pattern in them are referenced.

Special Character	Effect
.	Matches on any one possible character in a pattern
*	Matches on repeated characters in a pattern
[]	Matches on classes of characters, a set of characters, in the pattern
^	References the beginning of a line
$	References the end of a line
/<	References the start of a word

Table 22-2. _Vi Editor Commands_ (continued)

Special Character	Effect
>/	References the end of a word

Substitution Command	Effect
s/*pattern***/***replacement***/**	Locates *pattern* on a line and substitutes *pattern* with *replacement* pattern
s/*pattern***/***replacement***/g**	Substitutes all instances of a pattern on a line with the replacement pattern
Num–Num **s/***pattern***/***replacement***/**	Performs substitutions on the range of lines specified
1,$ s/*pattern***/***replacement***/g**	Substitutes all instances of a pattern in the file with the replacement pattern

Table 22-2. *Vi Editor Commands* (continued)

The Emacs Editor

Emacs can best be described as a working environment featuring an editor, a mailer, a newsreader, and a Lisp interpreter. The editor is tailored for program development, enabling you to format source code according to the programming language you use. Many versions of Emacs are currently available for use on Unix and Linux systems. The versions usually included with Linux distributions are either GNU Emacs or XEmacs. The current version for GNU Emacs is 20.*x*; it is X Window System capable, enabling GUI features such as menus, scroll bars, and mouse-based editing operations. (See Chapter 11 for a discussion of the GNU Emacs mailer, and Chapter 12 for one on its newsreader.) Check the update FTP sites for your distribution for new versions as they come out, and also check the GNU Web site at **www.gnu.org**, and the Emacs Web site at **www.emacs.org**. You can find out more information about XEmacs at its Web site, **www.xemacs.org**. Currently, GNU Emacs is distributed with Red Hat systems, and XEmacs is distributed with OpenLinux.

Emacs derives much of its power and flexibility from its capability to manipulate buffers. Emacs can be described as a buffer-oriented editor. Whenever you edit a file in any editor, the file is copied into a work buffer, and editing operations are made on the work buffer. Emacs can manage many work buffers at once, enabling you to edit several files at the same time. You can edit buffers that hold deleted or copied text. You can even create buffers of your own, fill them with text, and later save them to a file.

Emacs extends the concept of buffers to cover any task. When you compose mail, you open a mail buffer; when you read news, you open a news buffer. Switching from one task to another is simply a matter of switching to another buffer.

The Emacs editor operates much like a standard word processor. The keys on your keyboard represent input characters. Commands are implemented with special keys, such as control (CTRL) keys and alternate (ALT) keys. There is no special input mode, as is in Vi or Ed. You type in your text; and if you need to execute an editing command, such as moving the cursor or saving text, you use a CTRL key. Such an organization makes the Emacs editor easy to use. However, Emacs is anything but simple—it is a sophisticated and flexible editor with several hundred commands. Emacs also has special features, such as multiple windows. You can display two windows for text at the same time. You can also open and work on more than one file at a time, and display each on the screen in its own window. You invoke the Emacs editor with the command **emacs**. You can enter the name of the file you want to edit; or, if the file does not exist, it is created. In the next example, the user prepares to edit the file **mydata** with Emacs:

```
$ emacs mydata
```

Emacs is a full-screen editor that supports menus even when used on the command line. In the case of a newly created file, the screen is empty except for the bottom two lines. The cursor is positioned in the upper-left corner. The bottom line is called the *Echo area*, and it functions as a kind of Emacs command line. The *Echo area* is also used to display Emacs messages. The line above it is called the *mode line*; it is used to display status information about the text being edited. The mode line is highlighted in reverse video. The GNU version of Emacs also displays a list of menus at the top of the screen. If you are working from the shell, you can access the menu entries by pressing the F10 key. If you are working on a desktop, you can use your mouse (see Figure 22-3).

To enter text, simply start typing—you are always in the input mode. Editing commands, such as movement commands, are implemented with CTRL keys. For example, to move the cursor right, use CTRL-F; and to move the cursor left, use CTRL-B. To move up one line, use CTRL-P; and to move down one line, use CTRL-N. You can save your text at any time with the CTRL-X-CTRL-S command sequence. Many Emacs commands are made up of CTRL key combinations. The command sequence to quit the editor is CTRL-X-CTRL-C. When you finish editing the file, first save the file with CTRL-X-CTRL-S before quitting the editor with CTRL-X-CTRL-C.

Emacs provides several help utilities, such as an online manual and a tutorial. You access the help utilities through a CTRL-H sequence. CTRL-H followed by another CTRL-H lists the many possible options. An option of special note is the tutorial. CTRL-H-T places you into an online tutorial that provides you with special lessons on Emacs. Table 22-3 lists the Emacs help commands.

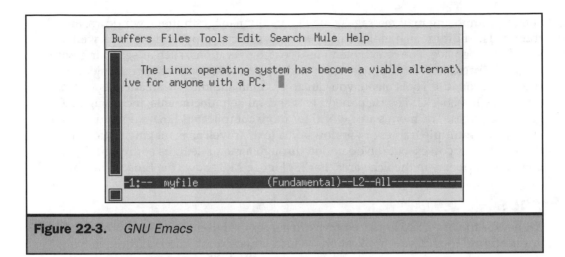

Figure 22-3. *GNU Emacs*

GNU Emacs X Windows Support

You can run GNU Emacs either from an X Windows window manager or from the shell command line. Many window managers or desktops may already have an entry in their main menu. If not, you can open a terminal window and enter the command **emacs**. When run from a terminal window, Emacs operate with X Windows support, enabling mouse-based editing and menu selection. You can also run Emacs from a standard shell command line, without X Windows. In this case, mouse-based operations are not enabled. However, the Emacs menu headings are still displayed at the top of the screen. You can access a menu by pressing F10. The screen will split, with the lower section listing menus and keys you press to access them. Once you select a menu, the items for that menu are listed with keys to press to select one. For example, to open a file, you press F10, the **f** to list the file menu items, and then the **o** to select the open item.

The GNU Emacs editor now supports an X Windows graphical user interface. To enable X Windows support, start Emacs within an X Windows environment, such as a KDE, Gnome, or FVWM desktop. The basic GUI editing operations are supported: selection of text with click-and-drag mouse operations; cut, copy, and paste; and a scroll bar for moving through text. The Mode line and Echo areas are displayed at the bottom of the window, where you can enter keyboard commands. The scroll bar is located on the left side. To move the scroll bar down, click it with the left mouse button. To move the scroll bar up, click it with the right mouse button.

From the menus at the top of the window, you can execute most file, edit, and buffer operations. The Buffers menu lists your active buffers. You can use it to switch to another buffer, in effect, switching to other files you are editing or to other tasks,

APPLICATIONS

such as composing mail messages. The File menu manages buffers, windows, and frames. The Edit menu handles edit operations like cut, copy, and paste, as well as search and replace. The Search menu lists search operations, such as searching with regular expressions. An Options menu enables you to set options for editing and printing. From the Tools menu, you can access mail and the newsreader, as well as perform spell-checks. The Help menu lists several help documents, including FAQs and Web pages. The menus are helpful for more complicated Emacs operations, such as opening multiple frames or windows on a text, as well as managing buffers and file buffers. When you execute an operation through a menu item, its equivalent keyboard command appears in the Echo area. Earlier Figure 22-3 shows the Emacs window.

XEmacs

XEmacs is the complete Emacs editor with a graphical user interface and Internet applications. The Internet applications, which you can easily access from the main XEmacs button bar, include a Web browser, a mail utility, and a newsreader. If an entry exists for XEmacs in the Desktop menu, you can use that to start it. Otherwise, you can open a terminal window and enter the **xemacs** command at the prompt. The main XEmacs window is displayed with a button bar across the top for basic editing operations and for Internet applications. XEmacs supports the basic GUI editing operations. Selection of text is done with click-and-drag mouse operations—cut, copy, and paste—and a scroll bar for moving through text. At the bottom of the XEmacs window, the Mode line and Echo areas are displayed as on the standard Emacs editor. You can enter keyboard commands in the Echo area, just as you would in the Emacs editor. From the XEmacs menus at the top of the window, you can execute most file, edit, and buffer operations. The File menu manages buffers, windows, and frames. The Edit menu handles edit operations like cut, copy, and paste, as well as search and replace. An Options menu enables you to set options for editing and printing. From the Apps menu, you can access other applications, like mail, the newsreader, and the Web browser. The Buffers menu lists your active buffers. The Help menu lists several help documents, including FAQs and Web pages. The XEmacs menus are helpful for more complicated Emacs operations, such as opening multiple frames or windows on a text, as well as managing buffers and file buffers. When you execute an operation through a menu item, its equivalent keyboard command appears in the Echo area.

Meta-Keys, Line Commands, and Modes

The Emacs editor operates much like any normal word processor. Only one mode, the input mode, exists. If you press any character key, you are entering data into the file. All character keys are input characters, not commands. A *character key* can be thought of as any key you type in directly, as opposed to CTRL keys or ALT keys. Character keys are any keys you could type in at a typewriter. Commands are assigned to CTRL keys, as well as meta-keys. In this version of Emacs, a *meta-key* may be either an ALT key sequence or an escape (ESC) key sequence. On other systems, they may be one or the other. ALT key sequences operate like CTRL keys. While you hold down the ALT key, you press another key, and then you let up on both. The ESC key sequence is slightly different. First, you press ESC and let up on it. Then you press another key. CTRL keys and meta-keys constitute only part of the many commands available in Emacs. All commands can be entered using command words typed in the Echo area. The meta-key commands ALT-X or ESC-X place you in the Echo area. Once in the Echo area, you execute a command by typing in the command and any of its arguments, and pressing ENTER. Table 22-3 lists the Emacs editing commands.

The mode line displays status information about the text being edited. The mode line is made up of several components, with the following form:

```
-ST-Emacs: BufferName   (major minor)------Place--
```

The first field, ST, indicates whether the file has been saved since the last change to the text. If the field displays two asterisks, ******, the text has been changed but not yet saved. If the field displays two dashes, **- -**, the text has not been changed since the last save. If the field displays two percent signs, **%%**, the file is read-only and cannot be modified.

The NAME field is the name of the buffer. In the case of files, this is the name of the file. The PLACE field indicates how far you are positioned in the file. For example, if the PLACE field is 40 percent, the text being displayed is 40 percent of the way through the file. In the next example, the mode line indicates the file has not been saved since the last change, the name of the buffer is **mytext**, and the cursor is positioned at the top of the file.

```
-**-Emacs: mytext       (text fill)----  --Top--
```

The MAJOR/MINOR field indicates the major and minor modes for editing the file. Emacs recognizes several major modes, the most common of which is the text mode. Different types of files require special editing configurations. A C program file, for example, may need special indentation features. For this reason, a special editing mode exists for C programs. Emacs recognizes other standard modes, such as nroff and Lisp. Emacs determines the mode by examining the extension used in the filename. A **.c** extension indicates a C program file. In that case, Emacs uses the C mode. If there is no extension, Emacs uses the text mode. If, for some reason, Emacs cannot determine the mode for the file, it uses the fundamental mode, which offers no special features. Emacs has three minor modes: fill, overwrite, and abbrev. The *fill mode* is usually the default and automatically wraps long lines in the file. The *overwrite mode* enables you to overwrite text, and the *abbrev mode* enables you to use abbreviations when entering text.

Keys	Effect
CTRL-B	Moves left one character (backward to the previous character)
CTRL-F	Moves right one character (forward to the next character)
CTRL-N	Moves down one line (the next line)
CTRL-P	Moves up one line (the previous line)
CTRL-V	Moves forward one screen
CTRL-Z	Moves backward one screen
CTRL-L	Moves to the center of screen
ALT-F	Moves forward one word
ALT-B	Moves backward one word
ALT-]	Moves to the next paragraph
ALT-[	Moves back to the previous paragraph
CTRL-A	Moves to the beginning of a line
CTRL-E	Moves to the end of a line
ALT-<	Moves to the beginning of buffer, usually beginning of file
ALT->	Moves to the end of buffer, usually end of file
ALT-*num*	Repeats the following command *num* number of times
ALT-X	Moves to the Echo area to enter a command
Deletion	**Effect**
DEL	Deletes the character before the cursor
CTRL-D	Deletes the character after the cursor
Kills and Yanks	**Effect**
CTRL-K	Removes the remainder of a line (kills the rest of the line)
CTRL-K-CTRL-K	Removes the remainder of a line and the newline character at the end

Table 22-3.   *Emacs Commands*

Kills and Yanks	Effect
ALT-D	Removes the word after the cursor
ALT-DEL	Removes the word before the cursor
ALT-K	Removes the remainder of a sentence
CTRL-W	Removes a region (deletes a block)
CTRL-Y	Inserts (yanks) the contents of a kill buffer into the text
CTRL-X-U	Undoes the previous command

Search and Replace	Effect
CTRL-S	Searches for a pattern forward in the text
CTRL-R	Searches for a pattern backward in the text (reverse)
ALT-CTRL-S	Searches for a regular expression forward in the text
ALT-CTRL-R	Searches for a regular expression backward in the text
replace *string*	Performs a global substitution
replace *regexp*	Performs a global substitution using regular expression
query-replace-*regexp*	Searches for a regular expression in query-and-replace operation
ALT-% *pattern* ENTER *replacement* ENTER	Queries and replaces a pattern: **Key** SPACEBAR　Replaces and moves to next instance DEL　　　　Does not replace and moves to next instance ESC　　　　Quits search-replace operation .　　　　　　Replaces and exits !　　　　　　Replaces all remaining instances ^　　　　　　Moves back to previous replacement

Region	Effect
CTRL-@ or CTRL-SPACEBAR	Marks a region (block)
CTRL-X-CTRL-X	Exchanges cursor (point) and marks
ALT-H	Marks a paragraph as a region
CTRL-X-CTRL-P	Marks a page as a region

Table 22-3.　*Emacs Commands* (continued)

Region	Effect
CTRL-X-H	Marks the entire text in buffer as a region
Text Format	**Effect**
auto-fill-mode	Sets fill mode option
ALT-*num* CTRL-X-F	Sets position of right margin
ALT-Q	Justifies a paragraph
Window Command	**Effect**
CTRL-X-2	Splits to a new window vertically
CTRL-X-5	Splits to a new window horizontally
CTRL-X-O	Selects other window
CTRL-X-P	Selects previous window
ALT-CTRL-V	Scrolls the other window
CTRL-X-0	Closes the current window
CTRL-X-1	Closes all but the current window
CTRL-X-^	Extends the current window vertically
CTRL-X-}	Extends the current window horizontally
File Buffer Command	**Effect**
CTRL-X-CTRL-F	Opens and reads a file into a buffer
CTRL-X-CTRL-S	Saves the contents of a buffer to a file
CTRL-X-CTRL-C	Quits the editor
CTRL-X-CTRL-V	Closes the current file and opens a new one (visiting a new file)
CTRL-X-I	Inserts contents of a file to a buffer
CTRL-X-CTRL-Q	Opens a file as read-only; you cannot change it.
CTRL-X-D	Enters the **dired** (directory editor) buffer that has a listing of your current directories; moves to different file and directory names; displays other directories; and selects and opens files

Table 22-3.   *Emacs Commands* (continued)

Buffer Command	Effect
CTRL-X-B	Changes to another buffer; you are prompted for the name of the buffer to change to (to create a new buffer, enter a new name).
CTRL-X-K	Deletes (kills) a buffer
CTRL-X-CTRL-B	Displays a list of all buffers
ALT-X **buffer-menu**	Selects different buffers from a list of buffers

Help Command	Effect
CTRL-H-CTRL-H	Lists possible help options
CTRL-H-I	Accesses the Emacs manual
CTRL-H-T	Runs the Emacs tutorial
CTRL-H-B	Displays keys and the commands they represent

Table 22-3. *Emacs Commands* (continued)

The
Complete
Reference

Linux

Part V

Servers

The
Complete
Reference

Linux

Chapter 23

Server Management

Reflecting the close relationship between Unix and the development of the Internet, Linux is particularly good at providing Internet services, such as the Web, FTP, and e-mail. In the case of the Web, instead of only accessing other sites, you can set up your own Linux system as a Web site. Other people can then access your system using Web pages you created or download files you provide for them. A system that operates this way is called a *server* and is known by the service it provides. You can set up your system to be a Web server or an FTP server, connecting it to the Internet and turning it into a site others can access. A single Linux system can provide several different services. Your Linux system can be a Web server and an FTP server, as well as a mail and news server, all at the same time. One user could download files using your FTP services, while another reads your Web pages. All you have to do is install and run the appropriate server software for each service. Each one operates as a continually running daemon looking for requests for its particular services from remote users. A *daemon* is any program that continually runs, checking for certain requests and performing appropriate actions.

When you install Linux, you have the option of installing several Internet servers, including Web and FTP servers. Linux was designed with Internet servers in mind. For many Linux distributions, a standard install installs these servers automatically and configures them for you (check to make sure the servers are included). Every time you start your system, you also start the Web and FTP server daemons. Then, to turn your Linux system into a Web server, all you have to do is create Web pages. For an FTP server, you only have to place the files you want to make available in the FTP directories.

You can operate your Linux system as a server on the Internet or an intranet (local area network), or you can set it up to service only the users on your own system. To operate servers as Internet servers, you must obtain a connection to the Internet and provide access to your system for remote users. Access is usually a matter of enabling anonymous logins to directories reserved for server resources. Linux systems are usually already configured to enable such access for Web and FTP users. Connections to the Internet that can accommodate server activity can be difficult to find. You may need a dedicated connection, or you may need to use a connection set up by an *Internet service provider* (*ISP*). You are no longer connecting only yourself to the Internet, but you are allowing many other users to make what could be a great many connections to you through the Internet. This will involve security risks to your system, and precautions should be taken to protect it (see Chapter 39). If you only want to provide the services to a *local area network* (*LAN*), you don't need a special connection. Also, you can provide these services to users by allowing them to connect over a modem and to log in directly. Users could dial into your system and use your Web pages or use FTP to download files. Furthermore, users with accounts on your own machine can also make use of the servers. In whatever situation you want to use these services, you need the appropriate server software installed and running. This chapter examines how servers are started and stopped on your system, as well as different ways of accessing the servers.

Starting Servers: Standalone and inetd/xinetd

A *server* is a daemon that runs concurrently with your other programs, continuously looking for a request for its services, either from other users on your system or from remote users connecting to your system through a network. When it receives a request from a user, a server starts up a session to provide its services. For example, if users want to download a file from your system, they can use their own FTP client to request that your FTP server start a session for them. In the session, they can access and download files from your system. Your server needs to be running for a user to access its services. For example, if you set up a Web site on your system with HTML files, you must have the **httpd** Web server program running before users can access your Web site and display those files. See Chapters 16 and 17 on how to install FTP and Web servers.

You can start a server in several ways. One way is to do it manually from the command line by entering the name of the server program and its arguments. When you press ENTER, the server starts, although your command line prompt reappears. The server runs concurrently as you perform other tasks. To see if your server is running, you can enter the following command to list all currently running processes. You should see a process for the server program you started. To refine the list, you can add a **grep** operation with a pattern for the server name you want. The second command lists the process for the Web server.

```
# ps -aux
# ps -aux | grep 'httpd'
```

On many Linux systems such as Red Hat and Caldera, you can also use special start-up scripts to start and stop your server manually. These scripts are located in the **/etc/rc.d/init.d** directory and have the same name as the server programs. For example, the **/etc/rc.d/init.d/httpd** script with the **start** option starts the Web server. Using this script with the **stop** option stops it. These scripts are explained in greater detail later in this chapter.

```
/etc/rc.d/init.d/httpd stop
/etc/rc.d/init.d/httpd start
```

Instead of manually executing all the server programs each time you boot your system, you can have your system automatically start the servers for you. You can do this in two ways, depending on how you want to use a server. You can have a server running continuously from the time you start your system until you shut it down, or you can have the server start only when it receives a request from a user for its services. If a server is being used frequently, you may want to have it running all the time. If it is used rarely, you may only want the server to start when it receives a request. For example, if you are running a Web site, your Web server is receiving requests all the time from remote hosts on the Internet. For an FTP site, however, you may receive requests infrequently, in which case you may want to have the FTP server start only when it receives a request. Of course, certain FTP sites receive frequent requests, which would warrant a continuously running FTP server.

A server that starts automatically and runs continuously is referred to as a *standalone* server. Red Hat and Caldera use the SysV Init procedure to start servers automatically whenever your system boots. This procedure uses special startup scripts for the servers located in the **/etc/rc.d/init.d** directory. Most Linux systems configured the Web server to start automatically and to run continuously by default. A script for it called **httpd** is in the **/etc/rc.d/init.d** directory.

To start the server only when a request for its services is received, you configure it using either the **inetd** daemon or **xinetd**. The **inetd** daemon (the term stands for the Internet Services Daemon) is commonly known as the *Internet Superserver.* **xinetd,** the Extended Internet Services Daemon, is meant to be the enhanced replacement for **inetd**. Since many Linux systems still use **inetd**, both are covered here.

If you add, change, or delete server entries in the **/etc/inetd.conf** or **/etc/xinetd** files, you will have to restart the **inetd** or **xinetd** daemons for these changes to take effect. On Red Hat and Caldera, you can restart the **inetd** daemon using the **/etc/rc.d/init.d/inetd** script with the **restart** argument, as shown here (use **/etc/rc.d/init.d/xinetd** for **xinetd**).

```
# /etc/rc.d/init.d/inet restart
```

You can also use the **inet** script to start and stop the **inetd** daemon. Stopping effectively shuts down all the servers that the **inetd** daemon manages (those listed in the **/etc/inetd.conf** file).

```
# /etc/rc.d/init.d/inet stop
# /etc/rc.d/init.d/inet start
```

You can also directly restart the **inetd** by sending its process a SIGHP signal, forcing it to restart. To do this, you use the **kill** command with the **-HUP** option and the process ID of the **inetd** daemon. You can find the process ID using the **ps -aux** command to list all processes and then use **grep** to locate the **inetd** entry as shown here. The process ID will also be held in the /**var/run/inetd.pid** file.

```
# ps -aux | grep inetd
# kill -HUP inetd-process-id
```

Standalone Server Tools

The System V Runlevel Editor, Linuxconf, Webmin, and the KDE System V Editor all provide simple interfaces you can use to choose what servers you want started up and how you want them to run.

The System V Runlevel Editor features a GUI interface to enable you to manage any daemons on your system easily—Internet servers as well as system daemons, such as print servers. The Runlevel Editor window is divided into three major panes. To the left is a scroll window labeled "available" that lists all the daemons available for use on your system. These include the daemons for Internet servers, such as **httpd**. Below are buttons for operations you can perform on the server daemons: add, remove, edit, and execute. To the right, taking up most of the window, are an upper pane and a lower pane. The upper pane has four scroll windows, one for each runlevel. These list the daemons currently configured to run in their respective runlevels. The lower pane also holds four scroll windows, one for each runlevel. These are daemons that will be shut down if you switch to that respective runlevel. System administrators can switch from one level to another. All the servers that start up under normal processing are listed in the start runlevel 3 scroll window.

To start or stop a server manually, click its entry in the available scroll window, and then click the Execute button. This displays a small window with the various options to start or stop the selected server. To stop the **httpd** server, click its entry in the available scroll window, and then click the Stop button in the displayed window. Do the same procedure to restart the server, clicking the Start button. You can also configure a server to start automatically when you boot at a certain runlevel. You can boot your system to operate at certain runlevels, each specified by a given number, such as the standard multiuser level (runlevel 3), a graphical login level (runlevel 5), and an administrative level (runlevel 1). See Chapter 29 for a discussion of runlevels. To have a server start at a given runlevel, select its entry in the available scroll window, and then click the Add button. A window appears where you can select the runlevel and whether you want to start or stop the server. To have a server automatically start up when you boot normally, make sure it is listed in the runlevel 3 start scroll window. If not, click its entry in the available window and select Start and runlevel 3 in the window that is displayed. The server is then added to the list in the runlevel 3 start scroll window. For example, if you don't want your Web server to start when you boot, click the **httpd** entry in the runlevel 3 start list and click the Remove button. To have the Web server start again whenever you boot, click its entry in the available window, and then click the Add button, selecting Start and runlevel 3 in the window that appears. **httpd** is then added to the runlevel 3 start list. Figure 23-1 shows the System V Runlevel Editor with the Execute and Add windows.

Servers that operate under **inetd** are not listed by the System V Runlevel Editor. The FTP wu-ftpd server is usually installed to run under **inetd**, so you won't find

Figure 23-1. *The System V Runlevel Editor with Execute and Add windows*

entries for them here. The System V Editor reads its list of servers from the server scripts in the **/etc/rc.d/init.d** directory. If you add a new script, you can have the System V Editor rescan that directory and then see it appear in the available list. Removing a server from a runlevel window only removes its link in the corresponding runlevel **rc.d** directory. It does not touch the startup script in the **init.d** directory. Adding in the server to the Start runlevel window puts the link back in that runlevel directory. Adding a server to a Stop window adds a *K* link in the corresponding **rc.d** directory, which stops a server when the system switches to that runlevel. For example, if you remove **httpd** from the runlevel 3 start window, then the **S85httpd** link in the **rc3.d** directory is deleted. Adding **httpd** back to the runlevel 3 start window recreates the **S85htppd** link in the **rc3.d** directory. Adding **httpd** to the runlevel 2 stop directory would create a **K85httpd** link in the **rc2.d** directory, shutting down the server when switching to runlevel 2.

You can also control the startup of a server using Linuxconf. The Control service activity panel, located in the Control Panel list, lists various services available on your system (see Figure 23-2). You can click check boxes to enable or disable them. Disabling

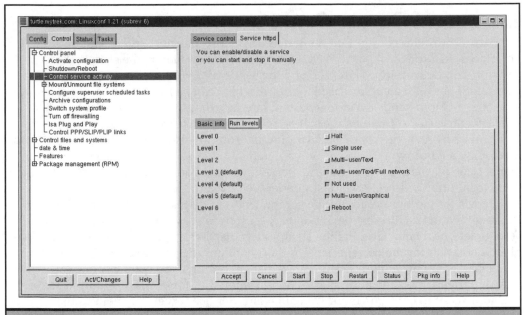

Figure 23-2.   *Linuxconf Control service activity panel*

a service removes its startup link in the **rc.d** directory. For example, disabling the Web server removes the **S85httpd** link in the **rc3.d** directory. Enabling the service restores that link.

With Webmin you can also select which servers to start and stop. The Bootup and Shutdown page, accessed from the System page, lists the daemons and servers that you can have automatically start when the system boots. They are listed as links, which you can click to open an Edit Action page for that daemon or server. On this page you can specify the runlevels to start or stop on. The startup script executed is also listed and you can edit it directly. Click the save button to save your settings.

Note   *If you change the configuration of a server, you may need to start and stop it several times as you refine the configuration. Several servers provide special management tools that enable you to perform this task easily. The **apachectl** utility enables you to start and stop the Apache Web server easily. It is functionally equivalent to using the **/tec/rc.d/init.d/httpd** script to start and stop the server. For the domain name server, the **ndc** utility enables you to start and stop the named server. It is, however, advisable not to mix the use of **init.d** scripts and the management tools.*

SERVERS

Linuxconf Server Configuration

Linuxconf provides configuration interfaces for most Internet servers. Configuration interfaces exist for the Apache Web server, the BIND domain name server, the Washington University FTP server, and the Sendmail mail server, among others. Linuxconf has both a cursor-based interface, which can be run from a shell command line, and a Gnome and X Window System interface that uses an expandable tree to display entries for different panels. If no menu entry exists, you can start a terminal window and enter the command **linuxconf**. You can also use a **netconf** command to display a window with panels only for network and server tasks. Click the server panel to display the list of buttons for servers you can configure. When using the main Linuxconf utility, select Server tasks under Networking.

Panels for various configuration components are displayed with entries for different features. Different panels display buttons for basic operations, such as accept, add, delete, and help. Clicking the Help button displays a window providing detailed documentation for the current panel and the configuration process for that server. Once you make your entries and click the Act/Changes button to accept the configuration, Linuxconf generates the appropriate configuration files for you. For example, if you use Linuxconf to configure your Domain Name Service server, it generates the **named.conf** file and any needed zone files. Configuring the wu-ftpd FTP server generates a new **/etc/ftpaccess** file. Configuring the Apache Web server generates new **httpd.conf**, **srm.conf**, and **access.conf** files. Many servers have an extensive set of features that only need to be turned on or off, rather than given a value. For these, Linuxconf provides check buttons, enabling you to include a feature by clicking its button. The server configurations currently require certain Linuxconf modules to be loaded: Mailconf, dnsconf, apache, and wu-ftpd. Current distributions configure Linuxconf to do this automatically. You can manually add modules by selecting the Linuxconf modules panel in the Control files and systems list and entering the module name. Figure 23-3 shows the panel for the Apache Web server configuration.

SysV Init: init.d Scripts

The startup and shutdown of server daemons is managed using special startup scripts located in the **/etc/rc.d/init.d** directory. These scripts often have the same name as the server's program. For example, for the **/usr/sbin/httpd** Web server program, a corresponding script is called **/etc/rc.d/init.d/httpd**. This script actually starts and stops the Web server. This method of using **init.d** startup scripts to start servers is called *SysV Init*, after the method used in Unix System V.

On Caldera you can use Webmin to create a new startup script by clicking on the "Create a new bootup or shutdown link" on the Bootup and Shutdown page.

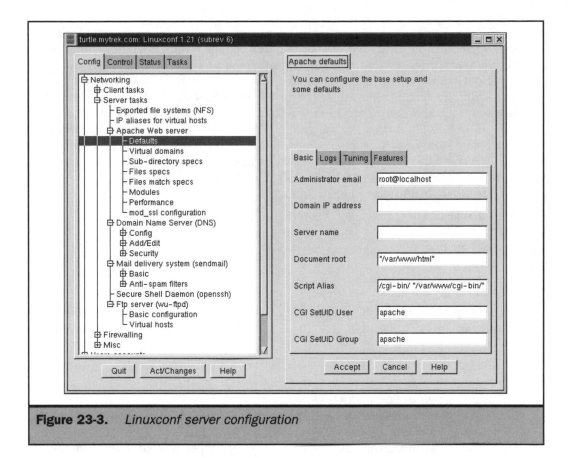

Figure 23-3.   *Linuxconf server configuration*

The startup scripts in the **/etc/rc.d/init.d** directory can be executed automatically whenever you boot your system. Be careful when accessing these scripts, however. These start essential programs, such as your network interface and your printer daemon. These init scripts are accessed from links in subdirectories set up for each possible runlevel. In the **/etc/rc.d** directory is a set of subdirectories whose names have the format **rc***N***.d**, where *N* is a number referring to a runlevel. The **rc** script detects the runlevel in which the system was started, and then executes only the startup scripts specified in the subdirectory for that runlevel. The default runlevel is 3, the multiuser level. When you start your system, the **rc** script executes the startup scripts specified in the **rc3.d** directory. The **rc3.d** directory holds symbolic links to certain startup scripts in the **/etc/rc.d/init.d** directory. So, the **httpd** script in the **/etc/rc.d/init.d** directory is actually called through a symbolic link in the **rc3.d** directory. The symbolic link for the **/etc/rc.d/httpd** script in the **rc3.d** directory is **S85httpd**. The *S* prefixing the link stands for *startup* and calls the corresponding **init.d** script with the start option. **S85httpd** invokes **/etc/rc.d/init.d/httpd** with the option **start**. The numbers in these links are simply there for ordering purposes. If you change the name of the link to start with a *K*, then the script is invoked with the **stop** option, stopping it. To have a server start automatically, first create a startup script for it in the **/etc/rc.d/init.d** directory, and then create a symbolic link to that script in the **/etc/rc.d/rc3.d** directory. The startup script **httpd** used on Red Hat systems is shown here. You can see the different options listed under the case statement: start, stop, status, restart, and reload. If no option is provided (*), then the script use syntax is displayed. The **httpd** script first executes a script to define functions used in these startup scripts. The **daemon** function with **httpd** actually executes the **/usr/sbin/httpd** server program.

```
echo -n "Starting httpd: "
   daemon httpd
   echo
   touch /var/lock/subsys/httpd
```

The **killproc** function shuts down the daemon. The lock file and the process ID file (**httpd.pid**) are then deleted.

```
   killproc httpd
   echo
   rm -f /var/lock/subsys/httpd
   rm -f /var/run/httpd.pid
```

The **daemon, killproc**, and **status** scripts are shell scripts defined in the **functions** script also located in the **inet.d** directory. The **functions** script is executed at the beginning of each startup script to activate these functions. A list of these functions is provided in Table 23-1.

```
. /etc/rc.d/init.d/functions
```

The beginning of the startup script holds tags used to configure the server. These tags, which begin with an initial #, are used to provide runtime information about the service to your system. The tags are listed in Table 23-1 along with the startup functions. You enter a tag with a preceding # symbol, the tag name with a colon, and then the tag arguments. For example, the processname tag will specify the name of the program being executed, in this example **httpd**.

```
# processname: httpd
```

Init Script Functions	Description
daemon [+/-*nicelevel*] *program* [*arguments*] [**&**]	Starts a daemon, if it is not already running.
killproc *program* [*signal*]	Sends a signal to the program; by default it sends a SIGTERM, and if the process doesn't stop, it sends a SIGKILL. It will also remove any PID files, if it can.
pidofproc *program*	Used by another function, it determines the PID of a program.
status *program*	Displays status information.
Init Script Tags	Description
# chkconfig: *startlevellist startpriority endpriority*	Required. Specifies the default start levels for this service as well as start and end priorities.
# description [*ln*]**:** *description of service*	Required. The description of the service, continued with '\' characters. Use an initial # for any added lines. With the *ln* option, you can specify the language the description is written in.
# autoreload: true	Optional. If this line exists, the daemon checks its configuration files and reloads them automatically when they change.
# processname: *program*	Optional, multiple entries allowed. Name of the program or daemon started in the script.
# config: *configuration-file*	Optional, multiple entries allowed. Specify a configuration file used by the server.
# pidfile: *pid-file*	Optional, multiple entries allowed. Specifies the PID file.
# probe: true	Optional, used *in place* of autoreload, processname, config, and pidfile entries to automatically probe and start the service.

Table 23-1.   *System V Init Script Functions and Tags*

SERVERS

If your script starts of more than one daemon, you should have a processname entry for each. For example, the Samba service starts up both the smdb and nmdb daemons.

```
# processname: smdb
# processname: nmdb
```

The end of the tag section is indicated by an empty line. After this line, any lines beginning with a # are treated as comments. The chkconfig line will list the default runlevels that the service should start up on, along with the start and stop priorities. The following entry lists runlevels 3, 4, and 5 with a start priority of 85 and a stop of 15.

```
# chkconfig: 345 85 15
```

With the description you enter a short description of the service, using the \ symbol before a newline to use more than one line. pidfile indicates the file where the server process ID is held. With config tags, you specify the configuration files the server may use. In the case of the Apache Web server, there may be three configuration files.

```
# config: /etc/httpd/conf/access.conf
# config: /etc/httpd/conf/httpd.conf
# config: /etc/httpd/conf/srm.conf
```

As an example, the Web server startup script is shown here. It has the same name as the Web server daemon, **httpd**.

/etc/rc.d/init.d/httpd

```
#!/bin/sh
#
# Startup script for the Apache Web Server
#
# chkconfig: 345 85 15
# description: Apache is a World Wide Web server.  It is used to serve \
#              HTML files and CGI.
# processname: httpd
# pidfile: /var/run/httpd.pid
# config: /etc/httpd/conf/access.conf
# config: /etc/httpd/conf/httpd.conf
# config: /etc/httpd/conf/srm.conf


# Source function library.
. /etc/rc.d/init.d/functions

# See how we were called.
```

```
case "$1" in
  start)
   echo -n "Starting httpd: "
   daemon httpd
   echo
   touch /var/lock/subsys/httpd
   ;;
  stop)
   killproc httpd
   echo
   rm -f /var/lock/subsys/httpd
   rm -f /var/run/httpd.pid
   ;;
  status)
   status httpd
   ;;
  restart)
   $0 stop
   $0 start
   ;;
  reload)
   echo -n "Reloading httpd: "
   killproc httpd -HUP
   echo
   ;;
  *)
   echo "Usage: $0 {start|stop|restart|reload|status}"
   exit 1
esac

exit 0
```

The RPM packaged versions for an Internet server include the startup script for that server. Installing the RPM package installs the script in the **/etc/rc.d/init.d** directory and creates its appropriate links in the runlevel directories, such as **/etc/rc.h/rc3.d**. If you decide, instead, to create the server using its source code files, you can then manually install the startup script. If no startup script exists, you first make a copy of the **httpd** script, renaming it, and then edit the copy to replace all references to **httpd** with the name of the server daemon program. Then, place the copy of the script in the **/etc/rc.d/init.d** directory and make a symbolic link to it the **/etc/rc.d/rc3.d** directory. Or you could use the System V Runlevel Editor to create the link in the **/etc/rc.d/rc3.d** directory. Have the editor scan the **init.d** directory by selecting Re-scan from the File menu, click the entry in the Available listing, click the Add button, and then select the Runlevel and Start options in the Add window. When you start your system now, the new server is automatically started up, running concurrently and waiting for requests.

If you want to change a server from using **inetd** to a standalone process, first create a startup script for it in the **/etc/rc.d/init.d** directory with a link to it in the **rc3.d** directory. Then you have to remove or comment out its entry in the **/etc/inetd.conf** configuration file. To change a server from a standalone process to using **inetd**, you first remove its link in the **/etc/rc.d/rc3.d** directory and any other runlevel directory, and then place an entry for it in the **inetd.conf** file. For example, the ProFTP FTP server can run as a standalone server or an **inetd** (or **xinetd**) server. If it is running as an **inetd** server, and you want to run it as a standalone server, you first set up a Sys V Init script for it in the **/etc/rc.d/init.d** directory (ProFTP provides one). Place a symbolic link for it in the **rc3.d** directory. The name of the standalone ProFTP server program is **proftpd**. Then disable **inetd** management of the ProFTP server by commenting out or removing its entry in the **inetd.conf** file. The server name used in this file is **in .proftpd** (see Chapter 24 for more on ProFTPD and wu-ftpd).

Extended Internet Services Daemon (xinetd)

If your system averages only a few requests for a specific service, you don't need the server for that service running all the time. You only need it when a remote user is accessing its service. The Extended Internet Services Daemon (**xinetd**) manages Internet servers, invoking them only when your system receives a request for their services. **xinetd** checks continuously for any requests by remote users for a particular Internet service; when it receives a request, it then starts the appropriate server daemon.

The **xinetd** program is designed to be a replacement for **inetd** and **tcpd**, providing security enhancements, logging support, and even user notifications. For example, with **xinetd** you can send banner notices to users when they are not able to access a service, telling them why. **xinetd** security capabilities can be used to prevent denial-of-service attacks, limiting remote hosts' simultaneous connections or restricting the rate of incoming connections. Furthermore, you do not have to have a service listed in the **/etc/services** file. **xinetd** can be set up to start any kind of special-purpose server. Many older Linux systems may still be using **inetd**.

The Red Hat Linux version provided with this book now uses **xinetd** instead of **inetd**. You can start and stop **xinetd** using its startup script in the **/etc/rc.d/init.d** directory, as shown here.

```
# /etc/rc.d/init.d/xinetd stop
# /etc/rc.d/init.d/xinetd start
```

The **xinetd.conf** file is the configuration file for **xinetd**. Entries in it define different servers to be activated when requested along with any options and security precautions. An entry consists of a block of attributes defined for different features such as the name of the server program, the protocol used, and security restrictions. Each block for an Internet service such as a server is preceded by the keyword *service* and the name by which you want to identify the service. A pair of braces enclose the block of attributes. Each attribute entry begins with the attribute name followed by an assignment operator such as = and then the value or values assigned. A special block specified by the keyword default contains default attributes for services. The syntax is shown here.

```
service <service_name>
{
<attribute> <assign_op> <value> <value> ...
      . . .
}
```

Most attributes take a single value for which you use the standard assignment operator, =. Some attributes can take a list of values. You can assign values with the = operator, but you can also add or remove items from these lists with the =+ and =− operators. Use the =+ to add values and =− to remove values. You often use the =+ and =− operators to add values to attributes that may have an initial value assigned in the default block.

Attributes are listed in Table 23-2. Certain attributes are required for a service. These include socket_type and wait. socket_type can be *stream* for stream-based service, *dgram* for datagram-based service, *raw* for service that requires direct access, and *seqpacket* service for sequential datagram transmission. The wait attribute can have a yes or no value to specify if the server is single-threaded (yes) or multithreaded (no). If yes, then **xinetd** will wait, calling the server initially and letting that server handle further requests until the server stops. If the value is no (multithreaded), the **xinetd** will continue to handle new requests for the server, generating new server processes to handle them. For a standard Internet service, you would also need to provide the user (user ID for the service), the server (name of the server program), and the protocol (protocol used by the server). With server_arguments, you can also list any arguments you want passed to the server program (this does not include the server name as with **tcpd**). If protocol is not defined, then the default protocol for the service is used.

```
service ftp
{
      socket_type        = stream
      wait               = no
      user               = root
      protocol           = ftp
      server             = /usr/sbin/in.ftpd
      server_args        = -l -a
}
```

You can further add a variety of other attributes such as logging information about connections and server priority (nice). In the following example, the log_on_success attribute will log the duration (DURATION) and the user ID (USERID) for connections to a service, log_on_failure will log the users that failed to connect, and nice will set the priority of the service to 10.

```
log_on_success      += DURATION USERID
log_on_failure      += USERID
nice                = 10
```

The default attributes defined in the defaults block often set global attributes such as default logging activity and security restrictions. log_type specifies where logging information is to be sent, such to a specific file (FILE) or to the system logger (SYSLOG). log_on_success will specify information to be logged when connections are made, and log_on_failure, when they fail.

```
log_type                = SYSLOG authpriv
log_on_success          = HOST PID
log_on_failure          = HOST RECORD
```

For security restrictions, you can use only_from to restrict access by certain remote hosts. no_access denies access by the listed hosts, but no others. These controls take as their values IP addresses. You can list individual IP addresses, or a range of IP addresses, or a network using the network address. The instances attributes will limit the number of server processes that can be active at once for a particular service. The following examples restrict access to a local network 192.168.1.0 and the localhost, deny access from 192.168.1.15, and use the instances attribute to limit the number of server processes at one time to 60.

```
only_from       = 192.168.1.0
only_from       = localhost
no_access       = 192.168.1.15
instances       = 60
```

A sample default block is shown here.

```
defaults
{
    instances       = 60
    log_type        = FILE /var/log/servicelog
    log_on_success = HOST PID
    log_on_failure = HOST RECORD
    only_from       = 192.168.1.0
    only_from       = localhost
    no_access       = 192.168.1.15
}
```

The **xinetd** program also provides several internal services including time, services, servers, and xadmin. The services service provides a list of currently active services, and servers provides information about servers. xadmin provides **xinetd** administrative support.

Several recent Linux distribution releases, such as Red Hat 7.0, now include **xinetd**. Other systems may still be using **inetd**. A sample **xinetd.conf** file shown here is based on the Red Hat version.

xinetd.conf

```
# Simple configuration file for xinetd

defaults
{
            instances               = 60
            log_type                = SYSLOG authpriv
            log_on_success          = HOST PID
            log_on_failure          = HOST RECORD
}

# default: off
# description: The Linuxconf system can also be accessed\
# via a web browser.  Enabling this service will \
# allow connections to Linuxconf running in web UI mode.
# Set disable to no to enable.
service linuxconf
{
    socket_type = stream
    wait        = yes
    user        = root
    server      = /sbin/linuxconf
    server_args = —http
    disable     = yes
}

# default: on
# description: rlogind is the server for the rlogin(1) program.  The server \
#provides a remote login facility with authentication based on \
#privileged port numbers from trusted hosts.
service login
{
    socket_type         = stream
    wait                = no
    user                = root
    log_on_success          += USERID
    log_on_failure          += USERID
    server                  = /usr/sbin/in.rlogind
}

# default: off
# description: SWAT is the Samba Web Admin Tool. Use swat \
#to configure your Samba server. To use SWAT, \
#connect to port 901 with your favorite web browser.
```

```
#Set disable to no to enable.
service swat
{
      port = 901
      socket_type      = stream
      wait = no
      only_from = localhost
      user = root
      server      = /usr/sbin/swat
      log_on_failure   += USERID
      disable = yes
}

# default: on
# description: The telnet server serves telnet sessions; it uses \
#unencrypted username/password pairs for authentication.
service telnet
{
      flags         = REUSE
      socket_type = stream
      wait          = no
      user          = root
      server              = /usr/sbin/in.telnetd
      log_on_failure   += USERID
}

# default: on
# description: The wu-ftpd FTP server serves FTP connections. It uses \
#normal, unencrypted usernames and passwords for authentication.
service ftp
{
      socket_type       = stream
      wait              = no
      user              = root
      server            = /usr/sbin/in.ftpd
      server_args       = -l -a
      log_on_success   += DURATION USERID
      log_on_failure   += USERID
      nice              = 10
}
```

Instead of having one large **xinetd.conf** file, you can split it into several configuration
files, one for each service. You do this by creating an **xinetd.conf** file with an includedir
attribute that specifies a directory to hold the different service configuration files. In the
following example, the **xinetd.d** directory will hold **xinetd** configuration files for
services like wu-ftpd. Red Hat 7.0 uses just such an implementation. This approach has
the advantage of letting you add services by just creating a new configuration file for it.
Modifying a service only involves editing its configuration file, not an entire
xinetd.conf file.

```
includedir /etc/xinetd.d
```

Attributes	Description
id	Identifies a service. By default, the service ID is the same as the service name.
type	Type of service: RPC, INTERNAL (provided by **xinetd**), UNLISTED (not listed in a standard system file).
flags	Possible flags include REUSE, INTERCEPT, NORETRY, IDONLY, NAMEINARGS (allows use of **tcpd**), NODELAY, DISABLE (disable the service). See the **xinetd.conf** man page for more details.
disable	Specify "yes" to disable the service.
socket_type	Specify stream for a stream-based service, dgram for a datagram-based service, raw for a service that requires direct access to IP, and the seqpacket service for reliable sequential datagram transmission.
protocol	Specify a protocol for the service. The protocol must exist in **/etc/protocols**. If this attribute is not defined, the default protocol employed by the service will be used.
wait	Specifies whether the service is single-threaded or multithreaded (yes or no). If yes the service is single-threaded, which means that **xinetd** will start the server and then stop handling requests for the service until the server stops. If no, the service is multithreaded and **xinetd** will continue to handle new requests for it.
user	Specifies the user ID (UID) for the server process. The user name must exist in **/etc/passwd**.
group	Specify the GID for the server process. The group name must exist in **/etc/group**.
instances	Specifies the number of server processes that can be simultaneously active for a service.

Table 23-2. *xinetd Attributes*

SERVERS

nice	Specifies the server priority.
server	Specifies the program to execute for this service.
server_args	Lists the arguments passed to the server. This does not include the server name.
only_from	Controls the remote hosts to which the particular service is available. Its value is a list of IP addresses. With no value, service is denied to all.
no_access	Controls the remote hosts to which the particular service is unavailable.
access_times	Specifies the time intervals when the service is available. An interval has the form hour:min-hour:min.
log_type	Specifies where the output of the service log is sent, either syslog facility (SYSLOG) or a file (FILE).
log_on_success	Specifies the information that is logged when a server starts and stops. Information you can specify includes: PID (server process ID), HOST (the remote host address), USERID (the remote user), EXIT (exit status and termination signal), DURATION (duration of a service session).
log_on_failure	Specifies the information that is logged when a server cannot be started. Information you can specify includes: HOST (the remote host address), USERID (user ID of the remote user), ATTEMPT (logs a failed attempt), RECORD (records information from the remote host to allow monitoring of attempts to access the server).
rpc_version	Specifies the RPC version for a RPC service.
rpc_number	Specifies the number for an UNLISTED RPC service.
env	Defines environment variables for a service.

Table 23-2.   *xinetd Attributes* (continued)

passenv	The list of environment variables from **xinetd**'s environment that will be passed to the server.
port	Specifies the service port.
redirect	Allows a TCP service to be redirected to another host.
bind	Allows a service to be bound to a specific interface on the machine.
interface	Synonym for bind.
banner	The name of a file to be displayed for a remote host when a connection to that service is established.
banner_success	The name of a file to be displayed at the remote host when a connection to that service is granted.
banner_fail	Takes the name of a file to be displayed at the remote host when a connection to that service is denied.
groups	Allow access to groups the service has access to (yes or no).
enabled	Specify the list of service names to enable.
include	Inserts the contents of a specified file as part of the configuration file.
includedir	Takes a directory name in the form of "includedir /etc/xinetd.d". Every file inside that directory will be read sequentially as an **xinetd** configuration file, combining to form the **xinetd** configuration.

Table 23-2.   *xinetd Attributes* (continued)

inetd Server Management

If your system averages only a few requests for a specific service, you don't need the server for that service running all the time. You only need it when a remote user is accessing its service. The **inetd** daemon manages Internet servers, invoking them only when your system receives a request for their services. **inetd** checks continuously for any requests by remote users for a particular Internet service; when it receives a request, it then starts the appropriate server daemon. For example, the Washington University FTP daemon, wu-ftpd, is usually installed to run using **inetd**, rather than as a standalone daemon. When **inetd** receives a request from a user to access FTP, it starts **in.ftpd**, the FTP daemon. **in.ftpd** then handles the request, enabling the remote user to download files.

For **inetd** to call the appropriate server daemon, it must be configured for that service. You place entries for that server in the **/etc/services** and **/etc/inetd.conf** files. The **/etc/services** file lists services available on your system. An entry in **/etc/services** consists of the name of the service followed by its port and protocol, separated by a slash. Entries for FTP as they appear in your **/etc/service** file are shown here. Other distributions may require only one entry for FTP.

```
ftp-data     20/tcp
ftp          21/tcp
```

Note *With Webmin, you can add and edit services for inetd. Select the Internet Services page, accessible from the Servers page. This page will list available services that you can run on inetd. Services that are listed in boldface are enabled. To enable or disable a service, click on its entry to display an Edit Internet Services page where you can select the Program enabled button. Then save the settings and return to the Internet Services page. You must then click Apply Changes to restart the inetd daemon.*

The **/etc/inetd.conf** file is the **inetd** configuration file. For its entries, you specify the service, its protocol, and the server program to invoke. An entry for FTP is shown here. Server paths and arguments may vary according to different Linux distributions. Some programs have a special script, link, or alternate program to use for **inet.d** activation, instead of directly using the program file. Such scripts or links begin with the prefix "in" and a period, followed by the program name. For example, the ProFTP server is called **proftpd**, but uses the **in.proftpd** as the program name in an **inetd.conf** entry. Other programs, such as the Apache Web server, use the same program name—in this case, **httpd**.

```
#<service> <sock_type> <proto> <flags> <user> <server_path>     <args>
ftp        stream      tcp      nowait  root  /usr/sbin/in.ftpd in.ftpd
```

For some services, the configuration lines may exist, but they may be commented out with a preceding # symbol. Remove the #. If no configuration entries exist, you need to add them. The standard entries in **inetd.conf** for Internet services are shown here:

```
# These are standard services.
#
ftp       stream   tcp   nowait   root   /usr/sbin/in.ftpd   in.ftpd -l -a
```

```
telnet    stream    tcp    nowait    root    /usr/sbin/in.telnetd    in.telnetd
gopher    stream    tcp    nowait    root    /usr/sbin/in.gn    gn
```

TCP Wrappers:tcpd

You can use the **tcpd** daemon to add another level of security to **inetd**-managed servers. In effect, the **tcpd** daemon will wrap a server with an intervening level of security, monitoring connections and controlling access. Such envelopment of a server is known as a *TCP wrapper*. **tcpd** will monitor a server connection made through **inetd**, verifying remote user identities and checking to make sure they are making valid requests. Connections are logged with the **syslogd** daemon (Chapter 29) and may be found in **syslogd** files such as **/var/log/secure**. With **tcpd**, you can also restrict access to your system by remote hosts. Lists of hosts are kept in the **hosts.allow** and **hosts.deny** files. Entries in these files have the format **service:hostname:domain**. The domain is optional. For the service, you can specify a particular service, such as FTP, or you can enter **ALL** for all services. For the hostname, you can specify a particular host or use a wildcard to match several hosts. For example, **ALL** will match on all hosts. Table 23-3 lists the available wildcards you can use. In the following example, the first entry allows access by all hosts to the Web service, **http**. The second entry allows access to all services by the **pango1.train.com** host. The third and fourth entries allow **rabbit.trek.com** and **sparrow.com** FTP access.

```
http:ALL
ALL:pango1.train.com
ftp:rabbit.trek.com
ftp:sparrow.com
```

The **hosts.allow** file holds hosts to which you allow access. If you want to allow access to all but a few specific hosts, you can specify **ALL** for a service in the **hosts.allow** file, but list the one you are denying access in the **hosts.deny** file. Using IP addresses instead of hostnames is more secure because hostnames can be compromised through the DNS records by spoofing attacks where an attacker pretends to be another host. The **tcpd** Man pages (**man tcpd**) provide more detailed information about **tcpd**.

To have **tcpd** monitor a server, you have to place the pathname for **tcpd** in the pathname field of a server's entry for the **inetd.conf** file. This is what has already been done for the **ftpd** server entry in the Red Hat **inetd.conf** file. Instead of the pathname for the **ftpd** program, **/usr/sbin/in.ftpd**, there is the pathname for the **tcpd** daemon, **/usr/sbin/tcpd**. The argument field that follows then lists the **in.ftpd** server program.

```
# <service> <sock_type> <proto> <flags> <user>  <server_path>    <args>
ftp          stream      tcp     nowait  root    /usr/sbin/tcpd   in.ftpd
```

Wildcard	Description
ALL	Matches all hosts
LOCAL	Matches any host specified with just a host name without a domain name. Used to match on hosts in the local domain.
UNKNOWN	Matches any user or host whose name or address is unknown.
KNOWN	Matches any user or host whose name or address is known.
PARANOID	Matches any host whose host name does not match its IP address.
EXCEPT	An operator that lets you provide exceptions to matches. It take the form of *list1* EXCEPT *list2* where those hosts matched in *list1* that are also matched in *list2* are excluded.

Table 23-3. *TCP Wrapper Wildcards*

When **inetd** receives a request for an FTP service, it calls the **tcpd** daemon, which then takes over and monitors the connection. Then it starts up the **in.ftpd** server program. By default, **tcpd** allows all requests. To allow all requests specifically for the FTP service, you would enter the following in your **/etc/hosts.allow** file. The entry **ALL:ALL** opens your system to all hosts for all services.

```
ftp:ALL
```

The standard Internet services listed in the **/etc/initd.conf** file all use the **tcpd** daemon, as shown here.

```
# These are standard services.
#
ftp      stream   tcp   nowait   root   /usr/sbin/tcpd   in.ftpd -l -a
telnet   stream   tcp   nowait   root   /usr/sbin/tcpd   in.telnetd
```

The Complete Reference

Chapter 24

FTP Servers

The *File Transfer Protocol* (*FTP*) is designed to transfer large files across a network from one system to another. Like most Internet operations, FTP works on a client/server model. FTP client programs can enable users to transfer files to and from a remote system running an FTP server program. Chapter 16 discusses FTP clients. Any Linux systems can operate as an FTP server. It only has to run the server software—an FTP daemon with the appropriate configuration. Transfers are made between user accounts on client and server systems. A user on the remote system has to log in to an account on a server and can then transfer files to and from that account's directories only. A special kind of user account, named *ftp*, allows any user to log in to it with the user name "anonymous." This account has its own set of directories and files that are considered public, available to anyone on the network who wants to download them. The numerous FTP sites on the Internet are FTP servers supporting FTP user accounts with anonymous login. Any Linux system can be configured to support anonymous FTP access, turning them into network FTP sites. Such sites can work on an intranet or on the Internet.

Note *On Red Hat and Caldera systems, the configuration files for anonymous FTP are in packages beginning with the term **anonftp**. Installing this package sets up your FTP directories and configures the FTP account.*

FTP Daemons

FTP server software consists of an FTP daemon and configuration files. The *daemon* is a program that continuously checks for FTP requests from remote users. When a request is received, it manages a login, sets up the connection to the requested user account, and executes any ftp commands the remote user sends. For anonymous FTP access, the FTP daemon allows the remote user to log in to the FTP account using anonymous or ftp as the user name. The user then has access to the directories and files set up for the FTP account. As a further security measure, however, the daemon changes the root directory for that session to be the FTP home directory. This hides the rest of the system from the remote user. Normally, any user on a system can move around to any directories open to him or her. A user logging in with anonymous FTP can only see the FTP home directory and its subdirectories. The remainder of the system is hidden from that user. This effect is achieved by the chroot operation (discussed later) that literally changes the system root directory for that user to that of the FTP directory. By default, the FTP server also requires a user be using a valid shell. It checks for a list of valid shells in the **/etc/shells** file. Most daemons have options for turning off this feature.

Several FTP server daemons are available for use on Linux systems. Most Linux distributions come with the Washington University FTP server called *wu-ftpd*. You can download RPM package updates for particular distributions from their FTP sites, such as **ftp.redhat.com**. The software package usually begins with the term **wu-ftpd**. You can obtain the original compressed archive from the Washington University archive at **http://wuarchive.wustl.edu/packages/wuarchive-ftpd**.

ProFTPD is a newer and popular FTP daemon based on an Apache Web server design. It features simplified configuration and support for virtual FTP hosts. Although not currently included with most distributions, you can download RPM packages from both Red Hat and Caldera. Check the **contrib** directories. The package begins with the term **proftpd**. The compressed archive of the most up-to-date version, along with documentation, is available at the ProFTPD Web site at **www.proftpd.net**. Another FTP daemon, **ncftpd**, is a commercial product produced by the same programmers who did the ncftp FTP client. ncftpd is free for academic use and features a reduced fee for small networks. Check **www.ncftpd.org** for more information.

Most distributions currently install the wu-ftpd server and the **anon** anonymous FTP package during installation. At that time, an **ftp** directory along with several subdirectories are created where you can place files for FTP access. The directories have already been configured to control access by remote users, restricting use to only the **ftp** directories and any subdirectories. The **ftp** directory is placed in different directories by different distributions. On Caldera OpenLinux, the **ftp** directory is placed in the **/home** directory, **/home/ftp**, whereas on Red Hat, the **ftp** directory is placed in the **/var** directory, **/var/ftp**. Place the files you want to allow access to in the **ftp/pub** directory. For example, on Red Hat this would be at **/var/ftp/pub**. You can also create subdirectories and place files there. Once connected to a network, a remote user can connect to your system and download files you placed in **ftp/pub** or any of its subdirectories. The **anon** FTP package implements a default configuration for those directories and their files. You can change these if you want. If you are installing an FTP server yourself, you need to know the procedures detailed in the following sections to install an FTP server and create its data directories.

The **anon** FTP package does not create a directory where users can upload files to the FTP site. Such a directory is usually named the incoming directory located at **ftp/pub/incoming**. If you want such as directory, you will have to create it, make it part of the **ftp** group, and then set its permissions to allow user's write access.

```
chgrp ftp /var/ftp/pub/incoming
chmod g+w /var/ftp/pub/incoming
```

Anonymous FTP: anon

An anonymous FTP site is essentially a special kind of user on your system with publicly accessible directories and files in its home directory. Anyone can log in to this account and access its files. Because anyone can log in to an anonymous FTP account, you must be careful to restrict a remote FTP user to only the files on that anonymous FTP directory. Normally, a user's files are interconnected to the entire file structure of your system. Normal users have write access that lets them create or delete files and directories. The anonymous FTP files and directories can be configured in such a way that the rest of the file system is hidden from them and remote users are given only read access. In ProFTPD, this is achieved through configuration directives placed in its configuration file. An older approach used by wu-ftpd and implemented by the **anon** package involves having copies of certain system configuration, command, and libraries files placed within subdirectories of the FTP home directory. Restrictions placed on those sudirectories then control access by other users. Within the FTP home directory, you then have a publicly accessible directory that holds the files you want to make available to remote users. This directory usually has the name **pub**, for public.

An FTP site is made up of an FTP user account, an FTP home directory, and certain copies of system directories containing selected configuration and support files. Newer FTP daemons, such as ProFTPD, do not need the system directories and support files. Most distributions, including Red Hat, have already set up an FTP user account when you installed your system. On systems that support RPM package installation, such as Red Hat and Caldera, you can use the **anon** RPM package to set up the home directory and the copies of the system directories. If you do not have access to the **anon** package, you may have to create these system directories yourself.

The FTP User Account: anonymous

To allow anonymous FTP access by other users to your system, you must have a user account named *FTP*. Most distributions, such as Caldera, have already created this account for you. If your system does not have such an account, you will have to create one. You can then place restrictions on the FTP account to keep any remote FTP users from accessing any other part of your system. You must also modify the entry for this account in your **/etc/passwd** file to prevent normal user access to it. The following is the entry you find in your **/etc/passwd** file on Red Hat systems that sets up an FTP login as an anonymous user:

```
ftp:*:14:50:FTP User:/var/ftp:
```

The asterisk in the password field blocks the account, which prevents any other users from gaining access to it, thereby, gaining control over its files or access to other parts of your system. The user ID, 14, is a unique ID. The comment field is FTP User. The login directory is **/var/ftp**. When FTP users log in to your system, this is the directory in which they are placed. If a home directory has not been set up, create one and then change its ownership to the FTP user with the chown command.

The group ID is the ID of the **ftp** group, which is set up only for anonymous FTP users. You can set up restrictions on the **ftp** group, thereby restricting any anonymous FTP users. Here is the entry for the **ftp** group you find in the **/etc/group** file. If your system does not have one, you should add it.

```
ftp::50:
```

Anonymous FTP Server Directories

As previously noted, on most distributions, the FTP home directory is named **ftp** and is usually placed in either the **/home** or **/var** directory. When users log in anonymously, they are placed in this directory. An important part of protecting your system is preventing remote users from using any commands or programs not in the restricted directories. For example, you would not let a user use your ls command to list filenames because ls is located in your **/bin** directory. At the same time, you want to let the FTP user list filenames using an ls command. Newer FTP daemons like ProFTPD solve this problem by creating secure access to needed system commands and files, while restricting remote users to only the FTP site's directories. Another more traditional solution, used by wu-ftpd, is to create copies of certain system directories and files needed by remote users and to place them in the **ftp** directory where users can access them. A **bin** directory is placed in the **ftp** directory and remote users are restricted to it, instead of the system's **bin** directory. Whenever they use the ls command, remote users are using the one in **ftp/bin**, not the one you use in **/bin**.

On systems that support RPM installation, such as Red Hat and Caldera, you can use the **anon** RPM package to set up these copies of system directories and files. Otherwise, you may have to create these directories and support files yourself. On Red Hat, the **anon** package installs **etc**, **bin**, and **lib** directories in the **/var/ftp** directory. These contain localized versions of system files needed to let an FTP client execute certain ftp commands, such as listing files or changing directories. The **ftp/etc** directory contains versions of the password and group configuration files, the **ftp/bin** directory contains copies of shell and compression commands, and the **ftp/lib** directory holds copies of system libraries. The directories set up by the **anon** package are shown here:

```
ftp
ftp/bin
ftp/etc
ftp/lib
ftp/pub
```

The **ftp/etc** directory holds a version of your **passwd** and **group** files specially configured for FTP access. Again, the idea is to prevent any access to the original files in the **/etc** directory by FTP users. The **ftp/etc/passwd** file should not include any entries for regular users on your system. All entries should have their passwords set to * to block access. The **group** file should not include any user groups and all passwords should be set to *.

ftp/etc/passwd
```
root:*:0:0:::
bin:*:1:1:::
```

```
operator:*:11:0:::
ftp:*:14:50:::
nobody:*:99:99:::
```

ftp/etc/group
```
root::0:
bin::1:
daemon::2:
sys::3:
adm::4:
ftp::50:
```

If, for some reason, you do not have access to the **anon** package, you can set up the anonymous FTP directories yourself. Again, remember, if you are using ProFTPD, you do not need any of these files, except for an FTP home directory. You must use the chmod command to change the access permissions for the directories so remote users cannot access the rest of your system. Create an **ftp** directory and use the chmod command with the permission 555 to turn off write access: **chmod 555 ftp**. Next, make a new **bin** directory in the **ftp** directory, and then make a copy of the ls command and place it in **ftp/bin**. Do this for any commands you want to make available to FTP users. Then create a **ftp/etc** directory to hold a copy of your **passwd** and **group** files. Again, the idea is to prevent any access to the original files in the **/etc** directory by FTP users. The **ftp/etc/passwd** file should be edited to remove any entries for regular users on your system. All other entries should have their passwords set to * to block access. For the **group** file, remove all user groups and set all passwords to *. Create an **ftp/lib** directory, and then make copies of the libraries you need to run the commands you placed in the **bin** directory. Some libraries make use of the **/dev/zero** file. For these, you have to create a **ftp/dev** directory and use **mknod** to make a copy of the **/dev/zero** device file and place it in this directory.

Anonymous FTP Files

A directory named **pub** located in the FTP home directory usually holds the files you are making available for downloading by remote FTP users. When FTP users log in, they are placed in the FTP home directory, such as **/var/ftp** on Red Hat, and they can then change to the **pub** directory to start accessing those files (**/var/ftp/pub** on Red Hat). Within the **pub** directory, you can add as many files and directories as you want. You can even designate some directories as upload directories, enabling FTP users to transfer files to your system.

Note *In each subdirectory set up under the **pub** directory to hold FTP files, you should create a **readme** file and an **index** file as a courtesy to FTP users. The **readme** file contains a brief description of the kind of files held in this directory. The **index** file contains a listing of the files and a description of what each one holds.*

Permissions

Technically, any remote FTP user gaining access to your system is considered a user and, unless restricted, could access other parts of your file system, create directories and files, or delete the ones already there. Permissions can be used to restrict remote users to simple read access, and the rest of your file system can be hidden from the FTP directories. The **anon** package and the ProFTPD daemon already implement these restrictions. If you are manually creating your anonymous FTP files, you must be sure to set the permission correctly to restrict access.

Normally, a Linux file structure interconnects all the directories and files on its system. Except where prevented by permissions set on a directory or file, any user can access any directory or file on your system. Technically, any remote FTP user gaining anonymous access is an anonymous user and, as a user, could theoretically access an unrestricted directory or file on your system. To restrict FTP users to the FTP home directory, such as **ftp**, and its subdirectories, the rest of the file structure must be hidden from them. In effect, the FTP home directory should appear to be the root directory as far as FTP users are concerned. On Red Hat, the FTP home directory **ftp** would appear to the remote FTP user as the root directory. The real root directory, /, and the rest of the directory structure remain hidden. The FTP daemon attains this effect by using the chroot command to make the FTP home directory appear as a root directory, with the FTP user as the argument. When a remote FTP user issues a cd / command to change to the root, they always change to the FTP home directory, not the system's root directory. For example, on Red Hat, the cd / command would change to **ftp**.

As a further restriction, all the directories that hold commands in the FTP home directory, as well as the commands themselves, should be owned by the root, not by the FTP user. In other words, no FTP user should have any control over these directories. The root has to own the FTP home directory's **bin** and **etc** subdirectories and all the files they contain (**/var/ftp/bin** and **/var/ftp/etc** on Red Hat). The **anon** package already has set the ownership of these directories to the root. If you need to set them manually, you can use the chown command. The following example changes the ownership of the **/var/ftp/bin** directory to the root:

```
# chown root  /home/ftp/bin
```

Permissions for the FTP directories should be set to allow access for FTP users. You recall that three sets of permissions exist—read, write, and execute for the owner, the group, and others. To allow access by FTP users, the group and other permissions for directories should be set to both read and execute. The execute permission allows FTP users to access that directory, and the read permission allows listing the contents of the directory. Directories should not allow write permission by FTP users. You don't want them to be able to delete your directories or make new ones. For example, the FTP **bin** directory needs both read and execute permissions because FTP users have to access and execute its commands. This is particularly true for directories, such as **pub**, which hold the files for downloading. It must have both read and execute permissions set.

You, as the owner of the directories, may need write permission to add new files or subdirectories. Of course, you only need this when you are making changes. To add further security, you could set these directories at just read and execute, even for the owner when you are not making changes. You can set all permissions to read and execute with the chmod command and the number 555 followed by the directory name. This sets the owner, group, and other permissions to read and execute. The permissions currently in place for the FTP directories set up by the **anon** package are designated by the number 755, giving the owner write permission.

```
# chmod 555 /var/ftp/bin
```

Permissions for files within the FTP **bin** directory and other special FTP directories can be more restrictive. Some files only need to be read, while others must be execute. Files in the FTP **bin** or **lib** directories only have to be execute. These could have their permissions set to 555. Files in the FTP **etc** directory such as **passwd** and **group** should have their permissions set to 111. They only have to be read. You always use the chmod command to set permissions for files, as shown in the following example. The **anon** package sets these permissions at read and execute, 555. For other distributions, you may have to set them yourself.

```
# chmod 111 /var/ftp/etc/passwd
```

FTP Server Tools

Both the wu-ftpd and ProFTPD daemons provide a set of FTP tools you can use to manage your FTP server. With the ftpshut command, you can smoothly shut down a running server, warning users of the shutdown well before it happens. ftpwho can tell you who is currently connected and what they are doing. ftpcount can give you the number of connections currently in effect. Although each daemon has its own set of tools, they perform the same action with much the same set of options. Tools provided by both ProFTPD and wu-ftpd have the same name and options, though ProFTPD provides more information on virtual hosts and has some added options.

ftpshut

With the ftpshut command, you can have the FTP server shut down at a given time, rather than suddenly shutting it down by killing its process. This gives you the chance to warn users the server is shutting down and not to start any long downloads. ftpshut takes several options for specifying the time and including a warning message. ftpshut takes as its arguments the time until the shutdown, followed by the warning message you want sent to users. The time can be a word such as "now" that effects an immediate shutdown, a + sign with the number of minutes remaining, or a specific time of day indicated by an HHMM format, where HH is the hour in a 24-hour cycle and MM is the minute. The following example shuts down the FTP server in ten minutes, issuing a warning to users:

```
ftpshut +10  "Shutdown in ten minutes"
```

Shutdown disables new FTP access ten minutes before a scheduled shutdown, though this can be changed using the -l option with the number of minutes you want. Five minutes before a scheduled shutdown, all current connections are disconnected. You can adjust the time with the -d options. The warning message is formatted at 75 characters and you can use special formatting symbols for in-place substitutions of certain values in the warning message, such as the shutdown time. These symbols are called *magic cookies.* For example, %s is the shutdown time, **%r** is the time when new connections are refused, **%d** is the time when current connections are cut, **%M** is the maximum number of users, and **%L** is the local hostname.

ftpwho and ftpcount

With the ftpwho command, you can find out who is currently connected to your FTP server. ftpwho shows the current process information for each user. The output displays five fields: the process ID, the tty connection, the status of the connection, the amount of CPU time used so far for the process, and the connection details. The status of the connection is *R* for running, *S* for sleeping, and *Z* for crashed. The connection details include the Internet address from where the connection is made, the user making the connection, and the task currently being performed, such as downloading a file. The field begins with the name of the FTP daemon, usually **ftpd**, followed by the different segments separated by colons.

ftpcount displays the number of users connected to your FTP server, broken down according to the classes specified in your **.ftpaccess** file. Along with the number of users, it shows the maximum number allowed to connect.

The Washington University FTP daemon: wu-ftpd

The Washington University FTP daemon is currently the most widely used FTP server on Linux systems. It is the FTP server installed by most Linux distributions. The name of the Washington University FTP daemon is wu-ftpd. The wu-ftpd options are shown in Table 24-1. wu-ftpd must be running to allow FTP access by remote users. As with other servers, you can start the FTP server at boot time, through **inetd** when a request is received, or directly from the command line. By default, the wu-ftpd server is installed to run using inetd. The use of inetd for the servers is described in detail in the previous chapter. The command name for the FTP server invoked by inetd is **in.ftpd**. This is a link to the wu-ftpd command. If you want to run your server continually (like a Web server), you have to configure it to start up initially with your system. On Red Hat and Caldera, this means creating an **init** script for it in the **/etc/rc.d/init.d** directory, so it starts when you boot your system. You can also start the FTP server directly from the command line by entering the wu-ftpd command with any options or arguments. The wu-ftpd server can be called with several options. Usually, it is called with the -l option that allows logins. The -t and -T options set timeouts for users, cutting off those that have no activity after a certain period of time. The -d option displays debugging information, and -u sets the umask value for uploaded files.

Option	Effect
`-d`	Writes debugging information to the **syslog**
`-l`	Logs each FTP session in the **syslog**
`-t`*seconds*	Sets the inactivity timeout period to specified seconds (default is 15 minutes)
`-T`*seconds*	The maximum timeout period allowed when timeout is set by user (default is two hours)
`-a`	Enables use of the **ftpaccess** configuration file
`-A`	Disables use of the **ftpaccess** configuration file
`-L`	Logs commands sent to the **ftpd** server to the **syslog**
`-xi`	Logs files received by **ftpd** to xferlog
`-o`	Logs files transmitted by **ftpd** to the **syslog**

Table 24-1.   *wu-ftpd Options*

Configuring the wu-ftpd Server with Linuxconf

Linuxconf includes an FTP configuration module for the wu-ftpd server. To configure the server, open the FTP server entry in the Server Tasks list under Networking in the Config panel (see Figure 24-1). For the Basic configuration entry, you will find two panels, one for Misc and one for Control. The Control panel has four subpanels, one of which, Anonymous, you use to set permissions for anonymous FTP users. You can also set permissions for Real users and Guests. The Misc panel lets you enter basic information such as the e-mail address of the administrator and the shutdown message to use. The Virtual hosts entry lets you create simple virtual FTP hosts on your server.

Note *You can also use Webin to configure the wu-ftpd server with pages for access, login, messages, among others.*

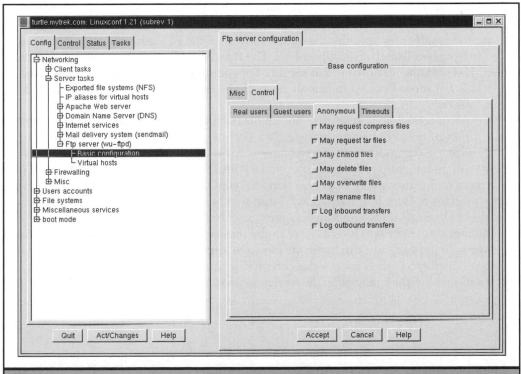

Figure 24-1. *Linuxconf configuration of the wu-ftpd FTP server*

SERVERS

wu-ftpd Server Configuration Files

You can use numerous configuration options to tailor your FTP server to your site's particular needs. wu-ftpd makes use of several configuration files located in the system's **/etc** directory. All begin with the pattern **ftp**. The primary configuration file is named **ftpaccess**. Here, you provide basic server information and access for specified directories. The **ftphosts**, **ftpusers**, and **ftpgroups** control access by systems, particular users, and groups. **ftpconversions** specifies how archive and compression operations are to be performed on files before or after they are transferred. **xferlog** is the log file that stores a running log of all transactions performed by the server. You can also configure your wu-ftpd server using Linuxconf.

ftpaccess

The **ftpaccess** file determines capabilities users have after they gain access to your FTP site. Access, information, permissions, logging, and several miscellaneous capabilities can be designated. You can have entries that create aliases for certain directories, display a message when FTP users login, or prevent anonymous users from deleting files. A **loginfails** entry determines the number of login tries a user can make before being cut off, and the **email** entry specifies the e-mail address of the FTP administrator. The Man page for **ftpaccess** lists the possible entries. The **ftpaccess** file with the configuration used on Red Hat systems is shown in this section. For commonly used **ftpaccess** entries, see Table 24-2. For more detailed information, check the **ftpaccess** Man page and wu-ftpd documentation.

In the **ftpaccess** file, you set capabilities for different types of users, called *classes*. Three different types of users exist: anonymous, guest, and real. *Anonymous users* are any users using the anonymous login name. *Guest users* are those given special guest access with **guestgroup** or **guestuser** options. A *real user* is one who has an account on the system and is using an FTP connection to access it. You can define your own class using the **class** option. In the **ftpaccess** file shown here, a class called **all** is created that consists of all users of the anonymous, guest, and real types.

The message entry specifies a file with the message to be displayed and when that message is to appear. You can have one message appear when users log in and other messages displayed when users enter certain directories. For example, the following entry will display the message in the **/welcome.msg** file when a user logs in:

```
message /welcome.msg            login
```

To set permissions, you use the command followed by a yes or a no and then a list of the user types or classes. An example of the **ftpaccess** file on Red Hat systems is shown here. In this example, all users can perform **tar** and **compress** operations, but anonymous and guest users are prohibited from using **chmod**, **delete**, **overwrite**, and **rename** operations. They also cannot erase files, modify them, or change their names or permissions.

/etc/ftpaccess

```
# define the class of users
class    all    real,guest,anonymous   *
# Email address of FTP managerm
email root@localhost
# Allow only 5 login failures per connection
loginfails 5
# Login and change directory README files
readme    README*    login
readme    README*    cwd=*
# Login and change directory message files
message /welcome.msg      login
message .message          cwd=*

# Set permissions
compress  yes        all
tar       yes        all
chmod     no         guest,anonymous
delete    no         guest,anonymous
overwrite no         guest,anonymous
rename    no         guest,anonymous

# Log file transfers, shutdown notice, password email address
log transfers anonymous,real inbound,outbound
shutdown /etc/shutmsg
passwd-check rfc822 warn
```

You can further modify your **ftpaccess** file to control access to particular users or groups of users by defining a class for them and placing restrictions on that class. For example, you could define a class for connections from a particular host as shown here:

```
class   manycons    192.168.1.55   *
```

Then apply controls such as limiting the number of connections from that host to 5. This would be helpful for cases where you know many users from a particular host are trying to user your FTP site.

```
limit manycons   5   Any
```

Access Capabilities	Description
autogroup *group classglob* [*classglob*...]	This allows access to a group's read-only files and directories by particular classes of anonymous users. *group* is a valid group from **/etc/group**.
class *class typelist addrglob* [*addrglob*...]	Defines *class* of users, with source addresses of the form *addrglob. typelist* is a comma-separated list of the user types: anonymous, guest, and real.
deny *host-addrglob message_file*	Always deny access to host(s) matching *host-addrglob. message_file* is displayed
guestgroup *groupname* [*groupname*...]	Allow guest access by a real user, where the user is a member of the specified group. A password entry for the guest user specifies a home directory within the FTP site directories.
guestuser *usrname* [*userpname*...]	Allow guest access by a real user.
limit *class n times message_file*	Limit class to *n* users at times—*times*, displaying *message_file* if access is denied.
noretrieve *file-list*	Deny retrieval ability of these files.
loginfails *number*	After *number* login failures, terminate the FTP connection. Default value is 5.
private *yes*	*no*	The user becomes a member of the group specified in the group access file **ftpgroups**.
Informational Capabilities	**Description**
banner *file*	The banner is displayed before login. File requires full pathname.
email *email-address*	Defines the e-mail address of the FTP manager.

Table 24-2.   */etc/ftpaccess wu-ftpd Configuration File*

Access Capabilities	Description
message *file* { *when* { *class* ...}}	FTP displays the contents of the *file* at login time or upon changing directories. The when parameter may be LOGIN or CWD=*dir*; *dir* specifies the directory that displays the message when entered. Magic cookies can be in the message file that cause the FTP server to replace the cookie with a specified text string, such as the date or the user name.
readme *file* { *when* { *class*}}	The user is notified at login time or upon using a change working directory command (cd) that *file* exists and was modified on such and such date.

Logging Capabilities

log commands *typelist*	Enables logging of individual commands by users.
log transfers *typelist* *directions*	Enables logging of file transfers. *directions* is a comma-separated list of the terms "inbound" and "outbound," and logs transfers for files sent to the server and sent from the server.

Miscellaneous Capabilities	Description
alias *string* *dir*	Defines an alias, *string*, for a directory.
cdpath *dir*	Defines an entry in cdpath. This defines a search path used when changing directories.
compress yes|no *classglob* [*classglob* **tar** yes|no *classglob* [*classglob*...]...]	Enables **compress** or **tar** capabilities for any class matching of *classglob*. The actual conversions are defined in the external file **ftconversion**.

Table 24-2.   */etc/ftpaccess wu-ftpd Configuration File* (continued*)*

Access Capabilities	Description
shutdown *path*	If the file pointed to by *path* exists, the server checks the file regularly to see if the server is going to be shut down.
virtual *address* root|banner|logfile *path*	Enables the virtual FTP server capabilities.
Permission Capabilities	**Description**
	Allows or disallows the ability to perform the specified function. By default, all users are allowed.
chmod yes | no *typelist*	Allow or disallow changing file permissions.
delete yes | no *typelist*	Allow or disallow deleting files, **rm**.
overwrite yes | no *typelist*	Allow or disallow modifying files.
rename yes | no *typelist*	Allow or disallow renaming files, **mv**.
umask yes | no *typelist*	Allow or disallow file creation permissions.
passwd-check *none* | *trivial* | *rfc822* (*enforce* | *warn*)	Define the level and enforcement of password checking done by the server for anonymous FTP. rfc822 requires an e-mail address in a valid e-mail address format.
path-filter *typelist mesg allowed_charset* { *disallowed regexp...*}	For users in *typelist*, **path-filter** defines regular expressions that control what a filename can or cannot be. Multiple disallowed *regexps* may occur.
upload *root-dir dirglob* yes|no *owner group mode* ["dirs" | "nodirs"]	Define a directory with *dirglob*, which permits or denies uploads.

Table 24-2.   */etc/ftpaccess wu-ftpd Configuration File* (continued)

ftphosts

You use the **ftphosts** file to allow or deny access by other host computers to your FTP site. When the remote system accesses your systems, it does so by logging in as a registered user. Access is made through a user account already set up on your system. You allow the remote host to log in as a certain specific user or deny access as a certain user. You could use this kind of control to allow or deny anonymous access to the FTP user by a remote host.

The file **ftphosts** has two kinds of entries: one for allowing access and the other for denying access. Entries to allow access begin with the keyword **allow**, then the user account on your system to which the host is allowed access, followed by the address of the remote host. The address can be a pattern that can be used to match several hosts. You can use any of the filename generation symbols (see Chapter 9). Entries to deny access begin with the keyword **deny**, then the user account on your system to which the host is denied access, followed by the address of the remote host. The terms **deny** and **allow** can be misleading. **allow** is a much more restrictive control, whereas **deny** is a much more open control. **allow** only allows access from the remote host to the specified account. No other access is permitted. You could use **allow** to permit a remote host anonymous access only. **deny**, on the other hand, only denies access to the specified account. You could use **deny** to deny anonymous access by a certain system, but not any direct FTP access from one user to another.

ftpusers and ftpgroups

The **ftpusers** files list users that cannot access the FTP service. For example, the root user should not be accessible through an FTP connection, even if you knew the password. This file will initially hold a listing of all your system users such as **root**, **mail**, and **bin**. **ftpgroups** is a group access file that allows FTP users to become members of specified groups on your system. This file lists special group passwords. For these to work, the Private entry must be set to yes in the **ftpaccess** file.

ftpconversions

The **ftpconversions** file holds possible FTP conversions for compression and archive operations. It operates as an FTP conversions database, listing all possible conversions. A default **ftpconversions** file is included with the installation package that already has entries for the most common conversion operations. Each line in the file is a record of eight fields, with the fields separated by colons. The fields are Strip Prefix and Postfix, Addon Prefix and Postfix, External Command, Types, Options, and Description. The Prefix and Postfix fields refer to changes made to the filename after the specified action is performed. The Strip Postfix removes a specified suffix from a filename, and the Add Postfix adds a suffix. For example, a gzipped compressed file has a suffix of **.gz**. If the command is to compress a file with gzip, then the Add Postfix entry should have the **.gz** placed in it. When the file is compressed, **.gz** is added to the end. If you were decompressing a file with gunzip, then you would want to remove the **.gz** suffix. For this, you would place **.gz** in the Strip Postfix field. The Strip and Add Prefix fields perform the same kind of action, but for prefixes.

The external command is the command you would use to convert the file. You can list command options after the command. The filename you are operating on is specified with **%s**, usually placed after any options. For example, you would use the tar command to extract a **.tar** archived file and gunzip to decompress a **.gz** file. The Type field lists the type of files that can be operated on by the command. These can be regular files, character files, or directories as indicated by the entries **T_REG**, **T_ASCII**, and **T_DIR**. You can specify more than one entry by placing a | between them. The Options field specifies the type of operation the command performs. Currently, options exist for compression, decompression, and use of the tar command: **O_COMPRESS**, **O_UNCOMPRESS**, and **O_TAR**. You can list more than one by separating them with a | symbol. The description provides some documentation as to what the conversion operation does. Here is the **ftpconversion** file used on Red Hat systems:

```
:.Z:  :  :/bin/compress -d -c \
  %s:T_REG|T_ASCII:O_UNCOMPRESS:UNCOMPRESS
:   :  :.Z:/bin/compress -c %s:T_REG:O_COMPRESS:COMPRESS
:.gz:  :  :/bin/gzip -cd %s:T_REG|T_ASCII:O_UNCOMPRESS:GUNZIP
:   :  :.gz:/bin/gzip -9 -c %s:T_REG:O_COMPRESS:GZIP
:   :  :.tar:/bin/tar -c -f - %s:T_REG|T_DIR:O_TAR:TAR
:   :  :.tar.Z:/bin/tar -c -Z -f -
  %s:T_REG|T_DIR:O_COMPRESS|O_TAR:TAR+COMPRESS
:   :  :.tar.gz:/bin/tar -c -z -f -
  %s:T_REG|T_DIR:O_COMPRESS|O_TAR:TAR+GZIP
```

FTP log file: xferlog

This file contains log information about connections and tasks performed by your FTP server. On Red Hat systems, this file is found in the **/var/log** directory. On other systems, this file may be on the **/usr/adm** directory. The file is made up of server entries, one on each line. The entry is divided into several fields separated by spaces. The fields are current-time, transfer-time, remote-host, file-size, filename, transfer-type, special-action-flag, direction, access-mode, username, service-name, authentication-method, and authenticated-user-id. The *transfer-time* is the time in seconds for the transfer. The *remote-host* is the address of the remote system making the connection and *username* is the name of the user on that system. The *transfer-type* is either an *a* for ASCII or *b* for binary. The *access-mode* is the method by which the user logged in: *a* for anonymous, *g* for guest, and *r* for a real login (to another account on your system). The direction is either *o* for outgoing or *i* for incoming. The following example shows the file **mydoc** transferred by user **larisa**. The entry first shows the time, the FTP server host, and the size of the file along with the filename. The file transfer was binary, outgoing, and made by an anonymous user (b o a). The user's name (password) and the service used, **ftp**.

```
Sun Oct 29 11:15:40 2000 1 turtle.mytrek.com 55945 /var/
   ftp/pub/mydoc b o a larisa@turtle.mytrek.com ftp 0 * c
```

Professional FTP Daemon: ProFTPD

ProFTPD is based on the same design as the Apache Web server, implementing a similar simplified configuration structure and supporting such flexible features as virtual hosting. ProFTPD RPM packages are available from the Red Hat and Caldera FTP. Unlike other FTP daemons, you do not need to set up special subdirectories of system files in the FTP home directory. No special **bin** or **etc** files are needed. You can also set up ProFTPD to alternate automatically between inetd startups or as a standalone server constantly running, depending on the system load.

ProFTPD's tools operate in the same way as the wu-ftpd tools. **Ftpshut** shuts down the system at specified times with warnings. With ProFTPD, you can shut down a virtual host while the main server continues to run. **Ftpwho** displays a list of all remote users currently connected, broken down according to virtual hosts and servers. **Ftpcount** shows the number of current connections by server and virtual hosts. See the previous section on FTP tools for more information.

install and startup

If you install ProFTPD using a distribution RPM packages such as the one for Red Hat, the required configuration entries are made in your **proftpd.conf** files. If you installed from compiled source code, you may have to modify the entries in the default **proftpd.conf** file provided. Make sure the FTP user and group specified in the **proftpd.conf** file actually exist.

You can download ProFTPD from the ProFTPD Web site at **www.proftpd.net**. The RPM package version will contain three packages: a core application, a standalone version, and an inetd version. Download and install the core package first. Then, depending on whether you want to run ProFTPD as a standalone or inetd process, install either the inetd or standalone package.

```
proftpd-core-1.2.0pre10-1.i686.rpm
proftpd-inetd-1.2.0pre10-1.i686.rpm
proftpd-standalone-1.2.0pre10-1.i686.rpm
```

You can run ProFTPD either as a standalone process or from inetd. Make sure the appropriate entry is made in the ServerType directive in your **proftpd.conf** file. The standalone RPM package will install **proftpd** to run as a standalone server, setting the ServerType to standalone. **proftpd** options are listed in Table 24-3. On Red Hat and Caldera systems, a startup script named **proftpd** is placed in the **/etc/inet.d** directory that starts up the daemon when you boot your system. A standalone process is continually running. If you want to run **proftpd** as an inetd process, you first must change the ServerType to inetd and disable the **proftpd** startup script in the **/etc/rc.d/inet.d** directory.

When you run ProFTPD from inetd, make sure the appropriate entry is in the **inetd.conf** file. If you were running wu-ftpd previously, you must change this entry to run **proftpd**. The inetd RPM package implements an **in.proftpd** link to the **proftpd** daemon. Use this link to invoke ProFTPD in the **inetd.conf** file. The ProFTPD inetd entry looks like this:

```
ftp stream tcp nowait root  /usr/sbin/in.proftpd  in.proftpd
```

Most systems use TCP wrappers for their inetd entries. The inetd entry looks like this:

```
ftp stream tcp nowait root  /usr/sbin/tcpd  in.proftpd
```

Option	Description
-h,--help	Use description, including options.
-n,--nodaemon	Runs the proftpd process in standalone mode (must also specify standalone as ServerType in the configuration file).
-v,--version	Display ProFTPD version number.
-d,--debug *debuglevel*	Sets proftpd's internal debug level (1–5).
-c,--config *config-file*	Specifies alternate configuration file.
-p,--persistent 0|1	Disables (0) or enables (1) the default persistent password support, which is determined at configure time for each platform (see PersistentPasswd directive).
-l,--list	Lists all modules compiled into proftpd.

Table 24-3.   *ProFTPD Daemon Startup Options*

proftpd.config and .ftpaccess

ProFTPD uses only one configuration file, named **proftpd.conf**, located in the **/etc** directory. Configuration entries take the form of directives. This format is purposely modeled on Apache configuration directives. With the directives, you can enter basic configuration information, such as your server name, or perform more complex operations, such as implementing virtual FTP hosts. The design is flexible enough to enable you to define configuration features for particular directories, users, or groups.

To configure a particular directory, you can use an **.ftpaccess** file with configuration options placed within that directory. These **.ftpaccess** options take precedence over those in the **proftpd.conf** directory. **.fptaccess** files are designed to operate like **.htaccess** files in the Apache Web server that configure particular Web site directories. You can find a complete listing of ProFTPD configuration parameters at the ProFTPD Web site (**www.proftpd.net**) and in the ProFTPD documentation installed in **/usr/doc** as part of the ProFTPD software package. Several of the more commonly used parameters are listed in Table 24-4. When creating a new configuration, you should make a copy of the **proftpd.conf** configuration file and modify it. Then you can test its syntax using the proftpd command with the -c option and the name of the file.

```
proftpd -c newfile.conf
```

Different kinds of directives exist. Many set values, such as MaxClients, which set the maximum number of clients, or NameServer, which sets the name of the FTP server. Others create blocks that can hold directives that apply to specific FTP server components. Block directives are entered in pairs: a beginning directive and a terminating directive. The terminating directive defines the end of the block and consists of the same name, beginning with a slash. Block directives take an argument that specifies the particular object to which the directives will apply. For the Directory block directive, you must specify a directory name to which it will apply. The <Directory *mydir*> block directive creates a block whose directives within it apply to the *mydir* directory. The block is terminated by a </Directory> directive. <Anonymous *ftp-dir*> configures the anonymous service for your FTP server. You need to specify the directory on your system used for your anonymous FTP service, such as **/home/ftp**. The block is terminated with the </Anonymous> directive. The <VirtualHost *hostaddress*> block directive is used to configure a specific virtual FTP server and must include the IP or the domain name address used for that server. </VirtualHost> is its terminating directive. Any Directives you place within this block are applied to that virtual FTP server. The <Limit *permission*> directive specifies the kind of access you want to limit. It takes as its argument one of several keywords indicating the kind of permission to be controlled: **WRITE** for write access, **READ** for read access, **STOR** for transfer access (uploading), and **LOGIN** to control user login.

A sample of the standard **proftpd.conf** file installed as part of the ProFTPD software package is shown here. Notice the default ServerType is standalone. If you want to use inetd to run your server, you must change this entry to inetd. Detailed examples of **proftpd.conf** files, showing various anonymous FTP and virtual host configurations, can be found with the ProFTPD documentation, located in **/usr/doc**, and on the ProFPTD Web site at **www.proftpd.net**.

```
# This is a basic ProFTPD configuration file (rename it to
# 'proftpd.conf' for actual use.  It establishes a single server
# and a single anonymous login.  It assumes that you have a user/group
# "nobody" and "ftp" for normal operation and anon.

ServerName          "ProFTPD Default Installation"
ServerType          standalone
DefaultServer       on

# Port 21 is the standard FTP port.
Port          21
Umask         022
MaxInstances  30

# Set the user and group that the server normally runs at.
User          nobody
Group         nobody

# Normally, we want files to be overwriteable.
<Directory /*>
  AllowOverwrite      on
</Directory>

# A basic anonymous configuration, with one incoming directory.
<Anonymous ~ftp>
  User                ftp
  Group               ftp
  RequireValidShell   off
  MaxClients          10
  # We want clients to be able to login with "anonymous" as well as "ftp"
  UserAlias           anonymous ftp

  # We want 'welcome.msg' displayed at login, and '.message' displayed
  # in each newly chdired directory.
```

```
DisplayLogin            welcome.msg
DisplayFirstChdir       .message

# Limit WRITE everywhere in the anonymous chroot except incoming
<Directory *>
   <Limit WRITE>
       DenyAll
   </Limit>
</Directory>

<Directory incoming>
   <Limit WRITE>
     AllowAll
   </Limit>
   <Limit READ>
     DenyAll
   </Limit>
</Directory>

</Anonymous>
```

Anonymous Access

You use the Anonymous configuration directive to create an anonymous configuration block in which you can place directives that configure your anonymous FTP service. The directive includes the directory on your system used for the anonymous FTP service. The ProFTPD daemon executes a **chroot** operation on this directory, making it the root directory for the remote user accessing the service. By default, anonymous logins are supported, expecting users to enter their e-mail address as a password. You can modify an anonymous configuration to construct more controlled anonymous services, such as guest logins and required passwords.

For ProFTPD, your anonymous FTP directory does not require any system files. Before ProFTPD executes a ***chroot*** *operation, hiding the rest of the system from the directory, it accesses and keeps open any needed system files outside the directory.*

The following example shows a standard anonymous FTP configuration. The initial Anonymous directive specifies **/home/ftp** as the anonymous FTP home directory. The User directive specifies the user that the Anonymous FTP daemon will run as, and Group indicates its group. In both cases, FTP, the standard user name, is used on most systems for anonymous FTP. A Directory directive with the * file matching character then defines a Directory block that applies to all directories and files in **/home/ftp**.

The * symbol matches on all filenames and directories. Within the Directory directive is a Limit directive that you use to place controls on a directory. The directive takes several arguments including **READ** for read access and **WRITE** for write access. In this example, the Limit directive places restrictions on the write capabilities of users. Within the Limit directive, the DenyAll directive denies write permission, preventing users from creating or deleting files and effectively giving them only read access. A second Directory directive creates an exception to this rule for the incoming directory. An incoming directory is usually set up on FTP sites to let users upload files. For this directory, the first Limit directive prevents both **READ** and **WRITE** access by users with its DenyAll directive, effectively preventing users from deleting or reading files here. The second Limit directive lets users to upload files, however, permitting transfers only (**STOR**) with the AllowAll directive.

One important directive for anonymous FTP configurations is the RequireValidShell. By default, the FTP daemon first checks to see if the remote user is attempting to log in using a valid shell, such as the Bash shell or the C-shell. The FTP daemon obtains the list of valid shells from the **/etc/shells** file. If the remote user does not have a valid shell, a connection is denied. You can turn off the check using the RequireValidShell directive and the **off** option. The remote user can then log in using any kind of shell.

```
<Anonymous /home/ftp>
    User ftp
    Group ftp
    UserAlias anonymous ftp
    RequireValidShell off
  <Directory *>
      <Limit WRITE>
          DenyAll
      </Limit>
    </Directory>
     # The only command allowed in incoming is STOR
     # (transfer file from client to server)
    <Directory incoming>
      <Limit READ WRITE>
          DenyAll
      </Limit>
      <Limit STOR>
          AllowAll
      </Limit>
    </Directory>
  </Anonymous>
```

Recall that FTP was originally designed to let a remote user connect to an account of his or her own on the system. Users can log in to different accounts on your system using the FTP service. Anonymous users are restricted to the anonymous user account. However, you can create other users and their home directories that also function as anonymous FTP accounts with the same restrictions. Such accounts are known as *guest accounts*. Remote users are required to know the user name and, usually, the password. Once connected, they only have read access to that account's files; the rest of the file system is hidden from them. In effect, you are creating a separate anonymous FTP site at the same location with more restricted access.

To create a guest account, first create a user and the home directory for it. You then create an Anonymous block in the **proftpd.conf** file for that account. The Anonymous directive includes the home directory of the guest user you create. You can specify this directory with a ~ for the path and the directory name, usually the same as the user name. Within the Anonymous block, you use the **User** and **Group** directives to specify the user and group name for the user account. Set the AnonRequirePassword directive to on if you want remote users to provide a password. A UserAlias directive defines aliases for the user name. A remote user can use either the alias or the original user name to login. You then enter the remaining directives for controlling access to the files and directories in the account's home directory. An example showing the initial directives is listed here. The User directive specifies the user as **myproject**. The home directory is **~myproject**, which usually evaluates to **/home/myproject**. The UserAlias lets remote users log in either with the name **myproject** or **mydesert**.

```
<Anonymous ~myproject>
    User myproject
    Group other
    UserAlias mydesert myproject
    AnonRequirePassword on
    <Directory *>
```

You could just as easily create an account that requires no password, letting users enter in their e-mail addresses instead. The following example configures an anonymous user named **mypics**. A password isn't required and neither is a valid shell. The remote user still needs to know the user name, in this case **mypics**.

```
<Anonymous /home/mypics>
    AnonRequirePassword off
    User mypics
    Group nobody
    RequireValidShell off
    <Directory *>
```

The following example provides a more generic kind of guest login. The user name is **guest** with the home directory located at **~guest**. Remote users are required to know the password for the guest account. The first Limit directive lets all users log in. The second Limit directive allows write access from users on a specific network, as indicated by the network IP address, and denies write access by any others.

```
<Anonymous ~guest>
  User                      guest
  Group                     nobody
  AnonRequirePassword       on

  <Limit LOGIN>
    AllowAll
  </Limit>

  # Deny write access from all except trusted hosts.
  <Limit WRITE>
    Order       allow,deny
    Allow       from 10.0.0.
    Deny        from all
  </Limit>

</Anonymous>
```

Virtual FTP Servers

The ProFTPD daemon can manage more than one FTP site at once. Using a VirtualHost directive in the **proftpd.conf** file, you can create an independent set of directives that configure a separate FTP server. The VirtualHost directive is usually used to configure virtual servers as FTP sites. You can configure your system to support more than one IP address. The extra IP addresses can be used for virtual servers, not independent machines. You can use such an extra IP address to set up a virtual FTP server, giving you another FTP site on the same system. This added server would use the extra IP address as its own. Remote users could access it using that IP address, instead of the system's main IP address. Because such an FTP server is not running independently on a separate machine but is, instead, on the same machine, it is known as a *virtual FTP server* or *virtual host*. This feature lets you run what appear to others as several different FTP servers on one machine. When a remote user uses the virtual FTP server's IP address to access it, the ProFTPD daemon detects that request and operates as the FTP service for that site. ProFTPD can handle a great many virtual FTP sites at the same time on a single machine.

Note   *Given its configuration capabilities, you can also tailor any of the virtual FTP sites to specific roles, such as a guest site, an anonymous site for a particular group, or an anonymous site for a particular user.*

You configure a virtual FTP server by entering a <VirtualHost> directive for it in your **proftpd.conf** file. Such an entry begins with the VirtualHost directive and the IP address, and ends with a terminating VirtualHost directive, </VirtualHost>. Any directives placed within these are applied to the virtual host. For anonymous or guest sites, add Anonymous and Guest directives. You can even add Directory directives for specific directories. With the Port directive on a standalone configuration, you can create a virtual host that operates on the same system but connects on a different port.

```
<VirtualHost 10.0.0.1>
 ServerName "My virtual FTP server"
</VirtualHost>
```

Inetd and standalone configurations handle virtual hosts differently. Inetd detects a request for a virtual host, and then hands it off to an FTP daemon. The FTP daemon then examines the address and port specified in the request and processes the request for the appropriate virtual host. In the standalone configuration, the FTP daemon continually listens for requests on all specified ports and generates child processes to handle ones for different virtual hosts as they come in. In the standalone configuration, ProFTPD can support a great many virtual hosts at the same time.

The following example shows a sample configuration of a virtual FTP host. The VirtualHost directives use domain name addresses for its arguments. When a domain name address is used, it must be associated with an IP address in the network's domain name server. The IP address, in turn, has to reference the machine on which the ProFTPD daemon is running. On the **ftp.mypics.com** virtual FTP server, an anonymous guest account named **robpics** is configured that requires a password to log in. An anonymous FTP account is also configured that uses the home directory **/home/ftp/virtual/pics**.

```
<VirtualHost ftp.mypics.com>

 ServerName        "Mypics FTP Server"
 MaxClients        10
 MaxLoginAttempts  1
 DeferWelcome      on
 <Anonymous ~robpics>
   User            robpics
   Group           robpics
   AnonRequirePassword      on
```

```
<Anonymous /home/ftp/virtual/pics>

    User              ftp
    Group             ftp
    UserAlias         anonymous ftp


  </Anonymous>

</VirtualHost>
```

Directive	Description
AccessGrantMsg *message*	Response message sent to an FTP client indicating the user has logged in or anonymous access has been granted. The magic cookie '**%u**' is replaced with the user name specified by the client. Default: Dependent on login type Context: server config, <VirtualHost>, <Anonymous>, <Global>
Allow *["from"] "all"|"none"|host|network[, host|network[,...]]*	Used inside a <Limit> context to specify explicitly which hosts and/or networks have access to the commands or operations being limited. Used with Order and Deny to create access control rules. Default: Allow from all Context: <Limit>
AllowAll	Allows access to a <Directory>, <Anonymous> or <Limit> block Default: Default is to implicitly AllowAll, but not explicitly Context: <Directory>, <Anonymous>, <Limit>, .ftpaccess

Table 24-4. *ProFTPD Configuration Directives, proftpd.conf*

Directive	Description
AllowFilter *regular-expression*	Allows the configuration of a regular expression that must be matched for all commands sent to ProFTPD. Default: None Context: server config, <VirtualHost>, <Anonymous>, <Global>
AllowForeignAddress *on|off*	Allows clients to transmit foreign data connection addresses that do not match the client's address. Default: AllowForeignAddress off Context: server config, <VirtualHost&, <Anonymous>, <Global>
AllowGroup *group-expression*	List of groups allowed in a Limit block. Default: None Context: <Limit>
AllowUser *user-expression*	Users allowed access. Default: None Context: <Limit>
AnonRequirePassword *on|off*	Requires anonymous logins to enter a valid password that must match the password of the user that the anonymous daemon runs as. This is used to create guest accounts that function like anonymous logins but require a valid password. Default: AnonRequirePassword off Context: <Anonymous>
<Anonymous *root-directory>*	Create an anonymous FTP login, terminated by a matching </Anonymous> directive. The root directory parameters are the directory proftpd first moves to and then **chroot**, hiding the rest of the file system. Default: None Context: server config,<VirtualHost>

Table 24-4.   *ProFTPD Configuration Directives, proftpd.conf* (continued)

SERVERS

Directive	Description
AuthGroupFile *path*	Alternate group's file with the same format as the system **/etc/group** file. Default: None Context: server config, <VirtualHost>, <Global>
AuthUserFile *path*	Alternate **passwd** file with the same format as the system **/etc/passwd** file. Default: None Context: server config,<VirtualHost>, <Global>
Bind *address*	Allows additional IP addresses to be bound to a main or VirtualHost configuration. Multiple Bind directives can be used to bind multiple addresses. Default: None Context: server config, <VirtualHost>
DefaultRoot *directory [group-expression]*	Default root directory assigned to user on login. The group-expression argument restricts the DefaultRoot directive to a group or set of groups. Default: DefaultRoot /Context: server config, <VirtualHost>, <Global>
Deny *["from"] "all"|"none"|host|network[, host|network[,...]]*	List of hosts and networks explicitly denied access to a given <Limit> context block. **all** indicates all hosts are denied access, and **none** indicates no hosts are explicitly denied. Default: None Context: <Limit>
DenyAll	Deny access to a directory, anonymous FTP, or Limit block. Default: None Context: <Directory>, <Anonymous>, <Limit>, .ftpaccess

Table 24-4. *ProFTPD Configuration Directives, proftpd.conf* (continued)

Directive	Description
DenyFilter *regular-expression*	Specifies a regular expression, which must *not* match any command. Default: None Context: server config, <VirtualHost>, <Anonymous>, <Global>
DenyUser *user-expression*	Users denied access within a Limit block. Default: None Context: <Limit>
<Directory *pathname*>	Directory-specific configuration. Used to create a block of directives that apply to the specified directory and its subdirectories. Default: None Context: server config, <VirtualHost>, <Anonymous>, <Global>
DisplayFirstChdir *filename*	Specifies the text file displayed to a user the first time he or she changes into a given directory during an FTP session. Default: None Context: server config, <VirtualHost>, <Anonymous>, <Directory>, <Global>
DisplayLogin *filename*	Specifies the text file displayed to a user who logs in. Default: None Context: server config, <VirtualHost>, <Anonymous>, <Global>
<Global>	Global configuration block is used to create a set of configuration directives applied universally to both the main server configuration and all VirtualHost configurations. Default: None Context: server config, <VirtualHost>

Table 24-4.   *ProFTPD Configuration Directives, proftpd.conf* (continued)

Directive	Description
`<Limit command|command-group [command2 ..]>`	Access restrictions on FTP commands, within a given context. The **command-group** refers to groupings of commands as defined in the ProFTPD documentation. Default: None Context: server config, <VirtualHost>, <Directory>, <Anonymous>, <Global>, .ftpaccess
`LsDefaultOptions "options string"`	Default options for directory listings (as in the ls command). Default: None Context: server config, <VirtualHost>, <Global>
`MaxClients number|none message`	Maximum number of connected clients allowed. The message specified is displayed when a client is refused connection. Default: MaxClients none Context: server config, <Anonymous>, <VirtualHost>, <Global>
`MaxLoginAttempts number`	Maximum number of times a client may attempt to log in to the server during a given connection. Default: MaxLoginAttempts 3 Context: server config, <VirtualHost>, <Global>
`Order allow,deny|deny,allow`	Configures the order that Allow and Deny directives are checked inside of a <Limit> block. Default: Order allow,deny Context: <Limit>

Table 24-4. *ProFTPD Configuration Directives, proftpd.conf* (continued)

Directive	Description
PersistentPasswd *on/off*	When on, proftpd, during login, opens the system-wide **/etc/passwd**, **/etc/group** files, accessing them even during a **chroot** operation that changes the root directory. Default: Platform dependent Context: server config
RequireValidShell *on/off*	Allow or deny logins not listed in **/etc/shells**. By default, proftpd disallows logins if the user's default shell is not listed in **/etc/shells**. Default: RequireValidShell on Context: server config, <VirtualHost>, <Anonymous>, <Global>
ScoreboardPath *path*	Directory that holds proftpd runtime **Scoreboard** files. Default: ScoreboardPath /var/run Context: server config
ServerAdmin *"admin-email-address"*	E-mail address of the server or virtual host administrator. Default: ServerAdmin root@[ServerName] Context: server config, <VirtualHost>
ServerType *type-identifier*	The server daemon's operating mode, either inetd or standalone. Default: ServerType standalone Context: server config
TimeoutIdle *seconds*	Maximum number of seconds proftpd allows clients to stay connected without any activity. Default: TimeoutIdle 600 Context: server config

Table 24-4. *ProFTPD Configuration Directives, proftpd.conf* (continued)

Directive	Description
Umask *octal-mask*	Permissions applied to newly created file and directory within a given context. Default: None Context: server config, <Anonymous>, <VirtualHost>, <Directory>, <Global>, .ftpaccess
User *userid*	The user the proftpd daemon runs as. Default: None Context: server config, <VirtualHost>, <Anonymous>, <Global>
UserAlias *login-user userid*	Maps a login name used by a client to a user ID on the server. A client logging in as *login-user* is actually logged in as *user ID*. Often used inside an <Anonymous> block to allow specified *login-names* to perform an anonymous login. Default: None Context: server config, <VirtualHost>, <Anonymous>, <Global>
<VirtualHost *address*>	Configuration directives that apply to a particular hostname or IP address. Often used with virtual servers that run on the same physical machine. The block is terminated with a </VirtualHost> directive. By using the Port directive inside a VirtualHost block, creating a virtual server that uses the same address as the master server, but that listens on a separate TCP port, is possible. Default: None Context: server config

Table 24-4.   *ProFTPD Configuration Directives, proftpd.conf* (continued)

The
Complete
Reference

Chapter 25

Apache Web Server

The Apache Web server is a full-featured free HTTP (Web) server developed and maintained by the Apache Server Project. The aim of the project is to provide a reliable, efficient, and easily extensible Web server, with free open source code. The server software includes the server daemon, configuration files, management tools, and documentation. The Apache Server Project is maintained by a core group of volunteer programmers and supported by a great many contributors worldwide. The Apache Server Project is one of several projects currently supported by the Apache Software Foundation (formerly known as the Apache Group). This nonprofit organization provides financial, legal, and organizational support for various Apache open-source software projects, including the Apache HTTPD Server, Java Apache, Jakarta, and XML-Apache. The Web site for the Apache Software Foundation is at **www.apache.org**. Table 25-1 lists various Apache-related Web sites.

JAVA: Jakarta and Apache-Java

Apache was originally based on the NCSA Web server developed at the National Center for Supercomputing Applications, University of Illinois, Champaign-Urbana. Apache has since emerged as a server in its own right and has become one of the most popular Web servers in use. Although originally developed for Linux and Unix systems, Apache has become a cross-platform application with Windows and OS2 versions. Apache provides online support and documentation for its Web server at

Web Site	Description
www.apache.org	Apache Software Foundation
www.apache.org/httpd.html	Apache HTTP Server Project
java.apache.org	Java Apache Project
jakarta.apache.org	Jakarta Apache Project
gui.apache.org	Apache GUI Project
www.comanche.org	Comanche (Configuration Manager for Apache)
www.apache-ssl.org	Apache-SSL server
www.openssl.org	OpenSSL project (Secure Socket Layer)

Table 25-1.   *Apache-Related Web Sites*

www.apache.org/httpd.html. An HTML-based manual is also provided with the server installation. Several GUI configuration tools are also available to help configure your Apache server easily. They operate on any X Windows window manager, including Gnome and KDE. You can link to these Apache GUI configuration tools at **gui.apache.org**.

Other Web servers available for Linux include the Red Hat Secure Server (**www.redhat.com**), Apache-SSL (**www.apache-ssl.org**), Stronghold (**www.c2.net**), and Netscape Enterprise Server (**home.netscape.com**). *Apache-SSL* is an encrypting Web server based on Apache and OpenSSL (**www.openssl.org**). *Stronghold* is a commercial version of the Apache Web server featuring improved security and administration tools. You can also use the original NCSA Web server, though it is no longer supported (**hoohoo.ncsa.uiuc.edu**). AOLserver is America Online's Web server that is now available under the GPL license (**www.aolserver.com**).

The Java Apache Project develops open source Java software and has its Web site located at **java.apache.org**. Currently, the Java Apache Project support numerous projects, including JServ, JSSI, JMeter, and mod_java, among others. The Apache Jserv Project has developed a Java servlet engine compliant with the JavaSoft Java Servlet APIs 2.0 specification. The Apache JSSI project has developed a Java servlet for dynamic servlet output from HTML files through the <SERVLET> tag as designated by the JavaSoft Java Web Server. *JMeter* is a Java desktop application to test performance of server resources, such as servlets and CGI scripts. The MOD_JAVA project has developed a mod_java extension module for Apache Web servers that allows Apache modules to be written in Java instead of in C. It functions much like mod_perl (which allows modules to be written in Perl).

Jakarta is an Apache project to develop server-side Java capabilities on Linux. Jakarta's main product, called *Tomcat,* is an open-source implementation of the Java Servlet 2.2 and JavaServer Pages 1.1 Specifications. Tomcat is designed for use in Apache servers. The Jakarta Web site is at **jakarta.apache.org**.

Linux Distribution Apache Installations

Most distributions, such as Red Hat, Caldera, and SUSE, provide you with the option of installing the Apache Web server during your initial installation of your Linux system. All the necessary directories and configuration files are automatically generated for you. Then, whenever you run Linux, your system is already a fully functional Web site. Every time you start your system, the Web server will also start up, running continuously. On both Red Hat and Caldera systems, the directory reserved for your Web site data files is **/var/www/html**. Place your Web pages in this directory or in any subdirectories. Your system is already configured to operate as a Web server. All you need to do is perform any needed network server configurations, and then designate the files and directories open to remote users. You needn't do anything else. Once your Web site is connected to a network, remote users can access it.

SERVERS

The Web server installed on Red Hat and Caldera systems sets up your Web site in the **/var/www** directory. It also sets up several directories for managing the site. The **/var/www/cgi-bin** directory holds the CGI scripts, and **/var/www/html/manual** holds the Apache manual in HTML format. You can use your browser to examine it. Your Web pages are to be placed in the **/var/www/html** directory. Place your Web site home page there. Your configuration files are located in a different directory, **/etc/httpd/conf**. Table 25-2 lists the various Apache Web server directories and configuration files.

Web Site Directories	Description
/var/www	Directory for Apache Web site files on your Red Hat and Caldera systems
/var/www/html	Web site Web files
/var/www/cgi-bin	CGI program files
/var/www/html/manual	Apache Web server manual
Configuration Files	
.htaccess	Directory-based configuration files. An **.htaccess** file holds directives to control access to files within the directory in which it is located
/etc/httpd/conf	Directory for Apache Web server configuration files
/etc/httpd/conf/httpd.conf	Primary Apache Web server configuration file (from version 1.3.4, it holds all configuration directives)
/etc/httpd/conf/srm.conf	Older configuration file used to handle document specifications, configuring file types and locations
/etc/httpd/conf/access.conf	Older configuration file designed to hold directives that control access to Web site directories and files
Startup Scripts	
/etc/rc.d/init.d/httpd	Start up script for Web server daemon
/etc/rc.d/rc3.d/S85httpd	Link in runlevel 3 directory (**/etc/rc3.d**) to the **httpd** start up script in the **/etc/rc.d/init.d** directory

Table 25-2. *Apache Web Server Files and Directories (RPM Installation)*

Web Site Directories	Description
Application Files	
/usr/sbin	Location of the Apache Web server program file and utilities
/usr/doc/	Apache Web server documentation
/var/log/http	Location of Apache log files

Table 25-2. *Apache Web Server Files and Directories (RPM Installation)* (continued)

To upgrade your Apache server, look for recent Apache update files at your Linux distribution's FTP sites. There you can download RPM packages containing the latest version of the Apache Web server, specially configured for your Linux distribution. Then use the **rpm** command with the **-Uvh** options to install the upgrade (the **-U** option specifies an upgrade option, see Chapter 19).

```
rpm -Uvh apache-1.3.12-20.i386.rpm
rpm -Uvh apache-docs-1.3.12-20.i386.rpm
```

Alternatively, you can download the source code version for the latest Apache Web server directly from Apache and compile it on your system. You must decompress the file and extract the archive. Many of the same directories are created, with added ones for the source code. The server package includes installation instructions for creating your server directories and compiling your software. Make sure the configuration files are set up and installed.

Note *If you are installing Apache from the source code, notice that versions of the configuration files ending with the extension .conf-dist are provided. You have to make copies of these configuration files with the same prefix, but only with the extension .conf to set up a default configuration. The Web server reads configuration information only from files with a .conf extension.*

SERVERS

Starting and Stopping the Web Server

On most systems, Apache is installed as a standalone server, continually running. As noted in Chapter 23 in the discussion of **init** scripts, your system automatically starts up the Web server daemon, invoking it whenever you start your system. On Caldera and Red Hat systems, a startup script for the Web server called **httpd** is in the **/etc/rc.d/init.d** directory. A symbolic link through which the **rc** program runs is in the **/etc/rc.d/rc3.d** directory and is called **S85httpd**.

You can use this **httpd** script in the **/etc/rc.d/init.d** directory to start and stop the server manually. This may be helpful when you are testing or modifying your server. The **httpd** script with the **start** option starts the server and with the **stop** option stops it. You can also use the SysV Runlevel Manager, available on many systems, to start and stop the **httpd** daemon (see Chapter 23). Click the **httpd** entry in the Available list, and then click the Execute button. A menu is displayed with buttons to stop or start the daemon. Simply killing the Web process directly is not advisable.

```
/etc/rc.d/init.d/httpd stop
/etc/rc.d/init.d/httpd start
```

Apache also provides a control tool called **apachectl** (Apache control) for managing your Web server. With **apachectl** you can start, stop, and restart the server from the command line. **apachectl** takes several arguments: **start** to start the server, **stop** to stop it, **restart** to shut down and restart the server, and **graceful** to shut down and restart gracefully. In addition, you can use **apachectl** to check the syntax of your configuration files with the **config** argument. You can also use **apachectl** as a system startup file for your server in the **/etc/rc.d** directory.

Remember, **httpd** is a script that calls the actual **httpd** daemon. You could call the daemon directly using its full pathname. This daemon has several options. The **-d** option enables you to specify a directory for the **httpd** program if it is different from the default directory. With the **-f** option, you can specify a configuration file different from **httpd.conf**. The **-v** option displays the version.

```
/usr/sbin/httpd -v
```

To check your Web server, start your Web browser and enter the Internet domain name address of your system. For the system **turtle.trek.com,** the user enters **http://turtle.trek.com**. This should display the home page you placed in your Web root directory. A simple way to do this is to use **lynx**, the command line Web browser. Start **lynx,** and then press **g** to open a line where you can enter a URL for your own system. Then **lynx** displays your Web site's home page. Be sure to place an **index.html** file in the **/var/www/html** directory first.

Once you have your server running, you can check its performance with the **ab** benchmarking tool, also provided by Apache. **ab** shows you how many requests at a time your server can handle. Options include **-v,** which enables you to control the level of detail displayed, **-n,** which specifies the number of request to handle (default is 1), and **-t,** which specifies a time limit.

Alternatively, you can run the Web server as an **inetd** process. This is helpful for situations where you have limited resources and a low level of connection traffic. With **inetd** the Web server will be run only when it its services are requested. Also, when testing configurations you will not have to continually restart the server. Red Hat and Caldera, like most distributions, do not configure the Web server to run from **inetd**. If you want this done, place the appropriate entries in **/etc/services** and **/etc/inetd.conf**. You also must remove your Web server from the list of startup daemons in your system's autostart list (see Chapter 23 for details). If you want to have **httpd** called by the **inetd** daemon, place an entry for **httpd** in the **/etc/services** and **/etc/inetd.conf** files. The **/etc/services** file lists the different services available on your system. For a Web server, you enter **http** with a *port*/tcp specification.

```
http    80/tcp
```

The Web server entry in the **/etc/inetd.conf** file is similar to the entry for the FTP server. Use the pathname for the Web server installed on your system, usually **/usr/sbin/httpd**.

```
http stream tcp nowait nobody /usr/sbin/httpd  /usr/sbin/httpd
```

To have Web server requests monitored and controlled by **tcpd**, you place the **/usr/sbin/tcpd** pathname in place of the **/usr/sbin/httpd** pathname.

```
http stream tcp nowait nobody /usr/sbin/tcpd  /usr/sbin/httpd
```

You also have to specify the **inetd** value for the ServerType variable in your Apache **httpd.conf** file, **/etc/httpd/conf/httpd.conf**.

```
# ServerType is either inetd, or standalone.
ServerType inetd
```

Apache Configuration Files

Traditionally, configuration directives have been placed in their different configuration files: **httpd.conf**, **srm.conf**, and **access.conf**. These files are located in the **/etc/httpd/conf** directory. **srm.conf** and **access.conf** are designed to hold directives that configure your

Web site documents. **httpd.conf** is used to configure your server. The s**rm.conf** file handles document specifications, configuring file types and locations. The **access.conf** file is designed to hold directives that control access to Web site directories and files. This three-file organization was originally implemented to maintain compatibility with the NCAA Web server that preceded Apache.

With version 1.3.4, Apache recommends that all configuration directives be placed in one file, the **httpd.conf** file. Most current distributions currently comply with this recommendation, including Red Hat and Caldera. In fact, if you download the original source code version, both the **srm.conf** and **access.conf** files will be empty. Only the **httpd.conf** file is used. Directives even exist that prevent reading the **srm.conf** and **access.conf** files. By default, Apache still reads both the **srm.conf** and **access.conf** files, in case anything is in them, though **httpd.conf** is still considered the primary configuration file. The situation is complicated because some distributions still use all three configuration files.

Any of the directives in the main configuration files can be overridden on a per-directory basis using an **.htaccess** file located within a directory. Although originally designed only for access directives, the **.htaccess** file can also hold any resource directives, enabling you to tailor how Web pages are displayed in a particular directory. You can configure access to **.htaccess** files in the **httpd.conf** file.

Note	*Apache configuration directives, traditionally placed in the **srm.conf** or **access.conf** file, can now be placed in the **httpd.conf** file, and those files can be left empty. Still, the three-files organization does help to categorize files into primary directives, resources, and access controls. On the other hand, the Apache's capabilities have extended to the point that these categories no longer cover the current directives. For example, directives for virtual hosts are placed in the **httpd.conf** file, along with their access control directives. Directives should be thought of as independent of any particular file.*

Apache Directives

Apache configuration operations take the form of directives entered into the Apache configuration files. With the directives, you can enter basic configuration information, such as your server name, or perform more complex operations, such as implementing virtual hosts. The design is flexible enough to enable you to define configuration features for particular directories and different virtual hosts. Apache has a variety of different directives performing operations as diverse as controlling directory access, assigning file icon formats, and creating log files. Most directives set values such as DirectoryRoot, which holds the root directory for the server's Web pages, or Port, which holds the port on the system that the server listens on for requests. Table 25-3 provides a listing of the more commonly used Apache Directives (due to its length, Table 25-3 is shown at the end of this section). The syntax for a simple directive is shown here.

```
directive option option ...
```

Certain directives create blocks able to hold directives that apply to specific server components (also referred to as Sectional directives). For example, the **Directory** directive is used to define a block within which you place directives that apply only to a particular directory. Block directives are entered in pairs: a beginning directive and a terminating directive. The terminating directive defines the end of the block and consists of the same name beginning with a slash. Block directives take an argument that specifies the particular object to which the directives apply. For the **Directory** block directive, you must specify a directory name to which it will apply. The **<Directory *mydir*>** block directive creates a block whose directives within it apply to the *mydir* directory. The block is terminated by a **</Directory>** directive. The **<VirtualHost *hostaddress*>** block directive is used to configure a specific virtual Web server and must include the IP or domain name address used for that server. **</VirtualHost>** is its terminating directive. Any directives you place within this block are applied to that virtual Web server. The **<Limit *method*>** directive specifies the kind of access method, such as GET or POST, you want to limit. The access control directives located within the block list the controls you are placing on those methods. The syntax for a block directive is as follows.

```
<block-directive option … >
    directive option …
    directive option …
</block-directive>
```

Usually, directives are placed in one of the main configuration files. Directory directives in those files can be used to configure a particular directory. However, Apache also makes use of directory-based configuration files. Any directory may have its own **.htaccess** file that holds directives to configure only that directory. If your site has many directories or if any directories have special configuration needs, you can placed their configuration directives in their **.htaccess** files, instead of filling the main configuration file with specific Directory directives for each one. You can control what directives in an **.htaccess** file take precedence over those in the main configuration files. If your site allows user- or client-controlled directories, you may want to carefully monitor or disable the use of **.htaccess** files in them. (It is possible for directives in an **.htaccess** file to override those in the standard configuration files unless disabled with AllowOverride directives.)

Much of the power and flexibility of the Apache Web server comes from its use of modules to extend its capabilities. Apache is implemented with a core set of directives. Modules can be created that hold definitions of other directives. They can be loaded into Apache, enabling you to use those directives for your server. A standard set of modules is included with the Apache distribution, though you can download others and even create your own. For example, the mod_autoindex module holds the directives for automatically indexing directories (as described in the following section). The mod_mime module holds the MIME type and handler directives. Modules are loaded with the **LoadModule** directive. On Red Hat and Caldera Linux, you can find

LoadModule directives in the **httpd.conf** configuration file for most of the standard modules.

```
LoadModule mime_module   modules/mod_mime.so
```

The **apxs** application provided with the Apache package can be used to build Apache extension modules. With the **apxs** application, you can compile Apache module source code in C and create dynamically shared objects that can be loaded with the **LoadModule** directive. The **apxs** application requires the **mod_so** module be part of your Apache application. It includes extensive options such as **-n** to specify the module name, **-a** to add an entry for it in the **httpd.conf** file, and **-i** to install the module on your Web server.

You can find a complete listing of Apache Web configuration directives at the Apache Web site, **www.apache.org**, and in the Apache manual located in your site's Web site root directory. On Red Hat and Caldera systems, this is located at **/var/www/manual**. Many of the more commonly used directives are listed in Table 25-3.

Server Configuration

Certain directives are used to configure your server's overall operations. These directives are placed in the **httpd.conf** configuration file. Some require pathnames, whereas others only need to be turned on or off with the keywords **on** and **off**. Apache provides a default **httpd.conf** configuration file that is used by most distributions, including Red Hat and Caldera. The **httpd.conf** file already contains these directives. Some are commented out with a preceding # symbol. You can activate a directive by removing its # sign. Many of the entries are preceded by comments explaining their purpose. The following is an example of the **ServerAdmin** directive used to set the address where users can send mail for administrative issues. You replace the **you@your.address** entry with the address you want to use to receive system administration mail. On Red Hat and Caldera systems, this is set to **root@localhost**.

```
# ServerAdmin: Your address, where problems should be e-mailed.
ServerAdmin you@your.address
```

Some directives require specific information about your system. For example, **ServerName** holds the host name for your Web server. Specifying a hostname to avoid unnecessary DNS lookup failures that can hang your server is important. Notice the entry is commented with a preceding #. Simply remove the # and type your Web server's hostname in place of **new.host.name**.

```
# ServerName allows you to set a hostname which is sent
# back to clients for your server if it's different than the
# one the program would get (i.e. use
```

```
# "www" instead of the host's real name).

#ServerName new.host.name
```

On Red Hat and Caldera systems, entries have already been made for the standard Web server installation using **/var/www** as your Web site directory. You can tailor your Web site to your own needs by changing the appropriate directives. The **DocumentRoot** directive determines the home directory for your Web pages. The **ServerRoot** directive specifies where your Web server configuration, error, and log files are kept.

```
DocumentRoot /var/www/html
ServerRoot /etc/httpd
```

The **MaxClients** directive sets the maximum number of clients that can connect to your server at the same time.

```
MaxClients 150
```

Directory-Level Configuration: .htaccess and <Directory>

One of the most flexible aspects of Apache is its capability to configure individual directories. With the **Directory** directive, you can define a block of directives that apply only to a particular directory. Such a directive can be placed in the **httpd.conf** or **access.conf** configuration file. You can also use an **.htaccess** file within a particular directory to hold configuration directives. Those directives are then applied only to that directory. The name ".htaccess" is actually set with the **AccessFileName** directive. You can change this if you want.

```
AccessFileName .htaccess
```

A *Directory block* begins with a **<Directory *pathname*>** directive, where *pathname* is the directory to be configured. The ending directive uses the same <> symbols, but with a slash preceding the term "Directory": **</Directory>**. Directives placed within this block apply only to the specified directory. The following example denies access to only the **mypics** directory by requests from **www.myvids.com**.

```
<Directory /var/www/html/mypics>
    Order Deny,Allow
    Deny from www.myvids.com
</Directory>
```

With the **Options** directive, you can enable certain features in a directory, such as the use of symbolic links, automatic indexing, execution of CGI scripts, and content negotiation. The default is the All option, which turns on all features except content negotiation (multiviews). The following example enables automatic indexing (Indexes), symbolic links (FollowSymLinks), and content negotiation (Multiviews).

```
Options Indexes FollowSymLinks Multiviews
```

Configurations made by directives in main configuration files or in upper-level directories are inherited by lower-level directories. Directives for a particular directory held in **.htaccess** files and Directory blocks can be allowed to override those configurations. This capability can be controlled by the **AllowOverride** directive. With the **all** argument, **.htaccess** files can override any previous configurations. The **none** argument disallows overrides, effectively disabling the **.htaccess** file. You can further control the override of specific groups of directives. AuthConfig enables use of authorization directives, FileInfo is for type directives, Indexes is for indexing directives, Limit is for access control directives, and Options is for the **options** directive.

```
AllowOverride all
```

Access Control

With access control directives, such as **allow** and **deny**, you can control access to your Web site by remote users and hosts. The **allow** directive followed by a list of hostnames restricts access to only those hosts. The **deny** directive with a list of hostnames denies access by those systems. The argument **all** applies the directive to all hosts. The **order** directive specifies in what order the access control directives are to be applied. Other access control directives, such as **require,** can establish authentication controls, requiring users to log in. The access control directives can be used globally to control access to the entire site or placed within **Directory** directives to control access to individual directives. In the following example, all users are allowed access.

```
order allow,deny
allow from all
```

You can further qualify access control directives by limiting them to certain HTML access methods. HTML access methods are ways a browser interacts with your Web site. For example, a browser could get information from a page (GET) or send information through it (POST). You can control such access methods using the **<Limit>** directive. **Limit** takes as its argument a list of access methods to be controlled. The directive then pairs with a **</Limit>** directive to define a Limit block within which you can place access control directives. These directives only apply to the specified access methods. You can place such Limit blocks with a Directory block to set up controls of access methods for a specific directory. On the Red Hat distribution, the following Directory block in the **/etc/config/httpd.conf** file controls access methods for your Web site's home directory, **/var/www/html**.

```
# This should be changed to whatever you set DocumentRoot to.
<Directory /var/www/html>
Options Indexes FollowSymLinks
AllowOverride All
<Limit GET>
order allow,deny
allow from all
</Limit>
</Directory>
```

Controls are inherited from upper-level directories to lower-level ones. If you want to control access strictly on a per-directory basis to your entire Web site, you can use the following entry to deny access to all users. Then, in individual directories, you can allow access to certain users, groups, or hosts.

```
<Directory /var/www/html>
    Order Deny,Allow
    Deny from All
 </Directory>
```

URL Pathnames

Certain directives can modify or complete pathname segments of a URL used to access your site. The pathname segment of the URL specifies a particular directory or Web page on your site. Directives enable you to alias or redirect pathnames, as well as to select a default Web page. With the **Alias** directive, you can let users access resources located in other parts of your system, on other file systems, or on other Web sites. An alias can use a URL for sites on the Internet, instead of a pathname for a directory on your system. With the **Redirect** directive, you can redirect a user to another site.

```
Alias /mytrain /home/dylan/trainproj
Redirect /mycars  http://www.myautos.com/mycars
```

If Apache is given only a directory to access, rather than a specific Web page, it looks for an index Web page located in that directory and displays it. The possible names for a default Web page are listed by the **DirectoryIndex** directive. The name usually used is **index.html**, but you can add others. The standard names are shown here. When Apache is given only a Web directory to access, it looks for and displays the **index.html** Web page located in it.

```
DirectoryIndex index.html index.shtml index.cgi
```

Apache also enables a user to maintain Web pages located in a special subdirectory in the user's home directory, rather than in the main Web site directory. Using a ~ followed by the user name accesses this directory. The name of this directory is specified with the **UserDir** directive. The default name is **public_html**, as shown here. The site **turtle.trek.com/~dylan** accesses the directory **turtle.trek.com/home/dylan/public_html** on the host **turtle.trek.com**.

```
UserDir public_html
```

MIME Types

When a browser accesses Web pages on a Web site, it is often accessing many different kinds of objects, including HTML files, picture and sound files, and script files. To display these objects correctly, the browser must have some indication of what kind of objects they are. A JPEG picture file is handled differently from a simple text file. The server provides this type information in the form of MIME types (see Chapter 14). MIME types are the same types used for sending attached files through Internet mailers, such as Pine. Each kind of object is associated with a given MIME type. Provided with the Mime type, the browser can correctly handle and display the object.

The MIME protocol associates a certain type with files of a given extension. For example, files with a **.jpg** extension would have the MIME type image/jpeg. The **TypesConfig** directive holds the location of the **mime.types** file, which lists all the MIME types and their associated file extensions. DefaultType is the default MIME type for any file whose type cannot be determined. AddType enables you to modify the **mime.type** types list without editing the MIME file.

```
TypesConfig /etc/mime.types
DefaultType text/plain
```

Other type directives are used to specify actions to be taken on certain documents. **AddEncoding** lets browsers decompress compressed files on the fly. **AddHandler** maps file extensions to actions, **AddLanguage** enables you to specify the language for a document. The following example marks filenames with the **.gz** extension as gzip-encoded files and files with the **.fr** extension as French language files.

```
AddEncoding x-gzip gz
AddLanguage fr .fr
```

A Web server can display and execute many different types of files and programs. Not all Web browsers are able to display all those files, though. Older browsers are the most limited. Some browsers, such as Lynx, are not designed to display even simple graphics. To allow a Web browser to display a page, the server negotiates with it to determine the type of files it can handle. To enable such negotiation, you need to enable the multiviews option.

```
Option multiviews
```

CGI Files

Common Gateway Interface (*CGI*) files are programs that can be executed by Web browsers accessing your site. CGI files are usually initiated by Web pages that execute the program as part of the content they display. Traditionally, CGI programs were placed in a directory called **cgi-bin** and could only be executed if they resided in such a special directory. Usually, only one **cgi-bin** directory exists per Web site. Red Hat and Caldera systems set up a cgi-bin directory in the **/var/www** directory, **/var/www/cgi-bin**. Here, you place any CGI programs that can be executed on your Web site. The **ScriptAlias** directive specifies an alias for your **cgi-bin** directory. Any Web pages or browsers can use the alias to reference this directory.

```
ScriptAlias /cgi-bin/ /var/www/cgi-bin/
```

If you want to execute CGI programs that reside anywhere on your Web site, you can specify that files with a **.cgi** extension are treated as executable CGI programs. You do this with the **AddHandler** directive. This directive applies certain handlers to files of a given type. The handler directive to do this is included in the default **httpd.conf** file, provided with the Apache source code files, though commented out. You can remove the comment symbol (#) to enable it.

```
AddHandler cgi-script cgi
```

Automatic Directory Indexing

When given a URL for a directory instead of an HTML file, and when no default Web page is in the directory, Apache creates a page on the fly and displays it. This is usually only a listing of the different files in the directory. In effect, Apache indexes the items in the directory for you. You can set several options for generating and displaying such an index. If **FancyIndexing** is turned on, then Web page items are displayed with icons and column headers that can be used to sort the listing.

```
FancyIndexing on
```

Icon directives tell Apache what icon to display for a certain type of file. The **AddIconByType** and **AddIconByEncoding** directives uses MIME-type information to determine the file's type and then associate the specified image with it. **AddIcon** uses the file's extension to determine its type. In the next example, the **text.gif** image is displayed for text files with the extension **.txt**. You can also use **AddIcon** to associate an image with a particular file. The **DefaultIcon** directive specifies the image used for files of undetermined type.

```
AddIcon /icons/text.gif .txt
DefaultIcon /icons/unknown.gif
AddIconByType (VID,/icons/movie.gif) video/*
```

With the **AddDescription** directive, you can add a short descriptive phrase to the filename entry. The description can be applied to an individual file or to filenames of a certain pattern.

```
AddDescription "Reunion pictures" /var/www/html/reunion.html
```

Within a directory, you can place special files that can be used to display certain text both before and after the generated listing. The **HeaderName** directive is used to set the name of the file whose text is inserted before the listing. The **ReadmeName** directive sets the name of the file whose text is placed at the end of the listing. You can use these directives in an **.htaccess** files or a **<Directory>** block to select particular files within a directory. The **ReadmeName** directive is usually set to README, and **HeaderName**, to HEADER. In that case, Apache searches for files named **HEADER** and **README** in the directory.

```
HeaderName HEADER
ReadmeName README
```

With the **IndexOptions** directive, you can set different options for displaying a generated index. Options exist for setting the height and width of icons and filenames. The **IconsAreLinks** option makes icons part of filename anchors. The **ScanHTMLTitles** read the titles in HTML documents and use those to display entries in the index listing instead of filenames. Various options exist for suppressing different index display features such as sorting, descriptions, and header/readme inserts. You can set options for individual directories using a Directory block or an **.htaccess** file. Normally, options set in higher-level directories are be inherited by lower-level ones. If you use an **IndexOption** directive to set any new option, however, all previously inherited options are cleared. If you want to keep the inherited options, you can set options using the plus (+) or minus (–) symbols. These add or remove options. If you were also to set an option without the + or – symbols, though, all inherited options would be cleared.

```
IndexOptions IconsAreLinks FancyIndexing
IndexOptions +ScanHTMLTitles
```

Authentication

Your Web server can also control access on a per-user or per-group basis to particular directories on your Web site. You can require various levels for authentication. Access can be limited to particular users and require passwords, or expanded to allow members of a group access. You can dispense with passwords altogether or set up an anonymous type of access, as used with FTP.

To apply authentication directives to a certain directory, you place those directives either within a Directory block or the directory's **.htaccess** file. You use the **require** directive to determine what users can access the directory. You can list particular users or groups. The **AuthName** directive provides the authentication realm to the user, the name used to identify the particular set of resources accessed by this authentication process. The **AuthType** directive specifies the type of authentication, such as basic or digest. A **require** directive requires also **AuthType**, **AuthName**, and directives specifying the locations of group and user authentication files. In the following example, only the users **george**, **robert**, and **mark** are allowed access to the **newpics** directory:

```
<Directory /var/www/html/newpics
AuthType Basic
AuthName Newpics
AuthUserFile /web/users
AuthGroupFile /web/groups
<Limit GET POST>
    require users george robert mark
</Limit>
</Directory>
```

The next example allows group access by administrators to the CGI directory:

```
<Directory /var/www/html/cgi-bin
AuthType Basic
AuthName CGI
AuthGroupFile /web/groups
<Limit GET POST>
    require groups admin
</Limit>
</Directory>
```

To set up anonymous access for a directory, place the **Anonymous** directive with the user anonymous as its argument in the directory's Directory block or **.htaccess** file. You can also use the **Anonymous** directive to provide access to particular users without requiring passwords from them.

Apache maintains its own user and group authentication files specifying what users and groups are allowed to which directories. These files are normally simple flat files, such as your system's password and group files. They can become large, however, possibly slowing down authentication lookups. As an alternative, many sites have used database management files in place of these flat files. Database methods are then used to access the files, providing a faster response time. Apache has directives for specifying the authentication files, depending on the type of file you are using. The **AuthUserfile** and **AuthGroupFile** directives are used to specify the location of authentication files that have a standard flat file format. The **AuthDBUserFile** and **AuthDBGroupFile** directives are used for DB database files, and the **AuthDBMGUserFIle** and **AuthDBMGGroupFile** are used for DBMG database files.

The programs **htdigest**, **htpasswd**, and **dbmmanage** are tools provided with the Apache software package for creating and maintaining *user authentication files*, which are user password files listing users who have access to specific directories or resources on your Web site. **htdigest** and **htpasswd** manage a simple flat file of user authentication records, whereas **dbmmanage** uses a more complex database management format. If your user list is extensive, you may want to use a database file for fast lookups. **htdigest** takes as its arguments the authentication file, the realm, and the username, creating or updating the user entry. **htpasswd** can also employ encryption on the password. **dbmmanage** has an extensive set of options to add, delete, and update user entries. A variety of different database formats are used to set up such files. Three common ones are Berkeley DB2, NDBM, and GNU GBDM. **dbmanage** looks for the system libraries for these formats in that order. Be careful to be consistent in using the same format for your authentication files.

Log Files

Apache maintains logs of all requests by users to your Web site. By default, these logs include records using the *Common Log Format* (*CLF*). The record for each request takes up a line composed of several fields: host, identity check, authenticated user (for logins), the date, the request line submitted by the client, the status sent to the client, and the size of the object sent in bytes. Using the **LogFormat** and **CustomLog** directives, you can customize your log record to add more fields with varying levels of detail. These directives use a format string consisting of field specifiers to determine the fields to record in a log record. You add whatever fields you want, and in any order. A field specifier consists of a percent (%) symbol followed by an identifying character. For example, %h is the field specifier for a remote host, %b, for the size in bytes, and %s, for the status. See the documentation for the **mod_log_config** module for a complete listing. Table 25-4 lists several of the commonly used ones. You should quote fields

Format Specifier	Description
% a	Remote IP address
% A	Local IP address
% b	Bytes sent, excluding HTTP headers
% {*variable*}e:	The contents of the environment *variable*
% f	Filename
% h	Remote host
% l	Remote logname (from identd, if supplied)
% m	The request method
% P	The process ID of the child that serviced the request
% r	First line of request
% s	Status
% t	Time, in common log format time format (standard English format)
% u	Remote user
% U	The URL path requested
% v	The canonical ServerName of the server serving the request

Table 25-4.   *Apache Log Format Specifiers*

whose contents may take up more than one word. The quotes themselves must be quoted with a backslash to be included in the format string. The following example is the Common Log Format implemented as a **FormatLog** directive:

```
FormatLog "%h %l %u %t \"%r\" %s %b"
```

Instead of maintaining one large log file, you can create several log files using the **CustomLog** or **TransferLog** directive. This is helpful for virtual hosts where you may want to maintain a separate log file for each host. You use the **FormatLog** directive to define a default format for log records. The **TransferLog** then uses this default as its format when creating a new log file. **CustomLog** combines both operations, enabling you to create a new file and to define a format for it.

```
FormatLog "%h %l %u %t \"%r\" %s %b"
# Create a new log file called myprojlog using the FormatLog format
TransferLog myprojlog
# Create a new log file called mypicslog using its own format
CustomLog mypicslog "%h %l %u %t \"%r\" %s %b"
```

Certain field specifiers in the log format can be qualified to record specific information. The *%i specifier* records header lines in requests the server receives. The reference for the specific header line to record is placed within braces between the % and the field specifier. For example, User-agent is the header line that indicates the browser software used in the request. To record User-agent header information, use the conversion specifier %{User-agent}i.

To maintain compatibility with NCSA servers, Apache originally implemented **AgentLog** and **RefererLog** directives to record User-agent and Referer headers. These have since been replaced by qualified %i field specifiers used for the **LogFormat** and **CustomLog** directives. A referer header records link information from clients, detecting who may have links to your site. The following is an NCSA-compliant log format:

```
"%h %l %u %t \"%r\" %s %b\"%{Referer}i\" \"%{User-agent}i\"".
```

Apache provides two utilities for processing and managing log files. **logresolve** resolves IP addresses in your log file to host names. **rotatelogs** rotates log files without having to kill the server. You can specify the rotation time.

Directive	Description
AccessConfig *filename*	File to be read for more directives after reading the ResourceConfig file. *Filename* is relative to the ServerRoot. Default: AccessConfig **conf/access.conf** Context: server config, virtual host
AccessFileName *filename filename ...*	Default directory configuration filenames located within directories. Default: AccessFileName **.htaccess** Context: server config, virtual host

Table 25-3. *Apache Configuration Directives*

Directive	Description
Action *action-type cgi-script*	Adds an action, which activates *cgi-script* when *action-type* is triggered by the request. Context: server config, virtual host, directory, **.htaccess** Override: FileInfo Module: mod_actions
AddDescription *string file file ...*	Sets the description to display for a file. Can be a file extension, partial filename, wildcard expression, or full filename. String is enclosed in double quotes ("). Context: server config, virtual host, directory, **.htaccess** Override: Indexes Status: Base Module: mod_autoindex
AddHandler *handler-name extension extension ...*	Maps the filename extensions *extension* to the handler *handler-name*. Context: server config, virtual host, directory, **.htaccess** Override: FileInfo Status: Base Module: mod_mime
AddIcon *icon name name ...*	Specifies the icon to display next to a file ending in *name*. Context: server config, virtual host, directory, **.htaccess** Override: Indexes Status: Base Module: mod_autoindex
AddIconByEncoding *icon MIME-encoding MIME-encoding ...*	Specifies the icon to display next to files with *MIME-encoding* (FancyIndexing). Context: server config, virtual host, directory, **.htaccess** Override: Indexes Status: Base Module: mod_autoindex

Table 25-3.   *Apache Configuration Directives* (continued)

Directive	Description
AddIconByType *icon MIME-type MIME-type ...*	Specifies the icon to display next to files of type *MIME-type* (FancyIndexing). Context: server config, virtual host, directory, **.htaccess** Override: Indexes Status: Base Module: mod_autoindex
AddLanguage *MIME-lang extension extension ...*	Maps the given filename extensions to the specified content language. Context: server config, virtual host, directory, **.htaccess** Override: FileInfo Status: Base Module: mod_mime
AddModule *module module ...*	Enables use of modules compiled, but not in use. Context: server config
Alias *url-path directory-filename*	Enables access to documents stored in the local file system, other than under the DocumentRoot. Context: server config, virtual host Status: Base Module: mod_alias
allow *from host host ...*	Determines which hosts can access a given directory: all, partial, or full domain name, or IP address. Context: directory, **.htaccess** Override: Limit Status: Base Module: mod_access
AllowOverride *override override ...*	Directives that can be overridden by entries in an **.htaccess** file. All allows overrides, and none denies them. Default: AllowOverride All Context: directory

Table 25-3.   *Apache Configuration Directives* (continued)

Directive	Description
Anonymous *user user ...*	Users who are allowed access without password verification. *User* is usually anonymous (case-sensitive). Default: none Context: directory, **.htaccess** Override: AuthConfig Status: Extension Module: mod_auth_anon
Anonymous_Authoritative on | off	When on, there is no fall-through to other authorization methods. Default: Anonymous_Authoritative off Context: directory, **.htaccess** Override: AuthConfig Status: Extension Module: mod_auth_anon
AddType *MIME-type extension extension ...*	Maps the given filename extensions onto the specified content type. *MIME-type* is the MIME type to use for filenames containing *extension*. Context: server config, virtual host, directory, **.htaccess** Override: FileInfo Status: Base Module: mod_mime
AuthGroupFile *filename*	Sets the name of the file with the list of user groups for user authentication. Context: directory, **.htaccess** Override: AuthConfig Status: Base Module: mod_auth
AuthDBGroupFile *filename*	DB file containing the list of groups for user authentication. Context: directory, **.htaccess** Override: AuthConfig Status: Extension Module: mod_auth_db

Table 25-3.   *Apache Configuration Directives* (continued)

SERVERS

Directive	Description
AuthDBUserFile *filename*	DB file containing the list of users and passwords for user authentication. Context: directory, **.htaccess** Override: AuthConfig Status: Extension Module: mod_auth_db
AuthDBMGroupFile *filename*	DBM file containing the list of groups for user authentication. Context: directory, **.htaccess** Override: AuthConfig Status: Extension Module: mod_auth_dbm
AuthDBMUserFile *filename*	DBM file containing the list of users and passwords for user authentication. Context: directory, **.htaccess** Override: AuthConfig Status: Extension Module: mod_auth_dbm
AuthName *auth-domain*	The authorization realm for a directory. A realm is given to the client so the user knows which username and password to send. Context: directory, **.htaccess** Override: AuthConfig
AuthType *type*	Type of user authentication for a directory. Only Basic and Digest are currently implemented. Context: directory, **.htaccess** Override: AuthConfig
AuthUserFile *filename*	Sets the name of the file with the list of users and passwords for user authentication. Context: directory, **.htaccess** Override: AuthConfig Status: Base Module: mod_auth

Table 25-3. *Apache Configuration Directives* (continued)

Directive	Description
BindAddress *saddr*	Binds the server to a specified IP address. If the value is *, then the server listens for connections on every IP address; otherwise, the server only listens on the IP address specified. Only one BindAddress directive can be used. For more control over the address and ports listened to, use the **Listen** directive. Default: BindAddress * Context: server config
CheckSpelling on | off	Enables or disables spelling module. This module tries to find a matching document by comparing each document name in the requested directory against the requested document name, disregarding case and allowing up to one misspelling. Default: CheckSpelling Off Context: server config, virtual host, directory, **.htaccess** Override: Options Status: Base Module: mod_speling
ClearModuleList	Clears the built-in list of active modules. Context: server config
CustomLog *file-pipe format-or-nickname*	Creates a new log file with the specified format. Context: server config, virtual host Status: Base Compatibility: Nickname only available in Apache 1.3 or later Module: mod_log_config
DefaultIcon *url*	Specifies the icon to display for files when no specific icon is known (FancyIndexing). Context: server config, virtual host, directory, **.htaccess** Override: Indexes Status: Base Module: mod_autoindex

Table 25-3. *Apache Configuration Directives* (continued)

Directive	Description
DefaultLanguage *MIME-lang*	Specifies *MIME-lang* as the default file language. Context: server config, virtual host, directory, **.htaccess** Override: FileInfo Status: Base Module: mod_mime
DefaultType *MIME-type*	Default type for documents whose type cannot be determined by their MIME types mappings. Default: DefaultType text/html Context: server config, virtual host, directory, **.htaccess** Override: FileInfo
deny *from host host ...*	Determines hosts that can access a given directory: **all**, or partial or full domain name or IP address. Context: directory, **.htaccess** Override: Limit Status: Base Module: mod_access
<Directory *directory>* ... **</Directory>**	**<Directory>** and **</Directory>** directives operate as tags that enclose a group of directives applying only to the named directory and subdirectories of that directory. Context: server config, virtual host
<DirectoryMatch *regex>* ... **</DirectoryMatch>**	**<DirectoryMatch>** and **</DirectoryMatch>** enclose a group of directives that apply only to the named directory. It operates the same as **<Directory>,** but takes a regular expression as an argument. Context: server config, virtual host

Table 25-3.   *Apache Configuration Directives* (continued)

Directive	Description
DirectoryIndex *local-url local-url ...*	Specifies the list of resources to look for when the client requests an index of the directory by specifying a / at the end of a directory name (usually **index.html**). Default: DirectoryIndex **index.html** Context: server config, virtual host, directory, **.htaccess** Override: Indexes Status: Base Module: mod_dir
DocumentRoot *directory-filename*	The directory from which **httpd** serves files. Default: DocumentRoot **/usr/local/apache/htdocs** (**/var/www/html** on Red Hat and Caldera systems) Context: server config, virtual host
ErrorDocument *error-code document*	Redirects to a local or external URL to handle the problem/error. Context: server config, virtual host, directory, **.htaccess**
ErrorLog *filename* | *syslog*[:*facility*]	The file on which the server logs errors. Default: ErrorLog logs/error_log Context: server config, virtual host
FancyIndexing *Boolean*	Sets the FancyIndexing option for a directory. Boolean can be on or off. Context: server config, virtual host, directory, **.htaccess** Override: Indexes Status: Base Module: mod_autoindex
<Files *filename*> ... **</Files>**	Provides for access control by filename. Similar to the **<Directory>** directive and **<Location>** directive. **<Files>** sections are processed in the order they appear in the configuration file, after the **<Directory>** sections and **.htaccess** files are read, but before **<Location>** sections. **<Files>** can be nested inside **<Directory>** sections to restrict the portion of the file system to which they apply. Context: server config, virtual host, **.htaccess**

Table 25-3.   *Apache Configuration Directives* (continued)

SERVERS

Directive	Description
<FilesMatch *regex>* ... **</FilesMatch>**	Provides for access control by filename like the **<Files>** directive, but uses a regular expression. Context: server config, virtual host, **.htaccess**
Group *unix-group*	Sets the group for the server. The standalone server must be run initially as root. The recommendation is you set up a new group specifically for running the server. Default: Group #-1 Context: server config, virtual host
HeaderName *filename*	Specifies the name of the file to be inserted at the top of the index listing (FancyIndexing). Context: server config, virtual host, directory, **.htaccess** Override: Indexes Status: Base Module: mod_autoindex
HostNameLookups on | off | double	Enables DNS lookups so host names can be logged. Double refers to double-reverse DNS. Default: HostNameLookups off Context: server config, virtual host, directory
IdentityCheck *Boolean*	Enables RFC 1413–compliant logging of the remote user name for each connection. Default: IdentityCheck off Context: server config, virtual host, directory
<IfDefine [!]*parameter-name>* ... **</IfDefine>** Default: NoneContext: all	The **<IfDefine test>...</IfDefine>** section specifies conditional directives. Directives within an **IfDefine** section are processed if the test is true and are ignored otherwise. The test consists of a parameter name, which is true if the parameter is defined, and false if undefined. A ! placed before the parameter makes the test true if the parameter is undefined (not).

Table 25-3.   *Apache Configuration Directives* (continued)

Directive	Description
<IfModule [!]*module-name*> ... **</IfModule>**	The **<IfModule test>...</IfModule>** section specifies conditional directives. The test checks to see if a module is compiled in Apache. It is true if present, and false if not. A !*module-name* is true if the module is not present.
Include *filename*	Inclusion of other configuration files. Context: server config
IndexOptions [+	-]*option* [+	-]*option* ...	Set options for directory indexing: FancyIndexing, IconHeight, IconsAreLinks, IconWidth, NameWidth, ScanHTMLTitles, SuppressDescription. Context: server config, virtual host, directory, **.htaccess** Override: Indexes Status: Base Module: mod_autoindex
KeepAlive on/off	Enables persistent connections, "Off" to disable. Default: KeepAlive On Context: server config
KeepAliveTimeout *seconds*	The number of seconds Apache waits for another request before closing the connection. Default: KeepAliveTimeout 15 Context: server config
<Limit *method method* ... > ... **</Limit>**	**<Limit>** and **</Limit>** specify a group of access control directives that apply only to the specified access methods, any valid HTTP method. Access control directive appearing outside a **<Limit>** directive apply to all access methods. Method names are GET, POST, PUT, DELETE, CONNECT, or OPTIONS
<LimitExcept *method method* ... > ... **</LimitExcept>**	**<LimitExcept>** and **</LimitExcept>** specify a group of access control directives, which then apply to any HTTP access method *not* listed in the arguments

Table 25-3.   *Apache Configuration Directives* (continued)

Directive	Description
LimitRequestBody *number*	Limits the size of an HTTP request message body. Default: LimitRequestBody 0 Context: server config, virtual host, directory, **.htaccess**
LimitRequestFields *number*	Limits the number of request header fields allowed in an HTTP request. Default: LimitRequestFields 100 Context: server config
Listen [*IP address:*]*port number*	Listens to more than one IP address or port. By default, it responds to requests on all IP interfaces, but only on the port given by the Port directive. Context: server config
ListenBacklog *backlog*	The maximum length of the queue of pending connections. Default: ListenBacklog 511 Context: server config
LoadFile *filename filename ...*	Links in the named object files or libraries when the server is started or restarted. Used to load additional code required for some module to work Context: server config Status: Base Module: mod_so
LoadModule *module filename*	Links in the object file or library filename and adds the module structure named *module* to the list of active modules. Context: server config Status: Base Module: mod_so
<Location *URL***>** ... **</Location>**	The **<Location>** directive provides for access control by URL. Similar to the **<Directory>** directive. Context: server config, virtual host
<LocationMatch *regex***>** ... **</LocationMatch>**	Provides access control by URL, in an identical manner to **<Location>**, using a regular expression an argument. Context: server config, virtual host

Table 25-3. *Apache Configuration Directives* (continued)

Directive	Description
LockFile *filename*	Path to the lockfile used when Apache is compiled. Default: LockFile logs/accept.lock Context: server config
LogFormat *format* [*nickname*]	Sets the format of the default logfile named by the TransferLog directive Default: LogFormat "%h %l %u %t \"%r\" %s %b" Context: server config, virtual host Status: Base Module: mod_log_config
LogLevel *level*	Adjusts the verbosity of the messages recorded in the error logs. Default: LogLevel error Context: server config, virtual host
MaxClients *number*	Limits the number of simultaneous requests that can be supported. Any connection attempts over the MaxClients limit are normally queued, up to a number based on the **ListenBacklog** directive. Default: MaxClients 256 Context: server config
MaxKeepAliveRequests *number*	Limits the number of requests allowed per connection when KeepAlive is on Default: MaxKeepAliveRequests 100 Context: server config
NameVirtualHost *addr*[*:port*]	Specifies the address a name-based virtual host name resolves. If you have multiple name-based hosts on multiple addresses, repeat the directive for each address. Required for configuring name-based virtual hosts. Although *addr* can be a hostname, the recommendation is for you always to use an IP address. Context: server config

Table 25-3.   *Apache Configuration Directives* (continued)

Directive	Description
`Options` [+	-]*option* [+	-]*option* ...	Controls the server features available in a particular directory. If set to None, then none of the extra features are enabled. **All** All options except for MultiViews. This is the default setting. **ExecCGI** Execution of CGI scripts is permitted. **FollowSymLinks** The server follows symbolic links in this directory. **Includes** Server-side includes are permitted. **IncludesNOEXEC** Server-side includes are permitted, but the #exec command and #include of CGI scripts are disabled. **Indexes** Returns a formatted listing of the directory for directories with no DirectoryIndex. **MultiViews** Content negotiated MultiViews are allowed. **SymLinksIfOwnerMatch** The server only follows symbolic links for which the target file or directory is owned by the same user ID as the link. Context: server config, virtual host, directory, **.htaccess** Override: Options
`order` *ordering*	Controls the order in which allow and deny directives are evaluated Default: order deny, allow Context: directory, **.htaccess** Override: Limit Status: Base Module: mod_access
`PidFile` *filename*	File in which the server records the process ID of the daemon. Default: PidFile logs/httpd.pid Context: server config

Table 25-3. *Apache Configuration Directives* (continued)

Directive	Description
Port *number*	If no **Listen** or **BindAddress** directives exist, then a port directive sets the network port on which the server listens. Ports for a virtual host are set by the **VirtualHost** directive. Default: Port 80 Context: server config
ReadmeName *filename*	Specifies the name of the file to be appended to the end of the index listing. Context: server config, virtual host, directory, **.htaccess** Override: Indexes Status: Base Module: mod_autoindex
Redirect [*status*] *url-path url*	Maps an old URL into a new one. Context: server config, virtual host, directory, **.htaccess** Override: FileInfo Status: Base Module: mod_alias
RemoveHandler *extension extension* ...	Removes handler associations for files with the given extensions. This allows **.htaccess** files in subdirectories to undo any associations inherited from parent directories or the server configuration files. Context: directory, **.htaccess** Status: Base Module: mod_mime
require *entity-name entity entity* ...	Selects the authenticated users that can access a directory. *entity-name* is either the user or group, followed by a list of users or groups. require user *userid userid* ... require *group group-name group-name* ... Context: directory, **.htaccess**Override: AuthConfig
ResourceConfig *filename*	Server reads this file for more directives after reading the **httpd.conf** file. Default: ResourceConfig conf/srm.conf Context: server config, virtual host

Table 25-3.   *Apache Configuration Directives* (continued)

Directive	Description
Satisfy *directive*	Access policy if both allow and require are used. The parameter can be either 'all' or 'any'. Syntax: Satisfy 'any' or 'all' Default: Satisfy all Context: directory, **.htaccess**
ScoreBoardFile *filename*	Specifies the ScoreBoardFile file. Default: ScoreBoardFile logs/apache_status Context: server config
Script *method cgi-script*	Adds an action, which activates *cgi-script* when a file is requested using the method of *method*, which can be one of GET, POST, PUT, or DELETE. Context: server config, virtual host, directory Status: Base Module: mod_actions
ScriptAlias *url-path directory-filename*	Marks the target directory as containing CGI scripts. Context: server config, virtual host Status: Base Module: mod_alias
ScriptInterpreterSource 'registry' or 'script'	Finds the interpreter used to run CGI scripts. The default method is to use the interpreter pointed to by the #! line in the script. Default: ScriptInterpreterSource script Context: directory, **.htaccess**
ServerAdmin *e-mail-address*	The e-mail address included in any error messages sent to a client. Context: server config, virtual host
ServerAlias *host1 host2 ...*	Sets the alternate names for a host, for use with name-based virtual hosts. Context: virtual host
ServerName *fully qualified domain name*	Sets the host name of the server. This is only used when creating redirection URLs. If it is not specified, then the server attempts to deduce it from its own IP address. Context: server config, virtual host

Table 25-3. *Apache Configuration Directives* (continued)

Directive	Description
ServerPath *pathname*	Sets the legacy URL pathname for a host, for use with name-based virtual hosts. Context: virtual host
ServerRoot *directory-filename*	Sets the directory in which the server resides. Default: ServerRoot /usr/local/apache Context: server config
ServerSignature Off | On | EMail	Configures a trailing footer line under server-generated documents, such as error messages. Default: ServerSignature Off Context: server config, virtual host, directory, **.htaccess**
ServerType *type*	Sets how the server is executed by the system. *type* can be either inetd or standalone. Default: ServerType standalone Context: server config
SetHandler *handler-name*	Forces all matching files to be parsed through the handler given by *handler-name*. Context: directory, **.htaccess** Status: Base Module: mod_mime
StartServers *number*	Sets the number of child server processes created on startup. Default: StartServers 5 Context: server config
TimeOut *number*	Sets the timeout in seconds for receiving GET requests, receipt of POST and PUT requests, and TCP packet transmissions acknowledgments. Default: TimeOut 300 Context: server config
TransferLog *file-pipe*	Adds a log file in the format defined by the most recent **LogFormat** directive or Common Log Format if default is specified. Default: none Context: server config, virtual host Status: Base Module: mod_log_config

Table 25-3.   *Apache Configuration Directives* (continued)

SERVERS

Directive	Description
TypesConfig *filename*	Sets the location of the MIME types configuration file. Default: TypesConfig conf/MIME.types Context: server config Status: Base Module: mod_mime
User *unix-userid*	Specifies the user ID for the server. The standalone server must be run as root initially. You can use a user name or a user ID number. The user should have no access to system files. The recommendation is for you to set up a new user and group specifically for running the server. Default: User #-1 Context: server config, virtual host
UserDir *directory/filename*	Sets the real directory in a user's home directory to use when a request for a document for a user is received. Default: UserDir public_html Context: server config, virtual host Status: Base Module: mod_userdir
<VirtualHost *addr*[*:port*] ...> ... <**/VirtualHost**>	**<VirtualHost>** and **</VirtualHost>** specify a group of directives that apply only to a particular virtual host. When the server receives a request for a document on a particular virtual host, it uses the configuration directives enclosed in the **<VirtualHost>** section. *Addr* can be an IP address of the virtual host or its fully qualified domain name. Each VirtualHost must correspond to a different IP address, a different port number, or a different host name for the server. Context: server config

Table 25-3.   *Apache Configuration Directives* (continued)

Virtual Hosting

Virtual hosting allows the Apache Web server to host multiple Web sites as part of its own. In effect, the server can act as several servers, each hosted Web site appearing separate to outside users. Apache supports both IP address and name-based virtual hosting. IP address virtual hosts use valid registered IP addresses, whereas name-based virtual hosts use fully qualified domain addresses. These domain addresses are provided by the Host header from the requesting browser. The server can then determine the correct virtual host to use on the basis of the domain name alone. Note, SSL servers require IP Virtual Hosting. See **www.apache.org/docs/vhost** for more information.

IP Address Virtual Hosts

In the IP address virtual hosting method, your server must have a different IP address for each virtual host. The IP addresses you use is already set up to reference your system. Network system administration operations can set up your machine to support several IP addresses. Your machine could have separate physical network connections for each one, or a particular connection could be configured to listen for several IP addresses at once. In effect, any of the IP addresses can access your system.

You can configure Apache to run a separate daemon for each virtual host, separately listening for each IP address, or you can have a single daemon running that listens for requests for all the virtual hosts. To set up a single daemon to manage all virtual hosts, use **VirtualHost** directives. To set up a separate daemon for each host, also use the **Listen** and **BindAddress** directives.

A **VirtualHost** directive block must be set up for each virtual host. Within each **VirtualHost** block, you place the appropriate directives for accessing a host. You should have **ServerAdmin**, **ServerName**, **DocumentRoot**, and **TransferLog** directives specifying the particular values for that host. You can use any directive within a **VirtualHost** block, except for **ServerType**, **StartServers**, **MaxSpareServers**, **MinSpareServers**, **MaxRequestsPerChild**, **BindAddress**, **Listen**, **PidFile**, **TypesConfig**, **ServerRoot**, and **NameVirtualHost**.

Although you can use domain names for the address in the **VirtualHost** directive, using the actual IP address is preferable. This way, you are not dependent on your domain name service to make the correct domain name associations. Be sure to leave an IP address for your main server. If you use all the available IP addresses for your machine for virtual hosts, then you can no longer access your main server. You could, of course, reconfigure your main server as a virtual host. The following example shows two IP-based virtual hosts blocks: one using an IP address and the other, a domain name that associates with an IP address:

```
<VirtualHost 192.168.1.23>
    ServerAdmin webmaster@mail.mypics.com
    DocumentRoot /groups/mypics/html
    ServerName www.mypics.com
    ErrorLog /groups/mypics/logs/error_log
    …..
</VirtualHost>

<VirtualHost www.myproj.org>
    ServerAdmin webmaster@mail.myproj.org
    DocumentRoot /groups/myproj/html
    ServerName www.myproj.org
    ErrorLog /groups/myproj/logs/error_log
    ....
</VirtualHost>
```

Name-Based Virtual Hosts

With IP-based virtual hosting, you are limited to the number of IP addresses your system supports. With name-based virtual hosting, you can support any number of virtual hosts using no additional IP addresses. With only a single IP address for your machine, you can still support an unlimited number of virtual hosts. Such a capability is made possible by the HTTP/1.1 protocol, which lets a server identify the name by which it is being accessed. This method requires the client, the remote user, to use a browser that supports the HTTP/1.1 protocol, as current browsers do (though older ones may not). A browser using such a protocol can send a host: header specifying the particular host to use on a machine.

To implement name-based virtual hosting, use a **VirtualHost** directive for each host and a **NameVirtualHost** directive to specify the IP address you want to use for the virtual hosts. If your system has only one IP address, you need to use that address. Within the **VirtualHost** directives, you use the **ServerName** directive to specify the domain name you want to use for that host. Using **ServerName** to specify the domain name is important to avoid a DNS lookup. A DNS lookup failure disables the virtual host. The **VirtualHost** directives each take the same IP address specified in the **NameVirtualHost** directive as its argument You use Apache directives within the **VirtualHost** blocks to configure each host separately. Name-based virtual hosting uses the domain name address specified in a host: header to determine the virtual host to use. If no such information exists, the first host is used as the default. The following example implements two name-based virtual hosts. Here **www.mypics.com**

and **www.myproj.org** are implemented as name-based virtual hosts, instead of IP-based hosts:

```
ServerName turlte.trek.com

NameVirtualHost 192.168.1.5

<VirtualHost 192.168.1.5>
    ServerName www.mypics.com
    ServerAdmin webmaster@mail.mypics.com
    DocumentRoot /var/www/mypics/html
    ErrorLog /var/www/mypics/logs/error_log
    ...
</VirtualHost>

<VirtualHost 192.168.1.5>
    ServerName www.myproj.org
    ServerAdmin webmaster@mail.myproj.org
    DocumentRoot /var/www/myproj/html
    ErrorLog /var/www/myproj/logs/error_log
    ....
</VirtualHost>
```

If your system has only one IP address, then implementing virtual hosts prevents access to your main server with that address. You could no longer use your main server as a Web server directly; you could only use it indirectly to manage your virtual host. You could configure a virtual host to manage your main server's Web pages. You would then use your main server to support a set of virtual hosts that would function as Web sites, rather than the main server operating as one site directly. If your machine has two or more IP addresses, you can use one for the main server and the other for your virtual hosts. You can even mix IP-based virtual hosts and name-based virtual hosts on your server. You can also use separate IP addresses to support different sets of virtual hosts. You can further have several domain addresses access the same virtual host. To do so, place a **ServerAlias** directive listing the domain names within the selected **VirtualHost** block.

```
ServerAlias www.mypics.com www.greatpics.com
```

Requests sent to the IP address used for your virtual hosts have to match one of the configured virtual domain names. To catch requests that do not match one of these virtual hosts, you can set up a default virtual host using *_default_:*. Unmatched requests are then handled by this virtual host.

```
<VirtualHost _default_:*>
```

Dynamic Virtual Hosting

If you have implemented many virtual hosts on your server that have basically the same configuration, you can use a technique called *dynamic virtual hosting* to have these virtual hosts generated dynamically. The code for implementing your virtual hosts becomes much smaller, and as a result, your server accesses them faster. Adding yet more virtual hosts becomes a simple matter of creating appropriate directories and adding entries for them in the DNS server.

To make dynamic virtual hosting work, the server uses commands in the mod_vhost_alias module (supported in Apache version 1.3.6 and up) to rewrite both the server name and the document root to those of the appropriate virtual server (for older Apache versions before 1.3.6, you use the mod_rewrite module). Dynamic virtual hosting can be either name-based or IP-based. In either case, you have to set the **UseCanonicalName** directive in such a way as to allow the server to use the virtual host name instead of the server's own name. For name-based hosting, you simply turn off **UseCanonicalName**. This allows your server to obtain the host name from the host: header of the user request. For IP-based hosting, you set the **UseCanonicalName** to DNS. This allows the server to look up the host in the DNS server.

```
UseCanonicalName  Off
UseCanonicalName DNS
```

You then have to enable the server to locate the different Document root directories and CGI bin directories for your various virtual hosts. You use the **VirtualDocumentRoot** directive to specify the template for virtual hosts' directories. For example, if you place the different host directories in the **/var/www/hosts** directory, then you could set the **VirtualDocumentRoot** directive accordingly.

```
VirtualDocumentRoot    /var/www/hosts/%0/html
```

The %0 will be replaced with the virtual host's name, when that virtual host is accessed. It is important that you create the dynamic virtual host's directory using that host's name. For example, for a dynamic virtual host called **www.mygolf.org**, you would create a directory named **/var/www/hosts/www.mygolf.org**. Then create subdirectories for the Document root and CGI programs as in **/var/www/hosts/www.mygolf.org/html**. For the CGI directory, use the **VirtualScriptAlias** directive to specify the CGI subdirectory you use.

```
VirtualScriptAlias    /var/www/hosts/%0/cgi-bin
```

A simple example of name-based dynamic virtual hosting directives follows.

```
UseCanonicalName Off
VirtualDocumentRoot /var/www/hosts/%0/html
VirtualScriptAlias    /var/www/hosts/%0/cgi-bin
```

To make this example implement IP-based dynamic virtual hosting instead, simply set the **UseCanonicalName** to DNS instead of Off.

```
UseCanonicalName DNS
VirtualDocumentRoot /var/www/hosts/%0/html
VirtualScriptAlias    /var/www/hosts/%0/cgi-bin
```

One drawback of dynamic virtual hosting is that you can only set up one log for all your hosts. However, you can create your own shell program to simply cut out the entries for the different hosts in that log.

```
LogFormat "%V %h %l %u %t \"%r\" %s %b" vcommon
CustomLog logs/access_log vcommon
```

Implementing IP-based dynamic virtual hosting in the standard way as shown previously will slow down the process, as your server will have to perform a DNS lookup to discover the name of your server using its IP address. You can avoid this step by simply using the IP address for your virtual host's directory. So for IP virtual host **192.198.1.6**, you would create a directory **/var/www/hosts/192.198.1.6**, with an **html** subdirectory for that host's Document root. The directive will look the same, but now the IP address can be mapped directly to the Document root directory name, no longer requiring a DNS lookup. Also be sure to include the IP address in your log, **%A**.

```
UseCanonicalName DNS
LogFormat "%A %h %l %u %t \"%r\" %s %b" vcommon
CustomLog logs/access_log vcommon

VirtualDocumentRoot /var/www/hosts/%0/html
VirtualScriptAlias    /var/www/hosts/%0/cgi-bin
```

You can mix these commands in with other Virtual host entries as you need them. For example, to specify the Document root directory for a non–dynamic name based virtual host, you could simply use the **VirtualDocumentRoot** directive. In other words, you can simply use the same directories for both dynamic and nondynamic virtual hosts. You could still specify other directories for different nondynamic virtual hosts as you wish. In the following example, the **www.mypics.com** name-based virtual host uses the dynamic virtual host directive **VirtualDocumentRoot** to set its document root directory. It now uses **/var/www/www.mypics.com/html** as its document root directory. The CGI directory, however, is set as a nondynamic directory, **/var/www/mypics/cgi-bin**.

```
UseCanonicalName Off

NameVirtualHost 192.168.1.5

<VirtualHost 192.168.1.5>
    ServerName www.mypics.com
    ServerAdmin webmaster@mail.mypics.com
    VirtualDocumentRoot /var/www/%0/html
    ScriptAlias   /var/www/mypics/cgi-bin
    ...
</VirtualHost>
```

Server Side Includes

Server-side includes (*SSIs*) are designed to provide a much more refined control of your Web site content, namely the Web pages themselves. Server-side includes are Apache directives placed within particular Web pages as part of the page's HTML code. You can configure your Apache Web server to look for SSI directives in particular Web pages and execute them. First, you have to use the Options directive with the include option to allow SSI directives.

```
Options Includes
```

You need to instruct the server to parse particular Web pages. The easiest way to enable parsing is to instruct Apache to parse HTML files with specified extensions. Usually, the extension **.shtml** is used for Web pages that have SSI directories. In fact, in the default Apache configuration files, you can find the following entry to enable parsing for SSI directives in HTML files. The **AddType** directive here adds the **.shtml** type as an HTML type of file, and the **AddHandler** directive specifies that **.shtml** files are to be parsed (server-parsed).

```
# To use server-parsed HTML files
AddType text/html .shtml
AddHandler server-parsed .shtml
```

Instead of creating a separate type of file, you can use the **XBitHack** directive to have Apache parse any executable file for SSI directives. In other words, any file with execute permission (see Chapter 9) will be parsed for SSI directives.

SSI directives operate much like statements in a programming language. You can define variables, create loops, and use tests to select alternate directives. An SSI directive consists of an element followed by attributes that can be assigned values. The syntax for a SSI directive is shown here.

```
<!--#element attribute=value …  -->
```

You can think of an element as operating much like a command in a programming language and attributes as its arguments. For example, to assign a value to a variable, you use the **set** element with the variable assignment as its attribute. The **if** directive displays any following text on the given Web page. The **if** directive takes as its attribute **expr**, which is assigned the expression to test. The test is able to compare two strings using standard comparison operators like **<=**, **!=**, or **=**. Variables used in the test are evaluated with the **$** operator.

```
<!--#set myvar="Goodbye"  -->
<!--#if expr="$myvar = Hello"  -->
```

Other helpful SSI elements are **exec**, which executes CGI programs, or **shell** commands, which read the contents of a file into the Web page and also execute CGI files. The **echo** element displays values such as the date, the document's name, and the page's URL. With the **config** element, you can configure certain values, such as the date or file size.

Apache GUI Configuration Tools: Comanche and Linuxconf

The Apache GUI Project (**gui.apache.org**) provides a set of GUI tools for configuring and managing your Apache Web server. Its currently active projects are Comanche and TkApache. An older Comanche module comes with the Red Hat distribution. In the Linuxconf utility, you can also configure your Apache Web server. Webmin provides a very complete Apache Web server module.

Comanche (Configuration Manager for Apache) is an easy-to-use, full-featured Apache configuration utility that runs on any X Windows window manager. You can download the current version and documentation from the Comanche Web site at **www.comanche.org**. Comanche uses a simple, directory tree–like structure to enable you to access and configure your main Web server, and any virtual server you have set up. Currently, Comanche can only configure the server on your local machine, but in the future, it may be able to configure remote servers.

When you first start the program, a window displayed where you enter in information about your Web server. This includes a description you want to give it, along with the locations of the server executable file, its configuration files, and the document root directory (see Figure 25-1). You can also define aliases for commands such as those to start and stop the server.

The main Comanche window is divided into two panes: The left pane is a tree of Apache servers, and the right pane show the items in the selected entry in the tree (see Figure 25-2). Unlike in ordinary programs, the menus are in the form of pop-up menus activated on entries in the server tree, not from the menu bar at the top of the window. This menu bar only has an entry for quitting the program and accessing help.

The server tree in the upper pane of the Comanche main window initially only shows one entry, the name of your server with a computer icon. Click the plus sign to the left to expand the tree to show the different services you can configure. Expand the Networking entry to list the Apache server. Expand the tree for the server entry to display Server Management and Default Web server entries. To perform actions on any of these entries, you use pop-up menus that you activate by right-clicking the entry. A right-click on the Server Management entry displays a pop-up menu with items to Start, Stop, Restart, and Query the server status, as well as to save your configuration. Any changes you make with Comanche are not made in your Apache configuration files until you explicitly save the configuration by selecting this item in the Server Management pop-up menu. Be sure to save before you quit. To see what actual entries are going to be made in the Apache configuration files, choose the server entry,

Figure 25-1.   *Comanche Server Information*

Figure 25-2. *The Comanche Apache configuration tool*

right-click, and select the Conf entry in the pop-up menu. This displays a version of the **httpd.conf** configuration file that reflects your current configuration selections. When you save your configuration, this version overwrites your **httpd.conf** file.

Initially, only one server is listed, labeled Default Web Server. If you add virtual hosts, they are listed at the same level. Servers have a ball icon placed next to them. To create a virtual host, access the pop-up menu for the New Apache Server by right-clicking the computer icon. Then select New on the pop-up menu. This activates a drop-down menu with a Virtual Host entry. Select the Virtual Host entry to create your virtual host.

If you double-click the server icon, the tree expands to list server locations. These are the root directory, your Web server home directory, the CGI program directory, and the documentation directory. To create new directories, right-click the blue ball icon in the Web server entry and select the New item in the menu that pops up. Then select Directory in the drop-down menu displayed. If you want to delete it later, right-click its entry and select Delete from the pop-up menu.

To configure a server or directory, right-click its entry and select the Properties item from the pop-up menu displayed. This opens a new window for configuring your selection, as shown in Figure 25-3. The window is divided into two panes: a left pane that shows a tree of configuration items and a right pane that displays the

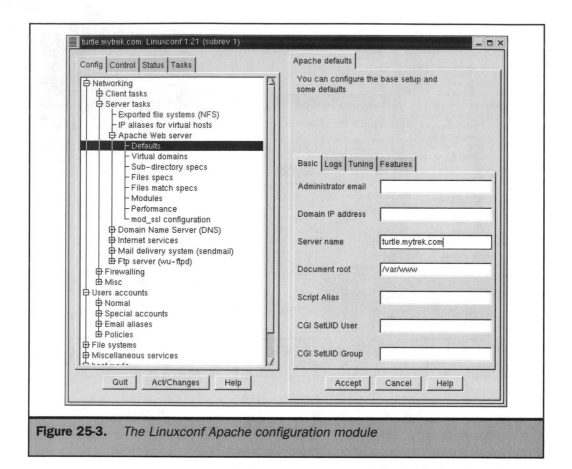

Figure 25-3. *The Linuxconf Apache configuration module*

configuration dialog windows for these items. The structure is similar to the Netscape preferences interface. For example, by selecting the Basic configuration entry you can display text boxes for entering items such as the Document root directory and the name of your server. Other entries let you set server options, Proxy settings, and Indexing formats.

Linuxconf provides configuration capabilities for most standard features of the Apache Web server. You can locate the Apache Web server configuration entries under the Server tasks heading with the Networking item in the Config panel. Apache has several entries covering such aspects as the server defaults, virtual domains, subdirectory configuration, and module selection. A panel is displayed for each entry with fields where you can enter your values or buttons to click to select features. The Defaults entry displays several panels (Basic, Logs, Tuning, and Features) listing field for the directives used to configure your server defaults. For example, in the Basic panel there are fields where you can enter the Administrator's e-mail address, the Server name, and the Document root directory. The subdirectory entry enables you to configure particular directories, using buttons to select controls you want to place on them. With virtual domains, you can create and configure virtual hosts, entering directive values into displayed fields and selecting controls from a list of buttons.

If you installed Apache as part of your installation, Linuxconf may already have its Apache module loaded. Otherwise, to use Linuxconf to configure your Apache server, you may have to load the Linuxconf Apache module first into the Linuxconf utility. To do this, first select the Control tab, and then select Control files and systems, and, finally, select the Linuxconf modules entry. This displays a panel where you can select various Linuxconf modules you want added, including the one for Apache.

| Note | *You can also configure Apache with Webmin. Select the Apache Web Server page from the Servers page. You can then perform operations including setting limits, configuring modules, defining MIME types, and setting up virtual servers.* |

Web Server Security—SSL

Web server security deals with two different tasks, protecting your Web server from unauthorized access and providing security for transactions carried out between a Web browser client and your Web server. To protect your server from unauthorized access, you use a proxy server such as Squid. Squid is a GNU proxy server often used with Apache on Linux systems. (See Chapter 28 for a detailed explanation of the Squid server.) Apache itself has several modules that provide security capabilities. These include mod_access for mandatory controls; mod_auth, mod_auth_db, mod_auth_digest, and mod_auth_dbm that provide authentication support; and mod_auth_anon for anonymous FTP–like logging (see previous sections on access control and authentication).

To secure transactions, you need to add encryption capabilities to your server. Transactions between a browser and your server can then be encrypted, with the browser and your server alone able to decrypt the transmissions. The protocol most often used with Linux Apache Web servers is the Secure Sockets Layer (SSL) protocol, which was originally developed by Netscape for secure transactions on the Web. Like the Secure Shell (SSH) described in Chapter 39, SSL uses a form of public and private key encryption. Data is encrypted with the public key but can only be decrypted with the private key.

A free version of SSL called OpenSSL is available for use with Apache (see **www.openssl.org**). It is based on SSLeay from Eric A. Young and Tim J. Hudson. However, U.S. government restrictions prevent the Apache Web server from being freely distributed with SSL capabilities built-in. You have to separately obtain SSL and update your Apache server to incorporate this capability.

The U.S. government maintains export restrictions on encryption technology over 40 bits. SSL, however, supports a number of ciphers using 168-, 128-, and 40-bit keys (128 is considered secure, and so by comparison the exportable 40-bit versions are useless). This means that if Apache included SSL, it cannot be distributed outside the U.S. Outside the U.S., however, there are projects that do distribute SSL for Apache using OpenSSL. These are free for noncommercial use in the U.S., though export

SERVERS

restrictions apply. The Apache-SSL project freely distributes Apache with SSL built-in, apache+ssl. You can download this from their Web site at **www.apache-ssl.org** (though there are restrictions on exporting encryption technology, there is none on importing it). In addition, the mod_ssl project provides an SSL module with patches that you can use to update your Apache Web server to incorporate SSL (**www.modsll.org**). mod_ssl is free for noncommercial use in the U.S. and free for all uses in other countries.

There is, however, a further restriction on the use of encryption patents and certificates. Currently, many companies in the U.S. are using an implementation of SSL that use encryption methods patented by RSA Data Security. This is a private product available only with licensing fees. Instead of obtaining the licensing directly, you can simply buy a commercial version of Apache that includes RSA licensing such as Stronghold and Raven (**www.covalent.net**). This restriction only applies to the use of RSA technology in the U.S., where it is patented. OpenSSL does use RSA methods and does require licensing if you are going to use it for commercial use in the U.S.

In addition to encryption capability, you also need to set up a server certificate. This is an official identification of your server, certifying that you are who you say you are. You need to obtain the certificate from a certificate authority such as Verisign and have your server officially approved. Again, a commercial vendor such as Stronghold can do this for you. Outside the U.S., although you do not need any RSA licensing, you still need to obtain an official certificate.

Apache Web Server Configuration File

An edited version of the current **httpd.conf** configuration file for Red Hat is shown here. It is strongly recommended that you consult this file on your system. It contains detailed documentation and default entries for Apache directives.

httpd.conf

```
##
## httpd.conf -- Apache HTTP server configuration file
##


#
# Based upon the NCSA server configuration files originally by Rob McCool.
#
# This is the main Apache server configuration file.  It contains the
# configuration directives that give the server its instructions.
# See <URL:http://www.apache.org/docs/> for detailed information about
# the directives.
#
#
# The configuration directives are grouped into three basic sections:
# 1. Directives that control the operation of the Apache server process
# as a whole (the 'global environment').
# 2. Directives that define the parameters of the 'main' or 'default' server,
#    which responds to requests that aren't handled by a virtual host.
```

```
#        These directives also provide default values for the settings
#        of all virtual hosts.
# 3. Settings for virtual hosts, which allow Web requests to be sent to
#        different IP addresses or hostnames and have them handled by the
#        same Apache server process.
#

### Section 1: Global Environment
#
# The directives in this section affect the overall operation of Apache,
# such as the number of concurrent requests it can handle or where it
# can find its configuration files.

# ServerType is either inetd, or standalone.
# Inetd mode is only supported on Unix platforms.
#
ServerType standalone


#
# ServerRoot: The top of the directory tree under which the server's
# configuration, error, and log files are kept.
# Do NOT add a slash at the end of the directory path.
#
ServerRoot "/etc/httpd"


#
# The LockFile directive sets the path to the lockfile used when Apache
# is compiled with either USE_FCNTL_SERIALIZED_ACCEPT or
# USE_FLOCK_SERIALIZED_ACCEPT. This directive should normally be left at
# its default value.
#
LockFile /var/lock/httpd.lock


# PidFile: The file in which the server should record its process
# identification number when it starts.
#
PidFile /var/run/httpd.pid


# ScoreBoardFile: File used to store internal server process information.
# Not all architectures require this.
ScoreBoardFile /var/run/httpd.scoreboard


#
# In the standard configuration, the server will process this file,
# srm.conf, and access.conf in that order.  The latter two files are
# now distributed empty, as it is recommended that all directives
# be kept in a single file for simplicity.  The commented-out values
# below are the built-in defaults.  You can have the server ignore
# these files altogether by using "/dev/null" (for Unix) or
# "nul" (for Win32) for the arguments to the directives.
#
#ResourceConfig conf/srm.conf
#AccessConfig conf/access.conf
```

```
# Timeout: The number of seconds before receives and sends time out.
#
Timeout 300

# KeepAlive: Whether or not to allow persistent connections (more than
# one request per connection). Set to "Off" to deactivate.
#
KeepAlive On

# MaxKeepAliveRequests: The maximum number of requests to allow
# during a persistent connection. Set to 0 to allow an unlimited amount.
# We recommend you leave this number high, for maximum performance.
#
MaxKeepAliveRequests 100

# KeepAliveTimeout: Number of seconds to wait for the next request from
# the same client on the same connection.
#
KeepAliveTimeout 15

# Server-pool size regulation.
MinSpareServers 5
MaxSpareServers 20

# Number of servers to start initially
#
StartServers 8

# Limit on total number of servers running
#
MaxClients 150

#
# MaxRequestsPerChild: the number of requests each child process is
# allowed to process before the child dies.
#
MaxRequestsPerChild 100

#
# Listen: Allows you to bind Apache to specific IP addresses and/or
# ports, in addition to the default. See also the <VirtualHost>
# directive.
#
#Listen 3000
#Listen 12.34.56.78:80
Listen 80

#
# BindAddress: You can support virtual hosts with this option. This directive
# is used to tell the server which IP address to listen to. It can either
# contain "*", an IP address, or a fully qualified Internet domain name.
# See also the <VirtualHost> and Listen directives.
#
```

```
#BindAddress *

#
# Dynamic Shared Object (DSO) Support
#
# To be able to use the functionality of a module which was built as a
# DSO you have to place corresponding `LoadModule' lines at this location
# so the directives contained in it are actually available _before_ they
# are used.
#
# Note: The order is which modules are loaded is important.  Don't change
# the order below without expert advice.
#
# Example:
# LoadModule foo_module modules/mod_foo.so

#LoadModule mmap_static_module modules/mod_mmap_static.so
LoadModule vhost_alias_module modules/mod_vhost_alias.so
LoadModule env_module            modules/mod_env.so
LoadModule config_log_module  modules/mod_log_config.so
LoadModule mime_module           modules/mod_mime.so
.............................. .
#LoadModule bandwidth_module   modules/mod_bandwidth.so
#LoadModule put_module          modules/mod_put.so
<IfDefine HAVE_PERL>
LoadModule perl_module          modules/libperl.so
</IfDefine>
<IfDefine HAVE_PHP>
LoadModule php_module           modules/mod_php.so
</IfDefine>
.............................. .
<IfDefine HAVE_SSL>
LoadModule ssl_module           modules/libssl.so
</IfDefine>

#   Reconstruction of the complete module list from all available modules
#   (static and shared ones) to achieve correct module execution order.
#   [WHENEVER YOU CHANGE THE LOADMODULE SECTION ABOVE UPDATE THIS, TOO]
ClearModuleList
#AddModule mod_mmap_static.c
AddModule mod_vhost_alias.c
AddModule mod_env.c
AddModule mod_log_config.c
.............................. .
AddModule mod_setenvif.c
#AddModule mod_bandwidth.c
#AddModule mod_put.c
.............................. .
<IfDefine HAVE_PERL>
AddModule mod_perl.c
</IfDefine>
<IfDefine HAVE_PHP>
AddModule mod_php.c
</IfDefine>
```

```
...............................
<IfDefine HAVE_SSL>
AddModule mod_ssl.c
</IfDefine>

#
# ExtendedStatus: controls whether Apache will generate "full" status
# information (ExtendedStatus On) or just basic information (ExtendedStatus
# Off) when the "server-status" handler is called. The default is Off.
#
#ExtendedStatus On

### Section 2: 'Main' server configuration
#
# The directives in this section set up the values used by the 'main'
# server, which responds to any requests that aren't handled by a
# <VirtualHost> definition.  These values also provide defaults for
# any <VirtualHost> containers you may define later in the file.
#
# All of these directives may appear inside <VirtualHost> containers,
# in which case these default settings will be overridden for the
# virtual host being defined.

# Port: The port to which the standalone server listens. For
# ports < 1023, you will need httpd to be run as root initially.
#
Port 80

# If you wish httpd to run as a different user or group, you must run
# httpd as root initially and it will switch.
#
# User/Group: The name (or #number) of the user/group to run httpd as.
#
User apache
Group apache

#
# ServerAdmin: Your address, where problems with the server should be
# e-mailed.
#
ServerAdmin root@localhost

#
# ServerName: allows you to set a host name which is sent back to clients for
# your server if it's different than the one the program would get (i.e., use
# "www" instead of the host's real name).
#
#ServerName localhost

#
# DocumentRoot: The directory out of which you will serve your
# documents. By default, all requests are taken from this directory, but
# symbolic links and aliases may be used to point to other locations.
#
```

```
DocumentRoot "/var/www/html"

## Each directory to which Apache has access, can be configured with
# respect to which services and features are allowed and/or disabled in
# that directory (and its subdirectories).
#
# First, we configure the "default" to be a very restrictive set of
# permissions.
#
<Directory />
    Options FollowSymLinks
    AllowOverride None
</Directory>

## Note that from this point forward you must specifically allow
# particular features to be enabled - so if something's not working as
# you might expect, make sure that you have specifically enabled it
# below.

# This should not require changing.
#
<Location "/">

## This may also be "None", "All", or any combination of "Indexes",
# "Includes", "FollowSymLinks", "ExecCGI", or "MultiViews".
#
# Note that "MultiViews" must be named *explicitly* --- "Options All"
# doesn't give it to you.
#
    Options Indexes Includes FollowSymLinks

## This controls which options the .htaccess files in directories can
# override. Can also be "All", or any combination of "Options", "FileInfo",
# "AuthConfig", and "Limit"
#
    AllowOverride None

## Controls who can get stuff from this server.
#
    Order allow,deny
    Allow from all
</Location>

## UserDir: The name of the directory which is appended onto a user's home
# directory if a ~user request is received.
#
UserDir public_html

# Control access to UserDir directories.  The following is an example
# for a site where these directories are restricted to read-only.
#
#<Directory /var/*/public_html>
#    AllowOverride FileInfo AuthConfig Limit
```

```
#       Options MultiViews Indexes SymLinksIfOwnerMatch IncludesNoExec
#       <Limit GET POST OPTIONS PROPFIND>
#           Order allow,deny
#           Allow from all
#       </Limit>
#       <Limit PUT DELETE PATCH PROPPATCH MKCOL COPY MOVE LOCK UNLOCK>
#           Order deny,allow
#           Deny from all
#       </Limit>
#</Directory>

# DirectoryIndex: Name of the file or files to use as a pre-written HTML
# directory index.  Separate multiple entries with spaces.
#
DirectoryIndex index.html index.htm index.shtml index.php\
index.php4 index.php3 index.cgi

# AccessFileName: The name of the file to look for in each directory
# for access control information.
#
AccessFileName .htaccess

#
# The following lines prevent .htaccess files from being viewed by
# Web clients.
#
<Files ~ "^\.ht">
    Order allow,deny
    Deny from all
</Files>

# CacheNegotiatedDocs: By default, Apache sends "Pragma: no-cache" with
# each document that was negotiated on the basis of content. This asks
# proxy servers not to cache the document. Uncommenting the following line
# disables this behavior, and proxies will be allowed to cache the documents.
#
#CacheNegotiatedDocs

#
# UseCanonicalName:  (new for 1.3)  With this setting turned on, whenever
# Apache needs to construct a self-referencing URL (a URL that refers back
# to the server the response is coming from) it will use ServerName and
# Port to form a "canonical" name.  With this setting off, Apache will
# use the hostname:port that the client supplied, when possible.  This
# also affects SERVER_NAME and SERVER_PORT in CGI scripts.
#
UseCanonicalName On

# TypesConfig describes where the mime.types file (or equivalent) is
# to be found.
#
TypesConfig /etc/mime.types
```

```
## DefaultType is the default MIME type the server will use for a document
#
DefaultType text/plain

# The mod_mime_magic module allows the server to use various hints from the
# contents of the file itself to determine its type.  The MIMEMagicFile
# directive tells the module where the hint definitions are located.
#
<IfModule mod_mime_magic.c>
    MIMEMagicFile share/magic
</IfModule>

## HostnameLookups: Log the names of clients or just their IP addresses
# e.g., www.apache.org (on) or 204.62.129.132 (off).
#
HostnameLookups Off


#
# ErrorLog: The location of the error log file.
#
ErrorLog /var/log/httpd/error_log

# LogLevel: Control the number of messages logged to the error_log.
#
LogLevel warn

# The following directives define some format nicknames for use with
# a CustomLog directive (see below).
#
LogFormat "%h %l %u %t \"%r\" %>s %b \"%{Referer}i\"\
\"%{User-Agent}i\"" combined
LogFormat "%h %l %u %t \"%r\" %>s %b" common
LogFormat "%{Referer}i -> %U" referer
LogFormat "%{User-agent}i" agent

# The location and format of the access logfile (Common Logfile Format).
#
CustomLog /var/log/httpd/access_log common

# If you would like to have agent and referer logfiles, uncomment the
# following directives.
#
#CustomLog /var/log/httpd/referer_log referer
#CustomLog /var/log/httpd/agent_log agent

# If you preter a single logfile with access, agent, and referer information
# (Combined Logfile Format) you can use the following directive.
#
#CustomLog /var/log/httpd/access_log combined

# Optionally add a line containing the server version and virtual host
# name to server-generated pages (error documents, FTP directory listings,
# mod_status and mod_info output etc., but not CGI generated documents).
```

```
# Set to one of:  On | Off | EMail
#
ServerSignature On

# Aliases: Add here as many aliases as you need (with no limit). The format is
# Alias fakename realname
#
Alias /icons/ "/var/www/icons/"

<Directory "/var/www/icons">
    Options Indexes MultiViews
    AllowOverride None
    Order allow,deny
    Allow from all
</Directory>

# ScriptAlias: This controls which directories contain server scripts.
#
ScriptAlias /cgi-bin/ "/var/www/cgi-bin/"

# "/var/www/cgi-bin" should be changed to whatever your ScriptAliased
# CGI directory exists, if you have that configured.
#
<Directory "/var/www/cgi-bin">
    AllowOverride None
    Options ExecCGI
    Order allow,deny
    Allow from all
</Directory>

# Redirect allows you to tell clients about documents which used to exist in
# your server's namespace, but do not anymore. This allows you to tell the
# clients where to look for the relocated document.
# Format: Redirect old-URI new-URL

#
# Directives controlling the display of server-generated directory listings.
#

## FancyIndexing: whether you want fancy directory indexing or standard
#
IndexOptions FancyIndexing

## AddIcon* directives tell the server which icon to show for different
# files or filename extensions.  These are only displayed for
# FancyIndexed directories.
#
AddIconByEncoding (CMP,/icons/compressed.gif) x-compress x-gzip

AddIconByType (TXT,/icons/text.gif) text/*
AddIconByType (IMG,/icons/image2.gif) image/*
AddIconByType (SND,/icons/sound2.gif) audio/*
AddIconByType (VID,/icons/movie.gif) video/*
```

```
AddIcon /icons/binary.gif .bin .exe
AddIcon /icons/binhex.gif .hqx
AddIcon /icons/tar.gif .tar
AddIcon /icons/world2.gif .wrl .wrl.gz .vrml .vrm .iv
AddIcon /icons/compressed.gif .Z .z .tgz .gz .zip
AddIcon /icons/a.gif .ps .ai .eps
AddIcon /icons/layout.gif .html .shtml .htm .pdf
AddIcon /icons/text.gif .txt
AddIcon /icons/c.gif .c
AddIcon /icons/p.gif .pl .py
AddIcon /icons/f.gif .for
AddIcon /icons/dvi.gif .dvi
AddIcon /icons/uuencoded.gif .uu
AddIcon /icons/script.gif .conf .sh .shar .csh .ksh .tcl
AddIcon /icons/tex.gif .tex
AddIcon /icons/bomb.gif core

AddIcon /icons/back.gif ..
AddIcon /icons/hand.right.gif README
AddIcon /icons/folder.gif ^^DIRECTORY^^
AddIcon /icons/blank.gif ^^BLANKICON^^

## DefaultIcon: which icon to show for files which do not have an icon
# explicitly set.
#
DefaultIcon /icons/unknown.gif

## AddDescription: allows you to place a short description after a file in
# server-generated indexes.  These are only displayed for FancyIndexed
# directories.
# Format: AddDescription "description" filename
#
#AddDescription "GZIP compressed document" .gz
#AddDescription "tar archive" .tar
#AddDescription "GZIP compressed tar archive" .tgz

## ReadmeName: the name of the README file the server will look for by
# default, and append to directory listings.
#
# HeaderName: the name of a file which should be prepended to
# directory indexes.
#
ReadmeName README
HeaderName HEADER

# IndexIgnore: a set of filenames which directory indexing should ignore
# and not include in the listing.  Shell-style wildcarding is permitted.
#
IndexIgnore .??* *~ *# HEADER* README* RCS CVS *,v *,t

# AddEncoding: allows you to have certain browsers (Mosaic/X 2.1+) uncompress
# information on the fly. Note: Not all browsers support this.
# Despite the name similarity, the following Add* directives have nothing
# to do with the FancyIndexing customization directives above.
```

```
#
AddEncoding x-compress Z
AddEncoding x-gzip gz tgz

# AddLanguage: allows you to specify the language of a document.
AddLanguage en .en
AddLanguage fr .fr

# LanguagePriority: allows you to give precedence to some languages
LanguagePriority en fr

# AddType: allows you to tweak mime.types without actually editing it, or
# to make certain files to be certain types.
#
# The following is for PHP4 (conficts with PHP/FI, below):
<IfModule mod_php4.c>
  AddType application/x-httpd-php .php4 .php3 .phtml .php
  AddType application/x-httpd-php-source .phps
</IfModule>


AddType application/x-tar .tgz

# AddHandler: allows you to map certain file extensions to "handlers",
# actions unrelated to filetype. These can be either built into the server
# or added with the Action command (see below)
#
# If you want to use server side includes, or CGI outside
# ScriptAliased directories, uncomment the following lines.
#
# To use CGI scripts:
#
AddHandler cgi-script .cgi

# To use server-parsed HTML files
#
AddType text/html .shtml
AddHandler server-parsed .shtml

# Uncomment the following line to enable Apache's send-asis HTTP file
# feature
#
#AddHandler send-as-is asis

# If you wish to use server-parsed imagemap files, use
#
AddHandler imap-file map

# To enable type maps, you might want to use
#
#AddHandler type-map var


#
# Action: lets you define media types that will execute a script whenever
```

```
# a matching file is called. This eliminates the need for repeated URL
# pathnames for oft-used CGI file processors.
# Format: Action media/type /cgi-script/location
# Format: Action handler-name /cgi-script/location
#

# MetaDir: specifies the name of the directory in which Apache can find
# meta information files. These files contain additional HTTP headers
# to include when sending the document
#
MetaDir .web

# MetaSuffix: specifies the file name suffix for the file containing the
# meta information.
#
MetaSuffix .meta


# If the perl module is installed, this will be enabled.
<IfModule mod_perl.c>
  Alias /perl/ /var/www/perl/
  <Location /perl>
    SetHandler perl-script
    PerlHandler Apache::Registry
    Options +ExecCGI
  </Location>
</IfModule>


# Allow access to local system documentation from localhost
Alias /doc/ /usr/share/doc/
<Location /doc>
  order deny,allow
  deny from all
  allow from localhost
  Options Indexes FollowSymLinks
</Location>

#
# Proxy Server directives. Uncomment the following lines to
# enable the proxy server:
#
#<IfModule mod_proxy.c>
#ProxyRequests On
#
#<Directory proxy:*>
#    Order deny,allow
#    Deny from all
#    Allow from .your_domain.com
#</Directory>

#
#
# To enable the cache as well, edit and uncomment the following lines:
```

```
# (no cacheing without CacheRoot)
#
#CacheRoot "/var/cache/httpd"
#CacheSize 5
#CacheGcInterval 4
#CacheMaxExpire 24
#CacheLastModifiedFactor 0.1
#CacheDefaultExpire 1
#NoCache a_domain.com another_domain.edu joes.garage_sale.com

#</IfModule>
# End of proxy directives.

### Section 3: Virtual Hosts
#
# VirtualHost: If you want to maintain multiple domains/hostnames on your
# machine you can setup VirtualHost containers for them.
# Please see the documentation at <URL:http://www.apache.org/docs/vhosts/>
# for further details before you try to setup virtual hosts.
# You may use the command line option '-S' to verify your virtual host
# configuration.

## If you want to use name-based virtual hosts you need to define at
# least one IP address (and port number) for them.
#
#NameVirtualHost 12.34.56.78:80
#NameVirtualHost 12.34.56.78

## VirtualHost example:
# Almost any Apache directive may go into a VirtualHost container.
#
#<VirtualHost ip.address.of.host.some_domain.com>
#    ServerAdmin webmaster@host.some_domain.com
#    DocumentRoot /www/docs/host.some_domain.com
#    ServerName host.some_domain.com
#    ErrorLog logs/host.some_domain.com-error_log
#    CustomLog logs/host.some_domain.com-access_log common
#</VirtualHost>

#<VirtualHost _default_:*>
#</VirtualHost>

<IfDefine HAVE_SSL>
##
## SSL Virtual Host Context
##

# Apache will only listen on port 80 by default.  Defining the virtual server
# (below) won't make it automatically listen on the virtual server's port.
Listen 443

<VirtualHost _default_:443>

# General setup for the virtual host
DocumentRoot "/var/www/html"
```

Chapter 26

Domain Name System

The *Domain Name System* (*DNS*) is an Internet service that converts domain names into their corresponding IP addresses. As you may recall, all computers connected to the Internet are addressed using an *Internet Protocol* (*IP*) address. This consists of a number composed of four segments separated by periods. Depending on the type of network, several of the first segments are used for the network address and several of the last segments are used for the host address. In a standard Class C network used in smaller networks, the first three segments are the computer's network address and the last segment is the computer's host ID. For example, in the address 192.168.1.2, 192.168.1 is the network address and **2** is the computer's host ID within that network. Together, they make up an IP address with which the computer can be addressed from anywhere on the Internet. IP addresses, though, are difficult to remember and easy to get wrong. Early on, IP addresses were associated with corresponding names called fully qualified domain names. A *fully qualified domain name* is composed of three or more segments: the first segment is the name to identify the host, and the remaining segments are for the network in which the host is located. The network segments of a fully qualified domain name are usually referred to simply as the domain name, while the host part is referred to as the host name (though this is also used to refer to the complete fully qualified domain name). In effect, subnets are referred to as domains. The fully qualified domain name, **www.linux.org**, has an IP address 198.182.196.56, where 198.182.196 is the network address and 56 is the host ID. Computers can be accessed only with an IP address. So, a fully qualified domain name must first be translated into its corresponding IP address to be of any use. The parts of the IP address that make up the domain name and the hosts can vary. See Chapter 38 for a detailed discussion of IP addresses, including network classes and *Classes Interdomain Routing* (*CIDR*).

Any computer on the Internet can maintain a file that manually associates IP addresses with domain names. On Linux and Unix systems, this file is called the **/etc/hosts** file. Here, you can enter the IP addresses and domain names of computers you commonly access. Using this method, however, each computer needs a complete listing of all other computers on the Internet, and that listing must be updated constantly. Early on, this became clearly impractical for the Internet, though it is still feasible for small isolated networks. The Domain Name System has been implemented to deal with the task of translating the domain name of any computer on the Internet to its IP address. The task is carried out by interconnecting servers that manage the Domain Name System (also referred to either as DNS servers, or as name servers). These DNS servers keep lists of fully qualified domain names and their IP addresses, matching one up with the other. This service that they provide to a network is referred to as the Domain Name Service. The Internet is composed of many connected subnets called *domains*, each with its own Domain Name System (DNS) servers that keep track of all the fully qualified domain names and IP addresses for all the computers on its network. DNS servers are hierarchically linked to root servers, which, in turn, connect to other root servers and the DNS servers on their subnets throughout the Internet. The section of a network for which a given DNS server is responsible is called a *zone.* Although a zone may correspond to a domain, many zones may, in fact, be within a domain, each with its own name server. This is true for large domains where too many systems exist for one name server to manage.

When a user enters a fully qualified domain name to access a remote system, a resolver program queries the local network's DNS server requesting the corresponding IP address for that remote system. The names of the DNS servers that service a host's network are kept in the host's **/etc/resolv.conf** file.

If you are setting up a DNS server for a *local area network* (*LAN*) that is not connected to the Internet, you should use a special set of IP numbers reserved for such non-Internet networks (also known as *private networks* or *intranets*). This is especially true if you are implementing IP masquerading, where only a gateway machine has an Internet address, and the others make use of that one address to connect to the Internet. For a class C network (254 hosts or less), these are numbers that have the special network number 192.168, as used in these examples. If you are setting up a LAN, such as a small business or home network, you are free to use these numbers for your local machines. You can set up an private network, such as an intranet, using network cards such as Ethernet cards and Ethernet hubs, and then configure your machines with IP addresses starting from 192.168.1.1. The host segment can range from 1 to 254, where 255 is used for the broadcast address. If you have three machines on your home network, you can give them the addresses 192.168.1.1, 192.168.1.2, and 192.168.1.3. You can then set up domain name services for your network by running a DNS server on one of the machines. This machine becomes your network's DNS server. You can then give your machines fully qualified domain names and configure your DNS server to translate the names to their corresponding IP addresses. As shown in Figure 26-1, for example, you could give the machine 192.168.1.1 the name **turtle.mytrek.com**, and the machine 192.168.1.2 the name **rabbit.mytrek.com**. You can also implement Internet services on your network such as FTP, Web, and mail services by setting up servers for them on your machines. You can then configure your DNS server to let users access those services using fully qualified domain names. For example, for **mytrek.com** network, the Web server could be accessed using the name **www.mytrek.com**. Instead of a domain name service, you could have the **/etc/hosts** files in each machine contain the entire list of IP addresses and domain names for all the machines in your network. But, for any changes, you would have to update each machine's **/etc/hosts** file.

Numbers are also reserved for Class A and Class B non-Internet local networks. Table 26-1 lists these addresses. The possible addresses available span from 0 to 255 in the host segment of the address. For example, Class B network addresses range from 172.16.0.0 to 172.16.255.255, giving you a total of 65,534 possible hosts. The Class C network ranges from 192.168.0.0 to 192.168.255.255, giving you 254 possible subnetworks, each with 254 possible hosts. The number 127.0.0.0 is reserved for a system's loopback interface, which allows it to communicate with itself, as it enables users on the same system to send messages to each other.

Figure 26-1. *DNS server and network*

Address	Networks
10.0.0.0	Class A network
172.16.0.0	Class B network
192.168.0.0	Class C network
127.0.0.0	Loopback network (for system self-communication)

Table 26-1. *Non-Internet Private Network IP Addresses*

BIND

The DNS server software currently in use on Linux systems is *Berkeley Internet Name Domain* (*BIND*). BIND was originally developed at the University of California, Berkeley, and is currently maintained and supported by *the Internet Software Consortium* (*ISC*). You can obtain BIND documentation and current software releases from its Web site at **www.isc.org**. The site includes online Web page documentation and manuals, including the *BIND Operations Guide* (*BOG*). RPM packages are available at Red Hat and Caldera FTP sites. The BIND directory in **/usr/share/doc** contains extensive documentation, including Web page manuals and examples. The Linux HOW-TO for the Domain Name Service, DNS-HOWTO, provides detailed examples. Documentation, news, and DNS tools can be obtained from the DNS Resource Directory at **www.dns.net/dnsrd**.

The BIND DNS server software consists of a name server daemon called **named**, several sample configuration files, and resolver libraries. As of 1998, a new version of BIND, beginning with the series number 8.*x*, implemented a new configuration file using a new syntax. Recently version 9.0 was released. Older versions, which begin with the number 4.*x*, use a different configuration file with an older syntax. In effect, two versions are now in use with different configuration files. All Linux distributions currently install the newer 8.*x* version of BIND.

The name of the BIND name server daemon is **named**. To operate your machine as a name server, simply run the **named** daemon with the appropriate configuration. The **named** daemon listens for resolution requests and provides the correct IP address for the requested host name. You can use the **ndc** utility provided with BIND to start, stop, restart, and check the status of the server as you test its configuration. **ndc** with the **stop** command stops **named** and, with the **start** command, starts it again, reading your **named.conf** file. **ndc** with the **help** command provides a list of all **ndc** commands. Once your name server is running, you can test it using the **nslookup** utility, which queries a name server, providing information about hosts and domains. If you start **nslookup** with no arguments, it enters an interactive mode where you can issue different **nslookup** commands to refine your queries. Numerous other DNS tools are also available, such as Dig and host. Check the DNS Resource Directory at **www.dns.net/ dnsrd** for a listing.

On Red Hat and Caldera systems, the **named** daemon is started using a startup script in the **/etc/rc.d/init.d** directory called **named**. You can use this script to start and stop the daemon using the **stop** and **start** arguments. **named** runs as a standalone daemon, constantly running. If you don't want **named** to run, you can use the System V Runlevel Editor or Linuxconf to change its status.

Domain Name System Configuration

You configure a DNS server using a configuration file, several zone files, and a cache file. The part of a network for which the name server is responsible is called a zone. A *zone* is not the same as a domain, because in a large domain, you could have several zones, each with its own name server. You could also have one name server service several zones. In this case, each zone has its own zone file. The zone files hold resource records that provide host name and IP address associations for computers on the network for which the DNS server is responsible. Zone files exist for the server's network and the local machine. The most commonly used zone types are described here.

- **Master zone** This is the primary zone file for a network. It holds the mappings from domain names to IP addresses for all the hosts on the network.

- **Slave zone** These are references to other DNS servers for your network. Your network can have a master DNS server and several slave DNS servers to help carry the workload. A slave DNS server automatically copies its configuration files, including all zone files, from the master DNS server. Any changes to the master configuration files trigger an automatic download of these files to the slave servers. In effect, you only have to manage the configuration files for the master DNS server, as they are automatically copied to the slave servers.

- **Forward zone** The forward zone lists name servers outside your network that should be searched if your network's name server fails to resolve an address.

Zone entries are defined in the **named.conf** file. Here you place zone entries for your master, slave, and forward DNS servers. In addition, you also need to make entries for a couple of special zones, described here.

- **IN-ADDR.ARPA zone** For each master zone entry, a corresponding reverse mapping zone entry named IN-ADDR.ARPA also exists, as well as one for the localhost. This entry performs reverse mapping from an IP address to its domain name. The name of the zone entry uses the domain IP address, which is the IP address with segments listed starting from the host, instead of the network. So, for the IP address 192.168.1.4 where 4 is the host address, the corresponding domain IP address is 4.1.168.192, listing the segments in reverse order. The reverse mapping for the localhost is 0.0.127.

- **. zone** This zone entry defines a hint zone specifying the root name servers.

DNS Servers

There are several kinds of DNS server, each designed to perform a different type of task under the Domain Name System. The basic kind of DNS server is the *master* server. Each network must have at least one master server that is responsible for resolving names on the network. Large networks may need several DNS servers. Some of these can be *slave* servers that can be updated directly from a master server. Others may be *alternative master* servers that hosts in a network can use. Both are commonly referred to as *secondary* servers. For DNS requests a DNS server cannot resolve, the request can be forwarded to specific DNS servers outside the network, say on the Internet. DNS servers in a network can be set up to perform this task and are referred to as Forwarder servers. To help bear the workload, local DNS servers can be set up within a network that operate as caching servers. Such a server merely collects DNS lookups from previous requests it sent to the main DNS server. Any repeated requests can then be answered by the caching server.

A server that can answer DNS queries for a given zone with authority is known as an *authoritative* server. An authoritative server holds the DNS configuration records for hosts in a zone that will associate each host's DNS name with an IP address. For example, a master server is an authoritative server. So are slave and stealth servers (see the list that follows). A caching server is not authoritative. It only holds whatever associations it picked up from other servers and cannot guarantee that the associations are valid.

- **Master server** This is the primary DNS server for a zone.
- **Slave server** A DNS server that receives zone information from the master server.
- **Forwarder server** A server that forwards unresolved DNS requests to outside DNS servers. Can be used to keep other servers on a local network hidden from the Internet.
- **Caching only server** Caches DNS information it receives from DNS servers and uses it to resolve local requests.
- **Stealth server** A DNS server for a zone not listed as a name server by the master DNS server.

Linuxconf DNS Configuration

As an alternative to making entries in the configuration files manually, you can use the Linuxconf DNS server configuration panels. You can use the **dnsconf** command to start up Linuxconf to perform only the Domain Name configuration tasks. This command displays a window with buttons for the different DNS server configuration panels. If you use the main Linuxconf window, select the Domain Name Server entry in the Servers Tasks list located under Networking. Linuxconf provides panels for primary (master), secondary (slave), reverse mapping, and forwarder zone entries. You can also configure features such as access control and logging. When you finish configuration, Linuxconf generates new **named.conf** and zone files. Use the domain panel to create zone files, and the IP reverse mapping panel to create corresponding reverse mapping zone files. In this panel, be sure to use only the network part of the IP address for the network number. Figure 26-2 shows the DNS server panel.

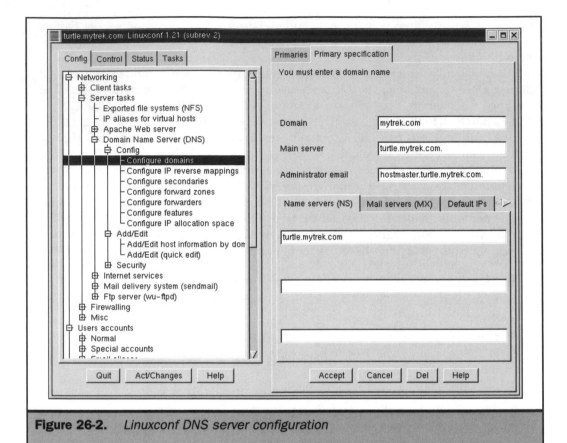

Figure 26-2. Linuxconf DNS server configuration

named.conf

The configuration file for the **named** daemon is **named.conf**, located in the **/etc** directory. It uses a flexible syntax similar to C programs. The format enables easy configuration of selected zones, enabling features such as access control lists and categorized logging. The **named.conf** file consists of BIND configuration commands with attached blocks within which specific options are listed. A configuration command is followed by arguments and a block that is delimited with braces. Within the block are lines of option and feature entries. Each entry is terminated with a semicolon. Comments can use the C, C++, or Shell/Perl syntax: enclosing /* */, preceding //, or preceding #. The following example shows a **zone** command followed by the zone name and a block of options that begin with an opening brace, {. Each option entry ends with a semicolon. The entire block ends with a closing brace, also followed by a semicolon.

```
// a caching only nameserver config
//
zone "." {
      type hint;
      file "named.ca";
};
```

The **named.conf** file is a new feature implemented with BIND version 8.*x*. The older BIND 4.*x* versions use a file called **named.boot**. This file is no longer used by version 8.*x*. The syntaxes used in these configuration files differ radically. If you upgrade to 8.*x*, you can use the **named-bootconf.pl** Perl script provided with the BIND software to convert your **named.boot** file to a **named.conf** file.

The **zone** command is used to specify the domains the name server will service. You enter the keyword **zone,** followed by the name of the domain placed within double quotes. Do not place a period at the end of the domain name. In the following example, a period is within the domain name, but not at the end, **"mytrek.com"**; this differs from the zone file, which requires a period at the end of a complete domain name.

After the zone name, you can specify the class **in**, which stands for Internet. You can also leave it out, in which case **in** is assumed (there are only a few other esoteric classes that are rarely used). Within the zone block, you can place several options. Two essential options are **type** and **file**. The **type** option is used to specify the zone's type. The **file** option is used to specify the name of the zone file to be used for this zone. You can choose from several types of zones: master, slave, stub, forward, and hint. *Master* specifies that the zone holds master information and is authorized to act on it. A master server was called a primary server in the older 4.*x* BIND configuration. *Slave* indicates that the zone needs to update its data periodically from a specified master name server. You use this entry if your name server is operating as a secondary server for another primary (master) DNS server. A *stub zone* only copies other name server entries, instead of the entire zone. A *forward zone* directs all queries to name servers specified in a forwarders statement. A *hint zone* specifies the set of root name servers used by all Internet DNS servers. You can also specify several options that can override any global options set with the **options** command. Table 26-2 lists the BIND zone types. The following example shows a simple **zone** command for the **mytrek.com** domain. Its class is Internet, "in," and its type is master. The name of its zone file is usually the same as the zone name, in this case, **"mytrek.com"**.

```
zone "mytrek.com" in {
      type master;
      file "mytrek.com";
};
```

Type	Description
master	Primary DNS zone.
slave	Slave DNS server. Controlled by a master DNS server.
hint	Set of root DNS Internet servers.
forward	Forwards any queries in it to other servers.
stub	Like a slave zone, but only holds names of DNS servers.

Table 26-2. *DNS BIND Zone Types*

Other commands, such as **acl**, **server**, **control**, and **logging**, enable you to configure different features for your name server. The **server** statement defines the characteristics to be associated with a remote name server, such as the transfer method and key ID for transaction security. The **control** statement defines special control channels. The **key** statement defines a key ID to be used in a server statement that associates an authentication method with a particular name server. The **logging** statement is used to configure logging options for the name server, such as the maximum size of the log file and a severity level for messages. To control access by other hosts, you use the **acl** command. **allow** and **deny** options with access control host lists enable you to deny or allow access by specified hosts to the name server. Table 26-3 lists the **BIND** commands.

Statements	Description
/ comment */*	BIND comment in C syntax
// comment	BIND comment in C++ syntax
# comment	BIND comment in Unix shell and Perl syntax
acl	Defines a named IP address matching list
include	Includes a file
key	Specifies key information for use in authentication and authorization

Table 26-3. *Common BIND Configuration Statements and Options*

Statements	Description
logging	Specifies what the server logs and where the log messages are sent
options	Global server configuration options and defaults for other statements
controls	Declares control channels to be used by the **ndc** utility
server	Sets certain configuration options for the specified server basis
trusted-keys	Defines DNSSEC keys preconfigured into the server and implicitly trusted
zone	Defines a zone
type	Specifies a zone type
file	Specifies the zone file for the zone
directory	Specifies a directory for zone files.
forwarders	Lists hosts for DNS servers where requests are to be forwarded
masters	Lists hosts for DNS master servers for a slave server
allow-transfer	Specifies which hosts are allowed to receive zone transfers
allow-query	Specifies hosts that are allowed make queries
notify	Allows master servers to notify their slave servers when the master zone data changes and updates are needed

Table 26-3.   *Common BIND Configuration Statements and Options* (continued)

The **options** statement defines global options and can be used only once in the configuration file. An extensive number of options cover such components as forwarding, name checking, directory path names, access control, and zone transfers, among others. A complete listing can be found in the BIND documentation. A critically important option found in most configuration files is the **directory** option, which

SERVERS

holds the location of the name server's zone and cache files on your system. The following example is taken from the Red Hat **/etc/named.conf** file. This example specifies the zone files are located in the **/var/named** directory. In this directory, you can find your zone files, including those used for your local system.

```
options {
        directory "/var/named";
        forwarders { 192.168.1.34;
                     192.168.1.47;
                     };
};
```

Another commonly used global option is the **forwarders** option. With the **forwarders** option, you can list several DNS servers to which queries can be forwarded if they cannot be resolved by the local DNS server. This is helpful for local networks that may need to use a DNS server connected to the Internet. The **forwarders** option can also be placed in forward zone entries.

With the **notify** option turned on, the master zone DNS servers send messages to any slave DNS servers whenever their configuration has changed. The slave servers can then perform zone transfers in which they download the changed configuration files. Slave servers always use the DNS configuration files copied from their master DNS servers. **notify** takes one argument, **yes** or **no**, where **yes** is the default. With the **no** argument, you can have the master server not send out any messages to the slave servers, in effect, preventing any zone transfers.

The following example is a simple **named.conf** file based on the example provided in the BIND documentation. This example shows samples of several of the configuration commands. The file begins with comments using C++ syntax, **//**. The **options** command has a directory entry that sets the directory for the zone and cache files to **/var/named**. Here, you find your zone files, such as **named.local** and reverse mapping files, along with the cache file, **named.ca**. The first **zone** command (**.**) defines a hint zone specifying the root name servers. The cache file listing these servers is **named.ca**. The second **zone** command defines a zone for the **mytrek.com** domain. Its type is master, and its zone file is named **"mytrek.com"**. The next zone is used for reverse IP mapping of the previous zone. Its name is made up of a reverse listing of the **mytrek.com** domain's IP address with the term **in-addr.arpa** appended. The domain address for **mytrek.com** is 192.168.1, so the reverse is 1.168.192. The **in-addr.arpa** domain is a special domain that supports gateway location and Internet address to host mapping. The last **zone** command defines a reverse mapping zone for the loopback interface, the method used by the system to address itself and enable communication between local users on the system. The zone file used for this local zone is **named.local**.

named.conf

```
//
// A simple BIND 8 configuration
//
```

```
logging {
        category cname { null; };
};

options {
   directory "/var/named";
   };
};

zone "." {
   type hint;
   file "named.ca";
};

zone "mytrek.com" {
   type master;
   file "mytrek.com";
};
zone "1.168.192.IN-ADDR.ARPA" {
   type master;
   file "192.168.1";
};

zone "0.0.127.in-addr.arpa" {
   type master;
   file "named.local";
};
```

When BIND is initially installed, it creates a default configuration for what is known as a caching only server. A *caching only server* copies queries made by users and saves them in a cache, for use later if the queries are repeated. This can save DNS lookup response times. The cache is held in memory and only lasts as long as **named** runs. The following example is the **named.conf** file initially installed for a caching only server. Only the local and cache zones are defined.

named.conf (caching only server)

```
// generated by named-bootconf.pl

options {
   directory "/var/named";
};

//
// a caching only nameserver config
//
zone "." {
   type hint;
   file "named.ca";
};
```

```
zone "0.0.127.in-addr.arpa" {
   type master;
   file "named.local";
};
```

Resource Records

Your name server holds domain name information about the hosts on your network in resource records placed in zone and reverse mapping files. Resource records are used to associate IP address with fully qualified domain names. You need a record for every computer in the zone that the name server services. A record takes up one line, though you can use parentheses to use several lines for a record, as is usually the case with SOA records. A resource record uses the Standard Resource Record Format as shown here:

```
name [<ttl>] [<class>] <type> <rdata> [<comment>]
```

Here, *name* is the name for this record. It can be a domain name for a fully qualified domain name. If you only specify the host name, the default domain is appended. If no name entry exists, then the last specific name is used. If the @ symbol is used, the name server's domain name is used. *ttl* (time to live) is an optional entry that specifies how long the record is to be cached. *class* is the class of the record. The class used in most resource record entries is IN, for Internet. By default, it is the same as that specified for the domain in the **named.conf** file. *type* is the type of the record. *rdata* is the resource record data. The following is an example of a resource record entry. The name is **rabbit.mytrek.com**, the class is Internet (IN), the type is a host address record (A), and the data is the IP address 192.168.1.2.

```
rabbit.mytrek.com.   IN   A      192.168.1.2
```

Different types of resource records exist for different kinds of hosts and name server operations (see Table 26-4 for a listing of resource record types). A, NS, MX, PTR, and CNAME are the types commonly used. *A* is used for host address records that match domain names with IP addresses. NS is used to reference a name server. MX specifies the host address of the mail server that services this zone. The name server has mail messages sent to that host. The PTR type is used for records that point to other resource records and is used for reverse mapping. CNAME is used to identify an alias for a host on your system.

Start of Authority: SOA

A zone and reverse mapping files always begin with a special resource record called the *Start of Authority record* (SOA). This record specifies that all the following records are authoritative for this domain. It also holds information about the name server's

Type	Description
A	Host address, maps host name to IP address
NS	Authoritative name server for this zone
CNAME	Canonical name, used to define an alias for a host name
SOA	Start of Authority, starts DNS entries in zone file, specifies name server for domain and other features like server contact and serial number
WKS	Well-known service description
PTR	Pointer record, for performing reverse domain name lookups, maps IP address to host name
RP	Text string that contains contact information about a host
HINFO	Host information
MINFO	Mailbox or mail list information
MX	Mail exchanger, informs remote site of your zone's mail server
TXT	Text strings, usually information about a host

Table 26-4. *Domain Name System Resource Record Types*

domain, which is to be given to other name servers. An SOA record has the same format as other resource records, though its data segment is arranged differently. The format for an SOA record follows:

```
name    {ttl}    class    SOA Origin    Person-in-charge (
                                            Serial number
                                            Refresh
                                            Retry
                                            Expire
                                            Minimum )
```

Each zone has its own SOA record. The SOA begins with the zone name specified in the **named.conf** zone entry. This is usually a domain name. An @ symbol is usually used for the name and acts like a macro expanding to the domain name. The *class* is usually the Internet class, IN. *SOA* is the type. *Origin* is the machine that is the origin of the records, usually the machine running your name server daemon. The *person-in-charge* is the e-mail address for the person managing the name server (use dots, not @, for the

SERVERS

e-mail address, as this symbol is used for the domain name). Several configuration entries are placed in a block delimited with braces. The first is the *serial number.* You change the serial number when you add or change records, so that it is updated by other servers. The serial number can be any number, as long as it is incremented each time a change is made to any record in the zone. A common practice is to use the year-month-day-number for the serial number, where number is the number of changes in that day. For example, 1999120403 would be the year 1999, December 4, for the third change. Be sure to update it when making changes.

Refresh specifies the time interval for refreshing SOA information. *Retry* is the frequency for trying to contact an authoritative server. *Expire* is the length of time a secondary name server keeps information about a zone without updating it. *Minimum* is the length of time records in a zone live. The times are specified in the number of seconds.

The following example shows an SOA record. The machine running the name server is **turtle.mytrek.com,** and the e-mail address of the person responsible for the server is **hostmaster.turtle.mytrek.com**.

> **Note** *Notice the periods at the end of these names. For names with no periods, the domain name is appended.* **turtle** *would be the same as* **turtle.mytrek.com***. When entering full host names, be sure to add the period so that the domain is not appended.*

```
@    IN    SOA    turtle.mytrek.com. hostmaster.turtle.mytrek.com.
(
                                    1997022700 ; Serial
                                    28800      ; Refresh
                                    14400      ; Retry
                                    3600000    ; Expire
                                    86400 )    ; Minimum
```

Name Server: NS

The name server record specifies the name of the name server for this zone. These have a resource record type of NS. If you have more than one name server, list them in NS records. These records usually follow the SOA record. As they usually apply to the same domain as the SOA record, their name field is often left blank to inherit the server's domain name specified by the @ symbol in the previous **SOA** record.

```
                IN        NS    turtle.mytrek.com.
```

You can, if you wish, enter the domain name explicitly as shown here.

```
mytrek.com.     IN        NS    turtle.mytrek.com.
```

Address Record: A

Resource records of type A are address records that associate a fully qualified domain name with an IP address. Often, only their host name is specified. Any domain names without a terminating period automatically have the domain appended to it. Given the domain mytrek.com, the turtle name in the following example is expanded to **turtle.mytrek.com**.

```
rabbit.mytrek.com.  IN      A       192.168.1.2
turtle              IN      A       192.168.1.1
```

Mail Exchanger: MX

The Mail Exchanger record, MX, specifies the mail server that is used for this zone or for a particular host. The mail exchanger is the server to which mail for the host is sent. In the following example, the mail server is specified as turtle.mytrek.com. Any mail sent to the address for any machines in that zone will be sent to the mail server, which in turn will send it to the specific machines. For example, mail sent to a user on rabbit.mytrek.com will first be sent to turtle.mytrek.com, which will then send it on to rabbit.mytrek.com. In the following example, the host 192.168.1.1 (turtle.mytrek.com) is defined as the mail server for the mytrek.com domain.

```
mytrek.com. IN      MX      10      192.168.1.1
```

You could also inherit the domain name from the SOA record, leaving the domain name entry blank.

```
            IN      MX      10      192.168.1.1
```

An MX record recognizes an additional field that specifies the ranking for a mail exchanger. If your zone has several mail servers, you can assign them different rankings in their MX records. The smaller number has a higher ranking. This way, if mail cannot reach the first mail server, it can be routed to an alternate server to reach the host. In the following example, mail for hosts on the mytrek.com domain is first routed the mail server at 192.168.1.1 (turtle.mytrek.com), and if that fails, then it is routed to the mail server at 192.168.1.2 (rabbit.mytrek.com).

```
mytrek.com.    IN      MX      10      turtle.mytrek.com
               IN      MX      20      rabbit.mytrek.com
```

You can also specify a mail server for a particular host. In the following example, the mail server for **lizard.mytrek.com** is specified as **rabbit.mytrek.com**.

```
lizard.mytrek.com.   IN   A            192.168.1.3
                     IN   MX    10     rabbit.mytrek.com.
```

Aliases: CNAME

Resource records of type CNAME are used to specify alias names for a host in the zone. Aliases are often used for machines running several different types of servers, such as both Web and FTP servers. They are also used to locate a host when it changes its name. The old name becomes an alias for the new name. In the following example, **ftp.mytrek.com** is an alias for a machine actually called **turtle.mytrek.com**.

```
ftp.mytrek.com.           IN           CNAME   turtle.mytrek.com.
```

The term CNAME stands for canonical name. The canonical name is the actual name of the host. In the example above the canonical name is turtle.mytrek.com. The alias, also know as the CNAME, is ftp.mytrek.com. In a CNAME entry, the alias points to the canonical name. Aliases cannot be used for NS (name server) or MX (mail server) entries.

A more stable way to implement aliases is simply to create another address record for it. You can have as many host names for the same IP address as you want, provided they are certified. For example, to make **www.mytrek.com** an alias for **turtle.mytrek.com**, you only have to add another address record for it, giving it the same IP address as **turtle.mytrek.com**.

```
turtle.mytrek.com.   IN   A    192.168.1.1
www.mytrek.com.      IN   A    192.168.1.1
```

Pointer Record: PTR

A PTR record is used to perform reverse mapping from an IP address to a host. PTR records are used in the reverse mapping files. The name entry holds a reversed IP address and the data entry holds the name of the host. The following example maps the IP address 192.168.1.1 to **turtle.mytrek.com**.

```
1.1.168.192      IN   PTR       turtle.mytrek.com.
```

Host Information: HINFO, RP, MINFO, and TXT

The HINFO, RP, MINFO, and TXT records are used to provide information about the host. The RP record enables you to specify the person responsible for a certain host. The HINFO record provides basic hardware and operating system identification. The

TXT record is used to enter any text you want. MINFO provides a host's mail and mailbox information.

Zone Files

A DNS server uses several zone files covering different components of the DNS. Each zone uses two zone files: the principal zone file and a reverse mapping zone file. The *zone file* contains the resource records for hosts in the zone. A *reverse mapping file* contains records that provide reverse mapping of your domain name entries, enabling you to map from IP addresses to domain names. The name of the file used for the zone file can be any name. The name of the file is specified in the **zone** command's file entry in the **named.conf** file. If your server supports several zones, you may want to use a name that denotes the specific zone. Most systems use the domain name as the name of the zone file. For example, the zone **mytrek.com** would have a zone file also called **mytrek.com**. These could be placed in a subdirectory called **zones** or **master**. The zone file used in the following example is called **mytrek.com**. The reverse mapping file can also be any name, though it is usually the reverse IP address domain specified in its corresponding zone file. For example, in the case of **mytrek.com** zone file, the reverse mapping file might be called **192.168.1**, the IP address of the **mytrek.com** domain defined in the **mytrek.com** zone file. This file would contain reverse mapping of all the host addresses in the domain, allowing their host name addresses to be mapped to their corresponding IP addresses. In addition, BIND sets up a cache file and a reverse mapping file for the localhost. The cache file holds the resource records for the root name servers to which your name server connects. The cache file can be any name, although it is usually called **named.ca**. The localhost reverse mapping file holds reverse IP resource records for the local loopback interface, localhost. Although localhost can be any name, it usually has the name **named.local**.

Zone Files for Internet Zones

A zone file holds resource records that follow a certain format. The file begins with general directives to define default domains or to include other resource record files. These are followed by a single SOA, name server, and domain resource records, and then resource records for the different hosts. Comments begin with a semicolon and can be placed throughout the file. The @ symbol operates like a special macro, representing the domain name of the zone to which the records apply. The @ symbol is used in the first field of a resource or SOA record as the zone's domain name. Multiple names can be specified using the * matching character. The first field in a resource record is the name of the domain to which it applies. If the name is left blank, the next previous explicit name entry in another resource record is automatically used. This way, you can list several entries that apply to the same host without having to repeat the host name. Any host or domain name used throughout this file that is not terminated with a period has the zone's domain appended to it. For example, if the zone's domain is **mytrek.com** and a resource record has only the name **rabbit** with no trailing period, the zone's domain is automatically appended to it, giving you **rabbit.mytrek.com.** Be sure to include the trailing period whenever you enter the complete fully qualified domain name as in **turtle.mytrek.com..** You can also use several directives to set global attributes. $ORIGIN sets a default domain name to append to address names that do not end in a period. $INCLUDE includes a file. $GENERATE can generate records whose domain or IP addresses differ only by an iterated number.

A zone file begins with an SOA record specifying the machine the name server is running on, among other specifications. The @ symbol is used for the name of the SOA record, denoting the zone's domain name. After the SOA, the name server resource records (NS) are listed. Just below the name server records are resource records for the domain itself. Resource records for hosts addresses (A), aliases (CNAME), and mail exchangers (MX) follow. The following example shows a sample zone file, which begins with an SOA record and is followed by an NS record, resource records for the domain, and then resource records for individual hosts.

```
; Authoritative data for turle.mytrek.com
;
@    IN   SOA turtle.mytrek.com. hostmaster.turtle.mytrek.com. (
                                   93071200    ; Serial number
                                   10800       ; Refresh 3 hours
                                   3600        ; Retry  1 hour
                                   3600000     ; Expire  1000 hours
                                   86400 )     ; Minimum 24 hours
              IN   NS              turtle.mytrek.com.
              IN   A               192.168.1.1
              IN   MX      10      turtle.mytrek.com.
              IN   MX      15      rabbit.mytrek.com.

turtle        IN   A               192.168.1.1
              IN   HINFO   PC-686  LINUX
gopher        IN   CNAME           turtle.mytrek.com.
ftp           IN   CNAME           turtle.mytrek.com.
www           IN   A               192.168.1.1

rabbit        IN   A               192.168.1.2

lizard        IN   A               192.168.1.3
              IN   HINFO   MAC     MACOS
localhost     IN   A               127.0.0.1
```

The first two lines are comments about the server for which this zone file is used. Notice that the first two lines begin with a semicolon. The class for each of the resource records in this file is IN, indicating these are Internet records. The SOA record begins with an @ symbol that stands for the zone's domain. In this example, it is **mytrek.com**. Any host or domain name used throughout this file that is not terminated with a period has this domain appended to it. For example, in the following resource record, **turtle** has no period, so it automatically expands to **turtle.mytrek.com**. The same happens for **rabbit** and **lizard**. These are read as **rabbit.mytrek.com** and **lizard.mytrek.com**. Also, in the SOA, notice that the e-mail address for host master uses a period instead of an @ symbol; @ is a special symbol in zone files and cannot be used for any other purpose.

The next resource record specifies the name server for this zone. Here, it is **mytrek.com**. Notice the name for this resource record is blank. If the name is blank, a resource record inherits the name from the previous record. In this case, the NS record inherits the value of @ in the SOA record, its previous record. This is the zone's domain and the NS record specifies **turtle.mytrek.com** is the name server for this zone.

```
                IN   NS        turtle.mytrek.com.
```

Here the domain name is inherited. The entry can be read as the following. Notice the trailing period at the end of the domain name.

```
  mytrek.com.       IN   NS        turtle.mytrek.com.
```

The following address records set up an address for the domain itself. This is often the same as the name server, in this case 192.168.1.1 (the IP address of **turtle.mytrek.com**). This enables users to reference the domain itself, rather than a particular host in it. A mail exchanger record follows that routes mail for the domain to the name server. Users can send mail to the **mytrek.com** domain and it will be routed to **turtle.mytrek.com.**

```
                IN   A         192.168.1.1
```

Here the domain name is inherited. The entry can be read as the following.

```
  mytrek.com.       IN   A         192.168.1.1
```

The next records are mail exchanger records (MX) listing **turtle.mytrek.com** and **fast.mytrek.com** as holding the mail servers for this zone. You can have more than one mail exchanger record for host. More than one host may exist through which mail can be routed. These can be listed in mail exchanger records for which you can set priority rankings (smaller number ranks higher). In this example, if **turtle.mytrek.com** cannot be reached, its mail is routed through **rabbit.mytrek.com**, which has been set up also to handle mail for the **mytrek.com** domain.

```
         IN   MX      100    turtle.mytrek.com.
         IN   MX      150    rabbit.mytrek.com.
```

Again the domain name is inherited. The entries can be read as the following.

```
mytrek.com.      IN   MX      100    turtle.mytrek.com.
mytrek.com.      IN   MX      150    rabbit.mytrek.com.
```

The following resource record is an address record (A) that associates an IP address with the fully qualified domain name **turtle.mytrek.com**. The resource record name only holds **turtle** with no trailing period, so it is automatically expanded to **turtle.mytrek.com.** This record provides the IP address to which **turtle.mytrek.com** can be mapped.

```
turtle   IN      A       192.168.1.1
```

Several resource records immediately follow that have blank names. These inherit their names from the preceding full record, in this case **turtle.mytrek.com.** In effect, these records also apply to that host. Using blank names is an easy way to list additional resource records for the same host (notice that an apparent indent occurs). The first record is an information record, providing the hardware and operating system for the machine.

```
         IN   HINFO   PC-686    LINUX
```

If you are using the same machine to run several different servers, such as Web, FTP, and Gopher servers, you may want to assign aliases to these servers to make accessing them easier for users. Instead of using the actual domain name, such as **turtle.mytrek.com,** to access the Web server running on it, users may find using the following is easier: for the Web server, **www.mytrek.com**; for the Gopher server, **gopher.mytrek.com**; and for the FTP server, **ftp.mytrek.com**. In the DNS, you can implement such a feature using alias records. In the example zone file, two CNAME alias records exist for the **turtle.mytrek.com machine**: FTP, and Gopher. The next record implements an alias for **www** using another address record for the same machine. None of the name entries end in a period, so they are appended automatically with the domain name **mytrek.com**. **www.mytrek.com**, **ftp.mytrek.com**, and **gopher.mytrek.com** are all aliases for **turtle.mytrek.com**. Users entering those URLs automatically access the respective servers on the **turtle.mytrek.com** machine.

Address and main exchanger records are then listed for the two other machines in this zone: **rabbit.mytrek.com** and **lizard.mytrek.com**. You could add HINFO, TXT, MINFO, or alias records for these entries. The file ends with an entry for localhost, the special loopback interface that allows your system to address itself.

Reverse Mapping File

Reverse name lookups are enabled using a reverse mapping file. *Reverse mapping files* map fully qualified domain names to IP addresses. This reverse lookup capability is unnecessary, but it is convenient to have. With reverse mapping, when users access remote hosts, their domain name address can be used to identify their own host, instead of only the IP address. The name of the file can be anything you want. On most current distributions, it is the zone's domain address (the network part of a zone's IP address). For example, the reverse mapping file for a zone with the IP address of 192.168.1.1 is 192.168.1. Its full pathname would be something like **/var/named/192.168.1**. On some systems using older implementations of BIND, the reverse mapping filename may consist of the root name of the zone file with the extension **.rev**. For example, if the zone file is called **mytrek.com,** the reverse mapping file would be called something like **mytrek.rev**. The zone entry for a reverse mapping in the **named.conf** file uses a special domain name consisting of the IP address in reverse, with an **in-addr.arpa** extension. This reverse IP address becomes the zone domain referenced by the @ symbol in the reverse mapping file. For example, the reverse mapping zone name for a domain with the IP address of **192.168.43** would be **43.168.192.in-addr.arpa**. In the following example, the reverse domain name for the domain address **192.168.1** is **1.168.192.in-addr.arpa**.

```
zone "1.168.192.in-addr.arpa" in {
        type master;
        file "192.168.1";
};
```

A reverse mapping file begins with an SOA record, which is the same as that used in a forward mapping file. Resource records for each machine defined in the forward mapping file then follow. These resource records are PTR records that point to hosts in the zone. These must be actual hosts, not aliases defined with CNAME records. Records for reverse mapping begin with a reversed IP address. Each segment in the IP address is sequentially reversed. Each segment begins with the host ID, followed by reversed network numbers. If you list only the host ID with no trailing period, the zone domain is automatically attached. In the case of a reverse mapping file, the zone domain as specified in the **zone** command is the domain IP address backward. The 1 expands to **1.1.168.192**. In the following example, **turtle** and **lizard** inherit the domain IP address, whereas **rabbit** has its explicitly entered.

```
;     reverse mapping of domain names 1.168.192.in-addr.arpa
;
@    IN  SOA turtle.mytrek.com. hostmaster.turtle.mytrek.com. (
                              92050300   ; Serial (yymmddxx format)
                              10800      ; Refresh   3hHours
                              3600      ; Retry      1 hour
                              3600000    ; Expire   1000 hours
                              86400 )    ; Minimum   24 hours
@             IN   NS    turtle.mytrek.com.
1             IN   PTR   turtle.mytrek.com.
2.1.168.192   IN   PTR   rabbit.mytrek.com.
3             IN   PTR   lizard.mytrek.com.
```

Localhost Reverse Mapping

A localhost reverse mapping file implements reverse mapping for the local loopback interface known as *localhost*, whose network address is **127.0.0.1**. This file can be any name. On most systems, localhost is given the name **named.local**. On other systems, localhost may use the network part of the IP address, **127.0.0**. This file allows mapping the domain name localhost to the localhost IP address, which is always **127.0.0.1** on every machine. The address **127.0.0.1** is a special address that functions as the local address for your machine. It allows a machine to address itself. In the **zone** command for this file, the name of the zone is **0.0.127.in-addr.arpa**. The domain part of the IP address is entered in reverse order, with **in-addr.arpa** appended to it, **0.0.127.in-addr.arpa**. The **named.conf** entry is shown here:

```
zone "0.0.127.in-addr.arpa" {
    type master;
    file "named.local";
};
```

The name of the file used for the localhost reverse mapping file is usually **named.local**, though it can be any name. The NS record specifies the name server localhost should use. This file has a PTR record that maps the IP address to the localhost. The 1 used as the name expands to append the zone domain—in this case, giving you **1.0.0.127**, a reverse IP address. The contents of the **named.local** file are shown here. Notice the trailing periods for localhost.

```
@       IN      SOA     localhost. root.localhost.  (
                                    1997022700 ; Serial
                                    28800      ; Refresh
                                    14400      ; Retry
                                    3600000    ; Expire
                                    86400 )    ; Minimum
        IN      NS      turtle.mytrek.com.
1       IN      PTR     localhost.
```

Subdomains and Slaves

Adding a subdomain to a DNS server is a simple matter of creating an added master entry in the **named.conf** file, and then placing name server and authority entries for that subdomain in your primary DNS server's zone file. The subdomain, in turn, has its own zone file with its SOA record and entries listing hosts, which are part of its subdomain, including any of its own mail and news servers.

The name for the subdomain could be a different name altogether or a name with the same suffix as the primary domain. In the following example, the subdomain is called **beach.mytrek.com**. It could just as easily be called **mybeach.com**. The name server to that domain is on the host **crab.beach.mytrek.com**, in this example. Its IP address is 192.168.1.33 and its zone file is **beach.mytrek.com**. The **beach.mytrek.com** zone file holds DNS entries for all the hosts being serviced by this name server. The following example shows zone entries for its **named.conf**.

```
zone "beach.mytrek.com" {
   type master;
   file "beach.mytrek.com";
};

zone "1.168.192.IN-ADDR.ARPA" {
   type master;
   file "192.168.1";
};
```

On the primary DNS server, in the example **turtle.mytrek.com**, you would place entries in the master zone file to identify the subdomain server's host and designate it as a name server. Such entries are also known as glue records. In this example, you would place the following entries in the **mytrek.com** zone file on **turtle.mytrek.com**.

```
beach.mytrek.com.         IN   NS     beach.mytrek.com.
beach.mytrek.com.         IN   A      192.168.1.33.
```

URL references to hosts serviced by **beach.mytrek.com** can now be reached from any host serviced by **mytrek.com**, which does not need to maintain any information about the **beach.mytrek.com** hosts. It simply refers such URL references to the **beach.mytrek.com** name server.

A slave DNS server is tied directly to a master DNS server and periodically receives DNS information from it. You use a master DNS server to configure its slave DNS servers automatically. Any changes you make to the master server are automatically transferred to its slave servers. This transfer of information is called a *zone transfer.* Zone transfers are automatically initiated whenever the slave zone's refresh time is reached or the slave server receives a notify message from the master. The *refresh time* is the second argument in the zone's SOA entry. A notify message is automatically sent by the master whenever changes are made to the master zone's configuration files and the named daemon is restarted. In effect, slave zones are automatically configured by the master zone, receiving the master zone's zone files and making them their own.

Using the previous examples, suppose you want to set up a slave server on **rabbit.mytrek.com**. Zone entries, as shown in the following example, are set up in the **named.conf** configuration file for the slave DNS server on **rabbit.mytrek.com**. The slave server is operating in the same domain as the master, and so it has the same zone name, **mytrek.com**. Its SOA file is named **slave.mytrek.com**. The term "slave" in the filename is merely a convention that helps identify it as a slave server configuration file. The masters statement lists its master DNS server, in this case, 192.168.1.1. Whenever the slave needs to make a zone transfer, it transfers data from that master DNS server. The entry for the reverse mapping file for this slave server lists its reverse mapping file as "slave.192.168.1".

```
zone "mytrek.com" {
    type slave;
    file "slave.mytrek.com";
    masters { 192.168.1.1;
            };
};

zone "1.168.192.IN-ADDR.ARPA" {
    type slave;
    file "slave.192.168.1";
    masters { 192.168.1.1;
            };
};
```

On the master DNS server, the master SOA zone file has entries in it to identify the host that holds the slave DNS server and to designate it as a DNS server. In this example, you would place the following in the **mytrek.com** zone file.

```
        IN   NS    192.168.1.2
```

You would also place an entry for this name server in the **mytrek.com** reverse mapping file.

```
        IN   NS    192.168.1.2
```

The master DNS server can control which slave servers can transfer zone information from it using the **allow-transfer** command. Place the command with the list of IP addresses for the slave servers for which you want to allow access. Also, the master DNS server should be sure the **notify** option is not disabled. The **notify** option is disabled by a "notify no" statement in the options or zone **named.conf** entries. Simply erase the "no" argument to enable notify.

IP Virtual Domains

IP-based virtual hosting allows more than one IP address to be used for a single machine. If a machine has two registered IP addresses, either one can be used to address the machine. If you want to treat the extra IP address as another host in your domain, you need only create an address record for it in your domain's zone file. The domain name for the host would be the same as your domain name. If you want to use a different domain name for the extra IP, however, you have to set up a virtual domain for it. This entails creating a new **zone** command for it with its own zone file. For example, if the extra IP address is **192.168.1.42** and you want to give it the domain name **sail.com**, you must create a new **zone** command for it in your **named.conf** file with a new zone file. The **zone** command would look something like this. The zone file is called **sail.com**.

```
zone "sail.com" in {
        type master;
        file "sail.com";
};
```

In the "**sail.com**" file, the name server name is **turtle.mytrek.com** and the e-mail address is **hostmaster@turtle.mytrek.com**. In the name server record (NS), the name server is **turtle.mytrek.com.** This is the same machine using the original address that the name server is running as. **turtle.mytrek.com** is also the host that handles mail addressed to **sail.com** (MX). An address record then associates the extra IP address **192.168.1.42** with the **sail.com** domain name. A virtual host on this domain is then defined as **jib.sail.com**. Also, **www** and **ftp** aliases are created for that host, creating **www.sail.com** and **ftp.sail.com** virtual hosts.

```
; Authoritative data for sail.com
;
@      IN   SOA   turtle.mytrek.com. hostmaster.turtle.mytrek.com. (
```

```
93071200    ; Serial (yymmddxx)
                                10800      ; Refresh 3 hours
                                3600       ; Retry   1 hour
                                3600000    ; Expire  1000 hours
                                86400 )    ; Minimum 24 hours
        IN   NS         turtle.mytrek.com.
        IN   MX   10    turtle.mytrek.com.
        IN   A          192.168.1.42   ;address of the sail.com domain

jib   IN   A          192.168.1.42
www   IN   A          jib.sail.com.
ftp   IN   CNAME      jib.sail.com.
```

In your reverse mapping file (**/var/named/1.168.192**), add PTR records for any virtual domains.

```
42.1.168.192    IN      PTR    sail.com.
42.1.168.192    IN      PTR    jib.sail.com.
```

You also have to configure your network connection to listen for both IP addresses on your machine (see Chapter 28).

Cache File

The *cache file* is used to connect the DNS server to root servers on the Internet. The file can be any name. On many systems, the cache file is called **named.ca**. Other systems may call the cache file **named.cache** or **roots.hints**. The cache file is usually a standard file installed by your BIND software, which lists resource records for designated root servers for the Internet. You can obtain a current version of the **named.ca** file from the rs.internic.net FTP site. The following example shows sample entries taken from the **named.ca** file:

```
; formerly NS.INTERNIC.NET
;
.                          3600000  IN  NS   A.ROOT-SERVERS.NET.
A.ROOT-SERVERS.NET.        3600000      A    198.41.0.4
;
; formerly NS1.ISI.EDU
;
.                          3600000      NS   B.ROOT-SERVERS.NET.
B.ROOT-SERVERS.NET.        3600000      A    128.9.0.107
```

If you are creating an isolated intranet, you need to create your own root DNS server until you connect to the Internet. In effect, you are creating a fake root server. This can be another server on your system pretending to be the root or the same name server.

*BIND version 4.x uses a different kind of configuration file called the **named.boot** file. The entries in this file consist of one-line records corresponding to entries in a **named.conf** file. You can always convert a **name.boot** file to a **named.conf** file using the **named-bootconf.pl** Perl script provided with BIND 8.x. You can learn more about BIND version 4.x from **www.isc.org** and BIND documentation.*

The
Complete
Reference

Linux

Chapter 27

Mail Servers: SMTP, POP, and IMAP

685

Mail servers provide Internet users with electronic mail services. They have their own TCP/IP protocols such as *Simple Mail Transfer Protocol* (*SMTP*), the *Post Office Protocol* (*POP*), and the *Internet Mail Access Protocol* (*IMAP*). Messages are sent across the Internet through mail servers that service local domains. A *domain* can be seen as a subnet of the larger Internet, with its own server to handle mail messages sent from or received for users on that subnet. When a user mails a message, it is first sent from his or her host system to the mail server. The mail server then sends the message to another mail server on the Internet, the one servicing the subnet on which the recipient user is located. The receiving mail server then sends the message to the recipient's host system.

At each stage, a different type of operation takes place using different agents (programs). A *mail user agent* (*MUA*) is a mail client program, such as mail or Elm. With an MUA, a user composes a mail message and sends it. Then a *mail transport agent* (*MTA*) transports the messages over the Internet. MTAs are mail servers that use the *Simple Mail Transfer Protocol* (*SMTP*) to send messages across the Internet from one mail server to another, transporting them from one subnet to another. On Linux and UNIX systems, the commonly used MTA is Sendmail, a mail server daemon that constantly checks for incoming messages from other mail servers and sends outgoing messages to appropriate servers. Incoming messages received by a mail server are then distributed to a user with *mail delivery agents* (*MDAs*). Most Linux systems use procmail as their MDA, taking messages received by the mail server and delivering them to user accounts (see **www.procmail.org** for more information).

Most Linux distributions automatically install and configure Sendmail for you. On starting your system, you can send and receive messages over the Internet using Sendmail. You can also set up your Linux system to run a POP server. POP servers hold user's mail until they log in to access their messages, instead of having mail sent to their hosts directly.

Messages sent within a single standalone system require a loopback interface. Most Linux distributions do this automatically for you during the installation process. A *loopback interface* enables your system to address itself, allowing it to send and receive mail to and from itself. A loopback interface uses the hostname **localhost** and a special IP address reserved for use by local systems, **127.0.0.1**. You can examine your **/etc/hosts** file to see if your loopback interface has been configured as the local host. You see **127.0.0.1 localhost** listed as the first entry. If, for some reason, no entry exists for "localhost," you may have to create a loopback interface yourself using the **ifconfig** and **route** commands as shown here (**lo** is the term for *loopback*):

```
ifconfig lo 127.0.0.1
route add -net 127.0.0.0
```

Sendmail

Sendmail operates as a server to both receive and send mail messages. Sendmail listens for any mail messages received from other hosts and addressed to users on the network hosts it serves. At the same time, Sendmail handles messages users are sending out to remote users, determining to what hosts to send them. You can learn more about Sendmail at **www.sendmail.org**, including online documentation and current software packages. The Sendmail newsgroup is **comp.mail.sendmail**. You can also obtain a commercial version from **www.sendmail.com**.

The domain name server for your network designates the host that runs the Sendmail server. This is your mail host. Messages are sent to this host, whose Sendmail server then sends the message to the appropriate user and its host. In your domain name server configuration file, the mail host entry is specified with an MX entry. To print the mail queue of messages for future delivery, you can use **mailq** (or **sendmail -v -q**). This runs Sendmail with instructions to print the mail queue.

Sendmail supports the use of aliases for either sent or received mail. It checks an **aliases** database file called **aliases.db** that holds alias names and their associated e-mail addresses. This is often used for administrator mail, where mail may be sent to the system's root user and then redirected to the mail address of the actual system administrator. You can also alias host addresses, enabling you to address hosts on your network using only their aliases. Aliases entries are kept in the **/etc/aliases** file. This file consists of one-line alias records, beginning with the address of the user or host, followed by a colon and a list of aliases for that entry. You can edit this file to add new entries or to change old ones. They are then stored for lookup in the **aliases.db** file using the command **newaliases**, which runs Sendmail with instructions to update the **aliases.db** file. The following is an example of an alias entry for the system administrator address:

```
# Basic system aliases -- these MUST be present.
MAILER-DAEMON:    postmaster
postmaster:    root
# Person who should get root's mail
#root:       richlp
```

Sendmail Configuration

The main Sendmail configuration file is **sendmail.cf**, located in the **/etc** directory. This file consists of a sometimes lengthy list of mail definitions that set general options, designate MTAs, and define the address rewrite rules. A series of options set features such as maximum size of mail messages or the name of host files. The MTAs are those mailers through which Sendmail routes messages. The rewrite rules "rewrite" a mail address to route through the appropriate Internet connections to its destination (these rules can be complex). Check the Sendmail HOW-TO and the online documentation for a detailed explanation.

The **sendmail.cf** definitions can be complex and confusing. To simplify the configuration process, Sendmail supports the use of macros you can use to generate the **sendmail.cf** file using the m4 preprocessor (this requires installation of the sendmail-cf package). Macros are placed in the **sendmail.mc** file. Here, you can use macros to designate the definitions and features you want for Sendmail, and then the macros are used to generate the appropriate definitions and rewrite rules in the **sendmail.cf** file. As part of the Sendmail package, several specialized versions of the **sendmail.mc** file are made available. These begin with a system name and have the suffix **.mc**. For example, a **redhat.mc** file exists for Red Hat systems and a **generic-solaris2.mc** for Sun Solaris files. In Red Hat systems, the **redhat.mc** file is already installed as your **sendmail.mc** file.

Once you configure your **sendmail.mc** file, you use the following command to generate a **sendmail.cf** file (be sure first to back up your original **sendmail.cf** file). You can rename the **sendmail.mc** file to reflect the specific configuration. You can have as many different **.mc** files as you want and use them to implement different configurations.

```
m4 sendmail.mc > /etc/sendmail.cf
```

You can also use Linuxconf to configure Sendmail. This requires that Linuxconf have its mailconf module loaded. Under the Networking heading, open the Server Tasks listing and select the Mail Delivery System entry. This opens a lengthy list of entries for panels that configure Sendmail on your system. Click its entry to display a panel (see Figure 27-1). Once you configure Sendmail, you can then have Linuxconf generate a **sendmail.cf** file. You can also use the **mailconf** command to display a window with buttons for the different Linuxconf Sendmail panels.

   You can also perform basic Sendmail configuration using Webmin.

In the **sendmail.mc** file, you configure different aspects of Sendmail using either a **define** command to set the value of Sendmail variables or a Sendmail macro that has already been defined to set a particular Sendmail feature. For example, to assign the PROCMAIL_PATH variable the directory **/usr/bin/procmail**, you would use the following:

```
define(`PROCMAIL_MAILER_PATH',`/usr/bin/procmail')
```

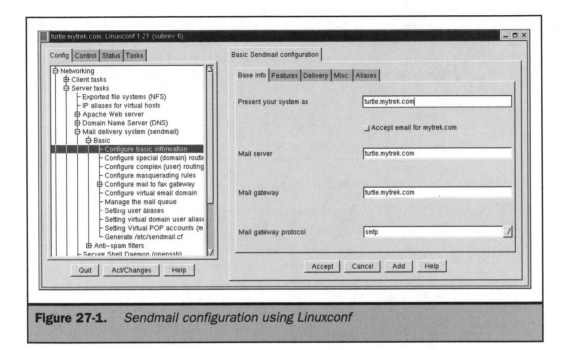

Figure 27-1.   *Sendmail configuration using Linuxconf*

Similarly, if there are variables that you do not want defined, you can remove them with the **undefine** command:

```
undefine(`UUCP_RELAY')
```

To specify the type of operating system that your Sendmail server is running on, you would use the OSTYPE Sendmail macro. The following example specifies the Linux operating system:

```
OSTYPE(`linux')
```

The MAILER macro specifies the mail delivery agents (MDAs) to be used. You may have more than one. Usually, you will need a mail delivery agent such as procmail for delivering mail to hosts on your network. In addition, Sendmail in effect operates as an MDA to receive messages from hosts in its local network, which it will then send out to the larger network.

```
MAILER(procmail)
MAILER(smtp)
```

Sendmail also supports an extensive number of features that you need to explicitly turn on. You can do this with the Sendmail FEATURE macro. See Table 27-1 for a list of Sendmail features. The following example turns on the redirect feature, which is used to inform a sender that a recipient is now at a different address:

```
FEATURE(redirect)
```

Feature	Description
use_cw_file	Check for alternate names for a host specified in the **/etc/sendmail.ct** file.
use_ct_file	Read a list of users from the **/etc/sendmail.ct** file. These users are trusted users that can change the sender name for their messages.
redirect	Reject all mail addressed to "address.REDIRECT," providing forwarding address is placed in the **/etc/aliases** file.
nouucp	Do nothing special with UUCP addresses.
nocanonify	Don't pass addresses for canonification.
mailertable	Use a mailer table in the **/etc/mailtertable** file to override routing for particular domains.
domaintable	Use a domain table in the **/etc/domaintable** file to map one domain to another. Useful if you change your domain name.
uucpdomain	Domain feature for UUCP hosts.
always_add_domain	Add the local host domain to local mail on your system (those for which you would only need a user name).
allmasquerade	Cause recipient addresses to also masquerade as being from the masquerade host.
masquerade_entire_ domain	Masquerade all hosts within the domain specified in MASQUERADE_AS.

Table 27-1.　*Sendmail Features*

Feature	Description
masquerade_envelope	Masquerade envelope sender and recipient along with headers.
virtusertable	For virtual domains, maps addresses to user names.
nullclient	Turn a Sendmail server into a null client, which simply forwards mail messages to a central mail server for processing.
local_lmtp	Use an LMTP-capable local mailer.
local_procmail	Use procmail as the local mailer.
smrsh	Use the Sendmail Restricted SHell (smrsh) for mailing.
promiscuous_relay	Allow you to relay mail—mail is received from outside your domain and sent on to hosts outside your domain.
relay_entire_domain	Allow any host in your domain to relay mail (default limits this to hosts in the access database).
relay_hosts_only	Check for relay permission for particular hosts instead of domains.
accept_unqualified_ senders	Allow sender e-mail address to be single user names instead of just fully qualified names that include domain names.
accept_unresolvable_ domains	Allow Sendmail to accept unresolvable domain names. Useful for those users in a local network blocked by a firewall from the full DNS namespace. By default, Sendmail requires domains in addresses to be resolvable with DNS.
access_db	Accept or reject mail from domains and hosts in the **access** database.
blacklist_recipients	Block mail to certain users, such as those that should never receive mail—like the users nobody, host, and yp.
rbl	Reject hosts in the Realtime Blackhole List. Managed by MAPS (Mail Abuse Prevention System LLC), designed to limit transport of unwanted mass e-mail. **maps.vix.com/rbl/**.

Table 27-1. *Sendmail Features* (continued)

SERVERS

In addition, you can set certain configuration options. These are variables beginning with the prefix "conf" that you can set and assign values to using the **define** command. There are an extensive number of configuration options, most of which you will not need to change. Table 27-2 lists several of the commonly used ones. The following example defines the confAUTO_REBUILD configuration option, which will automatically rebuild the **aliases** database if needed.

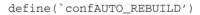

```
define(`confAUTO_REBUILD')
```

Option	Description
confMAILER_NAME	The sender name used for internally generated outgoing messages.
confDOMAIN_NAME	Your domain name. Used only if your system cannot determine your local domain name.
confCF_VERSION	Appended to the configuration version name.
confCW_FILE	File that holds alternate hostnames for server.
confCT_FILE	File that holds trusted users.
confCR_FILE	File that holds relay domains.
confUSERDB_SPEC	Specify the user database.
confALIAS_WAIT	Time to wait to rebuild **aliases** database.
confMIN_FREE_BLOCKS	Minimum number of free blocks needed on file system for Sendmail to accept new mail.
confMAX_MESSAGE_SIZE	The maximum size of messages that will be accepted (in bytes).
confDELIVERY_MODE	Default delivery mode.
confAUTO_REBUILD	Automatically rebuild **alias** file if needed.
confERROR_MODE	Error message mode.
confERROR_MESSAGE	Error message header/file.
confBIND_OPTS	Default options for DNS resolver.
confLOG_LEVEL	Set the Sendmail log level.

Table 27-2.   *Sendmail Configuration Options*

Option	Description
confTO_CONNECT	The timeout waiting for an initial connect to complete.
confME_TOO	Include sender in group expansions.
confTO_INITIAL	The timeout waiting for a response on the initial connect.
confTO_IDENT	The timeout waiting for a response to an IDENT query.
confTO_QUEUERETURN	The timeout before a message is returned as undeliverable.
confTRY_NULL_MX_LIST	If the server is the best MX for a host and hasn't made other arrangements, try connecting to the host directly.
confDEF_USER_ID	Default user ID.
confDOUBLE_BOUNCE_ADDRESS	If an error occurs when sending an error message, send that "double bounce" error message to this address.
confDONT_PROBE_INTERFACES	If set, Sendmail will *not* insert the names and addresses of any local interfaces into the list of known "equivalent" addresses.
confMAX_RCPTS_PER_MESSAGE	Allow no more than the specified number of recipients in an SMTP envelope.

Table 27-2.   *Sendmail Configuration Options* (continued)

Certain macros and types of macros need to be placed in the **sendmail.mc** file in a particular sequence, as shown next. Notice that MAILER is toward the end and OSTYPE at the beginning. Local macro definitions (**define**) and FEATURE entries follow the OSTYPE and DOMAIN entries.

```
VERSIONID
OSTYPE
DOMAIN
define
```

```
FEATURE
local macro definitions
MAILER
LOCAL_RULE_*
LOCAL_RULESETS
```

The local macro and configuration option definitions that affect a particular feature need to be entered before the FEATURE entry. For example, the redirect feature uses the **aliases** file. Any local definition of the **aliases** file needs to be entered before the redirect feature.

```
define('ALIAS_FILE','/etc/aliases')
FEATURE(redirect)
```

If you are implementing a mail server on a local network that may be connected to the Internet with a single gateway/firewall host, you will need to masquerade mail sent from the local hosts out to the Internet. To do this, you use the MASQUERADE_AS macro. This macro makes it appear that the mail is originating from a single host—the gateway—when, in fact, it is originating from different local hosts. The following example shows MASQUERADE_AS takes as its argument the name of the local domain:

```
MASQUERADE_AS(mytrek.com)
```

This will masquerade the headers only. To masquerade the sender and recipient addresses within the envelope (the message), you have to set the masquerade_envelope feature as well.

```
FEATURE(`masquerade_envelope')
```

You need to be careful how you enter comments into a **sendmail.mc** file. This file is read as a stream of macros—ignoring all white spaces, including newlines. There are no special comment characters that are looked for. Instead, you have to simulate comment indicators using the **dnl** or **divert** commands. The **dnl** command instructs that all characters following that **dnl** command up to and including the next newline are to be ignored. If you place a **dnl** command at the beginning of a text line in the **sendmain.mc** file, it has the effect of turning that line into a comment, ignoring everything on that line—including its newline. Even empty lines will require a **dnl** entry to ignore the newline character.

```
dnl you will have to /etc/sendmail.cf by running this the m4
dnl macro config through preprocessor:
dnl
```

Alternatively, you can use the **divert** command. The **divert** command will ignore all data until another **divert** command is reached.

```
divert(-1)
 This is the macro config file used to generate
 the /etc/sendmail.cf file. If you modify the file regenerate
 you will have to regenerate /etc/sendmail.cf by running the m4
 macro
divert(0)
```

For Sendmail to work at all, it only requires that the OSTYPE and MAILERS macros, and any needed features and options, be defined. A very simple Sendmail file is shown here.

mysendmail.mc

```
dnl My sendmail.mc file
OSTYPE('linux')
define('PROCMAIL_MAILER_PATH','/usr/bin/procmail')
FEATURE(redirect)
MAILER(procmail)
MAILER(smtp)
```

A **sendmail.mc** file usually contains many more entries, particularly for parameters and features. The default Red Hat **sendmail.mc** file is shown here.

/etc/sendmail.mc

```
dnl This is the macro config file used to generate the /etc/sendmail.cf
dnl file. If you modify the file you will have to regenerate the
dnl /etc/sendmail.cf by running this configuration through the m4
dnl preprocessor:
dnl
dnl         m4 /etc/sendmail.mc > /etc/sendmail.cf
dnl
include(`/usr/lib/sendmail-cf/m4/cf.m4')
VERSIONID(`linux setup for Red Hat Linux')dnl
OSTYPE(`linux')
define(`confDEF_USER_ID',``8:12'')dnl
undefine(`UUCP_RELAY')dnl
undefine(`BITNET_RELAY')dnl
define(`confAUTO_REBUILD')dnl
define(`confTO_CONNECT', `1m')dnl
define(`confTRY_NULL_MX_LIST',true)dnl
define(`confDONT_PROBE_INTERFACES',true)dnl
```

```
define(`PROCMAIL_MAILER_PATH',`/usr/bin/procmail')dnl
define(`ALIAS_FILE',`/etc/aliases')dnl
define(`STATUS_FILE', `/var/log/sendmail.st')dnl
define(`UUCP_MAILER_MAX', `2000000')dnl
define(`confUSERDB_SPEC', `/etc/mail/userdb.db')dnl
FEATURE(`smrsh',`/usr/sbin/smrsh')dnl
FEATURE(`mailertable',`hash -o /etc/mail/mailertable')dnl
FEATURE(`virtusertable',`hash -o /etc/mail/virtusertable')dnl
FEATURE(redirect)dnl
FEATURE(always_add_domain)dnl
FEATURE(use_cw_file)dnl
FEATURE(local_procmail)dnl
FEATURE(`access_db')dnl
FEATURE(`blacklist_recipients')dnl
FEATURE(`accept_unresolvable_domains')dnl
MAILER(smtp)dnl
MAILER(procmail)dnl
```

Sendmail Configuration Operators: sendmail.cf

It is not advisable that you modify the **sendmail.cf** file directly. However, it may be helpful to know how it is set up. This section describes the type of entries you will find there. Table 27-3 lists the basic Sendmail configuration operators found in the **sendmail.cf** file. These operators consist of a single uppercase character, some with no spaces separating their arguments. The *D* operator defines macros. These are often used for specific information, such as the name of a host. The macro name usually consists of one character. Uppercase macro names are reserved for use by Sendmail, whereas lowercase macro names are used for user-defined macros. The following example defines a macro called *T* for **turtle.mytrek.com**. You can then reference the macro anywhere in other operations by preceding it with a $, as in $T. To have a macro name longer than one character, encase the name within braces, as shown here for "rabbit." To evaluate the rabbit macro, use ${rabbit}.

```
DTturtle.mytrek.com
D{rabbit}rabbit.mytrek.com
```

Much of the **sendmail.cf** file consists of options that are specified by the *O* operator followed by the option and its arguments. For example, the following entries determine the location of the **alias** file and the maximum size of a message.

```
O AliasFile=/etc/aliases
O HelpFile=/usr/lib/sendmail.hf
O MaxMessageSize=1000000
```

The *H* operator is used to define mail headers. The *P* operator is used to define the priority of mail messages based on keywords, such as the term "bulk" in the mail header. The *K* operator specifies the location of key database files, such as the **aliases** databases. The *C* operator is used to define a class, such as a collection of hosts, while the *F* operator is used to define a class from names read from a file.

```
# file containing names of hosts for which we receive email
Fw/etc/sendmail.cw
```

The *M* operator is used to define the mailers used by Sendmail. The *S* and *R* operators are used to define rulesets and rewriting rules. Rulesets and rewriting rules are used to determine how a message is to be routed and, if necessary, to rewrite its address so Sendmail's MTAs can handle it. You can think of *rulesets* as functions in a program, which are called as needed to work on message addresses—and can themselves call yet other rulesets. A ruleset consists of a set of rules, much like a function consists of a set of programming statements. Each ruleset is labeled with a number defined by an initial *S* operator. The rules making up the ruleset are then defined by *R* operators. Sendmail uses the rulesets first to format an address into a standard form. Then, for messages being sent, it determines the MTA to use. Special rules called *rewriting rules* can rewrite the address into a form that can be better handled by the MTA. Rewriting rules consist of a left-hand and a right-hand pattern. An address that matches the pattern on the left-hand side is rewritten in the format of the pattern on the right-hand side.

Operator	Action
D	Define a macro.
C	Define a class.
F	Define a class read from a file.
H	Define mail header.
O	Set an option.
P	Set message priority.
V	Specify version level of **sendmail.cf** file.
K	Specify key file.
M	Specify mailer.
S	Label and start a ruleset.
R	Define a rule.
#	Comment.

Table 27-3. *Sendmail Configuration Operators*

POP Servers

The *Post Office Protocol* (*POP*) allows a remote server to hold mail for users who can then fetch their mail from it when they are ready. Unlike Sendmail and procmail, which deliver mail messages directly to a user account on a Linux system, the POP protocol holds mail until a user accesses his or her account on the POP server. The POP server then transfers any received messages to the user's local mailbox. Servers are often used by ISPs to provide Internet mail services for users. Instead of sending mail directly to a user's machine, the mail resides in the POP server until it's retrieved.

You can access the POP server from different hosts; however, when you do, all the messages are transferred to that host. They are not kept on the POP server. The POP server simply forwards your messages on the requesting host. When you access your messages from a certain computer, they will be transferred to that computer and erased from the POP server. If you access your POP server again from a different computer, those previous messages will be gone.

The POP protocol provides a set of commands you can use to directly test a POP server. You can access the POP server on port 110 using telnet and then enter a series of POP commands to check the server's performance. The following example connects to the **mypopserver.mytrek.com** POP server using telnet on port 110:

```
telnet mypopserver.mytrek.com 110
```

You can then log into an account using the **USER** and **PASSWORD** commands. The **LIST** command will list messages and the **RETR** command will display a message. Use **DELE** to delete a message. Use the **QUIT** command to the session.

> **Note** *The current version of the POP protocol is known as POP3, whereas POP2 is an earlier one that still may be in use in some places.*

Qpopper is the current version of the Berkeley POP server (popper). Qpopper is supported by Qualcomm, makers of Eudora e-mail software. The Qpopper Web page is **www.eudora.com/free/qpop.html**. You can obtain a current source code version from **ftp.qualcomm.com/eudora/servers/unix**. RPM package versions are located at distribution sites such as **ftp.redhat.com** for Red Hat.

You can install Qpopper software on your Linux system and have it operate as a POP server for your network. It consists of both the **qpopper** daemon and the popauth program, which manages an authentication database with password encryption for secure user access. popauth creates a database file called **/etc/pop.auth**. To add a user, enter the **popauth** command with the options **-user** and **user name**. You are then prompted for a password with which the user can access his or her POP account.

If you download the source code version, you use the ./configure, make, and make install sequence to configure, compile, and install the server. For the configure stage, you may need to enter several options to make Qpopper compatible with your system.

For example, if your system uses shadow passwords (as most do), you will need to use the **--enable-specialauth** option. The **--enable-apop** option enables the use of the APOP (Authenticated POP) extension to provide encryption that is managed by the **popauth** command.

```
./configure --enable-specialauth -enable-apop
```

Qpopper is usually run through inetd or xinetd. For inetd, you can find the following entries in the **/etc/inetd.conf** file:

```
pop-3  stream  tcp  nowait root  /usr/sbin/tcpd  /usr/bin/popper
```

Be sure that the pop-3 service is listed in **/etc/services** along with its port, 110.

```
pop-3     110/tcp
```

You can also use the University of Washington POP server (**ftp.cac.washington.edu/imap**), which is part of the University of Washington's imap RPM package. Simply install the package, which is already done as part of the standard install (both POP2 and POP3 servers are installed). The Server daemons are called **ipop2d** and **ipop3d**. Your Linux system then runs as a POP2 and POP3 server for your network. These servers are usually run through inetd or xinetd. For inetd, you can find the following entries for them in the **/etc/inetd.conf** file:

```
pop-2  stream  tcp   nowait  root   /usr/sbin/tcpd   ipop2d
pop-3  stream  tcp   nowait  root   /usr/sbin/tcpd   ipop3d
```

IMAP

The *Internet Mail Access Protocol* (*IMAP*) allows a remote server to hold mail for users who can then log in to access their mail. Unlike the POP servers, IMAP servers retain user mail messages. Users can even save their mail on the IMAP mail server. This has the advantage of keeping a user's mail in one centralized location, accessible from anywhere on the network. Users can log into the mail server from any host on the network and read, send, and save their mail. This interactive connection requires more connect time than the POP protocol and is best suited to an Ethernet LAN where users are always connected, rather than dial-up access through a modem.

Unlike POP, IMAP allows users to set up multiple folders on their mail server in which they can organize their mail. IMAP also supports the use of shared folders to which several users have access to mail on a given topic.

SERVERS

The Washington University IMAP server is available as an RPM software package, beginning with the name "imap." The name of the server daemon is **imapd**. The server is run through inetd or xinetd, and you can find a line for it in the **/etc/inetd.conf** file.

```
imap    stream  tcp     nowait  root    /usr/sbin/tcpd   imapd
```

The
Complete
Reference

Linux

Chapter 28

News, Proxy,
and Search Servers

News servers provide Internet users with Usenet news services. They have their own TCP/IP protocol, *Network News Transfer Protocol (NNTP)*. In addition, servers exist that provide better access to Internet resources. Proxy servers speed Web access by maintaining current copies of commonly accessed Web pages, speeding access times by eliminating the need to access the original site constantly. They also perform security functions, protecting servers from unauthorized access. The search and indexing server ht:/Dig enables document searches of Web and FTP sites. With it, you can index documents and carry out complex search requests. Table 28-1 lists different news, proxy, and search servers.

News Servers: INN

The *InterNetNews (INN)* news server accesses Usenet newsfeeds, providing news clients on your network with the full range of newsgroups and their articles. Newsgroup articles are transferred using the NNTP, and servers that support this protocol are known as *NNTP servers*. INN was written by Rich Salz, and is currently maintained and supported by the *Internet Software Consortium (ISC)*. You can download current versions from its Web site at **www.isc.org**. INN is also included with most Linux distributions, and the documentation directory for INN in **/usr/share/doc** contains extensive samples. The primary program for INN is the **innd** daemon. Various INN configuration files can be found in **/etc/news**, including **innd**, **inn.conf**, **rnews**, **nnrp.access**, and **hosts.nntp**. **inn.conf** sets options for INN, and the **hosts.nntp** file holds the hosts from which you receive newsfeeds. Place entries for remote hosts in the **nnrp.access** file to allow them access to your news server. Correct configuration of INN can be a complex and time-consuming process, so be sure to consult references and online resources, such as the HOW-TO documents. An **innd** script is in the **/etc/rc.d/init.d** directory, which has similar arguments to the Web **httpd** script. You can use start and stop arguments with the **innd** script to start and stop the INN server.

Web Site	Description
www.isc.org	InterNetNews news server, INN
www.leafnode.org	Leafnode news server
squid.nlanr.net	Squid proxy server
www.htdig.org	ht://Dig search and indexing server

Table 28-1.   *News, Proxy, and Search Servers*

Most Linux systems have already created a **news** user with a news group for use by your INN daemon. On other systems, you may have to create the **news** user and group. On all systems, you must create a news home directory, such as **/home/news**. INN software also installs **cron** scripts, which are used to update your news server, removing old articles and fetching new ones. These are usually placed in the **/etc/cron.daily** directory, though they may reside anywhere. **inn-cron-expire** removes old articles and **inn-cron-rnews** retrieves new ones. **inn-cron-nntpsend** sends articles posted from your system to other news servers.

Leafnode News Server

Leafnode is a NTTP news server designed for small networks that may have slow connections to the Internet. You can obtain the Leafnode software package along with documentation from its Web site at **www.leafnode.org**. You can also download it from software repositories like **freshmeat.net** or **linuxapps.com**. Along with the Leafnode NNTP server, the software package includes several utilities such as Fetchnews, Texpire, and Newsq. Fetchnews retrieves and sends articles to your upstream news servers. Texpire deletes old news, and Newsq shows articles waiting to be sent out.

Leafnode is tailored to very low usage requirements. Only newsgroups that users on your local network have accessed within the last week are actually downloaded. Newsgroups not accessed in over a week are no longer downloaded. The usage levels of Leafnode are comparable to a news client, accessing only the news that users on your network want. For a small network, this means having the advantages of a news service with few of the disadvantages. Much less disk space is used and less time is needed to download newsfeeds.

Configuring Leafnode is a relatively simple process. You need to enter news server information in the Leafnode configuration file and make sure that there is an entry for Leafnode in the **inetd.conf** or **xinetd.conf** file, so that users on your network can access it. The Leafnode configuration file is **/etc/leafnode/config**. You can edit this file directly or use one of several GUI Leafnode configuration utilities, such as Keafnode or leafwa. Keafnode is a KDE program that provides a simple dialog box to configure your Leafnode servers, expire messages in selected newsgroups, and control download operations. leafwa provides a Web page-based interface, letting you configure Leafnode using any Web browser.

You can think of Leafnode as more of a news client that provides news server services to a small local network. It assumes that you already have a connection to a larger network such as the Internet and to an NNTP news server on that network. You then configure Leafnode to download newsgroup articles from that NNTP news server. In the Leafnode configuration file, you need to specify the name of that NNTP news server in the server entry as shown here:

```
server = mynewsever.mynet.com
```

If you have access to other news servers, you can list them in the supplement entry.

```
supplement = myothernewserver.mynet.com
```

If you need a user name and password to access the news server, you can list them in user name and password entries following the server entry.

```
username = mylogin
password = mypassword
```

In the configuration file, you can also specify a default expiration time for unread newsgroup articles.

```
expire = 20
```

The Leafnode server does not perform the task of downloading articles. For this task, use Fetchnews. Fetchnews will download articles for specified newsgroups from the NNTP news server and send posted articles to it submitted by users on your local network. Similarly, you use the Texpire application to expire articles that have been previously downloaded. You can further automate these operation by scheduling them in a Leafnode crontab file, **leafnode.crontab**.

To allow users on your network to access the Leafnode server set up for them, you place an entry for it in the **inetd.conf** or **xinetd.conf** file.

```
nntp steap tcp nowait news /usr/sbin/tcpd  /usr/local/sbin/leafnode
```

Squid Proxy-Caching Server

Squid is a proxy-caching server for Web clients, designed to speed Internet access and provide security controls for Web servers. It implements a proxy-caching service for Web clients that caches Web pages as users make requests. Copies of Web pages accessed by users are kept in the Squid cache; and, as requests are made, Squid checks to see if it has a current copy. If Squid does have a current copy, it returns the copy from its cache instead of querying the original site. In this way, Web browsers can then use the local Squid cache as a proxy HTTP server. Squid currently handles Web pages supporting the HTTP, FTP, Gopher, SSL, and WAIS protocols (Squid cannot be used with FTP clients). Replacement algorithms periodically replace old objects in the cache.

As a proxy, Squid does more that just cache Web objects. It operates as an intermediary between the Web browsers (clients) and the servers they access. Instead of connections being made directly to the server, a client connects to the proxy server. The proxy then relays requests to the Web server. This is useful for situations in which a Web server is placed behind a firewall server, protecting it from outside access. The proxy is accessible on the firewall, which can then transfer requests and responses back and forth between the client and the Web server. The design is often used to allow Web servers to operate on protected local networks and still be accessible on the Internet. Technically, you could use a proxy server to simply manage traffic between a Web server and the clients that want to communicate with it, without doing caching at all. Squid combines both capabilities as a proxy-caching server.

Squid also provides security capabilities that let you exercise control over hosts accessing your Web server. You can deny access by certain hosts and allow access by others. Squid also supports the use of encrypted protocols such as SSL (see Chapter 39). Encrypted communications are tunneled (passed through without reading) through the Squid server directly to the Web server.

Squid is supported and distributed under a GNU public license by the *National Laboratory for Applied Network Research* (*NLANR*) at the University of California, San Diego. The work is based on the Harvest Project to create a Web indexing system that included a high-performance cache daemon called *cached*. You can obtain current source code versions and online documentation from the Squid home page at **http://squid.nlanr.net** and the Squid FTP site at **ftp.nlanr.net**. The Squid software package consists of the Squid server, a domain name lookup program called dnsserver, an FTP client called ftpget, and a cache manager script called **cachemgr.cgi**. The dnsserver resolves IP addresses from domain names, and the ftpget program is an FTP client Squid uses to retrieve files from FTP servers. **cachemgr.cgi** lets you view statistics for the Squid server as it runs.

The Squid configuration file is **squid.conf**, located in the **/etc/squid** directory. The default version provided with Squid software includes detailed explanations of all standard entries, along with commented default entries. Entries consist of tags that specify different attributes. For example, maximum_object_size and maximum_object set limits on objects transferred.

```
maximum_object_size 4096 KB
```

Security

Squid can use its role as an intermediary between Web clients and a Web server to implement access controls, determining who can access the Web server and how. Squid does this by checking access control lists (ACLs) of hosts and domains that have had controls placed on them. When it finds a Web client from one of those hosts attempting to connect to the Web server, it executes the control. Squid supports a number of controls with which it can deny or allow access to the Web server by the remote host's Web client (see Table 28-2). In effect, Squid sets up a firewall just for the Web server.

The first step in configuring Squid security is to create ACLs. These are lists of hosts and domains for which you want to set up control. You define ACLs using the **acl** command, with which you create labels for the systems on which you are setting

Option	Description
src *ip-address/netmask*	Client's IP address
src *addr1-addr2/netmask*	Range of addresses
dst *ip-address/netmask*	Destination IP address
myip *ip-address/netmask*	Local socket IP address
srcdomain *domain*	Reverse lookup, client IP
dstdomain *domain*	Destination server from URL. For **dstdomain** and **dstdom_regex**, a reverse lookup is tried if an IP-based URL is used.
srcdom_regex [-i] *expression*	Regular expression matching client name
dstdom_regex [-i] *expression*	Regular expression matching destination
time *[day-abbrevs] [h1:m1-h2:m2]*	Time as specified by day, hour, and minutes. Day-abbreviations: S – Sunday, M – Monday, T – Tuesday, W – Wednesday, H – Thursday, F – Friday, A – Saturday
url_regex [-i] *expression*	Regular expression matching on whole URL
urlpath_regex [-i] *expression*	Regular expression matching on URL path
port *ports*	Specify a port or range of ports
proto *protocol*	Specify a protocol, such as HTTP or FTP
method *method*	Specify methods, such as GET and POST
browser [-i] regexp	Pattern match on user-agent header
ident *username*	String match on **ident** output
src_as *number*	Used for routing of requests to specific caches
dst_as *number*	Used for routing of requests to specific caches
proxy_auth *username*	List of valid user names
snmp_community *string*	A community string to limit access to your SNMP agent

Table 28-2. *Squid ACL Options*

controls. You then use commands, such as **http_access**, to define these controls. You can define a system, or a group of systems, based on several **acl** options, such as the source IP address, the domain name, or even the time and date (see Table 28-2). For example, the **src** option is used to define a system or group of systems with a certain source address. To define a **mylan acl** entry for systems in a local network with the addresses 192.168.1.0 through to 192.168.1.255, use the following ACL definition:

```
acl mylan src 192.168.1.0/255.255.255.0
```

Once defined, you can use an ACL definition in a **Squid** option to specify a control you want to place on those systems. For example, to allow access by the mylan group of local systems to the Web through the proxy, use a **http_access** option with the **allow** action specifying **mylan** as the **acl** definition to use, as shown here.

```
http_access allow mylan
```

By defining ACLs and using them in **Squid** options, you can tailor your Web site with the kind of security you want. The following example allows access to the Web through the proxy by only the mylan group of local systems, denying access to all others. Two **acl** entries are set up: one for the local system and one for all others. **http_access** options first allow access to the local system, and then deny access to all others.

```
acl mylan src 192.168.1.0/255.255.255.0
acl allsystems src 0.0.0.0/0.0.0.0
http_access allow mylan
http_access deny allsystems
```

The order of the **http_access** options is important. Squid starts from the first and works its way down, stopping at the first **http_access** option with an ACL entry that matches. In the previous example, local systems that match the first **http_access** command are allowed, whereas others fall through to the second **http_access** command and are denied.

For systems using the proxy, you can also control what sites they can access. For a destination address, you create an **acl** entry with the **dst** qualifier. The **dst** qualifier takes as its argument the site address. Then you can create an **http_access** option to control access to that address. The following example denies access by anyone using the proxy to destination site **rabbit.mytrek.com**. If you have a local network accessing the Web through the proxy, you can use such commands to restrict access to certain sites.

```
acl myrabbit dst rabbit.mytrek.com
http_access deny myrabbit
```

You can also qualify addresses by domain. Often Web sites can be referenced using only the domain. For example, a site called **www.mybeach.com** can be referenced using just the **domain mybeach.com**. To create an **acl** entry to reference a domain, use either the **dstdomain** or **srcdomain** options for destination and source domains, respectively. Remember, such a reference refers to all hosts in that domain. An **acl** entry with the **dstdomain** option for **mybeach.com** restricts access to sites called **www.mybeach.com**, **ftp.mybeach.com**, **surf.mybeach.com**, and so on. The following example restricts access to the **www.mybeach.com** site, along with all other **.mybeach.com** sites and any hosts in the **mybeach.com** domain.

```
acl thebeach dstdomain .mybeach.com
http_access deny thebeach
```

You can list several domains or addresses in an **acl** entry to reference them as a group, but you cannot have one domain that is a subdomain of another. For example, if **mybeachblanket.com** is a subdomain of **mybeach.com**, you cannot list both in the same **acl** list. The following example restricts access to both **mybeach.com** and **mysurf.com**:

```
acl beaches dstdomain .mybeach.com .mysurf.com
http_access deny beaches
```

An **acl** entry can also use a pattern to specify certain addresses and domains. In the following example, the access is denied to any URL with the pattern "chocolate," and allows access from all others:

```
acl Choc1 url_regex chocolate
http_access deny Choc1
http_access allow all
```

Squid also supports ident and proxy authentication methods to control user access. The following example only allows the users **dylan** and **chris** to use the Squid cache:

```
ident_lookup on
acl goodusers user chris dylan
http_access allow goodusers
http_access deny all
```

Caches

Squid uses the *Internet Cache Protocol* (*ICP*) to communicate with other Web caches. Using the ICP protocols, your Squid cache can connect to other Squid caches or other cache servers, such as Microsoft proxy server, Netscape proxy server, and Novell

BorderManager. This way, if your network's Squid cache does not have a copy of a requested Web page, it can contact another cache to see if it is there, instead of accessing the original site. You can configure Squid to connect to other Squid caches by connecting it to a cache hierarchy. Squid supports a hierarchy of caches denoted by the terms *child*, *sibling*, and *parent*. Sibling and child caches are accessible on the same level and are automatically queried whenever a request cannot be located in your own Squid's cache. If these queries fail, then a parent cache is queried, which then searches its own child and sibling caches—or its own parent cache, if needed—and so on. Use `cache_host` to set up parent and sibling hierarchical connections.

```
cache_host sd.cache.nlanr.net    parent 3128 3130
```

You can set up a cache hierarchy to connect to the main NLANR server by registering your cache using the following entries in your **squid.conf** file:

```
cache_announce 24
announce_to sd.cache.nlanr.net:3131
```

Squid keeps several logs. **access.log** holds requests sent to your proxy, **cache.log** holds Squid server messages such as errors and startup messages, and **store.log** holds information about the Squid cache such as objects added or removed. You can use the cache manager (**cachemgr.cgi**) to manage the cache and view statistics on the cache manager as it runs. To run the cache manager, use your browser to execute the **cachemgr.cgi** script (this script should be placed in your Web server's **cgi-bin** directory). You can also monitor Squid using the Multi Router Traffic utility.

Dig Server

Dig, known officially as *ht:/Dig*, is a Web indexing and search system designed for small networks or intranets. Dig is not considered a replacement for full-scale Internet search systems, such as Lycos, Infoseek, or Alta Vista. Unlike Web server–based search engines, Dig can span several Web servers at a site. Dig was developed at San Diego State University and is distributed free under the GNU public license. You can obtain information and documentation at **www.htdig.org**, and you can download software packages—including RPM packages—from **ftp.htdig.org**.

Dig supports simple and complex searches, including complex Boolean and fuzzy search methods. *Fuzzy searching* supports a number of search algorithms, including exact, soundex, and synonyms. Searches can be carried out on both text and HTML documents. HTML documents can have keywords placed in them for more accurate retrieval, and you can also use HTML templates to control how results are displayed.

Searches can be constrained by authentication requirements, location, and search depth. To protect documents in restricted directories, Dig can be informed to request a specific user name and password. You can also restrict a search to retrieve documents in a certain URL, search subsections of the database, or retrieve only documents that are a specified number of links away.

All the ht:/Dig programs use the same configuration file, **htdig.conf**, located in the **/etc/htdig** directory. The configuration file consists of attribute entries, each beginning with the attribute line and followed by the value after a colon. Each program takes only the attributes it needs.

```
max_head_length:      10000
```

You can specify attributes such as allow_virtual_hosts, which index virtual hosts (see Chapter 25) as separate servers, and search_algorithm, which specifies the search algorithms to use for searches.

Dig consist of five programs: **htdig**, **htmerge**, **htfuzzy**, **htnotify**, and **htsearch**. **Htdig**, **htmerge**, and **htfuzzy** generate the index, while *htsearch* performs the actual searches. First, **htdig** gathers information on your database, searching all URL connections in your domain and associating Web pages with terms. The **htmerge** program uses this information to create a searchable database, merging the information from any previously generated database. **Htfuzzy** creates indexes to allow searches using fuzzy algorithms, such as soundex and synonyms. Once the database is created, users can use Web pages that invoke **htsearch** to search this index. Results are listed on a Web page. You can use META tags in your HTML documents to enter specific htdig keywords, exclude a document from indexing, or provide notification information such as an e-mail address and an expiration date. **Htnotify** uses the e-mail and expiration date to notify Web page authors when their pages are out-of-date.

Htsearch is a CGI program that expects to be invoked by an HTML form, and it accepts both the GET and POST methods of passing data. The **htsearch** program can accept a search request from any form containing the required configuration values. Values include search features such as config (configuration file), method (search method), and sort (sort criteria). For the Web page form that invokes **htsearch**, you can use the default page provided by **htdig** or create your own. Output is formatted using templates you can modify. Several sample files are included with the htdig software: **rundig** is a sample script for creating a database, **searchform.html** is a sample html document that contains a search form for submitting **htdig** searches, **header.html** is a sample header for search headers, and **footer.html** is for search footers.

The
Complete
Reference

Linux

Part VI

Administration

Chapter 29

Basic System Administration

Linux is designed to serve many users at the same time, as well as to provide an interface among the users and the computer with its storage media, such as hard disks and tapes. Users have their own shells through which they interact with the operating system, but you may need to configure the operating system itself in different ways. You may need to add new users, printers, and even file systems. Such operations come under the heading of system administration. The person who performs such actions is referred to as either a *system administrator* or a *superuser*. In this sense, two types of interaction with Linux exist: regular users' interaction and the superuser, who performs system administration tasks. The chapters in the "Administration" section cover operations such as changing system states, managing users, configuring printers, and compiling the kernel. You perform most of these tasks, such as adding a new printer or mounting a file system, rarely. Other tasks, such as adding users, you perform on a regular basis. Basic system administration covers topics such as system access by superusers, selecting the run level to start, system configuration files, performance monitoring, and loading different operating systems. These are discussed in detail in this chapter.

Although system administration can become complex, basic administration tasks, such as adding users or mounting files systems, are easy to perform, particularly if you use a configuration tool such as COAS, Webmin, or Linuxconf. Red Hat uses Linuxconf as its primary administration tool, though it also still provides the set of older specialized Red Hat tools used in previous Red Hat releases. Caldera systems use COAS and Webmin, and SuSE uses YaST, though Linuxconf can also be used on all these systems. Webmin is a browser-based administration tool that uses a Web page interface to directly modify system configuration files. Most tools have a cursor-based interface, as well as an X Windows–based interface that use menus, windows, and buttons with which you can make entries. You can run the cursor-based interface from the command line, using ARROW keys, the SPACEBAR, and the ENTER key to make choices. All are operated as front ends for making entries in Linux configuration files. You can edit these files and make entries directly, if you want. The underlying administration tasks are the same. Configuration using Linuxconf is discussed throughout the book where appropriate, with Chapter 30 examining how you can better configure and use the Linuxconf utility. The traditional Red Hat administration tools are usually accessed through a Control Panel entry on your desktop menu. These Control Panel tools are discussed in Chapter 30.

System Management: Superuser

To perform system administration operations, you must first have the correct password that enables you to log in as the root user, making you the superuser. Because a superuser has the power to change almost anything on the system, such a password is usually a carefully guarded secret given only to those whose job is to manage the system. With the correct password, you can log in to the system as a system administrator and configure the system in different ways. You can start up and shut down the system, as well as change to a different operating mode, such as a single-user mode. You can also add or remove users, add or remove whole file systems, back up and restore files, and even designate the system's name. To become a superuser, you log in to the root user account. This is a special account reserved for system management operations with unrestricted access to all components of your Linux operating system. When you log in to the system as the root user, you are placed in a shell from which you can issue administrative Linux commands. The prompt for this shell is a sharp sign, **#**. In the next example, the user logs in to the system as the root user. The password is, of course, not displayed.

```
login: root
password:
#
```

As the root user, you can use the **passwd** command to change the password for the root login, as well as for any other user on the system.

```
# passwd root
New password:
Re-enter new password:
#
```

While you are logged in to a regular user account, it may be necessary for you to log in to the root and become a superuser. Ordinarily, you would have to log out of your user account first, and then log in to the root user account. Instead, you can use the **su** command (switch user) to log in directly to the root user account while remaining logged in to your user account. A CTRL-D or **exit** command returns you to your own login. When logged in as the root, you can use **su** to log in as any user, without providing the password. In the next example, the user is logged in already. The **su** command then logs the user in to the root user account, making the user a superuser. Some basic superuser commands are shown in Table 29-1.

```
$ pwd
/home/chris
$su
 password:
# cd
# pwd
/root
# exit
$
```

Command	Description
su root	Logs a superuser into the root from a user login; the superuser returns to the original login with a CTRL-D
passwd *login-name*	Sets a new password for the login name
crontab *options file-name*	With *file-name* as an argument, installs crontab entries in the file to a **crontab** file; these entries are operations executed at specified times: **-e** Edits the **crontab** file **-l** Lists the contents of the **crontab** file **-r** Deletes the **crontab** file
init *state*	Changes the system state (see Table 29-2)
lilo *options Config-file*	Reinstalls the Linux Loader (LILO)
shutdown *options time*	Shuts down the system; similar to CTRL-ALT-DEL
date	Sets the date and time for the system

Table 29-1. *Basic System Administration*

Note *For security reasons, Linux distributions do not allow the use of **su** in a telnet session to access the root user.*

System Configuration

Although many different specialized components go into making up a system, such as servers, users, and devices, some operations apply to the system in general. These include setting the system date and time, specifying shutdown procedures, and determining the services to start up and run whenever the system boots. In addition, you can use numerous performance analysis tools to control processes and check on resource use.

System Time and Date

You can use several different tools to set the system time and date, depending on the distribution you use. On all distributions, you can set the system time and date using the shell **date** command. Most users prefer to use a configuration tool. On Red Hat and other distributions, you can use Linuxconf or the Control Panel Time tool. Recall that you set the time and date when you first installed your system. You should not need to do so again. If you entered the time incorrectly or moved to a different time zone, though, you could use this utility to change your time.

You can use the **date** command on your root user command line to set the date and time for the system. As an argument to date, you list (with no delimiters) the month, day, time, and year. In the next example, the date is set to 2:59 P.M., March 6, 2000 (03 for March, 06 for the day, 1459 for the time, and 00 for the year 2000):

```
# date 0306145900
Mon Mar  6 02:59:27 PST 2000
```

To set the system time and date with Linuxconf, select the Time and Date entry under Control. This displays a panel with boxes for the date and time (see Figure 29-1). Linuxconf is configured to read your system's time and date directly from the CMOS, the time and date set on your motherboard's BIOS. On Webmin, select the hardware panel and then click on the System Time icon to open a page where you can check and edit the time and date.

Figure 29-1. *Linuxconf system date and time*

You can also use the Red Hat TimeTool, included on many distributions. An icon exists for it in the Control Panel. Double-click the TimeTool icon or select its menu entry to open the Time Configuration window. You can make changes to any part of the time you want. On COAS, you can select the System Clock entry in the System Administration menu or window. This displays a System Time window with a box displaying the current time and a pop-up menu for selecting your time zone.

Scheduling Tasks: crontab

Although it is not a system file, a crontab file is helpful in maintaining your system. A *crontab* file lists actions to take at a certain time. The cron daemon constantly checks the user's crontab file to see if it is time to take these actions. Any user can set up a crontab file of his or her own. The root user can set up a crontab file to take system administrative actions, such as backing up files at a certain time each week or month.

A crontab entry has six fields: the first five are used to specify the time for an action, while the last field is the action itself. The first field specifies minutes (0–59), the second field specifies the hour (0–23), the third field specifies the day of the month (1–31), the fourth field specifies the month of the year (1–12), and the fifth field specifies the day of the week (0–6), starting with 0 as Sunday. In each of the time fields, you can specify a range, a set of values, or use the asterisk to indicate all values. For example, 1–5 for the day-of-week field specifies Monday through Friday. In the hour field, 8, 12, 17 would specify 8 A.M., 12 noon, and 5 P.M. An * in the month-of-year field indicates every month. The following example backs up the **projects** directory at 2:00 A.M. every weekday:

```
0 2 1-5 * * tar cf  /home/chris/backp  /home/chris/projects
```

You use the **crontab** command to install your entries into a crontab file. To do this, you first create a text file and type your crontab entries. Save this file with any name you want, such as **mycronfile**. Then, to install these entries, enter **crontab** and the name of the text file. The **crontab** command takes the contents of the text file and creates a crontab file in the **/var/spool/cron** directory, adding the name of the user who issued the command. In the next example, the root user installs the contents of the **mycronfile** as the root's crontab file. This creates a file called **/var/spool/cron/root**. If a user named **justin** installed a crontab file, it would create a file called **/var/spool/cron/justin**. You can control use of the **crontab** command by regular users with the **/etc/cron.allow** file. Only users with their names in this file can create crontab files of their own.

```
# crontab mycronfile
```

Never try to edit your crontab file directly. Instead, use the **crontab** command with the **-e** option. This opens your crontab file in the **/var/spool/cron** directory with the standard text editor, such as Vi. **crontab** uses the default editor as specified by the

EDITOR shell environment variable. To use a different editor for **crontab**, change the default editor by assigning the editor's program name to the EDITOR variable and exporting that variable. Running **crontab** with the **-l** option displays the contents of your crontab file, and the **-r** option deletes the entire file. Invoking **crontab** with another text file of crontab entries overwrites your current crontab file, replacing it with the contents of the text file.

You can also schedule tasks with crontab using Webmin (see Figure 29-2). On Webmin, select the Scheduled Cron Jobs icon on the System panel. This opens a page listing the scheduled jobs in your crontab file. There are also links to create a new cron job and to control user access. To edit a job, click on it to open an Edit Cron Job page where you can set crontab features such as the time, date, and command options.

System States: init and shutdown

Your Linux system has several states, numbered from 0 to 6, and a single-user state represented by the letters *s* and *S*. When you power up your system, you enter the

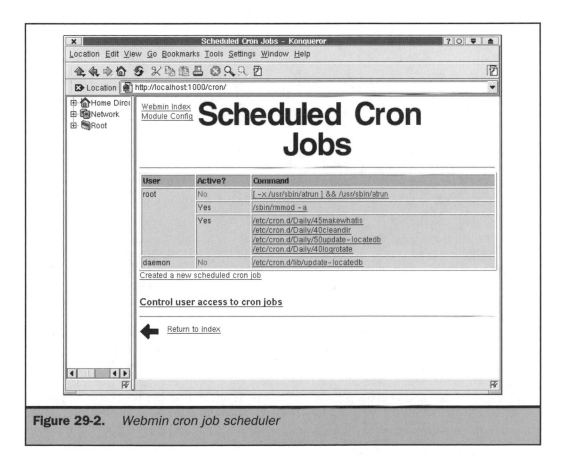

Figure 29-2.   *Webmin cron job scheduler*

default state. You can then change to other states with the **init** command. For example, state 0 is the power-down state. The command **init 0** shuts down and powers off your system. State 6 stops the system and reboots. Other states reflect how you want the system to be used. State 1 is the administrative state, allowing access only to the superuser. This enables you, as administrator, to perform administrative actions without interference from others. State *s* is a single-user state that allows use of the system by only one user. State 2 is a partial multiuser state, allowing access by many users, but with no remote file sharing. State 3, the default state for the command line interface, is the multiuser state that implements full remote file sharing. State 5 is the default state for graphical logins using display managers, such as gdm or xdm. If you choose to use graphical logins during installation, this will be your default state. You can change the default state by editing the **/etc/inittab** file and changing the **init** default entry. The states are listed in Table 29-2.

No matter what state you start in, you can change from one state to another with the **init** command. If your default state is 2, you power up in state 2, but you can change to, say, state 3 with init 3. In the next example, the **init** command changes to state *s*, the single-user state:

```
# init s
```

 Note *To change between a GUI startup state (5) and a command line state (3), you should use one of the system administration tools such as Linuxconf (Config panel under boot mode) or Webmin (see Chapter 30). This is safer than trying to edit the /etc/inittab file directly.*

Use the **runlevel** command to see what state you are currently running in. In the next example, the system is running in state 3. The word "runlevel" is another term for state.

```
# runlevel
N 3
```

Although you can power down the system with the **init** command and the 0 state, you can also use the **shutdown** command or the Shutdown panel in Linuxconf. On Linuxconf, select the Shutdown/Reboot entry in the Control Panel under Control. This displays a panel that shows the entries for entering a shutdown message and specifying how long to wait before shutting down.

The **shutdown** command has a time argument that gives users on the system a warning before you power down. You can specify an exact time to shut down or a period of minutes from the current time. The exact time is specified by *hh:mm* for the hour and minutes. The period of time is indicated by a + and the number of minutes. The shutdown command takes several options with which you can specify how you want your system shut down. The **-h** option, which stands for halt, simply shuts down the system, whereas the **-r** option shuts down the system and then reboots it. In the

State	Description
init *state*	Changes the system state; you can use it to power up or power down a system, or allow multiuser or single-user access; the **init** command takes as its argument a number representing a system state

System States

0	Halt (do *not* set the default to this); this shuts down the system completely
1	Administrative single-user mode; denies other users access to the system, but allows root access to the entire multiuser file system
2	Multiuser, without NFS (the same as 3, if you do not have networking)
s or S	Single user; only one user has access to the system; used when you want all other users off the system or you have a single-user personal system
3	Full multiuser mode with login to command line interface; allows remote file sharing with other systems on your network
4	Unused
5	Graphical login (X11) for full multiuser mode; allows remote file sharing with other systems on your network (same as 3, but with graphical login)
6	Reboots; shuts down and restarts the system (do *not* set the default to this)

Table 29-2. *Runlevel States*

next example, the system is shut down after ten minutes. The shutdown options are listed in Table 29-3.

```
# shutdown -h +10
```

To shut down the system immediately, you can use **+0** or the word **now**. The following example has the same effect as the CTRL-ALT-DEL method of shutting down

Command	Description
shutdown [-rkhncft] *time* [*warning-message*]	Shuts the system down after the specified time period, issuing warnings to users; you can specify a warning message of your own after the time argument; if neither **-h** nor **-r** is specified to shut down the system, the system sets to the administrative mode, runlevel state 1
Argument	
Time	Has two possible formats: it can be an absolute time in the format *hh:mm*, with *hh* as the hour (one or two digits) and *mm* as the minute (in two digits); it can also be in the format +*m*, with *m* as the number of minutes to wait; the word now is an alias for +0
Option	
-t *sec*	Tells init to wait *sec* seconds between sending processes the warning and the kill signals, before changing to another runlevel
-k	Doesn't actually shut down; only sends the warning messages to everybody
-r	Reboots after shutdown, runlevel state 6
-h	Halts after shutdown, runlevel state 0
-n	Doesn't call init to do the shutdown; you do it yourself
-f	Does a *fast* reboot
-c	Cancels an already running shutdown; no time argument

Table 29-3. *System Shutdown Options*

your system, as described in Chapter 3. It shuts down the system immediately, and then reboots.

```
# shutdown -r now
```

With the **shutdown** command, you can include a warning message to be sent to all users currently logged in, giving them time to finish what they are doing before you shut them down.

```
# shutdown -h +5  "System needs a rest"
```

If you do not specify either the **-h** or the **-r** options, the **shutdown** command shuts down the multiuser mode and shifts you to an administrative single-user mode. In effect, your system state changes from 3 (multiuser state) to 1 (administrative single-user state). Only the root user is active, allowing the root user to perform any necessary system administrative operations with which other users might interfere.

Note *You can also shutdown your system from the Gnome or KDE desktops as well as from Linuxconf (shutdown entry in the Control panel) and Webmin (Bootup and shutdown page under System).*

System Directories and Files

Your Linux system is organized into directories whose files are used for different system functions. Directories with "bin" in the name are used to hold programs. The **/bin** directory holds basic user programs, such as login, shells (bash, tcsh, and zsh), and file commands (cp, mv, rm, ln, and so on). The **/sbin** directory holds specialized system programs for such tasks as file system management (fsck, fdisk, mkfs) and system operations like shutdown and startup (lilo, init). The **/usr/bin** directory holds program files designed for user tasks. The **/usr/sbin** directory holds user-related system operation, such as useradd to add new users. The **/lib** directory holds all the libraries your system makes use of, including the main Linux library, **libc**, and subdirectories such as **modules**, which holds all the current kernel modules.

```
# ls /
bin boot dev etc home lib lost+found mnt proc root sbin tmp usr var
```

The **/etc** directory holds your system, network, server, and application configuration files. Here you can find the **fstab** file listing your file systems, the **hosts** file with IP addresses for hosts on your system, and **lilo.conf** for the boot systems provided by LILO. This directory includes various subdirectories, such as **apache** for the Apache Web server configuration files and **X11** for the X Window System and window manager configuration files.

The **/mnt** directory is usually used for mount points for your CD-ROM, floppy, or Zip drives. These are file systems you may be changing frequently, unlike partitions on fixed disks. The **/home** directory holds user home directories. When a user account is set up, a home directory for it is set up here, usually with the same name as the user. On many systems, the **/home** directory also holds server data directories, such as **/home/httpd** for the Apache Web server Web site files or **/home/ftpd** for your FTP site files. The **/var** directory holds subdirectories for tasks whose files change frequently, such as lock files, log files, or printer spool files. Red Hat currently places its server data directories in the **/var** directory. The **/tmp** directory is simply a directory to hold any temporary files programs may need to perform a particular task.

The **/usr** directory holds programs for user-related operations. The **/usr/lib** directory holds many of the libraries for particular applications. The **/usr/X11R6** directory holds the X Window System programs and libraries for revision 6 of the X Window System. The **/usr/X11R6/lib/X11** directory is a link to the **/etc/X11** directory, which holds the X Window System configuration files. The **/usr/src** directory holds source files; in particular, **/usr/src/linux** holds the kernel source files you use to update the kernel. The **/usr/doc** directory holds documentation that is usually installed with different applications. Here you can also find HOW-TO documents. The **/usr/local** directory is used for programs meant to be used only on this particular system. The **/usr/opt** directory is where optional packages are installed.

```
# ls /usr
X11R6 bin cgi-bin dict doc etc games include info lib libexec local man sbin
share src tmp
```

Standard system directories and configuration files are shown in Tables 29-4 and 29-5. See Chapter 36 for network configuration files.

Directories	Description
/bin	System-related programs
/sbin	System programs for specialized tasks
/lib	System libraries
/etc	Configuration files for system and network services and applications
/home	The location of user home directories and server data directories, such as Web and FTP site files
/mnt	The location where CD-ROM and floppy disk files systems are mounted

Table 29-4.   *System Directories*

Directories	Description
/var	The location of system directories whose files continually change, such as logs, printer spool files, and lock files
/usr	User-related programs and files; includes several key subdirectories, such as **/usr/bin**, **/usr/X11**, and **/usr/doc**
/usr/bin	Programs for users
/usr/X11	X Window System programs and files
/usr/share/doc	Documentation for applications
/tmp	Directory for system temporary files

Table 29-4. *System Directories* (continued)

File	Description
/etc/inittab	Sets the default state, as well as terminal connections
/etc/passwd	Contains user password and login configurations
/etc/shadow	Contains user-encrypted passwords
/etc/group	Contains a list of groups with configurations for each
/etc/fstab	Automatically mounts file systems when you start your system
/etc/lilo.conf	The LILO configuration file for your system
/etc/conf.modules	Modules on your system to be automatically loaded
/etc/printcap	Contains a list of each printer and its specifications
/etc/termcap	Contains a list of terminal type specifications for terminals that could be connected to the system
/etc/gettydefs	Contains configuration information on terminals connected to the system
/etc/skel	Directory that holds the versions of initialization files, such as **.bash_profile**, which are copied to new users' home directories

Table 29-5. *Configuration Files*

File	Description
/etc/ttys	List of terminal types and the terminal devices to which they correspond
/etc/services	Services run on the system and the ports they use
/etc/profile	Default shell configuration file for users
/etc/shells	Shells installed on the system that users can use
/etc/motd	System administrator's message of the day

Table 29-5.   *Configuration Files* (continued)

System Startup Files: /etc/rc.d

Each time you start your system, it reads a series of startup commands from system initialization files located in your **/etc/rc.d** directory (on SuSE Linux, these are located in **/sbin/init.d**). These initialization files are organized according to different tasks. Some are located in the **/etc/rc.d** directory itself, while others are located in a subdirectory called **init.d**. You should not have to change any of these files. The organization of system initialization files varies among Linux distributions. The Red Hat organization is described here. Some of the files you find in **/etc/rc.d** are listed in Table 29-6.

The **/etc/rc.d/rc.sysinit** file holds the commands for initializing your system, including the mounting of your file systems. Kernel modules for specialized features or devices can be loaded in an **rc.modules** file. The **/etc/rc.d/rc.local** file is the last initialization file executed. You can place commands of your own here. If you look at this file, you see the message displayed for you every time you start the system. You can change that message if you want. When you shut down your system, the **halt** file, which contains the commands to do this, is called. The files in **init.d** are then called to shut down daemons, and the file systems are unmounted. In the current distribution of Red Hat, **halt** is located in the **init.d** directory. For other distributions, it may be called **rc.halt** and located in the **/etc/rc.d** directory.

The **/etc/rc.d/init.d** directory is designed primarily to hold scripts that both start up and shut down different specialized daemons. Network and printer daemons are started up here. You also find files here to start font servers and Web site daemons. These files perform double duty, starting a daemon when the system starts up and shutting down the daemon when the system shuts down. The files in **init.d** are designed in a way to make it easy to write scripts for starting up and shutting down specialized applications. On Caldera systems, the **skeleton** file is a sample file for how to write scripts for this directory. It uses functions defined in the **functions** file, as do many of the other **init.d** files. Many of these files are set up for you automatically. You needn't change them. If you do change them, be sure you know how these files work first. Chapter 15 describes this process in detail.

When your system starts up, several programs are automatically started and run continuously to provide services such as Web site operations. Depending on what kind of services you want your system to provide, you can add or remove items in a list of services to be automatically started. In the installation process, you could determine what services those would be. For example, the Web server is run automatically when your system starts up. If you are not running a Web site, you would have no need, as yet, for the Web server. You could have the service not started, removing an extra task the system does not need to perform. Several of the servers and daemons perform necessary tasks. The **sendmail** server enables you to send messages across networks, while the **lpd** server performs printing operations.

When your system starts up, it uses links in special runlevel directories in the **/etc/rc.d/** directory to run the startup scripts in the **/etc/rc.d/init.d** directory. A runlevel directory bears the number of its runlevel, as in **/etc/rc.d/rc3.d** for runlevel 3. To have a service not start up, remove its link from that runlevel directory. You can use any of these scripts to start and stop a daemon manually at any time by using the stop argument to stop it, the start argument to start it again, and the restart argument to restart the daemon.

Most administration tools provide interfaces displaying a simple list of services from which you can select the ones you want to start up. On Linuxconf, the Control Service Activity panel lists different daemons and servers that you can have start by just clicking a check box. On Webmin, select Bootup and Shutdown on the System panel to display a list of available services that you can then configure to start up. On COAS, you select Enable/Disable System Services from the System Administration menu. This lists the different services you can have start up. Those with checks in their check boxes are already selected. Click a box to toggle the service on or off. On the Red Hat Setup menu, select System Services and then choose from the list of servers and daemons provided. Toggle an entry on or off with the SPACEBAR.

Webmin Index
Module Config

Bootup and Shutdown

Bootup and Shutdown			
amd	atd	bigfs	cameleo
cron	gpm	halt	httpd
inet	ipx	keytable	ldap
local	lpd	mta	netmount
network	nis-client	ntp	portmap
reboot	rmnologin	rstatd	single
skeleton	skipped	syslog	urandom
webmin	/etc/rc.d/rc.local		

Create a new bootup or shutdown action

Reboot System	Click on this button to immediately reboot the system. All currently logged in users will be disconnected and all services will be re-started.
Shutdown System	Click on this button to immediately shutdown the system. All services will be stopped, all users disconnected and the system powered off (if your hardware supports it).

In addition, many distributions also provide a System V Init utility that you can use to determine which servers and daemons are to start and stop at what runlevel. You can choose from several System V Init utilities. Sys V Init Manager is an X-based utility that provides an easy-to-use GUI interface for managing the servers and daemons in your **/etc/rc.d/init.d** directory. You can stop, start, and assign servers to different runlevels. There is also a KDE System V init utility called the Sys V Init Editor, (**ksysv**) with many of the same features (see Figure 29-3). The Sys V Init Editor is easier to use because it supports drag-and-drop operations. To assign a server to a particular runlevel, drag its entry from the Services box to the appropriate Runlevel box. To remove it from a particular runlevel, drag its entry out of that Runlevel box to the Trash icon. To start and stop a daemon manually, right-click it and select either the Stop or Start entry from the pop-up menu.

On Red Hat systems, configuration and startup information is also kept in the **/etc/syslog** directory. Here you will find files containing definitions of system variables used to configure devices such as your keyboard and mouse. These entries were defined for you when you configured your devices during installation. You will also find network definitions, as well as scripts for starting and stopping your network connections. A sample of the keyboard file is shown here.

/etc/sysconfig/keyboard

```
KEYBOARDTYPE="pc"
KEYTABLE="us"
```

System Logs: /var/log and syslogd

Various system logs kept for tasks performed on your system are kept in the **/var/log** directory. Here you can find logs for mail, news, and all other system operations. The **/var/log/messages** file is a log of all system tasks not covered by other logs. This

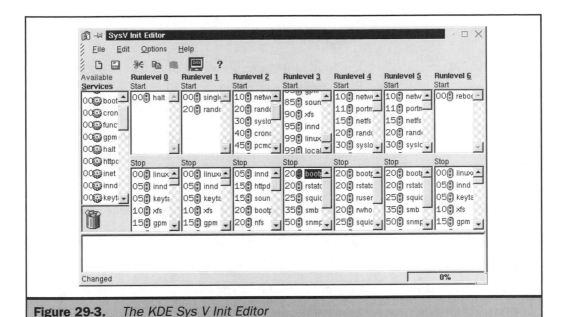

Figure 29-3.   *The KDE Sys V Init Editor*

File	Description
/etc/sysconfig	Directory on Red Hat Linux that holds system configuration files
/etc/rc.d	Directory that holds system startup and shutdown files
/etc/rc.d/rc.sysinit	Initialization file for your system
/etc/rc.config	Configuration file for your system on SuSE
/etc/rc.d/rc.local	Initialization file for your own commands; you can freely edit this file to add your own startup commands; this is the last startup file executed
/etc/rc.d/rc.modules	Loads kernel modules (not implemented by default on Red Hat Linux)
/etc/rc.d/init.d	Directory that holds many of the daemons, servers, and scripts such as httpd for Web servers and networks to start up network connections

Table 29-6.   *System Startup Files*

File	Description
/sbin/init.d	On SuSE Linux, this is the directory that holds many of the daemons, servers, and scripts such as httpd for Web servers and networks to start up network connections.
/etc/rc.d/rcnum**.d**	Directories for different runlevels, where *num* is the runlevel. The directories hold links to scripts in the **/etc/rc.d/init.d** directory (on SuSE **/sbin/init.d/rc**num**.d**).
/etc/rc.d/init.d/halt	Operations performed each time you shut down the system, such as unmounting file systems; called **rc.halt** in other distributions.
/etc/rc.d/init.d/lpd	Start up and shut down the lpd daemon.
/etc/rc.d/init.d/inet	Operations to start up or shut down the inetd daemon.
/etc/rc.d/init.d/network	Operations to start up or shut down your network connections.
/etc/rc.d/init.d/httpd	Operations to start up or shut down your Web server daemon, httpd.

Table 29-6. *System Startup Files* (continued)

usually includes startup tasks, such as loading drivers and mounting file systems. If a driver for a card failed to install at startup, you find an error message for it here. Logins are also logged in this file, showing you who attempted to log in to what account. The **/var/log/maillog** file logs mail message transmissions and news transfers.

Logs are managed by the **syslogd** daemon. This daemon will manage all the logs on your system, as well as coordinating with any the logging operations of other systems on your network. Configuration information for **syslogd** is held in the **/etc/syslog.conf** file. This file contains the names and locations for your system log files. Here you find entries for **/var/log/messages** and **/var/log/maillog**, among others. An entry consists of two fields: a selector and an action. The selector is the kind of service to be logged such as mail or news and the action is the location where messages are to be placed. The action is usually a log file, but it can also be a remote host or a pipe to another program. The kind of service is referred to as a facility. **Syslogd** has several terms it uses to specify certain kinds of service (see Table 29-7). A facility can be further qualified by a priority. A priority specifies

ADMINISTRATION

Facilities	Description
auth–priv	Security/authorization messages (private)
cron	Clock daemon (cron and at) messages
daemon	Other system daemon messages
kern	Kernel messages
lpr	Line printer subsystem messages
mail	Mail subsystem messages
mark	Internal use only
news	Usenet news subsystem messages
syslog	Syslog internal messages
user	Generic user-level messages
uucp	UUCP subsystem messages
local0 through local7	Reserved for local use
Priorities	**Description**
debug	7, Debugging messages, lowest priority
info	6, Informational messages
notice	5, Notifications, normal, but significant, condition
warning	4, Warnings
err	3, Error messages
crit	2, Critical conditions
alert	1, Alerts, action must be taken immediately
emerg	0, Emergency messages, system is unusable, highest priority
Operators	**Description**
*	Matches all facilities or priorities in a sector
=	Restrict to a specified priority

Table 29-7. *Syslogd Facilities, Priorities, and Operators*

Facilities	Description
!	Exclude specified priority and higher ones
/	A file to save messages to
@	A host to send messages to
|	FIFO pipe to send messages to

Table 29-7.   *Syslogd Facilities, Priorities, and Operators* (continued)

the kind of message generated by the facility. **Syslogd** uses several designated terms to indicate different priorities. A sector is constructed from both the facility and priority, separated by a period. For example, to save error messages generated by mail systems, you use a sector consisting of the mail facility and the **err** priority, as shown here.

```
mail.err
```

To save these messages to the **/var/log/maillog** file, you specify that file as the action, giving you the following entry:

```
mail.err                          /var/log/maillog
```

Syslogd also supports the use of * as a matching character to match either all the facilities or priorities in a sector. cron.* would match on all cron messages no matter what the priority, *.err would match on error messages from all the facilities, and *.* would match on all messages. The following example saves all mail messages to the **/var/log/maillog** file and all critical messages to the **/var/log/mycritical** file:

```
mail.*                           /var/log/maillog
*.crit                           /var/log/mycritical
```

When you specify a priority for a facility, that will in fact include all the messages with a higher priority. So the **err** priority also includes the **crit**, **alret**, and **emerg** priorities. If you just want to select the message for a specific priority, you qualify the priority with the = operator. For example, **mail.=err** will select only error messages, not **crit**, **alert**, and **emerg** messages. You can also restrict priorities with the ! operator. This will eliminate messages with the specified priority and higher. For example, **mail.!crit** will exclude **crit** messages and the higher **alert** and **emerg** messages. To specifically exclude all the messages for an entire facility, you use the **none** priority. **mail.none** excludes all mail messages. This is usually used when you defining several sectors in the same entry.

You can list several priorities or facilities in a given sector by separating them with commas. You can also have several sectors in the same entry by separating them with semicolons. The first example saves to the **/var/log/messages** file all messages with **info** priority, excluding all mail, news, and authentication messages (**authpriv**). The second saves all **crit** messages and higher for the **uucp** and **news** facilities to the **/var/log/spooler** file:

```
*.info;mail.none;news.none;authpriv.none      /var/log/messages
uucp,news.crit                                /var/log/spooler
```

For the action field, you can specify files, remote systems, users, or pipes. An action entry for a file must always begin with a **/** and specify its full path name, such as **/var/log/messages**. To log messages to a remote host, you simply specify the hostname preceded by an **@** sign. The following example saves all kernel messages on **rabbit.trek.com**:

```
kern.*                          @rabbit.trek.com
```

For users, you just list the login names of the users you want to receive the messages. The following example will send critical news messages to the consoles for the user's **chris** and **aleina**:

```
news.=crit                              chris,aleina
```

You can also output messages to a named pipe (FIFO). The pipe entry for the action field begins with a **|**. The following example pipes kernel debug messages to the name pipe **|/usr/adm/debug**:

```
kern.=debug              |/usr/adm/debug
```

Whenever you make changes to the **syslog.conf** file you need to restart the **syslogd** daemon using the following command:

```
/etc/rc.d/init.d/syslog restart
```

The default **/etc/syslog.conf** file for Red Hat systems is shown here. Messages are logged to various files in the **/var/log** directory.

/etc/syslog.conf

```
# Log all kernel messages to the console.
# Logging much else clutters up the screen.
#kern.*                                 /dev/console

# Log anything (except mail) of level info or higher.
# Don't log private authentication messages!
*.info;mail.none;news.none;authpriv.none     /var/log/messages

# The authpriv file has restricted access.
authpriv.*                              /var/log/secure

# Log all the mail messages in one place.
mail.*                                  /var/log/maillog

# Everybody gets emergency messages, plus log them on another
# machine.
*.emerg                                        *

# Save mail and news errors of level err and higher in a
# special file.
uucp,news.crit                          /var/log/spooler

# Save boot messages also to boot.log
local7.*                                /var/log/boot.log

#
# INN
#
news.=crit                              /var/log/news/news.crit
news.=err                               /var/log/news/news.err
news.notice                             /var/log/news/news.notice
```

Performance Analysis Tools and Processes

Each task performed on your system is treated by Linux as a process, and is assigned a number and a name. You can examine these processes and even stop them. From the command line, you can use the **ps** command to list processes. With the **-aux** command, you can list all processes. Piping the output to a **grep** command with a pattern enables you to search for a particular process. The following command lists all X Window System processes:

```
ps -aux | grep 'X'
```

A number of utilities on your system provide detailed information on your processes, as well as other system information such as CPU and disk use. Although these tools were designed to be used on a shell command line, displaying output in text lines, several now have KDE and Gnome versions that provide a GUI interface for displaying results and managing processes. The **vmstat** command outputs a detailed listing indicating the performance of different system components, including CPU, memory, I/O, and swap operations. A report is issued as a line with fields for the different components. If you provide a time period as an argument, it repeats at the specified interval—usually a few seconds. The **top** command provides a listing of the processes on your system that are the most CPU intensive, showing what processes are using most of your resources. The listing is in real time and updated every few seconds. Commands are provided for changing a process's status, such as its priority. The **free** command lists the amount of free RAM memory on your system, showing how much is used and how much is free, as well as what is used for buffers and swap memory. Xosview is an X Window System tool showing the load, CPU, and memory. You can also use Linuxconf to display basic system information, such as memory and disk use. Select Viewing System State under Control. iostat will display your disk usage, and sar will show system activity information.

The K Desktop provides two utilities for viewing and managing your processes: the KDE Task Manager (KTop, shown in Figure 29-4) and the KDE Process Manager (kpm). On both utilities, you can sort the processes according to their fields by clicking the field's button at the top of the process list. If you select a process, you can then choose to perform several different actions on it, such as ending it (killing the process) or suspending it (putting it to sleep). A right-click on a process entry displays a pop-up menu with the different actions you can take. You can further refine your process list by choosing to view only your own processes, system processes, or all processes.

KTop provides both list and tree views. With the tree view, you can see what processes are dependent on others. For example, the desktop relies on the X Window System process. A Performance Meters panel displays system information, such as memory use and CPU load.

On the Gnome System Manager (GTop), you can also sort the processes according to their fields by clicking the field's button at the top of the process list. If you right-click an entry, a pop-up menu displays with actions you can perform on it (see Figure 29-5). System statistic summary graphs are displayed at the top of the window showing the CPU load, memory use, and disk use. You can add more graphs or change their display features, such as the colors used. The GTop window displays three tabbed panels for detailed reports showing processes, memory use, and file system use. You can add more, showing customized reports such as only the user processes. Process lists can be further refined to show user, system, or all processes. To configure Gtop, you select the Preferences entry in the Settings menu. This displays a menu with tabbed panels for specifying the update frequency for different statistics, determining the summaries you want displayed, and what process fields to show. You can find the Gnome System Manager in the Utilities menu.

On Webmin, the Running Processes page accessible from the System panel lists current processes. You can click on any process name and display a page providing

Figure 29-4. *The KDE Task Manager*

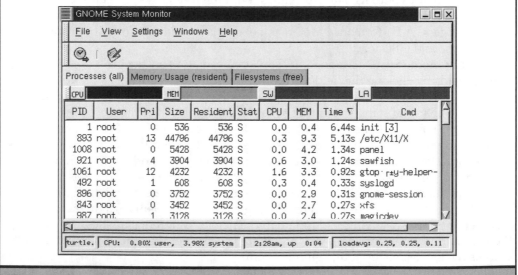

Figure 29-5. *Gnome system monitor*

detailed information. On this page, you can select a signal to send the process, such as kill to end it.

LILO

If you have installed two or more operating systems on your computer's hard disks, you need to use a boot manager to enable you to choose the one you want to use whenever your computer starts up. Most Linux distributions provide the *Linux Loader* (*LILO*) as its boot manager, which you can install as part of the installation process. LILO currently has one important limitation: on hard disks greater than 8 gigs, any operating system boot partitions need to be located within the first 8 gigs of the hard disk. Other partitions can then be located anywhere else, including the gigs after the first 8 gigs. A boot partition is a primary partition. Keep in mind that on PC systems you are still limited to only four primary or extended partitions per hard disk. Boot partitions can be relatively small. For example, on a 30-gig hard drive, you could have a 1-gig partition for the Linux boot partition somewhere in the first 8 gigs and another 10 gig Linux extended partition anywhere else. You could have a 3-gig primary partition in the first 8 gigs and a large extended partition located anywhere else. This is known as the 1,024-cylinder limit, where the boot partition must be located within the first 1,024 cylinders. For large hard disks, you would specify the LINEAR global option in the **lilo.conf** file to ensure LILO can access vary large partitions.

You can modify your LILO configuration either by using an administration tool like Linuxconf or Webmin, or by editing the **/etc/lilo.conf** configuration file directly. To change LILO configuration with Webmin, first select the Webmin Hardware panel, and then select the Linux Bootup Configuration icon. This opens a Linux Bootup Configuration screen where you can modify the current LILO configuration, add a new kernel or operating system to boot, and change global options (see Figure 29-6). Your changes are not made until you click the Apply Configuration button. Each kernel or system that LILO currently can boot will be listed with it own icon. To change the options for starting just that system, click on its icon. This opens an Edit Boot Kernel page for that system.

On Linuxconf, you select Lilo from the Boot mode entry in the Config panel. Here you can set global options (defaults), configure your Linux boot entry or those of other systems, and add new kernel boot entries.

If you need to change your LILO configuration, you can easily do so by either modifying the **/etc/lilo.conf** configuration file or executing the command **lilo**. If you examine your **/etc/lilo.conf** file, you find it organized into different segments called *stanzas*, one for each operating system that LILO is to start up. If your Linux system shares your computer with a DOS system, you should see two stanzas listed in your **/etc/lilo.conf** file: one for Linux and one for Windows. Each stanza indicates the hard disk partition on which the respective operating system is located. It also includes an entry for the label. This is the name you enter at the LILO prompt to start that operating system.

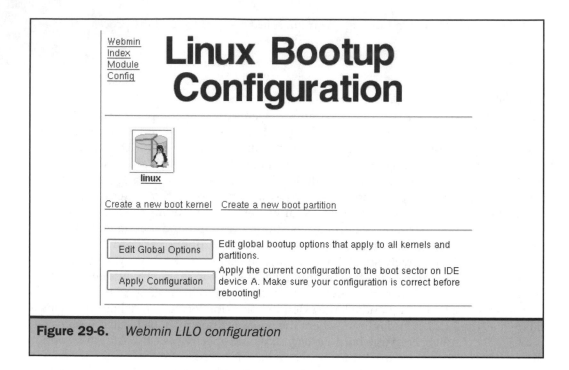

Figure 29-6. *Webmin LILO configuration*

Entries in the **lilo.conf** file consist of options to which you assign values with the = operator. At the beginning of the file, you enter global options. The entries you need will already be generated for you if you have already set up Lilo during installation or with an administration utility like Linuxconf or Webmin. An example of a Linux global entry follows. To set the timeout period when Lilo waits for you make an entry before starting the default, you create a timeout entry and assign to it the number of seconds you want to wait.

```
timeout = 200
```

Another useful global entry is **default,** with which you can set the default operating system to start. It takes as its argument the label for the stanza. In the following example, the stanza labeled **win** will be executed by default, in this case, starting Windows:

```
default = win
```

Then you start a Linux stanza for an operating system with an image or other option to which you assign the boot image file or boot image partition for that system. The next example starts a stanza for Linux loading a Linux 2.2.16-22:

```
image = /boot/vmlinuz-2.2.16-22
```

You can then enter options for that stanza, such as its label and the partition that holds its root device:

```
label = linux
root = /dev/hda4
```

The stanza continues until another image or other option is reached, starting a new stanza. You can, if you want, make changes directly to the **/etc/lilo.conf** file using a text editor. Whenever you make a change, you must execute the **lilo** command to have it take effect. Type **lilo** and press ENTER.

```
# lilo
```

You can also configure LILO using the LILO panels in Linuxconf. You can add segments and specify options there. When you activate your changes in Linuxconf, the **/etc/lilo.conf** file is updated and the **lilo** command is run.

/etc/lilo.conf

```
# general section
boot = /dev/hda
# wait 20 seconds (200 10ths) for user to select the entry to load
timeout = 200
message = /boot/message
prompt
linear
# default entry
default = win
vga = normal
map=/boot/map
install=/boot/boot.b
image = /boot/vmlinuz-2.2.16-22
          label = linux
          root = /dev/hda4
          read-only
other = /dev/hda1
            label = win
          table=/dev/hda
```

Unless specified by the default entry, the default operating system LILO boots is the one whose segment is the first listed in the **lilo.conf** file. Because the Linux stanza is the first listed, this is the one LILO boots if you don't enter anything at the LILO prompt. If you want to have your Windows system be the default, you can use **lilo** with the **-D** option to reset the default or you can edit the **lilo.conf** file to assign a value to default. You could also use a text editor to place the DOS stanza first, before the Linux stanza. Be sure to execute **lilo** to have the change take effect. The next time you start your system, you could press ENTER at the LILO prompt to have Windows loaded, instead of typing **win**.

```
# lilo -D win
```

You can set a number of LILO options using either command line options or making entries in the **lilo.conf** file. These options are listed in Table 29-8.

If you are booting an operating system from a location other than the first hard disk, you need to include a loader line for the **chain.b** file in its stanza.

```
loader=/boot/chain.b
```

Command Line Options	lilo.conf Options	Description
-b *bootdev*	boot=*bootdev*	Boot device
-c	compact	Enable map compaction; speeds up booting
-d *dsec*	delay=*dsec*	Timeout delay to wait for you to enter the label of an operating system at the LILO prompt when you boot up
-D *label*	default=*label*	Use the kernel with the specified label, instead of the first one in the list, as the default kernel to boot
-i *bootsector*	install=*bootsector*	File to be used as the new boot sector
-f *file*	disktab=*file*	Disk geometry parameter file

Table 29-8. *LILO Options for the Command Line and **lilo.conf** Entries*

Command Line Options	lilo.conf Options	Description
-1	linear	Generate linear sector addresses, instead of sector/head/cylinder addresses (for large hard disks. This option can cause a conflict with compact)
-m *mapfile*	map=*mapfile*	Use specified map file instead of the default
-P fix	fix-table	Fix corrupt partition tables
-P ignore	ignore-table	Ignore corrupt partition tables
-s *file*	backup=*file*	Alternate save file for the boot sector
-S *file*	force-backup=*file*	Allow overwriting of existing save file
-v	verbose=*level*	Increase verbosity
-u		Uninstall LILO, by copying the saved boot sector back
-V		Print version number
-t		Test only. Do not actually write a new boot sector or map file. Use together with **-v** to learn what LILO is about to do
-I *label*		Display label and pathname of running kernel. Label is held in BOOT_IMAGE shell variable
	timeout=*dsec*	Timeout delay to wait for you to enter the label of an operating system at the LILO prompt when you boot up
	image=*Linux-kernel*	Pathname for boot image of a Linux kernel
	other=*os-boot-image*	Pathname for boot image of a non-Linux operating system
	read-only	Boot Linux kernel as read-only (system startup remounts as read/write)

Table 29-8.   *LILO Options for the Command Line and **lilo.conf** Entries*

The Complete Reference

Linux

Chapter 30

Administration Tools

With system administration tools, you can perform almost all your administration tasks with the user-friendly screen-based or X Window System interfaces. Some tools are commonly found on particular distributions, whereas other are independent efforts designed to be used on any system. Linuxconf and Webmin are administration tools designed to be used with any Linux distributions. You can download current versions from their distribution sites. Currently Linuxconf is distributed with Red Hat and Webmin with Caldera OpenLinux. Linuxconf is an independent effort available under the GNU public license, though it has been adopted by Red Hat as its official configuration tool. It aims to be a comprehensive administration tool covering tasks such as user and file system configuration, as well as server configurations. Its modular design allows its capabilities to be enhanced easily. Webmin is another comprehensive administration tool that uses a simple Web page–based interface to update system configuration files.

Several administration tools are associated with particular distributions. YaST is yet another system administration tool used on SuSE systems. Red Hat provides several X Window System configuration tools accessible from a Control Panel window. It also includes a setup utility that lets you change any of the settings you made during installation, such as specifying your keyboard or mouse type. Caldera, on OpenLinux systems, provides the Caldera Open Administration System (COAS) tool. COAS is a comprehensive administration tool that covers most system administration tasks such as file system, user, and module configuration.

These tools are only available to the root user. You first have to log in as the root user and provide the password. You can run most of these tools either from the desktop or from a shell command line. Webmin has to be run using a Web browser such as Netscape. Tools that run on the shell command line use a screen-based interface from which you can select entries using the arrow keys and the TAB key. From a window manager or desktop, most tools provide an X Window interface with menus, icons, and buttons. Your root user's main menu will display entries for these tools, listed in Table 30-1.

Configuration Tool	Command	Description
Linuxconf	`linuxconf`	The Linuxconf configuration tool providing comprehensive configuration for users, networks, file systems, servers, and LILO. Designed for all Linux and Unix systems.

Table 30-1. *Linux Configuration Tools*

Configuration Tool	Command	Description
Webmin	**http://localhost:1000**	The Webmin configuration tool providing comprehensive configuration for users, networks, file systems, servers, and LILO. Designed for all Linux and Unix systems.
COAS	**coastool**	Caldera Open Administration System (COAS) provides time zone, network, user, group, printer, file system, and LILO configuration, as well as software package management. Used on OpenLinux.
YaST	**yast**	Yet Another System Administration Tool provides user, network, file system, module, and LILO configuration. Used on SuSE.
Control Panel	**control-panel**	Red Hat collection of X configuration tools for networking, modules, printers, time settings, etc.
Setup	**setup**	Collection of Red Hat setup utilities for specifying device types, time zone, and X Window configuration (screen-based only)

Table 30-1.   *Linux Configuration Tools* (continued)

Linuxconf

Linuxconf is a comprehensive configuration tool for almost all your administrative tasks, including user and file system management, as well as network services (see the list of features in Table 30-2). Linuxconf is designed to work on any Linux distribution and is currently, compatible with Caldera, Red Hat, SuSe, Slackware, and Debian. Both compressed archive and RPM versions of the software are provided. You can download the current version from the Linuxconf Web site at **www.solucorp.qc.ca/linuxconf**. Here you can also find documentation and links to any added packages.

Linuxconf currently has three interfaces: text, GUI, and HTML. The *text interface* provides cursor-based full screens that can be run from any shell command line. You use the TAB key to move between boxes, lists, and buttons, and you use the arrow keys to select entries in a list. The text mode also operates as a command line mode, enabling you to place Linuxconf commands in the shell scripts. The *GUI interface* is an X Window System interface that runs on any window manager or desktop, including Gnome and KDE. It provides a menu tree with which you can easily select panels for different configuration tasks. The *HTML interface,* shown in Figure 30-1, is a Web page interface that lists options as links to other Web pages. It provides boxes and check boxes with which you can make your entries. To access the HTML interface, enter your system's hostname with the port 98, written as :98 attached to the end of the hostname, for example **http://turtle.mytrek.com:98**. Be sure to first permit access by setting permissions for the user you want to use (such as **root**) in the Linuxconf Network Access panel in the Misc list under Networking. All the interfaces provide context-level help. On each screen, panel, or page is a Help button that displays detailed information about the current task.

Features	Description
User accounts and groups	User and group configuration, passwords, and permissions
Networking	TCP/IP, NIS, PPP, IPX, DHCP, DNS, IP-aliasing, UUCP, hosts, routing, and gateways
Servers	Apache, Squid, ProFTP, wu-ftpd, DHCPD, Samba, DNS, and sendmail
File systems	fstab, NFS, NIS
LILO	LILO boot options and entries

Table 30-2. *Linuxconf Configuration Features*

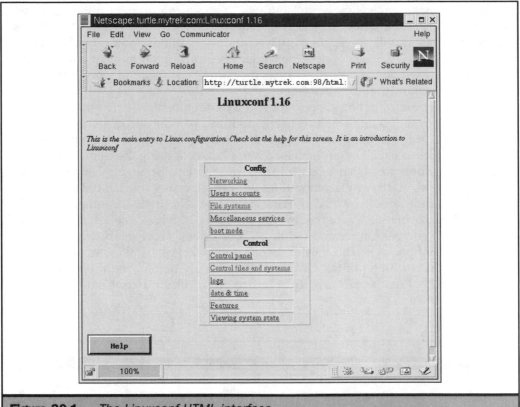

Figure 30-1. *The Linuxconf HTML interface*

In the GUI interface, the main Linuxconf window displays a window with two frames. On the left are four panels configuration tasks (Config), system controls (Control), system information such as logs (Status), and task helpers (Tasks). Each displays an expandable list of items. The list is organized into categories and subcategories you can expand to list entries or to shrink to show only the category heading. Small boxes to the left of the category headings show small minus (–) signs when expanded and plus (+) signs when entries are not displayed. Initially, all entries for each category are displayed. Clicking a category box displays or hides the entries. The two major panels are Config and Control. You use the Config entries to configure almost all components on your systems, including users, file systems, networking, servers, and LILO. Among the servers supported are Apache, Squid, wu-ftpd, DHCPD, Samba, and sendmail. The Control entries enable you to perform tasks such as setting the time, adding modules, selecting servers to start up, and mounting file systems.

Using the main window shown in Figure 30-2, you select an administration task by clicking its entry. A panel for that task is then displayed on the right frame. Most tasks have several panels with panel tabs displayed at the top of the window. Click a tab to display that panel. If you do not close the window before selecting another administration task, then a new window is opened on top of the current one. You can move from one task to another by clicking the respective entries.

Much of the configuration support for specific components, such as the Apache Web server or Squid, is implemented using modules. You can add or remove modules as you choose. Modules are usually included with the Linuxconf software package. You can then select which modules to load into Linuxconf using the Configure Linuxconf Modules panel in the Control Files And Systems list under Control Panel. This panel shows all the available modules with check boxes you can use to toggle whether a module should be loaded. For example, to add firewall configuration panels to Linuxconf, make sure the firewall module check box is selected. Table 30-3 shows a list of current Linuxconf modules. Those listed as core modules are included in the Linuxconf package. Those listed as pkg are packages installed separately and usually located at different sites. Links are available on the Linuxconf Web site, and most are also kept on the FTP site, **ftp.solucorp.qc.ca/pub/linuxconf/modules**.

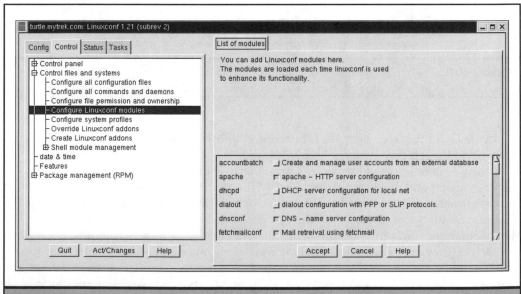

Figure 30-2. *Linuxconf GUI interface and modules*

ADMINISTRATION

Module	Status	Description
apache	core	Configuration of the Apache Web server
dhcpd	core	Configuration of the ISC dhcpd server
dialout	core	PPP dialout configuration. Alternative to redhatppp
dnsconf	core	Configuration of bind 4 and 8 DNS
firewall	core	Configuration of the kernel 2.0 packet filter, including support for masquerading, port redirection, and accounting
inittab	core	Control editing of the **/etc/inittab** file
isdnadmin	pkg	Manages an ISDN adapter, **www.terminator.net/isdnadmin**
ldapconf	pkg	Configures an ldap server and clients, **www.terminator.net/ldapconf**
mailconf	core	Configuration of sendmail
managerpm	pkg	Manipulates RPM packages
mgettyconf	pkg	Configuration of the mgetty serial port manager
motd	core	Edits the message of the day file
mrtg	core	Configuration for the mrtg package
netadm	core	Configures PPP connections
pppdialin	core	Configures a PPP session
proftpd	pkg	Manages the pro-ftp daemon, **http://lie-br.conectiva.com.br/~marcelo**
rarp	core	Configures the kernel RARP table
redhatppp	core	PPP/SLIP/PLIP configuration compatible with Red Hat netcfg utility
samba	core	Configuration of the Samba SMB file server

Table 30-3.   *Linuxconf Modules*

Module	Status	Description
shellmod	pkg	Writes Linuxconf modules and standalone utilities using the shell (**/bin/sh**)
squid	core	In development. Provides basic support for the configuration of the squid
status	core	Reports various items of information about the system
treemenu	core	Pulls all menu/submenu options into a single large tree
updpass	pkg	Updates password
userinfo	pkg	Adds custom fields to the user account dialog box
usermenu	core	Custom views of the Linuxconf menu access privileges
usersbygroup	pkg	Enables user account management by group
virtual	pkg	In development. Provides a unified view of all services supporting virtual hosting, to configure a virtual host in one dialog box
wuftpd	core	Configuration of the wu-ftpd FTP server
xterminals	core	Management of Linux-based X terminals

Table 30-3.   *Linuxconf Modules* (continued)

You can also access Linuxconf using specialized windows for the particular service you want to configure: userconf, fsconf, dnsconf, netconf, and mailconf. These are special Linuxconf commands that call Linuxconf using an interface listing option for a particular service. For example, to add a new user to your system, you could use the **userconf** command to display a special Linuxconf window. This window displays buttons and icons for accessing the different Linuxconf user and group configuration panels. These are the same panels you can access through the main Linuxconf interface. The **netconf** command displays a window listing the icons for the different network configuration panels. Another panel on this same window lists icons for the different server configuration panels. The **dnsconf** command displays a window with buttons for accessing the Domain Name Service (named) configuration panels. The **mailconf** command enables you to access panels directly for configuring your mail server (sendmail). The **liloconf** command provides a window with buttons for panels that enable you to configure LILO, adding new boot entries and editing current ones. You have to open a terminal window, and then enter and execute their commands at the prompt.

Note   *Some distributions may include versions of Linuxconf that do not contain all the modules (such as dnsconf for Red Hat 7.0). In that case you can download and install the current Linuxconf RPM package for your distribution from the Linuxconf Web site.*

Linuxconf saves its configuration information in files located in the **/etc/linuxconf/ archive** directory. When you activate changes with new configuration information, Linuxconf both updates your system configuration files and saves the information in its own files. In effect, Linuxconf maintains its own set of your system's configuration files and can detect if its information does not correspond to your system's configuration files. Linuxconf also includes a sophisticated translation system that enables you to implement Linuxconf in the language of your choice.

Linuxconf enables you to create multiple system configurations that you can load, activating or deactivating features and services. You can have one set of configurations for your office and one for home, or even one for, say, a Web server. A home configuration might have your Web server turned off, whereas a Web server configuration might have it running. If you have Linux running on a portable PC, you could switch networking configurations just by switching Linuxconf system configurations. Different configurations are placed in subdirectories in the **/etc/linuxconf/archive** directory. Their names are the same as those subdirectories. Linuxconf provides two for you by default: Office and Home-Office. Various Linuxconf startup commands appear in Table 30-4.

Command	Description
linuxconf	Start Linuxconf in the main window
netconf	Network configuration window for configuring your network and servers; accesses network and server panels directly
userconf	User configuration window; accesses user and group configuration panels directly
fsconf	File system configuration window; accesses file system configuration panels directly
dnsconf	Domain Name Service configuration window; accesses DNS configuration panels directly
mailconf	Mail (sendmail) configuration window; accesses sendmail configuration panels directly

Table 30-4.   *Linuxconf Startup Commands*

System Profile Versioning

With system profile versioning, you can create customized configurations for your entire system. For example, you could have a set of configurations for your home and another for your office, save your working version and create a new one to experiment with, or keep a version you know works safely with all your devices just in case your current version freezes. Linuxconf enables you to switch easily from one configuration to another. You can even set up shared configurations where you can partially switch from one to another. A history of changes is kept for each configuration.

A specific configuration consists of a set of configuration files collected into a subsystem. In effect, a *subsystem* is a particular system configuration. A subsystem consists of a key name and a description. The configuration files Linuxconf uses are located in the subsystem for the configuration currently in use. Subsystems are the archiving unit for Linuxconf, holding all configuration files.

Configuration files are connected to a subsystem dynamically, where the configuration file consists of the subsystem key name. You can even define a module to include configuration files for specific subsystems.

A profile version specifies the families in which each subsystem is to be archived. A family is composed of configuration files for different subsystems. A family name is given to a subdirectory in **/etc/linuxconf/archive**, where you find directories and configuration files that duplicate those on your system, such as **/etc/ppp**. For example, Linuxconf will set up two families for you, Office and Home-Office, both as subdirectories in **/etc/linuxconf/archive**. The profile has a default family in which added subsystems are placed. Profiles that share the same subsystem configurations will share the same families. If you do not want a subsystem archived, you give it the family "none."

You can switch from one version to another at any time during a session or when you boot up. When you switch, the version currently in use is archived and the new one is activated. If the new one shares subsystems in the same family, those subsystems are left alone. The original subsystems remain. A log of all operations is maintained for you to check.

An archive is saved in the **/etc/linuxconf/archive/** and given the name of the profile version. Within the directory is a directory tree of standard Linux configuration directories and files. Directories like **etc**, **var**, and **dev** are listed. The configuration files have the extension *,v*, the extension for an RCS file. Configuration files are actually archived with the **cfgarchive** command, which normally uses the RCS system to archive a file, provided RCS is installed on your Linux system. If not, then the most recent file is simply stored on disk.

Boot Time Control

Linuxconf has the boot time control feature that enables users to select the kind of interface they want to boot to, such as the command line or the graphical user interface, such as Gnome. With boot time control, users can easily select an interface, boot to administration level, select a Linuxconf profile version, or view the boot messages. With the boot time control feature installed, Linuxconf runs an **askrunlevel** command at boot time. This command is located in the **/etc/rc.d/rc.sysinit** startup file on RedHat systems.

```
/sbin/askrunlevel
```

The **runlevel** command offers a menu to users (timed out by default at 20 seconds). The menu lists the following options:

```
Start graphic & network
Start graphic only
Start in X terminal mode
Start in text mode & network
Start in text mode only
System maintenance (single user mode)
Configure the workstation
Select configuration version
View the boot logs
```

The graphic mode starts the GUI interface (runlevel 5), whereas the text mode starts with the command line interface (runlevel 3). The Configure the workstation entry lets the user log in as the root user and perform configurations before the boot process finishes. This is helpful when installing a computer on a different network. The Select configuration version enables you to switch at startup to a different system profile version. You can choose from a menu of the list of available profile versions. The View the boot logs entry list the boot messages that normally scroll by onscreen at startup.

Network Administration System

With its network administration system, you can use Linuxconf to administer Linux systems on remote machines. You first define an admin group that consists of the machines sharing configuration files. In effect, they are sharing subsystems, parts of the Linuxconf configuration. And in effect, each machine has its own system profile version.

The configuration files and directories for a particular machine are placed in an administration tree. This is a subdirectory in the Linuxconf **admtrees** directory. These files and directories include copies of the machine's configuration files and directories, such as **/etc/passwd, /etc/hosts**, and **/etc/ppp**. Linuxconf works entirely within this admtree, as these files are the same as those on the machine.

To manage a remote machine, you use the netadm module. Currently, this connects to the remote host with a GUI front end. The command line version of netadm has several options you can use. The **-import** option installs configuration files received for an administration host. The **-remadm** option enables remote administration. A GUI front end starts up and connects to Linuxconf on a remote host. If you do not specify a host on the command line, then a menu is displayed of the different hosts you can access.

Webmin

Webmin is a Web-based interface for Unix and Linux system administration tasks. You can use any Web browser that supports tables and forms to access Webmin and perform extensive administrative operations (see Figure 30-3). Webmin itself is composed of a simple Web server with CGI Perl programs with which you can directly update system configuration files such as **/etc/passwd** and **/etc/inetd.conf**. Webmin is available free of charge under the BSD license. You can find out more about Webmin at **www.webmin.com**.

Webmin is an extensible application designed to be enhanced by modules that any users can write and plug into their versions. A number of standard modules, listed in Table 30-5, are provided with Webmin that cover areas such as user account setup, LILO modification, and server configuration. Numerous third-party modules are under development. You can access them at **www.thirdpartymodules.com/webmin**.

Figure 30-3. *Webmin*

When you first use Webmin, you are asked to enter a valid login and password. As the system administrator, you could log in as root and then enter root as your login and your root password. In the Webmin configuration, you can change the username and password to whatever you want. You can also configure Webmin to allow certain users the ability to perform configuration operations, limiting them to certain modules.

Module	Description
Webmin Configuration	Change the admin username/password, Web server port, and list of allowed hosts for the Webmin server
Webmin Help	Webmin's help system
Webmin Servers Index	List all Webmin servers on a network
Webmin Users	Create Webmin users and configure which modules and features they are allowed to access.
Bootup and Shutdown	Control system startup and shutdown processes, including servers you want to start up.
Disk and Network Filesystems	List and manipulate locally mounted file systems
NFS Exports	Add, delete, and edit NFS exported file systems
Running Processes	List running processes and control them
Scheduled Cron Jobs	Display, edit, and create cron jobs
Software Packages	Graphical interface for installing packages with RPM
Users and Groups	Manage users and groups
Apache Webserver	Configure the Apache Web server
BIND 8 DNS Server	Configure the BIND 8 domain name server
DHCP Server	Configure the DHCP server
FTP Server	Configure the access control, anonymous FTP, and other options of wu-ftpd

Table 30-5.   *Webmin Standard Modules*

Module	Description
Internet Services and Protocols	Manage Internet services
Majordomo List Manager	Create and configure mailing lists using majordomo
PPP Usernames and Passwords	Configure PPP users
Samba Windows File Sharing	Configure the SAMBA server
Sendmail Configuration	Configure sendmail server
Squid Proxy Server	Configure the Squid proxy/caching server
Linux Bootup Configuration	Add or modify LILO entries
Network Configuration	Control NIC and network configuration
Partitions on Local Disks	Add, edit, and delete local disk partitions
Printer Administration	Manage local and remote printers and queues
System Time	Set system and hardware clocks
Custom Commands	Create custom commands to execute from Webmin
File Manager	View, edit, and change permissions on files and directories on your system with a Windows-like file manager
Telnet Login	Log into your system with telnet.

Table 30-5. *Webmin Standard Modules* (continued)

COAS

The Caldera Open Administration System (COAS) provides an effective and easy-to-use interface for performing most system and network administration functions. COAS is available for use by any distribution, although it currently is included with Caldera's OpenLinux. COAS has both a GUI interface and a cursor-based interface. You can operate the GUI interface on any window manager, as well as the KDE or Gnome desktop. The cursor-based interface can be used in a command line shell and displays a series of screens on which you can use arrow and TAB keys to make selections.

On the OpenLinux KDE desktop, you will find an entry for COAS on the main menu, as well as an icon for it in the panel. Clicking either displays a main COAS menu from which you can select the kind of tasks you want to perform, including system administration, kernel configurations, and software management (see Figure 30-4). Selecting System Administration displays entries for administration operations such as Account Administration, Filesystem Administration, and the System Clock. Here you can manage users or mount file systems, including CD-ROMs and floppy disks. Kernel Modules allows you to install modules for different devices and services that you are adding to your system. Menus at the top of COAS windows let you edit or delete selected entries as well as add new ones. You can use the Exit entry in the File menu to close the window.

The COAS command is **coastool**. Entering this command in a shell command line will start the cursor-based COAS interface. You use the TAB and arrow keys to move to different entries. To access the menu, press the F8 key. You can then use the RIGHT ARROW and LEFT ARROW keys to move to the menu you want. Press ENTER to display the menu and use arrow keys to move to the entry you want. Press ESC to shift back to the main window. At any point you can press the F1 key to bring up a box with an explanation of the current choice.

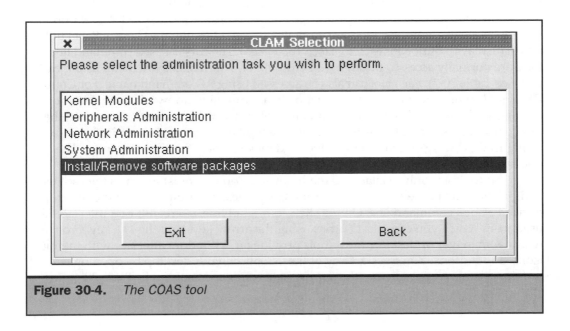

Figure 30-4.   *The COAS tool*

YaST

The Yet Another System Tool (YaST) is administrative tool for SuSE Linux. The original cursor-based version is called simply YaST, and a GUI version is called YaST2. YaST makes special used of function keys to perform operations such as getting help, editing entries, and selecting menus. Use arrow keys to move from one selection to another. The TAB key moves you to the buttons at the bottom of the screen for OK, Cancel, or Continue to the next screen. From the main window, you can click the System Administration entry to display a pop-up menu of administration functions. Use your arrow keys to move to the one you want and select it.

Red Hat Control Panel Tools

Red Hat has traditionally provided several easy-to-use configuration interfaces for most system administration tasks. Most of these tasks have been superceded by Linuxconf, which is now the official Red Hat administration tool. The older Red Hat tools described here, however, are still included with Red Hat distributions, and many user prefer them. Some provide an easy way to perform simple tasks, such as selecting a new keyboard or changing the time zone.

Two sets of administration tools exist, classified by the type of interface: X Window System–based configuration tools and cursor-based command line tools. Each set is commonly identified by the utility through which it is ordinarily accessed. The X Window System–based configuration tools are normally accessed through the Control Panel utility, which displays a button for each tool (see Table 30-6). The cursor-based command line tools are normally accessed through the Setup utility, which displays a menu listing each tool (see Table 30-7). Each tool can also be accessed using its command name. For Control Panel tools, you can enter their commands in a terminal window. You can run the cursor-based interface from the command line using arrow keys, the SPACEBAR, and the ENTER key to make choices. The tools are simple front ends for making entries in Linux configuration files. You can edit these files and make entries directly if you want. The underlying administration tasks are the same.

These tools are only available to the root user. You first must log in as the root user and provide the password. You can run most of these tools either from the desktop or from a shell command line. On the shell command line, a screen-based interface is used from which you can select entries using the arrow keys and the TAB key. From a window manager or desktop, most tools provide an X Window interface with menus, icons, and buttons. You can start any of these tools on your desktop by opening a terminal window and entering the appropriate command as listed in Table 30-6.

Tool	Description
tksysv	Starts and stops servers and daemons
timetool	Sets the system date and time
printtool	Configures a printer, creating a printer device and printcap entry for the printer
netcfg	Configures your network interfaces (see Chapter 21)
kernelcfg	Kernel Configurator: loads and configures kernel modules
modemtool	Selects your modem's device name (sets the /etc/modem link to the modem's port)
helptool	Searches for documentation, man pages, and info pages
linuxconf	Linuxconf configuration tool for user, networking, LILO, servers, file systems, and so forth

Table 30-6. *Red Hat Control Panel Tools*

You can access the X Window–based configuration tools using the Control Panel window on your root user desktop. An entry for the Control Panel is in a window manager or the desktop's main menu under System or Administration. As shown in Figure 30-5, the Control Panel provides icons for accessing a variety of configuration tools.

Figure 30-5. *Red Hat Control Panel*

Currently, tools exist for such tasks as setting the time and date, network administration, and kernel module management. Many of these tools have their own entries in the System or Administration menus. You can also invoke them from a terminal window using their command names. The **netcfg** utility enables you to configure your network interfaces (discussed in detail in Chapter 25). With **timetool**, you can set the system time and date (see Chapter 20). Using PrintTool, you can configure new printers, interfacing them with your system (see Chapter 26). The **helptool** enables you to search for documentation on your system using a keyword search (see this chapter). The **helptool** displays man, HOW-TO, and info documentation. The Sys V Init Editor enables you to start and stop servers and daemons (see Chapter 15). With the Kernel Configurator, you can manually add and remove modules. Many system tasks, including user, server, and file system management, are provided by the Linuxconf, which is accessible by clicking the icon labeled System, which shows a picture of a music conductor waving a baton. Table 30-6 lists these tools.

The *tksysv* tool is used to configure the System V daemon configuration, enabling you to determine what daemons to start up at boot time. It also enables you to start or stop daemons manually. Daemons include your Internet daemons, such as the FTP or Web servers, as well as services, such as your printer daemon. See Chapter 23 for a more detailed discussion and figure.

With *timetool*, you can configure all aspects of the system date and time . For example, select the hour entry to change the hour. You use the two triangles below the time and date display to increase or decrease the time or date entry. If you select the hour, clicking the upper triangle sets the time forward to the next hour. The bottom inverted triangle moves the hour backward. The same is true for the date. Once you set the new time and date, click the Set System Clock button at the bottom of the window. Then click the Exit Time Machine button to exit the Time Configuration window.

PrintTool is an easy interface for setting up and managing your printers (see Chapter 33 for more details and a figure). Using only PrintTool, you can easily install a printer on your Linux system. You can start PrintTool either by selecting its entry in the System menu or clicking its icon in the Red Hat Control Panel. In the PrintTool window, select the Add button. This opens an Edit window that displays several fields in which you enter printer configuration information. In the Names field, you enter the names you want to use for the printer. Each name is separated from the next by a |. A default name for your first printer is **lp**. In the Spool directory fields, the default spool directory is already entered for you. You can change this to another directory if you want. For the Device field, enter the name of the device your printer uses. Four devices have already been set up for parallel printers: **/dev/lp0**, **/dev/lp1**, **/dev/lp2**, and **/dev/lp3**. These correspond to first, second, third, and fourth parallel ports. If you have a serial device, you must use a serial device name, such as **/dev/ttyS1**, for the second serial port.

For the Input Filter, you can click Select to display a window with three fields. Each field has a Select button by it that displays a set of currently available options. The Select button for the PrinterType field opens a menu of printers from which you can choose. The Select button for the Resolution field lists several possible resolutions. The Select button for the PaperSize field lists paper sizes, such as letter and legal. When you finish, click OK to close the window and do the same for the Edit window. You then see your printer listed in the PrintTool window. Choose the Quit item from the PrintTool menu to quit PrintTool. You are now ready to print. For a detailed explanation of printer installation, see the **Printing-HOWTO** file in **/usr/share/doc/HOWTO**.

Red Hat provides an easy-to-use network configuration tool called *netcfg* (see Chapter 36 for more details and a figure). On the Red Hat Control Panel, an icon is labeled Network Configuration. You can also start it from the desktop or the window manager's program menus, usually with the entry Network Configuration. The netcfg window consists of four panels and a button bar at the top for each one: Name, Hosts, Interfaces, and Routing. Clicking a button displays its panel. Basic configuration of your network requires you to specify the hostname and IP address of your own system, the IP addresses of your network's name servers and gateway, the network netmask, and your network interfaces. Using the netcfg tool, you can enter all this information easily. The Name panel is where you enter your own system's hostname and your network's name server addresses. The Hosts panel lists host IP addresses and their domain names, including those for your own system. On the Interfaces panel, you add and configure your network interfaces, such as an Ethernet or PPP interface. The Routing panel is where you specify special routing hosts, including your gateway system. If you already configured your network during installation, entries are now in these panels.

The **kernelcfg** utility provides an interface for **kerneld** or **kmod** daemons with which you can load and unload kernel modules. You use kernel modules to add different capabilities to your system, particularly support for hardware devices. The modules your system need are usually determined during installation, based on the kind of configuration information you provided. For example, if your system uses an Ethernet card whose type you specified during installation, then the system loads the module for that card. You can, however, manually control what modules are to be loaded for your system. This, in effect, enables you to customize your kernel whatever way you want. Be careful not to remove any necessary modules. *Modules* are essentially extensions of the kernel and they are often critical for providing the needed support for your system.

For a modem, you should make sure there is a link by the name of **/dev/modem** to your modem device, which is usually one of the **/dev/ttyS**num devices, where *num* is in the range of 0–3. For example, a modem on the second serial port would have a device name of **/dev/ttyS1**, and **/dev/modem** would be a link to the **/dev/ttyS1** device file. This is usually done for you during installation. You can use the modem configuration tool **modemtool** to create this link. Many modem programs and PPP configuration programs look for the **/dev/modem** file by default. **modemtool** provides a simple way to create this link. It displays four entries, one for each serial port. Click the one that applies to your system.

The **helptool** enables you to search for documentation on your system using a keyword search. It displays man, HOW-TO, and info documentation. Any user can use **helptool**. It is not limited to system administration.

Red Hat Setup Configuration Tools

Red Hat also provides a **setup** utility with which you can configure different devices and system settings, such as your keyboard, mouse, and time zone. **setup** is useful if you have changed any of your devices—say, installed a new mouse, keyboard, or sound card. Start the **setup** utility with the command **setup**, which you enter at a shell command line. On the desktop, you can open a terminal window and enter the command. A menu of configuration choices is displayed. Use the arrow keys to select one, and then press the TAB key to move to the Run Tool and Quit buttons. Figure 30-6 Shows the initial Setup menu.

The Setup utility is actually an interface for running several configuration tools (see Table 30-7). You can call any of these tools separately using their commands. For example, the **kbdconfig** command starts the keyboard configuration utility that enables you to select the type of keyboard, while the **mouseconfig** command enables you to select the type of mouse.

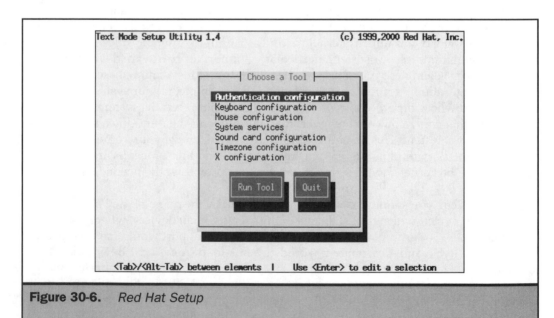

Figure 30-6.   *Red Hat Setup*

Tools	Description
`setup`	Red Hat Setup interface listing configuration tools for system and device setting
`authconfig`	Authentication options, such as enabling NIS, shadow passwords, and MD5 passwords
`kbdconfig`	Selects the keyboard type
`mouseconfig`	Selects the mouse type
`ntsysv`	Selects servers and daemons to start up at boot time
`sndconfig`	Detects and configures your sound card
`timeconfig`	Selects the time zone
`Xconfigurator`	Configures your X Window System for your video card and monitor

Table 30-7.   *Setup Tools*

Authentication configuration displays a simple dialog box, shown next, for enabling the *Network Information Service* (*NIS*) and Password encryption. You find an entry for NIS, and entries for the shadow and MD5 password security methods.

With **kbdconfig**, you can select the type of keyboard you are using. A cursor-based dialog box appears with a list of different keyboard types.

With **mouseconfig**, you can select the type of mouse you are using. A cursor-based dialog box appears with a list of different mouse device types. Your system is automatically probed for the type of mouse connected to your system, and the cursor is positioned at that entry. If you have a two-button mouse, you can select the three-button emulation option to let a simultaneous click on both the left and the right mouse buttons emulate a third mouse button.

The **ntsysv** utility is a simple utility for specifying which servers and services should be automatically started at boot time (see Chapter 15). The dialog box lists the possible servers and services to choose from. Move to the entry you want and use the SPACEBAR to toggle it on or off. An entry with an asterisk next to it is selected and is started automatically the next time you boot your system.

The **sndconfig** utility enables you to select and configure your sound card. It initially tries to detect your sound card automatically. If the automatic detection fails, a dialog box appears with a listing of different sound cards. Select the one on your system. Another dialog box appears where you need to enter the setting for your sound card. **sndconfig** then tries to play sample sound and MIDI files to test the card. As an alternative to **sndconfig,** you can obtain, load, and configure sound drivers yourself (see Chapter 26).

You can use the simple **timeconfig** utility to specify your system's time zone. This is useful if your system has moved to a different time zone.

One important utility is the X Window System setup provided by Xconfigurator. If you have trouble with your X Window System configuration, you can use the **Xconfigurator** command to configure it again. Xconfigurator is also helpful for updating X Windows if you change your video card. Run Xconfigurator again and select the card. When you download a new version of XFree86, the packages includes a compatible version of Xconfigurator.

Chapter 31

Managing Users

Linux is designed to serve many users at the same time, as well as provide an interface between the users and the computer with its storage media, such as hard disks and tapes. Users have their own shells through which they interact with the operating system. As a system administrator, you can manage user logins on your system. You can add or remove users, as well as add and remove groups. You also have access to system initialization files you can use to configure all user shells. And you have control over the default initialization files copied into an account when it is first created. With them, you can decide how accounts should initially be configured.

You can find out which users are currently logged in with the **who** command. Add the **-u** option to display information about each connected user, such as from where they have logged in and how long they have been inactive. The command displays the login name, the login port, the date and time of login, the length of inactivity (if still active), and the process ID for the login shell. For example:

```
# who -u
root        console      Oct 12 10:34       .        1219
valerie     tty1         Oct 12 22:18       10       1492
```

Any utility to add a user, such as Linuxconf, makes use of certain default files, called configuration files, and directories to set up the new account. A set of path names is used to locate these default files or to know where to create certain user directories. For example, **/etc/skel** holds initialization files for a new user. A new user's home directory is placed in the **/home** directory. A list of the path names follows:

Directory	Description
/home	Location of the user's own home directory
/etc/skel	Holds the default initialization files for the login shell, such as **.bash_profile** and **.cshrc**
/etc/shells	Holds the login shells, such as BASH or TCSH
/etc/passwd	Holds the password for a user
/etc/group	Holds the group to which the user belongs

The /etc/passwd File

When you add a user, an entry for that user is made in the **/etc/passwd** file, commonly known as the *password file*. Each entry takes up one line that has several fields separated by colons. The fields are as follows:

Field	Description
Username	Login name of the user
Password	Encrypted password for the user's account
User ID	Unique number assigned by the system
Group ID	Number used to identify the group to which the user belongs
Comment	Any user information, such as the user's full name
Home directory	The user's home directory
Login shell	Shell to run when the user logs in; this is the default shell, usually **/bin/bash**.

The following is an example of a **/etc/passwd** entry. The entry for **chris** has a * in its Password field, indicating a password has not yet been created for this user. For such entries, you must use **passwd** to create a password. Notice also that user IDs in this particular system start at 500 and increment by one.

```
dylan:YOTPd3Pyy9hAc:500:500:User:/home/dylan:/bin/bash
chris:*:501:501:User:/home/chris:/bin/bash
```

The **/etc/passwd** file is a text file you can edit using a text editor. You can change fields in entries and even add new entries. The only field you cannot effectively change is the password, which must be encrypted. To change the Password field, you should always use the **passwd** command.

Although you can make entries directly to the **/etc/passwd** file, an easier and safer way is to use the userconf, adduser, and useradd utilities. These programs not only make entries in the **/etc/passwd** file, but they also create the home directory for the user and install initialization files in the user's home directory.

The **/etc/passwd** file is a simple text file and is vulnerable to security breaches. If anyone gains access to the **/etc/password** file, they might be able to decipher or brute force crack the passwords. On most Linux distributions , the shadow suite of applications implements a greater level of security. These include versions of useradd, groupadd, and their corresponding update and delete programs. Most other user configuration tools support shadow security measures. With shadow security, passwords are no longer kept in the **/etc/password** file. Instead, passwords are kept in a separate file called **/etc/shadow** and are heavily encrypted. Access is restricted to the root user. A corresponding password file, called **/etc/gshadow**, is also maintained for groups that require passwords.

Managing User Environments: /etc/skel

Each time a user logs in, two profile scripts are executed. A system profile script is the same for every user, and each user has the **.bash_profile** script in his or her home directory. The system profile script is located in the **/etc** directory and named **profile** with no preceding period. As a superuser, you can edit the profile script and put in any commands you want executed for each user when he or she logs in. For example, you may want to define a default path for commands, in case the user has not done so. Or, you may want to notify the user of recent system news or account charges.

When you first add a user to the system, you must provide the user with a skeleton version of their login shell initialization file. For the BASH shell, this would be a **.bash_profile** file. The **useradd** command adds this file automatically by searching for a **.bash_profile** file in the directory **/etc/skel** and copying it to the user's new home directory. The **/etc/skel** directory contains a skeleton initialization file for **.bash_profile** files or, if you are using the C shell as your login shell, **.login** and **.logout** files. It also provides initialization files for BASH and C shells: **.bashrc** and **.cshrc**. The **/etc/skel** directory also contains default files and directories for your desktops. These include an **.Xdefaults** file for the X Window System, a **.kderc** file for the KDE Desktop, and a Gnome Desktop directory that contains default configuration files for the Gnome Desktop.

As a superuser, you can configure the **.bash_profile** file in **/etc/skel** any way you want. Usually, basic system variable assignments are included that define pathnames for commands, system prompts, mail pathnames, and terminal default definitions. In short, the **PATH, TERM, MAIL**, and **PS1** variables are defined. Once users have their own **.bash_profile** files, they can redefine variables or add new commands as they choose.

Login Access

You can control user login access to your system with the **/etc/login.access** file. The file consists of entries listing users, whether they are allowed access, and from where they can access the system. A record in this file consists of three colon-delimited fields: a plus (+) or minus (–) sign indicating whether users are allowed access, user login names allowed access, and the remote system (host) or terminal (tty device) from which they are trying to log in. The following enables the user **dylan** to access the system from the **rabbit.mytrek.com** remote system:

```
+:chris:rabbit.mytrek.com
```

You can list more than one user or location. You can also use the ALL option in place of either users or locations to allow access by all users and locations. The ALL option can be qualified with the EXCEPT option to allow access by all users except certain specified ones. The following entry allows any user to log in to the system using the console, except for the users **larisa** and **aleina**:

```
+:ALL EXCEPT larisa aleina:console
```

Other access control files are used to control access for specific services, such as the **hosts.deny** and **hosts.allows** files used with **tcpd** daemon for inetd-supported servers.

Controlling Access to Directories and Files

Recall from Chapter 12 that you can control access to your files and directories by user, group, or others. This is a capability given to all users for their own files and directories. Access in each of these categories can be controlled according to write, read, and execute permissions. Write access lets users modify a file, read access lets them display it, and execute access (used for programs) lets them run it. For directories, write access lets them delete it, read access will list its contents, and execute access will let users change to that directory. You could allow anyone on the system to read one of your files by assigning a read access to its other permission. Chapter 12 describes how you can use the **chmod** command to set permissions, using the **u** for user, **g** for group, and **o** for other, as well as **r** for read, **w** for write, and **x** for execute. The following command provides read and write group permissions for the file **ourdraft1**:

```
chmod g+rx ourdraft1
```

In Gnome, you can set a directory or file permission using its Permissions panel in the Properties window (see Figure 31-1). Right-click the file or directory entry in the file manager window and select Properties. Then select the Permissions panel. Here you will find a table of boxes with columns for read, write, and execute, along with rows for user, group, and other. Check the appropriate box for the permission you want. Normally, the read and write boxes for user permission will already be set. You can specify the group you want access provided to from the Group drop-down menu. This displays the groups a user belongs to.

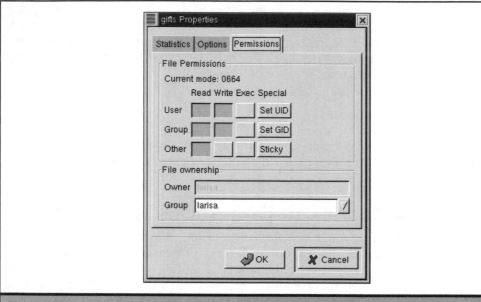

Figure 31-1. *File and directory permissions in Gnome*

Managing Users with Linuxconf

Most administration tools let you easily add, remove, or change users. This chapter will cover Linuxconf and Webmin. Currently, for Red Hat distributions, it is recommended you use Linuxconf to manage user accounts. You can access Linuxconf user configuration panels either through the main Linuxconf interface or through a special user-configuration interface invoked with the **userconf** command. With the main Linuxconf interface, select the User Accounts entry in the Normal list under the User Accounts heading, which is under Config. This displays a panel listing all your user accounts, including those used for special system purposes, such as FTP and news (see Figure 31-2). Each entry has four fields: the account name, the login name, the account ID, and the group to which it belongs. With the **userconf** command, you are first presented with a window showing icons for User, Group, and Password Configuration. Click the User icon to display a window with several tabbed panels, the first being a list of all users on the system.

To add a new user, click Add on this panel. This displays a User Information panel that contains several tabbed panels labeled Base Info, Params, Mail Settings, and Privileges. To create a user account, all you have to do is enter the login name you want to give the user and the user's full name. Linuxconf will use default entries for the remaining fields, adding in a home directory, group, login shell (command interpreter), and user ID. Click the Accept button to create the user. You can select values for these fields yourself, if you wish. The home directory has the default consisting of **/home** and

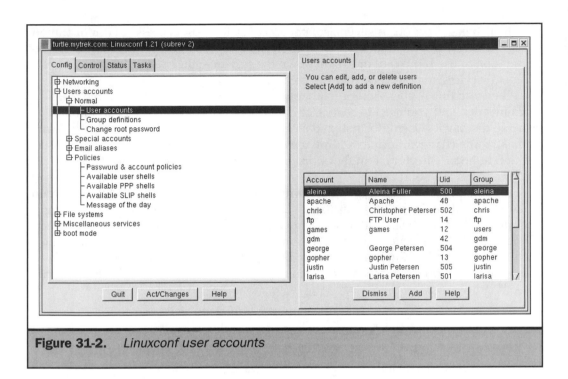

Figure 31-2. *Linuxconf user accounts*

the user's login name, as in **/home/aleina**. Both the group and the shell have drop-down menus listing available groups and shells from which to choose. To give the user an initial password, click the Password button. A Changing Password panel is displayed in which you can enter the new password.

There are entries for both a default group and supplementary groups. The default group (also known as the primary group) is determined by the files and processes the user account needs to have access to. For user accounts, this has traditionally been the group named **users**. Alternatively, the new user can be assigned to a special group set up for just that user and given the user's same name. So, the new user **dylan** is given a default group also called **dylan**. The group **dylan** will also show up in the listing of groups. This method of assigning default user groups is called the User Private Group (UPG) scheme. UPG is currently used on Red Hat systems and is shown in the Linuxconf figures in this chapter. The supplementary groups are additional groups that the user may want to belong to. Traditionally, users were all assigned to one group named **users** that would subject all users to the group permission controls for the **users** group. With UPG, each user has its own group, with its own group permissions.

In the Params panel, you can require that a user change his or her password in a specified period of time. You can also shut down an account at a specified time, issuing a warning to the user. The Mail Settings panel lets you manage mail aliases for the user.

The Privileges panel has several subpanels controlling user access to administration tasks. On the General System's Control panel, you can give the user superuser access, or permission to use Linuxconf or to shut down the system. Other panels let you control access to services, mail servers, and user accounts.

When you finish, click Accept. You now see the new user displayed in the User Accounts panel. If you need to change or delete a user, double-click its entry in this panel to display its User Information panel. To remove the user, click DEL. If you want to make some changes, such as adding the user to a different group or giving the user a different home directory, edit the appropriate entries and click Accept. The user information is then updated.

From the User Information panel, shown in Figure 31-3, you can also schedule certain tasks you want performed for this user at specific times, such as backup or printing operations. Click the Tasks button to display the Schedule Jobs panel. You can then create job definitions. In the Schedule Job Definitions panel, you can enter the command along with the time and date for the command to be executed. Boxes are there for the month, day, hour, and minute. The scheduling operation works much like the UNIX **at** command.

Figure 31-3.   *Linuxconf user information*

You can also deactivate an account, denying all access to it and its files. The files for this account remain intact; and when you decide to reactivate the account, the files can then be accessed. The check box labeled The Account Is Enabled in the user's User Information panel is a toggle that activates and deactivates the user account. When recessed and dark, the user account is activated.

Managing Users with Webmin

To manage users with Webmin, select the Users And Groups entry in the System panel. This displays a listing of all your users and groups (see Figure 31-4). To create a new user, click the Create A New User link below the list of users.

The Create User page displays segments for User Details, Password Options, and Group Memberships. For User Details, you enter the Username (login name), the Real Name, the Shell (login shell), home directory, and Password (see Figure 31-5). For the Shell entry, you can choose the shell you want from a drop-down menu. For the home directory, you can type in the directory name or click the button next to the entry box labeled with three dots. This opens a file manager interface where you can click to the directory and file you want.

Webmin
Index
Help..
Module
Config

Users and Groups

Local Users

Username	User ID	Real name	Home directory	Shell
root	0	root	/root	/bin/bash
bin	1	bin	/bin	
daemon	2	daemon	/sbin	
adm	3	adm	/var/adm	
lp	4	lp	/var/spool/lpd	
sync	5	sync	/sbin	/bin/sync
shutdown	6	shutdown	/sbin	/sbin/shutdown
halt	7	halt	/sbin	/sbin/halt
mail	8	mail	/var/spool/mail	
news	9	news	/var/spool/news	
uucp	10	uucp	/var/spool/uucp	

Figure 31-4.   *Webmin users*

Figure 31-5. *Webmin user details*

For the password options, you can specify the period when the user needs to change the password and even set an expiration date. For Group Membership, you can select the primary (default) group (usually users), and add any secondary groups.

Once a group is created, an entry for it will appear in the Users And Groups page. The user name will appear as a link. To make any changes or to delete group, simply click on its name. The Edit User page will appear with entries for changing the password, changing secondary groups, or deleting the user.

Managing Users with COAS, YaST, and kuser

OpenLinux and SuSE provide user configuration as part of their configuration utilities, COAS and YaST. With COAS, you select the Account Administration entry in the System Administration menu. This displays a User Accounts window listing all the users on your system, including special system users' setup for system tasks like FTP. From the View menu, you can select display options such as displaying only regular users. To add a new user, select the Add entry from the Actions menu. This displays an Edit User dialog box with boxes for entering user information such as the login name, home directory, and password. To change any user information, select its entry in the User Accounts window and choose Edit from the Actions menu. To remove a user, select it and choose Delete.

ADMINISTRATION

Yet Another Setup Tool (YaST), used on SuSE, provides a similar interface, providing a full-screen interface for adding, deleting, and editing users. Start up YaST and select Systems Administration, and then User Administration. This displays a screen with fields for user information. Press F3 to display a selection list of users.

The K Desktop also provides a simple user management utility called kuser that works much like Linuxconf. You can use it to manage both users and groups. The window is divided into two panes: one for users and the other for groups. Add, Edit, and Delete icons easily enable you to add new users, change their configuration, or remove them. When you add a new user, a new window opens with entries such as the shell and home directory. To add the password, click Password and enter the password in the window displayed.

Adding Users with adduser

You can also add a new user to the system with the **adduser** command. This command is entered on your command line and is easy to use. Different versions of adduser exist. This version of adduser takes as its argument the user name for the account you are creating. When you press ENTER, it then creates the new account using default values. You can use **passwd** to create a password for the new account. This adduser program is a shell script located in the **/usr/sbin** directory. If you are familiar with shell programming, you can edit this script to change its default values.

With different versions of adduser found on other Linux distributions, it is best to enter the **adduser** command without any arguments. You are then prompted for each piece of information needed to set up a new user. At the end of each prompt, within brackets, adduser displays a default value. To accept this default value as your entry, press ENTER. After you type all your entries, adduser creates the new account. Once you add a new user login, you need to give the new login a password. The login is inaccessible until you do.

Adding and Removing Users with useradd, usermod, and userdel

Most distributions of Linux also provide the **useradd**, **usermod**, and **userdel** commands to manage user accounts. All these commands take in all their information as options on the command line. If an option is not specified, they use predetermined default values. With the **useradd** command, you enter values as options on the command line, such as the name of a user to create a user account. It then creates a new login and directory of that name using all the default features for a new account.

```
# useradd chris
```

The **useradd** utility has a set of predefined default values for creating a new account. The default values are the group name, the user ID, the home directory, the **skel** directory, and the login shell. The *group name* is the name of the group in which the new account is placed. By default, this is *other*, which means the new account belongs to no group. The user ID is a number identifying the user account. This starts at 1 with the first account and increments automatically for each new account. The **skel** directory is the system directory that holds copies of initialization files. These initialization files are copied into the user's new home directory when it is created. The login shell is the pathname for the particular shell the user plans to use. You can display these defaults using the **useradd** command with the **-D** option. The **useradd** command has options that correspond to each default value. Table 31-1 holds a list of all the options you can use with the **useradd** command. You can use specific values in place of any of these defaults when creating a particular account. Once you add a new user login, you need to give the new login a password. The login is inaccessible until you do. In the next example, the group name for the **chris** account is set to intro1 and the user ID is set to 578:

```
# useradd chris -g intro1 -u 578
```

The **usermod** command enables you to change the values for any of these features. You can change the home directory or the user ID. You can even change the user name for the account.

When you want to remove a user from the system, you can use the **userdel** command to delete the user's login. In the next example, the user **chris** is removed from the system:

```
# userdel -r chris
```

Command	Description
adduser *username*	Adds a new user, creating a password file entry and home directory with initialization files; uses **passwd** command to create a password for the user
useradd *username options*	Adds new users to the system

Table 31-1. *User and Group Management Commands*

Command	Description
usermod *username options*	Modifies a user's features
userdel -r *username*	Removes a user from the system
useradd, usermod **Options**	
-u *userid*	Sets the user ID of the new user (The default is the increment of the highest number used so far.)
-g *group*	Sets a group or name
-d *dir*	Sets the home directory of the new user
-s *shell*	Sets the login shell directory of the new user
-c *str*	Adds a comment to the user's entry in the system password file: **/etc/passwd**
-k *skl-dir*	Sets the skeleton directory that holds skeleton files, such as **.profile** files, which are copied to the user's home directory automatically when it is created (The default is **/etc/skel**.)
-D	Displays defaults for all settings
Group Management Commands	
groupadd	Creates a new group
groupdel	Removes a group
groupmod *option*	Modifies a group **-g** Changes a group ID **-n** Changes a group name

Table 31-1.   *User and Group Management Commands* (continued)

Managing Groups

You can manage groups using either shell commands or window utilities like Linuxconf. The system file that holds group entries is called **/etc/group**. The file consists of group records, with one record per line and its fields separated by colons. A group record has four fields: a group name, a password, its ID, and the users who are part of this group. The Password field can be left blank. The fields for a group record are as follows:

Group name	Name of the group; must be unique
Password	Usually an asterisk to allow anyone to join the group (A password can be added to control access.)
Group ID	Number assigned by the system to identify this group
Users	List of users that belong to the group

Here is an example of an entry in an **/etc/group** file. The group is called **engines**; there is no password; the group ID is 100; and the users who are part of this group are **chris**, **robert**, **valerie**, and **aleina**.

```
engines::100:chris,robert,valerie,aleina
```

As in the case of the **/etc/passwd** file, you can edit the **/etc/group** file directly using a text editor. Instead of using either Linuxconf or groupdel, you could simply delete the entry for that group in the **/etc/group** file. This can be risky, however, if you make accidental changes.

As for users, you can also create a home directory for a group. Several administration utilities like Linuxconf support this feature. To do so manually, you simply create a directory for the group in the **/home** directory and change its group to that of the group, along with allowing access by any member of the group. The following example creates a directory called **engines** and changes its group to that of the **engines** group:

```
mkdir /home/engines
chgrp engines /home/engines
```

Then the read, write, and execute permissions for the group level should be set:

```
chmod g+rwx /home/engines
```

Any member of the **engines** group can now access the **/home/engines** directory and any shared files placed therein. This directory becomes a shared directory for the group. You can, in fact, use the same procedure to make other shared directories at any location in the file system.

Files within the shared directory should also have their permissions set to allow access by other users in the group. When a user places a file in a shared directory, permissions on that file need to be changed to allow other members of the group to access it. A read permission will let others display it, write lets them change it, and execute lets then run it (used for scripts and programs). The following example first changes the group for the **mymodel** file to **engines**. Then it copies the **mymodel** file to the **/home/engines** directory, and sets the group read and write permission for the **engines** group.

```
$ chgrp engines mymodel
$ cp mymodel /home/engines
$ chmod g+rw /home/engines/mymodel
```

Managing Groups Using Linuxconf

You can add, remove, and modify any groups easily with the Linuxconf utility on your root user desktop. To manage groups using Linuxconf, select the Group Definitions entry in the Normal list under User Accounts in Config. This displays a User Groups panel that lists all the groups currently on your system (see Figure 31-6). Each entry has three fields: the group name, the group ID, and the list of users who are part of this group.

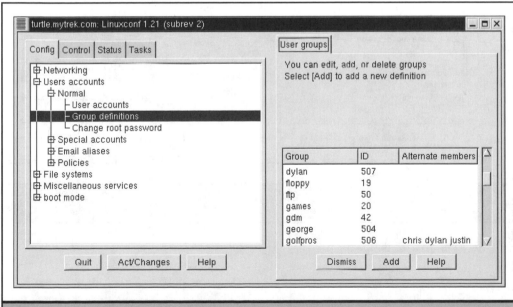

Figure 31-6.   *The Linuxconf Group panel*

To add a new group, click Add. This displays a Group Specification panel in which you can enter the name for the new group and the group ID (see Figure 31-7). A default group ID is already listed. To add users to this group, just enter their login names in the Alternate Members field. You can edit or delete any group by first double-clicking its entry in the User Groups panel to display its Group Specification panel. To remove the group, click DEL. For changes, edit any of the entries and click Accept. For example, to add certain users to a group, bring up the group's Group Specification panel and enter the users you want to add.

To create a home directory for this group, switch to the Directories panel. Here you will find entries labeled Home Base Directory and Creation Permissions. In the Home Base Directory box, enter the pathname for the group's home directory. This is usually **/home/**groupname, where groupname is the name of the group. In Figure 31-8 a group directory called **/home/gophpros** is created for the **golphpros** group.

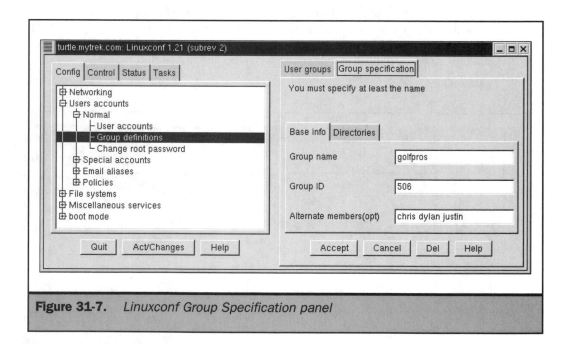

Figure 31-7. *Linuxconf Group Specification panel*

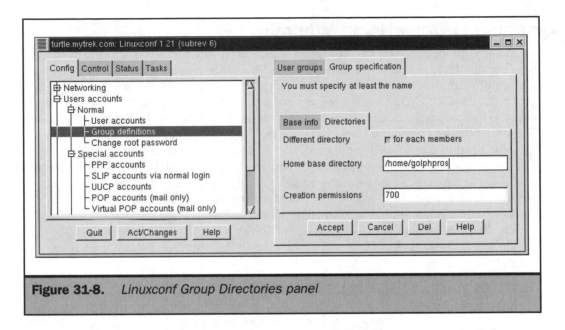

turtle.mytrek.com: Linuxconf 1.21 (subrev 6)

Config | Control | Status | Tasks

- Networking
- Users accounts
  - Normal
    - User accounts
    - Group definitions
    - Change root password
  - Special accounts
    - PPP accounts
    - SLIP accounts via normal login
    - UUCP accounts
    - POP accounts (mail only)
    - Virtual POP accounts (mail only)

Quit   Act/Changes   Help

User groups | Group specification

You must specify at least the name

Base info | Directories

Different directory   ☐ for each members

Home base directory   /home/golphpros

Creation permissions   700

Accept   Cancel   Del   Help

Figure 31-8.   *Linuxconf Group Directories panel*

Be sure to check the permissions and group ownership for any group directory that you create. The group permissions need to be set to read, write, and execute for full access. The read permission will let users list files in the directory, the write will let users add and remove files, and the execute permission lets users change to that directory. As the root user, you can use **chmod** to set these permissions:

```
chmod 775 /home/golphpros
```

Then, to change the group ownership, you use **chgrp**, as shown here:

```
chgrp golphpros  /home/golphpros
```

In Gnome, you can check and change permission with the Gnome file manager by right-clicking the directory name and selecting Properties. Then select the Permissions panel. For full access, make sure the row of Group Permission buttons are selected. Also, select the group from the list of groups in the Group drop-down menu—in this example, **golphpros**.

Managing Groups Using Webmin

To manage groups in Webmin, you select the Users And Groups entry in the Systems panel to display the Users And Groups page. Move down to the group listings. Here, groups are listed with their names functioning as links to an Edit Group page for that group. In the Edit Group page, you can add a password, change the ID, or add new users to the group. To create a group, click the Create New Group link following the Group list on the Users And Groups page. This opens a Create Group page where you can add a group name, add a password, and add users to the group (see Figure 31-9). The group ID is provided for you, which you can then change if you wish. When you add users to a group, a new window opens up with two panes, one listing all users and the other for the users you have selected for this group. Each user name is a link. Clicking a user name in the All Users lists adds it to the Selected Users list. Clicking a name in the Selected Users list removes it from that list. When you click the OK button, the names you have selected will appear in the Members box on the Create Group page.

Figure 31-9. *Webmin Create Groups page*

Managing Groups
Using groupadd, groupmod, and groupdel

On many Linux distributions, you can manage groups with the **groupadd**, **groupmod**, and **groupdel** commands. With the **groupadd** command, you can create new groups. When you add a group to the system, the system places the group's name in the **/etc/group** file and gives it a group ID number. The **groupadd** command only creates the group category. Users are individually added to the group. In the next example, the **groupadd** command creates the **engines** group:

```
# groupadd engines
```

You can delete a group with the **groupdel** command. In the next example, the **engines** group is deleted:

```
# groupdel engines
```

You can change the name of a group or its ID using the **groupmod** command. Enter **groupmod -g** with the new ID number and the group name. To change the name of a group, you use the **–n** option. Enter **groupmod -n** with the new name of the group, followed by the current name. In the next example, the **engines** group has its name changed to "trains":

```
# groupmod -n trains engines
```

Disk Quotas

With disk quotas, you can control how much disk space a particular user makes use of on your system. On your Linux system, unused disk space is held as a common resource that all users can access as they need it. As usera create more files, they take the space they need from the pool of available disk space. In this sense, all the users are sharing this one resource of unused disk space. However, if one user were to use up all the remaining disk space, then none of the other users would be able to create files or even run programs. To counter this problem, you can create disk quotas on particular users, limiting the amount of available disk space they can use.

In Linuxconf, you can enable disk quotas and set general controls. To enable quotas for a disk, first select the disk in the Access Local Drive panel under File Systems in the Config panel. Then click the disk's Options panel, and click the User Quota Enabled and Group Quota Enabled check boxes. Once you Accept and activate the changes, you can then access the Set Quota Defaults panel under File systems. Here, you can set user and group defaults for disk space and file limits, as well as grace periods (see Figure 31-10).

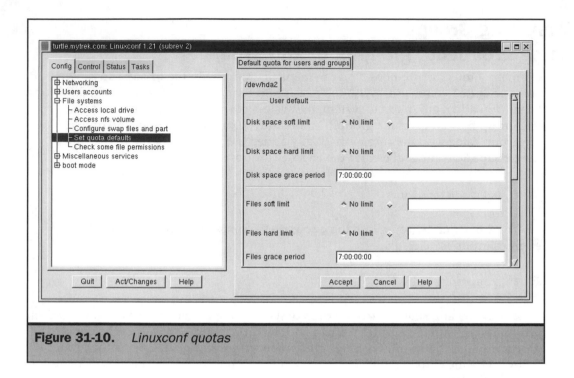

Figure 31-10. *Linuxconf quotas*

Quotas are enabled using the **quotacheck** and **quotaon** programs. They are executed in the **/etc/rc.d/rc.sysinit** script, which is run whenever you start up your system. Each partition then needs to be mounted with the quota options, **usrquota** or **grpquota**. **usrquota** enables **quota** controls and users, and **grpquota** works for groups. These options are usually placed in the mount entry in the **/etc/fstab** file for a particular partition. For example, to mount the **/dev/hda6** hard disk partition to the **/home** directory with support for user and group quotas, you would require a mount entry like the following:

```
/dev/hda6    /home    ext2    defaults,usrquota,grpquota    1    1
```

You also need to create **quota.user** and **quota.group** files for each partition for which you enable quotas. These are the quota databases used to hold the quota information for each user and group. You can create these files by running the **quotacheck** command with the **–a** option or the device name of the file system in which you want to enable quotas.

The limit you set for a quota can be hard or soft. A hard limit will deny a user the ability to exceed his or her quota, whereas a soft limit will just issue a warning. For the soft limit, you can designate a grace period, during which time the user has the chance to reduce his or her disk space below the limit. If the disk space still exceeds the limit after the grace period expires, then the user can be denied access to his or her account.

You can set disk quotas using the **edquota** command or the User Account panels in Linuxconf. In Linuxconf, select a user from the User Accounts listing and then select that user's Disk Quota panel. Here, you can enter the hard and soft limits, along with the grace period. You can also select a default for these limits. The default is set using the Set Quota Defaults panel in the File System menu. There are entries for both group and user soft and hard defaults. Linuxconf will allow you to place limits on both the disk size and the number of files.

The **edquota** command is run from the command line. With it you can access the quota record for a particular user and group, which is maintained in the disk quota database. You can also set default quotas that will be applied to any user or group in the file system for which quotas have not been set. **edquota** will open the record in your default editor, and you can use your editor to make any changes. To open the record for a particular user, use the **-u** option and the user name as an argument for **edquota** (see Table 31-2). The following example opens the disk quota record for the user **larisa**:

```
edquota -u larisa
```

The quota record begins with the hard disk device name and the blocks of memory and inodes in use. The Limits segments have parameters for soft and hard limits. If these entries are 0, then there are no limits in place. You can set both hard and soft limits, using the hard limit as a firm restriction. Blocks in Linux are currently about 1,000 bytes. The inodes are used by files to hold information about the memory blocks making up a file. To set the time limit for a soft limit, you use the **edquota** command with the **-t** option. The following example displays the quota record for **larisa**:

```
Quotas for user larisa:
/dev/hda3: blocks in use: 9000, limits (soft = 40000, hard = 60000)
           inodes in use: 321, limits (soft = 0, hard = 0)
```

These records are maintained in the quota database for that partition. Each partition that has quotas enabled will have its own quota database. You can check the validity of your quota database with the **quotacheck** command. You can turn quotas on and off using the **quotaon** and **quotaoff** commands. When you start up your system, **quotacheck** is run to check the quota databases and then **quotaon** is run to turn on quotas.

As the system administrator, you can use the **repquota** command to generate a summary of memory usage, checking to see what users are approaching or exceeding quota limits. Individual users can use the **quota** command to check their memory use and how much disk space they have left in their quota (see Table 31-2).

Option	Description
edquota	
-u	Edit the user quota. This is the default.
-g	Edit the group quota.
-p	Duplicate the quotas of the prototypical user specified for each user specified. This is the normal mechanism used to initialize quotas for groups of users.
-t	Edit the soft time limits for each file system.
quota	
-g	Print group quotas for the group of which the user is a member.
-u	Print the user's quota.
-v	Will display quotas on file systems when no storage is allocated.
-q	Print information on file systems where usage is over quota.

Table 31-2. *The options* **edquota** *and* **quota**

Chapter 32

File System
Administration

Files reside on physical devices such as **hard** drives, CD-ROMs, or floppy disks. The files on each device are organized into a file system. To access files on a device, you attach its file system to a specified directory. This is called *mounting* the file system. For example, to access files on a floppy disk, you first mount its file system to a particular directory. This chapter discusses how you can access CD-ROMs, floppy disks, and hard disk partitions. You can even access an MS-DOS hard drive partition or floppy disk, as well as file systems on a remote server (see Chapter 37). Archives are used to back up files or to combine them into a package, which can then be transferred as one file over the Internet or posted on an FTP site for easy downloading. The standard archive utility used on Linux and UNIX systems is **tar**, for which several GUI front ends exist. You have several compression programs to choose from, including GNU zip (**gzip**), Zip, bzip, and compress.

Local File Systems

Your Linux system is capable of handling any number of storage devices that may be connected to it. You can configure your system to access multiple hard drives, partitions on a hard drive, CD-ROM disks, floppy disks, and even tapes. You can elect to attach these storage components manually or have them automatically mount when you boot. For example, the main partition holding your Linux system programs is automatically attached whenever you boot, whereas a floppy disk must be manually attached when you put one in your floppy drive. You can configure this access to different storage devices either by manually editing configuration files, such as **/etc/fstab**, or by using a file system configuration tool such as the Linuxconf's fsconf. You can use administration tools such as Linuxconf or Webmin to configure the file system, as well as Caldera's COAS and SuSE's YaST.

File Systems

Although all the files in your Linux system are connected into one overall directory tree, the files themselves reside on storage devices such as hard drives or CD-ROMs. The Linux files on a particular storage device are organized into what is referred to as a *file system*. Your Linux directory tree may encompass several file systems, each on different storage devices. On a hard drive with several partitions, you would have a file system for each partition. The files themselves are organized into one seamless tree of directories, beginning from the root directory. Although the root may be located in a file system on a hard drive partition, a pathname leads directly to files located on the file system for your CD-ROM.

The files in a file system remain separate from your directory tree until you specifically connect them to it. A file system has its files organized into its own directory tree. You can think of this as a *subtree* that must be attached to the main directory tree. For example, a floppy disk with Linux files has its own tree of directories. You need to attach this subtree to the main tree on your hard drive partition. Until they are attached, you cannot access the files on your floppy disk.

Attaching a file system on a storage device to your main directory tree is called *mounting the device.* The mount operation attaches the directory tree on the storage device to a directory you specify. You can then change to that directory and access those files. The directory in the file structure to which the new file system is attached is referred to as the *mountpoint*. For example, to access files on a CD-ROM, first you have to mount the CD-ROM.

Currently, Linux systems have several ways to mount a file system. You can use Linuxconf to select and mount a file system easily. If you are using either Gnome or the K Desktop, you can use special desktop icons to mount a file system. From a shell command line, you can use the **mount** command. Mounting file systems can only be done as the root user. This is a system administration task and cannot be performed by a regular user. To mount a file system, be sure to log in as the root user (or use the su operation). As the root user, you can, however, make a particular device like a CD-ROM user mountable. In this way, any user could put in a CD-ROM and mount it. You could do the same for a floppy drive.

For a file system to be accessible, it must be mounted. Even the file system on your hard disk partition must be mounted with a **mount** command. When you install your Linux system and create the Linux partition on your hard drive, however, your system is automatically configured to mount your main file system whenever it starts. Floppy disks and CD-ROMs must be explicitly mounted. Remember, when you mount a CD-ROM or floppy disk, you cannot then simply remove it to put in another one. You first have to unmount it. In fact, the CD-ROM drive remains locked until you unmount it. Once you unmount a CD-ROM, you can then take it out and put in another one, which you then must mount before you can access it. When changing several CD-ROMs or floppy disks, you are continually mounting and unmounting them.

The file systems on each storage device are formatted to take up a specified amount of space. For example, you may have formatted your hard drive partition to take up 300MB. Files installed or created on that file system take up part of the space, while the remainder is available for new files and directories. To find out how much space you have free on a file system, you can use the **df** command or, on Gnome, you can use the Gnome Disk Free utility, shown in Figure 32-1. *Gnome DiskFree* displays a list of meters showing how much space is used on each partition and how much space you have left. kdf, a KDE utility, provides similar information.

Figure 32-1.   *Gnome DiskFree*

The **df** command lists all your file systems by their device names, how much memory they take up, and the percentage of the memory used, as well as where they are mounted. The **df** command is also a safe way to obtain a listing of all your partitions, instead of using **fdisk**. The command only shows mounted partitions, however, whereas **fdisk** shows all partitions.

```
$ df
Filesystem      1024-blocks   Used Available Capacity Mounted on
/dev/hda3          297635    169499    112764    60%    /
/dev/hda1          205380    182320     23060    89%    /mnt/dos
/dev/hdc           637986    637986         0   100%    /mnt/cdrom
```

You can also use **df** to tell you to what file system a given directory belongs. Enter **df** with the directory name or **df .** for the current directory.

```
$ df .
Filesystem      1024-blocks   Used Available Capacity Mounted on
/dev/hda3          297635    169499    112764    60%    /
```

To make sure nothing is wrong with a given file system, you can use the **fsck** command to check it. However, be sure that the file system is unmounted. **fsck** should not be used on a mounted file systems. To use **fsck**, enter **fsck** and the device name that references the file system. Table 32-1 lists the **fsck** options. The following examples check the disk in the floppy drive and the primary hard drive:

```
# fsck   /dev/fd0
# fsck   /dev/hda1
```

Filesystem Hierarchy Standard

Linux organizes its files and directories into one overall interconnected tree, beginning from the root directory and extending down to system and user directories (refer Chapter 11). The organization and layout for the system directories is determined by the Filesystem Hierarchy Standard (FHS). The FHS provides a standardized layout that all Linux distributions should following setting up their system directories. For example, there must be an **/etc** directory to hold configuration files and a **/dev** directory for device files. You can find out more about FHS, including the official documentation, at **www.pathname.com/fhs**. The current release is FHS 2.1, which is the successor to FSSTND 1.2, a precursor to FHS. Linux distributions, developers, and administrators all follow the FHS to provide a consistent organization to the Linux file system.

Linux uses a number of specifically named directories for specialized administration tasks. All these directories are directories at the very top level of your main Linux file system, the file system root directory represented by a single slash, /.

Options	Description
file-system	Specifies the file system to be checked. Use file system's device name, such as **/dev/hda3**.
-A	Checks all file systems listed in **/etc/fstab** file.
-V	Verbose mode. List actions that **fsck** takes.
-t *file-system-type*	Specifies the type of file system to be checked.
-a	Automatically repairs any problems.
-l	Lists the names of all files in the file system.
-r	Asks for confirmation before repairing file system.
-s	Lists superblock before checking file system.

Table 32-1.   *The **fsck** Options for Checking and Repairing File Systems*

For example, the **/dev** directory holds device files, the **/etc** directory holds configuration files, and the **/home** directory holds the user home directories and all their user files. You only have access to these directories and files as the system administrator. You need to log in as the root user, placing you in a special root user administrative directory called **/root**. From here, you can access any directory on the Linux file system, both administrative and user.

The directories held in the root directory, **/**, are listed in Table 32-2, along with other useful subdirectories. Ones that you may commonly access as an administrator

Directory	Function
/	Begins the file system structure—called the root.
/boot	Holds the kernel image files and modules loaded when your system boots up.
/home	Contains users' home directories.
/sbin	Holds administration level commands and any used by the root user.

Table 32-2.   *Linux File System Directories*

Directory	Function
/dev	Holds file interfaces for devices such as the terminal and printer.
/etc	Holds system configuration files and any other system files.
/etc/opt	Holds system configuration files for applications in **/opt**.
/etc/X11	Holds system configuration files for the X Window System and its applications.
/bin	Holds the essential user commands and utility programs.
/lib	Holds essential shared libraries and kernel modules.
/lib/modules	Holds the kernel modules.
/mnt	Used to hold directories for mounting file systems like CD-ROMs or floppy disks that are mounted only temporarily.
/opt	Holds added software applications (for example, KDE on some distributions).
/proc	Process directory, a memory-resident directory containing files used to provide information about the system.
/tmp	Holds temporary files.
/usr	Holds those files and commands used by the system; this directory breaks down into several subdirectories.
/var	Holds files that vary, such as mailbox files. On Red Hat, these also hold Web and FTP server data files.

Table 32-2. *Linux File System Directories* (continued)

are the **/etc** directory which holds configuration files, the **/dev** directory that holds device files, and the **/var** directory that holds server data files for DNS, Web, mail, and FTP servers, along with system logs and scheduled tasks. For managing different versions of the kernel, you may need to access the **/boot** and **/lib/modules** directories.

The **/boot** directory will hold the kernel image files for any new kernels you install and the **/lib/modules** directory will hold modules for your different kernels.

The **/usr** directory contains a multitude of important subdirectories used to support users, providing applications, libraries, and documentation (see Table 32-3). **/usr/bin** holds numerous user-accessible applications and utilities. **/usr/sbin** holds user-accessible administrative utilities. The **/usr/share** directory holds architecture-independent data that includes an extensive number of subdirectories, including those for the documentation such as Man, info, and doc files.

The **/var** directories are designed to hold data that changes with the normal operation of the Linux system (see Table 32-4). For example, spool file for documents that you are printing are kept here. A spool file is created as a temporary printing file and is removed after printing. Other files, like system log files, are changed constantly.

The **/proc** file system is a special file system that is generated in system memory (see Table 32-5). It does not exist on any disk. **/proc** contains files that provide important

Directory	Description
/usr/bin	Holds most user commands and utility programs.
/usr/sbin	Holds nonessential administrative applications.
/usr/lib	Holds libraries for applications, programming languages, desktops, etc.
/usr/games	Games and educational program.
/usr/include	C programming language header files (**.h**).
/usr/doc	Holds Linux documentation.
/usr/local	Directory for locally installed software.
/usr/share	Architecture independent data such as documentation like Man and info pages.
/usr/src	Holds source code, including the kernel source codes.
/usr/X11R6	X Window System–based applications and libraries.

Table 32-3. */usr Directories*

Directory	Description
/var/account	Process accounting logs.
/var/cache	Application cache data for Man pages, Web proxy data, fonts, or application-specific data.
/var/crash	System crash dumps.
/var/games	Varying games data.
/var/lib	Holds state information for particular applications.
/var/local	Used for data that changes for programs installed in **/usr/local**.
/var/lock	Holds lock files that indicate when a particular program or file is in use.
/var/log	Hold log files such as **/var/log/messages** that contain all kernel and system program messages.
/var/mail	User mailbox files.
/var/opt	Variable data for applications installed in **/opt**.
/var/run	Information about system's running processes.
/var/spool	Holds application's spool data such as that for mail, news, and printer queues, as well as cron and at jobs.
/var/tmp	Holds temporary files that should be preserved between system reboots.
/var/yp	Network Information Service (NIS) data files.

Table 32-4.   */var Directories*

information about the state of your system. For example, **/proc/cpuinfo** holds information about your computer's CPU processor. **/proc/devices** will list those devices currently configured to run with your kernel. **/proc/filesystems** will list the file systems.

Files	Description
/proc/*num*	There is a directory for each process labeled by its number. **/proc/1** is the directory for process 1.
/proc/cpuinfo	Contains information about the CPU, such as its type, make, model, and performance.
/proc/devices	List of the device drivers configured for the currently running kernel.
/proc/dma	Displays the DMA channels currently used.
/proc/filesystems	File systems configured into the kernel.
/proc/interrupts	Displays the interrupts in use.
/proc/ioports	Shows the I/O ports are in use.
/proc/kcore	Holds an image of the physical memory of the system.
/proc/kmsg	Messages generated by the kernel.
/proc/ksyms	Symbol table for the kernel.
/proc/loadavg	The system 'load average'.
/proc/meminfo	Memory usage.
/proc/modules	Lists the kernel modules currently loaded.
/proc/net	Status information about network protocols.
/proc/stat	System operating statistics, such as page fault occurrences.
/proc/uptime	The time the system has been up.
/proc/version	The kernel version.

Table 32-5. */proc Directories and Files*

Device Files: /dev

To mount a file system, you have to specify its device name. The interfaces to devices that may be attached to your system are provided by special files known as *device* files. The names of these device files are the device names. Device files are located in the **/dev** directories and usually have abbreviated names ending with the number of device. For example, **fd0** may reference the first floppy drive attached to your system.

On Linux systems operating on PCs, the hard disk partitions have a prefix of **hd**, followed by an alphabetic character that labels the hard drive, and then a number for the partition. For example, **hda2** references the second partition on the first hard drive. In most cases, you can use the **man** command with a prefix to obtain more detailed information about this kind of device. For example, **man sd** displays the Man pages for SCSI devices. A complete listing of all device names can be found in the **devices** file located in the **linux/doc/device-list** directory at the **www.kernel.org** Web site. Table 32-6 lists several of the commonly used device names.

The device name for your floppy drive is **fd0** and is located in the directory **/dev**. **/dev/fd0** references your floppy drive. Notice the numeral **0** after **fd**. If you have more than one floppy drive, they are represented by **fd1**, **fd2**, and so on.

Device Name	Description
hd	IDE hard drives, 1–4 are primary partitions, and 5 and up are logical partitions
sd	SCSI hard drives
sr	SCSI CD-ROM drives
fd	Floppy disks
st	SCSI tape drives
ht	IDE tape drives
tty	Terminals
lp	Printer ports
pty	Pseudoterminals (used for remote logins)
js	Analog joy sticks
midi	Midi ports
ttyS	Serial ports
cua	Callout devices (COM ports)
cdrom	Link to your CD-ROM device file
modem	Link to your modem device file
floppy	Link to your floppy device file

Table 32-6.   *Device Name Prefixes*

IDE hard drives use the prefix **hd**, while SCSI hard drives use the prefix **sd**. The prefix for a hard disk is followed by an alphabetic character that labels the hard drive and a number for the partition. For example, **hda2** references the second partition on the first IDE hard drive, and **sdb3** refers to the third partition on the second SCSI hard drive. To find the device name, you can use **df** to display your hard partitions or examine the **/etc/fstab** file.

The device name for your CD-ROM drive varies depending on the type of CD-ROM you have. The device name for an IDE CD-ROM has the same prefix as an IDE hard disk partition, **hd**, and is identified by a following character that distinguishes it from other IDE devices. For example, an IDE CD-ROM connected to your secondary IDE port may have the name **hdc**. An IDE CD-ROM connected as a slave to the secondary port may have the name **hdd**. The actual name is determined when the CD-ROM is installed, as happened when you installed your Linux system. SCSI CD-ROM drives use a different nomenclature for their device names. They begin with **sd** for SCSI drive and are followed by a distinguishing character. For example, the name of a SCSI CD-ROM could be **sdb** or **sda**. The name of your CD-ROM was determined when you installed your system. You can find out what it is either by examining the **/etc/fstab** file or using Linuxconf on your root user desktop.

Mount Configuration: /etc/fstab

Although you can mount a file system directly with only a **mount** command, you can simplify the process by placing mount information in the **/etc/fstab** configuration file. Using entries in this file, you can have certain file systems automatically mounted whenever your system boots. For others, you can specify configuration information, such as mountpoints and access permissions, which can be automatically used whenever you mount a file system. You needn't enter this information as arguments to a **mount** command as you otherwise must. This feature is what allows mount utilities on Gnome, KDE, and Linuxconf to enable you to mount a file system simply by clicking a button. All the mount information is already in the **/etc/fstab** file. For example, when adding a new hard disk partition to your Linux system, you most likely want to have it automatically mounted on startup, and then unmounted when you shut down. Otherwise, you must mount and unmount the partition explicitly each time you boot up and shut down your system. To have Linux automatically mount the file system on your new hard disk partition, you only need to add its name to the **fstab** file. You can do this by directly and carefully editing the **/etc/fstab** file to type in a new entry, or you can use Linuxconf as described in the next section.

An entry in a **fstab** file contains several fields, each separated by a space or tab. The first field is the name of the file system to be mounted. This usually begins with **/dev**, such as **/dev/hda3** for the third hard disk partition. The next field is the directory in your file structure where you want the file system on this device to be attached. The third field is the type of file system being mounted. Table 32-7 provides a list of all the different types you can mount. The type for a standard Linux hard disk partition is

Types	Description
minux	Minux file systems (filenames are limited to 30 characters)
ext	Earlier version of Linux file system, no longer in use
ext2	Standard Linux file system supporting large filenames and file sizes
xiaf	Xiaf file system
msdos	File system for MS-DOS partitions (16-bit)
vfat	File system for Windows 95, 98, and Millennium partitions (32-bit)
ntfs	NT and Windows2000 file systems
hpfs	File system for OS/2 high-performance partitions
proc	Used by operating system for processes
nfs	NFS file system for mounting partitions from remote systems
umsdos	UMS-DOS file system
swap	Linux swap partition or swap file
sysv	UNIX System V file systems
iso9660	File system for mounting CD-ROM

Table 32-7.   *File System Types*

ext2. The next example shows an entry for the main Linux hard disk partition. This entry is mounted at the root directory, */*, and has a file type of **ext2**.

```
/dev/hda3  /  ext2  defaults  0  1
```

The field after the file system type lists the different options for mounting the file system. You can specify a default set of options by simply entering **defaults**. You can list specific options next to each other separated by a comma (no spaces). The **defaults** option specifies a device is read/write, asynchronous, block, ordinary users cannot mount on it, and programs can be executed on it. By contrast, a CD-ROM only has a few options listed for it: **ro** and **noauto**. **ro** specifies this is read-only; and **noauto** specifies this is not automatically mounted. The **noauto** option is used with both CD-ROMs and floppy drives, so they won't automatically mount because you do not know if you have anything in them when you start up. At the same time, the entries for both the CD-ROM and the floppy drive specify where they are to be mounted when you decide to mount them. Table 32-8 lists the options for mounting a file system. An example of CD-ROM and floppy drive entries follows. Notice the type for a CD-ROM file system is different from a hard disk partition, **iso9660**. The floppy drive also has all the **default** options of the hard disk partitions.

```
/dev/fd0    /mnt/floppy   ext2     defaults,noauto  0  0
/dev/hdc    /mnt/cdrom    iso9660  ro,noauto        0  0
```

Options	Description
async	All I/O to the file system should be done asynchronously.
auto	Can be mounted with the **-a** option.
defaults	Use default options: **rw**, **suid**, **dev**, **exec**, **auto**, **nouser**, and **async**.
dev	Interpret character or block special devices on the file system.
noauto	Can only be mounted explicitly. The **-a** option does not cause the file system to be mounted.
exec	Permit execution of binaries.
nouser	Forbid an ordinary (that is, nonroot) user to mount the file system.
remount	Attempt to remount an already mounted file system. This is commonly used to change the mount flags for a file system, especially to make a read-only file system writable.
ro	Mount the file system read-only.
rw	Mount the file system read-write.

Table 32-8.   *Mount Options for File Systems: -o and /etc/fstab*

Options	Description
suid	Allow set-user-identifier or set-group-identifier bits to take effect.
sync	All I/O to the file system should be done synchronously.
user	Enable an ordinary user to mount the file system. Ordinary users always have the following options activated: **noexec**, **nosuid**, and **nodev**.
nodev	Do not interpret character or block special devices on the file system.
nosuid	Do not allow set-user-identifier or set-group-identifier bits to take effect.

Table 32-8.   *Mount Options for File Systems: -o and /etc/fstab* (continued)

The last two fields consist of an integer value. The first one is used by the **dump** command to determine if a file system needs to be dumped, backing up the file system. The last one is used by **fsck** to see if a file system should be checked at reboot and in what order. If the field has a value of 1, it indicates a boot partition, and 2 indicates other partitions. The 0 value means the **fsck** needn't check the file system.

A copy of an **/etc/fstab** file is shown here. Notice the first line is comment. All comment lines begin with a **#**. The entry for the **/proc** file system is a special entry used by your Linux operating system for managing its processes, and it is not an actual device. To make an entry in the **/etc/fstab** file, you can either edit the **/etc/fstab** file directly or use Linuxconf, which prompts you for information and then makes the correct entries into your **/etc/fstab** file. You can use the **/etc/fstab** example here as a guide to show how your entries should look. The **/proc** and **swap** partition entries are particularly critical.

/etc/fstab

```
# <device>     <mountpoint>    <filesystemtype>   <options>          <dump><fsck>
/dev/hda3      /               ext2               defaults           0     1
/dev/hdc       /mnt/cdrom      iso9660            ro,noauto          0     0
/dev/fd0       /mnt/floppy     ext2               defaults,noauto    0
/proc          /proc           proc               defaults
/dev/hda2      none            swap               sw
/dev/hda1      /mnt/windows    vfat               defaults           0     0
```

You can mount either MS-DOS or Windows95 partitions used by your MS-DOS or Windows operating system onto your Linux file structure, just as you would mount any Linux file system. You only have to specify the file type of **vfat** for Windows95 and **msdos** for MS-DOS. You may find it convenient to have your Windows partitions automatically mounted when you start up your Linux system (the same is true for MS-DOS partitions). To do this, you need to put an entry for your Windows partitions in your **/etc/fstab** file. You make an entry for each Windows partition you want to mount, and then specify the device name for that partition followed by the directory in which you want to mount it. The **/mnt/windows** directory would be a logical choice (be sure the **windows** directory has already been created in **/mnt**). For the file system type, enter vfat. The next example shows a standard MS-DOS partition entry for an **/etc/fstab** file. Notice the last entry in the **/etc/fstab** file example was an entry for mounting an Windows partition.

```
/dev/hda1 /mnt/windows  vfat  defaults  0  0
```

If your **/etc/fstab** file ever becomes corrupt—say, a line gets deleted accidentally or changed—then your system will boot into a maintenance mode, giving you read-only access to your partitions. To gain read/write access so you can fix your **/etc/fstab** file, you have to remount your main partition. The following command performs such an operation:

```
# mount -n -o remount,rw  /
```

File systems listed in the **/etc/fstab** file are automatically mounted whenever you boot, unless this feature is explicitly turned off with the **noauto** option. Notice the CD-ROM and floppy disks have a **noauto** option. Also, if you issue a **mount -a** command, all the file systems without a **noauto** option are mounted. If you would want to make the CD-ROM user mountable, add the user option.

```
/dev/hdc    /mnt/cdrom    iso9660   ro,noauto,user  0   0
```

Linuxconf Configuration for Local File Systems

Unless you are familiar with the **fstab** file, using Linuxconf to add and edit entries is easier, instead of editing entries directly. Linuxconf is available on Red Hat systems and can be installed on any major distribution (see Chapter 30). With Linuxconf, you can choose many of the configuration options using drop-down menus and check boxes. Once you finish making your entries, you can have Linuxconf generate a new **/etc/fstab** file incorporating your changes.

You can start Linuxconf from a window manager, a desktop, or a shell command line. The figures here show Linuxconf panels as they are displayed in Gnome. Other desktops and window managers show the same display. A Linuxconf shell command shows cursor-based lists and boxes. To access the Linuxconf file system configuration panels, you can select its entry in the main Linuxconf interface, or you can use the

fsconf command to invoke a specialized window showing only file system options (see Chapter 4 for an example of the **fsconf** interface). Using the main Linuxconf interface, you select the Access local drive entry in the file systems list under the Config heading. This displays the information about the different file systems accessible on your local system. The source is the device name for the storage device. The name begins with **/dev**, the directory where device files are kept. For example, the name given to the first partition on the first hard drive is **hda1**. Its device filename is **/dev/hda1**. On most Linux distributions, a CD-DROM is given the device name **/dev/cdrom**. Names for additional CD-ROMS vary, depending on whether they are SCSI or IDE devices. On PCs, a second IDE CD-ROM could have the name **/dev/hdd**. The mountpoint and file system type are shown along with the size, partition type, and whether it is mounted. Figure 32-2 shows the Linuxconf Access local drive panel.

To add a new entry, click the Add button. This displays panels for file system information and options. The Base tab prompts you to enter in the file system's device name, its file system type, and its mountpoint, as shown in Figure 32-3. The box labeled Partition is where you enter the file system's device name. This box holds a drop-down menu listing the different hard disk partitions on your hard drive. If you are making an entry for one of those partitions, you can select it from there. If you are making an entry for a CD-ROM or floppy drive, you must enter the name yourself. The Type box is where you enter the file system type. The box contains a drop-down menu that lists the different file system types from which you can choose. Select the type from this menu. See Table 32-7 for a listing of file system types supported. The Mountpoint box is where you enter the mountpoint—the directory on your main file system where you attach this file system. For example, a floppy disk is usually attached to the

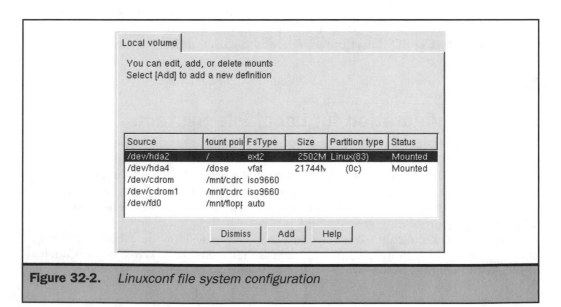

Figure 32-2. *Linuxconf file system configuration*

ADMINISTRATION

/mnt/floppy directory. When you mount a floppy disk, you find its files in that directory. The directory can actually be any directory on your file system. If the directory does not exist, then Linuxconf asks to create it for you. Figure 32-3 shows an example of the Base tab for a Linux partition. The device name in this example is /dev/hda2, the file system type is ext2 (standard for Linux), and the mountpoint is / (this is the root directory). If you were mounting a windows file system, you would use the vfat type, and for DOS partitions you would use msdos.

The Options tab lists different mount options in the form of check boxes. You can select options, such as whether you don't want the file system automatically mounted at boot, or if you want to let normal users mount it. Figure 32-4 shows the Options tab. The example here show entries you may make for a CD-ROM. The CD-ROM is read-only, not mounted at boot time, and can be mounted by any user.

If your Linux system shares a hard drive with a Windows system, you may want to add mount entries for the Windows partition. This way, those partitions would be accessible by your Linux system. Linux can access any file on an Windows partition, though it cannot run its programs. For example, files could be downloaded by your

Figure 32-3.   *Linuxconf Local Volume Base tab for adding or editing file systems*

| Base | Options | Dos options | Misc. |

Options

☐ Read only

☐ User mountable

☐ Mountable by device owner

☐ Not mount at boot time

☐ No program allowed to execute

☐ No special device file support

☐ No setuid programs allowed

☐ User quota enabled

☐ Group quota enabled

Dump frequency　　　　　　　0

Fsck priority　　　　　　　　0

Figure 32-4.　*Linuxconf Options tab*

Linux system and saved directly on a Windows partition. To create a mount entry for a Windows partition, you would enter its hard disk partition name in the Partition box, and enter **vfat** for its file system type.

When you finish, click the Accept button. This returns you to the Local volume panel and you then see the new entry displayed. Linuxconf does not actually implement these changes on your system until you click the Act/Changes button in the lower-left corner. When you do this, Linuxconf generates a new **/etc/fstab** file, replacing the previous one.

If you create an MS-DOS partition you may want to control access to it. As a single-user system, MS-DOS does not implement any of the user access controls found on a multiuser system like Linux. For this reason, MS-DOS systems are mounted by default with global access, allowing any user on your Linux system full read and write access to the partition. If you want to control access, say to a particular user, you need to specify the controls you want on the MS-DOS Options panel. Here you will find entries for the user and the group, and the default permissions for that user and group. This way you can limit access to a single user or to users belonging to a particular group. DOS and Linux implement files differently, particularly in the way the end-of-file indicator is represented. When copying a Linux text file to DOS directory, a DOS end-of-file character should be inserted in it so that it can be read in DOS.

Normally the translation setting is **auto**, which will translate text files but not binary ones, such as programs or archives (**text** will translate all files and **binary** will translate none).

You can change any of the current entries by simply double-clicking its entry. This displays the Volume specification panel for that entry. You can then change any of the options or the base configuration. For example, to use a different mountpoint, type in a new directory in the Mountpoint box. If you want to delete the entry, click the DEL button.

Webmin Configuration for Local File Systems

To use Webmin to administer your file system, you first select Disk and Network Filesystems on the System panel. This opens a page listing all the file systems listed in your **fstab** file (see Figure 32-5). The first column lists their mountpoints, and these are links to pages where you can configure individual entries.

To change any of the entries, you can click on their mountpoint directory to open an Edit Mount page (see Figure 32-6). Here you can set the mountpoint directory, the device mounted, and the different mountpoint options.

If you want to add a new file system, you first select the file system type from the pop-up menu at the bottom of the page. This menu will have as its default Linux Native Filesystem. Once you have selected the file system type, click on the Add Mount button next to it. This opens a page where you can enter the directory for the mountpoint, the device to be mounted, and the mount options.

Webmin
Index
Module
Config

Disk and Network Filesystems

Mounted As	Type	Location	In use?	Permanent?
/dev/pts	PTS Filesystem	devpts	Yes	Yes
/proc	Kernel Filesystem	proc	Yes	Yes
/mnt/cdrom	ISO9660 CD-ROM	/dev/cdrom	No	Yes
/mnt/floppy	Automatic	Floppy disk 0	No	Yes
/	Linux Native Filesystem	IDE device A partition 1	Yes	Yes
Virtual Memory	Virtual Memory	IDE device A partition 2	Yes	Yes
/auto	Automounter Filesystem	/etc/am.d/localdev	Yes	Yes

[Add mount] Type: Linux Native Filesystem ▾

Figure 32-5.   *Webmin file system management*

Figure 32-6. *Webmin Edit Mount page*

Mounting File Systems Using Linuxconf, Webmin, KDE, and Gnome

Once you enter a new file system configuration and activate the changes to implement it on your system, you can then actually mount the file system. By default, file systems are mounted automatically—though certain file systems, such as CD-ROMs and floppy disks, are normally mounted manually.

Both the Gnome and K Desktop provide easy-to-use desktop icons for mounting and unmounting your file systems. Normally, these are used for manually mounted devices, such as CD-ROMs, tapes, and floppy disks. Hard disk partitions are usually mounted automatically at boot time. If a CD-ROM or floppy device can be mounted with the user option, then normal users on your system can also have CD-ROM and floppy icons for mounting and unmounting CD-ROMs and floppy disks.

On Gnome, an icon is automatically generated for your CD-ROM devices when you first insert a CD-ROM disk. Right-clicking the icon displays a menu from which you can select an entry to mount or unmount the CD-ROM. For a floppy disk you right-click on the Floppy drive icon and select mount to mount the floppy. Be sure to unmount it before you remove the floppy disk. You can also install a Mount applet in a Gnome panel that enables you to mount a floppy, CD-ROM, or partition by simply clicking its Panel icon (See Chapter 9 for more details).

On the K Desktop, you can create a KDE desktop file for a particular CD-ROM or floppy device. To add a file for a new device, right-click the desktop and select the entry either for the CD-ROM or floppy device from the New entry in the pop-up menu. Enter a name for the desktop file in the General panel. In the Device panel, enter the device name, mountpoint, and file system type. You can also select a mount and unmount icon. See Chapter 8 and Figure 8-8 for an example showing a Device tab for a CD-ROM.

To mount a file system manually with Linuxconf, select Control Configured Local Drives in the Mount/Unmount File Systems list in the Control Panel. This displays a listing of your local file systems, as shown in Figure 32-7. When you click an entry, you are then asked if you want to mount the file system. You can also use this panel to unmount a file system. If a file system is already mounted, clicking it displays a dialog box asking if you want to unmount the file system. Remember, when you mount a CD-ROM or floppy disk, you cannot then simply remove it to put in another one. You first have to unmount the CD or floppy disk before you can take it out and put in another one.

Using the Access local drive configuration panel to mount a file system is also possible (see Figure 32-3). Click the Mount button in a file system's Volume

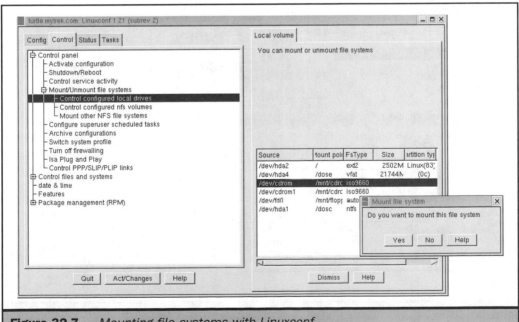

Figure 32-7. *Mounting file systems with Linuxconf*

Specification panel. An Unmount button also unmounts it. You can use this method when checking to see if a new system mounts correctly.

With Webmin, you first display the Disk and Network Filesystems page (accessible from the System panel). Click on the mount directory for the file system you want to mount and then select Mount in the Edit Mount page and save.

On OpenLinux, you can use COAS to mount and unmount file systems (shown in Figure 32-8). Select File System from the System Administration menu. This displays a File System window showing mountable devices on the left and the directories for mounted file systems on the right. To mount a file system, like a CD-ROM, select its device in the left list and click on the Mount button. An IDE CD-ROM will often have a device name like **hdc** or **hdd**. To check what a device is used for, click on it and then click on the Info button. When you mount a file system, a window opens showing the device name, the directory it will be mounted on, and the file system type. For a new device, you will have to enter a directory and type. CD-ROMs have the type **iso9660** and Linux floppy disks use **ext2**. Windows partitions have a type of **vfat**. You can further set options such as read-only or user mountable. You can also elect to have it added to the **fstab** file, which then makes it a permanent entry and easier to mount again later.

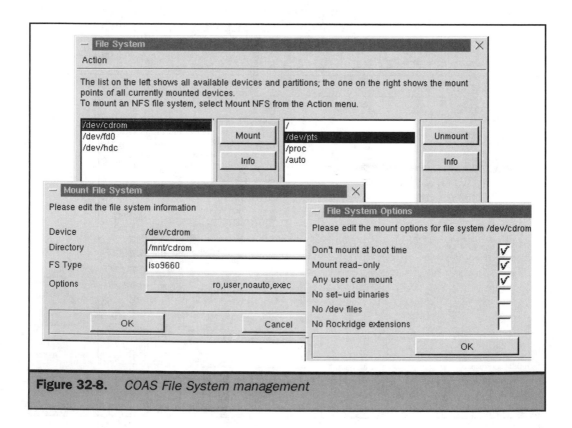

Figure 32-8. *COAS File System management*

The mount and umount Commands

You can also mount or unmount any file system using the **mount** and **umount** commands. You enter these commands on a shell command line. In a window manager or desktop, you can open a terminal window and enter the command there, or you can simply use your login shell. The mount operations discussed in the previous sections use the **mount** command to mount a file system. Normally, mounting file systems can only be done as the root user (unless the device is user mountable). This is a system administration task and cannot be performed by a regular user. To mount a file system, be sure to log in as the root user. Table 32-9 lists the different options for the **mount** command.

The **mount** command takes two arguments: the storage device through which Linux accesses the file system, and the directory in the file structure to which the new file system is attached. The *mountpoint* is the directory on your main directory tree where you want the files on the storage device attached. The *device* is a special device

Mount Option	Description
-f	Fakes the mounting of a file system. You use it to check if a file system can be mounted.
-v	Verbose mode. Mount displays descriptions of the actions it is taking. Use with **-f** to check for any problems mounting a file system, **-fv**.
-w	Mount the file system with read and write permission.
-r	Mount the file system with only read permission.
-n	Mount the file system without placing an entry for it in the **mstab** file.
-t *type*	Specify the type of file system to be mounted. See Table 32-7 for valid file system types.
-a	Mount all file systems listed in **/etc/fstab**.
-o *option-list*	Mount the file system using a list of options. This is a comma-separated list of options following **-o**. See Table 32-8 for a list of the options and the Man pages for mount for a complete listing.

Table 32-9. *The* **mount** *Command*

file that connects your system to the hardware device. The syntax for the **mount** command is as follows:

```
# mount device mountpoint
```

Device files are located in the **/dev** directories and usually have abbreviated names ending with the number of the device. For example, **fd0** may reference the first floppy drive attached to your system. On Linux systems operating on PCs, the hard disk partitions have a prefix of **hd**, followed by an alphabetic character that labels the hard drive, and then a number for the partition. For example, **hda2** references the second partition on the first hard drive. In most cases, you can use the **man** command with a prefix to obtain more detailed information about that kind of device. For example, **man sd** displays the Man pages for SCSI devices. The following example mounts a floppy disk in the first floppy drive device (**fd0**) to the **/mydir** directory. The mountpoint directory needs to be empty. If you already have a file system mounted there, you will receive a messages that another file system is already mounted there and that the directory is busy. If you mount a file system to a directory that already has files and subdirectories in it, then those will be bypassed, giving you access only to the files in the mounted file system. Unmounting the file system restores access to the original directory files.

```
# mount /dev/fd0   /mydir
```

For any partition with an entry in the **/etc/fstab** file, you can mount it using only the mount directory specified in its **fstab** entry. You needn't enter the device filename. The **mount** command looks up the entry for it in the **fstab** file, using the directory to identify the entry and, in that way, find the device name. For example, to unmount the **/dev/hda1** DOS partition in the previous example, the **mount** command only needs to know the directory it is mounted to—in this case, **/mnt/dos**.

```
# mount /mnt/dos
```

If you want to replace one mounted file system with another, you must first explicitly unmount the one already mounted. Say you have mounted a floppy disk, and now you want to take it out and put in a new one. You must unmount that floppy disk before you can put in and mount the new one. You unmount a file system with the **umount** command. The **umount** command can take as its argument either a device name or the directory where it was mounted. Here is the syntax:

```
# umount device-or-mountpoint
```

The following example unmounts the floppy disk mounted to the **/mydir** directory:

```
# umount /dev/fd0
```

Using the example where the device was mounted on the **/mydir** directory, you could use that directory to unmount the file system:

```
# umount /mydir
```

One important constraint occurs on the **umount** command. You can never unmount a file system in which you are currently working. If you change to a directory within a file system that you then try to unmount, you receive an error message saying the file system is busy. For example, suppose you mount the Red Hat CD-ROM on the **/mnt/cdrom** directory, and then change to that **/mnt/cdrom** directory. If you decide to change CD-ROMs, you first have to unmount the current one with the **umount** command. This will fail because you are currently in the directory in which it is mounted. You first have to leave that directory before you can unmount the CD-ROM.

```
# mount  /dev/hdc  /mnt/cdrom
# cd /mnt/cdrom
# umount /mnt/cdrom
umount: /dev/hdd: device is busy
# cd  /root
# umount /mnt/cdrom
```

If other users are using a file system you are trying to unmount, you can use the lsof or the fuser commands to find out who they are.

Mounting Floppy Disks

To access a file on a floppy disk, you first have to mount that disk onto your Linux system. The device name for your floppy drive is **fd0**, and it is located in the directory **/dev**. Entering **/dev/fd0** references your floppy drive. Notice the number **0** after **fd**. If you have more than one floppy drive, they are represented by **fd1**, **fd2**, and so on. You can mount to any directory you want. Red Hat creates a convenient directory to use for floppy disks, **/mnt/floppy**. The following example mounts the floppy disk in your floppy drive to the **/mnt/floppy** directory:

```
# mount /dev/fd0  /mnt/floppy
```

Remember, you are mounting a particular floppy disk, not the floppy drive. You cannot simply remove the floppy disk and put in another one. The **mount** command has attached those files to your main directory tree, and your system expects to find those files on a floppy disk in your floppy drive. If you take out the disk and put another one in, you get an error message when you try to access it.

To change disks, you must first unmount the floppy disk already in your disk drive; then, after putting in the new disk, you must explicitly mount that new disk. To do this, use the **umount** command. Notice no *n* is in the **umount** command.

```
# umount    /dev/fd0
```

For the **unmount** operation, you can specify either the directory it is mounted on or the **/dev/fd0** device.

```
# umount   /mnt/floppy
```

You can now remove the floppy disk, put in the new one, and then mount it.

```
# mount    /mnt/floppy
```

When you shut down your system, any disk you have mounted is automatically unmounted. You do not have to unmount it explicitly.

Mounting CD-ROMs

You can also mount CD-ROM disks to your Linux system using the **mount** command. On Red Hat, the directory **/mnt/cdrom** has been reserved for CD-ROM file systems. You see an entry for this in the **/etc/fstab** file. With such an entry, to mount a CD-ROM, all you have to do is enter the command **mount** and the directory **/mnt/cdrom**. You needn't specify the device name. Once mounted, you can access the CD-ROM through the **/mnt/cdrom** directory.

```
# mount /mnt/cdrom
```

As with floppy disks, remember you are mounting a particular CD-ROM, not the CD-ROM drive. You cannot just remove the CD-ROM and put in a new one. The **mount** command has attached those files to your main directory tree, and your system expects to find them on a disc in your CD-ROM drive. To change discs, you must first unmount the CD-ROM already in your CD-ROM drive with the **umount** command. Your CD-ROM drive will not open until you issue this command. Then, after putting in the new disc, you must explicitly mount that new CD-ROM. You can then remove the CD-ROM and put in the new one. Then, issue a **mount** command to mount it.

```
# umount   /mnt/cdrom
```

If you want to mount a CD-ROM to another directory, you have to include the device name in the **mount** command. The following example mounts the disc in your CD-ROM drive to the **/mydir** directory. The particular device name for the CD-ROM in this example is **/dev/hdc**.

```
# mount /dev/hdc  /mydir
```

To change discs, you have to unmount the CD-ROM already in your CD-ROM drive, and then, after putting in the new disc, you must explicitly mount that new CD-ROM.

```
# umount /mydir
```

You can now remove the CD-ROM and put in the new one. Then, issue a **mount** command to mount it.

```
# mount   /dev/hdc    /mydir
```

Mounting Hard Drive Partitions: Linux and Windows

You can mount either Linux or Windows hard drive partitions with the **mount** command. However, it is much more practical to have them mounted automatically using the **/etc/fstab** file as described in the next section. The Linux hard disk partitions you created during installation are already automatically mounted for you. To mount a Linux hard disk partition, enter the **mount** command with the device name of the partition and the directory to which you want to mount it. IDE hard drives use the prefix **hd**, and SCSI hard drives use the prefix **sd**. The next example mounts the Linux hard disk partition on **/dev/hda4** to the directory **/mnt/mydata**:

```
# mount -t ext2  /dev/hda4   /mnt/mydata
```

You can also mount a Windows partition and directly access the files on it. As with a Linux partition, you use the **mount** command, but you also have to specify the file system type as Windows. For that, use the **-t** option, and then type **vfat** (**msdos** for MS-DOS). In the next example, the user mounts the Windows hard disk partition **/dev/hda1** to the Linux file structure at directory **/mnt/windows**. The **/mnt/windows** directory is a common designation for Windows file systems, though you can mount it in any directory (**/mnt/dos** for MS-DOS). If you have several Windows partitions, you could create a Windows directory and then subdirectory for each drive using the drive's label for letter, such as **/mnt/Windows/a** or **/mnt/Windows/mystuff**. Be sure you have already created the directory.

```
# mount -t vfat  /dev/hda1   /mnt/windows
```

Formatting File Systems: mkfs

If you want to mount a new partition from either a new hard drive or your current
drive, you must first create that partition using the Linux **fdisk** and format it with
mkfs. Once created and formatted, you can then mount it on your system. To start
fdisk, enter **fdisk** on the command line. This brings up an interactive program you
can use to create your Linux partition. Be careful using Linux **fdisk**. It can literally
erase your entire hard disk if you are not careful. The Linux **fdisk** operates much as
described in the installation process discussed in Chapter 2. The command **n** creates a
new partition, and the command **t** enables you to set its type to that of a Linux type,
83. Table 32-10 lists the **fdisk** commands.

Hard disk partitions are named with **hd** (IDE drive) or **sd** (SCSI drives), followed
by an alphabetic letter indicating the hard drive, and then a number for the partition

Commands	Description
a	Sets and unsets the bootable flag for a partition.
c	Sets and unsets the DOS compatibility flag.
d	Deletes a partition.
l	List partition types.
m	Displays a listing of **fdisk** commands.
n	Creates a new partition.
p	Prints the partition table, listing all the partitions on your disk.
q	Quits without saving changes. Use this to abort an **fdisk** session if you made a mistake.
t	Select the file system type for a partition.
v	Verify the partition table.
w	Write partition table to disk and exit. At this point, the changes are made irrevocably.
x	Display a listing of advanced fdisk commands. With these, you can set the number of cylinders, sectors, and heads; print raw data; and change the location of data in the partition table.

Table 32-10. *The* **fdisk** *Commands*

on the hard drive. They can belong to any operating system, such as MS-DOS, OS/2, or Windows NT, as well as Linux. The first partition created is called **hda1**—the first partition on the first IDE hard drive, hda. If you add another partition, it will have the name **hda2**. If you add a new IDE hard drive, its first partition will have the name **hdb1**.

Once you create your partition, you have to format it. For this, use the **mkfs** command and the name of the hard disk partition. A hard disk partition is a device with its own device name in the **/dev** directory. You must specify its full pathname with the **mkfs** command. For example, the second partition on the first hard drive has the device name **/dev/hda4**. You can now mount your new hard disk partition, attaching it to your file structure. The next example formats that partition:

```
# mkfs -t ext2   /dev/hda4
```

To format a floppy disk, use the **mkfs** command. This creates a Linux file system on that disk. Be sure to specify the **ext2** file system type with the **-t ext2** option (see Table 32-11). Once formatted, you can then mount that file system. The **mkfs** command takes as its arguments the device name and the number of memory blocks on the disk (see Table 32-11). At 1,000 bytes per block, 1400 formats a 1.44MB disk. You do not

Options	Description
Blocks	Number of blocks for the file system. There are 1,440 blocks for a 1.44MB floppy disk.
-t *file-system-type*	Specify the type of file system to format. The default is the standard Linux file system type, **ext2**.
fs *–options*	Options for the type of file system specified.
-V	Verbose mode. Displays description of each action **mkvfs** takes.
-v	Instructs the file system builder program that **mkvfs** invokes to show actions it take.
-c	Checks a partition for bad blocks before formatting it (may take some time).
-l *file-name*	Reads a list of bad blocks.

Table 32-11. *The* **mkfs** *Options*

first mount the blank disk; you simply put it in your floppy drive and enter the **mkfs** command with its arguments. The next example formats a 1.44MB floppy disk:

```
# mkfs -t ext2 /dev/fd0   1400
```

If you have the K Desktop installed, you can use the kfloppy utility to format your floppy disks. Kfloppy enables you to choose an MS-DOS or Linux file system type. For MS-DOS disks, you can choose a quick or full format.

The mtools Utilities: msdos

Your Linux system provides a set of utilities, known as *mtools*, that enable you to access a floppy disk formatted for MS-DOS easily (see Table 32-12) . The **mcopy** command enables you to copy files to and from an MS-DOS floppy disk in your floppy drive. No special operations, such as mounting, are required. With mtools, you needn't mount an MS-DOS partition to access it. For an MS-DOS floppy disk, place the disk in your floppy drive, and you can then use mtool commands to access those files. For example, to copy a file from an MS-DOS floppy disk to your Linux system, use the **mcopy** command. You specify the MS-DOS disk with **a:** for the A drive. Unlike normal DOS pathnames, pathnames used with mtool commands use forward slashes instead of backslashes. The directory **docs** on the A drive would be referenced by the pathname **a:/docs**, not **a:\docs**. Unlike MS-DOS, which defaults the second argument to the current directory, you always need to supply the second argument for mcopy. The next example copies the file **mydata** to the MS-DOS disk, and then copies the **preface** file from the disk to the current Linux directory. Notice that, unlike DOS, mtools uses forward slashes instead of backward slashes.

```
$ mcopy mydata a:
$ mcopy a:/preface   .
```

You can use the **mdir** command to list files on your MS-DOS disk, and you can use the **mcd** command to change directories on it. The next example lists the files on the MS-DOS disk in your floppy drive, and then changes to the **docs** directory on that drive:

```
$ mdir a:
$ mcd a:/docs
```

Most of the standard MS-DOS commands are available as mtool operations. You can create MS-DOS directories with **mmd** and erase MS-DOS files with **mdel**. A list of mtool commands is provided in Table 32-12. For example, to display a file on drive **b:** on an MS-DOS 5 1/4-inch floppy drive, use **mtype** and the name of the file preceded by **b:/**.

```
$ mtype b:/readme
```

Commands	Execution
mcopy *filename filename*	Copies a file to and from an MS-DOS disk, or your Linux system. The following copies a file from an MS-DOS floppy disk to your Linux system: **mcopy a:**/*filename directory-or-filename* The following copies a file from Linux for an MS-DOS floppy disk in your floppy drive: **mcopy** *filename* **a:**/*filename*
mcd *directory-name*	Changes directory on your MS-DOS file system
mdir	Lists the files on an MS-DOS disk in your floppy drive
mattrib	Changes the attribute of a MS-DOS file
mdel *filename*	Deletes an MS-DOS file
mformat	Adds an MS-DOS file system to a floppy disk
mlabel	Makes a volume label
mmd *directory-name*	Makes an MS-DOS directory
mrd *directory-name*	Removes an MS-DOS directory
mread *filename filename*	Low-level read (copy) of an MS-DOS file to UNIX
mren *filename filename*	Renames an MS-DOS file
mtype *filename*	Displays contents of an MS-DOS file
mwrite *filename filename*	Low-level write (copy) a UNIX file to MS-DOS

Table 32-12. *The mtools Access Commands*

Access to MS-DOS partitions is configured by the **/etc/mtools.conf** file. This file lists several different default MS-DOS partitions and disk drives. Each drive or partition is identified with a particular device name. Entries for your floppy drives are already entered, using the device names **/dev/fd0** and **/dev/fd1** for the first and second floppy drives. An entry in the **/etc/mtools.conf** file takes the form of the drive label followed by the term "file" and the equal sign, and then the device name of the drive or partition you want identified with this label. The device name is encased in quotes. For example, assuming the first hard disk partition is an MS-DOS partition and has the device name of **/dev/hda1**, the following entry would identify this as the **c:** drive on an MS-DOS system:

```
drive c: file="/dev/hda1"
```

You must have the correct device name for your partition. These device names are listed in the **/etc/fstab** file and can also be viewed with the Linuxconf Local drive access panel on your root user desktop. If you have a SCSI hard disk, the hard disk partition has the form of **sd,** followed by a character for the hard drive and a number for the partition in it. For example, **sda1** refers to the first partition on the SCSI hard drive. IDE hard drives have the form of **hd**, also followed by a character and a partition number—**hda1** refers to the first partition on an IDE hard drive.

On most distributions, a default **/etc/mtools.conf** file is installed for you (see the following **/etc/mtools.conf** example). This file has commented entries for the **c:** drive: one for a SCSI hard disk partition and one for an IDE partition. Both are commented out with a preceding **#**. If you have an IDE hard drive (as most users do), you need to remove the preceding **#** symbol from the entry for the IDE hard disks partition and leave the preceding **#** symbol in front of the entry for the SCSI partition. Also, if your MS-DOS partition on your IDE hard drive is not the first partition, you must change the device name. For example, if the MS-DOS partition is the second partition, the device name will be **/dev/hda2**. If you have several MS-DOS partitions, you can add entries for each one, assigning a different label to each. The following example assigns the **d:** label to the fourth hard disk partition on an IDE drive:

```
drive d: file="/dev/hda4"
```

/etc/mtools.conf

```
# Linux floppy drives
drive a: file="/dev/fd0" exclusive 1.44m
drive b: file="/dev/fd1" exclusive 1.44m
# First SCSI hard disk partition
#drive c: file="/dev/sda1"
# First IDE hard disk partition
drive c: file="/dev/hda1"
drive d: file="/dev/hda5"
#dosemu floppy image
drive m: file="/var/lib/dosemu/diskimage"
#dosemu hdimage
drive n: file="/var/lib/dosemu/diskimage" offset=3840
#Atari ramdisk image
drive o: file="/tmp/atari_rd" offset=136
mtools_lower_case=1
```

Once the DOS hard disk partitions are referenced, you can then use their drive letters to copy files to and from them to your Linux partitions. The following command copies the file **mydoc.html** to the **c:** partition in the directory **webstuff** and renames it **mydoc.htm**. Notice the use of forward slashes instead of backward slashes.

```
$ mcopy mypage.html c:/webstuff/mypag.htm
```

Because of the differences in the way DOS and Linux handle newlines in text files, you should use the **-t** option whenever copying a DOS text file to a Linux partition. The following command copies the **mydoc.txt** file from the **c:/project** directory to the **/newdocs** directory:

```
$ mcopy -t c:/project/mydoc.txt   /newdocs
```

Archive Files and Devices: tar

The tar utility creates archives for files and directories. With tar, you can archive specific files, update them in the archive, and add new files as you want to that archive. You can even archive entire directories with all their files and subdirectories, all of which can be restored from the archive. The tar utility was originally designed to create archives on tapes. The term *tar* stands for tape archive. You can create archives on any device, such as a floppy disk, or you can create an archive file to hold the archive. The tar utility is ideal for making backups of your files or combining several files into a single file for transmission across a network.

On Linux, tar is often used to create archives on devices or files. You can direct tar to archive files to a specific device or a file by using the **f** option with the name of the device or file. The syntax for the **tar** command using the **f** option is shown in the next example. The device or filename is often referred to as the archive name. When creating a file for a tar archive, the filename is usually given the extension **.tar**. This is a convention only, and is not required. You can list as many filenames as you want. If a directory name is specified, then all its subdirectories are included in the archive.

```
$ tar optionsf archive-name.tar directory-and-file-names
```

To create an archive, use the **c** option. Combined with the **f** option, **c** creates an archive on a file or device. You enter this option before and right next to the **f** option. Notice no preceding dash is before a tar option. Table 32-13 lists the different options you can use with tar. In the next example, the directory **mydir** and all its subdirectories are saved in the file **myarch.tar**. In this example, the **mydir** directory holds two files, **mymeeting** and **party**, as well as a directory called **reports** that has three files: **weather**, **monday**, and **friday**.

```
$ tar cvf myarch.tar mydir
mydir/
mydir/reports/
```

```
mydir/reports/weather
mydir/reports/monday
mydir/reports/friday
mydir/mymeeting
mydir/party
```

The user can later extract the directories from the tape using the **x** option. The **xf** option extracts files from an archive file or device. The tar extraction operation

Commands	Execution
tar *options files*	Backs up files to tape, device, or archive file
tar *options*f *archive_name filelist*	Backs up files to a specific file or device specified as *archive_name. filelist*; can be filenames or directories
Options	
c	Creates a new archive
t	Lists the names of files in an archive
r	Appends files to an archive
u	Updates an archive with new and changed files; adds only those files modified since they were archived or files not already present in the archive
--delete	Removes a file from the archive
w	Waits for a confirmation from the user before archiving each file; enables you to update an archive selectively
x	Extracts files from an archive
m	When extracting a file from an archive, no new timestamp is assigned
M	Creates a multiple-volume archive that may be stored on several floppy disks

Table 32-13.   *File Backups:* **tar**

Commands	Execution
f *archive-name*	Saves the tape archive to the file archive name, instead of to the default tape device; when given an archive name, the **f** option saves the **tar** archive in a file of that name
f *device-name*	Saves a **tar** archive to a device such as a floppy disk or tape, **/dev/fd0** is the device name for your floppy disk; the default device is held in **/etc/default/tar-file**
v	Displays each filename as it is archived
z	Compresses or decompresses archived files using **gzip**

Table 32-13.   *File Backups:* **tar**   (continued)

generates all subdirectories. In the next example, the **xf** option directs **tar** to extract all the files and subdirectories from the **tar** file **myarch.tar**.

```
$ tar xvf myarch.tar
mydir/
mydir/reports/
mydir/reports/weather
mydir/reports/monday
mydir/reports/friday
mydir/mymeeting
mydir/party
```

You use the **r** option to add files to an already created archive. The **r** option appends the files to the archive. In the next example, the user appends the files in the **letters** directory to the **myarch.tar** archive. Here the directory **mydocs** and its files are added to the **myarch.tar** archive:

```
$ tar rvf myarch.tar mydocs
mydocs/
mydocs/doc1
```

If you change any of the files in your directories you previously archived, you can use the **u** option to instruct **tar** to update the archive with any modified files. The **tar** command compares the time of the last update for each archived file with those in the user's directory and copies into the archive any files that have been changed since they were last archived. Any newly created files in these directories are also added to the archive. In the next example, the user updates the **myarch.tar** file with any recently modified or newly created files in the **mydir** directory. In this case, the **gifts** file was added to the **mydir** directory.

```
tar uvf myarch.tar mydir
mydir/
mydir/gifts
```

If you need to see what files are stored in an archive, you can use the **tar** command with the **t** option. The next example lists all the files stored in the **myarch.tar** archive:

```
tar tvf myarch.tar
drwxr-xr-x root/root           0 2000-10-24 21:38:18 mydir/
drwxr-xr-x root/root           0 2000-10-24 21:38:51 mydir/reports/
-rw-r--r-- root/root          22 2000-10-24 21:38:40 mydir/reports/weather
-rw-r--r-- root/root          22 2000-10-24 21:38:45 mydir/reports/monday
-rw-r--r-- root/root          22 2000-10-24 21:38:51 mydir/reports/friday
-rw-r--r-- root/root          22 2000-10-24 21:38:18 mydir/mymeeting
-rw-r--r-- root/root          22 2000-10-24 21:36:42 mydir/party
drwxr-xr-x root/root           0 2000-10-24 21:48:45 mydocs/
-rw-r--r-- root/root          22 2000-10-24 21:48:45 mydocs/doc1
drwxr-xr-x root/root           0 2000-10-24 21:54:03 mydir/
-rw-r--r-- root/root          22 2000-10-24 21:54:03 mydir/gifts
```

To back up the files to a specific device, specify the device as the archive. For a floppy disk, you can specify the floppy drive. Be sure to use a blank floppy disk. Any data previously placed on it will be erased by this operation. In the next example, the user creates an archive on the floppy disk in the **/dev/fd0** device and copies into it all the files in the **mydir** directory:

```
$ tar cf /dev/fd0 mydir
```

To extract the backed-up files on the disk in the device, use the **xf** option:

```
$ tar xf /dev/fd0
```

If the files you are archiving take up more space than would be available on a device such as a floppy disk, you can create a **tar** archive that uses multiple labels. The **M** option instructs tar to prompt you for a new storage component when the current one is filled. When archiving to a floppy drive with the **M** option, tar prompts you to put in a new floppy disk when one becomes full. You can then save your tar archive on several floppy disks.

```
$ tar cMf /dev/fd0 mydir
```

To unpack the multiple-disk archive, place the first one in the floppy drive, and then issue the following **tar** command using both the **x** and **M** options. You are then prompted to put in the other floppy disks as they are needed.

```
$ tar xMf /dev/fd0
```

The **tar** operation does not perform compression on archived files. If you want to compress the archived files, you can instruct tar to invoke the **gzip** utility to compress them. With the lowercase **z** option, tar first uses **gzip** to compress files before archiving them. The same **z** option invokes **gzip** to decompress them when extracting files.

```
$ tar czf  myarch.tar.gz mydir
```

Remember, a difference exists between compressing individual files in an archive and compressing the entire archive as a whole. Often, an archive is created for transferring several files at once as one tar file. To shorten transmission time, the archive should be as small as possible. You can use the compression utility **gzip** on the archive tar file to compress it, reducing its size, and then send the compressed version. The person receiving it can decompress it, restoring the tar file. Using **gzip** on a **tar** file often results in a file with the extension **.tar.gz**. The extension **.gz** is added to a compressed **gzip** file. The next example creates a compressed version of **myarch.tar** using the same name with the extension **.gz**:

```
$ gzip myarch.tar
$ ls
$ myarch.tar.gz
```

If you have a default device specified, such as a tape, and you want to create an archive on it, you can simply use **tar** without the **f** option and a device or filename. This can be helpful for making backups of your files. The name of the default device is held in a file called **/etc/default/tar**. The syntax for the **tar** command using the default tape device is shown in the following example. If a directory name is specified, all its subdirectories are included in the archive.

```
$ tar option directory-and-file-names
```

In the next example, the directory **mydir** and all its subdirectories are saved on a tape in the default tape device:

```
$ tar c mydir
```

In this example, the **mydir** directory and all its files and subdirectories are extracted from the default tape device and placed in the user's working directory:

```
$ tar x  mydir
```

Note   *There are other archive programs you can use such as cpio and shar. However, **tar** is the one most commonly used for archiving application software.*

Midnight Commander (Gnome) and konqueror (KDE)

Both file managers in Gnome and the K Desktop have the capability to display the contents of a **tar** archive file automatically. The contents are displayed as though they were files in a directory. You can list the files as icons or with details, sorting them by name, type, or other fields. You can even display the contents of files. Clicking a text file opens it with a text editor and an image is displayed with an image viewer. If the file manager cannot determine what program to use to display the file, it prompts you to select an application. Both file managers can perform the same kind operation on archives residing on remote file systems, such as **tar** archives on FTP sites. You can obtain a listing of their contents and even read their **readme** files. The Midnight Commander file manager (Gnome) can also extract an archive. Right-click the Archive icon and select extract.

Desktop Archivers: guiTAR, Ark, KDAT, and Xtar

Several desktop applications provide a GUI interface for creating and extracting archives. These archivers provide simple methods for managing archives, enabling you to select files and set options easily. The guiTAR archiver is Gnome-based. When creating an archive, you can choose from several compression methods, including **tar**, rar, and zip. You can open an archive with a drag-and-drop operation, dragging an archive file from the file manager window to the guiTAR window (see Figure 32-9). Files listed in an archive can be sorted by different fields by clicking the buttons across the top of the list.

Ark is a K Desktop archiver. To open a new archive, you enter a name with the **.tar.gz** extension. Once an archive is open, you can add to it by dragging files from a file manager window to the Ark window. To extract an archive, first open it, and then select Extract. KDAT is a tape archiver for the K Desktop. You can use it to back up files to a tape drive. You can specify a root directory or create a tape profile listing specific files and directories. The Xtar archiver is an X Window System application that can run on any file manager and provides much the same functionality as the other archivers. Once you select the **tar** archive to open, all the files making up the **tar** archive are then listed in the main window. With Xtar, you have the option of either unpacking the entire **tar** archive or only a few files within it. Options also has a View item for displaying short text files, such as a **readme** file.

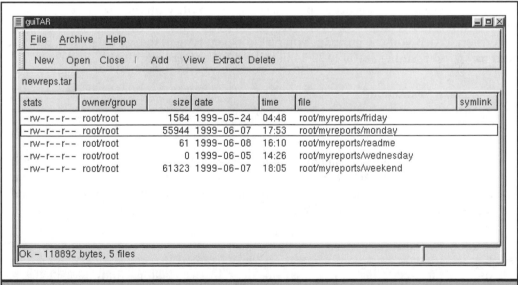

Figure 32-9.   *The guiTAR Gnome archiver*

File Compression: gzip, bzip2, and zip

Several reasons exist for reducing the size of a file. The two most common are to save space or, if you are transferring the file across a network, to save transmission time. You can effectively reduce a file size by creating a compressed copy of it. Anytime you need the file again, you decompress it. Compression is used in combination with archiving to enable you to compress whole directories and their files at once. Decompression generates a copy of the archive file, which can then be extracted, generating a copy of those files and directories.

Several compression utilities are available for use on Linux and UNIX systems. Most software for Linux systems use the GNU **gzip** and **gunzip** utilities. The **gzip** utility compresses files and **gunzip** decompresses them. To compress a file, enter the command **gzip** and the filename. This replaces the file with a compressed version of it, with the extension **.gz**.

```
$ gzip mydata
$ ls
mydata.gz
```

To decompress a **gzip** file, use either **gzip** with the **-d** option or the command **gunzip**. These commands decompress a compressed file with the **.gz** extension and replace it with a decompressed version with the same root name, but without the **.gz** extension. When you use **gunzip**, you needn't even type in the **.gz** extension. **gunzip** and **gzip -d** assumes it. Table 32-14 lists the different **gzip** options.

```
$ gunzip mydata.gz
$ ls
mydata
```

Suppose you want to display or print the contents of a compressed file without first having to decompress it. The command **zcat** generates a decompressed version of a file and sends it to the standard output. You can then redirect this output to a printer or display a utility such as **more**. The original file remains in its compressed state.

```
$ zcat mydata.gz | more
```

You can also compress archived **tar** files. This results in files with the extensions **.tar.gz**. Compressed archived files are often used for transmitting extremely large files across networks.

```
$ gzip myarch.tar
$ ls
myarch.tar.gz
```

Option	Execution
-c	Sends compressed version of file to standard output; each file listed is separately compressed: **gzip -c** mydata preface > myfiles.gz
-d	Decompresses a compressed file; or, you can use gunzip: **gzip -d** myfiles.gz **gunzip** myfiles.gz
-h	Displays help listing.
-l *file-list*	Displays compressed and uncompressed size of each file listed: **gzip -l** myfiles.gz.
-r *directory-name*	Recursively searches for specified directories and compresses all the files in them; the search begins from the current working directory; when used with **gunzip**, compressed files of a specified directory are uncompressed.
-v *file-list*	For each compressed or decompressed file, displays its name and the percentage of its reduction in size.
-num	Determines the speed and size of the compression; the range is from −1 to −9. A lower number gives greater speed but less compression, resulting in a larger file that compresses and decompresses quickly; −1 gives the quickest compression, but with the largest size; −9 results in a very small file that takes longer to compress and decompress. The default is −6.

Table 32-14. *The* `gzip` *Options*

You can compress **tar** file members individually using the **tar z** option that invokes **gzip**. With the **z** option, **tar** invokes **gzip** to compress a file before placing it in an archive. Archives with members compressed with the **z** option, however, can neither be updated nor is it possible to add to them. All members must be compressed and all must be added at the same time.

You can also use the **compress** and **uncompress** commands to create compressed files. They generate a file that has a **.Z** extension and use a different compression format than **gzip**. The **compress** and **uncompress** commands are not that widely used, but you may run across **.Z** files occasionally. You can use the **uncompress** command to decompress a **.Z** file. The **gzip** utility is the standard GNU compression utility and should be used instead of **compress**.

Another popular compression utility is **bzip2**. It compresses files using the Burrows-Wheeler block-sorting text compression algorithm and Huffman coding. The command line options are similar to **gzip** by design, but they are not exactly the same. See the **bzip2** Man page for a complete listing. You compress files using the **bzip2** command and decompress with **bunzip2**. The **bzip2** command creates files with the extension **.bz2**. You can use **bzcat** to output compressed data to the standard output. The **bzip2** command compresses files in block and enables you to specify their size (larger blocks give you greater compression). Like **gzip**, you can use **bzip2** to compress **tar** archive files. The following example compresses the **mydata** file into a **bzip** compressed file with the extension **.bz2**:

```
$ bzip2 mydata
$ ls
mydata.bz2
```

To decompress, use the **bunzip2** command on a **bzip** file.

```
$ bunzip2 mydata.bz2
```

zip is a compression and archive utility modeled on **pkzip**, which was used originally on DOS systems. **zip** is a cross-platform utility used on Windows, Mac, MSDOS, OS/2, UNIX, and Linux systems. **zip** commands can work with archives created by PKZIP and PKZIP programs and can use Zip archives. You compress a file using the **zip** command. This creates a Zip file with the **.zip** extension. If no files are listed, **zip** outputs the compressed data to the standard output. You can also use the **–** argument to have **zip** read from the standard input. To compress a directory, you include the **-r** option. The first example archives and compresses a file:

```
$ zip mydata
$ ls
mydata.zip
```

The next example archives and compresses the **reports** directory:

```
$ zip -r reports
```

A full set of archive operations is supported. With the **-f** option, you can update a particular file in the zip archive with a newer version. The **-u** option replaces or adds files, and the **-d** option deletes files from the zip archive. Options also exist for encrypting files, and DOS to UNIX end-of-line translations, and including hidden files. To decompress and extract the Zip file, you use the **unzip** command.

```
$ unzip mydata.zip
```

Chapter 33

Devices

ll devices, such as printers, terminals, and CD-ROMs, are connected to your Linux operating system through special files called *device files.* Such a file contains all the information your operating system needs to control the specified device. This design introduces great flexibility. The operating system is independent of the specific details for managing a particular device; the specifics are all handled by the device file. The operating system simply informs the device what task it is to perform, and the device file tells it how. If you change devices, you only have to change the device file, not the whole system.

To install a device on your Linux system, you need a device file for it, software configuration such as provided by a configuration tool, and kernel support, usually supplied by a module or already built into the kernel. A extensive number of device files are already set up for different kinds of devices. You usually only need to choose one of these. For kernel support, you may have to load a kernel module or recompile the kernel, both simple procedures. In most cases, support is already built into the kernel. Configuration of your device may be provided by desktop configuration tools such as the Gnome Control Center, system configuration tools such as Linuxconf, or a module configuration interface such as that provided for sound modules.

Device Files

The name of a device file is designed to reflect the task of the device. Printer device files begin with **lp** for "line print." Because you could have more than one printer connected to your system, the particular printer device files are distinguished by two or more numbers or letters following the prefix **lp**, such as **lp0**, **lp1**, **lp2**. The same is true for terminal device files. They begin with the prefix **tty**, for "teletype," and are further distinguished by numbers or letters such as **tty0**, **tty1**, **ttyS0**, and so on. You can obtain a complete listing of the current device filenames and the devices for which they are used from the **kernel.org** Web site at

```
http://www.kernel.org/pub/linux/docs/device-list/devices.txt
```

All of these filenames will be implemented as device files in your **/dev** directory. Here you can find printer, CD-ROM, hard drive, SCSI, and sound device files, along with many others. Certain link files bear common device names that are often linked to the actual device file used. For example, a **/dev/cdrom** symbolic link links to the actual device used for your CD-ROM. If your CD-ROM is an IDE device, it may use the device file **hdc**. In this case, **/dev/cdrom** would be a link to **/dev/hdc**. In effect, **/dev/cdrom** is another name for **/dev/hdc**. You can use **/dev/cdrom** to reference your CD-ROM's device file, instead of **/dev/hdc**. A **/dev/modem** link file also exists for your modem. If your modem is connected to the second serial port, its device file would be **/dev/ttyS1**. In this case, **/dev/modem** would be a link to that device file. Applications can then use **/dev/modem** to access your modem, instead of having to know the actual device file used. A listing of commonly used device links is shown in Table 33-1.

Link	Description
/dev/mouse	Current mouse device
/dev/tape	Current tape device
/dev/cdrom	Current CD-ROM device
/dev/cdwriter	Current CD-writer device
/dev/scanner	Current scanner device
/dev/modem	Current dial-out device, modem port
/dev/root	Current root file system
/dev/swap	Current swap device

Table 33-1.   *Device Links*

Two types of devices are in Linux: block and character. A *block device,* such as a hard disk, transmits data a block at a time. A *character device,* such as a printer or modem, transmits data one character at a time, or rather as a continuous stream of data, not as separate blocks. Device driver files for character devices have a *c* as the first character in the permissions segment displayed by the **ls** command. Device driver files for block devices have a *b.* In the next example, **lp0** (the printer) is a character device and **hda1** (the hard disk) is a block device.

```
# ls -l hda1 lp0
brw-rw----   1 root      disk      3,   1 Sep  7  1994 hda1
crw-r-----   1 root      daemon    6,   0 Dec 31  1979 lp0
```

Although most distributions include an extensive set of device files already set up for you, you can create your own. You use the **mknod** command to create a device file, either a character or block type. The **mknod** command has the following syntax:

mknod *options device device-type major-num minor-num*

The device type can be either *b, c, p,* or *u.* As already mentioned, the *b* indicates a block device, and *c* is for a character device. The *u* is for an unbuffered character device, and the *p* is for a FIFO device. Devices of the same type often have the same name, for example, serial interfaces all have the name *ttyS.* Devices of the same type are then uniquely identified by a number attached to the name. This number has two components: the major number and the minor number. Devices may further have the same major number, but if so, the minor number is always different. This major and minor structure is designed to deal with situations in which several devices may be dependent on one larger device, such as several modems connected to the same I/O card. All would have the same major number that would reference the card, but each modem would have a unique minor number. Both the minor and major numbers are required for block and character devices (*b*, *c*, and *u*). They are not used for FIFO devices, however.

For example, Linux systems usually provide device files for three parallel ports (lp0–2). If you need more, you can use the **mknod** command to create a new one. Printer devices are character devices and must be owned by the root and daemon. The permissions for printer devices are read and write for the owner and the group, 660 (see Chapter 12 for a discussion of file permissions). The major device number is set to 6, while the minor device number is set to the port number of the printer, such as 0 for LPT1 and 1 for LPT2. Once the device is created, you use **chown** to change its ownership to **root.daemon**. In the next example, a parallel printer device is made on a fourth parallel port, **/dev/lp3**. The **–m** option specifies the permissions, in this case, 660. The device is a character device, as indicated by the *c* argument following the device name. The major number is 6, and the minor number is 3. If you were making a device at **/dev/lp4**, the major number would still be 6, but the minor number would be 4. Once the device is made, the **chown** command then changes the ownership of the parallel printer device to **root.daemon**. Be sure to check if a spool directory has been created for your device. If not, you need to make one.

```
# mknod -m 660 /dev/lp3 c 6 3
# chown root.daemon /dev/lp3
```

Valid device names along with their major and minor numbers are listed in the **devices.txt file** located in the documentation directory for the kernel source code, **/usr/src/linux**. When creating a device, you use the major and minor numbers as well as the device name prefix for the particular kind of device you are creating. Most of these devices are already created for you and are listed in the **/etc/dev** directory.

Device Information: /proc

The **/proc** filesystem (see Chapter 32) maintains special information files for your devices. The **/proc/devices** file lists all your installed character and block devices along with their major numbers. IRQs, DMAs, and I/O ports currently used for devices are listed in the **interrupts**, **dma**, and **ioports** files respectively. Certain files list information covering several devices, such as **pci**, which lists all your PCI devices, and **sound**, which lists all your sound devices. The sound file will list detailed information about your sound card. Several subdirectories, such as **net**, **ide**, and **scsi**, contain information files for different devices. Table 33-2 lists several device-related **/proc** files (Chapter 32 details other entries).

File	Description
/proc/devices	List of the device drivers for configured for the currently running kernel
/proc/dma	Displays the DMA channels currently used
/proc/interrupts	Displays the IRQs (interrupts) in use
/proc/ioports	Shows the I/O ports in use
/proc/pci	Lists PCI devices
/proc/sound	Lists sound devices
/proc/scsi	Directory for SCSI devices
/proc/ide	Directory for IDE devices
/proc/net	Directory for network devices

Table 33-2.   */proc Device Information Files*

Installing and Managing Printers

Setting up a printer interface is fairly simple: determine which device file to use and place printer configuration entries in your **printcap** file. You may also have to set up printing filters. You can use several configuration tools to enable you to set up and configure your printer easily. Red Hat systems provide the PrintTool utility.

Most distributions of Linux create three device names for parallel printers automatically during installation: **lp0**, **lp1**, and **lp2**. (Most systems currently use **lp0**.) The number used in these names corresponds to a parallel port on your PC. **lp0** references the LPT1 parallel port usually located at address 0x03bc, **lp1** references the LPT2 parallel port located at 0x0378, and **lp2** references LPT3 at address 0x0278. If you are unsure at what address your parallel port is located, you can use the **msd.exe** command on your DOS system to find it. **lp0** connects to an XT bus, and **lp1** connects to an AT bus. For a detailed explanation of printer installation, see the **Printing-HOWTO** file in **/usr/doc/HOWTO**.

The Red Hat Print Manager: PrintTool

The PrintTool utility provided on Red Hat distributions is an easy interface for setting up and managing your printers. Using only PrintTool, you can easily install a printer on your Linux system. You can start PrintTool either by selecting its entry in the System menu or by clicking its icon in the Red Hat Control Panel. In the PrintTool window, select the Add button. This opens an Edit window that displays several fields in which you enter printer configuration information. In the Names field, enter the names you want to use for the printer (see Figure 33-1). Each name is separated by a |. You should include lp as one of your names. The **lpr** command used without a specified printer name uses the printer named **lp** (actually the first entry in the **/etc/printcap** file). In the Spool directory fields, the default spool directory is already entered for you. You can change it to another directory if you want. For the Device field, entering **/dev/lp0** is customary. This is the parallel printer device for computers that use an AT bus, which most computers today use. If you have a serial device, you must use a different device name.

For the Input Filter, you can click Select to display the Configure Filter window (see Figure 33-2). The left pane of this window is a listing of different printer types. Scroll through the list and select your printer. On the right side of the window are panes for different printer configurations, labeled Printer Driver Description, Resolution, Color Depth, Printing Options, and Margins. You can select a particular resolution for your printer, set the margins, and choose the printing speed. When you finish, click OK to close the window. You then see your printer listed in the PrintTool window, as shown in Figure 33-2. Choose the Quit item from the PrintTool menu to quit PrintTool. You are now ready to print. For a detailed explanation of printer installation, see the **Printing-HOWTO** file in **/usr/doc/HOWTO**.

Figure 33-1. *PrintTool*

ADMINISTRATION

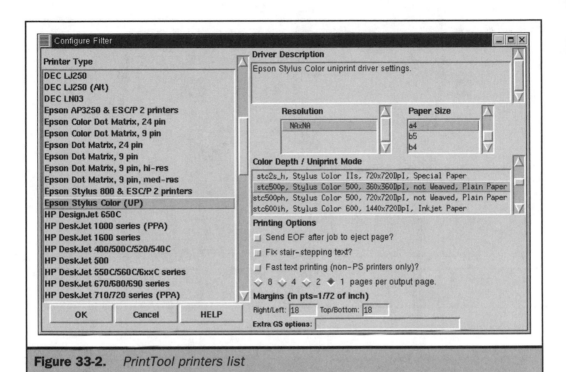

Figure 33-2. *PrintTool printers list*

Setting Up Printers with Linuxconf

To set up a printer using Linuxconf, select Add/Edit printers under the Miscellaneous services/Printer menu in the Config panel (be sure you are using the full version of Linuxconf). This opens a Printer Setup panel listing all the printers installed on your system. Click the Add button to open an Adding a printer panel where you can enter the printer name and specify whether it is a local or remote printer (see Figure 33-3).

Once the printer is added, you can then double-click its entry in the Printer Setup panel to open a Printer Properties panel with panels for General, Printertype, and Filter options. In the Printertype panel, you select the device file to use for this printer, such as /dev/lp0. In the Filter options panel, you can choose options such as resolution, paper size, and color depth (see Figure 33-4). To select your printer type, click the Filter button to open a listing of printers to choose from.

Setting Up Printers with Webmin

To manage printers with Webmin, you select Printer Administration from the Hardware panel. To add a printer, click the Add a new printer link on the Printer Administration page to display the Create Printer page. Here you can enter the printer name and description as well as enable the printer and specify the port. For a local printer, you can then select the appropriate driver (see Figure 33-5).

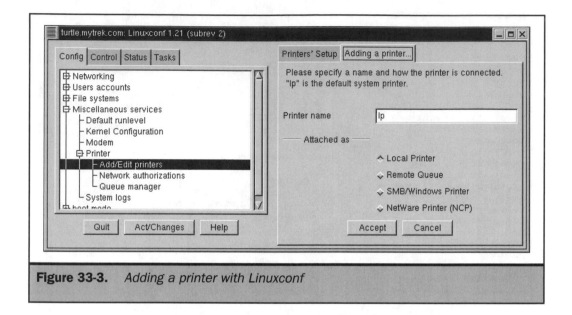

Figure 33-3. *Adding a printer with Linuxconf*

Figure 33-4. *Linuxconf Printer Properties*

Figure 33-5. *Webmin Create Printer*

Setting Up Printers with COAS

On OpenLinux, you use COAS or LISA to configure printers. For COAS, select Printer Administration from the Peripherals Administration menu. This opens a Printer Attributes window with boxes for entering printer information such as device, speed, and type. Many of the boxes have drop-down menus from which you can select entries. The Type drop-down list will list all the supported printers. The list for Device will list the currently available devices. You can also select features such as resolution, paper size, and speed.

Printer Devices and /etc/printcap

When your system prints a file, it makes use of special directories called *spool directories.* A print job is a file to be printed. When you print a file to a printer, a copy of it is made and placed in a spool directory set up for that printer. The location of the spool directory is obtained from the printer's entry in the **/etc/printcap** file. In the spool directory, two files are made for each print job. One file, which begins with **df,** is the data file containing the copy of the file to be printed. The other file begins with **cf** and is the control file for the print job. This second file contains information about the print job, such as the user to whom it belongs.

The **/etc/printcap** file holds entries for each printer connected to your system. A *printcap entry* holds information, such as the pathname for a printer's spool directory and the device name of the printer port the printer uses. The first field in a printcap entry is a list of possible names for the printer. These are names you can make up yourself, and you can add others if you want. Each name is separated by a |. You use these names to identify the printer when entering various printer commands or options, such as the **-P** option. These names are also used for special shell variables, such as the **PRINTER** variable, used in many initialization scripts.

The fields following the list of names set different fields for your printer. The fields have two-letter names and are usually assigned a value using **=**. These assignments are separated by colons. Three of the more important fields are **lp**, **sd**, and **of**. The **lp** field is set to the device name the printer uses. The **sd** field is set to the pathname of the spool directory, and **of** is set to the particular filter used for this printer. Some have Boolean values and simply list the field name with no assignment for a true value. You can find a complete listing of the printcap fields in the **printcap** man pages: **man 8 printcap**. An example of a printcap entry follows.

```
##PRINTTOOL## LOCAL djet500c 600x600 letter {}
 hp1|lp:\
    :sd=/var/spool/lpd/lp:\
    :mx#0:\
    :lp=/dev/lp1:\
    :if=/var/spool/lpd/lp/filter:
```

Instead of making your own entries in the **/etc/printcap** file, you can use a printer configuration tool such as the PrintTool utility, Linuxconf, or COAS to make them for you automatically.

Printing on your system is handled by a print daemon called **lpd**, which is constantly running, waiting for print jobs, and then managing their printing procedures. The **lpd** daemon takes its print jobs from a print queue, which you can list using the **lpq** command. The **lpq** command places a job on the print queue, and **lpq** then takes it in turn and prints it. **lpq** takes as its argument the name of a file. You can also feed data to **lpq** through the standard input, piping in the data to be printed from another operation. The **-P** option enables you to specify a particular printer. In the next example, the user first prints the file **preface**. Then she uses the **cat** command to generate combined output of the files **intro** and **digest**. This is piped to the **lpq** command, which then prints it. Finally, the user prints the file **report** to the printer with the name **hp1**.

```
$ lpr preface
$ cat intro digest | lpr
$ lpr -Php1 report
```

You can also print directly to the printer by simply redirecting output to the printer's device file. This does not place anything on the print queue. The print operation becomes a command to be immediately executed. However, your system is occupied until the file completes printing. The following example uses this technique to print the **report** file to a printer connected to device **lp1**.

```
$ cat report > /dev/lp1
```

Remote Printers

To install a remote (network or remote host–attached) printer, you place remote entries for the printer host and device in the printer's **/etc/printcap** file entry. An **:rm** entry identifies the remote host that controls the remote printer, and an :rp entry specifies the device name of the remote printer. In the following example, the remote printer is located at **rabbit.mytrek.com** and is called **lp1**.

```
:rm=rabbit.mytrek.com
:rp=lp1
```

You can also use PrintTool to set up a remote printer (see Figure 33-6). When you add a printer, you are presented with a dialog box listing several types of printers: Local, Remote UNIX Queue, SMB, and NetWare. For a remote printer, select Remote Queue. This displays a dialog box for configuring the remote printer with entries for the Remote Host and the Remote Queue. For the Remote Host, enter the host name for the system that controls the printer. For the Remote Queue, enter the device name on that host for the printer.

On Linuxconf, you can also set up a remote printer. When adding a printer, you determine if it is a local, remote, SMB/Windows, or NetWare printer (see Figure 33-3).

Figure 33-6. *PrintTool remote printer configuration*

When you open the Printer properties panel for that printer, the Printertypes options panel will display entry boxes where you can enter the remote host and the remote queue for that printer.

The Linux system controlling the printer should, in turn, list the hosts permitted access to its printer in the **/etc/hosts.lpd** file. For example, the **/etc/hosts.lpd** file on **rabbit.mytrek.com** should hold the host name **turtle.mytrek.com** to enable users on **turtle.mytrek.com** to use its printer. If you want to provide access by remote hosts to your local printer, you can enter that host's name in your own **/etc/hosts.lpd** file. You can also use Linuxconf to list them in the Allowed hostnames panel in the Network authorizations entry under Printer.

An SMB remote printer is one located on a Windows network. To access an SMB remote printer, you need to install Samba and have the Server Message Block services enabled using the smbd daemon. Printer sharing must, in turn, be enabled on the Windows network. In the PrintTool SMB configuration dialog box, you need to enter the remote system's name, its IP address, the name of the printer, and the printer user name and password. You can then use the **smbclient** (Samba) command to send print jobs to the Window printer.

The Print Queue

To manage the printing jobs on your printer or printers, you can use either Linuxconf or the **lpc** command. With Linuxconf, select the Queue manager entry under Printer in the Config panel. Then select the printer whose queue you want to manage. This opens a list of buttons for actions such as enabling or stopping the queue (see Figure 33-7). Click the List jobs button to list all print jobs currently in that printer's queue.

To use **lpc**, enter the command **lpc** at the shell prompt. You are then given an LPC> prompt at which you can enter **lpc** commands to manage your printers and their jobs. The status command with the name of the printer displays whether the printer is ready, how many print jobs it has, and so on. The **stop** and **start** commands can stop a printer and start it back up.

```
# lpc
lpc> status hp1
hp1|lp1:
    queuing is enabled
    printing is enabled
    1 entry in spool area
```

You can manage the print queue using the **lpq** and **lprm** commands. The **lpq** command lists the printing jobs currently on the print queue. With the **-P** option and the printer name, you can list the jobs for a particular printer. If you specify a user name, you can list the print jobs for that user. With the **-l** option, **lpq** displays detailed information about each job. If you want information on a specific job, simply use that job's ID number with **lpq**.

Figure 33-7.   *Managing a printer queue with Linuxconf*

With the **lprm** command, you can remove a printing job from the queue, erasing the job before it can be printed. The **lprm** command takes many of the same options as **lpq**. To remove a specific job, use **lprm** with the job number. To remove all printing jobs for a particular user, enter **lprm** with the user name. To remove all printing jobs for a particular printer, use the **-P** option with the printer name.

The **lprm** command has a special argument indicated by a dash, **-**, that references all print jobs for the user who issues the command. For example, to remove all your own print jobs, enter **lprm -**. If you logged in as the root user, then **lprm -** removes all print jobs for all printers and users from the print queue, emptying it completely.

You should not use **lprm** to kill a printing job that has already started printing. Instead, you may have to use the **kill** command on the print job process. You can display processes using the **ps -ax** command, and then use **kill** and the number of the process to end it. For a job that is already printing, you see a process for its filter. This is the process to kill. If the process does not end, you can force its termination by using the **-s** option and the kill signal number, 9.

Table 33-3 shows various printer commands; Table 33-4 includes **lpc** commands.

Printer Management	Description
lpr *options file-list*	Prints a file; copies the file to the printer's spool directory, and places it on the print queue to be printed in turn. **-P***printer* Prints the file on the specified printer
lpq *options*	Displays the print jobs in the print queue **-P***printer* Prints queue for the specified printer **-l** Prints a detailed listing
lprm *options Printjob-id* or *User-id*	Removes a print job from the print queue; you identify a particular print job by its number as listed by **lpq**; if you use *User-id*, it removes all print jobs for that user **-** Refers to all print jobs for the logged-in user; if the logged-in user is the root, it refers to all print jobs **-P***printer* Removes all print jobs for the specified printer
lpc	Manages your printers; at the **LPC>** prompt, you can enter commands to check the status of your printers and take other actions

Table 33-3.   *Printer Commands*

Command	Operation
help [*command ...*]	Prints a short description of each command
abort *printers*	Terminates an active spooling daemon on the local host immediately, and then disables printing for the specified printers; use **all** to indicate all printers
clean *printers*	Removes any temporary files, data files, and control files that cannot be printed
disable *printers*	Turns the specified printer queues off; new jobs are not accepted

Table 33-4.   *lpc Commands*

Command	Operation
down *printers message*	Turns the specified printer queue off, disables printing, and puts *message* in the printer status file
enable *printers*	Enables spooling for the listed printers; allows new jobs into the spool queue
quit or **exit**	Exits from **lpc**
restart *printers*	Starts a new printer daemon; used if the printer daemon, **lpd**, dies, leaving jobs yet to be printed
start *printers*	Enables printing and starts a spooling daemon for the listed printers
status *printers*	Displays the status of daemons and queues on the local machine
stop *printers*	Stops a spooling daemon after the current job completes and disables printing
topq *printer* [*jobnum* ...] [*user* ...]	Places the jobs in the order listed at the top of the printer queue
up *printers*	Enables everything and starts a new printer daemon; undoes the effects of **down**

Table 33-4. *lpc Commands* (continued)

Installing and Managing Terminals and Modems

With a multiuser system such as Linux, you might have several users logged in at the same time. Each user would, of course, need his or her own terminal through which to access the Linux system. The monitor on your PC acts as a special terminal called the *console*, but you can add other terminals either through the serial ports on your PC or a special multiport card installed on your PC. The other terminals can be standalone terminals or PCs using terminal emulation programs. For a detailed explanation of terminal installation, see the **Term-HOWTO** file in **/usr/doc/HOWTO**. A brief explanation is provided here.

The serial ports on your PC are referred to as COM1, on up to COM4. These serial ports correspond to the terminal devices **/dev/ttyS0** through **/dev/ttyS3**. Note, several of these serial devices may already be used for other input devices, such as your mouse, and for communications devices, such as your modem. If you have a serial printer, one of these serial devices is already used for that. If you installed a multiport card, you have many more ports from which to choose. For each terminal you add, you must create a character device on your Linux system. As with printers, you use the **mknod** command to create terminal devices. The permissions for a terminal device are 660. *Terminal devices* are character devices with a major number of 4 and minor numbers usually beginning at 64.

Terminal devices are managed by your system using the getty program and a set of configuration files. When your system starts, it reads a list of connected terminals in the **inittab** file and then executes an **/etc/getty** program for each one. The getty program sets up the communication between your Linux system and a specified terminal. It obtains from the **/etc/gettydefs** file certain parameters, such as speed and the login prompt, as well as any special instructions.

```
# Format: <speed># <init flags> # <final flags> #<login
    string>#<next-speed>
# 38400 fixed baud Dumb Terminal entry
DT38400# B38400 CS8 CLOCAL # B38400 SANE -ISTRIP CLOCAL #@S login:
    #DT38400
```

The **/etc/inittab** file holds instructions for your system on how to manage terminal devices. A line in the **/etc/inittab** file has four basic components: an ID, a runlevel, an action, and a process. Terminal devices are identified by ID numbers, beginning with 1 for the first device. The runlevel at which the terminal operates is usually 1. The action is usually *respawn,* which says to run the process continually. The process is a call to **/etc/getty** with the baud rate and terminal device name. The **/etc/ttys** file associates the type of terminal used with a certain device.

The **/etc/termcap** file holds the specifications for different terminal types. These are the different types of terminals users could use to log into your system. Your **/etc/termcap** file is already filled with specifications for most of the terminals currently produced. An entry in the **/etc/termcap** file consists of various names that can be used for a terminal separated by a | , and then a series of parameter specifications, each ending in a colon. You find the name used for a specific terminal type here. You can use more to display your **/etc/termcap** file, and then use a search, /, to locate your terminal type. You can set many options for a terminal device. To change these options, use the **stty** command instead of changing configuration files directly. The **stty** command with no arguments lists the current setting of the terminal.

When a user logs in, having the terminal device initialized using the **tset** command is helpful. Usually the **tset** command is placed in the user's **.bash_profile** file and is automatically executed whenever the user logs into the system. You use the **tset** command to set the terminal type and any other options the terminal device requires. A common entry of **tset** for a **.bash_profile** file follows. The **-m dialup:** option prompts the user to enter a terminal type. The type specified here is a default type that is displayed in parentheses. The user presses ENTER to choose the default. The prompt looks like this: TERM=(vt100)?

```
eval 'tset -s -Q -m dialup:?vt00'
```

Input Devices

Input devices, such as mice and keyboards, are displayed on several levels. Initial configuration is performed during installation where you select the mouse and keyboard types. You can change that configuration with your administration configuration tool, such as Red Hat Setup (see Chapter 30). Red Hat provides a keyboard configuration tool called **kbdconfig** and a mouse configuration tool called **mouseconfig**. Both can be run from any command line interface. Special configurations also exist for mice and keyboard for the X Window System, and for the KDE and Gnome desktops. You select the keyboard layout and language, as well as configure the speed and display of the mouse.

Installing Sound, Network, and Other Cards

For you to install a new card, your kernel must be configured to support it. Support for most cards is provided in the form of modules that can be dynamically loaded in and attached to the kernel, running as its extension. Installing support for a card is usually a simple matter of loading a module that includes the drives for it. For example, drivers for the Sound Blaster sound card are in the module **sb.o**. Loading this module makes your sound card accessible to Linux. Most distributions automatically detect the cards installed on your system and load the needed modules. If you change cards, you may have to load the module you need manually, removing an older conflicting one. For example, if you change your Ethernet card, you may have to unload the module for your previous card and load in the one for your new card. Certain utilities, such as **Linuxconf** and **netcfg,** enable you to choose a new Ethernet card and have the module loaded for you. You can, however, load modules manually. The section "Modules" later in this chapter describes this process. Device files for most cards are already set up for you in the **/dev** directory. For example, the device name for your sound card is **/dev/audio**.

Multimedia Devices: Sound, Video, and DVD

Currently, most Linux sound drivers are developed as part of the Open Sound System and freely distributed as OSS/Free. These are installed as part of Linux distributions. The OSS device drivers are intended to provide a uniform API for all Unix platforms, including Linux. They support Sound Blaster– and Windows Sound System–compatible sound cards (ISA and PCI). OSS is a commercial version called the *Open Sound System* (*OSS*). OSS is also available for a nominal fee and features configuration interfaces for device setup. A listing of the different OSS/Free sound devices is provided in Table 33-5. On Red Hat, you can use the **sndconfig** utility to install most sound cards on Linux. Some sound cards may require more specialized support (see Table 33-6). For sound cards, you can tell what your current sound configuration is by listing the contents of the **/dev/sndstat** file. You can test your card by simply redirecting a sound file to it, as shown here:

```
cat sample.au  >  /dev/audio.
```

The Linux *Musical Instrument Digital Interface* (*MIDI*) and Sound Pages currently at **www.xdt.com/ar/linux-snd** hold links to Web and FTP sites for Linux sound drivers for various sound cards. They also include links to sites for Linux MIDI and sound software. Currently, most Linux sound drivers have been developed as part of the Open Sound System and are freely distributed as OSS/Free. These are installed as part of most Linux distributions. The OSS device drivers are intended to provide a uniform API for all Unix platforms, including Linux. They support Sound Blaster– and Windows Sound System–compatible sound cards (ISA and PCI).

The *Advanced Linux Sound Architecture* (*ALSA*) project is developing a modular sound driver, API, and configuration manager that aims to be a better alternative to OSS, while maintaining compatibility with it. ALSA is a GNU project and is entirely free; its Web site at **www.alsa-project.org** contains extensive documentation, applications, and drivers. Currently under development are the ALSA sound driver,

Device	Description
/dev/sndstat	Sound driver status
/dev/audio	Audio output device
/dev/dsp	Sound sampling device
/dev/mixer	Control mixer on sound card
/dev/music	High-level sequencer
/dev/sequencer	Low-level sequencer
/dev/midi	Direct MIDI port

Table 33-5. *Sound Devices*

Driver Site	Description
Linux MIDI and Sound Pages	Information and links to Linux Sound projects and site: **www.xdt.com/ar/linux-snd**
Advanced Linux Sound Architecture (ALSA)	The Advanced Linux Sound Architecture project (ALSA) is developed on Linux under the GPL: **www.alsa-project.org**
Open Sound System/Free	The standard Linux sound drivers formerly known as USS/Lite, TASD, and Voxware are now called OSS/Free: **www.opensound.com**
Open Sound System/Linux	OSS/Linux is a commercial version of the Linux sound drivers: **www.opensound.com**
Linux Ultra Sound Project	Drivers for the Gravis Ultrasound: **www.perex.cz/~perex/ultra**
PC Serial Port MIDI Driver	Linux MIDI driver for IBM-PC serial ports: **http://crystal.apana.org.au/ghansper/midiaxis.html**

Table 33-6.   *Linux Sound Driver Sites*

the ALSA Kernel API, the ALSA library to support application development, and the ALSA manager to provide a configuration interface for the driver. ALSA evolved from the Linux Ultra Sound Project.

The Linux Ultra Sound Project has developed drivers for Gravix Ultrasound sound cards. Although Gravis Ultrasound is supported by OSS/Free, the Linux Ultra Sound Project drivers offer many more features. See Table 33-6 for a listing of sites providing sound drivers. Included are drivers for Turtle Beach sound cards and Sound Blaster AWE native support.

Several projects are underway to provide TV, Video, and DVD support for Linux (see Table 33-7). The site **linuxtv.org** provides detailed links to DVD, Digital TV (DVD), and Analog TV Linux projects. Several projects have already developed applications. The Video 4 Linux project has created the Video4Linux software package, which enables you to play Mpeg1 video sources on Linux. Video4Linux is included with

Device Name	Type of Device
/dev/video	Video capture interface
/dev/vfx	Video effects interface
/dev/codec	Video codec interface
/dev/vout	Video output interface
/dev/radio	AM/FM radio devices
/dev/vtx	Teletext interface chips
/dev/vbi	Data services interface

Table 33-7. *Video Devices (V4L and V4L2)*

Linux distributions. Currently under development is Video for Linux Two (V4L2). This is a separate project that established a set of APIs and standards for handling video devices on Linux, providing a common API for video and tuning sources, teletext, and other TV-related VBI data. V4L2 includes a suite of related driver specifications for different types of video devices and video-related data. It is intended as a replacement for Video for Linux.

Drivers for DVD and TV decoders are also under development (see Table 33-8). mga4linux is developing video support for the Matrox Multimedia cards like the Marvel G200. The *General ATI TV and Overlay Software* (*GATOS*) is developing drivers for the currently unsupported features of ATI video cards, specifically TV features. The BTTV Driver Project has developed drivers for the Booktree video chip. Creative Labs sponsors Linux drivers for the Creative line of DVD DXR2 decoders (**opensource.creative.com**).

Project	Description
linuxtv.org	Links to Video, TV, and DVD sites
video4linux	Video for Linux
video4linux 2	Video for Linux Two
LiViD	The Linux Video and DVD Project **www.linuxvideo.org**

Table 33-8. *Video, TV, and DVD Projects and Drivers*

Project	Description
LinuxDVD	The LinuxDVD Project **linuxdvd.corepower.com**
LSDVD	LSDVD Linux Player Project **www.csh.rit.edu/projects/lsdvd/**
mga4linux	Driver for Matrox Multimedia Cards **www.cs.brandeis.edu/~eddie/mga4linux/**
GATOS	The Gneral ATI TV and Overlay Software **www.core.binghamton.edu/~insomnia/gatos**
BTTV	BTTV Driver Project for cards with Booktree video chips
DVD DXR2	Drivers for Creative DVD DXR2 decoders **opensource.creative.com**.

Table 33-8. *Video, TV, and DVD Projects and Drivers* (continued)

Modules

Beginning with Linux kernel 2.0, the Linux kernel adopted a modular structure. In earlier kernel versions, support for specific features and devices had to be included directly into the kernel program. Adding support for a new device, say, a new kind of sound card, required you to create a new version of your kernel program that included the code for supporting that device. This involved a sometimes lengthy configuration, followed by compiling and installing the new kernel program, as well as making sure it was called properly when your system booted up.

As an alternative to this rebuilding of the kernel, Linux now supports the use of modules. *Modules* are components of the Linux kernel that can be loaded and attached to it as needed. To add support for a new device, you can now simply instruct a kernel to load its module. In some cases, you may have to recompile only that module to provide support for your device. The use of modules has the added advantage of reducing the size of the kernel program. The kernel can load modules in memory only as they are needed. For example, the module for the PPP network interface used for a modem only needs to be used when you connect to an ISP.

The modules your system needs are usually determined during installation, based on the kind of configuration information you provided. For example, if your system uses an Ethernet card whose type you specified during installation, then the system loads the module for that card. You can, however, manually control what modules are to be loaded for your system. This, in effect, enables you to customize your kernel whatever way you want. You can use several commands, configuration tools, and daemons to manage kernel modules. The 2.2 Linux kernel includes the Kernel Module Loader, which has the capability to load modules automatically as they are needed. In addition, several tools enable you to load and unload modules manually, if you must. Red Hat provides a user interface called **kernelcfg** that enables you to load and unload modules manually. The Kernel Module Loader uses certain kernel commands to perform the task of loading or unloading modules. The **modprobe** command is a general-purpose command that calls **insmod** to load modules and **rmmod** to unload them. These commands are listed in Table 33-9.

The filename for a module has the extension **.o**. Modules reside in the **/lib/modules/**_version_ directory, where _version_ is the version number for your current module. The directory for the 2.2 kernel is **/lib/modules/2.2.16-17**. As you install new kernels on your system, new module directories are generated for them. One trick to access the directory for the current kernel is to use the **uname -r** command to generate the kernel version number. This command needs to have backquotes.

```
cd /lib/modules/`uname -r`
```

In this directory, several subdirectories are where the modules reside. These subdirectories serve to categorize your modules, making them easier to locate. For example, the **net** directory holds modules for your Ethernet cards, and the **misc** directory contains sound card modules.

Command	Description
lsmod	Lists modules currently loaded
insmod	Loads a module into the kernel
rmmod	Unloads a module currently loaded
depmod	Creates a dependency file listing all other modules on which the specified module may rely
modprobe	Loads a module with any dependent modules it may also need. Uses the file of dependency listings generated by **depmod**

Table 33-9.   *Kernel Module Commands*

Managing Modules with Red Hat Kernel Configurator

The Red Hat Kernel Configurator utility (kernelcfg) shown in Figure 33-8 provides an X interface for loading and unloading modules. The Kernel Configurator uses the Kernel Module Loader capability of the kernel (incorporated with 2.2 kernel) to load modules. The Kernel Configurator window lists all the modules currently loaded. Each entry has three fields: its type, its module name, and its arguments. For example, the module 3c59x, which provides support for 3c59x 3Com Ethernet cards, has the type eth0 (the Ethernet interface), 3c59x (its name), and no arguments. You can add new entries by clicking Add. A window opens where you can enter the module type, the name, and any arguments. A new entry is not immediately loaded to the kernel. Entries are saved to the **/etc/modules.conf** file. To load the new entry, click Restart to read the **/etc/modules.conf** file, which now has the new entry. To remove a module, select its entry and click Remove. To edit an entry, say, to add arguments, select its entry and click Edit.

Managing Modules with COAS

On OpenLinux, you can use COAS to unload and load modules. Select Kernel Modules from the COAS menu to display the Kernel Modules window shown in Figure 33-9. The window is divided into two scrollable lists. The left list consists of available modules not yet loaded. The right list shows modules already loaded. To load a module, just select it from in the left list and click Load. Modules are listed by their filenames, which can be obscure. To find out what a module is used for, select it and click Info. If you should want to unload a module, select its name in the right list and click Unload.

Figure 33-8. *The Red Hat Kernel Configurator*

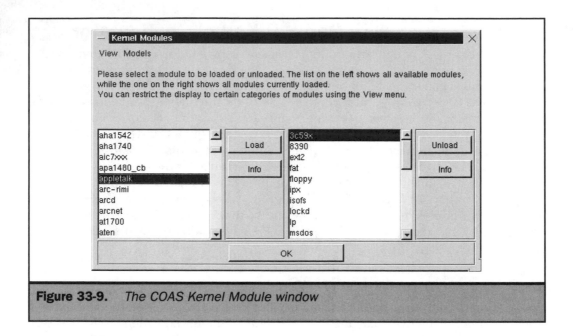

Figure 33-9. *The COAS Kernel Module window*

If a module requires configuration, then a window opens up with entries for different configuration options. For example, with sound cards, you may have to specify the IRQ, DMA, and I/O settings. When you add the Sound Blaster sound module, **sb.o**, a window opens up with entries for the different sound card settings.

Managing Modules with the Module Commands

The **lsmod** command lists the modules currently loaded into your kernel. You can add a new one using the **insmod** command and the module name. With **rmmod,** you can unload a module. See Table 33-9 for kernel module commands. It is often the case, however, that a given module requires other modules to be loaded. For example, the module for the Sound Blaster sound card, **sb.o**, requires the **sound.o** module to be loaded also. Instead of manually trying to determine what modules a given module depends on, you use the **modep** command to detect the dependencies for you. The **modep** command generates a file that lists all the modules on which a given module depends. The **modep** command generates a hierarchical listing, noting what modules should be loaded first and in what order. Then, to load the module, you use the **modprobe** command using that file. **modprobe** reads the file generated by **modep** and loads any dependent modules in the correct order, along with the module you want. You need to execute **modep** with the **-a** option once, before you ever use **modprobe**. Entering **modep -a** creates a complete listing of all module dependencies. This command creates a file called **modules.deb** in the module directory for your current kernel version, **/lib/modules/***version*.

```
modep -a
```

To install a module, you use the **modprobe** command and the module name. You can add any parameters the module may require. The following command installs the Sound Blaster sound module with the I/O, IRQ, and DMA values. **modprobe** also supports the use of the * character to enable you to use a pattern to select several modules.

```
modprobe sb io=0x220 irq=5 dma=1
```

You can use the **-1** option to list modules and the **-t** option to look for modules in a specified subdirectory. In the next example, the user lists all modules that begin with "sound" in the **misc** directory.

```
# modprobe -l -t misc sound*
/lib/modules/2.2.16-17/misc/soundlow.o
/lib/modules/2.2.16-17/misc/soundcore.o
/lib/modules/2.2.16-17/misc/sound.o
```

Options for the **modprobe** command are placed in the **/etc/conf.modules** file. Here, you can enter configuration options, such as default directories and aliases. An alias provides a simple name for a module. For example, the following entry enables you to reference the 3c59x.o Ethernet card module as eth0.

```
alias eth0 3c59x
```

Installing New Modules for the Kernel

The source code for your Linux kernel contains an extensive set of modules, of which only a few are actually used on your system. When you install a new device, you may have to install the kernel module that provides the drivers for it. This involves selecting the module you need from a listing, and then regenerating your kernel modules with the new module included. Then the new module is copied into the module library, installing it on your system. Then you can use **modprobe** to install it manually or to place an entry for it in **modules.conf** to have it loaded automatically. First, make sure you have installed the kernel source code in the **/usr/src/linux** directory (described in Chapter 34). If not, simply use your distribution's installation utility such as **rpm** or an RPM utility like **kpackage** or **gnomerpm** to install the kernel source RPM packages. The following command installs the kernel sources.

```
rpm -i kernel-source-2.2.16-17.i386.rpm
```

You can also download the source code version from **www.kernel.org**, as discussed in Chapter 34.

Now change to the **/usr/src/linux** directory. Then use the **make** command with the **xconfig** or **menuconfig** argument to display the kernel configuration menus, invoking them with the following commands. The **make xconfig** command starts an X Window System interface that needs to be run on your desktop from a terminal window.

```
make xconfig
make menuconfig
```

Using the menus, as described in the next section, select the modules you need. Make sure each is marked as a module, clicking the Module check box in **xconfig** or pressing M for **menuconfig**. Once the kernel is configured, save it and exit from the configuration menus. Then you create the modules with the following command:

```
make modules
```

This places the modules in the kernel source modules directory: **/usr/src/linux/ modules**. You can copy the one you want to the modules directory, **/lib/modules/** *version*, where *version* is the version number of your Linux kernel. A simpler approach is to reinstall all your modules, using the following command. This copies all the compiled modules to the **/lib/modules/***version* directory.

```
make modules-install
```

For example, if you want to provide AppleTalk support and your distribution did not create an AppleTalk module or incorporate the support into the kernel directly, then you can use this method to create and install the AppleTalk module. First, check to see if your distribution has already included it. The **appletalk.o** module should be in the **/lib/modules/***version***/misc** directory. If not, you can move to the **/usr/src/linux** directory, run **make xconfig**, and select AppleTalk as a module. Then generate the modules with the **make modules** command. You could then use the **make modules-install** command to install the new module, along with your other modules. Or, you can use the following command to copy **appletalk.o** to the module directory (**uname -r** is used here to generate the version number for the installed kernel).

```
cp /usr/src/linux/modules/appletalk.o   /lib/modules/`uname -r`/misc
```

The Complete Reference

Linux

Chapter 34

Kernel Administration

The *kernel* is the core of the operating system, the program that performs operating system functions. The version number for a Linux kernel consists of three segments: the major, minor, and revision numbers. The *major number* increments with major changes in the kernel. The *minor number* indicates stability. *Even numbers* are used for stable releases, whereas *odd numbers* are reserved for development releases, which may be unstable. New features first appear in the development versions. If stability is a concern, waiting for the stable version is best. The *revision number* refers to the corrected versions. As bugs are discovered and corrected, new revisions of a kernel are released. A development kernel may have numerous revisions. For example, kernel 2.2.16 has a major number of 2 and a minor number of 2, with a revision number of 16. On Red Hat systems, another number is added that refers to a Red Hat–specific set of patches applied to the kernel. For Red Hat 7.0, this is 2.2.16-22, with 22 being the patch number. The newest kernel is 2.4, which has a major number of 2 and a minor number of 4. This will be the most recent stable release of the Linux kernel. On systems that support RPM packages, you can use an RPM query to learn what version is installed, as shown here:

```
rpm -q kernel
```

The Linux kernel is being worked on constantly, with new versions released when they are ready. Red Hat includes the most up-to-date kernel in its releases. Linux kernels are kept at **www.kernel.org**. Also, RPM packages for a new kernel often are available at distribution update sites, such as **ftp.redhat.com**. One reason you may need to upgrade your kernel is to provide support for new hardware or for features not supported by the distribution's version. For example, you may need support for a new device not provided in the distribution's version of the kernel. Certain features may not be included in a distribution's version because they are considered experimental or a security risk.

Note *You probably don't need to install a new kernel only to add support for a new device. Kernels provide most device support in the form of modules, of which only those needed are installed with the kernel. Most likely your current kernel has the module you need. You simply have to install it. For this task, see the "Installing New Modules for the Kernel" section in Chapter 33.*

You can learn more about the Linux kernel from **www.kernel.org**, the official repository for the current Linux kernels. The most current source code, as well as documentation, is here. For Red Hat systems, **www.redhat.com** also provides online documentation for installing and compiling the kernel on its systems. Several Linux HOW-TOs also exist on the subject. You can find the HOW-TOs online at **www.linux.org** and at distribution Web sites. The kernel source code software packages also include extensive documentation. Kernel source code files are always installed in the **/usr/src/linux** directory. In this directory, you can find a subdirectory named **Documentation,** which contains an extensive set of files and directories documenting kernel features, modules, and commands. You can also consult the Web site **kernelnotes.org** for the latest information on kernel developments.

To install a new kernel, you need to download the software packages for that kernel to your system. You can download them either from your Linux distribution's FTP sites or from **www.kernel.org**. You can install a new kernel either by downloading a binary version from your distribution's Web site and installing it, or by downloading the source code, compiling the kernel, and then installing the resulting binary file. For Red Hat and Caldera, the binary version of the kernel is provided in the RPM package. You can install a new kernel using the Red Hat Package Manager, just as you would any other RPM software package.

The source code version is available either from your distribution site, such as **ftp.redhat.com** for Red Hat, or from **www.kernel.org**. Wherever you download a kernel version from, it is always the same. The source code downloaded for a particular kernel version from Red Hat is the same as the one for **www.kernel.org**. Patches for that version can be applied to any distribution. Though the basic procedures for creating a kernel using the source code is the same for both kernel versions 2.2 and 2.4, the 2.4 kernel provides a few configuration options that differ. This chapter describes the 2.4 kernel, though most of its features can be applied to the 2.2 kernel.

Precautionary Steps

You should retain a copy of your current kernel, so you can use it again in case something goes wrong with the new one. This simply involves making a backup copy of the kernel file. The kernel file is called **vmlinuz-***version* where *version* is the version number attached, as in **vmlinuz2.2-16**. It is located in the **/boot** directory. Also, there is a file called **/boot/vmlinuz**, which is only a symbolic link to the actual kernel file (on other distributions, the **vmlinuz** file may be the actual boot file). The new kernel is installed with a filename using its own version number. To be on the safe side, however, making a backup copy may be advisable. You should also make a backup of the **System.map** file. This file contains kernel symbols needed by modules to start kernel functions. In the case of kernel 2.2.16-22, this would be **System.map-2.2.16-22**. If you are going to compile the same version of the kernel, making a few changes, then you should also back up your modules located in the **/lib/modules/***version* directory, where *version* is the version number of the kernel. Otherwise, you will lose the modules already set up to work with the original kernel. For version 2.2.16-22, the libraries are located in **/lib/modules/2.2.16-22**. If you are compiling a different version, those libraries are placed in a new directory named with the new version number.

```
cp /boot/vmlinuz2.2.16-22  /boot/vmlinuz2.2.16-22.back
```

If you are using LILO, you should create a new entry for the old kernel in the **lilo.conf** file (see Chapter 29). You then make an entry for the new kernel in the

lilo.conf file. Leaving the entry for the old kernel is advisable in case something goes wrong with the new kernel. This way, you can always reboot and select the old kernel. In **lilo.conf**, add a new entry, similar to the one for the old kernel which references the new kernel in its image line. The **lilo.conf** entry would look something like the following code. Be sure to execute the `lilo` command to update LILO with the new **lilo.conf** entries. You could then use the label **oldlinux2.2-16** at the LILO prompt to launch the old kernel.

```
image = /boot/vmlinuz2.2-16.back
    label = oldlinux2.2-16
    root = /dev/hda3
    read-only
```

Also advisable is to have a boot disk ready, just in case something goes wrong with the installation. With a boot disk, you can start your system without using `lilo`. On Red Hat systems, you can create a boot disk using the mkbootdisk utility. Examine your **lilo.conf** file to learn the name of the boot image you are currently loading. The boot image is in the line beginning with **image =**, as in the previous code. The name of the boot file is **/boot/vmlinuz** (which is a link to the boot file). Use the boot image file to create your boot disk.

```
mkbootdisk --device /boot/vmlinuz
```

Installing a Distribution Kernel Binaries and Source: RPM

You can obtain RPM packages for the Linux kernel from your distribution's update sites. For example, to download a new kernel for Red Hat, locate the kernel RPM packages from **ftp://ftp.redhat.com** or its mirror sites. These will be located in the corresponding update directories for your Red Hat distribution, such as **6.2** or **7.0**. A series of RPM packages are there, all beginning with the term *kernel.* There are also other packages you may need, which contain updated system configuration files used by the new kernel. As an example, the kernel packages for the 2.4 kernel are listed in the following code. Only install one of the **kernel-*version*-ix86** packages and one of the **kernel-smp** packages. Choose the one for your machine—for example, i686 for a Pentium II, i586 for a Pentium, and i386 for other PCs. The following list shows the RPM packages for the Red Hat version of kernel 2.4:

```
kernel-2.4.0-0.26.i386.rpm
kernel-2.4.0-0.26.i586.rpm
kernel-2.4.0-0.26.i686.rpm
```

```
kernel-doc-2.4.0-0.26.i386.rpm
kernel-enterprise-2.4.0-0.26.i686.rpm
kernel-headers-2.4.0-0.26.i386.rpm
kernel-pcmcia-cs-2.4.0-0.26.i386.rpm
kernel-smp-2.4.0-0.26.i386.rpm
kernel-smp-2.4.0-0.26.i586.rpm
kernel-smp-2.4.0-0.26.i686.rpm
kernel-source-2.4.0-0.26.i386.rpm
kernel-utils-2.4.0-0.26.i386.rpm
```

To make sure a kernel RPM package was downloaded without any errors, you can use the **rpm** command with the **-K --nopgp** options to check it:

```
rpm -K --nopgp *rpm
```

You are now ready to install the new kernel. First, install any updated versions of other support packages. In Red Hat, these currently include mkinitrd, SysVinit, and initscripts. Use the **-Uvh** option to update those packages:

```
# rpm -Uvh mkinitrd*rpm SysVinit*rpm initscripts*rpm
```

Installing the source code and headers for the kernel is also essential. You use the source code to generate any modules and tailor the kernel to your own needs. For example, you can use the source code to generate modules containing device drivers for any uncommon devices you may have installed, as shown here:

```
# rpm -Uvh kernel-headers-2.4.0-0.26.i386.rpm
# rpm -Uvh kernel-source-2.4.0-0.26.i386.rpm
```

You can now install the kernel. On Red Hat systems, you install the kernel, kernel-ibcs, and the kernel-pcmia-cs packages. As a safety precaution, it is advisable to preserve your old kernel in case the new one does not work out for some reason. This involves installing with the install (**-i**) option instead of the update(**-U**) option, creating a separate RAM disk for the new kernel, and then modifying **lilo.conf** to have LILO start up using the new kernel.

```
# rpm -Uvh kernel-2.4.0-0.26.i686.rpm
# rpm -Uvh kernel-pcmcia-cs-2.4.0-0.26.386.rpm
# rpm -Uvh kernel-smp-2.4.0-0.26.i686.rpm
# rpm -Uvh kernel-utils-2.4.0-0.26.i386.rpm
```

On Red Hat and Caldera Linux, kernels are installed in the **/boot** directory. Performing an `ls -l` operation on this directory lists all the currently installed kernels. A file for your old kernel and a file for your new one now exist, as well as a link file called **vmlinuz**, which links to the new kernel file. If you took the precautions described in the previous section, you may have already renamed the older kernel. On Red Hat and Caldera, if you are using LILO, you needn't change the **lilo.conf** file because the entry to invoke the kernel still references the **/boot/vmlinuz** link, which now points to the new kernel. Red Hat boots the kernel using the **/boot/vmlinux** link to the kernel file. In your **lilo.conf** file, the image line for the kernel file references this link.

```
image = /boot/vmlinuz
```

Compiling the Kernel

You can compile a kernel using the Linux kernel source code. One advantage to compiling the kernel is you are able to customize its configuration, selecting particular devices you want supported by the kernel or the kind of networking support you want. You can have more control over exactly what your operating system can support. The 2.4 kernel is described here, though the 2.2 kernel still in use on many systems is very similar.

Installing Kernel Sources: tar.gz

You can obtain the most recent version of the source code from **www.kernel.org** or **www.linuxhq.com**. RPM packages of kernel sources are also available. If you are downloading a compressed archive (**.tar.gz**) package, be sure to unpack in the **/usr/src** directory. The archive extracts a directory named **linux** that holds the source code files. This way, the files are located in the **/usr/src/linux** directory. Links are already set up in the **/usr/include** directory to source files in the **/usr/src/linux** directory. They expect to find the source code in **/usr/src/linux**.

You can also download the compressed archive of the kernel source from **www.kernel.org** and its mirror sites. In this case, you first decompress and extract the archive with the following commands. *vnum* is the version number.

```
cd /usr/src
-tar xzvf linux-2.4.vnum.tar.gz
```

For some releases, you can simply update your current kernel source code files using patches. A *patch* modifies a source code file, making required changes. To install a patch, download the patch file and then execute the following command. The patch file is first decompressed, and then the **patch** command implements the changes.

```
cd /usr/src
gzip -cd patchvnum.gz | patch -p0
```

You may have to implement several patches, depending on how out-of-date your kernel is. In this case, you must execute a patch operation for each patch file needed. Patches need to be applied in sequence. The latest patch does not include any previous ones. So to apply patch 2.2.12, you would first have to apply patch 2.2.11. Or, you can use the patch-kernel script, which determines your kernel version and applies the patches needed.

```
cd /usr/src
linux/scripts/patch-kernel
```

Before you can install the kernel, you have to configure and compile it, as discussed in the next section.

Configuring the Kernel

Once the source is installed, you must configure the kernel. Configuration consists of determining the features for which you want to provide kernel-level support. This includes drivers for different devices, such as sound cards and SCSI devices. This process is referred to as *configuring the kernel*. You can configure features as directly included in the kernel itself or as modules the kernel can load as they are needed. You can also specifically exclude features. Features incorporated directly into the kernel make for a larger kernel program. Features set up as separate modules can also be easily updated. Documentation for many devices that provide sound, video, or network support can be found in the **/usr/share/doc** directory. Check the kernel-doc package to find a listing of the documentation provided.

```
rpm -ql kernel-doc
```

 *If you configured your kernel previously and now want to start over from the default settings, you can use the **make mrproper** command to restore the default kernel configuration.*

You can configure the kernel using one of several available configuration tools: config, menuconfig, and xconfig. They perform the same configuration tasks, but use different interfaces. The *config* tool is a simple configure script providing line-based prompts for different configuration options. The *menuconfig* tool provides a cursor-based menu, which you can still run from the command line. Menu entries exist for different configuration categories, and you can pick and choose the ones you want. To mark a feature for inclusion in the kernel, move to it and press the SPACEBAR. An asterisk appears in the empty parentheses to the left of the entry. If you want to make it a module, press M and an *M* appears in the parentheses. The *xconfig* tool runs on a window manager and provides a window interface with buttons and menus. You can use your mouse to select entries. A menu consists of configuration categories that are listed as buttons you can click.

You start a configuration tool by preceding it with the **make** command. Be sure you are in the **/usr/src/linux-***version* directory. The process of starting a configuration tool is a **make** operation that uses the Linux kernel **Makefile**. The xconfig tool should be started from a Terminal window on your window manager. The menuconfig and config tools are started on a shell command line. The following example lists commands to start xconfig, menuconfig, or config:

```
make xconfig
make menuconfig
make config
```

The xconfig tool opens a Linux Kernel Configuration window listing the different configuration categories. Figure 34-1 shows the configuration categories for the 2.4 kernel—the ones for the 2.2 kernel will be slightly different. Buttons at the right of the screen are used to save the configuration or to copy it to a file, as well as to quit. Clicking an entry opens a window that lists different features you can include. Three check boxes to the left of each entry enable you to choose to have a feature compiled directly into the kernel, created as a separate module that can be loaded at runtime, or not included at all. As a rule, features in continual use, such as network and file system support, should be compiled directly into the kernel. Features that could easily change,

Figure 34-1. *The xconfig Linux kernel configuration tool*

such as sound cards, or features used less frequently, should be compiled as modules. Otherwise, your kernel image file may become too large and slower to run.

Note *If you decide to include a feature directly into the kernel that was previously a module, be sure to check that the old module is removed from the /lib/modules/version directory. Otherwise, conflicts can occur between the module and its corresponding code, which is now directly part of the kernel.*

The xconfig and menuconfig tools provide excellent context-sensitive help for each entry. To the right of an entry is a Help button. Click it to display a detailed explanation of what that feature does and why you would include it either directly or as a module, or even exclude it. When in doubt about a feature, always use the Help button to learn exactly what it does and why you would want to use it. Some of the features are described here:

■ **Loadable Module Support**   In most cases, you should make sure your kernel can load modules. Click the Loadable Modules Support button to display a listing of several module management options (see Figure 34-2). Make sure Enable Loadable Module Support is Yes. This feature allows your kernel to load modules as they are needed. Kernel Module Loader should also be Yes, as this allows your daemons, like your Web server, to load any modules they may need. The Set Version Information entry enables you to use any modules set up for previous kernels.

■ **Processor Type and Features**   The Processor Type and Features window enables you to set up support for your particular system (see Figure 34-3). Here, you select the type of processor your have (486, 586, 686, Pentium III, and so forth), as well as the amount of maximum memory your system supports (up to 64 gigs with 2.4 kernel).

Figure 34-2.   *Loadable Modules Support window*

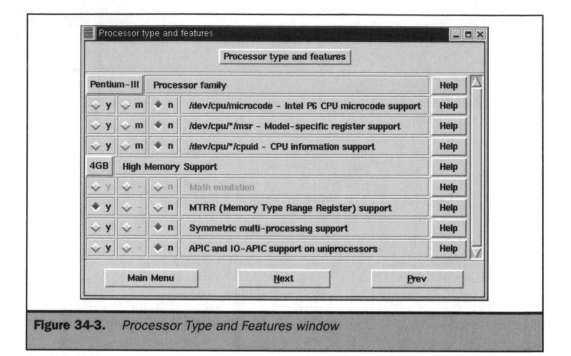

Figure 34-3. *Processor Type and Features window*

- **General Setup**   The General Setup window enables you to select general features, such as networking, PCI BIOS support, and Power management, as well as support for ELF and a.out binaries (see Figure 34-4).

- **Block Devices**   The Block Devices window lists entries that enable support for your IDE floppy drive, parallel port devices, and RAID drives. Special features, such as RAM disk support and the loopback device for mounting CD-ROM image files, are also there.

- **Networking Options**   The Networking Options window, shown in Figure 34-5, lists an extensive set of networking capabilities. The TCP/IP Networking entry must be set to enable any kind of Internet networking. Here, you can specify features that enable your system to operate as a gateway, firewall, or router. Network Aliasing enables support for IP aliases. Support also exists for other kinds of networks, including AppleTalk and IPX. AppleTalk must be enabled if you want to use NetaTalk to connect to a Macintosh system on your network.

- **ATA/IDE/MFM/RLL Support**   In the ATA/IDE/MFM/RLL Support window, you can click the IDE, ATA, and ATAPI Block Device button to open a window in which you can select support for IDE ATA hard drives and ATAPI CD-ROMs. Included here are IDE chipsets, such as HTP366 used for ATA66 drives (in kernel 2.2, these are in the Block Devices window).

Figure 34-4. *General Setup window*

Figure 34-5. *Networking Options window*

- **SCSI Support**   If you have any SCSI devices on your system, make sure the entries in the SCSI support window are set to Yes. You enable support for SCSI disks, tape drives, and CD-ROMs here. The SCSI Low-Level Drivers window displays an extensive list of SCSI devices currently supported by Linux. Be sure the ones you have are selected.

- **Network Device Support**   The Network Device Support window lists several general features for network device support. There are entries here for windows that list support for particular types of network devices, including Ethernet (10 or 100Mbit) devices, Token Ring devices, WAN interfaces, and Appletalk devices. Many of these devices are created as modules you can load as needed. You can elect to rebuild your kernel with support for any of these devices built directly into the kernel. Figure 34-6 shows the Ethernet (10 or 100Mbit) window listing Ethernet devices. Notice they are built as separate modules.

- **Character Devices**   The Character Devices window lists features for devices such as your keyboard, mouse, and serial ports. Support exists for both serial and bus mice.

- **File Systems**   The File Systems window, shown in Figure 34-7, lists the different types of file systems Linux can support. These include DOS, VFAT (Windows 95), and ISO9660 (CD-ROM) file systems. Network file systems— such as NFS, SMB (Samba), NCP (NetWare)—HFS (Macintosh), and NTFS (Windows NT—read-only with 2.2) are also listed. Note, the Linux file system type, ext2fs, must be included in the kernel, and is not compiled as a module.

- **Sound**   The Sound window lists different sound cards supported by the kernel. Select the one on your system. You also must provide the IRQ, DMA, and Base I/0 your sound card uses. These are compiled as separate modules, some of which you could elect to include directly in the kernel if you want (see Figure 34-8).

Figure 34-6.   *Ethernet (10 or 100Mbit) window*

Figure 34-7. *File Systems window*

Figure 34-8. *Sound window*

■ **Kernel Hacking**   The Kernel Hacking window lists features of interest to programmers who want to modify the kernel code. You can have the kernel include debugging information.

Once you set your options, save your configuration. You can also make a backup copy by clicking Save To File.

Compiling and Installing the Kernel

Now that the configuration is ready, you can compile your kernel. You first need to generate a dependency tree to determine what part of the source code to compile, based on your configuration. Use the following command:

```
make dep
```

A good idea is also to clean up any stale object and dependency files that may remain from a previous compilation. Use the following command to remove such files:

```
make clean
```

You can use several options to compile the kernel (see Table 34-1). The **bzImage** option simply generates a kernel file called **bzImage** and places it in the **/usr/src/linux/arch** directory. For Intel systems, you find **bzImage** in the **i386/boot** subdirectory, **/user/src/linux/arch/i386/boot**.

```
make bzImage
```

The **install** option both generates the kernel files and installs them on your system, as **vmlinuz**.

```
make install
```

The **zlilo** option installs the kernel file, as well, but also runs **lilo** to update LILO. The **zlilo** option is designed for use with systems that run LILO. If you are booting Linux from DOS using loadlin, you will need to copy the bzImage file to the loadlin directory on the DOS partition from which you are starting Linux.

To install a kernel **bzImage** file manually, copy the **bzImage** file to the directory in which the kernel resides, and give it the name used on your distribution—such as **vmlinuz** for Red Hat, Caldera, and SuSE. Remember to first back up the old kernel file. On Red Hat, SuSE, and Caldera, vmlinuz is a symbolic link to an actual kernel file that will have the term "vmlinuz" with the version name. So, to manually install a bzImage

Configuration Tool	Description
config	Line-based interface for kernel configuration
menuconfig	Screen-based interface for kernel configuration
xconfig	X Window System interface for kernel configuration

Maintenance Options	
checkhelp	Checks configuration for options not documented
checkconfig	Checks source tree for missing header files
clean	Removes old object files and dependencies
mrproper	Removes old object files and dependencies

Compiling Options	
zImage	Creates the kernel file called **zImage** located in the **/usr/src/linux/arch** or **arch/i386/boot** directory
install	Creates the kernel and installs it on your system
zlilo	Creates the kernel, installs it on your system, and runs LILO
zdisk	Creates a kernel file and installs it on a floppy disk (creates a boot disk)
bzImage	Creates a compressed kernel file and calls it **bzImage**
bzlilo	Creates and installs a compressed kernel and runs LILO
bzdisk	Creates a compressed kernel and installs it on a floppy disk (creates a boot disk)

Module Options	
modules	Creates kernel modules
modules-install	Installs kernel modules in the **/lib/modules** directory

Table 34-1. *Kernel Compile Options Used as Arguments to the* **make** *Command in* ***/usr/src/linux***

file on Red Hat, you copy it to the **/boot** directory with the name vmlinuz and the attached version number, such as vmlinuz-2.4-0. You then create a symbolic link from **/boot/vmlinuz** to **/boot/v'mlinuz-2.4-0**.

```
make bzImage
cp arch/i386/boot/bzImage /boot/vmlinuz-2.4-0
ln -s /boot/vmlinuz /boot/vmlinuz-2.4-0
```

The **bzImage** option and those options that begin with the letter *b*, like **bzlilo**, create a compressed kernel image. This kernel image may not work on older systems. If not, try using the **zImage** option to create a kernel file called **zImage**. Then install the **zImage** file manually. Bear in mind that support for **zImage** will be phased out eventually.

```
make zImage
```

The **bzlilo** option both installs the kernel file on your system and runs LILO. You should use this option if you receive an error saying your kernel is too large. The following command compiles the kernel, installs it on your system, and runs LILO for you. To install and update LILO, use the following:

```
make zlilo
```

If you receive an error saying the kernel is too large, try using a *b* version of the option, such as **bzlilo**, to further reduce its size.

```
make bzlilo
```

If you want to create a boot disk with the new kernel, use the **bzdisk** option. This option will install the kernel on a floppy disk placed in your floppy drive. The kernel will reside on the floppy disk. To use the kernel, boot your system with that floppy (the kernel is not installed on your root partition as it is with the **install** option).

```
make bzdisk
```

The previous options will create the kernel, but not the modules—those features of the kernel to be compiled into separate modules. To compile your modules, use the **make** command with the **modules** argument.

```
make modules
```

To install your modules, use the **make** command with the **modules_install** option. This installs the modules in the **/lib/modules/***version-num* directory, where *version-num* is the version number of the kernel. Making a backup copy of the old modules before you install the new ones may be advisable.

```
make modules_install
```

The commands for a simple compilation and installation are shown here:

```
make dep
make clean
make bzImage
make modules
make modules_install
make install
```

The following commands show a basic compilation and a manual installation. First, all previous binary files are removed with the **clean** option. Then, the kernel is created using the **bzImage** option. This creates a kernel program called **bzImage**, located in the **arch/i386/boot** directory. Copy this kernel file to the **/boot** directory and give it the name **vmlinuz-***version*, where *version* is the kernel version. Then create a symbolic link called **/boot/vmlinuz** to the kernel **vmlinuz-***version* file. Create the modules and install the modules:

```
make dep
make clean
make bzImage
make modules
make modules_install
cp arch/i386/boot/bzImage /boot/vmlinuz-2.4-0
ln -s /boot/vmlinuz /boot/vmlinux-2.4-0
```

Instead of installing the kernel on your system, you can simply place it on a boot disk and boot your system from that disk. In that case, you just have to create a boot disk using the **bzdisk** option. Be sure a formatted floppy disk is in the floppy drive. You will still have to create and install your modules. Be sure that the **bzImage** file is small enough to fit on a floppy disk. If not, you will have to reconfigure your kernel, compiling as many features as possible as modules instead of as part of the kernel.

```
make clean
make bzImage
```

```
make modules
make modules_install
make bzdisk
```

 If you are experimenting with your kernel configurations, it may be safer to put a new kernel version on a boot disk, rather than installing it on your system. If something goes wrong, you can always boot up normally with your original kernel still on your system.

LILO Configurations

If you are using LILO, you can configure your system to enable you to start any of your installed kernels. As seen in the "Precautionary Steps" section earlier in this chapter, you can create an added entry in the **lilo.conf** file for your old kernel. As you install new kernel versions, you could simply add more entries, enabling you to use any of the previous kernels. For example, you could install a developmental version of the kernel, along with a current stable version, while keeping your old version. In the image line for each entry, you would specify the filename of the kernel. Whenever you add a new entry, be sure to execute the **lilo** command to update LILO. Whenever you install the kernel on Red Hat using the RPM kernel package, the **/boot/vmlinuz** link is automatically changed to the new kernel. You can still create another LILO entry for your older kernel. In the next example, the **lilo.conf** file contains entries for two Linux kernels, one using the standard **/boot/vmlinuz** link, as well as windows.

/etc/lilo.conf
```
boot = /dev/hda
install = /boot/boot.b
message = /boot/message
prompt
timeout = 200
default = win
image = /boot/vmlinuz
        label = linux
        root = /dev/hda3
        read-only
image = /boot/vmlinuz-2.2.16
        label = linux-2.2
        root = /dev/hda3
        read-only
other = /dev/hda1
        label = win
        table = /dev/had
```

On Linuxconf, you can select an Add New Kernel entry in the list of LILO entries to add a new kernel entry for LILO. You can do the same for Webmin on the Linux Bootup Configuration page accessible from the Hardware page. Here, you can create a new kernel entry or edit a current one. On the Create Boot Kernel page, you can enter the kernel image file to boot along with any options.

Module RAM Disks

If your system requires certain modules to be loaded when you boot, you may have to create a RAM disk for them. For example, if you have SCSI hard drive or CD-ROMs, the SCSI drivers for them are often held in modules that are loaded whenever you start up your system. These modules are stored in a RAM disk from which the startup process reads. If you create a new kernel that needs to load modules to start up, then you must create a new RAM disk for those modules. When you create a new kernel, you also need to create its modules. You place the modules needed for startup, such as SCSI hard drive modules, in a new RAM disk. In the **lilo.conf** file, add an entry to load this RAM disk. You only need to create a new RAM disk if your kernel has to load modules at startup. If, for example, you use a SCSI hard drive, but you have incorporated SCSI hard drive and CD-ROM support (including support for the specific model) directly into your kernel, you needn't set up a RAM disk. Support for IDE hard drives and CD-ROMs is already incorporated directly into the kernel.

If you need to create a RAM disk, you can use the **mkinitrd** command to create a RAM disk image file or create a RAM disk device. See the Man pages for **mkinitrd** and RAM disk documentation for more details. In the **lilo.conf** segment for the new kernel, you would place an initrd entry specifying the new RAM disk.

```
# mkinitrd /boot/initrd-2.2.5-15.img 2.2.5-15
```

In your **lilo.conf** file, an initrd entry would exist for the kernel, specifying the RAM disk to use.

```
image=/boot/vmlinuz-2.2.5-15
        label=linux
        root=/dev/hda3
        initrd=/boot/initrd-2.2.5-15.img
        read-only
```

The
Complete
Reference

Chapter 35

The X Window System
and XFree86

877

Linux and Unix systems use the same standard underlying graphics utility known as the *X Window System,* also known as *X* or *X11.* This means that, in most cases, an X-based program can run on any of the window managers and desktops. X-based software is often found at Linux or Unix FTP sites in directories labeled **X11**. You can download these packages and run them on any window manager running on your Linux system. Some may already be in the form of Linux binaries that you can download, install, and run directly. Netscape is an example. Others are in the form of source code that can easily be configured, compiled, and installed on your system with a few simple commands. Some applications, such as Motif applications, may require special libraries.

The X Window System is designed for flexibility—you can configure it in various ways. You can run the X Window System on almost all the video cards currently available. The X Window System is not tied to any specific desktop interface. It provides an underlying set of graphical operations that user interface applications such as window managers, file managers, and even desktops can use. A window manager uses these operations to construct widgets for manipulating windows, such as scroll bars, resize boxes, and close boxes. Different window managers can construct them to appear differently, providing interfaces with different appearances. All window managers work on the X Window System. You can choose from a variety of different window managers, and each user on your system can run a different window manager, each using the same underlying X Window System graphic operations. You can even run X programs without any window or file managers.

To run the X Window System, you need to install an X Windows server. A free version of X Windows server software, known as *XFree86,* is used on most Linux systems, though commercial versions are available from MetroLink (**www.metrolink.com**) and Accelerated X. Once you install the XFree86 server, you must provide configuration information about your monitor, mouse, and keyboard. This information is then used in a configuration file called **/etc/X11/XF86Config**, which includes technical information best generated by an X Window System configuration program, such as Xconfigurator, xlizard, or XF86Setup. When you configured the X Window System when you installed your system, this file was automatically generated.

You can also configure your own X interface using the **.xinitrc** and **/etc/X11/xinit/xinitrc** configuration files, where window managers, file managers, and initial X applications can be selected and started. And, you can use a set of specialized X commands to configure your root window, load fonts, or configure X Window System resources, such as setting the color of window borders. You can also download X utilities from online sources that serve as Linux mirror sites, usually in their **/pub/Linux/X11** directory. If you have to compile an X application, you may have to use special procedures, as well as install support packages. An official source for X Window System news, tools, and window managers is **www.X11.org**. Here you can find detailed information about X Window System features, along with compliant desktops and window managers.

The X Window System was developed and is maintained by *The Open Group* (*TOG*), a consortium of over a hundred companies including Sun, HP, IBM, Motorola, Intel, and Microsoft (**www.opengroup.org**). Development is currently managed by the X.org group (**www.X.org**) on behalf of the TOG. *X.org* is a nonprofit organization that maintains the existing X Window System code. X.Org periodically provides free official Window System update releases to the general public. It controls the development of the X11R6 specifications, working with appropriate groups to revise and release updates to the standard, as required. The newest release is currently X11R6.4. *XFree86* is a free distributed version of X Window System servers used on most Linux systems. XFree86 incorporates X11R6.4 into its XFree86-4.0 release. You can find out more about XFree86 at **www.xfree86.org**.

The X Protocol

The *X protocol* was developed for Unix systems in the mid-1980s to provide a network-transparent graphical user interface. The X protocol organizes display operations into a client and server relationship, in which a client submits display requests to a server. The client is known as an *X client,* and the server, as an *X server.* The client, in this case, is an application and the server is a display. This relationship separates an application from the server. The application acts as a client sending requests to the server, which then does the actual work of performing the requested display operation. This has the advantage of letting the server interact with the operating system and its devices, whereas the application need know nothing of these details. An application operating as an X client can display on any system that uses an X server. In fact, a remote X client can send requests to have an X server on a local machine perform certain display operations. In effect, the X server/client relationship is, in a sense, inverted from the way we normally think of servers. Usually, several client systems access a single server. In the X server model, you would have each system operating as an X server that can access a single system that holds X client programs.

XFree86

The *XFree86 Project* (**www.xfree86.org**) is a nonprofit organization that provides free X Window System servers and supporting materials for several operating systems on PCs and other microcomputers. The X server, client programs, and documentation supplied by the XFree86 Project are commonly referred to as *XFree86*. The XFree86 server is available free and includes source code. The project is funded entirely by donations.

In releases 3.3 and earlier, XFree86 organized video card and monitor drivers into separate servers. You had to find the correct one to use and load it. With release 4.0, XFree86 now uses only one server, called the XFree86 X server, which includes all video card and monitor drivers. You only need to install the XFree86 X server package along with basic support packages such as those for fonts. The XFree86 X server will have support for given video cards and monitors implemented as static libraries or as modules it can load as needed. The XFree86 X server uses a built-in run-time loader, donated by **Metro Link**, that is operating system independent, though it is still hardware dependent. Currently the XFree86 X server supports the Intel, Alpha, PowerPC, and Sparc platforms.

The XFree86 server support a wide range of video cards and monitors, including Monochrome, VGA and Super VGA, and accelerated video cards. You can find a detailed listing of supported cards by checking the driver status for a particular release. To obtain information about a particular XFree86 release, just attach its release number to the **www.xfree86.org** site as in **www.xfree86.org/4.0** for information about release 4.0. To find out the driver status for release 4.0.1, go to **www.xfree86.org/4.0.1** and click the Driver Status link. This will list links for all video cards to pages detailing support for particular video card models. Also, you can consult the man pages for the different driver types such as nv for Nvidia cards, mga for Matrox, and ati for ATI graphics cards.

XFree86 configuration tools, such as Red Hat's Xconfigurator, Caldera's xlizard, SuSE's SaX2, and even XFree86's xf86cfg, make configuring your video card and monitor a simple process. They keep on hand an extensive list of video cards and monitors provided by Xfree86 from which you can select your own. If your video card or monitor is quite new, however, it may not be on this list. If this is the case, first check to see if a new release of XFree86 has come out. The new release may have support for your card or monitor. If not, you will need to enter certain hardware specifications, such as horizontal and vertical sync frequencies for monitors. If you must do this, be careful to enter the correct information. The wrong settings could damage both your card and your monitor.

Be sure to check for new releases of XFree86 servers periodically at the XFree86 Web site. You can download the new releases from there or from your distribution's update sites, such as **ftp.redhat.com/updates** for Red Hat or **ftp.calderasystems.com/updates** for Caldera. It's always preferable to download from your Linux distribution sites, since those packages may be modified to work better with your system. The entire XFree86 software release includes the XFree86 X server and its modules along with several supporting packages such as those for fonts and configuration files. Table 35-1 lists the current XFree86 packages. If you are downloading from the Xfree86 site, you first download and run Xinstall.sh to determine which packages are appropriate for your system. XFree86 provides versions for different platforms on its FTP site at **ftp.xfree86.org**. For downloads from the XFree86 site, it is strongly recommended that you use the Xinstall.sh installer. Xinstall.sh will query for installation information and then download and install all needed XFree86 packages. For Red Hat and Caldera systems, download and install the RPM packages from the Red Hat and Caldera FTP sites, instead of the ones at the XFree86 site.

In addition to the server, XFree86 includes support programs and development libraries. The entire XFree86 collection is installed in various directories, beginning with the pathname **/usr/X11R6**. Directories are here for X programs, development files,

Package	Description
Xinstall.sh	The installer script
extract	The utility for extracting tarballs
Xbin.tgz	X clients/utilities and run-time libraries
Xlib.tgz	Some data files required at run time
Xman.tgz	Manual pages
Xdoc.tgz	XFree86 documentation
Xfnts.tgz	Base set of fonts
Xfenc.tgz	Base set of font encoding data
Xetc.tgz	Run-time configuration files
Xvar.tgz	Run-time data
Xxserv.tgz	XFree86 X server
Xmod.tgz	XFree86 X server modules
Optional Package	**Description**
Xfsrv.tgz	Font server
Xnest.tgz	Nested X server
Xprog.tgz	X header files, config files, and compile-time libs
Xprt.tgz	X Print server
Xvfb.tgz	Virtual framebuffer X server
Xf100.tgz	100 dpi fonts
Xfcyr.tgz	Cyrillic fonts
Xflat2.tgz	Latin-2 fonts
Xfnon.tgz	Some large bitmap fonts
Xfscl.tgz	Scalable fonts (Speedo and Type1)
Xhtml.tgz	HTML version of the documentation
Xps.tgz	PostScript version of the documentation
Xjdoc.tgz	Documentation in Japanese

Table 35-1.   *XFree86 Packages*

libraries, man pages, and documentation. Configuration files are placed in the **/etc/X11** directory. Applications written to support *X* usually install in the **/usr/X11R6/bin** directory. You can also find the XFree86 servers and support programs here. Table 35-2 lists XFree86 configuration directories.

You can use X servers to run X Window System applications on a remote system. When you access a remote system, you can have the X server on that system generate a new display for you to run the remote X application. Every X server has a display name consisting of a hostname, a display number, and a screen number. These are used by an application to determine how to connect to the server and the screen it should use.

```
hostname:displaynumber.screennumber
```

The hostname is the host where the X server is physically located. The display number is the number of the display being managed by the X server. On a local workstation, there is usually only one display. But on a multiuser system where several terminals (each with its own keyboard and mouse) are connected to a single system, each terminal is its own display with its own display number. This way several users can be running X applications at the same time off the same X server. If your system has two or more monitors sharing the same keyboard and mouse, then a different screen number would be applied to each monitor, though they would have the same display number.

The display a user is currently using is listed the DISPLAY environment variable. On a single-user system, you will find that the display entry begins with a colon and

Directory	Description
/usr/X11R6/bin	Programs (X Window System clients and servers)
/usr/X11R6/include	Development files
/usr/X11R6/lib	Libraries
/usr/X11R6/man	man pages
/usr/X11R6/lib/X11/doc	Documentation
/etc/X11	Configuration files
/usr/X11R6/lib/X11/	Contains subdirectories for window manager program functions

Table 35-2. *XFree86 Directories*

is followed by a 0 as shown here. This indicates that the X server is on the local system (not a remote host) and has the display number of 0.

```
$ echo $DISPLAY
:0
```

To use a remote X application, you have to change the display name for the DISPLAY variable. You can do this manually by assigning a new hostname and display number to the variable, or you can use the **xon** script.

```
$ DISPLAY=rabbit.mytrek.com:0
$ export DISPLAY
```

You can also use the **-display** option when invoking an X application to specify the remote X server to use.

```
$ xterm -display rabbit.mytrek.com:0
```

XFree86 Configuration: /etc/X11/XF86Config

The XFree86 servers provide a wide range of hardware support, but it can be challenging to configure. You can consult the XFree86-HOWTO document at **www.linux.org** or in the **/usr/doc/HOWTO** directory for most distributions. There are also man pages for XFree86 and XF86Config, and documentation and FAQs are available at **www.xfree86.org**. The configuration file used for your XFree86 server is called **XF86Config**, located in the **/etc/X11** directory. **XF86Config** contains all the specifications for your graphics card, monitor, keyboard, and mouse. To configure the **XF86Config** file, you need specific information on hand about your hardware. For your monitor, you must know the horizontal and vertical sync frequency ranges and bandwidth. For your graphics card, you have to know the chipset, and you may even need to know the clocks. For your mouse, you should know whether it is Microsoft-compatible or some other brand, such as Logitech. Also, know the port to which your mouse is connected.

Although you could create and edit the file directly, using a configuration utility such as Xconfigurator, XF86Setup, lizardx or xf86config is better. (Table 35-3 lists these various configuration tools.) With these, you simply answer questions about your hardware or select options on the dialog window, and the program generates the appropriate **/etc/X11/XF86Config** file. xf86config provides line mode prompts where you type responses or enter a menu selection, and it provides explanations of each step. You can run it from any shell command line. Xconfigurator uses a cursor-based screen that also operates on a shell command line. You can use arrow keys, TAB, and the ENTER key to make your selections. xf86config also attempts to detect your card automatically, or you can select your monitor from a predetermined list. Lizardx is a Caldera tool described in Chapter 3. XF86Setup provides you with a full-screen

Tool	Description
xf86cfg	XFree86 Screen-based X Window System configuration tool
XFree86 -configure	XFree86 X Window System configuration tool that is built into the XFree86 X server
xlizard	Caldera GUI X Window System configuration tool
SaX2	SuSE GUI X Window System configuration tool
XF86Setup	GUI X Window System configuration tool. Use after installation process
Xconfigurator	Screen-based X Window System configuration tool (used in Red Hat install procedure)
xf86config	XFree86 command line X Window System configuration tool. Requires no screen-based support
lizardx	Caldera X Window System configuration tool
/etc/X11/XF86Config	The X Window System configuration file; edited by the configuration tools

Table 35-3. *X Window System Configuration Tools*

interface where you can easily select features for your mouse, keyboard, graphics card, and monitor. You need the horizontal and vertical frequency for your monitor. If you have problems configuring with XF86Setup, however, you can use xf86config, which presents you with a command line interface that prompts you for different settings. SaX (SuSE Advanced X Configuration) is another GUI X Window System configuration tool provided by the SuSE Linux distribution. It provides windows similar to XF86Setup for your mouse, keyboard, video card, and monitor. The monitor window lists supported monitor models.

The **/etc/X11/XF86Config** file is organized into several parts, as shown here. You can find a detailed discussion of all these sections and their entries in the XF86Config man page. All of these are set by the XF86Setup program. For example, the Monitor screen generates the Monitor section in the **XF86Config** file, the Mouse screen generates the Input Device section for the mouse, and so on. A section in the file begins with the keyword **Section,** followed by the name of the section in quotes. The section ends with the term **EndSection**. Comments have a # sign at the beginning of the line. The different kinds of sections are listed here.

Section	Description
Files	Directories for font and **rgb** files
Module	Dynamic module loading
ServerFlags	Miscellaneous options
Input Device	Mouse and keyboard configuration
Monitor	Monitor configuration (set horizontal and vertical frequencies)
Device	Video card configuration
Screen	Configure display, setting virtual screen, display colors, screen size, and other features
ServerLayout	Specify layout of screens and input devices

Entries for each section begin with a data specification, followed by a list of values. With release 4.0, many former data specifications are now implemented using the Option entry. You enter the keyword Options followed by the data specification and its value. For example, the keyboard layout specification, XkbLayout, is now implemented using an Options entry as shown here.

```
Option      "XkbLayout"  "us"
```

Although you can directly edit the file using a standard text editor, relying on the setup programs such as XF86Setup to make changes is always best. You won't ever have to touch most of the sections, but in some cases, you want to make changes to the Screen section, located at the end of the file. To do so, you would edit the file and add or change entries in the Screen section. In the Screen section, you can configure your virtual screen display and set the number of colors supported. Because the Screen section is the one you would most likely change, it is discussed first, even though it comes last, at the end of the file.

Screen

A Screen section begins with an Identifier entry to give a name to this Screen. After the Identifier entry, the Device and Monitor entries specify the monitor and video card you are using. The name given in the Identifier entry in these sections is used to reference those components.

```
Section "Screen"
    Identifier "Screen0"
    Device "Matrox|MGA G400 AGP"
    Monitor "C1025"
    DefaultDepth 24
    Subsection "Display"
       Depth 32
       Modes "1024x768"
    EndSubSection
    Subsection "Display"
       Depth 24
       Modes "1024x768"
    EndSubSection
EndSection
```

The Screen section has Display subsections, one for each depth supported. Whereas the previous sections configured hardware, the Display subsection configures display features, such as the number of colors displayed and the virtual screen size. Two main entries exist: Depth and Modes. The *Depth* entry is the screen resolution: 8, 16, and 24. You can add the DefaultDepth entry to set the default color depth to whatever your X server supports: 8 for 256K, 16 for 32K, and 24 for 16M. *Modes* are the modes allowed given the resolution. You can also add to the Virtual entry to specify the size of the virtual screen. You can have a virtual screen larger than your display area. When you move your mouse to the edge of the displayed screen, it scrolls to that hidden part of the screen. This way, you can have a working screen much larger than the physical size of your monitor. The physical screen size for a 17-inch monitor is usually 1,024 × 768. You could set it to 1,152 × 864, a 21-inch monitor size, with a Virtual entry.

Any of these features in this section can be safely changed. In fact, to change the virtual screen size, you must modify this section. Other sections in the **XF86Config** file should be left alone, however, unless you are certain of what you are doing.

Files, Modules, and ServerFlags

The Files section lists different directories for resources that XFree86 needs. For example, to specify the location where **rgb** color data is listed, a line begins with the data specification **RgbPath,** followed by the pathname for that **rgb** color data file. For fonts, you can specify either font files or a font server. In earlier versions of the X Window System, this section mostly listed the fonts available on your system. A font entry would begin with the data specification **FontPath** and was followed by the pathname for that font. A sample of these entries is shown here:

```
RgbPath      "/usr/X11R6/lib/X11/rgb"
FontPath     "/usr/X11R6/lib/X11/fonts/misc:unscaled"
```

To specify a font server, you enter the transport type, the hostname, and the port it is listening on (this is usually 7100). If the server is on your own system, you can leave the hostname blank.

```
transport/hostname:port
```

The *transport* can be either tcp for a TCP/IP connection (Internet) or unix for a Unix domain socket. On most systems, the **xfs** server manages fonts. Font paths for the **xfs** server are listed in the **/etc/X11/fs/config** file. A sample entry for the font server is shown here for a local font server listening on port 7100.

```
FontPath "unix/:7100"
```

If no FontPaths are specified, then the X server falls back on default font paths already compiled into the X server (see the XF86Config man page for more details).

The Module section specifies modules to be dynamically loaded, and the Load entry loads a module. It is used to load server extension modules and font modules. This is a feature introduced with version 4.0 that allows X server components that extend the functionality of the X server to be loaded as modules. This feature provides for easy updating, letting you upgrade modules without having to replace the entire X server. For example, the extmod module contains miscellaneous extensions to enable commonly used functions in the X server. In the following example, the extmod module is loaded that contains a set of needed extensions. See the XF86Config man page for more details.

```
Load "extmod"
```

Several flags can be set for the XFree86 server. With version 4.0, these are now implemented as Options. (You can find a complete listing in the XF86Config man page.) For example, the **BlankTime** value specifies the inactivity timeout for the screen saver. **DontZap** disables the use of CTRL-ALT-BACKSPACE to shut down the server. **DontZoom** disables switching between graphic modes. You create an Option entry with the flag as the option. The following example sets the server flag for the screen saver inactivity timeout.

```
Option "BlankTime " "30"
```

Intput Device

With 4.0, the Input Device section replaces the previous Keyboard, Pointer, and XInput sections. To provide support for an input device such as a keyboard, you create an Input Device section for it and enter Identifier and Driver entries for the device. For example, the following entry creates an Input Device section for the keyboard.

```
Section "Input Device"
             Identifier "keyboard 1"
             Driver "keyboard"
```

Any features are added as Options, such as keyboard layout or model. A large number of options exist for this section. Consult the XF86Config man pages for a complete listing. The following example shows an entire keyboard entry with autorepeat, keyboard model (XkbModel), and keyboard layout (XkbLayout) options entered.

```
Section "InputDevice"
    Identifier   "Keyboard 1"
    Driver       "keyboard"
    Option       "AutoRepeat" "500 5"
    Option       "XkbModel"   "pc104"
    Option       "XkbLayout"  "us"
EndSection
```

You create an Input Device section for your mouse and any other pointer devices. This section has only a few entries, with some tailored for specific types of mice. Features are defined using Option entries. The *Protocol* option specifies the protocol your mouse uses, such as PS/2, Microsoft, or Logitech. The *Device* option is the pathname for the mouse device. The following example shows a standard Pointer section for a three-button PS/2 mouse. The device file is **/dev/mouse**.

```
Section "InputDevice"
    Identifier   "Mouse 1"
    Driver       "mouse"
    Option       "Protocol"   "PS/2"
    Option       "Device"     "/dev/mouse"
    Option       "Emulate3Buttons" "off"
EndSection
```

The following is a listing of the Pointer section options:

Option	Description
Protocol	Mouse protocol (do man XF86Config for complete listing)
Device	Device path, such as **/dev/mouse** or **/dev/cua0**
BaudRate	Baud rate for serial mouse
Emulate3Buttons	Enables two-button mouse to emulate a third button when both left and right buttons are pressed at once
ChordMiddle	Three-button mouse configuration on some Logitech mice
ClearDTR and ClearRTS	Clear DTR and RTS lines, valid only for Mouse Systems mice
SampleRate	Set the sampling rate (Logitech)

Monitor

A Monitor section should exist for each monitor used on your system. The vertical and horizontal frequencies must be accurate, or you can damage your monitor. A *Monitor* section begins with entries that identify the monitor, such as vendor and model names. The HorizSync and VerRefresh entries are where the vertical and horizontal frequencies are specified. Most monitors can support a variety of resolutions. Those resolutions are specified in the Monitor section by ModeLine entries. A ModeLine entry exists for each resolution. The ModeLine entry has five values, the name of the resolution, its dot clock value, and then two sets of four values, one for the horizontal timing and one for the vertical timing, ending with flags. The flags specify different characteristics of the mode, such as Interlace, to indicate the mode is interlaced, and +hsync and +vsync to select the polarity of the signal.

```
ModeLine "name"  dotclock  horizontal-freq  vertical-freq  flags
```

A sample of a ModeLine entry is shown here. Leaving the entire Monitor section alone is best; rely, instead, on the entries generated by XF86Setup.

```
Modeline  "800x600"   50.00 800 856 976 1040 600 637 643 666 +hsync +vsync
```

Commonly used entries for the Monitor section are listed here.

Option	Description
Identifier	A name to identify the monitor
VendorName	Manufacturer
ModelName	The make and model
HorizSync	The horizontal frequency; can be a range or series of values
VerRefresh	Vertical refresh frequency; can be a range or series of values
Gamma	Gamma correction
ModeLine	Specifies a resolution with dotclock, horizontal timing, and vertical timing for that resolution

A sample monitor section is shown here:

```
Section "Monitor"
   Identifier "C1025"
   VendorName "Unknown"
   ModelName  "Unknown"
   HorizSync 30 - 95
   VertRefresh 50 - 160
EndSection
```

Device

The *Device* section specifies your video card. It begins with an Identifier entry and an entry for the video card driver. The following example creates an Identifier for a Matrox card called "MGA 1" and then specifies that the **mga** driver is to be used for it.

```
Identifier " Matrox|MGA G400 AGP"
Driver     "mga"
```

Further entries identify the card, such as VendorName, BoardName, and Chipset. The amount of video RAM is indicated in the VideoRam entry. The *Clocks* entry lists your clock values. Many different entries can be made in this section, such as Ramdac for a Ramdac chip, if the board has one, and MemBase for the base address of a frame buffer, if it is accessible. See the XF86Config man pages for a detailed list and descriptions.

Although you could safely change a VideoRam entry—for example, if you added more memory to your card—changing the Clocks entry is not safe. If you get the clock values wrong, you could easily destroy your monitor. Rely on the clock values generated by XF86Setup or other XFree86 setup programs. If the clock values are missing, it means that the server will automatically determine them. This may be the case for newer cards. A sample Device entry is shown here.

```
Section "Device"
    Identifier "Matrox|MGA G400 AGP"
    Driver "mga"
    BoardName "Unknown"
EndSection
```

ServerLayout

A ServerLayout has been added with release 4.0 to let you specify the layout of the screens and the selection of input devices. The ServerLayout sections may also include options that are normally found in the ServerFlags section. You can set up several ServerLayout sections and select them from the command line. The following example shows a simple ServerLayout section for a basic configuration.

```
Section "ServerLayout"
    Identifier "XFree86 Configured"
    Screen        0   "Screen0" 0 0
    InputDevice      "Mouse0" "CorePointer"
    InputDevice      "Keyboard0" "CoreKeyboard"
EndSection
```

X Window System Command Line Arguments

You can start up any X Windows application either within an **.xinitrc** or **.xsession** script or on the command line in an Xterm window. Some distributions, including Red Hat, place X Windows startup applications in an **.Xclients** file that is read by the **.xinitrc** script. Most X Windows applications take a set of standard X Windows arguments used to configure the window and display the application uses. You can set the color of the window bars, give the window a specific title, and specify the color and font for text, as well as position the window at a specific location on the screen. Table 35-4 lists these X Windows arguments. They are discussed in detail in the X man pages, man X.

One commonly used argument is **-geometry**. This takes an additional argument that specifies the location on the screen where you want an application's window displayed. In the next example, the xclock X Windows application is called with a geometry argument. A set of up to four numbers specifies the position. The value +0+0

X Windows Application Configuration Arguments	(See the X man pages for detailed explanations.)
–bw *num*	Border width of pixels in frame
–bd *color*	Border color
–fg *color*	Foreground color (for text or graphics)
–bg *color*	Background color
–display *display-name*	Displays client to run on; displays name consisting of hostname, display number, and screen number (see X man pages)
–fn *font*	Font to use for text display
–geometry *offsets*	Location on screen where X Windows application window is placed; offsets are measured relative to screen display
–iconic	Starts application with icon, not with open window
–rv	Switches background and foreground colors
–title *string*	Title for the window's title bar
–name *string*	Name for the application
xrm *resource-string*	Specifies resource value

Table 35-4.   *Configuration Options for X Window System–Based Applications*

references the upper left-hand corner. There, you see the clock displayed when you start up the X Window System. The value –0–0 references the upper right-hand corner.

```
& xclock -geometry +0+0 &
```

With the **–title** option, you can set the title displayed on the application window. Notice the use of quotes for titles with more than one word. You set the font with the **–fn** argument and the text and graphics color with the **–fg** argument. **–bg** sets the background color. The following example starts up an Xterm window with the title

"My New Window" in the title bar. The text and graphics color is green, and the background color is gray. The font is Helvetica.

```
$ xterm -title "My New Window"  -fg green -bg gray  -fn /usr/fonts/helvetica  &
```

X Window System Commands and Configuration Files

The X Window System uses several configuration files, as well as X commands to configure your X Window System. Some of the configuration files belong to the system and should not be modified. Each user can have her own set of configuration files, however, such as **.xinitrc**, **.xsession**, and **.Xresources**, that can be used to configure a personalized X Windows interface. Some distributions, like Red Hat, also use an **.Xclients** file to hold X Window startup applications. These configuration files are automatically read and executed when the X Window System is started up with either the **startx** command or an X display manager, such as xdm, kdm, or gdm. Within these configuration files, you can execute X commands used to configure your system. With commands such as **xset** and **xsetroot**, you can add fonts or control the display of your root window. Table 35-5 provides a list of X Window System configuration files and commands. You can obtain a complete description of your current X configuration using the **xdypinfo** command. The X man page provide a detailed introduction to the X commands and configuration files.

X Resources

Several X commands, such as **xrdb** and **xmodmap,** configure your X Windows interface. X Windows graphic configurations are listed in a resource file called **.Xresources**. Each user can have a customized **.Xresources** file in his home directory, configuring the X Window System to particular specifications. The **.Xresources** file contains entries for configuring specific programs, such as the color of certain widgets. A systemwide version called **/etc/X11/xinit/.Xresources** also exists. (Notice, unlike **/etc/X11/xinit/xinitrc**, a period is before Xresources in the **/etc/X11/xinit/.Xresources** filename.) The **.Xdefaults** file is a default configuration loaded by all programs, which contains the same kind of entries for configuring resources as **.Xresources**. An **.Xdefaults** file is accessible by programs on your system, but not by those running on other systems. The **/usr/X11R6/lib/X11/app-defaults** directory holds files that contain default resource configurations for particular X applications, such as Xterm, Xclock, and Xmixer. The Xterm file holds resource entries specifying how an Xterm window is displayed. You can override any of these defaults with alternative entries in an **.Xresources** file in your home directory. You can create an **.Xresources** file of your own in your home directory and add resource entries to it. You can also copy the **/etc/X11/xinit/.Xresources** file and edit the entries there or add new ones of your own.

Configuration is carried out by the **xrdb** command, which reads both the system's .**Xresources** file and any .**Xresources** or .**Xdefaults** file in your home directory. The **xrdb** command is currently executed in the **/etc/X11/xinit/xinitrc** script and the **/etc/X11/xdm/Xsession** script. If you create your own .**xinitrc** script in your home directory, be sure it executes the **xrdb** command with at least your own .**Xresources** file or the **/etc/X11/xinit/.Xresources** file (preferably both). You can ensure this by simply using a copy of the system's **xinitrc** script as your own .**xinitrc** file, and then modifying that copy as you want. See the man pages on **xrdb** for more details on resources. Also, you can find a more detailed discussion of Xresources, as well as other X commands, in the man pages for *X*.

An entry in the .**Xresources** file consists of a value assigned to a resource, a class, or a group of resources for an application. Usually, resources are used for widgets or classes of widgets in an application. The resource designation typically consists of three elements separated by periods: the application, an object in the application, and the resource. The entire designation is terminated by a colon, and the value follows. For example, suppose you want to change the color of the hour hand to blue in the oclock application. The application is oclock, the object is clock, and the resource is hour: oclock.clock.hour. This entry looks like this:

```
oclock.clock.hour: blue
```

The object element is actually a list of objects denoting the hierarchy leading to a particular object. In the oclock example, only one object exists, but in many applications, the object hierarchy can be complex. This requires a lengthy set of objects listed to specify the one you want. To avoid this complexity, you can use the asterisk notation to reference the object you want directly, using an asterisk in place of the period. You only need to know the name of the resource you want to change. The following example sets the oclock minute and hour hands to green.

```
oclock*hour: green
oclock*minute: green
```

You can also use the asterisk to apply a value to whole classes of objects. Many individual resources are grouped into classes. You can reference all the resources in a class by their class name. Class names begin with an uppercase character. In the Xterm application, for example, the background and pointer color resources are both part of the Background class. The reference **XTerm*Background** would change all these resources in an Xterm window. However, any specific references always override the more general ones.

You can also use the asterisk to change the values of a resource in objects for all your applications. In this case, you place an asterisk before the resource. For example, to change the foreground color to red for all the objects in every application, you enter

```
*foreground: red
```

If you want to change the foreground color of the scroll bars in all your applications, you use

```
*scrollbar*foreground: blue
```

The **showrgb** command lists the different colors available on your system. You can use the descriptive name or a hexadecimal form. Values can also be fonts, bitmaps, and pixmaps. You could change the font displayed by certain objects in, or for, graphic applications as well as changing background or border graphics. Resources vary with each application. Applications may support different kinds of objects and the resources for them. Check the man pages and documentation for an application to learn what resources it supports and the values accepted for it. Some resources take Boolean values that can turn features on or off, while others can specify options. Some applications have a default set of resource values that is automatically placed in your system's **.Xresources** or **.Xdefaults** file.

The **Xmodmap** file holds configurations for your input devices, such as your mouse and keyboard (for example, you can bind keys such as BACKSPACE or reverse the click operations of your right and left mouse buttons). The **Xmodmap** file used by your display manager is in the display manager configuration directory, such as **/etc/X11/xdm**, whereas the one used by **startx** is located in **/etc/X11/xinit**. Each user can create a custom **.Xmodmap** file in her home directory to configure the system's input devices. This is helpful if users connect through their own terminals to your Linux system. The **.Xmodmap** file is read by the **xmodmap** command, which performs the configuration. The **xmodmap** command first looks for an **.Xmodmap** file in the user's home directory and uses that. If no **.Xmodmap** is in the home directory, it uses the one for your display manager or **startx** command. You see entries for the **xmodmap** command in the **/etc/X11/xinit/xinitrc** file and the display manager's **Xsession** file. If you have your own **.xinitrc** or **.xsession** script in your home directory, it should execute the **xmodmap** command with either your own **.Xmodmap** file or the system's **Xmodmap** file. See the man pages on **xmodmap** for more details.

X Commands

Usually, an **.xinitrc** or **.xssesion** script has X Window System commands, such as **xset** and **xsetroot,** used to configure different features of your X Windows session. The **xset** command sets different options, such as turning on the screen saver or setting the volume for the bell and speaker. You can also use **xset** to load fonts. See the **xset** man pages for specific details. With the **b** option and the **on** or **off** argument, **xset** turns your speaker on or off. The following example turns on the speaker.

```
xset b on
```

You use **xset** with the **-s** option to set the screen saver. With the **on** and **off** arguments, you can turn the screen saver on or off. Two numbers entered as arguments specify the length and period in seconds. The length is the number of seconds the screen saver waits before activating and the period is how long it waits before regenerating the pattern.

The **xsetroot** command enables you to set the features of your root window (setting the color or displaying a bitmap pattern—you can even use a cursor of your own design). Table 35-5 lists the different **xsetroot** options. See the man pages for **xsetroot** for options and details. The following **xsetroot** command uses the **-solid** option to set the background color of the root window to blue.

```
xsetroot -solid blue
```

Fonts

Your X Window System fonts are located in a directory called **/usr/X11R6/lib/X11/fonts**. X Window System fonts are loaded using the **xfs** command. **xfs** reads the **/etc/X11/fs/config** configuration file that lists the font directories in an entry for the term **catalogue**. The XMan pages provides a detailed discussion on fonts. To install a set of fonts automatically, place them in a directory whose path you can add to the catalogue entry. You can also separately install a particular font with the **xset** command and its **+fp** option. Fonts for your system are specified in a font path. The *font path* is a set of filenames, each holding a font. The filenames include their complete path. An example of the catalogue entry in the **/etc/X11/config** file follows. This is a comma-delimited list of directories. These are directories where the X Window System first looks for fonts.

```
catalogue = /usr/X11R6/lib/X11/fonts/misc/,
/usr/X11R6/lib/X11/fonts/Speedo/,/usr/X11R6/lib/X11/fonts/Type1/,
/usr/X11R6/lib/X11/fonts/75dpi/,/usr/X11R6/lib/X11/fonts/100dpi/
```

Before you can access newly installed fonts, you must first index them with the **mkfontdir** command. From within the directory with the new fonts, enter the **mkfontdir** command. You can also use the directory path as an argument to **mkfontdir**. After indexing the fonts, you can then load them using the **xset** command with the **fp rehash** option. To have the fonts automatically loaded, add the directory with the full pathname to the catalogue entry in the **xfs** configuration file. The following shows how to install a new font and then load it:

```
$ cp newfont.pcf  ~/myfonts
$ mkfontdir ~/myfonts
$ xset fp rehash
```

Within a font directory, several special files hold information about the fonts. The **fonts.dir** file lists all the fonts in that directory. In addition, you can set up a **fonts.alias** file to give other names to a font. Font names tend to be long and complex. A **fonts.scale** file holds the names of scalable fonts. See the man pages for **xfs** and **mkfontdir** for more details.

With the **xset +fp** and **-fp** options, you can specifically add or remove particular fonts. The **fn** option with the **rehash** argument then loads the fonts. With the default argument, the default set of fonts is restored. The **+fp** option adds a font to this font path. For your own fonts, you can place them in any directory and specify their filenames, including their complete path. The next example adds the **myfont** font in the **/usr/local/fonts** directory to the font path. Then the **fp** option with the **rehash** argument loads the font.

```
xset +fp  /usr/local/fonts/myfont
xset fp rehash
```

To remove this font, use **xset -fp /usr/home/*myfont*** and follow it with the **xset fp rehash** command. If you want to reset your system to the set of default fonts, enter the following:

```
xset fp default
xset fp rehash
```

With **xlsfonts**, you can list the fonts currently installed on your system. To display an installed font to see what it looks like, use **xselfonts**. You can browse through your fonts, selecting the ones you like.

Table 35-5 lists common X Window System commands, whereas Table 35-6 lists the configuration files and directories associated with the X Window System.

X Window Command	Explanation
xterm	Opens a new terminal window
xset	Sets X Windows options; see man pages for complete listing **-b** Configures bell **-c** Configures key click **+fp** *fontlist* Adds fonts **-fp** *fontlist* Removes fonts **led** Turns on or off keyboard LEDs **m** Configures mouse **p** Sets pixel color values **s** Sets the screen saver **q** Lists current settings

Table 35-5.   *X Window System Commands*

X Window Command	Explanation
xsetroot	Configures the root window **-cursor** *cursorfile maskfile* Sets pointer to bitmap pictures when pointer is outside any window **-bitmap** *filename* Sets root window pattern to bitmap **-gray** Sets background to gray **-fg** *color* Sets color of foreground bitmap **-bg** *color* Sets color of background bitmap **-solid** *color* Sets background color **-name** *string* Sets name of root window to string
xmodmap	Configures input devices; reads the **.Xmodmap** file **-pk** Displays current keymap **-e** expression Sets key binding keycode NUMBER = KEYSYMNAME Sets key to specified key symbol keysym KEYSYMNAME = KEYSYMNAME Sets key to operate the same as specified key pointer = NUMBER Sets mouse button codes
xrdb	Configures X Windows resources; reads the **.Xresources** file
xdm	X Windows Display Manager; runs the XFree86 server for your system; usually called by **xinitrc**
startx	Starts X Windows by executing **xinit** and instructing it to read the **.Xclients** file
xfs *config-file*	The X Windows font server
mkfontdir *font-directory*	Indexes new fonts, making them accessible by the font server
xlsfonts	Lists fonts on your system

Table 35-5. *X Window System Commands* (continued)

X Window Command	Explanation
xfontsel	Displays installed fonts
xdpyinfo	Lists detailed information about your X Windows configuration
xinit	Starts X Windows, first reading the system's **xinitrc** file; when invoked from **startx**, it also reads the user's **.Xclients** file; **xinit** is not called directly, but through **startx**
xmkmf	Creates a Makefile for an X Windows application using the application's Imakefile; invokes **imake** to generate the Makefile (never invoke **imake** directly)
xauth	Reads **.Xauthority** file to set access control to a user account through xdm from remote systems

Table 35-5. *X Window System Commands* (continued)

Configuration File	Explanation
.Xmodmap	User's X Windows input devices configuration file
.Xresources	User's X Windows resource configuration file
.Xdefaults	User's X Windows resource configuration file
.xinitrc	User's X Windows configuration file read automatically by **xinit**, if it exists
.Xclients or .Xsessions	User's X Windows configuration file (used on Red Hat and other Linux distributions)

Table 35-6. *X Window System Configuration Files*

Configuration File	Explanation
.Xauthority	User's access controls through xdm GUI login interface
/usr/X11R6/	Directory where the X Window System release 6 commands, applications, and configuration files are held
/usr/X11R6/lib/X11/	Link to the **/etc/X11** directory that holds X Window System release 6 configuration file and subdirectories
/etc/X11/	Directory that holds X Window System release 6 configuration file and subdirectories
/usr/X11R6/lib/X11/	Directory that holds X Window System configuration files and subdirectories for the version currently installed on your system. On Red Hat, this is a link to the **/etc/X11** directory
/etc/X11/xinit/xinitrc	System X Windows initialization file; automatically read by **xinit**
/etc/X11/xinit/Xclients	System X Windows configuration file (used on Red Hat and other Linux distributions)
/etc/X11/xinit/.Xresources	System X Windows resources file; read by **xinitrc**
/etc/X11/xinit/.Xmodmap	System X Windows input devices file; read by **xinitrc**
/etc/X11/rgb.txt	X Windows colors. Each entry has four fields: the first three fields are numbers for red, green, and blue; the last field is the name given to the color

Table 35-6. *X Window System Configuration Files* (continued)

X Window System Startup Methods: startx and Display Managers

You can start up your X Window System in two different ways. You can start Linux with the command line interface and then, once you log in, use the **startx** command to start the X Window System and your window manager and desktop. You can also use a display manager that automatically starts the X Window System when you boot your computer, displaying a login window and a menu for selecting the window manager or desktop you want to use. Options for shutting down your system are also there. Currently, you can use three display managers: The K Display Manager is a display manager provided with the KDE. The Gnome Display Manager comes with the Gnome desktop. The X Display Manager is the original display manager used on Linux system.

Each method uses its own startup script. The **startx** command uses the **xinit** command to start the X Window System; its startup script is **/etc/X11/xinit/xinitrc**. Startup scripts for display managers are found in their respective directories. For **xdm**, the startup script is **/etc/X11/xdm/Xsession**. **kdm** and **gdm** have their own configuration directories, **/etc/X11/kdm** and **/etc/X11/gdm**. Here you find files for configuring their login window and menus. The gdm application as currently implemented on Red Hat uses the Xdm **Xsession** script, whereas kdm uses an **Xsession** script in its own directory.

As an enhancement to either **startx** or a display manager, you can use the *X session manager* (*xsm*). You can use it to launch your X Window System with different sessions. A *session* is a specified group of X applications. Starting with one session might start Gnome and Netscape, while starting with another might start KDE and KOffice. You can save your session while you are using it or when you shut down. The applications you are running become part of a saved session. When you start, xsm displays a session menu for you to choose from, listing previous sessions you saved. For xsm to work, it must be the last entry in your **.xsessions** or **.Xclients** file and you shouldn't have any other applications started in these files.

startx, xinit, and .xinitrc

The X Window System can be started from the command line interface using the **xinit** command. You do not invoke the **xinit** command directly, but through the **startx** command, which you always use to start the X Window System. Both of these commands are found in the **/usr/X11R6/bin** directory, along with many other X-based programs. The **startx** command is a shell script that executes the **xinit** command. The **xinit** command, in turn, first looks for an X Window System initialization script called **.xinitrc**, in the user's home directory. If no **.xinitrc** script is in the home directory, **xinit** uses **/etc/X11/xinit/xinitrc** as its initialization script. Both **.xinitrc** and

/etc/X11/xinit/xinitrc have commands to configure your X Windows server and to execute any initial X commands, such as starting up the window manager. You can think of the **/etc/X11/xinit/xinitrc** script as a default script. In addition, many systems use a separate file named **Xclients**, where particular X applications, desktop, or window manager can be specified. These entries can be directly listed in an **xinitrc** file, but a separate file makes for a more organized format. The Xclients files are executed as shell scripts by the **xinitrc** file. A user version as well as a system version exist: **.Xclients** and **/etc/X11/init/Xclients**. On Red Hat systems, the user's home directory is checked for the **.Xclients** file and, if missing, the **/etc/X11/xinit/Xclients** file is used.

Most distributions, including Red Hat, do not initially set up any **.xinitrc** or **.Xclients** scripts in any of the home directories. These must be created by a particular user who wants one. Each user can create a personalized **.xinitrc** script in her home directory, configuring and starting up the X Window System as wanted. Until a user sets up an **.xinitrc** script, the **/etc/X11/xinit/xinitrc** script is used and you can examine this script to see how the X Window System starts. Certain configuration operations required for the X Window System must be in the **.xinitrc** file. For a user to create his own **.xinitrc** script, copying the **/etc/X11/xinit/xinitrc** first to his home directory and naming it **.xinitrc** is best. Then each user can modify the particular **.xinitrc** file as required. (Notice the system **xinitrc** file has no preceding period in its name, whereas the home directory **.xinitrc** file set up by a user does have a preceding period.) The following example shows a simple system **xinitrc** file that starts the Window Maker window manager and an Xterm window. System and user **.Xresources** and **.Xmodmap** files are executed first to configure the X Window System.

/etc/X11/xinit/xinitrc

```
#!/bin/sh
userresources=$HOME/.Xresources
usermodmap=$HOME/.Xmodmap
sysresources=/usr/X11R6/lib/X11/xinit/.Xresources
sysmodmap=/usr/X11R6/lib/X11/xinit/.Xmodmap

# merge in defaults and keymaps
if [ -f $sysresources ]; then
    xrdb -merge $sysresources
fi
if [ -f $sysmodmap ]; then
    xmodmap $sysmodmap
fi
if [ -f $userresources ]; then
    xrdb -merge $userresources
fi
if [ -f $usermodmap ]; then
    xmodmap $usermodmap
fi
# start some nice programs
xterm &
exec wmaker &
```

On Red Hat, if a user only wants to add startup applications, then the user can simply create an **.Xclients** file, instead of a complete **.xinitrc** file. Be sure commands are in the system **xinitrc** file to check for and run a user's **.Xclients** file. The following example shows the code used in the Red Hat **xinitrc** file to execute a user's **.Xclients** script and, failing that, the system **Xclients** script. If this fails, the FVWM2 window manager is started and, if that fails, then the twm file manager is started.

```
if [ -f $HOME/.Xclients ]; then
    exec $HOME/.Xclients
elif [ -f /etc/X11/xinit/Xclients ]; then
    exec /etc/X11/xinit/Xclients
else
        # failsafe settings.  Although we should never get here
         xclock -geometry 100x100-5+5 &
        xterm -geometry 80x50-50+150 &
        if [ -f /usr/X11R6/bin/fvwm2 ]; then
                exec fvwm2
        else
                exec twm
        fi
fi
```

Display Managers: xdm, kdm, and gdm

When a system configured to run a display manager starts up, the X Window System starts up immediately and displays a login dialog box. The dialog box prompts the user to enter a login name and a password. Once they are entered, a selected X Windows interface starts up, say with Gnome, KDE, or some other desktop or window manager. When the user quits the window manager or desktop, the system returns to the login dialog box and remains there until another user logs in. You can shift to a command line interface with the CTRL-ALT-F1 keys and return to the display manager login dialog box with CTRL-ALT-F7. A display manager can do much more than provide a GUI login window. You can also use it to control access to different hosts and users on your network. The **.Xauthority** file in each user's home directory contains authentication information for that user. A display manager like xdm supports the *X Display Manager Control Protocol* (*XDMCP*). They were originally designed for systems like workstations that are continually operating, but they are also used to start up X Windows automatically on single-user systems when the system boots.

A display manager is automatically run when your system starts up at runlevel 5. Recall that your system can run at different runlevels; for example, runlevel 3 is the standard multiuser level, whereas runlevel 2 is a nonnetwork user level, and runlevel 1 is a system administration level. Runlevel 5 is the same as the standard multiuser level (runlevel 3), except it automatically starts up the X Window System on connected machines and activates the display manager's login screen.

During installation, you could choose whether you wanted to start with the display manager (runlevel 5) or not (runlevel 3). In this case, your system automatically starts at runlevel 5, activating the display manager. If, instead, you are starting with a standard line-mode login prompt (runlevel 3), you can change to the display manager by changing your default runlevel. To do this, you can either specify your startup runlevel with an administration utility like Linuxconf, Webmin, or COAS (see Chapter 4 and Chapter 29), or you can edit the system's **/etc/inittab** file. Editing the **/etc/inittab** file can be dangerous. You should do this with great care. The entry for your default runlevel in the **/etc/inittab** file should look like the following:

```
id:3:initdefault:
```

You can change the 3 to a 5:

```
id:5:initdefault:
```

To test your display manager, you can change to runlevel 5 with the **init** command as shown here:

```
init 5
```

Xsession

A display manager refers to a user's login and startup of a window manager and desktop as a session. When the user quits the desktop and logs out, the session ends. When another user logs in, a new session starts. The X Window System never shuts down; only desktop or window manager programs shut down. Session menus on the display manager login window list different kinds of sessions you can start, in other words, different kinds of window managers or desktops. For each session, the **Xsession** script is the startup script used to configure a user's X Window System display and to execute the selected desktop or window manager. Although this script is unnecessary for gdm, it is still used in the gdm Red Hat implementation.

Xsession is the display manager session startup script used by xdm, kdm, and also by the Red Hat implementation of gdm. It contains many of the X commands also used the **xinitrc** startup script. **Xsession** usually executes the same **xmodmap** and **xrdb** commands using the **.Xmodmap** and **.Xrsources** files in the **/etc/X11/xinit** directory. Shown here is the **Xsession** script used by gdm on Red Hat systems, which is located in the **/etc/X11/xdm** directory.

```
#!/bin/bash -login
# (c) 1999 Red Hat Software, Inc.

xsetroot -solid #356390
```

```
# redirect errors to a file in user's home directory if we can for errfile
# in "$HOME/.xsession-errors" "${TMPDIR-/tmp}/xses-$USER" "/tmp/xses-$USER"
do
    if ( cp /dev/null "$errfile" 2> /dev/null )
    then
    chmod 600 "$errfile"
    exec > "$errfile" 2>&1
    break
     fi
done


# clean up after xbanner
if [ -f /usr/X11R6/bin/freetemp ]; then
    freetemp
fi


userresources=$HOME/.Xresources
usermodmap=$HOME/.Xmodmap
sysresources=/usr/X11R6/lib/X11/xinit/.Xresources
sysmodmap=/usr/X11R6/lib/X11/xinit/.Xmodmap


# merge in system defaults and keymaps
if [ -f $sysresources ]; then
    xrdb -merge $sysresources
fi


if [ -f $sysmodmap ]; then
    xmodmap $sysmodmap
fi


# merge in user defaults and keymaps
if [ -f $userresources ]; then
    xrdb -merge $userresources
fi


if [ -f $usermodmap ]; then
    xmodmap $usermodmap
fi


#see if xdm/gdm/kdm has asked for a specific environment case $# in 1
# for failsafe just open an xterm window
# for Gnome, start Gnome with gnome-session
```

```
# for KDE, start KDE with startkde
  case $1 in
    failsafe)
    exec xterm -geometry 80x24-0-0
    ;;
    gnome)
    exec gnome-session
    ;;
    kde)
    exec startkde
    ;;
    esac
esac
```

If users want to set up their own startup files, you can reprogram the kdm **Xsession** file first to check for an *.xsession* file in the user's home directory and execute that. A user could copy the **Xsession** file to her own *.xsession* and then edit it, as well as replace the case statement with a single invocation of the desktop she wants. The following example shows a simple **Xsession** script that executes the user's *.xsession* script if it exists. The user's *.xsession* script is expected to start a window manager or desktop.

```
#
# Xsession
#
# This is the program that is run as the client
# for the display manager.


startup=$HOME/.xsession
resources=$HOME/.Xresources

if [ -f "$startup" ]; then
        exec "$startup"
   else
       if [ -f "$resources" ]; then
           xrdb -load "$resources"
       fi
       fvwn2 &
       exec xterm -geometry 80x24+10+10 -ls
  fi
```

The following example shows a simple **.xsession** script to start Window Maker:

```
wmaker &
xrdb -merge "$HOME/.Xresources"
xterm -geometry -0+50 -ls
```

The X Display Manager (xdm)

The *X Display Manager* (*xdm*) manages a collection of X displays either on the local system or remote servers. xdm's design is based on the *X Consortium standard X Display Manager Control Protocol* (*XDMCP*). The xdm program manages user logins, providing authentication and starting sessions. For character-based logins, a session is the lifetime of the user shell that is started up when the user logs in from the command line interface. For xdm and other display managers, the session is determined by the session manager. The session is usually the duration of a window manager or desktop. When the desktop or window manager terminates, so does the session.

The xdm program displays a login window with boxes for a login name and password. The user logs in, and a window manager or desktop starts up. When the user quits the window manager, the X Window System restarts automatically, displaying the login window again. Authentications to control access for particular users are kept in their **.Xauthority** file.

The xdm configuration files are located in the **/usr/X11R6/lib/X11/xdm/** directory, although on Red Hat this is a link to the **/etc/X11/xdm** directory. The main xdm configuration file is **xdm-config**. Files such as **Xresources** configure how the dialog box is displayed, and **Xsetup** enables you to specify a root-window image or other windows to display. You can use the **xbanner** program to choose a graphic to display with the login dialog box. When the user starts up a session, the **Xsession** script is run to configure the user's X Window System and execute the user's window manager or desktop. This script usually calls the **.xsession** script in the user's home directory, if there is one (though this is not currently the case for Red Hat Xsession scripts). It holds any specific user X commands.

If you want to start xdm from the command line interface, you can enter it with the **-nodaemon** option. CTRL-C then shuts down xdm:

```
xdm -nodaemon
```

Table 35-7 lists the configuration files and directories associated with xdm. **xdm-errors** will contain error messages from xdm and the scripts it runs such as **Xsession** and **Xstartup**. Check this file if you are having any trouble with xdm.

The Gnome Display Manager

The *Gnome Display Manager* (*gdm*) manages user login and GUI interface sessions. gdm can service several displays and generates a process for each. The main gdm process

Filename	Description
/usr/X11R6/lib/X11/xdm	xdm configuration directory. On Red Hat, this is **/etc/X11/xdm**
xdm-config	xdm configuration file
Xsession	Startup script for user session
Xresource	Resource features for xdm login window
Xsetup	Sets up the login window and xdm login screen
Xstartup	Session startup script
xdm-errors	Errors from xdm sessions
.xsession	User's session script in the home directory. Usually executed by **Xsession**
Xreset	Resets the X Window System after a session ends
.Xauthority	User authorization file where xdm stores keys for clients to read

Table 35-7. *The xdm Configuration Files and Directories*

listens for XDMCP requests from remote displays and monitors the local display sessions. gdm displays a login window with boxes for entering a login name and password, and also displays a pop-up menu labeled options with entries for Sessions and Shutdown submenus. The Sessions menu displays different window managers and desktops you can start up. On Red Hat, you can find entries for Gnome, kde, and AnotherLevel (fvwm2). You can easily add entries to this menu by adding files for them in the gdm configuration directory, **/etc/X11/gdm/Sessions**.

The gdm configuration files are located in the **/etc/X11/gdm** directory. Its main configuration file is **gdm.conf**, where you can set various options, such as the logo image and welcome text to display. The **gdm** directory also contains four directories: **Init**, **Sessions**, **PostSession**, and **PreSession**. You can easily configure gdm by placing or editing files in these different directories. The **Init** directory contains scripts that are executed when gdm starts up. On Red Hat, this directory contains a Default script that holds X commands, such as setting the background. These are applied to the screen showing the gdm login window.

The Sessions directory hold session scripts. These become entries in the session menu displayed on the gdm login window options menu. For example, you could have a script called **kde** that contains the command **startkde** to run the KDE desktop. The term "kde" appears in the gdm session menu. Selecting kde executes this script and starts KDE. Currently on Red Hat, these scripts contain calls to the **/etc/X11/xdm/Xsession** script, using the filename as its argument. In the **Xsession** script, this name is used to start that particular kind of session. For example, when you select kde, the term "kde" is passed to the **Xsession** script, which then uses it to execute the **kde** command to start KDE. For example, the **gnome** script consists of only the following lines of code. The term "gnome" is passed to the **Xsession** script, which then uses it to execute the **gnome-session** command to start Gnome. This design has the advantage of not having to repeat any X configuration commands, such as **xmodmap**.

```
#!/bin/bash -login
/etc/X11/xdm/Xsession gnome
```

The **PreSession** directory holds any presession commands to execute, while the **PostSession** directory holds scripts for commands you want executed whenever a session ends. Neither the **Init**, **PreSession**, or **PostSession** scripts are necessary (Red Hat currently does not include **PreSession** or **PostSession** scripts).

For gdm, the login window is generated by a program called *the greeter*. Initially, the greeter looks for icons for every user on the system, located in the **.gnome/photo** file in users' home directories. Clicking the icon automatically displays the name of the user in the login box. The user can then enter the password and click the Login button to log in.

Table 35-8 lists the configuration files and directories associated with gdm.

Filename	Description
/etc/X11/gdm	gdm configuration directory
gdm.conf	gdm configuration file
Init	Startup scripts for configuring gdm display
Sessions	Holds session scripts whose names appear in session menu
PreSession	Scripts execute at start of session
PostSession	Scripts execute when session ends

Table 35-8.   *The gdm Configuration Files and Directories*

The K Display Manager (kdm)

The *K Display Manager* (*kdm*) also manages user logins and starts X Window System sessions. kdm is derived from the xdm Display Manager, using the same configuration files. The kdm login window displays a list of user icons for users on the system. A user can click his icon and that user's name then appears in the login box. Enter the password and click Go to log in. The session menu is a drop-down menu showing possible sessions. Click the Shutdown button to shut down the system.

You configure kdm using the KDM Configuration Manager located on the KDE root user desktop (see Chapter 4). Log in as the root user, and then start the KDM Configuration Manager by selecting KDM login manager in the Applications menu located in the Settings menu. Panels exist for configuring the background, logo, and welcome message, as well as for adding icons for users on the system. To add a new session entry in the session menu, enter the name for the entry in the New Type box on the Sessions panel and click Add. The name you enter is then passed as an argument to the kdm **Xsession** script.

When you select a session and click Go, kdm runs the **/etc/X11/kdm/Xsession** script, passing the name of the session as an argument. In the **Xsession** script, this name is used to start that particular kind of session. For example, when you select kde, the term "kde" is passed to the **Xsession** script, which then uses it to execute the **kde** command to start KDE. The kdm program uses the same configuration files as xdm. A directory called **/etc/X11/kdm** is created with kdm versions of the xdm files. Here, you find an **xdm.conf** file along with **Xsession**, **Xresources**, and **Xsetup**, among others. The resources used to control how the kdm login window is displayed are set in the **/opt/kde/share/config/kdmrc** file.

Starting Window Managers

As noted in Chapter 4, the X Window System is started either automatically using a display manager with a login window or from the command line by entering the **startx** command. Your X Window System server then loads, followed immediately by the window manager. You exit the window manager by choosing an exit or quit entry in the desktop workspace menu. The display manager and some window managers, such as FVWM2 and Window Maker, give you the option of starting other window managers. If you get into trouble and the window manager hangs, you can forcibly exit the X Window System with the keys CTRL-ALT-BACKSPACE.

The window manager you start is the default window manager set up by your Linux distribution when you installed your system. Many distributions now use either Gnome or KDE as their default. For Gnome and the K Desktop, different window managers are used: kwm for the K Desktop and Enlightenment for Gnome. You can run Gnome or KDE applications on most window managers. To have Gnome use a particular window manager, you need to select it using the Gnome Control Center. You can also use a window manager in place of kwm for KDE. Check the window manager's Web site for current information on Gnome and KDE compatibility.

Currently, Enlightenment is fully Gnome compliant, and AfterStep and Window Maker are nearly so. Normally, distributions include several window managers on their CD-ROM, which you can install and run on your system. Red Hat provide Window Maker, Enlightenment, AfterStep, kwm, and FVWM2, with FVWM2 as the default.

To use a different window manager, first install it. RPM packages install with a default configuration for the window manager. If you are installing from source code you compiled, follow the included installation instructions. You can then configure Gnome or KDE to use that window manager, provided it is compliant with them. See Chapters 8 and 9 on how to configure the KDE and Gnome desktops. Or, you can configure your system to start a particular window manager without either desktop. To do this, you have to place an entry for your window manager in an X Window System startup file. Different startup files exist for the display manager and the **startx** command.

startx and .xinitrc

The system X Window System startup file is called **/etc/X11/xinit/xinitrc**. For the **startx** command, users can also set up their own **.xinitrc** files in their home directories in place of the system's **xinitrc** file. To create your own **xinitrc** file, you can copy the one from the system. In addition, Red Hat enables users to specify their own X clients, such as window managers and desktops, in a startup file called **.Xclients**. This way, you needn't bother with a complex **.xinitrc** file. These startup files are discussed in more detail earlier in this chapter.

The following command generates a user's **.xinitrc** file using the system's **xinitrc** file. Be sure you are in your home directory. Notice the **.xinitrc** file has a preceding dot as part of its name, whereas the system's **xinitrc** file does not.

```
$ cp /etc/X11/xinit/xinitrc  .xinitrc
```

The invocation of the window manager is always the last command in the **.xinitrc** script. The X Window System exits after finishing the execution of whatever the last command in the **.xinitrc** script is. By making the window manager the last command, exiting the window manager shuts down your X Windows session. Any other programs you want to start up initially should be placed before the window manager command. You must place the command to start the window manager you want at the end of your **.xinitrc** file. Be sure to comment out any other window managers by placing a # at the beginning of the lines that hold their commands or simply remove them. Also best is to use the full pathname of a window manager program. These pathnames are usually located in the **/usr/X11R6/bin** directory or in the **/usr/bin** directory. Leave the rest of the file alone. The following example runs Window Maker:

```
exec /usr/X11R6/bin/wmaker
```

If you also want to load other programs automatically, such as a file manager, you can place their commands before the command for the window manager. Put an ampersand (&) after the command. The following example starts the Xterm window when the Window Maker window manager starts up:

```
xterm &
exec /usr/X11R6/bin/wmaker
```

If you are planning extensive changes, making them a few at a time is advisable, testing as you go. A simple **.xinitrc** file is shown here:

.xinitrc

```
#!/bin/sh

userresources=$HOME/.Xresources
usermodmap=$HOME/.Xmodmap
sysresources=/usr/X11R6/lib/X11/xinit/.Xresources
sysmodmap=/usr/X11R6/lib/X11/xinit/.Xmodmap

# merge in defaults and keymaps

# load system X resources
if [ -f $sysresources ]; then
    xrdb -merge $sysresources
fi

# load system modmap
if [ -f $sysmodmap ]; then
    xmodmap $sysmodmap
fi

# load user X resources
if [ -f $userresources ]; then
    xrdb -merge $userresources
fi

# load user modmap
if [ -f $usermodmap ]; then
    xmodmap $usermodmap
fi


# if the window maker is installed, run it.
if [ -f /usr/X11R6/bin/wmaker ]; then
            exec /usr/X11R6/bin/wmaker
     else
            exec fvwm2
     fi
```

Red Hat uses a rather complex startup procedure designed to configure window managers automatically with the complete set of Red Hat menus for applications installed by its distribution. Support exists for FVWM2, Window Maker, and AfterStep. Red Hat's global **Xclients** file searches for a file called **.wm_style** in a user's home directory. This is where the name of your preferred window manager is placed if you select an alternative from the FVWM2 or AfterStep menus. You can also manually edit this file with a text editor and type in one. The **.wm_style** file holds a single name, such as FVWM2, AfterStep, Window Maker, or LessTiff. Xclients then calls the **/usr/X11R6/bin/RunWM** script with an option for the window manager to start. The RunWM script checks to see if the window manager is installed, and then starts it up with helpful options. As the system administrator, you can edit this file to add new entries, if you want. Or, you can create your own **.xinitrc** file to bypass this procedure.

Display Managers and Xsession

To invoke a window manager using a display manager like xdm, KDE, or gdm, you first have to create an entry for it in the login window's session menu. You can do this in different ways for kdm and gdm. You then must edit the session startup script and add code to select and start up that window manager. The startup script used for the Red Hat implementation of gdm is **/etc/X11/xdm/Xsession**.

Gnome Display Manager: gdm

First, create an entry for the window manager in the session menu displayed in the gdm login window's option's menu. Here you find files for other items listed in this menu. Simply create a file with the name of the entry you want displayed in the **/etc/X11/gdm/Sessions** directory (you can copy one of the scripts already there). On Red Hat, these scripts invoke the **/etc/X11/xdm/Xsession** script with an option for the particular window manager or desktop chosen. For example, to create an entry for Window Maker, you can create a file called **winmaker** as shown here.

/etc/X11/gdm/Sessions/winmaker

```
#!/bin/bash -login

/etc/X11/xdm/Xsession wmaker
```

You then must edit the **/etc/X11/xdm/Xsession** file to insert the code for selecting and starting the new window manager. **Xsession** contains detailed code, most of which you can ignore. In it is a case statement that lists the different window managers and desktops. Here you can enter a case entry for **wmaker** that the "wmaker" argument to Xsession will match on. The entry will execute the Window Maker program, **wmaker**.

```
# now, we see if xdm/gdm/kdm has asked for a specific environment
case $# in
1)
    case $1 in
    failsafe)
        exec xterm -geometry 80x24-0-0
```

```
        ;;
    gnome)
        exec gnome-session
    ;;
    kde)
    exec startkde
    ;;
    wmaker)
    exec wmaker
    ;;
    anotherlevel)
        # we assume that switchdesk is installed.
    exec /usr/share/apps/switchdesk/Xclients.anotherlevel
    ;;
    esac
esac
```

KDE Display Manager: kdm

To start a new window manager or desktop from the kdm login window, you first must add an entry for it to the session menu. You do this using the kdm configuration tool, described in Chapter 4. Log in as the root user and start the KDM Configuration Manager by selecting KDM login manager in the Applications menu located in the Settings menu, and then display the Sessions panel. Enter the new session entry in the box labeled New Type and click Add. The entry is added to the session menu on the kdm login window. The name you give the session entry is the argument passed to the kdm **Xsession** script.

You then need to edit the kdm **Xsession** script and add code that checks for the name of this new session, and then execute your new window manager. The KDE display manager (kdm) uses its own **Xsession** file, **/etc/X11/kdm/Xsession**. The code is added to the case statement in the **Xsession** script that chooses which window manager or desktop to run for the user. The following example shows an entry for Window Maker added to the kdm **Xsession** script.

```
case $# in
1)
    case $1 in
    kde)
       KDEDIR=/opt/kde; export KDEDIR
       PATH=$KDEDIR/bin:$PATH
       exec /etc/X11/xinit/kdeinitrc
       ;;
```

```
    wmaker)
       exec wmaker
       ;;
    failsafe)
       exec xterm -geometry 80x24-0-0
          ;;
    esac
  esac
```

Compiling X Window System Applications

To compile X Window System applications, you should first make sure the XFree86 development package is installed, along with any other development package you may need. These contain header files and libraries used by X Window System programs. The name of such packages contain the term **devel**, for example, **XFree86-devel**. Also, many X Windows applications may need special shared libraries. For example, some applications may need the **xforms** library or the **qt** library. Gnome applications require the Gnome development libraries, while KDE applications require the KDE development libraries. You may have to obtain some of these from online sites, though most are available as part of the standard Red Hat installation.

Many X Window System applications use configure scripts that automatically detect your system's configuration and generate a Makefile, which can then be used to compile and install the program. An applications configure script is located in its source code directory. Simply change to that directory and execute the **configure** command. Be sure to include a preceding *./* to specify the configure script in that directory. Afterward, the command **make** compiles the program, and **make install** installs the program on your system. Check an application's README and INSTALL files for any special instructions.

```
./configure
make
make install
```

For older applications that do not have configure scripts, use the **xmkmf** command. A Makefile must be generated that is configured to your system. This is done using an Imakefile provided with the application source code. The **xmkmf** command installed on your system can take an Imakefile and generate the appropriate Makefile. Once you have the Makefile, you can use the **make** command to compile the application. The **xmkmf** command actually uses a program called **imake** to generate the Makefile from the Imakefile; however, you should never use **imake** directly. Consult the man pages for **xmkmf** and **make** for more details.

The
Complete
Reference

Part VII

Network Administration

The Complete Reference

Chapter 36

Configuring Network Connections

Most distributions enable you to configure your network during installation. If you did so, then your system is ready to go. If you need to change your configuration later, you may find the information in this chapter helpful. Administering and configuring a TCP/IP network on your Linux system is not particularly complicated. Your system uses a set of configuration files to set up and maintain your network. Table 38-2 in Chapter 38 provides a complete listing.

Instead of manually editing configuration files, you can use the GUI or cursor-based configuration tools included in many distributions that prompt you for network information. Many distributions incorporate this kind of network configuration into the installation process. If you chose not to configure your network during configuration or you need to make changes to it, you may find it easier and safer to use a network configuration tool. On Red Hat, you can use either Linuxconf or netcfg to configure your network.

Many networks now provide a service that automatically configures a system's network interface. They use a protocol called DHCP (Dynamic Host Configuration Protocol). If your network is configuring your system with DHCP, you will not have to configure it manually. All necessary information will be automatically entered into your network configuration files.

If your system does not have a direct hardware connection to a network, such as an Ethernet connection, and you dial into a network through a modem, you will probably have to set up a PPP connection. Several GUI tools are available for use with Linux that you can use to configure your PPP connection. These include Linuxconf, netcfg, and Kppp. You can even initiate PPP connections from the command line.

Network Startup Script

On Red Hat and Caldera, your network interface is started up using the network script in the **/etc/rc.d/init.d** directory. You can manually shut down and restart your network interface using this script, and the **start** or **stop** options. The following commands shut down and then start up your network interface:

```
/etc/rc.d/init.d/network stop
/etc/rc.d/init.d/network start
```

To test if your interface is working, use the **ping** command with an IP address of a system on your network, such as your gateway machine. The **ping** command continually repeats until you stop it with a CTRL-C. For example, if you have a host on your network with the IP address **192.168.1.42**, you could enter:

```
ping 192.168.1.42
```

Hardware Specifications

In addition to your configuration files, you may also have to configure support for your networking hardware, such as Ethernet cards and modems. Ethernet cards use different modules. During installation, most Linux systems automatically detect your Ethernet card type and have the appropriate module loaded whenever you boot up. If you change your Ethernet card, you may have to change the module. On most Linux distributions, you can use Linuxconf to select a new Ethernet module. You can also manually load a module using the **insmod** command.

For a modem, you should make sure a link by the name of **/dev/modem** exists to your modem device, which is usually one of the **/dev/ttyS**num devices, where num is in the range of 0–3. For example, a modem on the second serial port has a device name of **/dev/ttyS1**, and **/dev/modem** is a link to the **/dev/ttyS1** device file (see Chapter 33). On most distributions, this is usually done for you during installation. On many systems, you can use a modem configuration tool called modemtool to create this link for you. Many modem programs and PPP configuration programs look for the **/dev/modem** file by default.

Dynamic Host Configuration Protocol (DHCP)

The Dynamic Host Configuration Protocol (DHCP) provides configuration information to systems connected to a TCP/IP network, whether the Internet or an intranet. The machines on the network operate as DHCP clients, obtaining their network configuration information from a DHCP server on their network. A machine on the network runs a DHCP client daemon that automatically downloads its network configuration information from its network's DHCP server. The information includes its IP address, along with the network's name server, gateway, and proxy addresses, including the netmask. Nothing has to be entered manually on the local system. This has the added advantage of centralizing control over network configuration for the different systems on the network. A network administrator can manage the network configurations for all the systems on the network from the DHCP server.

A DHCP server also supports several methods for IP address allocation: automatic, dynamic, and manual. Automatic allocation assigns a permanent IP address for a host. Manual allocation assigns an IP address designated by the network administrator. With dynamic allocation, a DHCP server can allocate an IP address to a host on the network only when the host actually needs to use it. Dynamic allocation takes addresses from a pool of IP addresses that hosts can use when needed and release when they are finished.

A variety of DHCP servers and clients are available for different operating systems. For Linux, you can obtain DHCP software from the Internet Software Consortium (ISC) at **www.isc.org**. The software package includes a DHCP server, client, and relay agent.

Linux includes a DHCP server and client. The DHCP client is called dhcpcd, and the server is called dhcpd. The network information a DHCP client downloads is kept in its own network configuration files in the **/etc/dhcpc** directory. For example, here you can find a **resolv.conf** file for your network's name servers.

On Red Hat and Caldera systems, you can stop and start the DHCP server using the **dhcpd** command in the **/etc/rc.d/init.d** directory. The following example starts the DHCP server. Use the **stop** argument to shut it down.

```
/etc/rc.d/init.d/dhcpd start
```

Configuration files for the DHCP server are kept in the **/etc/dhcpd** directory. Here is kept the primary configuration file **dhcpd.conf**, where you specify parameters that define how different DHCP clients on your network are accessed by the DHCP server. Global parameters apply to all clients. You can further create declarations that reference a particular client or different groupings of clients. Within these declarations you can enter parameters that will apply only to those clients. Declarations are implemented using different statements for different kinds of client groups. For example, to define a declaration for a particular host, you use the **host** statement as shown here.

```
host  192.168.1.2  {
             parameters
             }
```

You use the subnet statement to inform the DHCP server of the possible IP addresses encompassed by a given subnet. The subnet statement includes the netmask for the subnet.

```
subnet 192.168.1.0 netmask 255.255.255.0 {
```

With the range statement, you specify a range of addresses that can be dynamically allocated to clients. You enter the first and last addresses in the range.

```
range 192.168.1.5 192.168.1.128 {
```

With parameters, you can specify how the server is to treat clients. For example, default-lease-time parameter sets the number of seconds a lease is assigned to a client. The filename parameter specifies the boot file to be used by the client. The server-name parameter informs the client of the host from which it is booting. The fixed-address parameter can be used to assign a static IP address to a client. See the man page for **dhcpd.conf** for a complete listing.

Clients can further be provided with information they may need to access network services, such as the domain name servers that client uses or the broadcast address. This information is provided by option statements as shown here.

```
option broadcast-address 192.168.1.255;
option domain-name-servers 192.168.1.1, 192.168.1.4;
option domain-name "mytrek.com";
```

A sample **dhcpd.conf** file is shown here.

/etc/dhcpd.conf

```
subnet 192.168.1.0 netmask 255.255.255.0 {
          option routers                  192.168.0.1;
          option subnet-mask              255.255.255.0;

          option domain-name              "mytrek.com ";
          option domain-name-servers      192.168.1.1;

          range     192.168.0.5 192.168.0.128;
          default-lease-time    21600;
          max-lease-time    43200;

          # we want the name server to appear at a fixed address
          host mynameserver {
                  next-server turtle.mytrek.com;
                  hardware ethernet 08:00:2b:4c:29:32;
                  fixed-address 192.168.1.1;
          }
}
```

Note *With Webmin you can configure your DHCP server easily, entering options and parameters for subnets and hosts as well as globally.*

Linuxconf Network Configuration

Linuxconf provides panels for entering network configuration information settings that are saved to the appropriate network configuration files when you activate the changes. You use the Basic host information panel to enter your system's hostname and interface information. Select the panel from the Client tasks list under the Networking heading under Config. This panel has several tabbed subpanels for the hostname and for different adapters. On the Hostname panel, enter your system's fully qualified domain name (see Figure 36-1). You can also enter the **netconf** command in a terminal window to display a Linuxconf window for only the network configuration panels (see Chapter 6).

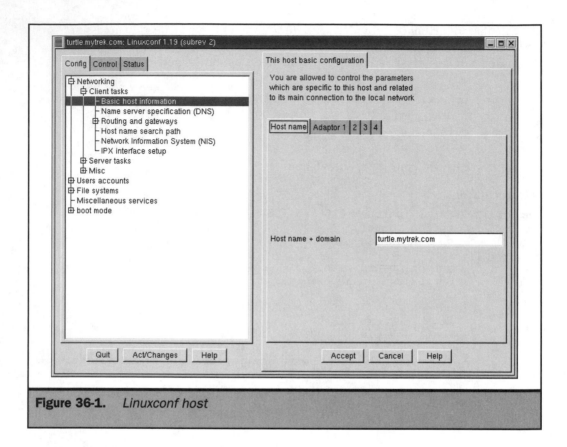

Figure 36-1. *Linuxconf host*

You then use a different Adapter panel for each network interface on your system. Most systems have only one interface, usually an Ethernet or PPP interface. To configure an interface, click an Adapter tab to display an Adapter panel (Figure 36-2). On the Adapter panel, you can use a BOOTP, DHCP, or manual configuration. If the network to which this interface connects provides BOOTP or DHCP configuration services, then your network information is automatically set up for you. Your system is configured with an IP address, name server and gateway addresses, and the network netmask. If such configuration services are not provided, you must enter your network information manually.

On the Adaptor panel, several boxes are for network interface information, some of which have drop-down menus for selecting entries. In the Primary name + domain box, enter your system's fully qualified domain name, and in the IP Address box, enter your system's IP address. In the Aliases box, you can enter nicknames (these are not IP aliases). For the Netmask box, include your network's netmask. In the Net Device box, enter the name of your network interface. The Net Device box has a drop-down menu listing the different interface devices available. You can select an entry from this menu

NETWORK
ADMINISTRATION

Figure 36-2. *Linuxconf Adaptor panel*

to make your entry. For example, for an Ethernet card, you can select eth0 from the drop-down menu, or for a modem, you could select **ppp0**. The Kernel module box is where you enter the name of the module used for your interface's device. This is usually used for the many modules available for different Ethernet cards. This box has a long drop-down menu listing all the kernel modules available for your system. Choose the one appropriate for your card and, when you finish, click the Accept button. If the interface is active, the check box labeled Enabled at the top of the panel is darkened and recessed. If the interface is inactive, the check box is lighter and stands out. Click this check box to toggle the interface on and off.

You also must specify your network's domain name servers and search domains. Enter this information in the Resolver configuration panel. Select Name server specification (DNS) from the Client tasks list under the Networking heading. You then find three boxes for name server Internet addresses, starting with the first name server for your network (see Figure 36-3). Enter the IP address for your primary name server in the name server1 box, and enter the secondary name server in the name server 2 box. Enter your search domains in the search domains boxes. If your network is connected to the Internet, it has a gateway system. You enter the IP address for the gateway in the default gateway box on the Defaults panel in the Routing and gateways list. This is located in the Client tasks list under the Networking heading.

Figure 36-3. *Linuxconf name server specification*

If you use a modem instead of an Ethernet card to connect to a network, you need to configure a dial-up interface. With Linuxconf, you can configure a PPP, SLIP, or PLIP interface (see following section on PPP and SLIP). Most *Internet service providers* (*ISPs*) set up connections over a modem using PPP interfaces. To configure such an interface, click the PPP/SLIP/PLIP entry in the Routing and gateways list under Client tasks in Networking. This displays a PPP/SLIP/PLIP panel. When you add an interface, it displays another panel where you can choose the interface you want. If you select PPP, a PPP interface panel is displayed with boxes for the dial-up phone number, the interface device, and the login name and password you use to connect to your ISP (see Figure 36-4). If you click the Customize button, four more tabbed panels are displayed for Hardware, Communications, Networking, and PAP (the Password Authentication Protocol). On the Hardware panel, you can set communication speeds and the modem port, along with PPP options. The Communications panel enables you to set the modem initialization string, phone number, and dial-up command, as well as the Expect/Send script used for the ISP login operation. Here, you can specify what

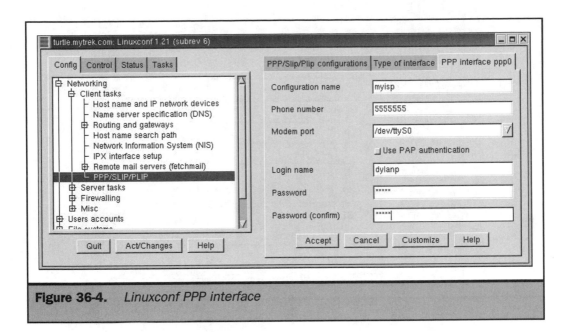

Figure 36-4.   *Linuxconf PPP interface*

password and login prompt to expect. When you finish, click Accept. When you click the Linuxconf Activate/Changes button, it saves your dial-up configuration to appropriate files, generating any needed scripts. For a PPP connection, it generates a chat script to dial the connection and an Expect/Send script for login. To use Linuxconf to connect to your ISP, click the Control PPP/SLIP/PLIP links entry in the Control panel list under Control (not Config). This displays a panel in which you can click a Connect button to have your modem dial up and connect to the ISP. You can also use the PPP/SLIP/PLIP entry in the Routing and gateways list under Client tasks in Networking. For a PPP connection, select the PPP interface panel and click the Connect button. When you finish, click the Disconnect button.

COAS, Webmin, and YaST (SuSE) Network Configuration

OpenLinux and SuSE provide network configuration as part of their configuration utilities, COAS and YaST. To configure a network connection with COAS (Caldera Open Adminstration System), you select Network Administration from the COAS menu. You can then further select Ethernet Interfaces to enter your network settings. This displays a window where you can enter your IP, Gateway, and Broadcast addresses, along with your Netmask, as well as the name of your Ethernet device (see Figure 36-5). When finished, you can then select the Hostname Resolution entry in the Network Administration menu to open a window where you can enter your domain name server addresses. For PPP connections, you use a PPP configuration tool like Kppp.

Figure 36-5. *COAS Network Configuration*

Yet Another Setup Tool (YaST) used on SuSE, provides a similar interface, prompting you to enter various network addresses for your system. Start up YaST and select "Systems administration" and then "Network configuration." From here, you can select "Basic network configuration" to list your network interfaces that you can then configure with your host and gateway IP addresses.

To configure your network with Webmin, you select the Network Configuration page from the Hardware page. On this page you can choose to configure interfaces, gateways and routes, client DNS (**resolv.conf**), and Host addresses. On the Network configuration page, you can configure network interfaces such as Ethernet connections, adding new ones and editing current ones (see Figure 36-6). Each interface name is a link that will display a configuration page for that interface. Here you can change entries or delete the entire interface configuration.

Red Hat Network Configuration Tool: netcfg

Red Hat provides an easy-to-use network configuration tool called netcfg. Other systems may also have this tool. On the Red Hat control panel, an icon is labeled Network Configuration. You can also start netcfg from the desktop or window manager's program menus, usually with the entry Network Configuration. The netcfg window consists of four panels and a button bar at the top for each one: Name, Hosts,

Webmin Index
Module Index

Network Interfaces

Interfaces Active Now

Name	Type	IP Address	Netmask	Status
eth0	Ethernet	192.168.1.1	255.255.255.0	Up
lo	Loopback	127.0.0.1	255.0.0.0	Up

Add a new interface

Interfaces Activated at Boot Time

Name	Type	IP Address	Netmask	Activate at boot?
eth0	Ethernet	192.168.1.1	255.255.255.0	Yes
eth1	Ethernet	0.0.0.0	255.255.255.0	Yes
lo	Loopback	127.0.0.1	255.0.0.0	Yes
plip0	PLIP	10.0.0.1	Automatic	Yes

Add a new interface

Figure 36-6.   *Webmin Network Configuration*

Interfaces, and Routing (see Figure 36-7). Clicking a button displays its panel. Basic configuration of your network requires you to specify the hostname and IP address of your own system, the IP addresses of your network's name servers and gateway, the network netmask, and your network interfaces. Using the netcfg tool, you can easily enter all this information. The Name panel is where you enter your own system's hostname and your network's name server addresses. The Hosts panel lists host IP addresses and their domain names, including those for your own system. On the Interfaces panel, you add and configure your network interfaces, such as an Ethernet or PPP interface. The Routing panel is where you specify special routing hosts, including your gateway system. If you already configured your network during installation, your entries are already in these panels.

The Names panel has two boxes at the top, labeled Hostname and Domain. Here, you enter your system's fully qualified domain name and your network's domain name. For example, **turtle.mytrek.com** is the fully qualified domain name, and **mytrek.com** is the domain name. The panel has two panes, one for search domains and another for name server addresses. For the search domain, you enter specific domains you want searched for an Internet address. In the name server pane, you enter the IP addresses for your network's name servers. Both the search domain and the name server addresses are saved in the **/etc/resolv.conf** file. The hostname is saved to your **/etc/HOSTNAME** file.

Figure 36-7. *The netcfg Names panel*

The Hosts panel has a single pane with Add, Edit, and Remove buttons. This panel lists entries that associate hostnames with IP addresses. You can also add aliases (nicknames). The Hosts panel actually displays the contents of the **/etc/hosts** file and saves any entries you make to that file. To add an entry, click the Add button. A window opens with boxes for the hostname, IP address, and nicknames. When you click OK, the entry is added to the Hosts list. To edit an entry, click the Edit button and a similar window opens, enabling you to change any of the fields. To delete an entry, select it and click the Remove button.

The Interfaces panel lists configured network interfaces on your system (shown in Figure 36-8). Making entries here performs the same function as ifconfig. An entry shows the interface name, its IP address, preferences, whether it is made active whenever you boot, and whether it is currently active. Use the Add, Edit, Alias, and Remove buttons to manage the interface entries. You use the Activate and Deactive buttons to connect or disconnect the interface with the network. To add an interface, click the Add button. A window opens—the Choose Interface window—listing possible interfaces, including Ethernet or PPP. Select one and its appropriate interface window appears.

For example, if you choose Ethernet, the Edit Ethernet Interface window appears. Here, you enter the IP address for your machine and your network's netmask. You can choose further if you want the interface to start automatically at boot time and whether you want to use the BOOTP or DHCP protocols to configure the interface. When you finish, you see your new entry displayed on the Interfaces panel. To activate your new entry, click the Activate button. To make any changes, select it and click the Edit button. The Alias button enables you to create IP aliases for the interface. This enables you to assign two IP addresses to the same interface, instructing your system to listen on that interface
for packets and messages addressed to either IP address. In effect, you are giving your system two IP addresses.

The Routing panel has boxes at the top for your network's gateway system. In the Default Gateway box, enter the IP address of gateway system, and in the Default Gateway Device box, specify the interface through which you connect to the network serviced by that gateway. This is usually the same interface you use to connect to your network. For example, the device for an Ethernet card would be **eth0**. If your network

Figure 36-8.   *The netcfg Interfaces pane*

uses more than one gateway, you can add the others here by clicking the Add button. If you are on a *local area network* (*LAN*) with no connection to the Internet, you do not have a gateway and needn't make any entries here.

When you finish and are ready to save your configuration, click the Save button. If you want to abandon the changes you made, you can Quit without saving. You can run netcfg at any time to make changes in your network configuration or to connect or disconnect manually from a network using the Activate or Deactivate buttons on the Interfaces panel.

PPP and SLIP

As an alternative to hardwired network connections such as Ethernet, you can use a modem with telephone lines to connect to a network. Two protocols can transmit IP communications across the telephone lines. These are the *Serial Line Internet Protocol* (*SLIP*) and the *Point-to-Point Protocol* (*PPP*). SLIP is an older protocol, whereas PPP is newer and has become predominant. Most high-speed connections used by current ISPs use PPP. The SLIP and PPP protocols are especially designed for users who connect their systems to the Internet over a modem and a telephone line. Usually, a connection is made to an ISP, which then connects the system to the Internet through its own systems. An ISP supports either SLIP or PPP on a given line. Find out which protocol your ISP supports. You need to use one or the other. Setting up a SLIP or PPP connection can be a complicated process. For more detailed explanations, see the PPP-HOWTO and the Net-2-HOWTO documents in **/usr/share/doc/HOWTO**. Web page instructions are in **/usr/share/doc/HTML**, and you can also, check the **/usr/doc/ppp-***version* where version is the PPP package version.

PPP Connection Utilities: Kppp, gnomeppp, and rp3

You can use several graphical PPP configuration utilities on your Linux desktop to create and manage a PPP connection. For a simple PPP connection, you can use the Red Hat PPP Dialer utility known as *rp3*. For more complex connections, you can use the KDE PPP tool called *Kppp,* a Gnome PPP tool called *gnomeppp,* and several X Windows–based tools such as *xisp* and *easyppp.* All the tools offer the same kind of interface, providing panels for login information, modem configuration, and dial-up connections. You can also use netcfg and Linuxconf to manage a PPP connection. Although their interfaces are somewhat different, netcfg and Linuxconf do perform many of the same tasks as described here for Kppp.

For simple connections on Red Hat systems, you only need to use the Red Hat PPP Dialer (rp3). Select its entry in the Internet submenu on the Gnome desktop. If you do not have any Internet connections set up already, the Add New Internet Connection dialog box starts up. First, you are asked to configure your modem, selecting its serial device, speed, and sound level. Next, you are asked to enter ISP connection information, such as your login name, password, and phone number. Each time you want to connect, select the Red Hat PPP Dialer entry from the Gnome Internet menu or enter the command **/usr/bin/rp3** on the command line. To change your setting or to add a new connection, select the Red Hat Dialup Configuration Tool entry in the Internet menu. The Edit button opens a window with panels for modifying connection and modem information. These tools are covered in more detail in Chapter 6.

This section discusses the Kppp PPP utility in detail. You can use Kppp as a model for using the other PPP tools. During Kppp configuration, you are presented with a set of tabbed panels in which you enter Internet and modem information. Once configured, connecting is simply a matter of clicking a button labeled Connect. The Kppp tool runs fine from the root user, but it needs permission set on certain files to allow use by other users on your system. See the documentation in the **/usr/doc/kppp*** directory, which also includes a detailed tutorial you can view with your Web browser.

To configure a connection, click the Setup button. This brings up the Configuration window, which has several panels. One panel appears in the front, with tabs for the others showing at the top. Six panels are in the Configuration window: one for accounts, other panels for device and modem settings, and one for PPP features. Accounts hold your Internet information. You can have more than one account, depending on how many different ISPs you subscribe to (most users have only one). To create an account, click the New button. This brings up a New Accounts window with a set of panels for Internet information. The Dial panel is where you enter connection information, such as the phone number you use to connect to the provider. Be sure to enter a name for the connection, which can be anything you want. The Arguments button brings up another window for entering PPP arguments. These are options for the PPP daemon. Figure 36-9 shows the Configuration and New Account windows.

The IP panel is where you enter any local and remote IP addresses, as well as a netmask. Each entry has Dynamic and Static check buttons; the Dynamic check buttons are already set by default. If your ISP gives you dynamic addresses and a netmask, as most do these days, you can leave this panel alone. If, on the other hand, you have a static local or remote address, you must bring up the panel and enter the address(s). Click the tab labeled DNS to bring up the Domain Name Server panel. Here, you enter in the IP addresses of your ISP's domain name servers. Click the box labeled IP Address and type the address. Then, click Add to add the address to the list of name servers.

You then have to create a login script in which you provide the user name and password you use to connect to your ISP. To do this, click the Login Script tab to bring up the Script panel. You then see a frame called Edit Script with several buttons and boxes (see Figure 36-10). You need to create a simple script that performs the following task using two instructions: send and receive:

```
receive       ogin:
send          username
receive       word:
send          password
```

You see a button labeled Expect. This is actually a pop-up menu with several entries listing possible login instructions. The entry you select is shown when the

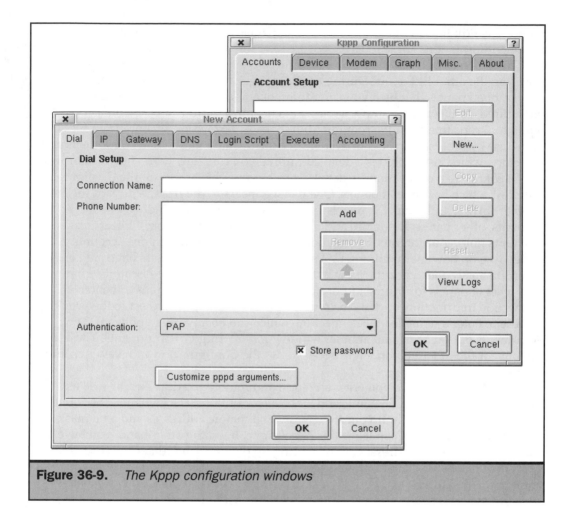

Figure 36-9. *The Kppp configuration windows*

pop-up menu collapses. Five entries exist: Expect, Send, Pause, Hangup, and Answer. The instructions usually used to send a string or to expect receiving a string are Send and Expect. If you want a send instruction, select the Send entry. If you want a receive instruction, select the Expect entry. The box to the right of this button is where you enter text on which the instruction operates. For example, for the instruction to receive the text ogin:, select the Expect entry and type **ogin:** into this box. To place it in the script, click the Add button. Both the term expect and the text ogin: appear in the script frame below the Add button. If you make a mistake, you can click the entry and then click the Remove button to delete it. If you need to insert an instruction instead of having it placed at the end, use the Insert button.

Most login scripts only need two pairs of Send and Expect instructions: one for the login name and one for the password. The first instruction expects the text ogin: and

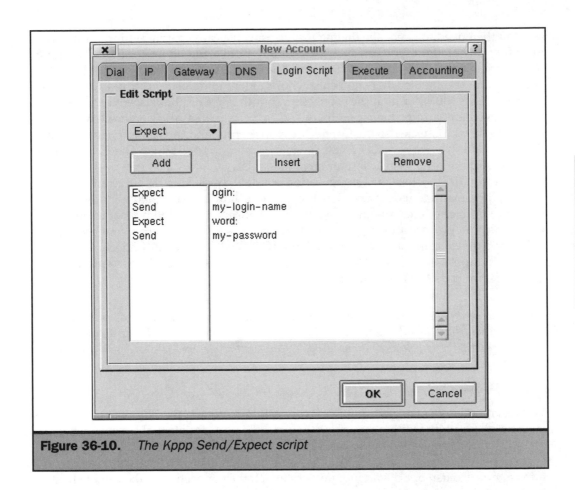

Figure 36-10.   *The Kppp Send/Expect script*

the second instruction sends text consisting of the login name. The third instruction expects the text word: and the fourth sends the text consisting of the password. This may vary depending on how you connect to your ISP. The previous Figure 36-10 shows a sample login script, where my-login-name is your user name and my-password is the password you use.

After you finish entering the Internet information, click OK to close the Script and New Accounts windows. At the Configure window, click the Modem tab to bring up the Modem panel. Make sure the modem port is correct. Usually, this is **/dev/modem**, where modem is a link to the actual modem port device. In most cases, you needn't change this. Modem port devices begin with the name **/dev/ttyS** with an attached number from 0 to 3. On your PC, you have four ports from which to choose: 1 through 4. Usually, a modem is connected to either port 2 or port 4. The names for these would be **/dev/ttyS1** and **/dev/ttyS3** (the count is from 0, so port 1 is ttyS0 and port 2 is ttyS1). If you already set up a modem alias for the port, you can use **/dev/modem**.

You then need to check the dialing prefix, as well as any special settings you may need for your modem. You can click the Edit button to bring up a window with a long list of boxes with settings for your modem. They should already have default settings entered. The first box is where you enter your modem initialization string, adding such instructions as M0 to turn off the connection sound. The third box, labeled Dial String, is where you enter your dialing prefix. ATDT is the default already entered, which most people use. Check also the Connect response entry and the Hangup string. The default connect response is CONNECT, which is valid for most ISPs. The *Hangup string* is a standard hang-up instruction for most modems.

After you finish, close the Configuration window by clicking the OK button. You are then ready to use Kppp. Click the Connect button in the main window. If you have problems, click the show log window to bring up a window that displays the connection process and any errors that occur. When Kppp makes a connection, it displays the amount of time connected and the speed at which it connected. The Connect button is changed to Disconnect. To end your session, click Disconnect. Clicking Quit ends the Kppp program.

*Each individual user can create his or her own accounts, using the steps described previously. This information is held in a .kppprc file in the user's **home** directory. In fact, different users could use Kppp to connect to different ISPs.*

Manual PPP Connections

You can manually create your own PPP connection, invoking the PPP program directly on the command line with **chat** scripts to make the appropriate dial-up connections. The PPP program is called pppd. The pppd program neither makes the initial connection nor does it dial up through your modem and provide login and password information. To use pppd, you first must establish the connection to the remote host. You can make such a connection using the chat program, which has its own options and format. The chat program first makes the connection, and then pppd configures it. You needn't call chat first, and then call pppd, however. The pppd program is designed to take as its argument a program that can make the connection—in this case, chat. You simply specify **chat** along with its options on the command line with **pppd**.

Static and dynamic IP addresses are distinguished by pppd by whether you include a set of IP addresses as an argument on the command line and by the use of the **noipdefault** option. If you do include the IP addresses, then pppd assumes you have a static connection and that the addresses you enter are the remote and local addresses to use to establish that connection. If you do not specify any addresses as arguments, then pppd assumes a default remote and local address. The default local address is the IP address of your system, as specified in your **/etc/hostname** file. A default remote address tries to be determined from remote addresses in your **/etc/hosts** file. The pppd program assumes you use dynamic addresses and looks for them when a connection is made. To have pppd assume dynamic addresses, you use the

noipdefault option and you do not specify any addresses. The **noipdefault** option instructs pppd not to use default addresses. When no address is specified, pppd then assumes dynamic addresses are going to be received from the remote host.

The local and remote static addresses are entered next to each other, separated by a colon. The local address is entered first. The following example specifies a local address of **192.168.1.72** and remote address of **163.179.4.22**.

```
192.168.1.72:163.179.4.22
```

If you use a dynamic remote address, but your own local address, you can specify only your local address, followed by the colon. The pppd program then uses your local address and dynamically receives your remote address.

```
192.168.1.72:
```

Because your local address as specified in your **/etc/hostname** file is your default local address, you needn't even enter it on the command line. You could enter only the **pppd** command with no addresses. The pppd program uses your hostname address as your local address and receives a remote address from the remote host.

 Note   *Most ISPs that use dynamic addresses provide you with both the local and remote address. In this case, you do not enter any addresses at all and you do have to specify the* **noipdefault** *option. The* **noipdefault** *option prevents the use of the hostname address as the default local address. Lacking any addresses, pppd obtains both from the remote host.*

Chat Scripts

The best way to use chat is to invoke a **chat** script. To make a connection, **chat** has to specify all the connection information: the telephone number, the login prompt and user ID, the password prompt and password, and any connect strings. You could enter this as a string after the **chat** command on the command line, but this makes for a long and complex command line. Instead, you can create a file with the chat information in it and then use the **-f** option and the filename with the **chat** command. Such files are called **chat** scripts.

A **chat** *script* consists of one line organized into different segments for the parts of the connection procedure. Each segment consists of an expect-reply pair of strings. The first string is what you expect to receive, while the second string is what you are sending. If you expect to receive nothing, then you use a null string, "". Each expect-reply pair performs a specific task in the login process. You can start with an initialization of your modem, if you need to do this. Many users can simply use the default settings. Then, the number is dialed to make the connection and you can check to see if the connection was made. A login name is provided at the login prompt, and finally, a password is sent at the password prompt.

NETWORK
ADMINISTRATION

If you decide to initialize your modem, you need to start with an expect-reply entry to perform this task. You expect nothing at first, so the expect string is only an empty string, two double quotes, **""**. For the reply string, you specify the codes for your modem initialization. When entering the codes for your initialization string, you need to escape any code beginning with **&**. For chat, the **&** is a break and stops the process. See Table 36-1 for a list of **chat** options and special characters.

The next expect-reply entry dials the phone number. If you have an initialization string before the next expect-reply entry, then its expect string is the word OK. This is the response from your modem indicating no problem occurred initializing your modem. You usually receive a connect string indicating you have connected to the remote system. This can vary from system to system, and there may not even be a connect string at all. On many systems, the connect string is the word CONNECT; on others, the connect string is the baud rate, or speed. In this example, the user receives the speed as the connect string. The response to a connect string is usually nothing, though it can also be a newline. Recall that you represent no response with an empty string—two double quotes, **""**. The newline is represented in a **chat** script with a \n.

After the connect string, the remote system usually sends the login prompt. This is often the word "login" with a colon. You only need the last few characters, **ogin:** and don't forget the colon. In reply, you send your user ID. Depending on your ISP, you may have to add **\n** to the user ID to enter a newline, as in **mylogin**\n.

```
ogin:  mylogin
```

After the login, you can expect the password prompt. Again, you only need the last few characters, **word:**. In response, you send your password. If needed, be sure to add the **\n** to enter the newline.

```
word: mypass
```

All this fits together on just one line. You have a sequence of words that indicate alternating received and sent text:

```
"" AT\&F2V1L0 OK  ATDT8888888 CONNECT \n ogin: mylogin  word: mypass
```

If you did not initialize your modem, it looks slightly different:

```
"" ATDT8888888 CONNECT  \n  ogin:  mylogin  word:  mypass
```

If your ISP does not require you to send a return character on receiving the connect string, you can leave that out, reducing the **chat** script as shown here:

```
"" ATDT8888888 ogin:  mylogin  word:  mypass
```

In a **chat** script, you can break the expect and reply pairs into separate lines, one pair to a line, with the strings for each pair separated by a space or tab. You could also put it all on the first line if you want. The filename for the script has the extension **.chat**. The next example shows the **/etc/ppp/ppp.chat** script with pairs entered on separate lines.

ppp.chat

```
"  "        AT\&F2V1L0
OK          ATDT4448888
CONNECT     \n
ogin:       mylogin
word:       mypass
```

You can then call the **chat** script with the **chat** command and the **-f** option, as shown here. The chat program uses the information in the **chat** script to initialize your modem, to dial up your remote host, and then to log in with your user ID and password.

```
chat -f  /etc/ppp/ppp.chat
```

Many remote systems and modes send error messages if something goes wrong in the connection process. You can use the special expect string, ABORT, followed by a key term to detect such an error message. If such a term is received, **chat** cancels the connection procedure. If you are using a command line only, you can enter abort strings either where you would expect them to occur in the connection process or at the beginning. Within a **chat** script, as shown here, the abort strings are placed at the beginning. The next example would expect a NO CARRIER or a BUSY response before the login prompt. In either case, an initial connection failed, and **chat** will cancel the remaining steps. Notice the quotes around NO CARRIER. If a string has a space in it, you have to quote it.

ppp.chat

```
ABORT       'NO CARRIER'
ABORT       BUSY
"  "        AT\&F2V1L0
OK          ATDT5558888
CONNECT     \n
ogin:       mylogin
word:       mypass
```

You need to incorporate the **chat** operation into your invocation of the **pppd** command. The entire **chat** operations is encased in single quotes and entered on the same line as the **pppd** command. The **chat** program uses the information in the **chat** script to initialize your modem, dial up your remote host, and then log in with your user ID and password. The **chat** script makes the connection, and then **pppd** configures it. The

Point-to-Point Protocol daemon (**pppd**) is invoked with several possible options. Its standard syntax is

> **pppd** *options serial-device-name speed local:remote-addresses ppp-options*

The *serial-device-name* is the device name for your modem. This is likely to be **/dev/ttyS** with a number attached, usually from 0 to 3, depending on the port you are using for your modem. Port 1 is ttyS0, port 2 is ttyS2, and so on. The *speed* is the baud rate. For a 14.4 modem, this is 14,400. For a v.36 modem, this is 38,400, or even 56,700. Check with your ISP and your modem documentation for the highest speed you can support.

The options specify configuration features, such as your MTU size and whether you are receiving a dynamic IP address. The **connect** option instructs **pppd** to make a connection and takes as its argument a Linux command that can actually make the connection—usually the **chat** command. You enter **pppd,** followed by the **connect** option, and the **chat** command with its **-f** option and **chat** script filename. The **chat** command and its **-f** option with the chat filename are all enclosed in quotes to distinguish them from other **pppd** options. In the next example, the user invokes **pppd** with the **chat** command using the **mycon.chat chat** script. The modem is connected to port 4, **/dev/ttyS1**, and the speed is 57,600 baud.

> # **pppd connect 'chat -f /etc/ppp/ppp.chat' /dev/ttyS1   57600**

To disconnect your PPP connection, you invoke **pppd** with the **disconnect** option. You must use **chat** to instruct your modem to hang up. For this, you may have to send a modem command, such as **H0**. You can also use the **ppp-off** script to disconnect. You might find a chat file is a more convenient to place the **chat** commands, as shown here:

> # **pppd disconnect 'chat -f turnoff.chat'**

turnoff.chat
```
—  \d+++\d\c    OK
   ATH0   OK
```

PPP Options

The **pppd** command has a great many options. The more commonly used ones are listed in Table 36-2. See the **pppd** Man pages for a complete list. For example, the **mru** option sets the maximum receive unit size. The **pppd** command instructs the remote system to send packets no larger than this size. The default is 1500, and 296 or 542 is recommended for slower modems. The **defaultroute** option instructs **pppd** to set up the PPP connection as the default route. The lack of any addresses combined with

Option	Description
-f *filename*	Executes **chat** commands in the **chat** script with name *filename*
-l *lockfile*	Makes UUCP (Unix-to-Unix Copy Protocol) style like file using *lockfile*
-t *num*	Timeout set to *num* seconds
-v	A description of all chat actions are output to the **/log/messages** file; use **tail**, **cat**, or **more** on this file to display the descriptions: **tail /log/messages**

Special Characters

BREAK	Sends break to modem
''	Sends null string with single newline character
\b	BACKSPACE
\c	Suppresses newline sent after reply string
\d	Makes chat wait for one second
\K	Sends break; when specifying string for modem initialization, and codes beginning with *K* may have to be escaped
\n	Sends newline characters
\N	Sends null character
\p	Pauses for 1/10 of a second
\q	String does not appear in **syslog** file
\r	Sends or expects a new line
\s	Sends or expects a space
\t	Sends or expects a tab
\\	Sends or expects a backslash
\\nnn	Specifies a character in octal
^C	Specifies a control character

Table 36-1.   *The* **Chat** *Options and Special Characters*

the **noipdefault** option instructs **pppd** to detect and use a dynamic IP address from the ISP remote system. You have to specify this option if you have an ISP that supplies dynamic IP addresses. The **crtscts** option uses hardware flow control, while the **modem** option uses the modem control lines. You can list the options after the speed on the command line, as shown here:

```
# pppd connect 'chat -f /etc/ppp/ppp.chat' /dev/ttyS1 57600
    mru 1500 defaultroute noipdefault crtscts modem
```

In the following command, the presence of addresses instructs **pppd** to use these addresses to establish a static connection. The local address is **192.168.1.72**, and the remote address is **163.179.4.22**.

```
# pppd connect 'chat -f /etc/ppp/ppp.chat' /dev/ttyS1 57600
      192.168.1.72:163.179.4.22 mru 1500 defaultroute crtscts modem
```

This can make for a lengthy and complex command line, depending on how many options you need. As an alternative, **pppd** enables you to enter options in the file **/etc/ppp/options,** as well as in a **.ppprc** file. The **pppd** option automatically reads and uses the options specified in these files each time it is invoked. You can specify as many options as you want, entering each on a separate line. With the **#** symbol, you can also enter comments, explaining the options and their settings. The **/etc/ppp/options** file contains system default options for **pppd**. You create this file as the root user, and it is the first options file called when **pppd** is invoked. Each user can have a **.ppprc** file in her own **home** directory. These options are specified by a particular user and are read after the system's **/etc/ppp/options** file.

/etc/ppp/options

```
crtscts
defaultroute
modem
mru 1500
asyncmap 0
netmask 255.255.255.0
noipdefault
```

Now when you invoke **pppd**, you needn't enter any of these options on the command line. With your options specified in the **/etc/ppp/options** file, you then only need to enter the **pppd** command with the **chat** invocation, the device name for your modem, and the modem speed.

```
$ pppd connect 'chat -f /etc/ppp/ppp.chat' /dev/ttyS1 57600
```

You can reduce your entry even further by placing the **pppd** invocation in a shell script, and then executing the shell script. Recall that a shell script is a text file you create with any text editor (see Chapter 11). You type the command invocation with all its arguments as you would on the command line. Be sure to precede the **pppd** command with an **exec** command. The **exec** command runs **pppd** from your command line shell, not the script's shell. You then make the script executable with the command **chmod 755** *script-name.* Now, to execute your **pppd** operation, enter the script name on the command line and press ENTER. In the next example, the **pppd** connect operation is placed in a shell script called **pppcon**, and the user simply enters **pppcon** to invoke **pppd**.

pppcon

```
exec pppd connect 'chat -f /etc/ppp/ppp.chat' /dev/ttyS1 57600$ pppcon
```

You are now ready to try **pppd** to connect to your remote system. Any number of things may go wrong. You may not have the right connect string, or the modem may be initializing wrong. The **pppd** command logs descriptions of all the steps it is taking in the **/var/log/messages** file. You can use **tail** to list these descriptions even as **pppd** is operating. For a successful connection, you see the local and remote IP addresses listed at the end, as shown here:

```
$ tail /var/log/messages
```

To receive an ongoing display of messages as they are entered in the **/var/log/messages** file, use the **tail** command with the **–f** option, as shown here. Use a CTRL-C to end the process.

```
$ tail -f /var/log/messages
Mar 23 20:01:03 richlp pppd[208]: Connected...
Mar 23 20:01:04 richlp pppd[208]: Using interface ppp
Mar 23 20:01:04 richlp kernel: ppp: channel ppp mtu=1500, mru=1500
Mar 23 20:01:04 richlp kernel: ppp: channel ppp open
Mar 23 20:01:04 richlp pppd[208]: Connect: ppp ~/dev/ttyS3
Mar 23 20:01:09 richlp pppd[208]: local  IP address 204.32.168.68
Mar 23 20:01:09 richlp pppd[208]: remote IP address 163.179.4.23
```

The ppp RPM package installed on Red Hat systems includes a sample login PPP script called **ppp-on** in the **/usr/doc/ppp-***version***/scripts** directory, where version is the pppd version. You can use a text editor to set the correct values to certain variables, such as TELEPHONE, ACCOUNT, and PASSWORD. You also must be careful to set the correct arguments and options for both the **chat** and the **pppd** commands. If you

Option	Description
device-name	Uses the specified device; if the device name does not have **/dev** preceding it, pppd adds it for you
speed *num*	Sets the modem speed (baud rate)
asyncmap *map*	Sets the async character map that specifies what control characters cannot be sent and should be escaped
auth	Requires the remote host to authenticate itself
connect *Connection-operation*	Uses the connection operations to set up the connection; the Linux command here is usually **chat**, which makes the actual connection
crtscts	Uses hardware flow control
xonxoff	Uses software flow control
defaultroute	**pppd** sets a default route to the remote host.
disconnect *Linux-command*	Runs the specified command after **pppd** cuts its connection; usually a chat operation
escape *c,c,...*	Causes the specified characters to be escaped when transmitted
file *filename*	Reads **pppd** options from the specified file
lock	Uses UUCP-style locking on the serial device
mru *num*	Sets the maximum receive units to *num*
netmask *mask*	Sets the PPP network interface mask
noipdefault	For dynamic IP addresses provided by ISP; searches the incoming data stream from the remote host for both the local and remote IP addresses assigned to your system for that Internet session; must have this option to connect with a dynamic IP address

Table 36-2.   *The **pppd** Options*

Option	Description
passive	Makes **pppd** wait for a valid connection instead of failing when it can't make the connection immediately
silent	**pppd** waits for a connection to be made by a remote host

Table 36-2.   *The **pppd** Options* (continued)

have already set options in the **/etc/ppp/options** file, you can remove most of the options you would normally specify on the command line. Also, be sure to set the correct speed and device name for the modem. The default used on the script is 38,400. For a 56K modem, change it to 57,600. Once it is working, all you must enter then is **ppp-on** to establish your PPP connection. If you have trouble disconnecting, try the **ppp-off** command.

You can also configure your system to be a PPP server, allowing remote systems to dial into yours and make PPP connections. You only need to create one special account and a script to invoke **pppd** with the **-detach** and **silent** options. The script is usually called **ppplogin**—here is an example:

/etc/ppp/ppplogin

```
exec pppd -detach silent modem crtscts
```

With the **-detach** option, **pppd** won't detach itself from the line on which it is located. The **silent** option makes **pppd** wait for a remote system to make a link to your system. The **modem** option monitors the modem lines, and **crtscts** uses hardware flow control. The special account has the name ppp. The **/etc/passwd** entry for the ppp account appears as follows:

```
ppp:*:501:300:PPP Account:/tmp:etc/ppp/ppplogin
```

PPP Security: CHAP

To ensure security for PPP connections, you have to use additional protocols. Two have been developed for PPP: the *Password Authentication Protocol* (*PAP*) and the *Challenge Handshake Authentication Protocol* (*CHAP*). CHAP is considered a more secure protocol because it uses an encrypted challenge system that requires the two connected systems to authenticate each other continually. The keys for the encryption are kept in the **/etc/ppp/chap-secrets** file. To use CHAP in your PPP connections, you include the **auth** option when you invoke **pppd**. Also, you must enter the required information for the remote host into the **/etc/ppp/chap-secrets** file. The following is an example of a **/etc/ppp/chap-secrets** entry. Entries for the PAP in **/etc/ppp/pap-secrets** have the same format.

etc/ppp/chap-secrets

```
pango1.train.com      turtle.trek.com        "my new hat"
 *                    turtle.trek.com         "confirmed tickets"
turtle.trek.com       pango1.train.com     "trek on again"
```

A CHAP secrets entry has up to four fields: the client's host name, the server's host name, a secret key, and a list of IP possible addresses. For a particular computer trying to make a connection to your system, you can specify that it supply the indicated secret key. Instead of specifying a particular computer, you can use a ***** to indicate any computer. Any system that knows the designated secret key can connect to your system. In the first entry in the following example, the server is the user's own system, **turtle.trek.com**. The server allows **pango1.train.com** to connect to it if it provides the secret key specified. In the next entry, any remote system can connect to **turtle.trek.com** if it knows the secret key "confirmed tickets."

```
pango1.train.com      turtle.trek.com      "my new hat"
 *                    turtle.trek.com      "confirmed tickets"
```

You also have to make entries for remote systems you want to access. In that case, the remote system is the PPP server and you are the client. In the next example, **turtle** can connect to **pango1** with the secret key "trek on again."

```
turtle.trek.com pango1.train.com "trek on again"
```

SLIP: dip

Two types of SLIP connections exist: the standard one referred to simply as *SLIP,* and the newer *Compressed SLIP* (*CSLIP*). Be sure you know which type of connection your ISP is giving you. You must specify one or the other as your protocol mode when you connect. Except for specifying the mode, the connection procedure is the same for both. References to SLIP apply to both SLIP and CSLIP, unless specifically noted. You use the dip program to manage and set up your SLIP connection. The *dip program* operates like an interpreter. In a file called a **dip** script, you specify certain commands needed to log into the ISP and make the connection. The dip program then reads the commands in this file, executing them one by one. With Linux, not only can you make a SLIP connection to a remote system, but other systems can also make their own SLIP connections to your system. Another system can dial into your system and make a SLIP connection. If you have provided an account for a user on that remote system, then the user could dial in a SLIP connection and log in to that account. Such remote dial-up SLIP connections are managed by **dip** with the **-i** option. This places dip in a dial-in mode to receive incoming connections. In the dial-in mode, dip prompts a remote user for a user ID and a password, and then makes the SLIP connection.

Chapter 37

Samba, NFS, NIS, and Appletalk

L inux provides several tools for accessing files on remote systems connected to a network. The *Network File System* (*NFS*) enables you to connect to and directly access resources such as files or devices like CD-ROMs that reside on another machine. The *Network Information Service (NIS)* maintains configuration files for all systems on a network. With Samba, you can connect your Windows clients on a Microsoft Windows network to services such as shared files, systems, and printers controlled by the Linux Samba server. Netatalk enables you to connect your Linux systems to an AppleTalk network, enabling you to access remote Macintosh file systems directly, as well as to access any Apple printers such as LaserWriters.

Network File Systems: NFS and /etc/exports

NFS enables you to mount a file system on a remote computer as if it were local to your own system. You can then directly access any of the files on that remote file system. This has the advantage of allowing different systems on a network to access the same files directly, without each having to keep its own copy. Only one copy would be on a remote file system, which each computer could then access.

NFS operates over a TCP/IP network. The remote computer that holds the file system makes it available to other computers on the network. It does so by exporting the file system, which entails making entries in an NFS configuration file called **/etc/exports**, as well as by running three daemons to support access by other systems: **rpc.mountd, rpc.nfsd,** and **rpc.portmapper. rpc.nfsd** receives NFS requests from remote systems and translates them into requests for the local system. **rpc.mountd** performs requested mount and unmount operations. **rpc.portmapper** maps remote requests to the appropriate NFS daemon. In addition, **rpc.statd** provides locking services when a remote host reboots, and **rpc.quotad** provides user disk quota management. You can use the `rpcinfo` command with the `-p` options to see if the daemons are running. It is advisable to use NFS on a local secure network only. If used over the Internet, NFS would open your system up to nonsecure access.

An entry in the **/etc/exports** file specifies the file system to be exported and the computers on the network that can access it. For the file system, enter its *mountpoint,* the directory to which it was mounted on the host system. This is followed by a list of computers that can access this file system. A comma-separated list of mount options placed within a set of parentheses may follow each computer. For example, you might want to give one computer read-only access and another read and write access. If only the options are listed, they are applied to anyone. A list of mount options is provided in Table 37-1. Examples of entries in an **/etc/exports** file are shown here. Read-only access with no security check is given to all computers to the file system mounted on the **/pub** directory, a common name used for public access. Read and write access is given to the **ant.trek.com** computer for the file system mounted on the **/home/foodstuff** directory. The next entry would allow access by **butterfly.trek.com** to your CD-ROM. The last entry denies anyone access to **/home/richlp**.

General Options	Description
`secure`	Requires authentication. This is on by default.
`ro`	Allows only read-only access.
`rw`	Allows read-write access. This is the default.
`noaccess`	Makes everything below the directory inaccessible for the named client.
`link_absolute`	Leaves all symbolic links as they are. This is the default operation.
`link_relative`	Converts absolute symbolic links (where the link contents start with a slash) into relative links by prepending the necessary number of slashes (/) to get from the directory containing the link to the root on the server.

User ID Mapping	Description
`squash_uids` `squash_gids`	Specifies a list of uids and gids that should be subject to anonymous mapping.
`all_squash`	Maps all uids and gids to the anonymous user. Useful for NFS-exported public FTP directories, news spool directories, and so forth.
`no_all_squash`	The opposite option to **all_squash**, and is the default setting.
`root_squash`	Maps requests from uid/gid 0 to the anonymous uid/gid.
`no_root_squash`	Turns off root squashing. Does not map requests from uid/gid 0. This is the default.
`anonuid` `anongid`	Set explicitly the uid and gid of the anonymous account. Primarily useful for PC/NFS clients, where you might want all requests to appear to be from one user.
`map_daemon`	Turns on dynamic uid/gid mapping. The uids in NFS requests are translated to the equivalent server uids. The uids in NFS replies are mapped the other way. The default setting is map identity, which leaves all uids untouched.

Table 37-1.   *The /etc/exports Options*

/etc/exports

```
/pub                    (ro,insecure,all_squash)
/home/foodstuff         ant.trek.com(rw)
/mnt/cdrom              butterfly.trek.com(ro)
/home/richlp            (noaccess)
```

Instead of editing the **/etc/exports** file directly, you can use Linuxconf's Exported File Systems panel in the Server Tasks list under the Networking heading in Config. Click the Add button to add a new entry. Figure 37-1 shows the panel with the **butterfly** example.

Once an NFS file system is made available, different computers on the network must first mount it before they can use the file system. You can mount an NFS file system either by an entry in the **/etc/fstab** file or by an explicit **mount** command. An NFS entry in the **/etc/fstab** file has a mount type of NFS. An NFS file system name consists of the hostname of the computer it is located on, followed by the pathname of the directory where it is mounted. The two are separated by a colon. For example, **rabbit.trek.com:/home/project** specifies a file system mounted at **/home/project** on the **rabbit.trek.com** computer.

You can also include several NFS-specific mount options with your NFS entry. You can specify the size of datagrams sent back and forth, and the amount of time your computer waits for a response from the host system. You can also specify whether a file system is to be hard-mounted or soft-mounted. For *a hard-mounted file system*, your computer continually tries to make contact if for some reason the remote system fails to respond. A *soft-mounted file system,* after a specified interval, gives up trying to make contact and issues an error message. A hard-mount is the default. A system making a hard-mount attempt that continues to fail will stop responding to user input as it tries continually to achieve the mount. For this reason soft-mounts may be preferable as

Figure 37-1. *Linuxconf Exported File Systems panel*

they will simply stop attempting a mount that continually fails. Table 37-2 and the Man pages for **mount** contain a listing of these NFS client options. They differ from the NFS server options indicated previously.

An example of an NFS entry follows. The remote system is **rabbit.trek.com** and the file system is mounted on **/home/projects**. This file system is to be mounted on the local system's **/home/dylan** directory. The type of system is NFS and the **timeo** option specifies the local system waits up to 20-tenths of a second (two seconds) for a response.

```
rabbit.trek.com:/home/projects      /home/dylan       nfs     timeo=20
```

Options	Description
rsize=n	The number of bytes NFS uses when reading files from an NFS server. The default is 1,024 bytes.
wsize=n	The number of bytes NFS uses when writing files to an NFS server. The default is 1,024 bytes.
timeo=n	The value in tenths of a second before sending the first retransmission after a timeout. The default value is seven-tenths of a second.
retry=n	The number of times to retry a backgrounded NFS **mount** operation before giving up. The default is 10,000 times.
soft	Mount system using soft-mount.
hard	Mount system using hard-mount. This is the default.
intr	Allow NFS to interrupt the file operation and return to the calling program. The default is not to allow file operations to be interrupted.
bg	If the first mount attempt times out, continue trying the mount in the background. The default is to fail without backgrounding.
tcp	Mount the NFS file system using the TCP protocol, instead of the default UDP protocol.

Table 37-2. *NFS Options*

You can also use the **mount** command with the **-t nfs** option to mount an NFS file system explicitly. To mount the previous entry explicitly, use the following command:

```
# mount -t nfs -o timeo=20   rabbit.trek.com:/home/projects   /home/dylan
```

Instead of editing the **/etc/fstab** file directly, you can use Linuxconf's Access nfs volume in the File Systems list under Config. Figure 37-2 shows the Access NFS Volume panel.

Clicking the Add button displays Volume Specification panels for Base entries, standard file options, and NFS options. In the Base tab, boxes exist for the remote server, the remote directory (Volume), and the directory on your local system where the remote directory is to be attached (Mountpoint). Figure 37-3 shows the Volume Specification panel where the remote server is rabbit.trek.com and the remote directory is /home/projects. The local mountpoint directory is **/home/dylan**.

NFS file systems are mounted automatically by **/etc/fstab**. On Red Hat and Caldera systems, you can mount and unmount all the NFS file systems manually—you can do so with the **/etc/rc.d/init.d/netfs** script. This script reads the **/etc/fstab** file and copies the NFS entries, using them to manage the file systems. Using the **stop** argument unmounts the file systems and, with the **start** argument, you mount them again. The **restart** argument first unmounts and then remounts the file systems.

```
/etc/rc.d/init.d/netfs stop
```

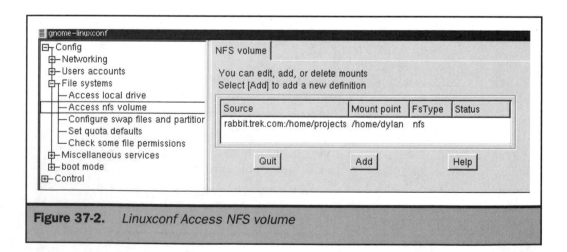

Figure 37-2.   *Linuxconf Access NFS volume*

Figure 37-3.   *Linuxconf Volume Specification panel for NFS*

You can also use the **/etc/rc.d/init.d/nfs** script to start up or shut down the NFS daemons, starting and stopping NFS services.

```
/etc/rc.d/init.d/nfs stop
```

Network Information Service: NIS

On networks supporting NFS, many resources and devices are shared by the same systems. Normally, each system would need its own configuration files for each device or resource. Changes would entail updating each system individually. However, NFS provides a special service called *Network Information Services* (*NIS*) that maintains such configuration files for the entire network. For changes, you only need to update the NIS files. NIS works for information required for most administrative tasks, such as those relating to users, network access, or devices. For example, you can maintain password information with an NIS service, having only to update those NIS password files.

NIS was developed by Sun Microsystems and was originally known as Sun's *Yellow Pages* (*YP*). NIS files are kept on an NIS server (NIS servers are still sometimes referred to as *YP servers*). Individual systems on a network use NIS clients to make requests from the NIS server. The NIS server maintains its information on special database files called *maps*. Linux versions exist for both NIS clients and servers. Linux NIS clients easily connect to any network using NIS.

Most Linux distributions contain both the Linux NIS client and server software in RPM packages that install with default configurations. The NIS client is installed as part of the initial installation on most Linux distributions. You can use the Linuxconf Network Information Service panel in the Client Tasks list under Networking to specify the remote NIS server on your network. NIS client programs are ypbind (the NIS client daemon), ypwhich, ypcat, yppoll, ypmatch, yppasswd, and ypset. Each has its own Man page with details of its use. The NIS server programs are ypserv, ypinit, yppasswdd, yppush, ypxfr, and netgroup—each also with its own Man page. A detailed NIS HOW-TO document is available in the **/usr/share/doc/HOWTO** directory.

The **/var/yp/securenets** file enables access by hosts to your NIS server. Hosts can be referenced by network or individually. Entries consist of subnet mask and an IP address. For example, you could give access to all the hosts in a local network with the following entry:

```
255.255.255.0  192.168.1.0
```

For individual hosts you can use the mask 255.255.255.255 or just the term "host", as shown here:

```
host    192.168.1.4
```

Controlling how different hosts access NIS shared data is determined in the **/etc/ypserv.conf**.

Each NIS client host on your network then has to run the ypbind NIS client to access the server. In the client's **/etc/yp.conf** file, you need to specify the NIS server it will use. The following entry would reference the NIS server at 192.168.1.1:

```
ypserver 192.168.1.1
```

To ensure that the client accesses the NIS server, you should specify nis in the **/etc/nsswitch.conf** file. This file specifies where a host should look for certain kinds of information. For example, the following entry says to check the NIS server (nis) first and then the local configuration files (files) for passwords data:

```
passwd:   nis files
```

Samba

Whereas most UNIX and Linux systems use the TCP/IP protocol for networking, Microsoft networking with Windows uses a different protocol, called the *Server Message Block* (*SMB*) protocol, that implements a *local area network* (*LAN*) of PCs running Windows. SMB makes use of a network interface called *Network Basic Input Output System* (*NetBIOS*) that allows Windows PCs to share resources, such as printers and disk space. One Windows PC on such a network can access part of another Windows PC's disk drive as if it were its own. SMB was originally designed for small LANs. To connect it to larger networks, including those with UNIX systems, Microsoft developed the *Common Internet File System* (*CIFS*). CIFS still uses SMB and NetBIOS for Windows networking. Andrew Tridgell wrote a version of SMB he called *Samba*. Samba also allows UNIX and Linux systems to connect to such a Windows network, as if they were Windows PCs. UNIX systems can share resources on Window's systems as if they were just another Windows PC. Windows PCs can also access resources on UNIX systems as if they were Windows systems. Samba, in effect, has become a professional level, open source, and free version of CIFS. It also runs twice as fast. Samba effectively enables you to use a Linux or UNIX server as a network server for a group of Windows machines operating on a Windows network. You can also use it to share files on your Linux system with other Windows PCs or to access files on a Windows PC from your Linux system, as well as between Windows PCs. On Linux systems, an **smbfs** file system enables you, in effect, to mount a remote SMB-shared directory on to your own file system. You can then access it as if it were a directory on your local system.

You can obtain extensive documentation and current releases from the Samba Web and FTP sites at **www.samba.org** and **ftp.samba.org**. RPM packages can be obtained from respective distribution FTP sites, such as **ftp.redhat.com**. Samba is also included on most Linux distributions. Other information can be obtained from the SMB newsgroup, **comp.protocols.smb**. Extensive documentation is provided with the software package and installed on your system, usually in the **/usr/share/doc** directory under a subdirectory bearing the name of the Samba release. Here, you can find extensive documentation in HTML and text format, as well as numerous examples and the current FAQs. The examples include sample **smb.conf** files for different kinds of configuration. The home page of the SWAT configuration utility also provides Web page-based Samba documentation, as well as context-level help for different features.

The Samba software package consists of two server daemons and several utility programs: **smbd, nmbd, smbclient, smbmount, smbumount, smbstatus,** and **testparm** (see Table 37-3). One daemon, **smbd**, provides file and printer services to SMB clients and other systems, such as Windows, that support SMB. The nmbd utility is a daemon that provides NetBIOS name resolution and service browser support. The smbclient utility provides FTP-like access by Linux clients to Samba services. The **smbclient** utility provides FTP-like access by Linux clients to Samba services. **smbmount** and **smbumount** enable Linux clients to mount and unmount Samba-shared directories. The smbstatus utility displays the current status of the smb server and who is using it. You use testparm to test your Samba configuration. **smbtar** is a shell script that backs up SMB/CIFS-shared resources directly to a UNIX tape drive. You use **nmblookup** to map the NetBIOS name of a Windows PC to its IP address. Included also with the package is the *Samba Web administration tool* (*SWAT*). This enables you to use a Web page interface to create and maintain your Samba configuration file, **smb.conf**.

Application	Description
smbd	Samba server daemon that provides file and printer services to SMD clients.
nmbd	Samba daemon that provides NetBIOS name resolution and service browser support.
smbclient	Provides FTP-like access by Linux clients to Samba services.
smbmount	Mounts Samba share directories on Linux clients.
smbumount	Unmounts Samba share directories mounted on Linux clients.
smbpasswd	Changes SMB-encrypted passwords on Samba servers.
smbstatus	Displays the current status of the SMB network connections.
smbrun	Interface program between smbd and external programs.
testparm	Tests the Samba configuration file, **smb.conf**.
smbtar	Backs up SMB/CIFS-shared resources directly to a UNIX tape drive.
nmblookup	Maps the NetBIOS name of a Windows PC to its IP address.
SWAT	Samba Web administration tool for configuring **smb.conf** with a Web browser. Enables you to use a Web page interface to create and maintain your Samba configuration file, **smb.conf**.

Table 37-3.   *Samba Applications*

Samba provides four main services: file and printer services, authentication and authorization, name resolution, and service announcement. The SMB daemon, **smbd**, provides the file and printer services, as well as authentication and authorization for those services. This means users on the network can share files and printers. You can control access to these services by requiring users to provide a password. When users try to access a shared directory, they are prompted for a password. Control can be implemented in share mode or user mode. The *share mode* sets up one password for the shared resource, and then enables any user who has that password to access it. The *user mode* provides a different password for each user. Samba maintains its own password file for this purpose, **smbpasswords**.

Name resolution and service announcements are handled by the nmbd server. Name resolution essentially resolves NetBIOS names with IP addresses (Microsoft plans to have this handled by DNS in the future). Service announcement, also known as *browsing*, is the way a list of services available on the network is made known to the connected Windows PCs (and Linux PCs connected through Samba).

Setting Up Samba

For a simple Samba setup, you should be able to use the default **smb.conf** file installed with the Linux distribution package of Samba. If you need to make changes, however, you must restart the Samba server to have the changes take effect. You can do so using the smb startup script, as shown here:

```
/etc/rec.d/init.d/smb restart
```

To test your connection from a Linux system, you can use the **smbclient** command to query the Samba server. To access the home directory of a user on the Samba server, use the IP or hostname address of the Samba server, along with the homes section. With the **–U** option, specify a user to connect to on the system, as shown here:

```
smbclient '//turtle.mytrek.com/homes' -U dylan
```

You are then prompted for a password. If the client password is different from the server password, use the server password. Once connected, you are presented with the smb client prompt as shown here. You can then access the files on the user's home directory.

```
smb: \>
```

To set up a connection for a Window client, you need to specify the Windows workgroup name and configure the password. The workgroup name is the name that appears in the Entire Network window in the Network Neighborhood on the Windows desktop. In the **smb.conf** file, you specify the workgroup name in the **workgroup=** entry in the **global** section. The workgroup name should be uppercase, no more than eight characters, and with no spaces.

You can then restart the Samba server. On a Windows client, you see the workgroup name appeared in the Entire Network folder in your Network Neighborhood. Within the workgroup is an icon for the Samba server, and within that is an icon for the user directory, as specified in the homes section of the **smb.conf** file.

Samba configuration options are kept in the **/etc/smb.conf** file. You edit this file to make changes to the configuration. Once you finish making any changes, you should test your **smb.conf** file using the **testparm** program. The **testparm** program checks the validity of your configuration entries. By default, **testparm** uses the **/etc/smb.conf** file, although you can supply a different configuration file as an argument.

```
testparm
```

To check your network connections, use the **smbstatus** command. This command returns a listing of all active smb connections.

Samba Configuration: smb.conf

You configure the Samba daemon using the **smb.conf** file located in the **/etc** directory. The file is separated into two basic parts: one for global options and the other for shared services. A *shared service*, also know as *shares*, can either be filespace services (used by clients as an extension of their native file systems) or printable services (used by clients to access print services on the host running the server). The *filespace service* is a directory to which clients are given access and can use the space in it as an extension of their local file system. A printable service provides access by clients to print services, such as printers managed by the Samba server.

The **/etc/smb.conf** file holds the configuration for the various shared resources, as well as global options that apply to all resources. Linux installs a **smb.conf** file in your **/etc** directory. The file contains default settings used for your distribution. You can edit the file to customize your configuration to your own needs. Many entries are commented with either a semicolon or a **#** sign, and you can remove the initial comment symbol to make them effective. Instead of editing the file directly, you may want to use the SWAT configuration utility, which provides an easy-to-use, full-screen Web page interface for entering configurations for shared resources. The SWAT configuration utility also provides extensive help features and documentation. For a complete listing of the Samba configuration parameters, check the Man page for **smb.conf**. An extensive set of sample **smb.conf** files is located in the **/usr/doc/samba*** directory in the **examples** subdirectory.

In the **smb.conf** file, global options are set first, followed by each shared resource's configuration. The basic organizing component of the **smb.conf** file is a section. Each resource has its own section that holds its service name and definitions of its attributes. Even global options are placed in a section of their own: labeled **global**. For example, each section for a filespace share consists of the directory and the access rights allowed to users of the filespace. The section of each share is labeled with the name of the shared resource. Special sections, called **printers** and **homes**, provide default descriptions for user directories and printers accessible on the Samba server. Following the special sections, sections are entered for specific services, namely access to specific directories or printers. The basic organizing component is a section. Global options are placed in a section of their own labeled **global**.

A section begins with a section label consisting of the name of the shared resource encased in brackets. Other than the special sections, the section label can be any name you want to give it. Following the section label, on separate lines, different parameters for this service are entered. The parameters define the access rights to be granted to the user of the service. For example, for a directory, you may want it to be browsable, but read-only and to use a certain printer. Parameters are entered in the format *parameter name = value*. You can enter a comment by placing a semicolon at the beginning of the comment line.

A simple example of a section configuration follows. The section label is encased in brackets and followed by two parameter entries. The **path** parameter specifies the directory to which access is allowed. The **writable** parameter specifies whether the user has write access to this directory and its filespace.

```
[mysection]
        path = /home/chris
        writable = true
```

A printer service has the same format, but requires certain other parameters. The **path** parameters specify the location of the printer spool directory. The **read-only** and **printable** parameters are set to true, indicating the service is read-only and printable. **Public** indicates anyone can access it.

```
[myprinter]
        path = /var/spool/samba
        read only = true
        printable = true
        public = true
```

Parameter entries are often synonymous, different entries that have the same meaning. For example, **read only = no**, **writable = yes**, and **write ok = yes**, all mean the same thing, providing write access to the user.

SWAT and smb.conf

SWAT is a network-based Samba configuration tool that uses a Web page interface to enable you to configure your **smb.conf** file. SWAT is, by far, the easiest and simplest way to configure your Samba server. SWAT provides a simple-to-use Web page interface with buttons, menus, and text boxes for entering values. A simple button bar across the top enables you to select the sections you want to configure. A button bar button is even there to add passwords. To see the contents of the **smb.conf** file as SWAT changes it, click the View button. The initial screen (HOME) displays the index for Samba documentation (see Figure 37-4). One of SWAT's more helpful features is its context-sensitive help. For each parameter and option SWAT displays, you can click a Help button to display a detailed explanation of the option and examples of its use.

On most Linux distributions, SWAT in installed with Samba. SWAT is an inetd or xinetd service. As an inetd service, it will be listed in the **/etc/services** and **/etc/inetd.conf** files. In the **/etc/inetd.conf** file, the entry for SWAT will be commented. You will have to edit this file and remove the preceding **#** comment symbol. The SWAT entry looks like this:

```
swat        stream  tcp     nowait.400      root /usr/sbin/swat swat
```

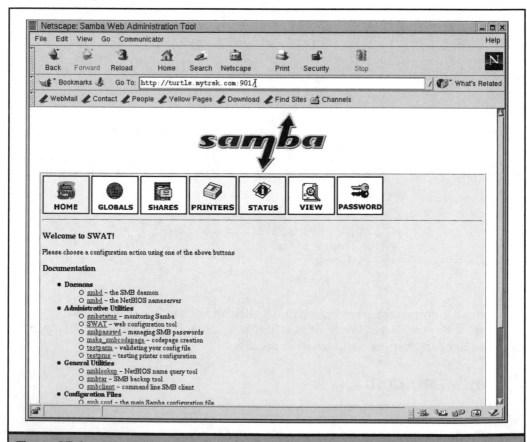

Figure 37-4. *SWAT home page*

Once you remove the comment, you must restart the inetd server to have the change take effect. On Red Hat and Caldera systems, you can do this simply using the **inetd** script, as shown here:

```
/etc/rc.d/init.d/inetd restart
```

As an xinetd service, it will be listed in the **xinetd.conf** file, having its own block entry. To restart xinetd, you use the **xinetd** script instead of the **inetd** script.

```
service swat
{
    port             = 901
    socket_type      = stream
    wait             = no
    only_from        = localhost
    user             = root
    server           = /usr/sbin/swat
    log_on_failure  += USERID
    disable          = no
}
```

The SWAT program uses port 901, as designated in the **/etc/services** file. Before you use SWAT, back up your current **smb.conf** file. SWAT overwrites the original, replacing it with a shorter and more concise version of its own. The **smb.conf** file originally installed lists an extensive number of options with detailed explanations. This is a good learning tool, with excellent examples for creating various kinds of printer and directory sections. Simply make a backup copy.

```
cp /etc/smb.conf   /etc/smb.bk
```

You start up SWAT by entering the address of the Samba server it is running on, along with its port (901) into a Web browser. The following URL entered into a Web browser, such as Netscape, displays the Web page interface for SWAT on the **turtle.mytrek.com** Samba server:

```
http://turtle.mytrek.com:901
```

If you are logged in to the Linux system that is operating the Samba server, you could simply use localhost as the URL.

```
http://localhost:901
```

You are first asked to enter a user name and a password. To configure Samba, you need to enter **root** and the root password. (If you are connecting from a remote system, it is NOT advisable to enter the root password in clear text, see Chapter 31.) The main SWAT page is displayed with a button bar, with buttons for links for HOME, GLOBAL, SHARES, PRINTERS, STATUS, VIEW, and PASSWORD. You can use STATUS to list your active SMB network connections.

For the various sections, SWAT can display either a basic or advanced version. The basic version shows only those entries needed for a simple configuration, whereas the advanced version shows all the possible entries for that type of section. A button—labeled Advanced View and Basic View, respectively—is at the top of the section page for toggling between the advanced or basic versions (see Figure 37-5). Section pages for Printers and Shares have added buttons and a menu for selecting the particular printer or share you want to configure. The term "share," as it's used here, refers to directories you want to make available through Samba. When you click the SHARES button, you initially see only a few buttons displayed at the top of the

Figure 37-5.   SWAT Share page showing Homes section

SHARES page. You use these buttons to create new sections or to edit sections already set up for shares. For setting up a new Share section, you enter its name in the box next to the Create Share button, and then click that button. The new share name appears in the drop-down menu next to the Choose Share button. Initially, this button is blank. Click it to display the list of current Share sections. Select the one you want, and then click the Choose Share button. The page then displays the entries for configuring a share. For a new share, these are either blank or hold default values. For example, to select the Homes section that configures the default setting for user home directories, click the drop-down menu where you find a Homes entry. Select it, and then click the Choose Share button. The entries for the Homes section are displayed. The same process works for the Printers page, where you can select either the Printers section or Create sections for particular printers.

In Figure 37-6, notice the Help links next to each entry. Such a link displays a Web page showing the Samba documentation for **smb.conf**, positioned at the appropriate entry. In this figure, the Guest OK part of the documentation is displayed after the user clicks the Help link next to the Guest OK entry.

Figure 37-6. *SWAT Help*

When you finish working on a section, click the Commit Changes button on its page to save your changes. Do this for each separate page you work on, including the GLOBALS page. Clicking the Commit Changes button generates a new version of the **smb.conf** file. To have the Samba server read these changes, you then have to restart it.

```
/etc/rec.d/init.d/smb restart
```

You can, of course, edit the **/etc/smb.conf** file directly. This is a simple text file you can edit with any text editor. You still must restart the smb server to have the changes take effect.

The following example shows an **smb.conf** file generated by SWAT for a simple configuration. This is much smaller than the comment-intensive versions originally installed with Samba.

```
# Samba config file created using SWAT
# from UNKNOWN (24.0.67.231)
# Date: 2000/02/11 01:08:09

# Global parameters
[global]
     workgroup = MYGROUP
     server string = Samba Server
     username map = /etc/smbusers
     log file = /var/log/samba/log.%m
     max log size = 50
     socket options = TCP_NODELAY SO_RCVBUF=8192 SO_SNDBUF=8192
     dns proxy = No

[homes]
     comment = Home Directories
     read only = No
     browseable = No

[printers]
     comment = All Printers
     path = /var/spool/samba
     print ok = Yes
     browseable = No
```

Global Section

The *Global* section determines configuration for the entire server, as well as specifying default entries to be used in the home and directory segments. In this section, you find entries for the workgroup name, password configuration, and directory settings.

Several of the more important entries are discussed here. Figure 37-7 shows the Global Variables page on the SWAT that you can use to set global options. The Basic View of this page lists the options you would most likely need.

The workgroup entry specifies the workgroup name you want to give to your network. This is the workgroup name that appears on the Windows client's Network Neighborhood window. The default workgroup entry in the **smb.conf** file is shown here:

```
[global]

# workgroup = NT-Domain-Name or Workgroup-Name
   workgroup = MYGROUP
```

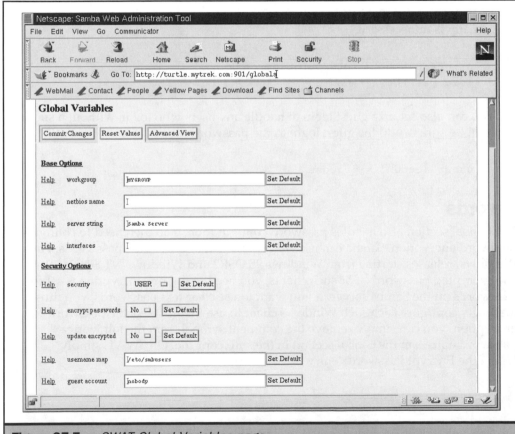

Figure 37-7. *SWAT Global Variables page*

The server string entry holds the descriptive name you want displayed for the server on the client systems. On Windows systems, this is the name displayed on the Samba server icon.

```
# server string is the equivalent of the NT Description field
server string = Samba Server
```

As a security measure, you can restrict access to SMB services to certain specified local networks. On the host's network, type the network addresses of the local networks for which you want to permit access. The localhost (127) is always automatically included. The next example allows access to two local networks:

```
hosts allow = 192.168.1. 192.168.2.
```

To enable printing, allow Samba to load the printer descriptions from your **printcap** file. Although you can specify a particular print system type with the printing entry, this usually is unnecessary.

```
printcap name = /etc/printcap
load printers = yes
```

You can also set up a guest login to handle any users who log in without a specific account. Be sure to add the guest login to the **password** file.

```
guest account = pcguest
```

Passwords

The Global section also handles password configuration. You then need to configure password encryption. Samba can use either clear text or encrypted passwords. For Windows, releases starting from Windows 95 OSR2 and Windows NT Service Pack 3 use encrypted passwords. For such clients, you need to be sure encryption is set for passwords on the Samba server. If you want to use clear text passwords, you must manually configure each such Windows client to use them. To enable password encryption, you can simply remove the comment symbol from the following password entries in the Global section in the **smb.conf** file. On SWAT, simply toggle the Encrypt Passwords entry to Yes.

```
encrypt passwords = yes
```

Users are usually prompted for a password when they try to access a client. You can have Samba maintain a list of default passwords in the **/etc/smbpasswd** file, however. If you want, you can use the **smb passwd** file entry to specify a different password file.

```
# smb passwd file = /etc/smbpasswd
```

To add a password for a particular user, you use the **smbpasswd** command with the **–a** option and the user's name.

```
smbpasswd –a dylan
```

On SWAT, you manage passwords on the Server Password Management page, as shown in Figure 37-8. Click Add New User to add a new user. As the root user on the Samba server, you can add new passwords, as well as enable or disable current ones. Users can also use the Password page to change their own passwords.

Server Password Management

User Name :	root
New Password :	
Re-type New Password :	

[Change Password] [Add New User] [Disable User] [Enable User]

Client/Server Password Management

User Name :	root
Old Password :	
New Password :	
Re-type New Password :	
Remote Machine :	

[Change Password]

Figure 37-8.   *SWAT Server Password Management page*

If, instead, you want to use clear text passwords, you must manually edit the Windows registry of each Windows client. In the registry, change the EnablePlainTextPassword entry to 1. For Windows 95 and 98, it is located in **HKEY_LOCAL_MACHINES\System\CurrentContorlSet\Services\VxD\VNETSUP**. If this entry is not there, you must make one. Select Edit | New | DWORD Value from the regedit menu bar and rename the entry from New Value #1 to EnablePlainTextPassword. For Windows 2000 and NT, check the **.reg** files in the **/usr/doc/Samba**version directory, in the **docs** subdirectory. Clear passwords, of course, present a security risk.

Homes Section

The *Homes* section specifies default controls for accessing a user home directory through the SMB protocols by remote users. Setting the Browsable entry to No prevents the client from listing the files with the browser, such as that used by a file manager to display files and directories (for example, Explorer on Windows). The Writable entry specifies whether a user has read and write control over files in his home directory. On SWAT, you simply select the SHARES page, select the Homes entry from the drop-down menu, and click Choose Share (see Figure 37-5).

```
[homes]
    comment = Home Directories
    browseable = no
    writable = yes
```

Printer Section

The *Printer* section specifies the default controls for accessing printers. These are used for printers for which no specific sections exist. In this case, Samba uses printers defined in the server's **printcap** file.

In this context, setting Browsable to No simply hides the Printer section from the client, not the printers. The path entry specifies the location of the spool directory Samba will use for printer files. To enable printing at all, the printable entry must be set to Yes. To allow guest users to print, set the Guest OK entry to Yes. The Writable entry set to No prevents any kind of write access, other than the printer's management of spool files. On SWAT, select the PRINTER page and the Printers entry in the drop-down menu, and then select Choose Printers (see Figure 37-6). A standard implementation of the Printers section is shown here:

```
[printers]
  comment = All Printers
  path = /var/spool/samba
  browseable = no
```

```
# Set public = yes to allow user 'guest account' to print
   guest ok = no
   writable = no
   printable = yes
```

If you can't print, be sure to check the Default Print entry. This specifies the command the server actually uses to print documents.

Shares

Sections for specific shared resources, such as directories on your system, are usually placed after the Homes and Printers sections. For a section defining a shared directory, enter a label for the system. Then, on separate lines, enter options for its pathname and the different permissions you want to set. In the **path =** options, specify the full pathname for the directory. The **comment =** option holds the label to be given the share. You can make a directory writable, public, or read-only. You can control access to the directory with the Valid Users entry. With this entry, you can list those users permitted access. For those options not set, the defaults entered in the Global, Home, and Printer segments are used.

On SWAT, you use the SHARES page to create and edit shared directories. Select the one you want to edit from the drop-down menu and click Choose Share. The Basic View shows the commonly used entries. For entries such as Valid Users, you need to select the Advanced View. Be sure to click Commit Changes before you move on to another Share or Printer section.

The following example is found in the original **smb.conf** file and shows a simple Share section for a directory **fredsdir** where only the user **fred** has access:

```
[fredsdir]
   comment = Fred's Service
   path = /usr/somewhere/private
   valid users = fred
   public = no
   writable = yes
   printable = no
```

For public access, set Public Entry to Yes, with no valid user's entry. If you want guest users to have access, you can also set the Only Guest entry to Yes.

```
   [public]
     path = /usr/somewhere/else/public
```

```
public = yes
only guest = yes
writable = yes
printable = no
```

To set up a directory that can be shared by more than one user, where each user has control of the files he or she creates, simply list the users in the Valid Users entry. Permissions for any created files are specified by the Create Mask entry. In this example, the permissions are set to 765, which provides read/write/execute access to owners, read/write access to members of the group, and only read/execute access to all others:

```
[myshare]
    comment = Mary's and Fred's stuff
    path = /usr/somewhere/shared
    valid users = mary fred
    public = no
    writable = yes
    printable = no
    create mask = 0765
```

Printers

For a printer, you need to include the printer and printable entries. With the Printer entry, you name the printer, and by setting the Printable entry to Yes, you allow it to print. You can control access to specific users with the Valid Users entry and by setting the Public Entry to No. For public access, set the Public Entry to Yes. On SWAT, you can create individual Printer sections on the PRINTER page. Default entries are already set up for you.

The following example sets up a printer accessible only by the user **fred** (you could add other users if you want). User's need to have write access to the printer's spool directory. In this example, **fred**'s home directory is used.

```
[fredsprn]
    comment = Fred's Printer
    valid users = fred
    path = /homes/fred
    printer = freds_printer
    public = no
    writable = no
    printable = yes
```

Linuxconf, Webmin, and KSamba

You also can edit the **smb.conf** file using the Linuxconf Samba File Server panel in the Server Tasks list under Networking in Config. Five entries correspond to global options: (Default), the Homes section (Default setup for user home directories), the Printers section (Default setup for printers), net login (Netlogon setup), and individual shared resources (Disk shares).

Linuxconf uses a set of panels for each kind of section, organizing parameters into different categories. For example, Figure 37-9 shows the Share Setup panel for configuring a shared resource. The panel contains several tabbed panels for configuring access, users, and features. Entries here correspond to the possible parameters you can enter in a share's section in the **smb.conf** file.

> **Note** *Though SWAT is preferred, you can also use Webmin to configure Samba. Select the Samba entry on the Servers page. On KDE, you can use KSamba to configure your Samba server.*

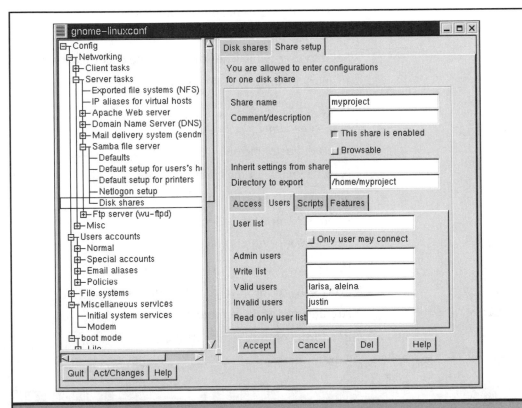

Figure 37-9. *Linuxconf Samba configuration*

Variable Substitutions

For string values assigned to parameters, you can incorporate substitution operators. This provides greater flexibility in designating values that may be context-dependent, such as user names. For example, suppose a service needs to use a separate directory for each user who logs in. The path for such directories could be specified using the **%u** variable that substitutes the name of the current user. The string **path = /tmp/%u** would become **path = /tmp/justin** for the **justin** user and **/tmp/dylan** for the **dylan** user. Table 37-4 lists several of the more common substitution variables.

Variable	Description
%S	Name of the current service
%P	Root directory of the current service
%u	User name of the current service
%g	Primary group name of the user
%U	Session user name (the user name the client wanted)
%G	Primary group name of session user
%H	Home directory of the user
%v	Samba version
%h	Internet hostname on which Samba is running
%m	NetBIOS name of the client machine
%L	NetBIOS name of the server
%M	Internet name of the client machine
%N	Name of your NIS home directory server
%p	Path of the service's home directory
%d	Process ID of the current server process
%a	Architecture of the remote machine
%I	IP address of the client machine
%T	Current date and time

Table 37-4. *Samba Substitution Variables*

Testing the Samba Configuration

After you make your changes to the **smb.conf** file, you can then use the testparm program to see if the entries are correctly entered. **testparm** checks the syntax and validity of Samba entries. By default, testparm checks the **/etc/smb.conf** file. If you are using a different file as your configuration file, you can specify it as an argument to testparm. You can also have testparm check to see if a particular host has access to the service set up by the configuration file.

With the **smbstatus** command, you can check on current Samba connections on your network.

To check the real-time operation of your Samba server, you can log in to a user account on the Linux system running the Samba server and connect to the server.

Domain Logons

Samba also supports domain logons whereby a user can log on to the network. Logon scripts can be set up for individual users. To configure such netlogin capability, you need to set up a netlogon share in the **smb.conf file**. The following sample is taken from the original **smb.conf file.** This share holds the **netlogon** scripts, in this case, the **/home/netlogon** directory, which should not be writable, but it should be accessible by all users (Guest OK).

```
[netlogon]
   comment = Network Logon Service
   path = /home/netlogon
   guest ok = yes
   writable = no
   share modes = no
```

The Global section would have the following parameters enabled:

```
domain logons = yes
logon script = %U.bat
```

The logon scripts would be DOS batch scripts (**.bat**), which you should edit on a DOS or a Windows system.

Accessing Samba Services with Clients

Client systems connected to the SMB network can access the shared services provided by the Samba server. Windows clients should be able to access shared directories and services automatically through the Network Neighborhood and the Entire Network icons on a Windows desktop. For other Linux systems connected to the same network,

Samba services can be accessed using special Samba client programs. With smbclient, a local Linux system can connect to a shared directory on the Samba server and transfer files, as well as run shell programs. With smbmount, directories on the Samba server can be mounted to local directories on the Linux client.

smbclient

smbclient operates like FTP to access systems using the SMB protocols. Whereas with an FTP client you can access other FTP servers or UNIX systems, with smbclient you can access SMB-shared services, either on the Samba server or on Windows systems. Many smbclient commands are similar to FTP, such as **mget** to transfer a file or **del** to delete a file. The smbclient program has several options for querying a remote system, as well as connecting to it (see Table 37-5). See the smbclient Man page for a complete list of options and commands. The smbclient program takes as its argument a server name and the service you want to access on that server. A double slash precedes the server name and a single slash separates it from the service. The service can be any shared resource, such as a directory or a printer. The server name is its NetBIOS name, which may or may not be the same as its IP name. For example, to specify the **myreports** shared directory on the server named **turtle.mytrek.com**, use **//turtle.mytrek.com/myreports**. If you must specify a pathname, use backslashes for Windows files and forward slashes for UNIX/Linux files.

```
//server-name/service
```

You can also supply the password for accessing the service. Enter it as an argument following the service name. If you do not supply the password, you are prompted to enter it.

You can then add several options, such as the remote user name or the list of services available. With the **-I** option, you can specify the system using its Domain Name Service name. You use the **-U** option and a login name for the remote login name you want to use on the remote system. Attach **%** with the password if a password is required. With the **-L** option, you can obtain a list of the services provided on a server, such as shared directories or printers. To access a particular directory on a remote system, enter the directory as an argument to the smbclient command, followed by any options. For Windows files, you use backslashes for the pathnames, and for UNIX/Linux files you use forward slashes.

Once connected, an **smb** prompt is displayed and you can use smbclient commands such as **get** and **put** to transfer files. The **quit** or **exit** commands quit the smbclient program. In the following example, smbclient accesses the directory **myreports** on the **turtle.mytrek.com** system, using the **dylan** login name:

```
smbclient //turtle.mytrek.com/myreports -I 192.168.0.1 -U dylan
```

Option	Description
password	The password required to access the specified service on the server—if no password is supplied, the user is prompted to enter one
-s *smb.conf*	Specify the pathname to **smb.conf** file
-B *IP_address*	Specify the broadcast IP address
-O *socket_options*	List the socket options
-R *name resolve order*	Use these name resolution services only
-M *host*	Send a winpopup message to the host
-i *scope*	Use this NetBIOS scope
-N	Don't ask for a password
-n *netbios name*	Use this name as my NetBIOS name
-d *debuglevel*	Set the debug level
-P	Connect to the service as a printer
-p *port*	Connect to the specified port
-l *log basename*	Base name for log/debug files
-h	Print this help message
-I *IP_address*	Specify the IP address to connect to
-E	Write messages to stderr instead of stdout
-U *username*	Specify the user to log in to on the remote system
-L *host*	List the shares available on the specified host
-t *terminal code*	Terminal i/o code used {sjis I euc I jis7 I jis8 I junet I hex}
-m *max protocol*	Set the max protocol level
-W *workgroup*	Set the workgroup name
-T<c I x>	Command line **tar** operation
-D *directory*	Start from this directory
-c *command_string*	Execute semicolon-separated commands
-b *xmit/send buffer*	Changes the transmit/send buffer (default: 65520)

Table 37-5.   *smbclient Options*

In most cases, you can simply use the server name to reference the server, as shown here:

```
smbclient  //turtle.mytrek.com/myreports -U dylan
```

If you are accessing the home directory of a particular account on the Samba server, you can simply specify the **homes** service. In the next example, the user accesses the home directory of the **aleina** account on the Samba server, after being prompted to enter that account's password:

```
smbclient  //turtle.mytrek.com/homes -U aleina
```

Once logged in, you can execute smbclient commands to manage files and change directories. The smbclient commands are listed in Table 37-6. Shell commands can be executed with the **!** operator. To transfer files, you can use the **mget** and **mput** commands, much as they are used in the FTP program. The **recurse** command enables you to turn on recursion to copy whole subdirectories at a time. You can use file-matching operators, referred to here as *masks,* to select a certain collection of files. The file-matching (mask) operators are *****, **[]**, and **?** (see Chapter 7). The default mask is *****, which matches everything. The following example uses **mget** to copy all files with a **.c** suffix, as in **myprog.c**:

```
smb> mget *.c
```

During transfers, you can have smbclient either prompt you for each individual file, or simply transfer all the selected ones. The **prompt** command toggles this file, prompting on and off.

smbmount

With the **smbmount** command, a Linux or a UNIX client can mount a shared directory onto its local system. The syntax for the **smbmount** command is similar to the **smbclient** command, with many corresponding options. The **smbmount** command takes as its arguments the Samba server and shared directory, followed by the local directory to which you want to mount the directory. The following example mounts the **myreports** directory onto the **/mnt/myreps** directory on the local system:

```
smbmount  '//turtle.mytrek.com/myreports' '/mnt/myreps' -U dylan
```

To unmount the directory, use the **smbmount** command with the local directory name, as shown here:

```
smbumount  /mnt/myreps
```

Command	Description
? *[command]*	With no command argument, lists of all available commands are displayed. Use command argument to display information about a particular command.
! *[shell command]*	With no shell command argument, runs a local shell. If a shell command is provided, it executes that command.
cd *[directory name]*	Change directory on server. With no directory specified, the name of the current working directory is displayed.
del *mask*	Request the server delete all files matching mask from the current working directory on the server.
dir *mask*	A list of the files matching the mask in the current working directory on the server is retrieved from the server and displayed.
exit	Terminate the connection with the server and exit from the program.
get *remote filename [local filename]*	Copy a file from the server to the local system. You can rename the local system copy. Transfer is binary.
help *[command]*	With no command argument, lists of all available commands are displayed. Use command argument to display information about a particular command. Same as **!**.
lcd *[directory name]*	Change directories on the local system. With no argument, the local directory name is displayed.

Table 37-6.   *smbclient Commands*

Command	Description
lowercase	Toggle lowercasing of filenames for the **get** and **mget** commands. When lowercasing is toggled ON, local filenames are converted to lowercase when using the **get** and **mget** commands. This is often useful when copying (say) MS-DOS files from a server because lowercase filenames are the norm on UNIX systems.
ls *mask*	A list of the files matching the mask in the current working directory on the server is retrieved from the server and displayed. Same as **dir**.
mask *mask*	This command enables the user to set up a mask that is used during recursive operation of the **mget** and **mput** commands. The masks specified to the **mget** and **mput** commands act as filters for directories, rather than files when recursion is toggled ON. The value for mask defaults to blank (equivalent to *****) and remains so until the **mask** command is used to change it.
md *directory name*	Create a new directory on the server (user access privileges permitting) with the specified name. Same as **mkdir**.
mget *mask*	Copy all files matching mask from the server to the machine running the client. Note, mask is interpreted differently during recursive operation and nonrecursive operation—refer to the **recurse** and **mask** commands for more information. Transfers are binary.
mkdir *directory name*	Create a new directory on the server (user access privileges permitting) with the specified name.

Table 37-6. *smbclient Commands (continued)*

Command	Description
mput *mask*	Copy all files matching mask in the current working directory on the local system to the current working directory on the server. Transfers in are binary.
print *filename*	Print the specified file from the local machine through a printable service on the server.
printmode *graphics or text*	Set the print mode for either binary data (graphics) or text. Subsequent print commands use the currently set print mode.
prompt	Toggle prompting for filenames during operation of the **mget** and **mput** commands.
put *local filename [remote filename]*	Copy a file on the local system to the server. You can rename the server copy. Transfers are binary.
queue	Displays the print queue, showing the job ID, name, size, and current status.
quit	Terminate the connection with the server and exit from the program. Same as **exit** command.
rd *directory name*	Delete the specified directory (user access privileges permitting) from the server. Same as **rmdir** command.
recurse	Toggle directory recursion for the commands **mget** and **mput**. When toggled ON, the **mget** and **mput** commands will copy any subdirectories and files. Files can be selected by a mask specified with the **mget** and **mput** commands. The mask for directories is specified with the **mask** command. When toggled OFF, only files from the current working directory are copied.

Table 37-6.   *smbclient Commands* (continued)

Command	Description
rm *mask*	Delete all files matching mask from the current working directory on the server.
rmdir *directory name*	Delete the specified directory (user access privileges permitting) from the server.
tar *c	x [IXbgNa]*	Performs a **tar** operation. See the **-T** command-line option in Table 25-5. Behavior may be affected by the **tarmode** command.
blocksize *blocksize*	Specify blocksize. Must be followed by a valid (greater than zero) block size. Causes **tar** file to be written out in blocksize*TBLOCK (usually 512 byte) blocks.
tarmode *full	inc	reset	noreset*	Changes **tar**'s behavior regarding archive bits. In full mode, **tar** backs up everything, regardless of the archive bit setting (this is the default mode). In incremental mode, **tar** only backs up files with the archive bit set. In reset mode, **tar** resets the archive bit on all files it backs up (implies read/write share).
setmode *filename perm=[+	\-]rsha*	A version of the DOS **attrib** command to set file permissions. For example: **setmode myfile +r** would make **myfile** read-only

Table 37-6. *smbclient Commands* (continued)

To mount the home directory of a particular user on the server, specify the **homes** service and the user's login name. The following example mounts the home directory of the user **larisa** to the **/home/chris/larisastuff** directory on the local system:

```
smbmount '//turtle.mytrek.com/homes' '/home/chris/larisastuff' –U larisa
```

smb.conf

A listing of the **/etc/smb.conf** file installed initially by Samba is listed in the following pages. The file includes extensive comments for each entry, but it is still only a simple configuration, with most entries commented with a semicolon. To activate an entry, remove its preceding semicolon. Default values are already assigned to the entries. You can change them as you want. Several sections, such as the **fredsdir** section, are meant only to be examples. Use them as a guide for making your own sections for shared services. Most global entries may be left as is. The essential ones are already uncommented.

smb.conf

```
# This is the main Samba configuration file. You should read the
# smb.conf(5) manual page in order to understand the options listed
# here. Samba has a huge number of configurable options (perhaps too
# many!) most of which are not shown in this example
#
# Any line which starts with a ; (semi-colon) or a # (hash)
# is a comment and is ignored. In this example we will use a #
# for commentary and a ; for parts of the config file that you
# may wish to enable
#
# NOTE: Whenever you modify this file you should run the command
# "testparm" to check that you have not many any basic syntactic
# errors.
#======================= Global Settings =========================
[global]

# workgroup = NT-Domain-Name or Workgroup-Name
   workgroup = MYGROUP

# server string is the equivalent of the NT Description field
   server string = Samba Server

# This option is important for security. It allows you to restrict
# connections to machines which are on your local network. The
# following example restricts access to two C class networks and
# the "loopback" interface. For more examples of the syntax see
# the smb.conf man page
;   hosts allow = 192.168.1. 192.168.2. 127.

# if you want to automatically load your printer list rather
# than setting them up individually then you'll need this
   printcap name = /etc/printcap
   load printers = yes

# It should not be necessary to spell out the print system type unless
# yours is non-standard. Currently supported print systems include:
# bsd, sysv, plp, lprng, aix, hpux, qnx
;   printing = bsd
```

```
# Uncomment this if you want a guest account, you must add this to
# /etc/passwd otherwise the user "nobody" is used
;   guest account = pcguest

# this tells Samba to use a separate log file for each machine
# that connects
    log file = /var/log/samba/log.%m

# Put a capping on the size of the log files (in Kb).
    max log size = 50

# Security mode. Most people will want user level security. See
# security_level.txt for details.
    security = user
# Use password server option only with security = server
;    password server = <NT-Server-Name>

# Password Level allows matching of _n_ characters of the password
# for all combinations of upper and lower case.
;   password level = 8
;   username level = 8

# You may wish to use password encryption. Please read
# ENCRYPTION.txt, Win95.txt and WinNT.txt in the Samba documentation.
# Do not enable this option unless you have read those documents
;   encrypt passwords = yes
;   smb passwd file = /etc/smbpasswd

# The following are needed to allow password changing from Windows to
# update the Linux system password also.
# NOTE: Use these with 'encrypt passwords' and 'smb passwd file'
# above.
# NOTE2: You do NOT need these to allow workstations to change only
#        the encrypted SMB passwords. They allow the Unix password
#        to be kept in sync with the SMB password.
;   unix password sync = Yes
;   passwd program = /usr/bin/passwd %u
;   passwd chat = *New*UNIX*password* %n\n *ReType*new*UNIX*password*
%n\n *passwd:*all*authentication*tokens*updated*successfully*

# Unix users can map to different SMB User names
;   username map = /etc/smbusers

# Using the following line enables you to customize your
# configuration on a per machine basis. The %m gets replaced with the
# netbios name of the machine that is connecting
;    include = /etc/smb.conf.%m

# Most people will find that this option gives better performance.
# See speed.txt and the manual pages for details
    socket options = TCP_NODELAY SO_RCVBUF=8192 SO_SNDBUF=8192
```

```
# Configure Samba to use multiple interfaces
# If you have multiple network interfaces then you must list them
# here. See the man page for details.
;    interfaces = 192.168.12.2/24 192.168.13.2/24

# Configure remote browse list synchronization here
#   request announcement to, or browse list sync from:
#   a specific host or from / to a whole subnet (see below)
;     remote browse sync = 192.168.3.25 192.168.5.255
# Cause this host to announce itself to local subnets here
;     remote announce = 192.168.1.255 192.168.2.44

# Browser Control Options:
# set local master to no if you don't want Samba to become a master
# browser on your network. Otherwise the normal election rules apply
;     local master = no

# OS Level determines the precedence of this server in master browser
# elections. The default value should be reasonable
;     os level = 33

# Domain Master specifies Samba to be the Domain Master Browser. This
# allows Samba to collate browse lists between subnets. Don't use
# this if you already have a Windows NT domain controller doing this
# job
;     domain master = yes

# Preferred Master causes Samba to force a local browser election on
# startup and gives it a slightly higher chance of winning the
# election
;     preferred master = yes

# Use only if you have an NT server on your network that has been
# configured at install time to be a primary domain controller.
;     domain controller = <NT-Domain-Controller-SMBName>

# Enable this if you want Samba to be a domain logon server for
# Windows95 workstations.
;     domain logons = yes

# if you enable domain logons then you may want a per-machine or
# per user logon script
# run a specific logon batch file per workstation (machine)
;     logon script = %m.bat
# run a specific logon batch file per username
;     logon script = %U.bat

# Where to store roving profiles (only for Win95 and WinNT)
#         %L substitutes for this servers netbios name, %U is username
#         You must uncomment the [Profiles] share below
;     logon path = \\%L\Profiles\%U
```

```
# All NetBIOS names must be resolved to IP Addresses
# 'Name Resolve Order' allows the named resolution mechanism to be specified
# the default order is "host lmhosts wins bcast". "host" means use the unix
# system gethostbyname() function call that will use either /etc/hosts OR
# DNS or NIS depending on the settings of /etc/host.config, /etc/nsswitch.conf
# and the /etc/resolv.conf file. "host" therefore is system configuration
# dependant. This parameter is most often of use to prevent DNS lookups
# in order to resolve NetBIOS names to IP Addresses. Use with care!
# The example below excludes use of name resolution for machines that are NOT
# on the local network segment
# - OR - are not deliberately to be known via lmhosts or via WINS.
; name resolve order = wins lmhosts bcast

# Windows Internet Name Serving Support Section:
# WINS Support - Tells the NMBD component of Samba to enable it's WINS Server
;    wins support = yes

# WINS Server - Tells the NMBD components of Samba to be a WINS Client
#    Note: Samba can be either a WINS Server, or a WINS Client, but NOT both
;    wins server = w.x.y.z

# WINS Proxy - Tells Samba to answer name resolution queries on
# behalf of a non WINS capable client, for this to work there must be
# at least one WINS Server on the network. The default is NO.
;    wins proxy = yes

# DNS Proxy - tells Samba whether or not to try to resolve NetBIOS names
# via DNS nslookups. The built-in default for versions 1.9.17 is yes,
# this has been changed in version 1.9.18 to no.
   dns proxy = no

# Case Preservation can be handy - system default is _no_
# NOTE: These can be set on a per share basis
;  preserve case = no
;  short preserve case = no
# Default case is normally upper case for all DOS files
;  default case = lower
# Be very careful with case sensitivity - it can break things!
;  case sensitive = no

#============================ Share Definitions ============================
[homes]
   comment = Home Directories
   browseable = no
   writable = yes

# Un-comment the following and create the netlogon directory for Domain Logons
; [netlogon]
;   comment = Network Logon Service
;   path = /home/netlogon
```

```
;    guest ok = yes
;    writable = no
;    share modes = no

# Un-comment the following to provide a specific roving profile share
# the default is to use the user's home directory
;[Profiles]
;      path = /home/profiles
;      browseable = no
;      guest ok = yes

# NOTE: If you have a BSD-style print system there is no need to
# specifically define each individual printer
[printers]
    comment = All Printers
    path = /var/spool/samba
    browseable = no
# Set public = yes to allow user 'guest account' to print
    guest ok = no
    writable = no
    printable = yes

# This one is useful for people to share files
;[tmp]
;      comment = Temporary file space
;      path = /tmp
;      read only = no
;      public = yes

# A publicly accessible directory, but read only, except for people in
# the "staff" group
;[public]
;      comment = Public Stuff
;      path = /home/samba
;      public = yes
;      writable = yes
;      printable = no
;      write list = @staff

# Other examples.
#
# A private printer, usable only by fred. Spool data will be placed in fred's
# home directory. Note that fred must have write access to the spool directory,
# wherever it is.
;[fredsprn]
;      comment = Fred's Printer
;      valid users = fred
;      path = /homes/fred
;      printer = freds_printer
;      public = no
;      writable = no
;      printable = yes
```

```
# A private directory, usable only by fred. Note that fred requires write
# access to the directory.
;[fredsdir]
;    comment = Fred's Service
;    path = /usr/somewhere/private
;    valid users = fred
;    public = no
;    writable = yes
;    printable = no

# a service which has a different directory for each machine that connects
# this allows you to tailor configurations to incoming machines. You could
# also use the %u option to tailor it by user name.
# The %m gets replaced with the machine name that is connecting.
;[pchome]
;    comment = PC Directories
;    path = /usr/pc/%m
;    public = no
;    writable = yes

# A publicly accessible directory, read/write to all users. Note that all files
# created in the directory by users will be owned by the default user, so
# any user with access can delete any other user's files. Obviously this
# directory must be writable by the default user. Another user could of course
# be specified, in which case all files would be owned by that user instead.
;[public]
;    path = /usr/somewhere/else/public
;    public = yes
;    only guest = yes
;    writable = yes
;    printable = no

# The following two entries demonstrate how to share a directory so that two
# users can place files there that will be owned by the specific users. In this
# setup, the directory should be writable by both users and should have the
# sticky bit set on it to prevent abuse. Obviously this could be extended to
# as many users as required.
;[myshare]
;    comment = Mary's and Fred's stuff
;    path = /usr/somewhere/shared
;    valid users = mary fred
;    public = no
;    writable = yes
;    printable = no
;    create mask = 0765
```

Netatalk: AppleTalk

Netatalk implements the AppleTalk network protocol on UNIX and Linux systems. It provides support for sharing files' systems, accessing printers, and routing AppleTalk. Netatalk allows a Mac machine connected to an AppleTalk network to access a Linux system as if it were an AppleTalk file and print server. Linux systems can also use Netatalk to access Mac machines connected to an AppleTalk network. AppleTalk is the network protocol used for Apple Macintosh computers. AppleTalk supports file sharing and network printing, where different Macs can share each other file systems and printers. For example, if you have a LaserWriter connected to a Macintosh, you can have your Linux system access it and print on that LaserWriter. You can also access any shared file systems that may be set up on the Macintoshes on the network. The current Netatalk Web site is **www.umich.edu/~rsug/netatalk/**, with a FAQ site at **threepio.hitchcock.org/netatalk/**.

The name of the Netatalk daemon is **atalkd**. It performs much the same function as **routed** and **ifconfig**. Several programs manage printing. The papd program lets Macs spool to a Linux printer. The pap program lets Linux systems print to an AppleTalk printer. The psf program is a PostScript printer filter for pap, and psorder enables you to print PostScript pages in reverse. The apfd program provides an interface to the Linux file system, while the nbplkup program lists all AppleTalk objects on the network. For example, **nbplkup :LaserWriter** lists the LaserWriters available. You would use the pap program to access and print to a LaserWriter. To use Linux commands to access a printer, you need to make an entry for the command in the **/etc/printcap** file, and create spool, status, and lock files for it.

Netatalk requires kernel-level support for the AppleTalk Datagram Delivery Protocol (DDP). If your kernel does not currently support it, you either must rebuild the kernel including AppleTalk support or use a loadable module for AppleTalk. Current kernels for most distributions include AppleTalk support.

Netatalk uses five configuration files, as shown in Table 37-7. The software package includes default versions you can modify. The RPM packages include the **config** file that contains documented default entries for use by the **atalk** startup script. Check the variable entries for any parameters you may want to change, such as the maximum number of allowed simultaneous users (default is 5).

Configuration files are automatically installed for you by the RPM package versions of Netatalk, such as those for Red Hat or OpenLinux. If you are installing from the source distribution, you need to install these from default files in the source directory. Also, make sure the following lines are in your **/etc/services** file (RPM packages add these automatically):

```
rtmp 1/ddp # Routing Table Maintenance Protocol
nbp 2/ddp # Name Binding Protocol
echo 4/ddp # AppleTalk Echo Protocol
zip 6/ddp # Zone Information Protocol
```

Netatalk is started using a startup script called **atalk**. RPM packages, such as those for Red Hat and OpenLinux, install **atalk** in the **/etc/rc.d/init.d** directory. You can also use a System V Init run-level editor to manage startup and shutdown operations. A link is set up to start the **atalk** script when you boot. You can also use **start** and **stop**

Filename	Description
AppleVolumes.default	List of shared directories, including optional names.
AppleVolumes.system	Maps of file extensions to Mac OS types.
afpd.conf	Configuration file for **afpd** daemon (AppleTalk File system and printer daemon).
atalkd.conf	Controls the interfaces to which Netatalk binds, enabling you to specify network numbers or zones. If empty, Netatalk detects the interfaces itself.
papd.conf	Provides AppleTalk access to Linux print queues. If empty, uses **/etc/printcap**.

Table 37-7. *Netatalk Configuration Files*

arguments directly with **atalk**. The source code distribution uses a startup script called **rc.atalk** and installs it in the **/usr/local/atalk/etc** directory.

```
/etc/rc.d/init.d/atalk  start
```

The Complete Reference

Linux

Chapter 38

Administering TCP/IP Networks

L inux systems are configured to connect into networks that use the TCP/IP protocols. These are the same protocols that the Internet uses, as do many *local area networks* (*LANs*). In Chapter 23, you were introduced to TCP/IP, a robust set of protocols designed to provide communications among systems with different operating systems and hardware. The TCP/IP protocols were developed in the 1970s as a special DARPA project to enhance communications between universities and research centers. These protocols were originally developed on Unix systems, with much of the research carried out at the University of California, Berkeley. Linux, as a version of Unix, benefits from much of this original focus on Unix. Currently, the TCP/IP protocol development is managed by *the Internet Engineering Task Force* (*IETF*), which, in turn, is supervised by the *Internet Society* (*ISOC*). The ISOC oversees several groups responsible for different areas of Internet development, such as the *Internet Assigned Numbers Authority* (*IANA*), which is responsible for Internet addressing (see Table 38-1). Over the years, TCP/IP protocol standards and documentation have been

Group	Title	Description
ISOC	Internet Society	Professional membership organization of Internet experts that oversees boards and task forces dealing with network policy issues **www.isoc.org**
IESG	The Internet Engineering Steering Group	Responsible for technical management of IETF activities and the Internet standards process **www.ietf.org/iesg.html**
IANA	Internet Assigned Numbers Authority	Responsible for Internet Protocol (IP) addresses. **www.iana.org**
IAB	Internet Architecture Board	Defines the overall architecture of the Internet, providing guidance and broad direction to the IETF. **www.iab.org**
IETF	Internet Engineering Task Force	Protocol engineering and development arm of the Internet **www.ietf.org**

Table 38-1. *TCP/IP Protocol Development Groups*

issued in the form of *Requests for Comments (RFC)* documents. Check the most recent ones for current developments at the IETF Web site at **www.ietf.org**.

The TCP/IP protocols suite actually consists of different protocols, each designed for a specific task in a TCP/IP network. The three basic protocols are the *Transmission Control Protocol (TCP)*, which handles receiving and sending; out communications; the *Internet Protocol (IP)*, which handles the actual transmissions, and the *User Datagram Protocol (UPD)*, which also handles receiving and sending packets. The IP protocol, which is the base protocol that all others use, handles the actual transmissions, handling the packets of data with sender and receiver information in each. The TCP protocol is designed to work with cohesive messages or data. This protocol checks received packets and sorts them into their designated order, forming the original message. For data sent out, the TCP protocol breaks the data into separate packets, designating their order. The UDP protocol, meant to work on a much more raw level, also breaks down data into packets but does not check their order. The TCP/IP protocol is designed to provide stable and reliable connections that ensure that all data is received and reorganized into its original order. UDP, on the other hand, is designed to simply send as much data as possible, with no guarantee that packets will all be received or placed in the proper order. UDP is often used for transmitting very large amounts of data of the type that can survive the loss of a few packets, for example, temporary images, video, and banners displayed on the Internet.

Other protocols provide various network and user services. The *Domain Name Service (DNS)* provides address resolution. The *File Transfer Protocol (FTP)* provides file transmission, and *Network File System (NFS)* provides access to remote file systems. Table 38-2 lists the different protocols in the TCP/IP protocol suite. These protocols make use of either the TCP or UDP protocol to send and receive packets, which, in turn, uses the IP protocol for actually transmitting the packets.

Transport	Description
TCP	Transmission Control Protocol; places systems in direct communication
UDP	User Datagram Protocol
IP	Internet Protocol; transmits data
ICMP	Internet Control Message Protocol; status messages for IP
Routing	**Description**
RIP	Routing Information Protocol; determines routing

Table 38-2. *TCP/IP Protocol Suite*

NETWORK ADMINISTRATION

Routing	Description
OSPF	Open Shortest Path First; determines routing
Network Addresses	**Description**
ARP	Address Resolution Protocol; determines unique IP address of systems
DNS	Domain Name Service; translates hostnames into IP addresses
RARP	Reverse Address Resolution Protocol; determines addresses of systems
User Services	**Description**
FTP	File Transfer Protocol; transmits files from one system to another using TCP
TFTP	Trivial File Transfer Protocol; transfers files using UDP
TELNET	Remote login to another system on the network
SMTP	Simple Mail Transfer Protocol; transfers e-mail between systems
RPC	Remote Procedure Call; allows programs on remote systems to communicate
Gateway	**Description**
EGP	Exterior Gateway Protocol; provides routing for external networks
GGP	Gateway-to-Gateway Protocol; provides routing between Internet gateways
IGP	Interior Gateway Protocol; provides routing for internal networks
Network Services	**Description**
NFS	Network File System; allows mounting of file systems on remote machines
NIS	Network Information Service; maintains user accounts across a network

Table 38-2. *TCP/IP Protocol Suite* (continued)

Network Services	Description
BOOTP	Boot Protocol; starts system using boot information on server for network
SNMP	Simple Network Management Protocol; provides status messages on TCP/IP configuration
DHCP	Dynamic Host Configuration Protocol; automatically provides network configuration information to host systems

Table 38-2. *TCP/IP Protocol Suite* (continued)

In a TCP/IP network, messages are broken into small components, called *datagrams*, which are then transmitted through various interlocking routes and delivered to their destination computers. Once received, the datagrams are reassembled into the original message. Datagrams themselves can be broken down into smaller packets. The *packet* is the physical message unit actually transmitted among networks. Sending messages as small components has proved to be far more reliable and faster than sending them as one large, bulky transmission. With small components, if one is lost or damaged, only that component must be re-sent; whereas if any part of a large transmission is corrupted or lost, the entire message has to be re-sent.

The configuration of a TCP/IP network on your Linux system is implemented using a set of network configuration files. Table 38-2 provides a complete listing. Many of these can be managed using administrative programs, such as Linuxconf or **netcfg,** on your root user desktop (see Chapter 29). You can also use the more specialized programs, such as **netstat, ifconfig,** and **route.** Some configuration files are easy to modify yourself using a text editor.

TCP/IP networks are configured and managed with a set of utilities: **ifconfig, route,** and **netstat.** The **ifconfig** utility operates from your root user desktop and enables you to configure your network interfaces fully, adding new ones and modifying others. The **ifconfig** and **route** utilities are lower-level programs that require more specific knowledge of your network to use effectively. The **netstat** utility provides you with information about the status of your network connections.

IPv4 and IPv6

Traditionally, a TCP/IP address is organized into four segments, consisting of numbers separated by periods. This is called the *IP address.* The IP address actually represents a 32-bit integer whose binary values identify the network and host. This form of IP addressing adheres to Internet Protocol, version 4, also known as IPv4. IPv4, the kind of IP addressing described here, is still in wide use.

Currently, a new version of the IP protocol called Internet Protocol version 6 (IPv6) is gradually replacing the older IPv4 version. IPv6 expands the number of possible IP addresses using a 128-bit address. It is fully compatible with systems still using IPv4. IPv6 addresses are represented differently, using a set of eight 16-bit segments, each separated by a colon. Each segment is represented by a hexadecimal number. A sample address would be

```
FEDC:0:0:200C:800:BA98:7654:3210
```

IPv6 features simplified headers that allow for faster processing. It also provides support for encryption and authentication. Its most significant advantage is extending the address space to cover 2 to the power of 128 possible hosts (billions of billions of billions—a lot). This extends far beyond the 4.2 billion supported by IPv4.

TCP/IP Network Addresses

As noted previously, the traditional IPv4 TCP/IP address is organized into four segments, consisting of numbers separated by periods. This kind of address is still in wide use and is what people commonly refer to as an *IP address.* Part of an IP address is used for the network address, and the other part is used to identify a particular interface on a host in that network. You should realize that IP addresses are assigned to interfaces—such as Ethernet cards or modems—and not to the host computer. Usually a computer has only one interface and is accessed using only that interface's IP address. In that regard, an IP address can be thought of as identifying a particular host system on a network, and so the IP address is usually referred to as the *host address.*

In fact, though, a host system could have several interfaces, each with its own IP address. This is the case for computers that operate as gateways and firewalls from the local network to the Internet. One interface usually connects to the LAN and another to the Internet, as by two Ethernet cards. Each interface (such as an Ethernet card) has its own IP address. For example, when you use Linuxconf to specify an IP address for an Ethernet card on your system, the panel for entering your IP address is labeled as Adapter 1 and three other panels are there for other Ethernet cards that have their own IP addresses. Currently, the Linux kernel can support up to four network adapters. If you use a modem to connect to an ISP, then you would set up a PPP interface that would also have its own IP address (usually dynamically assigned by the ISP). Remembering this distinction is important if you plan to use Linux to set up a local or home network, using Linux as your gateway machine to the Internet (see the section "IP Masquerading" later, in Chapter 39).

Network Addresses

The IP address is divided into two parts: one part identifies the network, and the other part identifies a particular host. The network address identifies the network of which a particular interface on a host is a part. Two methods exist for implementing the network and host parts of an IP address: the original class-based IP addressing and the current *Classless Interdomain Routing* (*CIDR*) addressing. Class-based IP addressing designates officially predetermined parts of the address for the network and host addresses, whereas CIDR addressing allows the parts to be determined dynamically using a netmask.

Class-Based IP Addressing

Originally, IP addresses were organized according to classes. On the Internet, networks are organized into three classes depending on their size—classes A, B, and C. A class A network uses only the first segment for the network address and the remaining three for the host, allowing a great many computers to be connected to the same network. Most IP addresses reference smaller, class C, networks. For a class C network, the first three segments are used to identify the network, and only the last segment identifies the host. Altogether, this forms a unique address with which to identify any network interface on computers in a TCP/IP network. For example, in the IP address 192.168.1.72, the network part is 192.168.1 and the interface/host part is 72. The interface/host is a part of a network whose own address is 192.168.1.0.

In a class C network, the first three numbers identify the network part of the IP address. This part is divided into three network numbers, each identifying a subnet. Networks on the Internet are organized into subnets, beginning with the largest and narrowing to small subnetworks. The last number is used to identify a particular computer referred to as a *host*. You can think of the Internet as a series of networks with subnetworks; these subnetworks have their own subnetworks. The rightmost number identifies the host computer, and the number preceding it identifies the subnetwork of which the computer is a part. The number to the left of that identifies the network the subnetwork is part of, and so on. The Internet address 192.168.187.4 references the fourth computer connected to the network identified by the number 187. Network 187 is a subnet to a larger network identified as 168. This larger network is itself a subnet of the network identified as 192. Here's how it breaks down:

192.168.187.4   IP address

192.168.187   Network identification

4   Host identification

Netmask

Systems derive the network address from the host address using the netmask. You can think of an IP address as a series of 32 binary bits, some of which are used for the network and the remainder for the host. The *netmask* has the network set of bits set to 1s, with the host bits set to 0s (see Figure 38-1). In a standard class-based IP address, all the numbers in the network part of your host address are set to **255**, and the host part is set to **0**. This has the effect of setting all the binary bits making up the network address to 1s. This, then, is your netmask. So, the netmask for the host address **192.168.1.72** is **255.255.255.0**. The network part, **192.168.1**, has been set to **255.255.255**; and the host part, **72**, has been set to **0**. Systems can then use your netmask to derive your network address from your host address. They can determine what part of your host address makes up your network address and what those numbers are.

For those familiar with computer programming, a bitwise AND operation on the netmask and the host address results in zeroing the host part, leaving you with the network part of the host address. You can think of the address as being implemented as a four-byte integer with each byte corresponding to a segment of the address. In a class C address, the three network segments correspond to the first three bytes, and the host segment corresponds to the fourth byte. A netmask is designed to mask out the host part of the address, leaving the network segments alone. In the netmask for a standard class C network, the first three bytes are all 1s and the last byte consists of 0s. The 0s in the last byte mask out the host part of the address, and the 1s in the first three bytes leave the network part of the address alone. Figure 38-1 shows the bitwise operation of the netmask on the address 192.168.1.4. This is a class C address to the mask, which consists of 24 1s making up the first three bytes and eight 0s making up the last byte. When it is applied to the address 192.168.1.4, the network address

Class-based Addressing

IP Address   192.168.1.4

	Network			Host
binary	11000000	10101000	00000001	00000100
numeric	192	168	1	4

Netmask   255.255.255.0

binary	11111111	11111111	11111111	00000000
numeric	255	255	255	000

Network Address   192.168.1.0

binary	11000000	10101000	00000001	00000000
numeric	192	168	1	0

Netmask Operation

IP Address	11000000	10101000	00000001	00000100
Netmask	11111111	11111111	11111111	00000000
Net Address	11000000	10101000	00000001	00000000

Figure 38-1.   *Class-based netmask operations*

remains (192.168.1) and the host address is masked out (4), giving you 192.168.1.0 as the network address.

Classless Interdomain Routing (CIDR)

Currently, the class-based organization of IP addresses is being replaced by the CIDR format. CIDR was designed for mid-sized networks, those between a class C, and classes with numbers of hosts greater than 256 and smaller than 65,534. A class C network–based IP address using only one segment for hosts uses only one segment, an 8-bit integer, with a maximum value of 256. A class B network–based IP address uses two segments, which make up a 16-bit integer whose maximum value is 65,534. You can think of an address as a 32-bit integer taking up four bytes, where each byte is eight bits. Each segment conforms to one of the four bytes. A class C network uses three segments, or 24 bits, to make up its network address. A class B network, in turn, uses two segments, or 16 bits, for its address. With this scheme, allowable host and network addresses are changed an entire byte at a time, segment to segment. With CIDR addressing, you can define host and network addresses by bits, instead of whole segments. For example, you can use CIDR addressing to expand the host segment from eight bits to nine, rather than having to jump it to a class B 16 bits (two segments).

CIDR addressing notation achieves this by incorporating netmask information in the IP address (the netmask is applied to an IP address to determine the Network part of the address). In the CIDR notation, the number of bits making up the network address is placed after the IP address, following a slash. For example, the CIDR form of the class C 192.168.187.4 IP address is

```
192.168.187.4/24
```

The netmask as used in *Classless Interdomain Routing* (*CIDR*) is much more flexible than a class-based netmask. Instead of having the size of the network address and its mask determined by the network class, it is determined by a number attached to the end of the IP address. This number simply specifies the size of the network address, how many bits in the address it takes up. For example, in an IP address whose network part takes up the first three bytes (segments), the number of bits used for that network part is 24—eight bits to a byte (segment). Instead of using a netmask to determine the network address, the number for the network size is attached to the end of the address with a slash, as shown here:

```
192.168.1.72/24
```

CIDR gives you the advantage of specifying networks that are any size bits, instead of only three possible segments. You could have a network whose address takes up 14 bits, 22 bits, or even 25 bits. The host address can use whatever bits are left over. An IP address with 21 bits for the network can cover host addresses using the remaining 11 bits, 0 to 2047.

Figure 28-2 shows an example of a CIDR address and its network mask. The IP address is 192.168.1.6 with a network mask of 22 bits, 192.168.1.6/22. The network

```
CIDR Addressing

IP Address   192.168.4.6/22
                               Network                    Host
              binary  11000000  10101000  000001 00   00000110
              numeric    192       168       4            6

Netmask  255.255.252.0      22 bits

              binary  11111111  11111111  111111 00   00000000
              numeric    255       255      252          000
```

Figure 38-2.   *CIDR addressing*

address takes up the first 22 bits of the IP address and the remaining 10 bits are used for the host address. The host address is taking up the equivalent of a class-based IP address's 4th segment (8 bits) and two bits from the 3rd segment.

Table 38-3 lists the different CIDR network masks available along with the maximum number of hosts. Both the short form and the full form of the netmask are listed.

The network address for any standard class C IP address takes up the first three segments, 24 bits. If you want to create a network with a maximum of 512 hosts, you can give them IP addresses where the network address is 23 bits and the host address takes up 9 bits (0–511). The IP address notation remains the same, however, using the four eight-bit segments. This means a given segment's number could be used for both a network address and a host address. Segments are no longer wholly part of either the host address or the network address. Assigning a 23-bit network address and a 9-bit host address means that the number in the third segment is part of both the network address and the host address, the first seven bits for the network and the last bit for the host. In this following example, the third number, 145, is used as the end of the network address and as the beginning of the host address.

```
192.168.145.67/23
```

This situation complicates CIDR addressing; and, in some cases, the only way to represent the address is to specify two or more network addresses. Check RFC 1520 at **www.ietf.org** for more details.

Note   *A simple way to calculate the number of hosts a network can address is to take the number of bits in its host segment as a power of 2 and then subtract 2, that is, 2 to the number of host bits, minus 2. For example, an eight-bit host segment would be 2 to the power of 8, which equals 256. Subtract 2, one for the broadcast address, 255, and one for the zero value, 000, to leave you with 254 possible hosts.*

Short Form	Full Form	Maximum Number of Hosts
/8	/255.0.0.0	16,777,215 (A class)
/16	/255.255.0.0	65,535 (B class)
/17	/255.255.128.0	32,767
/18	/255.255.192.0	16,383
/19	/255.255.224.0	8,191
/20	/255.255.240.0	4,095
/21	/255.255.248.0	2,047
/22	/255.255.252.0	1,023
/23	/255.255.254.0	511
/24	/255.255.255.0	255 (C class)
/25	/255.255.255.128	127
/26	/255.255.255.192	63
/27	/255.255.255.224	31
/28	/255.255.255.240	15
/29	/255.255.255.248	7
/30	/255.255.255.252	3

Table 38-3.   *CIDR Network Masks*

CIDR also allows a network administrator to take what is officially the host part of an IP address and break it up into subnetworks with fewer hosts. This is referred to as subnetting. A given network will have its official IP network address recognized on the Internet or by a larger network. The network administrator for that network could, in turn, create several smaller networks within it using CIDR network masking. A classic example is to take a standard class C network with 254 hosts and break it up into two smaller networks, each with 64 hosts. You do this by using a CIDR netmask to take a bit from the host part of the IP address and use it for the subnetworks. Numbers within the range of the original 254 addresses whose first bit would be set to 1 would represent one subnet; and the others, whose first bit would be set to 0, would constitute the remaining network. In the network whose network address is 192.168.187.0, where the last segment is used for the hostnames, that last host segment could be further split into two subnets, each with its own hosts. For two subnets, you would use the first bit in the last eight-bit segment for the network. The remaining seven bits could then be used for host addresses, giving you a range of 127 hosts per network. The subnet whose bit is set to 0 would have a range of 1 to 127, with a CIDR netmask of 25. The eight-bit segment for the first host would be 00000001. So the host with the address of 1 in that network would have this IP address:

```
192.168.187.1/25
```

For the subnet where the first bit is 1, the first host would have an address of 129, with the CIDR netmask of 25, as shown here. The eight-bit sequence for the first host would be 10000001.

```
192.168.187.129/25
```

Each subnet would have a set of 126 addresses, the first from 1 to 126, and the second from 129 to 254. 127 is the broadcast address for the first subnet, and 128 is the network address for the second subnet.

Subnetworks	CIDR Address	Binary Mask
First subnet network address	.0/25	00000000
Second subnet network address	.128/25	10000000
First subnet broadcast address	.127/25	01111111
Second subnet broadcast address	.255/25	11111111
First address in first subnet	.1/25	00000001
First address in second subnet	.129/25	10000001
Last address in first subnet	.126/25	01111110
Last address in second subnet	.254/25	11111110

Obtaining an IP Address

IP addresses are officially allocated by IANA, which manages all aspects of Internet addressing (**www.iana.org**). IANA oversees *Internet Registries* (*IR*), which, in turn, maintain Internet addresses on regional and local levels. The Internet Registry for the Americas is the *American Registry for Internet Numbers* (*ARIN*), whose Web site is at **www.arin.net**. These addresses are provided to users by Internet service providers (ISPs). You can obtain your own Internet address from an ISP; or, if you are on a network already connected to the Internet, your network administrator can assign you one. If you are using an ISP, the ISP may temporarily assign one from a pool it has on hand with each use.

Certain numbers are reserved. The numbers 127, 0, or 255 cannot be part of an official IP address. The number 127 is used to designate the network address for the loopback interface on your system. The loopback interface enables users on your system to communicate with each other without having to route through a network connection. Its network address would be 127.0.0.0 and its IP address 127.0.0.1. For class-based IP addressing, the number 255 is a special broadcast identifier you can use to broadcast messages to all sites on a network. Using 255 for any part of the IP address references all nodes connected at that level. For example, 192.168.255.255 broadcasts a message to all computers on network 192.168, all its subnetworks, and their hosts. The address 192.168.187.255 broadcasts to every computer on the local network. If you use 0 for the network part of the address, the host number references a computer within your local network. For example, 0.0.0.6 references the sixth computer in your local network. If you want to broadcast to all computers on your local network, you can use the number 0.0.0.255. For CIDR IP addressing, the broadcast address may appear much like a normal IP address. As indicated in the previous section, CIDR addressing allows the use of any number of bits to make up the IP address for either the network or the host part. For a broadcast address, the host part must have all its bits set to 1 (see Figure 31-3).

A special set of numbers is reserved for use on non-Internet LANs (RFC 1918). These are numbers that begin with the special network number 192.168 (for class C networks), as used in these examples. If you are setting up a LAN, such as a small business or a home network, you are free to use these numbers for your local machines. You can set up an intranet using network cards, such as Ethernet cards and Ethernet hubs, and then configure your machines with IP addresses starting from 192.168.1.1. The host segment can go up to 256. If you have three machines on your home network, you could give them the addresses 192.168.1.1, 192.168.1.2, and 192.168.1.3. You can implement Internet services, such as FTP, Web, and mail services, on your local machines and use any of the Internet tools to make use of those services. They all use the same TCP/IP protocols used on the Internet. For example, with FTP tools, you can transfer files among the machines on your network; with mail tools, you can send

Class-based Broadcast Addressing

Broadcast Address 192.168.1.255

binary	11000000	10101000	00000001	11111111
numeric	192	168	1	255

CIDR Broadcast Addressing

Broadcast Address 192.168.7.255/22

		Network		Host
binary	11000000	10101000	000001 11	11111111
numeric	192	168	7	255

Figure 38-3. *Class-based and CIDR Broadcast Addressing*

messages from one machine to another; and with a Web browser, you can access local Web sites that may be installed on a machine running its own Web servers. If you want to have one of your machines connected to the Internet or some other network, you can set it up to be a gateway machine. By convention, the gateway machine is usually given the address 192.168.1.1. With a method *called IP masquerading,* you can have any of the non-Internet machines use a gateway to connect to the Internet.

Numbers are also reserved for class A and class B non-Internet local networks. Table 38-4 lists these addresses. The possible addresses available span from 0 to 255 in the host segment of the address. For example, class B network addresses range from 172.16.0.0 to 172.31.255.255, giving you a total of 32,356 possible hosts. The class C network ranges from 192.168.0.0 to 192.168.255.255, giving you 256 possible

Private Network address	Network Class
10.0.0.0	Class A network
172.16.0.0 to 172.31.255.255	Class B network
192.168.0.0	Class C network
127.0.0.0	Loopback network (for system self-communication)

Table 38-4. *Non-Internet Local Network IP Addresses*

subnetworks, each with 256 possible hosts. The network address 127.0.0.0 is reserved for a system's loopback interface, which allows it to communicate with itself, enabling users on the same system to send messages to each other.

Broadcast Addresses

The *broadcast address* allows a system to send the same message to all systems on your network at once. With class-based IP addressing, you can easily determine the broadcast address using your host address: the broadcast address has the host part of your address set to **255**. The network part remains untouched. So, the broadcast address for the host address **192.168.1.72** is **192.168.1.255** (you combine the network part of the address with **255** in the host part). For CIDR IP addressing, you need to know the number of bits in the netmask. The remaining bits are set to 1 (see Figure 38-1). For example, an IP address of 192.168.4.6/22 has a broadcast address of 192.168.7.255/22. In this case, the first 22 bits are the network address and the last 10 bits are the host part set to the broadcast value (all 1s).

In fact, you can think of a class C broadcast address as merely a CIDR address using 24 bits (the first three segments) for the network address, and the last eight bits (the fourth segment) as the broadcast address. The value 255 expressed in binary terms is simply eight bits that are all 1s. 255 is the same as 11111111.

IP Address	Broadcast Address	IP Broadcast Number	Binary Equivalent
192.168.1.72	192.168.1.255	255	11111111
192.168.4.6/22	192.168.7.255/22	7.255 (last 2 bits in 7)	1111111111

Gateway Addresses

Some networks have a computer designated as the gateway to other networks. Every connection to and from a network to other networks passes through this gateway computer. Most local networks use gateways to establish a connection to the Internet. If you are on this type of network, you must provide the gateway address. If your network does not have a connection to the Internet, or a larger network, you may not need a gateway address. The *gateway address* is the address of the host system providing the gateway service to the network. On many networks, this host is given a host ID of **1**: the gateway address for a network with the address **192.168.1** would be **192.168.1.1**; but this is only a convention. To be sure of your gateway address, ask your network administrator.

Name Server Addresses

Many networks, including the Internet, have computers that provide a Domain Name Service (DNS) that translates the domain names of networks and hosts into IP addresses. These are known as the network's *domain name servers*. The DNS makes your computer identifiable on a network, using only your domain name, rather than your IP address. You can also use the domain names of other systems to reference them, so you needn't know their IP addresses. You must know the IP addresses of any domain name servers for your network, however. You can obtain the addresses from your system administrator (often more than one exists). Even if you are using an ISP, you must know the address of the domain name servers your ISP operates for the Internet.

TCP/IP Configuration Files

A set of configuration files in the **/etc** directory, shown in Table 38-5, are used to set up and manage your TCP/IP network. These configuration files specify such network information as host and domain names, IP addresses, and interface options. The IP addresses and domain names of other Internet hosts you want to access are entered in these files. If you configured your network during installation, you can already find that information in these files. The netcfg, Linuxconf, and the netconfig configuration tools described in the next section provide easy interfaces for entering the configuration data for these files.

Identifying Hostnames: /etc/hosts

Without the unique IP address the TCP/IP network uses to identify computers, a particular computer cannot be located. Because IP addresses are difficult to use or remember, domain names are used instead. For each IP address, a domain name exists. When you use a domain name to reference a computer on the network, your system translates it into its associated IP address. This address can then be used by your network to locate that computer.

Originally, every computer on the network was responsible for maintaining a list of the hostnames and their IP addresses. This list is still kept in the **/etc/hosts** file. When you use a domain name, your system looks up its IP address in the **hosts** file. The system administrator is responsible for maintaining this list. Because of the explosive growth of the Internet and the development of more and more large networks, the responsibility for associating domain names and IP addresses has been taken over by domain name servers. The **hosts** file is still used to hold the domain names and IP addresses of frequently accessed hosts, however. Your system normally checks your **hosts** file for the IP address of a domain name before taking the added step of accessing a name server.

The format of a domain name entry in the **hosts** file is the IP address followed by the domain name, separated by a space. You can then add aliases for the hostname. After the entry, on the same line, you can enter a comment. A comment is always preceded by a **#** symbol. You can already find an entry in your **hosts** file for localhost with the IP address **127.0.0.1**. *Localhost* is a special identification used by your computer to enable users on your system to communicate locally with each other. The IP address **127.0.0.1** is a special reserved address used by every computer for this purpose. It identifies what is technically referred to as a *loopback device*.

/etc/hosts

```
127.0.0.1          turtle.trek.com          localhost
192.168.1.72       turtle.trek.com
192.168.196.56     pango1.train.com
202.211.234.1      rose.berkeley.edu
```

Network Name: /etc/networks

The **/etc/networks** file holds the domain names and IP addresses of networks you are connected to, not the domain names of particular computers. Networks have shortened IP addresses. Depending on the type of network, they use one, two, or three numbers for their IP addresses. You also have your localhost network IP address **127.0.0.0**. This is the network address used for the loopback device.

   The IP addresses are entered, followed by the network domain names. Recall that an IP address consists of a network part and a host part. The network part is the network address you find in the **networks** file. You always have an entry in this file for the network portion of your computer's IP address. This is the network address of the network to which your computer is connected.

/etc/networks

```
loopback 127.0.0.0
trek.com 192.168.1.0
```

/etc/HOSTNAME

The **/etc/HOSTNAME** file holds your system's hostname. To change your hostname, you change this entry. Configuration tools like Linuxconf and netcfg enable you to change your hostname and places the new name in **/etc/HOSTNAME**. Instead of displaying this file to find your hostname, you can use the **hostname** command.

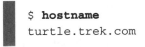

```
$ hostname
turtle.trek.com
```

/etc/services

The **/etc/services** file lists network services available on your system, such as FTP and telnet, and associates each with a particular port. Here, you can find out what port your Web server is checking or what port is used for your FTP server. You can give a service an alias, which you specify after the port number. You can then reference the service using the alias.

/etc/protocols

The **/etc/protocols** file lists the TCP/IP protocols currently supported by your system.

/etc/sysconfig/network

The **/etc/sysconfig/network** file contains system definitions for your network configuration. These include definitions for your domain name, gateway, and hostname, among others.

Address	Description
Host address	IP address of your system; includes a network part to identify the network you are on and a host part to identify your own system
Network address	IP address of your network
Broadcast address	IP address for sending messages to all hosts on your network at once
Gateway address	IP address of your gateway system, if you have one (usually the network part of your host IP address with the host part set to **1**)
Domain name server addresses	IP addresses of domain name servers your network uses
Netmask	Used to determine the network and host parts of your IP address
Files	**Description**
/etc/hosts	Associates hostnames with IP addresses
/etc/networks	Associates domain names with network addresses
/etc/host.conf	Lists resolver options
/etc/nsswitch.conf	Lists resolver options

Table 38-5.   *TCP/IP Configuration Addresses and Files*

Address	Description
/etc/hosts	Lists domain names for remote hosts with their IP addresses
/etc/resolv.conf	Lists domain name server names, IP addresses (nameserver), and domain names where remote hosts may be located (search)
/etc/protocols	Lists protocols available on your system
/etc/services	Lists available network services, such as FTP and telnet, and the ports they use
/etc/HOSTNAME	Holds the name of your system
/etc/sysconfig/network	Network configuration information

Table 38-5.   *TCP/IP Configuration Addresses and Files* (continued)

Domain Name Service (DNS)

Each computer connected to a TCP/IP network, such as the Internet, is identified by its own IP address. IP addresses are difficult to remember, so a domain name version of each IP address is also used to identify a host. As described in Chapter 10, a domain name consists of two parts, the hostname and the domain. The hostname is the computer's specific name, and the domain identifies the network of which the computer is a part. The domains used for the United States usually have extensions that identify the type of host. For example, **.edu** is used for educational institutions and **.com** is used for businesses. International domains usually have extensions that indicate the country they are located in, such as **.de** for Germany or **.au** for Australia. The combination of a hostname, domain, and extension forms a unique name by which a computer can be referenced. The domain can, in turn, be split into further subdomains.

As you know, a computer on a network can still only be identified by its IP address, even if it has a hostname. You can use a hostname to reference a computer on a network, but this involves using the hostname to look up the corresponding IP address in a database. The network then uses the IP address, not the hostname, to access the computer. Before the advent of large TCP/IP networks, such as the Internet, it was feasible for each computer on a network to maintain a file with a list of all the hostnames and IP addresses of the computers connected on its network. Whenever a hostname was used, it was looked up in this file and the corresponding IP address was located. You can still do this on your own system for remote systems you access frequently.

As networks became larger, it became impractical—and, in the case of the Internet, impossible—for each computer to maintain its own list of all the domain names and IP addresses. To provide the service of translating domain addresses to IP addresses, databases of domain names were developed and placed on their own servers. To find the IP address of a domain name, you send a query to a name server, which then looks up the IP address for you and sends it back. In a large network, several name servers can cover different parts of the network. If a name server cannot find a particular IP address, it sends the query on to another name server that is more likely to have it.

If you are administering a network and you need to set up a name server for it, you can configure a Linux system to operate as a name server. To do so, you must start up a name server daemon, and then wait for domain name queries. A name server makes use of several configuration files that enable it to answer requests. The name server software used on Linux systems is the *Berkeley Internet Name Domain* (*BIND*) server distributed by the Internet Software Consortium (**www.isc.org**). Chapter 18 describes the process of setting up a domain name server in detail.

Name servers are queried by resolvers. These are programs specially designed to obtain addresses from name servers. To use domain names on your system, you must configure your own resolver. Your local resolver is configured with your **/etc/host.conf** and **/etc/resolv.conf** files. You can use **--/etc/nsswitch** in place of **/etc/host.conf**.

host.conf

Your **host.conf** file lists resolver options (shown in the following table). Each option can have several fields, separated by spaces or tabs. You can use a # at the beginning of a line to enter a comment. The options tell the resolver what services to use. The order of the list is important. The resolver begins with the first option listed and moves on to the next ones in turn. You can find the **host.conf** file in your **/etc** directory, along with other configuration files.

Option	Description
`order`	Specifies sequence of name resolution methods: **hosts** Checks for name in the local **/etc/host** file **bind** Queries a DNS name server for address **nis** Uses Network Information Service protocol to obtain address
`alert`	Checks addresses of remote sites attempting to access your system; turned on or off with the **on** and **off** options

Option	Description
nospoof	Confirms addresses of remote sites attempting to access your system
trim	Checks your local host's file; removes the domain name and checks only for the hostname; enables you to use only a hostname in your host file for an IP address
multi	Checks your local hosts file; allows a host to have several IP addresses; turned on or off with the **on** and **off** options

In the next example of a **host.conf** file, the **order** option instructs your resolver first to look up names in your local **/etc/hosts** file, and then, if that fails, to query domain name servers. The system does not have multiple addresses.

/etc/host.conf

```
#  host.conf file
#  Look up names in host file and then check DNS
order bind host
# There are no multiple addresses
multi off
```

/etc/nsswitch.conf: Name Service Switch

Different functions in the standard C Library must be configured to operate on your Linux system. Previously, database-like services, such as password support and name services like NIS or DNS, directly accessed these functions, using a fixed search order. For GNU C Library 2.*x*, used on current versions of Linux, this configuration is carried out by a scheme called the *Name Service Switch* (*NSS*), which is based on the method of the same name used by Sun Microsystems Solaris 2 OS. The database sources and their lookup order are listed in the **/etc/nsswitch.conf** file.

The **/etc/nsswitch.conf** file holds entries for the different configuration files that can be controlled by NSS. The system configuration files that NSS supports are listed in Table 38-6. An entry consists of two fields: the service and the configuration specification. The service consists of the configuration file followed by a colon. The second field is the configuration specification for that file, which holds instructions on how the lookup procedure will work. The configuration specification can contain service specifications and action items. Service specifications are the services to search. Currently, valid service specifications are nis, nis-plus, files, db, dns, and compat (see Table 38-7). Not all are valid for each configuration file. For example, the dns service is only valid for the **hosts** file, whereas nis is valid for all files. An action item specifies the action to

Files	Description
aliases	Mail aliases, used by sendmail
ethers	Ethernet numbers
group	Groups of users
hosts	Hostnames and numbers
netgroup	Network-wide list of hosts and users, used for access rules (C libraries before glibc 2.1 only support netgroups over NIS.)
network	Network names and numbers
passwd	User passwords
protocols	Network protocols
publickey	Public and secret keys for SecureRPC used by NFS and NIS+
rpc	Remote procedure call names and numbers
services	Network services
shadow	Shadow user passwords

Table 38-6.   *NSS Supported Files*

take for a specific service. An action item is placed within brackets after a service. A configuration specification can list several services, each with its own action item. In the following example, the entry for the network file has a configuration specification that says to check the NIS service and, if not found, to check the **/etc/networks** file.

```
networks:        nis [NOTFOUND=return] files
```

An action item consists of a status and an action. The status holds a possible result of a service lookup, and the action is the action to take if the status is true. Currently, the possible status values are SUCCESS, NOTFOUND, UNAVAIL, and TRYAGAIN (service temporarily unavailable). The possible actions are **return** and **continue**: **return** stops the lookup process for the configuration file, whereas **continue** continues on to the next listed service. In the previous example, if the record is not found in NIS, the lookup process ends.

Service	Description
files	Checks corresponding **/etc** file for the configuration (for example, **/etc/hosts** for hosts); valid for all files
db	Checks corresponding **/var/db** databases for the configuration; valid for all files except **netgroup**
compat	Valid only for passwd, group, and shadow files
dns	Checks the DNS service; valid only for **hosts** file
nis	Checks the NIS service; valid for all files
nisplus	NIS version 3
hesoid	Use for lookup

Table 38-7.   *NSS Configuration Services*

Shown here is a copy of the current Red Hat **/etc/nsswitch.conf** file. Comments and commented-out entries begin with a # sign.

/etc/nsswitch.conf

```
#
# /etc/nsswitch.conf
#
# An example Name Service Switch config file. This file should be
# sorted with the most-used services at the beginning.
#
# The entry '[NOTFOUND=return]' means that the search for an
# entry should stop if the search in the previous entry turned
# up nothing. Note that if the search failed due to some other reason
# (like no NIS server responding) then the search continues with the
# next entry.
#
# Legal entries are:
#
#    nisplus or nis+          Use NIS+ (NIS version 3)
#    nis or yp          Use NIS (NIS version 2), also called YP
#    dns          Use DNS (Domain Name Service)
#    files          Use the local files
#    db          Use the local database (.db) files
#    compat          Use NIS on compat mode
#    hesiod          Use Hesiod for user lookups
#    [NOTFOUND=return]     Stop searching if not found so far
```

```
#
# To use db, put the "db" in front of "files" for entries you want to
# be looked up first in the databases
#
# Example:
#passwd:     db files nisplus nis
#shadow:     db files nisplus nis
#group:      db files nisplus nis

passwd:      files nisplus nis
shadow:      files nisplus nis
group:       files nisplus nis

hosts:       files nisplus nis dns

# Example - obey only what nisplus tells us...
#services:   nisplus [NOTFOUND=return] files
#networks:   nisplus [NOTFOUND=return] files
#protocols:  nisplus [NOTFOUND=return] files
#rpc:        nisplus [NOTFOUND=return] files
#ethers:     nisplus [NOTFOUND=return] files
#netmasks:   nisplus [NOTFOUND=return] files

bootparams: nisplus [NOTFOUND=return] files

ethers:      files
netmasks:    files
networks:    files
protocols:   files
rpc:         files
services:    files

netgroup:    nisplus

publickey:   nisplus

automount:   files nisplus
aliases:     files nisplus
```

Network Interfaces and Routes: ifconfig and route

Your connection to a network is made by your system through a particular hardware interface, such as an Ethernet card or a modem. Data passing through this interface is then routed to your network. The **ifconfig** command configures your network interfaces, and the **route** command sets up network connections accordingly. If you configure an interface with a network configuration tool, such as netcfg, Linuxconf, or YaST, you needn't use **ifconfig** or **route**. If you are using another Linux system, the

netconfig utility also performs the same configuration as netcfg. However, you can directly configure interfaces using **ifconfig** and **route**, if you want. Every time you start your system, the network interfaces and their routes must be established. This is done automatically for you when you boot up by **ifconfig** and **route** commands executed for each interface by the **/etc/rc.d/init.d/network** initialization file, which is executed whenever you start your system. If you are manually adding your own interfaces, you must set up the network script to perform the **ifconfig** and **route** operations for your new interfaces.

On Red Hat, your network interface is started up using the network script in the **/etc/rc.d/init.d** directory. You can manually shut down and restart your network interface using this script and the **start** or **stop** options. The following commands shut down and then start up your network interface:

```
/etc/rc.d/init.d/network stop
/etc/rc.d/init.d/network start
```

To test whether your interface is working, use the **ping** command with an IP address of a system on your network, such as your gateway machine. The **ping** command continually repeats until you stop it with a CTRL-C.

```
ping 192.168.1.42
```

ifconfig

The **ifconfig** command takes as its arguments the name of an interface and an IP address, as well as options. The **ifconfig** command then assigns the IP address to the interface. Your system now knows that such an interface exists and that it references a particular IP address. In addition, you can specify whether the IP address is a host address or a network address. You can use a domain name for the IP address, provided the domain name is listed along with its IP address in the **/etc/hosts** file. The syntax for the **ifconfig** command is as follows:

```
# ifconfig  interface  -host_net_flag  address  options
```

The *host_net_flag* can be either **-host** or **-net** to indicate a host or network IP address. The **-host** flag is the default. The **ifconfig** command can have several options, which set different features of the interface, such as the maximum number of bytes it can transfer (**mtu**) or the broadcast address. The **up** and **down** options activate and deactivate the interface. In the next example, the **ifconfig** command configures an Ethernet interface:

```
# ifconfig eth0  204.32.168.56
```

For a simple configuration such as this, **ifconfig** automatically generates a standard broadcast address and netmask. The standard broadcast address is the network address with the number **255** for the host address. For a class C network, the standard netmask is **255.255.255.0**; whereas for a class A network, the standard netmask is 255.0.0.0. If you are connected to a network with a particular netmask and broadcast address, however, you must specify them when you use **ifconfig**. The option for specifying the broadcast address is **broadcast**; for the network mask, it is **netmask**. Table 38-8 lists the different **ifconfig** options. In the next example, **ifconfig** includes the netmask and broadcast address:

```
# ifconfig eth0 204.32.168.56    broadcast 204.128.244.127\
  netmask 255.255.255.0
```

Once you configure your interface, you can use **ifconfig** with the **up** option to activate it and with the **down** option to deactivate it. If you specify an IP address in an **ifconfig** operation, as in the previous example, the **up** option is implied.

```
# ifconfig eth0 up
```

Point-to-point interfaces such as *Parallel IP* (*PLIP*), *Serial Line IP* (*SLIP*), and *Point-to-Point Protocol* (*PPP*) require you to include the **pointopoint** option. A PLIP interface name is identified with the name plip with an attached number. For example, plip0 is the first PLIP interface. SLIP interfaces use slip0. PPP interfaces start with ppp0. Point-to-point interfaces are those that usually operate between only two hosts, such as two computers connected over a modem. When you specify the **pointopoint** option, you need to include the IP address of the host. In the next example, a PLIP interface is configured that connects the computer at IP address **192.168.1.72** with one at **204.166.254.14**. If domain addresses were listed for these systems in **/etc/hosts**, those domain names could be used in place of the IP addresses.

```
# ifconfig  plip0  192.168.1.72  pointopoint 204.166.254.14
```

If you need to, you can also use **ifconfig** to configure your loopback device. The name of the loopback device is **lo**, and its IP address is the special address **127.0.0.1**. The following example shows the configuration:

```
# ifconfig lo 127.0.0.1
```

The **ifconfig** command is useful for checking on the status of an interface. If you enter the **ifconfig** command, along with the name of the interface, information about that interface is displayed.

```
# ifconfig eth0
```

To see if your loopback interface is configured, you can use **ifconfig** with the loopback interface name, lo.

```
# ifconfig lo
lo        Link encap:Local Loopback
          inet addr:127.0.0.1  Bcast:127.255.255.255  Mask:255.0.0.0
          UP BROADCAST LOOPBACK RUNNING  MTU:2000  Metric:1
          RX packets:0 errors:0 dropped:0 overruns:0
          TX packets:12 errors:0 dropped:0 overruns:0
```

Option	Description
Interface	Name of the network interface, such as eth0 for the first Ethernet device or ppp0 for the first PPP device (modem)
aftype	Address family for decoding protocol addresses; default is inet, currently used by Linux
up	Activates an interface; implied if IP address is specified
down	Deactivates an interface
-arp	Turns ARP on or off; preceding—turns it off
-trailers	Turns on or off trailers in Ethernet frames; preceding—turns it off
-allmulti	Turns on or off the promiscuous mode; preceding—turns it off; allows network monitoring
metric *n*	Cost for interface routing (not currently supported)
mtu *n*	Maximum number of bytes that can be sent on this interface per transmission

Table 38-8.   *The ifconfig Options*

Option	Description
dstaddr *address*	Destination IP address on a point-to-point connection
netmask *address*	IP network mask; preceding—turns it off
broadcast *address*	Broadcast address; preceding—turns it off
point-to-point *address*	Point-to-point mode for interface; if address included, it is assigned to remote system
hw	Sets hardware address of interface
Address	IP address assigned to interface

Table 38-8.   *The **ifconfig** Options* (continued)

Routing

A packet that is part of a transmission takes a certain *route* to reach its destination. On a large network, packets are transmitted from one computer to another until the destination computer is reached. The route determines where the process starts and to what computer your system needs to send the packet for it to reach its destination. On small networks, routing may be static—that is, the route from one system to another is fixed. One system knows how to reach another, moving through fixed paths. On larger networks and on the Internet, however, routing is dynamic. Your system knows the first computer to send its packet off to, and then that computer takes the packet from there, passing it on to another computer, which then determines where to pass it on. For dynamic routing, your system needs to know little. Static routing, however, can become complex because you have to keep track of all the network connections.

Your routes are listed in your routing table in the **/proc/net/route** file. To display the routing table, enter **route** with no arguments (the **netstat -r** command will also display the routing table).

```
# route
Kernel routing table
Destination      Gateway   Genmask          Flags Metric  Ref   Use Iface
loopback           *       255.0.0.0          U     0      0      12  lo
pango1.train.com   *       255.255.255.0      U     0      0       0  eth0
```

Each entry in the routing table has several fields, providing information such as the route destination and the type of interface used. The different fields are listed in the following table.

Field	Description
Destination	Destination IP address of the route
Gateway	IP address or hostname of the gateway the route uses; * indicates no gateway is used
Genmask	The netmask for the route
Flags	Type of route: U = up, H = host, G = gateway, D = dynamic, M = modified
Metric	Metric cost of route
Ref	Number of routes that depend on this one
Window	TCP window for AX.25 networks
Use	Number of times used
Iface	Type of interface this route uses

You should have at least one entry in the routing table for the loopback interface. If not, you must route the loopback interface using the **route** command. The IP address for an interface has to be added to the routing table before you can use that interface. You add an address with the **route** command and the **add** option.

```
route  add  address
```

The next example adds the IP address for the loopback interface to the routing table:

```
route add 127.0.0.1
```

With the **add** argument, you can add routes either for networks with the **–net** option or with the **–host** option for IP interfaces (hosts). The **–host** option is the default. In addition, you can then specify several parameters for information, such as the netmask (**netmask**), the gateway (**gw**), the interface device (**dev**), and the default route (**default**). If you have more than one IP interface on your system, such as several Ethernet cards, you must specify the name of the interface using the **dev** parameter. If your network has a gateway host, you use the **gw** parameter to specify it. If your system is connected to a network, at least one entry should be in your routing table that specifies the default route. This is the route taken by a message packet when no other route entry leads to its destination. The following example is the routing of an Ethernet interface:

```
# route add 192.168.1.2 dev eth0
```

If your system has only the single Ethernet device as your IP interface, you could leave out the **dev eth0** parameter.

```
# route add 192.168.1.2
```

You can delete any route you establish by invoking **ifconfig** with the **del** argument and the IP address of that route, as in this example:

```
# route del 192.168.1.2
```

You also need to add routes for networks that an IP interface can access. For this, you use the **-net** option. In this example, a route is set up for a system's LAN at **192.168.1.0**:

```
# route add -net  192.168.1.0 dev eth0
```

For a gateway, you first add a route to the gateway interface, and then add a route specifying that it is a gateway. The address of the gateway interface in this example is **192.168.1.1**:

```
# route add 192.168.1.1
# route add default gw  192.168.1.1
```

If you are using the gateway to access a subnet, add the network address for that network (in this example, **192.168.23.0**).

```
 # route add -net 192.168.23.0 gw dev eth1
```

To add another IP address to a different network interface on your system, use the **ifconfig** and **route** commands with the new IP address. The following command configures a second Ethernet card (eth1) with the IP address **192.168.1.3**.

```
ifconfig eth1 192.168.1.3
route add 192.168.1.3 dev eth1
```

Network Startup Script: /etc/rc.d/init.d/network

On OpenLinux and Red Hat systems, the **/etc/rc.d/init.d/network** file performs the startup operations for configuring your network. The network script uses a script called **ifup** to activate a network connection, and **ifdown** to shut it down. These scripts make use of special configuration files located in the **/etc/sysconfig/network-scripts** directory that bear the names of the network interfaces currently configured. These files define shell variables that hold information on the interface, such as whether to start them at boot time. The **ifdown** and **ifup** scripts hold the `ifconfig` and `route` commands to activate scripts using these special variables. As noted previously, you can use the network script to activate and deactivate your network interfaces at any time. Use the `start` option to activate interfaces, and `stop` to deactivate them.

Monitoring Your Network: ping and netstat

With the ping program, you can check to see if you can actually access another host on your network. The ping program sends a request to the host for a reply. The host then sends a reply back, and it is displayed on your screen. The ping program continually sends such a request until you stop it with a break command, a CTRL-C. You see one reply after another scroll by on your screen until you stop the program. If ping cannot access a host, it issues a message saying the host is unreachable. If ping fails, this may be an indication that your network connection is not working. It may only be the particular interface, a basic configuration problem, or a bad physical connection. ping uses the Internet Control Message Protocol (ICMP) discussed in Chapter 39. Networks may block these protocols as a security measure, also preventing ping from working. A ping failure may simply indicate a security precaution on the part of the queried network.

To use ping, enter `ping` and the name of the host. You can also use the KDE network utilities on the K Desktop and gfinger on the Gnome desktop (see Chapter 15).

```
$ ping pango1.mytrain.com
```

The netstat program provides real-time information on the status of your network connections, as well as network statistics and the routing table. The netstat program has several options you can use to bring up different sorts of information about your network (see Table 38-9).

```
# netstat
Active Internet connections
Proto Recv-Q Send-Q Local Address        Foreign Address        (State)        User
tcp      0       0  turtle.mytrek.com:01 pango1.mytrain.com.:ftp ESTABLISHED dylan
Active UNIX domain sockets
```

```
Proto RefCnt Flags      Type          State       Path
unix  1      [ ACC ]    SOCK_STREAM   LISTENING   /dev/printer
unix  2      [ ]        SOCK_STREAM   CONNECTED   /dev/log
unix  1      [ ACC ]    SOCK_STREAM   LISTENING   /dev/nwapi
unix  2      [ ]        SOCK_STREAM   CONNECTED   /dev/log
unix  2      [ ]        SOCK_STREAM   CONNECTED
unix  1      [ ACC ]    SOCK_STREAM   LISTENING   /dev/log
```

The **netstat** command with no options lists the network connections on your system. First, active TCP connections are listed, and then the active domain sockets are listed. The domain sockets contain processes used to set up communications among your system and other systems. The various fields are described in Table 38-9. You can use **netstat** with the **-r** option to display the routing table, and **netstat** with the **-i** option displays the uses of the different network interfaces.

Option	Description
-a	Displays information about all Internet sockets, including those sockets that are only listening
-i	Displays statistics for all network devices
-c	Displays network status continually every second until the program is interrupted
-n	Displays remote and local addresses as IP addresses
-o	Displays timer states, expiration times, and backoff state for network connections
-r	Displays the kernel routing table
-t	Displays information about TCP sockets only, including those that are listening
-u	Displays information about UDP sockets only
-v	Displays version information
-w	Displays information about raw sockets only
-x	Displays information about Unix domain sockets

Table 38-9. *The netstat Options*

IP Aliasing

In some cases, you may want to assign a single Linux system that has only one network interface to two or more IP addresses. For example, you may want to run different Web sites that can be accessed with separate IP addresses on this same system. In effect, you are setting up an alias for your system, another address by which it can be accessed. In fact, you are assigning two IP addresses to the same network interface, for example, assigning a single Ethernet card two IP addresses. This procedure is referred to as *IP aliasing* and is used to set up multiple IP-based virtual hosts for Internet servers. This method enables you to run several Web servers on the same machine using a single interface (or more than one on each of several interfaces). See Chapters 16 and 17 for FTP and Web server information about virtual hosts, and Chapter 18 for Domain Name Service configuration.

Setting up an IP alias is a simple matter of configuring a network interface on your system to listen for the added IP address. Your system needs to know what IP addresses it should listen for and on what network interface. You set up IP aliases using either Linuxconf or the **ifconfig** and **route** commands. For Linuxconf, select the IP aliases for virtual hosts under Server tasks. This opens a panel that lists available interfaces. Click one to open a panel where you can enter added IP addresses for it.

To add another address to the same interface, you need to qualify the interface by adding a colon and a number. For example, if you are adding another IP address to the first Ethernet card (eth0), you would add a :0 to its interface name, eth0:0. The following example shows the **ifconfig** and **route** commands for the Ethernet interface **192.168.1.2** and two IP aliases added to it: **192.168.1.100** and **192.168.1.101**. To add yet another IP address to this same interface, you would use **eth0:1**, incrementing the qualifier, and so on. The first **ifconfig** command assigns the main IP address, **192.168.1.2**, to the first Ethernet device, eth0. Then, two other IP addresses are assigned to that same device. In the first **route** command, the network route is set up for the Ethernet device, and then routes are set up for each IP interface. The interfaces for the two aliases are indicated with **eth0:0** and **eth0:1**.

```
ifconfig eth0 192.168.1.2
ifconfig eth0:0 192.168.1.100
ifconfig eth0:1 192.168.1.101
route add -net 192.168.1.0 dev eth0
route add -host 192.168.1.2 dev eth0
route add -host 192.168.1.100 dev eth0:0
route add -host 192.168.1.101 dev eth0:1
```

IP aliasing must be supported by the kernel before you can use it. If your kernel does not support it, you may have to rebuild the kernel, including IP aliasing support, or use loadable modules to add IP aliasing.

The Complete Reference

Linux

Chapter 39

Network Security: Firewalls and Encryption

Most systems currently connected to the Internet are open to attempts by outside users to gain unauthorized access. Outside users can try either to gain access directly by setting up an illegal connect or to intercept valid communications from users remotely connected to the system. Firewalls and encryption are ways of protecting against such attacks. A *firewall* prevents any direct unauthorized attempts at access, and *encryption* protects transmissions from authorized remote users. The current Linux kernel incorporates support for firewalls. There are two firewall packages currently in use, *ipchains* for kernel 2.2 and its replacement, *Netfilter* (iptables), for kernel 2.4. To implement a firewall, you simply provide a series of rules to govern what kind of access you want to allow on your system. If that system is also a gateway for a private network, then the system's firewall capability can effectively help protect the network from outside attacks. To provide protection for remote communications, transmission can be simply encrypted. For Linux systems, you can use the *Secure Shell* (*SSH*) suite of programs to encrypt any transmissions, preventing them from being read by anyone else. The SSH programs are meant to replace the remote tools such as **rsh** and **rcp** (see Chapter 18), which perform no encryption and include security risks such as transmitting passwords in clear text. In addition, Kerberos authentication provides another level of security whereby individual services can be protected. Table 39-1 lists several network security applications commonly used on Linux.

Outside users may also try to gain unauthorized access through any Internet services you may be hosting, such as a Web site. In such a case, you can set up a proxy to protect your site from attack. For Linux systems, use Squid proxy software to set up a proxy to protect your Web server (see Chapter 28).

Web Site	Security Application
netfilter.kernelnotes.org/ipchains	IP-Chains firewall
netfilter. kernelnotes.org	Netfilter project, iptables and NAT
www.ssh.com	Secure SHell encryption
www.squid.org	Squid Web Proxy server
web.mit.edu/kerberos	Kerberos network authentication

Table 39-1.   *Network Security Applications*

Firewalls: IP Chains and IP Tables

A good foundation for your network's security is to set up a Linux system to operate as a firewall for your network, protecting it from unauthorized access. You can use a firewall to implement either packet filtering or proxies. *Packet filtering* is simply the process of deciding whether a packet received by the firewall host should be passed on into the local network. The packet filtering software checks the source and destination addresses of the packet and sends the packet on, if it's allowed. Even if your system is not part of a network but connects directly to the Internet, you can still use the firewall feature to control access to your system. Of course, this also provides you with much more security. With proxies, you can control access to specific services, such as Web or FTP servers. You need a proxy for each service you want to control. The Web server has its own Web proxy, while an FTP server has an FTP proxy. Proxies can also be used to cache commonly used data, such as Web pages, so that users needn't constantly access the originating site. The proxy software commonly used on Linux systems is Squid, discussed in Chapter 28.

The tool used to implement packet filtering on firewalls for the Linux 2.2 kernel is ipchains. For the 2.4 kernel, this was changed to iptables, provided by the Netfilter Project (**netfilter.kernelnotes.org**). The main difference between iptables and ipchains is that ipchains performs both packet filtering and Network Address Translation (NAT) tasks such as redirection and IP masquerading, whereas in iptables these tasks are separated. NAT and IP masquerading redirect packets to appropriate destinations. The iptables program is a pure packet filtering tool; IP masquerading and redirection are no longer considered part of it. Instead, you use NAT table operations to implement IP masquerading and redirection. Still, NAT operations are implemented using iptables with the **-nat** command option.

Iptables includes backward-compatible modules for both ipfwadm and ipchains. In fact, iptables is very similar to ipchains. As the 2.4 kernel is still somewhat new and is also very similar to ipchains, ipchains is featured here.

IP Chains (kernel 2.2)

The Linux Web site for ipchains, which is the successor to ipfwadm used on older versions of Linux, is currently **netfilter.kernelnotes.org/ipchains/**. Support for ipchains is already implemented on the Linux 2.2 kernel. For earlier versions, you must enable support in the kernel, rebuilding it with Network Firewalls and IP Firewalling features (see Chapter 34). The IP chains HOWTO, located in your **/usr/doc/ipchains** directory, provides an excellent introduction and tutorial to ipchains and how you use it to implement a firewall. The HOWTO is in Web page format and can be viewed with any Web browser. The HOWTO features specific examples on how to guard against several standard attacks, such as IP spoofing, the ping of death, and teardrop.

The process of setting up and maintaining firewall chains can be complex. To simplify the process, you can use a GUI-based firewall configuration tool, such as Linuxconf or **fwconfig**. Linuxconf provides a configuration interface for maintaining simple chain rules, as well as loading special kernel ipchains modules for services such as FTP, Quake, and IRC. Select Firewalling under Networking, and then choose the panel for the kind of chain rules you want to configure: Input , Forward, and Output. See Chapter 7 for more details.

IP Chains Rules

The kernel uses chains to manage packets it receives. A *chain* is simply a checklist of rules. These rules specify what action to take for packets containing certain headers. The rules operate with an if-then-else structure. If a packet does not match the first rule, the next rule is then checked, and so on. If the packet does not match any rules, then the kernel consults chain policy. Usually, at this point the packet is rejected. If the packet does match a rule, it is passed to its target, which determines what to do with the packet. The standard targets are listed in Table 39-2. If a packet does not match any of the rules, then it is passed to the chain's default target.

Target	Function
ACCEPT	Allow packet to pass through the firewall.
DENY	Deny access by the packet (changed to DROP in iptables).
REJECT	Deny access and notify the sender.
MASQ	Masquerade the packet. Used only in the forward chain or chains called from the forward chain. Replaces sender's address with firewall host address (changed to MASQUERADE in iptables and to a NAT task).
REDIRECT	Redirect the packet to a local socket or process on the firewall. Used only in the input chain or chains called from the forward chain (changed to a NAT task in iptables).
RETURN	Jump to the end of the chain and let the default target process it.

Table 39-2.   *ipchains Targets*

A *target* could, in turn, be another chain of rules, even a chain of user-defined rules. A packet could be passed through several chains before finally reaching a target. In the case of user-defined chains, the default target is always the next rule in the chains from which it was called. This sets up a procedure or function call–like flow of control found in programming languages. When a rule has a user-defined chain as its target, then, when activated, that user-defined chain is executed. If no rules are matched, execution returns to the next rule in the originating chain.

The kernel uses three firewall chains: input, output, and forward. When a packet is received through an interface, the input chain is used to determine what to do with it. The kernel then uses its routing information to decide where to send it. If the kernel sends the packet to another host, then the forward chain is checked. Before the packet is actually sent, the output chain is also checked.

You add and modify chain rules using the **ipchains** commands. An **ipchains** command consists of the keyword **ipchains**, followed by an argument denoting the command to execute. For example, **ipchains -A** is the command to add a new rule, whereas **ipchains -D** is the command to delete a rule. The **ipchains** options are listed in Table 39-3. The following command simply lists the chains along with their rules currently defined for your system. The output shows the default values created by **ipchains** commands.

```
ipchains -L
Chain input (policy ACCEPT):
Chain forward (policy ACCEPT):
Chain output (policy ACCEPT):
```

Following the command, list the chain to which the rule applies, such as the input, output, or forward chain, or else a user-defined chain. Next, list different options that specify the actions you want taken. Options exist to specify the address a rule is to match on (**-s, -d**) and to specify the target the rule is to execute (**-j**). The **-s** option specifies the *source* address attached to the packet, while the **-d** option specifies the *destination* address attached to the packet (where it is coming from and where it is going to). The **-j** option, which stands for *jump,* is used to specify the target to *jump* to and execute. This is the target that is executed if the packet in a chain matches all the options. The standard targets used for a firewall are ACCEPT and DENY. The ACCEPT target will allow a packet to pass, whereas a DENY target will refuse access. Table 39-4 lists the available options.

In the following example, the user adds a rule to the input chain to accept all packets originating from the address 192.168.1.55. Any packets that are received (input) whose source address (**-s**) matches 192.168.1.55 are accepted and passed through as specified by the ACCEPT target, **-j ACCEPT**.

```
ipchains -A input -s 192.168.1.55 -j ACCEPT
```

Option	Function
-A *chain*	Append a rule to a chain.
-D *chain*	Delete matching rule from a chain.
-D *chain rulenum*	Delete rule *rulenum* (1 = first) from *chain*.
-I *chain* [*rulenum*]	Insert in *chain* as *rulenum* (default 1 = first).
-R *chain rulenum*	Replace rule *rulenum* (1 = first) in *chain*.
-L [*chain*]	List the rules in *chain* or all chains.
-F [*chain*]	Delete (flush) all rules in *chain* or all chains.
-Z [*chain*]	Zero counters in *chain* or all chains.
-C *chain*	Test this packet on *chain*.
-N *chain*	Create a new user-defined chain.
-X *chain*	Delete a user-defined chain.
-P *chain target*	Change policy on *chain* to *target*.
-M -L	List current masquerading connections (not valid for iptables).
-M -S *tcp tcpfin udp*	Set masquerading timeout values (not valid for iptables).
-h	Display list of commands.
--v*ersion*	Display version.

Table 39-3.   *ipchains Options*

To deny access from a particular site, simply specify the DENY target (in iptables this was changed to DROP). Alternatively, you can send a packet back to where it came from using the REJECT target instead of the DENY target. In the following example, any packet received from **www.myjunk.com** is rejected.

```
ipchains -A input -s www.myjunk.com -j DENY
```

You can specify an individual address using its domain name or its IP number. For a range of addresses, you can use the IP number of their network and the network IP

Option	Function
-b	Execute the rule bidirectionally (whether a packet is coming in or going out). Actually, insert two rules where the second one has the sender (**-s**) and destination (**-d**) reversed.
-p [!] *proto*	Specify a protocol, such as TCP, UDP, ICMP, or ALL.
-s [!] *address* [**/***mask*] [!] [*port* [**:***port*]]	Source address to match. With the *port* argument, you can specify the port.
--source-port [!] [*port* [**:***port*]]	Source port specification. You can specify a range of ports using the colon, *port:port*.
-d [!] *address* [**/***mask*] [!] [*port* [**:***port*]]	Destination address to match. With the *port* argument, you can specify the port.
--destination-port [!] [*port* [**:***port*]]	Destination port specification.
--icmp-type [!] *typename*	Specify ICMP type.
-i [!] *name* [**+**]	Specify a network interface using its name (for example, eth0). The **+** symbol functions as a wildcard. The **+** attached to the end of the name matches all interfaces with that prefix (**eth+** matches all Ethernet interfaces) (indicate input interface only in iptables).
-j *target* [*port*]	Specify the target for a rule (specify [*port*] for REDIRECT target).
-m [**+-**]*mark*	Number to mark on matching packet.
-n	Numeric output of addresses and ports, used with **-L**.

Table 39-4.   *ipchains Options*

Option	Function
-l	Turn on kernel logging for matching packets, logging them in the syslog.
-o [*maxsize*]	Output matching packet to netlink device (changed to output device in iptables).
-t and xor	Specify and/xor masks for Type of Service (TOS) field.
-v	Verbose mode, used with **-L**.
-x	Expand numbers (display exact values), used with **-L**.
[!] -f	Match second through last fragments of a fragmented packet.
[!] -y	Match SYN TCP packets only (TCP packets requesting connections). A ! placed before **-y** rejects all other packets except SYN TCP packets (changed to **--syn** in iptables).
[!] -V	Print package version.
!	Negates an option or address.

Table 39-4.   *ipchains Options* (continued)

mask. The IP mask can be an IP number or simply the number of bits making up the mask. For example, all of the addresses in network 192.168.0 can be represented by 192.168.0.0/225.255.255.0 or by 192.168.0.0/24. To specify any address, you can use 0.0.0.0/0.0.0.0 or simply 0/0. By default, rules reference any address if no **-s** or **-d** specification exists. The following example accepts messages coming in that are from (source) any host in the 192.168.0.0 network and that are going (destination) anywhere at all (the **-d** option is left out or could be written as **-d 0/0**).

```
ipchains -A input -s 192.168.0.0/24  -j ACCEPT
```

If your system is hosting an Internet service, such as a Web or FTP server, you can use ipchains to control access to it. You can specify a particular service by specifying the port it uses. For a Web server, the port would be www. The names of services and the ports they use are listed in the **/etc/services** file, which maps ports to particular services. For a domain name server, the port would be **domain**. You can also use the port number if you want, preceding the number with a colon. The following example accepts all messages to the Web server located at 192.168.0.43.

```
ipchains -A input -d 192.168.0.43 www -j ACCEPT
```

Inverse Operations

With the **!** operator, you can change the effect of a rule to its inverse. The **!** operator works like a "not" logical operator in programming languages. Placing a **!** operator before a **-s** entry matches on any address that is not the specified address: **! -s 192.168.1.66** matches on any packet whose address is not 192.168.1.66. The operator is helpful if you want to restrict by only a few selected sites. The following example restricts access to 192.168.1.66, denying access to all others.

```
ipchains -A input ! -s 192.168.1.66 -j DENY
```

The inverse can apply also to ports, protocols, and devices. For example, to allow access to any port except the Ethernet device eth2, you would use

```
ipchains -A input ! eth2 -j ACCEPT
```

The following example denies access to any port except the Web server.

```
ipchains -A input ! www -j DENY
```

SYN Packets

If you are designing a firewall that is meant to protect your local network from any attempts to penetrate it from an outside network, you may want to restrict packets coming in. Simply denying access by all packets is unfeasible because users connected to outside servers, say, on the Internet, must receive information from them. You can, instead, deny access by a particular kind of packet used to initiate a connection. The idea is that an attacker must initiate a connection from the outside. The headers of these kinds of packets have their SYN bit set on and their FIN and ACK bits empty. The **ipchains -y** option matches on any such SYN packet. By specifying a DENY target for such packets, you deny access by any packet that is part of an attempt to make a connection with your system. Anyone trying to connect to your system from the outside is unable to do so. Users on your local system who have initiated connections with outside hosts can still communicate with them.

```
ipchains -A input -y -j DENY
```

You make this a qualification of a rule with an ACCEPT target by preceding the **-y** with a **!** symbol. This turns the rule into its inverse. For example, to accept all messages except the SYN messages, you could use the following rule. This says to accept all input messages except those that are new connections.

```
ipchains -A input ! -y -j ACCEPT
```

Firewalls often block certain *Internet Control Message Protocol* (*ICMP*) messages. ICMP redirect messages in particular can take control of your routing tasks. You need to enable some ICMP messages, however, such as those needed for ping, traceroute, and particularly destination-unreachable operation. In most cases, you always need to make sure destination-unreachable packets are allowed; otherwise, domain name queries could hang. Some of the common ICMP packet types are listed in Table 39-5. You can enable an ICMP type of packet with the **-icmp-type** option, which takes as its argument a number or a name representing the message. The following example enables the use of echo-reply messages, which have the number 3 and the name **destination-unreachable**.

```
ipchains -A input -icmp-type destination-unreachable -j ACCEPT
```

IP Chains Scripts

You can enter **ipchains** commands from the shell command line. When you shut down your system, however, these commands will be lost. To save your commands, you can use the **ipchains-save** script to save them to a file. The recommended file to use is **/etc/ipchains.rules**. The **ipchains-save** command outputs rules to the standard

Number	Name	Required by
0	echo-reply	Ping
3	destination-unreachable	Any TCP/UDP traffic
5	redirect	Routing if not running routing daemon
8	echo-request	Ping
11	time-exceeded	Traceroute

Table 39-5. *Common ICMP Packets*

output. To save them in a file, you must redirect the output to a file with the redirection operator, **>**, as shown here.

```
ipchains-save > /etc/ipchains.rules
```

Then, to restore the rules, use the **ipchains-restore** script to read the ipchains commands from that saved file.

```
ipchains-restore < /etc/ipchains.rules
```

An example of the output from the **ipchains-save** script is shown here.

```
[root@turtle /root]# cat /etc/ipchains.rules
:input DENY
:forward ACCEPT
:output ACCEPT
-A input -s ! 192.168.1.0/255.255.255.0 -d 0.0.0.0/0.0.0.0 -i eth1 -j DENY -l
-A input -s 192.168.1.0/255.255.255.0 -d 0.0.0.0/0.0.0.0 -i ! eth1 -j DENY -l
-A input -s 127.0.0.0/255.0.0.0 -d 0.0.0.0/0.0.0.0 -i ! lo -j DENY -l
-A input -s 0.0.0.0/0.0.0.0 -d 0.0.0.0/0.0.0.0 -i lo -j ACCEPT
-A input -s 0.0.0.0/0.0.0.0 -d 10.0.0.2/255.255.255.255 80:80 -i eth0 -p 6 -j ACCEPT
-A input -s 0.0.0.0/0.0.0.0 -d 10.0.0.1/255.255.255.255 -i eth0 -p 6 -j DENY -l -y
-A input -s 0.0.0.0/0.0.0.0 -d 10.0.0.1/255.255.255.255 -i eth0 -p ! 1 -j ACCEPT
-A input -s 192.168.1.0/255.255.255.0 -d 0.0.0.0/0.0.0.0 -i eth1 -j ACCEPT
-A input -s 0.0.0.0/0.0.0.0 0:0 -d 10.0.0.1/255.255.255.255 -i eth0 -p 1 -j ACCEPT
-A input -s 0.0.0.0/0.0.0.0 8:8 -d 10.0.0.1/255.255.255.255 -i eth0 -p 1 -j ACCEPT
-A input -s 0.0.0.0/0.0.0.0 3:3 -d 10.0.0.1/255.255.255.255 -i eth0 -p 1 -j ACCEPT
-A forward -s 192.168.1.0/255.255.255.0 -d 0.0.0.0/0.0.0.0 -i eth0 -j MASQ
-A output -s 10.0.0.2/255.255.255.255 80:80 \
        -d 192.168.1.0/255.255.255.0 -i eth0 -p 6 -j DENY -y
```

To have ipchains start up automatically at boot time, you can create a packetfilter script and place it in the **/etc/rc.d/init.d** directory. Make a symbolic link to it, such as **S39packetfilter**, in the appropriate **rc*n*.d** directory.

packetfilter

```
#! /bin/sh
# Script to control packet filtering.

# If no rules, do nothing.
 [ -f /etc/ipchains.rules ] || exit 0

case "$1" in
```

```
    start)
        echo -n "Turning on packet filtering:"
        /sbin/ipchains-restore < /etc/ipchains.rules || exit 1
        echo 1 > /proc/sys/net/ipv4/ip_forward
        echo "."
        ;;
    stop)
        echo -n "Turning off packet filtering:"
        echo 0 > /proc/sys/net/ipv4/ip_forward
        /sbin/ipchains -X
        /sbin/ipchains -F
        /sbin/ipchains -P input ACCEPT
        /sbin/ipchains -P output ACCEPT
        /sbin/ipchains -P forward ACCEPT
        echo "."
        ;;
    *)
        echo "Usage: /etc/init.d/packetfilter {start|stop}"
        exit 1
        ;;
esac

exit 0
```

Using this startup script, you can then manually start and stop **ipchains** with the start and stop arguments.

```
/etc/init.d/packetfilter start
/etc/init.d/packetfilter stop
```

Instead of manually typing in each **ipchains** command on the command line, you can create a shell script of these commands and then simply run the script. This technique is useful if you want to create several different firewall configurations, each with different levels of control. Running the script is the same as entering the rules, one by one. Once you run the script, the rules take effect. If you are using the **packetfilter** startup script, you can then use **ipchains-save** to make those ipchains script rules your startup configuration.

The following example shows a simple ipchains script called **mychains**. It configures a simple firewall for a private network (check the ipchains HOWTO for a more complex example). If you have a local network, you could adapt this script to it. In this configuration, all remote access initiated from the outside is blocked, but two-way communication is allowed for connections that users in the network make with outside systems. In this example, the firewall system functions as a gateway for a private network whose network address is 192.168.1.0. The Internet address is, for the sake of this example, 10.0.0.1. The system has two Ethernet devices: one for the private network (eth1) and one for the Internet (eth0). The gateway firewall system also supports a Web server at address 10.0.0.2. Entries in this example that are too large to fit on one line are continued on a second line, with the newline quoted with a backslash.

mychains

```
# Firewall Gateway system IP address is 10.0.0.1 using Ethernet device eth0
# Private network address is 192.168.1.0 using Ethernet device eth1
# Web site address is 10.0.0.2

# turn off IP forwarding
echo 0 > /proc/sys/net/ipv4/ip_forward

# Flush chain rules
ipchains -F input
ipchains -F output
ipchains -F forward

# set default rules
ipchains -P input DENY
ipchains -P output ACCEPT
ipchains -P forward ACCEPT

# IP spoffing, deny any packets on the internal network
# that has an external source address.
ipchains -A input -j DENY  -i eth1 \! -s 192.168.1.0/24  -l
# IP spoofing, deny any outside packets (any not on eth1)
# that have the source address of the internal network
ipchains -A input -j DENY \! -i eth1 -s 192.168.1.0/24 -l
# IP spoofing, deny any outside packets with localhost address
# (packets not on the lo interface (any on eth0 or eth1) that
#  have the source address of  localhost
ipchains -A input -j DENY  -i \! lo  -s  127.0.0.0/255.0.0.0 -l

# allow all  incoming  messages for users on firewall gateway
ipchains -A input -j ACCEPT  -i lo

# allow  communication to the Web server (address 10.0.0.2), port www
ipchains -A input  -j ACCEPT -p tcp -i eth0  -d 10.0.0.2 www
# Deny new connections from Web server to internal network
ipchains -A output -j DENY -p tcp -i eth0  -y -s 10.0.0.2 www  -d 192.168.1.0/24

# prevent outside initiated connections, allow established ones
ipchains -A input -j DENY -p tcp -i eth0  -y -d 10.0.0.1 -l
# allow outside communication to the firewall, except for ICMP packets
 ipchains -A input -j ACCEPT -p \! icmp -i eth0  -d 10.0.0.1

# allow all local communication to and from the firewall eth1 interface
ipchains -A input -j ACCEPT -p all -i eth1 -s 192.168.1.0/24

# Set up masquerqading to allow internal machines access
# to outside network, enable FORWARD chain
ipchains -A forward -j MASQ -p all -i eth0  -s 192.168.1.0/24
```

```
# Accept ICMP Ping (0 and 8) and Destination ureachable (3)  messages
# Others will be rejected by input and output DENY policy
ipchains -A input -j ACCEPT  -p icmp -i eth0 —icmp-type echo-reply -d 10.0.0.1
ipchains -A input -j ACCEPT  -p icmp -i eth0 —icmp-type  echo-request -d 10.0.0.1
ipchains -A input -j ACCEPT -p icmp -i eth0 —icmp-type \
  destination-unreachable -d 10.0.0.1

# Turn on IP Forwarding
echo 1 > /proc/sys/net/ipv4/ip_forward
```

Initially, in the script you would clear your current ipchains with the flush option (**-F**), and then set the policies (default targets) for the nonuser-defined rules. IP Forwarding should also be turned off while the chain rules are being set.

```
echo 0 > /proc/sys/net/ipv4/ip_forward
```

One way to protect the private network from IP spoofing any packets is to check for any outside addresses on the Ethernet device dedicated to the private network. In this example, any packet on device eth1 (dedicated to the private network) whose source address is not that of the private network (**! -s 192.168.1.0**) is denied. Also, check to see if any packets coming from the outside are designating the private network as their source. In this example, any packets with the source address of the private network on any Ethernet device other than for the private network (eth1) are denied. The same strategy can be applied to the local host.

```
# IP spoffing, deny any packets on the internal network
# that has an external source address.
ipchains -A input -j DENY  -i eth1 \! -s 192.168.1.0/24  -l
# IP spoofing, deny any outside packets (any not on eth1)
# that have the source address of the internal network
ipchains -A input -j DENY \! -i eth1 -s 192.168.1.0/24 -l
# IP spoofing, deny any outside packets with localhost address
ipchains -A input -j DENY  -i \! lo  -s  127.0.0.0/255.0.0.0 -l
```

Note *Notice that the ! is escaped with a backslash (\). ! is also a shell operator and, as part of the shell script, needs to be quoted with a \ to prevent the shell from executing it instead of ipchains.*

Then you would set up rules to allow all packets sent and received within your system (localhost) to pass.

```
ipchains -A input -j ACCEPT  -i lo
```

For the Web server, you want to allow access by outside users, but to block access by anyone attempting to initiate a connection from the Web server into the private network. This prevents anyone from breaking into the local network through the Web server, which is open to outside access. In the next example, all messages are accepted to the Web server, but the Web server cannot initiate contact with the private network (**! -y**). Established connections are allowed, permitting the private network to use the Web server.

```
# allow  communication to the Web server (address 10.0.0.2), port www
ipchains -A input  -j ACCEPT -p tcp -i eth0  -d 10.0.0.2 www
# Deny new connections from Web server to internal network
ipchains -A output -j DENY -p tcp -i eth0  -y -s 10.0.0.2 \
          www  -d 192.168.1.0/24
```

To prevent outsiders from initiating any access to your system, create a rule to block access by SYN packets (new connections) from the outside. The following rules uses the **-y** option to specify SYN packets.

```
# prevent outside initiated connections, allow established ones
ipchains -A input -j DENY -p tcp -i eth0  -y -d 10.0.0.1 -l
```

To allow access by the firewall to outside networks, you allow input by all packets except for ICMP packets. These are handled later. The firewall address is designated as the input destination.

```
# allow outside communication to the firewall, except for ICMP packets
 ipchains -A input -j ACCEPT -p \! icmp -i eth0  -d 10.0.0.1
```

To allow interaction by the internal network with the firewall, you allow input by all packets on the internal Ethernet connection, eth1. The valid internal network addresses are designated as the input source.

```
# allow all local communication with the firewall eth1 interface
ipchains -A input -j ACCEPT -p all -i eth1 -s 192.168.1.0/24
```

To implement masquerading, where systems on the private network can use the gateway's Internet address to connect to Internet hosts, you simply create a MASQ target for the forward rule.

```
ipchains -A forward -j MASQ -p all -i eth0  -s 192.168.1.0/24
```

In addition, to allow ping and destination-reachable ICMP packets, you enter input rules with the firewall as the destination. To enable ping operations, you use both echo-reply and echo-request ICMP types, and for destination unreachable, you use the destination-unreachable type.

```
# Accept ICMP Ping (0 and 8) and Destination ureachable (3)  messages
# Others will be rejected by input DENY policy
ipchains -A input -j ACCEPT  -p icmp -i eth0 \
         --icmp-type echo-reply -d 10.0.0.1
ipchains -A input -j ACCEPT  -p icmp -i eth0 \
         --icmp-type  echo-request -d 10.0.0.1
ipchains -A input -j ACCEPT -p icmp -i eth0 \
         --icmp-type destination-unreachable -d 10.0.0.1
```

At the end, IP forwarding is turned on again:

```
echo 1 > /proc/sys/net/ipv4/ip_forward
```

A listing of these **ipchains** commands shows the different rules for each command, as shown here.

```
[root@turtle /root]# ipchains -L
Chain input (policy DENY):
target prot opt     source          destination ifname  ports
DENY   all  ----1- !192.168.1.0/24 anywhere     eth1    n/a
DENY   all  ----1- 192.168.1.0/24  anywhere     !eth1   n/a
DENY   all  ----1- 127.0.0.0/8     anywhere     !lo     n/a
ACCEPT all  ------ anywhere        anywhere     lo      n/a
ACCEPT tcp  ------ anywhere        10.0.0.2     eth0    any->www
DENY   tcp  -y--1- anywhere        10.0.0.1     eth0    any->any
ACCEPT !icmp ------ anywhere       10.0.0.1     eth0    any->any
ACCEPT all  ------ 192.168.1.0/24  anywhere     eth1    n/a
ACCEPT icmp ------ anywhere        10.0.0.1     eth0    echo-reply
ACCEPT icmp ------ anywhere        10.0.0.1     eth0    echo-request
ACCEPT icmp ------ anywhere        10.0.0.1     eth0
           destination-unreachable
Chain forward (policy ACCEPT):
target prot opt     source          destination ifname ports
MASQ   all  ------ 192.168.1.0/24  anywhere     eth0    n/a
Chain output (policy ACCEPT):
target prot opt     source          destination     ifname ports
DENY   tcp  -y---- 10.0.0.2        192.168.1.0/24 eth0    www->any
```

Netfilter:iptables and NAT (kernel 2.4)

Netfilter implements firewalls using a packet filtering tool called iptables. Unlike ipchains, iptables is a pure packet filtering tool without the added baggage of Network Address Translation (NAT) tasks such as IP masquerading, redirection, and forwarding. iptables is the replacement for ipchains in the 2.4 kernel. The Netfilter software is developed by the Netfilter Project, which you can find out more about at **netfilter.kernelnotes.org**. iptables is very similar to ipchains, using many of the same principles, with several syntax changes for certain commands. You can still use ipchains and the earlier ipfwadm commands by loading the ipchains.o or ipfwadm.o modules provided with the Netfilter software. These provide full backward compatibility. The iptables software can be built directly into the 2.4 kernel or loaded as a kernel module, iptable_filter.o. Unlike its predecessor, ipchains, Netfilter is designed to be modularized and extensible. Capabilities can be added in the form of modules such as the state module, which adds connection tracking analysis.

IP Tables (iptables)

Netfilter is essentially a framework for packet mangling that can check packets for particular network protocols and notify parts of the kernel listening for them. Built on the Netfilter framework is the packet selection system implemented by IP Tables. With IP Tables, different tables of rules can be set up to select packets according to differing criteria. Packet filtering is implemented using a filter table that holds rules for dropping or accepting packets. Network Address Translation operations such as IP masquerading are implemented using the NAT table that holds IP masquerading rules. Pre-route packet mangling uses the mangle table. This structure is extensible in that new modules can define their own tables with their own rules. It also greatly improves efficiency. Instead of all packets checking one large table, they only access the table of rules they need to.

IP Table rules are managed using the **iptables** command. For this command, you will need to specify the table you want to manage. The default is the filter table, which need not be specified.

Note *In iptables commands, chain names have to be entered in uppercase. This means that the chain names INPUT, OUTPUT, and FORWARD have to be written in uppercase.*

Packet filtering rules are very similar to those used in **ipchains** with few exceptions. To add a new rule to a chain, you use **-N**. Use **-D** to remove it, and **-R** to replace it. Following the command, list the chain to which the rule applies, such as the INPUT, OUTPUT, or FORWARD chain, or else a user-defined chain. Next, you list different options that specify the actions you want taken. Most are the same as those used for ipchains, with a few exceptions. The **-s** option specifies the source address attached to the packet, **-d** specifies the destination address, and the **-j** option specifies

NETWORK ADMINISTRATION

the target. The ACCEPT target will allow a packet to pass. The **-i** option now indicates the input device and can only be used with the INPUT and FORWARD chains. The **-o** option indicates the output device and can only be used for OUTPUT and FORWARD chains. Table 39-6 lists several basic options. Many are similar to the ipchains options, but some, like **-i**, are different and others are missing (like **-y**).

Option	Function
-p [!] *proto*	Specify a protocol, such as TCP, UDP, ICMP, or ALL
-s [!] *address* [*/mask*] [!] [*port* [*:port*]]	Source address to match. With the *port* argument, you can specify the port
--sport [!] [*port* [*:port*]]	Source port specification. You can specify a range of ports using the colon, *port:port*
-d [!] *address* [*/mask*] [!] [*port* [*:port*]]	Destination address to match. With the *port* argument, you can specify the port
--dport [!] [*port* [*:port*]]	Destination port specification
--icmp-type [!] *typename*	Specify ICMP type
-i [!] *name* [+]	Specify an input network interface using its name (for example, eth0). The **+** symbol functions as a wildcard. The **+** attached to the end of the name matches all interfaces with that prefix (**eth+** matches all Ethernet interfaces). Can only be used with the INPUT chain
-j *target* [*port*]	Specify the target for a rule (specify [*port*] for REDIRECT target)
-n	Numeric output of addresses and ports, used with **-L**

Table 39-6.   *iptables Options*

Option	Function
-o **[!]** *name***[+]**	Specify an output network interface using its name (for example, eth0). Can only be used with FORWARD and OUTPUT chains.
-t *table*	Specify a table to use, as in **-t nat** for the NAT table.
-v	Verbose mode, shows rule details, used with **-L**
-x	Expand numbers (display exact values), used with **-L**
[!] -f	Match second through last fragments of a fragmented packet
[!] -V	Print package version
!	Negates an option or address
-m	Specify a module to use, such as state
--state	Specify options for the **state** module such as NEW, INVALID, RELATED, and ESTABLISHED. Used to detect packets state. NEW references SYN packets (new connections).
--syn	SYN packets, new connections.
--tcp-flags	Tcp flags: SYN,ACK,FIN,RST,URG,PS, and ALL for all flags.
--limit	Option for the **limit** module (**-m limit**). It is used to control the rate of matches, matching a given number of times per second
--limit-burst	Option for the **limit** module (**-m limit**). Specify maximum burst before the a limit kicks in. Used to control Denial of service attacks.

Table 39-6.   *iptables Options* (continued)

In the following example, the user adds a rule to the INPUT chain to accept all packets originating from the address 192.168.1.55. Any packets that are received (**INPUT**) whose source address (**-s**) matches 192.168.1.55 are accepted and passed through (**-j ACCEPT**).

```
iptables -A INPUT -s 192.168.1.55 -j ACCEPT
```

There are two built-in targets, DROP and ACCEPT. DROP is the same as the ipchains DENY target. Other targets can be either user-defined chains or extensions added on such as REJECT. There are two special targets used to manage chains, RETURN and QUEUE. RETURN indicates the end of a chain and returns to the chain it started from. QUEUE is used to send packets to userspace (replaces **-o** in ipchains).

```
iptables -A INPUT -s www.myjunk.com -j DROP
```

You can turn a rule into its inverse with a **!** symbol. For example, to accept all incoming packets except those from a specific address, place a **!** symbol before the **-s** option and that address. The following example will accept all packets except those from the IP address 192.168.0.45:

```
iptables -A INPUT -j ACCEPT ! -s 192.168.0.45
```

You can specify an individual address using its domain name or its IP number. For a range of addresses, you can use the IP number of their network and the network IP mask. The IP mask can be an IP number or simply the number of bits making up the mask. For example, all of the addresses in network 192.168.0 can be represented by 192.168.0.0/225.255.255.0 or by 192.168.0.0/24. To specify any address, you can use 0.0.0.0/0.0.0.0 or simply 0/0. By default, rules reference any address if no **-s** or **-d** specification exists. The following example accepts messages coming in that are from (source) any host in the 192.168.0.0 network and that are going (destination) anywhere at all (the **-d** option is left out or could be written as **-d 0/0**).

```
iptables -A INPUT -s 192.168.0.0/24  -j ACCEPT
```

The iptables rules are usually applied to a specific network interface such as the Ethernet interface used to connect to the Internet. For a single system connected to the Internet, you will have two interfaces, one that is your Internet connection and a localhost interface (lo) for internal connections between users on your system. The network interface for the Internet is referenced using the device name for the interface. For example, an Ethernet card with the device name **/dev/eth0** would be referenced by the name eth0. A modem using PPP protocols with the device name **/dev/ppp0** would have the name ppp0. In iptables rules, you use **-i** option to indicate the input device; it can only be used with the INPUT and FORWARD chains. The **-o** option indicates the output device and can only be used for OUTPUT and FORWARD chains. Rules can then be applied to packets arriving and leaving on particular network devices. In the following examples, the first rule references the Ethernet device eth0, and the second, the localhost.

```
iptables -A INPUT -j DROP -i eth0 -s 192.168.1.45
iptables -A INPUT -j ACCEPT  -i lo
```

If your system is hosting an Internet service, such as a Web or FTP server, you can use iptables to control access to it. You can specify a particular service by using the source port (**---sport**) or destination port (**--dport**) options with the port that the service uses. iptables lets you use names for ports such as **www** for the Web server port. The names of services and the ports they use are listed in the **/etc/services** file, which maps ports to particular services. For a domain name server, the port would be **domain**. You can also use the port number if you want, preceding the number with a colon. The following example accepts all messages to the Web server located at 192.168.0.43.

```
iptables -A INPUT -d 192.168.0.43 --dport www -j ACCEPT
```

Iptables is designed to be extensible, and there are number of options with selection criteria that can be included with iptables. For example, the TCP extension includes the **--syn** option that checks for SYN packets. The ICMP extension provides the **--icmp-type** option for specifying ICMP packets as those used in ping operations. The limit extension includes the **--limit** option with which you can limit the maximum number of matching packets in a specified time period, like a second.

One of the more useful extensions is the state extension, which can easily detect tracking information for a packet. You need to specify the state module first with **-m state**. Then you can use the **--state** option. Here you can specify any of the following states.

States	Description
NEW	A packet that creates a new connection
ESTABLISHED	A packet that belongs to an existing connection
RELATED	A packet that is related to, but not part of, an existing connection, such as an ICMP error or a packet establishing an FTP data connection
INVALID	A packet that could not be identified for some reason

If you are designing a firewall that is meant to protect your local network from any attempts to penetrate it from an outside network, you may want to restrict packets coming in. Simply denying access by all packets is unfeasible because users connected to outside servers, say, on the Internet, must receive information from them. You can, instead, deny access by a particular kind of packet used to initiate a connection. The idea is that an attacker must initiate a connection from the outside. The headers of these kinds of packets have their SYN bit set on and their FIN and ACK bits empty. The **state** module's **NEW** state matches on any such SYN packet. By specifying a DROP target for such packets, you deny access by any packet that is part of an attempt to make a connection with your system. Anyone trying to connect to your system from the outside is unable to do so. Users on your local system who have initiated connections with outside hosts can still communicate with them. The following example will drop any packets trying to create a new connection on the eth0 interface, thought they will be accepted on any other interface.

```
iptables -A INPUT -m state --state NEW -i eth0 -j DROP
```

You can use the ! operator on the eth0 device combined with an ACCEPT target to compose a rule that will accept any new packets except those on the eth0 device. If the eth0 device is the only one that connects to the Internet, this still effectively blocks outside access. At the same time, input operation for other devices such as your localhost are free to make new connections. This kind of conditional INPUT rule is used to allow access overall with exceptions. It usually assumes that a later rule such as a chain policy will drop remaining packets.

```
iptables -A INPUT -m state --state NEW ! -i eth0 -j ACCEPT
```

The next example will accept any packets that are part of an established connection or related to such a connection on any interface.

```
iptables -A INPUT -m state --state ESTABLISHED,RELATED -j ACCEPT
```

Network Address Translation (NAT)

IP masquerading is really an form of Network Address Translation (NAT). NAT is the process whereby a system will change the destination or source of packets as they pass through the system. A packet will traverse several linked systems on a network before it reaches its final destination. Normally they will simply pass the packet on. However, if one of these systems performs a NAT on a packet, it can change the source or destination. A packet sent to a particular destination could have its destination address changed. To make this work, the system also needs to remember such changes so that the source and destination for any reply packets are altered back to the original addresses of the packet being replied to.

NAT is often used to provide access to systems that may be connected to the Internet through only one IP address. Such is the case with networking features like IP masquerading, support for multiple servers, and transparent proxying. As we have seen, with IP masquerading, NAT operations will change the destination and source of a packet moving through a firewall/gateway linking the Internet to computers on a local network. The gateway has a single IP address that the other local computers can use through NAT operations. If you have multiple servers but only one IP address, you can use NAT operations to send packets to the alternate servers. You can also use NAT operations to have your IP address reference a particular server application such as a Web server (transparent proxy).

Packet selection rules for NAT operations are added to the NAT table managed by the iptables command. To add rules to the NAT table, you have to specify the NAT table with the **-t** option. Thus to add a rule to the NAT table, you would have to specify the NAT table with the **-t nat** option as shown here:

```
iptable -t nat
```

In addition, there are two types of NAT operations, source NAT, specified as SNAT target, and destination NAT, specified as DNAT target. SNAT target is used for rules that alter source addresses, and DNAT target for those that alter destination addresses.

Three rules in the NAT table are used by the kernel for NAT operations. These are PREROUTING, POSTROUTING, and OUTPUT. PREROUTING is used for Destination NAT (DNAT) rules. These are packets that are arriving. POSTROUTING is used for Source NAT (SNAT) rules. These are for packets leaving. OUTPUT is used for Destination NAT rules for locally generated packets.

As with packet filtering, you can specify source (**-s**) and destination (**-d**) addresses, as well as the input (**-i**) and output (**-o**) devices. The **-j** option will specify a target such as MASQUERADE. You would implement IP masquerading by adding a MASQUERADE rule to the POSTROUTING chain.

```
# iptables -t nat -A POSTROUTING -o eth0 -j MASQUERADE
```

To change the source address of a packet leaving your system, you would use the POSTROUTING rule with the SNAT target. For the SNAT target, you use the **--to** option to specify the source address.

```
# iptables -t nat -A POSTROUTING -o eth0 -j SNAT --to 192.168.1.4
```

To change the destination address of packets arriving on your system, you would use the PREROUTING rule with the DNAT target.

```
# iptables -t nat -A PRETROUTING -i eth0 -j DNAT --to 192.168.1.3
```

To redirect an packet, you use the REDIRECT target on the PREROUTING chain.

```
# iptables -t nat -A PREROUTING -i eth1 --dport 80 -j REDIRECT --to-port 3128
```

The targets only valid for the NAT table are shown here:

SNAT	Modify source address
DNAT	Modify destination address
REDIRECT	Redirect a packet
MASQUERADE	IP masquerading

Differences Between IP chains and IP Tables/NAT

There are important differences between iptables and ipchains as delineated in the following list provided by the Netfilter Project.

- First, the names of the built-in chains have changed from lowercase to uppercase, because the INPUT and OUTPUT chains now get only locally destined and locally generated packets. They used to see all incoming and all outgoing packets, respectively.

- The **-i** flag now means the incoming interface, and it only works in the INPUT and FORWARD chains. Rules in the FORWARD or OUTPUT chains that used **-i** should be changed to **-o**.

- TCP and UDP ports now need to be spelled out with the **--source-port** or **--sport** (or **--destination-port**/**--dport**) options, and they must be placed after the **-p tcp** or **-p udp** options, as this loads the TCP or UDP extensions, respectively.

- The TCP **-y** flag is now **--syn**, and it must follow **-p tcp**.

- The DENY target is now DROP.

- Zeroing single chains while listing them works.

- Zeroing built-in chains also clears policy counters.

- Listing chains gives you the counters as an atomic snapshot.

- REJECT and LOG are now extended targets, meaning they are separate kernel modules.

- Chain names can be up to 31 characters.

- MASQ is now MASQUERADE and uses a different syntax. REDIRECT, while keeping the same name, has also undergone a syntax change.

- The **-o** option is no longer used to direct packets to the userspace device (see the previous **-i** item). Packets are now sent to userspace via the QUEUE target.

IP Tables Scripts

You can enter **iptables** commands from the shell command line. When you shut down your system, however, these commands will be lost. To save your commands, you can place them in a script (the **iptables-save** and **iptables.res**tore commands are currently under development). You can create a script called **/etc/iptables.rules** and place your **iptables** commands in it. You now have enough information to create a simple iptables script that will provide basic protection for a single system connected to the Internet. The following script provides an IP Tables filtering process to protect a local network and a Web site from outside attacks. It is the iptables version of the ipchains **mychains** script listed in the previous section on IP Chains. First a DROP policy is set up for INPUT and FORWARD built-in IP chains. This means that if a packet does not meet a criterion in any of the rules to let it pass, it will be dropped. Then both IP spoofing attacks and any attempt from the outside to initiate connections (SYN packets) are rejected. Outside connection attempts are also logged. This is a very basic configuration that can easily be refined to your own needs by adding IP Tables rules.

myfilter

```
# # Firewall Gateway system IP address is 10.0.0.1 using Ethernet device eth0
# Private network address is 192.168.1.0 using Ethernet device eth1
# Web site address is 10.0.0.2

# modprobe iptable_filter
# turn off IP forwarding
echo 0 > /proc/sys/net/ipv4/ip_forward

# Flush chain rules
iptables -F INPUT
iptables -F OUTPUT
iptables -F FORWARD

# set default (policy) rules
iptables -P INPUT DROP
iptables -P OUTPUT ACCEPT
iptables -P FORWARD ACCEPT

# IP spoffing, deny any packets on the internal network that has an external
# source address.
iptables -A INPUT -j LOG  -i eth1 \! -s 192.168.1.0/24
iptables -A INPUT -j DROP  -i eth1 \! -s 192.168.1.0/24
# IP spoofing, deny any outside packets (any not on eth1) that have the
# source address of the internal network
iptables -A INPUT -j DROP \! -i eth1 -s 192.168.1.0/24
# IP spoofing, deny any outside packets with localhost address
# (packets not on the lo interface (any on eth0 or eth1) that have the source
# address of localhost)
iptables -A INPUT -j DROP  -i \! lo  -s  127.0.0.0/255.0.0.0
```

```
# allow all incoming messages for users on your firewall system
iptables -A INPUT -j ACCEPT  -i lo

# allow  communication to the Web server (address 10.0.0.2), port www
iptables -A INPUT  -j ACCEPT -p tcp -i eth0  —dport www -s 10.0.0.2
# Allow  established connections from Web servers to internal network
iptables -A INPUT -m state —state ESTABLISHED,RELATED -i eth0 \
    -p tcp  —sport www -s 10.0.0.2 -d 192.168.1.0/24  -j ACCEPT
# Prevent new  connections from Web servers to internal network
iptables -A OUTPUT -m state —state  NEW -o eth0 -p tcp \
    —sport www -d 192.168.1.1.0/24  -j DROP

# allow established and related outside communication to your system
# allow outside communication to the firewall,except for ICMP packets
iptables -A INPUT -m state —state ESTABLISHED,RELATED \
    -i eth0 -p \! icmp -j ACCEPT
# prevent outside initiated connections
iptables -A INPUT -m state —state NEW -i eth0 -j DROP

# allow all local communication to and from the firewall on eth1
# from the local network
iptables -A INPUT -j ACCEPT -p all -i eth1 -s 192.168.1.0/24

# Set up masquerqading to allow internal machines access to outside network
iptables -t nat -A POSTROUTING -o eth0 -j MASQUERADE

# Accept ICMP Ping (0 and 8) and Destination ureachable (3)  messages
# Others will be rejected by INPUT and OUTPUT DROP policy
iptables -A INPUT -j ACCEPT  -p icmp -i eth0 \
    —icmp-type  echo-reply -d 10.0.0.1
iptables -A INPUT -j ACCEPT  -p icmp -i eth0 \
    —icmp-type  echo-request -d 10.0.0.1
iptables -A INPUT -j ACCEPT -p icmp -i eth0 \
    —icmp-type  destination-unreachable -d 10.0.0.1

 # Turn on IP Forwarding
echo 1 > /proc/sys/net/ipv4/ip_forward
```

Initially, in the script you would clear your current iptables with the flush option (**-F**), and then set the policies (default targets) for the non-user-defined rules. IP Forwarding should also be turned off while the chain rules are being set.

```
echo 0 > /proc/sys/net/ipv4/ip_forward
```

One way to protect the private network from IP spoofing any packets is to check for any outside addresses on the Ethernet device dedicated to the private network. In this

example, any packet on device eth1 (dedicated to the private network) whose source
address is not that of the private network (**! -s 192.168.1.0**) is denied. Also, check
to see if any packets coming from the outside are designating the private network as
their source. In this example, any packets with the source address of the private network
on any Ethernet device other than for the private network (eth1) are denied. The same
strategy can be applied to the local host.

```
# IP spoffing, deny any packets on the internal network
# that has an external source address.
iptables -A INPUT -j LOG  -i eth1 \! -s 192.168.1.0/24
iptables -A INPUT -j DROP  -i eth1 \! -s 192.168.1.0/24
# IP spoofing, deny any outside packets (any not on eth1)
# that have the source address of the internal network
iptables -A INPUT -j DROP \! -i eth1 -s 192.168.1.0/24
# IP spoofing, deny any outside packets with localhost address
# (packets not on the lo interface (any on eth0 or eth1)
# that have the source address of localhost)
iptables -A INPUT -j DROP  -i \! lo  -s  127.0.0.0/255.0.0.0
```

Then you would set up rules to allow all packets sent and received within your
system (localhost) to pass.

```
iptables -A INPUT -j ACCEPT  -i lo
```

For the Web server, you want to allow access by outside users, but to block access
by anyone attempting to initiate a connection from the Web server into the private
network. In the next example, all messages are accepted to the Web server, but the
Web server cannot initiate contact with the private network. This prevents anyone
from breaking into the local network through the Web server, which is open to outside
access. Established connections are allowed, permitting the private network to use the
Web server.

```
# allow  communication to the Web server (address 10.0.0.2), port www
iptables -A INPUT  -j ACCEPT -p tcp -i eth0  --dport www -s 10.0.0.2
# Allow  established connections from Web servers to internal network
iptables -A INPUT -m state --state ESTABLISHED,RELATED -i eth0 -p tcp  \
  --sport www -s 10.0.0.2 -d 192.168.1.0/24  -j ACCEPT
# Prevent new  connections from Web servers to internal network
iptables -A OUTPUT -m state --state  NEW -o eth0 -p tcp  \
  --sport www -d 192.168.1.1.0/24  -j DROP
```

To allow access by the firewall to outside networks, you allow input by all packets except for ICMP packets. These are handled later. The firewall is specified by the firewall device, eth0. First, allow established and related connections to proceed.

```
# allow outside communication to the firewall,
# except for ICMP packets
iptables -A INPUT -m state --state ESTABLISHED,RELATED \
        -i eth0 -p \! icmp -j ACCEPT
```

To prevent outsiders from initiating any access to your system, create a rule to block access by SYN packets from the outside using the state option with NEW. Drop any new connections on the eth0 connection (assumes only eth0 is connected to the Internet or outside network).

```
# prevent outside initiated connections
iptables -A INPUT -m state --state NEW -i eth0 -j DROP
```

To allow interaction by the internal network with the firewall, you allow input by all packets on the internal Ethernet connection, eth1. The valid internal network addresses are designated as the input source.

```
iptables -A INPUT -j ACCEPT -p all -i eth1 -s 192.168.1.0/24
```

To implement masquerading, where systems on the private network can use the gateway's Internet address to connect to Internet hosts, you create a NAT table (**-t nat**) POSTROUTING rule with a MASQUERADE target.

```
iptables -t nat -A POSTROUTING -o eth0 -j MASQUERADE
```

In addition, to allow ping and destination-reachable ICMP packets, you enter INPUT rules with the firewall as the destination. To enable ping operations, you use both echo-reply and echo-request ICMP types, and for destination unreachable, you use the destination-unreachable type.

```
iptables -A INPUT -j ACCEPT  -p icmp -i eth0 --icmp-type \
   echo-reply -d 10.0.0.1
iptables -A INPUT -j ACCEPT  -p icmp -i eth0 --icmp-type \
   echo-request -d 10.0.0.1
iptables -A INPUT -j ACCEPT -p icmp -i eth0 --icmp-type \
   destination-unreachable -d 10.0.0.1
```

INPUTAt the end, IP forwarding is turned on again:

```
echo 1 > /proc/sys/net/ipv4/ip_forward
```

A listing of these **iptables** options shows the different rules for each option, as shown here.

```
[root@turtle fire]# iptables -L
Chain INPUT (policy DROP)
target prot source             destination      in
LOG    all  !192.168.1.0/24 anywhere         eth1
DROP   all  !192.168.1.0/24 anywhere         eth1
DROP   all  192.168.1.0/24  anywhere         !eth1
DROP   all  127.0.0.0/8      anywhere         !lo
ACCEPT all  anywhere         anywhere         lo
ACCEPT tcp  10.0.0.2         anywhere         eth0  tcp dpt:www
ACCEPT tcp  10.0.0.2         192.168.1.0/24 eth0
                             state RELATED,ESTABLISHED tcp spt:www
ACCEPT !icmp anywhere        anywhere         eth0  state
RELATED,ESTABLISHED
DROP   all  anywhere         anywhere         eth0  state NEW
ACCEPT all  192.168.1.0/24  anywhere         eth1
ACCEPT icmp anywhere         10.0.0.1         eth0  icmp echo-reply
ACCEPT icmp anywhere         10.0.0.1         eth0  icmp echo-request
ACCEPT icmp anywhere         10.0.0.1         eth0  icmp
                                              destination-unreachable

Chain FORWARD (policy ACCEPT)
target prot source         destination      in

Chain OUTPUT (policy ACCEPT)
target prot source         destination      in
DROP   tcp  anywhere       192.168.1.0/24 eth0  state NEW tcp spt:www
```

IP Masquerading

On Linux systems, you can set up a network in which you can have one connection to the Internet, which several systems on your network can use. This way, using only one IP address, several different systems can connect to the Internet. This method is called *IP masquerading*, where a system masquerades as another system, using that system's IP address. In such a network, one system is connected to the Internet with its own IP address, while the other systems are connected on a *local area network* (*LAN*) to this system. When a local system wants to access the network, it masquerades as the Internet-connected system, borrowing its IP address.

IP masquerading is implemented on Linux using the ipchains firewalling tool. In effect, you set up a firewall, which you then configure to do IP masquerading. Currently, IP masquerading—as does ipchains firewalling—supports all the common network services, such as Web browsing, telnet, ping, and gopher. Other services, such as IRC, FTP, and Real Audio, require the use of certain modules. Any services you want local systems to access must also be on the firewall system because request and response actually are handled by services on that system.

You can find out more information on IP masquerading at the IP Masquerade Resource Web site at **http://ipmasq.cjb.net/**. In particular, the Linux IP Masquerade mini-HOWTO provides a detailed, step-by-step guide to setting up IP masquerading on your system. IP masquerading must be supported by the kernel before you can use it. If your kernel does not support it, you may have to rebuild the kernel including IP masquerade support or use loadable modules to add it. See the IP Masquerade mini-HOWTO for more information.

With IP masquerading, as implemented on Linux systems, the machine with the Internet address is also the firewall and gateway for the LAN of machines that use the firewall's Internet address to connect to the Internet. Firewalls that also implement IP masquerading are sometimes referred to as *MASQ gates*. With IP masquerading, the Internet-connected system (the firewall) listens for Internet requests from hosts on its LAN. When it receives one, it replaces the requesting local host's IP address with the Internet IP address of the firewall and then passes the request out to the Internet, as if the request were its own. Replies from the Internet are then sent to the firewall system. The replies the firewall receives are addressed to the firewall using its Internet address. The firewall then determines the local system to whose request the reply is responding. It then strips off its IP address and sends the response on to the local host across the LAN. The connection is transparent from the perspective of the local machines. They appear to be connected directly to the Internet.

IP Masquerading with ipchains

You need to specify forwarding rules for use by **ipchains** to implement IP masquerading. (See the **mychains** file in the previous section for another example of an ipchains masquerade entry.) The following example assumes the Internet connect host, the firewall, uses its first Ethernet device to connect to the Internet, eth0. If you are using a modem to dial up a connection to an ISP, then the interface used would probably be the first PPP interface, ppp0. The second command appends (**-A**) the forward rule to the target (**-j**) **MASQ** (masquerade) for the interface (**-i**) eth0. The host machines on the LAN must specify the connected system as their gateway machine. The last command enables IP forwarding. To enable IP masquerading using Linuxconf's firewalling entries, select Forward Firewalling and click the Do masquerade check box for any firewall forwarding rules you add that you want to apply to IP masquerading.

```
ipchains -P forward DENY
 ipchains -A forward -i eth0 -j MASQ
 echo 1 > /proc/sys/net/ipv4/ip_forward
```

IP masquerading is often used to allow machines on a private network to access the Internet. These could be machines in a home network or a small LAN, say, for a small business. Such a network might have only one machine with Internet access and, as such, only the one Internet address. The local private network would have IP addresses chosen from the Private Network allocations (**10.**, **172.16.**, or **192.168.**). Ideally, the firewall has two Ethernet cards: one for an interface to the LAN (say, **eth1**) and one for an interface to the Internet, such as **eth0** (for dial-up ISPs, this would be ppp0 for the modem). The card for the Internet connection (**eth0**) would be assigned the Internet IP address. The Ethernet interface for the local network (**eth1**, in this example) is the firewall Ethernet interface. Your private LAN would have a network address like **192.168.1**. Its Ethernet firewall interface (**eth1**) would be assigned the IP address **192.168.1.1**. In effect, the firewall interface lets the firewall operate as the local network's gateway. The firewall is then configured to masquerade any packets coming from the private network. Your LAN needs to have its own domain name server, identifying the machines on your network, including your firewall. Each local machine needs to have the firewall specified as its gateway. Try not to use IP aliasing to assign both the firewall and Internet IP addresses to the same physical interface. Use separate interfaces for them, such as two Ethernet cards, or an Ethernet card and a modem (**ppp0**).

IP Masquerading with Netfilter (NAT and iptables)

In Netfilter, IP masquerading is a NAT operation and is no longer integrated with packet filtering as in ipchains. IP masquerading commands are placed on the NAT table and treated separately from the packet filtering commands. To implement IP masquerading with Netfilter, first make sure that the **iptable_nat** module is loaded (you can have this operation built into the kernel).

```
modprobe iptable_nat
```

Then use iptables to place a masquerade rule on the NAT table. First reference the NAT table with the **-t nat** option. Then add a POSTROUTING command with the **-o** option specifying the output device and the **-j** option with the MASQUERADE command.

```
iptables -t nat -A POSTROUTING -o eth0 -j MASQUERADE
```

Then turn on IP forwarding as you normally would.

```
echo 1 > /proc/sys/net/ipv4/ip_forward
```

Bear in mind that with iptables, masquerading is no longer combined with the FORWARD chain, as it is with ipchains. So if you specify a DROP policy for the FORWARD chain, you will also have to specifically enable FORWARD operations for the network that is being masqueraded. You will need both a POSTROUTING rule and FORWARD rules.

Secure Shell (SSH)

Although a firewall can protect a network from attempts to break in to it from the outside, the problem of securing legitimate communications to the network from outside sources still exists. A particular problem is one of users who want to connect to your network remotely. Such connections could be monitored, and information such as passwords and user IDs used when the user logs into your network could be copied and used later to break in. One solution is to use SSH for remote logins. SSH encrypts any communications between the remote user and a system on your network. The SSH programs are meant to replace remote tools such as **rsh** and **rcp** (see Chapter 18), which perform no encryption and introduce security risks such as transmitting passwords in clear text.

SSH encryption makes use of two keys: a public key and a private key. The *public key* is used to encrypt data, while the *private key* decrypts it. Each host or user has her own public and private keys. The public key is freely distributed to other hosts, who can then use it to encrypt data that only the host's private key can decrypt. For example, when a host sends data to a user on another system, the host encrypts the data with a public key, which it previously received from that user. The data can only be decrypted by the user's corresponding private key. The public key can safely be sent in the open from one host to another, allowing it to be installed safely on different hosts. You think of the process as taking place between a client and a server. The client (a user) connects to a server (a remote system). Each has its own pair of public and private keys. To enable an SSH connection, the client and server have to exchange their public keys, though each always retains its private keys. The client needs the server's public key, and the server needs the client's public key. When the client sends data to the server, it first encrypts the data using the server's public key. The server can then decrypt the data using its own private key. The server, in turn, can encrypt data using the client's public key, which the client can then decrypt using the client's private key. In fact, encryption uses a combination of both the sender's private key and the recipient's public key. This encryption can only be decrypted using the combination of the recipient's private key and the sender's public key.

SSH uses strong encryption methods for which rexport from the United States may be illegal. Currently, SSH can deal with the following kinds of attacks:

- IP spoofing, where a remote host sends out packets that pretend to come from another, trusted host

- IP source routing, where a host can pretend an IP packet comes from another, trusted host

- DNS spoofing, where an attacker forges name server records

- Interception of clear text passwords and other data by intermediate hosts

- Manipulation of data by people in control of intermediate hosts

- Attacks based on listening to *X* authentication data and spoofed connections to the X11 server

The official developer of SSH is SSH Communications Security, whose Web site is **www.ssh.com**. It actually supports several security products, including the IPSEC and IKE toolkits. IPSEC is an *Internet Engineering Task Force* (*IETF*) standard for protecting IP transmission using cryptography on IP packets. The *Internet Key Exchange* (*IKE*) *Protocol* is a method for managing keys used in an encrypted transmission.

The site for SSH Communications Security's Secure Shell product is **www.ssh.org**. Here, you can find links to download a free version of SSH for use on a variety of platforms. You can also find a link to the SSH FAQ, which answers most questions (**www.ssh.org/faq.html**). The FAQ also provides a list of links to the SSH tutorials, such as Purdue University's SSH tutorial, currently located at **csociety.ecn.purdue.edu/ ~sigos/projects/ssh/**.

SSH Communications Security provides SSH free for noncommercial use and sells SSH for commercial use through Datafellows. Numerous alternative free versions of SSH are being developed or are currently available for several different platforms, including Macintosh, Windows, Java, and, of course, Linux. All use the SSH protocols as supported by SSH Communications Security. See the FAQ for a current listing.

SSH1 and SSH2

Two different implementations of SSH currently use what are, in effect, two different and incompatible protocols. The first version of SSH, known as SSH1, uses the original SSH protocol, whereas version 2.0, known as SSH2, uses a completely rewritten version of the SSH protocol. Encryption is performed in different ways, encrypting different parts of a packet. SSH1 uses server and host keys to authenticate systems, whereas SSH2 only uses host keys. Furthermore, certain functions, such as sftp, are only supported by SSH2.

Although SSH2 is more secure, it has stronger licensing restrictions. SSH1 is available free to anyone for noncommercial purposes. For SSH1, the term "noncommercial" is interpreted broadly and businesses can use it for their private networks. SSH2, on the other hand, is free only for educational and personal use. All other uses require a license to be purchased from Datafellows, which controls commercial distribution for SSH Communications Security. For this reason, most networks still make use of SSH1.

SSH Applications

The official distribution site for SSH is at the Helsinki University of Technology at **ftp.cs.hut.fi/pub/ssh/**, though you can easily download it from a variety of mirror sites or use the SSH Web site at **www.ssh.com**. From these sites, you can download a compressed archive (**.tar.gz**) of the most recent version, either version 1 or version 2. Decompress and unpack with the **gunzip** and **tar xvf** commands, and then check the README file for detailed instructions on creating and installing the SSH applications. Be sure your development libraries and C compiler are installed on your system. The **./configure**, **make**, and **make install** commands generate the applications and install them by default on the **/usr/local/bin** directory. You can either place this directory in your **PATH** in the **/etc/profile** file or simply copy the applications to the **/usr/bin** directory.

The SSH applications are listed in Table 39-7. They include several client programs and the ssh server. The ssh server (**sshd**) provides secure connections to anyone from the outside using the ssh client to connect. With ssh, users can remotely log in and execute commands using encrypted transmissions. In the same way, with scp, users can copy files from one host to another securely. The ssh server can also invoke the **sftp-server** to provide encrypted FTP transmissions to those using the sftp client. This client, which only works with ssh version 2.0, operates much like ftp, with many of the same commands (see Chapter 16). Several configuration utilities are also included, such as **ssh-add**, which adds valid hosts to the authentication agent, and **ssh-keygen**, which generates the keys used for encryption.

SSH was originally designed to replace remote access operations, such as rlogin, rcp, and telnet (see Chapter 18). The ssh-clients package contains corresponding SSH clients to replace these applications. With slogin or ssh, you can log in from a remote host to execute commands and run applications, much as you can with rlogin and rsh. With scp, you can copy files between the remote host and a network host, just as with rcp.

For version 2.0, names of the actual applications have a 2 suffix to indicate they are version 2.0 programs. Version 1.0 applications have a 1 as their suffix. During installation, however, links are set for each application to use only the name with the suffix. For example, if you have installed version 2.0, there is a link called scp to the scp2 application. You can then use the link to invoked the application. Using scp starts scp2. Table 39-7 specifies only the link names, as these are the same for each version. Remember, though, some applications, such as sftp, are only available with version 2.0.

Application	Description
ssh	ssh client
sshd	ssh server (daemon)
sftp	sftp client. Version 2 only. Use **?** to list **sftp** commands
sftp-server	sftp server. Version 2 only
scp	scp client
ssh-keygen	Utility for generating keys. **-h** for help
ssh-add	Add identities to the authentication agent
ssh-agent	SSH authentication agent
ssh-askpass	X Window System utility for querying passwords
ssh-signer	Signs host-based authentication packets. Version 2 only. Must be suid root (performed by installation)
slogin	Remote login (Version 1)

Table 39-7. *SSH Applications*

SSH Setup

Each user who intends to use SSH applications first needs to create the public and private keys to use for the encryption process. You do this using the **ssh-keygen** command. The **ssh-keygen** command prompts you for a pass-phrase, which it will use as a kind of password to protect your private key. The pass-phrase should be several words long. The **ssh-keygen** command generates the public key and places it in your **.ssh/identity.pub** file; it places the private key in the **.ssh/identity** file. If you need to change your pass-phrase, you can do so with the **ssh-keygen** command and the **-p** option. Each user will have her own SSH configuration directory, called **.ssh**, located in her own home directory. The public and private keys, as well as SSH configuration files, are placed here. If you build from the source code, then the make install operation will automatically run **ssh-keygen**. Table 39-8 lists the SSH configuration files.

File	Description
$HOME/.ssh/known_hosts	Records host keys for all hosts the user has logged in to (that are not in **/etc/ssh/ssh_known_hosts**).
$HOME/.ssh/random_seed	Used for seeding the random number generator.
$HOME/.ssh/identity	Contains the RSA authentication identity of the user.
$HOME/.ssh/identity.pub	Contains the public key for authentication (public part of the identity file in human-readable form). The contents of this file should be added to **$HOME/.ssh/authorized_keys** on all machines where you want to log in using RSA authentication.
$HOME/.ssh/config	The per-user configuration file.
$HOME/.ssh/authorized_keys	Lists the RSA keys that can be used for logging in as this user.
/etc/ssh/ssh_known_hosts	Systemwide list of known host keys.
/etc/ssh/ssh_config	Systemwide configuration file. This file provides defaults for those values not specified in the user's configuration file.
$HOME/.rhosts	This file is used in **.rhosts** authentication to list the host/user pairs permitted to log in. Note, this file is also used by rlogin and rsh, which makes using this file insecure.
$HOME/.shosts	This file is used exactly the same way as **.rhosts**. The purpose for having this file is to use rhosts authentication with **ssh** without permitting login with rlogin or rsh.

Table 39-8. *SSH Configuration Files (SSH2 files are placed in /etc/ssh2 and .ssh2 directories)*

File	Description
/etc/hosts.equiv	This file is used during **.rhosts** authentication. It contains canonical hosts' names, one per line. If the client host is found in this file, login is automatically permitted, provided client and server user names are the same.
/etc/ssh/shosts.equiv	This file is processed exactly as **/etc/hosts.equiv**. This file may be useful to permit logins using **ssh** but not using rsh/rlogin.
/etc/ssh/sshrc	System default. Commands in this file are executed by **ssh** when the user logs in just before the user's shell (or command) is started.
$HOME/.ssh/rc	Commands in this file are executed by **ssh** when the user logs in just before the user's shell (or command) is started.

Table 39-8.   *SSH Configuration Files (SSH2 files are placed in /etc/ssh2 and .ssh2 directories)* (continued)

A public key is used to identify a user and its host. You use the public key on a remote system to allow that user access. The public key is placed in the remote user account's **.ssh/authorized_keys** file. Recall that the public key is held in the **.ssh/identity.pub** file. If a user wants to log in remotely from a local account to an account on a remote system, he would first place his public key in the **.ssh/authorized_keys** file in the account on the remote system he wants to access. If the user larisa on **turtle.mytrek.com** wants to access the aleina account on **rabbit.mytrek.com,** larisa's public key from **/home/larisa/.ssh/identity.pub** first must be placed in aleina's authorized_keys file, **/home/aleina/.ssh/authorized_keys**.

If you regularly make connections to a variety of remote hosts, you can use the **ssh-agent** command to place private keys in memory where they can be accessed quickly to decrypt received transmissions. The **ssh-agent** command is intended for use at the beginning of a login session. If you are using a shell in your work, use that shell as the argument for the **ssh-agent** command. If you are using the X Window System (Gnome or KDE), use the **startx** command as your argument. That way, any applications you start inherit a connection to **ssh-agent**. For a graphical login, such as GDM, place the **ssh-agent** command in your *.xsession* file.

Although the **ssh-agent** command enables you to use private keys in memory, you also must specifically load your private keys into memory using the **ssh-add** command. **ssh-add** with no arguments loads your private key from your *.ssh/identity* file. You are prompted for your pass-phrase for this private key. To remove the key from memory, use **ssh-add** with the **-d** option. If you have several private keys, you can load them all into memory. **ssh-add** with the **-l** option lists those currently loaded.

SSH also supports the original rhosts form of authentication where hosts and users that are permitted access are placed in an *.rhosts* or *.shosts* file. However, this method is not considered secure.

ssh

With ssh, you can remotely log in from a local client to a remote system on your network operating as the SSH server. The term *local client* here refers to one outside the network such as your home computer, and the term *remote* refers to a host system on the network to which you are connecting. In effect, you connect from your local system to the remote network host. It is designed to replace rlogin, which performs remote logins, and rsh, which executes remote commands. With **ssh**, you can log in from a local site to a remote host on your network and then send commands to be executed on that host. ssh is also capable of supporting X Window System connections. This feature is automatically enabled if you make an **ssh** connection from an X Window System environment, such as Gnome or KDE. A connection is set up for you between the local X server and the remote X server. The remote host sets up a dummy X server and sends any X Window System data through it to your local system to be processed by your own local X server.

The ssh login operation function is much like the **rlogin** command. You enter the **ssh** command with the address of the remote host, followed by an **-l** option and the login name (user name) of the remote account you are logging into. The following example logs into the aleina user account on the **rabbit.mytrek.com** host.

```
ssh rabbit.mytrek.com -l aleina
```

A variety of options are available to enable you to configure your connection (see Table 39-9). Most have corresponding configuration options that can be set in the configuration file. For example, with the **-c** option, you can designate which encryption method you want to use. With the **-i** option, you can select a particular private key to use. The **-C** option enables you to have transmissions compressed at specified levels.

Option	Description
-a	Disables forwarding of the authentication agent connection
-c idea | des | 3des | blowfish | arcfour | none	Selects the cipher to use for encrypting the session. idea is used by default and is believed to be secure. none disables encryption entirely; it is only intended for debugging and renders the connection insecure
-e *ch* | ^*ch* | none	Sets the escape character for sessions with a pty (default: ~). The escape character is only recognized at the beginning of a line. The escape character followed by a dot (.) closes the connection, followed by CTRL-Z suspends the connection, and followed by itself sends the escape character once. Setting the character to "none" disables any escapes and makes the session fully transparent
-f	Requests ssh to go to background after authentication is done and forwardings are established
-i *identity_file*	Selects the file from which the identity (private key) for RSA authentication is read. Default is **.ssh/identity** in the user's home directory
-k	Disables forwarding of the Kerberos tickets
-l *login_name*	Specifies the user to log in as on the remote machine
-n	Redirects stdin from **/dev/null** (actually, prevents reading from stdin). Used when ssh is run in the background. Used to run X11 programs in a remote machine

Table 39-9. *ssh Command Options*

Option	Description
-o *option*	Specifies options
-p *port*	Port to connect to on the remote host
-q	Quiet mode, suppresses warning and diagnostic messages
-P	Uses nonprivileged port
-t	Forces pseudo-tty allocation
-v	Verbose mode
-V	Displays version number
-g	Allows remote hosts to connect local port forwarding ports
-x	Disables X11 forwarding
-C	Requests compression of all data. The compression algorithm is the same used by gzip and the level can be controlled by the CompressionLevel option
-L *port*:*host*:*hostport*	Specifies that the given port on the local (client) host is to be forwarded to the given host and port on the remote side
-R *port*:*host*:*hostport*	Specifies that the given port on the remote (server) host is to be forwarded to the given host and port on the local side

Table 39-9.   *ssh Command Options* (continued)

scp

You use **scp** to copy files from one host to another on a network. Designed to replace rcp, scp actually uses ssh to transfer data and employs the same authentication and encryption (see Table 39-10). If authentication requires it, **scp** requests a password or pass-phrase. **scp** operates much like rcp. Directories and files on remote hosts are specified using the user name and the host address before the filename or directory. The user name specifies the remote user account that **scp** is accessing, and the host is the remote system where that account is located. You separate the user from the host address with a @, and you separate the host address from the file or directory name

Option	Description
-q	Turns off statistics display
-Q	Turns on statistics display
-r	Recursively copies entire directories
-v	Verbose mode
-B	Selects batch mode (prevents asking for passwords or pass-phrases)
-C	Compression-enabled
-P *port*	Specifies the port to connect to on the remote host
-S *path-to-ssh*	Specifies the path to **ssh** program

Table 39-10.   *scp Options*

with a colon, **:**. The following example copies the file **party** from a user current directory to the user **aleina**'s **birthday** directory, located on the **rabbit.mytrek.com** host.

```
scp party aleina@rabbit.mytrek.com:/birthday/party
```

Of particular interest is the **-r** option (recursive), which enables you to copy whole directories. In the next example, the user copies the entire **reports** directory to the user **justin**'s **projects** directory.

```
scp -r reports justin@rabbit.mytrek.com:/projects
```

Port Forwarding

If, for some reason, you can only connect to a secure host by going through an unsecure host, ssh provides a feature called port forwarding. With *port forwarding*, you can secure the unsecure segment of your connection. This involves simply specifying the port at which the unsecure host is to connect to the secure one. This sets up a direct connection between the local host and the remote host, through the intermediary unsecure host. Encrypted data is passed through directly.

You can set up port forwarding to a port on the remote system or your local system. To forward a port on the remote system to a port on your local system, use the **ssh -R** option, followed by an argument holding the local port, the remote host address, and the remote port to be forwarded, each separated by a colon. This works by allocating a socket to listen to the port on the remote side. Whenever a connection is made to this port, the connection is forwarded over the secure channel, and a connection is made to a remote port from the local machine. In the following example, port 22 on the local system is connected to port 23 on the **rabbit.mytrek.com** remote system.

```
ssh -R 22:rabbit.mytrek.com:23
```

To forward a port on your local system to a port on a remote system, use the **ssh -L** option, followed by an argument holding the local port, the remote host address, and the remote port to be forwarded, each two arguments separated by a colon. A socket is allocated to listen to port on the local side;whenever a connection is made to this port, the connection is forwarded over the secure channel and a connection is made to the remote port on the remote machine. In the following example, port 22 on the local system is connected to port 23 on the **rabbit.mytrek.com** remote system.

```
ssh -L 22:rabbit.mytrek.com:23
```

You can use the **LocalForward** and **RemoteForward** options in your **.ssh/config** file to set up port forwarding for particular hosts or to specify a default for all hosts you connect to.

SSH Session

An SSH session can be implemented as a pseudoterminal, much like a telnet connection, or it can be transparent, as is the case with X server connections. With a psuedoterminal, the user can control the connection with a set of escape characters, each beginning with a tilde (~). To end the connection, use a "~." escape sequence. A **~Ctrl-Z** suspends the session. The escape sequence must be entered in a line of its own. The **~?** lists the available escape sequences you can use.

If no pseudoterminal is set up, the session is transparent. Usually, setting the escape character to "none" makes the session transparent. Binary data can safely be transmitted during transparent sessions. A transparent session ends when the shell or command on the remote system ends and all connections have been closed. X Window System connections are automatically set up as transparent connections. SSH sets up a proxy X server on the remote system.

SSH Configuration

The SSH configuration file for each user is in her **.ssh/config** file. The **/etc/sys_config** file is used to set sitewide defaults. In the configuration file, you can set various options, as listed in Table 39-11. The configuration file is designed to specify options for different remote hosts to which you might connect. It is organized into segments where each segment begins with the keyword HOST, followed by the IP address of the

Option	Description
Host *hostname*	Specifies the host to which the following options apply. All options apply to this host until the next Host entry. You can specify a range of hosts by using the * and ? pattern-matching wildcard symbols. A host specified as only '*' matches on all hosts and can be used to specify global options.
BatchMode (yes | no)	If set to **yes**, pass-phrase/password querying is disabled. This option is useful in scripts and other batch jobs where you have no user to supply the password. The argument must be **yes** or **no**.
Cipher *cipher*	Specifies the cipher to use for encrypting the session, such as idea, des, 3des, blowfish, arcfour, and none. The default is idea (or 3des if idea is not supported by both hosts). Using "none" (no encryption) renders the connection insecure and is intended only for debugging.
ClearAllForwardings (*yes* | *no*)	Clears all forwardings after reading all config files and parsing the command line. This is useful to disable forwardings in config files when you want to make a second connection to the host having forwardings in the config file. **scp** sets this on by default, so it does not fail, even if you have some forwardings set in a config file.
Compression (yes | no)	Specifies whether to use compression.

Table 39-11. *SSH Configuration Options*

host. The following lines hold the options you have set for that host. A segment ends at the next HOST entry. Of particular interest are the **User** and **Cipher** options. Use the **User** option to specify the names of users on the remote system that are allowed

Option	Description
CompressionLevel *(1–9)*	Specifies the compression level. The argument must be an integer from 1 (fast) to 9 (slow, best). The default level is 6
ConnectionAttempts *num*	Specifies the number of tries (one per second) to make
EscapeChar	Sets the escape character (default: ~). The argument should be a single character, ^, followed by a letter or **none** to disable the escape character entirely (making the connection transparent for binary data)
FallBackToRsh *(yes ǀ no)*	Specifies if connecting with **ssh** fails because no **sshd** is on the remote host, **rsh** should automatically be used instead
ForwardAgent *(yes ǀ no)*	Specifies whether the connection to the authentication agent should be forwarded to the remote machine
ForwardX11 *(yes ǀ no)*	Specifies whether X11 connections should be automatically redirected over the secure channel and DISPLAY set
GatewayPorts *(yes ǀ no)*	Specifies that remote hosts may connect to locally forwarded ports
GlobalKnownHostsFile *file*	Specifies a file to use instead of **/etc/ssh/ssh_known_hosts**
HostName *hostname*	Specifies the real host name to log into. This can be used to specify nicknames or abbreviations for hosts
IdentityFile *file*	Specifies the file from which the user's RSA authentication identity is read (default **.ssh/identity** in the user's home directory)

Table 39-11. *SSH Configuration Options* (continued)

Option	Description
KeepAlive (yes | no)	Specifies whether the system should send keepalive messages to the other side. Used to detect if connection fails
KerberosAuthentication (yes | no)	Specifies whether Kerberos V5 authentication should be used
KerberosTgtPassing (yes | no)	Specifies whether a Kerberos V5 TGT is to be forwarded to the server
LocalForward *host host:port*	Specifies a TCP/IP port on the local machine be forwarded over the secure channel to given host:port from the remote machine. The first argument must be a port number, and the second must be *host:port*
NumberOfPasswordPrompts *num*	Specifies the number of password prompts before giving up
PasswordAuthentication (yes | no)	Specifies whether to use password authentication
PasswordPromptHost (yes | no)	Specifies whether to include the remote host name in the password prompt
PasswordPromptLogin (yes | no)	Specifies whether to include the remote login name in the password prompt
Port	Specifies the port number to connect on the remote host. Default is 22
ProxyCommand *command*	Specifies the command to use to connect to the server
RemoteForward *host host:port*	Specifies a TCP/IP port on the remote machine be forwarded over the secure channel to given host:port from the local machine. The first argument must be a port number, and the second must be *host:port*

Table 39-11.   *SSH Configuration Options* (continued)

Option	Description
RhostsAuthentication (yes | no)	Specifies whether to try rhosts-based authentication
RhostsRSAAuthentication (yes | no)	Specifies whether to try rhosts-based authentication with RSA host authentication
RSAAuthentication (yes | no)	Specifies whether to try RSA authentication
StrictHostKeyChecking (yes | no | *ask*)	If this flag is set to yes, **ssh** never automatically adds host keys to the **$HOME/.ssh/known_hosts** file and refuses to connect hosts whose host key has changed
TISAuthentication (yes | no)	Specifies whether to try TIS authentication
UsePrivilegedPort (yes | no)	Specifies whether to use a privileged port when connecting to other end
User *username*	Specifies the user to log in as
UserKnownHostsFile *file*	Specifies a file to use instead of **$HOME/.ssh/known_hosts**
UseRsh (yes | no)	Specifies rlogin/rsh should be used for this host if it does not support the ssh protocol

Table 39-11.   *SSH Configuration Options* (continued)

access. With the **Cipher** option, you can select which encryption method to use for a particular host (see Table 39-12). The following example allows access from larisa at **turtle.mytrek.com** and uses blowfish encryption for transmissions.

```
Host turtle.mytrek.com
     User larisa
     Compression no
     Cipher blowfish
```

Method	Description
idea	Believed to be secure
des	The data encryption standard, but this is breakable by governments, large corporations, and major criminal organizations
3des (triple-des)	Encrypt-decrypt-encrypt triple with three different keys. Presumably more secure than DES and used as the default if both sites do not support IDEA
blowfish	128-bit keys encryption algorithm invented by Bruce Schneier
arcfour	Equivalent with the RC4 cipher from RSA Data Security (RC4 is a trademark of RSA Data Security). This is the fastest algorithm currently supported
Twofish	Version 2 only
Arcfour	Version 2 only
Cast128-cbc	Version 2 only

Table 39-12.   *SSH2 Encryption Methods*

To specify global options that apply to any host you connect to, create a HOST entry with the asterisk as its host, HOST *. This entry must be placed at the end of the configuration file because an option is changed only the first time it is set. Any subsequent entries for an option are ignored. Because a host matches on both its own entry and the global one, its specific entry should come before the global entry. The asterisk, *, and the question mark, ?, are both wildcard matching operators that can enable you to specify a group of hosts with the same suffix or prefix.

```
Host *
  FallBackToRsh yes
  KeepAlive no
  Cipher idea
```

Kerberos Authentication and Encryption

Kerberos is a network authentication protocol that provides encrypted authentication to connections between a client and a server. As an authentication protocol, Kerberos requires a client to prove his or her identity using encryption methods before they can access a server. Once authenticated, the client and server can conduct all communications using encryption. Whereas firewalls only protect from outside attacks, Kerberos is designed to also protect from attacks from those inside the network. Users already within a network could try to break in to local servers. Kerberos places protection around the servers themselves, rather than an entire network or computer. A free version is available from the Massachusetts Institute of Technology at **web.mit.edu/kerberos** under the MIT Public License, which is similar to the GNU Public License. The name Kerberos comes from Greek mythology and is the name of the three-headed watchdog for Hades.

The key to Kerberos is a Kerberos server through which all requests for any server services are channeled. The Kerberos server then authenticates a client, identifying the client and validating the client's right to use a particular server. The server maintains a database of authorized users. Kerberos then issues the client an encrypted ticket that the client can use to gain access to the server. For example, if a user needs to check his mail, a request for use of the mail server is sent to the Kerberos server, which then authenticates the user and issues him a ticket that is then used to access the mail server. Without a Kerberos-issued ticket, no one can access any of the servers. Originally this process required that the user undergo a separate authentication procedure for each server he or she wanted to access. However, users now only need to perform an initial authentication that is valid for all servers.

This process actually involves the use of two servers, an authentication server (AS) and a ticket granting server (TGS). Together they make up what is known as the Key Distribution Center (KDC). In effect, they distribute keys used to unlock access to services. The authentication server first validates a user's identity. The AS issues a ticket called the ticket granting ticket (TGT) that allows the user to access the ticket granting server. The TGS then issues the user another ticket to actually access a service. This way, the user never has any direct access of any kind to a server during the authentication process. The process is somewhat more complex than described. An authenticator using information such as the current time, a checksum, and an optional encryption key is sent along with the ticket and is decrypted with the session key. This authenticator is used by a service to verify your identity.

The authentication server validates a user using information in its user database. Each user needs to be registered in the authentication server's database. The database will include a user password and other user information. To access the authentication server, the user provides the user name and the password. The password is used to generate a user key with which communication between the AS and the user is encrypted. The user will have its own copy of the user key with which to decrypt communications.

Accessing a service with Kerberos involves the following steps:

1. First the user has to be validated by the authentication server and granted access to the ticket granting server with a ticket access key. The user does this by issuing the **kinit** command, which will ask you enter your Keberos user name and then send it on to the Authentication server (the Keberos user name is usually the same as your user name).

   ```
   kinit
   ```

2. The AS generates a ticket granting ticket with which to access the ticket granting server. This ticket will include a session key that will be used to let you access the TGS server. The TGT is sent back to you encrypted with your user key (password).

3. The **kinit** program then prompts you to enter your Keberos password, which it then uses to decrypt the TGT.

4. Now you can use a client program such as a mail client program to access the mail server, for instance. When you do so, the TGT is used to access the TGS server, which then will generate a ticket for accessing the mail server. The TGS will generate a new session key for use with just the mail server. This will be provided in the ticket sent to you for accessing the mail server. In effect, there is a TGT sessions key used for accessing the TGS server, and a mail session key used for accessing the mail server. The ticket for the mail server is sent to you encrypted with the TGS session key.

5. The client then uses the mail ticket received from the TGS server to access the mail server.

6. If you want to use another service such as FTP, when your FTP client send a request to the TGS server for a ticket, the TGS server will automatically obtain authorization from the authentication server and issue an FTP ticket with an FTP session key. This kind of support remains in effect for limited period of time, usually several hours, after which you again have to use kinit to undergo the authentication process and access the TGS server.

Installing and configuring a Keberos server can be a complex process. Carefully check the documentation for installing the current versions. Some of the key areas are listed here. In the Kerberos configuration file, **krb5.conf**, you can set such features as the encryption method used and the database name. When installing Kerberos, be sure to carefully follow the instructions for providing administrative access. The

/etc/services file should contain a listing of all Kerberized services. These are services such as kftp or klogin that provide Kerberos FTP and login services. To run Keberos, you start the Keberos server with the **krb5kdc** and **kadmin** commands.

Setting up a particular service to use Kerberos (known as Kerberizing) can be a complicated process. A Kerberized service needs to check the user's identity and credentials, check for a ticket for the service, and, if one is not present, obtain one. Once they are set up, use of Kerberized services is nearly transparent to the user. Tickets are automatically issued and authentication carried out without any extra effort by the user.

The Complete Reference

Linux

Part VIII

Programming

Chapter 40

Shell Programming

A shell program combines Linux commands in such a way as to perform a specific task. The Linux shell provides you with many programming tools with which to create shell programs. You can define variables and assign values to them. You can also define variables in a script file and have a user interactively enter values for them when the script is executed. There are loop and conditional control structures that repeat Linux commands or make decisions on which commands you want to execute. You can also construct expressions that perform arithmetic or comparison operations. All these programming tools operate like those found in other programming languages.

You can combine shell variables, control structures, expressions, and Linux commands to form a shell program. Usually, the instructions making up a shell program are entered into a script file that can then be executed. You can create this script file using any standard editor. To run the shell program, you then execute its script file. You can even distribute your program among several script files, one of which will contain instructions to execute others. You can think of variables, expressions, and control structures as tools you use to bring together several Linux commands into one operation. In this sense, a shell program is a new, complex Linux command that you have created. The BASH, TCSH, and Z shells that are supported on Linux distributions each have their own shell programming language with slightly different syntax. This chapter discusses BASH shell programming.

Shell Scripts: Commands and Comments

A shell script is a text file that contains Linux commands, which you enter using any standard editor. You can then execute the commands in the file by using the filename as an argument to any **sh** or dot command (**.**). They read the commands in shell scripts and execute them. You can also make the script file itself executable and use its name directly on the command line as you would use the name of any command. To better identify your shell scripts, you can add the **.sh** extension to them, as in **hello.sh**. However, this is not necessary.

You make a script file executable by setting its execute permission using the **chmod** command. The executable permission for the **chmod** command can be set using either symbolic or absolute references. The symbolic reference **u+x** sets the execute permission of a file. The command **chmod u+x hello** will set the execute permission of the **hello** script file. You can now use the script filename **hello** as if it were a Linux command. You only need to set the executable permission once. Once set, it remains set until you explicitly change it.

hello
```
echo "Hello, how are you"
```

```
$ chmod u+x hello
$ hello
Hello, how are you
$
```

An absolute reference will set read and write permission at the same time that it sets the execute permission. See Chapter 12 for a more detailed explanation of absolute and symbolic permission references. In brief, a 700 will set execute as well as read and write permission for the user; 500 will set only execute and read permission; 300 only execute and write permission; and 400 only execute permission. Users most often set 750 or 550. In the next example, the user sets the execute permission for both the user and the group using an absolute reference.

```
$ chmod 750 hello
$ hello
Hello, how are you
$
```

It is often helpful to include in a script file short explanations describing what the file's task is as well as describing the purpose of certain commands and variables. You can enter such explanations using comments. A *comment* is any line or part of a line preceded by a sharp (or hash) sign, #, with the exception of the first line. The end of the comment is the next newline character, the end of the line. Any characters entered on a line after a sharp sign will be ignored by the shell. The first line is reserved for identification of the shell, as noted in the following discussion. In the next example, a comment describing the name and function of the script is placed at the head of the file.

hello

```
# The hello script says hello
echo "Hello, how are you"
```

You may want to be able to execute a script that is written for one of the Linux shells while you are working in another. Suppose you are currently in the TCSH shell and want to execute a script you wrote in the BASH shell that contains BASH shell commands. First you would have to change to the BASH shell with the **sh** command, execute the script, and then change back to the TCSH shell. You can, however, automate this process by placing, as the first characters in your script, **#!**, followed by the pathname for the shell program on your system.

Your shell always examines the first character of a script to find out what type of script it is—a BASH, PDKSH, or TCSH shell script. If the first character is a space, the script is assumed to be either a BASH or PDKSH shell script. If there is a **#** alone, the script is a TCSH shell script. If, however, the **#** is followed by a **!** character, then your shell reads the pathname of a shell program that follows. A **#!** should always be followed by the pathname of a shell program identifying the type of shell the script works in. If you are currently in a different shell, that shell will read the pathname of the shell program, change to that shell, and execute your script. If you are in a different shell, the space or **#** alone is not enough to identify a BASH or TCSH shell script. Such identification works only in their own shells. To identify a script from a different shell, you need to include the **#!** characters followed by a pathname.

For example, if you put **#!/bin/sh** at the beginning of the first line of the **hello** script, you could execute it directly from the TCSH shell. The script will first change to the BASH shell, execute its commands, and then return to the TCSH shell (or whatever type of shell it was executed from). In the next example, the **hello** script includes the **#!/bin/sh** command. The user then executes the script while in the TCSH shell.

hello
```
#!/bin/sh
# The hello script says hello
echo "Hello, how are you"
```

```
> hello
Hello, how are you
```

Variables and Scripts

In the shell, you can create shell programs using variables and scripts. Within a shell program, you can define variables and assign values to them. Variables are used extensively in script input and output operations. The **read** command allows the user to interactively enter a value for a variable. Often **read** is combined with a prompt notifying the user when to enter a response. Another form of script input, called the Here document, allows you to use lines in a script as input to a command (discussed later). This overcomes the need to always read input from an outside source such as a file.

Definition and Evaluation of Variables: =, $, set, unset

A variable is defined in a shell when you first use the variable's name. A variable name may be any set of alphabetic characters, including the underscore. The name may also include a number, but the number cannot be the first character in the name. A name may not have any other type of character, such as an exclamation point, ampersand, or even a space. Such symbols are reserved by a shell for its own use. A name may not include more than one word, because a shell uses spaces to parse commands, delimiting command names and arguments.

You assign a value to a variable with the assignment operator. You type the variable name, the assignment operator, **=**, and then the value assigned. Note that you cannot place any spaces around the assignment operator. Any set of characters can be assigned to a variable. In the next example, the greeting variable is assigned the string "Hello".

```
$ greeting="Hello"
```

Once you have assigned a value to a variable, you can then use that variable to reference the value. Often you use the values of variables as arguments for a command. You can reference the value of a variable using the variable name preceded by the **$** operator. The dollar sign is a special operator that uses a variable name to reference a variable's value, in effect, evaluating the variable. Evaluation retrieves a variable's value—a set of characters. This set of characters then replaces the variable name on the command line. Thus, wherever a **$** is placed before the variable name, the variable name is replaced with the value of the variable.

In the next example, the shell variable greeting is evaluated and its contents, **"Hello"**, are then used as the argument for an **echo** command. The **echo** command simply echoes or prints a set of characters to the screen.

```
$ echo $greeting
Hello
```

Tip *You can obtain a list of all the defined variables with the **set** command. If you decide that you do not want a certain variable, you can remove it with the **unset** command.*

Variable Values: Strings

The values that you assign to variables may consist of any set of alphabetic and numeric characters. These characters may be a character string that you explicitly type in, or the result obtained from executing a Linux command. In most cases, you will need to quote your values using either single quotes, double quotes, backslashes, or back quotes. Single quotes, double quotes, and backslashes allow you to quote strings in different ways. Back quotes have the special function of executing a Linux command and using the results as arguments on the command line.

Although variable values can be made up of any characters, problems occur when you want to include characters that are also used by the shell as operators. Your shell has certain special characters that it uses in evaluating the command line. If you want to use any of these characters as part of the value of a variable, you must first quote them. Quoting a special character on a command line makes it just another character.

- A space is used to parse arguments on the command line.
- The asterisk, question mark, and brackets are special characters used to generate lists of filenames.
- The period (dot) represents the current directory.
- The dollar sign is used to evaluate variables, and the greater-than and less-than characters are redirection operators.
- The ampersand is used to execute background commands, and the vertical bar pipes execute output. Double and single quotes allow you to quote several

special characters at a time. Any special characters within double or single quotes are quoted. A backslash quotes a single character—the one that it precedes. If you want to assign more than one word to a variable, you need to quote the spaces separating the words. You can do so by enclosing the words within double quotes. You can think of this as creating a character string to be assigned to the variable. Of course, any other special characters enclosed within the double quotes will also be quoted.

The following examples show three ways of quoting strings. In the first example, the double quotes enclose words separated by spaces. Because the spaces are enclosed within double quotes, they are treated as characters, not as delimiters used to parse command line arguments. In the second example, single quotes also enclose a period, treating it as just a character. In the third example, an asterisk is also enclosed within the double quotes. The asterisk is considered just another character in the string and is not evaluated.

```
$ notice="The meeting will be tomorrow"
$ echo $notice
The meeting will be tomorrow

$ message='The project is on time.'
$ echo $message
The project is on time.

$ notice="You can get a list of files with ls *.c"
$ echo $notice
You can get a list of files with ls *.c
```

Double quotes, however, do not quote the dollar sign—the operator that evaluates variables. A **$** next to a variable name enclosed within double quotes will still be evaluated, replacing the variable name with its value. The value of the variable will then become part of the string, not the variable name. There may be times when you want a variable within quotes to be evaluated. In the next example, the double quotes are used so that the winner's name will be included in the notice.

```
$ winner=dylan
$ notice="The person who won is $winner"

$ echo $notice
The person who won is dylan
```

You can always quote any special character, including the **$** operator, by preceding it with a backslash. The backslash is useful when you want to evaluate variables within a string and also include **$** characters. In the next example, the backslash is placed before the dollar sign in order to treat it as a dollar sign character, **\$**. At the same time, the variable **$winner** is evaluated, since double quotes do not themselves quote the **$** operator.

```
$ winner=dylan
$ result="$winner won \$100.00""
$ echo $result
dylan won $100.00
```

Values from Linux Commands: Back Quotes

Though you can create variable values by typing in characters or character strings, you can also obtain values from other Linux commands. However, to assign the result of a Linux command to a variable, you first need to execute the command. If you place a Linux command within back quotes on the command line, that command is first executed and its result becomes an argument on the command line. In the case of assignments, the result of a command can be assigned to a variable by placing the command within back quotes to first execute it.

Think of back quotes as a kind of expression that contains both a command to be executed and its result, which is then assigned to the variable. The characters making up the command itself are not assigned.

In the next example, the command **ls *.c** is executed and its result is then assigned to the variable **listc**. The command **ls *.c** generates a list of all files with a .c extension, and this list of files will then be assigned to the **listc** variable.

```
$ listc=`ls *.c`
$ echo $listc
main.c prog.c lib.c
```

Script Input and Output: echo, read, and <<

Within a script, you can use the **echo** command to output data and the **read** command to read input into variables. Also within a script, the **echo** command will send data to the standard output. The data is in the form of a string of characters. As you have seen, the **echo** command can output variable values as well as string constants. The **read** command reads in a value for a variable. It is used to allow a user to interactively input a value for a variable. The **read** command literally reads the next line in the standard input. Everything in the standard input up to the newline character is read in and assigned to a variable. In shell programs, you can combine the **echo** command with the **read** command to prompt the user to enter a value and then read that value into a variable. In the **greetvar** script in the next example, the user is prompted to enter a value for the greeting variable. The **read** command then reads the value the user typed and assigns it to the greeting variable.

greetvar

```
echo Please enter a greeting:
read greeting
echo "The greeting you entered was $greeting"
```

```
$ greetvar
Please enter a greeting:
hi
The greeting you entered was hi
$
```

If the value of a variable is a special character and the variable's value is referenced with a **$**, then the special character will be evaluated by the shell. However, placing the evaluated variable within quotes prevents any evaluation of special characters such as **$**. In the **greetvar** script, **$greeting** was placed within a quoted string, preventing evaluation of any special characters. If **$greeting** is not quoted, then any special characters it contains will be evaluated.

The Here operation is a redirection operation, redirecting data within a shell script into a command. It is called Here because the redirected data is here in the shell script, not somewhere else in another file. The Here operation is represented by two less-than signs, **<<**. The **<<** operator can be thought of as a kind of redirection operator, redirecting lines in a shell script as input to a command. The **<<** operator is placed after the command to which input is being redirected. Lines following the **<<** operator are then taken as input to the command. The end of the input can be specified by an end-of-file character, **CTRL-D**. Instead of using an end-of-file character, you can specify your own delimiter. A word following the **<<** operator on the same line is taken to be the ending delimiter for the input lines. The delimiter can be any set of symbols. All lines up to the delimiter are read as input to the command.

In the next example, a message is sent to the user mark. The input for the message is obtained from a Here operation. The delimiter for the Here operation is the word **myend**.

mailmark

```
mail mark << myend
Did you remember the meeting
    robert
myend
```

Script Command Line Arguments

Like Linux commands, a shell script can take arguments. When you invoke a script, you can enter arguments on the command line after the script name. These arguments can then be referenced within the script using the **$** operator and the number of its position on the command line. Arguments on the command line are sequentially numbered from 1. The first argument is referenced with **$1**, the second argument with **$2**, and so on. The argument **$0** will contain the name of the shell script, the first word on the command line.

Note *These argument references can be thought of as referencing read-only variables. For those familiar with programming terminology, you can think of words on the command line as arguments that are passed into argument variables, $1 through $9.*

The argument variables are read-only variables. You cannot assign values to them. Once given the initial values, they cannot be altered. In this sense, argument variables function more as constants—constants determined by the command line arguments. Each word on the command line is parsed into an argument unless it is quoted. If you enter more than one argument, you can reference them with each corresponding argument number. In the next example, four arguments are entered on the command line.

greetargs

```
echo "The first argument is: $1"
echo "The second argument is: $2"
echo "The third argument is: $3"
echo "The fourth argument is: $4"
```

```
$ greetargs Hello Hi Salutations "How are you"
The first argument is: Hello
The second argument is: Hi
The third argument is: Salutations
The fourth argument is: How are you
$
```

A set of special arguments allows you to reference different aspects of command line arguments, such as the number of arguments or all the arguments together: **$***, **$@**, **$#**. The **$#** argument contains the number of arguments entered on the command line. This is useful when you need to specify a fixed number of arguments for a script. The argument **$*** references all the arguments in the command line. A command line may have more than nine arguments. The **$@** also references all the arguments on the command line but allows you to separately quote each one. The difference between **$*** and **$@** is not clear until you use them to reference arguments using the **for-in** control structure. For this reason, they are discussed only briefly here and more extensively in the section on control structures later in the chapter.

Export Variables and Script Shells

When you execute a script file, you initiate a new process that has its own shell. Within this shell you can define variables, execute Linux commands, and even execute other scripts. If you execute another script from within the script currently running, the current script suspends execution, and control is transferred to the other script. All the commands in this other script are first executed before returning to continue with the suspended script. The process of executing one script from another operates much like a function or procedure call in programming languages. You can think of a script calling another script. The calling script waits until the called script finishes execution before continuing with its next command.

Any variable definitions that you place in a script will be defined within the script's shell and only known within that script's shell. Variable definitions are local to their own shells. In a sense, the variable is hidden within its shell. Suppose, however, you want to be able to define a variable within a script and use it in any scripts it may call. You cannot do this directly, but you can export a variable definition from one shell to another using the **export** command. When the **export** command is applied to a variable, it will instruct the system to define a copy of that variable for each new subshell generated. Each new subshell will have its own copy of the exported variable. In the next example, the **myname** variable is defined and exported.

```
$ myname="Charles"
$ export myname
```

Note   *It is a mistake to think of exported variables as global variables. A shell can never reference a variable outside of itself. Instead, a copy of the variable with its value is generated for the new shell. An exported variable operates to some extent like a scoped global parameter. It is copied to any shell derived from its own shell. Any shell script called directly or indirectly after the exported variable's shell will be given a copy of the exported variable with the initial value.*

In the BASH shell, an environment variable can be thought of as a regular variable with added capabilities. To make an environment variable, you apply the **export** command to a variable you have already defined. The **export** command instructs the system to define a copy of that variable for each new subshell generated. Each new subshell will have its own copy of the environment variable. This process is called *exporting variables*.

In the next example, the variable **myfile** is defined in the **dispfile** script. It is then turned into an environment variable using the **export** command. The **myfile** variable will consequently be exported to any subshells, such as that generated when **printfile** is executed.

dispfile

```
myfile="List"
export myfile
echo "Displaying $myfile"
pr -t -n $myfile
printfile
```

printfile

```
echo "Printing $myfile"
lp $myfile &
```

```
$ dispfile
Displaying List
1 screen
2 modem
3 paper
Printing List
$
```

Arithmetic Shell Operations: let

The **let** command is the BASH shell command for performing operations on arithmetic values. With **let**, you can compare two values or perform arithmetic operations such as addition or multiplication on them. Such operations are used often in shell programs to manage control structures or perform necessary calculations. The **let** command can be indicated either with the keyword **let** or with a set of double parentheses. The syntax consists of the keyword **let** followed by two numeric values separated by an arithmetic or relational operator, as shown here:

```
$ let value1 operator value2
```

You can use as your operator any of those listed in Table 40-1. The **let** command automatically assumes that operators are arithmetic or relational. You do not have to quote shell-like operators. The **let** command also automatically evaluates any variables and converts their values to arithmetic values. This means that you can write your arithmetic operations as simple arithmetic expressions. In the next example, the **let** command multiplies the values 2 and 7. The result is output to the standard output and displayed.

Arithmetic Operators	Function
*	multiplication
/	division
+	addition
–	subtraction
%	modulo—results in the remainder of a division
Relational Operators	
>	greater-than
<	less-than
>=	greater-than-or-equal-to
<=	less-than-or-equal-to
=	equal in expr
==	equal in let
!=	not-equal
&	logical AND
|	logical OR
!	logical NOT

Table 40-1. *BASH Shell Operators*

```
$ let 2*7
14
```

If you want to have spaces between operands in the arithmetic expression, you must quote the expression. The **let** command expects one string.

```
$ let "2 * 7"
```

You can also include assignment operations in your **let** expression. In the next example, the result of the multiplication is assigned to **res**.

```
$ let "res = 2 * 7"
$ echo $res
```

14
$

You can also use any of the relational operators to perform comparisons between numeric values, such as checking to see whether one value is less than another. Relational operations are often used to manage control structures such as loops and conditions. In the next example, **helloprg** displays the word "hello" three times. It makes use of a **let** less-than-or-equal operation to manage the loop, **let "again <= 3 "**, and to increment the again variable, **let "again = again + 1"**. Notice that when **again** is incremented, it does not need to be evaluated. No preceding **$** is needed. The **let** command will automatically evaluate variables used in expressions.

<u>helloprg</u>

```
again=1
while let "again <= 3"
          do
          echo $again Hello
          let "again = again + 1"
          done
```

$ **helloprg**
1 Hello
2 Hello
3 Hello

Control Structures

You can control the execution of Linux commands in a shell program with control structures. Control structures allow you to repeat commands and to select certain commands over others. A control structure consists of two major components: a test and commands. If the test is successful, then the commands are executed. In this way, you can use control structures to make decisions as to whether commands should be executed.

There are two different kinds of control structures: *loops* and *conditions.* A loop repeats commands, whereas a condition executes a command when certain conditions are met. The BASH shell has three loop control structures: **while**, **for**, and **for-in**. There are two condition structures: **if** and **case**.

The **while** and **if** control structures are more for general purposes, such as performing iterations and making decisions using a variety of different tests. The **case** and **for** control structures are more specialized. The **case** structure is a restricted form of the **if** condition and is often used to implement menus. The **for** structure is a limited type of loop. It runs through a list of values, assigning a new value to a variable with each iteration.

The **if** and **while** control structures have as their test the execution of a Linux command. All Linux commands return an exit status after they have finished executing. If a command is successful, its exit status will be 0. If the command fails for any reason, its exit status will be a positive value referencing the type of failure that occurred. The **if** and **while** control structures check to see if the exit status of a Linux command is 0 or some other value. In the case of the **if** and **while** structures, if the exit status is a zero value, then the command was successful and the structure continues.

The test Command

Often you may need to perform a test that compares two values. Yet the test used in control structures is a Linux command, not a relational expression. There is, however, a Linux command called **test** that can perform such a comparison of values. The **test** command will compare two values and return as its exit status a 0 if the comparison is successful.

With the **test** command, you can compare integers, compare strings, and even perform logical operations. The command consists of the keyword **test** followed by the values being compared, separated by an option that specifies what kind of comparison is taking place. The option can be thought of as the operator, but is written, like other options, with a minus sign and letter codes. For example, **-eq** is the option that represents the equality comparison. However, there are two string operations that actually use an operator instead of an option. When you compare two strings for equality you use the equal sign, **=**. For inequality you use **!=**. Table 40-2 lists all the options and operators used by **test**. The syntax for the **test** command is shown here:

```
test value -option value
test string = string
```

In the next example, the user compares two integer values to see if they are equal. In this case, you need to use the equality option, **-eq**. The exit status of the **test** command is examined to find out the result of the test operation. The shell special variable **$?** holds the exit status of the most recently executed Linux command.

```
$ num=5
$ test $num -eq 10
$ echo $?
1
```

Instead of using the keyword **test** for the **test** command, you can use enclosing brackets. The command **test $greeting = "hi"** can be written as

```
$ [ $greeting = "hi" ]
```

Integer Comparisons	Function
`-gt`	Greater-than
`-lt`	Less-than
`-ge`	Greater-than-or-equal-to
`-le`	Less-than-or-equal-to
`-eq`	Equal
`-ne`	Not-equal
String Comparisons	
`-z`	Tests for empty string
`-n`	Tests for string value
`=`	Equal strings
`!=`	Not-equal strings
`str`	Tests to see if string is not a null string
Logical Operations	
`-a`	Logical AND
`-o`	Logical OR
`!`	Logical NOT
File Tests	
`-f`	File exists and is a regular file
`-s`	File is not empty
`-r`	File is readable
`-w`	File can be written to, modified
`-x`	File is executable
`-d`	Filename is a directory name
`-h`	Filename is a symbolic link
`-c`	Filename references a character device
`-b`	Filename references a block file

Table 40-2.   *BASH Shell Test Operators*

Similarly, the test command **test $num -eq 10** can be written as

```
$ [ $num -eq 10 ]
```

The brackets themselves must be surrounded by white space: a space, TAB, or newline. Without the spaces, it would be invalid.

The **test** command is used extensively as the Linux command in the test component of control structures. Be sure to keep in mind the different options used for strings and integers. Do not confuse string comparisons and integer comparisons. To compare two strings for equality, you use **=**; to compare two integers, you use the option **-eq**.

Conditions: if, if-else, elif, case

The BASH shell has a set of conditional control structures (see Table 40-3) that allow you to choose what Linux commands to execute. Many of these are similar to conditional control structures found in programming languages, but there are some differences.

Condition Control Structures: if, else, elif, case	Function
if *command* **then** *command* **fi**	**if** executes an action if its test command is true

if *command* **then**
    command
else
    command
fi
	if-else executes an action if the exit status of its test command is true; if false, then the **else** action is executed

if *command* **then**
    command
elif *command* **then**
    command
else
    command
fi
	elif allows you to nest **if** structures, enabling selection among several alternatives; at the first true **if** structure, its commands are executed and control leaves the entire **elif** structure

case *string* **in** *pattern* **)** *command***;;** **esac**	**case** matches the string value to any of several patterns; if a pattern is matched, its associated commands are executed

Table 40-3.   *BASH Shell Control Structures*

Condition Control Structures:
if, else, elif, case

Function

command **&&** *command*	The logical AND condition returns a true 0 value if both commands return a true 0 value; if one returns a non-zero value, then the AND condition is false and also returns a non-zero value
command **||** *command*	The logical OR condition returns a true 0 value if one or the other command returns a true 0 value; if both commands return a non-zero value, then the OR condition is false and also returns a non-zero value
! *command*	The logical NOT condition inverts the return value of the command

Loop Control Structures:
while, until, for, for-in, select

while *command* **do** *commands* **done**	**while** executes an action as long as its test command is true
until *command* **do** *commands* **done**	**until** executes an action as long as its test command is false
for *variable* **in** *list-values* **do** *commands* **done**	**for-in** is designed for use with lists of values; the variable operand is consecutively assigned the values in the list
for *variable* **do** *commands* **done**	**for** is designed for reference script arguments; the variable operand is consecutively assigned each argument value
select *string* **in** *item-list* **do** *commands* **done**	**select** creates a menu based on the items in the *item-list*; then it executes the command; the command is usually a **case**

Table 40-3. *BASH Shell Control Structures* (continued)

The **if** condition tests the success of a Linux command, not an expression. Furthermore, the end of an **if-then** command must be indicated with the keyword **fi**, and the end of a **case** command is indicated with the keyword **esac**.

if-then

The **if** structure places a condition on commands. That condition is the exit status of a specific Linux command. If a command is successful, returning an exit status of 0, then the commands within the **if** structure are executed. If the exit status is anything other than 0, then the command has failed and the commands within the **if** structure are not executed.

The **if** command begins with the keyword **if** and is followed by a Linux command whose exit condition will be evaluated. This command is always executed. After the command, the keyword **then** goes on a line by itself. Any set of commands may then follow. The keyword **fi** ends the command. Often, you need to choose between two alternatives based on whether or not a Linux command is successful. The **else** keyword allows an **if** structure to choose between two alternatives. If the Linux command is successful, then those commands following the **then** keyword are executed. If the Linux command fails, then those commands following the **else** keyword are executed. The syntax for the **if-then-else** command is shown here:

```
if Linux Command
    then
         Commands
    else
         Commands
fi
```

The **elsels** script in the next example executes the **ls** command to list files with two different possible options, either by size or with all file information. If the user enters an **s**, files are listed by size; otherwise, all file information is listed.

elsels

```
echo Enter s to list file sizes,
echo otherwise all file information is listed.
echo -n "Please enter option: "
read choice
if [ "$choice" = s ]
    then
      ls -s
    else
         ls -l
```

```
fi
echo Good-bye
```

```
$ elsels
Enter s to list file sizes,
otherwise all file information is listed.
Please enter option: s
total 2
     1 monday      2 today
$
```

The **elif** structure allows you to nest **if-then-else** operations. The **elif** structure stands for "else if." With **elif**, you can choose between several alternatives. The first alternative is specified with the **if** structure, followed by other alternatives, each specified by its own **elif** structure. The alternative to the last **elif** structure is specified with an **else**. If the test for the first **if** structure fails, control will be passed to the next **elif** structure, and its test will be executed. If it fails, control is passed to the next **elif** and its test checked. This continues until a test is true. Then that **elif** has its commands executed and control passes out of the **if** structure to the next command after the **fi** keyword.

The Logical Commands: && and ||

The logical commands perform logical operations on two Linux commands. The syntax is as follows:

```
command && command
command || command
```

In the case of the logical AND, **&&**, if both commands are successful, then the logical command is successful. For the logical OR, **||**, if either command is successful, then the OR is successful and returns an exit status of 0. The logical commands allow you to use logical operations as your test command in control structures.

case

The **case** structure chooses among several possible alternatives. The choice is made by comparing a value with several possible patterns. Each possible value is associated with a set of operations. If a match is found, the associated operations are performed. The **case** structure begins with the keyword **case**, an evaluation of a variable, and the keyword **in**. A set of patterns then follows. Each pattern is a regular expression terminated with a closing parenthesis. After the closing parenthesis, commands associated with this pattern are listed, followed by a double semicolon on a separate

line, designating the end of those commands. After all the listed patterns, the keyword
esac ends the **case** command. The syntax looks like this:

```
case string in
    pattern)
        commands
        ;;
    pattern)
        commands
        ;;
    *)
        default commands
        ;;
    esac
```

A pattern can include any shell special characters. The shell special characters are
the *****, **[]**, **?**, and **|**. You can specify a default pattern with a single ***** special character.
The ***** special character matches on any pattern and so performs as an effective default
option. If all other patterns do not match, the ***** will. In this way, the default option is
executed if no other options are chosen. The default is optional. You do not have to
put it in.

Loops: while, for-in, for

The BASH shell has a set of loop control structures that allow you to repeat Linux
commands. They are the **while**, **for-in**, and **for** structures. Like the BASH **if**
structure, **while** and **until** test the result of a Linux command. However, the **for**
and **for-in** structures do not perform any test. They simply progress through a list
of values, assigning each value in turn to a specified variable. Furthermore, the **while**
and **until** structures operate like corresponding structures found in programming
languages, whereas the **for** and **for-in** structures are very different. The loop control
structures are listed in Table 40-3.

while

The **while** loop repeats commands. A **while** loop begins with the keyword **while**
and is followed by a Linux command. The keyword **do** follows on the next line. The
end of the loop is specified by the keyword **done**. Here is the syntax for the **while**
command:

```
while Linux command
    do
        commands
    done
```

The Linux command used in **while** structures is often a test command indicated by enclosing brackets. In the **myname** script, in the next example, you are asked to enter a name. The name is then printed out. The loop is controlled by testing the value of the variable again using the bracket form of the **test** command.

myname

```
again=yes
while [ "$again" = yes ]
do
    echo -n "Please enter a name: "
    read name
    echo "The name you entered is $name"
    echo -n "Do you wish to continue? "
    read again
done
echo Good-bye
```

```
$ myname
Please enter a name: George
The name you entered is George
Do you wish to continue? yes
Please enter a name: Robert
The name you entered is Robert
Do you wish to continue? no
Good-bye
```

for-in

The **for-in** structure is designed to reference a list of values sequentially. It takes two operands—a variable and a list of values. The values in the list are assigned one by one to the variable in the **for-in** structure. Like the **while** command, the **for-in** structure is a loop. Each time through the loop, the next value in the list is assigned to the variable. When the end of the list is reached, the loop stops. Like the **while** loop, the body of a **for-in** loop begins with the keyword **do** and ends with the keyword **done**. The syntax for the **for-in** loop is shown here:

```
for variable in list of values
    do
    commands
    done
```

In the **mylistfor** script, the user simply outputs a list of each item with today's date. The list of items makes up the list of values read by the **for-in** loop. Each item is consecutively assigned to the grocery variable.

mylistfor

```
tdate=`date +%D`
for grocery in milk cookies apples cheese
do
    echo "$grocery
      $tdate"
done
```

```
$ mylistfor
milk        10/23/00
cookies     10/23/00
apples      10/23/00
cheese      10/23/00
$
```

The **for-in** loop is handy for managing files. You can use special characters to generate filenames for use as a list of values in the **for-in** loop. For example, the * special character, by itself, generates a list of all files and directories, and ***.c** lists files with the **.c** extension. The special character * placed in the **for-in** loop's value list will generate a list of values consisting of all the filenames in your current directory.

```
for myfiles in *
    do
```

The **cbackup** script makes a backup of each file and places it in a directory called **sourcebak**. Notice the use of the * special character to generate a list of all filenames with a **.c** extension.

cbackup

```
for backfile in *.c
do
    cp $backfile sourcebak/$backfile
    echo $backfile
done
```

```
$ cbackup
io.c
lib.c
main.c
$
```

for

The **for** structure without a specified list of values takes as its list of values the command line arguments. The arguments specified on the command line when the shell file is invoked become a list of values referenced by the **for** command. The variable used in the **for** command is set automatically to each argument value in sequence. The first time through the loop, the variable is set to the value of the first argument. The second time, it is set to the value of the second argument.

The **for** structure without a specified list is equivalent to the list **$@**. **$@** is a special argument variable whose value is the list of command line arguments. In the next example, a list of C program files is entered on the command line when the shell file **cbackuparg** is invoked. In **cbackuparg**, each argument is automatically referenced by a for loop, and **backfile** is the variable used in the for loop. The first time through the loop, **$backfile** holds the value of the first argument, **$1**. The second time through, it holds the value of the second argument, **$2**.

cbackuparg

```
for backfile
do
    cp $backfile sourcebak/$backfile
    echo "$backfile "
done
$ cbackuparg  main.c  lib.c  io.c

    main.c
    lib.c
    io.c
```

The Complete Reference

Chapter 41

Compilers, Libraries, and Programming Tools

An *application* is an executable program created by a programmer using one of several programming languages. Linux provides several utilities with which a programmer can control development of an application. Foremost among these is the **gcc** utility, which invokes the compiler for the C and C++ programming languages, generating an executable version of a program. Most Linux applications are written in the C or C++ programming language.

Application development often makes extensive use of libraries. You can create your own libraries or choose from specialized libraries. You can use libraries such as the X Windows library to program X Window displays, or the gdbm library, with which you can have database access to files. Libraries have become more flexible and can now be shared or loaded dynamically.

Other utilities allow you to better manage the development of your applications. The **gdb** symbolic debuggers help you to locate runtime errors. **indent** and **cproto** help you prepare your source code. Autoconf and RPM help you package your software for distribution. There are also compilers for all the major programming languages. There are compilers for Pascal, Lisp, Ada, Fortran, Basic, and Modula-2.

Getting Information: info

Though there are man pages for all the compilers and their tools, much more detailed information is available through the GNU info system. These are files located in the **/usr/info** directory that contain detailed descriptions and examples for various GNU tools. They are the equivalent of compact online manuals. There are info documents for the **gcc** compiler, the C and C++ libraries, and the Autoconf utility. Other applications may have their own local directories with info files such as the **/usr/TeX/info** directory that holds info files for LaTeX. You invoke the main menu of info documents by entering the command **info**.

```
$ info
```

You then use the SPACEBAR to page down the menu. When you find a topic you want, you press the **m** key. This opens up a line at the bottom of the screen where you can type in the name of the menu item. When you press ENTER, that document comes up. Pressing **b** pages you back to the beginning, and **U** puts you up to the previous menu. The command **info info** will bring up a tutorial on how to use **info**.

The C Compiler: gcc

There is a special relationship between the Unix operating system and the C programming language. The C programming language was developed specifically as a tool for programming the Unix operating system. The code for the Unix operating system is actually written in C. Linux has the same kind of special relationship. Most

Linux systems include the GNU version of the C compiler, **gcc**. The C programming language is a very complex language with many different features. This section briefly describes the basic components of the C programming language and uses them to construct a useful programming example. With an example program, we can then examine the different ways you can compile C programs.

You invoke the GNU C compiler on your Linux system with the **gcc** command. The **gcc** command, in turn, calls four other components. The first is the preprocessor. A C program contains special preprocessor commands that modify the code before it is sent to the compiler. The second component is the compiler itself. The compiler will process the code and generate an assembly code version of the program. The third component is the assembler. The assembler will use the assembly code version of the program to generate an object code version. The fourth component is the linker. The linker uses the program's object code to generate an executable file. The default name of this executable file is **a.out**. Normally, you should give the executable file a name of your own choosing. The **-o** option takes a filename as its argument. This filename will be the name of the executable file instead of the default, **a.out**. A list of **gcc** options is provided in Table 41-1. In the next example, the **gcc** command compiles the program **greet.c**. The user names the executable file "greet." The executable file is run by entering it at the Linux prompt as if it were a command.

```
$ gcc greet.c -o greet
$ greet
Hello, how are you
```

With multiple-file programs, you need to keep in mind the difference between the C compiler and the linker. The purpose of a C compiler is to generate object code, whereas the purpose of a linker is to build an executable file using object code files. The C compiler will individually compile each source code file, generating a separate object code file for each one. These object code files will have the extension **.o** instead of **.c**. You compile and link multiple file programs using the same **gcc** command. Simply list the source code filenames as arguments on the command line. In the next example, the user compiles the bookrecs program by invoking **gcc** with the source code files that make it up. The **-o** option specifies that the executable file will be called **bookrecs**.

```
$ gcc main.c io.c -o bookrecs
```

You can use the **gcc** utility to perform just a link operation by only listing object code files as its arguments. An object code file has an **.o** extension. In the next example, the user just performs a link operation. No compiling takes place. Of course, this operation assumes that the object code files have been previously generated.

```
$ gcc main.o io.o
```

Command	Description
gcc	The **gcc** utility creates an executable program using a preprocessor, a compiler, an assembler, and a linker. The preprocessor executes preprocessing commands found in the source code file. Such commands perform simple text substitutions. The compiler compiles a source code file into assembly code. The assembler then compiles assembly code files into object code files. The linker then links object code files into an executable file. **gcc** takes as possible arguments source code, object code, and assembly code files, as well as several options. **gcc** recognizes a file by its extension: .c C source code files .o Object code files .s Assembly code files .C C++ files .cpp C++ files

Option	Function
-S	Output only assembly code. Assembly code versions of compiled files have extension **.s**. The example will generate a file called **greet.s**.
-P	Output result of preprocessor.
-c	Create object code file only. Object code versions of compiled files have extension **.o**.
-g	Prepare compiled program for use with symbolic debugger.
-o *filename*	Name the executable file *filename*. Default is **a.out**.
-O	Optimize compilation.
-l*filename*	Link system library by name of filename. The filename is preceded by **lib** and has an extension of **.a**. Neither is included on the **gcc** command line. The **-l** options must always be placed after source code and object code filenames on the command line.
-I*dir*	Directories to be searched for files to include, such as header (**.h**) files.
-L*dir*	Directories to be searched for libraries.

Table 41-1. *The **gcc** Utility: The C Compiler*

As you develop and debug your program, you will be making changes to source code files and then recompiling your program to see how it runs. If you have a very large program made up of many source code files, it would be very inefficient to recompile all of them if you only made changes to just a few of them. Those to which you made no changes do not need to be recompiled, just linked. You can direct the **gcc** utility to do just that, by mixing source code files and object code files as arguments on the command line. Source code files have a **.c** extension, and object code files have a **.o** extension. **gcc** will compile the source code files you specified on the command line, but will only use the object code files with the linker. This has the advantage of being able to compile only those files in which changes have been made. If changes were made in **main.c**, but not in **io.c**, **io.c** would not have to be compiled. You would then specify the source code file **main.c** and the object code file **io.o** on the command line. In the next example, **io.o** will not be compiled, whereas **main.c** will be compiled.

```
$ gcc main.c io.o -o bookrecs
```

ELF and a.out Binary Formats

There are two possible formats for binary files such as executable programs. The first is the **a.out** format that is the original format used on Unix systems as well as early Linux systems. The term **a.out** comes from the default name given to an executable file by the Unix C compiler. As shared libraries came into use, difficulties arose with the **a.out** format. Adapting an **a.out** format for use as a shared library is a very complex operation. For this reason, a new format was introduced for Unix System 5 release 4 and for Solaris. It is called the Executable and Linking Format (ELF). Its design allowed for the easy implementation of shared libraries.

The ELF format has been adopted as the standard format for Linux systems. All binaries generated by the **gcc** compiler are in ELF format (even though the default name for the executable file is still **a.out**). Older programs that may still be in the **a.out** format will still run on a system supporting ELF.

C++ and Objective C: g++

The **gcc** utility is also a C++ compiler. It can read and compile any C++ program. However, it will not automatically link with the C++ Class library. You would have to invoke it on the command line. Alternatively, you can use the command **g++**, which invokes the **gcc** compiler with the C++ Class library.

C++ source code files have a different extension than regular C files. Several different extensions are recognized for C++: C, cc, cxx, or cpp. Other than this difference, you compile C++ programs just as you would C programs. Instead of **gcc**, it is preferable to use the **g++** command. The following example compiles a C++ program, **myprog.cpp**.

```
$ g++  myprog.cpp  -o myprog
```

The **gcc** compiler also supports Objective-C programs. Objective-C is an object-oriented version of C originally developed for NeXt systems. To compile a program in Objective-C, you use the **gcc** command with the **-lobjc** option, which links to the Objective-C library, **libobjc.so**.

Other Compilers: Pascal, Ada, Lisp, and Fortran

A great many programming languages are supported on your Linux system. Many are available on your OpenLinux CD-ROM. In addition to C and C++, you can compile Pascal, ADA, Lisp, Basic, and Fortran programs. In several cases, the compiling is handled by the **gcc** compiler, which is designed to recognize source code files for other programming languages. For example, G77 is the GNU Fortran compiler. This compiler is integrated with the **gcc** compiler. The command **g77** will compile a Fortran program by invoking the **gcc** compiler with options to recognize Fortran code, using the G77 features of **gcc**. The ADA 95 compiler is called **gnat**. The info file on ADA provides detailed information on **gnat**. You can compile an ADA program using the command **gnatmake** with the filename.

Creating and Using Libraries: Static, Shared, and Dynamic

There are usually functions used in a C program that rarely need to be compiled and are used repeatedly. There may also be functions that you may want to use in different programs. Often, such functions perform standardized tasks such as database input/output operations or screen manipulation. You can precompile such functions and place them together in a special type of object code file called a *library*. The functions in such a library file can be combined with a program by the linker. They save you the trouble of having to recompile these functions for each program you develop.

Different types of applications make use of specialized libraries that are placed in system directories and made available for use in developing programs. For example, there is a library, libdbm, that contains dbm functions for implementing database access to files. You can use these functions in your own programs by linking to that library. Mathematical applications would use the math library, libm, and X Window applications would use the Xlib library, libX11. All programs make use of the standard C library, libc, that contains functions to perform tasks such as memory management and I/O operations (a new version of the GNU libc library, 2.0, is now available). These libraries are placed within system directories such as **/usr/lib**, where they can be accessed by anyone on the system. You can also create your own library just for use with your own particular program, or make one that you would want to be accessed by others.

Libraries can be static, shared, or dynamic. A *static* library is one whose code is incorporated into the program when it is compiled. A *shared* library, however, has its code loaded for access whenever the program is run. When compiled, such a program simply notes the libraries it needs. Then, when the program is run, that library is loaded and the program can access its functions. A *dynamic* library is a variation on a shared library. Like a shared library, it can be loaded when the program is run. However, it does not actually load until instructions in the program tell it to. It can also be unloaded as the program runs, and another could be loaded in its place. Shared and dynamic libraries make for much smaller code. Instead of a program including the library as part of its executable file, it only needs a reference to it.

Most libraries currently developed are shared libraries. Shared libraries were made feasible by the implementation of the ELF binary format, though there is an older **a.out** format for shared (tagged) libraries. ELF is currently the standard format used for all binary files in Linux.

The GNU libraries are made available under a Library GNU Public License (LGPL). The conditions of this license differ from the standard GNU license in that you are free to charge for programs developed using these libraries. However, you do have to make available the source code for those libraries you used.

Libraries made available on your system reside in the **/usr/lib** and **/lib** directories. The names of these libraries always begin with the prefix **lib** followed by the library name and a suffix. The suffix differs, depending on whether it is a static or shared library. A shared library has the suffix **.so** followed by major and minor version numbers. A static library simply has an **.a** extension. A further distinction is made for shared libraries in the old **a.out** format. These have the extension **.sa**.

```
libname.so.major.minor
libname.a
```

The *name* can be any string, and it uniquely identifies a library. It can be a word, a few characters, or even a single letter. The name of the shared math library is **libm.so.5**, where the math library is uniquely identified by the letter **m** and the major version is 5. **libm.a** is the static math library. The name of the X Windows library is **libX11.so.6**, where the X Windows library is uniquely identified with the letters **X11** and its major version is 6.

You can link libraries to your programs using the **gcc** compiler. For example, the **libc.so.5 library** contains the standard I/O functions. This library is automatically searched and linked whenever the linker generates an executable file. The standard I/O library contains numerous functions that include input/output operations such as **printf**. There are other system libraries that you can access, such as the math library. Though the **libc.so.5** library is automatically linked, most other system libraries need to be explicitly referenced on the command line.

Most shared libraries are found in the **/usr/lib** and **/lib** directories. These will always be searched first. Some shared libraries are located in special directories of their own. A listing of these is placed in the **/etc/ld.conf** configuration file. These directories will also be searched for a given library. By default, Linux will first look for shared libraries, then static ones. Whenever a shared library is updated or a new one installed, you need to run the **ldconfig** command to update its entries in the **/etc/ld.conf** file, as well as links to it (if you install from an RPM package, this is usually done for you).

To reference a library file in one of these searchable directories when you invoke the **gcc** compiler, you use the **-l** option followed by the unique part of a system library's name: **-l**_name_. To instruct the linker to use the standard math library, you enter **-lm** on the **gcc** command line. **-l** will look first for a **lib**_name_**.so** file, in this case, **libm.so**. This is a link to the actual library file. In the next example, the **bookrecs** program is created and linked to the math library. Notice the **-lm** option.

```
$ gcc main.c io.c -o bookrecs -lm
```

Many different libraries are currently available for your use. One of the more popular is the **libncurses.a** library, which contains simple cursor movement routines. You would reference the **libncurses.so** library on the command line with **-lncurses**. In the next example, the user invokes both the math and curses libraries.

```
$ gcc main.c io.c -o bookrecs -lm -lncurses
```

To reference a library in another directory, you have to specify that directory using the **-L**_dir_ option. This options adds the specified directory to the list of directories that will be searched with the **-l** option. In the following example, the user links to a library in the **mydir** directory called **myio.so**. For a shared library, you will first have to have the dl and ld link names set up, such as libmyio.so and libmyio.so.1 for a **libmyio.so.1.0** file (see the next section).

```
gcc main.c -o bookrecs -Lmydir -lmyio
```

The gdb Symbolic Debugger

The gdb program is the symbolic debugger available on your Linux system. If you run your program and it crashes for some reason, you can use a symbolic debugger to track down the error. A symbolic debugger allows you to step through your program line by line, displaying the source code for each line as you execute it. You can decide to stop in specific functions and display the contents of active variables. You can even check specific addresses and the contents of the stack.

To be able to use an executable file with a symbolic debugger, you need to compile and link your program using the **-g** option. In the next example, a program is compiled and prepared for the symbolic debuggers. Once you have a prepared executable file, you can then use it with the symbolic debugger.

```
$ gcc -g main.c io.c
```

You invoke the gdb debugger with the keyword **gdb** and the name of the executable file. In the next example, the name of the executable file is **a.out**.

```
$ gdb a.out
```

The **gdb** command will place you in the debugger, replacing the Linux prompt (**$**), with the gdb prompt (**gdb**). You run your program in the debugger by typing at the prompt the command **run**:

```
(gdb) run
```

If your program has in it an **fopen** or **open** statement, it means it will be using a data file at some point in the program. If this is so, then gdb also needs to know the name of such a data file. When you type **run** in gdb to run your program, you must also supply the actual names of such data files.

```
(gdb) run filename
```

When you have finished, leave the debugger with the quit command, **q** or **quit**.

```
(gdb) quit
```

Most gdb commands have a single-letter equivalent consisting of the first letter of the command. Instead of entering the command **run**, you can enter just **r**. For **quit**, you can enter the letter **q**, for **print** just **p**, and for **next** the letter **n**. The gdb commands are listed in Table 41-2.

You display the contents of a variable using the **print** command. Enter the word **print** followed by the variable name. In the next example, the user displays the contents of the **count** variable.

```
(gdb) print count
10
```

PROGRAMMING

Running Programs in gdb

`r`	`run`	Run the program.
`q`	`quit`	Quit gdb.

Displaying Variables and Arguments

`p` *var*	`print` *var*	Display the contents of a variable.
`p` &*var*	`print` &*var*	Display the address of a variable.
`set` *var* = *value*		Assign a value to a variable during the gdb session.
`where`		Display a stack trace showing a sequence of function calls with function names and their arguments.
	`info locals`	Display defined variables and arguments.

Displaying Lines

`l` *linenum*	`list` *linenum*	Display lines beginning the specified line number.
`l` *func*	`list` *func*	Display lines in a function.
`l` *num,num*	`list` *num,num*	Display a range of lines.

Stepping and Continuing Execution

`n`	`next`	Single-step execution line by line, executing the current line and displaying the next line to be executed.
`s`	`step`	Single-step execution line by line, executing the current line and displaying the next line to be executed.
`c`	`cont`	Continue execution of the program.

Table 41-2.   *The **gdb** Symbolic Debugger*

Setting and Deleting Breakpoints

b	**break**	Set breakpoint at current line.
	break *line*	Set breakpoint at specified line.
	break *func*	Set breakpoint at first line in the specified function.
	info break	List all breakpoints.
d *num*	**delete** *num*	Delete breakpoints. You need to specify the number of the breakpoint.
	delete	Delete all breakpoints.

Table 41-2.   *The gdb Symbolic Debugger* (continued)

With the **where** command, you can display the function names and arguments of the functions that have been called at any point in your program. In the next example, the user is currently in the **calc** function. Entering the **where** command displays the functions **main**, as well as **calc** and its arguments.

```
(gdb) where
#3  calc(newcost = 2.0) at calc.c:25
#1  main () at main.c:19
#2  0x8000455 in ___crt_dummy__ ()
```

You can obtain a listing of all the variables and arguments defined in a function. The **info locals** command will display variable and argument values currently defined. In the next example, the user displays the defined variables.

```
(gdb) info locals
cost = 2
name = "Richard\000\000"
count = 10
count2 = 10
nameptr = 0x8000570 "petersen"
countptr = (int *) 0xbffffde8
```

You can set breakpoints in your program using the **break** command. When you reach a breakpoint, your program will stop. You can then step through your program line by line using the **next** or **step** command. When you wish, you can advance to the next breakpoint by using the **cont** command.

xxgdb

The xxgdb program provides an easy-to-use X Windows access to the gdb debugger. xxgdb is organized into a set of vertically positioned subwindows. Initially five subwindows are displayed. A top subwindow, called the file window, has the name of the file currently being displayed. The next subwindow displays the program's source code file and is called the source window. A scroll bar to the left allows you to scroll through the text. Below that is the message window for displaying gdb status and error messages. The bottom subwindow, called the dialog window, is used for entering gdb commands and displaying their results. A scroll bar to the left allows you to view previous commands and their results. Above the dialog window is the command window. This is a subwindow that lists a series of buttons for different gdb commands. To execute a command such as **run** or **step**, just click that button. You can horizontally change the size of any window using the small squares located to the right on the dividers between subwindows.

Programming Tools

Many tools are available to help you prepare and organize your source code. The **indent** utility will indent the braces used for blocks in a consistent format, making the code easier to read. **cproto** generates a list of function declarations for all your defined functions for use in header files. **f2c** and **p2c** can translate Fortran and Pascal programs into C programs. **xwpe** is an X Windows programming environment similar to Turbo C. Many more tools are available.

Once you have finished developing your software, you may then want to distribute it to others. Ordinarily, you would pack your program into a tar archive file. People would then download the file and unpack it. You would have to have included detailed instructions on how to install it, and where to place any supporting documentation and libraries. If you were distributing the source code, users would have to figure out how to adapt the source code to their systems. There are any number of variations that may stop compilation of a program.

The Red Hat Package Manager (RPM) and Autoconf are designed to automate these tasks. Autoconf is used to automatically configure source code to a given system. The Red Hat Package Manager will automatically install software on a system in the designated directories, along with any documentation, libraries, or support programs. Both have very complex and powerful capabilities, making them able to handle the most complex programs. Several Linux distributions like Red Hat and Caldera support RPM packages.

Development Tools

An application is an executable program created by a programmer using one of several programming languages. Linux provides several utilities with which a programmer can control development of an application. Foremost among these is the **make** utility. The **make** utility interfaces with the Linux operating system to provide an easy way to maintain and compile programs. The RCS utility allows you to better control program changes. It organizes changes into different versions that can be stored and later accessed. You can even use the **man** utility to create your own online documentation for your applications. All of these utilities are complex and powerful tools.

The Make Utility

You will often be working with a program that has many source code files. As you develop the program, making modifications, you will need to compile the program over and over again. However, you need only compile those source code files in which you made changes. The linker then links the newly generated object code files with previously compiled object code files, creating a new executable file. The fact that only a few of your source files are actually compiled drastically cuts down on the work of the compiler. Each time you need a new executable program, you do not need to recompile each source code file.

It can be very difficult in large programs with many source code files to keep track of which files have been changed and need to be compiled, and which files need only to be linked. The **make** utility will do this for you. **Make** was designed for a development environment in which different source code files in a program are constantly being modified. **Make** keeps track of which source files have been changed and which have not. It then recompiles only those that have been changed, linking them with the rest of the object code files to create a new executable file. In the next example, the user enters the command **make** on the command line to invoke the **make** utility. **Make** then compiles those files that have recently been modified and creates a new executable file. **make** displays each Linux command it executes.

```
$ make
gcc -c main.c
gcc -c io.c
gcc main.o io.o
```

To understand how the **make** utility works, you need to realize that it uses a source code file's time stamp to determine whether or not it should be compiled. Whenever a file is created, re-created, or modified in any way, a new time stamp is placed on it by the Linux operating system. If you create a file at 1:00, that file is stamped with the time 1:00. If you then change the file at 6:00, the file is restamped with the time 6:00. When you are compiling a program, only those source code files that have been changed need to be recompiled. Since a change in any file changes the time stamp, the time stamp can be used to determine which files need to be compiled. In this way, **make** knows which files need to be compiled and actually selects the files to be compiled for the programmer.

A dependency line specifies a dependency relationship between files. **make** operates in terms of dependencies. A source code file is used to create an object code file, which in turn is used to create a runnable program. The program can be said to be dependent on the object code file, which in turn is dependent on the source code file. You need to specify the dependency relationship between a source code file and an object code file in a dependency line. In another dependency line, you need to specify the dependency relationship between an executable file and all its object code files.

A dependency line can be thought of as a kind of conditional statement. The dependency relationship is its test condition. If an object code file depends on a source code file and the source code file has been recently modified, then the test condition is true and the file is then recompiled. However, the syntax for a dependency line is a bit more complex than a standard conditional statement. A dependency line consists of three components: a target file, a list of dependency files, and a Linux command. If any of the dependency files has been modified more recently than the target file, then the Linux command is executed. The target file and the dependent files are written on the same line, separated by a colon. You can either place the Linux command on the same line, separated from the dependent files by a semicolon, or you can place the Linux command on the next line preceded by a tab. You can list more than one Linux command if you wish. When entering Linux commands on the same line, you separate them with semicolons. Entered on a separate line, each Linux command has to be preceded by a tab. The dependency line ends with a following empty line. In these examples, the Linux command is an invocation of the **gcc** compiler, compiling a source code file or linking object code files. The syntax for a dependency line is as follows:

```
target file : dependent files ; Linux command
empty line

target file : dependent files
tab    Linux command
empty line
```

In the following **makefile**, we construct the dependency lines for a C program consisting of two source code files: **main.c** and **io.c**. In such a two-file program, there are really five files to manage. For each .c file, there is a corresponding .o file. There is the executable file, **a.out**. You need to set up your **makefile** with dependency lines to manage all of these files, specifying dependencies for each. An object code file (.o) is dependent on a source code file (.c). An executable file, **a.out**, is dependent on several object code files (.o). In this example, **a.out** is dependent on (made up of) the two object code files **main.o** and **io.o**. Each object code file is, in turn, dependent on their respective source code files—**main.o** on **main.c**, and **io.o** on **io.c**.

In the **makefile**, three dependency lines are needed for the **a.out**, **main.o**, and **io.o** files, respectively. Notice that the linking and compilation of the program are split up among the different dependency lines. The Linux command for the **a.out** target only links the two object code files, creating a new executable file. It invokes **gcc** with only object code files (**.o**), causing only the linker to be invoked. The Linux commands for the **main.o** and **io.o** targets only compile, creating **.o** object files. The **-c** option used with **gcc** means that no linking is done, only compilation, generating the object code file for this source code file.

makefile

```
a.out : main.o io.o
gcc main.o io.o

main.o : main.c
gcc -c main.c

io.o : io.c
gcc -c io.c
```

You can also create dependency lines for special operations such as printing files or installing an application. Many software packages that you create with **make** will also have an install target to install the application program on your system.

```
$ make install
```

The Revision Control System: RCS

When you work on a major project, you are continually changing source code. You may detect bugs, or you may add other features. Sometimes changes may unintentionally result in new bugs. A record of all the changes to your program may help you track down bugs and any possible design errors. The Revision Control System (RCS) is a Linux utility that keeps track of all changes that you have made to a program. In effect, RCS provides you with a set of prior versions for your program. You can view each version and examine the changes made for each.

RCS is very helpful in a situation in which a team of programmers is working on the same program. Each programmer may make changes to the program at different times. RCS can record each change a programmer makes and when it was made. It can even include notes about a change.

RCS stores an original version of a file and then records all changes to the file. Using this information, it can generate any one of several possible versions of a file. RCS does not actually store separate full versions of a file. Instead, it uses the change information and the original file to create a full version of the file. The commands that manage RCS files are listed in Table 41-3.

Command	Description
RCS	The Revision Control System (RCS) allows you to control the development of a program. With RCS, you can establish different versions of your program as you make changes. You can later retrieve different versions or obtain a record of how your program developed. An RCS file is created with the **ci** command and managed with the **rcs** command. Versions are retrieved with the **co** command, and versions are erased with the **rcs -o** command.
ci	The **ci** command updates an RCS file, creating new versions. If the RCS file does not already exist, **ci** will create it using the extension **,v**. You usually use **ci** to save an edited copy of a file that you previously retrieved using **co** with the **-l** option. Saving this edited copy will create a new version for the file within the RCS file. `$ ci main.c`

Table 41-3. *The RCS Utility*

Command	Description
	Options
ci	**-r**_version_ — This option will allow you to specify the release and version number you want to begin with when creating a new version. `$ ci -r5.2 main.c`
co	The **co** command retrieves a version of an RCS file. With no option, it retrieves a read-only version. If no version number is specified, then the most recent version is retrieved.
	Options
	-l — This option will retrieve an editable version of an RCS file, locking the file to prevent others from changing it. The file remains locked until you use **ci** to check it back in. `$ co -e main.c`
rcs	The **rcs** command manages RCS files and can be used to control access to an RCS file by other users.
	Options
	-a_user-name_ — This option will add _user-name_ to the list of users that can access a specified RCS file. `$ rcs -arobert main.c`

Table 41-3. *The RCS Utility* (continued)

Command	Description	
rcs	-euser-name	This option will remove *user-name* from the list of users that can access a specified RCS file. `$ rcs -erobert main.c`
	-lrelease	This option will lock a specific release for everyone but the creator of the file. `$ rcs -l2 main.c`
	-urelease	This option will unlock a specific release. `$ rcs -u2 main.c`
	-Lrelease	This option will lock a specific release for everyone, including the creator of the file. `$ rcs -L2 main.c`
	-Urelease	This option will unlock a specific release for everyone, including the creator of the file. `$ rcs -U2 main.c`
	-orelease	This option will delete a version from an RCS file. `$ rcs -o2.3 main.c`
rlog	The **rlog** command outputs information about the different releases and versions in a RCS file. Without an argument, it outputs summary information for each version.	

Table 41-3.   *The RCS Utility* (continued)

Command	Description	
	Options	
`rlog`	**-r***version*	This option will output information about a specific version. `$ rlog -r2 main.c`
	-d*date*	This option will output information about versions created on a specified date. The format for the date is year, month, day separated by slashes, and hour, minute, second separated by colons. All except the year are optional. `$ rlog -d93/04/12 main.c`
	-d<	Followed by a less-than sign, this option will output information that is earlier than a specified date. `$ rlog -d<93/04/12 main.c`
	-d<	Preceded by a greater-than sign, this option will output information that is later than a specified date. `$ rlog ->d93/04/12 main.c`

Table 41-3.   *The RCS Utility* (continued)

A set of recorded changes to a file is called a *version*. Each version is assigned a version number that has several components, the first two of which are the release and level numbers. By default, the first version is assigned a release number of 1 and a level number of 1. A version is often referred to by its release and level numbers. The first version is called version 1.1 or delta 1.1. Subsequent versions will have the same release number with an incremented level number. The next version will be 1.2, then 1.3, and so on. You can also change the release number manually.

To create an RCS file, you first create an RCS directory. Within this directory are placed the RCS files for your programs. You can then create an RCS file with the **ci** command. The **ci** command (which stands for check in) takes one argument, the name of the original file. The RCS file will be created in the RCS directory with the extension **,v**. A **main.c** file will have an RCS file called **main.c,v** in the RCS directory. If your program is initially made up of several source code files, you need to create an RCS file for each one, including its source code suffix. In the next example, the user creates an RCS file for the **main.c** program.

```
$ ci main.c
RCS/main.c,v    main.c
enter description, terminated with single '.' or end of file:
NOTE: This is NOT the log message!
>> Bookrecs main program
>> .
initial revision: 1.1
done
```

To edit your source code file using RCS, you must first have RCS generate a copy of the source code file. This copy will have the same name as RCS file, but without the **,v** suffix. For the **main.c,v** file, RCS will generate a file called **main.c**. To save the copy once you have made changes, you simply register any changes you make to the RCS file.

The RCS **co** command (which stands for check out) generates a copy of the source code file. The **co** command has several options. The **co** command with no options simply generates a read-only copy of the source code file. The **-l** option generates a copy of the source code file that you can edit; **-l** stands for lock, and when you use this option, the **main.c** program in the RCS **main.c,v** file is locked. The locking mechanism used by RCS permits only one programmer at a time to change a given file. When you have finished your modifications, you "check in" the program code, registering your changes and unlocking it for use by others. In the next example, the **co** command generates an editable copy of the source code file **main.c,v**.

```
$ co -l main.c
RCS/main.c,v   -->   main.c
revision 1.1 (locked)
done
```

Once you have finished editing your source code file, you then register your changes in the RCS file with the **ci** command. You enter the keyword **ci** followed by the name of the RCS file. You are then prompted to enter comments. In effect, editing a copy of the file generated with **co** creates a new version of the source code file, a new set of changes constituting a new version. The new version number (1.2) is displayed. In the next example, the user saves the changes to **main.c** by generating a new version, 1.2.

```
$ ci main.c
RCS/main.c,v   main.c
new revision: 1.2; previous revision: 1.1
enter log message, terminated with single '.' or end of file:
>> Added prompts
>> .
done
```

The Concurrent Versions System: CVS

The Concurrent Versions Systems (CVS) has become a popular alternative to RCS, primarily because it is easy to use for program development over the Internet. CVS allows several developers to work on a file at the same time. This means that CVS supports parallel development, where programmers around the world can work on the same task at the same time. Developed originally as a front end to RCS, CVS shares many of the same commands (see Table 41-5). You can find out more about CVS from **www.cvshome.org**.

CVS is structured along the same lines as RCS, using check-in and check-out procedures for projects. To use CVS, you first create a directory to hold your project files, and then use the import option to install your project files there. In the following example, the **/home/projects** directory is designated as the CVS repository directory. You use the command **cvs** with the **-d** option and the name of the directory along with the **init** option.

```
$ cvs -d /home/projects init
```

You can set the CVSROOT shell variable to the path of the repository directory and then export the variable. The **cvs** command, whenever executed, will automatically check this variable for the location of the repository.

```
CVSROOT=/home/projects
export CVSROOT
```

PROGRAMMING

Commands	Description
`commit,ci`	The **commit** command updates a CVS file, creating new versions.

Options

*-**r**version*	This option will allow you to specify the release and version number you want to begin with when creating a new version.

Commands	Description
`checkout,co`	The **checkout** command retrieves a version of a CVS file.

Options

*-**D**date*	Check out revisions for a specific date.
*-**d**dir*	Check out to a specified directory.

Commands	Description
`import`	Import files to CVS repository.
`login`	Log into a remote CVS repository.
`logout`	Log out from a remote CVS repository.
`rdiff`	Show the differences between releases.
`remove`	Remove an entry from a repository.
`update, up`	Update from a repository.
`init`	Create a CVS repository.
`admin`	Administer files in the repository.

Options

*-**l**release*	Lock a revision.
*-**u**release*	Unlock a revision.
*-**o**release*	Delete revision from the repository.

Table 41-4.   *CVS Commands and Options*

To install files in the repository directory, you use the **import** option. You can install them to a subdirectory in the repository. A CVS repository can support multiple projects, each in its own subdirectory. You will also need to provide arguments specifying the supplier and the release. The following example will import all the files in the current working directory to the **myproject** directory in the CVS repository (**/home/projects/myproject**). The supplier is **richp**, and the release is the first release, as indicated by the **start** argument. If the current directory holds the file **main.c**, then the **main.c** file will be installed in the **/home/projects/myproject** directory, along with any other files in the current directory.

```
$ cvs import myproject richp start
```

To work on a file, you must first retrieve it from the repository using the check-out option, **co**. You work on it in your local directory. When you are ready to check the file back into the repository, you use the **commit** option. The following example will extract the **main.c** file from the CVS repository.

```
$ cvs co myproject/main.c
```

In the current directory, you can then edit and change **main.c**. To check it back into the CVS repository, you would use the following command.

```
$ cvs commit
```

To see my changes, you can use the **diff** option. The **rdiff** option lets me see any changes to the entire release.

```
$ cvs diff
```

As you work on a project with numerous files, you can use the update option, **up**, to check out just the ones you need.

```
$ cvs up myproject/main.c
```

To access a repository on the Internet, you simply specify as the repository root the Internet site and the remote directory for that repository. You can do this by assigning the repository to the CVSROOT shell variable. The format for specifying the remote repository is as follows:

```
:method:user@hostname:/path/to/repository
```

The following example assigns the repository for KDE to the CVSROOT variable.

```
export CVSROOT=:pserver:anonymous@anoncvs.kde.org:/home/kde
```

To access the remote repository, you first log in with the login option.

```
$ cvs login
```

Then you use the standard check-out and commit options to check out and check in projects. When doing so, you may want to use the compression options such as **-z4** to speed transmission time.

If you want to set up a repository on your own system that is accessible over the Internet, you need to install and configure the CVS server.

Online Manuals for Applications: man

As you develop a program for use on Linux, you may need to document it. If it is a large application worked on by several programmers at once, documentation may become essential. Documentation often takes the form of a manual describing different commands and features of a program. Many times an application is broken down into separate programs. It is very helpful to both users and program developers to be able to retrieve and display appropriate sections of an application's manual. Such an online manual provides instant access to documentation by all users and developers. The **man** command provides access to an online manual for Linux commands. You can also use the **man** command to manage your own online manual for your own applications. You can create **man** documents using special **man** text processing macros. You can then instruct the **man** command to read these documents.

One of the more common uses today of gnroff is the creation of online manual documents. The online manual that you find on your Linux system is actually a gnroff document. You use a set of macros called the man macros to create your own online manual entries. If you create a new command and want to document it, you can create a manual document for it and read this document with the **man** command.

When you call the **man** command with the name of a document, the **man** command uses gnroff to format the document and then display it. The actual document that you create is an unformatted text file with the appropriate man macros. The man macros, which are very similar to the ms macros, are described in the next section. You can actually format and display a manual document directly by using the **gnroff** command with the **-man** option. In the next example, both commands display the manual document for the **ls** command.

```
$ man ls
$ gnroff -man /usr/man/man1/ls | more
```

Man Document Files

You can create a **man** document file using any standard text editor. The name that you give to the text file is the name of the command or topic it is about with a section number as an extension. The name of a document about the **who** command would be called **who.1**. In the example described here, the document is about the **bookrec** command and has a section number **1**. Its name is **bookrec.1**. Section numbers are discussed in the next section on **man** directories.

A man document is organized into sections with a running title at the top. The sections may be named anything you wish. By convention, a man document for Linux commands is organized into several predetermined sections such as NAME, SYNOPSIS, and DESCRIPTION. You are, however, free to have as many sections as you want and to give them names of your own choosing. The actual document that you create is an unformatted text file with the appropriate **man** macros. A manual document requires at least two different **man** macros: **TH** and **SH**. **TH** provides a running title that will be displayed at the top of each page displayed for the document, as well as the document's section number. You use the **SH** macro for each section heading. You can add other macros as you need them, such as a **PP** macro for paragraph formatting or an IP macro for indented paragraphs. The man macros are listed in Table 41-5.

You enter a macro in your document at the beginning of a line and preceded by a period. Any text that you enter in the lines after the macro will be formatted by it. A macro stays in effect until another macro is reached. Some macros, like **SH** and **TH**, take arguments. You enter in arguments after the macro on the same line. The **SH** macro takes as its argument the name of a section. You enter the section name on the same line as the **SH** macro. The body of the section then follows. The body of the section text is entered in as a series of short lines. These lines will later be formatted by **man** into a justified paragraph. In the next example, the user enters in the **SH** macro and follows it with the section name DESCRIPTION. In the following lines, the user enters in the text of the section.

```
.SH DESCRIPTION
.I  bookrec
 allows the user to input a title and price
for a book.  Then both elements
of the record are displayed
```

Your man document is organized into a series of section heading macros with their names and text. The following template below gives you an idea of how to organize your man document. It is the organization usually followed by the online manual for Linux commands.

```
.TH COMMAND    Section -number

.SH NAME
```

```
command and brief description of function
.SH SYNOPSIS
command and options.  Each option is encase in brackets.  This section is
sometimes called the SYNTAX.
.SH DESCRIPTION
 Detailed description of command and options.  Use paragraph macros for new
paragraphs: PP, LP, and IP
.SH OPTIONS
 .Options used for the command
.SH EXAMPLES
 .Examples of how a command is used
.SH FILE
 .File uses by the command
.SH "SEE ALSO"
 References to other documentation or manual documents
.SH DIAGNOSTICS
 Description of any unusual output.
.SH WARNINGS
 Warning about possible dangerous uses of the command
.SH BUGS
 Surprising features and bugs.
```

Within the text of a section, you can add other macros to perform specific text processing operations. You enter in these macros on a line by themselves. Some will also take arguments. The **.PP** macro starts a new paragraph. The **.IP** macro starts an indented paragraph and is usually used to display options. You enter in the option as an argument to the **.IP** macro, and then the following text is indented from it. The **.I** macro underlines text. The **.B** macro will boldface text. Both the **.B** macro and **.I** macro take as their argument the word you want to boldface or underline. By convention, the command name and options in the NAME section are set in boldface with the **.B** macro. Any other use of command names is usually underlined with the **.I** macro. If you use any hyphens, you need to quote them with a backslash.

In the next example, the user creates an online document for the bookrec program described earlier. Notice how the text is formatted into justified paragraphs. The options are displayed using indented paragraphs specified by the **.IP** macro.

bookrec.1—man document file man output

```
.TH    BOOKREC    1
.SH NAME
bookrec  \-Input and display a book record
.SH SYNOPSIS
.B bookrec
```

```
[ \-t ] [ \-p] [ \-f]
.SH DESCRIPTION
.I  bookrec
 allows the user to input a title and price
for a book.  Then both elements
of the record are displayed
.SH  OPTIONS
.IP t
Display only the title
.IP p
Display only the price.
.IP f
Save the record to a file
.SH FILES
  The command uses no special files.
.SH "SEE ALSO"
    printbook (1)
.SH DIAGNOSTICS
 Date output has the form of m/d/y.
.SH BUGS
 The program can only read and display one record.
.br
 It does not as yet allow you to read records from a file.
```

The **man** utility looks for a particular manual document in a system directory set aside for manual documents such as **/usr/man**. The **/usr/man** directory itself does not contain manual documents. Rather, it contain subdirectories called section directories, which in turn contain the documents. The name of a section directory begins with the word **man** and ends with the section number. **man1** is the name of the first section directory in a manual. There are usually about seven section directories, beginning with **man1** and ending with **man7**. In your own manual directory, you can have as many or as few section directories as you want, though you always have to have a **man1** directory.

Section directories allow you to create several documents of varying complexity and subject matter for the same command or topic. For example, the document in section 1 for the **man** command gives only a general description, whereas the document in section 7 for the **man** command lists all the man macros. These documents are identified by section numbers and reside in the appropriate section directory. The section number of a document, as noted previously, is entered as an argument to the **.TH** macro. To retrieve an online document from a particular section, enter the section number before the command name. The next example displays the document on the **bookrec** command that is in the third section directory. If you enter no section number, the first section is assumed.

```
$ man 3 bookrec
```

Command and Options	Description
man	The manual command can search and display online manual documents. You can create your own online manual documents and instruct **man** to search for them. The **man** command searches for documents in section directories specified by the word man followed by a section number, man1. When you create your own manual directories, be sure to include section directories.
man *command-name*	Search for and display online manual documents. `man who`
MANPATH	Shell special variable that holds the directory path name the **man** command automatically searches. You can add new path names with an assignment operation. `$ MANPATH=$MANPATH:/$HOME/man`
Options	
num	Search only specified section for a manual document. `$ man 3 bookrec`
-M *directory-name*	Search only specified directory for manual documents. `$ man -M $HOME/man bookrec`
The man Macros	
.TH *title sec-num*	Used to enter running title of the online document.
.SH *section-name*	Used to enter section headings.
.B *word*	Used to boldface words such as command names.
.I *word*	Used to underline words.
.IP *option*	Format indented paragraph. Used to enter options in the OPTIONS section.
.PP	Format paragraph. Starts a new paragraph.

Table 41-5.   **man** *Command and Macros for Creating Online Documents*

The Complete Reference

Linux

Chapter 42

Perl

The Practical Extraction and Report Language (Perl) is a scripting language originally designed to operate on files, generating reports and handling very large files. Perl was designed as a core program to which features could be easily added. Over the years, Perl's capabilities have been greatly enhanced. It can now control network connections, process interaction, and even support a variety of database management files. At the same time, Perl remains completely portable. A Perl script will run on any Linux system, as well as most other operating systems such as Unix, Windows, and Mac. Perl is also used extensively for implementing CGI scripts on Web sites. There are extensive and detailed man pages on Perl, discussing all aspects of the language with a great many examples. The man pages begin with the term **perl**; for example, **perlfunc** discusses the built-in Perl functions and **perlsyn** describes the different control structures. You can also use the **www.perl.com** site to access and search documentation including the reference manual, the online man pages, and FAQs.

There are extensive Internet resources for Perl. On the Perl Web site at **www.perl.com**, you can access documentation, software, newsgroups, and support. The site has programming and reference sections where you can access detailed FAQs on topics such as CGI, modules, and security. You can also access software archives and more detailed documentation.

Specialized Perl Web sites focus on programming, conferences, and reference resources. The Comprehensive Perl Archive Network (CPAN) maintains FTP sites that hold an extensive collection of utilities, modules, documentation, and current Perl distributions. You can also link to a CPAN site through the Perl Web sites. Several of the Perl Web sites are listed here:

- www.perl.com
- www.perlmongers.org
- www.perl.org
- republic.perl.com
- www.perlreference.net
- www.perl.com/CPAN/CPAN.html

The Perl advocacy group known as the perlmongers can be located at **www.perl.org** or **www.perlmongers.org**. The **republic.perl.com** site lets you join the Programming Republic of Perl. There are also several Usenet newsgroups that discuss different Perl issues. You can use them to post questions and check out current issues. Here is a listing of the current newsgroups:

- comp.lang.perl.announce
- comp.lang.perl.misc
- comp.lang.perl.modules
- comp.lang.perl.tk

Perl Command Line Operations

You can execute any Perl command from the shell command line by using the command **perl** with the **-e** option. The Perl command you want to execute should then be entered and quoted within single quotes. The following Perl operation prints the string "hello" using the Perl **print** command. The command ends with a semicolon.

```
perl -e  'print "hello";'
```

You can use Perl this way for simple operations, much as you would use single-line **gawk** commands. Perl will not read input from the standard input unless you explicitly instruct it to with a **while** loop. Unlike **gawk**, it does not read the standard input by default. The following example searches for the pattern "Dickens." The file **books** is first read by the **cat** command and piped to the **perl** command as standard input.

```
cat books | perl -e 'while(<STDIN>){ if(/Dickens/){ print; }}'
```

Note   *This command line use of Perl is rarely used. Normally, Perl commands are placed in script files that are then executed, much like shell scripts.*

Perl Scripts

Usually, Perl commands are placed in a file that is then read and executed by the **perl** command. In effect, you are creating a shell in which your Perl commands are executed. Files containing Perl commands must have the extension **.pl**. This identifies a file as Perl script that can be read by the **perl** command. There are two ways that you can use the **perl** command to read Perl scripts. You can enter the **perl** command on the shell command line, followed by the name of the Perl script. Perl will read and execute the commands. The following example executes a Perl script called **hello.pl**:

```
$ perl hello.pl
```

You can also include the invocation of the **perl** command within the Perl script file, much as you would for a shell script. This automatically invokes the Perl shell and will execute the following Perl commands in the script. The path **/usr/bin/perl** is the location of the **perl** command on the OpenLinux system. On other systems, it could be located in **/usr/local/bin** directory. The command **which perl** will return the location of Perl on your system. Place the following shell instruction on the first line of your file.

```
#!/usr/bin/perl
```

Then, to make the script executable, you would have to set its permissions to be executable. The **chmod** command with the **755** option sets executable permissions for a file, turning it into a program that can be run on the command line. You only have to do this once per script. You do not have to do this if you use the **perl** command on the command line, as noted previously. The following example sets the executable permissions for the **hello.pl** script.

```
$ chmod 755 hello.pl
```

As in C, Perl commands end with a semicolon. There is a **print** command for outputting text. Perl also uses the same escape sequence character to output newlines, **\n**, and tabs, **\t** (see Table 42-1). Comments are lines that begin with a **#**. The following is an example of a Perl script. It prints out the word "hello" and a newline. Notice the invocation of the **perl** command on the first line:

Escape Character	Description
\a	Bell
\b	Backspace
\cC	Control character C. \cD is CTRL-D
\f	Form feed
\e	Escape character
\n	Newline
\r	Return
\t	Tab
\\	Backslash
\"	Quotes
\uC	Makes C uppercase
\lC	Make C lowercase
\Ltext\E	Makes all characters in text within the \L and \E pair lowercase
\Utext\E	Makes all characters in text within the \L and \E pair uppercase

Table 42-1.   *Perl Escape Characters*

helloprg

```
#!/usr/bin/perl

print "hello \n";
$ helloprg
hello
```

Though Perl is an interpreted language, the entire Perl script is first validated before it is executed, checking for errors ahead of time. Should there be any, they will be displayed on your screen, specifying line numbers and error messages. Many of the error messages can be obscure. The following are some of the more common errors.

- One of the more common errors is failing to enter semicolons at the end of a line. Perl commands look a lot like shell commands, which do not take semicolons, so it is easy to forget them.

- Control structures must have blocks; they cannot have just a single command, as is the case in C. A block is a set of commands encased in braces, **{ }**.

- Variables must always be prefixed with a **$** symbol. This is very different from **gawk** and C.

Perl Modules

Parts of a Perl program can be split into separate files and then read into a main file with the **use** command. Such files end with the extension **.pm** and are referred to as either *packages* or *modules*. Often, they contain enhanced operations for tasks such as file handling or text searches. A standard set of Perl modules and packages is located in the **/usr/lib/perl5** directory. The **perlmod** man page has a detailed discussion of Perl packages and modules, including dynamically loaded modules. The following command reads in the **find.pm** module that provides a Perl version of the shell **find** command for searching directories:

```
use /usr/lib/perl5/File/find.pm ;
```

An extensive number of Perl modules have been written for various tasks such as network management, Web server support, and database interfacing. You can locate these at the Comprehensive Perl Archive Network (CPAN) sites at **www.perl.com/CPAN/modules**.

To use a module in your Perl script, enter the **use** command followed by the module name. The module entry will consist of the module's category, two colons, and the module's specific name. So the module for the cryptographic cipher Blowfish will be Crypt::Blowfish. In fact, the entry specifies a directory where the module is located, in this case Crypt, followed by the module name, Blowfish.pm. To use this module in your script, you would use the following command.

```
use Crypt::Blowfish
```

You can download modules in source code format. If you download the source code, you will have to compile it and then install it. You can also use the CPAN script installed with Perl to automatically access CPAN and select, download, and install a Perl module onto your system. Just enter the following command.

```
perl -MCPAN -e shell
```

Perl comes with a standard set of modules already installed. These make up the perlmodlib package. Check the documentation on **perlmodlib** for a listing of these modules or the module list at **www.perl.com/CPAN/modules**.

Perl Input and Output:<> and print

A Perl script can accept input from many different sources. It can read input from different files, from the standard input, and even from pipes. Because of this, you have to identify the source of your input within the program. This means that, unlike with **gawk** but like with a shell program, you have to explicitly instruct a Perl script to read input. A particular source of input is identified by a file handle, a name used by programs to reference an input source such as a particular file. Perl already sets up file handles for the standard input and the standard output, as well as the standard error. The file handle for the standard input is **STDIN**.

The same situation applies to output. Perl can output to many different destinations, whether they be files, pipes, or the standard output. File handles are used to identify files and pipes when used for either input or output. The file handle **STDOUT** identifies the standard output, and **STDERR** is the file handle for the standard error. We shall first examine how Perl uses the standard input and output, and later discuss how particular files are operated on.

Perl can read input from the standard input or from any specified file. The command for reading input consists of the less-than (<) and greater-than (>) symbols. To read from a file, a file handle name is placed between them, **<MYFILE>**. To read from the standard input, you can simply use the STDIN file handle, **<STDIN>**, which is similar to the **read** command in the BASH shell programming language.

```
<STDIN>
```

To use the input that **<STDIN>** command reads, you assign it to a variable. You can use a variable you define or a default variable called **$_**, as shown in the next example. **$_** is the default for many commands. If the print command has no argument, it will print the value of **$_**. If the **chomp** command has no argument, it operates on **$_**, cutting off the newline. The *myread* script that follows illustrates the use of **$_** with the standard input.

<u>myread</u>

```
#!/usr/bin/perl
# Program to read input from the keyboard and then display it.

$_ = <STDIN>;                          #Read data from the standard input
print "This is what I entered: $_"; #Output read data as part of a string
$ myread
larisa and aleina
This is what I entered: larisa and aleina
```

You can use the **print** command to write data to any file or to the standard output. File handle names are placed after the **print** command and before any data such as strings or variables. If no file handle is specified, then **print** outputs to the standard output. The following examples both write the "hello" string to the standard output. The explicit file handle for the standard output is **STDOUT**. If you do not specify an argument, then **print** will output whatever was read from the standard input.

```
print STDOUT "hello";
print "hello";
```

> **Tip** *A null file handle, <>, is a special input operation that will read input from a file listed on the command line when the Perl script is invoked. Perl will automatically set up a file handle for it and read. If you list several files on the command line, then Perl will read the contents of all of them using the null file handle. You can think of this as a cat operation in which the contents of the listed files are concatenated and then read in to the Perl script.*

PROGRAMMING

Perl File Handles

You use the **open** command to create a file handle for a file or pipe. The **open** command takes two arguments, the name of the file handle and the filename string. The name of the file handle is a name you make up. By convention, it is uppercase. The filename string can be the name of the file or a variable that holds the name of the file. This string can also include different modes for opening a file. By default, a file is opened for reading. But you can also open a file for writing, or for appending, or for both reading a writing. The syntax for **open** follows:

```
open (file-handle, filename-string);
```

In the next example, the user opens the file reports, calling the file handle for it **REPS**:

```
open (REPS, "reports");
```

Often the filename will be held in a variable. You then use the **$** with the variable name to reference the filename. In this example, the filename **"reports"** is held in the variable **filen**:

```
filen = "reports";
open (REPS, $filen );
```

To open a file in a specific mode such as writing or appending, you include the appropriate mode symbols in the filename string before the filename, separated by a space. The different mode symbols are listed in Table 42-2. The symbol **>** opens a file

Perl Command Line Options	
-e	Enter one line of a Perl program.
-n	Read from files listed on the command line.
-p	Output to standard output any data read.
Perl File Commands	
open (*file-handle,* *permission-with-filename*)	Open a file.
close (*file-handle*)	Close a file.
< *filename>*	Read from a file.
<STDIN>	Read from the standard input.
<>	Read from files whose filenames are provided in the argument list when the program was invoked.
print <file-*handle> text***;**	Write to a file. If no file handle is specified, write to standard output. If no text is specified, write contents of **$_**.
printf < handle> " *Format-str* ", *values* **;**	Write formatted string to a file. Use conversion specifiers to format values. If no file handle is specified, write to standard output. If no values are specified, use contents of **$_**.
sprintf *str-var* " *Format-str* ", *values* **;**	Write formatted values to a string. Use conversion specifiers to format values. If no values are specified, use contents of **$_**.

Table 42-2.   *Perl File Operations and Command Line Options*

Permissions for Opening Files

< filename	Read-only
> filename	Write-only
+> *filename*	Read and write
>> *filename*	Append (Written data is added to the end of the file.)
command **|**	An input pipe, reading data from a pipe
| *command*	An output pipe, sending data out through this pipe

Table 42-2.   *Perl File Operations and Command Line Options* (continued)

PROGRAMMING

for writing, and **+>** opens a file for both reading and writing. In the next example, the reports file is opened for both reading and writing.

```
open (REPS, "+> reports");
```

If you are using a variable to hold the filename, you can include the evaluated variable within the filename string, as shown here:

```
open (REPS, "+> $filen");
```

To read from a file using that file's file handle, you simply place the file handle within the **<** and **>** symbols. **<REPS>** reads a line of input from the reports file. In the **myreport** program, the reports file is opened and its contents are displayed.

myreport.pl

```
#!/usr/bin/perl
# Program to read lines from the reports file and display them

open(REPS, "< reports");              # Open reports file for reading only
while ( $ldat = <REPS> )              # Read a line from the reports file
    {
    print $ldat;                      # Display recently read line
    }
close REPS;                           # Close file
```

Perl also has a full set of built-in commands for handling directories. They operate much like the file functions. The **opendir** command opens a directory, much as a file is opened. A directory handle is assigned to the directory. The **readdir** command will read the first item in the directory, though, when in a list context, it will return all the file and directory names in that directory. **Closedir** closes the directory, **chdir** changes directories, **mkdir** creates directories, and **rmdir** removes directories.

Perl Variables and Expressions

Perl variables can be numeric or string variables. Their type is determined by context, the way they are used. You do not have to declare them. A variable that is assigned a numeric value and is used in arithmetic operations is a numeric variable. All others are treated as strings. To reference a variable in your program, you precede it with a **$** symbol, just as you would for a shell variable.

You can use the same set of operators with Perl variables as with C variables, with the exception of strings. Strings use the same special comparison terms as used in the Bourne shell, not the standard comparison operators. Those are reserved for numeric variables. However, other operators such as assignment operators work on both string and numeric variables. In the next example, the variable **myname** is assigned the string "Larisa". The assignment operator is the **=** symbol (see Table 42-3).

```
$myname = "Larisa";
```

For a numeric variable, you can assign a number. This can be either an integer or a floating-point value. Perl treats all floating-point values as double precision.

```
$mynum = 45;
$price = 54.72;
```

Perl also supports arithmetic expressions. All the standard arithmetic operators found in other programming languages are used in Perl. Expressions can be nested using parentheses (see Table 42-3). Operands can be numeric constants, numeric variables, or other numeric expressions. In the following examples, **$mynum** is assigned the result of an addition expression. Its value is then used in a complex arithmetic expression whose result is assigned to **$price**.

```
$mynum = 3 + 6;
$price = ( 5 * ($num / 3);
```

Perl supports the full range of assignment operators found in **gawk** and C. The **++** and **--** operators will increment or decrement a variable. The **+=** and **-=** operators and their variations will perform the equivalent of updating a variable. For example, **i++** is the same as **i = i + 1**, and **i += 5** is the same as **i= i + 5**. Increment operations such as **i++** are used extensively with loops.

Arithmetic Operators	Function
*	Multiplication
/	Division
+	Addition
–	Subtraction
%	Modulo—results in the remainder of a division
**	Power
Relational Operators	
>	Greater than
<	Less than
>=	Greater than or equal to
<=	Less than or equal to
==	Equal in let
!=	Not equal
Increment Operators	
++	Increment variable by one.
– –	Decrement variable by one.
Arithmetic Assignment Operators	
+=	Increment by specified value.
–=	Decrement by specified value.
/=	Variable is equal to itself divided by value.
*=	Variable is equal to itself multiplied by value.
%=	Variable is equal to itself remaindered by value.

Table 42-3.   *Arithmetic, Relational (Numeric), and Assignment Operators*

You can easily include the value of a variable within a string by simply placing the variable within it. In the following example, the value of **$nameinfo** would be the string "My name is Larisa \n":

```
print "The number of items is $mynum \n"
$nameinfo = "My name is $myname \n"
```

To assign data read from a file to a variable, just assign the result of the read operation to the variable. In the next example, data read from the standard input is assigned to the variable **$mydata**:

```
$mydata = <STDIN>;
```

When reading data from the standard input into a variable, the carriage return character will be included with the input string. You may not want to have this carriage return remain a part of the value of the variable. To remove it, you can use the **chomp** command, which removes the last character of any string. With data input from the keyboard, this happens to be the carriage return.

```
chomp $myinput;
```

In the next example, the user inputs his or her name. It is assigned to the **myname** variable. The contents of **myname** is then output as part of a string. **chomp** is used to remove the carriage return from the end of the **$myname** string before it is used as part of another string.

readname.pl

```
#!/usr/bin/perl
$myname = <STDIN>;
chomp $myname;

print "$myname just ran this program\n";
$ myread.pl
larisa Petersen
larisa Petersen just ran this program
```

Arrays and Lists

In Perl, you create an array by assigning it a list of values. A list in Perl consists of a set of values encased in parentheses and separated by colons. The following example is a list of four values:

```
( 23, 41, 92, 7)
```

You assign this list to the array you wish to create, preceding the array name with an **@** sign. This assignment will initialize the array sequentially, beginning with the first value in the list.

```
@mynums = (23, 41, 92, 7);
```

Once the array has been created, you can reference its individual elements. The elements start from 0, not 1. The **mynums** array has four elements, numbered from 0 to 3. You can reference individual elements using an index number encased within brackets. **[0]** references the first element, and **[2]** references the third element. The following example prints out the first element and then the fourth element. Notice that the array name is prefixed with a **$**.

```
print $mynums[0] ;
print $mynums[2] ;
```

You can change the value of any element in the array by assigning it a new value. Notice that you use a **$**, not an **@** sign, preceding an individual array element. The **@** sign references the entire array and is used when you are assigning whole lists of values to it. The **$** sign references a particular element, which is essentially a variable.

```
$mynums[2] = 40;
```

There is no limit to the number of elements in the array. You can add more by simply referencing a new element and assigning it a value. The following assignment will add a fifth element to the **mynums** array:

```
$mynums[4] = 63;
```

Each array will have a special variable that consists of a **#** and the name of the array. This variable is the number of elements currently in the array. For example, **#mynums** holds the number of elements in the **mynums** array. The following example prints out the number of elements. Notice the preceding **$**.

```
print  "$#mynums";
```

When assigning a list to an array, the values in a list do not have to be of the same type. You can have numbers, strings, and even variables in a list. Similarly, elements of the array do not have to be of the same type. One element could be numeric, and another a string. In the next example, the list with varied elements is assigned to the **myvar** array.

```
@myvar = ( "aleina", 11, 4.5, "a new car");
```

You can reference the entire set of elements in an array as just one list of values. To do this, you use the array name prefixed by the **@** sign. The following example will output all the values in the **mynums** array:

```
print @mynums;
```

The **@** is used here instead of the **$**, because the array name is not a simple variable. It is considered a list of values. Only the individual elements are variables. This means that to just reference all the values in an array, you use the **@** sign, not the **$**. This is even true when you want to assign one array to another. In the next example, the values of each element in **mynums** are assigned to corresponding elements in **newnums**. Notice the **@** used for **mynums**. You can think of **@mynums** as evaluating to a list of the values in the **mynums** array, and this list being then assigned to **newnums**.

```
@newnums = @mynums;
```

The list of values referenced by an array name can be used in a string, just as the value of a variable can. In the next example, the values of the elements in the **mynums** array are incorporated into a string. This string is then assigned to the **myreport** variable. Notice the use of the **@** as a prefix to the array name, **@mynums**.

```
$myreport = "Here are the numbers I have: @mynums \n";
print $myreport;
```

However, individual elements of an array are variables and need to be referenced using an index and the **$** sign. The following example uses the value of the third element in the **mynums** array:

```
$myelement= "This is the value of the third element: $mynums[2] \n";
print $myelement;
```

Array Management Functions: List Operations

Perl has a set of functions designed to help you to easily manage arrays. With simple commands you can perform common array operations such as listing the contents of an array, sorting an array, or sequentially referencing each element one by one. In this respect, you can think of an array as a list, and these functions as performing list operations. Table 42-4 lists the array and list functions.

Both **push** and **pop** operate on the end of an array, adding or removing the last element. You can think of them as adding or removing an element at the end of a list. The **push** function adds an new element to the end of the array; it takes as its arguments the array, followed by a list of values that you want added as elements to

Scalar Array Operations, @*array*	Action
push(*array, value-list*)	Add elements to the end of the array.
pop(*array*)	Remove the last element from the end of an array.
shift(*array, value-list*)	Add an element to the beginning of the array.
unshift(*array*)	Remove an element from the beginning of an array.
sort(*array*)	Sort in ascending order (alphabetic).
reverse(*array*)	Sort in descending order (alphabetic).
split(*delim, str*)	Split a string into an array of elements. Delimiter can be either a pattern or a string. It is used as the delimiter to separate the string into element values.
join(*delim, array*)	Combine array elements into one string.
grep(*array, pattern*)	Search the elements in an array for the pattern.
splice (*array, index*)	Use **splice** to delete an element from an array. Index numbered from 0.
splice(*array, index, num*)	Use **splice** to delete num consecutive number of elements from an array.
splice(*array, num,* **0,** *str*)	Use **splice** to insert an element to an array with the value of `str`.
splice(*array,* $#*argv,* **0,** *str*)	Use **splice** to add a new element to the end of an array.
Associative Arrays Operations, %*array*	
keys(%*assoc-array*)	Generate a list of all the index strings in an associative array.
values(%*assoc-array*)	Generate a list of all the values of the elements in an associative array.

Table 42-4. *Perl Array Operations*

Scalar Array Operations, @*array*	Action
each(%*assoc-array*)	Return both the value of the next element and its index string.
delete(%*assoc-array*, *index- string*)	Delete an element with the specified index from an associative array.
General Arrays Operations	
undef(*array*)	Delete an entire array (scalar or associative).

Table 42-4.   *Perl Array Operations*

the array. It can add several new elements at a time. The **pop** function removes the last element from an array. It will return as its value that last element. The **shift** and **unshift** operators work on the beginning of a list. The **shift** operator will remove the first element in a list, making the next element the first one. The **unshift** operator adds an new element to the beginning of the list. **shift** takes as its argument an array and returns the value of the first element it removes. **unshift** takes as its argument an array followed by the value of element you want to add. It then returns the total number of elements now in the array. The **sort** operation will sort the elements in an array according to the system's character set, usually the ASCII character set. **sort** will arrange elements in ascending order. The **sort** operation returns the list of sorted values. The **split** operation is used to create an array and assign it values derived from a string. The values are determined by a specified delimiter that is used to segment the string, forming the different values that will be assigned to elements in the array. **split** is often used with lines of input data that are already arranged into fields that are separated by a delimiter such as a comma or colon. You can use the **grep** function to search an array or any list. This function operates much like the Linux utility grep. It takes as its arguments a pattern and a list, usually an array. **grep** returns the value of the element matched.

Associative Arrays

An associative array uses strings to index elements in an array, instead of numbers. You can think of the index string as a keyword that you can use to find an element. In Perl, an associative array is defined with a **%** prefixing the array name. The list of values that it is assigned consists of an index string and element value pairs. An index string is followed by the element's value, which is then followed by the next index string and element value, and so on. In the next example, the associative array **city** is defined with four elements, each having an integer value and each indexed with the name of a city.

```
% city = ('Sacramento', 4,
     'Fallon', 86,
     'Napa', 7,
     'Alameda', 53 ) ;
```

You reference an element in an associative array using its index string. The index string is encased in single quotes and braces (not brackets).

```
print  $city{'Fallon'};
```

To add a new element in an associative array, you need to provide both the string to be used as the index for this element and the element's value.

```
$city{'LA'} = 45;
```

To reference the list of values for an associative array, you use the **%** sign with the array name. The following example prints out all values of the **city** array:

```
print %city ;
```

Perl also has a set of list operations designed to work on associative arrays. With these operations, you can generate lists of keys or values. They are helpful for easily iterating through an associative array. Unlike in a normal array, the strings used to index elements of an associative array are not readily known. For a scalar array, you know that the index always starts from 0 and runs consecutively to the last element. For an associative array, the indexes may be any arbitrary strings. To print out an associative array, you would need to know what these index strings are. You have to use them to reference the array elements. With the **keys** operation, you can generate a list of just the index strings in an associative array. You can then use this list to index the array itself. The **keys** operation takes as its argument an associative array and returns a list of all the index strings used to reference the elements in that array. Having obtained the index strings, you can then use them to reference each element in the array. In the next example, the **keys** operation on the **city** array generates a list of that array's index strings. Each index string in this list is then assigned, in turn, to the **myindex** variable. The **myindex** variable is then used to index the **city** array in a print operation.

```
foreach $myindex ( keys(%city) )
     {
     print " $city($myindex) \n ";
     }
```

The **each** operation works much like the **keys** operation. However, it returns both the index string for an element and the value of the element itself. **each** takes as its argument an array. When called, it returns the next element of the array and its index string. Placing it in a loop, you can use **each** to reference every element in the array. The next example assigns the index string and the value of the first element of the **myvar** array to the **myindex** and **myval** variables.

```
($myindex, $myval) = each (%ciry);
```

Placing it in a loop, you can use **each** to reference each element in the array. In the next example, **each** is used to obtain the value of each element, in turn.

```
while ( ($myindex, $myval) = each (%city) )
        {
        print "$myval  $myindex\n ";
        }
```

The **values** operation returns a list of all the values in an associative array. You can use this to easily print out the elements in an associative array, dispensing with the need for index strings.

You use the **delete** operation to remove an element from an associative array. **delete** takes as its argument the index string of the element you want to remove. It will then return the contents of that element. In the next example, **delete** is used to remove the element with the index string **"Sacramento"**.

```
delete(%myarr,"Sacramento");
```

Note *To remove the entire array, you use the **undef** operation. **undef** works on either scalar or associative arrays. It eliminates the array completely, releasing its memory.*

Control Structures

Perl has a set of control structures similar to those used in the **gawk**, TCSH shell, and C programming languages. Perl has loops with which you can repeat commands, and conditions that allow you to choose among specified commands. For the test expressions, there are two different sets of operators for use with strings and numeric values. Table 42-3 lists the numeric relational operators, and Table 42-5 lists the string operators. You can also use pattern operations that allow the use of regular expressions. Table 42-6 lists the Perl control structures with their syntax.

String Comparisons	Function
`gt`	Greater than
`lt`	Less than
`ge`	Greater than or equal to
`le`	Less than or equal to
`eq`	Equal
`ne`	Not equal

Logical Operations	
expression **&&** *expression* expression **and** *expression*	The logical AND condition returns a true 0 value if both expressions return a true 0 value; if one returns a non-zero value, then the AND condition is false and also returns a non-zero value. Execution stops at the first false expression. The **and** operation is the same as **&&** but has a lower precedence.
expression || *expression* expression **or** *expression*	The logical OR condition returns a true 0 value if one or the other expression returns a true 0 value; if both expressions return a non-zero value, then the OR condition is false and also returns a non-zero value. Evaluation stops at the first true expression. The **or** operation is the same as || but has a lower precedence.
! *command* **not** *command*	The logical NOT condition inverts the true or false value of the expression. The **not** operation is the same as **!** but has a lower precedence.

Table 42-5.   *String, Logical, File, and Assignment Operators*

PROGRAMMING

File Tests	Function
-e	File exists.
-f	File exists and is a regular file.
-s	File is not empty.
-z	File is empty, zero size.
-r	File is readable.
-w	File can be written to, modified.
-x	File is executable.
-d	Filename is a directory name.
-B	File is a binary file.
-T	File is a text file.
Assignment Operator	
=	Assign a value to a variable.

Table 42-5. *String, Logical, File, and Assignment Operators* (continued)

Control Structures	Description
*LABEL:***{** *statements;* **}**	Block is a collection of statements enclosed within opening and closing braces. The statements are executed sequentially. The block can be labeled.
Conditional Control Structures: if, else, elsif, case	
if(*expression* **) {** *statements;* **}**	**if** executes statements if its test expression is true. Statements must be included within a block.

Table 42-6. *Perl Conditions, Loops, and Functions*

if (*expression*) {
statements;
  }
 else (*expression*) {
statements;
  }
	if-else executes statements if the test expression is true; if false, then the **else** statements are executed.

if (*expression*) {
statements;
  }
 elsif (*expression*) {
statements;
  }
else (*expression*) {
statements;
  }
	elsif allows you to nest **if** structures, enabling selection among several alternatives; at the first true **if** expression, its statements are executed and control leaves the entire **elsif** structure.

unless (*expression*) {
statements;
  }
	unless executes statements if its test expression is false.

test **?** *stat1* **:** *stat2*	Conditional expression. If true executes *stat1*, **else** *stat2*.

LABEL **:** {
if (*expr*)
{*statements;* **last** *LABEL*};
}
	Simulate a **switch** structure by using listed **if** statements within a block with the **last** statement referencing a label for the block.

**Loop Control Structures:
while, until, for, foreach**

LABEL:**while** (*expression*) {
statements;
}
	while executes statements as long as its test expression is true. LABEL is optional.

do { *statements;* } **until** (*expression*)	**until** executes statements as long as its test expression is false.

foreach *variable* (*list-values*)
{
statements;
}
	foreach is designed for use with lists of values such as those generated by an array; the variable operand is consecutively assigned the values in the list.

Table 42-6.   *Perl Conditions, Loops, and Functions* (continued)

PROGRAMMING

for (*init-expr*; *test-expr*; *incr-expr*) **{** *statements*; **}**	The **for** control structure executes statements as long as *test-expr* is true. The first expression, *init-expr* is executed before the loop begins. The third expression, *incr-expr*, is executed within the loop after the statements.
LABEL: *block-or-loop*	Label a block or loop. Used with the **next**, **last**, and **redo** commands.
next	Skip remainder of loop and start next iteration. Like the C **continue** command. Will execute any continue block.
continue { *statements*; }	Execute continue block as last statements in a loop. Is executed even if a **next** statement starts next iteration.
redo *LABEL*	Reexecute loop even if test fails. Skips continue block.
last *LABEL*	Exit block or loop. Skips continue block, if any. Like the C **break** statement.

Functions

sub *function-name* ;	Declare a function.
sub *function-name* **{** *statements*; **}**	Define a function with the name *function-name*.
& *function-name* (*arg-list*)	Call a function with arguments specified in the argument list.
@_	Holds the values of arguments passed to the current function. **$_** and index references an argument. **$_**[0] is the first argument.
$#_	Number of arguments passed to the current function.

Table 42-6. *Perl Conditions, Loops, and Functions* (continued)

Test Expressions

Perl has different sets or operators for numeric and string comparisons. You have to be careful not to mix up the different operators. The string operators are two-letter codes similar to those used in the BASH shell. For example, the **eq** operator tests for the equality of two strings, and the **gt** operator tests to see if one is greater than the other. Numeric comparisons, on the other hand, use as operators symbols similar to those found in programming languages. For example, **>** stands for greater-than, and **==** tests for equality. These are essentially the same comparison operators used for the C programming language.

There are two important exceptions, patterns and string-patterns. The string-pattern operator, **=~**, tests for a pattern in a string variable. The right-hand operand is the pattern, and the left-hand operand is the string. The pattern can be any regular expression, making this a very flexible and powerful operation.

Patterns perform pattern matching on either a string or the contents of the **_$** special variable. The pattern operator consists of two slashes that enclose the pattern searched for, */pattern/*. The pattern can be any regular expression. Regular expression are discussed in detail in the section on pattern matching.

Perl supports the AND, OR, and NOT logical operations. There are two implementations of these operations, the standard operators and those with list processing capabilities. The standard logical operators are **&&**, **||**, and **!**. The **&&** operator implements an AND operation, **||** an OR, and **!** a NOT. They take as their operands expressions, just as they do in the C programming language. Their syntax is as follows:

```
(expression) && (expression)
(expression) || (expression)
!(expression)
```

In the case of the logical AND, **&&**, if both commands are successful, then the logical command is true. For the logical OR, **||**, if either command is successful, then the OR is true. You can extend these commands with added **&&** or **||** commands, creating complex AND or OR operations. The logical commands allow you to use logical operations as your test command in control structures. You can also use them independently.

The logical operators are usually used in test expressions for control structures such as **while** and **if**. But they can also be used independently as their own statements. In effect, they provide a simple way to write a conditional operation. In Perl scripts, you may often see an OR operation used with a file open command. In an OR operation, if the first expression fails, then the second one is checked. If that second one is the **die** command to end the program, then in effect there is an operation to end the program if the file open operation fails (the first expression fails).

```
open (REPS, "+> $filen") or die "Can't open $filen";
```

The AND operation works similarly, except that if the first expression is true, then the second one is checked. The following looks for an empty line and, if it finds it, prints the message.

```
/^$/ && print "Found empty line";
```

Loops

Perl loops are the **while**, **do-until**, **for**, and **foreach** loops. The **while** loop is the more general-purpose loop, whereas the **for** and **foreach** loops provide special capabilities. The **foreach** is particularly helpful in processing lists and arrays. The **while**, **do-until**, and **for** loops operate much like their counterparts in the C programming language. The **for** loop, in particular, has the same three expression formats as the C **for** loop. The **foreach** loop is similar to its counterpart in the C-shell, able to easily handle lists of items.

You can easily adapt the **while** loop for use with arrays. The variable used to control a loop can also be used, inside the loop, to index an array. In the next example, the elements of the title array are assigned the value of each title. Then, the contents of each element are printed out using a **for** loop. Notice that the **$#num** holds the count of elements in the array. **$#num** is used as the upper bound in the **for** loop test expression in order to check when the loop should stop.

titlearr.pl

```
#!/usr/bin/perl
# Program to define and print out a scalar array

@title = ( "Tempest", "Iliad", "Raven");        # define array with 3 elements

for($i = 0; $i <= $#title; $i++)                 # Loop through array, $#title is size
        {
        print "$title[$i] \n";          # Print an element of the title array
        }
```

```
$ titlearr.pl
Tempest
Iliad
Raven
```

The **foreach** loop is useful for managing arrays. In the **foreach** loop, you can use the array name to generate a list of all the element values in the array. This generated list of values then becomes the list referenced by the **foreach** loop. You can also specify a range of array elements, using only those values for the list, or a set of individual elements. In the next example, the array name **@mylist** is used to generate a list of its values that the **foreach** loop can operate on, assigning each one to **$mynum** in turn.

mynumlist.pl

```
#!/usr/bin/perl
# Program to use foreach to print out an array

@mylist = ( 34, 21, 96, 85);                    # define array of 4 elements

foreach $mynum ( @mylist )                      # Assign value of each element to $mynum
        {
        print "$mynum \n";
        }
```

Using the **@ARGV** array, you can specify the command-line arguments as a list of values. The arguments specified on the command line when the program was invoked become a list of values referenced by the **foreach** loop. The variable used in the **foreach** loop is set automatically to each argument value in sequence. The first time through the loop, the variable is set to the value of the first argument. The second time, it is set to the value of the second argument, and so on.

> **Tip**   *The number of arguments that a user actually enters on the command line can vary. The #ARGV variable will always hold the number of arguments that a user enters. This is the number of elements that are in the ARGV array. If you want to reference all the elements in the ARGV array using their indexes, you will need to know the number of elements, #ARGV. For example, to use the foreach loop to reference each element in the ARGV array, you would use the .. operator to generate a list of indexes. 0 .. $#ARGV generates a list of numbers beginning with 0 through to the value of $#ARGV.*

Perl has a set of special commands designed to give you more refined control over loops and blocks. They correspond to similar commands used in the C programming language. These commands need to make use of labels. If you use them within a loop, you need to label that loop; then when one of these commands is used, it references that loop.

The **last** command corresponds to the C **break** command. It stops execution of a loop. It can also be used to break out of a block. **last** is used with blocks to simulate switch structures. The **next** command skips over the remaining statements in the loop. It is similar to the C **continue** command. It is designed to work with the continue block. A continue block consists of the command **continue** followed by a block. This block is executed at the end of the loop. Even if a **next** command skips over the remaining statements, the continue block is always executed. You can use it to ensure that operations like increments are performed. The **redo** command will reexecute a loop, even if its test proves false. It has no corresponding C command. Both the **redo** and **last** commands will ignore any continue block.

Conditions: if, elsif, unless, and switch

Perl supports if-else operations much as they are used in other programming languages. The **if** structure with its **else** and **elsif** components allows you to select alternative actions. You can use just the **if** command to choose one alternative, or combine that with **else** and **elsif** components to choose among several alternatives. The **if** structure has a test expression encased in parentheses followed by a block of statements. If the test is true, the statements in the block are performed. If not, the block is skipped. Unlike in other programming languages, only a block can follow the test, and any statements, even just one, has to be encased with it. The following example tests to see if an **open** operation on a file was successful. If not, then it will execute a **die** command to end the program. The NOT operator, **!**, will make the test true if **open** fails, thereby executing the **die** command.

```
if (!(open (REPS, "< $filen"))) {
    die "Can't open $filen";
}
else {
        print "Opened $filen successfully";
        }
```

String Functions

Perl provides several functions and operators for manipulating strings (see Table 42-7). The **length**, **index**, and **substr** functions perform standard string operations such as obtaining the length of a string or copying a substring from a string. **split** performs a special task. It generates an array from a string, cutting the string into array element values. It is similar to the **split** function used in **gawk**. **split** was discussed previously with the array list operations. The dot operator concatenates strings, and the **x** operator generates strings consisting of repeated characters.

You use the dot operator, **.**, to concatenate two strings. The following example adds a ".dat" suffix to a root filename. If the contents of **$curfile** is myaddress, then **$newfile** would be "myaddress.dat".

```
$newfilename = $curfile . ".dat" ;
```

With the repetition operator, **x**, you can repeat a string any number of times. You precede the **x** operator with the string to be repeated and then follow the **x** operator with the number of times you want to repeat the string. The string can be single characters or any number of characters. You can also use the **x** operator to generate a list whose members all have the same value, and then use that list to initialize an array.

String Operations	Descriptions
str **.** *str*	The dot operator concatenates strings.
str **x** *num*	Repeat a string or character *num* number of times.
String Functions	
chomp(*str*)	Remove trailing newline.
substr(*str*, *start-pos*, *length*)	Return a substring of the specified string, beginning at the start position for the length specified.
substr(*str*, *start-pos*, *length*) **=** *string*	Replace the specified section of the string with the assigned string.
length(*str*)	Find the length of a string.
index(*str*, *pattern*)	Find the position of a pattern in a string.
rindex(*str*, *pattern*)	Find the last position of a pattern in a string.

Table 42-7. *String Operations*

PROGRAMMING

In the next example, an array is assigned a list of five zeros (0, 0, 0, 0, 0). But instead of your typing out the list, the list is generated by an **x** operator, **(0) x 5**.

```
@myarray = (0) x 5 ;
```

Pattern Matching

Perl can search for a pattern on a given line. Such a search pattern is indicated by a enclosing slashes. **/Dickens/** searches for the pattern "Dickens" in a line. By default, a pattern search operates on the contents of the **_$** special variable. This variable usually holds the contents of the recently read line of input, wherever that may come from. If the recent input command was **<STDIN>**, then **_$** will hold a line read from the standard input, and a following pattern search will search that line. In the next example, the user reads a line from the standard input, then searches for the pattern **/Dickens/** in it.

```
$_ = <STDIN>;
/Dickens/;
```

To search the contents of a variable for a pattern, you use the **=~** operator with the pattern search operation. You use the variable name as the left-hand operand, and the pattern search operation as the right-hand operand. Table 42-8 lists Perl pattern matching operators and options. The following example looks for the pattern "Christmas" in the **$title** variable.

```
$title =~ /Christmas/
```

Perl supports the full range of regular expressions in its pattern matching, including extended special characters. The *****, **+**, **?**, **{}**, **.**, **^**, **$**, and **[]** special characters can all be used to construct complex search operations. Chapter 14 discusses regular expressions in depth. In addition, Perl has a set of escape characters used in regular

Pattern Matching Operators	Action
var **=~** /*reg-expr*/	Find the occurrence of the regular expression in the string variable.
var **!~** /*reg-expr*/	Check if the regular expression does not occur in string variable.
/*reg-expres*/	Match a pattern using a regular expression.
Pattern Matching Options	
i	Do case-insensitive pattern matching.
m	Treat string as multiple lines.
s	Treat string as single line.
x	Extend your pattern's legibility with white space and comments.

Table 42-8. *Pattern Matching Operators and Options*

expressions that operate as a shorthand for many of the commonly used patterns. For example, **\w** matches on any alphanumeric character and is equivalent to the regular expression **[A-Ba-b0-9]+**. The sequence **\d** matches on numbers, and **\s** on white space characters. The sequence **\b** prefixing a word lets you search for a word, rather than any pattern. Uppercase versions perform negative matches. The sequence **\W** matches on anything other than alphanumeric characters, and **\D** on anything other than numbers. Table 42-9 lists the special characters available for use in Perl regular expressions.

Special Characters	Description
^	Beginning of a line
$	End of a line
*c**	Match on zero or more sequential instances of the preceding character, *c*.
.	Match on any single character.
c+	Match on at least one or more sequential instances of the preceding character, *c*.
c?	Match on zero or just one instance of the preceding character, *c*.
c{*num*}	Specify the number of repeated sequential instances of the preceding character, *c*, to match on.
c{*min*,*max*}	Specify minimum and maximum numbers of repeated sequential instances of the preceding character, *c*, to match on.
[*char-list*]	Classes of characters
[*char-char*]	Ranges of characters
[^*char-list*] [^*char-char*]	Any characters NOT in the character list or the range specified

Table 42-9. *Regular Expressions*

Special Characters	Description
reg-exp | *reg-exp*	Match on any of the specified regular expressions. The regular expressions can be a simple string (functions as a logical OR operation).
(*pattern-segment*) \\ *n*	Specify a segment of a pattern that can then be referenced with the *n* code. **1** references the first segment, **2** the second, and so on. Used with s/// substitution.

Escape Character Regular Expressions

w	Any alphanumeric character, [a-bA-B0-9]+
d	Any digit (number), [0-9]+
s	White space characters (spaces, tabs, newlines, form feeds), [\\n\\t\\r\\f]+
bword	Words
W	Characters NOT alphanumeric, [^a-bA-B0-9]+
D	Characters NOT digits, [^0-9]+
S	Characters NOT white space characters, [^\\n\\t\\r\\f]+
Bpattern	Any pattern not a word

Table 42-9. *Regular Expressions* (continued)

Functions: sub

In your Perl script you can define subroutines, permitting you to better organize your program. Instead one long series of statements, you can define separate subroutines for specific tasks. Tasks you wish to be performed more than once do not have to have their code repeated in the program. You can just define a subroutine for it and call that subroutine as many times as you need to. Subroutines are defined with the **sub** command followed by the subroutine name and a block of statements. Within the block of statements, you can have any Perl statements you wish. Subroutines operate like functions do in C programs and procedures in other programs. They can take arguments and have parameters with predetermined names. Table 42-10 list the different components that can make up a Perl subroutine. The following example defines a subroutine called **dispfile**.

```
sub dispfile
    {
    print "Please enter in name of file to be displayed: ";
    chomp($filename = <STDIN>);
    system("cat $filename");
}
```

You can define Perl subroutines before or after the main statements in your script. It is helpful to place the main statements in a block of their own. However, if subroutines are called in statements that occur before the subroutine's definition, then you should

Subroutine Components	Description
@_	Array to hold list of arguments. Arrays are combined into single elements of this array.
sub *name* **{** *statements;* **}**	Subroutine definition
sub *name***;**	Subroutine declaration
sub *name* **(***type-list***);**	Prototype declaration
*function-name***;**	Function call
*function-name***(***arguments***);**	Function call
&*function-name arguments***;**	Function call
my(*object-list***)**	Local variable restricted to subroutine or block
Local(*object-list***)**	Local version of global object, known to current subroutine and block and all other subroutines called
\@*array-name*	Array reference (used in argument list to maintain integrity of an array)

Table 42-10.   *Perl Subroutines*

PROGRAMMING

place forward declarations of the subroutines in the code before the subroutine calls. Subroutine declarations operate like C function declarations. They consist of the **sub**command and the subroutine name followed by a semicolon, with no block of code. Usually you would place subroutine declarations at the beginning of the Perl script, following by the main block of statements and then your subroutine definitions. The following example is a subroutine declaration for **dispfile**.

```
sub dispfile;
```

With Perl 5, there are several ways to call subroutines. Traditionally, a subroutine is called with the subroutine name preceded by a **&**. For example, **&dispfile** would call the **dispfile** subroutine. You can also use parenthesis instead of the preceding **&**. With a preceding subroutine declaration, you can just use the function name itself. The following subroutine calls are equivalent, though using the name alone requires a subroutine declaration.

```
dispfile;
&dispfile;
dispfile();
```

Subroutines can have arguments passed to them and return values back to the calling statement. Arguments and return values are passed as lists. Arguments specified in a subroutine call are placed in a list and assigned to the **@_** array that is then passed to the subroutine. The **@_** array will hold the arguments for the subroutine currently being called. To access a particular argument, you use array or list operations to reference elements of the **@_** array, which is used in every subroutine to access that subroutine's arguments.

Arguments are arranged in the **@_** array, counting from 0, and are referenced as you would elements of any scalar array. The first argument would be referenced with **$_[0]**, the second with **$_[1]**, and so on. The following example, **dispfilearg**, is designed to receive as its argument the name of a file. It uses **$_[0]** to access a filename passed to it using the **@_** array.

```
sub dispfilearg
    {
    system("cat $_[0]");
}
```

The subroutine calls would be any of the following:

```
dispfilearg ("myfile");
&dispfilearg  "myfile";
```

For constants, the **@_** list holds only values. However, if you use a variable or array as an argument, then **@_** will reference those objects. In effect, with variables and arrays, call by reference is implemented. This means that references to elements of the **@_** array reference the original objects. Changes made by referencing these objects through the **@_** array will change the original object in the calling function. So, if a string variable is used as an argument to a function, and then that argument is referenced through **@_** and used in the assignment operation, then the value of that variable is changed.

Chapter 43

Tcl, Tk, and Expect

Tcl is general-purpose command language developed by John Ousterhout in 1987 at the University of California, Berkeley. Originally designed to customize applications, it has become a fully functional language in its own right. As with Perl and gawk, you can write Tcl scripts, developing your own Tcl programs. Tcl is a very simple language to use.

TK and Expect are Tcl applications that extend the capabilities of the language. The Tk application allows easy development of graphical interactive applications. You can create your own windows and dialog boxes with buttons and text boxes of your choosing. The Expect application provides easy communication with interactive programs such as FTP and telnet.

Tcl is often used in conjunction with Tk to create graphical applications. Tk is used to create the graphical elements such as windows, and Tcl performs the programming actions such as managing user input. Like Java, Tcl and Tk are cross-platform applications. A Tcl/Tk program will run on any platform that has the Tcl/Tk interpreter installed. Currently, there are Tcl/Tk versions for Windows, the Mac, and Unix systems, including Linux. You can write a Tcl application on Linux and run the same code on Windows or the Mac. The new versions of Tcl and Tk 8.0 even support a local look and feel for GUI widgets using Mac-like windows on the Mac, but Windows-like windows under Windows 98.

Tcl is an interpreted language operating, like Perl, within its own shell; **tclsh** is the command for invoking the Tcl shell. Within this shell, you can then execute Tcl commands. You can also create files within which you can invoke the Tcl shell and list Tcl commands, effectively creating a Tcl program. A significant advantage to the Tcl language and its applications is the fact that it is fully compatible with the C programming language. Tcl libraries can be incorporated directly into C programs. In effect, this allows you to create very fast compiled versions of Tcl programs.

When you install Tk and Tcl on your system, man pages for Tcl/Tk commands are also installed. Use the **man** command with the name of the Tcl or Tk command to bring up detailed information on that command. For example, **man switch** displays the manual page for the Tcl **switch** command, and **man button** displays information on the Tk **button** widget. Once you have installed Tk, you can run a demo program called **widget** that shows you all the Tk widgets available. The **widget** program uses Tcl/Tk sample programs and can display the source code for each. You can find the **widget** program by changing to the Tk **demos** directory as shown here. (**tk*** here matches on directory names consisting of **tk** and its version number, **tk4.1** for version 4.1 and **tk8.0** for version 8.0.)

```
cd /usr/lib/tk*/demos
```

From the Xterm window, just enter the command **widget**. You can also examine the individual demo files and modify them as you wish. If you have installed a version of Tk yourself into the **/usr/local/bin** directory rather than **/usr/bin**, then the **demos** directory will be located in **/usr/local/lib/tk***.

Tcl/Tk Extensions and Applications

Currently, both Tcl and Tk are being developed and supported as opensource projects by Tcl Core Team. The current release of both Tcl and Tk is 8.0, though version 8.1 will be ready soon. Current versions of Tcl and Tk, are available free of charge from the Tcl Developer Xchange Web site, **http://dev.scriptics.com**. Also available on this site is extensive documentation for each product in PostScript, Adobe PDF, and HTML formats. The HTML documentation can be viewed online. RPM packaged versions can also be found at distribution sites such as **ftp.redhat.com**. You will need both Tcl and Tk RPM packages, as well as the development packages for each. Current useful Tcl/TK site are listed here:

Tcl Developer Xchange	**dev.scriptics.com**
tcltk.com site for Tcl news and software	**www.tcltk.com**
Source Forge site for open source projects	**sourceforge.net**

Tcl/Tk has been enhanced by extensions that increase the capabilities of the language. Several commonly used extensions are TclX, [incr Tcl], and Oratcl. All these are currently available through links on the Tcl Developer Xchange Web site. Access the Tcl Software Resource page, and from there, you can access the Tcl Extensions page, listing those currently available (**dev.scriptics.com/software**). Most you can download and install for free. Most are also available at **http://sourceforge.net**. TclX extends capabilities such as file access, and time and date manipulation, many of which have been incorporated into recent Tcl releases. [incr Tcl] supports the easy implementation of higher-level widgets, using an object-oriented programming structure. BLT adds graph and bar widgets to Tk. Sybtcl and Oratcl implement database interfaces to the Sybase and Oracle databases. TclDP provides support for distributed programming across a network. With the Scotty Network Management Tools, you can develop network management applications. The TrfCrypt extension adds encryption that was removed from the standard Tcl/Tk release to make it exportable.

Numerous Tcl/Tk applications, development tools, and utilities are freely available for download from Internet sites. You can link to most of these through Tcl Developer Xchange site or through the **www.tcltk.com** site. Most products are also opensource projects available at **http://sourceforge.net**. If a site does not provide an RPM-packaged version of its software, be sure to check the appropriate distribution site, such as **ftp.redhat.com**. Of particular note is the Tcl/Tk Web page plugin that allows you to embed Tcl/Tk programs within a Web page. Such embedded Tcl/Tk programs are called Tclets. There is also a Tcl/Tk Web server called TclHttpd that can be easily embedded in applications, making them Web capable. You can configure and modify the server using Tcl/Tk commands. Several GUI builders are also available that let you build graphical user interfaces (GUIs). Free Visual Tcl, SpecTcl, VisualGIPSY, and XF SpecTclare GUI builders that have a window-based interface with menus and icons for easily creating Tcl/Tk widgets. They can generate both Tcl/Tk and Java code, and can be used to create standalone Tcl/Tk applications or Web Tclets. There are also editors

(TextEdit), desktops (TK Desk), multimedia (MBone), and specialized applications like Tik, a Tcl/Tk implementation of AOL Instant Messenger. Table 43-1 lists some of the available Tcl/Tk software.

Software Packages	Description
Tcl	The Tcl programming language and interpreter
Tk	The Tk programming language
Tcl/Tk Extensions	
TclX	Adds functions like date and time
BLT	Adds graph and bar chart widgets among others
[incr] Tcl	Implements higher-level widgets (object oriented)
Oratcl	Interface for Oracle database
Sybtcl	Interface for Sybase database
TrfCrypt	Adds encryption
TclDP	Supports distributed programming
Scotty Network Tools	Develops network management applications
Web Applications	
Tcl Plugin	The Tcl/Tk Web page plugin viewer for Tcl/Tk applications (Tclets)
Tik	AOL Instant Messenger
TclHttpd	Tcl/Tk Web server
GUI Builders	
Free Visual Tcl	Tcl/Tk GUI builder
SpecTcl	Tcl/Tk GUI builder
VisualGIPSY	Tcl/Tk GUI builder
XF	Tcl/Tk GUI builder
Applications	
TKDesk	Tk based desktop
MBone	Multimedia conferencing
Tcl Pro	Commercial Development Tools

Table 43-1. *Tcl/TK Software*

Tcl

Tcl is a simple-to-use programming language. Its statements consist of a command followed by arguments, though it also has a complete set of control structures including **while** and **for** loops. Commands can be terminated either by a semicolon or by a newline. You can think of a Tcl command as a function call where the command name operates like a function name, followed by arguments to the function. However, unlike with a function call, there are no parentheses or commas encasing the arguments. You simply enter the command name and then its arguments, separated only by spaces. A newline entered after the last argument will end the statement.

You can see the features in this format very clearly in the Tcl assignment command, **set**. To assign a value to a variable, you first enter the assignment command **set**. Then enter the name of the variable, followed by the value to be assigned. The command name, variable, and value are separated only by spaces. The newline at the end of the line ends the statement. The following statement assigns a string **"larisa"** to the variable **myname**, and the next statement assigns the integer value 11 to the variable **age**.

```
set myname  "larisa"
set age 11
```

Note *Variable types are determined by their use. A variable assigned an integer will be considered an integer, and one assigned a string will be a character array.*

The Tcl Shell and Scripts: tclsh

You execute Tcl commands within the Tcl shell. You can do this interactively, entering commands at a Tcl shell prompt and executing them one by one, or you can place the commands in a script file and execute them all at once. To start up the Tcl shell, you enter the command **tclsh**. This starts up the Tcl shell with the % prompt. You can then enter single Tcl commands and have them evaluated when you press ENTER. You leave the Tcl shell by entering either an **exit** command or a CTRL-D.

```
$ tclsh
% set age 11
% puts $age
11
% exit
$
```

You can run a Tcl script either as a standalone program or as a file explicitly read by the Tcl shell command **tclsh**. A Tcl script has the extension **.tcl**. For example, the **myread.tcl** Tcl script would be read and executed by the following command:

```
$ tclsh myread.tcl
```

PROGRAMMING

To create a standalone script that operates more like a command, you need to invoke the **tclsh** command within the script. You can do this using an explicit pathname for the **tclsh** command. This is placed on the first line of the script.

```
#!/usr/bin/tclsh
```

Expressions

Expressions are also handled as commands. The command **expr** evaluates an expression and returns its resulting value as a string. It takes as its arguments the operands and operator of an expression. Tcl supports all the standard arithmetic, comparison, and logical operators. The result of an arithmetic expression will be the same form as its operands. If the operands are real numbers, the result will be a real number. You can mix operands of different types and Tcl will convert one to be the same as the other. In the case of real and integer operands, the integer will be converted to a real. In the next statement, the addition of 4 and 3 is evaluated by the **expr** command. The following statement multiplies 25 and 2.

```
expr 4 + 3
expr 25 * 2
```

You can create complex expressions using parentheses. The most deeply nested expressions are evaluated first. In the following example, 25 * 2 is evaluated and the result, 50, has 20 subtracted from it.

```
expr (25 * 2) - 20
```

   *The resulting value returned by any Tcl command is always a string. In the case of arithmetic operations, the arithmetic value is converted first to a string, which is then returned by the **expr** command.*

Embedded Commands

You can combine commands by embedding one within the other. Embedding is commonly used for assigning the result of an expression to a variable. This involves two commands, the **set** command to perform the assignment, and the **expr** command to evaluate an expression. You embed commands using brackets. An embedded command is another Tcl command whose result is used as an argument in the outer Tcl command. The embedded command is executed first, and its result is used as the argument to the outer command. The following statement assigns the result of the arithmetic operation, 25 * 2, to the variable **num**. **expr 25 * 2** is a command embedded within the **set** command. First the embedded command is executed, and its result, 50, is assigned to the variable **num**.

```
set num [expr 25 * 2]
```

In the following example, the **exec** command executes the Linux **date** command. The returned date is assigned to the variable **mydate**. Then the **ls -l** command will be output by the **puts** command to the standard output (the screen).

```
set mydate [ exec date ]
puts [exec ls -l]
```

Variables

Tcl supports numeric and string variables as well as arrays, including associative arrays. All variables hold as their contents a string. However, though the content of a variable is a string, that string can be used as an integer or real value in an arithmetic expression, provided that the string consists of numbers. Whenever such a variable is used as an operand in an arithmetic expression, its contents are first converted to an integer or real value. The operation is performed on the arithmetic values, and the result returned by **expr** is then converted back to a string. This means that you do not have to worry about declaring the type of variable, or even defining a variable. All variables are automatically defined when they are first used in a statement.

As we have seen, variables can be assigned values using the **set** command. The **set** command takes as its argument the variable name and the value assigned. A variable's name can be any set of alphabetic or numeric characters and the underscore. Punctuation and other characters are not allowed.

When you need to use the value of a variable within a statement, you need to evaluate it. Evaluating a variable substitutes its name with its value. The **$** placed before a variable name performs such an evaluation. To use a variable's value as an operand in an expression, you need to evaluate the variable by preceding its name with the **$**. In the next example, the value 5 is assigned to the **mynum** variable. Then **mynum** is evaluated in an expression, **$mynum**, providing its value, 5, as an operand in that expression.

```
set mynum 5
expr  10 * $mynum
```

Should you want to make the value of a variable part of string, you only need to evaluate it within that string. The value of the variable becomes part of the string. In the following statement, the value of the variable **myname** is used as part of a string. In this case, the string will be "My name is Larisa".

```
set myname "Larisa"
set mystr "My name is $myname"
```

Certain commands are designed to operate on variables. The **append** command concatenates a string to a variable. The **incr** command will increment an integer, and the **unset** command will undefine a variable. The different commands that operate on variables are listed in Table 43-2.

Arrays

Array elements are defined and assigned values using the **set** command with the index encased in parentheses. The following example assigns the string **"rain"** as the second element in the **weather** array.

```
set weather(2) rain
```

You can then reference the element using its index encased in parentheses with the array name preceded with a **$**.

```
puts $weather(2)
rain
```

Tcl allows the use of any word string as an index, in effect supporting associative arrays. The string used as the index is encased within parentheses next to the array name. The following statements add two elements to the **city** array with the index strings Napa and Alameda.

```
set city(Napa) 34
set city(Alameda) 17
```

Command	Description
set	Assign a value to a variable
global	Declare global variables
incr	Increment a variable by an integer value
unset	Delete variables
upvar	Reference a variable in a different scope
variable	Declare namespace variables
array	Array access operations like searches
expr	Math expressions

Table 43-2.   *Assignments and Variables*

The elements of an associative array are referenced using a preceding **$** and the index string encased in parentheses.

```
puts $city(Napa)
34
```

Note   *You can search array elements one by one using the* **startsearch**, **nextelement**, *and* **anymore** *options, with the* **donesearch** *option ending your search.*

Lists

Tcl supports a type of widget not found in most programming languages, the list. A list is a set of words, strings, or numbers encased in parentheses. Tcl includes a set of very flexible list commands that you can use to manipulate lists, combining them, separating them, or adding and deleting elements from them (see Table 43-3). To reference a list,

Command	Description
set *list values*	Create a list and assign values to it
lsearch *list pattern*	Search for pattern in elements of a list
lindex *list index*	Return the value of the indexed element in a list
llength *list*	Return the number of elements in a list
lrange *list first last*	Return a subrange of the list specified by *first* and *last*
linsert *list index value-list*	Insert a new element into a list after the index
lreplace *list index value-list*	Replace element indexed with new value
lappend *list-name value-list*	Append new values to the end of the list
concat *lists*	Combine elements of several lists into one list
list *lists*	Combine lists into a larger list whose elements are the respective lists
split *str delim*	Split a string into a list using *delim*iter to separate values
join *list*	Join elements of a list into a string
lsort *list*	Sort the list alphabetically or numerically

Table 43-3.   *Tcl List Operations*

you can either use the name of the variable it was assigned to or delineate the list's elements encased in parentheses.

To assign a list to a variable, you place a set of words, numbers, or strings within a set of braces and assign this list to a variable using the **set** command. The following example assigns a list of three words to the variable **weather**. Notice that only spaces separate the components of a list.

```
set weather {sun rain wind}
```

To access and operate on the list, you use a set of list commands. Many of these commands can reference a particular element according to its place in the list. The elements are indexed from 0 for the first element. The value 1 would reference the second element, and so on. In the weather list, the index for sun is 0, for rain it is 1, and for wind it is 2.

The **lindex** command returns an element from a list using its index. It takes two arguments, the list and the index for the element you want. The **lreplace** command will replace elements of a list at a specified position with new elements. **lreplace** takes as its arguments the list, a beginning index, an ending index, and the new elements. The following statement replaces the second element, **blue**, with **green** (starting index of 1, and ending index of 1). This statement will return the list **{red green yellow }**.

```
% lreplace {red blue yellow} 1 1 green
```

The **lreplace** command can replace several elements at once. If the number of elements is larger than the remainder of the list, then the list is simply expanded to include the new elements. The next statement returns the list **{red purple aqua tan}**.

```
% lreplace {red blue yellow} 1 2 purple aqua tan
red purple aqua tan
```

You could also use array notation on the list, referencing the second element with **(1)**.

```
set mycolors(1) green
```

Control Structures

Tcl has a set of control structures similar to those used in the Perl, gawk, C shell, and C programming languages. Tcl has loops with which you can repeat commands and conditions that allow you to choose among specified commands. Table 43-4 lists the Tcl control structures. Control structures in Tcl often make use of a block of Tcl commands.

Control Structure	Description
if	Conditional command, extend with **else** and **elseif** blocks
switch	Switch selection structure
while	The **while** loop
for	The **for** loop, like the C **for** loop
foreach	Loop through a list, or lists, of values
break	Forced loop exit
continue	Skip remainder of block and continue with next loop iteration

Table 43-4.   *Tcl Control Structures*

A block of commands consists of Tcl commands enclosed in braces. The opening brace
({) will begin on the same line as that of the control structure that uses it. On following
lines, there can be several Tcl commands, each on its own line. The block ends with a
closing brace (}) on a line by itself. A block is literally an argument to a Tcl command.
The block is passed to a control structure command, and the control structure will
execute the commands in that block.

if

The **if** control structure allows you to select alternative actions. The **if** command
takes two arguments—a test expression, and a Tcl command or block of commands.
Each is encased in its own set of braces. The test expression is used to determine
whether the Tcl commands will be executed. If the test expression is true, the
commands are performed. If not, the commands are skipped. Below is the syntax for
the **if** structure. You can specify alternative commands to execute if the expression is
false by attaching an **else** block with those Tcl commands. You can nest **if** structures
using the **elseif** command.

```
if {test-expression} {
    Tcl commands
} elseif {test expression} {
        Tcl commands
        } else {
                Tcl commands
                }
```

*Keep in mind that the **else** and **elseif** keywords must be on the same line as the closing brace of the previous block, as in **} elseif { test-expression} {** . The opening brace of the next block must also be on the same line.*

switch

The **switch** structure chooses among several possible alternatives. The choice is made by comparing a string value with several possible patterns. Each pattern has its own block of Tcl commands. If a match is found, the associated block is executed. The **default** keyword indicates a pattern that matches anything. If all of the other matches fail, then the block associated with the **default** keyword is executed. The **switch** structure begins with the keyword **switch** and the options prefixed with **-**, and then the string pattern to be matched, followed by a block containing all the patterns with their blocks. The syntax for the **switch** structure is described next.

```
switch  -options string-pattern  {
     pattern  {
          Tcl commands
          }
     pattern {
          Tcl commands
          }
     default {
          Tcl commands
          }
      }
```

Options specify the pattern-matching capabilities. The following options are supported:

Option	Description
-exact	Use exact matching when comparing string to a pattern. This is the default.
-glob	When matching string to the patterns, use glob style matching.
-regexp	When matching string to the patterns, use regular expression matching (i.e., the same as implemented by the **regexp** command).
--	Marks the end of options. The argument following this one will be treated as a string even if it starts with a **-**.

The **-regexp** option lets you match any regular expression, whereas **-glob** lets you use the shell filename matching methods. With **-glob**, the shell special characters

*, [], and **?** let you easily match on part of a string. With the **-regexp** option, you can match on complex alternative strings, specifying multiple instances of characters, the beginning or end of a string, and classes of characters (see Chapter 11). For example, to match on all filenames with the **.c** extension, you would use the following command.

```
switch  -glob *.c
```

To match on words that end with a number, like "report17" and "report32," you could use the following command.

```
switch  -regexp  report[0-9]*
```

A **switch** structure is often used to implement menus. In the program **lschoice**, the user is asked to enter a choice for listing files in different ways. Notice the default option that warns of invalid input:

```
#!/usr/bin/tclsh

# Program to allow the user to select different ways of
#    listing files

    puts " s. List Sizes"
    puts " l. List All File Information"
    puts " c. List C Files"

    puts "Please enter choice: "
    gets stdin choice

    switch $choice {
        s {
        puts [exec ls -s]
            }
        l  {
        puts [exec ls -l]
            }
        c {
        puts [exec ls *.c]
            }
            default {
              puts "Invalid Option"
                }
        }
```

Here is a run of the **lschoice** program:

```
$ lschoice
s. List Sizes
l. List All File Information
c. List C Files
Please enter choice:
c
main.c    lib.c    file.c
```

while

The **while** loop repeats commands. In Tcl, the **while** loop begins with the **while** command and takes two arguments—an expression and either a single Tcl command or a block of Tcl commands. The expression is encased in braces. A block of Tcl commands begins with an opening brace on the same line as the **while** command. Then, on following lines are the Tcl commands that will be repeated in the loop. The block ends with a closing brace, usually on a line by itself. The syntax for the **while** loop with a single statement is described here:

```
while {expression } {
       Tcl commands
       }
```

for

The **for** loop performs the same tasks as the **while** loop. However, it has a different format. The **for** loop takes four arguments, the first three of which are expressions and the last of which is a block of Tcl commands. The first three arguments are expressions that incorporate the initialization, test, and increment components of a loop. These expressions are each encased in braces. The last argument, the block of Tcl commands, begins with an opening brace and then continues with Tcl commands on the following lines, ending with a closing brace.

```
for {expression1} {expression2} {expression3} {
    Tcl commands;
    }
```

foreach

The **foreach** structure is designed to sequentially reference a list of values. It is very similar to the C shell's **for-in** structure. The **foreach** structure takes three arguments: a variable, a list, and a block of Tcl commands. Each value in the list is assigned to the variable in the **foreach** structure. Like the **while** structure, the

foreach structure is a loop. Each time through the loop, the next value in the list is assigned to the variable. When the end of the list is reached, the loop stops. As in the **while** loop, the block of Tcl commands is encased in braces. The syntax for the **foreach** loop is described next.

```
foreach variable ( list of values ) {
     tcl commands
     }
```

Tcl Procedures: proc

The **proc** command allows you to create your own Tcl commands for use within a program. In effect, you are creating new procedures, much like procedures or functions in other programming languages. You can think of a **proc** command as defining a Tcl command, much as you would define a function in C. The **proc** command takes three arguments: the name of the new procedure, the arguments that the procedure will take, and a block of commands that the procedure will execute. The arguments are variables that will receive the values passed to them when the procedure is used. The arguments are placed after the procedure name within braces. An opening brace then begins the block of Tcl commands for this procedure. The syntax for the **proc** command follows:

```
proc procedure-name  { arguments } {
     Tcl commands
  }
```

The following example implements the **lsearch** command that searches a list for a pattern:

```
proc mysearch { mylist pat } {
    set i 0
    set len [length $mylist]
    while { $i < $len } {
        if { [lindex $mylist $i] == $pat }
            return $i
    }
    }
```

Tcl String Commands: string

The Tcl **string** command is used to perform different operations on strings. It takes various options, depending upon the task you want to perform. You can search, extract a substring, or obtain the length of a string. The option is entered as a word after the **string** command. Arguments will vary according to the option you choose. Table 43-5 includes the Tcl string commands.

Command	Description
binary	Convert between strings and binary data
regexp	Match on string using regular expressions
regsub	Perform substitutions using patterns with regular expressions
split	Split a string up into list elements
string	Operate on strings
subst	Perform substitutions on a string

Table 43-5. *Tcl String Operations*

With the **string match** command, you can perform basic matching on a string, though regular expressions are not supported by this command. It does support *****, **?**, and **[]**, special characters for simple pattern matching as used in the shell for filename matching. It takes two arguments, the pattern to match and the string to search.

```
string match report* $fname
```

The **string range** command returns a substring of a specified string. It takes three arguments: the string, and the beginning and end indexes. The count starts from 0. The term "end" used for the end index will automatically copy the remainder of the string. The first example here returns "ave", and the second returns "ven".

```
string range "Raven" 1 3
string range "Christmas Carol" 2 end
```

The **string index** command returns a single character from a string at a specified index. It takes two arguments: the string and the index of the character to be returned.

```
string index $mystring 5
```

The **string length** command returns the length of a string.

```
string length $mystring
```

Regular expression pattern matching is implemented with the **regexp** command. **regexp** has full extended regular expression–matching capabilities, similar to **egrep**.

It takes two arguments: the regular expression pattern and the string to be searched. It returns a 1 if the pattern is found in the string, and 0 if it isn't. The following looks for any numbers in **mystring**:

```
regexp [0-9]+ $mystring
```

The **regsub** command is the Tcl substitute command. It matches a regular expression like **regsub** but then replaces the matched string with a specified replacement string, placing the entire modified string in a new variable. **regsub** takes four arguments. The first two are the same as **regexp**, the regular expression pattern and the string to be searched. The third argument is the replacement string, and the fourth is the variable where the modified string will be placed.

Tcl Input and Output: gets and puts

Tcl can read input from the standard input or a file using the **gets** command, and write output to the standard output with the **puts** command. The following command reads a line from the standard input, usually the keyboard. The input is placed in the variable line.

```
gets line
```

The **puts** command outputs a string to the standard output or to a file. It takes as its argument the string to be output.

```
puts $line.
```

gets reads a line into the variable specified as its argument. You can then use this variable to manipulate whatever has been read. For example, you can use **line** in a **puts** command to display what was input.

<u>myread</u>

```
#!/usr/bin/tclsh
gets line
puts "This is what I entered: $line"
```

```
$ myread
larisa and aleina
This is what I entered: larisa and aleina
```

You can use the **puts** command to write data to any file or to the standard output. File handle names are placed after the **puts** command, and before any data such as strings or variables. If no filename is specified, then **puts** outputs to the standard output.

To output formatted values, you can use the results of a format command as the argument of a **puts** command. **format** performs a string conversion operation on a set of values, formatting them according to conversion specifiers in a format string.

```
puts [format "%s" $myname]
```

If you want to output different kinds of values in a **puts** operation, you can use the format command to first transform them into a single string. The **puts** command will only output a single string. In the following example, the contents of the **$firstname** and **$age** variables are output as a single string by first using the format command with two string specifiers, **"%s %d"**, to make them one string. **%d** will transform a numeric value into its corresponding character values.

```
puts [format "%s %d" $firstname  $age]
```

For string values, you can just make them part of the single string by placing them within double quotes. In this example, **firstname** and **lastname** are made part of the same string.

```
puts "$firstname  $lastname"
```

Tcl File Handles

You use the **open** command to create a file handle for a file or pipe (see Table 43-6 for a list of Tcl file commands). The **open** command takes two arguments, the filename and the file mode, and returns a file handle that can then be used to access the file. The filename argument can be the name of the file or a variable that holds the name of the file. The file mode is the permissions you are opening the file with. This can be **r** for read-only, **w** for write-only, and **a** for append only. To obtain both read and write permission for overwriting and updating a file, you attach a **+** to the file mode. **r+** gives you read and write permission. The syntax for **open** follows:

```
open (filename-string, file-mode );
```

You would usually use the **open** command in a **set** command so that you can assign the file handle returned by **open** to a variable. You can then use that file handle in that variable in other file commands to access the file. In the next example, the user opens the file **reports** with a file mode for reading, **r**, and assigns the returned file handle to the **myfile** variable.

```
set myfile [open  "reports" r]
```

File Access Command	Description
`file`	Obtain file information.
`open`	Open a file.
`close`	Close a file.
`eof`	Check for end of file.
`fcopy`	Copy from one file to another.
`flush`	Flush output from a file's internal buffers.
`glob`	Match filenames using glob pattern characters.
`read`	Read blocks of characters from a file.
`seek`	Set the seek offset of a file.
`tell`	Return the current offset of a file.
`socket`	Open a TCP/IP network connection.
Input/Output Command	**Description**
`format`	Format a string with conversion specifiers, like sprintf in C.
`scan`	Read and convert elements in a string using conversion specifiers, like scanf in C.
`gets`	Read a line of input.
`puts`	Write a string to output.

Table 43-6.   *Tcl File Access and Input/Output Commands*

Often, the filename will be held in a variable. You then use the **$** with the variable name to reference the filename. In this example, the filename "**reports**" is held in the variable **filen**.

```
set myfile [open  $filen r]
```

Once you have finished with the file, you close it with the **close** command. **close** takes as its argument the file handle of the file you want to close.

```
close $myfile
```

With the **gets** and **puts** commands, you can use a file handle to read and write from a specific file. **gets** takes two arguments: a file handle and a variable. It will read a line from the file referenced by the file handle and place it as a string in the variable. If no file handle is specified, then **gets** reads from the standard input. The following command reads a line from a file using the file handle in the **myfile** variable. The line is read into the **line** variable.

```
gets $myfile line
```

The **puts** command also takes two arguments: a file handle and a string. It will write the string to the file referenced by the file handle. If no file handle is specified, then **puts** will write to the standard output. In the following example, **puts** writes the string held in the **line** variable to the file referenced by the file handle held in **myfile**. Notice that there is a **$** before **line** in the **puts** command, but not in the previous **gets** command. **puts** operates on a string, whereas **gets** operates on a variable.

```
puts $myfile $line
```

myreport
```
#!/usr/bin/tclsh
    set reps [open "reports" r ]
    while ( gets $reps line)
        {
        puts $line;
        }
    close reps
```

You can use the **file** command to check certain features of files, such as whether they exist or they are executable. You can also check for directories. The **file** command takes several options, depending the action you want to take. The **exist** option checks whether a file exists, and the **size** option tells you its size. The **isdirectory** option determines whether the file is a directory, and **isfile** checks to see whether it is a file. With the executable, readable, and writable options, you can detect whether a file is executable, can be read, or can be written to. The **dirname** option displays the full pathname of the file, and the **extension** and **root name** options show the extension or root name of the file, respectively. The **atime**, **mtime**, and **owned** options display the last access time and the modification time, and whether it is owned by the user.

```
file exits reps
file isfile reps
file size reps
file executable myreport
```

Often filenames will be used as arguments to Tcl programs. In this case, you can use the **argv** list to obtain the filenames. The **argv** command lists all arguments entered on the command line when the Tcl script was invoked. You use the **lindex** command to extract a particular argument from the **argv** list. Many programs use filenames as their arguments. Many also specify options. Remember that the **lindex** command indexes a list from 0. So the first argument in the **argv** list would be obtained by the following (be sure to precede **argv** with the **$**):

```
lindex $argv 0
```

You can, if you wish, reference an argument in the **argv** list within the **open** command. Here, the **lindex** operation is enclosed in braces, in place of the filename. The **lindex** command will return the filename from the **argv** list.

```
set shandle [ open {lindex $argv 1}  r ]
```

Tk

The Tk application extends Tcl with commands for creating and managing graphic objects such as windows, icons, buttons, and text fields. Tk commands create graphic objects using the X Window System. It is an easier way to program X Window objects than using the X11 toolkit directly. With Tk, you can easily create sophisticated window-based user interfaces for your programs.

The Tk language is organized according to different types of graphic objects such as windows, buttons, menus, and scroll bars. Such objects are referred to as *widgets*. Each type of widget has its own command with which you can create a widget. For example, you can create a button with the **button** command or a window with the **window** command. A type of widget is considered a class, and the command to create such a widget is called a *class command*. The command will create a particular instance of that class, a particular widget of that type. **button** is the class command for creating a button. Graphical objects such as buttons and frames are also often referred to as widgets. Table 43-7 lists the different widgets available in Tk.

Note *Several currently available Tcl/Tk GUI builders are Free Visual Tcl, SpecTcl, VisualGIPSY, and XF. These are freely available, and you can download them from their Web sites or from the Tcl Developer Xchange.*

PROGRAMMING

Widget	Description
button	A button
canvas	A window for drawing objects
checkbutton	A check button
entry	An input box
frame	A frame is a simple widget. Its primary purpose is to act as a spacer or container for complex window layouts.
image	Create image objects for displaying pictures
label	A label
listbox	A list box with a selectable list of items
menu	A menu bar
menubutton	A menu button to access the menu
message	Create and manipulate message widgets
radiobutton	A radio button
scrollbar	A scroll bar
text	An editable text box
scale	A scale

Table 43-7. *Standard TK Widgets*

The wish Shell and Scripts

Tk operates under the X Window System. Within the X Window System, Tk uses its own shell, the wish shell, to execute Tk commands. To run Tk programs, you first start up your X Window System and then start up the wish shell with the command **wish**. This will open up a window in which you can then run Tk commands.

You execute Tk commands within the wish shell interactively, entering commands and executing them one by one, or you can place the commands in a script file and execute them all at once. Usually, Tk commands are placed in a script that is then run with the invocation of the **wish** command. Like Tcl scripts, Tk scripts usually have the extension **.tcl**. For example, a Tk script called **mydir.tcl** would be read and executed by the following command entered in an Xterm window:

```
$ wish mydir.tcl
```

To create a standalone script that operates more like a command, you need to invoke the **wish** command within the script. Ordinarily, the **wish** command will open an interactive Tk shell window whenever executed. To avoid this, you should invoke wish with the **-f** option.

```
#!/usr/bin/wish -f
```

 Note *When creating a standalone script, be sure to change its permissions with the **chmod** command to allow execution. You can then just enter the name of the script to run the program.*

```
$ chmod 755 mydir1
$ ./mydir1
```

Tk Widgets

Tk programs consist of class commands that create various graphic widgets. The class command takes as its arguments the name you want to give the particular widget, followed by configuration options with their values (see Table 43-8). Tk commands have a format similar to Tcl. You enter a Tk class command on a line, beginning with the name of the command and followed by its arguments. Tk commands are more complicated than Tcl commands. Graphic interface commands require a significant amount of information about a widget to set it up. For example, a button requires a name, the text it will display, and the action it will take.

Many Tk commands can take various options indicating different features of a widget. Table 43-9 lists several options commonly used for Tk widgets. In the following example, a button is created using the **button** command. The **button** command takes as its first argument the name of the button widget. Then, different options define various features. The **-text** option is followed by a string that will be the text displayed by the button. The **-command** option is followed by the command that the button executes when it is clicked. This **button** command will display a button with the text "Click Me." When you click it, the Tk shell will exit.

```
button .mybutton -text "Click Me" -command exit
```

Event Operations	Description
bind	Associate Tcl scripts with X events
bindtags	Bind commands to tags
selection	Object or text selected by mouse
Geometry Managers	
pack	Pack widgets next to each other
place	Place widgets in positions in frame
grid	Place widgets in a grid of rows and columns
Window Operations	
destroy	Close a TK window
toplevel	Select the top-level window
wm	Set window features
uplevel	Move up to previous window level

Table 43-8. *Tk Commands*

Button	Description
-activebackground	Specifies background color to use when drawing active elements
-activeborderwidth	Width of the 3-D border drawn around active elements
-activeforeground	Foreground color to use when drawing active elements
-anchor	How information is displayed in the widget; must be one of the values n, ne, e, se, s, sw, w, nw, or center

Table 43-9. *Tk Standard Options*

Button	Description
-background	The normal background color to use when displaying the widget
-bitmap	A bitmap to display in the widget
-borderwidth	The width of the 3-D border to draw around the outside of the widget
-cursor	The mouse cursor to be used for the widget
-disabledforeground	Foreground color to use when drawing a disabled element
-font	The font to use when drawing text inside the widget
-foreground	The normal foreground color to use when displaying the widget
-geometry	Specifies the desired geometry for the widget's window
-highlightbackground	The color to display in the traversal highlight region when the widget does not have the input focus
-highlightcolor	The color to use for the traversal highlight rectangle that is drawn around the widget when it has the input focus
-highlightthickness	The width of the highlight rectangle to draw around the outside of the widget when it has the input focus
-image	Specifies an image to display in the widget
-insertbackground	Color to use as background in the area covered by the insertion cursor
-insertborderwidth	Width of the 3-D border to draw around the insertion cursor
-insertofftime	Number of milliseconds the insertion cursor should remain "off" in each blink cycle

Table 43-9.   *Tk Standard Options* (continued)

Button	Description
-insertontime	Number of milliseconds the insertion cursor should remain "on" in each blink cycle
-jump	For widgets with a slider that can be dragged to adjust a value
-justify	Justifies multiple lines of text displayed in a widget
-orient	Orientation for widgets that can position themselves, such as scroll bars
-padx	Specifies how much extra space to request for the widget in the X-direction
-pady	Specifies how much extra space to request for the widget in the Y-direction
-relief	Specifies the 3-D effect desired for the widget
-repeatdelay	Specifies the number of milliseconds a button or key must be held down before it begins to auto-repeat
-selectbackground	Specifies the background color to use when displaying selected items
-selectborderwidth	Specifies width of the 3-D border
-selectforeground	Foreground color
-text	String to be displayed inside the widget
-troughcolor	Color to use for the rectangular trough areas in widgets such as scroll bars and scales
-underline	Specifies the integer index of a character to underline in the widget
-wraplength	The maximum line length for word wrapping

Table 43-9.   *Tk Standard Options* (continued)

Button	Description
-xscrollcommand	Command used to communicate with horizontal scroll bars
-yscrollcommand	Command used to communicate with vertical scroll bars
Button Options	
-command	Specifies a Tcl command to associate with the button
-selectimage	Image to display when the checkbutton is selected
-height	Height for the button
-selectcolor	Background color to use when the button is selected
-state	Specifies one of three states for the radiobutton: normal, active, or disabled
-variable	Global variable to set to indicate whether or not this button is selected
-width	Width for the button

Table 43-9.   *Tk Standard Options* (continued)

PROGRAMMING

To set up a working interface, you need to define all the widgets you need to perform a given task. Some widgets are designed to manage other widgets; for instance, scroll bars are designed to manage windows. Other widgets, such as text input fields, may interact with a Tcl program. A menu choice may take the action of running part of a Tcl program.

Widgets are organized hierarchically. For example, to set up a window to input data, you may need a frame, within which may be text field widgets as well as buttons. Widget names reflect this hierarchy. The widget contained within another widget is prefixed with that widget's name. If the name of the frame is **report** and you want to call the text input field **monday**, then the text input field will have the name **report.monday**. A period separates each level in the hierarchy. A button that you want to call **ok** that is within the **report** frame would be named **report.ok**.

Once you have created your widgets, their geometry has to be defined. The geometry determines the size of each widget in relation to the others, and where they are placed in the window. Tk has three geometry managers, **pack**, **place**, and **grid**. The **pack** command is used in these examples. When you have defined your widgets, you issue a geometry manager command on them to determine their size and shape on the screen.

Note   *Your widgets cannot be displayed until their geometry is determined.*

The following determines the geometry of the **.mybutton** widget using the **pack** command.

```
pack .mybutton
```

The **mydir1** program is a simple Tcl/Tk program to display a list of file and directory names in a Tk listbox widget with an attached scroll bar. Figure 43-1 shows this list box. With a listbox widget, you can display a list of items that you can then easily scroll through. Using the mouse, you can select a particular item. If a scroll bar is attached, you can scroll through the displayed items, if more than can fit in the designated size of the list box. First, the scroll bar is defined using the **scrollbar** command, giving it the name **.scroll** and binding it with the command "**.list yview**". This instructs the scroll bar to be attached to the list box on a y-axis, vertical.

```
scrollbar .scroll -command ".list yview"
```

Figure 43-1.   *The **mydir1** Tk list box*

Then, the list box is defined with the **listbox** command, giving it the name **.list** and a y-axis scroll capability provided by the **.scroll** widget. The list box will appear sunken with the specified width and height.

```
listbox .list -yscroll ".scroll set"  -relief sunken -width 15 \
   -height 15 -setgrid yes
```

The two widgets are then created with the **pack** command and positioned in the window. They are placed on the left side of the window and will always expand to fill the window. The anchor is on the west side of the window, **w**. The list box, **.list**, is placed first, followed by the scroll bar, **.scroll**.

```
pack .list .scroll   -side left  -fill both -expand yes -anchor w
```

A Tcl **if** test then follows that checks if the user entered an argument when the program was invoked. The **if** test checks to see whether if there is a first element in the **argv** list in which any arguments are held. If there are no arguments, then the current directory is used, as represented by the period. This chosen directory is assigned to the **dir** variable. A Tcl **foreach** operation is then used to fill the list box. The shell **ls** command, as executed with the **exec** command, obtains the list of files and directories. Each is then placed in the list box with the Tk **insert** operation for the **.list** widget. The **insert** command takes a position and a value. Here, the value is a filename held in **$i** that is placed at the **end** of the list.

```
.list insert end $i
```

The CTRL-C character is then bound to the **exit** command to allow you to easily close the window.

mydir1

```
#!/usr/bin/wish -f
# Create a scroll bar and listbox
scrollbar .scroll -command ".list yview"
listbox .list -yscroll ".scroll set"  -relief sunken -width 15 -height 15 \
   -setgrid yes
pack .list .scroll   -side left  -fill both -expand yes -anchor w
# If user enters a directory argument use that, otherwise use current
# directory.
if {$argc > 0} then {
    set dir [lindex $argv 0]
    } else {
          set dir "."
          }
# Fill the listbox (.list) with the list of files and directories obtained
```

```
# from ls
 cd $dir
 foreach i [exec ls -a ] {
    if [file isfile $i] {
    .list insert end $i
    }
    }
# Set up bindings for the file manager.  Control-C closes the window.
bind all <Control-c> {destroy .}
```

To run the **mydir1** program, first make it executable using the **chmod** command to set the executable permissions, as shown here.

```
chmod 755 mydir1
```

Then, within a terminal window on your desktop or window manager, just enter the **mydir1** command at the prompt. You may have to precede it with a **./** to indicate the current directory.

```
./mydir1
```

A window will open with a list box displaying a list of files in your current working directory (see Figure 43-1). Use the scroll bar to display any filenames not shown. Click the window close box to close the program.

Events and Bindings

A Tk program is event driven. Upon running, it waits for an event, such as a mouse event or a keyboard event. A mouse event can be a mouse click or a double-click, even a mouse down or up. A keyboard event can be a CTRL key or meta key, even the ENTER key at the end of input data. When the program detects a particular event, it takes an action. The action may be another graphical operation, such as displaying another menu, or it may be a Tcl, Perl, or shell program.

Bindings are the key operational component of a Tk program. Bindings detect the events that drive a Tk program. You can think of a Tk program as an infinite loop that continually scans for the occurrence of specified events (bindings). When it detects such an event, such as a mouse click or control key, then it executes the actions bound to that event. These actions can be any Tcl/Tk command or series of commands. Usually, they call functions that can perform complex operations. When finished, the program resumes its scanning, looking for other bound events. This scanning continues indefinitely until it is forcibly broken by an **exit** or **destroy** command, as is done with the CTRL-C binding. You can think of bindings as multiple entry points where different parts of the program begin. It is not really the same structure as a traditional hierarchical sequential program. You should think of a binding as starting its own sequence of commands, its own program. This means that to trace the flow of control for a Tk program, you start with the bindings. Each binding has its own path, its own flow of control.

Actions are explicitly bound to given events using the **bind** command. The **bind** command takes as its arguments the name of a widget or class, the event to bind, and the action to bind to that event. Whenever the event takes place within that widget, the specified action is executed.

```
bind .myframe  <CTRL-H>   {.myframe delete insert }
```

You use the **bind** command to connect events in a Tk widget with the Tcl command you want executed. In a sense, you are dividing your Tcl program into segments, each of which is connected to an event in a Tk widget. When an event takes place in a Tk widget, its associated set of Tcl commands are executed. Other Tk commands, as well as Tcl commands, can be associated with an event bound to a Tk widget. This means that you can nest widgets and their events. The Tcl commands executed by one Tk event may, in turn, include other Tk commands and widgets with events bound to yet other Tcl commands.

The **mydir2** program shown in Figure 43-2 illustrates functions and widget bindings. The previous **mydir1** program is enhanced with the capability to display two list boxes, one for directories and one for files. Each has its own scroll bars. The directory list box is named **.listdir**, and its scroll bar **.scrolldir**. Each list box

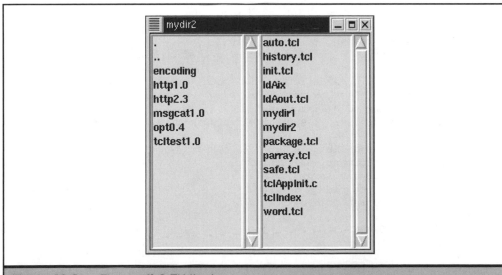

Figure 43-2.   *The mydir2 TK list box*

PROGRAMMING

and scroll bar is defined and then created, **.listdir** and **.scrolldir** first so that they will be placed on the left side of the window.

The Tcl function **listdirsfuncs** is then defined to fill both list boxes. This function takes as its argument a directory. The **cd** command will change to that directory, providing the capability of listing different directories. The **isdirectory** test checks for directories, placing them in the **.listdir** list box. Following the definition of this function, there is a function call for it. **listdirsfuncs** needs to be called once to initially fill up the list boxes with the contents of the current directory.

There is now a binding for the **.listdir** widget. The double-click of the left mouse button, Double-Button-1, is bound to a call of the **listdirfuncs** function for the **.listdir** list box. This binding makes any double-click on the **.listdir** list box have the effect of calling the **listdirsfuncs** function. As there is no binding for the **.list** list box, a double-click on that box will have no effect.

There are two actions bound to **.listdir** with the double-click. These are encased in braces. To have more than one action executed with a binding, you have to place them within braces. The first action is an operation to obtain the selected directory name from the list box. When you click an item in a list box, you select it. The **[selection get]** operation will return the selected item, in this case, a directory name. The directory name is assigned to the variable **i**. This variable is then used as an argument in the function call of **listdirsfuncs**, the second action. These two actions illustrate how you can obtain values and pass them as arguments to a function, all within a binding. First, you obtain the values, assigning them to variables; then, you use the contents of these variables as arguments in the function call.

mydir2

```
#!/usr/bin/wish -f
# Create scroll bar and listbox for directories
scrollbar .scrolldir -command ".listdir yview"
listbox .listdir -yscroll " .scrolldir set" -relief sunken -width 15 -height \
  15 -setgrid yes
pack .listdir .scrolldir -side left -fill both -expand yes -anchor w
# Create scroll bar and listbox for files
scrollbar .scroll -command ".list yview"
listbox .list -yscroll ".scroll set" -relief sunken -width 15 -height 15 \
  -setgrid yes
pack .list .scroll -side left -fill both -expand yes -anchor w
# Check to see if an argument was entered
if $argc>0 {set dir [lindex $argv 0]} else {set dir "."}
# Function to list directories and files.
#Current entries are first deleted
proc listdirsfunc dir {
    .listdir delete 0 end
    .list delete 0 end
    cd $dir
    foreach i [exec ls -a ] {
        if [file isdirectory $i] {
            .listdir insert end $i
            } else {
```

```
                    .list insert end $i
                }
        }
    }
# Display directories and files the first time
listdirsfunc $dir
# Set up bindings for the browser. Directories are bound to the Mouse \
  double-click
bind all <Control-c> {destroy .}
bind .listdir <Double-Button-1> {set i [selection get]
                                 listdirsfunc  $i}
```

To run the **mydir1** program, first make it executable using the **chmod** command to set the executable permissions, as shown here.

```
chmod 755 mydir1
```

Then, within a terminal window on your desktop or window manager, just enter the **mydir1** command at the prompt. You may have to precede it with a **./** to indicate the current directory.

```
./mydir2
```

A window will open up with two list boxes displaying a list of directories on the left and on the right (see Figure 43-2). Use the scroll bars to display any filenames or directories not shown. Change to another directory by double-clicking its name. Then the subdirectories and files in that directory are displayed. To move back up to the parent directory, double-click the **..** entry in the directory list box. Click the window close box to close the program.

Expect

Expect has several commands that you can use to automatically interact with any Unix program or utility that prompts you for responses. For example, the login procedure for different systems using FTP or telnet can be automatically programmed with Expect commands. Expect is designed to work with any interactive program. It waits for a response from a program and will then send the response specified in its script. You can drop out of the script with a simple command and interact with the program directly.

Three basic Expect commands are the **send, expect,** and **interact** commands. The **expect** command will wait to receive a string or value from the application you are interacting with. The **send** command will send a string to that application. The **interact** command places you into direct interaction with the application, ending the Expect/Tcl script. In the following script, Expect is used to perform an anonymous login with FTP. The **spawn** command starts up the FTP program. The Internet address of the FTP site is assumed to be an argument to this script, and as such, will be held in the **argv** list. In place of **$argv** you could put the name of a particular FTP site.

myftp.expect

```
#!/usr/bin/expect
spawn ftp
send "open $argv\r"
expect "Name"
send "anonymous\r"
expect "word:"
send "richlp@turtle.mytrek.com\r"
interact
```

To run Expect commands, you have to first enter the Expect shell. In the previous **myftp.expect** script, the Expect shell is invoked with the command **#!/usr/bin/expect**. Be sure to add execute permission with **chmod 755 myftp.expect**:

```
$myftp ftp.calderasystems.com
```

The **expect** command can take two arguments, the pattern to expect and an action to take if the pattern is matched. **expect** can also take as its argument a block of pattern/action arguments. In this case, **expect** can match on alternative patterns, executing the action only for the pattern it receives. For example, the **ftp** command may return a "Connection refused" string instead of a "Name" string. In that case, you would want to issue this message and exit the Expect script. If you want more than one action taken for a pattern, you can encase them in braces, separated by semicolons.

Another useful Expect command is **timeout**. You can set the **timeout** command to a number of seconds, and then have **expect** check for the **timeout**. To set the number of seconds for a **timeout**, you use **set** to assign it to the **timeout** variable (the default is 10 seconds). To have the **expect** command detect a **timeout**, you use the word **timeout** as the **expect** command's pattern. With the **timeout**, you can add an action to take. An example of an **expect** script follows:

```
set timeout 20
end "open $argv\r"
expect {
    timeout {puts "Connection timed out\n"; exit }
    "Connection refused"  {puts "Failed to connect\n"; exit}
    "Unknown host" {puts "$argv is unknown\n"; exit}
    "Name"
}
```

Expect can run with any kind of program that requires interaction. All you need to do is to determine the sequence of prompts and responses you want.

The Complete Reference

Linux

Chapter 44

Gawk

Gawk is a programming language designed to let Linux users create their own shell filters. A filter operates within a Linux shell such as BASH or TCSH. It reads information from an input source such as a file or the standard input, modifies or analyzes that information, and then outputs the results. Results can be a modified version of the input or an analysis. For example, the **sort** filter reads a file and then outputs a sorted version of it, generating output that can be sorted alphabetically or numerically. The **wc** filter reads a file and then calculates the number of words and lines in it, outputting just that information. The **grep** filter will search a file for a particular pattern, outputting the lines the pattern is found on. With Gawk, you can design and create your own filters, in effect creating your own Linux commands. You can instruct Gawk to simply display lines of input text much like **cat**, or search for patterns in a file like **grep**, or even count words in a file like **wc**. In each case, you could add your own customized filtering capabilities. You could display only part of each line, or search for a pattern in a specific field, or count only words that are capitalized. This flexibility lets you use Gawk to generate reports, detecting patterns and performing calculations on the data.

You can use Gawk directly on the shell command line, or you can place Gawk within a shell file that you can then execute. The name of the shell file can be thought of as a new filter that you have created. In effect, with Gawk, you can define your own filters. In this sense, there are two ways of thinking about Gawk. Gawk is itself a filter that you can invoke on the command line like any other filter, and Gawk is a programmable filter that you can use to create your own filters. This chapter will examine both aspects of Gawk. First, we will examine Gawk as a filter, with all its different features. Then we will see how you can use Gawk to define your own filters.

The Gawk utility has all the flexibility and complexity of a programming language. Gawk has a set of operators that allow it to make decisions and calculations. You can also declare variables and use them in control structures to control how lines are to be processed. Many of the programming features are taken from the C programming language and share the same syntax. All of this makes for a very powerful programming tool.

Gawk is the GNU version of the Unix Awk utility. Awk was originally created as a standard utility for the Unix operating system. One of its creators is Brian Kernighan, who developed the Unix operating system. An enhanced version of Awk, called Nawk, was developed later to include file handling. With Nawk, you can access several files in the same program. Gawk is a further enhancement, including the added features of Nawk, as well as the standard capabilities of Awk.

The gawk Command

The **gawk** command takes as its arguments a Gawk instruction and a list of filenames. The Gawk instruction is encased in single quotes and is read as one argument. The Gawk instruction itself consists of two segments, a pattern and an action. The action is enclosed in brackets. The term "pattern" can be misleading. It is perhaps clearer to think of the pattern segment as a condition. The pattern segment can be either a pattern search or a test condition of the type found in programming languages. The Gawk utility has a full set of operators with which to construct complex conditions. You can think of a pattern search as just one other kind of condition for retrieving records. Instead of simply matching patterns, as in the case of **grep**, the user specifies a condition. Records that meet that condition are then retrieved. The actions in the action segment are then applied to the record. The next example shows the syntax of a Gawk instruction, which you can think of as **condition {action}**.

```
pattern {action}
```

The Gawk utility operates on either files or the standard input. You can list filenames on the command line after the instruction. If there are no filenames listed, then input is taken from the standard input. The next example shows the structure of the entire Gawk instruction. The invocation of Gawk consists of the **gawk** keyword followed by a Gawk instruction and filenames. As with the **sed** commands, the instruction should be placed within single quotes to avoid interpretation by the shell. Since the condition and action are not separate arguments for Gawk, you need to enclose them both in one set of quotes. The next example shows the syntax of a **gawk** command:

```
$ gawk 'pattern action { }' filenames
```

You can think of the pattern in a Gawk instruction as referencing a line. The Gawk action is then performed on that line. The next two examples print all lines with the pattern "Penguin." The pattern segment is a pattern search. A pattern search is denoted by a pattern enclosed in slashes. All records with this pattern are retrieved. The action segment in the first example contains the **print** command. The **print** command outputs the line to the standard output.

books

```
Tempest     Shakespeare   15.75   Penguin
Christmas   Dickens        3.50   Academic
Iliad       Homer         10.25   Random
Raven       Poe            2.50   Penguin
```

```
$ gawk '/Penguin/{print}' books
Tempest     Shakespeare   15.75   Penguin
Raven       Poe            2.50   Penguin
```

Tip   *Both the action and pattern have defaults that allow you to leave either of them out. The print action is the default action. If an action is not specified, the line is printed. The default pattern is the selection of every line in the text. If the pattern is not specified, the action is applied to all lines.*

In the second example, there is no action segment. The default action is then used, the **print** action.

```
$ gawk '/Penguin/' books
Tempest     Shakespeare  15.75   Penguin
Raven       Poe           2.50   Penguin
```

Pattern Searches and Special Characters

Gawk can retrieve lines using a pattern search that contains special characters. The pattern is designated with a beginning and ending slash, and placed in the pattern segment of the Gawk instruction.

```
/pattern/ {action}
```

The pattern search is performed on all the lines in the file. If the pattern is found, the action is performed on the line. In this respect, Gawk performs very much like an editing operation. Like **sed**, a line is treated as a line of text and the pattern is searched for throughout the line. In the next example, Gawk searches for any line with the pattern "Poe." When a match is found, the line is output.

```
$ gawk '/Poe/{print}' books
Raven       Poe           2.50    Penguin
```

You can use the same special characters for Gawk that are used for regular expressions in the **sed** filter and the Ed editor. The first example here searches for a pattern at the beginning of the line. The special character ^ references the beginning of a line. The second example searches for a pattern at the end of a line using the special character **$**.

```
$ gawk '/^Christmas/{print}' books
Christmas   Dickens      3.50    Academic

$ gawk '/Random$/{print}' books
Iliad       Homer       10.25    Random
```

As in Ed and **sed**, you can use special characters to specify variations on a pattern. The period matches any character, the asterisk matches repeated characters, and the brackets match a class of characters: **.**, *****, and **[]**. In the next example, the period is used to match any pattern in which a single character is followed by the characters "en":

```
$ gawk '/.en/{print}' books
Tempest      Shakespeare 15.75   Penguin
Christmas    Dickens      3.50   Academic
Raven        Poe          2.50   Penguin
```

The next example uses the brackets and asterisk special characters to specify a sequence of numbers. The set of possible numbers is represented by the brackets enclosing the range of numeric characters, [0–9]. The asterisk then specifies any repeated sequence of numbers. The context for such a sequence consists of the characters ".50." Any number ending with .50 will be matched. Notice that the period is quoted with a backslash to treat it as the period character, not as a special character.

```
$ gawk '/[0-9]*\.50/ {print}' books
Christmas    Dickens      3.50   Academic
Raven        Poe          2.50   Penguin
```

Gawk also uses the extended special characters: **+**, **?**, and **|**. The **+** and **?** are variations on the ***** special character. The **+** matches one or more repeated instances of a character. The **?** matches zero or one instance of a character. The **|** provides alternative patterns to be searched. In the next example, the user searches for a line containing either the pattern "Penguin" or the pattern "Academic":

```
$ gawk '/Penguin|Academic/ {print}' books
Tempest      Shakespeare 15.75   Penguin
Christmas    Dickens      3.50   Academic
Raven        Poe          2.50   Penguin
```

Variables, Operators, and Arrays

Gawk provides for the definition of variables and arrays. It also supports the standard kind of arithmetic and assignment operators found in most programming languages such as C. Relational operators are also supported and discussed later in the section "Control Structures."

Variables, Constants, and Patterns

In Gawk, there are three types of variables: field variables, special Gawk variables, and user-defined variables. Gawk automatically defines both the field and special variables. The user can define his or her own variables. You can also define arithmetic and string constants. Arithmetic constants consist of numeric characters, and string constants consist of any characters enclosed within double quotes.

Field variables are designed to reference fields in a line. A field is any set of characters separated by a field delimiter. The default delimiter is a space or tab. As with other database filters, Gawk numbers fields from 1. Gawk defines a field variable for each field in the file. A field variable consists of a dollar sign followed by the number of the field. **$2** references the second field. The variable **$0** is a special field variable that contains the entire line.

A variable may be used in either the pattern or action segment of the Gawk instruction. If more than one variable is listed, they are separated by commas. Notice that the dollar sign is used differently in Gawk than in the shell.

In the next example, the second and fourth fields of the books file are printed out. The **$2** and **$4** reference the second and fourth fields.

books

```
Tempest     Shakespeare  15.75  Penguin
Christmas   Dickens       3.50  Academic
Iliad       Homer        10.25  Random
Raven       Poe           2.50  Penguin
```

```
$ gawk '{print $2, $4}' books
Shakespeare  Penguin
Dickens      Academic
Homer        Random
Poe          Penguin
```

In the next example, the user outputs the line with the pattern "Dickens" twice—first reversing the order of the fields and then with the fields in order. The **$0** is used to output all the fields in order, the entire line.

```
$ gawk '/Dickens/ {print $4, $3, $2, $1; print $0}' books
Academic  3.50  Dickens  Christmas
Christmas Dickens  3.50  Academic
```

Gawk defines a set of special variables that provide information about the line being processed. The variable **NR** contains the number of the current line (or record).

The variable **NF** contains the number of fields in the current line. There are other special variables that hold the field and record delimiters. There is even one, **FILENAME**, that holds the name of the input file. The Gawk special variables are listed in Table 44-1.

Both special variables and user-defined variables do not have a dollar sign placed before them. To use such variables, you only need to specify their names. The next example combines both the special variable **NR** with the field variables **$2** and **$4** to print out the line number of the line followed by the contents of fields two and four. The **NR** variable holds the line number of the line being processed.

```
$ gawk '{print NR, $2, $4}' books
1 Shakespeare   Penguin
2 Dickens       Academic
3 Homer         Random
4 Poe           Penguin
```

You can also define your own variables, giving them any name you want. Variables can be named using any alphabetic or numeric characters, as well as underscores. The name must begin with an alphabetic character. A variable is defined when you first use it. The type of variable is determined by the way it is used. If you use it to hold numeric values, then the variable is considered arithmetic. If you use it to hold characters, then the variable is considered a string. You need to be consistent in the way in which you use a variable. String variables should not be used in arithmetic calculations, and vice versa.

Variable	Description
NR	Record number of current record
NF	Number of fields in current record
$0	The entire current record
$n	The fields in the current record, numbered from 1—for example, $1
FS	Input field delimiter; default delimiter is space or tab
FILENAME	Name of current input file

Table 44-1. *Gawk Special Variables*

You assign a value to a variable using the assignment operator, **=**. The left-hand side of an assignment operation is always a variable and the right-hand side is the value assigned to it. A value can be the contents of a variable, such as a field, special, or other user variable. It can also be a constant, as described in the next section. In the next example, the user assigns the contents of the second field to the variable **myfield**:

```
$ gawk '{myfield = $2; print myfield}' books
Shakespeare
Dickens
Homer
Poe
```

By default, Gawk separates fields by spaces or tabs. However, if you want to use a specific delimiter, you need to specify it. The **-F** option allows Gawk to detect a specific delimiter. The **-F** option actually sets a Gawk special variable called **FS**, which stands for field separator. With the **-F** option, you can use any character you want for your delimiter.

Arithmetic and Assignment Operations

Gawk has a full set of arithmetic operators. You can perform multiplication, division, addition, subtraction, and modulo calculations. The arithmetic operators are the same as those used in the C programming language, and they are listed in Table 44-2 along with the assignment operators, which will be discussed shortly.

You can perform arithmetic calculations on numeric values represented by numeric patterns. A numeric pattern is any sequence of digits, and an arithmetic constant is an obvious numeric pattern. A field whose contents are digits is also a numeric pattern. Arithmetic constants, field variables, and user-defined variables whose values are numeric patterns can all be used as operands in arithmetic operations. There are also certain special Gawk variables that are defined as numeric, such as **NR** and **NF**. These can also be arithmetic operands.

Arithmetic operations can be used in either the action or pattern segment of the Gawk instruction. In the next example, the user outputs every even-numbered line. The percent sign (**%**) is a modulo operator that results in the remainder of a division. If 2 divides evenly into the line number with no remainder, then the line is an even-numbered line. Notice how parentheses are used to arrange the expression.

```
$ gawk '(NR % 2) == 0 {print NR, $0}' books
2 Christmas    Dickens    3.50    Academic
4 Raven        Poe        2.50    Penguin
```

Arithmetic Operators and Functions	Description
*	Multiplication
/	Division
+	Addition
-	Subtraction
%	Modulo; results in the remainder of a division
int(*num*)	Truncates a floating-point number, *num*, to its integer value
cos(*num*)	Returns the cosine of *num*
sin(*num*)	Returns the sine of *num*
log(*num*)	Returns the natural log of *num*
exp(*num*)	Returns the exponential of *num*
sqrt(*num*)	Returns the square root of *num*
rand()	Returns a random number
srand(*num*)	Uses *num* as a new seed for **rand**()

Assignment Operators

=	Assignment
++	Increment
--	Decrement
+=	Addition and assignment; **i = i + 1** is the same as **i += 1**.
-=	Subtraction and assignment; **i = i - 1** is the same as **i -= 1**.
*=	Multiplication and assignment; **i = i * 1** is the same as **i *= 1**.
/=	Division and assignment; **i = i / 1** is the same as **i /= 1**.
%=	Modulo and assignment; **i = i % 1** is the same as **i %= 1**.

Table 44-2. *The Gawk Arithmetic and Assignment Operators*

With arithmetic operators and variables, you can easily perform calculations on a field in a database file. For example, you could sum the values of the same field in each line, just as you could sum up a column in a spreadsheet. The next example sums up the third field in the **books** file. The user-defined variable **tot** holds the sum, and the **END** condition then prints out the final value of the **tot** variable. Since variables are automatically initialized to 0, the **tot** variable begins with an initial value of 0.

```
$ gawk '{print; tot = tot + $3} END {print "Total=",tot}' books
Tempest     Shakespeare   15.75   Penguin
Christmas   Dickens        3.50   Academic
Iliad       Homer         10.25   Random
Raven       Poe            2.50   Penguin
Total= 32
```

In addition to the standard arithmetic operators, there is also a set of arithmetic assignment operators, listed in Table 44-2. These operators combine the assignment operation with an arithmetic operation. They are used as a kind of shorthand for specifying an operation that assigns a variable to the result of an expression in which that same variable is also an operand. The operation **tot = tot + 1** can be written with the arithmetic operator **+=** as **tot += 1**. You do not have to specify the **tot** variable in the arithmetic expression because the arithmetic assignment operation assumes it. The operation **i = i * 2** can be written as **i *= 2**. The following command produces the same result as the previous example using an arithmetic assignment operation:

```
$ gawk '{print; tot += $3} END {print "Total=", tot}' books
```

Arrays and Associative Arrays

A subscript enclosed in brackets and placed next to an array name references an element in the array. Like variables, the first use of a subscript in Gawk also defines the array. Unlike programming languages, arrays are not declared, and no maximum size needs to be given for an array. An array will dynamically expand as elements are referenced.

In the following example, the array **titles** is defined. Each element of **titles** is assigned the value of the first field of a line. There will be only as many elements in the array as there are values assigned. The variable **num** is used to reference each element of the array, and it is incremented after each use. At the end, the last element in the array is printed out.

```
$ gawk '{titles[num] = $1; num++} END{print titles[num - 1]}' books
Raven
```

Suppose, however, that you want to assign each field in a particular record to an array. You could do this through individual assignment operations for each field, but Gawk provides a shortcut. You can assign fields to array elements with the **split** function. The **split** function takes as its arguments a line, an array, and a field separator. The field separator is specified by a string—to use a colon as a field separator, you would specify the string ":". The field separator is optional, and if no field separator is entered, either a tab or a space is assumed by default.

The **split** function can also operate on any string. **split("9-10-92", date,"-")** assigns **9** to **date[1]**, **10** to **date[2]**, and **92** to **date[3]**. In the following example, each field in a line is assigned to an element of the **myrec** array. The line assigned is selected by the search pattern **/Dickens/**. The fields are then output in reverse order.

```
$ gawk '/Dickens/ {split($0, myrec); print myrec[4], myrec[3],
myrec[2], myrec[1]}' books
Academic   3.50  Dickens    Christmas
```

Gawk also allows you to define *associative arrays*. An associative array allows strings to be array subscripts. Suppose you want to reference an author's publisher by the author's name. In the next example, the user assigns publishers to an array indexed by the author's name. The second field is the author name and the fourth field is the publisher name. In this case, the Dickens publisher is printed. Notice the double quotes around **"Dickens"**. When you use a string constant as a subscript in an associative array, you need to enclose the string within double quotes.

```
$ gawk '{publ[$2] = $4} END{ print publ["Dickens"]}' books
Academic
```

Pattern Segment as a Condition

What is known as the pattern segment of a Gawk instruction can be thought of as a test condition. Control structures in programming languages have test expressions that are tested for truth or falsity. If the test is true, the control structure's statements are executed. In the same way, a pattern in Gawk can be considered a test expression. If the pattern makes a successful match, then it is true and its Gawk action is executed. In this respect, a pattern is a condition for the action's execution.

In programming languages, test expressions can be made up of complex subexpressions using relational and logical operators, as well as arithmetic expressions and function calls. Like such test expressions, a Gawk pattern can also contain subpatterns using relational, logical, and even arithmetic operations. In this sense, a pattern can be thought of as another term for "expression." However, whereas in programming languages the operands used in expressions are numbers or characters, in the Gawk pattern, the operands are considered patterns. In Gawk, a relational operation compares a value to a pattern. A logical operation will have subexpressions that compare patterns. In fact, the subexpressions are technically referred to as "patterns," and a complex logical operation can be referred to as a "compound pattern."

Equality and Relational Operators

You can construct simple conditions using equality operators, field variables, and constants. The equality operators are the same as those in the C programming language. The equality operator consists of two equal symbols, **==**. This is slightly different from other programming languages. A single equal symbol is the assignment operator, **=**. It is easy to confuse the two. The inequality operator is the exclamation point with the equal symbol, **!=**. In the next example, only those lines whose last field is equal to the string "Penguin" are printed. Notice that a string constant is used here instead of a pattern encased in slashes. A pattern encased in slashes is a pattern search operation, whereas a string is a simple value.

```
$ gawk '$4 == "Penguin" {print}' books
Tempest      Shakespeare   15.75    Penguin
Raven        Poe            2.50    Penguin
```

You can also use relational operators to construct conditions. Gawk has the same relational operators used in other programming languages: **>**, **<**, **>=**, **<=**. They are listed in Table 44-3. However, unlike the C language versions, Gawk relational operators can compare strings. The strings are ranked by alphabetic order. "Aleina" is less than "Larisa." In the next example, the user lists all books that cost more than 10.00. Notice that an arithmetic constant is used for the operand.

```
$ gawk '$3 > 10.00 {print}' books
Tempest      Shakespeare   15.75    Penguin
Iliad        Homer         10.25    Random
```

*An operand in a Gawk condition may also be a value returned by a function. In the next example, the **length** function is used to print out only those records whose second field has a length greater than 5.*

```
$ gawk 'length($2) > 5 {print}' books
Tempest      Shakespeare   15.75    Penguin
Christmas    Dickens        3.50    Academic
```

Operator	Description
>	Greater than
<	Less than
>=	Greater than or equal
<=	Less than or equal
==	Equal
!=	Not equal
&&	Logical AND
||	Logical OR
!	Logical NOT
str ~ regular expr	Matches regular expression; right operand is a regular expression.
str !~ regular expr	Does not match regular expression; right operand is a regular expression.
Initial and Terminating Patterns	
BEGIN	Execute operations before Gawk begins processing.
END	Execute operations after Gawk finishes processing.

Table 44-3.   *Gawk Test Operators*

Logical Operators

Gawk has a set of logical operators that you can use to create complex conditions. The logical operators are the same as those used in the C programming language. The logical operator for AND is a double ampersand, **&&**. The logical operator for OR is a double bar, **||**. The logical operator for NOT is a single exclamation point, **!**. The operands for logical operators are themselves conditions. These are each usually enclosed within parentheses. In the next example, all books published by Penguin that cost over $10.00 are output. This involves comparing the fourth field to "Penguin" and testing to see if the third field is greater than 10.00.

```
$ gawk '($4 == "Penguin") && ($3 > 10.00) {print}' books
Tempest      Shakespeare  15.75  Penguin
```

In the next example, the user retrieves books that are published either by Penguin or Academic. This involves checking to see if the fourth field is equal either to the string "Penguin" or to the string "Academic."

```
$ gawk '($4 == "Penguin") || ($4 == "Academic") {print}' books
Tempest      Shakespeare  15.75  Penguin
Christmas    Dickens       3.50  Academic
Raven        Poe           2.50  Penguin
```

Pattern Search Operators

With Gawk, you can also search a specific field for a pattern. You use the special operators ~ and !~ to carry out pattern searches on fields. Instead of using the equality operator to compare the entire field to a string, you can use the ~ operator to see if a certain pattern exists within the field. When using these operators to search fields, the right operand is the pattern and the left operand is the field to be searched. In the next example, the first field is searched for "mas":

```
$ gawk '($1 ~ /mas/) {print}' books
Christmas    Dickens    3.50   Academic
```

The next example retrieves all records whose first field does not contain the pattern "mas".

```
$ gawk '($1 !~ /mas/) {print}' books
Tempest      Shakespeare  15.75  Penguin
Iliad        Homer        10.25  Random
Raven        Poe           2.50  Penguin
```

Just as you can use special characters in a general pattern search, you can also use special characters to search fields. In the next example, the user matches both uppercase and lowercase versions of "Penguin" in the fourth field. The brackets special character is used to define a class for uppercase and lowercase "P."

```
$ gawk '($4 ~ /[Pp]enguin/) {print}' books
Tempest     Shakespeare  15.75   Penguin
Raven       Poe           2.50   Penguin
```

BEGIN and END Patterns

The Gawk instruction has two special patterns that allow the user to specify actions to be executed before and after processing lines in the input. The **BEGIN** pattern specifies actions to be performed before lines are processed. The **END** pattern specifies actions to be performed after lines are processed. In the next example, the heading " Book List " is output before any lines are processed. After processing, the value of **NR** is printed. Since **NR** increments with each line, after processing, **NR** will hold the total count of the records in the file.

```
$ gawk 'BEGIN {print "Book List"} {print} END{ print "Total records is ", NR}' books
Book List
Tempest     Shakespeare  15.75   Penguin
Christmas   Dickens       3.50   Academic
Iliad       Homer        10.25   Random
Raven       Poe           2.50   Penguin
Total records is 4
```

Gawk Instruction Files

As Gawk instructions become more complex, it is easier to handle them by placing them in a file that can then be read by Gawk. If you need to ever make any changes, you only need to modify the file. The **-f** option allows Gawk to read Gawk instructions from a file instead of the command line. In the next example, the Gawk instructions to list books published by Penguin are placed in a file called **findbk.gawk**. Gawk is then invoked with the **-f** option and the **findbk.gawk** filename. The Gawk instruction will then be read from the file **findbk.gawk**.

 *To better keep track of your Gawk instruction files, it is helpful to label them with the extension **.gawk**, as in **findbk.gawk**. The extension is, however, in no way necessary.*

findbk.gawk

```
BEGIN {print "Book List";
       count = 1;
       }
$4 ~ /Penguin/ {
```

```
            count = count + 1;
            print;
            }
END {
    print "Total records found is ", count
    }
```

```
$ gawk -f findbk.gawk  books
Book List
Tempest      Shakespeare  15.75   Penguin
Raven        Poe           2.50   Penguin
Total records found is 2
```

Tip	*Notice that you do not need any single quotes around the instruction. You can organize different parts of your instruction on separate lines, making for a more readable instruction. This feature is very helpful when using control structures, as we shall see.*

Control Structures

Gawk operates like a programming language. You can define variables, construct expressions, and assign values. Gawk also includes a set of control structures to provide iteration and selection capability. There are three control structures that construct loops in Gawk: the **while**, **for**, and **for-in** loops. There is one selection control structure, the **if** structure. The Gawk control structures are listed in Table 44-4. With the exception of the **for-in** loop, these control structures are similar to those in the C programming language. Table 44-4 lists the various input and output commands used in Gawk.

The while Loop

The **while** loop consists of the keyword **while**, followed by a test expression encased in parentheses. A Gawk action follows the test expression. Several Gawk actions can be combined into a block of actions with braces, each action separated by a semicolon. Placing a block of actions after the test expression of a **while** loop executes all those actions within the loop. Below is the syntax for a **while** loop:

```
while ( test expression )
        {
        gawk-actions;
        }
```

Most loops require three components to work properly: an initialization, a test, and an increment. All components operate on a variable used to control the loop. In the **threefields.gawk** file that follows, the first three fields of each record are printed out.

Control Structure	Description
{ *actions* }	A block is formed by opening and closing braces. A block groups actions, making them subject to a control structure, such as a loop, or enclosing the actions in the Gawk instruction proper.

if (*expression*)
  action
else
  action
	The **if** control structure executes an action if its expression is true. If false, then the **else** action is executed.

while (*expression*) *action*	The **while** control structure executes an action as long as its expression is true.
for (*exp1*; *exp2*; *exp3*) *action*	The **for** control structure executes an action as long as *exp2* is true. The first expression, *exp1*, is executed before the loop begins. The third expression, *exp3*, is executed within the loop after the action.
for (*variable* **in** *arrayname*) *action*	The **for-in** control structure is designed for use with associative arrays. The variable operand is consecutively assigned the strings that index the array.
next	The **next** statement stops operations on the current record and skips to the next record.
exit	The **exit** statement ends all processing and executes the **END** command if there is one.

Table 44-4.   *Gawk Control Structures*

The variable **i** is used to control the loop. It is incremented by 1 inside the loop. The increment of **i** is placed within a block enclosed within braces. The variable is then tested in a relational operation with the loop's test expression in order to determine when to stop the loop. The value of the **i** variable is used to reference each field in the record. The first time through the loop, the value of **i** will be 1. **$i** will reference the first field variable for the record. As **i** is incremented, its value will change and **$i** will consecutively reference each field variable for the line in turn up to the third field, at which point the loop cuts off.

threefields.gawk

```
{
i=1;
while(i <= 3)
    {
    printf("%s\t", $i);
    i++
    }
printf("\n");
}
```

This is the run of the **threefields.gawk** script:

```
$ gawk -f threefields.gawk books
Tempest     Shakespeare  15.75
Christmas   Dickens       3.50
Iliad       Homer        10.25
Raven       Poe           2.50
```

The for Loop

The **for** loop performs the same tasks as the **while** loop. However, it has a different format. The initialization, test, and increment components of a loop have all been incorporated into the **for** loop expressions. The **for** loop has three expressions encased within parentheses and separated by semicolons.

```
for(expression1; expression2; expression3)
    {
    gawk-actions;
    }
```

The first expression is usually reserved for initializations. This expression is executed before the loop is actually entered. It usually consists of an initialization of a variable used to control the loop. The second expression is the test expression such as a relational expression that controls the loop. The third expression is the expression executed within and at the end of the loop. It is usually used for incrementing the variable used to control the loop. Following the expressions is the Gawk action to be executed within the loop. This action can be a block of actions encased in braces. The third expression, usually the increment, is executed after the Gawk action.

```
for(initialization; test expression; increment)
    {
    gawk-actions;
    }
```

In the **field3for** file, the first three fields are printed out using a **for** loop. Notice how much more compact the **for** loop is than the **while** loop.

```
{
for(i=1;(i <= 3);i++)
      {
      printf("%s\t", $i);
   }
printf("\n");
}
```

The following example shows a run of the **field3for** script.

```
$ gawk -f field3for books
Tempest    Shakespeare  15.75
Christmas  Dickens       3.50
Iliad      Homer        10.25
Raven      Poe           2.50
```

The for-in Loop

Though a numeric variable was used in previous examples to reference elements in an array, it is of no help when you need to reference elements of an associative array. Elements of an associative array are referenced by strings, not numbers. Gawk has a special loop control structure that allows you to reference an associative array. This loop structure also begins with the keyword **for**; however, it is very different from the **for** loop. It has only one specialized expression that uses as its operator the keyword **in**. For this reason, the loop for associative arrays can be best described as a **for-in** loop, rather than just a **for** loop. The first operand in the **for-in** loop's expression is a variable, and the second operand is the name of the array. As the loop executes, the string that indexes each element is assigned to this variable. You can then use the contents of this variable to index an element in the array. No other type of expression is allowed. The **for-in** loop for an associative array is very restrictive in this regard. Next is the syntax for the **for-in** loop:

```
for(variable in array-name)
    {
    gawk-actions;
    }
```

In the following **bkcoun.gawkt** script, each element of the **bookcnt** array is printed out after the lines have been processed. During processing, the index for the **bookcnt** array is the fourth field of the record, the name of the publisher. In the **for** loop, string variable **pubname** is used for the index of the **bookcnt** array, not a numeric variable. Each time the loop is executed, the string that references the next element is assigned to **pubname**. **pubname** is then used to index that array element. Both the index and the array element are printed.

bkcount.gawk

```
{ bookcnt[$4] = bookcnt[$4] + 1 }

END {
    for(pubname in bookcnt)
        {
        print bookcnt[pubname], pubname;
        }
}
```

```
$ gawk -f bkcount.gawk books
2   Penguin
1   Academic
1   Random
```

The if Control Structure

Gawk also has a selection control structure, the **if** structure, that allows you to select alternative actions. The **if** structure has a test expression encased in parentheses. Following the test is a Gawk action. If the test is true, the action is performed. If not, the action is skipped. Here is the syntax for the **if** structure:

```
if(test-expression)
    {
    gawk-actions;
    }
```

The **if** structure also has an **else** component. Another Gawk action follows the **else** keyword. If the test expression of the **if** structure is false, the action following the else is executed. In this respect, the **if-else** structure can be thought of as a branch. If the test is true, one action is taken; if false, the other action is taken. Next is the syntax for the **if-else** structure. Take special note that there is no semicolon at the end of the gawk-action that comes before the **else**. The Gawk **if-else** structure is similar to the C programming language **if-else** structure with this one exception. If you use programming languages, you may inadvertently add a semicolon in. This will be taken as an error since a semicolon in Gawk separates actions. In the **markup.gawk** script that follows, the third field of the books file is a price. If the price is over 10.00, it is raised by 10 percent; otherwise, it is raised by 20 percent. Notice that there is no semicolon at the end of the action before the **else**.

markup.gawk

```
{
if($3 > 10.00)
   $3 = $3 + (0.10 * $3 )
else
   $3 = $3 + (0.20 * $3 );
print $0
}
```

Gawk as User-Defined Filters

You can use Gawk to define your own filters by placing the whole Gawk instruction in a script file. You can then make the file executable, and the filename becomes a new Linux command. Within the script file, Gawk instructions must be quoted. A script file literally contains a Linux command that will be executed in the shell. Within the script file, you need to write the instruction as if you were going to execute it on the command line. You can write the Gawk pattern and actions on their own lines, but any carriage returns need to be enclosed within the Gawk instruction's beginning and end quotes. This means that the first line of the Gawk operation will begin with the keyword **gawk**, followed on the same line by a single quote. Then you can enter the pattern and actions of the Gawk instruction using different lines. However, the end of the action needs to be terminated by a single quote, followed on the same line by any filename arguments. The syntax for such a format follows:

```
gawk ' pattern {
          gawk-actions;
} ' filenames
```

In the next example, the user has placed the entire Gawk instruction in a script file called **field3**. The instruction prints out the first three fields in each line. Notice that the Gawk instruction is quoted. Once you have set the execution permission for the script file with the **chmod** command, you can then execute the file by simply entering the script file's name.

field3

```
gawk '{
for(i=1;(i <= 3);i++)
   {
   printf("%s\t", $i);
   }
printf("\n");
}' books
```

```
$ chmod 755 field3
$ field3
Tempest     Shakespeare  15.75
Christmas   Dickens       3.50
Iliad       Homer        10.25
Raven       Poe           2.50
```

String Functions

The Gawk utility provides a set of string functions that can operate on fields, patterns, or variables. Several of the more commonly used string functions are **length**, **index**, **substr**, and **split** (see Table 44-5).

String Function	Description
length(str)	Returns the number of characters in a string, **str**. If **length** has no argument, it calculates the length of the current record in characters.
index(str1, str2)	Determines if **str1** is contained in **str2** and, if so, returns the position in **str2** where **str1** begins. If not, it returns 0.
split(str, arr, delim)	Copies segments of **str** that are separated by the delimiter **delim** into elements of the array **arr**. It returns the number of elements in the array. (See the section, "Arrays and Associative Arrays.").
substr(str, pos, len)	Returns a substring of **str**. Characters in the string are numbered from 1. The **pos** argument is a number that references the character where the substring begins. The **len** argument is a number that indicates how many characters from the **pos** character the substring will use.

Table 44-5. *Gawk String Functions*

The
Complete
Reference

Linux

Part IX

Appendix

Linux

Appendix

About the CD-ROMS

The two Linux distribution CD-ROMs, Red Hat Linux 7.*x* and Caldera eDesktop 2.*x* Linux, are included with this book. Standard installation also installs and configures the Apache Web server and an FTP server, automatically configuring your Linux system to be a Web and FTP site. You can find recent information about Red Hat from **www.redhat.com** and about OpenLinux from **www.caldera.com**. You can find detailed installation and reference manuals at each site.

The CDs include both the Gnome and the K Desktop Environment (KDE) GUI user interfaces, along with an extensive number or Gnome and KDE applications. Red Hat installs both Gnome and KDE, whereas Caldera installs KDE. Both distributions include a comprehensive set of Linux software applications including the GNU software packages (graphics, communications, publishing, editing, programming, and games), as well as development tools, and Internet servers (FTP, Web, mail, news, and DNS). Both distributions also install a complete set of Internet clients such as mail, news, FTP, and Web browsers, including Netscape Communicator. There are clients for both the Gnome and KDE desktops, as well as for shell and window manager interfaces.

For added functionality, you can also download free personal editions of the StarOffice office suite from **www.stardivision.com** and WordPerfect from **linux.corel.com**. Also, the Java Development Kit is available for free through **www.blackdown.org**. Databases are available from their respective Web sites, such as Oracle from **www.oracle.com**. Numerous applications, in the easy-to-install RPM package format, are available for download from the Red Hat and Caldera sites. You can both download and install these applications using either the Gnome or KDE file manager. Gnome and KDE applications can be downloaded from the Gnome and KDE sites at **www.gnome.org** and **apps.kde.com**. In addition, numerous software packages are available at Linux software repositories such as **rpmfind.net, freshmeat.net**, **www.linuxapps.com**, and **sourceforge.net**. Several popular Internet sites where you can easily obtain Linux applications are listed here.

Linux Applications	Internet site
Java Development Kit	**www.blackdown.org**
Window manager and desktop themes	**www.themes.org**
Gnome applications	**www.gnome.org**
KDE applications	**apps.kde.com**
Netscape Communicator and Navigator	Any distribution site such as **ftp.redhat.com** or **ftp.caldera.com**
StarOffice	**www.sun.com**
Tcl/TK applications	**dev.scriptics.com**
Perl applications	**www.perl.com**

Linux Applications	Internet site
Linux applications	**www.linuxapps.com**
Linux applications in RPM packages	**www.rpmfind.net**
New Linux applications	**www.freshmeat.net**
Linux Documentation Project	**www.linuxdoc.org**
WordPerfect	**linux.corel.com**

Both the OpenLinux and Red Hat distributions install a professional-level and very stable Linux system with KDE and Gnome GUI interfaces, providing you with all the advantages of a Unix workstation on your PC combined with the same ease of use and versatility found on GUI systems like Windows and Mac/OS. An extensive set of Internet servers is also included that is automatically installed, along with flexible and easy-to-use system configuration tools like Linuxconf and Webmin.

Index

X

redhat®

www.redhat.com